Pharmaceutical Economics

The International Library of Critical Writings in Economics

This series is an essential reference source for students, researchers and lecturers in economics. It presents by theme a selection of the most important articles across the entire spectrum of economics. Each volume has been prepared by a leading specialist who has written an authoritative introduction to the literature included.

Wherever possible, the articles in these volumes have been reproduced as originally published using facsimile reproduction, inclusive of footnotes and pagination to facilitate ease of reference.

For a list of all Edward Elgar published titles visit our website at
www.e-elgar.com

Pharmaceutical Economics

Edited by

William S. Comanor

Professor of Health Policy and Management
Director, Research Program on Pharmaceutical Economics and Policy
Fielding School of Public Health, University of California at Los Angeles
Professor of Economics
University of California, Santa Barbara, USA

and

Stuart O. Schweitzer

Professor of Health Policy and Management
Associate Director, Research Program on Pharmaceutical Economics and Policy
Fielding School of Public Health, University of California at Los Angeles
USA

THE INTERNATIONAL LIBRARY OF CRITICAL WRITINGS IN ECONOMICS

An Elgar Research Collection
Cheltenham, UK • Northampton, MA, USA

Published by
Edward Elgar Publishing Limited
The Lypiatts
15 Lansdown Road
Cheltenham
Glos GL50 2JA
UK

Edward Elgar Publishing, Inc.
William Pratt House
9 Dewey Court
Northampton
Massachusetts 01060
USA

A catalogue record for this book is available from the British Library

Library of Congress Control Number: 2013944946

MIX
Paper from responsible sources
FSC® C013056

ISBN 978 0 85793 449 9

Printed and bound in Great Britain by T.J. International Ltd, Padstow

Contents

Acknowledgements

The editors and publishers wish to thank the authors and the following publishers who have kindly given permission for the use of copyright material.

American Economic Association for articles: Willard G. Manning, Joseph P. Newhouse, Naihua Duan, Emmett B. Keeler, Arleen Leibowitz and M. Susan Marquis (1987), 'Health Insurance and the Demand for Medical Care: Evidence from a Randomized Experiment', *American Economic Review*, **77** (3), June, 251–77; Ernst R. Berndt (2002), 'Pharmaceuticals in U.S. Health Care: Determinants of Quality and Price', *Journal of Economic Perspectives*, **16** (4), Fall, 45–66; Mark Duggan and Fiona Scott Morton (2010), 'The Effect of Medicare Part D on Pharmaceutical Prices and Utilization', *American Economic Review*, **100** (1), March, 590–607.

American Journal of Health-System Pharmacy for article: Scott Gottlieb (2008), 'Biosimilars: Policy, Clinical, and Regulatory Considerations', *American Journal of Health-System Pharmacy*, **65** (14 Supplement 6), July 15, S2–S8.

Blackwell Publishing Ltd for article: Ernst R. Berndt, Robert S. Pindyck and Pierre Azoulay (2003), 'Consumption Externalities and Diffusion in Pharmaceutical Markets: Antiulcer Drugs', *Journal of Industrial Economics*, **LI** (2), June, 243–70.

Brookings Institution for article: Richard E. Caves, Michael D. Whinston and Mark A. Hurwitz (1991), 'Patent Expiration, Entry, and Competition in the U.S. Pharmaceutical Industry', *Brookings Papers on Economic Activity. Microeconomics 1991*, 1–48, 64–66.

Cambridge University Press for excerpts and article: William S. Comanor (2007), 'The Economics of Research and Development in the Pharmaceutical Industry', in Frank A. Sloan and Chee-Ruey Hsieh (eds), *Pharmaceutical Innovation: Incentives, Competition, and Cost–Benefit Analysis in International Perspective*, Chapter 3, 54–72, notes, references; Henry Grabowski (2007), 'Competition between Generic and Branded Drugs', in Frank A. Sloan and Chee-Ruey Hseih (eds), *Pharmaceutical Innovation: Incentives, Competition, and Cost–Benefit Analysis in International Perspective*, Chapter 8, 153–73, notes, references; Daniel Carpenter and Gisela Sin (2007), 'Policy Tragedy and the Emergence of Regulation: The Food, Drug, and Cosmetic Act of 1938', *Studies in American Political Development*, **21** (2), Fall, 149–80.

Elsevier for articles: Joseph A. DiMasi, Ronald W. Hansen, Henry G. Grabowski and Louis Lasagna (1991), 'Cost of Innovation in the Pharmaceutical Industry', *Journal of Health Economics*, **10** (2), July, 107–42; Patricia M. Danzon and Li-Wei Chao (2000), 'Cross-national

Price Differences for Pharmaceuticals: How Large, and Why?', *Journal of Health Economics*, **19** (2), March, 159–95; Patricia M. Danzon, Sean Nicholson and Nuno Sousa Pereira (2005), 'Productivity in Pharmaceutical–Biotechnology R&D: The Role of Experience and Alliances', *Journal of Health Economics*, **24** (2), March, 317–39; David Granlund (2010), 'Price and Welfare Effects of Pharmaceutical Substitution Reform', *Journal of Health Economics*, **29** (6), December, 856–65.

Health Affairs and Project HOPE — The People-to-People Health Foundation, Inc. for articles: F.M. Scherer (2001), 'The Link between Gross Profitability and Pharmaceutical R&D Spending', *Health Affairs*, **20** (5), September, 216–20; Frank R. Lichtenberg and Shawn X. Sun (2007), 'The Impact of Medicare Part D on Prescription Drug Use by the Elderly', *Health Affairs*, **26** (6), November, 1735–44; Stuart O. Schweitzer and William S. Comanor (2011), 'Prices of Pharmaceuticals in Poor Countries are Much Lower than in Wealthy Countries', *Health Affairs*, **30** (8), August, 1553–61.

Henry J. Kaiser Family Foundation for article: Meredith B. Rosenthal, Ernst R. Berndt, Julie M. Donohue, Arnold M. Epstein and Richard G. Frank (2003), *Demand Effects of Recent Changes in Prescription Drug Promotion*, Report of the Henry J. Kaiser Family Foundation #6085, June, 1–33.

Informa Healthcare and *Expert Opinion* for article: Joel W. Hay (2004), 'Evaluation and Review of Pharmacoeconomic Models', *Expert Opinion in Pharmacotherapy*, **5** (9), September, 1–14 [1867–80].

Massachusetts Medical Society via the Copyright Clearance Center's RightsLink service for article: Steven Kozlowski, Janet Woodcock, Karen Midthun and Rachel Behrman Sherman (2011), 'Developing the Nation's Biosimilars Program', *New England Journal of Medicine*, **365** (5), August, 385–88.

MIT Press Journals for article: Z. John Lu and William S. Comanor (1998), 'Strategic Pricing of New Pharmaceuticals', *Review of Economics and Statistics*, **80** (1), February, 108–18.

Nature Publishing Group for article: Bernard Munos (2009), 'Lessons from 60 Years of Pharmaceutical Innovation', *Nature Reviews/Drug Discovery*, **8**, December, 959–68.

Oxford University Press, USA for excerpt: Stuart O. Schweitzer (2007), 'The Timing of Drug Approvals in the United States and Abroad', in *Pharmaceutical Economics and Policy*, Second Edition, Chapter 9, 191–206.

RAND Journal of Economics for articles: Rebecca Henderson and Iain Cockburn (1996), 'Scale, Scope, and Spillovers: The Determinants of Research Productivity in Drug Discovery', *RAND Journal of Economics*, **27** (1), Spring, 32–59; Fiona M. Scott Morton (1999), 'Entry Decisions in the Generic Pharmaceutical Industry', *RAND Journal of Economics*, **30** (3), Autumn, 421–40.

SAGE Publications, Inc. for article: Michele M. Spence, Stephanie S. Teleki, T. Craig Cheetham, Stuart O. Schweitzer and Mirta Millares (2005), 'Direct-to-Consumer Advertising of COX-2 Inhibitors: Effect on Appropriateness of Prescribing', *Medical Care Research and Review*, **62** (5), October, 544–59.

Springer Science and Business Media BV for article: Henry Grabowski, John Vernon and Joseph A. DiMasi (2002), 'Returns on Research and Development for 1990s New Drug Introductions,' *PharmacoEconomics*, **20** (3 Supplement), December, 11–29.

University of Chicago Press for excerpt and articles: Davina C. Ling, Ernst R. Berndt and Margaret K. Kyle (2002), 'Deregulating Direct-to-Consumer Marketing of Prescription Drugs: Effects on Prescription and Over-the-Counter Product Sales', *Journal of Law and Economics*, **XLV**, October, 691–723; Frank R. Lichtenberg (2003), 'Pharmaceutical Innovation, Mortality Reduction, and Economic Growth', in Kevin M. Murphy and Robert H. Topel (eds), *Measuring the Gains from Medical Research: An Economic Approach*, Chapter 3, 74–109; Jayanta Bhattacharya and William B. Vogt (2003), 'A Simple Model of Pharmaceutical Price Dynamics', *Journal of Law and Economics*, **XLVI** (2), October, 599–626.

John Wiley and Sons, Inc. for articles: Iain Cockburn and Rebecca Henderson (1994), 'Racing to Invest? The Dynamics of Competition in Ethical Drug Discovery', *Journal of Economics and Management Strategy*, **3** (3), Fall, 481–519; Richard G. Frank and David S. Salkever (1997), 'Generic Entry and the Pricing of Pharmaceuticals', *Journal of Economics and Management Strategy*, **6** (1), Spring, 75–90.

John Wiley and Sons Ltd for articles: Patricia M. Danzon, Andrew Epstein and Sean Nicholson (2007), 'Mergers and Acquisitions in the Pharmaceutical and Biotech Industries', *Managerial and Decision Economics*, **28** (4–5), June–August, 307–28; Adrian Towse (2007), 'If It Ain't Broke, Don't Price Fix It: The OFT and the PPRS', *Health Economics*, **16** (7), July, 653–65.

Every effort has been made to trace all the copyright holders but if any have been inadvertently overlooked the publishers will be pleased to make the necessary arrangement at the first opportunity.

In addition the publishers wish to thank the Library at the University of Warwick, UK, and the Library at Indiana University, Bloomington, USA, for their assistance in obtaining these articles.

Introduction: Pharmaceutical Economics and Policy

William S. Comanor, Stuart O. Schweitzer and Karleen Giannitrapani

Introduction

Pharmaceutical Economics encompasses the economics of the pharmaceutical industry, but it is far more than that. Because pharmaceuticals have an important impact on public health, government actions also play a major role in determining market outcomes. In this volume, we present a series of particularly important published articles that span both subject areas. We also offer an introductory chapter, which reviews the extensive literature on these subjects and provides a setting through which the importance of the reprinted articles can be seen.

There are important features that distinguish the pharmaceutical industry from most others. The first is its unique regulatory structure, which follows from its importance for public health. Not only must new products be approved by the Food and Drug Administration (FDA) but even approved products face continued regulatory review. More significantly, the approval process gave rise to two separate and distinct pharmaceutical industries, which compete vigorously with each other: the branded and the generic pharmaceutical industries. They are largely comprised of different firms with different business plans, who are frequent rivals and opponents. No other major industry has had this type of structure imposed by the regulatory system.

A second distinguishing feature is the industry's distinctive payment system. As with other health care products and services, pharmaceuticals are largely purchased and paid for by one set of buyers, such as insurance companies and other payers, but actually consumed by a second set of buyers – the patients. To complicate matters still further, products are prescribed by a third set of entities, hospitals and physicians, who often have little economic stake in the outcome. In these circumstances, product flows and payment flows generally follow different routes than those observed in most other industries.

This payment system has impacted the pharmaceutical industry and led to many of its unique characteristics. A consequence of the separation between prescriber, payer, and consumer is that decision-making has evolved in distinct ways. Historically, physicians were the decision-makers who selected medicines for their patients. However, with the evolving roles of insurance companies, Health Maintenance Organizations (HMOs) and government payers, these buyers have become far more involved in prescribing decisions and selection. In addition, the expanding role of the Internet has provided consumers with access to information that was never previously available. This broadening of decision-making has changed the manner by which pharmaceuticals are sold and marketed.

The third distinctive feature of the pharmaceutical industry is its continually changing menu of products, which relies on high expenditures for research and development. There are two effects of the rapid pace of new product development. The first is that prices for branded products greatly exceed marginal costs. These prices are often more than twice their marginal production costs (Berndt, this volume, Chapter 24). While this feature is not unique to the pharmaceutical industry, it has important implications for behavior and performance.

Another implication of the rapid pace of new product introduction is the increased importance of the information provided by drug manufacturers to payers, prescribers, and consumers. As a result, there is greater need for information by all decision-makers about the features and characteristics of the new products. This factor has contributed to the branded industry's heavy expenditures on advertising and promotion.

The Regulatory Structure

The modern pharmaceutical industry has been shaped by more than a century of legislation. In response to contaminated smallpox vaccines, the US federal government passed The Biologics Act of 1902 that first provided the federal government with authority to require pre-market approval for all drugs sold (Miller, 2000, pp. 11–12). It was followed by the Pure Food and Drug Act of 1906, which among other things, established standards for the strength, quality and purity of drug products.[1] While new drugs would be assessed for quality and safety, no regulatory body was created. Instead, the relevant state officials would carry out examinations.

This structure was maintained until 1938 when a newly introduced sulfa drug, elixir sulfonamide, led to a reported 107 deaths (Boslaugh, 2008, p. 395). In this case, the active ingredient had been approved for its quality and safety, but its solvent diethylene glycol, commonly known as antifreeze, was toxic. In response, a new government agency, which evolved into the Food Drug Administration (FDA), was established to confirm the safety of food and drug products (Carpenter and Sin, 2007, p. 170). This authority became the agency's mission in the period of the modern pharmaceutical industry, starting at the end of the Second World War.

In the early 1960s, another scandal led to further regulation. In 1957, Thalidomide was introduced in Germany as a sedative for morning sickness during the first trimester of pregnancy. By 1962 its use had spread to 46 countries. Fortunately, Thalidomide was only an investigational drug in the United States when it became known that it led to major birth defects. This episode is recounted in Carpenter and Sin (2007). Even though the US had largely escaped the Thalidomide tragedy, the worldwide pandemonium that was created set the stage for further regulation. Paradoxically, the new law did not address the safety issues that lay at the heart of the Thalidomide episode, but rather emphasized the dubious efficacy of many new drugs.

In the early post-war years, large numbers of new drugs had been introduced which may have been safe but were often not very efficacious. This fact raised few regulatory issues because at the time, the FDA confirmed the safety of new drugs but not their efficacy. However, the 1962 Kefauver–Harris Amendments changed the FDA's mandate (Peltzman, 1973). It was now charged with monitoring the efficacy as well as the safety of all new drugs.

That was more than 50 years ago and we now take for granted those extended FDA responsibilities. However, they were not part of the original legislation and represented a major policy shift when enacted. Following the 1962 amendments, the FDA adopted new rules and procedures, which led ultimately to the current system of clinical trials and New Drug Applications (NDAs) required for drug approvals. While these amendments eliminated the introduction of large numbers of non-efficacious drugs, they also led to greatly increased research and testing costs for drug introductions.

Twenty-two years later, another major piece of regulatory legislation was enacted – the Hatch–Waxman Act of 1984. There were two parts of the new law. The first part extended the patent lives of drugs to account for the fact that patent protection began when a drug was discovered rather than when it was approved by the FDA. The lengthening period during which the FDA processed an NDA had shortened the period of market exclusivity granted by the patent, sometimes substantially. To compensate for this regulatory delay, the new law extended pharmaceutical patents by as much as five years.

A second response to the problem of regulatory delay was the passage of the Prescription Drug User Fee Act (PDUFA) of 1992. Prior to enacting this law, the FDA was taking an average of 30 months to approve new molecules (Schweitzer, 2007, p. 196). To hasten the regulatory process, the branded industry agreed to pay substantial user fees to be used specifically for the review process. The law had its intended effect; and review times have greatly diminished. See further discussion of these issues in Schweitzer (2007).

Although not anticipated at the time, the second part of the Hatch–Waxman Act had far greater implications for the pharmaceutical industry. It authorized Abbreviated New Drug Applications (ANDAs) under which manufacturers of imitative drugs could seek approval following expiration of the patent covering the original product. For this approval, new entrants needed only to demonstrate that their active ingredient was the same as that used in the branded product ('chemical equivalence') and also that the active ingredient entered the body with the same effects as that of the previously approved drug ('bio-equivalence') (Karki, 2005).

Previously, the FDA had considered an innovator's NDA as proprietary material which could be applied only to that company's products and not used by rivals seeking authorization for a competing but equivalent product. That policy changed with the new law. Most importantly, this provision triggered the striking growth of the generic pharmaceutical industry. Although the Hatch–Waxman Act contained various other provisions, its primary substantive one was that new entrants wishing to produce and market a drug that no longer had patent protection would now face only minor regulatory hurdles (Grabowski, Chapter 13, this volume). The result was the emergence of a second pharmaceutical industry, whose business strategy and objectives differed sharply from those of the first.

The growth of the generic drug industry coincided with increasing concerns over health care costs. Payers encouraged their subscribers to purchase lower-cost generic drugs whenever possible. By 2010, 78% of all US prescriptions were filled generically (IMS Health, 2011, p. 22). Because branded products are much more costly than generics, these shares look different when measured by product revenues. Branded pharmaceuticals accounted for 83% of total pharmaceutical revenues in 2010, with only 17% left for generic drugs (IMS Health, 2012, p. 22).

The regulatory burden imposed on the branded pharmaceutical industry arose from the FDA's early decision to minimize Type I errors (the error of approving a drug that in fact is dangerous or ineffective) at the expense of tolerating higher Type II errors (the error of rejecting a drug although it is actually safe and effective). Because the FDA has focused so strongly on minimizing Type I errors, Intriligator (1996) points out that there was less attention paid to the regulatory effect on Type II errors.

To minimize Type I errors, the FDA mandated a series of (human) clinical trials which have become increasingly expensive. Study populations expanded so that trials which earlier took place in one or two centers are now carried out in many sites throughout the world (DiMasi et al., Chapter 4, this volume, 2003). By 2000, average out-of-pocket research and development (R&D) costs per approved chemical entity had increased to $282 million, not including the opportunity cost of the capital employed in the R&D process. Including those capitalized costs effectively doubles average R&D outlays per new product introduction (Scherer, 2010, p. 534). Whatever the gains achieved from demonstrating safety and efficacy, FDA requirements have imposed greatly increased costs on the branded industry.

An integral part of the current regulatory structure is its focus on 'indications.' An NDA identifies not only the drug itself but also a specific therapeutic purpose, called an 'indication.' The NDA applies only to that indication. What this means is that drugs are not approved for 'general' use, but only for the specific purposes evaluated during the drug's clinical trials. That approach raises no issues when a proposed drug has only a single indication, which is frequently not the case. Many drugs provide useful therapy for more than one symptom or disease, and for more than one type of patient.

A critical factor is that physicians are not bound by FDA approvals. They can prescribe a drug for any indications, even one not approved by the FDA, if they believe it will benefit their patients (Stafford, 2008). This distinction creates a hole in the regulatory structure, but it is not one easily closed. To serve their patients, physicians require the authority to employ whatever drugs are available that they deem useful. Because the FDA has paid minimal attention to Type II errors, where a drug is effective but still not approved, there may be various unapproved indications that are therapeutically useful in particular circumstances. For this reason, there are good reasons not to limit physicians' authority in this area.

Furthermore, the FDA understandingly emphasizes the experience of the average patient in its regulatory decision-making. In contrast, physicians deal with individual patients who may or may not reflect average responses; and there is evidence that patient responses to particular drugs can differ widely (Ma and Lu, 2011). For this reason as well, physicians are not limited to authorized indications. Indeed, a recent study reported that in a sample of 160 common drugs, approximately 21% of their prescriptions were written for off-label uses (Stafford, 2008, p. 1427).

Prescribing a drug for a non-approved indication is called 'off-label' use since the product's label reflects only its approved indications. However, off-label prescribing puts pharmaceutical companies in a quandary. Seeking approval for multiple indications is costly, and in many cases a drug is already being prescribed for different 'off-label' uses. Although seeking approval from the FDA for other indications might lead to greater sales, there is a risk in doing so. New clinical trials might show that the drug is *ineffective* for the second indication, a finding which would reduce sales. New trials might even reveal a safety issue pertaining to the original use of the drug. Since there is always uncertainty over what a new clinical trial will demonstrate, and because these trials are very costly, there are strong incentives for drug companies to rest on existing product authorizations.

However, the widespread sale of pharmaceuticals for 'off-label' uses creates legal risks for the company. Under the current regulatory structure, manufacturers may sell but not advertise or market a drug for 'off-label' uses (Carpenter, 2010, p. 619). This distinction, however, is hardly clear or precise. Often, even the FDA has difficulty in defining what drug representatives can and cannot say, and what materials can and cannot be given to physicians pertaining to a product.

This regulatory structure has been called into question by a 2012 decision by a US Court of Appeals. The Court deals directly with the problem that 'certain speech [delivered by drug companies and their agents] about off-label use of drugs [...] is prohibited, even though the off-label use itself is not' (*US v. Caronia*, 2012, p. 15). Since 'speech in aid of pharmaceutical marketing [...] is protected by the First Amendment' (*US v. Caronia*, 2012, p. 14, quoting *Sorrell v. IMS Health*, 2011), the Court ruled that the FDA could not prohibit pharmaceutical manufacturers from marketing off-label indications. As observed by the dissenting judge, this decision 'calls into question the very foundation of our century-old system of drug regulation' (*US v. Caronia*, dissenting opinion, p. 18).

Not only did the 1984 legkjislation establish the ANDA structure but it also created incentives for generic producers to enter the market rapidly. The first producer with an approved ANDA receives six months of exclusivity from competition from other generic producers; a restriction that is enforced by the FDA. This incentive has encouraged generic entry into many markets, even though there can still be a dearth of generic products for drugs with low prospective demand (Gray, 2012, p. 158).

Another facet of the current regulatory structure is that it rests on a model of pharmaceutical products that is centered on small molecule drugs produced through chemical processes. For such drugs, production methods can be specified with sufficient precision that products are uniform from one batch to another, and from one manufacturer to another. Testing one batch of products for bio-equivalence is sufficient to justify regulatory approval for both the facility and the product. Under these circumstances, bio-equivalence can readily be determined.

However, that model does not fully apply to large molecule drugs, which are produced by biological rather than chemical processes. The growth of biotechnology has led to a rapid increase in the development and sale of such drugs. In 2007 biologic drug sales were $75 billion out of total pharmaceutical sales of $712 billion, or just over 10% of the total (Fierce Biotech, 2013). This percentage is expected to rise in the future and may approach 17% of total spending by 2016 (IMS, 2012, pp. 4–5). A critical feature of biologicals is that the methods used to produce them are not nearly as precise as their chemical counterparts. Their therapeutic characteristics can vary across facilities, and even across batches in the same facility. Merely demonstrating the adequacy of the production processes may therefore not confirm therapeutic equivalence.

This factor has implications for the regulatory process. See the discussions, reprinted here, in both Gottlieb (Chapter 17) and Kozlowski et al. (Chapter 16). In particular, the concepts of chemical equivalence and bio-equivalence on which the ANDA process rests are called into question. If batches of the same drug, even those produced by the same manufacturer, can have different therapeutic properties, so that repeated testing is required, what chance is there to determine bio-equivalence between different producers? The key to this issue is determining how much variation is acceptable therapeutically, and how much is unacceptable, as between the products of the branded originator and a generic imitator.

In this context, the relevant regulatory concept has shifted from bio-equivalence to 'biosimilars.' What now appears relevant to the FDA for approving new versions of large-molecule drugs is whether they are 'interchangeable' in use with the original version. How this question is answered is critical for determining whether the current regulatory structure can be applied to biologicals (Chapter 16, this volume). In 2005, the European Medicines Agency (EMA) approved a pathway for generic biological product approvals (Wiecek and Mikhail, 2006). More recently, the FDA has proposed draft guidelines for biosimilar products. However, guidelines have not been approved and the issue remains unsettled.

Public Reimbursement for Pharmaceuticals

Public reimbursement offers a separate route through which government affects market outcomes in the pharmaceutical industry. Currently, nearly 60% of all prescriptions in the United States are filled for beneficiaries of Medicare, Medicaid and other government programs (Duggan and Scott Morton, Chapter 9, this volume). Since the mechanisms employed for these purchases affect market outcomes, they require attention. In this section, we look first at the Medicare Program, and especially its expansion in 2006 to cover outpatient pharmaceuticals for the elderly. We also review that reimbursement program for drugs covered through the Medicaid programs, and then offer a brief review of other programs.

Even prior to the expansion of Medicare pharmaceutical coverage in 2003, most of its beneficiaries already had coverage through supplementary plans (Davis et al., 1999, p. 235). These plans, authorized in 1997, permitted Medicare beneficiaries to join managed care organizations. As a result, as many as two-thirds of Medicare beneficiaries had coverage for pharmaceuticals when Medicare, Part D was created.

The original 1966 legislation creating this program contained a 'non-interference provision' which prohibited Medicare from negotiating pharmaceutical prices with drug manufacturers regarding hospital, in-patient drugs. That provision was carried forward into the 2003 law which created Part D pharmaceutical coverage. Apparently, the legislative commitment to use private markets to set drug prices was thought to outweigh any savings that might accrue from allowing price negotiations to proceed (Gellad et al., 2008).

Under the new Part D program, previously uninsured consumers who had paid cash prices for their drugs could now enroll in private insurance plans paid for by Medicare. As Duggan and Scott Morton (Chapter 9) point out, the direct effect of this program was to move large numbers of Medicare enrollees from being individual cash buyers to being members in an insured group. However, rather than seeing more inelastic demands with greater insurance coverage, as might have been expected, they found that aggregate demand was more elastic. As a result, the prices paid for drugs declined with enhanced coverage. Duggan and Scott Morton's explanation, offered in their paper reprinted here (Chapter 9), is that cash buyers could not 'move market share' as individuals, but when brought together in a large group and represented by insurers and PBMs, they can have this effect and drive prices down.

The effect of Part D coverage on pharmaceutical quantities is more expected. Lichtenberg and Sun report, in a paper reprinted here (Chapter 19), that the number of prescriptions filled in 2006 by the elderly increased by nearly 13% and drug expenditures grew by over 18%.

They estimated that about 70% of Part D expenditures would have been made anyway even if this law had not been enacted.

The expansion of Medicare insurance coverage also created an incentive for firms to alter their R&D efforts specifically to capture the increased demand by elderly patients. Blume-Kohout and Sood studied this effect and found significant increases in R&D outlays directed at therapeutic areas with greater potential Medicare sales (Blume-Kohout and Sood, 2013, pp. 327–36). In this manner, the extended Medicare coverage for pharmaceuticals had broader implications than expected.

In 1966, the US created the Medicaid program along with Medicare. That program is actually a group of 50 state health insurance programs for low-income people, which are supported by federal funds. Strikingly, drug payments under those programs are quite different than under Medicare Part D; the government here retains more control over the prices actually paid. Under Medicaid, affiliated state programs pay the manufacturer for drugs provided to beneficiaries on the basis of the average manufacturer price (AMP). In addition, the manufacturer pays a rebate to the Medicaid program. The rebate is the higher of either a fixed percentage of the AMP or the difference between the AMP and the lowest price the firm had negotiated with another purchaser. An implication of this procedure is that a manufacturer who agrees to a low-cost purchasing agreement with an insurance company or pharmacy benefit manager (PBM) is then constrained to offer a similar lower price to the Medicaid program. This pricing scheme thereby gives manufacturers an incentive to refrain from discounting prices to private payers.

Duggan and Scott Morton (2006) study the effect of this incentive. Following an empirical analysis of the leading 200 drugs in 1997 and 2002, they report that a 10% increase in the Medicaid market share is associated with a 7% to 10% increase in the average price of a prescription. What is implied is that government procurement practices lead to higher equilibrium prices in the private sector.

Finally, there are other federal government purchasing programs of which the Departments of Veterans Affairs (VA) and of Defense (DOD) are the most important. The VA has obtained relatively low pharmaceutical prices by requiring competitive bids for national contracts, which then determines DOD prices as well. Both agencies pay lower prices for branded drugs than are paid under either the Medicare or Medicaid programs (CBO, 2005).

What this discussion emphasizes is that pharmaceutical prices and quantities depend not only on product characteristics and competition among sellers, but also on the particular buyers involved. Who the buyers are for individual drugs is a relevant factor for industry behavior.

Prices and Quantities in Two Industries

In 1960, early in the growth of the modern pharmaceutical industry, more than 95% of the costs of prescribed drugs were paid directly by consumers. Drugs were purchased like most other commodities; after receiving a prescription from his or her physician, the consumer filled it at a neighborhood pharmacy and paid for it directly. By 2000, just 40 years later, the situation had reversed. Only about one-fourth of these costs were paid by consumers 'out of pocket,' with the rest covered by insurance companies, employers, HMOs or government agencies (Chapter 24, this volume; Danzon and Pauly, 2002, p. 587).

This shift in payment, from consumers to payers, has major implications for pharmaceutical prices and quantities. In the first place, it has meant that product flows and payment flows follow different paths. For most consumer items, product and payment flows move in similar paths but in opposite directions. Products move from the manufacturer to pharmacy to consumer, while payments move from consumer to pharmacy to manufacturer. That picture still characterizes cash purchase of pharmaceuticals today.

For most drug purchases, however, payment flows follow a more circuitous route. Pharmacies acquire their pharmaceutical products from manufactures, typically via one of the major drug wholesalers, at an established price that is often termed the Wholesale Acquisition Cost (WAC). That price is paid before the pharmacy knows who will be the drug's ultimate consumer and what price the consumer will eventually pay. The pharmacy's acquisition costs are therefore the same for all customers.

To cover its drug costs on insured sales along with its own direct costs and profits, a pharmacy receives payments from two sources: from the consumer directly in the form of a 'co-pay,' and from the health plan or other payer, generally via a PBM serving as the payer's agent, in the form of a 'reimbursement.' Since each PBM and/or payer makes its own contract with the affiliated pharmacies, both consumer co-pays and payer reimbursements can differ significantly across sales. As a result, a pharmacy can receive quite different amounts from different customers of the same product. Moreover, these amounts can differ substantially from those paid by cash customers. This payment structure facilitates a system of price discrimination in which the same product is sold at very different prices to different customers.

Although the pharmacy receives two payment streams, only one is made directly by consumers. From the consumer's vantage point, the relevant price of a drug is the co-pay charged at the pharmacy (Esposito, 2006). Although patients and their employers may have paid premiums to a health plan, those premiums generally cover the costs of hospitals and physicians as well, with only about 10% to 15% used for pharmaceuticals (Esposito, 2006, pp. 85–7). There is also no direct link between the pharmaceuticals received and the premiums paid. Strikingly, in pharmaceutical markets for sales made to insured consumers, consumer prices take the form of co-pays which are set by payers in conjunction with their PBMs. For most retail sales of pharmaceuticals, drug companies do not set the prices that consumers actually pay.

Until recently, co-pays have followed a tiered structure which is only loosely related to the product's cost. The lowest co-pay is charged for generic drugs, with a somewhat higher one charged for branded drugs on the plan's formulary. Formulary status is typically reserved for drugs where the payer pays a discounted price. The highest co-pay is then charged for non-formulary, branded drugs. More recently, some payers have added a fourth tier that is tied directly to the manufacturer's price, but this tier has generally been limited to high-priced pharmaceuticals. Except for this fourth tier, the striking feature of the typical co-pay structure is that consumer prices are not linked to the price paid by the manufacturer for the drug in question.

In the retail market for insured pharmaceuticals, there are two types of pharmacies, each employing a different payment mechanism. There are conventional ('brick-and-mortar') and also mail-order pharmacies. Networks of conventional pharmacies are organized by PBMs.

These networks are reimbursed for the drugs supplied to subscribers of their affiliated health plans. For mail-order pharmacies, however, the leading PBMs reserve this business for themselves by refusing to affiliate with independent mail-order operations.

Through negotiations with their client health plans and other payers, the leading PBMs have established unit co-pay amounts which are lower than the corresponding co-pays at conventional pharmacies. For maintenance drugs, they also permit mail-order sales for three-month supplies while limiting sales at conventional pharmacies to a one-month supply. Consumers are thereby incentivized to use mail-order pharmacies for maintenance drugs which do not require immediate supply. Although the number of prescriptions filled via mail order is still much lower than those filled at conventional pharmacies, these sales have increased rapidly in recent years (Stat. Abs U.S., 2011, Table 15.9) and now represent a major source of PBM revenues and profits.

Even though consumers pay lower co-pays to the mail-order pharmacies owned by the largest PBMs, that arrangement is a mixed blessing for their affiliated payers. In most cases, the PBMs charge less to health plans for drugs supplied via their integrated mail-order affiliates than for those provided at conventional pharmacies. However, these charges could be still lower, to the benefit of the payers, if independent mail-order pharmacies were allowed to compete. The result of this process is that drug costs for health plan and other payers are greater than they would be otherwise because of the exclusionary actions of the largest PBMs.

Another feature of the payment system for pharmaceuticals supplied to insured consumers is the role of rebates through which drug companies return some of the revenues received for their drugs from pharmacies and wholesalers to PBMs and payers. In this manner, pharmaceuticals can be sold at different prices to different payers. Although the actual prices paid by pharmacies to drug companies are the same, the rebate amounts frequently differ between PBMs and payers so that sellers can reap the benefits of price discrimination. Since no rebates are paid on cash sales, those prices are the highest. Moreover, PBMs typically retain about 30% of the rebates received, and transmit about 70% to their affiliated plans (Langenfeld and Maness, 2003, p. 4).

This circuitous payment system means that the prices paid by pharmacies for their drug supplies overstate the true level of sales made to insured customers. Only with cash sales do those amounts indicate accurately the volume of pharmaceutical sales. Since cash sales provide at most one fourth of the total, reported levels of pharmaceutical prices and sales are likely to be substantially overstated.

Not only does pharmaceutical price setting differ between cash and insured sales, it also differs between branded and generic products. In the branded industry, new products are priced strategically where prices depend on the therapeutic improvement offered by the new drug. See the paper reprinted here by Lu and Comanor (Chapter 25). For drugs reflecting important therapeutic advances, particularly those indicated for acute conditions, manufacturers generally pursue a skimming strategy. They set relatively high prices at introduction but then reduce them over time as their products face increasing competition from available alternatives. In contrast, 'me too' drugs (those similar therapeutically to products already on the market but sold by a different company) often pursue a penetration strategy. In that case, sellers set a low price originally to gain market acceptance but then raise their price over time with growing consumer recognition. This process is described in their paper reprinted here (Chapter 25). See also a theoretical explanation for this pricing pattern in a paper reprinted here by

Bhattacharya and Vogt (Chapter 26). Whichever strategy is employed, the therapeutic advance embodied in a new product is the major factor affecting the price charged for a new pharmaceutical.

To determine the therapeutic value of new products, payers often employ pharmacoeconomic models through which a product's cost-effectiveness can be determined. In a paper reprinted here (Chapter 23), Hay reviews and evaluates these models. Since most pharmaceuticals are cost-effective at some price, the company's goal is generally to set the highest price at which this appraisal can be reached.

Not only does the therapeutic advance embodied in the new product affect its price, but it also affects the quantities sold, and thereby product revenues. These revenues are strongly influenced by the relevant elasticity of demand. Manning et al. (Chapter 18) find an industry elasticity of approximately –0.2. This result implies that higher prices lead generally to higher revenues, but also that competitive forces have forced average prices below monopolistic levels.

A striking feature of the branded industry is the considerable skewness in profitability across pharmaceutical products. Although a few 'blockbuster' products generate high returns, most provide much lower returns. Grabowski and Vernon (1994, p. 399) find that 60% of new pharmaceuticals do not cover average R&D costs, and only the leading 20% of introductions exceed these costs, with most of aggregate returns concentrated in the top 10%. To a great extent, industry profits result predominantly from a small number of drugs, known generally as 'blockbusters.' Large numbers of new products are introduced whose returns exceed their marginal costs but apparently not their fixed costs.

Another important factor in the pricing of branded pharmaceuticals is competition among and between patented, sole-source products. Their order of entry within a therapeutic class of drugs frequently conveys substantial advantages, which sometimes can be overcome by aggressive marketing efforts. This process is described by Ling, Berndt and Kyle in Chapter 21. See also Bond and Lean (1979).

The number of rivals in a therapeutic market is also relevant. When the number of rival products is large, firms compete and prices are lower. The presence of 'me-too' products thereby serves the important market function of imposing competitive discipline on pharmaceutical prices. The introduction of drugs similar therapeutically to those already on the market is therefore not counter-productive, as is sometimes claimed (Kessler et al., 1994, pp. 1350–53). Instead, it leads to lower prices for branded drugs through enhanced competition in addition to giving clinicians more choice in product selection.

An interesting analysis of many of these factors appears in Berndt et al., reprinted here as Chapter 30. The authors emphasize the important role played by consumption externalities in which product evaluations are strongly influenced by others' previous use. Among their important conclusions is that 'past sales have an economically significant effect on the rate of [a product's] diffusion.' As a result, while pioneering brands benefit from having a larger installed base, second entrants can also succeed by gaining more rapid rates of product diffusion.

Competition from generic rivals plays a very different role. As Scott Morton reports in a paper reprinted here (Chapter 14), the presence of lower regulatory barriers has led to the rapid entry of generic rivals following the branded product's patent expiration. Moreover, the rate of entry depends primarily on the size of the market, and also is greater with more sales made to hospitals and for drugs treating chronic conditions. Of considerable importance also is the prior experience and capabilities of the entering firms.

The impact of generic entry on branded products is more strongly found in its effects on relative quantities. For the most part, branded producers do not compete with generic rivals on price. On the contrary, prices of branded products sometimes rise following generic entry as their sellers seek to maximize revenues from customers unwilling to accept different versions of their product (Scott Morton, 2000; see also, Chapter 15 and Chapter 26). However, there are other cases where branded companies compete by offering greater rebates which limits their decline in both units sold and revenues received (Comanor and Schweitzer, 2007, p. 367). For the most part, generic producers still set lower prices than their branded rivals and acquire most sales of the molecule. These results are described by Grabowski (Chapter 13).

Similar results were reported for Sweden when reforms were enacted to require pharmacists to substitute generics for prescribed branded pharmaceuticals. See the results provided by Granlund in his paper reprinted here (Chapter 31).

Although the prices of branded pharmaceuticals are largely determined by demand considerations, primarily the therapeutic value of the product, that is not so for generic drugs where equilibrium prices are largely cost determined. While prices for both types of drugs are affected by the number of rival sellers, the economic processes leading to this result are different. The first generic seller generally sets a price that is only 10% to 20% below that charged for the branded product, but then prices decline as the number of generic sellers increase (Reiffen and Ward, 2005). With five or six generic sellers, no further price declines typically occur and a stable level is reached, which approximate marginal costs.

When the prospective sales of a generic product are limited, the number of firms intent on producing the product is also limited. In that case, prices following generic entry can exceed marginal production and distribution costs. As with many markets, the size of the market can have a major impact on both the number of rivals and the resulting prices.

The branded and generic industries differ not only in terms of their pricing policies but also in terms of supply conditions. That issue has become significant as supply shortages for some essential drugs have appeared in the generic industry, often for sterile injectibles. Although branded drugs are generally available, generic drugs may sometimes not be available at any price.

Unlike the branded industry, generic firms operate on limited profit margins as firms compete by setting the lowest possible price. Furthermore, generic product lives extend for as long as there is sufficient demand for the product. For both reasons, generic firms are frequently unwilling to bear the cost required to prevent supply disruptions, either by maintaining large inventories or constructing redundant productive capacity.

These problems are exacerbated by the structure of the generic industry. Most of these suppliers do not engage in the manufacturing side of their business but rather purchase their supplies of active pharmaceutical ingredients (APIs) from specialized suppliers often located outside the United States (Schweitzer, 2013). When manufacturing problems arise, it can be a long and difficult road to recovery, particularly for sterile injectibles.

Generic sellers are largely engaged in producing pharmaceuticals in dosage form, and then marketing and distributing their final products. This focus stands in contrast to the supply chain in the branded industry where much of the manufacturing process is done in-house. An important distinction between the two industries is that the branded industry maintains greater control over its supply chain than does the generic industry.

Branded firms frequently have redundant capacity to meet the demand for their products. They also generally hold larger inventories. While costly, branded sellers take both steps because the cost of forgone sales, were supply problems to arise, are even higher. In contrast, the smaller margins found in the generic industry make such actions prohibitively costly, and therefore there are increased prospects for supply disruptions.

Although the prices of branded pharmaceuticals may substantially exceed production costs, that does not mean that prices necessarily exceed total costs. To introduce and sell large numbers of new products, branded suppliers spend large sums on both R&D and on marketing and promotion. However, even when these outlays are accounted for, reported US industry profit rates for major pharmaceutical firms appear relatively high. In 1999, for example, the profit rate on assets for the largest branded suppliers was the highest reported of all industries at 15.4% (Reinhart, 2001, p. 183).

A substantial portion of these high returns, however, was due to the accounting convention of expensing both R&D and marketing expenditures even though they actually represent investments on which profits are earned over time (Clarkson, 1977; Reinhart, 2001). For this reason, an alternate approach towards measuring profitability is that followed by Grabowski and colleagues (Chapter 8).

Rather than looking at firm data, Grabowski et al. examine the returns earned from introducing new pharmaceuticals. Although drug companies engage in other commercial activities as well, developing, marketing and selling new products is their core business. Their sample of products includes 118 new chemical entities introduced into the United States between 1990 and 1994, which represented nearly all those introduced during these years (Chapter 8).

For each new drug in the sample, they constructed worldwide sales profiles, which were then converted to after-tax profits using industry profit margins and R&D investment data. Internal rates of return were calculated for this portfolio of new products. The authors stated their conclusion succinctly (Chapter 8): 'The IRR [internal rate of return] is 11.5% and can be compared with our cost-of-capital estimate of 11%. Hence, the industry mean performance is positive but only by a small amount.'

That conclusion is broadly consistent with one reached in an earlier government study which surveyed new chemical entities introduced between 1981 and 1983. This study reported:

> the average revenue per compound was $36 million more in NPV (net present value) than was needed to bring forth the research on the drugs introduced. [But however,] this excess would be eliminated if annual revenues per compound were reduced by 4.3 percent. (USOTA, 1993, p. 94)

Large drug companies earned rates of return on their investment generally about two or three percentage points higher than the real cost of their financial capital.

This discussion of pharmaceutical prices and quantities applies to the United States, which is the largest national market but still accounts for only just over one third of worldwide pharmaceutical sales (IMS Health, 2012). Other countries, particularly those with government administered health systems, operate differently. Frequently, those government systems act as monopsonistic buyers who negotiate prices with drug manufacturers. Although dealing with each of these systems individually is beyond the scope of this chapter, we do reprint an interesting evaluation of the British price regulation scheme (Towse, Chapter 32). What we report instead are average price and quantities that arise across the various national systems.

Such comparisons are confounded by two problems. The first is deciding what exchange rate should be used to express prices in the same currency. Market exchange rates are strongly influenced by international capital flows, which make them a poor measure of the relative prices that buyers actually pay. More applicable are 'purchasing power parity' exchange rates, which are designed to reflect buyer costs. However, those exchange rates can differ widely across commodity groups so that the appropriate rate for one group of commodities may not be applicable for another. What is required are purchasing power parity exchange rates specifically for pharmaceuticals.

Fortunately, the Organization of Economic Cooperation and Development (OECD) has calculated these exchange rates for the leading developed countries (Miller and Frech, 2004, pp. 2–30). Applying these exchange rates, these authors provide average per capita expenditures on pharmaceuticals in 1990.

Their findings are striking. When relative prices are accounted for correctly, the US is not a particularly large consumer of pharmaceuticals. In a list of 18 developed countries, the US stands in sixth place, and France and Italy spend the most per capita. Indeed, the simple average of real pharmaceutical spending per capita across countries was \$238 in 1990 as compared to the US value of \$240 (Miller and Frech, 2004, Table A-5).

Using a different metric, Danzon and Furukawa place the US even lower with regard to the quantities of pharmaceuticals actually consumed. They compare the number of standard units of pharmaceuticals consumed per capita in 2005 across eight developed countries. In this comparison, the US is the second lowest behind Canada, France, Germany, Spain, the UK and Japan (Danzon and Furukawa, 2008, Ex. 2). Overall, these findings do not indicate that US quantities are greater than those found elsewhere.

Although the quantities of pharmaceuticals consumed in the United States may not be so different from those found elsewhere on a per capita basis, the prices charged for branded drugs may be higher. International comparisons of pharmaceutical prices require the calculation of price indices. However, because consumption patterns can vary greatly between different countries, price indices used to describe average prices can also vary widely. Prices which are higher using one consumption pattern may not appear higher using another.

Seeking to untangle these issues, Danzon and colleagues compare US pharmaceutical prices with those found elsewhere (Chapter 28; Danzon and Furukawa, 2008). Their studies report that US prices are generally higher than those found elsewhere, although much depends on which bundle of goods is used for the comparison. Using US bundles, prices are not much higher in the US than found elsewhere, although they appear much higher using foreign bundles (see Chapter 28). An important factor is that US consumption is more heavily concentrated in new products. Danzon and Furukawa write that 'US per capita use is higher than in all other countries for molecules within ten years of global launch, particularly for the newest molecules within five years of global launch' (p. 224). Since new products are frequently priced higher than older ones, this factor leads to higher reported prices within the United States for branded drugs.

Pointing in the opposite direction, however, the US has more generic availability for molecules at least 12 years old than any other country. It also has a higher percentage of 'unbranded generics' which are marketed under the molecular name and where competition is driven largely by price. The relative importance of generic products in US pharmaceutical markets makes international comparisons of branded product prices less revealing.

A related issue concerns pharmaceutical prices charged in poorer countries. Comparing pharmaceutical price indices in the US with those constructed for less developed countries, one finds that prices in poorer countries are far lower than in the US and on average do not exceed marginal costs. Although the prices set for branded pharmaceuticals in the United States exceed total costs, including research and marketing costs, that is not the case in poorer countries where average prices approach average production costs. These results are described by Schweitzer and Comanor in Chapter 27.

Advertising and Promotion

Not only does the branded pharmaceutical industry spend large amounts on R&D but it also spends large sums on advertising and promoting its products. In 2007, pharmaceutical companies with sales exceeding $50 million allocated between 17% and 18% of sales on R&D but spent more than 40% on selling, general and administrative expenses (Weiss et al., 2009, p. 534). In the latter category, selling expense represents at least half of the total. In this section, we consider the implications of these substantial outlays for industry performance.

Although branded companies spend large sums on advertising and promotion, generic pharmaceutical firms spend minimal amounts for these purposes. Once they enter the market, the product's therapeutic properties are already known and the generic producer has already met the FDA's requirement for bio-equivalence. What matters to prospective buyers is the dependability of the seller to provide a high-quality product. While some selling efforts may go towards demonstrating these factors, those amounts are minimal as compared with those spent by their branded counterparts.

For a branded pharmaceutical company, intent on introducing a new product, the marketing task is substantial. Both medical professionals and payers must be informed of the drug's availability and its therapeutic usefulness. This process is modeled by Bhattacharya and Vogt (Chapter 26, this volume) who derive the optimal path of advertising outlays over a drug's life cycle. Because the impact of these expenditures is greatest when knowledge of the product is lowest, it is optimal to spend more at the time of product introduction and then reduce expenditures over time as the value of incremental knowledge declines.

The empirical evidence supports these conclusions. Advertising expenditures are highest in therapeutic areas where more new products are introduced (Leffler, 1981, p. 57) and where the product's therapeutic advance is greatest (Bond and Lean, 1979, pp. 67–8). Moreover, Caves et al. (Chapter 12, this volume, p. 40) report 'significant declines in advertising levels due to the impending and actual entry of generic drugs.' For various reasons, advertising and promotional outlays are strongly concentrated toward the early years of a product's life cycle.

In the early post-war years, advertising and promotion was heavily concentrated in 'detailing' activities. As recently as 1989, about 79% of these outlays took this form, in which company representatives reached out in person to physicians and other health care providers. The other major category was advertising in medical journals which accounted for 23% (IMS Health, 2012). No other efforts were substantial.

More recently, these proportions have shifted as 'direct to consumer' (DTC) advertising has become prominent. In 2000, DTC advertising accounted for nearly 16% of all advertising outlays while 'detailing,' including the retail value of samples offered to providers, retained its leading position at nearly 82%. However, about half of reported promotional outlays were accounted for by the value of the samples dispensed. That value is greatly over-stated because firms value the samples that are distributed by their retail values rather than their production costs. See the paper by Rosenthal et al. (2003), reprinted here as Chapter 20.

Although most products are not promoted via DTC advertising, its demand effects can be substantial where employed. Rosenthal et al. estimate the promotional elasticity of DTC advertising is approximately 0.1, indicating that a 10% increase in these outlays leads to about a 1% increase in sales. In contrast, their estimated effects of detailing on sales suggest much smaller elasticities of between 0.02 and 0.03, considerably smaller (Rosenthal et al., pp. 15–16). Apparently, where DTC advertising can be effective, its impact is much greater than promotional efforts directed at physicians.

While DTC advertising may lead to increased sales of particular pharmaceuticals, that result does not mean that its use either is or is not excessive. Spence and colleagues (Chapter 22), address the issue of whether consumers who act upon DTC ads are more or less likely to be prescribed drugs they actually need. The authors report that DTC advertising improved prescribing quality for some patients but worsened it for others. Strikingly, they suggest that the unnecessary use of the advertised products increased more often than the necessary use. It appears that when patients ask their doctor for a particular product, physicians generally comply with the request, even though not always to the patient's benefit (see Chapter 22).

Research and Development

Since the years immediately following the Second World War, the modern pharmaceutical industry has spent heavily on R&D. The leading firms used these expenditures to develop and introduce a vast array of new patented products for which high prices could be charged; and these higher price levels generated the funds needed to support expanding R&D budgets.

For many decades, the system worked as planned. Large numbers of compounds were tested in industry laboratories for their therapeutic properties (Carpenter, 2010, p. 130). Even when the 1962 Drug Amendments were passed, which led to a sharp decline in the number of new products introduced (Peltzman, 1973), the industry prospered. Indeed, the leading companies benefited from the new regulations as competition from non-efficacious products declined.

In contrast, the leading companies were negatively impacted by the Hatch–Waxman Act of 1984. Under the new law, finding new and effective drugs to replace older ones that were going off-patent became more critical. The branded industry responded by spending increasing amounts on R&D in an effort to maintain or expand the rate of new product introduction. From total industry R&D expenditures in the United States of about $7 billion in 1970 (in 2000 dollars), these outlays grew to over $30 billion by 2002, or by nearly five times over a 40-year period (Cockburn, 2004, p. 11). Furthermore, these trends have continued, and R&D outlays have approached nearly $40 billion by 2008 (CBO, 2009, p. 3).

However, the number of newly approved molecules did not increase correspondingly. From a base of 16 new molecules approved in 1970, the number reached a peak of more than 50 in 1996, but has declined since then. By 2002, the number of new molecules approved had fallen to less than 25 (Cockburn, 2004, p. 11). Moreover, the number of approvals has continued to decline (CBO, 2009, p. 2). As Munos points out (see Chapter 11), the number of new pharmaceuticals introduced has been fairly constant over a 30-year period despite industry efforts to see it increased.

Over this extended period, the contrast between the increasing volume of R&D inputs and the stable rate of new molecules is striking. A direct result of these trends has been greatly increased R&D costs for each new product introduced. DiMasi and colleagues estimated these costs at $231 million per new product introduced in 1987, a figure that includes both the cost of unsuccessful products and the opportunity costs of the funds invested in the R&D process (DiMasi et al., 2003). By 2000, these costs had risen to $803 million per introduction, or by nearly 3.5 times over only a 13-year period (DiMasi et al., 2003).

Another way of documenting this result has been a sharp decline in the productivity of pharmaceutical R&D. As Cockburn has observed in a series of papers, research productivity in the pharmaceutical industry has fallen sharply in recent years (Henderson and Cockburn, Chapter 5, this volume). However characterized, what is apparent is that the rate of new product introduction has not kept pace with the rate of expenditures designed for this purpose. A critical issue for pharmaceutical economics is how to explain this discrepancy.

A relevant factor is the process by which R&D budgets are set. Rather than linked to the expected returns of individual projects, they are largely determined by available cash flows. Scherer offers this type of model and provides evidence supporting its applicability to the R&D budgeting process (Chapter 6). As available cash expands, research-based firms have traditionally allocated increasing shares to their research efforts; while when cash flows decline, they do the opposite and restrict their outlays.

This description differs from the conventional picture of investment decision-making. That account emphasizes the likely returns from a prospective investment project, and concludes that funds are allocated to a project so long as its expected return exceeds its cost of capital. The critical factors are the prospective rates of return on individual research projects.

However, when future returns cannot be estimated because of the overwhelming uncertainty in the research process, another approach is required. What Scherer's analysis describes is an allocation process for R&D outlays which is more likely to occur. An implication of the available cash-flow picture of this budgetary process is that returns at the margin can vary widely. Projects are pursued so long as there are available funds, and returns depend on both the viability of the projects undertaken and the volume of investable funds.

Pharmaceutical research and development includes two distinct sets of activities, commonly labeled Discovery and Development (Cockburn and Henderson, Chapter 2, this volume). The former describes the scientific efforts made to discover new therapeutic agents. In the early years of the modern industry, this research was largely an empirical activity where large numbers of molecules were tested for their medicinal properties with relatively little science involved. As observed at the time, 'the research and development of new drugs [...] differs from other forms of scientific research in its unusually heavy dependence on empirical exploration and inference' (Schwartzman, 1976, p. 32).

Much changed with the advent of bio-technology, which represented a major shift in the technology of pharmaceutical research (Scriabine, 1999). The new technology has led to the enhanced prominence of biologicals, which are large molecule drugs produced by different methods from the small molecule drugs on which the industry had relied. Bio-technology offered a scientific foundation for drug Discovery which was not present before.

The increasing role of smaller companies in Discovery research is revealed in Scherer's study of the origins of 85 new medical entities approved by the Food and Drug Administration (FDA), between 2001 and 2005. Examining the patents associated with NDAs submitted to the FDA, he reports that 47% were issued to firms or non-profit entities with names different from those of the ultimate FDA approval recipient. Although some of these mismatches may have involved subtle cross-ownership ties, he concludes that the leading pharmaceutical companies rely increasingly on outsiders for the pharmaceutical innovations they eventually bring to market (Scherer, 2010, p. 552).

To be sure, the large drug companies often pursue Discovery activities in their own laboratories, sometimes concurrently with externally supported work. Cockburn and Henderson provide detailed descriptions of the internal Discovery activities pursued in ten large companies during the 1980s (Chapters 2 and 5). Among their findings is that large companies support on average about ten substantial Discovery programs per year, which are directed towards particular therapeutic objectives and which often span the entire range of pharmaceutical research.

In contrast, Development stage activities are more costly and account for about two-thirds of total R&D expenditures (Cockburn and Henderson, 2001). These activities primarily consist of the animal and human testing required by the FDA to demonstrate both the safety and efficacy of the proposed drugs. Once an agent has survived animal testing, it is subject to various phases of clinical trials. Both Phases I and II involve relatively small numbers of subjects, first to test for toxicity and then to provide a preliminary indication of efficacy. For agents that successfully pass the earlier trials, more extensive Phase III clinical trials are required.

The latter investigations employ large numbers of subjects, often at various locations, and can last for several years. Their goal is to determine the agent's efficacy for a particular indication in different populations. The FDA requires randomized testing under which neither the patient nor the treating physician knows whether a particular patient is receiving the drug being evaluated. With these detailed requirements, Phase III trials can cost more than $200 million each (DiMasi et al., 2003).

Although, originally, the major drug companies carried out most Discovery and Development activities within their own facilities, they now outsource considerable portions of these efforts. What has occurred is a large degree of vertical disintegration of the pharmaceutical R&D process. Even so, the major pharmaceutical companies have retained an essential role in the overall process. They continue to provide oversight of the FDA approval process, including preparing and maintaining final authority over the clinical testing process needed for new drug approval. This process is described by Comanor (Chapter 3).

Just as important are their interactions with smaller biotech firms. Those companies typically enjoy the advantages of a rapidly advancing scientific base, Ph.D.-intensive staffs, and an array of unexploited medical possibilities, all in sharp contrast to the growing obsolescence of the small-molecule discovery techniques on which the major companies have traditionally relied. By comparison, the major companies have the resources and expertise needed to supervise the regulatory approval process.

A further advantage of the larger firms is their access to substantial financial resources. This complements an important gap for the smaller companies where years are often spent conducting research on a single product without any income to cover their costs. As the product research period lengthens, the smaller firms increasingly need further financing.

Such complementarities offer strong incentives for collaboration. Some linkages take the form of outright mergers, although there can be difficulties in assimilating the loosely structured, basic science-oriented researchers of biotech companies with the more bureaucratic and applications-oriented laboratories of the traditional large pharmaceutical companies. More common collaborations take the form of alliances in which the major companies provide financial support for ongoing research activities in return for a licensing arrangement for whatever new drugs result from the process.

The decisions by Big Pharma companies on which biotech research to support can have a major impact on whether particular drugs are introduced. Even though there may be large numbers of similar research efforts carried on within smaller companies at any moment in time, only a relatively few receive the follow-on industry funding and support needed for large–scale testing and commercial success.

Danzon, Nicholson and Pereira (Chapter 7), studied the productivity of these alliances. For the period from 1988 through 2000, they report that R&D success probabilities are negatively correlated with the size of the relevant therapeutic category. More importantly, they find that the probability of product success in Phase II and III trials is greater for products developed in an alliance, particularly if the licensee is a large company.

Despite the changes that have marked the R&D process, the social benefits from this process remain substantial. In an important study presented here as Chapter 10, Lichtenberg estimates the effect of new drug introductions on reduced mortality. Using a benchmark estimate of $25,000 per life-year saved, he estimates a social rate of return from pharmaceutical innovation at roughly 68% per annum. That return is nearly six times Grabowski's figure for the private returns from pharmaceutical research and development.

Lichtenberg acknowledges various extenuating factors related to this estimate. The first is its sensitivity to the assumed value of an additional life-year produced. If life-years were valued instead at $10,000, the estimated social return from pharmaceutical innovation would instead be 27%. However, a second factor points in the opposite direction. Since new drugs convey many benefits beyond reduced mortality, including reduced sickness and morbidity, fewer workdays and schooldays lost, and an improved quality of life, these returns are greatly understated. Since those factors are not included in the empirical analysis, Lichtenberg concludes that the social returns from new drug development may be even greater than the 68% return he reported originally (Chapter 10).

These high returns exacerbate the social costs due to the steady decline in research productivity, and the diminished pace of pharmaceutical innovation. One reason may have been the increasing concentration of the branded, research-oriented pharmaceutical industry resulting from the ongoing merger wave (Comanor and Scherer, 2013).

That conclusion is broadly consistent with one reached by Danzon and colleagues (Chapter 1) of pharmaceutical mergers and acquisitions. Following their empirical analysis, they write:

> This evidence supports the hypothesis that mergers are frequently the response to expected excess capacity that is triggered by patent expirations and gaps in the product pipeline [...] [Furthermore] we find no evidence that mergers create positive long term value. This suggests that mergers [...] motivated to address R&D gaps through cost saving and economics of scale are unsuccessful in the long run. (Danzon et al., p. 325, Chapter 1, this volume)

What we observe is that the major branded companies have continued to fall behind their generic rivals in the number of prescriptions filled even if not in sales revenues. At some point, the current model of research-based companies could prove untenable, but we are not there yet.

Note

1. This was accomplished by recognizing the 'US Pharmacopeia and National Formulary,' a privately produced encyclopedia already in use as representing the official US government standards.

References

Blume-Kohout, M. E. and Sood, N. (2013). Market Size and Innovation: Effects of Medicare Part D on Pharmaceutical Research and Development, *Journal of Public Economics*, 97, 327–36.

Bond, R. S. and Lean, D. F. (1979). Sales, Promotion, and Products Differentiation in Two Prescription Drug Markets, *Staff Report to the FTC*, 46.

Boslaugh, S. (2008). *Encyclopedia of Epidemiology*, Sage Publications, Thousand Oaks, CA, p. 395.

Carpenter, D. (2010). *Reputation and Power: Organizational Image and Pharmaceutical Regulation at the FDA*, Princeton University Press, Princeton, NJ.

Carpenter, D. and Sin, G. (2007). Policy Tragedy and the Emergence of Regulation: The Food, Drug, and Cosmetic Act of 1938, *Studies in American Political Development*, 21(02), 149–80.

Clarkson, K. (1977). *Intangible Capital and Rates of Return: Effects of Research and Promotion on Profitability*, American Enterprise Institute for Public Policy Research.

Cockburn, I. M. (2004). The Changing Structure of the Pharmaceutical Industry, *Health Affairs*, 23(1), 10.

Cockburn, I. M. and Henderson, R. (2001). Scale and Scope in Drug Development: Unpacking the Advantages of Size in Pharmaceutical Research, *Journal of Health Economics*, 751, 1–25.

Comanor, W. S. and Scherer, F. M. (2013). Mergers and Innovation in the Pharmaceutical Industry, *Journal of Health Economics*, 32, 106–13.

Comanor, W. S. and Schweitzer, S. O. (2007). Determinants of Drug Prices and Expenditures, *Managerial and Decision Economics*, 28, 358–70.

Danzon, P. M. and Furukawa, M. F. (2008). International Prices and Availability of Pharmaceuticals in 2005, *Health Affairs*, 27(1), 221–33.

Danzon, P. M. and Pauly, M. (2002). Health Insurance and the Growth of Pharmaceutical Expenditures, *Journal of Law and Economics*, XLV, 587–613.

Davis, M., Poisal, J., Chulis, G., Zarabozo, C. and Cooper, B. (1999). Prescription Drug Coverage, Utilization, and Spending Among Medicare Beneficiaries, *Health Affairs*, 18(1), 231–43.

DiMasi, J. A., Hansen, R. W. and Grabowski, H. G. (2003). The Price of Innovation: New Estimates of Drug Development Costs. *Journal of Health Economics*, 22(2), 151–85.

Duggan, M. and Scott Morton, F. (2006). The Distortionary Effects of Government Procurement: Evidence from Medicaid Prescription Drug Purchasing, *Quarterly Journal of Economics*, 121(1), 1–29.

Esposito, D. (2006). *Copayments and the Demand for Perscription Drugs*. Routledge, Abingdon, Oxon, UK and New York, NY.

Fierce Biotech. (2013). The Biotech Market Share Report. Available at: http://www.fiercebiotech.com/special-reports/biotech-marketshare-report.
Gellad, W. F., Schneeweiss, S., Brawarsky, P., Lipsitz, S. and Hass, J. (2008). What if the Federal Government Negotiated Pharmaceutical Prices for Seniors? An Estimate of National Savings, *Journal of General Internal Medicine*, 23(9), 1435–40.
Grabowski, H. G. and Vernon, J. M. (1994). Returns to R&D on New Drug Introductions in the 1980s, *Journal of Health Economics*, 13(4), 383–406.
Gray, A. and Manasse, H. R. (2012). Shortages of Medicines: A Complex Global Challenge, *Bulletin of the World Health Organization*, 90, 158–158A.
IMS Institute for Healthcare Informatics (2011). The Use of Medicines in the United States: Review of 2010, April.
IMS Institute for Healthcare Informatics (2012). The Global Use of Medicines: Outlook Through 2016, July.
Intriligator, M. (1996). Drug Evaluations: Type I vs Type II Errors. Research Program in Pharmaceutical Economics and Policy, UCLA. May.
Karki, L. (2005). Review of FDA Law Related to Pharmaceuticals: The Hatch–Waxman Act, Regulatory Amendments and Implications for Drug Patent Enforcement, *Journal of the Patent & Trademark Office Society*. 87, 602–20.
Kessler, D., Rose, J. L., Temple, R. J., Schapiro, R. and Griffen, J. P. (1994). Therapeutic-Class Wars – Drug Promotion in a Competitive Marketplace, *New England Journal of Medicine*, 331, 1350–53.
Langenfeld, J. and Maness, R. (2003). The Cost of PBM 'Self-Dealing' Under A Medicare Prescription Drug Benefit, Unpublished Paper.
Leffler, K. B. (1981). Persuasion or Information? The Economics of Prescription Drug Advertising, *Journal of Law & Economics*, 24(1), April, 45–74.
Ma, Q. and Lu, A. Y. H. (2011). Pharmacogenetics, Pharmacogenomics, and Individualized Medicine, *Pharmacological Reviews*, 63(2), 437.
Miller, H. I. (2000). *To America's Health: A Proposal to Reform the Food and Drug Administration*, Hoover Institution Press, Stanford, CA.
Miller, R. D., Jr. and Frech, H. E. III (2004). *Healthcare Matters: Pharmaceuticals, Obesity and the Quality of Life*, American Enterprise Institute, 2–30.
Peltzman, S. (1973). An Evaluation of Consumer Protection Legislation: The 1962 Drug Amendments, *Journal of Political Economy*, 81(5), 1049–91.
Reiffen, D. E. and Ward, M. E. (2005). Generic Drug Industry Dynamics, *Review of Economics and Statistics*, 87, 37–49.
Reinhart, U. (2001). Perspectives on the Pharmaceutical Industry, *Health Affairs*, 20(5), 136–49.
Scherer, F. M. (2010). 'Pharmeceutical Innovation,' in Hall, B. and Rosenberg, N., eds, *Handbook of the Economics of Technological Industry*, North Holland, 552.
Schwartzman, D. (1976). *Innovation in the Pharmaceutical Industry*, The Johns Hopkins University Press, Baltimore, MD.
Schweitzer, S. O. (2007). *Pharmaceutical Economics and Policy*, 2nd edition, Oxford University Press, Oxford.
Schweitzer, S. O. (2013). How the US Food and Drug Administration Can Solve the Prescription Drug Shortage Problem, *American Journal of Public Health*, Public Health Policy Briefs, e1–e5.
Scott Morton, F. (2000). Barriers to Entry, Brand Advertising, and Generic Entry in the US Pharmaceutical Industry, *International Journal of Industrial Organization*, 18(7), 1085–104.
Scriabine, A. (1999). 'The Role of Biotechnology in Drug Development,' in Landau, R. et al., eds, *Pharmaceutical Innovation*, Chemical Heritage Press, 271–97.
Sorrell v. IMS Health, Inc. (2011). 131 S. Ct. 2653, 2659, 180 L. Ed. 2d 544.
Stafford, R. S. (2008). Regulating Off-Label Drug Use – Rethinking the Role of the FDA, *New England Journal of Medicine*, 358(14), 1427–29.
United States Congress, Office of Technology Assessment (USOTA) (1993). Pharmaceutical R&D: Costs, Risks and Rewards. OTA-H-522. US Government Printing Office, Washington, D.C.
United States Congressional Budget Office (CBO) (2005). Prices for Brand-Name Drugs Under Selected Federal Programs. US Government Printing Office, Washington, D.C.

United States Congressional Budget Office (CBO) (2009). Pharmaceutical R&D and the Evolving Market for Prescription Drugs. US Government Printing Office, Washington, D.C.
United States v. Caronia (2012). WL 5992141 (US Court of Appeals, 2d Cir., Dec. 3, 2012).
United States, Statistical Abstract of the United States (Stat. Abs U.S.) (2011). US Government Printing Office, Washington, D.C.
Weiss, D., Naik, P. and Weiss, R. (2009). The 'Big Pharma' Dilemma: Develop New Drugs or Promote Existing Ones? *Nature Reviews/Drug Discovery*, 8, 533.
Wiecek, A. and Mikhail, A. (2006). European Regulatory Guidelines for Biosimilars, *Nephrology Dialysis Transplantation*, 21: Suppl 5, v17–v20.

Part I
The Industry

A
The Structure of the Industry

[1]

MANAGERIAL AND DECISION ECONOMICS
Manage. Decis. Econ. **28:** 307–328 (2007)
Published online in Wiley InterScience
(www.interscience.wiley.com) DOI: 10.1002/mde.1343

Mergers and Acquisitions in the Pharmaceutical and Biotech Industries

Patricia M. Danzon[a,*], Andrew Epstein[b] and Sean Nicholson[c]

[a] *University of Pennsylvania, USA*
[b] *Yale University, USA*
[c] *Cornell University, USA*

We examine the determinants and effects of M&A activity in the pharmaceutical/ biotechnology industry using SDC data on 383 firms from 1988 to 2001. For large firms, mergers are a response to expected excess capacity due to patent expirations and gaps in a firm's product pipeline. For small firms, mergers are primarily an exit strategy in response to financial trouble (low Tobin's q, few marketed products, low cash–sales ratios). In estimating effects of mergers, we use a propensity score to control for selection based on observed characteristics. Controlling for merger propensity, large firms that merged experienced a similar change in enterprise value, sales, employees, and R&D, and had slower growth in operating profit, compared with similar firms that did not merge. Thus mergers may be a response to trouble, but they are not a solution. Copyright © 2007 John Wiley & Sons, Ltd.

INTRODUCTION

A significant body of economic research has examined the reasons for mergers and their effects—whether mergers add, destroy or merely redistribute value. Economic theory suggests several, not mutually exclusive reasons for mergers, including economies of scale and scope, acquisition of specific assets, and the market for corporate control. These general theories have difficulty explaining the fact that mergers have historically occurred in industry-specific waves. To explain these waves, several authors have suggested shocks, due to such factors as technological advances or deregulation, that are often industry specific and create excess capacity or other inefficiencies in the current configuration of resources, which leads to within-industry correlation in merger activity (for example, Jensen, 1993; Mitchell and Mulherin, 1996; Hall, 1999; Andrade and Stafford, 2004). These studies shed some light on cross-industry variation in merger activity but they do not address within-industry variation.

Assuming that mergers are intended to create value, there is no consensus on whether expectations at the time of merger are actually realized in the longer term and, if so, how this value is created. In their review of empirical evidence on mergers, Andrade *et al.* (2001) report a quasi difference-in-differences estimate of operating margin before and after merger, for merged firms versus the industry average. They conclude that 'mergers improve efficiency and that the gains to shareholders at announcement accurately reflect improved expectations of future cash flow performance. ... (But) the underlying sources of gains from mergers have not been identified.'

In this paper, we examine the determinants and effects of M&A activity in the pharmaceutical–biotechnology industry during 1988–2001. The value of M&A during this period exceeded $500

*Correspondence to: Patricia M. Danzon, Celia Moh Professor, Health Care Department, The Wharton School, University of Pennsylvania, 207 Colonial Penn Center, 3641 Locust Walk, Philadelphia, PA 19104, USA.

billion, which led to a significant increase in the 10-firm share of global sales, from 20% in 1985 to 48% in 2002. Pharmaceutical mergers are often rationalized by claims of economies of scale and scope in R&D and marketing. The pharmaceutical industry is research-intensive, with an average R&D to sales ratio of 18%, compared to 4% for US manufacturing industry overall (Pharmaceutical Researchers and Manufacturers of America, 2003). However, despite rising R&D spending, the number of compounds approved per year by the Food and Drug Administration (FDA) has deteriorated since 1996, and the share of these compounds originated by large firms has decreased. This evidence of apparently declining R&D productivity, particularly for large firms, casts doubt on the effectiveness of mergers and the economies of scale hypothesis more generally.

Two recent event studies of pharmaceutical mergers found mixed evidence of abnormal stock returns at the time of merger announcement. Ravenscraft and Long (2000) performed an event study of 65 pharmaceutical mergers between 1985 and 1996. They found abnormal stock returns around the announcement date of 13.3% for the target firm, −2.1% for the bidding firm, but effects not significantly different from zero for the combined firm. For large horizontal mergers and cross-border mergers, however, the combined abnormal returns were positive.[1] Ravenscraft and Long show that target firms experienced negative cumulative stock return in the 18 months prior to merger, compared to an index of non-merging pharmaceutical firms; however, they do not analyze the firm-specific determinants of mergers nor whether the positive expectations at announcement are actually realized in the longer term and, if so, how shareholder value is created.

Higgins and Rodriguez (2005) focus on mergers as a means to outsource R&D in a sample of about 60 public firms that formed at least one strategic alliance between 1994 and 2001. In this selected sample, they find that firms with a high 'desperation index' (expected years of patent life, including marketed and pipeline products) were more likely to acquire another firm. Among 160 acquisitions that were selected as being R&D-related, they find positive announcement period abnormal returns to both the acquirer (3.9%) and to the target firm (16.0%), and that these returns are positively correlated with prior alliances between the parties. Higgins and Rodriguez also find that 71% of acquirers maintained or improved their product pipelines in the first year post-merger. They conclude that pre-merger alliances are a means of reducing information asymmetries and hence increasing the value of M&A undertaken to outsource R&D. While this analysis provides insights for a selected subset of pharma–biotech mergers, it does not address the longer term effects of these mergers, the broader set of mergers that are not included in the study, and does not control firm characteristics that affect the probability of merging.

We study a more comprehensive sample of pharma–biotech mergers and use a two-part estimation strategy. The first stage tests various hypothesized determinants of M&A activity. The second stage measures the effects of merger on firm performance, using a propensity score to control for probability that each firm would merge. Specifically, our sample includes 383 firms in the pharma–biotech industry and 165 'transforming mergers', defined as transactions that are sufficiently large that post-merger integration will require reorganization and potentially have an observable impact on accounting measures of performance. The analysis distinguishes between small biotech firms and large pharmaceutical firms, because small firms, which account for almost half the firms in our sample, face very different production and cost functions.

Our analysis is designed to test several hypotheses to explain mergers based on existing literature (for example, Jensen, 1986; Holmstrom and Kaplan, 2001), including: economies of scale or scope; specific assets or capacities (for example, foreign subsidiaries) that can be acquired more efficiently than through internal growth; imperfect agency controls that permit acquisitions by managers with excess cash; and the market for corporate control, in which acquisition is a mechanism to transfer assets to more efficient uses and/or management.

We also test a variant of the excess capacity theory of mergers as applied to large pharmaceutical firms. Previous literature has suggested that excess capacity is a rationale for merger to restructure assets in industries that experience shocks due to technological change or deregulation (Jensen, 1993; Mitchell and Mulherin, 1996; Hall, 1999; Andrade and Stafford, 2004). We argue that an analogous but firm-specific capacity-adjustment motive for merging occurs when a pharmaceutical firm experiences patent expirations and gaps in its pipeline of new drugs that make

DOI: 10.1002/mde

current levels of human and physical capital potentially excessive. Essentially, a fully-integrated pharmaceutical firm has two production activities. The first is R&D, which uses labor, capital, and various technologies to discover new compounds and obtain regulatory approval.[2] R&D investment by itself generates no revenue, and is characterized by a high degree of *ex ante* uncertainty regarding the ultimate scientific and market potential of new compounds. The second activity is production, marketing and sales, for which approved compounds, obtained from internal R&D, in-licensing or acquisition, are an essential input. Patent protection on new drugs on average lasts for roughly 12 years after market approval. Once the patent expires, in the US generic competitors usually rapidly erode the originator firm's sales.[3] Since a few blockbuster drugs often account for 50% or more of a firm's revenues, patent expiration on one or more of these compounds can decimate the firm's revenues within a few months, unless the firm can replace the patent-expired compounds with new compounds. Thus, if a firm is faced with patent expirations and has failed to generate or in-license new compounds to replace them, its investment in specialized labor and capital in sales and marketing becomes unproductive. Since large firms finance their R&D almost exclusively from current earnings (Vernon, 2005), patent expirations may also disrupt the funding of R&D.

For an integrated pharmaceutical company that faces patent expirations and gaps in its pipeline, merging with a firm that has pipeline drugs but lacks adequate marketing and sales capacity to optimally launch these drugs may create value.[4] Merger may also permit elimination of duplicative functions, thereby offering cost savings in the short term to offset the negative effect of declining revenues on net profits and generating economies of scale in the longer run. Although a pharmaceutical firm that faces excess capacity due to lack of compounds could reduce staff and sell assets without merging, this may entail loss of quasi-rents on investments in firm-specific human and physical capital, if this capital has specialized skills and the compound shortfall is expected to be transitory (Oi, 1962). The loss of quasi-rents may be reduced if the cuts are made in the context of a merger that brings in new compounds and facilitates restructuring that permits the elimination of duplicative functions and selection of the best people for those jobs remain.[5]

Our analysis of determinants of M&A uses a multinomial logit to distinguish being an acquirer, a target or involved in a pooling of equals. For large pharmaceutical firms, we find evidence supporting the hypothesis that mergers are, in part, a response to expectations of excess capacity that will decrease future productivity. Large firms with a relatively low Tobin's q (the ratio of the market to book value of a firm's assets), and thus firms with a low expected growth rate of cash flows, are more likely to acquire other firms. Andrade and Stafford (2004), on the other hand, find that over the 1970–1994 period firms (from the pharma–biotech as well as other industries) with a high Tobin's q were more likely to undertake both mergers and non-merger investment. Controlling for the age of a firm's portfolio of drugs, which is a more direct measure of expected excess capacity than the Tobin's q, the coefficient on the 'drug age' variable is positive and significant and the Tobin's q coefficient remains negative but is insignificant. This is consistent with the hypothesis that the anticipation of patent expirations and the associated shock to revenues and excess labor capacity is a significant motive for acquisitions. Relatively large firms, as measured by market value, are more likely to acquire another firm, be acquired, and be involved in a pooling merger. This suggests that if achieving economies of scale is a rationale for merging, firms perceive that optimum scale exceeds the mean size in our large-firm sample. Firms that experienced a relatively large increase in operating expenses in the prior three years were more likely to be involved in a pooling merger, suggesting that merging may be a useful context for eliminating excess costs and/or that mergers transfer assets to firms with (more) competent management.[6]

For relatively small firms (firms with at least $20 million in sales for at least one year between 1988 and 2000 but with an enterprise value always less than $1 billion), our results suggest that firms that are financially weak are at risk of being acquired. Financially strong firms (as measured by relatively high Tobin's q, number of marketed drugs and high ratio of cash to sales) are more likely not to engage in M&A at all.

Our analysis of post-merger performance tests for effects on growth in inputs (employment and R&D investment) and accounting performance (growth in sales, operating profit and market value) for up to four years after the event.

DOI: 10.1002/mde

We use accounting data rather than an event study to examine post-merger performance for two reasons. First, almost three-quarters of the mergers in our sample involve a private firm or a subsidiary of a public firm. Analysis based on accounting data can include these mergers, whereas an event study would be restricted to transactions between public firms, or subsidiaries of public firms that report a separate stock price. Second, we are interested in measuring long term performance effects of mergers, and identifying the factors that contribute to performance changes, if any, whereas event studies at best capture expectations of future net revenue growth, measured at the time of merger announcement.

The results strongly confirm the importance of controlling for pre-merger firm characteristics. If we assume mergers are exogenous, we would conclude that merged firms have low growth rates of sales and R&D expenditures in the first year following a merger, relative to firms that do not merge. However, firms with a high merger propensity experience low growth of sales, employees, and R&D expenditures in the subsequent one, two, and three years, regardless of whether they actually merge. Controlling for the merger propensity, mergers have very little effect on a firm's subsequent growth in sales, employees, R&D expenditures, and enterprise value for large firms. For a large firm with the mean merger propensity, however, a merger is predicted to reduce operating profit by 52.3% in the third year following a merger relative to an otherwise similar firm that did not merge. This suggests that post-merger integration may absorb more resources and managerial effort than anticipated by most managers.

In the small firm sample, firms with a high merger propensity experienced relatively low growth in employees and R&D regardless of whether they merged, consistent with the earlier finding that strong firms tend not to engage in M&A. Merger was not an effective growth strategy for a firm with the mean propensity of merging. For such a firm, we predict that a merger would result in a 29% reduction in R&D in the first full year following a merger relative to an otherwise similar firm that did not merge. This suggests that resources may be diverted from R&D immediately post-merger. Conversely, for firms with a very high merger propensity, merging is predicted to increase employees and R&D investments by 21 and 30%, respectively, in the first full year following a merger, compared to similar firms that did not merge. Thus, small firms that faced the greatest distress appeared to increase inputs following a merger, possibly because the merger provided access to resources that these small firms lacked. There is no evidence of improved performance, however, at least by the measures and time frame included in this study.

BACKGROUND AND RELATED RESEARCH

Previous studies of pharmaceutical mergers by Ravenscraft and Long (2000) and Higgins and Rodriguez (2006) were described earlier. Both analyze a more limited sample of mergers and use an event study of abnormal returns to measure expected merger impact at the time of merger announcement, rather than measuring long term performance controlling for selection bias. Moreover, neither study tests alternative hypotheses of determinants of mergers.

Most similar to our study is Hall's (1999) analysis of the determinants of mergers and the real effects of mergers for a large, multi-industry sample of manufacturing firms between 1957 and 1995, using a propensity score to control for pre-merger characteristics when estimating the effects of merger. She uses a Cox proportional hazards model, treating merger, going private and bankruptcy as competing methods of exit, and separate logit models for probability of acquiring or being acquired. She finds that in general firms that were acquired by other public firms do not differ significantly from firms that remained independent. For the sample as a whole, there is no significant effect of merger on R&D investment, but for firms with the highest propensity to merge, those that did merge experienced more rapid post-merger growth in R&D than those that did not merge.[7] By contrast, in previous work on an earlier sample without controlling for pre-merger characteristics (propensity to merge), Hall (1988) found little effect of mergers on R&D, which she interpreted as evidence against economies of scale in R&D. Like many other industries, the pharmaceutical industry experienced a high rate of M&A activity in the 1980s and 1990s. Only three of the top 10 US companies have not been involved in a major horizontal acquisition during the last 15 years. However, Hall (1999) cites the pharmaceutical industry as an exception to the norm of restructuring driven by excess capacity and low market value-to-book value ratios (Tobin's *q*), but does not offer other reasons for pharmaceutical mergers.

Several studies have addressed the issue of self-selection and endogeneity of the decision to change corporate structure when measuring the effects of such changes. Similar to Hall (1999), Dranove and Lindrooth (2003) use a propensity score approach to control for self-selection when estimating the effects of hospital mergers. In a multi-industry study of returns to firm diversification, Campa and Kedia (2002) use instrumental variables, firm fixed effects and a Heckman selection correction as alternative econometric techniques to control for endogeneity of the decision to diversify. They show that controlling for self-selection reduces estimates of the discount on diversified firms that are found in studies that fail to control for selection. Similarly, Villalonga (2004) finds that using a propensity score to control for *ex ante* firm characteristics eliminates evidence of a diversification discount.

Our study contributes to the evidence on determinants of mergers by testing several competing hypotheses to explain a broad sample of pharmaceutical and biotechnology mergers. We also restate the excess capacity hypothesis for the context of large pharmaceutical firms and find consistent supporting evidence. We estimate the effects of mergers on several measures of inputs and financial performance over a three-year period post merger, controlling for *ex ante* observable characteristics using a propensity score. We find no evidence that merger improves firm performance but we do show that failure to control for *ex ante* conditions leads to overestimates of the negative effects of mergers.

EVIDENCE AND HYPOTHESES FOR PHARMACEUTICAL MERGERS

Table 1 reports the number of unique transforming mergers by year between 1998 and 2000 for our sample of biotech and pharmaceutical firms.[8] There were a total of 165 transforming mergers, defined as mergers of $500 million or more, or transactions that represent 20% or more of a firm's pre-merger enterprise value.[9] These acquisitions accounted for over $500 billion dollars (in 1999 dollars). The number of transforming mergers and the market value of the mergers increased throughout the 1990s. Six percent of firms were

Table 1. Merger and Acquisition Activity by Year

Year	Number of firms in sample	Number of unique transforming mergers	percent of firms involved in transforming merger (%)	Total market value of mergers ($ million)	Merger value as a percent of industry's market value (%)	Mean merger value as percent of acquiring firm's value (%)	Mean merger value as percent of target firm's value (%)
1988	121	3	2.5	1309	0.6	33.2	n/a
1989	125	12	7.2	27971	11.8	44.7	121.0
1990	134	9	5.2	15843	5.1	28.8	60.6
1991	190	6	4.2	1924	0.4	16.7	112.0
1992	196	3	2.6	1325	0.2	32.5	92.2
1993	212	5	1.9	8385	1.2	16.7	n/a
1994	216	18	9.7	37174	5.9	22.8	110.0
1995	243	12	6.2	36732	5.2	19.4	n/a
1996	267	13	5.2	36714	4.0	29.4	88.4
1997	286	16	5.2	20492	1.7	35.7	54.0
1998	288	21	8.3	67741	4.5	27.3	79.1
1999	302	25	9.6	157708	7.7	38.7	118.0
2000	228	22	10.8	100750	5.0	37.2	124.0
Total/average		165	6.5	514068	4.4	29.1	96.9

Note: We define a transforming merger as one where the price exceeded $500 million or represented at least 20% of the buying and/or selling firm's market value. If a merger involves two firms in the sample, we record it in this table as a single unique merger, but in the regression analysis as a merger for both firms. The market value of a firm is defined as the market value of its equity plus the book value of its long-term debt. 'n/a', or not available, indicates the data are missing. The number of firms involved in transforming merger can differ from the number of unique mergers if two firms from the sample were involved in a merger and/or if a single firm was involved in multiple mergers in a particular year.

DOI: 10.1002/mde

involved in a merger in a year, on average, and the value of the acquisition represented 29% of the acquirer's market value.

Several standard economic hypotheses are relevant to understanding the pharmaceutical–biotech merger experience. Pharmaceutical acquisitions of biotech companies are consistent with an asset-specific motive, as are cross-national acquisitions, assuming that it is cheaper, quicker and more effective to buy a local company with established connections than to build a foreign subsidiary. The horizontal mergers between large pharmaceutical companies are often rationalized by economies of scale and scope but the validity of these claims remains questionable, given the growing share of new compounds produced by smaller companies and the recent relatively high valuations of these smaller firms compared to larger pharmaceutical companies. The market power hypothesis is implausible, given the low overall level of concentration in this industry; although concentration is higher at the therapeutic category level (e.g. cardiovascular), the US and European Union competition authorities frequently require divestiture of compounds in therapeutic areas where the merger might significantly lessen competition. Thus, these theories seem inadequate to explain the horizontal mergers between large pharmaceutical firms.

An alternative hypothesis to explain these larger pharmaceutical mergers is the threat of excess capacity due to patent expirations and gaps in the firm's pipeline of compounds, which makes current levels of human and physical capital potentially excessive. This hypothesis is analogous to the excess capacity hypothesis proposed by Hall (1999, citing Blair, Shary and others), except that the causes of excess capacity in the pharmaceutical industry are firm-specific and reflect the atypically critical role of patents in defining product lifecycles and particularly end of economic life for pharmaceutical products. Hall argues that firms in the 1980s engaged in various forms of restructuring as a response to finding their existing capital stock excessive relative to the returns it could generate, as measured by values of Tobin's q less than one. The precipitating factors for the industries studied by Hall—increased foreign competition and high real interest rates—cannot explain pharmaceutical mergers.

Excess capacity due to looming patent expirations is less relevant for small biotech firms, which typically specialize in R&D devoted to either drug discovery or discovery-related technologies that may be of value to larger firms. The small firms raise capital through external offerings of private or public equity or alliances with larger companies, since they often have no products to generate retained earnings. For those firms that experience shocks that undermine their ability to raise cash, selling the firm and its technologies may be an attractive exit strategy for the seller and an efficient growth strategy for the acquirer. By the mid 1990s, the more mature biotech firms no longer specialized in discovery but had become fully integrated, manufacturing and marketing their own products, hence they faced the same pipeline issues as large pharmaceutical companies.

DATA

Our analysis draws on a number of different data sets. We define an initial universe of pharmaceutical and biotech firms as any company in the Standard & Poor's Compustat or Global Vantage databases with a primary biotechnology or pharmaceutical SIC code (2834,2835, or 2836). We then added firms listed in the Merrill Lynch Pharma Industry Report, which tracks the largest pharmaceutical and biotech firms, in order to include pharmaceutical divisions of conglomerate companies where the company's primary SIC code is outside of the pharmaceutical and biotech industries.[10] After removing firms with missing financial information, we were left with a universe of 896 pharmaceutical and biotech firms.

To limit our sample to firms with significant economic value, we excluded firms that never had net sales of at least S20 million (1999 dollars) in any year during the sample period and never had an enterprise value of at least $1 billion. This restriction reduced our universe of firms to 383. We then split these firms into two sub-samples. 'Large' firms are those that reached the $1 billion enterprise value threshold ($n = 213$) in at least one year during our study period, whereas 'small' firms had sales of at least $20 million in at least one year but never had an enterprise value of $1 billion or more ($n = 170$). Financial data are from the Standard & Poor's Compustat Industrial files and GlobalVantage Industrial/Commercial files for 1985–2001.[11] Information on the number of drugs a firm is selling and the year the drugs were

DOI: 10.1002/mde

Table 2. Sample Means and Standard Deviations

	Large-firm sample ($n = 1591$ firm years)		Small-firm sample ($n = 1492$ firm years)	
	Mean	Standard deviation	Mean	Standard deviation
Tobin's q, top-coded at 20	3.17	2.60	2.88	2.82
Indicator for Tobin's $q > 20$	0.006	0.075	0.014	0.118
Number of marketed drugs	3.53	7.35	0.082	0.442
Indicator for no marketed drugs	0.560	0.497	0.951	0.216
Percent of drugs launched 9–14 years ago	13.3	24.4	1.08	9.95
log(enterprise value), $millions	7.35	1.92	4.48	1.21
Foreign firm indicator	0.362	0.481	0.209	0.407
Ratio of cash to sales	3.11	8.46	2.68	7.65
Percent change in sales, $t-3$ to $t-1$	25.7	49.4	25.1	60.6
Indicator: sales data missing	0.151	0.359	0.212	0.409
Percent change in operating expenses, $t-3$ to $t-1$	25.3	36.6	24.4	44.0
Indicator: operating expenses missing	0.155	0.362	0.199	0.399

Notes: Large firms had an enterprise value (market value of equity plus book value of debt) exceeding $1 billion at least once during the sample period. Small firms had sales of at least $20 million at least once during the sample period but never had an enterprise value exceeding $1 billion.

approved come from five sources: the Food and Drug Administration (FDA), the First DataBank National Drug Data File, the Electronic Product Catalog, the Lehman Brother's Pipeline reports, and Chemdex. Sample means and standard deviation are reported in Table 2, separately for the large-firm and small-firm sub-samples.

We extracted merger transactions data for 1988–2001 from the Securities and Data Corp.'s (SDC) Worldwide Mergers and Acquisitions database. We use information from the SDC database to classify the role that a firm played in a transforming event as one of the following: (1) acquirer: the firm purchased part or all of another firm; (2) target: the firm sold a substantial portion or all of itself to another firm; or (3) partner in a pooling merger: the firm pooled its assets with another firm or merged with another firm of approximately equal size.[12] Because financial data are collected by fiscal year and fiscal years sometimes differ from calendar years, we linked the transaction to the firm's fiscal year based on the transaction announcement date and the firm's fiscal year calendar.

We restrict our formal analysis to 'transforming' mergers—transactions that are sufficiently large that post-merger integration will require reorganization of a firm's research, development, marketing and/or sales processes and potentially have an observable impact on accounting measures of performance. We consider a transaction to be transforming if the transaction value was $500 million or more, or if the transaction value represents 20% or more of a firm's pre-merger enterprise value (the value of the firm at the conclusion of the prior fiscal year). In the handful of cases where firms engaged in multiple transforming mergers in the same fiscal year, we recorded the largest transaction only. Of the 202 transforming mergers, 97 were classified as acquisitions, 59 as targets, and 46 as pooling.

Some mergers are recorded as a transforming event for both the seller and the buyer if both firms are in our sample. In a few cases a transaction was not recorded as a transforming merger for the buyer because the transaction represented less than 20% of its enterprise value, but was recorded as transforming event for the seller because it represented more than 20% of its enterprise value. In other cases, it was a transforming event for the buyer but the seller is simply not in our database, because it is either a privately held (usually small) firm or a foreign firm that in not traded in the US and not listed in Global Vantage. This underscores our assumption that an event is 'transforming' with respect to a specific participant; what is transforming to the seller may not necessarily be transforming to the buyer. Thus in our empirical analysis the number of acquirer and target observations is not identical.

DOI: 10.1002/mde

Most prior studies of M&A in other industries have focused on outright acquisitions that result in the exit of the target firm. However, outright acquisition is one extreme variant of the range of pharmaceutical-biotech and biotech-biotech relationships, including purchase of a major equity stake (e.g. Roche-Genentech), product-specific drug development alliances and/or marketing alliances. This continuum of activity makes the definition of a merger/acquisition somewhat arbitrary. Our definition of transforming mergers excludes major product licensing deals that were potentially transforming for one of the partners, such as Millenium's portfolio deals with Bayer and Monsanto.[13]

METHODS

Two-stage Model

Our analysis proceeds in two stages. To analyze the determinants of a firm's decision to engage in a transforming merger in each year between 1988 and 2001, we estimate a multinomial logit model with four possible outcomes: the firm acquires another firm in a transforming merger, is acquired by another firm, is involved in a pooling merger, or does not undertake any merger activity. In the second stage we examine the effects of these transforming mergers on several measures of firm investment and performance, using a propensity score to control for *ex ante* observable firm characteristics. Estimating the effect of mergers simply by comparing post-merger performance of merged firms to an industry mean for non-merged firms leads to biased estimates if the decision to engage in acquisition is related to expected future performance, as confirmed by our first-stage results. In particular, if firms that anticipate poor earnings growth, due to patent expirations or other pipeline shocks, are more likely to merge than firms with strong growth prospects, then the subsequent performance of the merged firms may be inferior to that of the non-merged firms, but still better than it would have been in the absence of merger.

Determinants of Merger

The unit of observation for the first stage analysis is a firm-year and the sample size is 3083 firm-years, of which 1591 are in the large-firm sample and 1492 are in the small-firm sample. We model the probability that a firm will engage in each of the three types of merger activity or not be involved in any merger activity in year t as a function of firm characteristics in years $t-3$, $t-2$, and $t-1$.[14] Our explanatory variables are selected to test a number of hypotheses regarding reasons for merger, as follows:

Excess Capacity due to Pipeline Gaps. The first hypothesis is that for large integrated pharmaceutical/biotech firms, mergers are motivated by the expectation of a gap in the product pipeline. Such gaps cause a decline in the expected growth of future revenue and create expected excess capacity in the firm's marketing, sales, and manufacturing departments. The excess capacity motivation for mergers should be less relevant for small firms that have yet to invest in large sales, marketing, and manufacturing capabilities whose productivity requires a steady stream of compounds to sell.

We use four variables to measure a firm's expected excess capacity: Tobin's q, the lagged percent change in sales, and the percentage of a firm's marketed drugs that are old and therefore likely to lose patent protection in the near future. Tobin's q is the ratio of the market value (the sum of book value of long-term debt and market value of equity) to the book value of a firm's assets at the end of a fiscal year.[15] The market value of a firm's equity will be a function of its current and expected future cash flows, while the book value of assets is a contemporaneous measure. Since the balance sheet records the book value of physical assets, whereas most of a pharmaceutical–biotech firm's assets are associated with patents and other intangible capital, Tobin's q is likely to be very sensitive to fluctuations in the value of this intangible capital. Specifically, a firm with large expected growth opportunities due to a promising pipeline of products will have a large Tobin's q. Conversely, a firm that will soon lose patent protection on key products and/or has few promising products in late-stage clinical trials will have lower expected future cash flows and a lower Tobin's q. The excess capacity hypothesis predicts that acquisitions and pooling mergers are negatively related to (lagged) Tobin's q.

On the other hand, firms with a high Tobin's q should be able to finance an acquisition relatively easily due to their relatively high stock price. If the financing effect of an abnormally high share value

DOI: 10.1002/mde

is important to the timing of acquisitions, we expect Tobin's q to be positively associated with being an acquirer. Thus, since Tobin's q may reflect both excess capacity effects and financing effects, the net effect for acquirers (and possibly pooling) will be negative if the excess capacity effect dominates the financing effect. Tobin's q is predicted to be negatively associated with being a target if firms tend to be acquired when the market undervalues them relative to some subjective estimates.

We also include the percentage change in sales between year $t-3$ and year $t-1$ since a relatively slow sales growth rate suggests aging of the product portfolio and hence that the productivity of quasi-fixed factors is or soon will be declining. Sales grew by 25%, on average, over a two-year period for both the large and small firms (Table 2), but with considerable variation across firms, as indicated by the high standard deviations. The excess capacity motivation for mergers predicts that acquisitions will be negative related to lagged sales growth.

Our most direct measure of expected excess capacity is the percentage of a firm's drugs that were approved by the FDA between nine and 14 years previously, which is a proxy for the percent of the firm's product portfolio that is approaching patent expiration. Although the normal patent term for drugs marketed during our analysis period was 17–20 years, years of sales under patent protection is usually 9–14, because many years of patent life are typically lost due to clinical trials and regulatory approval.[16] For large firms, 13% of their drugs had been approved between nine and 14 years ago (Table 2), and as before the standard deviation is almost twice as large as the mean. Table 2 indicates that for firms in the large-firm sample the mean number of marketed drugs is only 3.5, with 56% of firm years reporting no marketed drugs. This count reflects only new chemical entities (excluding reformulations, combinations, etc.) and assigns each product to a single firm, whereas in fact reformulations are numerous and many products are shared through licensing agreements. Small firms were marketing an approved drug in only 5% of the firm years, although they may be generating revenue through out-licensed products or technologies and/or services performed for other firms. Thus a firm may have revenues and a high market value despite no reported approved drugs. The excess capacity motivation for mergers predicts that acquisitions will be positively related to the percent of a firm's drugs approved 9–14 years ago. Both the sales and product portfolio measures are less inclusive than Tobin's q because they do not reflect the future value of pipeline products, licensed products and other revenue sources.

Finally, we include the percentage change in operating expenses between years $t-3$ and $t-1$. Under the excess capacity hypothesis, a firm that anticipates patent expirations or experiences a pipeline shock may respond initially by reducing costs, in order to maintain net revenue growth (John *et al.*, 1992). If this strategy is exhausted before the firm's pipeline produces new products, the firm may consider an acquisition as a means to obtain further expense reductions. If so, pharmaceutical firms with relatively low lagged expense growth rates would be more likely to acquire another firm or engage in a pooling merger.

Economies of Scale. If achieving economies of scale is a significant motive for merger in the pharmaceutical/biotech industry, smaller firms are expected to be more active as acquirers than larger firms that are operating at the minimum efficient scale. We measure a firm's size by the logarithm of its enterprise value and by the number of approved drugs that it markets.

Note that the excess capacity and economies of scale motives for mergers are not mutually exclusive and ideally they should be complementary. That is, if a firm faced with pipeline gaps were to engage in acquisition in order to achieve short run cost savings, this would be an extremely shortsighted strategy if in the long run the post-merger scale of operations were less efficient than the pre-merger scale.

The Market for Corporate Control. Another function of M&A is to transfer assets from ineffective to effective managers. A low value of Tobin's q could indicate that a firm's value is below its potential value. This would predict that firms with a low Tobin's q are more likely to be targets. As an alternative measure of managerial performance we include the percentage change in operating expenses and sales, respectively, between year $t-3$ and year $t-1$. According to the 'corporate control' hypothesis, firms with relatively high lagged operating expense growth rates and relatively low sales growth rates will be more likely to

DOI: 10.1002/mde

be acquired. As discussed above, the excess capacity hypothesis predicts that firms with relatively low lagged expense growth rates would be more likely to acquire another firm or merge through pooling. The mean two-year change in operating expenses is about 25% in both samples, approximately equal to the percentage change in sales (Table 2).

Specific Asset Acquisition. Another explanation for mergers is they are the most sensible way for firms to acquire specific assets. For example, a foreign pharmaceutical firm that wants to establish a presence in the US market may acquire a US firm that already has an established sales force and relationships with customers and with the FDA. We include an indicator variable for foreign firms in order to test the hypothesis that foreign-domiciled firms are more likely to merge to improve their access to the US market. One-third of the large firms and one-fifth of the small firms are foreign (Table 2). However, this is far from the universe of foreign pharmaceutical and biotech firms, because many are not listed in our data sets.

Financing/Agency Issues. Some have argued that mergers occur when managers have aspirations to run a larger company, they have considerable cash, and agency controls are imperfect. We include a variable measuring the ratio of cash to sales. A high ratio of cash to sales would be positively related to acquisitions if either imperfect agency concerns are significant or availability of financing is a significant constraint on mergers that are undertaken for other reasons.

Effects of Mergers

In the second stage we examine the effect of transforming mergers on several measures of firm performance between 1989 and 2000:[17] the annual percentage change in sales, operating profit, and enterprise value.[18] To shed light on mechanisms whereby mergers may affect value, we also examine the effects on annual percentage change in employees and R&D investment. Because post-merger integration takes time and results may not be evident immediately, we examine the impact of a merger in year t on the change in outcomes from $t+1$ to $t+2$, $t+2$ to $t+3$, and $t+3$ to $t+4$. Examining actual changes in a firm's financial and operating performance following a merger, rather than abnormal returns in stock prices around the merger announcement date, provides insights into the effects that were actually realized in longer term performance, while evidence on inputs provides evidence on the mechanism for any change in performance.

The hypotheses regarding motivations for merger imply related predictions for effects of merger. Under the excess capacity hypothesis, mergers are expected to facilitate restructuring and cost reductions. This would predict that employees (and possibly R&D) should grow less at firms that merged than at firms that did not merge and, assuming that the strategy is successful, operating profit should grow more rapidly than would have been predicted based on the acquiring firm's pre-merger condition. Similarly, if mergers are a means of achieving economies of scale or scope, merged firms should experience relatively slow growth in employees and/or R&D, and improved operating profit. Thus empirically the predicted outcomes of the excess capacity and economies of scale hypotheses are similar, which is not surprising because, as noted earlier, these two motives for mergers are not mutually exclusive and ideally should be complementary; that is, a merger could yield both short and long run cost savings if the post-merger scale of operations is more efficient than the pre-merger scale. As discussed earlier, the first stage estimates may enable us to distinguish between these hypotheses: in particular, if Tobin's q is inversely related to the probability of acquisition, this is consistent with the excess capacity motive but not with simple economies of scale. Both hypotheses would also be consistent with a relatively large growth in sales due to increased productivity of the combined sales forces and/or acquisition of new compounds for the sales force to market. Hall (1999) suggests that merger may actually reduce R&D, due to short-term management distraction and because the funds used to finance an acquisition may be diverted from R&D. This hypothesis predicts that R&D growth will be relatively low for firms that merge. However, this hypothesis is empirically indistinguishable from the economies of scale hypothesis.

Both the specific asset acquisition hypothesis and the market for corporate control predict that merged firms should experience relatively rapid growth of sales and/or operating profit. These two hypotheses are thus indistinguishable at the second stage but not at the first stage.

DOI: 10.1002/mde

Note that if firms that merge experience a relatively large (small) subsequent increase in enterprise value, this would imply that the market underestimates (overestimates) the impact of mergers on performance. However, such evidence cannot distinguish whether mergers actually changed profitability or merely changed profitability relative to the expectations at the time of the merger announcement, nor the means by which profitability was changed.

Controlling for Selection. Our goal is to estimate the effect of a merger on various measures of post-merger performance and inputs. Specifically, let Y_{i1} be the percentage change from year $t+1$ to year $t+2$ for one of the five variables of interest if firm i participated in a transforming merger in year t, and let Y_{i0} be the percentage change if the firm did not merge in year t. The effect of merger (treatment effect) for firms that merge is

$$E(Y_{i1}|M_{it}=1)-E(Y_{i0}|M_{it}=0), \quad (1)$$

where $M_{it}=1$ if firm i merged in year t. Since we only observe Y_{i0} for firms that do not merge, the estimated treatment effect from Equation (1) will be biased if Y_{i0} differs systematically for firms that do and do not merge. For example, if firms that anticipate poor earnings growth due to upcoming patent expirations are more likely to merge than firms with strong growth prospects, then the subsequent performance of the merged firms may be inferior to that of the non-merged firms even if there were no mergers. Failure to account for this type of selection would bias downward the estimated effect of a merger on the subsequent change in sales and operating profit. The descriptive data in Table 3 strongly suggest significant differences in observed characteristics between firms that were involved in M&A and those that were not.

Our analysis of effects of mergers controls for selection based on observed characteristics using a propensity score method to identify firms that are expected to have similar outcomes regardless of

Table 3. Differences in the Characteristics of Merging and Non-merging Firms

Panel A: Large-firm sample ($n=1049$ firm years)

	Mean for firms that merged	Mean for firms that did not merge	t-statistic for difference in means
Tobin's q, top-coded at 20	2.62	2.92	1.24
Indicator for Tobin's $q>20$	0.00	0.0062	3.01**
Number of marketed drugs	9.72	2.29	4.94**
Indicator: no marketed drugs	0.278	0.586	7.49**
Percent of drugs launched 9–14 years ago	23.4	10.3	3.63**
log(enterprise value), $ millions	8.60	6.82	5.49**
Foreign firm indicator	0.391	0.359	0.71
Ratio of cash to sales	1.36	3.34	3.56**
Change in sales, $t-3$ to $t-1$	23.7	24.2	0.08
Indicator: sales data missing	0.053	0.161	4.97**
Change in operating expenses, $t-3$ to $t-1$	23.5	24.6	0.23
Indicator: operating expenses missing	0.068	0.163	4.00**

Panel B: Small-firm sample ($n=1000$)

	Mean for firms that merged	Mean for firms that did not merge	t-statistic for difference in means
Tobin's q, top-coded at 20	2.34	3.04	1.67*
Indicator for Tobin's $q>20$	0.00	0.015	4.62**
Number of marketed drugs	0.091	0.070	0.23
Indicator: no marketed drugs	0.900	0.954	1.49
Percent of drugs launched 9–14 years ago	0.00	1.25	3.61**
log(enterprise value), $ millions	4.11	4.34	1.02
Foreign firm indicator	0.174	0.211	0.78
Ratio of cash to sales	2.13	3.24	1.05
Change in sales, $t-3$ to $t-1$	41.9	26.1	1.28
Indicator: sales data missing	0.101	0.218	3.05**
Change in operating expenses, $t-3$ to $t-1$	45.1	27.0	1.82*
Indicator: operating expenses missing	0.073	0.205	4.00**

Notes: ** = difference in sample means is significantly different from zero at the 5-percent level. The sample for this table is smaller than for Tables 3 and 4 because we include only firm-year observations that are included in the second stage regressions.

whether or not they actually merged. The propensity score is a summary measure of the likelihood of merging based on a vector of firm characteristics. The propensity to merge, $p(M_i)$, is the probability firm i will merge in year t conditional on observed characteristics X

$$p(M_{it}) = \Pr(M_{it} = 1|\mathrm{X}_{i,t-1}). \quad (2)$$

Rosenbaum and Rubin (1983) show that if the outcomes (Y_{i1} and Y_{i0}) are independent of the assignment to the treatment (merging firm) and control (non-merging firm) groups, conditional on the observed covariates, then classifying observations by their propensity score balances the observed covariates (X); within a subclass with a similar $p(M)$, the distribution of X is the same between the treatment and control groups. The treatment effect of a merger for firms with a specific propensity score is the difference in the mean outcomes between the treatment and control groups

$$E(Y_{i1}|p(M_{it}), M_{it} = 1) - E(Y_{i0}|p(M_{it}), M_{it} = 0), \quad (3)$$

where the expectation is taken with respect to the distribution of $p(M)$. Consider two firms with the same probability of merging in a particular year where one firm merged and the other did not. The firm that did not merge can serve as a control for the firm that did merge since the expected difference in their outcomes is equal to the average treatment effect of a merger.[19]

To estimate the propensity score, we estimate Equation (2) using a multinomial logit regression that distinguishes situations where a firm acquires another, is acquired, is involved in a pooling merger, or is not involved in any M&A activity. Although the propensity-generating model is similar in structure and includes all the variables in the model used to report first stage results, in order to achieve balance of the propensities the propensity generating equation also includes year indicators, lagged measures of employees, lagged ratio of R&D expenses to sales, lagged ratio of operating profit to sales, interaction terms between many pairs of variables, and quadratic terms of the continuous variables. We sum the predicted probability that a firm will acquire another company and the probability a firm will be involved in a pooling merger to derive the M&A propensity score. We omit the predicted probability that a firm will be acquired because firms that are acquired generally do not appear in our second-stage sample. We then sort firm-years by the propensity score and assign them to three separate groups, or tertiles: low, medium, and high merger propensity.[20]

We use a two-way analysis of variance model to determine if the propensity score balances each covariate between the treatment (merged) and control (did not merge) groups. Each covariate that appears in the multinomial logit model is regressed on indicator variables for the three propensity tertiles, an indicator for whether or not the firm actually merged in that year, and interactions between the propensity and merged indicator variables. We then calculate F-statistics to determine whether the covariates differ between merging and non-merging firms—overall and within each tertile—once we control for the firms' propensity to merge using the tertile indicator variables. In fact, once we control for a firm's merger propensity, none of the covariates from the first stage model differ significantly between firms that do and do not merge. For example, although firms in the large-firm sample that merge have considerably more marketed drags than firms that do not merge, within each of the three propensity tertiles there is no statistical difference in this variable between merging and non-merging firms.[21]

Our second stage estimates regress Y_i, the percentage change in a firm performance measure from $t+1$ to $t+2$, on a firm's propensity score for year t, an indicator that equals one if the firm merged in year t, year indicators, and an indicator for foreign firms.[22] We also include an interaction between the propensity score and the merger indicator to test whether the effect of a merger differs according to the firm's propensity to merge.[23]A firm facing a substantial loss of sales due to patent expiration, for example, may have a high propensity score and may reduce employees substantially if it were to acquire another firm, whereas a firm that was less distressed might alter staffing less aggressively if it were to merge. Since post-merger integration takes time and results may not be evident immediately, we report three second-stage regressions to measure the impact of mergers on firm performance one, two, and three years following a merger. That is, we define Y_i as the percentage change in a firm's performance from $t+1$ to $t+2$, from $t+2$ to $t+3$, and from $t+3$ to $t+4$ (where the merger of interest occurred in year t).

DOI: 10.1002/mde

As a robustness check, we also estimate a second-stage model based on the approach suggested by Hirano *et al.* (2000). Rather than including the propensity score as a regressor in the second stage regression, we perform weighted ordinary least squares where the weights for firms that merged are $1/p_i$, and the weights for firms that did not merge are $1/(1 - p_i)$.[24] Thus firms that did not merge are given a greater weight if they had a high propensity score (i.e. they appeared similar to firms that did merge based on observables), and firms that did merge are given a greater weight if they have a low propensity score (i.e. they appear similar to firms that aid not merge). The results using this method are qualitatively similar to those reported in Tables 6 and 7.[25]

The propensity score method controls for selection based on observed firm characteristics, including the number and age of approved drugs, enterprise value and Tobin's q, which should capture many factors affecting the expected growth of a firm's cash flow based on pre-merger conditions. Using growth rates in the second stage controls for unobserved fixed firm characteristics that might affect performance levels in both the pre- and post-merger periods. However, if mergers are systematically related to unobserved characteristics that also affect post-merger growth, our estimate of the impact of a merger may be biased.

RESULTS

Characteristics of Merging and Non-Merging Firms

Table 3 reports the means of the firm characteristics separately for firms that did and did not merge, as well as two-sample t-statistics of the differences in the means. Among the 1049 firm-years in the large-firm sample (panel A), firms that actually merged were marketing more drugs, were less likely to have no approved drugs, had a greater percentage of drugs at risk of patent expiration, had a larger enterprise value, a lower cash-to-sales ratio, and were less likely to have a top-coded Tobin' s q (our outlier control) and missing sales data relative to firms that did not merge.[26] Among the 1000 firm-years in the small-firm sample (panel B of Table 3), firms that merged had a lower Tobin's q, had fewer drugs at risk of patent expiration, experienced a relatively large increase in operating expenses in the prior two years, and were less likely to have a top-coded Tobin's q, missing sales data, and missing expense data relative to firms that did not merge.

Multinomial Logit Analysis of M&A Activity

Tables 4 and 5 report marginal effects of the four distinct outcomes for the large-firm sample and the small-firm sample, respectively. The marginal effects, which are the change in the probability of an event (e.g. the probability a firm acquires another) associated with a unit increase in the independent variable, are calculated at the means of the independent variables and sum to zero for each independent variable across all four possible outcomes. We report robust standard errors adjusted for clustering within firm over time.

Focusing first on acquisitions, the results in Table 4 support the hypothesis that large pharmaceutical–biotech firms that expect to have relatively high excess productive capacity are more likely to engage in acquisition. Recall that we use four different variables to measure expected excess capacity: Tobin's q, which is the most comprehensive; the percentage of a firm's drugs that were launched 9–14 years previously (and are thus approaching patent expiration); lagged change in sales; and lagged change in operating expense. When the number and age profile of a firm's marketed drugs are omitted (regressions not reported here), firms with a relatively low Tobin's q are significantly more likely to acquire other firms. This is consistent with the hypothesis that firms with relatively low expected earnings growth rates (as reflected in a low market value relative to book value of assets) use acquisition as a source of either cost reductions and/or new compounds to apply to their pipeline.

When the number and age profile of the firm's products are included, to provide a more direct measure of expected excess capacity (Table 4), the marginal effect of a change in Tobin' s q on the likelihood of acquiring another firm is still negative but is no longer significant. However, firms with a relatively old portfolio of drugs are more likely to acquire another firm, as predicted, and this marginal effect is concave. A one standard deviation increase in the percentage of a firm's drugs that are between 9 and 14 years old (from 13.3 to 37.7%) is associated with a 1.8 percentage point increase in the probability a firm will

Manage. Decis. Econ. **28:** 307–328 (2007)
DOI: 10.1002/mde

Table 4. Marginal Effects of the Probability of Participating in M&A Activity: Large-Firm Sample

	Acquirer	Target	Pooling merger	No M&A activity
Tobin's q	−0.276	−0.0027**	0.030	0.248
	(0.186)	(0.0012)	(0.044)	(0.18)
Number of marketed drugs	−0.0349	−0.00029	−0.012	0.047
	(0.047)	(0.00038)	(0.020)	(0.053)
Percent of drugs launched 9–14 years ago	0.104**	−0.00033	0.0012	−0.105**
	(0.051)	(0.00028)	(0.014)	(0.052)
% drugs 9–14, squared	−0.0013**	2.8×10^{-6}	−0.000035	0.0014**
	(0.00057)	(4.6×10^{-6})	(0.00015)	(0.00057)
% Change in sales, $t-3$ to $t-1$	−0.0042	−0.000022	−0.0032	0.0074
	(0.013)	(0.000085)	(0.0041)	(0.014)
Enterprise value (Ln)	1.00**	0.0035**	0.321**	−1.33*
	(0.315)	(0.0015)	(0.144)	(0.347)
% Change in operating expenses $t-3$ to $t-1$	0.0094	0.000066	0.011**	−0.020
	(0.017)	(0.00011)	(0.0047)	(0.018)
Foreign firm indicator	0.294	−0.0084**	−0.324	0.038
	(0.815)	(0.0042)	(0.296)	(0.847)
Ratio of cash to sales	0.0035	−0.00036	−0.069	0.066
	(0.051)	(0.00030)	(0.053)	(0.071)
Mean of dependent variable (percentage points)	4.65	1.76	1.95	91.6
Observations (firm-years)	74	28	31	1458

Notes: The marginal effects are based on a multinomial logit regression where the dependent variable takes on the value one if a firm was involved in a particular type of merger activity in year t, and zero otherwise. The marginal effects are presented as percentage point changes in the probability of an outcome. The regression also includes indicator variables for firms with missing data on operating expenses and sales, for firms with a Tobin's q above 20, and for firms with no marketed drugs in year $t-1$.

Table 5. Marginal Effects of the Probability of Participating in M&A Activity: Small-Firm Sample

	Acquirer	Target	Pooling merger	No M&A activity
Tobin's q	−0.079	−0.068**	7.4×10^{-6}	0.147*
	(0.070)	(0.029)		(0.076)
Number of marketed drugs	0.135	−5.02**	-1.7×10^{-6}	4.89**
	(0.206)	(1.41)	(6.1×10^{-6})	(1.42)
Percent of drugs launched 9–14 years ago	−1.22**	−0.120**	1.2×10^{-6}	1.34**
	(0.273)	(0.037)	(1.6×10^{-6})	(0.273)
% drugs 9–14, squared	0.010**	0.00027**	-9.2×10^{-9}	−0.011**
	(0.0023)	(0.000083)		(0.0023)
% Change in sales, $t-3$ to $t-1$	−0.00021	−0.00027	6.9×10^{-8}	0.00049
	(0.0025)	(0.0016)		(0.0029)
Enterprise value (Ln)	−0.077	0.190**	5.7×10^{-6}**	−0.113
	(0.108)	(0.053)	(2.4×10^{-6})	(0.123)
% Change in operating expenses, $t-3$ to $t-1$	0.0046	−0.00037	-1.5×10^{-7}	−0.0042
	(0.0028)	(0.0018)		(0.0034)
Foreign firm indicator	0.143	−0.070	−0.385**	0.312
	(0.336)	(0.129)	(0.166)	(0.403)
Ratio of cash to sales	−0.0069	−0.029**	-1.3×10^{-6}	0.036*
	(0.014)	(0.015)	(1.8×10^{-6})	(0.020)
Mean of dependent variable (percentage points)	1.54	2.08	1.01	95.4
Observations (firm-years)	23	31	15	1423

Notes: The marginal effects are based on a multinomial logit regression where the dependent variable takes on the value one if a firm was involved in a particular type of merger activity in year t, and zero otherwise. The marginal effects are presented as percentage point changes in the probability of an outcome. The regression also includes indicator variables for firms with missing data on operating expenses and sales, for firms with a Tobin's q above 20, and for firms with no marketed drugs in year $t-1$. The standard errors for four of the coefficients in the pooling arm of the multinomial logit are so small that they are reported to be zero by the Stata program. The point estimates for these four coefficients are also very small.

DOI: 10.1002/mde

acquire another.[27] Since the probability a firm acquires another in a particular year is 0.0465 (bottom row of Table 4), this represents a 38% increase in the likelihood of acquiring another firm. The lagged percent change in sales is negative but insignificant.[28]

Firms with a relatively low Tobin's q are more likely to be acquired, suggesting that the acquirer values the target's assets more highly than does the market, which is consistent with acquisition being a mechanism to transfer assets to more effective managers. Also consistent with this hypothesis is the finding that firms that experienced relatively rapid growth of operating expenses are more likely to be involved in pooling. However, since this variable is insignificant in the target equation, this interpretation is tentative.

If firms merged in part to achieve economies of scale, smaller firms would be more likely to merge. Contrary to expectations, larger firms, as measured by enterprise value, are more likely to be involved in all three types of merger activity. This suggests that, if economies of scale are a motive for merger, even the firms at the sample mean perceive advantages in growing larger. A 100% increase in a firm's enterprise value (or an increase of one in the log of its enterprise value, which is about one-half of a standard deviation) is associated with a 1.0 and 0.32 percentage point increase in the likelihood of acquiring another firm and being involved in a pooling merger, respectively, which is approximately a 20% increase in the probabilities. Firms with larger enterprise values are also more likely to be targets.

The coefficient on the indicator for foreign firms is positive but insignificant in the acquisition equation, suggesting that foreign firms do not disproportionately engage in merger as means to enter the US market. Our estimates suggest that foreign firms are less likely to be acquired than domestic firms, however this may simply reflect a US-bias in our data set, which may not capture all the acquisitions of foreign firms by other foreign firms. The coefficient on the ratio of cash to sales is insignificant. Thus there is no evidence of imperfect agency, that is, that managers acquire companies merely because they have the means to do so. There is also no evidence that financing is a constraint on M&A.

Table 5 reports the marginal effects from the multinomial regression analysis of determinants of mergers for the small firm sample.[29] For these relatively small firms, our variables have more success predicting the probability of being a target than an acquirer. The results are more consistent with merger being an exit strategy for firms in financial trouble in general, not specifically a response to expected excess capacity associated with patent expirations. This is as expected, since the great majority of these small firms had no marketed drugs, hence were not exposed to patent expirations and the associated risk of underutilized marketing and manufacturing assets. Nevertheless, most of these firms engage in R&D and would be heavily dependent on external financing through public or private equity or alliances with larger firms. If such firms experience R&D setbacks that result in a decline in their Tobin's q and inability to raise additional cash, being acquired may be the best alternative.

We find that small firms with a relatively low Tobin's q, implying a relatively low expected growth rate of earnings, are more likely to be acquired, as in the large firm sample. This is consistent with transfer of underperforming assets to other managers, A one-standard deviation increase in a firm's Tobin's q is associated with a 0.19 percentage point decrease in the predicted probability a firm will be acquired. The mean probability that a small firm will be acquired in a particular year is 0.021 (bottom row of Table 5), so this represents a 9% reduction in the predicted probability. By contrast, small firms with a relatively high value of Tobin's q, large number of drugs, and high ratio of cash to sales are less likely to engage any type of M&A activity. As further evidence that the causes of financial distress are different for small firms, we find that small firms with a large percentage of drugs at risk of losing patent protection are less likely to be involved in M&A activity, whereas the opposite effect was found for larger firms (Table 4).[30]

Small firms with relatively large enterprise value are more likely to be acquired and be involved in a pooling merger, whereas firm size has no effect on the probability that a small firm is an acquirer, in contrast to the large firm sample. A 100% increase in a small firm's enterprise value (which is slightly smaller than one standard deviation) is associated with a 0.19 percentage point, or 9%, increase in the predicted probability of being acquired. These results are consistent with larger firms being relatively attractive targets, presumably as a means whereby the acquiring firm can achieve economies

DOI: 10.1002/mde

of scale in an existing capability or acquire new technologies and expertise.

Although being in financial trouble puts a firm at risk for acquisition, there is no evidence that having the ability to finance a merger tends to precipitate acquisition. Firms with a relatively high cash-to-sales ratio are less likely to be involved in any M&A activity. The finding that small firms with relatively high Tobin's q (an indicator of ability to finance an acquisition through equity) are less likely to engage in M&A provides further evidence that financing is neither a constraint on acquisition nor a precipitating factor. In summary, for small firms the results suggest that financial weakness puts a firm at risk as a target, but financially strong firms (as measured by relatively high Tobin's q, number of marketed drugs and high ratio of cash to sales) are less likely to engage in any M&A.

Effect of Merger on Subsequent Performance

The evidence of means in Table 3 and the analysis of determinants of merger in Tables 4 and 5 demonstrate that merger in the pharmaceutical–biotech industry is not a random event but is related to observable firm characteristics. If post-merger performance is also a function of pre-merger observed characteristics, then estimates of post-merger performance that fail to control for these prior characteristics would produce biased estimates of the effects of mergers. We include the propensity to merge as a summary measure of the firm's likelihood of merging based on its prior observable characteristics (see the Methods section above). Once we control for the firm's merger propensity, none of the covariates in Table 3 differs significantly between firms that do and do not merge. Focusing on growth rates in the second stage allows us to control for unobserved firm fixed effects that may influence the levels of these outcome variables.

Table 6 reports estimates from 30 separate second-stage regressions for the large-firm sample. In the first three rows we regress the percentage change from $t+1$ to $t+2$ for each of the five firm performance measures on an indicator variable that equals one if a firm merged in year t, year indicators, and an indicator for foreign firms.[31] The coefficient on the merger indicator is the impact of a merger if one assumes mergers are exogenous. For each of the five dependent variables, we then report a second regression that includes the propensity score for the firm-year and an interaction between the merger indicator and the propensity score. This specification tests whether any merger effects are significant after controlling for the merger propensity and whether any effects of a merger differ according to the firm's prior likelihood of engaging in M&A activity. Finally, we repeat these two regressions for each dependent variable, using the percentage changes between $t+2$ and $t+3$ (rows 4–6 of Table 6) and $t+3$ and $t+4$ (rows 7–9) to examine the impact two and three years after the merger.

For large firms, in the first year post-merger, the merger has no significant effect on employees, operating profit, or enterprise value. The latter result is consistent with investors correctly incorporating, on average, the subsequent impact of a merger into the company's valuation at the announcement date or shortly thereafter. If one were to assume that mergers are exogenous, one would conclude that merger results in slower growth in sales and in R&D expenditures in the first full year after a merger (the first equation for each dependent variable in Table 6). However, the negative and frequently significant coefficient on the propensity score variable in the regressions for growth in sales, employees, and R&D highlights the importance of controlling for prior characteristics that are likely to be associated with future performance. Firms with a relatively high likelihood of merging in a particular year experience relatively small growth in sales, employees, and R&D, on average, over the next three years, regardless of whether or not they actually merge. This supports our hypothesis that many large firms merge to try to improve a bad situation. Firms that don't merge but share similar characteristics as firms that do merge, also perform relatively poorly on the three aforementioned dimensions. It is unsurprising that the propensity score coefficients are insignificant in the enterprise value regressions because a company's current stock price should incorporate expectations of its future performance, and those expectations should include the same firm characteristics as the propensity score.

Controlling for a firm's propensity to merge increases the coefficient on the merger indicator variable in 12 of the 15 regressions in Table 6 and eliminates the finding of significant difference in the growth in sales and R&D expenses between

DOI: 10.1002/mde

Table 6. Effect of a Merger on Firm Performance, Large-Firm Sample Change (Percentage Points) Between Year t and $t+1$

	Operating profit		Enterprise value		Sales		Employees		R&D	
1st year after a merger										
Merged in $t-1$	−10.72	−5.36	1.60	10.34	−5.590*	0.15	−3.25	1.57	−8.514*	−7.39
	(8.20)	(12.74)	(7.75)	(13.58)	(3.07)	(4.03)	(2.75)	(4.59)	(5.01)	(7.25)
Merged in $t-1\times$ propensity score		−12.64		−37.35		−11.78		5.87		32.18
		(56.04)		(39.39)		(20.02)		(16.64)		(20.47)
Propensity score, $t-1$		−19.31		−9.78		−20.99		−40.64***		−40.60***
		(28.60)		(17.23)		(14.95)		(10.77)		(11.17)
Mean of dependent variable	4.11	4.11	17.30	17.30	13.80	13.80	9.50	9.50	13.40	13.40
Observations	993	993	996	996	992	992	911	911	967	967
R^2	0.01	0.01	0.13	0.13	0.03	0.03	0.05	0.06	0.04	0.05
2nd year after a merger										
Merged in $t-2$	3.99	21.16	−2.89	−5.66	−6.25	−5.49	−6.107**	−5.66	−0.48	2.32
	(11.71)	(16.82)	(6.64)	(10.12)	(4.11)	(7.21)	(2.50)	(4.64)	(4.15)	(7.27)
Merged in $t-2\times$ propensity score		−90.77		12.61		14.33		19.28		0.64
		(58.28)		(37.29)		(24.01)		(16.24)		(23.77)
Propensity score, $t-2$		−5.77		3.66		−25.2*		−30.2***		−21.9*
		(20.89)		(16.02)		(14.50)		(9.49)		(12.97)
3rd year after a merger										
Merged in $t-3$	−28.01	−60.705**	−1.08	−8.874	−4.00	6.36	−8.09	−0.13	−0.65	−0.52
	(17.14)	(30.20)	(9.32)	(15.82)	(5.47)	(5.71)	(5.50)	(7.87)	(5.03)	(6.74)
Merged in $t-3\times$ propensity score		219.43**		57.83		−40.78		−32.71		16.02
		(102.69)		(54.06)		(30.43)		(33.88)		(43.18)
Propensity score, $t-3$		−40.97		−17.19		−26.198*		−18.50*		−22.97
		(38.79)		(18.84)		(14.27)		(10.29)		(14.14)

Notes: The results of 30 separate ordinary least squares regressions are reported in this table. The dependent variable is the change between t and $t+1$ in a firm performance measure, measured in percentage points relative to the midpoint between the two years. The regressions also include a constant, an indicator for foreign firms, and year indicators. Operating profit is sales minus manufacturing, selling, general, and administrative expenses (operating profit is pre-tax and excludes R&D expenses). The means of the dependent variables and the R^2 values are similar for the regressions analyzing the impact of mergers in the second and third year following the merger. There are about 120 and 240 fewer observations for the latter two sets of regressions.

merging and non-merging firms in the first full year following a merger. This confirms that failure to control for pre-merger characteristics leads to biased estimates of the effects of mergers.

The results for the second and third full years following a merger (rows 4–6 and rows 7–9 of Table 6, respectively) are similar to those for the first full year for all of the dependent variables except for employees and operating profit. In the second year post-merger, employee growth appears to be more negative for firms that merged, as expected if mergers facilitate cost reductions through restructuring. However, once we control for the propensity to merge, employee growth is not significantly different between firms that did and did not merge. Thus, firms that were in trouble either cut or slowed the growth of employees within the next two years, regardless of whether or not they merged.

Mergers are associated with relatively low growth in operating profit in the third year after a merger. Controlling for a firm's propensity to merge, a firm with the sample average propensity (0.038) is predicted to experience a 52.3% reduction in operating profit in the third year following a merger relative to an otherwise similar firm that did not merge.[32] This reduction is significantly different from zero at a 6% level. This suggests that post-merger integration may absorb more resources and managerial effort than anticipated by most managers, although not relative to market expectations given the insignificant result for the forward-looking enterprise value measure. However, the positive and significant coefficient of 219 on the merged-propensity score interaction indicates that mergers had a more beneficial effect on operating profit for firms with a relatively high probability of merging. A merger is predicted to increase the operating profit for a firm with a very high propensity score by 10.2% in the third year following a merger relative to an otherwise similar firm that did not

DOI: 10.1002/mde

Table 7. Effect of a Merger on Firm Performance, Small-Firm Sample Change (Percentage Points) Between Year t and $t+1$

	Operating profit		Enterprise value		Sales		Employees		R&D	
1st year after a merger										
Merged in $t-1$	−40.49*	−53.87*	2.83	8.35	−4.03	−13.83	−6.08	−15.51	−13.52	−38.32**
	(23.86)	(31.17)	(10.17)	(12.14)	(6.34)	(8.82)	(7.59)	(9.98)	(14.72)	(17.72)
Merged in $t-1\times$ propensity score		94.97		1.83		116.81**		161.11***		301.30***
		(164.37)		(71.71)		(52.53)		(43.52)		(87.86)
Propensity score, $t-1$		30.72		−70.68		−44.45		−99.22***		−146.04***
		(79.35)		(54.58)		(43.43)		(25.68)		(36.80)
Mean of dependent variable	−19.3	−19.3	5.72	5.72	12.6	12.6	7.49	7.49	8.37	8.37
Observations	930	930	934	934	922	922	887	887	841	841
R^2	0.03	0.03	0.07	0.07	0.02	0.02	0.02	0.06	0.01	0.03
2nd year after a merger										
Merged in $t-2$	−9.27	−8.15	−23.96	−18.69	−4.60	−13.25	4.11	−0.60	−3.26	−7.15
	(22.76)	(27.29)	(15.25)	(21.96)	(10.30)	(15.20)	(5.49)	(8.00)	(7.47)	(11.14)
Merged in $t-2\times$ propensity score		70.72		−31.21		130.29		87.25**		99.01
		(189.31)		(130.87)		(81.81)		(40.74)		(72.98)
Propensity score, $t-2$		−125.03		−35.11		−62.57		−58.79**		−93.47*
		(88.87)		(55.50)		(40.16)		(28.89)		(51.03)
3rd year after a merger										
Merged in $t-3$	4.61	−6.04	−13.65	−2.09	1.57	7.27	−5.64	−13.14	−3.19	−9.27
	(26.50)	(42.50)	(14.19)	(14.96)	(4.65)	(7.68)	(7.29)	(9.72)	(15.57)	(30.22)
Merged in $t-3\times$ propensity score		201.82		−217.70*		−61.40		153.55		112.94
		(475.00)		(110.32)		(97.04)		(128.55)		(295.18)
Propensity score, $t-3$		−66.41		69.68		−46.52		−61.38		−53.62
		(97.51)		(59.65)		(62.07)		(46.67)		(44.67)

Notes: The results of 30 separate ordinary least squares regressions are reported in this table. The dependent variable is the change between t and $t+1$ in a firm performance measure, measured in percentage points relative to the midpoint between the two years. The regressions also include a constant, an indicator for foreign firms, and year indicators. Operating profit is sales minus manufacturing, selling, general, and administrative expenses (operating profit is pre-tax and excludes R&D expenses). The means of the dependent variables and the R^2 values are similar for the regressions analyzing the impact of mergers in the second and third year following the merger. There are about 120 and 240 fewer observations for the latter two sets of regressions.

merge, although this effect is not significantly different from zero at conventional levels.[33]

Estimates from the same set of second-stage regressions are reported in Table 7 for the sample of small firms. In Table 5 we found that merging is an exit strategy for relatively small biotech firms in financial trouble, whereas strong firms, as measured by high Tobin's q, number of marketed drugs and high ratio of cash to sales, are more likely not to engage in M&A at all. Firms that merged had significantly lower growth in operating profit in the year following the merger, and controlling for the propensity to merge makes this effect more, not less, negative. In subsequent years there was no significant difference in operating profit between firms that did and did not merge, suggesting that post-merger integration is easier for small firms than for large firms, which is not surprising.

Small firms with high propensity scores experienced relatively low growth in employees and R&D regardless of whether they merged, consistent with the earlier finding that strong firms tend not to engage in M&A. As with the large-firm sample, this highlights the importance of controlling for the likelihood of a firm's expected performance when estimating the impact of mergers. Relative to an otherwise similar firm that did not merge, we predict that a merger reduces the growth rate of sales, employees, and R&D by 10.2, 10.6, and 29.1%, respectively, in the first full year following a merger for a firm with the mean propensity (0.031). Only the change in R&D is statistically significant, which indicates resources may be diverted from R&D immediately post-merger.

As in the operating profit regression discussed above, the positive coefficients on the merged-propensity score interactions for these three regressions indicate that mergers may be a more effective growth strategy for firms with high

DOI: 10.1002/mde

propensity scores. A merger is predicted to increase sales, employees, and R&D by 12.8, 21.2, and 30.3%, respectively, in the first full year following a merger for a firm with a very high propensity score relative to an otherwise similar firm that did not merge.[34] The results for employees and R&D are significantly different from zero at a 10-percent level, and the predicted effect of a merger is significantly larger for firms with very high propensity scores relative to those with the sample mean propensity score for all three of these dependent variables. Thus, firms that face the greatest distress appear to grow following a merger, possibly because the merger provided access to financial resources that these small firms lacked.

With two exceptions, the insignificant coefficients in most of the second- and third-year regressions indicate that the impact of a merger for small firms appears to be concentrated in the first full year following a merger. For a firm with the sample mean propensity, a merger is predicted to have no statistically significant effect on its employees two years following a merger or its enterprise value three years following a merger. By contrast, for a firm with a very high propensity score, we predict that a merger increases its employees by 16.5% in the second year and reduces its enterprise value by 48.7% in the third year post merger relative to an otherwise similar firm that did not merge.[35] This suggests that the long-run impact of merger fell short of investors' expectations for these distressed firms.

CONCLUSIONS

We analyzed the determinants and effects of significant M&A transactions across the entire pharma–biotech industry over the period 1988–2000. Specifically, we used a multinomial logit model to test several competing hypotheses to explain firm-specific merger activity and to generate a measure of each firm's propensity to participate in a merger in each eligible year. Then we measured the effects of mergers on a range of performance measures controlling for the firms' *ex ante* propensity to merge.

Among large firms (over $20 million in sales and $1 billion in market value), we find that firms with a low Tobin's q, hence with low expected earnings growth, are more likely to acquire another firm. This effect remains negative but becomes insignificant when we control for the percent of their product portfolio that is approaching patent expiration. Thus for large firms this evidence supports the hypothesis that mergers are frequently the response to expected excess capacity that is triggered by patent expirations and gaps in the product pipeline which render marketing resources unproductive. The excess capacity created by gaps in the pipeline of revenue-generating products creates a motive for merger and restructuring in the research-based pharmaceutical industry that is analogous to the role of technological and regulatory shocks that create a motive for merger and restructuring in other industries. We find that firms with high enterprise value are more likely to engage in merger, confirming that there is a perception of economies of scale in this industry. Whereas Higgins and Rodriguez (2005) find that mergers between firms that had a prior licensing relationship create value, however, in our larger sample that is not restricted to firms with a prior R&D relationship, we find no evidence that mergers create positive long term value. This suggests that mergers that are motivated to address R&D gaps through cost savings and economies of scale are unsuccessful in the long run.

For small firms mergers appear to be primarily an exit strategy for firms that are in financial trouble, as measured by low Tobin's q, few products and low cash–sales ratio. Because most of these small firms do not have marketed products, this financial trouble is more likely caused by unobserved R&D shocks rather than excess capacity due to patent expirations. Conversely, small firms with a relatively high Tobin's q, marketed products and cash/sales ratios are more likely to remain independent and less likely to engage in any M&A activity. We find no evidence that the availability of financing, either cash or relatively high value of equity, raises the probability of acquisitions for large or small firms; thus at least by this measure, we find no evidence that mergers are the result of imperfect agency by managers with cash available.

Our analysis of merger effects strongly confirms the importance of controlling for a firm's prior characteristics, as reflected in the merger propensity. For both the large- and small-firm samples, firms with relatively high merger propensity tend to have slower growth of sales, employees and R&D, consistent with merger being a response to

DOI: 10.1002/mde

distress. Controlling for merger propensity, large firms that merged were not significantly different from non-merging firms in growth in enterprise value, sales, employees, and R&D expenses in the three years following a merger. Firms that merged experienced slower operating profit growth in the third year after merger. For small firms, those that merged experienced relatively slow growth of R&D in the first year compared to similar firms that did not merge, suggesting that post-merger integration may absorb the cash that is necessary to finance R&D. Thus, although merger in the pharma–biotech industry is a response to being in trouble for both large and small firms, there is no evidence that it is a solution.

Acknowledgements

This research was supported by a grant from the Merck Company Foundation and a grant from the Huntsman Center at the Wharton School. The opinions expressed are those of the authors and do not necessarily reflect the views of the research sponsors.

NOTES

1. The remaining categories were partial, hostile and vertical acquisition.
2. Compounds must demonstrate safety and efficacy in human clinical trials, in order to obtain marketing approval from the FDA in the US or similar regulatory agencies in other countries. In the US, roughly 4 out of 5 drugs fail in clinical trials, and some are withdrawn post launch if adverse events occur once on the market. Taking a compound through discovery, development and regulatory approval takes on average 12 years.
3. Recent experience is that generics take over 80% of prescription volume within the first year of patent expiration, due to their much lower prices and strong incentives of patients and pharmacists to substitute generics.
4. In-licensing individual drugs from other companies is an alternative to merging. However, for a firm experiencing patent expiration and gaps in its pipeline, including both self-originated and in-licensed products, in-licensing additional late-stage (in phase III clinical trials) or marketed products may be prohibitively costly because there are relatively few late-stage products for sale. The majority of licensing deals involve compounds that have not reached human trials or are in phase 1, implying that they still face great uncertainty and many years before approval (Nicholson *et al.*, 2005).
5. According to a survey of US pharmaceutical firms conducted in 2000, 35% of personnel were in marketing, 22% in production and quality control, 21% in R&D, 12% in administration, and 10% in other functions (*Pharmaceutical Industry Profile*, Pharmaceutical Researchers and Manufacturers of America, 2003).
6. In theory, acquisition rather than pooling would be a more effective mechanism for transferring control, since acquisition clearly establishes who is in control. However, pooling may be a preferred means to implement such acquisitions due to the perceived accounting advantages of pooling rather man an outright acquisition at the time of our data.
7. Hall (1999), following Rosenbaum and Rubin (1983), constructs a cohort of merged firms and a matched cohort of firms that did not merge but that were similar in their predicted probability of merging, based on a logit regression (other forms of exit are presumably included in the non-merger group). The difference in differences in R&D growth of these two cohorts is used to estimate the effects of merger. The test is based on medians and other distribution-free tests.
8. To be included in our sample a firm had to have sales in excess of $20 million or a market value in excess of $1 billion for at least one year between 1988 and 2000. If two pharmaceutical/biotech firms in our sample merge, we record this in Table 1 as a single unique merger.
9. If firm A acquires 20% or more of firm B, firm A is required to incorporate firm B's results into its financial reporting. By our definitions, if a large firm buys a 50% share in a smaller firm, this may be a transforming acquisition for the small firm but not necessarily for the large firm.
10. We added four additional firms not identified in the two steps described in the text but known to be in the pharmaceutical or biotech sector: American Cyanamid, Warner-Lambert, Pharmacopeia, and Affymetrix, and excluded four firms more appropriately described as outside the pharmaceutical/biotech industry: Dupont, 3M, Procter & Gamble and BASF. Twenty more firms were excluded because they were old entries, *pro forma* entries, Indian subsidiaries, or duplicates.
11. Foreign currency values from the Global Vantage files were converted to US dollars, using monthly exchange rates from Global Vantage. All monetary values were then adjusted for inflation using the U.S. domestic manufacturing Producer Price Index (index year is 1999). To maximize our sample size, we imputed some financial data, but only for observations where other key financial variables were non-missing in order to be certain that the firm was active in that year. Because some firms were listed in both the Compustat and Global Vantage files, we extracted financial data on a firm-by-firm basis from the source that reported more years for a given firm, and we filled in missing data from the otherwise unused source.
12. The SDC database tracks up to three firms on the acquirer side of the transaction and up to three firms on the selling side. Each merger was credited to all of the relevant firms in our sample. Most transactions were credited to a single firm on the acquirer side. For transactions that involve the acquisition of

DOI: 10.1002/mde

a relatively small firm that is not listed in Compustat, we lack financial data on the target firm. However, for some transactions we were able to match both acquirer- and seller-side firms, and for others only seller-side firms. We excluded all divestiture transactions where the phamiaceutical–biotech firm in our sample was selling a division.

13. Our measure of a firm's portfolio of drugs assigns each drug to one firm, hence it omits royalty payments received by originators from licensee firms that market the drugs; it also excludes products in the pipeline, whether self-originated or in-licensed.
14. In a preliminary analysis not reported here, we tested whether the 4-outcome model, which treats pooling mergers as a separate category, is superior to a 3-outcome model, which includes only being an acquirer, a target and no M&A activity. We rejected the 3-outcome model in favor of the 4-outcome model because the pooling mergers vector of coefficients was significantly different from the other outcomes. Because the sample of pooling mergers is so small, our estimation does not distinguish acquirers and targets within this category, although SDC does designate one firm in a pooling as the acquirer and another as the target.
15. Book value of long-term debt should be close to its market value.
16. Firms file for patent protection during the pre-clinical stage, well before the FDA approves a drug.
17. Because 2001 is the last year of our financial data, 2000 is the last year for which we can calculate an annual percent change.
18. We calculate percentage changes using an arc formula. Operating profit is defined as sales—cost of goods sold—selling/general and administrative expenses. We exclude R&D expenses since increases in R&D expenses are often perceived to increase the future value of biotech and pharmaceutical firms.
19. See Imbens (2004) for a review of methods for estimating the treatment effect of a binary treatment when there is selection on observable characteristics.
20. Cochrane (1968) shows that grouping observations into five subclasses according to their propensity score often removes over 90% of the bias due to the covariates. Since mergers are infrequent in our sample (about five percent of the firms merge in a particular year), we would have a small number of mergers in each quintile and therefore use tertiles.
21. Using the propensity score enables us to include a more complete control for prior characteristics than would be possible if we simply included lagged values in the second stage regression. Given the relatively small number of observations (2000) at the second stage, the model would be over fitted if we included all the covariates that are included in the propensity generating equation.
22. We cannot compare performance of merged firms, pre- and post-merger, with a matched sample of non-merging firms over the same time period, because we lack pre-merger accounting data for one component of the merged entity for a significant fraction of our mergers. This occurs primarily due to partial acquisitions (where reported data pertains to the entire corporate entity, not just the division acquired), and acquisitions involving foreign firms and private companies that are not covered by Compustat or Global Vantage. We include the acquiring firm's propensity score in the second stage rather than averaging the propensity scores of the two merging firms because some of the target firms are not included in the first stage regression, due to missing accounting data.
23. We condition on the propensity score in a regression rather than estimating an average treatment effect within propensity score blocks, or strata, for two reasons. First, with a total of only 200 mergers, it would be difficult to estimate precisely the effect of a merger in the low-propensity score strata. Second, the mergers occurred over a 13-year period, and a regression framework allows us to control for year effects that are expected to have a substantial impact on second-stage outcomes. Imbens (2004) and D'Agostino (1998) describe the method of estimating the treatment effect conditional on the propensity score in a regression framework.
24. Finkelstein (2003) also uses this method in her study of vaccine development.
25. Results of the weighted least squares regressions are available upon request. In these specifications we do not include an interaction term between the merger indicator variable and the propensity score.
26. Observations may be included in the analysis of determinants of mergers in Tables 3 and 4 but not in the second stage regressions if mergers occurred in 2000 or 2001, hence are missing data on post-merger performance, or if there are missing values for the second stage dependent variables. Table 5 includes only the firm-year observations that are included in the second stage regressions.
27. $24.4(0.104) + (24.4)^2(-0.0013) = 1.8$.
28. In preliminary analyses, we also included an indicator variable for whether the firm formed an alliance or joint venture with another firm in the prior year, or a categorical variable counting the number of such alliances, as a rough test of the hypothesis that alliances may be a substitute for acquisitions. The alliance variables are omitted from the specifications in Tables 4 and 5 because the coefficients were insignificant, possibly because most alliances involve early-stage compounds and the alliance data from SDC were insufficiently precise to control for development stage of in-licensed compounds. Taken at face value, the results are consistent with the expectation that in-licensing is a long-term strategy but not an effective short-term solution to patent expiration problems.
29. The standard errors for four of the coefficients in the pooling merger arm of the multinomial logit are so small that the Stata software program reports them as zero. These standard errors are omitted in Table 4. The point estimates of these four coefficients are also very small, as is the frequency of pooling mergers in the small-firm sample.

DOI: 10.1002/mde

30. The number of marketed drugs is positive for only 4.9% of the firm-year observations in the small-firm sample. However, among these firm-years, there is considerable variation in the number of marketed drugs (ranges from one to four), and the percentage of drugs that were approved 9–14 years ago (ranges from 0 to 100, with a mean of 22).
31. Some of the year indicators were significant, suggesting industry-wide growth trends, but these coefficients are not reported here.
32. $-60.7 + (0.038)(219) = -52.3$.
33. The 10.2% predicted increase in operating profit is based on a firm with a propensity score of 0.323, which is one-standard deviation higher than the mean propensity score for firms that actually merged. The predicted impact of a merger on the operating profit of a firm with the mean propensity versus a firm with a very high propensity is statistically different from one another at a 5% level.
34. These predictions are based on a firm with a propensity score of 0.223, which is one-standard deviation higher than the mean propensity score for firms that actually merged.
35. Both of the predicted effects for firms with very high propensity scores are significantly different from zero at a 5-percent level. The predictions are based on a firm with a propensity score that is one-standard deviation higher than the mean propensity score for firms that actually merged.

REFERENCES

Andrade G, Mitchell M, Stafford E. 2001. New evidence and perspectives on mergers. *Journal of Economic Perspectives* **15**(2): 103–120.

Andrade G, Stafford E. 2004. Investigating the economic role of mergers. *Journal of Corporate Finance* **10**(1): 1–36.

Campa JM, Kedia S. 2002. Explaining the diversification discount. *Journal of Finance* **LVII**(4): 1731–1762.

Cochrane WG. 1968. The effectiveness of adjustment by subclassification in removing bias in observational studies. *Biometrics* **24**: 295–313.

D'Agostino RB. 1998. Tutorial in biostatistics: propensity score methods for bias reduction in the comparison of a treatment to a non-randomized control group. *Statistics in Medicine* **17**: 2265–2281.

Dranove D, Lindrooth R. 2003. Hospital consolidation and costs: another look at the evidence. *Journal of Health Economics* **22**(6): 983–997.

Finkelstein A. 2003. Health policy and technological change: evidence from the vaccine industry. *NBER Working Paper 9460*.

Hall BH. 1999. Mergers and R&D revisited. *Working Paper*.

Hall BH. 1988. The effect of takeover activity on corporate research and development. In *Corporate Takeovers: Causes and Consequences*, Auerbach AJ (ed.). University of Chicago Press: Chicago.

Higgins MJ, Rodriguez D. 2006. The outsourcing of R&D through acquisition in the pharmaceutical industry. *Journal of Financial Economics* **80**: 351–383.

Hirano K, Imbens GW, Ridder G. 2000. Efficient estimation of average treatment effects using the estimated propensity score. *NBER Technical Working Paper 251.*

Holstrom B, Kaplan SN. 2001. Corporate governance and merger activity in the United States: making sense of the 1980s and 1990s. *Journal of Economic Perspectives* **15**(2): 121–144.

Imbens G. 2004. Nonparametric estimation of average treatment effects under exogeneity: a review. *Review of Economics and Statistics* **86**(1): 4–29.

Jensen MC. 1986. Agency costs of free cash flow, corporate finance and takeovers. *American Economic Review* **76**: 323–329.

Jensen MC. 1993. The modern industrial revolution, exit, and control systems. *Journal of Finance* **48**: 831–880.

John K, Lang LHP, Netter J. 1992. The voluntary restructuring of large firms in response to performance decline. *Journal of Finance* **47**(3): 891–917.

Mitchell ML, Stafford E. 2000. Managerial decisions and long-term stock price performance. *Journal of Business* **73**(3): 287–329.

Mitchell M, Mulherin J. 1996. The impact of industry shocks on takeover and restructuring activity. *Journal of Financial Economics* **41**: 193–229.

Nicholson S, Danzon PM, McCullough J. 2005. Biotech–pharmaceutical alliances as a signal of asset and firm quality. *Journal of Business* **78**(4): 1433–1464.

Oi WY. 1962. Labor as a quasi-fixed factor. *Journal of Political Economy* **70**(6): 538–555.

Pautler PA. 2003. Evidence on mergers and acquisitions. *The Antitrust Bulletin* **48**(1): 119–221.

Pharmaceutical Researchers and Manufacturers of America. 2003. *Pharmaceutical Industry Profile 2003.* Washington, DC: PhRMA, March.

Ravenscraft DJ, Long WF. 2000. Paths to creating value in pharmaceutical mergers. In *Mergers and Productivity*, Kaplan SN (ed.). NBER Conference Report Series. University of Chicago Press: Chicago.

Rosenbaum PR, Rubin DB. 1983. The central role of the propensity score in observational studies for causal effects. *Biometrika* **70**(1): 41–55.

Vernon J. 2005. Examining the link between price regulation and pharmaceutical R&D investment. *Health Economics* **14**(1): 1–17.

Villalonga B. 2004. Does diversification cause the 'Diversification Discount'? *Financial Management* **33**(2): 5–27.

DOI: 10.1002/mde

B
Patented Pharmaceuticals and Innovation

[2]

Racing To Invest? The Dynamics of Competition in Ethical Drug Discovery

Iain Cockburn
University of British Columbia and NBER
Rebecca Henderson
Massachusetts Institute of Technology and NBER

Recent advances in the theoretical literature have greatly expanded our understanding of the forces that shape the competitive dynamics of research and development, but a paucity of sufficiently detailed empirical data has left these insights relatively untested. We draw on unusually detailed qualitative and quantitative internal data provided at the research program level by 10 major pharmaceutical firms to explore the usefulness of the modern literature as a source of insight into the dynamics of competition in ethical drug discovery.

Our analysis focuses on one particularly compelling aspect of the literature: the suggestion that in "winner take all situations," competition in R&D becomes a Prisoner's Dilemma, leading to overinvestment in research. Without adequate measures of the social return to innovation, we can say nothing about whether there is "too much" or "too little" research undertaken by the industry, but our results do not support the suggestion that R&D investment in drug discovery is driven by the "tit-for-tat" or simple reaction function models hinted at by the institutional literature. First, R&D investment is only weakly correlated across firms once common responses to exogenous shocks are accounted for, and second, rivals' R&D results are positively correlated with own research productivity, which we interpret as evidence for extensive R&D spillovers rather than the depletion externality implied by "winner take all" models.

These results are not, of themselves, sufficient to reject the hypothesis that investment behavior in the industry is driven by strategic considerations

This research was funded by the Sloan Foundation and by four pharmaceutical companies. Their support is gratefully acknowledged. We would also like to express our appreciation to all of those firms that contributed data to the study, and to Allan Afuah and Andrew Hoffman, who provided exceptional research assistance. We thank the editor and two particularly helpful referees, together with participants in seminars at the NBER, the UBC Summer IO Conference, Stanford, MIT, UCLA, and Berkeley for helpful comments and suggestions. The conclusions and opinions expressed in this paper are, however, our own, and any errors or omissions remain entirely our responsibility.

Journal of Economics & Management Strategy, Volume 3, Number 3, Fall 1994, 481–519

since there is theoretical support for a wide variety of observable behavior as equilibrium outcomes of strategic interaction. Nonetheless, they suggest that the more extreme forms of rent dissipation identified in the literature are probably poor characterizations of the reality of competition in pharmaceuticals. Our results point both to the need to develop theories that incorporate richer models of possible payoff structures, adjustment costs, and firm heterogeneity and to the need to collect empirical data that is comprehensive enough to enable one to test them.

1. Introduction

What drives a firm's decision to invest in research and development? Traditional industrial organization theory focused on market structure, demand, technological opportunity, and appropriability as determinants of the intensity and direction of R&D investment, and several empirical studies have demonstrated the fruitfulness of this approach (Levin and Reiss, 1988). More recent theoretical work has stressed strategic interaction among rivals as a primary determinant of investment decisions, and this approach has spawned a wealth of interesting and elegant theoretical models that have suggested some powerful insights into the dynamics of competition in R&D. Reinganum (1989) provides an excellent summary of this literature. For more recent work, see, for example, Dasgupta and Maskin (1987), Dixit (1988), D'Aspremont and Jacquemin (1988, 1990), Fraja (1993), and Suzumura (1992).

Despite the potential power of the game theoretic literature as a source of insight into the dynamics of competition, surprisingly little empirical research has attempted to build on its insights, and our understanding of the forces that drive R&D investment decisions in practice remains sketchy; Khanna (1993), Lerner (1991), Meron and Caves (1991), and Scherer (1992) are notable exceptions. One possible reason for this paucity of empirical work may be a lack of suitably detailed data. Whereas the early literature took the industry as its primary unit of analysis, more recent work focuses attention on the individual research project, or on the single-project firm, as the key competitive arena. The modern game theoretic literature says little about the determinants of aggregate investment in R&D at the level of the typical multiproduct, multiproject firm, and firm level data cannot be used to test its predictions without some heroic assumptions.

In this paper we use unusually detailed data on R&D investments and outcomes gathered at the level of individual research programs conducted within 10 pharmaceutical firms over a period of more than 17 years to explore the usefulness of the modern literature as a source of insight into the dynamics of competition in ethical drug discovery. These highly detailed data are well suited for examining R&D investment decisions, since they allow us to draw direct and meaningful comparisons between investment decisions made by different firms. The pharmaceutical industry also provides a particularly intriguing setting for this research, since competition in the industry has often been held up as a prime example of the types of strategic racing behavior predicted by the literature. Moreover, the industry is a relatively "pure play" in technological competition. Firms invest heavily in research and development, and successful research is a key contributor to commercial success. At the same time, since most firms invest in a wide range of technologies, we are able to compare competition across multiple "markets." It should be stressed that this paper examines ethical drug *discovery*—research intended to identify promising new drugs—rather than drug *development,* which is the application of these discoveries in the clinic. There may be important differences in the nature of competition in these two quite different stages of pharmaceutical R&D.

We begin the paper with a review of some of the modern literature on strategic competition in R&D. We argue that in general these models are very difficult to test. Investment behavior is critically dependent on a wide range of factors, including the nature of the payoff function, the spillover regime, the information structure of the game, and the extent and nature of asymmetries between players, all of which are rather difficult to capture empirically. Moreover, few of the models in the existing literature can be easily nested.

As a first step in the empirical analysis, we therefore focus on simple correlations in research investment and output across firms at the program level. We find investment levels are very weakly correlated across firms. This correlation is not robust to the inclusion of measures of technological opportunity and is consistent with the belief that levels of investment represent equilibrium responses to common shocks in demand and opportunity. Firm effects are quite significant, and investment levels are very highly autocorrelated. We interpret this as consistent with the hypothesis that adjustment costs and unobserved firm heterogeneities play a significant role in determining investment patterns.

To capture out of equilibrium behavior, we measure changes in investment levels using both first differences and a measure of "news" in investment. In contrast to previous studies that have explored correlations in first differences if investment across firms, we find no evidence of correlation in either first differences or "news" in investment across firms at the program level. We also find no evidence of correlation in the residuals of our best fitting investment equations across firms. These results suggest that simple reaction function or "tit-for-tat" models are not useful descriptions of competition in pharmaceutical research.

We draw on both qualitative and quantitative research to explore the degree to which the assumptions on which much of the racing literature is based are reasonable in the context of this industry. We find, for example, that the assumption that competition is for a single "prize" is probably not a useful one in this context. Our quantitative results suggest that research outputs are significantly positively correlated across firms, and that this correlation is robust to the inclusion of a number of measures of technical opportunity. Our qualitative work confirms that competing projects may well be complementary. The industry is characterized by substantial spillovers of knowledge and similar research can lead to related but significantly different outcomes.

Our results have implications both for our understanding of competition and for public policy. Our finding that the modern game theoretic literature is of only limited usefulness as an empirical guide points to the need not only to model R&D as a race with multiple prizes, but also to develop theories that incorporate richer models of adjustment costs and firm heterogeneity and to collect appropriately comprehensive and detailed data.

Our results also throw new light on our understanding of the relationship between investment behavior and social welfare. Many of the models that focus on strategic interaction raise the concern that free entry into R&D competition will result in overinvestment relative to both the private or social optima. Intuitively, these results are driven by the assumption that in deciding to invest research, firms consider only their own marginal return and do not take into account the externality that they impose on other firms in reducing their chances of success. In the extreme, these models suggest that entry will occur until all expected profits are dissipated (Dasgupta and Stiglitz, 1980b; Loury, 1979; Reinganum, 1982, 1989). While we cannot say anything definitive about the relationship between private levels of investment in research and social welfare in the pharmaceutical industry, our results suggest that the more extreme forms of rent dissipation identified in the literature are rather poor characterizations of the reality of competition in pharmaceuticals.

The paper begins with a review of the literature. Section 2 outlines our data, and Section 3 describes the history of the discovery of the ACE inhibitors as a source of qualitative insight into the nature of R&D competition in the industry. Section 4 presents our quantitative results, and the paper closes with a discussion of their significance and of possible directions for further work.

1.2 Literature Review

A large and lively theoretical tradition that traces its roots back to Schumpeter (1934, 1950) and Arrow (1962) has explored the relationship between market structure, strategic interaction, and R&D investment and has identified a number of conditions under which competitive markets may over-invest in R&D. Baldwin and Scott (1987) and Reinganum (1989) provide excellent surveys of a voluminous though disappointingly inconclusive literature.

Recent work has modeled R&D investment largely as games of timing. Two broad classes of model can be distinguished. The first, and most stark, are deterministic "auction" models (Scherer, 1967; Dasgupta and Stiglitz, 1980a, 1980b)). In these models, if firm i spends x_i on research, it will complete the invention at date $T_i = T(X_i)$. Assume that Π_m is the value of "winning" and that every other firm receives no return on its investment. Then if all firms have the same discount rate, r, a Nash equilibrium for the game involves two or more firms bidding x^*, where x^* is the largest value of x such that $\Pi_m e^{-rT(x)} - x = 0$. If the "winner" can appropriate all of the social returns to the invention, or if $\Pi_m = \Pi_s$, then all potential social returns from the invention will be dissipated through "overbidding."

Notice that within this framework there is no "racing" per se, since at equilibrium only one firm will actually invest x^*. However this class of models is unlikely to be a useful source of insight into the dynamics of competition in ethical drug discovery since it relies on a grossly inadequate characterization of the research technology. Pharmaceutical research is subject to enormous uncertainties (only 23% of all compounds entering clinical trials are eventually approved, and of the thousands of candidate compounds identified in the discovery phase, only a very small percentage enter the clinic [DiMasi et al., 1991]), and, thus, the deterministic R&D function fundamental to these models is an unacceptable characterization of the dynamics of research in the industry.

A second class of stochastic racing models that may be more appropriate for thinking about exploratory research allows the date of success to be stochastically related to the firm's level of R&D investment. These models yield qualitatively the same results as the deterministic auction model (Harris and Vickers, 1989; Loury, 1979; Lee and Wilde, 1980; Reinganum, 1982, 1989), but also rely on strong assumptions about the information available to the players and the stochastic nature of invention. In these models uncertainty leads to multiple entry, so that many firms invest in research. In the absence of effective barriers to entry or of collusion between firms in the industry, entry occurs until the expected returns from innovation are driven to zero, and all available social returns are dissipated through excessive entry.

These models capture some important aspects of competition in pharmaceuticals. This is an industry that is driven to a great extent by nonprice competition in R&D, and one of the few in which patents provide a very high degree of appropriability. Regulatory approvals or patent grants for new compounds represent particularly well-defined "prizes" in the R&D game, and the first and second firms to discover drugs usually capture the lion's share of the market. Since many major breakthroughs are triggered by advances in fundamental science, and since this knowledge is freely available, it is not unreasonable to believe that firms start each "race" in a symmetric position.

In the simplest version of one model representative of this tradition, n firms compete to perfect innovations from a common pool of undiscovered inventions, receiving the "leader's" payoff P_L if they are first to succeed, and the "follower's" payoff P_F otherwise (Reinganum, 1982). Two important features that add to the realism of this model are that rivals are free to change their level of investment over time and in response to changes in the state variables, and that the probability of success is a function of accumulated knowledge. Given that knowledge accumulates according to the expression

$$\frac{dz_i}{dt} = u_i(t,z(t)),$$

where $z_i(t)$ is firm i's knowledge stock at t, and $u_i(t,z)$ is firm i's rate of knowledge acquisition at (t,z), and assuming that $z_i(0) = 0$, and that the probability of success given a knowledge stock of z or less distributed is exponentially so that

$$F(z) = 1 - e^{(-\lambda z)},$$

then it is possible to explicitly compute each firm's payoff for any given strategy and aggregate rival hazard rate, and with some restrictions, to derive feedback Nash equilibrium strategies for each firm as functions of payoffs, elapsed time, and the number of players. For our purposes, the most significant propositions arising from these models are that

1. provided $P_L \gg P_F$, increases in rivalry have a positive impact on own investment

2. own success probability is negatively related to rivals' aggregate hazard of success.

However, a disappointingly comprehensive set of observed outcomes are consistent with one or more of these stochastic racing models, particularly when we recognize incentives to drop out of, or not to enter, races once a rival has established a big enough lead. Rival firms' optimizing responses to each other's moves could be to increase investment, decrease investment, or do nothing, depending on the structure of the "true" behavioral model, the determination of payoffs, the distribution of success probabilities, the nature of costs, and so on (Harris and Vickers, 1987; Scherer, 1967, 1992).

Discriminating empirically among these models is a daunting prospect, since theoretical models that attempt to account for the interactions between all possible factors simultaneously quickly become intractable. Equilibrium strategies for R&D investment can be computed, but signing the comparative statics results for, for example, the effect of an increase in rivalry upon equilibrium investment levels is difficult without knowing a great deal about payoffs in the product market and the nature of the asymmetries among players. Conclusions from these types of models are also rather fragile: Small changes in the timing of moves, the information structure of the game, or the treatment of spillovers can easily reverse or weaken any given theoretical result.

Notice, moreover, that these models are essentially models of industry *equilibrium:* Firms formulate R&D strategies based on anticipations of rival investment, and underlying demand and cost parameters. With perfect information, and absent any shocks to underlying demand and cost conditions, firms will not deviate from their equilibrium strategies. Investment will only be correlated across competitors as a common response to exogenous shocks. The simple tit-for-tat responses suggested by the anecdotal literature require a much more complicated framework incorporating, for example, heterogeneity of beliefs or private information.

Prior empirical research in this area has used firm-level investment data to test for reactions between "leaders" and "followers" in an industry. Grabowski and Baxter (1973), for example, found that in the chemical industry, the two largest firms responded quickly to changes in each other's R&D policies, while rivalry among the smaller firms in the industry was less clear-cut. Meron and Caves (1992) found that in a sample of 28 U.S. manufacturing industries, leaders and followers reacted positively to each others' increases in R&D expenditures, while fringe firms' investment decreased with their larger rival's investment, and Scherer (1992) found that firms with greater domestic sales in more concentrated U.S. markets were likely to react much more aggressively to increasing import competition than smaller firms or firms in less concentrated markets.

In this paper we look for evidence of racing behavior using disaggregated data on both investment and output at the research project or program level. This data set is described in the next section. We use the data to explore both correlation in investment levels and correlation in changes in investment levels across firms at the project level. We interpret the results of the first set of correlations as a test of the hypothesis that equilibrium strategies depend on underlying demand and cost parameters, rather than on rival's investment levels, while we interpret the results of the second as a test of the presence of simple-minded reaction function or tit-for-tat strategies.

We also use our data to explore the validity of the assumptions on which many of the racing models rely. Much of the literature assumes, for example, that firms race for a single prize, so that payoffs to investment have a "winner take all" quality and outputs will be negatively correlated across firms. To the degree that investments in research lay the groundwork for several, related innovations, or that success in one area increases the market for all innovation in that area, payoffs across firms may be positively correlated.

The strong implication of many of these models that free entry into research is unambiguously welfare-destroying is similarly subject to a number of caveats. Recent research has shown that it rests on at least five key assumptions: that there is total appropriability of consumer surplus and no spillover of knowledge between firms, that competing projects are perfect substitutes for each other, that there are no efficiency gains to multifirm competition, and that entry will occur until marginal private return has been driven to zero. Models of competition in which these assumptions are relaxed yield outcomes that are fundamentally indeterminate: Competitive industries may invest too much, too little, or just about the right amount in research.

For example, if firms pursue identical research projects, and if there is no transfer of information between firms, the entry of an additional firm into the industry unambiguously destroys social welfare. But if there are substantial spillovers of knowledge between firms, the entry of additional firms will increase the marginal productivity of existing players, reducing the negative externalities that lead to overinvestment. Spence (1984) shows that the effect on competition is difficult to predict, but in general, under plausible assumptions, the presence of spillovers will reduce R&D investments below their nonspillover levels. This conclusion has been confirmed by later work (D'Aspremont and Jacquemin, 1988, 1990; Fraja, 1993; Suzumura,

1992), which suggests that if the firms in an industry cooperate in setting their research investments, then the presence of spillovers may lead the industry to invest approximately the welfare maximizing amount. Similarly, if competing projects are better characterized as complements to each other—if, for example, any one of several approaches to a desired end is possible in theory, but there is great uncertainty as to which is likely to prove successful—then the entry of additional firms may enhance welfare as entry increases the odds that a discovery will be made (Dasgupta and Maskin, 1987).

Here we explore the validity of the assumptions on which the theoretical models rest using a combination of qualitative and quantitative data, focusing particularly on the degree to which competing projects are better characterized as substitutes or complements and on whether outputs are positively or negatively correlated across firms.

2. Sources and Construction of the Data Set

In order to explore these issues we rely on both qualitative and quantitative data drawn from a larger study of research productivity in the pharmaceutical industry. Data were obtained from public sources and from 10 major pharmaceutical firms. Although for reasons of confidentiality, we cannot describe the overall size or nature of the firms, we can say that they cover the range of major R&D-performing pharmaceutical manufacturers, and that they include both U.S. and European manufacturers. In aggregate, the firms in our sample account for approximately 25–30% of worldwide R&D and sales, and we believe that they are not markedly unrepresentative of the industry in terms of size, or of technical and commercial performance. In some therapeutic classes, our coverage is significantly higher, approaching 90% or more of industry R&D.

Pharmaceutical technology is enormously complex. Thus, we tried both to develop a general understanding of the history of research and development in the industry and to focus in detail on the scientific and technical history of the development of cardiovascular drugs.[1] We made extensive use of secondary sources such as the national press, reference texts, published articles, academic textbooks, and reports by both consultants and the Office of Technology Assess-

1. Cardiovascular drugs were chosen as the focus of the study for several reasons. Cardiovasculars are one of the largest and most rapidly growing classes of drugs. Moreover, the class includes both extraordinarily powerful agents whose mechanism of action—the precise biochemical means whereby the drug has a physiological effect—is well understood (such as the ACE inhibitors) and less effective agents that have been used for many years and whose precise mechanism of action has not been fully elucidated (drugs such as digitalis and some of the antiarrhythmic agents fall into this category).

ment. We combined this data with a program of extensive field interviews within the ten firms that make up our sample. Appendix 1 summarizes our qualitative research strategy.

The quantitative study draws upon data about spending and output at the research program level obtained from the internal records of 10 pharmaceutical firms. The choice of the "research program" as our fundamental unit of observation is important. A "program" is a level of aggregation of the data somewhere between individual research projects and the level of therapeutic classes, for example, "Thrombolytics" as opposed to "cardiovascular therapy" or "Compound 12345." We believe this is the most appropriate way of organizing the raw data provided to us by participating firms—though some detail about individual projects is lost for some of our firms, it does allow us to be consistent across firms and corresponds to the level of analysis at which firms organize their internal data and make strategic budgeting decisions. For each observation we have data on both inputs and outputs to the research process. Our primary measure of input is research spending on discovery, and our measures of output include patents, INDs, NDAs, new drug introductions, sales and market share. After carefully cleaning and matching these data, we were left with an unbalanced panel of 5,320 observations, indexed by firm, research program, and year.[2] The internal firm data are complemented by a variety of measures of scientific opportunity and pharmaceutical demand derived from public sources. Since our measure of scientific opportunity is only available after 1975, after matching to the R&D data the number of usable observations is reduced to 2,707. Table I presents descriptive statistics for this working sample drawn from our database. Full details of variable construction are given in Appendix 2.

3. A Qualitative Analysis: Racing in Pharmaceutical Research?

As a first step in the analysis, we exploit our qualitative data to explore the nature of competition in ethical drug discovery. At first glance, competition in the pharmaceutical industry seems to be a textbook

2. With a complete, rectangular, panel we would have 11,400 observations, made up of 10 firms, 38 detailed research areas, and up to 30 years of data. In practice not all of these observations are available: The average time period for which we have complete data is on average just under 20 years per firm, and not all firms are active in all research areas. Our working sample is drawn from a data base that currently has 5,320 observations, which after lagging variables leaves us with 4,930 observations covering the period 1961–1990.

TABLE I.
DESCRIPTIVE STATISTICS: SELECTED VARIABLES AT THE RESEARCH PROGRAM LEVEL

	Full Sample				
Variable	N	Minimum	Maximum	Mean	Std Dev
Discovery, 1986$M	2707	0.00	>20	1.29	2.68
Stock of discovery	2707	0.00	52.66	3.50	7.09
Own patents	2707	0.00	34.00	2.11	3.61
Stock of own patents	2707	0.00	96.18	8.08	12.63
Own patents in related programs	2707	0.00	38.00	3.37	5.25
News in own patents	2707	−11.41	23.97	0.49	2.32
Firm sales in program	2707	−0.06	>800	25.64	85.58
SCOPE: No. programs with disc > 500K	2707	2.00	19.00	10.36	4.58
SIZE: Total discovery spending this year	2707	1.97	>4	3.40	0.68
Papers	2707	0.00	37.00	1.62	5.05
Sum of competitors' discovery spending	2707	0.00	63.78	8.72	12.33
News in competitors' discovery spending	2707	−3.30	31.38	3.65	5.71
Competitors' patents in the same program	2707	0.00	300.00	44.91	47.82
Competitors patents in related programs	2707	4.00	353.00	131.53	82.23

example of "racing" behavior. Consider, for example, the case of captopril and the discovery of the ACE inhibitors.

In 1977, Cushman and Ondetti, two scientists working at the privately funded Squibb Institute, announced that they had synthesized an orally active inhibitor of the angiotensin-converting enzyme (Ondetti et al., 1977). The compound, subsequently named captopril, proved to be extraordinarily potent in the treatment of hypertension and triggered an explosion of interest in the medical and scientific communities (Laragh, 1984; Goodman et al., 1985).[3] By 1992, at least 12 other ACE inhibitors had been patented, all of them chemically related to the original molecule, and ACE inhibitors accounted for

3. Hypertension is a condition in which the patient's blood pressure is consistently greater than the normal level. Although in its early stages it has few symptoms, persistent high blood pressure severely damages the cardiovascular system, and hypertension, "the silent killer," is probably directly or indirectly responsible for 10–20% of all deaths (Julian, 1988).

nearly 30% of antihypertensive drugs sales.[4] Figure 1 outlines this history.

At first glance this would seem to be a clear case of "racing"—head to head competition between firms racing to be first using mere "molecular manipulation"—although the assumption that there is only one "prize" to the race is clearly violated. The identifiable

4. Data from *IMS America*.

1934-70: public sector researchers identify role of renin angiotensive system in controlling blood pressure

1965: pit-viper venom found to contain large numbers of compounds affecting heart muscle, vascular dilation, blood clotting, etc.

1971: Squibb publishes description of compound inhibiting production of Angiotensin Converting Enzyme, reduces blood pressure in rats, but research community skeptical

1977: Squibb patents captopril: orally active ACE inhibitor

Flurry of work on related compounds, results in

Generic Name	Firm	Date of first Patent	Date of first U.S. Patent
Captopril	Squibb	1977	1977
Enalapril	Merck	1980	1980
Lisinopril	Merck	1980	1980
Alacepril	Dainippon	1980	1980
Perindopril	French, public sector	1982	1982
Quinapril	Warner Lambert	1982	1982
Fosinopril	Squibb	1982	1982
Moveltipril	Chugai	1982	1982
Delapril	Takeda	1982	1983
Ramipril	Hoechst	1983	1986
Cilazapril	Hoffman La Roche	1983	1985
Benazepril	Ciba Geigy	?	?

1990 Captopril and Enalapril hold 82% of the U.S. market.

FIGURE 1. CASE STUDY: ACE INHIBITORS AND HYPERTENSION.

winners in the race, Squibb and Merck, currently market compounds that together comprise over 80% of the market for ACE inhibitors, and the other 10 patented compounds could be seen as evidence of socially wasteful overinvestment by the losers. However, a deeper exploration of the steps that led up to captopril's discovery calls into question some of the fundamental assumptions of many stochastic racing models.

Cushman and Ondetti's synthesis of captopril drew on many years of prior research in both the public and the private sectors. ACE inhibitors lower blood pressure by blocking a critical path in the renin angiotensive system (see Figure 2, derived from Julian, 1988). They are, literally, Angiotensin II converting enzyme inhibitors.

The idea that blocking the renin system might reduce high blood pressure originated with the work of Goldblatt and his colleagues (Goldblatt et al., 1934). However, serious interest in anti-renin system therapy as a potential treatment for hypertension only began with the publicly funded work of Laragh (Laragh et al., 1972), Gross (1968), and Erdos (1970), who first clarified the structure of the renin angiotensive system and its role in the control of blood pressure.

Although this research laid the groundwork for the subsequent

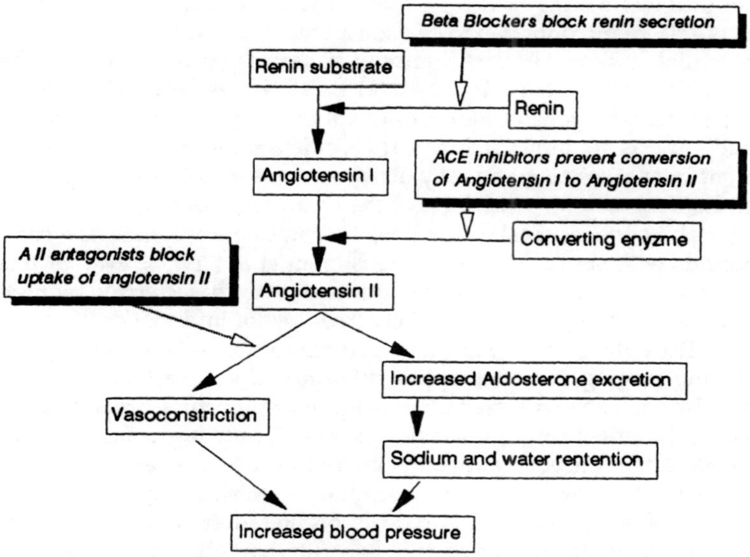

FIGURE 2. THE RENIN ANGIOTENSIN SYSTEM.

discovery of the ACE inhibitors, a great deal of further work was required to translate the fundamental scientific insight into therapeutically useful compounds. There was, initially, considerable skepticism that interference with the renin angiotensive system would reduce blood pressure, since the physiological and biochemical mechanisms that underlie hypertension are extraordinarily complex and interdependent. Many in the medical and scientific community believed that any reduction in blood pressure achieved by blocking the action of the renin angiotensin system would be automatically compensated by increased activity in other blood pressure regulating mechanisms. Even among those focusing on the system, there was disagreement about the most appropriate place in which to disrupt the chain. Some researchers explored the activity of propranolol and the other beta blockers, which inhibit renin secretion (Bühler et al., 1972), while others investigated the properties of Saralasin, a compound that interferes with the uptake of angiotensin II (Brunner et al., 1974). This work was undertaken by researchers working in both the public sector and in commercial firms (Pals et al., 1971).

Interest in inhibitors of the angiotensin II converting enzyme was aroused by the 1967 publication of results showing that a peptide isolated from the venom of a Brazilian snake blocked conversion of angiotensin I to angiotensin II (Hodge et al., 1967). Although this peptide was synthesized by Ondetti and his colleagues (Ondetti et al., 1971), there continued to be widespread doubt as to its therapeutic potential, and despite a sequence of papers exploring its role in the treatment of hypertension (Gavras et al., 1974, Case et al., 1976, 1977), there was little general interest in exploiting the discovery commercially. It was not until Cushman and Ondetti published their achievement in synthesizing an orally active enzyme inhibitor that research in the field took on something of the characteristics of the race, with several pharmaceutical companies attempting to synthesize compounds with similar properties (Cushman et al., 1977). Even at this late stage, research in the field continued to be characterized by high publication rates and the relatively free flow of information.

Thus, the discovery of the ACE inhibitors rested on over 20 years of wide-ranging and often apparently unproductive effort characterized by the extensive exchange of knowledge across firms and between the private and public sectors. It was only in the last stage of the work that the competitive dynamics took on the characteristics of a "race," and even then the description is misleading. On the one hand, it does not recognize that the proliferation of ACE inhibitors may have significant therapeutic benefits (Laragh, 1984). Enalapril, for example, appears to have a lower incidence of side effects such as rash and disturbance of taste in some patient groups (Goodman et al., 1985). Unlike captopril, enalapril is a "prodrug" that is not itself highly active, but must be converted in the body to the active principle, enalaprilate. The resulting differences in the rate at which enalapril is metabolized and excreted compared to captopril imply different dosing regimes, with benefits to some patients.

On the other hand, a characterization of this research as a "race" neglects the fact that many of the companies that subsequently entered continued to engage in the same kind of fundamental research and open exchange of information that characterized Squibb's program (Patchett et al., 1980). Moreover, the search for more effective therapies with fewer side effects based on regulation of the renin-angiotensin system continues. For example, Merck, the firm that introduced enalapril, continued to explore alternative hypertensive therapies, and in 1991 formed a joint venture with Dupont to exploit the latter's discovery of losartan, an angiotensin II receptor antagonist. All the firms in our sample continue to publish actively in this field in the open research literature, at rates exceeding those that accompanied the initial burst of scientific interest.

This pattern, which we believe to be relatively typical of the industry,[5] is confirmed by the accounts of those responsible for setting research strategy. In general, the managers whom we interviewed claimed that in planning their investment programs they focused on three criteria: the size of the unmet medical need, the scientific potential of a field, and the idiosyncratic capabilities of their researchers. Some also mentioned the views of their marketing departments and the need to service an existing franchise as critical factors in their decisions. But when pressed on the role of competitive investment in their criteria, the managers that we interviewed claimed that they tried to avoid head-to-head competition, or "racing," as inherently unproductive.

Although this evidence is suggestive, ultimately the degree to which competition in ethical drug discovery is well characterized as a rent-dissipating race is an empirical question, and, thus, we turn to the quantitative analysis.

5. Research in conditions that are less well understood, such as Alzheimer's or oncology (cancer), is probably even closer to a collaborative, diverse model, while research in the better understood areas such as the development of new anti-infective drugs is probably closer to a pure stochastic race.

4. Specification of the Econometric Model

Ideally, we would like to proceed by constructing a full structural model of R&D investment. However, although our data set is significantly more comprehensive and disaggregated than has been available to previous researchers, it is still neither sufficiently detailed nor complete enough to allow us to do this with any confidence. We would need to assume a structure for the payoff function, and accurately model the relative position of firms over time, the magnitude of spillovers, the nature of firm asymmetries, if any, as well as the evolution of the information structure of the game and the beliefs of each player. Quite apart from the usual concerns about functional form, whether or not we have the "true" model, etc., this places very serious demands on the data. Some of these variables are intrinsically difficult to measure, and in other cases we are limited by the availability of data. One of the most serious problems facing us is modeling payoffs: In the pharmaceutical industry, potential sales of a newly discovered compound are very difficult to assess ex ante and are only realized after long delays (five years or more) and the resolution of great uncertainty about regulatory approvals and the efficacy of the drug in clinical use. Interesting research is under way modeling demand and competition in the final product market (Suslow, 1992; Berndt, 1993), but we still know relatively little about the fundamental factors that determine the sales of new drugs or the dynamics of how new products displace existing drugs. The problem is particularly acute in the case of markets such as drug therapies for Alzheimer's disease where there is clearly great unmet medical need, but there are very few existing products and, thus, very limited information about potential demand, price elasticities etc. We attempted to capture some aspects of demand at the level of therapeutic classes by using data on firm and industry sales revenues, numbers of physicians practicing in relevant specialties, etc., but these variables are not very satisfactory. A further difficulty is that a test of a complete structural model would require a data set that included information about every player in each "race," and since we were only able to obtain data from a subsample of the industry, our analysis would be subject to very serious problems of selection bias. As a first step, therefore, we rely on reduced form analysis to explore some of the issues discussed above.

4.1 Investment Equation

We begin by looking for correlations in the level of research investments across competitors among the firms in our sample, using the research program as our primary unit of analysis and controlling for other exogenous factors that we think are driving investment decisions.

Our "base case" model is a reduced-form regression of each firm's own investment in discovery in each period in each program on internal, firm-specific variables such as lagged own investment and prior success in the program, as well as a number of measures of demand and technical opportunity intended to capture the dynamics that our qualitative research suggests are important to the determination of investment. In order to test for positively correlated investment across competitors, we then introduce suitably lagged measures of competitive investment in the area. Thus, we use the specification

$$R_{it} = \alpha + \beta_1 R_{i,t-1} + \beta_2 T_t + \beta_3 D_t + \beta_4 C_t + \epsilon_{it},$$

where T is a vector of variables capturing shocks to technological opportunity, D is variables capturing demand and perceived medical need, and C is measures of competitors' investment. This regression of the level of R&D investment on competitors' investment explores the degree to which investments are correlated across firms: A test of this hypothesis is simply whether $\beta_4 > 0$. Since we only have data for a sample of firms, and not for the industry, these competitor variables are not entirely satisfactory. However, we believe that our sample is not markedly unrepresentative of the industry as a whole, so these variables are probably a reasonable proportionate approximation to industry investment. Timing issues are clearly important here, and we addressed this empirically by trying a variety of models in which we include contemporaneous competitors' investment, the first and second lags, and a stock variable that can be thought of as a geometric distributed lag on subsequent lags. In the event our results are not significantly affected. Inclusion of both contemporaneous investment and the first or second lags reduces the significance of all three, but introduced alone neither is significantly more significant than the other.

Our proxies for demand do not work very well and are essentially collinear with therapeutic class dummies, so in the results reported here we attempt to capture demand as well as other unmeasured effects by including firm and therapeutic class dummies and a time trend. We measure scientific opportunity using counts of "important" scientific patents in the field, where importance is defined by the fact that they were included in ISI's list of the 100 most highly cited scientific papers in a given year. In most of the regressions we also include the stock of own discovery spending (calculated using the perpetual inventory formula with an assumed depreciation rate of 20%) to proxy for accumulated knowledge capital, and own sales in the program to try to capture some aspects of demand.[6]

There are a number of important econometric issues. First, since our dependent variable is truncated at zero—many firms choose to invest nothing in many areas and might indeed prefer to be disinvesting faster than the depreciation rate of knowledge capital—there is a potential for bias in the OLS estimates, and we therefore also estimate the equations where appropriate using Tobit analysis with appropriate corrections for heteroskedasticity in the error terms.[7] Second, this is a panel data set, and to the extent that there are significant unobserved program effects in the data, using a lagged dependent variable will induce bias in the parameter estimates (Anderson and Hsiao, 1982). This is not a serious problem here, since the bias is inversely proportional to the number of observations per program, which is fairly large here—on average we observe each program for just over 17 years.[8]

Note also that it is unclear that investment *levels* will necessarily show a strong correlation across firms even if racing behavior is an important factor. Recall that at equilibrium, investment levels should only be correlated across firms in the event of common responses to unobserved shocks in demand or in scientific opportunity. To the extent that realized investment levels reflect these equilibrium responses and rational beliefs about competitors, including competitive investment in the regression, does not introduce any additional information. Furthermore, our qualitative work suggests that adjustment costs are very significant, and that in the short term, firms are largely constrained to adjust spending at the margin. Building research capability requires sustained investments over time in both people and equipment, and organizational issues also limit the speed with which research resources can be reallocated within the firm. Therefore, we turn to an examination of the extent to which own investment reacts to *changes* in competitors' investment.

First, following previous research, we explore correlations in first differences across firms. Second, we use two different methods to

6. Own sales is also intended to proxy for the firm's investment in complementary assets such as specialized marketing capabilities. In interviews, some managers identified "the need to maintain a franchise" as an important factor in their investment decisions.

7. Assuming that heteroskedasticity is a result of variation in program size, the variance of the residual was modeled as a function of lagged investment: $\theta_i = \sigma \exp(\alpha R_i)$. Including other variables in this ancillary model had little effect on the results.

8. The telltale changes in parameter estimates moving from fixed effects to random effects models were not found in exploratory calculations.

decompose changes in investment into "anticipated" and "unanticipated" components. In the first place, we construct "news" variables, defined as the difference between this period's flow of investment, and the amount necessary to maintain the beginning of year stock given our assumed depreciation rate, or

$$News_t = R_t - 0.2 * K_t,$$

where K_t is stock of investment in research.

In the second place, we calculate a residual measure of unanticipated investment by taking residuals from a simple investment equation, summing them over competitors for each therapeutic class-year observation, and then including this measure in subsequent regressions.

4.2 Output Equation

Our qualitative analysis has already put the usefulness of one of the assumptions fundamental to much of the theoretical work in this area into doubt. The ACE inhibitor "race" led to the introduction of several compounds, several of them with significantly different therapeutic profiles from the first entrant, suggesting that, in this case at least, it may be inappropriate to characterize research competition as a single "winner take all" race.

We extend and generalize this analysis through a quantitative exploration of the correlation in research outputs across rivals. Recall that our discussion of the literature suggested that the entry of an additional firm into the research "race" is unambiguously welfare-destroying only under a number of quite strong assumptions, including the belief that competing projects are substitutes rather than complements and that there are no substantial spillovers of knowledge across firms. Our goal in this analysis is to explore the usefulness of these assumptions in the context of pharmaceutical research.

In previous work (Henderson and Cockburn, 1993), we estimated a number of research output equations in which competitors' research outcomes (as captured by "important" patents) were modeled as a measure of the spillover of knowledge across firms, entering the research production function with a strong positive coefficient. We interpreted this as evidence that competing research programs are complements rather than substitutes, and that on the whole competitors' success in a particular field does not represent a net "mining out" of opportunities. We reproduce some of these results here, with the addition of our measures of scientific opportunity to control for the possibility that the positive correlation of outputs obtained in previous work reflects common trends in research productivity induced by common shocks to opportunity. Since the dependent variable is a discrete count of important patents, we use Poisson regression.[9]

5. Results

5.1 Are Inputs Correlated?

Tables II to V present our results. As a basis for comparison, and to illustrate the pitfalls inherent in using aggregate data, we begin by exploring the correlation between own and competitive investment using data aggregated to the firm level. These results are shown in Table II. We regress own investment on investment in the previous period, stock of investment, firm sales, and "news" in patents obtained in the area. These regressions are dominated by the lagged dependent variable, which is highly significant, with a coefficient very close to unity. Firm dummies are jointly significant but add little to the explanatory power of the regression.

Models (4), (5), and (6) include competitors' investment in the equation. Competitors' investment in the current period is negatively and significantly correlated with own investment, while competitors' investment in the previous period is insignificant. Model (6) regresses the first difference in own investment on first differences in the explanatory variables, and again competitors' investment is negative and significant. Thus, at first blush our data appear to suggest that there are strong strategic effects operating between firms. However, given that the theory only tells us about competition at the level of research projects, and that we cannot control for technological opportunity in the aggregate analysis, it is not clear that this interpretation is warranted.

Tables IIIa, b, IV, and V report results using our disaggregated program level data. Table IIIa presents OLS estimates of simple investment equations, but these are badly misspecified because of the censoring of the dependent variable at zero. Table IIIb presents more satisfactory results from Tobit analysis. As in the firm-level data, investment at the level of the research program is overwhelmingly driven by investment in the previous period. Firm and therapeutic class dummies are jointly and individually significant. In Model (4) we control for technological opportunity, measured as shocks to the

9. See Henderson and Cockburn (1993) for a more detailed discussion of the specification and estimation of this equation, where similar results were obtained using Negative Binomial and Quasi-likelihood estimation.

TABLE II.
DETERMINANTS OF INVESTMENT IN DISCOVERY AT THE FIRM LEVEL

	(1)	(2)	(3)	(4)	(5)	Dep. Variable: Δ Inv.$_t$	(6)
Intercept	2.599**	0.453	0.775	3.230	1.713	Intercept	4.688**
	(0.920)	2.221	(2.275)	(2.228)	(2.206)		(1.073)
Research Investment$_{(t-1)}$	1.043**	0.986**	0.971**	0.963**	0.966**		
	(0.062)	(0.064)	(0.069)	(0.068)	(0.070)		
Stock of own Investment$_{(t-1)}$	0.000	−0.017	−0.017	−0.027	−0.021		
	(0.020)	(0.029)	(0.031)	(0.031)	(0.031)		
"News" in own patents$_{(t-1)}$			0.005	0.004	0.008	Δ Own patents$_t$	−0.009
			(0.024)	(0.023)	(0.023)		(0.026)
Firm Sales$_t$			0.002	0.001	0.001	Δ Own sales$_t$	−0.004
			(0.003)	(0.003)	(0.003)		(0.005)
Flow of Competitors' Investment$_{(t)}$				−0.046**		Δ Competitors' Investment$_t$	−0.082**
				(0.019)			(0.030)
Flow of Competitors' Investment$_{(t-1)}$					−0.024		
					(0.021)		
Firm dummies		Sig.	Sig	Sig.	Sig.		
Time	−0.357*	−0.340*	−0.449*	−0.523**	−0.444*	Time	−0.492
	(0.174)	(0.201)	(0.232)	(0.227)	(0.233)		(0.184)
Time * Time	0.0128*	0.020**	0.023**	0.049**	0.034**	Time * Time	0.021**
	(0.006)	(0.006)	(0.007)	(0.012)	(0.011)		(0.007)
R-squared	0.944	0.946	0.945	0.947	0.945	R-squared	0.049
Standard error of regression	5.128	5.078	5.102	5.043	5.101	Standard error of regression	5.100

OLS Regression. Dependent variable = Total firm investment in discovery, 171 observations.
Heteroskedastic-consistent standard errors in parentheses.
* Significant at the 5% level.
** Significant at the 1% level.

underlying science base, as captured by "news" in the publication rate of papers in any given area appearing on ISI's annual list of the 100 most significant papers published in the life sciences. This variable is only marginally significant—to a large extent the impact of variation in technological opportunity conditions is also being captured by therapeutic class dummies. In Table IV we again include competitors' investment in the equation. Regressing own investment onto competitors' investment alone, as in Model (1), suggests strong correlation between the two across firms, but once we control for own investment in the last period, this variable becomes insignificant. Neither controlling for technological opportunity (Models [3] and [4]) nor using contemporaneous versus lagged values of competitors' investment has any significant effect on the estimated coefficients. The difference between these program-level results and those obtained using data ag-

TABLE IIIA.
DETERMINANTS OF INVESTMENT IN DISCOVERY AT THE PROGRAM LEVEL

	(1)	(2)	(3)	(4)
Intercept	−0.020	0.080	0.029	0.053
	(0.815)	(0.828)	(0.835)	(0.832)
Flow of Investment in	0.987**	0.980**	0.976**	0.976**
Discovery$_{(t-1)}$	(0.034)	(0.039)	(0.039)	(0.039)
Stock of Investment in	−0.002	−0.005	−0.008	−0.009
Discovery$_{(t-1)}$	(0.012)	(0.013)	(0.013)	(0.013)
"News" in patients in this			0.008	0.008
class$_{(t-1)}$			(0.011)	(0.010)
Own sales in this class$_{(t)}$			0.0008	0.0007
			(0.0005)	(0.0006)
News in key papers in this class				0.002
				(0.007)
Class dummies		Sig.	Sig.	Sig.
Firm dummies	Sig.	Insig.	Insig.	Insig.
Time	−0.012	−0.010	−0.008	−0.010
	(0.079)	(0.078)	(0.078)	(0.079)
Time * Time	0.0007	0.0007	0.0007	0.0007
	(0.0019)	(0.0018)	(0.0019)	(0.0019)
R-squared	0.870	0.871	0.871	0.871
Standard error of regression	0.971	0.969	0.969	0.968

OLS Regression.
Dependent variable = investment in discovery, 2,707 observations.
Heteroskedastic-consistent standard errors in parentheses.
* Significant at the 5% level.
** Significant at the 1% level.

gregated to the firm level dramatically illustrates the danger of using aggregate, firm-level data to explore the validity of models derived from project level interactions.

Tables III and IV test for the presence of reactions across firms using data in levels. As argued above, however, expectations about competitive behavior should already be incorporated into investment strategy where they are reflected in the highly significant and positive coefficient on own investment in the previous period. In Table V we therefore explore the hypothesis that firms react strategically to (unanticipated) changes in competitive investment. As discussed above, we measure the unanticipated component of competitors' investment in three different ways—Models (1) and (2) estimate the investment equation in first differences, Models (3) and (4) use "news" versions of the key variables (the extent to which the current flow exceeds the

TABLE IIIB.
DETERMINANTS OF INVESTMENT IN DISCOVERY AT THE PROGRAM LEVEL

	(1)	(2)	(3)	(4)
Intercept	−2.162*	−2.120	−2.153	−2.034
	(1.105)	(1.147)	(1.148)	(1.170)
Flow of Investment in Discovery$_{(t-1)}$	1.190**	1.172**	1.175**	1.175**
	(0.024)	(0.024)	(0.025)	(0.025)
Stock of Investment in Discovery$_{(t-1)}$	0.029**	0.022**	0.014*	0.014*
	(0.006)	(0.006)	(0.007)	(0.007)
"News" in patents in this class$_{(t-1)}$			0.0004	0.0008
			(0.0109)	(0.0109)
Own sales in this class$_{(t)}$			0.001**	0.001**
			(0.0003)	(0.0002)
News in key papers in this class$_{(t-1)}$				0.012
				(0.007)
Class dummies		Sig.	Sig.	Sig.
Firm dummies	Sig.	Sig.	Sig.	Sig.
Time	0.089	0.096	0.098	0.084
	(0.100)	(0.106)	(0.106)	(0.108)
Time * Time	−0.002	−0.002	−0.002	−0.001
	(0.002)	(0.002)	(0.002)	(0.002)
Coefficient on Lagged Discovery in variance model	0.151**	0.152**	0.153**	0.152 **
	(0.005)	(0.005)	(0.005)	(0.005)
Sigma	0.848**	0.842**	0.842**	0.842**
	(0.011)	(0.011)	(0.011)	(0.012)
Log likelihood function	−2707.44	−2667.36	−2663.62	−2662.64

Heteroskedastic TOBIT Regression.
Dependent variable = Investment in discovery, 2,707 observations.
Heteroskedasticity modeled by $\theta_i = \sigma \exp(\alpha R_i)$.
BHHH Standard errors in parentheses.
* Significant at the 5% level.
** Significant at the 1% level.

amount necessary to maintain the previous period's stock unchanged), while Model (5) uses residuals from a "first-stage" regression of own investment onto lagged investment, sales, technological opportunity, and the usual firm and class dummies. In the first differences and "news" models, we find a weak correlation between changes in own and competitors' investment, but this result is not robust to the inclusion of firm and therapeutic class dummies. The residuals model also shows no evidence of correlated strategies once exogenous and predetermined variables have been partialed out. We

TABLE IV.
DETERMINANTS OF INVESTMENT IN DISCOVERY AT THE PROGRAM LEVEL

	(1)	(2)	(3)	(4)
Intercept	−1.263	−2.272*	−2.162*	−2.008
	(1.525)	(1.168)	(1.184)	(1.182)
Flow of Investment in Discovery$_{(t-1)}$		1.175**	1.175**	1.175**
		(0.025)	(0.025)	(0.025)
Stock of Investment in Discovery$_{(t-1)}$		0.012	0.012	0.012
		(0.007)	(0.007)	(0.007)
"News" in patents in this class$_{(t-1)}$		0.0004	−0.001	−0.001
		(0.011)	(0.011)	(0.011)
Own sales in this class$_{(t)}$		0.001**	0.001**	0.001**
		(0.0003)	(0.0003)	(0.0003)
News in key papers in this class$_{(t-1)}$			0.012	0.012
			(0.007)	(0.007)
Flow of Competitors' Investment in discovery in this class$_{(t)}$	0.028**	0.0025	0.0028	
	(0.004)	(0.0027)	(0.0027)	
Flow of Competitors' Investment in discovery in this class$_{(t-1)}$				0.0012
				(0.0029)
Class dummies	Sig.	Sig.	Sig.	Sig.
Firm dummies	Sig.	Sig.	Sig.	Sig.
Time	0.016	0.109	0.095	0.089
	(0.140)	(0.107)	(0.109)	(0.109)
Time * Time	−0.003	−0.002	−0.002	−0.002
	(0.003)	(0.003)	(0.003)	(0.003)
Coefficient on Lagged Discovery in variance model	0.279**	0.151**	0.151**	0.151**
	(0.008)	(0.005)	(0.005)	(0.005)
Sigma	1.1363**	0.843**	0.843**	0.843**
	(0.023)	(0.011)	(0.011)	(0.011)
Log likelihood function	−3574.47	−2663.20	−2662.10	−2662.56

Heteroskedastic TOBIT Regression.
Dependent variable = Investment in discovery, 2,707 observations.
Heteroskedasticity modeled by $\theta_i = \sigma \exp(\alpha R_i)$.
BHHH Standard errors in parentheses.
* Significant at the 5% level.
** Significant at the 1% level.

interpret these results as rejecting simple reaction-function or tit-for-tat models—they provide little evidence of strategic co-movements in inputs to the research process across firms above and beyond that induced by common exogenous shocks.

TABLE V.
DETERMINANTS OF INVESTMENT IN DISCOVERY AT THE PROGRAM LEVEL

Dependent Variable	(1) ΔInvest$_t$	(2) ΔInvest$_t$	(3) "News" in Invest$_t$	(4) "News" in Invest$_t$	(5) Residual from Invest$_t$ = $f\{.\ .\}$
Intercept	−0.024	−0.013	−0.143	−0.090	−0.0001
	(0.805)	(0.840)	(0.827)	(0.845)	(0.018)
Δ Investment$_{(t-1)}$	0.015	(0.004)			
	(0.057)	(0.057)			
"News" in own investment$_{(t-1)}$			0.832**	0.815**	
			(0.034)	(0.034)	
"News" in own patents$_{(t-1)}$	0.008	0.007	0.008	0.008	
	(0.011)	(0.011)	(0.011)	(0.011)	
"News" in papers$_{(t-1)}$	0.010	0.005	0.010	0.004	
	(0.008)	(0.008)	(0.008)	(0.008)	
Δ Competitors' Investment$_{(t-1)}$	0.024*	0.020			
	(0.012)	(0.012)			
News in Competitors' Investments$_{(t-1)}$			0.011*	0.007	
			(0.005)	(0.006)	
Competitors' Residual					−0.002
					(0.010)
Firm dummies		Partial Sig.		Partial Sig.	
Class Dummies		Sig.		Sig.	
Time	−0.008	−0.006		0.001	
	(0.077)	(0.080)		(0.080)	
Time * Time	0.001	0.001		0.000	
	(0.001)	(0.002)		(0.002)	
R-squared	0.006	0.007	0.627	0.629	0.00002
Standard error of regression	0.986	0.986	0.975	0.973	0.962

First differences, "News" and residuals.
OLS Regression. 2,707 observations.
Heteroskedastic-consistent standard errors in parentheses.
* Significant at the 5% level.
** Significant at the 1% level.

5.2 ARE OUTPUTS CORRELATED?

If firms are "racing" each other in the sense implicit in much of the theoretical literature, then outputs will be negatively correlated across firms—since if firms are racing for a single, well-defined goal, the odds that any firm will obtain it necessarily falls as others reach it successfully. Our qualitative discussion throws doubt on the assumption that pharmaceutical firms compete for a single goal. Here we explore this issue quantitatively.

In previous work (Henderson and Cockburn, 1993), we showed that at the program level, research outputs, as captured by "important" patents, were positively correlated across firms. However, in this analysis we failed to control for changes in technological opportunity, raising the possibility that the observed correlations across firms merely reflected exogenous shifts in opportunity that made it easier to obtain patents in any given class.

Table VI presents Poisson regression results that include controls for shifts in technological opportunity. The dependent variable is a count of important patents applied for (and subsequently granted) in the program area, where we define *importance* as filing in two or more major jurisdictions. Model (1) replicates results from previous work, using a somewhat larger sample, and illustrates the strongly significant and positive correlation between own output and the success of rival firm's efforts.[10] Models (2) and (3) are estimated from the smaller 1975–1988 sample used in the investment equation. Controlling for shocks to scientific opportunity (Model [3]) does *not* attenuate the positive correlation between own and rivals' research success.[11] Models (4) and (5) repeat the analysis for a much more limited subset of the data that covers cardiovascular drugs where we were able to use our knowledge of the scientific history of the field and consultation with experts to identify "Key Events"—those papers that had a seminal influence on the field and that represented order of magnitude changes in scientific opportunity. Again, this does not effect the estimated coefficient on competitors' research output. Far from being a "mining out" of opportunities, competitors' research appears to be a complementary activity to own R&D.

These results have several possible interpretations depending on the degree to which firms are engaged in closely related research projects. At one end of the spectrum, suppose firms investing in the same area are pursuing very different approaches. In this world positive correlation across outputs would reflect solely the spillover of knowledge across firms, and it might still be possible to model a particular race as having only a single reward. At the other end of the spectrum, suppose that firms are engaged in almost identical research.

10. Using competitors' discovery spending in place of their patents gives very similar results: Competitors' investment has a positive and significant impact on own research productivity.

11. An alternative measure of opportunity "cites to key papers" performed very similarly.

TABLE VI. DETERMINANTS OF PATENT OUTPUT AT THE PROGRAM LEVEL

	(1) Full sample 1961–1988	(2) Full sample 1975–1988	(3) Full sample 1975–1988	(4) C.V. only 1975–1988	(5) C.V. only 1975–1988
N	4930	2707	2707	438	438
Intercept	−2.257**	−0.380	−0.228	2.812*	2.420
	(0.134)	(0.621)	(0.625)	(1.309)	(1.329)
Ln(Investment)	0.024*	−0.014	−0.013	−0.038	−0.044
	(0.010)	(0.012)	(0.012)	(0.026)	(0.026)
Ln(Stock of Investment)	0.031**	0.036**	0.036**	0.108**	0.107**
	(0.010)	(0.010)	(0.011)	(0.036)	(0.036)
SCOPE: No. classes firm is active	0.104**	−0.012	−0.013	0.037	−0.046
	(0.016)	(0.034)	(0.034)	(0.072)	(0.072)
SCOPE * SCOPE	−0.006**	−0.001	−0.001	−0.020	−0.016
	(0.001)	(0.002)	(0.002)	(0.003)	(0.003)
Ln(SIZE): Total research spending by firm.	0.242**	0.201**	0.210**	0.454**	0.469**
	(0.042)	(0.066)	(0.067)	(0.139)	(0.140)
Stock own pats in this class	0.032**	0.033**	0.033**	0.034**	0.034**
	(0.001)	(0.001)	(0.001)	(0.002)	(0.002)
News in own patents in related classes$_t$	0.034**	0.026**	0.025**	0.028**	0.029**
	(0.003)	(0.005)	(0.005)	(0.009)	(0.009)
News in competitors' patents in this class$_t$	0.006**	0.004**	0.004**	0.017**	0.017**
	(0.001)	(0.001)	(0.001)	(0.002)	(0.002)
News in competitors' patents in related classes$_t$	0.002**	0.003**	0.003**	−0.002	−0.002
	(0.001)	(0.001)	(0.001)	(0.001)	(0.001)
News in Key papers$_{(t-1)}$			0.013**		
			(0.005)		
Key private sector C.V. papers$_t$					0.464**
					(0.167)
Key private sector C.V. papers$_{(t-1)}$					0.154
					(0.419)
Firm dummies	Sig.	Sig.	Sig.	Sig.	Sig.
Class dummies	Sig.	Sig.	Sig.		
Time	0.071**	−0.040	−0.060	−0.400**	−0.364**
	(0.008)	(0.060)	(0.061)	(0.128)	(0.130)
Time * Time	−0.003**	−0.002	−0.000	0.008	0.007
	(0.000)	(0.001)	(0.001)	(0.003)	(0.003)
Log-likelihood	−8194.3	−4444.2	−4440.8	−755.7	−752.2

Poisson Regression. Dependent variable = PATENTS.
Standard errors from analytical second derivatives in parentheses.
* Significant at the 5% level.
** Significant at the 1% level.

Then the finding that outputs are positively correlated would suggest both that there are significant spillovers of knowledge across programs and that any single "race" has several "rewards."

Our qualitative work suggests that the reality lies somewhere in between these two extremes: Some firms pursue different goals within the same general therapeutic area, while others compete more directly. In either case publication and the norms of professional disclosure appear to ensure the rapid exchange of knowledge across the industry. Thus, there are some grounds for believing that the entry of additional firms into the pharmaceutical research "race" is not unambiguously welfare-destroying. Competing projects are better described as complements rather than substitutes, and there are significant spillovers of knowledge across firms.

6. Conclusions

Recent advances in the theoretical literature have greatly expanded our understanding of the forces that shape the competitive dynamics of research and development, but a paucity of sufficiently detailed empirical data has left these insights relatively untested. In this paper we draw on unusually detailed qualitative and quantitative internal data provided at the research program level by 10 major pharmaceutical firms to explore the usefulness of the modern literature as a source of insight into the dynamics of competition in ethical drug discovery.

Our analysis focuses on one particularly compelling aspect of the literature: the suggestion that in winner take all situations, competition in R&D becomes a Prisoner's Dilemma, leading to overinvestment in research. Without adequate measures of the social return to innovation, we can say nothing about whether there is "too much" or "too little" research undertaken by the industry, but our results do not support the suggestion that R&D investment in drug discovery is driven by the "tit-for-tat" or simple reaction function models hinted at by the institutional literature.

Two key results were obtained from estimating simple reduced form models of R&D investment and R&D output from research program level data. First, R&D investment is only weakly correlated across firms once common responses to exogenous shocks are accounted for. Second, rivals' R&D results are positively correlated with own research productivity, which we interpret as evidence for extensive R&D spillovers rather than the depletion externality implied by winner take all models.

These results are not, of themselves, sufficient to reject the hypothesis that investment behavior in the industry is driven by strategic considerations. There is, after all, theoretical support for a very wide variety of observable behavior as equilibrium outcomes of strategic interaction. Nonetheless, knowledgeable critics of the industry have charged that "racing" is a useful characterization of industry dynamics, and our results provide little support for the most obvious form that we expect this to take. If "me too" or responsive investment occurs—and there is certainly qualitative evidence that it occurs occasionally—it appears not to be characteristic of the bulk of research investment. A better characterization, and one that is consistent with our qualitative research, is that investment decisions are driven by the heterogeneous capabilities of the firm, by adjustment costs, and by the evolution of technological opportunity.

Clearly, much additional work needs to be done to determine the nature of R&D competition in pharmaceuticals. Our results illustrate the potentially fruitful ways in which the modern game theoretic literature can frame the examination of complex strategic issues. However they also point to the need not only to model R&D as a race with multiple prizes, but also to develop theories that incorporate richer models of adjustment costs and firm heterogeneity, and to collect empirical data that is comprehensive and detailed enough to allow one to test them.

APPENDIX 1: QUALITATIVE RESEARCH STRATEGY

- Detailed study of secondary sources.
- Field interviews, 10 large pharmaceutical firms. Interviews were semi-structured in that each respondent had been provided with a list of key questions before the interview, and each interview lasted from one to three hours. These data were supplemented with interviews with a number of industry experts, including senior academics in the field. In all over 100 individuals were interviewed.

Company	1	2	3	4	5	6	7	8	9	10
General overview	X	X	X	X	X	X	X	X	X	X
Senior cardiovascular managers	X	X	X	X	X	X	X	X	X	X
Comprehensive interviews	X		X	X		X			X	

APPENDIX 2: SOURCES AND CONSTRUCTION OF QUANTITATIVE DATA

The data set used in this study is based on detailed data on R&D inputs and outputs at the research program (narrow therapeutic class) level for 10 ethical pharmaceutical manufacturers. Table A1 gives definitions of the variables used in the regression analysis. Their construction is described in detail below.

TABLE AI.
DEFINITION OF VARIABLES USED IN THE REGRESSION ANALYSIS

Measures of scientific opportunity	
Papers	Total papers in the class listed in the ISI list of "Top 100 papers" in the biological sciences
Key private papers (CV only)	Number of papers signaling major breakthroughs in the field published by authors employed by private firms
Key public papers (CV only)	Number of papers signaling major breakthroughs in the field published by authors employed by the public sector
Measures of demand	
Cases	Reported U.S. incidence of the disease
Deaths	Reported U.S. mortality
Doctors	Number of doctors identifying themselves as specialists in the area
US sales in class	Wholesale U.S. sales of drugs in the class
Measures of competitive activity	
Competitors' patents in this class	Important patents applied for by 28 major (worldwide) competitors
Competitors' patents in related classes	Important patents applied for by 28 major (worldwide) competitors in related classes
Competitors' investment in this class	Investment in discovery research by the other 9 firms in the core data base
Competitors' investment in related classes	Investment in discovery research by the other 9 firms in the core data base in related classes
Firm-specific variables	
Investment	Expenditures by this firm in this research area, relating primarily to production of new compounds, by year, in millions of constant 1986 dollars
Patents in this class	Important patents granted to this firm in this research area, by year, from the Derwent database. Note that throughout the analysis we count patents by year of *application*
Patents in related classes	Important patents granted to this firm in the related therapeutic class, net of the patents granted in this research area
Firm sales in class	Total U.S. sales in the class
Scope	The number of research areas in which this firm has spent at least $0.5m dollars on discovery this year
Total investment (size)	Total research expenditure by this firm in this year across all therapeutic classes

Observations are identified by (encoded) FIRM, CLASS, and YEAR.

Inputs

Our data on inputs to the drug discovery process is taken from the internal records of participating companies and consists primarily of annual expenditures on exploratory research and discovery by research program. Several issues arise in dealing with these data.

(A) Discovery versus Development The distinction between discovery and development is important. We define resources devoted to discovery as all preclinical expenditures within a therapeutic class, and development as all expenses incurred after a compound has been identified as a development candidate. Where exploratory research was attributable to a particular research program, this is included in the discovery category. Nonprogram exploratory research was included in the overhead allocation for each research program. Clinical grants are included in the figures for development, and grants to external researchers for exploratory research are included in the total for discovery.

In some cases, the companies supplied us with data already broken down by discovery versus development by research program. In others, we had to classify budget line items for projects/programs into the appropriate category. This was done based on the description of each item in the original sources, and the location of items within the structure of the company's reporting procedure.

(B) Overhead In order to maintain as much consistency in the data collection process as possible, we tried to ensure that these figures include appropriate overhead charges directly related to discovery activities, such as computing, R&D administration and finance, etc., but exclude charges relating to allocation of central office overhead, etc. The overhead also includes some expenditures on discipline-based exploratory research such as "molecular biology," which appeared not to be oriented toward specific therapies. Overhead was allocated across therapeutic classes according to their fraction of total spending.

(C) Licensing We treat up-front, lump-sum payments in respect of in-licensing of compounds, or participation in joint programs with other pharmaceutical companies, universities, or research institutes, as expenditure on discovery. Royalty fees and contingent payments are excluded.

Outputs

In this paper we focus on patent grants as our measure of research output. We count patents by year of application. Our interest here is on determinants of technical success, defined in terms of producing new potentially important compounds, rather than on the ultimate commercial success or failure of new drugs. Since patent examiners award grants based on slowly changing objective criteria of novelty, nonobviousness, and potential industrial application, we believe that patent grants are an appropriate basis for measuring research output in this industry. Pharmaceutical companies patent prolifically, and patents are, of course, a rather noisy measure of research success, in part because the significance of individual patents varies widely. We partially control for this by counting only "important" patents, where we define "importance" by the fact that the patent was granted in two of the three major markets: the United States, Japan, and the European Community.

These data were provided by Derwent Publications, Inc., who we asked to use their proprietary classification and search software to produce counts of "important" patents to us broken down by therapeutic class for 29 U.S., European, and Japanese pharmaceutical manufacturers for the 26 years preceding 1990. These firms were chosen to include the 10 firms that have given us data together with 19 other firms chosen on the basis of their absolute R&D expenditures, R&D intensity, and national "home base" to try to get a representative, rather than exhaustive, assessment of worldwide patenting activity. These 19 firms have been consistently in the top 30 worldwide pharmaceutical firms in terms of R&D dollars and sales.

Note that many of these patents will be "defensive" patents in that firms may patent compounds they do not intend to develop in the short term but that may have competitive value in the longer term. Alternative measures of "importance" include citation weighting and more detailed international filing data—"very" important patents are usually filed in nearly every major potential market. We hope to explore these alternative measures in later work.

Classification

Classification of inputs and outputs by therapeutic class is important because this drives our measure of spillovers. There are essentially two choices: to define programs by physiological mechanisms, for example, "prostaglandin metabolism," or by "indications" or disease states, for example, "arthritis." We have chosen to classify on the basis of indication, largely because this corresponds well to the internal divisions used by the companies in our sample (which is conceptually correct), but also because classification by mechanism is much more difficult (a practical concern.) In further work we intend to repeat the analysis using a "cut" by mechanism. We classified both inputs and outputs according to a scheme which closely follows the IMS World-wide classes. This scheme contains two tiers of aggregation: a detailed "research program" or "research area" level, and a more aggregated level that groups related programs into therapeutic classes. For example, the therapeutic class "CARDIOVASCULAR" includes the research programs "ANTI-HYPERTENSIVES," "CARDIOTONICS," "ANTITHROMBOLYTICS," "DIURETICS," etc.

There are some problems with this procedure. First, some projects and compounds are simply very difficult to classify. A particular drug may be indicated for several quite distinct therapies: consider serotonin, which has quite different physiological actions on either side of the blood-brain barrier. As a neurotransmitter it is believed to play important roles in mediating motor functions. As a systemic hormone it has a variety of effects on smooth muscle; for example, it functions as a vasoconstrictor. Some companies report expenditures in areas that are very difficult to assign to particular therapeutic classes: A company doing research using rDNA technology might charge expenditure to an accounting category listed as "Gene Therapy/Molecular Biology," which is actually specific research performed on, for example, cystic fibrosis, but we have no idea about which disease the research is directed toward treating, and are forced to include these expenditures in "overhead." Second, our two-tier classification scheme may not catch all important relationships between different therapeutic areas. We believe that we are undercounting, rather than overcounting in this respect, so that the importance of spillovers will be underestimated rather than overestimated. Third, where firms supplied us with "predigested" data, they may have used substantively different conventions in classifying projects. One firm may subsume antiviral research under a wider class of anti-infectives, while another may report antivirals separately. Not surprisingly there are major changes within companies in internal divisional structures, reporting formats, and so forth, which may also introduce classification errors. After working very carefully with these data, we recognize the potential for serious incorrect assignment of outputs to inputs, but we believe that such errors that remain are not serious. The use of patents as the output measure should reduce vulnerability to this problem, since we observe relatively large numbers, and a few misclassifications are unlikely to seriously affect our results. When we move to INDs and NDAs as our output measures, the much more sparsely distributed data are likely to increase our vulnerability.

Matching

Data series on inputs and outputs for each firm were matched at the research program level. This procedure appears to successfully match outputs and inputs unambiguously for the great majority of programs. In a very few cases, however, we ended up with research programs where patents, INDs, or NDAs were filed, but where there were no recorded expenditures. Of these the majority were obviously coding errors or reflected dilemmas previously encountered in the classification process, and appropriate corrections were made. In other cases, it was clear that these reflected "spillovers"—research done ostensibly in, for example, hypertension, may generate knowledge about the autonomic nervous system that prompts patenting of compounds that may be useful in treating secretory disorders (e.g., ulcers.) In such cases we set "own" inputs for the program equal to zero and included these observations in the data base.

Deflation

Since our data sources span many years, it is important to base the analysis on constant dollar expenditures. We used the R&D price deflator constructed by Edwin Mansfield (1987) for his Oil and Chemicals industry grouping. This index is based on wage rates for R&D employees, and a price index for equipment and instrumentation purchases, and though its movement is quite different from the CPI or the GNP deflator, it varies much less across industries, leading us to believe that it may be a reasonable approximation to the "correct" index for pharmaceuticals. Mansfield's index exists only for 1969–1983; we extended it backward to 1966 and forward to 1990 using movement in the CPI. The periods 1966–1969 and 1983–1990 saw relatively little price inflation, so this approximation is unlikely to be a serious problem. In a later paper we intend to exploit the information that some companies were able to give us on R&D inputs in units of labor hours to construct an index specifically for research costs in the pharmaceutical industry.

Demand

We attempt to measure cross-sectional and time series variation in the state of demand for drug treatments for the different therapeutic classes using a variety of publicly available data. First, we compiled statistics on disease incidence and mortality in the U.S. population from a variety of sources, including the information provided by bodies such as the National Institutes of Health and the National Cancer Institute. Unfortunately, these data are not entirely comprehensive and consistent. Some diseases or conditions are underreported because they are not sufficiently serious, or because of social stigma (e.g., depression). In many cases data only appear to have been gathered at five-year or longer intervals, and in others there were serious inconsistencies in series over time that presumably reflect differences in reporting requirements. There are also problems in comparing, for example, diseases that have low incidence but high mortality rates with those with high incidence and low mortality (thyroid cancer versus common cold), or indeed in comparing diseases that are merely uncomfortable with those that are life-threatening, or chronic conditions with acute conditions.

Second, we compiled data on the number of doctors in the United States belonging to various specialties. These data are at best only available at a rather high level of aggregation (cardiology versus neurology), and their usefulness is also limited by the classification of many doctors into specialties such as internal medicine or pediatrics, which have no information about therapeutic classes.

These data are far from satisfactory measures of demand: They are neither as detailed as we would like, nor do they show much variation over time (trend is driven by demographics), nor are they necessarily directly comparable in the cross section, nor do they capture the potential market size for, for example, drug therapies versus surgery. Our hope is that they pick up gross variation in levels of demand, or shocks to demand such as the appearance of AIDS. An alternative measure of demand is actual dollar sales of pharmaceuticals in the class. We compiled these data from the reports of IMS America (a market research firm) for each of the therapeutic classes in our data.

A final, and perhaps more fundamental, problem with these demand measures is that their usefulness as measures of incentives to do R&D may be rather limited. Ideally we would like some measure of the total consumer surplus available to be captured, based on market characteristics such as the price elasticity of demand, potential for drug therapies to enhance patients' quality of life or extend their life expectancy, the efficacy of currently available therapies, etc. Our measures fall far short of this ideal, but may be the best that we can do with limited time and resources.

Scientific Opportunity

We use two sources of data to measure "discrete" shocks to technological opportunity: bibliometric data based on the citation databases of ISI, and identification of key events in the evolution of the science base for particular therapeutic classes. The ISI publishes an annual list of the most significant papers published in the life sciences. For each year and each therapeutic class we noted the number of papers in that area that made the "Top 100" list and also how many times that those papers were subsequently cited in the next two years. Problems with these measures of shocks to opportunity include matching papers to therapeutic classes, which is often difficult if the paper refers to "generic" aspects of molecular biology or physiology rather than specific diseases or organ systems; failure of the scientific community to identify key advances until much time has passed; advances being of great importance to researchers in a narrowly defined field, but lacking sufficient general interest to attract enough citations to make the "Top 100" list, etc. However these measures have the advantage that they are consistent and comparable over time, and reasonably well matched to specific therapeutic classes.

For cardiovascular therapies, we attempted to identify "key events." This process is more subjective, but is hopefully more comprehensive. We examined standard texts on pharmacology, such as *Goodman and Gilman's The Pharmacological Basis for Therapeutics* (Gilman, A., et al, 1985) or accounts that focused particularly on cardiovascular therapies, including texts such as Hamer (1986), Schneeweiss (1986), and Morganroth and Moore (1981), and attempted to identify significant steps forward in scientific understanding, such as the discovery of entire classes of compounds showing desirable activity in vitro or in animal models, or the identification of important enzyme pathways.

References

Anderson, T.W. and C. Hsiao, 1982, "Formulation and Estimation of Dynamic Models Using Panel Data," *Journal of Econometrics*, 18, 47–88.

Arrow, K., 1962, "Economic Welfare and the Allocation of Resources for Invention," in R. Nelson, ed., *The Rate and Direction of Inventive Activity*, Princeton, NJ: Princeton University Press, pp. 609–619.

Baldwin, W.L and J.T. Scott, 1987, *Market Structure and Technological Change*, Chur, Switzerland: Harwood Academic Publishers.

Berndt, Ernst, 1993, "Price Indexes for Antihypertensive Drugs That Incorporate Quality Change; A Progress Report on a Feasibility Study." MIT Program on the Pharmaceutical Industry, Working Paper Number 6–92.

Dasgupta, P. and E. Maskin, 1987, "The Simple Economics of Research Portfolios," *Economic Journal*, 97, 581–595.

—— and J. Stiglitz, 1980a, "Industrial Structure and the Nature of Innovative Activity," *Economic Journal*, 90, 266–293.

—— and ——, 1980b, "Uncertainty, industry structure and the speed of R&D," *Bell Journal*, 11, 1–28.

D'Aspremont, C. and A. Jacquemin, 1988, "Cooperative and Noncooperative R&D in Duopoly with Spillovers," *American Economic Review*, 78, 1133–1137.

—— and ——, 1990, "Cooperative and Noncooperative R&D in Duopoly with Spillovers: Erratum," *American Economic Review*, 80, 641–642.

DiMasi, J. et al., 1991, "The Cost of Innovation in the Pharmaceutical Industry," *Journal of Health Economics*, 10, 107–142.

Dixit, Avinash, 1988, "A General Model of R&D Competition and Policy," *Rand Journal of Economics*, 19, 317–326.

Fraja, Giovanni, 1993, "Strategic Spillovers in Patent Races," *International Journal of Industrial Organization*, 11, 139–146.

Grabowski, Henry and Nevine Baxter, 1973, "Rivalry in Industrial Research and Development," *Journal of Industrial Economics*, 21, 209–235.

Harris, C. and J. Vickers, 1987, "Racing with Uncertainty," *Review of Economic Studies*, LIV, 1–22.

Henderson, Rebecca, and Iain Cockburn, 1993, "Scale, Scope, and Spillovers: Determinants of Research Productivity in Ethical Drug Discovery," NBER Working Paper #4476

Khanna, Tarun, 1993, "Racing Behavior: Technological Evolution in the High-End Computer Industry." Mimeo, Harvard Business School.

Lee, T.K. and L.L. Wilde, 1980, "Market Structure and Innovation: A Reformulation," *Quarterly Journal of Economics*, 94, 429–436.

Lerner, Joshua, 1991, "The Empirical Exploration of a Technology Race: The Winchester Disk Drive Industry, 1972–1988." Mimeo, Harvard Business School.

Levin, Richard C. and Peter C. Reiss, 1988, "Cost-reducing and Demand-creating R&D with Spillovers," *Rand Journal of Economics*, 19, 538–556.

Loury, Glenn, 1979, "Market Structure and Innovation," *Quarterly Journal of Economics*, 93, 395–410.

Meron, Amos and Richard E. Caves, 1991, "Rivalry among Firms in Research and Development Outlays," Paper presented at the 1991 UBC Summer IO Conference.

Reinganum, J.F., 1982, "A Dynamic Game of R and D: Patent Protection and Competitive Behavior," *Econometrica*, 50, 671–688.

——, 1989, "The Timing of Innovation: Research, Development and Diffusion," in Schmalensee, R. and R. Willig (eds.), *Handbook of Industrial Organization, Volume 1*, Amsterdam: North Holland, 1989.

Scherer, F.M., 1967, "Research and Development Resource Allocation Under Rivalry," *Quarterly Journal of Economics*, 81, 359–394.

——, 1992, *International High Technology Competition*, Cambridge, MA: Harvard University Press.

Schumpeter, J.A., 1934, *The Theory of Economic Development*, Cambridge, MA: Harvard University Press.

——, 1950, *Capitalism, Socialism and Democracy*, Cambridge, MA: Harvard University Press.

Spence, Michael, 1984, "Cost Reduction, Competition and Industry Performance," *Econometrica*, 52, 101–121.

Suslow, Valerie, 1992, "Are There Better Ways to Spell Relief: A Hedonic Pricing Analysis of Ulcer Drugs," University of Michigan, Working Paper #696.

Suzumura, K., 1992, "Cooperative and Noncooperative R&D in an Oligopoly with Spillovers," *American Economic Review*, 82, 1307–1320.

Scientific References

Bühler, F.R., J.H. Laragh, L. Baer, E.D. Vaughan Jr., and H.R. Brunner, 1972, "Propranolol Inhibition of Renin Secretion. A Specific Approach to Diagnosis and Treatment of Renin-dependent Hypertensive Diseases," *New England Journal of Medicine*, 287, 1209–1214.

Brunner, H.R., H. Gavras, J.H. Laragh, J.E. Sealey, I. Gavras, and R.A. Vukovitch, 1974, "Hypertension in Man. Exposure of the Renin and Sodium Components Using Angiotensin II Blockade," *Circulation Research* (Suppl. 1), 34–43.

Case, D.B et al., 1976, "Estimating Renin Participation in Hypertension. Superiority of Converting Enzyme Inhibitor over Saralasin," *American Journal of Medicine*, 1976, 790–796.

——, 1977, "Possible Role of Renin in Hypertension as Suggested by Renin-Sodium Profiling and Inhibition of Converting Enzyme," *New England Journal of Medicine*, 296, 641–646.

Cushman, D.W., H.S. Cheung, E.F. Sabo, and M.A. Ondetti, 1977, "Design of Potent Competitive Inhibitors of Angiotensin-Converting Enzyme. Carboxyalkanoyl and Mercaptoalkanoyl Amino Acids, *Biochemistry*, 16, 5484–5491.

Erdos, E.G. (ed.), 1970, "Bradykinin, Kallidin, and Kallikrein," *Handbuch der Experimentellen Pharmakologie*, Vol. 25, Berlin: Springer-Verlag.

Goldblatt, H.J., R.F. Lynch, R.F. Hanzal, et al., 1934, "Studies on Experimental Hypertension. Production of Persistent Elevation of Systolic Blood Pressure by Means of Renal Ischemia," *Journal of Experimental Medicine*, 49, 347–379.

Gavras et al., 1974, "An Angiotensin Converting Enzyme Inhibitor to Identify and Treat Vasoconstrictor and Volume Factors in Hypertensive Patients," *New England Journal of Medicine*, 291, 817–821.

Gilman, A.G., L.S. Goodman, T.W. Rall, and F. Murad, eds. 1985, *Goodman and Gilman's The Pharmacological Basis of Therapeutics*, New York: Macmillan.

Gross, F., 1968, "The Regulation of Aldosterone Secretion by the Renin-Angiotensin System Under Various Conditions," *Acta Endocrinol.* (Kbh.) (suppl. 124) 41–64.

Hodge, R.L., R.D. Lowe, and J.R. Vane, 1967, "Concurrent Measurement of Renin and Angiotensin in the Circulation of the Dog," *Nature*, 215, 853.

Julian, Desmond G., 1988, *Cardiology*, London: Bailliere Tindall.

Laragh, J.H. et al., 1972, "Renin, Angiotensin and Aldosterone System in Pathogenesis and Management of Hypertensive Vascular Disease," *American Journal of Medicine*, 52, 644–652.

——, 1984, "Concept of Anti-Renin System Therapy: Historic Perspective," *American Journal of Medicine*, 77(2A), 1–6.

Mansfield, E., 1987, "Price Indices for R&D Inputs, 1969–1983," *Management Science*, 33.

Ondetti, M.A., N.J. Williams, E.F. Sabo, J. Pluscec, E.R. Weaver, and O. Kocy, 1971, "Angiotensin-Converting Enzyme Inhibitors from the Venom of Bothrops Jararca: Isolation, Elucidation of Structure and Synthesis," *Biochemistry*, v 10, 4033–4039.

Ondetti, M.A., B. Rubin, and D.W. Cushman, 1977, "Design of Specific Inhibitors of

Angiotensin-Converting Enzyme. New Class of Orally Effective Antihypertensive Agents," *Science*, 196, 441–444.
Pals et al., 1971, "A Specific Competitive Antagonist of the Vascular Action of Angiotensin II," *Circulation Research*, 29, 664.
Patchett, A.A., E. Harris, E.W. Tristram, et al., 1980, "A New Class of Angiotensin-Converting Enzyme Inhibitors," *Nature*, 288, 280–282.

[3]

The Economics of Research and Development in the Pharmaceutical Industry

William S. Comanor

I. Introduction

In this chapter I return to the topic of my doctoral dissertation, completed in 1963 under the same title. My purpose then as now was to explore the importance of research and development (R&D) for new products in the pharmaceutical industry. Such products embody new medical advances and have a major impact on mortality and morbidity rates.

The structure of discovering and developing new drugs has shifted greatly over the past 20 years. In the early years of this industry, from its rebirth following the Second World War through roughly the end of the 1970s, the major pharmaceutical companies developed "in house" most of their primary products, largely by testing large numbers of available compounds. Scientific knowledge was obtained primarily from freely available sources. There were perhaps 40 highly integrated firms worldwide that contributed to this effort.[1]

Since then, the process of drug development and discovery has become increasingly complex. A new technology appeared, termed "biotechnology," which placed this process on a more scientific basis. A new set of firms appeared: smaller and interposed between the scientific community and the major pharmaceutical firms. It is reported that between 25% and 40% of sales by the major pharmaceutical companies currently are from products that originated in the biotech sector.

In this chapter I review the expanding economic literature that describes and explains the new structure for research. Along with the new scientific knowledge, I find an increasing degree of disintegration as the major companies have increasingly funded work carried out by others. I consider the costs and benefits of the new structure and explore the implication of current trends for the efficiency of the drug development process.

II. A New Technology for Pharmaceutical Research

Since the mid-1980s the pharmaceutical industry has been shaken by the rapid pace of technological change. Unlike most other industries, however, this change has had little effect on production processes used to produce new or existing products. It has not led to cost-saving innovations that permit lower production costs; indeed, it has had little to do with the manufacturing process. Instead the new technology relates to the process by which new products emerge in this industry.

At the same time, the new technology has not had so great an impact on the process by which new drugs are tested and evaluated. The extensive testing of new drugs required by the U.S. Food and Drug Administration (FDA) and similar agencies elsewhere has not been greatly affected by the new research methods.

At the dawn of the modern industry, in the 1950s and 1960s, the process of drug discovery was largely empirical and had little of a theoretical base. This fact was acknowledged in studies written during this era, such as the book by Jewkes, Sawyers, and Stillerman (1958). Those authors emphasized the distinction between systematic and empirical research. In the former, "the new idea has a certain completeness and unity from the outset," while in the latter, "the new idea is a nature of a discovery arising from a search, more or less informed, among many possibilities." The latter approach was characteristic of new discoveries in the chemical industry. Jewkes et al. suggested that "many modern chemical inventions . . . have risen from the vague intuition that a chemical compound with a given structure might have certain desirable properties, followed by the experimental verification of the hypothesis" (pp. 164–166).

This characterization was applied directly to pharmaceutical research during this era. Thus, a former medical director of a division within Pfizer stated in 1960:

> There can be no question that some very wonderful, exciting, extremely important, and productive research has been and is being done within the pharmaceutical industry. However, I do not think that it would detract in any way from these fine and worthwhile activities to point out that much that is called research in the pharmaceutical industry has little relationship to what most people engaged in academic and research activities would consider to be scientific research.[2]

If this picture applied to the early postwar years, it does not describe the pharmaceutical research process very well at the beginning of the twenty-first century. What was once a largely empirical discovery process has developed into a more theoretical activity. The science of pharmacology has become more advanced so that researchers can develop a greater understanding of how drugs work in the body. This greater understanding has shifted the character and setting for pharmaceutical research.

The shift to a more science-based process, however, is not fully complete. It occurred more rapidly in some therapeutic categories than in others, and in some pharmaceutical companies than in others. These two dimensions are, of course, not independent for companies whose work is more heavily concentrated in areas where science-driven activities have taken hold more fully and have in turn adopted the new approach more quickly. A striking feature about this technological shift has been the considerable heterogeneity in the adoption process. The diffusion of this change has not been rapid or complete.

One reason is that firms who want to employ the new technology cannot merely invest in basic research. Cockburn and Henderson (1998) emphasize that "it is also important for the firm to be actively connected to the wider scientific community" (p. 158). They developed the concept of "connectedness," as measured by the extent of collaboration in writing scientific papers across institutional boundaries, and conclude that "firms wishing to public sector research must do more than simply invest in in-house basic research: they must also actively collaborate with their public sector colleagues. . . . The extent of this collaboration . . . is positively related to private sector research productivity" (p. 180). The process by which firms acquire this new technology is not simple or direct, nor obtained without cost.

Cockburn, Henderson, and Stern (1999) emphasize the importance of organizational factors and the distribution of power relationships within the firm for the speed at which new research methods are employed. Some firms are more suited to the new technology than others. The authors note that all their informants emphasized "that differences in the historical experience of the firm, in their 'knowledge capital,' were critically important in shaping the adoption decision" (p. 19).

To examine the diffusion process empirically, Cockburn et al. explore the relationship between patenting and publishing by the company's scientific staff. When the older, more empirical approaches were employed, these activities were considered substitutes, and the publication of research findings not encouraged. In contrast, research organizations using more science-based methods saw the publication of research findings differently. These activities were encouraged as promoting increased interdependence with the scientific community. For this reason, patenting and publishing were now complements rather than substitutes in the research process.

Cockburn, Henderson, and Stern also study the manner by which the new technology was adapted. They find that the new technology was an important factor for pharmaceutical research and yet has been characterized by a relatively low rate of diffusion. The increasing importance of new biological discoveries for the design of pharmaceutical products required new capabilities.

As Gambardella (1995) notes, "Although a public good, science is not a 'free' good. Internal scientific capabilities are critical for taking advantage of the public good" (p. 103). From interviews with research personnel at various companies, he observes the different decisions taken at different companies to develop their scientific capabilities. Some made a major effort in this, while others did not. Where the new technology was employed, research personnel were encouraged to participate in the broader scientific community and publish their findings in the scientific literature. There was also increasing collaboration by industry researchers with nonindustry scientists located at university and government laboratories.

As part of these increasing interactions, there have been a greater number of research collaborations and agreements between drug companies and other scientific institutions. Gambardella provides a list of 59 such relationships between large U.S. companies and universities and other research institutions from the 1980s (pp. 49–54). While research institutions benefit from the infusion of industry funds,[3] the companies gain greater access to scientific discoveries.

To test these observations, Gambardella estimates the relationship between company patents and a lag structure of its scientific publications, together with the level of research expenditures. He reports that "scientific research and drug discovery appear to be intimately connected" (p. 115) and that "in the 1980s, the productivity of applied research increased which is related to significant advances in scientific knowledge and in the technology of experimentation (e.g., computerized drug design)" (p. 121). From his data, there were clear advantages to firms who adopt the new technology.

Cockburn and Henderson (1998) examine the importance of public funding for the development of the most important new drugs. Although they find that more than three-fourths of the leading 21 drugs introduced between 1965 and 1992 had at least some input from the public sector, this does not mean that public-sector research was sufficient for their development. Of these products, most relied on enabling discoveries from the public sector. However, for only 2 of the 21 did public-sector research contribute to the synthesis of the relevant compound. Even when creation of new drugs was facilitated by public research efforts, there were still important parts of the discovery process carried out in industry research laboratories. In large measure, industry and nonindustry research efforts are complementary.

To study this matter further, the authors investigate the extent to which scientists in industry research laboratories collaborated with their public-sector counterparts, using coauthorships as a measure. Not only did they find a large number of such collaborations but also that coauthorships are positively related to the number of important patents taken out by the firm. They conclude that "firms wishing to take advantage of public-sector research must do more than simply invest in in-house basic research: they must also actively collaborate with their public-sector colleagues. Further, . . . coauthorships across institutions are correlated with private sector research productivity . . . [so that there are] substantial differences across firms in their ability to access public knowledge" (Cockburn and Henderson 1998, p. 180). This is another factor affecting the rates of diffusion of the new science-based technology.

Although the trend in pharmaceutical research activities has been toward a more scientific basis, there remains a substantial empirical component to these activities. Schwartzman and Cognato (1996) argue that "pharmaceutical research remains empirical, notwithstanding the increase in knowledge." Even is cases where drugs were allegedly rationally designed, "it was essentially still a matter of following leads and not hypotheses suggested by general theories" (p. 850). Although acknowledging that pharmaceutical research efforts have become more structured in recent years, these writers suggest that it is still largely an empirical exercise.

An important corollary of these changes has been the growing connection between university and industry research activities. Schwartzman and Cognato report that the number of scientific publications authored by researchers at industry laboratories rose sharply in the years between 1973 and 1986. However, they indicate that this result does not apply to all companies (p. 850).

III. Biotechnology

The initial scientific discovery by Stanley Cohen and Herbert Boyer, leading to the new technology in 1973, provided the basic technique for recombinant DNA. As this discovery became increasingly understood, its commercial implications became recognized. New firms were created to employ this new technology.

Zucker, Darby, and Brewer (1998) observe that "the primary pattern in the development of the industry involved one or more scientist-entrepreneurs who remained on the faculty [of a research university] while establishing a business on the side. . . . We see the university as bringing about local industrial benefits by permitting its professors to pursue private commercial interests while their faculty appointments tie them to the area" (p. 291). These writers emphasize that the new scientific knowledge is not a "free good" usable by an unlimited number of potential users at little cost. Instead, it is a form of human capital that was held originally by only a small group of discoverers and co-workers who had gained this knowledge by working at the "bench-science level" (p. 291). Strikingly, this new technology was not immediately available to the major pharmaceutical firms.

At its outset, the new technology was the province of a host of small companies that typically focused on one or a few potential products. Scriabiane (1999) estimates that there were 1,308 such firms in the United States in 1996 (p. 271). Of these, only 260 were public corporations. Many startup firms had their roots in university science. Another survey reported that fully 1,100 new biotechnology companies were created between 1980 and 1994 from licenses granted by universities (p. 272).

Historically the new firms created to pursue this technology saw themselves as representing a different industry, distinct from the broader pharmaceutical industry. Their original goal was not only to discover new drugs but also to manufacture and sell them. But only a few actually reached that goal.[4] An important reason is that the discovery of a new drug is only the first step along the path to launching a new product successfully. The FDA requires extensive clinical testing for new drugs, and the costs of large-scale trials, particularly in Phases 2 and 3, can be substantial. As noted below, the costs of clinical trials and other product development efforts represent more than half of total research and development costs. Since the new startups had generally employed most of their resources in the more scientific, discovery phase of this research, they were often not prepared to support the additional testing costs that were required.

Furthermore, the marketing of a new drug is often as costly as its total research expenditures (Hurwitz and Caves 1988). Those outlays are typically concentrated in the first two years following a product's introduction. Marketing costs effectively double the total outlays required for a new product's launch. This level of resources was generally available only from the major pharmaceutical companies.

Increasingly, the large pharmaceutical companies formed partnerships and alliances with smaller biotechnology startups. In addition to providing needed capital, they facilitated the clinical trial process and supplied essential managerial support.

However, interactions between the two types of firms were often difficult as they developed from different cultures. A solution was the purchase of the more successful biotechnology firms by large pharmaceutical companies. These included the following acquisitions: Genentech by Hoffman-Laroche, Chiron by Ciba-Geigy (Novartis), Genetics Institute by American Home Products, Sphinx Biotechnologies by Lily, and Affymax by Glaxo. While some leading biotechnology firms remained independent, for example, Amgen, most joined the pharmaceutical industry. Prospects for an independent biotechnology industry soon disappeared.

Although the difficulty of raising sufficient capital from private investors was an important reason, there is also a second explanation, which resulted from the distinction between single-project and multiproject firms. As Guedj and Scharfstein (2004) observe, "the problem with single-project firms is that, if they have poor investment opportunities, they may still invest because managers are reluctant to return funds to shareholders. . . . This conflict is mitigated in an internal capital market to the extent that higher-level managers can retain funds for investment, but have a broader range of projects in which to invest" (pp. 1–2). Small biotechnology startups, which often have only a single research project, sometimes continue to invest funds even when prospects are relatively dim.

To test this proposition, Guedj and Scharfstein compare startup biotechnology firms with major firms that have a larger number of projects. They report that single-project firms were more likely to move their products from Phase 1 to Phase 2 trials within a two-year period than were mature firms. However, their products were also less likely to demonstrate good results in Phase 2 trials, and less likely to move into Phase 3 trials within a three-year period. The authors interpret these findings as suggesting an agency problem between investors and managers for smaller, single-project firms that often leads to overinvestment in research. Larger, multiproduct firms were therefore more efficient.

Although the early biotech firms had an advantage in their understanding of the new scientific technology, they faced the economic hurdle of raising sufficient capital to conduct their research, carry out the extensive trials required by FDA, and bring their products to market. As with other startups, they originally sought investor funding, although this was soon joined by contracts and grants from leading pharmaceutical companies. In return for providing the necessary funds, the larger companies sought alliances through which they would share in the returns from any new products that resulted.

An important feature of the biotechnology sector is the increasing formation of alliances between small startup firms and larger pharmaceutical companies. These alliances represent a middle ground between fully independent transactions and the acquisition of the smaller firm by the larger company. By the 1990s, funding by the leading pharmaceutical companies for their alliance partners became a major source of biotechnology financing. In four years – 1994, 1995, 1997, and 1998 – alliance funding represented more than half of the amounts received by startup biotechnology firms and exceeded 60% of total financing, although it was somewhat lower in other years.

While the new startup firms received financing, the large pharmaceutical companies came to rely increasingly on these alliances for their new product pipelines. Of the 691 new entities approved by the U.S. Food and Drug Administration between 1963 and 1999, fully 38% were in-licensed rather than developed fully in industry research laboratories (Nicholson, Danzon, and McCullough 2002, p. 2). Through this process, the major companies gained access to the new technology, and the new biotech products that resulted became important members of their overall menu of drugs.

These alliances required that smaller biotechnology firms accept diluted property rights in their new products. Not only would the returns be shared but decisions and control over the research process would now be negotiated with an outside partner. An obvious question is why they were willing to do so. One answer is that these steps were needed to raise capital that would not otherwise be available. However, if that were the only factor, other investors than the large pharmaceutical companies would have equal standing and be as likely to respond. This capital is typically provided by pharmaceutical companies, which suggests that other factors are also important.

To examine these matters, Danzon, Nicholson, and Pereira (2005) investigate the research performance of biotechnology alliances, paying particular attention to whether this performance varied with the experience of the originating and licensing companies. The issue studied was whether the gains from collaboration, and particularly the expertise that each firm brings to the alliance, exceed any likely disincentive effects following from the dilution of property rights. The latter might result because each firm's efforts were not fully internalized, and each bore only a portion of the research costs associated with bringing a product to market.

Danzon and colleagues collected information on nearly 200 compounds under development in the United States during 1988–2000. Nearly half of the compounds were developed within an alliance, both for large firms as well as for smaller and medium-sized ones. For Phase 1 trials, they report that the size of the originating firm was not related to the percentage developed within an alliance, which confirms the conventional wisdom that small firms generally have the same skills and resources needed for small-scale trials as larger firms. In contrast, they find that small and medium-sized originating firms more frequently had compounds in development through Phase 2 and 3 trials within an alliance than otherwise. The smaller firms seemed to require the resources and expertise of a major firm to pursue these larger and more expensive trials (p. 334 and Table 4).

The authors also examine the experience and size of the licensing firms. Again, they find that the number of past trials had little relationship with the prospects for success on Phase 1 trials, but the number of past trials did have a substantial positive effect on later phases of research. Having performed more trials in the past was predictive of greater success with the Phase 2 and 3 trials. They report that "large firms have higher success rates on in-licensed compounds than on compounds that they originate in-house" (p. 319). These findings suggest that large pharmaceutical companies have an advantage in carrying out latter-stage clinical trials as compared with new startups, but not in discovering new drugs or in performing Phase 1 trials. There appears to be an important division of labor by which biotechnology is employed to discover and develop new drugs.

Nicholson, Danzon, and McCullough (2002) examine the relationship between alliance payments and product features as related to the characteristics of the parties. They find that "biotechnology companies signing their first deal receive a 60% discount relative to firms that signed at least two prior deals, controlling for product characteristics and some measure of the rights transferred." Also, "the discount for inexperience declines to 30% on a biotech firm's second deal and is insignificant for subsequent deals" (pp. 5–6).

Learner and Merges (1998) review a sample of 200 alliances between smaller biotechnology firms and larger pharmaceutical companies, or among biotechnology firms, between 1980 and 1995. They seek to understand the role of control as between the two parties and report "evidence consistent with the hypothesis that the financial condition of R&D firms affects their ability to retain control rights in technology alliances" (p. 146). As expected, smaller biotechnology firms with more revenues prior to the alliance were less likely to negotiate away their control rights.

Learner and Tsai (2000) also consider the nature of biotechnology alliances and how they are influenced by whether or not they were formed in periods of sufficient external financing. They report that when external financing was more readily available, control was more frequently maintained by the smaller biotechnology company then when external financing was more limited.

This study also finds that when control was maintained by the smaller biotechnology firm, the alliance's performance was better as measured by the probability that their drug would advance to the next stage of testing or be finally approved. On the other hand, performance was "significantly worse" when control was assigned to the large corporation (p. 28). This issue is important because only when the research entity retains control is the project likely to be managed efficiently. However, when it does not have sufficient financial resources, and must transfer increased ownership to a pharmaceutical company, prospects for the larger project are reduced.[5]

IV. Scale and Scope of Pharmaceutical Research

These issues of scale and scope in regard to pharmaceutical R&D have been studied most extensively. The first concerns the relative productivity of different sized research efforts, and whether R&D dollars are more effective when aggregated together in large-scale enterprises or when divided among a larger number of smaller firms. The critical issue here is the importance of specialized people and equipment. Second is the issue of economics of scope, which refers to the advantages of specialization or diversification within research facilities, whether there are advantages within a given scale of research activities of concentrating on a limited number of research problems or alternatively in spreading the effort more broadly.

Forty years ago I published a paper that directly explored the scale effects of pharmaceutical R&D (Comanor 1965). In that paper, which used data for the years between 1955 and 1960, I found economies of scale for R&D carried out in smaller pharmaceutical firms but diseconomies for research undertaken within the largest companies.

These findings were disputed by Vernon and Gusen (1974), who instead report for the 1965–1970 period that larger firms were better at innovation than smaller firms (p. 294). To be sure, as those authors acknowledge, the latter period followed the introduction of the 1962 Drug Amendments that required demonstrations of efficacy as well as safety for the introduction of a new drug, while my earlier study preceded the new law. A possible explanation, therefore, for the reported differences was the new conditions under which pharmaceutical research was then carried out.[6]

Jensen (1987) reviewed these earlier studies and provided new estimates. She did not find that marginal product of research expenditures depended on firm size. Her results instead suggest that, except for the smallest firms, there is no particular advantage for new products of either large research scale or large firm size.

The current literature on this subject has advanced beyond these early studies. Much of the progress is attributable to the work of Cockburn and Henderson, who emphasize differences between the discovery and development of new drugs (2001, p. 3). Discovery includes both the basic science and the application of the science to the selection of candidate drugs. In this effort the research process is particularly risky in that only a few candidate drugs are actually continued into development. Drug development, on the other hand, largely includes the three phases of testing required by the FDA. Although outcomes are more certain than before, it remains a risky process in which many prospective drugs are discarded.

Although the development segment of pharmaceutical research has a lesser scientific component than the discovery phase, it remains a substantial undertaking that absorbs more than half of total industry research budgets. Cockburn and Henderson (2001, p. 6) report that the relative cost of development efforts has accounted for between 60% and 70% of pharmaceutical research activities since 1970. The costs of this work are largely determined by FDA requirements.

For their original study on this subject, Henderson and Cockburn (1996) gathered project level data from 10 large pharmaceutical companies, which together accounted for approximately one-fourth of total industry research and development. When their data are aggregated to the firm level, they report no evidence of scale economics: "the implied long-run elasticity of important patent output with respect to research spending in every model was between 0.4 and 0.5" (p. 46). However, their analysis of program-level data leads them to different conclusions. Although they report "quite sharply diminishing marginal returns to increasing investment in any single program,... programs embedded in larger and more diversified firms appear to be significantly more productive" (p. 48). Therefore, they find both economies of scale and scope at the firm level.

Cockburn and Henderson (2001) acknowledge that their early results pertain only to the discovery phase of pharmaceutical research, and not to development. To correct for this omission, they gathered additional data from the same 10 companies they had examined earlier. This information was for 708 development projects conducted between 1960 and 1990. On average, these firms undertook approximately 16 individual projects simultaneously, with average total spending per project exceeding $18 million. Over the 30-year period, mean expenditures per project roughly doubled (p. 1041). Furthermore, there was a wide range of product duration, running from 1 to 26 years, although 90% of them lasted 10 years or less. As expected, projects that failed to generate a new drug application (NDA) were concluded earlier than those that led to NDAs.

Their primary results were based on logit regression models used to explain the project's probability of success, where success was indicated by a new drug application. Their primary explanatory variables are: Scale – the firm's total development spending, Scope – the number of therapeutic classes in which the firm was active, and Experience – the stock of previously obtained NDAs. When these explanatory variables are included together in the estimating equation, the Scale effect was not statistically significant while the Scope effect has a major impact on the probability of the project's success. The firm's past success in the therapeutic class was also significantly and positively associated with successful outcomes. The authors conclude that "relocating the average project to a firm active in one more area would increase the probability of success by about 0.03" (p. 20). However, they also find that both of these purported effects disappear when firm dummy variables are introduced into the analysis, from which they conclude that "much of the variation in the scope measure is between rather than within firms" (p. 20).

The different ways in which research is organized as between firms in the Henderson-Cockburn sample have striking effects on the probability of success. The authors note the presence of "enduring idiosyncratic differences among firms in the organization and management of the drug development process. . . . Differences in development strategy – in the pace and timing of development spending, and in the formulation of research strategy that guides clinical development – [can be] important determinants of development productivity" (p. 21). That conclusion raises the question of why less efficient organizations and managements continue and are not replaced by more effective alternatives.

Overall, Cockburn and Henderson (1999) emphasize the presence of knowledge spillovers both within and across firms. The success of a given project is enhanced, they argue, by the success of a related program within the firm as well as in other firms. Even more important, they write:

The most statistically important determinant of a research program's success, however, is its past productivity. The keys to this determinant are the "knowledge capital" accumulated by the program as an organizational unit as well as the skills and experience of individual scientists.... The primary advantage of size has [therefore] become the ability to exploit internal returns to Scope – particularly the ability to exploit internal spillovers of knowledge – rather than any economy of Scale per se.... [Furthermore,] the benefits of spillovers can be realized only by incurring the costs of maintaining "absorptive capacity" – the ability to capture new spillovers." (1999, pp. 323–324)

The firm's scientific base, and the knowledge capital acquired by that base, they contend, dominates any simple economies of either scope or scale in determining the success or outcomes of a firm's research and development process. Scope and scale by themselves are less important than the knowledge capital accumulated by the firm.

The unique contributions of Henderson and Cockburn arise in part from the data set they have been able to acquire. While earlier studies used the firm as the observational unit, they probed within the firm to the level of the research project, and in doing so, provided rich insights that were not available earlier.

A dimension of the increasing disintegration of pharmaceutical R&D is the growing use of contract research organizations (CROs) to conduct clinical trials of new drugs. By 1999, 23% of trials were outsourced to CROs (Azoulay 2004, pp. 1593, 1600). In general, the more data-intensive projects are outsourced, while knowledge-intensive projects are more frequently undertaken within pharmaceutical companies (p. 1592).

V. Productivity and Costs

There are two ways of approaching the question of the productivity function and the cost function, which of course are duals of one another, and the economic literature deals with both. Except in perverse circumstances, conclusions regarding one have direct implications for the other. This principle applies to research costs and to research productivity. The increasing research cost of new drugs is directly related to the declining productivity of pharmaceutical R&D.

An important feature of pharmaceutical research in the past few decades is that despite the substantial scientific achievements that have occurred, and that are reflected in the increasing application of biotechnology to new drug development, the rate of new product generation has been fairly steady (Scherer 2000; Cockburn 2004). As Cockburn acknowledges, however, "counts of new molecular entities (NMEs) are a noisy measure. On average, over the long term, these numbers have been remarkably steady, but they fluctuate sharply from year to year, so that peak-to-trough changes over shorter time periods can be highly misleading" (p. 11).

To be sure, simple counts of new products introduced do not encompass either their medical or their economic importance. Some introductions are invariably more important than others. Indeed, as Grabowski and Vernon (1990, 1994) point out, there are major differences in sales among products so that the relevant distributions are highly skewed. Furthermore, pharmaceuticals have various indications, and the medical and/or economic importance of particular drugs can be more closely related to the number of approved indications than to the number of products.

In contrast, pharmaceutical industry spending on research and development has expanded greatly in the past few decades. From total spending of less than $5 billion in 1970, these outlays increased to $30 billion by 2002.[7] There has thus been an increasing discrepancy between the relatively stable number of new drugs approved and the increasing number of dollars spent on R&D to discover new drugs. The result, of course, has been declining research productivities in terms of the numbers of new products introduced, and also increasing costs for new drugs.

Berndt, Cockburn, and Grepin (2005) employ the number of medical indications to measure pharmaceutical innovation. A substantial share of industry research and development expenditures, estimated at between 25% and 30% (p. 45), is directed toward finding new indications for existing products. Berndt et al. use the term "incremental innovation" to describe these efforts. For the three therapeutic areas they examined, the number of FDA approvals for new indications increased substantially in the past decade (p. 27). In addition, the greater number of approved indications has led to increased utilizations of the drugs concerned (p. 41). On that basis, they maintain that reported declines in pharmaceutical research productivity are overstated.

An important feature of recent trends in pharmaceutical innovation is that they have accompanied the increasing disintegration of the research process. As noted earlier, an increasing share of pharmaceutical research is carried out in small biotechnology companies that deal with one or a small number of products. With increasing frequency, the major drug companies enter the process only at the development and testing phases. What seems clear, however, is that this new structure has not led to increased productivity or lower costs, at least in terms of the number of new products introduced, although it may have influenced the therapeutic properties of the new drugs. The shift of drug research to a more science-based mode has thus been associated with a substantial increase in research costs. What is unclear is whether these higher costs reflect the increased requirements of the science-based process or the effects of a more vertically disintegrated structure in which higher costs are borne or higher margins charged by participating firms.[8]

The reverse side of this same picture is, of course, the higher research costs of developing new drugs. There is a continuing literature on this question, which began with the 1979 paper by Hansen. Building on that foundation is the major study by DiMasi, Hansen, and Grabowski (1991). From a sample of 93 self-originated new chemical entities (NCEs) introduced by 12 companies in the 1970s and 1980s, they report mean cash outlays of $114 million per approved product (1987 dollars) and fully capitalized costs of $231 million. Because the R&D process is so lengthy, expenditures were just under half of total costs. Kettler (1999) updated DiMasi et al.'s estimates to 1997 values, based on the GDP implicit price deflator. Her resulting estimate is $312 million (pp. 14–15).

Because project-level data were available only for development and testing costs, DiMasi et al.'s estimates depended also on parameters derived from other sources. These included (1) an estimated success rate of 23% at which investigational NCEs gain approval, (2) an estimated ratio of 55.7% between preclinical and total R&D costs, (3) an estimated lag structure of 98.9 months between the initiation of clinical testing and NDA approval, and (4) a discount rate of 9% (pp. 121–126). All of these factors influenced their cost estimates.

Finding an appropriate discount rate is particularly important. Although the 9% rate used by DiMasi and colleagues may be appropriate for private firms making investment decisions, this rate may be much higher than is appropriate for public decision making. Fuchs and Zeckhauser (1987) argue that as long as future citizens are given equal weight to current ones, "the value of life-years to future generations should be discounted at the time-value-of-money rate" (p. 265). And Viscusi (1995) observes: "many cost-effectiveness studies currently use a real rate of discount of 5%, . . . [and] real rates of return of 3%, or even less, are more consistent with U.S. economic performance in the past decade" (p. 144). At lower discount rates, total research costs per new drug are much lower.

More recently, DiMasi, Hansen, and Grabowski (2003) employ a similar methodology to provide updated estimates of research costs. They examine development expenditures for a sample of 68 randomly selected new drugs introduced by 10 leading pharmaceutical companies during the 1990s. These firms accounted for 42% of industry R&D expenditures (p. 157). They then apply a real discount rate of 11% to capitalize costs to the point of marketing approval, which is a substantially higher rate than the 9% discount rate used earlier.

While their previous study estimated R&D expenditures per new drug at $231 million in 1987 dollars, their more recent one provides an estimate of $802 million in 2000 dollars. These figures indicate sharply higher costs for new product development. From this vantage point as well, the growth of a science-based research effort has not reduced research costs but led to higher ones.

VI. The Efficiency of Pharmaceutical Research: Some Conclusions

There are various perspectives from which to evaluate the efficiency of pharmaceutical research. One is whether the optimal amount of research is being conducted. Too many or too few resources could be allocated to this purpose. A second dimension is whether this research is carried out in the most effective manner so that output is maximized for given levels of input. In this section I consider both of these dimensions; the first is termed allocative efficiency, and the second is termed technical efficiency.

On the allocative efficiency of pharmaceutical research, there are theoretical reasons why there could be either under- or overinvestment in research. On the one hand, research activities, and particularly basic research, generate substantial positive externalities in that their total benefits to society exceed those accruing to the particular firm. As a result, firms do not incorporate their full measure of benefits when making their investment decisions.

On the other hand, there is more recent economic literature on racing behavior as applied to research activities. An important conclusion is that in a "winner take all" situation, there can be overinvestment in research activities. The reason is that the prospective gains may be less than the aggregate amount of the investment undertaken to achieve these gains.

Research spending in the pharmaceutical industry is carried out in the context of considerable interfirm rivalry. I emphasized that point in my first article on this topic (Comanor 1964) but provided no formal model of the process. Since that time, there have been more formal discussions of these issues. A particularly lucid one is offered by Cockburn and Henderson (1994), which emphasizes the competitive nature of the drug discovery process.

The authors first review the available theoretical literature on rivalrous research and emphasize its "winner take all" feature. In the case of pharmaceutical research, the firm completing the invention and receiving the patent wins the race. It gains most of the benefits from this research while others receive much lower returns on their investment. Although this picture is not always correct when applied to the pharmaceutical industry, it is largely so since the first and second entrants into a particular therapeutic market generally capture most of the net returns. Furthermore, firms understand that others are competing for the same prizes, and set their research strategies in anticipation of rival investment.

Cockburn and Henderson construct a data set to test the implications of this behavior. These data included the spending and output levels of individual research programs gathered from the internal records of 10 large pharmaceutical companies. Applying these data to an underlying model, they report that R&D investment is only weakly correlated across firms, but that R&D outcomes are positively correlated with the firm's own research productivity (p. 508). Although "me-too" investment occurs occasionally, it is not a major characteristic of this industry. In their judgment, "a better characterization . . . is that investment decisions are driven by the heterogeneous capabilities of the firm, by adjustment costs, and by the evolution of technological opportunity" (p. 509). Although strategic considerations may play some role, they argue that such factors do not drive investment decisions.

Cockburn and Henderson also note: "there are some grounds for believing that the entry of additional firms into the pharmaceutical research 'race' is not unambiguously welfare-destroying. Competing projects are better described as complements rather than substitutes, and there are significant spillovers of knowledge across firms" (p. 508). They conclude that rivalrous research activity is not the dominant factor behind the decision to invest in pharmaceutical research.

An alternate approach is not to examine variations in pharmaceutical research spending among firms but rather to consider the trends over time in total industry spending. Scherer (2001) employs this approach. His goal is to explain the long-term trend in real research spending, which had increased between 1962 and 1996 at a mean annual rate of 7.5% per year. In contrast, the growth rate of gross margins was 4.23% per year (pp. 217–218).

Rather than comparing these two series directly, Scherer computes the deviations of each series from its best-fitting linear trend. He finds a high correlation between these two sets of deviations and concludes that "the similarity of trend deviation patterns suggest that there was indeed cyclical co-movement in pharmaceutical industry growth margins and R&D

outlays" (p. 220). He goes on to explain: "As profit opportunities expand, [pharmaceutical] companies compete to exploit them by increasing R&D investments, and perhaps also promotional costs, until the increase in costs dissipate most, if not all, supranormal profit returns" (p. 220).

Consistent evidence is provided by Giaccotto, Santerre, and Vernon (2005), who estimate the influence of real drug prices on R&D intensity. Since drug prices are directly related to industry revenues, this study offers a similar picture of the process by which research spending is determined. These authors report "a 10% rise in the growth of real drug prices is associated with nearly a 6% increase in growth of R&D intensity" (pp. 204–205). What both these studies suggest is not an investment model at all, but rather one that employs available internally generated funds specifically for research and development purposes.

Where uncertainty levels are high, this process has the advantage of ensuring that all available funds are used for research purposes. What it does not demonstrate, nor could it do so, is whether this allocation process leads to an excess or insufficient spending on pharmaceutical research. What we observe is that spending has increased strongly in recent decades. New resources have flowed into the process by which new drugs are discovered, and there are no indications that promising avenues of research are neglected.

On this point, Grabowski and Vernon (1990, 1994) estimate rates of return from investment in pharmaceutical research and development, and report values slightly higher than the associated cost of capital. In their latter study they conclude: "the estimated mean return on pharmaceutical industry new chemical entity (NCE) introductions for the first half of the 1980s was 11.1% compared with the estimated (real) cost of capital of 10.5% over the same period" (p. 404). This finding also suggests that one is unlikely to find major unexploited opportunities. Still, without determining a social optimum, one cannot make firm conclusions about the sufficiency of resources directed toward these activities.

On the question of technical efficiency, results are also mixed. The productivity of pharmaceutical research funds has receded sharply in recent years, at least when measured by the number of new chemical entities introduced; and the cost of discovering and developing these products has correspondingly increased. The promise of a science-based research process has not led to the greater efficiency that was projected by its early proponents.

As Cockburn (2004) emphasizes, there are pluses and minuses to the process of disintegration of pharmaceutical research (pp. 17–20). One cannot conclude that the new structure of pharmaceutical research is the source of the higher costs and fewer products per research dollar that we observe. However, as Cockburn also suggests, "there is a genuine possibility . . . that the restructuring of the pharmaceutical industry will ultimately prove quite costly in terms of reduced productivity" (p. 21). Whether or not this concern is justified is unclear at this time.

Notes

1. The first therapeutic revolution that created the modern pharmaceutical industry is chronicled in Temin (1980), pp. 58–87.
2. Statement of Haskell J. Weinstein, Director of the Chest Hospital, Duarte, California, in Hearings, Part 18, p. 10243.
3. Industry critics argue that these organizations sacrifice their independence through such relationships. However, that charge presumes a more unbalanced relationship than is often the case.
4. By the end of the millennium, these companies included Amgen, Biogen, Chiron, Genentech, and Genzyme.
5. See Aghion and Tirole (1994) for a discussion of the underlying theoretical considerations.
6. Although Vernon and Gusin (1974) acknowledge the possibility of this factor, they reject it by reestimating one of their equations using data for the earlier period. However, these latter results are inconclusive.
7. These amounts describe worldwide research and development spending by member companies of the Pharmaceutical Research and Manufacturers of America and are expressed in constant 2002 dollars using the National Institutes of Health Biomedical R&D Price Deflator. See Cockburn (2004), p. 11.
8. For an interesting discussion of these issues, see Cockburn (2004).

References

Aghion, Philippe and Jean Tirole. 1994. 'The Management of Innovation.' *Quarterly Journal of Economics* 109: 1185–1209.

Azoulay, Pierre. 2004. 'Capturing Knowledge Within and Across Firm Boundaries: Evidence from Clinical Development.' *American Economic Review* 94(5): 1591–612.

Berndt, Ernst R., Iain M. Cockburn, and Karen A. Grepin. 2005. 'Biopharmaceutical R&D: Is the Productivity Decline Overstated?' Working paper, Conference on Health Reform in Europe and the U.S., Tufts Center, Talloues, France, July.

Cockburn, Iain M. 2004. 'The Changing Structure of the Pharmaceutical Industry.' *Health Affairs* 23(1): 10.

Cockburn, Iain M. and Rebecca Henderson. 1999. 'The Economics of Drug Discovery,' in Ralph Landau et al., eds, *Pharmaceutical Innovation*, 308–30, Philadelphia: Chemical Heritage Press.

Cockburn, Iain M. and Rebecca Henderson. 2001. 'Scale and Scope in Drug Development: Unpacking the Advantages of Size in Pharmaceutical Research.' *Journal of Health Economics* 20(6): 1033–57.

Cockburn, Iain M., Rebecca Henderson, and Scott Stern. 1999. 'The Diffusion of Science-Driven Drug Discovery: Organizational Change in Pharmaceutical Research', National Bureau of Economic Research Working Paper 7359.

Comanor, William. 1964. 'Research and Competitive Product Differentiation in the Pharmaceutical Industry in the United States.' *Economica* 31: 372–84.

Comanor, William. 1965. 'Research and Technical Change in the Pharmaceutical Industry.' *Review of Economics and Statistics* 47(2): 182–90.

Danzon, Patricia M., Sean Nicholson, and Nuno Sousa Pereira. 2005. 'Productivity in Pharmaceutical–Biotechnology R&D: The Role of Experience and Alliances.' *Journal of Health Economics* 24(2), March: 317–39.

DiMasi, Joseph A., Ronald W. Hansen, and Henry G. Grabowski. 2003. 'The Price of

Innovation: New Estimates of Drug Development Costs.' *Journal of Health Economics* 22(2): 151–85.
DiMasi, Joseph A., Ronald W. Hansen, Henry G. Grabowski, and Louis Lasagna. 1991. 'Cost of Innovation in the Pharmaceutical Industry.' *Journal of Health Economics* 10(2), July: 107–42.
Fuchs, Victor R. and Richard Zeckhauser. 1987. 'Valuing Health: A "Priceless" Commodity.' *American Economic Review* 77(2): 263–68.
Gambardella, Alfonso. 1995. *Science and Innovation: The US Pharmaceutical Industry During the 1980s*. Cambridge: Cambridge University Press.
Giaccotto, Carmelo, Rexford E. Santerre, and John A. Vernon. 2005. 'Drug Prices and Research and Development Investment Behavior in the Pharmaceutical Industry.' *Journal of Law and Economics* 48(1): 195–214.
Grabowski, Henry and John M. Vernon. 1990. 'A New Look at the Return and Risks to Pharmaceutical R&D.' *Management Science* 36: 804–21.
Grabowski, Henry and John M. Vernon. 1994. 'Returns on New Drug Introductions in the 1980s.' *Journal of Health Economics* 13(4): 383–406.
Guedj, Ilan and David Scharfstein. 2004. 'Organizational Scope and Investment: Evidence from the Drug Development Strategies and Performance of Biopharmaceutical Firms.' NBER Working Papers 10933, National Bureau of Economic Research, Inc.
Hansen, Ronald W. 1979. 'The Pharmaceutical Development Process: Estimates of Development Costs and Times and the Effects of Proposed Regulatory Changes,' in *Issues in Pharmaceutical Economics*, ed. Robert I. Chien, 151–87, Boston: Lexington Books.
Henderson, Rebecca and Iain Cockburn. 1996. 'Scale, Scope, and Spillovers: The Determinants of Research Productivity in Drug Discovery.' *RAND Journal of Economics* 27(1), Spring, 32–59.
Hurwitz, Mark and Richard Caves. 1988. 'Persuasion or Information? Promotion and the Shares of Brand Name and Generic Pharmaceuticals.' *Journal of Law and Economics* 31: 299–320.
Jensen, Elizabeth J. 1987. 'Research Expenditures and the Discovery of New Drugs.' *Journal of Industrial Economics* 36: 83–95.
Jewkes, John, David Sawers, and Richard Stillerman. 1958. *The Sources of Invention*. London: Macmillan.
Kettler, Hannah E. 1999. 'Updating the Cost of a New Chemical Entity.' London: Office of Health Economics.
Learner, Josh and Robert P. Merges. 1998. 'The Control of Technology Alliances: An Empirical Analysis of the Biotechnology Industry.' *Journal of Industrial Economics* 46: 125–56.
Learner, Josh and Alexander Tsai. 2000. 'Do Equity Financing Cycles Matter? Evidence from Biotechnology Alliances.' National Bureau of Economic Research Working Paper W7464.
Nicholson, Sean, Patricia M. Danzon, and Jeffrey McCullough. 2002. 'Biotech-Pharmaceutical Alliances as a Signal of Asset and Firm Quality.' NBER Working Papers 9007, National Bureau of Economic Research, Inc.
Scherer, F.M. 2000. 'The Pharmaceutical Industry,' in Culyer, B.J. and Newhouse J.P., eds, *Handbook of Health Economics*, Amsterdam: Elsevier Science, 1297–333.
Schwartzman, David and Antonio Cognato. 1996. 'Has Pharmaceutical Research Become More Scientific?' *Review of Industrial Organization*, 11: 841–51.
Scriabine, Alexander. 1999. 'The Role of Biotechnology in Drug Development,' in Landau, R. et al., eds, *Pharmaceutical Innovation*, Philadelphia: Chemical Heritage Press, 271–97.
Temin, Peter. 1980. *Taking Your Medicine: Drug Regulation in the United States*. Cambridge,

MA: Harvard University Press.

Vernon, John M. and Peter Gusen. 1974. 'Technical Change and Firm Size: Pharmaceutical Industry.' *Review of Economics and Statistics* 56: 294–302.

Viscusi, W. Kip. 1995. 'Discounting Health Effects for Medical Decisions,' in *Valuing Health Care*, ed. Frank Sloan, 125–47, Cambridge: Cambridge University Press.

Zucker, Darby, and Brewer. 1998. 'Intellectual Human Capital and the Birth of Biotechnology Enterprises.' *American Economic Review* 88(1): 290–306.

[4]

Journal of Health Economics 10 (1991) 107–142. North-Holland

Cost of innovation in the pharmaceutical industry*

Joseph A. DiMasi

Center for the Study of Drug Development, Tufts University, Boston, MA 02111, USA

Ronald W. Hansen

William E. Simon Graduate School of Business Administration, University of Rochester, Rochester, NY 14627, USA

Henry G. Grabowski

Department of Economics, Duke University, Durham, NC 27706, USA

Louis Lasagna

Center for the Study of Drug Developments, Tufts University, Boston, MA 02111, USA

Received June 1990, final version received November 1990

The research and development costs of 93 randomly selected new chemical entities (NCEs) were obtained from a survey of 12 U.S.-owned pharmaceutical firms. These data were used to estimate the pre-tax average cost of new drug development. The costs of abandoned NCEs were linked to the costs of NCEs that obtained marketing approval. For base case parameter values, the estimated out-of-pocket cost per approved NCE is $114 million (1987 dollars). Capitalizing out-of-pocket costs to the point of marketing approval at a 9% discount rate yielded an average cost estimate of $231 million (1987 dollars).

1. Introduction

Product innovation in the pharmaceutical industry is risky and time-consuming, with research and development (R&D) costs representing a high

*We are indebted to Gene Trimble who selected our sample of investigational drugs from a Center for the Study of Drug Development database and assisted in preparing our questionnaire. We are also grateful to Marianne Ulcickas for assistance with data entry. In addition, we wish to thank the Bradley Policy Research Center at the William E. Simon Graduate School of Business Administration of the University of Rochester and Duke University's Program in Pharmaceutical and Health Economics for partial support of expenses incurred by Ronald Hansen and Henry Grabowski, respectively. Finally, we thank the surveyed firms for providing proprietary data, and a number of individuals in those firms who graciously gave of their time when we requested clarification of responses.

proportion of sales revenues.[1] Although other forms of pharmaceutical innovation exist, new chemical entity (NCE) development is, on the whole, the most therapeutically and economically significant.[2,3] Typically, the R&D process for NCEs is spread over many years, and only a small proportion of these new drugs are eventually approved for marketing.

Empirical analyses of the cost to discover and develop NCEs are interesting on several counts. First, knowledge of R&D costs is important for analyzing issues such as the returns on R&D investment.[4] Second, the cost of a new drug has a direct bearing on the organizational structure of innovation in pharmaceuticals. In this regard, higher real R&D costs have been cited as one of the main factors underlying the recent trend toward more mergers and industry consolidation.[5] Third, R&D costs also influence the pattern of international resource allocation, and hence, international competitiveness.[6] Finally, the cost of R&D has become an important issue in its own right in recent policy deliberations involving regulatory requirements and the economic performance of the pharmaceutical industry.[7] In this paper we confine our analysis specifically to the study of R&D costs.

[1]The Pharmaceutical Manufacturers Association (PMA) Statistical Fact Book (1987) reports that, for member firms, U.S. pharmaceutical expenditures expressed as a percentage of U.S. pharmaceutical sales was 15.0% in 1986, up from 10.2% in 1965.

[2]An NCE is defined here as a new molecular compound not previously tested in humans. Excluded are new salts and esters of existing compounds; surgical and diagnostic materials; certain externally used compounds such as disinfectants, antiperspirants, and sunscreens; nutritional compounds such as natural forms of vitamins and sweetening agents; and certain biologic compounds such as vaccines, antigens, antisera, immunoglobulins, or purified extracts of existing drugs.

[3]Data in the PMA Annual Survey Report, 1987–1989, indicate that 82.9% of member firm company-financed human and veterinary use R&D expenditures in 1987 were spent on research for the advancement of scientific knowledge and development of new products and related services. The remainder was spent on research oriented to significant improvements and/or modification of existing products. This percentage has not varied much over the last few decades. The reason why such a high proportion of R&D is spent on new drugs is that a compound patent can usually be obtained covering the active ingredient. This patent confers protection from competition from any generic version of the drug.

[4]The two most recent rate of return analyses in the economics literature use cost estimates in Hansen (1979, 1980). Joglekar and Paterson (1985) estimates an after-tax rate of return for a hypothetical NCE first investigated in 1976. Grabowski and Vernon (1990) provides rate of return estimates for NCEs first marketed in the U.S. in the 1970s. The cost estimates used are applicable to NCEs first investigated in humans during the period 1963–1975. Future studies can benefit from cost estimates relevant to a later period.

[5]Within the past few years, there have been several major mergers and acquisitions in the pharmaceutical industry including SmithKline–Beecham, Bristol Myers–Squibb, Eastman Kodak–Sterling Drug, Merrell Dow–Marion Laboratories, and American Home Products–Robins.

[6]For studies of competitiveness in pharmaceuticals, see the analyses presented in the National Academy of Engineering (1983), Grabowski (1989), and especially Thomas (1990).

[7]In particular, Congressional concern has been focused on increases in relative drug prices and the role of increased R&D costs in explaining higher prices [U.S. Congress (1985, 1987, 1989)].

The ouput from our work can be applied to these various issues in subsequent research.

The approach to estimating an average pre-tax cost of new drug development used in this paper follows, for the most part, that found in Hansen (1979). Micro-level data on the cost and timing of development were obtained through a confidential survey of U.S. pharmaceutical firms for a random sample of NCEs first investigated in humans from 1970 through 1982. Reported development expenditures run through 1987. For every NCE that is approved, several others are abandoned at some point in the development process. Consequently, we associate the costs of failed projects with those of successful projects. R&D is also treated here as an investment with expenditures capitalized to the point of marketing approval.

In this paper, we examine the sensitivity of R&D costs to various parameters such as the clinical success rate and the economic discount rate. We also consider the sensitivity of R&D costs in reductions in Food and Drug Administration (FDA) regulatory review times and the lengths of various phases of NCE development. In addition, results are presented for the costs of developing approved new drugs categorized by an FDA measure of a new drug's medical significance.

The remainder of this paper is organized as follows: section 2 contains an outline of the new drug development process, which serves as background for the rest of the paper; section 3 provides a review of the literature on the cost of drug development; the cost estimation procedures we employ are described in section 4; a description of our sample data and the population from which they were drawn is given in section 5; baseline results on the average cost of NCE development are presented in section 6, while results for subsamples are given in section 7; section 8 contains an analysis using published aggregate pharmaceutical industry R&D data that serves as an external check on some of our baseline results; and some conclusions and prospects for future research are offered in section 9.

2. The new drug development process

New drug development is typically a sequential process. At several points in the process a pharmaceutical firm will review the status of testing on a drug and make a decision on whether to continue with its development.[8] In general, the decision depends on potential therapeutic benefits, the expected frequency and severity of adverse reactions, projected additional development, marketing, distribution, and production costs and estimates of a future revenue stream.

[8]The number and timing of these critical points in the life of an investigational drug vary by firm. See Wiggins (1981) for a discussion of when these decisions are usually made and what considerations are used in making them.

For drugs that make it all the way through to the point of FDA marketing approval, the sequence usually runs as follows. Prior to synthesis considerable discovery research is undertaken by chemists and biologists to develop concepts for new compounds. Once a new compound has been synthesized it will be screened for pharmacologic activity and toxicity in vitro, and then in animals. If, at this point, the drug is still considered a promising candidate for further development, the firm will file with the FDA an Investigational New Drug Application (IND).[9] Unless the FDA places a hold on this application, the firm may begin clinical (human) testing 30 days after filing. Clinical testing normally occurs over three distinct phases, each of which contributes different amounts and types of information on safety and efficacy.

Phase I testing is performed on a small number of (usually healthy) volunteers. These trials are conducted mainly to obtain information on toxicity and safe dosing ranges in humans. Data are also gathered on the drug's absorption and distribution in the body, its metabolic effects, and the rate and manner in which the drug is eliminated from the body.

In the second phase of human testing, phase II, the drug is administered to a larger number of individuals. The groups selected consist of patients for whom the drug is intended to be of benefit. Under the 1962 Amendments to the Food, Drug, and Cosmetics Act of 1938 (FD&C), substantial evidence of efficacy in the intended use of the drug is required before marketing approval can be granted. When successful, phase II trials usually provide the first significant evidence of efficacy. Additional safety data are also obtained during this phase.

The third, and final, premarketing clinical development phase, phase III, involves large-scale trials on patients. Additional evidence of efficacy is sought during this phase. The larger sample sizes increase the likelihood that actual benefits will be found to be statistically significant. Because many patients are typically enrolled in the trials, phase III testing is also useful in detecting adverse reactions that occur infrequently in patient populations. In addition, this testing may more closely approximate the manner in which the drug would be utilized after marketing approval.

Although extensive toxicology experimentation on animals occurs during the preclinical period, to detect teratologic and carcinogenic effects firms usually perform long-term animal testing concurrent with phases II and III. Long-term stability testing, and sometimes additional dosage formulation work and process development for manufacturing the compound in sufficient quantities for clinical testing, also occurs during the clinical period.

Once the clinical development phases have been completed and the firm believes that it has sufficient evidence for approval, it will submit a New

[9]See Mattison et al. (1988) for analysis of trends in the number of INDs filed by U.S. firms.

Drug Application (NDA) to the FDA for review. Marketing for approved uses may begin upon notification from the FDA.[10]

We designed our procedures for estimating average costs to utilize this categorization of drug development by phase. Not all new drug testing fits neatly into this framework, but the firms were able to allocate clinical costs satisfactorily to phases.

3. Previous estimates of new drug R&D costs

A number of studies, covering various time periods, have attempted to provide estimates of at least a portion of the R&D expenditures required to bring new drugs to market. Although comparing results from studies with different methodologies is risky, taken as a whole these analyses point to rising real R&D costs over time.

Table 1 presents the main results from these studies, the nature of the data analyzed, and the periods covered. Schnee (1974), Sarett (1974), and Clymer (1970) used out-of-pocket development cost data on limited groups of NCEs. Clymer's estimates for the late 1960s, exclusive of the costs of unsuccessful products, range from $2.5 to $4.5 million. This may be compared to Schnee's estimate of $0.5 million. If both estimates are correct, then R&D costs increased dramatically from the 1950s to the late 1960s.[11]

Mund (1970) and Baily (1972) used annual U.S. industry R&D expenditures and NCE introductions to estimate average costs, and also found a substantial increase in costs over time. An advantege to using aggregate data is that estimates will be based on information from a large group of firms. A serious disadvantage, though, is that aggregate expenditures cannot be associated in any precise manner with particular NCEs.[12]

Figure 1 shows the time pattern between 1963 and 1989 of annual U.S. pharmaceutical industry R&D expenditures and U.S. NCE approvals. As this figure shows, NCE approvals have changed only moderately over time, while real dollar pharmaceutical outlays have increased several times over this 25 year period. Aggregative industry data are therefore strongly suggestive of sharp increases in R&D cost over time, and this upward trend seems to have intensified in the 1980s. There are a number of difficulties, however,

[10]This contrasts with subsequent FDA approval of additional indications, dosage strengths, dosage forms, and delivery systems for the new drug. Further testing is required to obtain approval for such changes in the drug's labelling.

[11]Sarett's estimate for 1967 is also consistent with the Clymer range. A plausible hypothesis for explaining at least part of the large observed post-1962 change is that more extensive testing was required for approval following the implementation of the 1962 Amendments to the FD&C.

[12]Mund utilizes a simple 5-year fixed lag approach. Baily relates the average of aggregate R&D expenditures lagged 4 to 6 years to NCE introductions using a regression analysis framework. In computing the Baily cost estimates in table 1, we employ actual values of his independent variables, as opposed to the 'steady state' equilibrium value used in his article. The former is more appropriate for comparative purposes.

Table 1
Prior R&D cost studies.

Author	Sample	R&D cost/period	Notes
		(A) *Partial cost studies*	
Schnee	17 approved NCEs Single drug firm	0.5 mil/1950s–1960s	Discovery costs and unsuccessful NCEs ignored; no capitalization
Sarret	Successful NCEs Single drug firm	1.2 mil/1962 3.0 mil/1967 11.5 mil/1972	Discovery costs and unsuccessful NCEs ignored; no capitalization
Clymer	New drug candidates Single drug firm	10.5 mil/late 1960s	Discovery costs ignored; no capitalization
Mund	Aggregate industry data on R&D and NCEs	1.5 mil/1950s 10–20 mil/1960s	Five-year lag assumed between R&D and new drug introductions; no capitalization
Baily	Aggregate industry data on R&D and NCEs	2.3 mil/late 1950s 21.8 mil/late 1960s	Fixed lag regression analysis approach; no capitalization
		(B) *Full cost studies*	
Hansen	Representative sample of drugs tested in humans, 1963–1975	54 mil (1976 dollars)	Includes discovery and development costs capitalized to date of marketing introduction
Wiggins	Aggregate industry data on R&D and NCEs approved 1970–1985 (by therapeutic class)	125 mil (1986 dollars)	Fixed lag regression analysis approach; also uses selective parameter estimates from Hansen

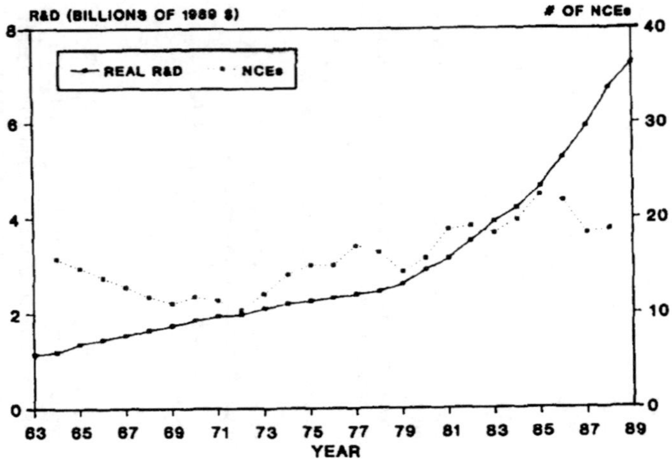

Fig. 1. Annual U.S. pharmaceutical industry real R&D expenditures and U.S. NCE approvals for the period 1963–1989. Expenditures are for PMA member firms and are indexed using the GNP Implicit Price Deflator. The NCE approval line is constructed from 3-year moving averages of annual approvals.

in using aggregate data to obtain precise estimates of R&D cost per approved NCE over particular subperiods. First, one must specify a lag structure between R&D inputs and output. This lag has been lengthening over time. Second, aggregate industry data cover compounds licensed from abroad, in addition to those that are U.S.-discovered. These two categories of drugs are likely to have vastly diferent R&D cost expenditure patterns within the United States.[13] For these reasons, R&D cost studies based on micro data at the individual project level are likely to produce much more accurate cost estimates.

The only prior R&D cost study that utilized multi-firm project level data for new drugs is Hansen (1979). Data were obtained from 14 firms on a large randomly selected group of NCEs first tested in humans during the period 1963 to 1975. Information was requested from surveyed firms on NCEs originated and developed by those firms. Time and cost data by development phase were gathered so that average phase lengths and costs could be computed. Costs of projects that were abandoned at some point in the clinical testing period were included and R&D was treated as an investment

[13]For example, the aggregate industry R&D cost data available from the PMA do not include the R&D expenditures performed abroad for licensed compounds originating in foreign countries. As we show later in the paper, where aggregate data are employed as a check on our results, average U.S. R&D costs for foreign licensed compounds are estimated to be small compared to the self-originated NCEs of U.S. firms. Of course, license fees account for much of the difference in R&D costs, but they are not publicly available.

with returns delayed until marketing approval. Hansen's R&D cost estimate of $54 million (in 1976 dollars) was larger than those of prior studies, but it was also more complete in the sense that it took account of discovery as well as development costs, the costs of failed projects, and the time value of funds invested in R&D.

The most recent drug R&D cost study is Wiggins (1987). It employs industry aggregates calculated at the therapeutic class level to compute an 'R&D production function'. Regression coefficient estimates are then used to infer an R&D cost value. This methodology is similar to that employed in Baily (1972). For NCEs approved during 1970–1985, Wiggins found an uncapitalized cost per NCE of $65 million in 1986 dollars. Wiggins then used the time profile for new drug development estimated in Hansen (1979) to provide capitalized cost estimates. For his base case, Wiggins used Hansen's preferred discount rate of 8% to determine capitalized cost to be $125 million in 1986 dollars. Woltman (1989), however, has pointed out that the Wiggins capitalized value should only be $108 million, given a proper analysis of the time profile utilized in Hansen (1979).[14]

When compared to Hansen's results, the corrected estimates reveal a relatively small real cost increase. General price inflation accounts for 80% of the increase in estimates ($54 million in 1976 dollars translates to $97 million in 1986 dollars). However, the time periods considered in the two studies also do not differ very much. Wiggins used data that were meant to be relevant to 1970–1985 NCE approvals. Given his imposed lag structure, R&D expenditures included run from 1965 through 1982. Hansen's R&D expenditures run from 1963 to the mid-1970s, with expenditures more concentrated in the latter half of this period.[15]

Even for identical periods, however, results from these two types of studies may not be comparable. Wiggins employed data that are a mixture of both licensed and self-originated NCEs, and this is likely to produce a lower R&D cost estimate than from a sample consisting of only U.S. self-originated NCEs.[16] In addition, Wiggins' (and Baily's) estimates, which are obtained from an R&D production function type analysis, are really marginal costs. They are estimates of the additional cost that would have been incurred if one more NCE had been approved during the sample

[14]To obtain capitalized costs, Wiggins multiplied his $65 million uncapitalized cost estimate by the ratio of capitalized to uncapitalized costs in Hansen (1979). Uncapitalized costs per marketed NCE are not presented in Hansen (1979), but can be determined from other data therein. Wiggins claimed that this figure is $28 million. The correct amount, however, is $32.5 million. This changes the Wiggins base amount to $108 million.

[15]Hansen's data are for a sample of NCEs first investigated in humans during 1963–1975. Some of the NCEs first investigated in the early part of this period had long development times with significant expenditures incurred late in the period.

[16]As noted in footnote 13, licensed compounds originating from foreign countries tend to have much lower *U.S.* costs than compounds originating in the U.S. from U.S.-owned firms.

period. Hansen's results, and those of the other studies listed in table 1, are average cost estimates. Unless constant returns to scale with respect to R&D effort exist at the industry level (at or near average expenditure levels for the sample period), marginal and average costs differ.

In summary, results from the studies discussed above suggest that new drug R&D costs have risen over time, at least relative to the pre-1962 Amendments period. However, only Hansen's study employs micro data, and none of the studies includes much data from the 1980s, a period during which real industry R&D expenditures have risen rapidly (fig. 1).[17] This study, like Hansen's, employs project level data, and a significant amount of the data used was taken from this recent time period.

4. Estimating the average cost of new drug development

We use project level data to obtain an estimate of the clinical period average cost per NCE tested in humans. A majority of these NCEs will not be approved for marketing. Our approach uses an estimated clinical approval success rate to link the R&D costs of failed projects to the costs of those NCEs that obtain marketing approval. A representative time profile for an NCE progressing through all testing phases to the point of marketing approval is also estimated and used to capitalize R&D expenditures. Preclinical discovery and development costs are accounted for and treated in a more refined manner than was the case in Hansen (1979).

Since the full R&D costs for licensed or acquired NCEs are not typically reflected in R&D budgets of the firms that acquired them, we restricted our analysis to self-originated NCEs. The various steps we use to determine an estimate of the total cost per approved self-originated NCE (inclusive of unsuccessful efforts, preclinical expenditures, and the opportunity cost of funds invested) are formally described below.

4.1. Expected out-of-pocket costs

Let h be the clinical period development cost of a randomly selected NCE tested in humans. This can be decomposed into a sum of random variables. Specifically, $h = x_{\mathrm{I}} + x_{\mathrm{II}} + x_{\mathrm{III}} + x_{\mathrm{A}}$, where x_{I}, x_{II} and x_{III} represent the NCE's development costs for phases I, II, and III, respectively, and x_{A} is its long-term animal testing cost. If the project was terminated prior to entering a phase, then the random variable for that phase assumes the value zero. The expected value of clinical period costs is then $E(h) = p_{\mathrm{I}}\mu_{\mathrm{I}|e} + p_{\mathrm{II}}\mu_{\mathrm{II}|e} + p_{\mathrm{III}}\mu_{\mathrm{III}|e} +$

[17]Data from the PMA Annual Survey Report, 1987–1989, can be used to compute growth rates for real pharmaceutical R&D expenditures for different time periods. From 1963 to 1979 real R&D expenditures grew at a 5.3% compound annual rate; from 1980 to 1989 expenditures grew at a 10.7% compound annual rate.

$p_A\mu_{A|e}$, where p_I, p_{II}, and p_{III} are the probabilities that a randomly selected NCE tested in humans will enter phases I, II, and III, respectively, p_A is the probability that long-term animal testing will be done, and $\mu_{I|e}$, $\mu_{II|e}$, $\mu_{III|e}$, and $\mu_{A|e}$ are conditional expectations. Specifically, $\mu_{I|e}$, $\mu_{II|e}$, $\mu_{III|e}$, and $\mu_{A|e}$ are the population mean costs for phases I, II, III, and long-term animal testing, respectively, for those NCEs that enter the respective phase.

The proportion of NCEs tested in humans that are taken through the various clinical period testing phases diminishes with each successive phase. As will be shown below, only a small minority undergo all testing phases. Thus, a simple random sample of this population will likely contain a good deal of information about NCEs that do not last very long in testing and little information about NCEs that reach the point of NDA submission or approval. Furthermore, we expect phase costs to be more variable for later testing phases. The later clinical trials are larger, last longer, and should be more subject to variability in size and duration depending on the type of drug tested and the condition it is meant to treat.

Therefore, to reduce overall sampling error, we grouped NCEs into strata according to the time spent in active testing if research was abandoned, whether research was still in progress, and whether an NDA had been submitted or approved. Successful NCEs were deliberately oversampled and unsuccessful NCEs lasting only a short time in active testing were undersampled. The sample percentage distribution for the strata was specified before sample selection. In preparing our estimates, we reweighted the responses to replicate the population.

The population from which our sample was selected consisted of a subset of the investigational NCEs contained in a Center for the Study of Drug Development (CSDD) database. The proportions of population NCEs that fall in our strata can be determined from information in this database. Thus, we were able to define a set of weights to be applied to the sample data that transform the sample from one that is unrepresentative with respect to the strata to one that is perfectly representative. Mean phase cost (in constant dollars), $\bar{x}_i$, and the probability that an NCE tested in humans will enter a phase, s_i, can then be estimated from the weighted sample (see appendices A and B for computational details). The expected clinical period cost per new drug tested in humans can be expressed as $\hat{E}=s_I\bar{x}_I+s_{II}\bar{x}_{II}+s_{III}\bar{x}_{III}+s_A\bar{x}_A$.

To estimate the expected cost per approved drug, C_u, one needs to multiply $\hat{E}$ by the ratio of the number of drugs taken into humans, n_T, to the number approved, n_a (i.e., $C_u=\hat{E}(n_T/n_a)$). Alternatively, C_u can be expressed as $\hat{E}/s$, where s is the successful rate for NCEs tested in humans (the ratio of n_a to n_T). Data from CSDD databases on investigational and approved NCEs for the survey firms can be used to estimate s.

The final step in estimating R&D costs is to incorporate preclinical expenditures. Firms are generally not able to allocate all preclinical costs to

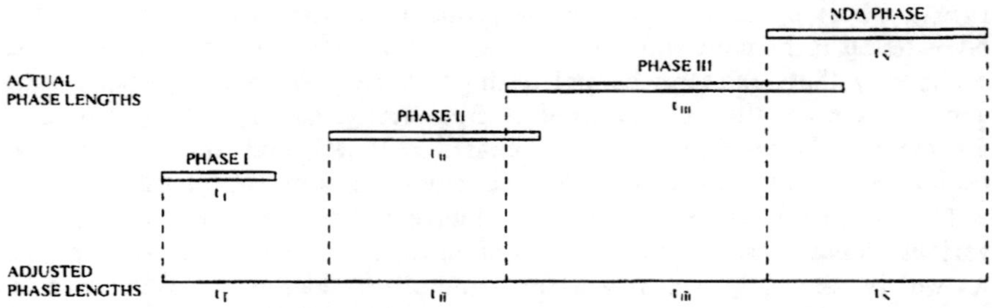

Fig. 2. Representative time profile for an NCE passing through all clinical development phases.

specific NCEs in a precise manner. Consequently, we use reported aggregate annual firm R&D expenditure data for the preclinical and clinical periods, and our previously estimated cost per approved NCE estimate, C_u, to derive P_u, the uncapitalized preclinical cost per approved NCE. Specifically, we use aggregate data to estimate the ratio of preclinical period to total expenditures, λ. We then estimate P_u from the identity $\lambda \equiv P_u/(C_u+P_u)$, or $P_u \equiv [\lambda/(1-\lambda)]C_u$. Estimated total uncapitalized cost per approved NCE is given as $C_u + P_u$.

4.2. *Expected capitalized costs*

To include the opportunity cost of funds invested in NCE R&D for a full cost estimate, we capitalize the mean phase costs to the point of marketing approval using a representative time profile for an NCE passing through all clinical period testing phases; use of a representative time profile yields a lower bound on costs. Weighted mean phase lengths, t_i, are calculated for our survey NCEs in the same manner as weighted mean phase costs.

It is generally not the case that a phase will begin exactly when the preceding phase ends. In many instances there is a significant overlap for successive phases. There can also be gaps between phases. To construct a time profile we reduce each calculated mean phase length by the weighted average overlap of that phase with the next (or add to the phase length for a gap).[18] Figure 2 depicts a hypothetical time profile. The adjusted mean phase lengths, $t_{\tilde{i}}$, are used to determine where in the time profile phase costs begin. Hence, the time from the start of phase I to NDA approval, T, is given as $T = t_{\tilde{I}} + t_{\tilde{II}} + t_{\tilde{III}} + t_{\tilde{N}}$, where $t_{\tilde{N}}$ is average NDA review time. We measure the time from the start of a phase to the expected approval date, z_j, as $z_j = \sum_{\tilde{i}=0}^{j-1} t_{\tilde{i}}$, with $t_0 = 0$.

Mean long-term animal testing time, t_A, is calculated in a manner identical

[18] For phase III the succeeding phase is the period during which the NDA is under review.

to that used for the actual mean durations of the clinical trial phases. The length of this phase, however, is not adjusted for an overlap (or gap) with other phases. We need to determine, though, how this testing fits into our representative time profile. The weighted mean time from the start of phase I to the start of long-term animal testing, t_{IA}, can be calculated. We then consider long-term animal testing costs to begin t_{IA} units of time after the start of phase I.

Phase costs are assumed to be distributed uniformly over actual mean phase lengths and capitalized at the discount rate r. Specifically, capitalized mean phase costs, c_j, are determined as follows, where the index values 1, 2, and 3 refer to phases I, II, and III, respectively.

$$c_j = \int_{z_j - t_j}^{z_j} (\bar{x}_j/t_j)\, e^{rt}\, dt \quad \text{for } j = 1, 2, 3. \tag{1}$$

Capitalized long-term animal testing costs, c_A, can be found in a similar fashion.[19]

An estimate of expected capitalized clinical period cost per NCE tested in humans, $\hat{c}$, can be obtained as $\hat{c} = s_I c_I + s_{II} c_{II} + s_{III} c_{III} + s_A c_A$. Transforming this into a cost per marketed NCE, C_c, requires only the approval success rate. In particular, we have $C_c = \hat{c}/s$.

Eq. (1) implies continuous compounding. The discount rate estimates we use are based on discrete compounding. It is possible, though, to find a continuous rate, r, that is equivalent to any discrete rate (with regard to monetary value after the same amount of time).[20]

Preclinical costs can be capitalized to the point of marketing approval in the same way that phase costs are in eq. (1). The average duration of the preclinical period, t_p, can be estimated using data on preclinical development times from a CSDD database on approved NCEs. Capitalized preclinical cost per approved NCE, P_c, can then be given as

$$P_c = \int_{T}^{T + t_p} (P_u/t_p)\, e^{rt}\, dt. \tag{2}$$

4.3. Cost of capital for pharmaceutical R&D

In selecting a baseline cost of capital for this analysis, we sought a

[19]Specifically, capitalized long-term animal testing costs can be computed as

$$c_A = \int_{t_A^L}^{t_A^U} (\bar{x}_A/t_i)\, e^{rt}\, dt, \quad \text{where } t_A^U = T - t_{IA} \text{ and } t_A^L = t_A^U - t_A.$$

[20]For example, if the relevant discrete rate is 10%, we use $r = 0.095$.

representative value for the pharmaceutical industry over the period spanned by the development of the drugs in our study. Our sample includes NCEs first tested in humans between 1970 and 1982. The marketing approval dates for this sample centers around the mid 1980s, with a few compounds still in active research. Hence, we want a cost of capital measure that essentially covers the period between 1975 and 1985 where the bulk of the expenditures are concentrated.

Our baseline analysis employs a 9% real cost of capital. This value is based on a recent study on R&D returns [Grabowski and Vernon (1990)]. The study applied the capital asset pricing model (CAPM) to a portfolio for a representative sample of pharmaceutical firms for each of the years from the mid 1970s to the mid 1980s. Over this period, the equity cost of capital for this representative group of firms clusters around 9%.[21] The capital structure of the pharmaceutical industry is overwhelmingly equity financed (in excess of 90%). Hence, their estimated 9% cost of equity capital offers a good proxy for the overall cost of capital.[22]

Hansen (1979) utilized an 8% cost of capital. That study focused on an earlier time period (i.e. R&D expenditures in the 1960s and 1970s). Although the 8% value was not based explicitly on a CAPM analysis, it is generally consistent with the values emerging from analyses for the relevant period of that study [see, e.g., Statman (1983)]. The slightly higher cost of capital utilized in the present study essentially reflects the trend toward higher real interest rates during the past decade [Feldstein (1988)]. Although a 9% real cost of capital measure is employed as our preferred estimate in the baseline analysis, we also perform sensitivity analysis using values significantly above and below this value.[23]

5. Data

Twelve U.S.-owned pharmaceutical firms agreed to participate in this study and provide, on a confidential basis, information on their self-

[21]An analysis of investment riskiness for this portfolio of pharmaceutical firms was undertaken and indicated that pharmaceutical firms generally had comparable riskiness to the market over the period (i.e. betas approximately equal to one). Long-term estimates on risk-free rates and market rates were obtained from Ibbotson Associates [Grabowski and Vernon (1990, p. 806)].

[22]One can compute a weighted cost of capital, taking account of how much debt relative to equity is held by pharmaceutical firms, as well as the tax deductibility of debt compared to equity [see Statman (1983)]. Since the percentage of capital held in the form of debt is minimal over this period, this does not change the computed 9% value in an appreciable manner.

[23]An alternative approach for estimating the cost of capital would be to utilize the arbitrage pricing model (APT). Some preliminary analysis applying the APT to the pharmaceutical industry by one of the authors suggests higher values for the cost of capital than that obtained from the CAPM. The hurdle rates employed by pharmaceutical firms also tend to suggest somewhat higher values for the cost of capital [Grabowski and Vernon (1990)].

originated NCE development activities (a copy of the questionnaire is available upon request).[24] These firms include a number of the largest in the U.S. pharmaceutical industry, as well as some that are small in size. From 1980 to 1986, these firms accounted for approximately 40% of U.S. industry R&D expenditures on ethical pharmaceuticals.[25]

We limited our study to self-originated NCEs since the full research and development expenditures for licensed and acquired NCEs would not be reflected in the acquiring firm's R&D accounts. The NCEs included in the study were first tested in humans during the period 1970–1982. Most of the NCEs from this period that eventually emerge as approved drugs will have entered the market in the 1980s or early 1990s. We did not extend the sample past 1982 since many of the later NCEs would still be in early testing at the time of the survey.

To construct a representative sample of NCEs tested during this period we used information from a CSDD database on investigational NCEs. This database, obtained from a triennial survey of the U.S. pharmaceutical industry,[26] provided us with information on the origin, therapeutic area, and development status of NCEs first tested in humans during the period 1970–1982. This information allowed us to identify the survey firm NCEs that met our study inclusion criteria (i.e. self-originated NCEs first tested in humans during the period 1970–1982), and to select a random sample of survey firm NCEs.[27] Detailed information was requested from each firm for the NCEs that we selected.

The firms provided data on 93 NCEs, or 19% of all NCEs in the CSDD database that met inclusion criteria. The NCE therapeutic class distributions for the sample and population are nearly identical. For the NCEs selected, firms provided clinical period phase beginning and ending dates, costs by year of clinical testing, and the date testing was suspended on those NCEs for which research was abandoned.

Aggregate pharmaceutical R&D expenditure data for the years 1970–1986 were also provided by the survey firms. The firms reported total annual pharmaceutical R&D expenditures broken down into expenditures on self-originated NCEs, on licensed or otherwise acquired compounds, and on existing approved products. For firms as a whole during the period 1970–

[24]A number of these firms had several major pharmaceutical divisions. Counting these as separate units, data were obtained from 15 divisions.

[25]One of the survey firms was not able to break out pharmaceutical R&D from total R&D expenditures for the 1970s. The industry level is the aggregate of PMA member firm real pharmaceutical R&D expenditures over the period 1980–1986 (computed from data in PMA Annual Survey Report, 1987–1989).

[26]At the time the sample was selected, 43 firms were included in the database, 34 of them U.S.-owned.

[27]The eligible NCEs were first stratified as described in section 4, and a random sample was selected from each strata.

Table 2

Average out-of-pocket clinical period costs for NCEs tested in humans (in thousands of 1987 dollars).[a]

Testing phase	Mean cost	Standard deviation of phase costs	Median cost	N^b	Probability of entering phase (%)	Expected cost
Phase I	2,134	4,519	960	87	100.0	2,134
Phase II	3,954	5,230	2,175	70	75.0	2,966
Phase III	12,801	13,974	7,888	36	36.2	4,634
Long-term animal	2,155	2,411	1,336	49	56.1	1,209
Other animal	648	1,183	129	15	15.8	102
Total						11,045

[a]All costs were deflated using the GNP Implicit Price Deflator. Weighted values were used in calculating means, standard deviations, medians and the probability of entering a phase.

[b]N = number of NCEs with full cost data for the phase.

1986, 73.7%, 16.3%, and 10.0% of total pharmaceutical R&D expenditures were spent on self-originated NCEs, existing approved products, and licensed and acquired compounds, respectively. Annual total expenditures for self-originated NCE R&D were further broken down according to whether they were incurred during the preclinical or clinical periods (since firms are generally unable to allocate all preclinical costs to individual NCEs, data were not obtained on preclinical expenditures for specific NCEs).

The firms did not provide full phase cost data for every NCE that entered a given phase, either because that phase was ongoing on the survey date or records were incomplete. Costs were not included in computations if the phase was ongoing or cost data were missing. Only nine NCEs were continuing in research on the survey date, and for each of them complete information is available for some phases.

6. Baseline cost estimates

6.1. Clinical cost per investigational NCE

Using the weighting procedure described in section 4, mean phase costs were calculated and are presented in table 2. All costs were deflated using the GNP Implicit Price Deflator and are given in 1987 dollars.[28] Since a

[28]The GNP Implicit Price Deflator measures changes in the prices of the nation's output. Ideally, we would want to use an index based on pharmaceutical R&D input prices. No such index, however, exists. Other indices which we considered were judged to be less appropriate than the GNP Implicit Price Deflator. The Producer Price Index is determined solely by manufacturing output prices. Mansfield (1987) develops an R&D input price index applicable to a number of industries for the years 1969–1983. The closest match to the pharmaceutical industry is the chemicals and oil category. Only a few pharmaceutical firms, however, were

number of firms reported clinical period animal testing other than the long-term animal tests, we reported their costs as other animal costs. On average, however, they constitute a very small portion of total costs.

The phase to phase attrition rates in column 6 of table 2 are roughly consistent with alternative estimates in an FDA study [Tucker et al. (1988)]. That study used FDA records to follow the progress of the new molecular entities (NMEs)[29] for which INDs were filed during the years 1976–1978. Based on their records and a mathematical model to project future outcomes, they found 70% of the NMEs entering phase II and 33% entering phase III.

Average costs vary substantially by clinical development phase. Phase II costs are nearly twice as large as phase I costs. The large-scale clinical trial costs of phase III are about six times as large as phase I costs. These are averages, however, and the third column of table 2 reveals substantial variation in individual NCE testing costs for each phase. The phase cost distributions are also positively skewed, as indicated by the differences between mean and median costs.

Since there is substantial attrition of NCEs prior to the more expensive phases II and III, expected phase costs rise less steeply than mean costs. For example, expected phase III costs are only slightly more than twice as large as expected phase I costs. Our estimate of the expected clinical period cost for NCEs tested in humans is $11.0 million in 1987 dollars.

6.2. Capitalized clinical cost per investigational NCE

To calculate the capitalized value of clinical period expenditures, we computed adjusted phase lengths and constructed a representative develop-

(footnote 28 continued)

included in the sample. We deemed the chemicals and oil index too broad-based to use. Extrapolation of the index through 1987 would also have been necessary. We also considered an index developed for biomedical R&D [U.S. Bureau of Economic Analysis (1986)], but judged it to be too dependent on the university research sector. However, we did apply alternative price indices to our cost data and found the following to be the case in general. The Producer Price Index resulted in overall cost estimates that were roughly 10% lower than those obtained with the GNP Deflator. We regressed Mansfield's chemicals and oil index on the GNP Deflator to obtain predicted Mansfield index values for 1983–1987. Applying the expanded Mansfield index resulted in overall costs that were approximately 10% higher than the GNP Deflator estimates. Use of the biomedical R&D index resulted in about a 10% increase in costs relative to those for the Mansfield index.

[29]The FDA definition of an NME differs somewhat from our definition of an NCE. One difference is that the FDA includes diagnostic agents and we do not. Another difference is that we include a few therapeutically significant biologics, whereas the FDA does not include any. Aside from the fact that we study a longer time period, an additional reason why the FDA study results are not precisely comparable to ours is that their drugs include some that were licensed or acquired. Presumably these drugs were prescreened to some extent, and so we might expect them to have success rates higher than those for self-originated new drugs. The impact of the other differences, however, is unclear.

Table 3

Average phase lengths and clinical period capitalized costs for NCEs tested in humans (in thousands of 1987 dollars).[a]

Testing phase	Mean phase length (actual)[b]	Mean phase length (adjusted)[b]	Time from phase start to approval[c]	Capitalized mean phase cost[d]	Capitalized expected phase cost
Phase I	15.5	16.2	98.9	4,103	4,103
Phase II	24.3	22.5	82.7	6,564	4,924
Phase III	36.0	29.9	60.2	17,370	6,288
Long-term animal	33.6	33.6	78.7	3,366	1,889
Other animal	33.6	33.6	78.7	1,012	159
Total					17,363

[a]All costs were deflated using GNP Implicit Price Deflator.

[b]Mean phase lengths and the time from the beginning of a phase to NDA approval are given in months. Weighted values were used in calculating mean phase lengths.

[c]The NDA review period was estimated to last 30.3 months. Animal testing was estimated to start 4.0 months into phase II.

[d]Costs were capitalized at a 9% discount rate.

ment time profile as described in section 4.2. The actual and adjusted phase lengths presented in table 3 indicate, on average, a very small gap (0.7 months) between the end of phase I and the beginning of phase II, and an overlap of phase III with both phase II (1.8 months) and the NDA review phase (6.1 months). The mean NDA review time for self-originated NCEs first tested in humans during 1970–1982 by U.S.-owned firms (30.3 months) was determined from a CSDD database. Long-term animal testing began, on average, 20.2 months after phase I testing commenced.[30] Our estimated time profile has a length of 98.9 months from the initiation of clinical testing to NDA approval. The time from the start of phase I testing to NDA submission is 68.6 months.

The expected capitalized cost per NCE tested in humans for the entire clinical period is $17.3 million in 1987 dollars. Of that amount, 36% is accounted for by interest costs.

6.3. Clinical costs per approved NCE

To relate costs to the number of approved NCEs, we need a clinical period approval success rate estimate. While phase success rates could only be obtained from information in our cost survey, approval success rate estimates can be obtained using a broader sample contained in CSDD databases on investigational and approved NCEs. Our methodology for estimating the

[30]Other animal testing sometimes occurred before long-term animal testing, sometimes after it, and at still other times both before and after it. No tendency in relation to the timing of long-term animal testing was apparent. As an approximation, then, we distributed other animal costs over the long-term animal testing period.

approval success rate is similar to that used in Sheck et al. (1984) and is described in appendix B. Evidence that the predictive power of our model is quite high is presented in the appendix.

The base clinical success rate for the cost survey firms (23%) is utilized to determine clinical cost *per approved NCE* from our prior estimates of clinical cost *per investigational NCE* presented in tables 2 and 3. In particular, dividing our prior cost estimates by the success rate of 23% yields estimates of clinical costs per approved NCE. Utilizing a 9% discount rate, the capitalized clinical cost per approved NCE is estimated to be $75 million, while the uncapitalized cost per approved NCE is $48 million. This contrasts with estimates of $17.3 and $11 million for capitalized and uncapitalized cost per investigational NCE, respectively.

6.4. Preclinical costs

In the preceeding sections we reported expected clinical period development costs calculated from project specific data. Many costs incurred during the preclinical period cannot be directly assigned to specific NCEs. Moreover, some specific development projects are abandoned prior to reaching the clinical stage. The activities in the preclinical period are essential to the eventual development of NCEs and the expenditures during this period should be allocated to approved NCEs to determine the total cost of developing a new pharmaceutical.

The activities during the preclinical period lead to a flow of NCEs into clinical testing. As described in section 4.1, we use the ratio of uncapitalized preclinical to clinical expenditures and our estimate of the uncapitalized clinical period cost per approved NCE to allocate preclinical costs to approved NCEs. In order to estimate λ, the preclinical period portion of total R&D costs, we need to confine our analysis to those expenditures that involve self-originated NCEs. Therefore, in our survey we requested annual expenditures on self-originated NCE R&D by preclinical and clinical periods for each of the survey firms for the years 1970–1986.

In the aggregate, 66.1% of total self-originated NCE R&D was spent during the preclinical period. Both the preclinical and clinical expenditure series, however, tend to increase in real terms over the survey period. Since clinical period expenditures lag behind preclinical costs, the ratio of preclinical period real R&D expenditures to total real R&D expenditures overestimates the true preclinical period contribution to the total. A lag structure for the aggregate data, based on average lengths of the preclinical and clinical periods, can be imposed to better estimate λ.

The mean length of the preclinical period for self-originated NCEs of U.S.-owned firms first tested in humans during 1970–1982 was estimated from data in a CSDD database on approved NCEs to be 42.6 months. Our

Table 4

Expected phase costs per marketed NCE (in millions of 1987 dollars).[a]

Testing phase[b]	Uncapitalized expected cost	Mean phase length (actual)	Capitalized expected cost[c]
Preclinical	65.5	42.6	155.6
Phase I	9.3	15.5	17.8
Phase II	12.9	24.3	21.4
Phase III	20.2	36.0	27.1
Long-term animal	5.3	33.6	8.2
Other animal	0.4	33.6	0.7
Total	113.6		230.8

[a]All costs were deflated using the GNP Implicit Price Deflator. A 23% clinical approval success rate was utilized.

[b]The NDA review period was estimated to last 30.3 months. Animal testing was estimated to start 4.0 months into phase II.

[c]Costs were capitalized at a 9% discount rate.

representative time profile suggests a clinical period duration (inclusive of phase III testing after NDA submission) of 74.7 months. We approximate the lag between preclinical and clinical period aggregate expenditures by computing the time between the midpoint of the preclinical period to the midpoint of the clinical period.[31] Thus, our base case lag is 5 years and the corresponding value of λ is 0.577. Hence, our previously estimated uncapitalized clinical cost is multiplied by a factor of 1.36 to obtain an estimate of uncapitalized preclinical cost ($P_u \equiv [\lambda/(1-\lambda)]C_u$).

Using the 5 year lag, uncapitalized and capitalized preclinical costs are $66 and $156 million, respectively. For lags of 4 and 6 years (adjusting at the same time the assumed duration of the preclinical period), the uncapitalized costs are $69 and $63 million and the capitalized costs are $152 and $166 million, respectively. Thus, our preclinical cost estimates are not very sensitive to reasonable variation in the lag.

6.5. Total expected cost per approved NCE

Given the preferred 5 year lag, discount rate of 9%, and clinical success rate of 23%, total capitalized cost per approved NCE is shown in table 4 as $230.8 million. Preclinical research activities, because they occur much earlier in time, entail significantly greater interst costs than do clinical activities. In particular, interest costs represent 58% of preclinical costs ($90 million of

[31]Survey data on phase costs were provided by year of clinical testing. Computing costs by year from the start of phase I testing revealed that the midway point of the clinical period (37.35 months) corresponds roughly to the time of maximum expected cost per NCE tested in humans.

Table 5

Preclinical, clinical, and total capitalized expected costs per marketed NCE at alternative approval success rates and discount rates (in millions of 1987 dollars).[a]

	Capitalized costs					
	0%	5%	8%	9%	10%	15%
(A) *Success rate*: 25%						
Preclinical	61	98	131	144	156	247
Clinical	44	57	66	69	73	93
Total	105	155	197	213	229	340
(B) *Success rate*: 23%						
Preclinical	66	107	142	156	170	269
Clinical	48	62	72	75	79	101
Total	114	169	214	231	249	370
(C) *Success rate*: 20%						
Preclinical	76	123	163	179	196	309
Clinical	55	71	83	86	91	116
Total	132	194	246	265	287	425

[a]All costs were deflated using the GNP Implicit Price Deflator. Clinical period expenditures were assumed to represent 42.3% of total R&D expenditures. The corresponding assumed preclinical phase length is 42.6 months.

$156 million), whereas they represent only 36% of clinical costs ($27 million of $75 million).

Table 5 allows us to examine how sensitive our estimate of total R&D cost per approved NCE is to variations in two key parameters – the clinical success rate and the discount rate. If we take as plausible ranges on these parameters a discount rate of 8 to 10% and a clinical success rate of 20 to 25%, the corresponding range in R&D cost per approved NCE is between $197 and $287 million. This provides some bounds around our estimate of $231 million per approved NCE by allowing for uncertainty in the values of these important parameters.

6.6. *Comparison with Hansen's analysis*

It is interesting to compare our base case average cost estimates with the preferred estimates in Hansen (1979), and measure the contribution to the apparent increase in costs of changes in several factors. In 1987 dollars Hansen's total capitalized cost estimate is $100.5 million, while his clinical period capitalized cost estimate is $39.2 million, Thus, in real terms, total capitalized costs are about 2.3 times larger here than in Hansen; clinical period capitalized costs are about 1.9 times larger. Assuming both sets of estimates are correct for their respective covered time periods, we can examine how much of the cost increases are due to differences in a given determinant of cost, holding all other determinants fixed.

Ignoring second-order interaction effects we may state the following. Table 5 reveals that the higher opportunity cost of capital used here (9% as opposed to 8%) results in an increase in cost amounting to 13.0% of the measured increase in total cost between the two studies.

R&D and regulatory review times are somewhat longer here. Our results show essentially no difference in phase II duration, but there is a 7.1 month increase in phase I duration and a 7.3 month increase for phase III. Regulatory review time and the preclinical period are 6.3 and 6.6 months longer here, respectively. Our longer development and regulatory review times result in total cost increases amounting to 23.9% of the measured increase in total costs.

The effects on total costs of changes in the discount rate and phase development times, taken together, constitute the change in time costs between the two studies. The residual proportion of the measured increase in total costs (63.1%) can be viewed as that part of the change in measured total costs that is due to changes in out-of-pocket costs. Out-of-pocket costs are dependent on the clinical approval success rate, the probabilities of entering the various phases, and the mean uncapitalized phase costs.

Mean uncapitalized preclinical period and clinical phase costs are substantially higher here and account for the bulk of the increase in out-of-pocket costs. In constant dollars, phases I, II, and III mean uncapitalized costs are 3.9, 1.4, and 2.5 times larger here than in the Hansen study. Similarly, long-term animal and preclinical costs are 1.6 and 3.7 times larger here, respectively. The phase-to-phase success rates estimated here are higher than those reported by Hansen,[32] but their cost increase effect is more than offset by the cost reducing effect of a higher clinical approval success rate.

6.7. Reductions in development and review times

Since our estimates of the full cost of developing a new pharmaceutical include an implicit interest charge, changes in the timing of expenditures will affect the full cost. Firms may be able to shorten development times by doing parallel, rather than sequential, studies. Clinical trial phase lengths may also

[32]Fewer drugs are screened out in phases I and II here relative to the earlier study. The probability of reaching phases II and III are 75% and 36% in this study and 50% and 19% in the Hansen study, respectively. The probability of approval conditional on reaching phase II has increased from 25% to 31%, but the approval probability conditional on entering phase III has remained virtually unchanged (65.8% previously vs. 63.5% currently).

Table 6

Impact on capitalized expected costs per marketed NCE of one-year reductions in average phase lengths (in millions of 1987 dollars).[a]

One-year reduction	Total capitalized expected cost[b]	Reduction in total cost
Preclinical	224	8
Phase I	218	13
Phase II	215	16
Phase III	213	18
NDA review	212	19

[a]All costs were deflated using the GNP Implicit Price Deflator. A 23% clinical approval success rate was utilized.
[b]Costs were capitalized at a 9% discount rate.

be shortened if the conferences now held between the FDA and sponsor firms during the development period provide firms with a better understanding of what will be necessary for approval. Reductions in the average length of the NDA review phase would shorten the time between R&D expenditures and marketing approval and so lower total costs.

In table 6 we present estimates of the effects of a 1-year reduction in phase duration (holding mean phase costs constant). The largest cost reduction ($19 million or 8.2% of total cost) is for a 1-year reduction in the NDA review phase. The reason the NDA phase carries the greatest impact is that a reduction in any phase length decreases the capitalized cost for that phase and for all prior phases.

Since preclinical costs are a large portion of the total cost, even a 1-year reduction in phase I produces savings of $13.5 million per approved NCE. Approval rates during the 1980s have averaged 19 per year. Thus, our results suggest that 1-year reductions in the clinical development or regulatory review phases would, holding all else constant, produce annual savings of $257 to $361 million in 1987 dollars.[33]

The activities required to shorten development times may require additional out-of-pocket costs. For example, doing studies in parallel may result in performing tests that would not have been performed had the results of the other tests been known. Shortening the NDA review period may require additional resources for the FDA. The cost of achieving a reduction in development times must be compared to the estimated savings in implicit interest costs. Within a broader context, one should also consider the effects on product lifetimes and associated sales revenues from having earlier marketing dates, and the benefits to society from having effective medications available for patient use sooner.

[33]It is worth noting that the entire FDA budget for fiscal year 1988 was $478 million, with $169 million spent on salaries and expenses for the human drugs and biologics divisions [U.S. Department of Health and Human Services (1990)].

7. Cost estimates for subsamples

7.1. Within-sample period effects

We examined whether it is possible to discern time trends in our data. The sample did not contain enough information to investigate costs on a year-to-year basis, so we divided the sample into two time periods (NCEs first tested in humans during the periods 1970–1976 and 1977–1982). The distribution of population NCEs over the strata used in the weighting scheme for the full sample differed by period. Consequently, we reweighted NCEs for each period according to the sample and population strata proportions for that period.

Mean phase III development time and cost are significantly lower for the more recent period, but these data are not complete. In particular, NCEs with long development times will be underrepresented in the late period. At this point, meaningful comparisons across periods of phase III costs cannot be undertaken. However, counting only phase I and phase II costs, the 1977–1982 period uncapitalized costs are 100.5% higher than those for the 1970–1976 period. This suggests a strong upward time trend in out-of-pocket clinical costs.

7.2. Clinical period costs for approved NCEs

The cost of development may differ between successful and unsuccessful projects. To investigate this, we examined costs for the approved NCEs in our sample. We had complete cost data on 22 of the 27 NCEs that had obtained marketing approval as of October 31, 1990. One of the 22 NCEs is an extreme outlier with respect to cost and was removed from the approved NCE subsample.[34] It was retained for the full sample results. Given the much larger sample size and the small weight this NCE received in the weighting scheme used for the full sample, its impact on the full sample results is minor.

Table 7 offers a comparison between mean phase costs and lengths for the approved NCEs and those for all sample NCEs. Development times are very similar. However, except for early clinical testing (phase I), phase costs are significantly higher for the approved NCEs. This may reflect a tendency to direct more resources, perhaps through conducting more studies concurrently, to the NCEs that early clinical testing suggests have the greatest promise of approval. Table 7 also shows that, as is the case for the full

[34]Both the uncapitalized and capitalized clinical costs of the outlier are roughly double those of the approved NCE with the next highest clinical costs.

Table 7

Clinical period average phase costs and phase lengths for approved NCEs and for all sample NCEs (in thousands of 1987 dollars).[a]

	Approved NCEs[b]			Full sample[c]		
Testing phase	Mean phase cost	Standard deviation of phase costs	Mean phase length (actual)	Mean phase cost	Standard deviation of phase costs	Mean phase length (actual)
Phase I	2,475	2,957	14.0	2,134	4,519	15.5
Phase II	5,629	4,138	25.9	3,954	5,230	24.3
Phase III	20,024	14,016	36.8	12,801	13,974	36.0
Long-term animal	3,646	3,065	37.4	2,155	2,411	33.6
Other animal	1,777	2,300	37.4	648	1,183	33.6

[a]All costs were deflated using the GNP Implicit Price Deflator.
[b]Estimates for approved NCEs are based on data for 21 of the 93 sample NCEs.
[c]Weighted values were used in calculating means and standard deviations for the full sample estimates.

sample, substantial variation exists in the costs of individual approved drugs for each phase.

The uncapitalized mean clinical period cost for the approved NCEs is \$31.9 million; the median cost is \$31.0 million. The 95% confidence interval for mean out-of-pocket clinical period cost is \$31.9±7.7 million.[35] Since we have approval dates for these drugs, it was not necessary to use a representative time profile; costs were capitalized to the point of actual marketing approval. Mean capitalized clinical period cost for approved NCEs is \$43.0 million; median capitalized cost is \$40.9 million. The 95% confidence interval is \$43.0±11.3 million.[36,37]

The FDA rates new drugs according to whether the drug represents an important therapeutic gain (A), a moderate therapeutic gain (B), or little or no therapeutic gain (C) over existing therapy. To get a sense for whether the cost of developing NCEs is related to their therapeutic importance, we

[35]A chi-squared goodness-of-fit test was used to compare the sample frequency distribution of uncapitalized clinical period costs to a normal probability distribution. The hypothesis of no difference in distributions could not be rejected. Hence, we used a *t*-distribution in constructing the confidence interval.

[36]As is the case with uncapitalized costs, the hypothesis that the capitalized costs were taken from a normal population cannot be rejected.

[37]Given the right-censored nature of the data, approved NCEs with very long development times may be somewhat under-represented in the sample. We found a moderate positive correlation between capitalized clinical period cost and the time from the start of clinical testing to NDA approval (Spearman rank correlation coefficient = 0.661). Thus, reported costs for the approved NCEs may be somewhat biased downward.

computed costs for approved NCEs according to their therapeutic ratings.[38] Mean and median capitalized clinical period costs for the A and B rated approved NCEs are $51.7 and $41.5 million, respectively.[39] Costs for the C rated approved NCEs are somewhat lower – mean and median capitalized clinical period costs are $36.5 and $36.2 million, respectively.

8. An external check on the results

As an external check on our results, we analyzed the R&D performance of the U.S. pharmaceutical industry to see if it was consistent with our analysis. In particular, our approach is to relate industry R&D expenditures to the NCE introductions of U.S. firms (see fig. 1) using the same lag structure and time period in our study. However, since our study focuses on the self-originated NCEs of U.S.-owned firms, it is necessary to make various transformations of the publicly available industry data before meaningful comparisons can be undertaken.

For the cost survey firms, we determined the proportions of their aggregate pharmaceutical R&D expenditures that were spent on self-originated NCEs (73.7%) and on licensed or acquired NCEs (10.0%). Published PMA industry R&D expenditure data, however, do not distinguish between what firms spend on self-originated NCEs and what they spend on licensed or acquired NCEs. The procedures we employ to estimate annual industry self-originated NCE R&D expenditures and how they can be related to annual NCE approvals are described in appendix C.

We averaged both lagged R&D expenditures and the number of approvals over the period 1979–1989.[40] Using an average of 7.3 industry self-originated approvals per year for this time frame, we found uncapitalized and capitalized cost estimates of $138 and $270 million, respectively. In 1983 there was only one approval of a self-originated NCE from a U.S.-owned firm. Excluding this outlier year yields 7.9 as an average annual number of

[38] Although the FDA gives an initial rating to investigational NCEs shortly after IND filing, we have information only on the final ratings for the approved NCEs in our sample. The FDA rating system must be viewed with caution when considered as a measure of therapeutic benefit since the FDA has rather limited information when it assigns the ratings. The ultimate clinical significance of some drugs may not become apparent until the drugs have been in widespread use for a number of years for the original approved indications, or until their effectiveness for additional indications has been noted in clinical practice.

[39] The A and B rated drugs were combined since there is only one A rated drug in the subsample. Of the remaining 20 approved NCEs, eight are B rated and 12 are C rated.

[40] Year-to-year cost estimates using aggregate data are highly variable because they are extremely sensitive to the denominator (number of self-originated NCE approvals) used for the calculations. Thus, to reduce variability in the estimate, we used average values for the numerator and denominator, as opposed to an average of the annual ratios of lagged expenditures to current approvals.

approvals, and reduces the uncapitalized and capitalized cost estimates to \$127 and \$250 million, respectively. Hence, our estimate of \$231 million is comparable to what one obtains from a comprehensive aggregate analysis.

9. Conclusions and prospects for future research

We have estimated the average cost of new drug development from a large sample of self-originated NCEs that were first tested in humans during 1970–1982. Data were obtained from a confidential survey of 12 U.S.-owned firms. The average cost of NCE development was estimated to be \$231 million in 1987 dollars (with \$114 million of that paid out-of-pocket). A representative time profile for an NCE passing through all phases of development from synthesis to marketing approval extended nearly 12 years.

Cost estimates are substantially higher here than in previous studies; some of which, however, did not measure R&D cost fully or adequately. Our period of analysis is also more recent than the periods used for these other analyses. In particular, this study is the only one to date that has reflected in its estimates much of the sharp increase in pharmaceutical R&D expenditures that occurred during the 1980s.

The most recent study on the cost of new drug development [Wiggins (1987)] used R&D expenditure data that covered the period 1965–1982, but with full weight placed only on expenditures from 1967 to 1980. This can partially explain why costs in that study are much lower than those found here. Another, perhaps more important, reason is that Wiggins used expenditure and approval data for all NCE approvals. In particular, he did not differentiate between self-originated and licensed or acquired NCEs. The R&D expenditures incurred on new drugs up to the point of licensing or sale will not be included in U.S. industry (PMA) data if the drug originated from an overseas operation of a foreign firm. Our analysis of industry data revealed substantially lower company expenditures per new drug on licensed or acquired NCEs than is the case for self-originated NCEs.

When results here are compared to those of a previous study [Hansen (1979)] with a similar methodology, total cost is seen to have increased 2.3 times in real terms. Development times are longer and a higher discount rate is used. The bulk of the increase in cost per approved NCE, however, can be attributed to large increases in out-of-pocket costs.

That clinical trial costs have risen sharply in recent years is attested to in F-D-C Reports: The Pink Sheet (1989), where an executive of a major pharmaceutical firm reports that the information required to support NDAs has increased dramatically. Clinical trials for one of the firm's anti-infective NCEs approved in 1979 used 1,493 patients; the trials for a related anti-infective that the firm is currently developing will require testing on 10,000 patients. Also mentioned as factors leading to rising costs are the complexity and scope of the research required and the adoption of expensive new technologies. Another factor often suggested to explain increased costs is that firms are now focusing development more on treatments for chronic and degenerative diseases, which typically require longer and more expensive testing.

In many applications that utilize pharmaceutical R&D cost estimates, the relevant concept is the after-tax cost (e.g., rate of return analyses). R&D is typically expensed immediately, rather than depreciated during the life of the marketed product. If the firm has sufficient profits against which to expense the R&D, the net cash flow required to finance the R&D will be reduced by the amount of the tax savings. However, in contrast to an investment in an asset such as a building, which can be depreciated over its useful life for tax purposes, the investment in R&D necessary to bring a product to market cannot be depreciated during the years in which sales occur. Thus, the effect of expensing rather than depreciating R&D is one of changing the time at which the deduction occurs.

The R&D tax credit, enacted in 1981, was in effect for only part of our study period. Depending on changes in firm spending levels, the credit had differential impacts across firms. In aggregate, though, the impact of the credit on our cost estimates is likely to be minor.[41] Since we were only interested here in estimating social cost, rather than rates of return, we did not adjust for the timing of taxes or the extra credits.[42]

Further research on the cost of new drug development could profitably be directed at a detailed analysis of differences in costs across therapeutic classes. We will address this issue in future research. Another interesting topic for future research is whether trade-offs exist on the margin between clinical trial expenditures and NCE failure rates.

Our analysis has been directed to the R&D cost of self-originated NCEs from U.S.-owned firms. In future research it would be interesting to analyze the R&D costs of NCEs originating in other countries. This would be especially the case for Japan. Aggregate data suggests that R&D costs per

[41]If we use U.S. pharmaceutical industry R&D expenditure data, we can obtain a rough upper bound estimate of the effect of the R&D tax credit. Until the Tax Reform Act of 1986 was enacted, the annual credit was 25% of the increase in covered R&D expenditures over the average of R&D expenditures for the previous three years. The Tax Reform Act of 1986 reduced the credit to 20%. Nominal U.S. pharmaceutical industry R&D expenditures grew at an 11.7% compound annual rate of growth from 1978 to 1986. This implies a 6.8% subsidy if all expenditures are covered and the credit is 25%. Much of our clinical cost data and the bulk of the related preclinical expenditures, though, predate the credit. Thus, the tax savings relevant to our study are likely much less than 6.8% of total expenditures.

[42]The impact of the tax rate in rate of return studies may not be substantial. Grabowski and Vernon (1989) found their results little affected when sensitivity analysis was conducted on the tax rate parameter.

NCE originating in Japan are significantly lower than those in the United States [Grabowski (1990)]. At the same time, pharmaceutical R&D in Japan has different characteristics from that undertaken in the United States, and has produced significantly fewer NCE introductions in major markets outside of Japan. Given the increased policy interest in international competitiveness, the cost and determinants of R&D performed in different countries is likely to be an important question for future research.

It would also be instructive to compare the total costs for U.S. firms of originating a new drug in-house versus licensing or acquiring one externally. Our survey data indicate that the R&D costs incurred by U.S. firms for a self-originated compound is several times what they spend for a licensed or acquired NCE. This raises the issue of whether the licensing fees and other costs for externally acquired compounds exactly offset the higher R&D costs of self-originated NCEs. This is what would be expected in equilibrium, if the market for licensed and acquired NCEs is perfectly competitive. Whether this in fact has been true of recent experience in the pharmaceutical industry is an interesting topic for future research.

Another important topic for future work is the effect of firm size and the scale of R&D activities on the costs of new drug introductions. This topic is also likely to have significant policy interest, given the recent tendency toward increased consolidation of the pharmaceutical industry. In this regard, it would be useful to know whether this consolidation is motivated in part by higher real R&D costs or potential R&D scale economies.

Our R&D cost estimates should be a useful input to studies of the returns to current new drug introductions. It should be emphasized that rising real R&D costs do not necessarily represent a problem for pharmaceutical innovative activity. In particular, if the higher costs are reflective of higher probabilities of commercial success and/or higher average sales per new drug introduction, then strong incentives to undertake pharmaceutical R&D can be maintained even in the face of rising R&D costs. Hence, it will be important in future research to examine trends in innovative output and sales revenues, as well as R&D costs.

Finally, it should be emphasized that while our estimates are presented in 1987 dollars, they are not estimates of the cost of developing a new drug in 1987. The drugs included in the sample were first tested in humans between 1970 and 1982, and many of the successful candidates from this sample are entering the market in the 1980s and 1990s (the mean approval date for approved drugs in the sample was in early 1983, with future approvals expected to raise the mean to early 1984). However, the expected cost of developing a new drug for which testing begins in the late 1980s or the 1990s will be affected by changes in the process which have occurred since our sample period. The trends suggest that the cost will be higher than our estimate.

Appendix A

Estimated weighted mean phase cost, $\bar{x}_i$, is determined as follows (where the index values 1, 2, 3 and A refer to phases I, II, III and long-term animal testing, respectively):

$$\bar{x}_i = \sum_{j=1}^{n} w_j x_{ij} \Big/ \sum_{j=1}^{n} w_j n_{ij} \quad \text{for } i = 1, 2, 3 \text{ and A}, \tag{A.1}$$

where

n = number of NCEs in the sample,

w_j = ratio of the % of population NCEs to the % of sample NCEs for the stratum in which NCE j falls,

$$x_{ij} = \begin{cases} j\text{th NCE phase } i \text{ cost} & \text{if the } j\text{th NCE has phase } i \text{ costs,} \\ 0 & \text{otherwise,} \end{cases}$$

$$n_{ij} = \begin{cases} 1 & \text{if the } j\text{th NCE has phase } i \text{ costs,} \\ 0 & \text{otherwise.} \end{cases}$$

For phases I, II, and III the estimated probability of entering a phase, s_i, is the product of the estimated conditional probability that the NCE will undergo testing in the phase given that the previous phase was entered, and the estimated probability of entering the preceding phase. For long-term animal testing, the estimate, s_A, is a weighted proportion of the sample NCEs that underwent that type of testing. Specifically, we have

$$s_i = \left(\sum_{g=1}^{G} \Theta_g \delta_{ig} \Big/ \sum_{g=1}^{G} \Theta_g \delta_{(i-1)g} \right) s_{i-1} \quad \text{for } i = 1, 2, 3, \tag{A.2}$$

$$s_A = \sum_{g=1}^{G} \Theta_g \delta_{Ag} \Big/ \sum_{g=1}^{G} \Theta_g \delta_g, \tag{A.3}$$

where

Θ_g = ratio of the % of population NCEs to the % of sample NCEs for stratum g,

δ_{ig} = number of sample NCEs in stratum g that entered phase i,

δ_g = number of sample NCEs in stratum g,

$s_0 = 1$,

$\delta_{0g} = \delta_g$.

With (A.1) and (A.2) an estimate of expected clinical period costs for a randomly selected NCE tested in humans, $\hat{E}$, can be expressed as $\hat{E} = s_I \bar{x}_I + s_{II} \bar{x}_{II} + s_{III} \bar{x}_{III} + s_A \bar{x}_A$. Given that the sample strata are prespecified, the weights, w_j and Θ_g are not random variables. We can see, then, that $\bar{x}_i$ and s_i are unbiased estimates of the population mean phase i cost and the population proportion of NCEs entering phase i, respectively. There is no reason to expect that the weighted mean cost for a phase and the weighted proportion of NCEs entering that phase are correlated across independent samples. Under the assumption that $\bar{x}_i$ and s_i are stochastically independent, it can easily be shown that $\hat{E}$ is an unbiased estimate of $E(h)$.

Appendix B

The problem of estimating an approval success rate for the population of cost survey firm NCEs that meet survey inclusion criteria is modelled in two stages. Since the ultimate fate of some NCEs first tested in humans from 1970 to 1982 is, to our knowledge, not yet determined, survival analysis should prove useful [see Cox and Oakes (1984)].

In the first stage we estimate the distribution of times that the NCEs are in residence. For NCEs that have either been abandoned or approved by the end of 1986, we define residence time to be the time from first testing in humans to either research abandonment or NDA approval. Some NCEs were continuing in research as of the end of 1986. Data for such NCEs are right-censored. Survival analysis techniques utilize the information provided by censored observations.

In the second stage of the model, we estimate the probability that an NCE will meet a given fate (research abandonment or NDA approval) as a function of residence time. Thus, the cumulative probability of success (NDA approval) as a function of residence time, t, can be given as

$$S(t)=\int_0^t f(u)P(u)\,\mathrm{d}u, \tag{B.1}$$

where $f(u)$ is the probability density function for residence time, and $P(u)$ is the probability that an NCE with a residence of u receives NDA approval at that time. The density function can be estimated by a nonparametric product-limit technique.

The data on approvals at various residence times indicate that the process may be adequately approximated by a sigmoidally shaped distribution. Thus, we applied the logit and probit models to estimate $P(u)$. Both the logit and probit models provided good fits and, in fact, were virtually indistinguishable from one another.[43] Computed values of the likelihood ratio index deve-

[43]The transformation suggested in Amemiya (1981) for comparing coefficients in logit and probit models showed very small differences in the coefficients. The results on cumulative success rates are also virtually the same when logit and probit specifications for $P(u)$ are used.

loped in McFadden (1974) shows the probit model to have a slightly superior fit, and so the success rate estimates utilize the probit specification for $P(u)$.[44]

The cost survey firms investigated in humans 279 NCEs that met cost survey inclusion criteria.[45] As of December 31, 1989, 17.2% of these NCEs had been approved. Our model predicts that approximately 23% of the population NCEs will have been approved 14 years after first testing in humans. By the end of 1986 only four NCEs had been in residence longer than 14 years, and information obtained in the cost survey indicated that two of these NCEs had been abandoned. We use 23% as our base case clinical approval success rate.

Evidence of the predictive power of eq. (B.1) can be obtained by focusing on one subclass of NCEs. Taking note of dates of research abandonment obtained from the cost survey and approvals after 1986, we were able to completely characterize the fate of all anti-infective NCEs. The model (using data through 1986) predicted an approval success rate of 31.7% for this class, which compares very well with the actual final cumulative success rate of 31.0%.

Appendix C

The PMA publishes R&D expenditure data for its member firms (PMA Annual Survey Report, various years). From these data it is possible to extract annual expenditures for human use ethical pharmaceuticals. These expenditures, in real terms for the years 1967–1987, are given in the first column of table C.1.

At our request, we also obtained information from the PMA on the percentage of total R&D expenditures accounted for by U.S.-owned member firms. The PMA had such data only for recent years. We utilized the 1987–1988 percentage (84.3%) to estimate annual R&D expenditures by U.S.-owned firms (column 2 of table C.1). There is some evidence of a slight decrease in this percentage over time. Given the downward trend in this percentage, the values in column 2 are likely to be conservative estimates.

We next subtract foreign expenditures from the values of U.S.-owned R&D expenditures to obtain their domestic R&D expenditures (column 3 of table C.1). We include only domestic expenditures in our analysis under the assumption that the foreign expenditures of U.S.-owned firms will be directed

[44]Specifically, we used an iteratively reweighted non-linear least squares routine to estimate $P(u)=F(\alpha+\beta u)$, where u represents residence time in months and $F(\cdot)$ is the cumulative distribution function of the standard normal random variable. The maximum likelihood estimates of α and β are -2.3720 and 0.0244, respectively.

[45]The information needed to conduct the survival analysis was available for 276 of these NCEs.

Table C.1

U.S. pharmaceutical industry real human use R&D expenditures 1967–1987 (millions of 1987 dollars).[a]

Year	(1) All PMA firms	(2) U.S.-owned PMA firms[b]	(3) U.S. R&D of (2)[c]	(4) Self-originated R&D of (3)
1967	1,363	1,149	972	670
1968	1,400	1,180	1,058	729
1969	1,492	1,258	1,135	782
1970	1,583	1,334	1,203	829
1971	1,663	1,402	1,264	871
1972	1,684	1,420	1,253	863
1973	1,785	1,505	1,247	859
1974	1,870	1,576	1,282	883
1975	1,928	1,625	1,338	922
1976	1,989	1,677	1,367	942
1977	2,061	1,737	1,393	960
1978	2,123	1,790	1,468	1,011
1979	2,275	1,918	1,501	1,034
1980	2,549	2,149	1,593	1,098
1981	2,762	2,328	1,771	1,220
1982	3,100	2,613	2,047	1,410
1983	3,462	2,918	2,324	1,601
1984	3,726	3,141	2,513	1,731
1985	4,142	3,492	2,774	1,911
1986	4,703	3,965	3,101	2,137
1987	5,310	4,476	3,508	2,417

[a]Expenditures on R&D for ethical pharmaceuticals intended for human use were obtained from the PMA Annual Survey Report (various years) and deflated using the GNP Implicit Price Deflator.

[b]The expenditures for all firms in a year were reduced by the average percentage of member firm R&D expenditures accounted for by U.S.-owned firms for 1987 and 1988 (source: Gary Persinger, PMA).

[c]Computed based on U.S.-owned firm aggregate expenditure levels and data contained in the PMA Annual Survey Report (various years).

primarily to non-U.S. introductions. This assumption will also tend to produce conservative estimates, since at least some of the foreign expenditures of U.S.-owned firms are obviously directed towards approval of new drugs in the United States and other major world markets.[46]

The last step in the analysis is to determine the percentage of R&D that is devoted to self-originated NCEs by U.S.-owned firms. In particular, we need to separate such R&D expenditures from those on licensed or acquired NCEs and on R&D for improvements in existing products. It would be

[46]Although some of the domestic R&D expenditures of U.S. firms may be targeted specifically to products only introduced abroad, our approach will produce a conservative estimate so long as these outlays are smaller in value than the foreign R&D expenditures of U.S. firms that are related to domestic introductions. This appears to be a reasonable presumption given the tendency of U.S. firms to prescreen compounds abroad for the U.S. market.

Table C.2

New chemical entity approvals in the United States, 1979–1989.

Year	Total NCEs	U.S.-owned PMA member firm NCEs	Self-originated NCEs of U.S.-owned PMA firms[a]
1979	13	13	9
1980	11	9	6
1981	23	15	6
1982	22	18	11
1983	12	6	1
1984	21	15	8
1985	26	16	12
1986	20	13	8
1987	18	13	10
1988	16	8	5
1989	21	10	4

[a]Information on the origin of compounds was obtained from a Center for the Study of Drug Development annual survey of firms with U.S. NCE approvals and supplemented, when necessary, with published sources.

inappropriate to assume that the firms who did not participate in our survey have the same pattern of R&D allocations as our survey firms. NCE output data show that non-survey U.S.-owned firms are somewhat more reliant on licensed or acquired NCEs.[47] We assume that the R&D effort necessary to produce a self-originated NCE relative to a licensed or acquired NCE is the same for the survey and non-survey firms.[48] Using this approach, we estimate that the non-survey U.S.-owned firms devoted 60.6% of their pharmaceutical R&D to self-originated NCEs. Given this estimate, and the fact that our cost survey firms account for 48.3% of the total pharmaceutical R&D expenditures of all U.S.-owned firms, we can compute a weighted

[47]For the cost survey firms, 66.7% of their NCE approvals during the period 1979–1989 are self-originated. For the same period, only 48.1% of the approvals of other U.S.-owned firms are self-originated.

[48]In particular, the ratio of expenditures on self-originated NCEs per approval of NCEs of this type to the expenditures on licensed or acquired NCEs per approval of such NCEs was estimated to be 3.7 for firms in our survey. In other words, it takes nearly four times the R&D outlays to produce a self-originated NCE compared to the R&D necessary for a licensed or acquired NCE for our survey firms (ignoring licensing and acquisition fees). We assume that this ratio is the same for the U.S.-owned firms that are not in our survey sample. We also assume that the group of foreign-owned PMA member firms spent the same proportion of their U.S. pharmaceutical R&D on new products as did the survey firms. We then used information available in the PMA Annual Survey Report (various years) to estimate that non-survey U.S.-owned firms spent 78.3% of their pharmaceutical R&D on new products. Using these two estimates, together with information on the breakdown of NCE approvals between self-originated and licensed or acquired NCEs for non-survey U.S.-owned firms, we estimated that these firms spent 60.6% of their pharmaceutical R&D for self-originated NCEs.

average estimate of the percentage of pharmaceutical R&D performed by U.S.-owned firms for self-originated NCEs (66.8%) and apply it to the previously calculated values in column 3 of table C.1.

We also performed a parallel analysis for the U.S. NCE approvals between 1979 and 1989. These results are presented in table C.2. We first separated total NCE approvals into those emanating from U.S.-owned PMA member firms and all other firms. The NCEs from U.S.-owned PMA firms (shown in column 2) were then further subdivided into self-originated versus licensed or acquired NCEs. To classify NCEs into these sub-categories, we used the CSDD annual survey of NCE approvals together with information from related sources. For the 1979–1989 period, the last column of table C.2 shows the annual number of self-originated NCEs accounted for by U.S.-owned PMA member firms. We found that approximately 39% of all U.S. NCE approvals for this period were for self-originated NCEs of U.S.-owned PMA firms.

For a lag structure, we use the phase time profile and cost levels found in this study. This implies that approvals in one year should be associated with R&D expenditures lagged 2 to 12 years. Monthly expenditures were calculated and spread over this period according to the phase time profile.[49] Weights to be attached to each of the lag years can then be determined,[50] and used to estimate uncapitalized cost per approval. Given the time profile, weights for capitalized cost estimates can also be calculated.

[49]Data from a CSDD database were used to determine that NCEs approved over the last 15 years received their approvals, on average, eight months into the year of approval. This was used to establish the endpoints of the time profile.

[50]If approval occurs in year t_0, then the weights for years t_{-2} to t_{-12} are 0.038, 0.059, 0.075, 0.083, 0.072, 0.058, 0.105, 0.163, 0.163, 0.163, and 0.020, respectively. These weights represent the proportions of out-of-pocket expenditures incurred in the years prior to approval.

References

Amemiya, T., 1981, Qualitative response models: A survey, Journal of Economic Literature 19, 1483–1536.

Baily, M.N., 1972, Research and development costs and returns: The U.S. pharmaceutical industry, Journal of Political Economy 80, no. 1, 70–85.

Clymer, H., 1970, The changing costs and risks of pharmaceutical innovation, in: J.D. Cooper, ed., The economics of drug innovation (American University, Washington, DC) 109–124.

Cox, D.R. and D. Oakes, 1984, Analysis of survival data (Chapman and Hall, London).

Feldstein, M., 1988, Halving the pain of budget balance, Wall Street Journal, May 28, 24.

F-D-C Reports: The Pink Sheet, 1989, Lilly estimates '3,300 person years' go into development of successful new molecular entity; current antibiotic project is requiring 10,000 patients, 51, nos. 51 & 52, 14.

Grabowski, H.G., 1989, An analysis of U.S. international competitiveness in pharmaceuticals, Managerial and Decision Economics (special issue), Spring, 27–33.

Grabowski, H.G., 1990, Innovation and international competitiveness in pharmaceuticals, in: A. Heertje and M. Perlman, eds., Evolving technology in market structure: Studies in Schumpeterian economics (University of Michigan Press, Ann Arbor) 167–185.

Grabowski, H.G. and J.M. Vernon, 1982, A sensitivity analysis of expected profitability of pharmaceutical research and development, Managerial and Decision Economics 3, no. 1, 36–40.
Grabowski, H.G. and J.M. Vernon, 1990, A new look at the returns and risks to pharmaceutical R&D, Management Science 36, no. 7, 804–821.
Grabowski, H.G., J.M. Vernon and L.G. Thomas, 1978, Estimating the effects of regulation on innovation: An international comparative analysis of the pharmaceutical industry, Journal of Law and Economics 21, no. 1, 133–163.
Hansen, R.W., 1979, The pharmaceutical development process: Estimates of current development costs and times and the effects of regulatory changes, in: R.I. Chien, ed., Issues in pharmaceutical economics (Lexington Books, Lexington, MA) 151–187.
Hansen, R.W., 1980, Pharmaceutical development costs by therapeutic categories, University of Rochester Graduate School of Management Working Paper No. GPB-80-6. March.
Joglekar, P. and M.L. Paterson, 1986, A closer look at the returns and risks of pharmaceutical R&D, Journal of Health Economics 5, 153–177.
Mansfield, E., 1987, Price indexes for R&D inputs, 1969–1983, Management Science 33, no. 1, 124–129.
Mattison, N., A.G. Trimble and L. Lasagna, 1988, New drug development in the United States, 1963–1984, Clinical Pharmacology and Therapeutics 43, 15–27.
McFadden, D., 1974, Conditional logit analysis of qualitative choice behavior, in: P. Zarembka, ed., Frontiers in econometrics (Academic Press, New York) 105–142.
Mund, V.F., 1970, The return on investment of the innovative pharmaceutical firm, in: J.D. Cooper, ed., The economics of drug innovation (American University, Washington, DC) 125–138.
National Academy of Engineering, 1983, The competitive status of the U.S. pharmaceutical industry (National Academy Press, Washington, DC).
Pharmaceutical Manufacturers Association, 1987, PMA statistical fact book (PMA, Washington, DC).
Pharmaceutical Manafacturers Association, Annual survey report, various years (1968–1989) (PMA, Washington, DC).
Sarett, L.H., 1974, FDA regulations and their influence on future research and development, Research Management, 18–20.
Schnee, J.E., 1972, Development costs: Determinants and overruns, Journal of Business, 347–374.
Sheck, L., C. Cox, H.T. Davis, A.G. Trimble, W.M. Wardell and R.W. Hansen, 1984, Success rates in the United States drug development system, Clinical Pharmacology and Therapeutics 36, 574–583.
Statman, M., 1983, Competition in the pharmaceutical industry (American Enterprise Institute, Studies in Health Policy, Washington, DC).
Thomas, L.G., 1990, Spare the rod and spoil the industry: Vigorous competition and vigorous regulation promote global competitive advantage, presented at the International Joseph Schumpeter Society Meetings, June, Charlottesville, VA.
Tucker, S.A., C. Blozan and P. Coppinger, 1988, The outcome of research on new molecular entities commencing clinical research in the years 1976–78, Office of Planning and Evaluation Study 77 (Food and Drug Administration, Rockville, MD).
U.S. Bureau of Economic Analysis, Government Division, 1986, The biomedical research and development price index: Revised and updated estimates (U.S. Government Printing Office, Washington, DC).
U.S. Congress, House, Subcommittee on Health and the Environment of the Committee on Energy and Commerce, 1985, Prescription drug price increases, 99th Congress, First Session, July 15, 1985 (U.S. Government Printing Office, Washington, DC).
U.S. Congress, House, Subcommittee on Health and the Environment of the Committee on Energy and Commerce, 1987, Medical devices and drug issues, 100th Congress, First Session, April 27, 1987 and May 4, 1987 (U.S. Government Printing Office, Washington, DC).
U.S. Congress, Senate, Special Committee on Aging, 1989, Prescription drug prices: Are we getting our money's worth?, Majority staff report (U.S. Government Printing Office, Washington, DC).

U.S. Department of Health and Human Services, 1990, Justification of appropriation estimates for committee on appropriations, Food and Drug Administration, Vol. 10 (U.S. Public Health Service, Hyattsville, MD).

Wiggins, S.N., 1981, The pharmaceutical research and development decision process, in: R.B. Helms, ed., Drugs and health: Issues and policy objectives (American Enterprise Institute, Washington, DC).

Wiggins, S.N., 1987, The cost of developing a new drug (Pharmaceutical Manufacturers Association, Washington, DC), June.

Woltman, H.R., 1989, Reviewing the bidding: R&D costs and profitability of new chemical entities, Journal of Research in Pharmaceutical Economics 1, no. 3, 49–65.

[5]

RAND Journal of Economics
Vol. 27, No. 1, Spring 1996
pp. 32–59

Scale, scope, and spillovers: the determinants of research productivity in drug discovery

Rebecca Henderson*

and

Iain Cockburn**

We examine the relationship between firm size and research productivity in the pharmaceutical industry. Using detailed internal firm data, we find that larger research efforts are more productive, not only because they enjoy economies of scale, but also because they realize economies of scope by sustaining diverse portfolios of research projects that capture internal and external knowledge spillovers. In pharmaceuticals, economies of scope in research are important in shaping the boundaries of the firm, and it may be worth tolerating the static efficiency loss attributable to the market power of large firms in exchange for their superior innovative performance.

1. Introduction

■ Are the research efforts of larger firms more productive than those of their smaller rivals, and if so, why? Answers to these questions speak directly to two central problems in the economics of industrial organization. In the first place, the relationship between the size of a firm and its innovative performance plays a central role in the analysis of industry structure, innovation, and the tradeoff between static and dynamic efficiency (Panzar, 1989; Baldwin and Scott, 1987). In the second place, economies of scope and scale in research and development (R&D) play an important role in the theory of the firm: well-known problems in the market for information imply that they are fundamental to the existence of multiproduct firms (Arrow, 1962; Teece, 1980; Cohen and Levinthal, 1989).

But despite the theoretical importance of these topics, quantitative evidence for the presence and sources of size advantages in R&D is mixed (Baldwin and Scott, 1987;

---

* Massachusetts Institute of Technology and NBER.

** University of British Columbia and NBER.

This research was funded by four pharmaceutical companies and by the Sloan Foundation. Their support is gratefully acknowledged. We would also like to express our deep appreciation to all the firms that contributed data to this project. We thank an Editor of this journal, two anonymous referees, and Richard Caves, Zvi Griliches, and Bronwyn Hall for their helpful comments and suggestions, as well as seminar participants at Carnegie Mellon, Columbia, MIT, the NBER, Northwestern, Stanford, UBC, and UCLA. The conclusions and opinions expressed in this article are our own, and any errors or omissions remain entirely our responsibility.

Cohen and Levin, 1989). Although much qualitative evidence is consistent with the belief that large firms are more effective in the conduct of industrial research (Freeman, 1982; Chandler, 1990), it has proved difficult to confirm this idea econometrically. Lack of sufficiently detailed data has made it difficult to control for industry effects or variation in technological opportunity, or to distinguish between economies of scale and economies of scope.

In this article we go inside the firm to examine the advantages of size in performing research. We use detailed data constructed at the level of the individual research program obtained from the internal records of ten major research-oriented pharmaceutical companies. As an unusually research-intensive and innovative industry whose products sometimes generate significant social returns (Sloan, 1995), pharmaceuticals present an interesting arena in which to study these issues. Moreover, the industry has recently undergone a dramatic shift from so-called "random" to "rational" drug discovery that may have changed the nature of the returns to scope and scale in research with potentially important consequences for both appropriate public policy and the competitive dynamics of the industry.

Our results suggest that there are significant returns to size in pharmaceutical research, but that only a small portion of these returns are derived from economies of scale per se. The primary advantage of large firms appears to be their ability to realize returns to scope: to sustain an adequately diverse portfolio of research projects, and to capture and use internal and external spillovers of knowledge. These effects appear to have become significantly more important as the industry has adopted a more science-based research technology.

We also use these data to explore the nature of spillovers between firms in the industry. Externalities arising from the public-goods aspect of knowledge have assumed a central role in modern growth theory (Romer, 1986; Grossman and Helpman, 1991), and R&D spillovers also play a key role in many models of market structure (Spence, 1984; Dasgupta and Stiglitz, 1980), but microeconometric evidence on their impact is disappointingly scarce (Griliches, 1992). Here we find evidence consistent with some quite substantial spillovers of knowledge between firms.

The article begins with a short literature review as background to the development of our hypotheses. In subsequent sections we discuss some of the estimation issues and describe the data on which the study is based. Section 5 outlines the empirical results, and the article closes with a brief discussion of their implications.

2. Hypothesis development and literature review

■ **Scale, scope, spillovers, and research productivity.** In principle, size confers three major advantages in performing R&D. First, in the absence of fully functioning markets for innovation, larger firms may be able to spread the fixed costs of research over a larger sales base. Second, large firms may have advantages in the financial markets over smaller firms: to the degree that they are able to mitigate problems of adverse selection and moral hazard in raising capital, they may be better positioned to fund risky projects. Third, larger firms may be able to exploit economies of scale and scope in the conduct of research itself (Panzar and Willig, 1981; Cohen and Levin, 1989; Schumpeter, 1950).

Early tests of these ideas attempted to establish a relationship between firm size and R&D intensity and were largely inconclusive (Baldwin and Scott, 1987; Cohen and Levin, 1989). The results of later work exploring the more appropriate relationship between research output and firm size have been similarly unconvincing. Bound et al. (1984) found that there was evidence of constant returns to scale for R&D programs between \$2 million and \$100 million when patents were used as a measure of research output, but their results were quite sensitive to specification assumptions. Acs and Audretsch (1988), using a measure of "major innovations" as a measure of output, found that in highly concentrated industries with high barriers to entry, large firms were likely to be the source of the majority of innovations. A study by Pavitt, Robson, and Townsend (1987), using a similar measure of output, suggested that both very small firms and very large firms were proportionately more innovative than more moderate-sized firms. Similarly, although the presence of economies of scope in production have been verified in many industries, including airlines, banking, and advertising (Caves, Christensen, and Tretheway, 1984; Glass and McKillop, 1992; Silk and Berndt, 1993), a lack of appropriately detailed data has meant that with some notable exceptions, we have very little empirical evidence as to their importance in research (Helfat, 1994).

Estimates of the impact of spillovers have also been difficult to obtain (Griliches, 1992). On the one hand, it is difficult to distinguish between the influence that spillovers from other industries have on research productivity through their unmeasured effect upon input costs and the influence that they have directly on research productivity by increasing the total stock of knowledge available to researchers. On the other hand, the accurate estimation of spillover effects depends on adequate measures of technological "distance" and of R&D capital, both constructs that have proved difficult to measure. Jaffe (1986) provides the best example of a careful attempt to account for these problems, and his work suggests that spillovers have important effects on research productivity, but there have been few attempts to duplicate his results using disaggregated data.

Turning to the pharmaceutical industry, prior research has also had inconclusive results. While Comanor (1965), Vernon and Gusen (1974), and Graves and Langowitz (1993) found evidence for decreasing returns to scale in R&D, Schwartzman (1976) suggested that there were significant economies of scale in pharmaceutical research, and Jensen (1987) found that beyond a (quite small) threshold, neither firm size nor the size of the research effort affected the marginal productivity of research and development. Furthermore, while Ward and Dranove (1995) and Gambardella (1992) have shown that in aggregate, private research productivity is significantly correlated with the generation of knowledge by the public sector, there has been no systematic study of the importance of spillovers between or within firms.

□ **Hypothesis formulation.** Pharmaceutical research and development takes place in two stages: drug discovery (hereafter "research") and drug development. The goal of the research phase is to find a chemical compound that has a desirable effect in a "screen" that mimics some aspect of a disease state in man, while the goal of the drug development process is to ensure that compounds identified through the research process are safe and effective in humans. These two activities require quite different sets of skills and resources, but prior research has relied on publicly available data in which this important distinction cannot be made. In this article we are able to focus exclusively on the determinants of productivity in the research phase.

Economies of scale. Pharmaceutical firms typically invest in approximately ten to fifteen distinct research programs. Each research program is targeted toward the discovery of therapies for a particular disease area—hypertension or depression, for example—and may have anywhere from one to more than a hundred full-time researchers associated with it. Research programs may be grouped in turn into therapeutic areas, such as cardiovascular disease or conditions of the central nervous system.

Conventional wisdom in the industry suggests that beyond a minimum threshold, under most circumstances there is little to gain from increasing the size of an individual research program, and our descriptive statistics (see below) are certainly consistent with this belief. The firms in our dataset sustain a large number of relatively small programs.

However, since pharmaceutical research often requires investment in substantial fixed costs, and since the complexity of the underlying science offers considerable scope for specialization, we hypothesize that there are probably significant economies of scale at the level of the entire research effort. For example, to the degree that inputs such as libraries, computer resources, or large pieces of equipment are fixed costs, we hypothesize that a larger research effort will gain economies of scale by spreading them over a larger base of research activity. Similarly, a larger firm may also be able to obtain economies of scale through its ability to support highly specialized scientific personnel. Thus,

Hypothesis 1. Individual programs are not subject to returns to scale.

But

Hypothesis 2. There are returns to scale in research at the firm level.

Economies of scope. We identify two kinds of returns to the scope of the firm's research effort. In the standard analysis of production, economies of scope are present when the costs of conducting two or more activities jointly are lower than if they are conducted separately. This occurs most obviously when activities can share inputs at no additional cost, which is an important aspect of pharmaceutical research. The public goods aspect of knowledge means that knowledge capital accumulated in one program may be utilized as a productive input to other related programs, at little or no additional cost to the firm.

Conceptually, a clear distinction can be drawn between these economies of scope and a second source of returns to the diversity of the research effort: internal spillovers of knowledge between programs that enhance each other's productivity. Economies of scope relate to research expenditures, whereas internal knowledge spillovers affect output irrespective of expenditures. We attempt to distinguish between these effects in our analysis but recognize that this may be empirically difficult.

Our qualitative work suggests that both types of returns to scope are critically important in shaping research productivity. Consider, for example, the benefits of investing in a centralized laboratory devoted to peptide chemistry. Economies of scale exist if the costs of the laboratory are partially fixed, and if the lab can serve a larger and larger research effort for a less-than-proportionate increase in cost. They will also exist if the laboratory can become more efficient as it has more work to do, possibly through the specialization of its members. Economies of scope exist if the work of a group of peptide chemists is potentially relevant to a wide range of applications, and can be utilized in any one of them without diminishing its usefulness to the others. Benefits of diversity may also arise if discoveries made in one program stimulate the output of another through cross-fertilization of ideas or other forms of knowledge spillovers. Several important central nervous system therapies, for example, were discovered as the result of the search for drugs active in the cardiovascular system. Hence,

Hypothesis 3. There are significant returns to scope in research.

We are agnostic as to whether economies of scale and scope should increase or decrease with firm size. While formal treatments of firm scale and scope suggest that increasing firm size should be unilaterally beneficial (Panzar, 1989), several researchers have suggested that beyond a certain point, escalating coordination costs and problems of agency lead to diseconomies of size (Holmström, 1989; Zenger, 1994).

The role of spillovers. Our qualitative research also leads us to believe that spillovers between firms play a major role in research productivity. The industry is characterized by high rates of publication in the open scientific literature, and many of the scientists with whom we spoke stressed the importance of keeping in touch with the science conducted both within the public sector and by their competitors.[1] Nearly all of them had a quite accurate idea of the nature of the research currently being conducted by their competitors, and they often described the ways in which their rivals' discoveries had been instrumental in shaping their own research. Thus,

Hypothesis 4. Research productivity is positively associated with knowledge spillovers between firms.[2]

Notice, though, that the impact of competing firms' efforts on own research productivity is ambiguous. On the one hand, in a world in which firms are in a first-past-the-post "race" with each other to reach a particular goal, all other things equal, rivals' success imposes an "exhaustion externality" on competitors, and own research productivity will be negatively correlated with competitors' efforts (Reinganum, 1989). On the other hand, a firm may benefit from competitors' research since, all other things equal, extensive spillovers of knowledge between firms can increase the productivity of its research teams.

In both theory and practice, of course, these two effects interact with each other in complex ways (Spence, 1984). In a related article (Cockburn and Henderson, 1994) we explore this issue in more detail. For the purposes of the analysis presented here, we hypothesize that, all other things equal, a positive correlation between research success in any given area across competing firms is consistent with the presence of significant spillovers or research complementarities between firms, while a negative correlation is consistent with a research environment in which rivals' research efforts are substitutes rather than complements, spillovers are limited, and research productivity is primarily driven by an exhaustion externality.

Changes over time. Over the course of the past twenty years, the process of drug research has been changed significantly by advances in the biological sciences. In popular terminology, the industry has moved away from a process of "random search" toward one of more "rational" drug design (Cocks, 1975; Gross, 1983; Spilker, 1989). This innovation in the technology of research may have significantly altered the relative importance of scale, scope, and spillovers in determining research productivity.

Thirty years ago, pharmaceutical research was principally a matter of the large-scale "random" screening of potentially therapeutic compounds. In general, the "mechanism of action" of most drugs—the specific biochemical and molecular pathways that were responsible for their therapeutic effects—was not well understood. Firms employed few scientific specialists beyond pharmacologists and medicinal chemists, and the most important spillovers between firms took the form of the knowledge that compounds of a particular type showed promise in the treatment of a particular disease.

More recently, significant advances in the understanding of both the mechanism of action of many existing drugs and of the biochemical roots of many diseases have made it possible to make this process considerably more precise (Henderson, 1994). The request "find me something that will lower blood pressure in rats" can be replaced with the request "find me something that inhibits the action of the angiotensin II converting enzyme," while at the same time firms have a much more precise idea of the kinds of compounds that might prove efficacious.

[1] Measuring the impact of upstream spillovers from the public sector, though very important, is beyond the scope of this article but will be addressed in future work.

[2] For example, when Squibb announced that it had found an orally active ACE inhibitor, a potent hypertensive therapy, several competing firms were able to take advantage of the announcement to focus their own research efforts (Henderson, 1994).

The impact of this change on scale economies is hard to determine *ex ante*. While the importance of the scale economies inherent in activities such as the random screening of thousands of compounds may have declined, the transition to mechanism-based research has also greatly increased both the number of scientific specialties that are central to pharmaceutical research and the pace of knowledge generation within the industry. Modern pharmaceutical research relies upon the input of scientists skilled in a very wide range of disciplines, many of which are advancing at an extraordinarily rapid rate. Thus we hypothesize that the opportunities to exploit economies of scale arising from specialization may well have increased.

Hypothesis 5. Economies of scale in pharmaceutical research may have increased in the last twenty years.

Our beliefs about the relative importance of returns to scope are much firmer. As drug research has become increasingly directed by an understanding of the fundamental physiological mechanisms, knowledge acquired in one area has become much more likely to have implications for research conducted elsewhere within the firm.

Hypothesis 6. Economies of scope in drug research have increased in the last twenty years.

Finally, we believe that there may have been a concomitant change in the role of spillovers in shaping research productivity. When one's competitors are merely screening compounds, there is little to be learned from them unless they find a particularly promising molecule. But when they are actively investing in the generation of new physiological and biochemical knowledge, even knowledge of their false starts and failures may help to shape one's own research program. Thus,

Hypothesis 7. The impact of interfirm spillovers on research productivity has significantly increased over the last twenty years.

3. Specification of the econometric model

■ We test these hypotheses by estimating a "knowledge production function" of the type proposed by Griliches (1984), in which new knowledge is generated using both accumulated "knowledge capital" and resources expended in the current period. Rather than look for economies of scope and scale in restrictions on the parameters of cost functions (Caves, Christensen, and Tretheway, 1984; Glass and McKillop, 1992; Silk and Berndt, 1993), we use direct measures of scope, scale, and spillovers as shift variables modifying the relationship between research expenditures and the generation of knowledge, where knowledge is measured as grants of "important" patents.[3]

Pharmaceutical companies patent prolifically, and patents are, of course, a rather noisy measure of research success, in part because the significance of individual patents varies widely. We control for this by counting only "important" patents, where an "important" patent is defined as one that was granted in two of three major jurisdictions: Japan, Europe, and the United States.[4] Applying this criterion screens out large numbers of patents: roughly 60 percent of the number filed in the United States in any given year are discarded.

[3] The use of reduced-form models of this type to explore the determinants of performance has been a matter of some debate (Rumelt, 1991). We employ it as a technique whose limitations are quite well understood and as a first step toward exploring a complex and multifaceted phenomenon.

[4] We would have preferred to use citation-weighted patents as our measure of output. Unfortunately, since the U.S. patent classifications do not map directly into our definitions of research programs, we would have had to buy citation data directly from Derwent Publications, which proved to be prohibitively expensive.

Patents are clearly only one possible measure of research output, and in later work we plan to explore the use of alternative measures such as the number of compounds obtaining the various levels of regulatory approval. However, preliminary analysis suggests that Investigational New Drug Applications are highly correlated with "important" patents, and previous work has found that patents are correlated with a variety of measures of economic return (Griliches, 1990; Mairesse and Mohnen, 1995). Moreover, some of the well-known problems inherent in using patents as a measure of research output are in the pharmaceutical industry. Intellectual property rights are particularly clearly defined, and acquiring comprehensive patent protection is a prerequisite for subsequent commercial success.

We hypothesize that patent counts are generated by a production function $Y = f(X, \beta)$ where Y is patent counts, X is a vector of inputs to the drug research process, and β is a vector of parameters. We have no priors about the "true" functional form, so the model estimated should be thought of as a local approximation.

Some previous studies have looked at the dynamics of the R&D-patents relationship by estimating a lag structure on the input variables. Rather than make assumptions about distributed lags (and have to throw out much of our data in order to have four or five lags present in every program), we include "stocks" of the input variables as explanatory variables. The annual flows are reasonably smooth, so this is equivalent in many senses to imposing a geometric lag structure, where we have assumed a depreciation rate rather than estimated one.[5]

Since the dependent variable in this relationship takes on nonnegative interger values only, some type of discrete dependent-variable model is dictated. We assume that patent counts are generated by a Poisson process, which is appropriate if we are prepared to model research results as the outcome of an unknown (but large) number of Bernoulli trials with a small probability of success. This model certainly captures some aspects of drug research, such as screening. It may be less appropriate for mechanism-based research, and below we explore the robustness of some of our results to the use of alternative estimation techniques.

We model the single parameter of the Poisson distribution function, λ, as an exponential function of explanatory variables, X, and parameters β in the standard fashion,

$$E[Y_{it}] = \lambda_{it} = \exp(X_{it}\beta), \tag{1}$$

to guarantee nonnegativity of λ, and estimate the parameters by maximum likelihood in the standard way. Research expenditures, R, are entered in logs, while the other explanatory variables, Z, are in levels to give

$$E[Y_{it}] = \lambda_{it} = \exp(\gamma \log(R_{it}) + \delta Z_{it}) = R_{it}^{\gamma} \cdot \exp(\delta Z_{it}), \tag{2}$$

an estimating equation in which there is a direct proportionate relationship between research expenditures and patent counts mediated by a set of multiplicative shift variables, which include our measures of scope, scale, and spillovers, a constant term, and firm and therapeutic class dummies.

This choice of functional form has some important implications: for variables entered in levels, the estimated elasticity is γZ, which varies with the magnitude of each variable by assumption; conversely, if a variable enters in logs, we impose a constant elasticity. For easy comparison with previous research, we maintain the null

[5] Note that given a smooth series for the flow variable, it will be difficult as a practical matter to identify the estimated coefficient on the stock variable separately from the depreciation rate, making our assumption of a particular depreciation rate a second-order problem.

hypothesis of constant elasticity of Y with respect to research expenditures. We have no strong priors about the appropriate way to include the other explanatory variables, and we report results obtained by entering these variables in levels.[6]

The assumption that the dependent variable is distributed Poisson is quite strong: as in most other data of this type, the mean = variance property of the Poisson distribution is violated here. In the presence of such overdispersion, although the parameters β will be consistently estimated, their standard errors will typically be underestimated, leading to spuriously high levels of significance. Overdispersion is often interpreted as evidence that the statistical model is misspecified, in the sense that there may be unobserved variables in the equation for λ,

$$E[Y_{it}] = \lambda_{it} = \exp(X_{it}\beta + \epsilon_{it}). \quad (3)$$

As is well known (Hausman, Hall, and Griliches, 1984; Hall, Griliches, and Hausman, 1986), if ϵ is distributed gamma, then it can be integrated out giving Y distributed as a negative binomial variate. If ϵ is not truly gamma, however, the maximum-likelihood estimates of the coefficients of the model will be inconsistent. Gourieroux, Montfort, and Trognon (1984) suggest using a quasi-generalized pseudo-maximum-likelihood estimator based on the first two moments of the distribution of Y, which gives consistent estimates for ϵ drawn from a wide variety of distributions. Their estimator is just weighted nonlinear least-squares estimates of the model

$$Y_{it} = \exp(X_{it}\beta) + \epsilon_{it}, \quad (4)$$

with weights derived from the relation $VAR[Y] = E[Y](1 + \eta^2 E[Y])$ using initial consistent estimates of β. Below we present alternate estimates of some of our regression models using maximum-likelihood estimation of the Poisson and negative binomial models, nonlinear least squares (with robust standard errors), and the Gourieroux, Montfort, and Trognon estimator.

4. The dataset

■ **Sources.** The larger study on which this article draws has both qualitative and quantitative components. The qualitative study draws upon the medical and scientific literature and upon a program of detailed field interviews, and was designed both to shape the choice of variables and hypotheses explored in the quantitative study and to explore the role of less easily measurable factors such as organizational structure in driving research productivity.

The quantitative study draws upon data about spending and output at the research program level obtained from the internal records of ten pharmaceutical firms. Although for reasons of confidentiality we cannot describe these firms, we can say that the sample covers the range of major R&D-performing pharmaceutical manufacturers. It includes relatively small as well as very large firms, and firms of both American and European origin, and we believe that it is not markedly unrepresentative of the industry in terms of size or technical or commercial performance.[7] Between them they represent about 25% of the pharmaceutical research conducted worldwide. This section offers a brief

[6] In exploratory work we tested for constant elasticity of output with respect to research expenditure and obtained very small and insignificant estimated coefficients on quadratic and higher powers of $\log(R)$. Entering the other explanatory variables in logs did not substantively change our results. Since many of them have substantial numbers of zeros, using levels also allowed us to avoid numerical estimation problems.

[7] The rate of growth in both sales and R&D for the firms in our sample, for example, is very similar to that reported for the members of the Pharmaceutical Manufacturers Association as a whole.

description of the variables used in the econometric analysis, and it presents descriptive statistics for the dataset.

The dataset used in this article is an unbalanced panel indexed by firm, research program, and year. With a complete, rectangular panel we would have 11,400 observations, made up of ten firms, 38 research programs, and up to 30 years of data. In practice not all of these observations are available: the average period for which we have complete data is on average just under 20 years per firm, and not all firms are active in all research areas. Our working sample is drawn from a database that has 5,543 potentially useful observations. After deleting missing values, grossly problematic data, and peripheral research areas, we are left with 4,930 observations. The number of observations per firm varies from over 1,000 to less than 100, with a mean of 489.8. For each observation we have data on both inputs and outputs to the research process. Our measures of input include person-years and research spending in research and development, and our measures of output include patents, regulatory filings such as Investigational New Drug applications (INDs) and New Drug Applications (NDAs), new drug introductions, sales, and market share.

Assembling the data in a consistent and meaningful format required considerable effort. In nearly every case the process of data collection was an iterative one, involving close collaboration between the researchers and key personnel from the participating companies. The majority of the data were collected specifically together for the purposes of this study. Each firm spent some months assembling its data, usually from primary documents, and the full data-collection effort took nearly two years. We worked hard to ensure that, as far as was possible, definitions of research program and of expense grouping were standard across firms, data were collected at the same level of aggregation, and overhead expenses were treated in a consistent way, and we took steps to ensure that, wherever possible, the data included worldwide research spending, not just U.S. facilities. (A more detailed discussion of these issues is given in the Appendix.)

□ **Construction of variables.** Table 1 gives a summary of variable names and definitions. Our primary variables are *RESEARCH,* defined as "expenditure relating primarily to the production of new compounds," which excludes both preclinical and clinical development work and is measured in constant dollars; and *PATENTS,* a count of "important" patents. We deflate research using the biomedical research and development price index issued by the National Institutes of Health. These measures of inputs and outputs are matched by year and research program. We count patents by their year of application, and define "importance" by the fact that the patent was granted in two of the three major markets: the United States, Japan, and the European Community. The first year in which we were able to obtain this data is 1961, and because patents grants may lag applications by as much as four years in the United States and six in Japan, we use observations for the years 1961–1988 only.

We measure the scale of the firm's research effort by *SIZE,* total research spending that year. There are some grounds for believing that the relevant measure of size is the scale of the entire firm, as captured by, for example, total sales or total employees, and this measure has been used in a number of previous studies of the industry. We experimented with these types of measures in exploratory work but obtained poor results. This is perhaps not surprising, given that any size effect captured by a variable such as total firm sales is likely to be confounded with factors such as demand (Jensen, 1987; Graves and Langowitz, 1993).

To test for economies of scope, we constructed a variety of measures of the diversity of the firm's research effort across therapeutic classes. *SCOPE* is a count of the number of research programs in which the firm spent more than $500,000, in constant

TABLE 1 Summary of Variables

Variable Name	Proxy for	Definition	Unit of Observation
PATENTS	Output of new knowledge in this program	Annual number of patent applications granted in at least two of U.S., Japan, EC; by worldwide priority date	Program-year
RESEARCH	Resources devoted to research in this program	Annual spending on drug research in millions of constant 1986 dollars, excluding clinical development	Program-year
SIZE	Overall scale of the firm's research effort	Total real annual firm research expenditures	Firm-year
SCOPE	Presence of scope economies	Number of research programs in which expenditure was more than $500,000 per year	Firm-year
SMALL	Diseconomies of scope: e.g., coordination costs	Number of research programs in which expenditure was less than $100,000 per year	Firm-year
HERF	"Focus" of research portfolio	Herfindahl index of *RESEARCH*	Firm-year
Stock of own patents in this program	Knowledge capital	"Capital stock" of *PATENTS* in previous years using perpetual inventory method and 20% depreciation rate	Program-year
News in own patents in related programs	Internal spillovers	See text	Program-year
News in competitors' patents in same program	External spillovers	See text	Program-year
News in competitors' patents in related programs	External spillovers	See text	Program-year
CLASS DUMMIES	Cross-sectional variation in technological opportunity and ease of obtaining patents	Dummy variables for 16 broad therapeutic classes	Program
FIRM DUMMIES	Cross-sectional variation in firms' accounting practices, patenting policies, etc.	Dummy variables for firm	Firm

1986 dollars per year. Our qualitative work led us to believe that this level—roughly equivalent to the employment of three to four fully funded Ph.D.-level scientists—was the minimum "critical mass" for a program run with the expectation of generating significant output. We experimented with a variety of alternative thresholds, but in general the use of different cutoff points yielded similar or insignificant results. We also constructed *SMALL*, a count of research programs in which the firm spent $100,000 or less, to test the hypothesis that diseconomies of scope could arise through the multiplication of coordination costs.

To explore a different dimension of diversification, we computed *HERF*, the Herfindahl index of research expenditures across the portfolio of programs, as a measure of the "focus" of the firm's research effort. Note that *SCOPE* and *HERF* are not simple transformations of each other. In general, larger firms run more programs and thus tend to have higher values of *SCOPE* and lower values of *HERF* by construction. Nonetheless, some of the smaller firms in the sample have very diverse portfolios, with activities spread evenly over a wide range of programs, and some of the larger firms concentrate their efforts in highly focused portfolios: the Pearson correlation coefficient between *SCOPE* and *HERF* is only .66.

We hypothesize that both *SCOPE* and *HERF* have nonlinear relationships to productivity: that both very highly focused and very disparate efforts will be on average less productive than those that are "appropriately" focused and "appropriately" diverse. Highly focused firms will be less productive, since they will be less able to take advantage of internal economies of scope, and very unfocused programs will be less productive, since they will incur higher coordination costs. Note that *SCOPE, HERF, SMALL,* and *SIZE* are unique only to firm and year, not to firm, year, and research program.

We then construct variables intended to capture the effects of spillovers both within and between firms. We use a "news" formulation of these variables, where *news in X* is defined by $N_t = X_t - \delta K_{t-1}$, where K is the stock of X and δ is the depreciation rate. This construction reduces potential measurement error problems and has an informative interpretation: own research productivity is higher when the output of spillover sources "spurts" beyond the level required simply to maintain their previous stock.[8] Our overall conclusions are not sensitive to this formulation.

To define spillovers, we distinguish between two tiers of aggregation: the detailed "research program" level and a more aggregated "therapeutic class" level that groups related programs into therapeutic areas. For example, the therapeutic class "Central Nervous System Drugs" includes the research programs "Depression," "Anxiety," and "Analgesics."

We use three spillover variables (see Figure 1): internal spillovers between related programs within the firm, external spillovers from programs in the same field at competing firms, and external spillovers from programs in the same therapeutic area. For each observation, we start with the basic data on each program's "own" annual flows of patents. *News in own patents in related classes*—spillovers internal to the firm—is constructed from the output of all the other research programs within the relevant broad therapeutic class. For example, in the case of a program in Depression we look for spillovers from the firm's other Central Nervous System programs. This is equivalent to using a binary measure of technological distance: programs within the same therapeutic class are assumed to be plausible sources of spillovers, whereas other programs are not.

We construct two measures of spillovers between firms. On the one hand, we count competitors' output in the same narrow research area in order to construct *News in competitors' patents in this program,* and on the other hand, we count competitors' output in all the other programs in the wider therapeutic class to construct *News in competitors' patents in related programs.*[9]

---

[8] In exploratory work we included both flow and stock versions of these spillover variables in the model, but in many instances we obtained equal but opposite-signed coefficients, suggesting that they were picking up the same underlying factor measured with error.

[9] For any given firm, "competitor's patents" are those generated by the other 9 firms in our dataset plus 19 others drawn from the world's top 40 research-oriented pharmaceutical manufacturers. Since we thus have a representative fraction of total spillovers generated within the industry rather than the entire pool, our estimated coefficients will tend to overstate the magnitude of this effect.

FIGURE 1

CONSTRUCTION OF THE SPILLOVER MEASURES

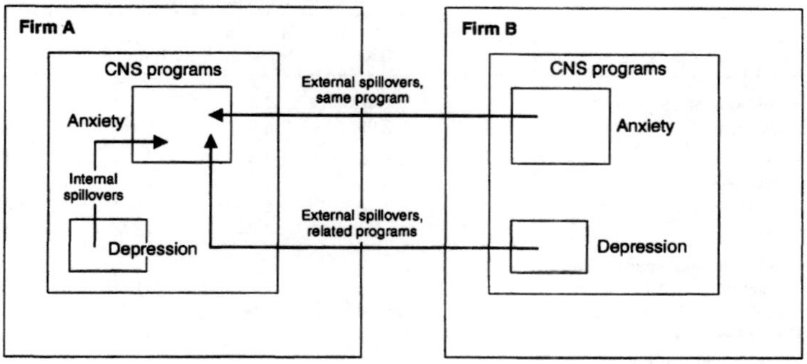

□ **Descriptive statistics.** Table 2 and Figures 2–4 present summary statistics describing the data. Averaging across all firms, research programs, and years, our firms spent on average $1.06 million in 1986 dollars on research per program per year for an average of 1.8 "important" patents. Each important patent, on average, thus costs about $600,000 in 1986 dollars. The average firm in our sample is highly diversified, investing substantially (more than $500,000) in just over ten programs a year. In addition, these firms on average invest more than $10,000 a year in a further six programs.

All of the key variables show a substantial amount of variation. Perhaps the most dramatic effect visible in the time-series aggregates is the continuing increase in research spending despite the fact that the mean cost per important patent rose dramatically from 1975 onwards. Figure 2 shows the evolution of mean research spending per program and mean important patents obtained per program over time. Mean research spending per program almost tripled in real terms over our sample period, from just over $.6 million in 1965 to around $1.9 million in 1988. This trend reflects both an expansion in the scale of the research effort and the change in its nature, as the adoption of rational drug discovery techniques increased the demand for sophisticated equipment and more highly skilled researchers. At the same time, mean patents obtained per program fell dramatically after 1978, from a high of just over 3 to less than .5 in 1988. In combination, these two trends imply that mean important patents per million real research dollars fell from a high of 2.4 in 1978 to less than .5 after 1986. The same trends are evident in data aggregated to the level of the firm: between 1965 and 1990, mean research spending per firm almost tripled in real terms, from just over $18 million in 1965 to around $54 million in 1990,[10] while mean important patents obtained per firm fell precipitously.

Part of this decline in patenting rates may reflect the general downward trend that has characterized U.S. and European firms over the last decade, some of which simply reflects institutional factors such as the resource constraints imposed on the U.S. Patent Office in the early 1980s (Griliches, 1992). However, the decline in patenting rates in our data is significantly steeper than that experienced by the rest of the U.S. economy, and we suspect that more fundamental factors may be at work.

[10] This number may seem surprisingly small, given the size of the research budgets reported by some of the larger firms in the industry in 1994. Recall that it is calculated as an arithmetic mean, that it is measured in 1986 dollars, and that it includes only resources spent on research, not clinical development.

TABLE 2 Descriptive Statistics
Selected Variables at the Research Program Level

	Regression Sample, N = 4,930			
Variable	Mean	Standard Deviation	Minimum	Maximum
Research, millions of 1986 dollars	1.06	2.31	0	20.18
Stock of research	2.99	6.42	0	55.19
Own patents	1.86	3.47	0	34.00
Stock of own patents	6.59	11.22	0	96.18
Own patents in related programs	3.56	6.26	0	60.00
News in own patents	.94	3.74	−13.60	33.97
SCOPE: Number of programs with research spending >$500,000	10.71	5.12	1.00	21.00
SCALE: Total research spending this year	33.54	22.96	4.97	>120
HERF: Herfindahl index of research spending across all programs	.18	.11	.07	.92
SMALL: Number of programs with research spending <$100,000	5.54	4.75	0	18.00
28 competitors' patents	38.62	44.79	0	300.00
News in competitors' patents	10.91	19.88	−91.84	128.26
Competitors' patents in related programs	116.79	81.45	0	353.00
News in competitors' patents in related programs	32.84	39.90	−106.61	172.92

One possibility is that the transition to more rational methods of drug research has led to a change in patenting strategies and an increase in the significance of each patent: real research output may have remained constant or even risen. Another possibility is that the industry is approaching technological exhaustion (Grabowski and Vernon, 1990) but rates of investment in research are continuing to accelerate despite the decline in patenting, perhaps as a strategic response to actions of competitors, or simply because changes in demand conditions were increasing the marginal revenue product of research.

Looking next at the program-level data, some surprising characteristics of the research portfolio emerge, illustrating the amount of detail lost in aggregating to the level

FIGURE 2

PATENTS AND RESEARCH PER PROGRAM

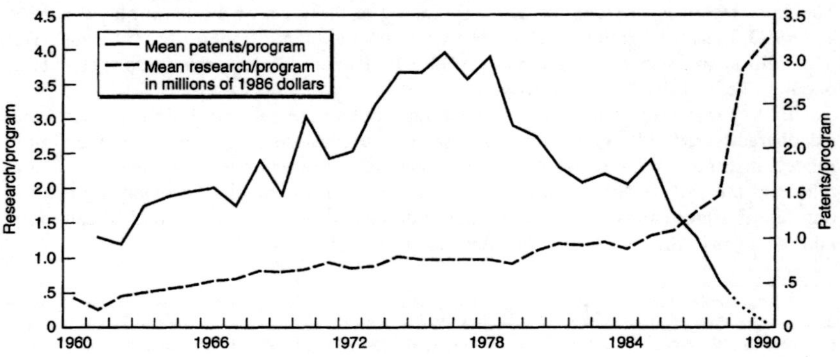

of the firm. Figure 3 presents the size distribution of research expenditures per research program. The mean firm in our sample invests heavily in a few large programs but also invests in a large number of much smaller programs. For over 44% of the program-years in our sample, no expenditures on research were recorded at all. To the best of our knowledge, these are "genuine" zeros and reflect intermittent expenditures over time, or programs that were "alive" in that the firm was consistently obtaining patents or was engaged in clinical development in the area.[11] Of the remainder, about one quarter of the program-year observations in our sample involved spending less than $.2 million in 1986 dollars per program per year, and about 40% spent less than our critical threshold of $.5 million in 1986 dollars per program per year. At the other tail of the distribution, just over 2% of cases involved expenditures of more than $10 million in 1986 dollars per program per year.

On the output side, the distribution of annual counts of important patents per program (Figure 4) is also highly skewed. About half of our observations show zero output per program-year, and almost 90% of the counts are less than 5 per year. Patent counts also vary significantly across firms, across therapeutic classes, and across time. While the mean number of patents per program is 1.7 per year, this varies across firms from 3.1 to .1 per year, and across therapeutic classes from .7 per year for work in the genito-urinary system to 3.7 per year for cardiac and circulatory products. There are also very substantial differences in the average level of expenditure across therapeutic classes: mean research expenditures per program range from roughly $900,000 per year in alimentary tract and metabolic research to over $4 million per year in anticancer research.

5. Empirical results

■ We begin by presenting results obtained by aggregating data to the firm level to allow comparison with previous work (Table 3). We then turn to analysis at the program level. Table 4 presents results obtained from the full sample, Table 5 explores the

FIGURE 3

RESEARCH/PROGRAM FREQUENCY DISTRIBUTION

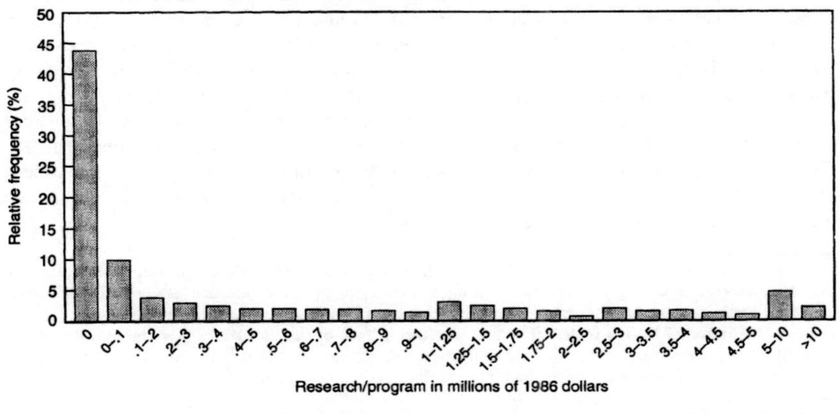

[11] Deleting these observations from the dataset does not substantially change either the magnitude or the significance of our estimated coefficients.

FIGURE 4

PATENTS/PROGRAM FREQUENCY DISTRIBUTION

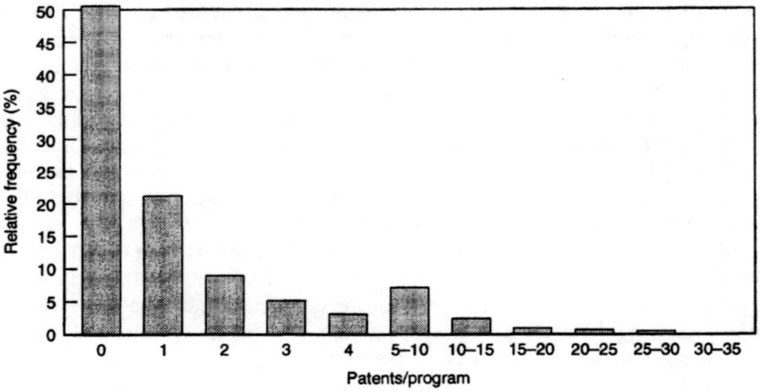

robustness of the Poisson specification, and Table 6 explores alternative measures of scope. In 1978, the number of patents obtained per discovery dollar by the firms in this sample appears to go into secular decline. In Tables 3 through 6 we control for any change in regime after 1978 by allowing for differences in the intercept and in the time trend, while in Table 7 we test for changes in the roles of scope, scale, and spillovers over time by splitting the sample into pre-1978 and post-1978 subsamples.[12]

□ **Analysis of firm-level data.** Table 3 presents results using data aggregated to the firm level. This aggregation generates a rather small sample, with only 181 observations on our 10 firms, and the results should therefore be treated with caution. In common with previous work, we find no evidence of returns to scale: the implied long-run elasticity of important patent output with respect to research spending in every model is between .4 and .5.[13]

These results also indicate that firm effects are a very important determinant of innovative performance: comparing equations (1) and (2), we see that including firm dummies increases the log-likelihood function very substantially, which corresponds to an increase in R^2 from .29 to .79.[14] To some extent these firm dummies are picking up factors such as systematic differences across firms in their propensity to patent, accounting practices, labor market conditions in different countries, and so forth, but their statistical importance also reflects more interesting types of heterogeneity among firms. For example, in these firm-level data we cannot control for the mix of investment across different therapeutic classes, which varies substantially across firms and has important implications for aggregate productivity.[15]

[12] 1978 was also the year following the publication of a seminal paper (Cushman et al., 1977) announcing the synthesis of an orally active ACE inhibitor, often cited as one of the first examples of successful "rational" drug design. Experimenting with alternative cutoff dates had little impact on the results.

[13] This is somewhat lower than estimates obtained in previous studies of the pharmaceutical industry as well as from much larger samples of manufacturing firms, but these results are not strictly comparable: we do not include development expenditures in our measure of research effort, and we count only "important" patents.

[14] R^2 is calculated as the squared correlation between observed values of Y and fitted values of Y from the Poisson regression.

[15] At the request of the firms supplying the data, we do not report the estimated coefficients on these

TABLE 3 Determinants of Patent Output at the Firm Level. Poisson Regression. Dependent Variable = Total Firm Patents. 181 Observations

	Equation				
	(1)	(2)	(3)	(4)	(5)
Intercept	2.090**	1.195**	1.069**	.597**	1.113**
	(.062)	(.115)	(.127)	(.142)	(.166)
Dum78	2.835**	2.779**	2.750**	2.830**	1.996**
	(.139)	(.141)	(.141)	(.142)	(.201)
ln(*SIZE*): Total firm research	.212**	.317**	.365**	.373**	.350**
	(.042)	(.043)	(.047)	(.047)	(.048)
ln(Total firm stock of research)	.221**	.120*	.155**	.157**	.068
	(.036)	(.051)	(.005)	(.053)	(.055)
SCOPE: Number of programs >500K, 1986$			−.016*	.087**	.103**
			(.007)	(.015)	(.015)
SCOPE-squared				−.005**	−.006**
				(.001)	(.001)
Stock of own patents					.002**
					(.001)
Firm dummies		Sig.	Sig.	Sig.	Sig.
Time	.038**	.043**	.042**	.042**	.024**
	(.003)	(.005)	(.005)	(.005)	(.006)
Time × Dum78	−.164**	−.160**	−.161**	−.167**	−.125**
	(.006)	(.007)	(.007)	(.007)	(.010)
Log-likelihood	−2,365	−1,219	−1,216	−1,185	−1,169

Notes: Standard errors in parentheses.
ln(variable) is set = 0 when variable = 0, and an appropriately coded dummy variable is included in the regression.
* Significant at the 5% level.
** Significant at the 1% level.

Equations (3) and (4) investigate the presence of returns to scope. In equation (3) our measure of scope enters the regression linearly, with an implausibly negative coefficient. Our preferred model allows for diminishing returns to scope by including a quadratic term, giving us a more plausible inverted-U relationship between scope and research productivity. The final column of Table 3 presents results conditioning on past innovative success by including the stock of past patents. The coefficient on research stock falls somewhat, but the coefficients for the scope variables are largely unchanged.

If we did not have access to program-level data we might stop here, noting that our finding that there are no returns to scale in research is consistent with the previous quantitative studies of the industry and with the qualitative evidence that suggests there are limited returns to increasing the size of specific research programs. The analysis of the program-level data that follows reveals how misleading such a conclusion would be.

□ **Analysis of program-level data.** Table 4 reestimates the models of Table 3 at the program level using the complete disaggregated dataset and introduces the spillover measures. We find no evidence for returns to scale at the level of the research

dummies here or in the tables, but they are jointly and separately highly significant in all of the models estimated. The ranking of firms according to these dummies conforms to our beliefs from our qualitative work about their relative innovative performance.

TABLE 4 **Determinants of Patent Output at the Research Program Level. Poisson Regression. Dependent Variable = Patents. 4,930 Observations**

	Equation					
	(1)	(2)	(3)	(4)	(5)	(6)
Intercept	.299**	−1.730**	−2.208**	−2.768**	−1.941**	−2.138**
	(.004)	(.088)	(.107)	(.128)	(.128)	(.130)
Dum78	2.644**	2.454**	2.520**	2.499**	1.307**	.613**
	(.139)	(.141)	(.142)	(.142)	(.146)	(.155)
ln(Research)	.177**	.111**	.099**	.096**	.036**	.024**
	(.010)	(.010)	(.010)	(.010)	(.009)	(.010)
ln(Stock of research)	.018*	.077**	.084**	.092**	.036**	.031**
	(.009)	(.009)	(.009)	(.009)	(.009)	(.009)
ln(*SIZE*): Total research spending by firm			.259**	.332**	.236**	.246**
			(.033)	(.043)	(.043)	(.043)
SCOPE: Number of programs >500K, 1986$				.082**	.115**	.114**
				(.015)	(.015)	(.015)
SCOPE-squared				−.005**	−.006**	−.007**
				(.001)	(.001)	(.001)
News in own patents in related programs				.026**	.032**	.034**
				(.002)	(.001)	(.003)
Stock of own patents in this program					.033**	.032**
					(.001)	(.001)
News in competitors' patents in this program						.006**
						(.001)
News in competitors' patents in related programs						.002**
						(.001)
9 firm dummies		Sig.	Sig.	Sig.	Sig.	Sig.
15 class dummies		Sig.	Sig.	Sig.	Sig.	Sig.
Time	.051**	.059**	.043**	.048**	.019**	.017**
	(.003)	(.003)	(.004)	(.004)	(.004)	(.004)
Time × Dum78	−.155**	−.144**	−.146**	−.149**	−0.089**	−.049**
	(.006)	(.007)	(.007)	(.007)	(.007)	(.007)
Log-likelihood	−12,312	−9,342	−9,311	−9,210	−8,346	−8,168

Notes: Standard errors in parentheses.
ln(variable) is set = 0 when variable = 0, and an appropriately coded dummy variable is included in the regression.
* Significant at the 5% level.
** Significant at the 1% level.

program. Indeed, the estimated coefficients imply quite sharply decreasing marginal returns to increasing investment in any single program. There do, however, appear to be economies of scale and scope at the level of the firm. *Ceteris paribus,* programs embedded in larger and more diversified firms appear to be significantly more productive.

Equations (1) and (2) demonstrate the importance of controlling for firm and therapeutic class effects. Including firm and class dummies in the regression leads to a very substantial increase in the log-likelihood function, which corresponds to an increase in R^2 from .10 to .46.[16] To save space we do not report here the coefficients on the 16 therapeutic class dummies, but with minor exceptions they are statistically distinguishable from each other as well as from zero. The coefficients on these variables are quite large: all else equal, programs in the most productive area (arthritis and related disorders) generate about 2.2 times as many important patents as programs conducted in the least productive field (anti-infectives), while programs conducted in the most successful firm in our sample are more than twice as productive as those in the least productive firm. Note though that the economic value of patents differs across therapeutic classes, and as stressed above, coefficients on firm dummies pick up factors such as firms' propensity to patent as well as "real" differences in research productivity.

While the firm dummies alone account for a substantial amount of the variance in the dependent variable, the research elasticities do not change much when they are included in the model. By contrast, the coefficients on the research variables fall by about a third when the class dummies are also included, highlighting the importance of controlling for cross-sectional differences in technological opportunity at this very detailed level.[17] Interestingly, even the largest firms in the sample do not invest in all therapeutic classes, although they clearly have the resources to do so if they wished: an important part of the firm effect identified in the firm-level data appears to lie in the firm's choice of research programs.

Equation (3) introduces our measure of scale into the analysis. *SIZE* enters with a positive and significant coefficient, suggesting that all other things equal, programs embedded in larger firms will be more productive than programs embedded in smaller rivals. This effect is quite large: at the mean, the elasticity of patent output with respect to *SIZE* is .26.

In equation (4) we introduce the measures designed to capture the effects of any economies of scope. Just as in the firm-level results, *SCOPE* has a significant and nonlinear impact on research productivity. At the mean, the elasticity of patent output with respect to *SCOPE* is .30, so that moving a program from the average firm to a firm that is running one more "critical mass" program raises its productivity by around 15%. *News in own patents in related programs* enters with a positive and strongly significant coefficient corresponding to an elasticity at the mean of .03, rising to .12 if related programs are generating spillovers at the rate of one standard deviation above the mean.

In equation (5) we condition on past success by including the stock of past patents, our measure of knowledge capital. This variable is highly significant and markedly improves the log-likelihood and the fit of the equation (R^2 increases from .47 to .67). While the *SIZE* and *SCOPE* effects are essentially unchanged, the coefficients on research fall sharply. This is consistent with the hypothesis that successful patent applications are driven by the available stock of knowledge capital, and that the better measure of this stock is innovative output rather than innovative input. However, it may also reflect two specification problems: the patent stock may be proxying for a variety of unobserved correlated effects, such as the quality of program-specific assets, or there may be a problem with the exogeneity of the research variables with respect

[16] Since the firm and therapeutic class dummies are not orthogonal (the first three canonical correlation coefficients between the two sets of variables are between .2 and .1), their separate contributions to explaining the dependent variable cannot easily be determined. Firm effects alone give an R^2 of .21, while class effects alone given an R^2 of .32.

[17] Notice that with both firm and therapeutic class dummies we are close to, but not quite, estimating a nonlinear panel data model with fixed (program) effects. A further problem is that the large number of dummy variables (10 firms and 16 therapeutic classes) limits our ability to obtain stable estimates if we try to, for example, use time dummies instead of trend variables.

to patents. Conditioning on past success may simply be purging the research coefficients of the part that is the endogenous response to past success.

In equation (6) we introduce our measures of external spillovers, *News in competitors' patents in this program* and *News in competitors' patents in related programs.* Both enter with positive and significant coefficients, with elasticities of about .1 at the mean. Again, though the coefficients may seem quite small, they can generate significant effects, and together they account for roughly 8% of the total variance across programs and firms. At the mean, for example, a program whose competitors' programs in the same and in related fields are roughly 10% more productive will be approximately 2% more productive itself.

Taken together, the results of Table 4 strongly support our first four hypotheses. As our qualitative analysis suggested, programs conducted within large firms are at a significant advantage, which flows as much from the opportunity to exploit returns to scope as from economies of scale.

Table 5 explores the sensitivity of our results to the use of the Poisson assumption by presenting alternative estimates of equation (6) using the various statistical models discussed in Section 2. (Equation (6) is duplicated from the previous table to allow easy comparison of results.) Equation (7) gives negative binomial estimates.[18] The coefficients are broadly comparable to those obtained in the Poisson model, with slightly inflated standard errors, though the coefficients on stock of patents and current research rise quite substantially and *News in competitors' patents in related programs* is no longer significant. Equation (8) is the consistent but not efficient nonlinear least squares model, $Y = \exp(X\beta) + \epsilon$, with robust (White) standard errors. In this model, the research variables lose their significance altogether, although by and large with the exception of the coefficient of *News in competitors' patents in this program,* the other results carry through from the Poisson specification. Finally, equation (9) gives the results from the weighted nonlinear least-squares estimator of Gourieroux, Montfort, and Trognon (1984), which, if the $\exp(X\beta)$ part of the model is correctly specified, will give consistent and efficient parameter estimates. Results are broadly comparable with the Poisson estimates, with slightly larger standard errors. To allow comparison with prior studies, in the remainder of the article we continue to report results obtained using the consistent Poisson estimator, but neither the magnitude nor the direction of our results changes significantly when we use the more computationally expensive estimation techniques.

In Table 6 we further investigate the effects of the diversity of the research effort on research productivity. Recall that the measure used in Table 4, *SCOPE,* is defined as the number of programs operating at greater than "critical mass," which we defined as an annual investment of $500,000 in 1986 dollars. In equation (10) we introduce *SMALL,* the number of programs that were smaller than $100,000 per year, to test the hypothesis that these much smaller programs affect productivity by imposing coordination costs. *SMALL* enters with a negative and significant coefficient, suggesting that all other things equal, programs embedded in firms that have many of these small programs may suffer from increased coordination costs, consistent with our interpretation of the negative effect of *SCOPE*-squared.

In equation (11) we include the Herfindahl of the research portfolio, *HERF,* to test for the impact of the focus of the research portfolio on program productivity. The coefficient of *HERF* is positive and highly significant, while *HERF*-squared enters negatively and significantly, suggesting that there is a substantial return to focus but,

[18] Cameron and Trivedi's (1986) Negbin II model, equivalent to adding an unobserved gamma distributed random program effect to the model, with the extra-Poisson variance modelled as a quadratic function of the mean.

TABLE 5 Determinants of Patent Output at the Research Program Level. Exploring Econometric Issues. Poisson Regression. Dependent Variable = Patents. 4,930 Observations

	Equation			
	Poisson (6)	Negative Binomial (7)	Nonlinear Least Squares (8)	Gourieroux, Montfort, and Trogrion (9)
Intercept	−2.138**	−2.350**	−1.223	−1.941**
	(.130)	(.190)	(.328)	(.243)
Dum78	.613**	.863	−.188	.248
	(.155)	(.240)	(.392)	(.256)
ln(Research)	.024**	.056**	.007	.042**
	(.010)	(.014)	(.021)	(.015)
ln(Stock of research)	.031**	.036**	.000	.049**
	(.009)	(.014)	(.021)	(.016)
ln(*SIZE*): Total research spending by firm	.246**	.127*	.303**	.200**
	(.043)	(.067)	(.092)	(.082)
SCOPE: Number of programs >500K, 1986$	.114**	.139**	.092**	.045*
	(.015)	(.023)	(.036)	(.024)
SCOPE-squared	−.007**	−.006**	−.005**	−.004**
	(.001)	(.001)	(.002)	(.001)
News in own patents in related programs	.034**	.042**	.021**	.048**
	(.003)	(.005)	(.005)	(.006)
Stock of own patents in this program	.032**	.053**	.027**	.054**
	(.001)	(.002)	(.002)	(.002)
News in competitors' patents in this program	.006**	.011**	.002	.009**
	(.001)	(.001)	(.002)	(.001)
News in competitors' patents in related programs	.002**	.001	.003**	.001
	(.001)	(.001)	(.001)	(.001)
9 firm dummies	Sig.	Sig.	Sig.	Sig.
15 class dummies	Sig.	Sig.	Sig.	Sig.
Time	.017**	.030**	−.016*	.025**
	(.004)	(.006)	(.010)	(.007)
Time × Dum78	−.049**	−.061**	−.006	−.038**
	(.007)	(.011)	(.018)	(.012)
Overdispersion parameter	N/A	1.888	N/A	.437
		(.096)		
Log-likelihood	−8,168	−7,208	R^2 = .577	−6,692
			SER = 2.274	

Notes: Standard errors in parentheses.
ln(variable) is set = 0 when variable = 0, and an appropriately coded dummy variable is included in the regression.
* Significant at the 5% level.
** Significant at the 1% level.

once again, that this return is only available up to a certain point. Equation (12) includes both *HERF* and *SCOPE*. While there does appear to be additional information in *HERF*, econometrically it is difficult to separate out the effects of *SIZE*, *SCOPE*, and *HERF*. These variables are measured at the firm level, and in general they move smoothly

TABLE 6 Determinants of Patent Output at the Research Program Level. Alternative Measures of *SCOPE*. Poisson Regression. Dependent Variable = Patents. 4,930 Observations

	Equation			
	(6)	(10)	(11)	(12)
Intercept	−2.138**	−1.705**	−2.135**	−1.624**
	(.130)	(.135)	(.192)	(.180)
Late, 1978 Dummy	.613*	.359	−.298	−.153*
	(.155)	(.171)	(.171)	(.174)
ln(Research)	.024**	.021*	.026**	.023**
	(.010)	(.010)	(.010)	(.010)
ln(Stock of research)	.031**	.028**	.027**	.029**
	(.009)	(.009)	(.009)	(.009)
ln(*SIZE*): Total research spending by firm	.246**	.276**	.101**	.309**
	(.043)	(.043)	(.030)	(.040)
News in own patents in related programs	.034**	.031**	.033**	.030**
	(.003)	(.003)	(.003)	(.003)
SCOPE: Number of programs >500K, 1986$	.114**	.112**		.009
	(.015)	(.015)		(.023)
SCOPE-squared	−.007**	−.007**		−.003**
	(.001)	(.001)		(.001)
SMALL: Number of programs <100K, 1986$		−.051**		−.049**
		(.005)		(.005)
HERF			9.029**	4.569**
			(.745)	(.789)
HERF-squared			−16.267**	−9.638**
			(1.354)	(1.340)
Stock of own patents in this program	.032**	.033**	.032**	.033**
	(.001)	(.001)	(.001)	(.001)
News in competitors' patents in this program	.006**	.006**	.006**	.006**
	(.001)	(.001)	(.001)	(.001)
News in competitors' patents in related programs	.002**	.003**	.003**	.003**
	(.001)	(.001)	(.001)	(.001)
9 firm dummies	Sig.	Sig.	Sig.	Sig.
15 class dummies	Sig.	Sig.	Sig.	Sig.
Time	.017**	−.004	−.006	−.018*
	(.004)	(.004)	(.004)	(.005)
Time × Dum78	−.049**	−.034**	.004	.006
	(.007)	(.008)	(.008)	(.009)
Log-likelihood	−8,168	−8,124	−8,147	−8,078

Notes: Standard errors in parentheses.
ln(variable) is set = 0 when variable = 0, and an appropriately coded dummy variable is included in the regression.
* Significant at the 5% level.
** Significant at the 1% level.

together over time. Moreover, most of the variance in *SCOPE* and *HERF* is between firms rather than within firms.

Throughout Tables 3 to 6, the continued significance of Dum78 and of Dum78 interacted with the time trend suggests that there was a significant shift of regime in

1978. In Table 7 we investigate the changing role of scale, scope, and spillovers over time by splitting the sample into two: 1961–1978 and 1979–1988. Equation (12) is included for comparison. Not surprisingly, given the large changes in the estimated coefficients, tests for equality of all coefficients across the two samples easily reject this hypothesis. This result is driven to a large extent by substantial differences in the coefficients of the therapeutic class dummies across subsamples, probably reflecting changes in technological opportunity across fields, but there are also significant differences in the estimated effects of our measures of scope, scale, and spillovers on research productivity.

Taken at face value, these results suggest that any returns to scale per se disappeared after 1978. In the short term there even appear to be negative marginal returns to increasing investment in any particular program, and the coefficient on *SIZE* falls to almost zero. Lower short-run returns to investment in research are consistent with the retooling necessary to adopt the techniques of rational drug design, but the collapse on the coefficient in *SIZE* is implausible given the qualitative evidence about the increasing importance of fixed costs and specialized scientific knowledge. We believe that this result reflects confounding between overall trends in the data rather than any real change in the relationship between *SIZE* and research productivity. All the firms in our sample increased their size over this period and did so at approximately the same rate, while patents per program fell dramatically across all firms and therapeutic classes (Figure 2). The strong negative correlation between these trends probably swamps any marginal effect of *SIZE* that might be discernable in the cross section, despite our efforts to control for, for example, an increase in the average "quality" of patents by including a time trend.[19] Limited cross-sectional variation in *SIZE* within the sample introduces another problem. As the small and medium firms have grown, it may be the case that they have reached the point at which the marginal effect of increasing *SIZE* is statistically undetectable.

We are more confident that the estimated relationship between the structure of the research portfolio and program productivity is a real economic phenomenon rather than an artifact of the measurement properties of the data, since while all the firms in our sample increased their investments in research more or less in concert, these larger research budgets were allocated in quite different ways. On average, firms deepened rather than widened their research efforts, but some firms grew by adding programs while others held the scope of their portfolio constant and altered its focus. Thus we interpret the greatly reduced coefficient on *SMALL* and the substantial increase in the coefficient of the internal spillover variable as consistent with our hypothesis that the transition from random to rational drug design increased the importance of the returns to scope realized by the more diversified firms.

At the same time, the influence of external spillovers on research productivity also changed. Although before 1978 the benefits of spillovers from competitors were realized primarily within narrow therapeutic areas, after 1978 the reverse appears to be true. Programs benefited primarily from work conducted by their competitors in related therapeutic areas, rather than from research focused on the same disease targets. This is consistent with our beliefs about the ways in which the transition to rational drug design has changed the nature of spillovers within the industry.

As pharmaceutical research has moved from a regime of "random" research to one of "rational" drug design, the evolution of biomedical science has placed an increasing premium on the ability to exchange information within the firm. The primary

[19] Exploratory calculations suggest that simple ways of controlling for changes in the "significance" or "quality" of patents may not have much impact: for example, there is no trend evident in the average number of citations per pharmaceutical patent between 1970 and 1985.

TABLE 7 Determinants of Patent Output at the Research Program Level. Exploring Changes over Time. Poisson Regression. Dependent Variable = Important Patents

	Equation		
Sample	1960–1988	1960–1978	1979–1988
N	4,930	2,482	2,448
	(12)	(13)	(14)
Intercept	−1.624**	−2.147**	−2.092
	(.180)	(.300)	(.345)
Late, 1978 Dummy	−.153*		
	(.174)		
ln(Research)	.023**	.061**	−.026*
	(.010)	(.015)	(.012)
ln(Stock of research)	.029**	.015	.033**
	(.009)	(.013)	(.013)
ln(*SIZE*): Total research spending by firm	.309**	.326**	.003
	(.040)	(.096)	(.102)
SCOPE: Number of programs >500K, 1986$	.009	.124**	.098*
	(.023)	(.04)	(.054)
SCOPE-squared	−.003**	−.006**	−.006*
	(.001)	(.001)	(.003)
News in own patents in related programs	.030**	.018**	.039**
	(.003)	(.003)	(.006)
SMALL: Number of programs <100K, 1986$	−.049**	−.051**	−.006
	(.005)	(.006)	(.010)
HERF	4.569**	7.048**	5.902**
	(.789)	(1.156)	(1.969)
HERF-squared	−9.638**	−10.627**	−9.290**
	(1.340)	(1.637)	(4.403)
Stock of own patents in this program	.033**	.030**	.036**
	(.001)	(.001)	(.001)
News in competitors' patents in this program	.006**	.008**	−.000
	(.001)	(.001)	(.001)
News in competitors' patents in related programs	.003**	.001	.005**
	(.001)	(.001)	(.001)
9 firm dummies	Sig.	Sig.	Sig.
15 class dummies	Sig.	Sig.	Sig.
Time	−.018*	−.027**	−.006
	(.005)	(.006)	(.010)
Time × Dum78	.006		
	(.009)		
Log-likelihood	−8,078	−4,382	−3,553

Notes: Standard errors in parentheses.

ln(variable) is set = 0 when variable = 0, and an appropriately coded dummy variable is included in the regression.

* Significant at the 5% level.

** Significant at the 1% level.

advantage of size has become the ability to exploit internal returns to scope—particularly the ability to exploit internal spillovers of knowledge—rather than any economy of scale per se. As Cohen and Levinthal (1989) have pointed out, the benefits of spillover can be realized only by incurring the costs of maintaining absorptive capacity, which take the form here of large numbers of small and apparently unproductive programs. We believe that these effects are what account for the presence of very large research oriented firms, despite sharply decreasing marginal returns to research spending at the level of the individual research program.

Interestingly, though our measures of the scope and scale of firms' research efforts are statistically significant, most of the variance in research productivity is attributable to idiosyncratic program, therapeutic class, and firm effects. Our measure of knowledge capital—the accumulated stock of patents obtained by the program in the past—is the single most important variable in our regressions, accounting for up to 20% of the variation in patenting across programs. Firm and therapeutic class dummies account for a further 30–40%, and some of their coefficients are remarkably large.

Note that it is difficult to use our estimates to speculate as to the optimal scale and scope of a modern pharmaceutical research effort. Interpreted literally, the results of Table 7 suggest that before 1978, for example, the optimal research portfolio has 9.8 programs of at least $500,000 each and a *HERF* of about .33, while after 1978 the optimal portfolio had only 8.3 "critical mass" programs and a *HERF* of about .32. But the effects that we have estimated are marginal effects. While doubling the size of an existing program or adding an additional program to the portfolio, for example, might increase the productivity of adjacent programs through its effects on scale and scope, the net effect of such a change on the productivity of the entire research effort is difficult to estimate. In reality one cannot add an average program to the average portfolio. Research programs are not homogeneous, and their heterogeneity—particularly the degree to which they have been successful in the past—has important implications for productivity, so that determining the size and shape of the optimal research portfolio requires solving a complex, nonlinear constrained optimization problem whose parameters are not fully known.

6. Discussion and conclusions

■ Debate about firm size and R&D performance dates back at least to Schumpeter and has important implications both for our understanding of the tradeoff between the static and dynamic efficiency properties of different industry structures and for theories of the determinants of the boundaries of the firm. Our results suggest that the inconclusive nature of previous empirical research on the relationship between firm size and innovation reflects its reliance on inappropriately aggregated data. By going within the firm and using data collected at the level of individual research programs, we have been able to control for variation in technological opportunity and to distinguish between economics of scale and economics of scope in the production of intellectual property.

At least in the pharmaceutical industry, large firms do appear to have an advantage in the conduct of research. *Ceteris paribus,* research programs located within larger firms are significantly more productive than rival programs located within smaller firms. This result gives added weight to the argument that in some circumstances it is worth trading the static efficiency loss attributable to the market power exercised by large firms for the dynamic efficiency gains that flow from their superior innovative performance.

Our second major finding is that this superior performance flows as much from economies of scope as it does from economies of scale per se. Research programs located in larger firms benefit more from the economies of scope arising from the public goods aspect of knowledge capital accumulated within the firm, and from the ability to internalize information externalities within the firm, than from economies of scale arising from such familiar sources as specialization and the sharing of fixed costs. In this research-intensive industry, one of the primary determinants of the boundaries of the firm is the search for internal economies of scope.

We also find evidence for significant spillovers of knowledge between firms. Modern theory ascribes a central role to interfirm spillovers as drivers of economic growth, so it is reassuring to find them present in a research-intensive industry such as pharmaceuticals.

The article opens up a number of questions for further research. Our results suggest that further exploration of research productivity using this kind of disaggregated data, particularly in other industries, may well prove fruitful. They also speak to the continuing debate about the nature and importance of firm heterogeneity (Lippman and Rumelt, 1982; Rumelt, 1991; Schmalensee, 1985). One of our most intriguing findings is the persistence of marked differences in research strategy across firms. Our results imply that quite small changes in the scale or scope of a research portfolio have a significant impact on productivity at the margin, yet differences in the structure of the portfolio across firms show great persistence over time. We also find very significant firm effects in research productivity, above and beyond those that can be attributed to the kinds of variation in the structure of the research portfolio that we examine here. We plan to explore these and related issues in further work.

Appendix

■ **Data sources and construction.** The dataset used in this study is based on detailed data on R&D inputs and outputs at the research program level for ten ethical pharmaceutical manufacturers. Data was collected by research program rather than by broad therapeutic class or by individual research project, since we believe that analyzing the problem in this way best reflects the dynamics of discovery research. A grouping by therapeutic class is too general: "cardiovascular research," for example, includes research into widely different areas, including hypertension, cardiotonics, antiarrhythmics, and hyperlipoproteinemia. However, analysis of data by individual project is difficult and misleading. Not only is it hard to assign effort to particular drug candidates with any accuracy, but the notion that research productivity is best measured at this level raises some conceptual difficulties. A research program typically continues over many years, and at the discovery stage the firm invests in the program, rather than in particular candidate compounds. The identification of a drug development candidate is an indication of the success of the program, and retrospectively assigning resources to its generation may introduce serious biases into the analysis.

□ **Inputs.** Our data on inputs to the drug research process are taken from the internal records of participating companies, and they consist primarily of annual expenditures on exploratory research and research by research program. Several issues arise in dealing with these data.

Research vs. development. We define resources devoted to research (or "discovery," in the terminology of the industry) as all preclinical expenditures within a therapeutic class, and development as all expenses incurred after a compound has been identified as a development candidate. We attributed exploratory research to a particular program wherever possible, but exploratory research that could not be so assigned was included in overhead. Clinical grants are included in the figures for development, and grants to external researchers for exploratory research are included in the total for research. In some cases, the companies supplied us with data already broken down by research versus development by research program. In others, we had to classify budget line items for projects/programs into the appropriate category. This was done based on the description of each item in the original sources, and the location of items within the structure of the company's reporting procedure.

Overhead. To maintain as much consistency as possible in the data-collection process, we tried to include appropriate overhead charges directly related to research activities, such as computing, R&D administration and finance, etc., but to exclude charges relating to allocation of central office overhead, etc. The overhead also includes some expenditures on discipline-based exploratory research, such as "molecular biology," which appeared not to be oriented toward specific therapies. Overhead was allocated across therapeutic classes according to their fraction of total spending.

Licensing. We treat up-front, lump sum payments in respect of in-licensing of compounds, or participation in joint programs with other pharmaceutical companies, universities, or research institutes, as expenditure on research. Royalty fees and contingent payments are excluded. Though increasing over time, expenditures on licensing are a vanishingly small fraction of research spending in this sample.

□ **Outputs.** In this article we use "important" patent grants as our measure of research output. We count patents by year of application, where we define "importance" by the fact that the patent was granted in two of the three major markets: the United States, Japan, and the European Community. These data were provided by Derwent Publications Inc., which used its proprietary classification and search software to supply us with counts of "important" patents broken down by therapeutic class for 29 U.S., European, and Japanese pharmaceutical manufacturers for the period 1961 to 1990. These firms were chosen to include the ten firms that have given us data, together with 19 other firms chosen on the basis of their absolute R&D expenditures, R&D intensity, and national "home base" to try to get a representative, rather than exhaustive, assessment of worldwide patenting activity. The 19 firms have been consistently in the top 40 worldwide pharmaceutical firms in terms of R&D dollars and sales.

Note that many of these patents will be "defensive" patents, in that firms may patent compounds they do not intend to develop in the short term but that may someday have competitive value, and that we were not able to exclude process patents. Alternative measures of "importance" such as citation weighting and more detailed international filing data proved prohibitively expensive to construct.

□ **Classification.** Classification of inputs and outputs by therapeutic class is important because this drives our measure of spillovers. There are essentially two choices: to define programs by physiological mechanisms, e.g., "prostaglandin metabolism," or by "indications" or disease states, e.g., "arthritis." We have chosen to classify on the basis of indication, largely because this corresponds well to the internal divisions used by the companies in our sample (which is conceptually correct), but also because classification by mechanism is much more difficult (a practical concern). We classified both inputs and outputs according to a scheme that closely follows the IMS Worldwide classes. This scheme contains two tiers of aggregation: a detailed research program level, and a more aggregated therapeutic class level, which groups related programs. For example, the therapeutic class "cardiovascular" includes the research programs "antihypertensives," "cardiotonics," "antithrombolytics," "diuretics," etc.

There are some problems with this procedure. First, some projects and compounds are simply very difficult to classify. A particular drug may be indicated for several quite distinct therapies. Consider serotonin, which has quite different physiological actions on either side of the blood-brain barrier: As a neurotransmitter, it is believed to play important roles in mediating motor functions. As a systemic hormone, it has a variety of effects on smooth muscle; for example, it functions as a vasoconstrictor. Some companies report expenditures in areas that are very difficult to assign to particular therapeutic classes: a company doing research using rDNA technology might charge expenditures to an accounting category called "Gene Therapy/Molecular Biology" that is actually specific research performed on, e.g., cystic fibrosis, but we were forced to include these expenditures in "overhead." Second, our two-tier classification scheme may not catch all important relationships between different therapeutic areas. We believe that we are undercounting, not overcounting, spillovers in this respect. Third, where firms supplied us with "predigested" data, they may have used substantively different conventions in classifying projects. One firm may subsume antiviral research under a wider class of anti-infectives, while another may report antivirals separately. Not surprisingly, there are major changes within companies in internal divisional structures, reporting formats, and so forth, which may also introduce classification errors. After working very carefully with these data, we recognize the potential for significant misassignment of outputs to inputs, but we believe such errors that remain are not serious. Using patents (as opposed to INDs or NDAs) as the output measure should reduce our vulnerability to this problem, since we observe relatively large numbers, and a few misclassifications are unlikely to seriously affect our results.

□ **Matching.** Data series on inputs and outputs for each firm were matched at the research program level. This procedure appears to successfully match outputs and inputs unambiguously for the great majority of programs. In a very few cases, however, we ended up with research programs where patents, INDs, or NDAs were filed, but where there were no recorded expenditures. Of these, the majority were obviously coding errors or reflected dilemmas previously encountered in the classification process, and appropriate corrections were made. In other cases, it was clear that these reflected spillovers—research done ostensibly in, for example, hypertension may generate knowledge about the autonomic nervous system, prompting patenting of compounds that may be useful in treating secretory disorders (e.g., ulcers). In such cases we set "own" inputs for the program equal to zero, and included these observations in the database.

□ **Deflation.** Since our data sources span many years, it is important to measure expenditures in constant dollar terms. We used the biomedical research and development price index constructed by James Schuttinga at the National Institutes of Health. The index is calculated using weights that reflect the pattern of NIH expenditures on inputs for biomedical research, and thus in large measure it reflects changes in the costs of conducting research at academic institutions. But since the firms in our sample compete directly with academic research laboratories for scientific talent, we believe that this index is likely to be the most appropriate publicly available index, and our results proved very robust to the use of alternate indices. In a later article we intend to exploit the information that some companies were able to give us on R&D inputs in units of labor hours to construct an index specifically for research costs in the pharmaceutical industry.

□ **Construction of stock variables.** Annual flows of research and expenditures were capitalized following the procedure described by Hall et al. (1988). In brief, we first assume a depreciation rate for "knowledge capital," δ, here equal to 20%. (This is consistent with previous studies, and as argued above it is not going to be very important in terms of its impact on the regression results, since no matter what number we chose, if the flow series is reasonably smooth we would still find it difficult to identify δ separately from the estimated coefficient on the stock variable.) We then calculate a starting stock for each class within firm based on the first observation on the annual flow: assuming that real expenditures have been growing since minus infinity at a rate g, we divide the first observed year's flow by $\delta + g$. Each year, the end-of-year stock is set equal to the beginning-of-year stock net of depreciation, plus that year's flow. For the cases where the annual flow was missing "within" a series of observations, we set it equal to zero. In almost all instances, these missing values occur after the expenditure flows have been declining toward zero. We are reasonably sure that these are "real" zeros and not missing data that should be interpolated. We used the same procedure to accumulate stocks of patents, based on the flow variables described above.

References

ACS, Z.J. AND AUDRETSCH, D.B. "Innovation in Large and Small Firms: An Empirical Analysis." *American Economic Review*, Vol. 78 (1988), pp. 678–690.

ARROW, K.J. "Economic Welfare and the Allocation of Resources for Invention." In R. Nelson, ed., *The Rate and Direction of Inventive Activity*. Princeton: Princeton University Press, 1962.

BALDWIN, W.L. AND SCOTT, J.T. *Market Structure and Technological Change*. Chur, Switzerland: Harwood Academic Publishers, 1987.

BOUND, J., CUMMINS, C., GRILICHES, Z., HALL, B.H., AND JAFFE, A. "Who Does R&D and Who Patents?" In Z. Griliches, ed., *R&D, Patents and Productivity*. Chicago: Chicago University Press, 1984.

CAMERON, A.C. AND TRIVEDI, P.K. "Econometric Models Based on Count Data: Comparisons and Applications of Some Estimators and Tests." *Journal of Applied Econometrics*, Vol. 1 (1986), pp. 29–53.

CAVES, D.W., CHRISTENSEN, L.R., AND TRETHEWAY, M.W. "Economies of Density versus Economies of Scale: Why Trunk and Local Service Airline Costs Differ." *RAND Journal of Economics*, Vol. 15 (1984), pp. 471–489.

CHANDLER, A.D. *Scale and Scope: The Dynamics of Industrial Capitalism*. Cambridge, Mass.: MIT Press, 1990.

COCKBURN, I.M. AND HENDERSON, R.M. "Racing to Invest? The Dynamics of Competition in Ethical Drug Discovery." *Journal of Economics and Management Strategy*, Vol. 3 (1994), pp. 481–519.

COCKS, D. "Product Innovation and the Dynamic Elements of Competition in the Ethical Pharmaceutical Industry." In R. Helms, ed., *Drug Development and Marketing*. Washington, D.C.: American Enterprise Institute, 1975.

COHEN, W.M. AND LEVIN, R.C. "Empirical Studies of Innovation and Market Structure." In R. Schmalensee and R.D. Willig, eds., *Handbook of Industrial Organization*. New York: North-Holland, 1989.

——— AND LEVINTHAL, D.A. "Innovation and Learning: The Two Faces of R&D." *Economic Journal*, Vol. 99 (1989), pp. 569–596.

COMANOR, W.S. "Research and Technical Change in the Pharmaceutical Industry." *Review of Economics and Statistics*, Vol. 47 (1965), pp. 182–190.

CUSHMAN, D.W., CHEUNG, H.S., SABO, E.F., AND ONDETTI, M.A. "Design of Potent Competitive Inhibitors of Angiotensin-Converting Enzyme." *Biochemistry*, Vol. 16 (1977), pp. 5484–5491.

DASGUPTA, P. AND STIGLITZ, J. "Industrial Structure and the Nature of Innovative Activity." *Economic Journal*, Vol. 90 (1980), pp. 266–293.

FREEMAN, C. *The Economics of Industrial Innovation*. 2d ed. Cambridge, Mass.: MIT Press, 1982.

GAMBARDELLA, A. "Competitive Advantages from In-House Scientific Research: The U.S. Pharmaceutical Industry in the 1980s." *Research Policy*, Vol. 21 (1992) pp. 391–407.

GLASS, J.C. AND MCKILLOP, D.G. "An Empirical Analysis of Scale and Scope Economies and Technical Change in an Irish Multiproduct Banking Firm." *Journal of Banking and Finance*, Vol. 16 (1992), pp. 423–437.

GOURIEROUX, C., MONFORT, A., AND TROGNON, A. "Pseudo Maximum Likelihood Methods: Applications to Poisson Models." *Econometrica*, Vol. 52 (1984), pp. 701–720.

GRABOWSKI, H. AND VERNON, J. "A New Look at the Returns and Risks to Pharmaceutical R&D." *Management Science*, Vol. 36 (1990), pp. 804–821.

GRAVES, S.B. AND LANGOWITZ, N. "Innovative Productivity and Returns to Scale in the Pharmaceutical Industry." *Strategic Management Journal*, Vol. 14 (1993), pp. 593–605.
GRILICHES, Z., ed. *R&D, Patents and Productivity*. Chicago: Chicago University Press, 1984.
———. "Patent Statistics as Economic Indicators: A Survey." *Journal of Economic Literature*, Vol. 28 (1990), pp. 1661–1707.
———. "The Search for R&D Spillovers." *Scandinavian Journal of Economics*, Vol. 94 (1992), pp. 29–47.
GROSS, F., ed. *Decision Making in Drug Research*. New York: Raven Press, 1983.
GROSSMAN, G.M. AND HELPMAN, E. *Innovation and Growth in the Global Economy*. Cambridge, Mass.: MIT Press, 1991.
HALL, B.H., GRILICHES, Z., AND HAUSMAN, J.A. "Patents and R and D: Is There a Lag?" *International Economic Review*, Vol. 27 (1986), pp. 265–283.
———, CUMMINS, C., LADERMAN, E.S., AND MUNDY, J. "The R&D Masterfiles Documentation." NBER Technical Working Paper no. 72, 1988.
HAUSMAN, J., HALL, B.H., AND GRILICHES, Z. "Econometric Models for Count Data With an Application to the Patents-R&D Relationship." *Econometrica*, Vol. 52 (1984), pp. 909–938.
HELFAT, C. "Know-how Complementarities and Knowledge Transfer Within Firms: The Case of R&D." Mimeo, Wharton Graduate School of Business, University of Pennsylvania, 1994.
HENDERSON, R.M. "The Evolution of Integrative Competence: Innovation in Cardiovascular Drug Discovery." *Industrial and Corporate Change*, Vol. 3 (1994), pp. 607–630.
HOLMSTRÖM, B. "Agency Costs and Innovation." *Journal of Economic Behavior and Organization*, Vol. 12 (1989), pp. 305–327.
JAFFE, A.B. "Technological Opportunity and Spillovers of R&D: Evidence from Firms' Patents, Profits, and Market Value." *American Economic Review*, Vol. 76 (1986), pp. 984–1001.
JENSEN, E.J. "Research Expenditures and the Discovery of New Drugs." *Journal of Industrial Economics*, Vol. 36 (1987), pp. 83–95.
LIPPMAN, S.A. AND RUMELT, R.P. "Uncertain Imitability: An Analysis of Interfirm Differences in Efficiency under Competition." *Bell Journal of Economics*, Vol. 13 (1982), pp. 418–438.
MAIRESSE, J. AND MOHNEN, P. "R&D and Productivity: A Survey of the Econometric Literature." Mimeo, INSEE, Paris, 1995.
PANZAR, J.C. "Technological Determinants of Firm and Industry Structure." In R. Schmalensee and R.D. Willig, eds., *Handbook of Industrial Organization*. New York: North-Holland, 1989.
——— AND WILLIG, R.D. "Economies of Scope." *American Economic Review*, Vol. 71 (1981), pp. 268–272.
PAVITT, K., ROBSON, M., AND TOWNSEND, J. "The Size Distribution of Innovative Firms in the U.K.: 1945–1983." *Journal of Industrial Economics*, Vol. 35 (1987), pp. 297–316.
REINGANUM, J.F. "The Timing of Innovation: Research, Development, and Diffusion." In R. Schmalensee and R.D. Willig, eds., *Handbook of Industrial Organization*. New York: North-Holland, 1989.
ROMER, P.M. "Increasing Returns and Long-Run Growth." *Journal of Political Economy*, Vol. 94 (1986), pp. 1002–1037.
RUMELT, R.P. "How Much Does Industry Matter?" *Strategic Management Journal*, Vol. 12 (1991), pp. 167–185.
SCHMALENSEE, R. "Do Markets Differ Much?" *American Economic Review*, Vol. 75 (1985), pp. 341–351.
SCHWARTZMAN, D. *Innovation in the Pharmaceutical Industry*. Baltimore: Johns Hopkins University Press, 1976.
SCHUMPETER, J.A. *Capitalism, Socialism and Democracy*. 3d ed. New York: Harper, 1950.
SILK, A.J. AND BERNDT, E.R. "Scale and Scope Effects on Advertising Agency Costs." *Marketing Science*, Vol. 12 (1993), pp. 53–72.
SLOAN, F.A., ed. *Valuing Health Care: Costs, Benefits, and Effectiveness of Pharmaceuticals and other Medical Technologies*. New York: Cambridge University Press, 1995.
SPENCE, M. "Cost Reduction, Competition, and Industry Performance." *Econometrica*, Vol. 52 (1984), pp. 101–121.
SPILKER, B. *Multinational Drug Companies: Issues in Drug Discovery and Development*. New York: Raven Press, 1989.
TEECE, D. "Economies of Scope and the Scope of the Enterprise." *Journal of Economic Behavior and Organization*, Vol. 1 (1980), pp. 223–247.
VERNON, J.M. AND GUSEN, P. "Technical Change and Firm Size: The Pharmaceutical Industry." *Review of Economics and Statistics*, Vol. 56 (1974), pp. 294–302.
WARD, M.R. AND DRANOVE, D. "The Vertical Chain of Research and Development in the Pharmaceutical Industry." *Economic Inquiry*, Vol. 33 (1995), pp. 70–87.
ZENGER, T.R. "Explaining Organizational Diseconomies of Scale in R&D: Agency Problems and the Allocation of Engineering Talent, Ideas, and Effort by Firm Size." *Management Science*, Vol. 40 (1994), pp. 708–729.

[6]

The Link Between Gross Profitability And Pharmaceutical R&D Spending

An analysis that answers the question: What does the pharmaceutical industry really do with its profits?

BY F.M. SCHERER

SINCE THE LATE 1950s, when the Kefauver Committee investigated the business practices of U.S. pharmaceutical companies, representatives of that industry have argued that its profits are an important stimulus to, and source of funding for, research and development (R&D)—which in turn leads to a stream of health-enhancing new products. Although the argument is plausible on its face, quantitative evidence on the robustness of the linkage has been scarce. This paper reports the results of a simple data analysis yielding surprising new insights.

Profitability and investments in R&D can, in principle, be linked in three rather different ways. First, successful R&D leads, with long and variable lags, to new products, which, depending upon their reception in the market, can add greatly to company profits. The distribution of profit outcomes, as research by Henry Grabowski and John Vernon has shown, is highly skewed.[1] A minority of new products confer blockbuster profits, while the majority return less than the capitalized cost of R&D, including the cost of failed projects.

Second, the profits earned by a company serve as a source of funds to support R&D investments, and some managers are known to set R&D budgets using rules of thumb emphasizing an indicator of current cash flow or sales. To be sure, as recent experience in biotechnology shows, funds for R&D can also be raised through new capital issues. Prior tests of the hypothesis of internally generated funds have yielded mixed results. For most well-established corporations, R&D spending is not greatly dependent upon internal cash flow, but small high-tech enterprises—before the 1990s venture capital boom—and the research-intensive pharmaceutical industry were probable exceptions.[2] Third, managers' expectations of future profit opportunities, which are tempered, inter alia, by contemporary market conditions, can exert a demand-pull influence on R&D investments.[3]

Testing how well these relationships hold for investments in pharmaceutical R&D is rendered difficult by the complex structure of the leading pharmaceutical companies. They operate within a wide variety of fields in addition to ethical drugs—for example, pharmacy benefit management, herbicides and pesticides, medical instruments and supplies, prosthetics, hair care products, dental products, and nutritional products. The more diversified companies almost never publish R&D outlay breakdowns subdivided among these fields, and they seldom report their operating margin results in enough detail to relate R&D indices with any precision to measures of profitability.

An alternative approach, and the one used here, is to analyze data on R&D investment and profits at the aggregated industry level.

F.M. Scherer is Aetna Professor of Public Policy Emeritus at Harvard University's Kennedy School of Government and a lecturer in public affairs at Princeton University.

The principal industry trade association, Pharmaceutical Research and Manufacturers of America (PhRMA), conducts an annual survey, from which one can obtain a continuous data series on PhRMA members' ethical drug R&D outlays extending back to the early 1960s (Exhibit 1).

■ **Time-series analysis.** Examination of Exhibit 1 reveals why the usual techniques of time-series analysis used by economists work poorly in ascertaining the links between R&D and profitability. Those methods focus on year-to-year changes in the variable of interest. But there are few sharp changes in the spending path from year to year and, accordingly, few true "degrees of freedom" necessary for a standard time series analysis.[4] Rather, one sees gradual swings in actual R&D spending around a best-fitting long-term R&D time trend, assuming steady exponential growth. The trend line implies growth in inflation-adjusted spending at an average rate of 7.5 percent per year.

The most closely comparable aggregate time-series measure of industry profitability is derived from *Census of Manufactures* and *Annual Survey of Manufactures* data from the U.S. Census Bureau. It is computed as sales less outside materials purchases, payroll outlays, and employee fringe benefits—including those mandated by law along with voluntary benefits. As such, it is best described as a measure of pharmaceutical manufacturing plants' gross margins—that is, the surplus of revenues over in-plant production costs available to cover R&D costs along with depreciation, marketing costs, central office costs, debt service costs, income taxes, and net profits. The coverage match between ethical drug R&D outlays and this gross margin measure is not perfect, as the census universe under the Standard Industrial Classification (SIC) code 2834—Pharmaceutical Preparations—also includes less research-intensive over-the-counter drugs, generic drugs, and some vitamin formulations.[5] Fringe benefit outlays, amounting to 3.68 percent of gross margins in 1967, had to be estimated by extrapolation for 1962–1966, imparting possible inaccuracies in the gross margin measure too small to affect the results reported here.

■ **Gross margins versus R&D outlays.** The growth rate of deflated gross margins was 4.23 percent per year—much lower than the 7.51 percent growth rate found for R&D outlays (Exhibit 2). The disparity of growth rates implies a likely slackening of R&D growth rates in the future. If R&D were covered solely by domestic gross margins, continuation of growth trends experienced since 1962

217

EXHIBIT 1
Pharmaceutical Industry Research And Development (R&D) Outlays Against Exponential Time Trend, 1962–1996

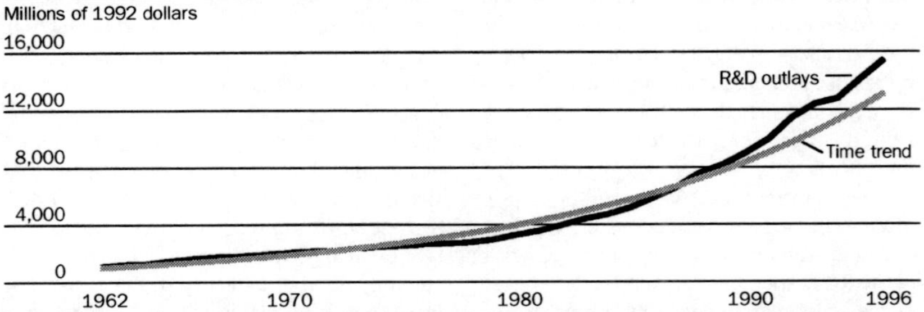

SOURCES: Pharmaceutical Research and Manufacturers of America, *Industry Profile: 1998* (Washington: PhRMA, July 1998); and PhRMA, *Annual Survey Report: 1983–85* (Washington: PhRMA, 1986).
NOTE: Outlays have been adjusted for inflation, using the deflator for U.S. gross domestic product, with 1992 as the base year.

EXHIBIT 2

Pharmaceutical Industry Gross Margins Against Exponential Time Trend, 1962–1996

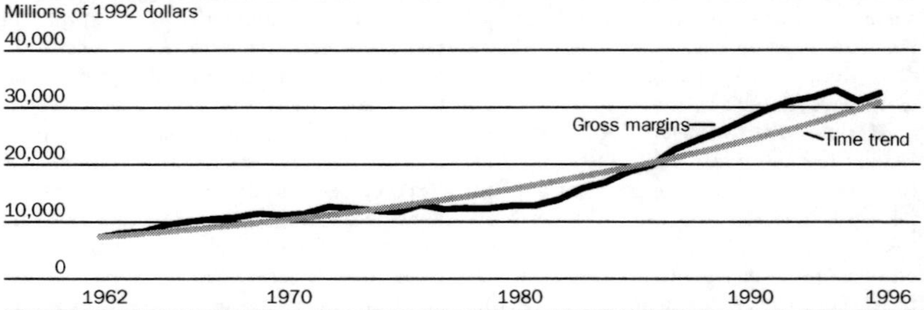

SOURCES: U.S. Bureau of the Census, *Census of Manufactures: 1992,* and *Annual Surveys of Manufactures*, various years.

would mean that R&D outlays would exceed gross margins in the year 2025. To be sure, profits from overseas sales also help to repay R&D costs, but since the United States is the largest single market for U.S. drug companies' products, retardation of R&D growth rates
218 seems likely in the long run.

As in the R&D time series, pharmaceutical industry gross margins exhibit long swings around their exponential time trend. To some extent, coincidence in the timing of the swings can be seen by comparing Exhibits 1 and 2. However, the relationships are brought into sharper focus by computing the percentage deviations of actual R&D outlays and gross margins from their exponential time trend values.[6] The resulting trend deviation series are juxtaposed in Exhibit 3.

The degree of coincidence was, at least to this investigator, surprisingly close. The simple Pearsonian correlation between the two time series is +0.92. Deviations from trend values rise and fall in tandem. The swings are so closely correlated that it would be implausible to infer a chain of causation running from R&D to profits, since lags of ten to fifteen years from peak R&D spending to peak profitability for new products are typical.[7] At two of the three clear turning points, reversals in the R&D spending series precede reversals in the gross margin series by a year or two. This is superficially inconsistent with a hypothesis that changes in gross margins drive changes in R&D spending. However, the paradox diminishes if decisionmakers are able to foresee changes in general industry conditions two or more years into the future—for example, recognizing that the "rational drug design" approaches, demonstrated by the introduction of Tagamet in 1977, presaged increasingly rich opportunities for profitable new product development.

Sensitivity tests revealed that the patterns observed in Exhibit 3 persist when domestic R&D outlays, a time series available only beginning in 1970, are substituted for worldwide R&D outlays, and when fringe benefit outlays, reported by the Census Bureau only beginning in 1967, are not deducted in calculating gross margins.

It is conceivable, as one referee suggested, that the cycles observed here reflect spuriously correlated changes in industry aggregates, for example, as a result of differences in sample coverage between the trade association and Census Bureau universes. To test this possibility, a further analysis correlated trend deviations in variables defined as ratios, with no intermingling of trade association and census universe data for a given ratio. For R&D, the relevant ratio was worldwide R&D outlays, divided by worldwide sales of trade association members in any given year. The PhRMA sales variable was not used in the previous analysis. For gross margins, the relevant ratio was the gross margin, as defined for

EXHIBIT 3
Percentage Deviations From Trend For Pharmaceutical Industry Gross Margins And Research And Development (R&D) Outlays, 1962–1996

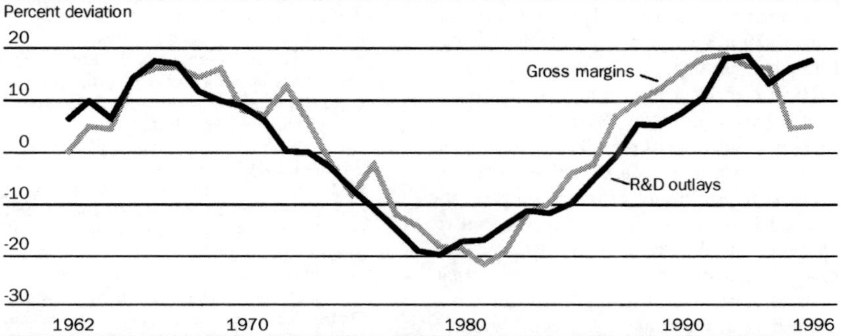

SOURCES: Pharmaceutical Research and Manufacturers of America, *Industry Profile: 1998* (Washington: PhRMA, July 1998), and *Annual Survey Report: 1983–85* (Washington: PhRMA, 1986); and U.S. Bureau of the Census, *Census of Manufactures: 1992*, and *Annual Surveys of Manufactures*, various years.
NOTE: Percentages were figured using constant 1992 dollars.

Exhibit 2, divided by the total value of plant shipments, a rough Census Bureau surrogate for sales, which can double-count interplant shipments. For the time series of each variable, a best-fitting linear trend was estimated. A linear trend was used because, as variables with a distinct upper bound, the two ratios could not plausibly sustain exponential growth for any extended period. Percentage deviations from these best-fitting linear trends were computed (Exhibit 4). Except during the early 1960s, their movements over 219

EXHIBIT 4
Percentage Deviations In Research And Development (R&D) As A Percentage Of Sales And Price-Cost Margins As A Percentage Of Census Sales, 1962–1996

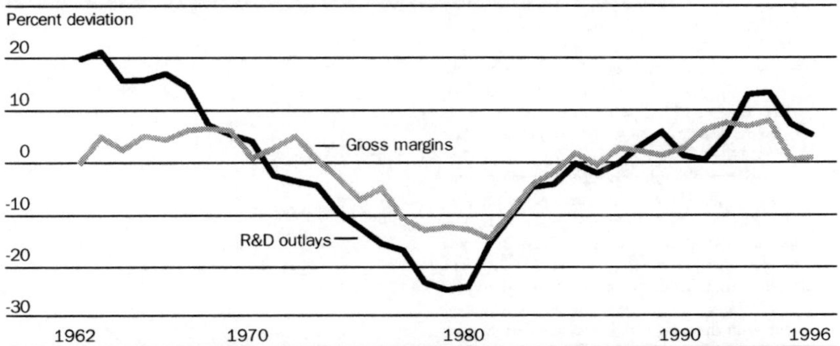

SOURCES: Pharmaceutical Research and Manufacturers of America, *Industry Profile: 1998* (Washington: PhRMA, July 1998), and *Annual Survey Report: 1983–85* (Washington: PhRMA, 1986); and U.S. Bureau of the Census, *Census of Manufactures: 1992*, and *Annual Surveys of Manufactures*, various years.
NOTE: Percentages were figured using constant 1992 dollars.

time are similar to and consistent with those of Exhibit 3. Their simple correlation is 0.863. Given the internally consistent industry sample frames but different trend measurement assumptions used for Exhibit 4 compared with Exhibit 3, the similarity of trend deviation patterns suggests that there was indeed cyclical comovement in pharmaceutical industry gross margins and R&D outlays.

■ **A virtuous rent-seeking model.** Thus, a robust pattern persists. Combined with evidence that profit rates of return on pharmaceutical industry R&D investments tend to exceed risk-adjusted capital costs by only modest amounts, the pattern suggests that pharmaceutical industry R&D is best described by a virtuous rent-seeking model.[8] That is, as profit opportunities expand, firms compete to exploit them by increasing R&D investments, and perhaps also promotional costs, until the increases in costs dissipate most, if not all, supranormal profit returns. If this is a correct interpretation of the industry's behavior, it has self-evident implications for policy interventions aimed at reducing industry prices and profits.

220

NOTES

1. H.G. Grabowski and J.M. Vernon, "A New Look at the Returns and Risks to Pharmaceutical R&D," *Management Science* (July 1990): 804–821.
2. See C.P. Himmelberg and B.C. Petersen, "R&D and Internal Finance: A Panel Study of Small Firms in High-Tech Industries," *Review of Economics and Statistics* (February 1994): 38–51; W.W. McCutchen Jr., "Estimating the Impact of the R&D Tax Credit on Strategic Groups in the Pharmaceutical Industry," *Research Policy* (August 1993): 337–351; and H.G. Grabowski, "The Determinants of Industrial Research and Development," *Journal of Political Economy* (March/April 1968): 292–306.
3. See J. Schmookler, *Innovation and Economic Growth* (Cambridge: Harvard University Press, 1966); and F.M. Scherer, "Demand-Pull and Technological Innovation: Schmookler Revisited," *Journal of Industrial Economics* (March 1982): 225–238.
4. Despite that difficulty, the use of standard year-to-year time series analysis yields results consistent with those reported here. See F.M. Scherer, *Industry Structure, Strategy, and Public Policy* (New York: HarperCollins, 1996), 388.
5. Extending the analysis into 1997 and especially beyond is problematic, since a new industry classification, the North American Standard Industrial Classification, was adopted by the U.S. Census Bureau in that year. Using splice data provided by the Census Bureau for 1997, one finds that constant-dollar gross margins for the industry, as defined in 1996, probably rose by approximately 11.9 percent relative to 1996. Constant-dollar R&D outlays rose by 10.6 percent. The census universe excludes production in Puerto Rico, which is an important source of U.S. pharmaceutical products.
6. For example, for R&D, the calculation is [(R&D−Trend)/Trend] × 100.
7. See U.S. Congress, Office of Technology Assessment, *Pharmaceutical R&D: Costs, Risks, and Rewards*, Pub. no. OTA-H-522 (Washington: U.S. Government Printing Office, February 1993), 20–22.
8. Ibid., chap. 1. For the pioneering theoretical analysis of such behavior, see Y. Barzel, "Optimal Timing of Innovations," *Review of Economics and Statistics* (August 1968): 348–355. For an application to pharmaceuticals, which at the time of writing was considered one of two plausible theoretical alternatives, see Scherer, *Industry Structure, Strategy, and Public Policy*, 365–366.

[7]

Available online at www.sciencedirect.com

SCIENCE @ DIRECT•

ELSEVIER

Journal of Health Economics 24 (2005) 317–339

JOURNAL OF HEALTH ECONOMICS

www.elsevier.com/locate/econbase

Productivity in pharmaceutical–biotechnology R&D: the role of experience and alliances

Patricia M. Danzon[1,*], Sean Nicholson[1], Nuno Sousa Pereira[1,2]

[1] *University of Pennsylvania, Health Care Management Department, The Wharton School, 3641 Locust Walk, Philadelphia, PA 19104, USA*

[2] *Universidade do Porto, Portugal*

Received 1 March 2003; received in revised form 1 July 2004; accepted 1 September 2004
Available online 25 January 2005

Abstract

Using data on over 900 firms for the period 1988–2000, we estimate the effect on phase-specific biotech and pharmaceutical R&D success rates of a firm's overall experience, its experience in the relevant therapeutic category, the diversification of its experience across categories, the industry's experience in the category, and alliances with large and small firms. We find that success probabilities vary substantially across therapeutic categories and are negatively correlated with mean sales by category, which is consistent with a model of dynamic, competitive entry. Returns to experience are statistically significant but economically small for the relatively straightforward phase 1 trials. We find evidence of large, positive and diminishing returns to a firm's overall experience (across all therapeutic categories) for the larger and more complex late-stage trials that focus on a drug's efficacy. There is some evidence that a drug is more likely to complete phase 3 if developed by firms whose experience is focused rather than broad (diseconomies of scope). There is evidence of positive knowledge spillovers across firms for phase 1. However, for phase 2 and phase 3 the estimated effects of industry-wide experience are negative, which may reflect either higher Food and Drug Administration (FDA) approval standards in crowded therapeutic categories or that firms in such categories must pursue more difficult targets. Products developed in an alliance tend to have a higher probability of success, at least for the more complex phase 2 and phase 3 trials, and particularly if the licensee is a large firm.

JEL classification: D2; L22; L23; L65; O32

Keywords: Pharmaceutical and biotechnology R&D; Alliances; Economics of scale and scope

* Corresponding author. Tel.: +1 215 898 5722; fax: +1 215 573 2157.
E-mail address: danzon@wharton.upenn.edu (P.M. Danzon).

0167-6296/$ – see front matter
doi:10.1016/j.jhealeco.2004.09.006

1. Introduction

Pharmaceutical firms invest a greater percentage of sales in research and development (R&D) than any other industry. R&D accounted for 15.6% of global sales in 2000 for the US research-based pharmaceutical industry, compared to 10.5% for computer software, 8.4% for electrical and electronics firms and 3.9% for U.S. companies overall, excluding drugs and medicines (Pharmaceutical Research Manufacturers Association, 2001). The average R&D cost per new chemical entity (NCE) brought to the market is estimated at US$ 802 million (DiMasi et al., 2003). The cost per NCE is high for three reasons: high input costs for both drug discovery and drug development, including human clinical trials that are required by the Food and Drug Administration (FDA) to establish proof of safety and efficacy;[1] the time value of money considering that it takes 12–15 years to advance a drug from discovery through regulatory approval; and high failure rates. For each new compound that is approved, roughly five enter human clinical trials and 250 enter preclinical testing. Thus, a key management challenge in increasing R&D productivity is to raise the percentage of compounds that succeed in clinical trials. Success rates are also critical in valuing an individual drug, a company's pipeline of drugs and a company as a whole.

Relatively little is known about the determinants of success rates in pharmaceutical R&D. Most of the published data come from the Tufts Center for Drug Development (CSDD), using a proprietary database that contains drug development histories for 24 large pharmaceutical firms. In a series of studies focusing on compounds that entered clinical trials between 1980 and 1992, DiMasi et al. (1991) and DiMasi (2000, 2001) report estimates of average success rates by development phase, by therapeutic category and for self-originated versus in-licensed drugs. Henderson and Cockburn (1996) and Cockburn and Henderson (2001) use proprietary data from 10 pharmaceutical firms to test for economies of scale and scope at the level of the firm and research program, for the period 1961–1990.

These studies largely predate recent developments that changed the nature of R&D, including the biotech and genomics revolution and the increasing importance of small and medium-sized firms; the horizontal mergers between large pharmaceutical firms that were supposed to improve R&D productivity through economies of scale and scope; and the growth of contract research organizations (CROs) that enable firms to outsource their clinical trials. Thus, the average success rates in DiMasi's studies and the scale and scope relationships identified by Henderson and Cockburn may not reflect current conditions. These studies also do not examine the role of biotech–pharmaceutical alliances.

In this paper, we develop more current and more detailed estimates of R&D success probabilities, by therapeutic category and firm size, using data from Adis International on over 1900 compounds developed in the US by over 900 firms between 1988 and 2000. Specifically, we estimate the effect on phase-specific success rates of a firm's overall

---

1 Firms must file an Investigational New Drug (IND) application with the FDA and receive approval before a drug can be taken into human clinical trials. Phase 1 clinical trials test whether the drug is safe in healthy subjects; phase 2 trials test whether the drug is effective in small samples of patients with the target disease; phase 3 trials test whether the drug is effective in a large sample of patients with the targeted disease. Upon completing phase 3, a company files a New Drug Application (NDA) with the FDA for regulatory review and approval.

experience; its experience in the relevant therapeutic category (e.g., cardiovascular disease); the diversification of its experience, as measured by a Herfindahl index; and its alliances with large and small firms. We measure overall and category-specific experience as the cumulative number of compounds with which the firms was involved as an originator or a licensee prior to the clinical trial of interest. Learning-by-doing may produce general and category-specific skills in designing and managing trials, and improved relationships with clinicians and regulators, thereby contributing to trial success rates.

A second focus of this paper is to describe the rich landscape of alliances between small and large firms, at different stages of drug development, and to examine the impact of alliances on R&D success rates. New technologies for drug discovery – including applied microbiology, genomics, high throughput screening, combinatorial chemistry and bioinformatics (see, for example, Carr, 1998) have revolutionized drug discovery and the types of drugs that emerge. Small firms, which have played a key role in developing these new technologies, often develop drug leads and then out-license these leads to large pharmaceutical firms, who then take the drug through development, clinical trials and ultimately regulatory approval. One rationale for these alliances is that the experience of large firms adds sufficient value to offset the costs of operating the alliance (Nicholson et al., 2003). We test whether alliances do in fact enhance success probabilities and how any effects vary depending on the experience of the licensing partners.

For phase 1 trials, which are small and relatively straightforward, we find that returns to experience are economically small. However, for the larger and more complex late-stage trials that focus on efficacy, we find evidence of large, positive and diminishing returns to a firm's overall experience (across all therapeutic categories). We find no evidence that scale improves productivity beyond a threshold size, although economies of scale and scope in R&D have often been cited as a major reason for recent horizontal mergers between large pharmaceutical firms. We also find no evidence that a drug's success probabilities are associated with the firm's therapeutic category-specific experience. However, the therapeutic experience of the entire industry is positively associated with the likelihood that a drug in that category will successfully complete phase 1, and negatively associated with the likelihood it will complete phase 2 and phase 3. The phase 1 result suggests that there may be category-specific spillover learning across firms in safety testing. The phase 2 and phase 3 results could reflect an increase in FDA approval standards as a category becomes crowded with candidate products; the results could also reflect diminishing scientific returns at the external margin, that is, finding new drugs in crowded categories requires going after increasingly risky prospects. Finally, drugs developed by firms whose experience is focused rather than broad (diseconomies of scope) are more likely to complete phase 3 successfully.

Our results confirm that drugs developed in alliances are more likely to succeed in clinical trials, especially for phase 2 and phase 3, and when the licensee has more drug development experience than the originator. Thus, any "lemons" or moral hazard effects associated with out-licensing appear to be dominated by gains from trade. Large firms have higher success rates on in-licensed compounds than on compounds that they originate in-house, which is further evidence against allegations of moral hazard on licensed products.[2] These results

[2] This is consistent with DiMasi (2001) and Arora et al. (2000), but not Pisano (1997).

are conditional on the existence of an alliance; our data are insufficient to analyze alliance formation, choice of partners or effects of specific contractual terms.

More generally, we find that success probabilities vary systematically across therapeutic categories and that these probabilities are negatively correlated with mean sales by category. Simple models of entry or of optimal allocation of a firm's R&D budget across drug candidates suggest that a profit-maximizing firm would be willing to accept a relatively low R&D success probability when expected sales, conditional on reaching the market, are large. Our findings are consistent with such behavior.[3] However, a complete model of dynamic equilibrium is beyond the scope of this paper.

2. Determinants of R&D productivity: theory and previous literature

2.1. *Experience and economies of scale and scope*

Several of the recent large horizontal mergers in the pharmaceutical industry have been rationalized at least in part by economies of scale in R&D, but evidence is limited on whether such economies exist and, if so, over what range. Henderson and Cockburn (1996) use up to 30 years of data from 10 U.S. and European pharmaceutical firms, which collectively accounted for 25% of worldwide pharmaceutical research, to test for returns to scale and scope in drug discovery/research and knowledge spillovers within and between firms. Their dependent variable is the number of patents filed by a disease-specific research program, such as depression or anxiety. For drug discovery, they find evidence of returns to scale (defined as total research spending) at the firm level but not at the research program level. Firms with diversified research activities (number of programs with expenditures over US$ 500,000 per year) also appear to file more patents, providing support for economies of scope. They also find evidence of knowledge spillovers within firms between related research programs (programs within the same therapeutic category), and between firms with the same and related programs.

Cockburn and Henderson (2001) use data from the same 10 firms to examine scale and scope economies in the clinical development phase of R&D. They measure scale as the firm's total development expenditures and scope as the number of research programs on which the firm's spending averages at least US$ 1 million per year. Their unit of observation is a development project that has started phase 1 trials and the dependent variable is one if the project produced a new drug application to the FDA and zero otherwise. They find evidence of returns to scope in development and returns to scale within a therapeutic category, but no evidence of overall scale economies. When firm fixed effects are included, however, the scope measure becomes statistically insignificant, which raises the possibility that firm-specific strategies, rather than breadth of development activities, explain the differential success rates. Moreover, since much of the scale and scope variation is within firms as they grew over time, rather than between firms, measures of scale and scope economies may be contaminated by technological and other time-related changes.

[3] Dranove and Meltzer (1994) find that important drugs, whether defined by size of potential market or therapeutic novelty, are developed faster. This is further evidence that R&D outcomes are to some extent endogenous.

2.2. Alliances

In our sample a majority of drugs in phase 2 and phase 3 are developed in an alliance, but the role of alliances in R&D productivity is not examined in either of the two Henderson and Cockburn studies. Theory suggests several reasons why firms may form alliances and hence why alliances may affect R&D productivity (see Kogut, 1988, for a summary). First, simple theory of contracting over property rights predicts that an originator firm will pursue drug development with a partner if the expected benefits exceed the transactions and other costs of licensure. Powell and Brantley (1992) argue that a single biotechnology firm rarely has all the necessary skills and organizational capabilities to succeed. Since drug development technology is changing rapidly and the sources of knowledge are dispersed across many companies, biotech firms will have strong incentives to enter into an array of alliances (Powell et al., 1996). This gains-from-trade theory predicts that alliances should have a positive effect on success probability, particularly when relatively inexperienced firms outlicense to relatively experienced firms, and for the more complex phase 2 and phase 3 trials. A second, not mutually exclusive hypothesis is that some biotech firms enter alliances to raise capital and to send a signal to the public and private capital markets that its management and science are high quality (Nicholson et al., 2003). This motive for alliances may have a positive effect on success probabilities if access to financing enables a biotech to conduct larger or better-designed trials.

The potential positive effects of alliances may be mitigated by the potential negative effects of moral hazard and adverse selection. Moral hazard with respect to effort may occur because each party's cost of effort is fully internalized, whereas the returns to effort are shared with the alliance partner. The moral hazard disincentive may be more problematic on early-stage deals (preclinical and phase 1) because the originating company typically receives only about 10% of gross sales as a royalty. The adverse selection or "lemons" theory articulated by Pisano (1997) posits that small firms take advantage of asymmetric information to out-license their least promising compounds, retaining their more promising candidates to develop independently. A market for alliances could still exist if alliance prices are appropriately reduced to reflect this adverse selection risk faced by in-licensing firms. Contractual terms are often designed to deter shirking and selection incentives, through milestone payments, royalties and other contingent or back-loaded forms of payment to the licensor. Both the moral hazard and the lemons hypotheses predict a negative effect of co-development on a drug's success probabilities, if these effects are large enough to dominate any gains from pooled experience and better financing.

These theories of alliances cannot explain why large firms would out-license, since they presumably have greater experience and lower financing costs than smaller firms. There are several reasons why large firms might out-license compounds. First, due to the stochastic nature of drug R&D, a firm may find itself with more potential compounds ready for development than can be accommodated by its in-house personnel. Handling this temporary excess by out-licensing avoids the fixed costs of hiring more personnel. Second, large companies typically apply a minimum threshold of expected sales to compounds that they develop in-house. Compounds that fall below this threshold may be out-licensed to smaller companies that apply lower expected sales thresholds; this enables the large firm to retain some stake in the compound, while committing fewer resources than would be required for in-house development. Third, a large firm may enter a development and marketing alliance with another large firm for compounds with very large market potential in order to share the marketing expense and/or diversify risk on the very large marketing investment required.

The empirical evidence on the impact of drug development alliances is mixed. Lerner and Tsai (2000) find that alliances formed during periods of unfavorable public and private equity markets assign most of the property rights to the licensing firm and these alliances are less likely to generate an approved drug than alliances signed in periods of more favorable financing. Arora et al. (2000) and Nicholson et al. (2003) conclude that drugs developed in alliances are more likely to advance in clinical trials than drugs developed by the originating company, while Pisano (1997) comes to the opposite conclusion using a smaller and older data set. Powell et al. (1999) find that R&D alliances help biotech firms establish a position within a network of firms, which in turn generates incremental patents, sales and non-operating income. All of the above studies use more limited data sets and none examine whether the performance of alliances varies according to the experience of the originating and licensing companies, as we do in this paper.

2.3. Hypotheses

This paper tests the following principal hypotheses with respect to the effect of firm experience and alliances on R&D productivity:

(1) Drugs developed by firms with relatively high overall and therapeutic-category specific experience are more likely to advance in clinical trials (economies of scale).
(2) Drugs developed by firms with relatively diversified experience across therapeutic categories are more likely to advance in clinical trials (economies of scope).
(3) Alliances increase R&D productivity, on average. Productivity gains are expected to be greater for alliances between inexperienced and more experienced firms than for alliances between two relatively experienced firms; and for the more complex phase 2 and phase 3 trials than for simple phase 1 trials.

3. Data and methodology

Our principal data source is the R&D Insight database from Adis International. It includes 1910 compounds developed by pharmaceutical and biotech firms in the US between 1988 and 2000, with most of the observations occurring after 1994. The data set contains information on characteristics of the compound, including allocation to one or more of 13 therapeutic category or categories (e.g., cardiovascular, central nervous system) and the indication(s) the drug is intended to treat (e.g., colon cancer, anxiety). Sample means and standard deviations are presented in Table 1.

Our unit of analysis is a specific indication for which a drug is being developed, rather than a drug or development project.[4] Since the FDA requires clinical trial evidence to estab-

[4] By contrast, Cockburn and Henderson (2001) and Henderson and Cockburn (1996) analyze output of an entire research program, which typically includes multiple compounds, each for multiple indications.

Table 1
Sample means and standard deviations

Observations (indications)	Phase 1	Phase 2	Phase 3
	2057	1275	861
Therapeutic categories			
Alimentary tract and metabolism products	0.145	0.156	0.150
Antithrombotic agents	0.073	0.085	0.081
Cardiovascular system	0.135	0.150	0.159
Antipsoriatics	0.116	0.120	0.115
Urologics and contraceptives	0.058	0.076	0.114
Hypothalamic hormones and analogues	0.009	0.016	0.029
Antivirals and antibacterials	0.175	0.185	0.223
Cytotoxic antibiotics and related substances	0.518	0.408	0.280
Antiinflammatory and antirheumatic products	0.135	0.149	0.166
Nervous system drugs	0.164	0.202	0.178
Agents against amoebiasis and other protozoal diseases	0.022	0.019	0.017
Respiratory system products	0.098	0.104	0.070
Carbonic anhydrase inhibitors	0.040	0.048	0.056
Drug is developed in an alliance	0.494	0.547	0.621
Average number of indications per compound	3.35 (2.88)	3.05 (2.50)	2.98 (2.23)
Firm's phase-specific Total Experience	7.26 (7.78)	8.72 (8.10)	9.38 (7.77)
Firm's phase-specific Therapeutic Experience	5.44 (5.99)	6.44(6.18)	7.51 (6.50)
Industry's phase-specific Therapeutic Experience	471 (375)	513 (459)	436 (311)
Scope of firm's R&D (HHI index across Therapeutic categories)	0.298 (0.260)	0.247 (0.220)	0.216 (0.192)
Screening Ratio (percentage of pre-clinical drugs that begin phase 1)	0.616 (0.258)	0.610 (0.228)	0.608 (0.209)

Note: Standard deviations are in parentheses for each continuous variable.

lish efficacy for each approved indication, an indication represents the most disaggregated unit of R&D output. Alliances between companies may also cover some but not all of a compound's indications. Since the indications that appear in our sample depend on strategic choices made by firms, the regression results should be interpreted as being conditional on a firm choosing to proceed with a clinical trial.[5] We include in our regression analysis the number of indications for which a compound is or has been tested. This variable may be a proxy for unmeasured "quality," assuming that more promising compounds are pursued for more indications and/or that success for a prior indication means that the compound has passed certain safety tests. In our database, phase 1 drugs were developed for 3.4 separate indications, on average, phase 2 drugs for 3.1 indications and phase 3 drugs for 3.0 indications. The Adis database assigns the same therapeutic categories to all indications for which a compound is being developed. We report robust standard errors to control for correlation of unobserved characteristics across indications for a given compound.

[5] A complete model of the R&D process would treat as endogenous the number of indications targeted, in addition to the existence of an alliance and the partner(s) chosen. Our data are insufficient to estimate such a complete model. We therefore, treat the number of indications, the existence of an alliance and type of partner as predetermined. All regression coefficients should be interpreted as conditional on these prior decisions.

We perform a series of logistic regressions to analyze the determinants of R&D productivity. Specifically, the dependent variable is one if a compound successfully completes a phase for a particular indication, conditional on starting that phase and zero if the trial for that indication is discontinued.[6] Our sample consists of 2057 observations for phase 1, 1275 observations for phase 2 and 861 observations for phase 3.

The data suffer from both left and right censoring. Left censoring occurs, for example, if we observe that a phase 2 trial was initiated for a particular indication but we have no information on the phase 1 trial. In this situation we include the observation in the phase 2 regression (and the phase 3 regression if the phase 2 trial is successful), but exclude it from the phase 1 regression. If we instead imputed a successful phase 1 trial and included this observation in the phase 1 regression, our advancement probabilities would likely be biased upward due to survival bias and incomplete reporting of drugs that fail in phase 1.[7] By including a drug only when we observe that it begins a development stage, we mitigate the potential survival bias that could result from incomplete reporting.

Right censoring occurs when we do not observe whether an indication completed a phase successfully or was discontinued. Rather than eliminating these observations from the regressions, we assume that an indication failed if it remained in a phase, without any further reported events, for more than a threshold value, defined as the maximum number of years observed for completion of each phase in the non-censored sample. These thresholds are 5 years for phase 1 and phase 3, and 6 years for phase 2. For example, if an indication entered phase 1 or phase 3 before 1996 and no further action is reported by 2000, we assume that it failed and code the dependent variable as a zero. Indications that entered phase 1 or phase 3 in or after 1996 or phase 2 in or after 1995 and contain no subsequent outcomes information are excluded from our regression analysis.

We define a firm's overall experience (Total Experience) as the (depreciated) total number of compounds in a particular phase (i.e., phase 1, phase 2 or phase 3) with which the firm was involved, either as an originator or a licensee, between 1988 and the date of the clinical trial of interest.[8] The firm's Total Experience thus varies over time and is phase-specific.[9] For the results reported, we depreciate experience by 10% per year to reflect the likely depreciation

[6] Information on the date at which an indication enters and completes a trial phase is incomplete. We therefore, cannot estimate the probability of approval of the first indication, similar to DiMasi et al. (2003) or estimate a hazard model of time to phase completion.

[7] Since Adis obtains its information from public announcements, interviews and other sources, it is likely to track a larger percentage of the universe of later-stage trials than early-stage trials because late-stage trials are more likely to be discussed at public conferences and by investment analysts. In that case, drugs that were discontinued in phase 1 may be underrepresented in the database, relative to drugs that completed phase 1.

[8] The experience measures might be subject to endogeneity bias if firms whose drugs are more likely to advance have more drugs under development, for example, because these firms are more attractive as licensing partners. However, since our experience measures include all compounds with which a firm was associated in clinical trials, regardless of whether the compound failed or succeeded, such bias should be minor.

[9] Adis updates firm names to reflect merger and acquisition information. A drug that was originated in 1992 by Upjohn, for example, will be credited to Pharmacia, reflecting the 1996 merger between Pharmacia and Upjohn. Although this could introduce some measurement error in our firm experience variable, the effect should be small because 83% of the observations in our analysis are from the 1996–2000 period, hence occur after many of the large mergers. To the extent that we overestimate experience of the largest firms, we may underestimate returns to experience for these firms.

of knowledge within a firm; results with undepreciated experience were very similar. The regressions include dummy variables for the year in which an indication exited a phase. These variables control for the secular increase in experience over the sample period, as well as any other time-specific effects such as changes in the FDA's approval standards or changes in types of compounds being developed. In some specifications, we classify firms as small, medium or large, in place of the continuous Total Experience measure. A small firm is defined as one with three or fewer compounds in development during the sample period, a medium-sized firm as one with between four and 24 compounds in development, and a large firm as one with 25 or more compounds in development. There are 961 firms in our sample, of which 776 are small, 163 medium-sized and 22 are large by these criteria. Some specifications include fixed effects for the 22 large firms. Controlling for experience and therapeutic class of the compound, these firm fixed effects test for firm-specific drug development proficiencies.

Our Total Experience measure will be highly correlated with firm size and hence, with other possible advantages of scale, such as spreading the fixed costs of capital equipment or information systems over a greater number of drug candidates. Further, large firms that can fund R&D from retained earnings may face a lower cost of capital than smaller firms that rely on external financing from private or public equity markets or alliances with larger firms (Myers and Majluf, 1984). Thus, to the extent that our experience measure is correlated with size, it may capture more traditional scale effects in addition to pure experience effects.

In order to examine whether experience in a therapeutic category matters, conditional on a firm's overall experience, we define therapeutic category-specific experience (Therapeutic Experience) as the number of compounds a firm has originated or in-licensed in the category of interest, separately for phase 1, phase 2 and phase 3. If multiple therapeutic categories are reported for a given compound, the firm's maximum experience across these therapeutic categories is assigned for that compound. Therapeutic and Total Experience are highly correlated (correlation of 0.78), which may make it difficult to precisely estimate each effect separately.

We also include a measure of total Industry Therapeutic Experience by phase and therapeutic category to test for spillover effects of experience across firms. If such cross-firm knowledge spillovers are positive, the effect of Industry Therapeutic Experience is expected to be positive. Conversely, success probabilities may decline in crowded therapeutic categories, either because firms must pursue progressively more difficult or risky prospects once the low hanging fruit in a category have been picked, or because the FDA implicitly requires higher benefit/risk ratios to approve new drugs in crowded categories.

To measure experience-based economies of scope (Scope), we define a Herfindahl–Hirschman index (HHI) as the proportion of the firm's compounds in each therapeutic category, squared and summed across all therapeutic categories in which the firm has been active.[10] Thus our experience and scope measures are based on numbers and distributions of compounds, whereas Cockburn and Henderson (2001) measure scale based on a firm's R&D expenditures and scope as the number of development projects with average annual

[10] When two or more companies are jointly developing a compound, we assign the experience and scope measures of the more experienced firm to the compound, assuming that the larger firm is likely to take on greater responsibility in managing the clinical trials (Lerner and Merges, 1988).

R&D expenditures in excess of US$ 1 million. Since we do not have expenditure data, we unfortunately cannot compare the predictive performance of these two approaches to measuring scale and scope.

Our data on alliances are from the three databases: Adis' R&D Insights, Windhover Information and Pharmaprojects. In order to test for the effects of alliances, we create an indicator variable (Alliance) that equals one if two or more firms were involved in the development trials for that indication.[11] This variable is phase-specific and includes only alliances that were formed prior to the conclusion of the development phase of interest, in order to avoid the potential for endogeneity bias that could result if more successful projects are more likely to be the subject of alliances. We create separate alliance indicator variables based on the experience of the originator firm and the licensee to test whether the effect of alliances varies by experience of either party. Our alliance databases do not report contractual terms in sufficient detail to permit testing the effects of specific assignment of rights on outcomes.

Estimating the effects of alliances on R&D success requires caution because alliances are formed by choice. If selection occurs based on unobserved (to the econometrician) drug characteristics, then our estimated effect of an alliance on the likelihood a drug will advance may not be the true causal effect. We control for this to the extent possible by including the therapeutic category of the indication in question. Nevertheless, our results should be interpreted as estimating the effect of an alliance, conditional on its occurrence prior to the phase under study.

Firms may differ in the quality of their drug candidates and in the stringency of their review criteria before taking a drug into human trials. On the one hand, it is often argued that small firms that are under pressure to provide results in order to raise external funds are more likely to take a compound into clinical trials than larger firms that typically use retained earnings to fund their R&D. On the other hand, researchers in large firms may apply less objective evaluation to their own compounds than that applied by financial markets to small firms seeking external funding. In order to control for the unobserved quality of a firm's compounds, due either to the firm's capabilities and/or its stringency in screening compounds prior to clinical trials, we calculate for each firm a Screening Ratio. This variable is defined as the number of compounds a firm takes into clinical trials divided by the sum of its compounds in clinical trials plus preclinical compounds that do not enter trials.[12] The Screening Ratio can range from zero to one. If product quality varies randomly across firms but some firms set higher standards in screening compounds to take into clinical trials, then Screening Ratio would be inversely related to success probability. However, if firms differ more in the underlying quality of their drugs than in the expected success probability they require to take a compound into clinical trials, then a low Screening Ratio would indicate

[11] The alliance variable is set equal to one if the database lists a licensee or two or more originators. When the database lists two or more originators but no licensee, we assume the company with the smallest number of drugs in development during our sample period is the originator and the larger firm is the licensee, because it is much more common for small firms to out-license to large firms than vice versa. When more than one licensee is listed, we assign licensee status to the largest firm.

[12] Drugs in the preclinical stage after 1998 are not included in the Screening Ratio because we do not observe these drugs for a long enough time to know whether they will enter clinical trials.

that a firm's preclinical drugs have relatively poor prospects. In that case Screening Ratio would be positively related to success probability. It is also possible that some firms take a larger fraction of their preclinical compounds into clinical trials because they are more competent and hence anticipate an above average success rate. In that case, Screening Ratio could be endogenous and could be positively correlated with Total Experience. In fact, the correlation between Screening Ratio and Total Experience is 0.19, plausibly because many small firms with only one or two compounds have a Screening Ratio of one. Nevertheless, as a check on bias in other coefficients due to possible endogeneity of Screening Ratio, we also estimate the equations without Screening Ratio.

4. Results

We begin by examining the extent to which development success rates vary across therapeutic categories. In Table 2 we report marginal effects from separate logit regressions for phase 1, phase 2 and phase 3, where the only regressors are therapeutic category indicator

Table 2
Marginal effects of therapeutic category indicators (in percentage points)

	Phase 1		Phase 2		Phase 3	
	Marginal effect	Standard error	Marginal effect	Standard error	Marginal effect	Standard error
A: Antithrombotic	0.42	(2.0)	3.6	(3.4)	−7.6	(5.2)
B: Blood	0.40	(2.5)	3.3	(4.2)	−19**	(6.8)
C: Cardiovascular	0.45	(2.0)	−8.4**	(3.9)	−18**	(5.1)
D: Antipsoriatics	3.8*	(2.1)	1.4	(4.0)	2.9	(5.7)
G: Urologics and contraceptives	8.3**	(1.8)	16**	(3.7)	13**	(5.2)
H: Hormonal preparations	5.9	(4.9)	21**	(5.5)	21**	(8.4)
J: Antivirals	−2.1	(1.9)	1.7	(3.3)	−2.2	(4.7)
L: Cytotoxics	4.4**	(1.5)	−12**	(2.8)	−19**	(4.2)
M: Antiinflammatory	2.9	(2.1)	5.0	(3.5)	3.2	(4.8)
N: Nervous system	0.41	(1.9)	−0.6	(3.3)	−22**	(4.9)
P: Parasitology	−0.63	(4.7)	9.6	(7.3)	0.45	(14)
R: Respiratory system	5.3**	(1.9)	−20**	(4.8)	−18**	(7.4)
S: Carbonic anhydrase	5.9**	(2.6)	13**	(4.5)	8.0	(7.5)
Mean of the dependent variable	88.2		72.5		61.2	

Note: Robust standard errors are in parentheses. The marginal effect for say category A is calculated as Prob[$Y = 1 \mid A = 1, X^*$] − Prob[$Y = 1 \mid A = 0, X^*$], where the X^* vector includes all variables evaluated at their means except the category A dummy, which is set to either 1 or 0. The marginal effect is thus the predicted probability of success for a drug with a category A indication, relative to the mean probability for drugs with no category A indication. With this approach the marginal effects need not average out to zero. There is no omitted therapeutic category in the regression because many compounds target multiple categories and hence the therapeutic category indicators are not mutually exclusive.

* Significantly different from zero at the 10% level.

** Significantly different from zero at the 5% level.

variables. Since the therapeutic categories are not mutually exclusive – a compound can target multiple therapeutic categories – all 13 therapeutic category indicators are included in the regressions. The marginal effects report the change in the probability that an indication will complete a phase if it targets that therapeutic category, relative to the overall average probability, measured in percentage points.

The predicted probability that an indication will advance differs from the overall average for five of the 13 therapeutic categories in phase 1, six of the therapeutic categories in phase 2 and seven of the therapeutic categories in phase 3. There is considerable variation across therapeutic categories in the likelihood of succeeding. For example, the predicted probability that an indication will be approved by the FDA, conditional on starting a phase 3 trial, is 22 percentage points below the sample average (61.2%) for central nervous system drugs and 21 percentage points above the average for hormonal preparations.

To calculate the predicted probability that the FDA will approve an indication, conditional on starting phase 1, we multiply the three phase-specific predicted probabilities of success for each therapeutic category. Drugs for respiratory indications have the lowest predicted probability of being approved (30%), whereas hormone preparations have the highest predicted probability (78%) (see Fig. 1). These large differences in success probabilities across therapeutic categories might seem inconsistent with a model in which firms initiate R&D until the expected return is equalized across therapeutic categories and is equal to the risk-adjusted cost of capital, unless offsetting differences exist across categories in costs or in expected revenues, conditional on reaching the market. In fact, total market size varies significantly across therapeutic categories. Given such variation, equalization of expected returns across categories could occur through several competitive mechanisms, including: smaller market shares per drug in large categories; lower prices in large categories, due to more intense price competition; shorter life-cycle of sales in large categories, due to cannibalization by successive entrants, as hypothesized by Acemoglu and Linn (2003); and lower success probabilities and/or higher costs of trials in large categories. Lower success probabilities could occur if either technological hurdles to creating new compounds rise once the easy compounds in a category have been developed, or if the FDA implicitly raises the standards required of new compounds in crowded categories.

Testing between these alternative hypotheses is beyond the scope of this paper; however our data do suggest the last two factors – lower success probabilities and higher costs in large therapeutic categories – play a role.[13] In Fig. 1, we plot the predicted probability that a drug will be approved in each therapeutic category, conditional on entering clinical trials, versus the market size of that therapeutic category, as measured by 1991 worldwide sales. Sales in 1991 are a reasonable proxy for expected sales at the time our sample compounds were in discovery testing. In Fig. 1, the correlation between the probability that a drug will reach the market and sales in the therapeutic category is −0.504 at the sample mean

[13] Differences in FDA requirements may contribute but are unlikely to fully explain the observed differences in success rates across classes. The FDA has Priority Review and Fast Track approval procedures for new drugs and biologics that are intended to treat life-threatening diseases and address unmet medical needs. These procedures are intended to affect the speed of review, not the probability of success. Success probabilities could be affected if the FDA accepts higher risks or lower benefits for diseases with no existing treatments. However, such diseases are much more narrowly defined than our therapeutic categories and probably exist in most categories.

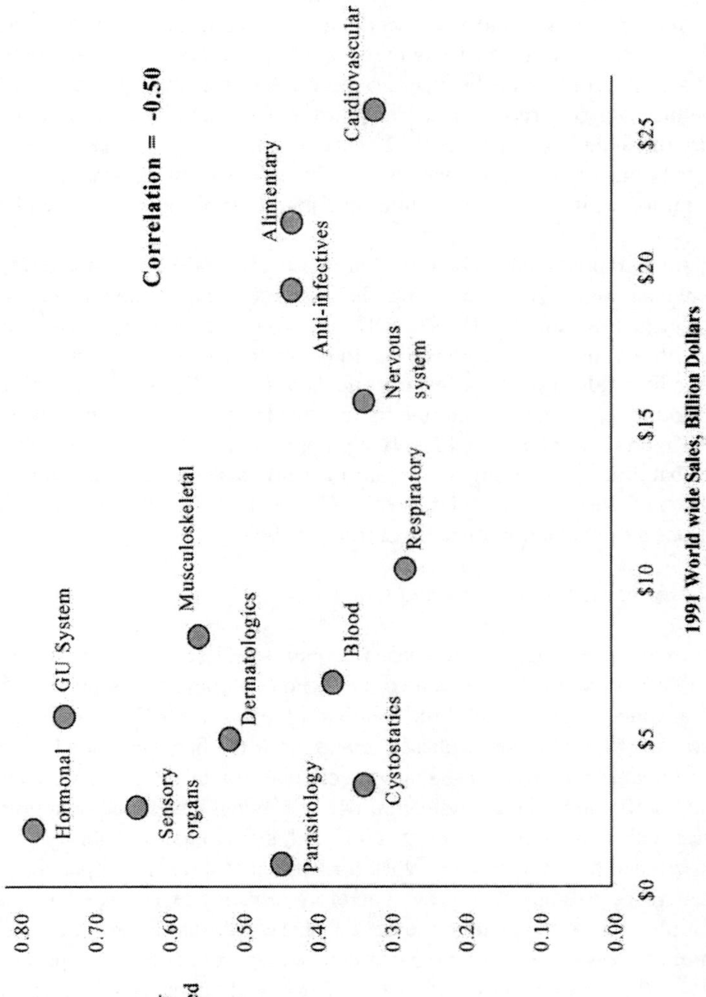

Source: Adis, Med Ad News.

Fig. 1. Relationship between size of market and probability a drug will reach the market by therapeutic class of drug.

probabilities, with a p-value of 0.079. Using 2001 worldwide sales by therapeutic category, the correlation is −0.642 with a p-value of 0.018. Thus, indications targeting relatively large categories (e.g., respiratory therapy, central nervous system, alimentary and cardiovascular) have relatively low predicted success probabilities. In other words, firms appear to be willing to develop drugs with a lower probability of success in therapeutic categories with greater sales potential. Firms also appear to be willing to incur higher costs on drugs with relatively large sales potential. The correlation between average R&D spending per development project by therapeutic category, reported in Cockburn and Henderson (2001), and 1991 worldwide sales by therapeutic category is 0.32. This evidence suggests that competition may reduce expected rents across categories on both the extensive margin (willingness to take on riskier conditions/drugs) and on the intensive margin (willingness to spend more per drug program).

Our indication-specific predicted probabilities of approval, conditional on entering human trials, are somewhat higher than the 20% probability across all therapeutic categories that DiMasi (2001) estimates using the Tufts CSDD data. This discrepancy probably results because our unit of observation is a specific indication or condition, whereas DiMasi's unit of observation is the first indication for a new chemical entity (NCE). As discussed earlier, if companies are more likely to target multiple indications for those compounds that have either already been approved or have a relatively high probability of being approved, then overall success probabilities will be higher for our measure based on all indications than for the first indication of a new compound. In our regression analysis below we include the number of indications a drug is targeting as a control variable.

4.1. Experience-based economies of scale and scope

We next test for evidence of experience-based economies of scale and scope in drug development in Table 3. In phase 1 there is a convex relationship between the probability an indication will advance to phase 2 and the originating firm's Total Experience (a contemporaneous measure of the number of phase 1 compounds the firm developed, either as an originator or as a licensee, between 1988 and the clinical trial of interest). As shown in Fig. 2, the predicted probability that an indication will advance if developed by a firm that has prior experience with a single phase 1 drug is 94%. This predicted probability declines gradually with experience to a minimum of 90% for firms that have developed 15 phase 1 drugs and then increases slightly thereafter. Therefore, a firm's experience has a small economic effect in phase 1: at the sample mean (7.3 phase 1 drugs), a unit increase in a firm's Total Experience is associated with a 0.5 percentage point reduction in the probability an indication will advance from a phase 1 to a phase 2 trial and this marginal effect is significantly different from zero at a 10% level.[14] Since a negative return to experience seems implausible, this may reflect more experienced firms applying more stringent scientific and economic screens in order to take a compound forward.

The returns to Total Experience are positive and more economically substantial for the more advanced clinical trials than for phase 1. In phase 2, the effect of Total Experience

[14] The marginal effect of a unit increase in Total Experience incorporates the coefficients on both the linear and quadratic Total Experience terms. The standard error of the marginal effect is calculated using the Delta Method.

Table 3
Experience-based economies of scale and scope in pharmaceutical/biotech drug development

	Phase 1		Phase 2		Phase 3	
	Marginal effect	Standard error	Marginal effect	Standard error	Marginal effect	Standard error
Firm's Total Experience	−0.49*	(0.29)	1.2*	(0.61)	2.0**	(1.0)
Firm's Therapeutic Experience	0.051	(0.17)	0.16	(0.38)	−0.35	(0.47)
Industry's Therapeutic Experience	0.0047*	(0.0025)	−0.011**	(0.0060)	−0.021**	(0.010)
Scope (HHI across therapeutic categories)	−0.98	(2.5)	12	(7.6)	23*	(12.0)
Co-development alliance	0.44	(1.1)	9.0**	(2.6)	14**	(3.8)
Number of indications for the compound	2.7**	(0.31)	2.8**	(0.66)	4.1**	(1.0)
Screening Ratio	4.9**	(2.1)	32**	(5.7)	9.4	(9.1)
Observations	2057		1275		861	
Pseudo R^2	0.12		0.12		0.15	
Percent correctly predicted	74.6		74.0		75	
Mean of the dependent variable	88.2		72.5		61.2	

Notes: Dependent variable is one if an indication successfully completes the development stage, and zero otherwise. The regressions also include a full set of therapeutic category and year indicators. The marginal effect is the change in the probability an indication will advance in clinical trials associated with a unit increase in the independent variable, holding the other regressors at their mean values, measured in percentage points.

* Significantly different from zero at the 10% level.

** Significantly different from zero at the 5% level.

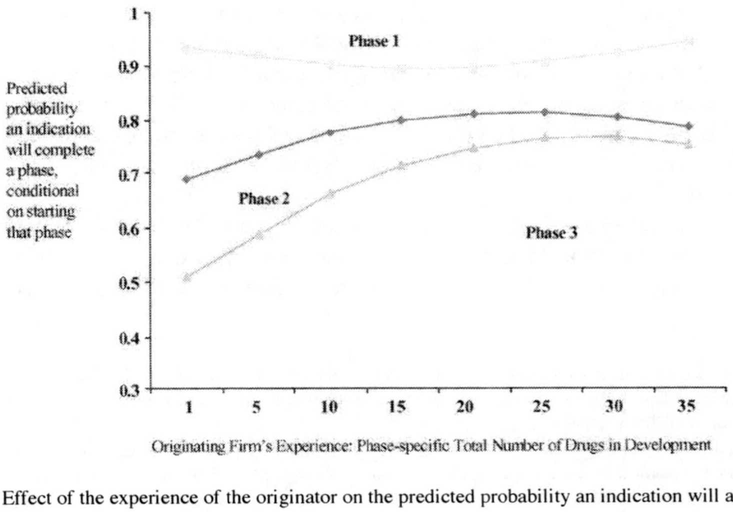

Fig. 2. Effect of the experience of the originator on the predicted probability an indication will advance.

on the likelihood of completing the phase is concave. The predicted probability of a phase 2 success for a firm that has previously participated in only one phase 2 trial is 69% (see Fig. 2). This predicted probability increases with the originator's experience to a maximum of 81% for a firm with experience in 25 phase 2 compounds and then decreases thereafter. At the sample mean (8.7 phase 2 drugs), a unit increase in Total Experience is associated with a 1.2 percentage point increase in the probability an indication will successfully complete a phase 2 trial and the marginal effect is significant at a 10% level.

In phase 3, the effect of Total Experience is concave as in phase 2. The predicted probability that an indication will complete phase 3 if the originating firm has previously developed a single phase 3 drug is 51% versus 81% for a firm that has developed 30 phase 3 drugs (see Fig. 2). At the sample mean (9.4 phase 3 drugs), a unit increase in a firm's Total Experience is associated with a 2.0 percentage point increase in the probability an indication will successfully complete a phase 3 trial and this marginal effect is significant at a 5% level.[15]

Our result that a firm's development experience does not substantially affect the likelihood that an indication will complete phase 1 but has a considerable effect in phase 2 and phase 3, is consistent with conventional wisdom: small firms are able to perform the relatively small and simple phase 1 trials for safety, whereas experience matters for the larger and more complex phase 2 and phase 3 trials, which require perfecting the dosage and establishing statistical evidence of efficacy in large patient samples.

We find no evidence of returns to therapeutic experience. Controlling for Total Experience, category-specific Therapeutic Experience (number of phase 1, phase 2 or phase 3 compounds the originator firm had developed in the same therapeutic category as the compound being evaluated) is insignificant in all three phases.[16]

The total Industry Therapeutic Experience in a therapeutic category is positively associated with the likelihood that a drug in that category will successfully complete phase 1 and negatively associated with the likelihood it will complete phase 2 and phase 3. Since year and therapeutic category indicators are included in the regressions, the coefficient on Industry Therapeutic Experience is identified by within-category changes in experience over time. The positive phase 1 marginal effect suggests positive knowledge spillovers across firms in safety testing. The negative phase 2 and phase 3 marginal effects are consistent with the hypotheses that either firms pursuing new drugs in crowded categories must go after more risky targets and/or that the FDA raises approval standards in therapeutic categories with multiple existing compounds. The phase 2 and phase 3 results are also consistent with our earlier finding that indications targeting categories with relatively large sales have relatively low success probabilities.

For phase 1 and phase 2, we find no evidence of returns to experience-based Scope, as measured by a Herfindahl index (HHI) of the squared shares of compounds in each therapeutic category in which the firm is active. In fact, the evidence suggests negative

[15] These results are robust to excluding Screening Ratio from the regressions, except that for phase 2 the marginal effect of Total Experience is insignificant when Screening Ratio is omitted. As noted earlier, the correlation between Screening Ratio and Total Experience is −0.19.

[16] Therapeutic and Total Experience are highly positively correlated. Omitting Therapeutic Experience has very little effect on the magnitude of the regression coefficients, although Total Experience is measured more precisely in such specifications.

returns to experience-based scope in phase 3. In other words, firms that focus their research efforts on a smaller number of therapeutic categories, and thus have a relatively high HHI measure, are more likely to have their indications complete phase 3. A one standard deviation increase in the HHI is associated with a 4.4 percentage point increase in the likelihood that an indication will complete a phase 3 trial. By contrast, Cockburn and Henderson (2001) find evidence of economies of scope but no evidence of economies of scale in drug development over the entire three development phases. These two sets of findings are not necessarily inconsistent because they pertain to different samples, different time periods and different measures of scale, scope and success.[17] In particular, it is plausible that specialization increases expertise for the small and medium size firms that dominate our sample but were excluded from the Cockburn and Henderson sample.

In Table 3, the number of conditions for which a drug is being developed is significantly positive, consistent with the hypothesis that multiple indications are more likely to be pursued for drugs that have already succeeded or are likely to succeed. The marginal effect for Screening Ratio is positive and significant for phase 1 and phase 2; firms that take a relatively large proportion of their preclinical drugs into human trials are more likely to experience successes in these trials. This suggests that this variable is measuring unobserved characteristics of a compound or unobserved ability of firms' managers, rather than different stringency levels of firms' internal review processes. The fact that coefficients on other variables are robust to excluding Screening Ratio indicates that these unobserved characteristics are not highly correlated with our measured variables.

Although the coefficients on the year indicator variables are jointly significant in all three phases, few of the individual coefficients are significantly different from zero and there is no clear trend in success rates over time.

We next explored whether large pharmaceutical firms differ in their productivity, conditional on their experience and the scope of their development activity. In regressions not reported here (available from the authors), we add to the regressions reported in Table 3 a vector of firm fixed effects for the 22 firms with 25 or more drugs under development during the sample period. The reference group for the firm coefficients is thus firms with 24 or fewer drugs under development during the period. We interact Total Experience and its quadratic with a Large Firm indicator variable for firms that developed 25 drugs or more, to test for differential effects of experience between small and large firms.

There is very little difference across firms in performance in phase 1. Only one of the 22 firm coefficients is significantly different from zero at the 10% level and the firm effects are not jointly significant. The experience coefficients for relatively small firms are insignificant when firm fixed effects are included for the largest firms. In phase 2, the firm fixed effects are jointly significant and seven of the 22 firm coefficients are significantly different from zero at the 10% level. The predicted probability that an indication will complete phase 2 varies by eight percentage points among the seven firms that have significant firm fixed effects. As in phase 1, the coefficients on experience for relatively small firms are insignificant.

[17] Cockburn and Henderson (2001) use a sample of 10 firms for 1961–1990, their measures of scale and scope are dollar outlays, their measure of success is the probability a drug was approved by the FDA conditional on starting phase 1, and they do not control for alliances. Our sample of almost 1000 firms includes many more observations on firms in the small- and medium-size range, where returns to experience are likely to be most important.

Firm fixed effects are also jointly significant in phase 3. Seven of the 22 firm indicators are significantly different from zero and the marginal effects for these firms range from 13 to 34 percentage points. As in phase 1 and phase 2, the Total Experience measures are very imprecisely estimated and become insignificant once we control for firm fixed effects.

4.2. Alliances

In Table 3, indications that are developed in an alliance are no more likely to complete phase 1 than drugs that are developed independently by the originating company. However, co-developed indications are significantly more likely to complete phases 2 and 3 than indications developed independently, and the marginal impact of an alliance is higher for phase 3 than phase 2. In phase 2, the probability a co-developed indication will advance is 9.0 percentage points higher than an indication that is developed by its originating company, other things equal. In phase 3, co-developed indications have a 14.1 percentage point higher predicted probability of advancing.

The finding that experience has a positive effect on the probability that an indication will complete phase 2 and phase 3 trials is consistent with the evidence from the distribution of alliances by phase, shown in Table 4. Table 4 reports the number and percentage of indications (e.g., anxiety) for which a drug is being developed that are out-licensed, by

Table 4
Alliance activity by development phase and experience of originator and licensee

Experience of originator	Total observations	Observations in alliances	Percentage in alliances (%)	Experience of licensee firm		
				Small	Medium	Large
Phase 1						
Small	635	314	49.4	112	121	81
Medium	673	357	53.0	36	144	177
Large	749	345	46.1	84	189	72
Total	2057	1016	49.4	232	454	330
Phase 2						
Small	322	202	62.7	50	82	70
Medium	400	241	60.3	29	74	138
Large	553	254	45.9	48	110	96
Total	1275	697	54.7	127	266	304
Phase 3						
Small	178	124	69.7	24	50	50
Medium	267	192	71.9	20	52	120
Large	416	219	52.6	30	97	92
Total	861	535	62.1	74	199	262

Note: A small firm had three or fewer drugs in development (drugs they originated plus drugs they in-licensed) during the 1988–2000 sample period; a medium-sized firm had between four and 24, and a large firm had 25 or more. There are 776 small firms in the sample, 163 medium-sized firms and 22 large firms.

experience of the originator, experience of the licensee and development phase. Forty-nine percent of the indications in phase 1 were developed in an alliance and large firms were almost as likely as small and medium-size firms to form an alliance. Recall that we define a small firm as one that had three or fewer drugs in development (drugs they originated plus drugs they in-licensed) during the 1988–2000 sample period; a medium-size firm as one with between four and 24 drugs; a large firm as one with 25 or more drugs. There is no strong pattern of alliances by size of the originator and licensee in phase 1: small firms often form alliances with other small firms (112 indications in panel A of Table 4) and large firms sometimes form alliances with small firms (84 indications in panel A of Table 4). For phase 2 and phase 3, a larger percentage of indications are co-developed and the licensees are more often medium and larger firms. Fifty-five percent and 62% of phase 2 and phase 3 indications, respectively, are co-developed. In phase 3, large firms in-license almost as many indications as small and medium firms combined, even though there are only 22 large firms in the data set (out of 961).

The data in Table 4, are generally consistent with the gains-from-trade theory: small and medium-size firms appear to have the skills and resources necessary to do the relatively simple and inexpensive phase 1 trials, but are more likely to seek a large pharmaceutical partner for the larger, more complex and more expensive phase 3 trials. Almost two-thirds (62.1%) of indications are under co-development by phase 3 and the majority of phase 3 licensees are medium or large firms.

In Table 3, we reported that drugs developed in alliances are more likely, on average, to successfully complete phase 2 and phase 3 trials relative to drugs developed by the originator firm. We next explore in more detail whether the impact of an alliance varies with the experience of the originator and licensee firms. In Table 5, we include indicator variables for indications originated by small and medium-size firms (large firms are the omitted group), and three separate indicator variables if small firms formed an alliance with a small, medium or large firm, and separate indicators if a medium-size firm formed an alliance with a small, medium or large firm. This specification allows us to test whether drugs originated by small and medium-size firms are more likely to succeed if they develop the drugs independently versus in an alliance with a small, medium or large firm. Since we found that experience has a positive effect on the probability that an indication will complete phase 2 and phase 3 trials, we also test whether drugs developed with a large licensee are more likely to advance relative to drugs developed with a small licensee. The regressions in Table 5 also include indicators for the therapeutic categories a drug is targeting and a variable measuring the number of conditions for which the drug is in trials.

For phase 1, drugs that small firms out-license to medium-sized firms have a 9.2 percentage point lower probability of advancing to phase 2 than the average of other indications.[18] This result may support the hypothesis that asymmetric information allows small companies to dump their "lemons" on unsuspecting partners (Pisano, 1997). Alternatively, small firms may invest less time in a partnership with small and medium-sized firms due to moral hazard.

[18] Furthermore, drugs that small firms out-license to other small firms have a lower probability of advancing than drugs that they develop independently.

Table 5
Effect of alliances on probability of advancing in a clinical trial

	Phase 1		Phase 2		Phase 3	
	Marginal effect	Standard error	Marginal effect	Standard error	Marginal effect	Standard error
Indication originated by small company						
Developed independently	3.9**	(1.5)	−0.17	(4.3)	2.2	(6.9)
Developed in alliance w/small licensee	−4.4	(4.2)	6.9	(6.5)	−6.7	(13)
Developed in alliance w/medium-size licensee	−9.2**	(4.8)	17**	(3.8)	8.6	(9.6)
Developed in alliance w/large licensee	−1.6	(4.0)	13**	(4.6)	7.1	(8.8)
Indication originated by medium-size company						
Developed independently	3.6**	(1.6)	−3.1	(4.1)	0.87	(6.5)
Developed in alliance w/small licensee	5.2	(3.7)	−4.0	(9.7)	−6.7	(14)
Developed in alliance w/medium-size licensee	1.9	(2.8)	−0.36	(6.8)	15**	(7.8)
Developed in alliance w/large licensee	−1.2	(3.0)	12**	(3.6)	15**	(6.3)
Indication originated by large company						
Developed independently	−3.0	1.0			−0.73	
Developed in an alliance	2.9*	(1.6)	2.2	(3.8)	11**	(4.7)
Number of indications for the compound	2.6**	(0.33)	3.2**	(0.64)	4.3**	(1.0)
Screening Ratio	4.9**	(2.4)	27**	(5.8)	−0.65	(9.3)
Observations	2057		1275		861	
R^2	0.06		0.12		0.13	
Mean of the dependent variable	88.2		72.5		61.2	

Notes: Dependent variable is one if an indication successfully completes the development stage, and zero otherwise. A small firm has 3 or fewer drugs in development during the sample period; a medium-sized firm has between 4 and 24, and a large firm has 25 or more. We include a full set of therapeutic category indicator variables in the regressions. The marginal effect is the change in the probability an indication will advance in clinical trials associated with a unit increase in the independent variable, holding the other regressors at their mean values, measured in percentage points. The marginal effect for large originators, which is the omitted group in the regression, is estimated by taking the difference from the predicted probability an indication will advance if originated by a large firm minus the predicted probability at the sample average of the regressors.

* Significantly different from zero at the 10% level.

** Significantly different from zero at the 5% level.

However, the insignificant marginal effects for small originators-small licensees and small originators-large licensees imply that this potential lemons or moral hazard problem does not apply to all alliances involving small originators. The drugs that small firms out-license to large firms and small firms do as well as the average of other drugs, but the drugs they out-license to medium-sized firms are less likely to complete phase 1. One possible explanation for this result is that large firms have sufficient experience in evaluating and managing deals to prevent a small firm from dumping its low-quality compounds or shirking in alliances with large firms. These data do not permit us to distinguish between the selection bias and gains-from-trade explanations of the difference between co-development with large versus smaller licensees. For compounds originated by medium and large firms, out-licensing has no significant effect on phase 1 success rates.[19]

In phase 2 (column 3 of Table 5), indications that small firms out-license to medium-size and large firms have a 17 and 13 percentage point higher predicted probability of completing phase 2, respectively, than the average indication. Medium-size originators benefit from an alliance for phase 2 trials only when the licensee is a large firm. If a medium-size firm develops an indication with a large firm, the predicted probability of completing phase 2 is 12 percentage points higher than for the average indication.[20] These results generally support the view that large, experienced firms are either competent at picking good drugs to in-license and/or competent at managing the alliances once they are formed, and that these positive effects of alliances dominate any negative selection or moral hazard effects.

For phase 3, indications that medium-size firms develop in an alliance with a large firm have a 15 percentage point higher probability of successfully completing phase 3 than indications medium-size firms develop independently.[21] Likewise, indications that large firms develop in an alliance (with all size firms) have an 11 percentage point higher probability of succeeding than the average indication. The perhaps surprising finding of no significant effects of alliances in phase 3 for indications originated by small firms, in contrast to the significant positive effects in phase 2, may reflect the relatively small sample of indications that are originated by small firms and enter phase 3 (178 enter phase 3 versus 322 that enter phase 2 and 635 that enter phase 1) and the small percentage (only 30%) of these that the small firms develop on their own. This small sample size makes the coefficient estimates imprecise. It may also be subject to biased selection, if small firms choose to undertake phase 3 trials without a partner only on those drugs for which they either have the necessary experience or are most confident in the quality of the compound.[22]

5. Conclusions

We examine whether success in biotech and pharmaceutical R&D varies according to the category of the drug, the experience of the originator firm, the experience of the entire industry, whether the drug is developed in an alliance, and the experience of the licensee. Our database reflects the experience of over 900 firms between 1988 and 2000, including many small and inexperienced firms as well as the large multinational companies. We find that success probabilities differ substantially across therapeutic categories. The significant

[19] In phase 1, for both small and medium-size originators the marginal effect of an alliance with a large licensee is not significantly larger than the marginal effect of an alliance with a small licensee.

[20] In phase 2, for a medium-size originator the marginal effect of an alliance is significantly greater if the licensee is large than if the licensee is small, whereas for small originators the difference in the marginal effects is not statistically significant.

[21] In phase 3, the marginal effect for a medium-size originator of an alliance with a large licensee is significantly larger than the marginal effect of an alliance with a small licensee, whereas for small originators the difference in the marginal effects is not statistically significant.

[22] The results in Table 5 are robust to excluding Screening ratio.

negative correlation between success probability and potential sales in a therapeutic category is consistent with a model of dynamic, competitive entry. That is, firms appear to be willing to undertake projects with lower probabilities of success in categories, where the expected sales, if successful, are relatively large.

Experience, measured by the number of compounds with which the firm was involved as an originator or licensee, does not appear to matter for phase 1 trials, which are small and relatively simple. However, for the larger and more complex phase 2 and phase 3 trials, there are positive returns to Total Experience up to a threshold. There is evidence of diseconomies of scope or breadth of experience in multiple therapeutic categories for phase 3 and no evidence of returns to category-specific experience in any phase. However, these returns to scale and scope are not robust to including firm fixed effects for the largest firms, which are jointly significant in phase 2 and phase 3. Phase 1 trials are more likely to succeed in therapeutic categories where the industry has considerable experience, which is consistent with knowledge spillovers for safety testing. The opposite is true for phase 2 and phase 3, however, which suggests that as a category becomes crowded, firms either must pursue more difficult phase 2 and phase 3 projects and/or the FDA raises approval standards. Finally, drugs developed by firms whose experience is focused rather than broad (diseconomies of scope) are more likely to complete phase 3 successfully.

Products developed in an alliance tend to have a higher probability of success, at least for the more complex phase 2 and phase 3 trials, particularly if the licensee is a large firm. This general finding that drugs developed in alliances are more likely to advance is consistent with DiMasi (2001) and Arora et al. (2000), but not Pisano (1997). Thus, the evidence on effects of alliances tends to confirm the direct evidence from the economies of experience measures: experience increases the probability of success for late-stage trials, whereas it is not necessary for the simpler, phase 1 trials. These productivity-enhancing effects of alliances with large firms dominate any lemons or moral hazard effects. Overall, these results suggest significant competitive entry into the market for pharmaceutical R&D, with extensive entry by small firms and effective use of alliances, as a source of both funding and expertise for small firms and a source of products for large firms.

Acknowledgements

We would like to thank ADIS International and Windhover for providing the data. We thank the Merck Foundation, the Leonard Davis Institute of Health Economics at the University of Pennsylvania and the Mack Center for Technological Innovation at the University of Pennsylvania and the Fundaçâo para a Ciência e Technologia, Portugal for financial support.

References

Acemoglu, D., Linn, J., 2003. "Market Size in Innovation: Theory and Evidence From the Pharmaceutical Industry. National Bureau of Economic Research Paper 10038.

Arora, A., Gambardella, A., Pammolli, F., Riccaboni, M., 2000. The Nature and the Extent of the Market for Technology in Biopharmaceuticals, mimeo.

Carr, G., 1998. The Alchemists. The Economist (February 21).
Cockburn, I.M., Henderson, R.M., 2001. Scale and scope in drug development: unpacking the advantages of size in pharmaceutical research. Journal of Health Economics 20 (6), 1033–1057.
DiMasi, J.A., Hansen, R.W., Grabowski, H.G., 2003. The price of innovation: new estimates of drug development costs. Journal of Health Economics 22 (2), 151–186.
DiMasi, J.A., Hansen, R.W., Grabowski, H.G., Lasagna, L., 1991. Cost of innovation in the pharmaceutical industry. Journal of Health Economics 10, 107–142.
DiMaisi, J.A., 2000. New Drug innovation and pharmaceutical industry structure: trends in the output of pharmaceutical firms. Drug Information Journal 34, 1169–1194.
DiMasi, J.A., 2001. Risks in new drug development: approval success rates for investigational drugs. Clinical Pharmacology & Therapeutics 69, 297–307.
Dranove, D., Meltzer, D., 1994. Do important drugs reach the market sooner? Rand Journal of Economics 25 (3), 402–423.
Henderson, R.M., Cockburn, I.M., 1996. Scale, scope, and spillovers: the determinants of research productivity in drug discovery. Rand Journal of Economics 27 (1), 32–59.
Kogut, B., 1988. Joint ventures: theoretical and empirical perspectives. Strategic Management Journal 9, 319–332.
Lerner, J., Tsai, A., 2000. Do Equity Financing Cycles Matter? Evidence From Biotechnology Alliances, NBER Working Paper number 7464.
Lerner, J., Merges, R.P., 1988. The control of technological alliances: an empirical analysis of the biotechnology industry. The Journal of Industrial Economics 46 (2), 125–156.
Myers, S., Majluf, N., 1984. Corporate financing and investment decisions when firms have information that investors do not have. Journal of Financial Economics 13, 187–221.
Nicholson, S., Danzon, P.M., Jeffrey McCullough, 2003. Biotech-pharmaceutical alliances as a signal of asset and firm quality. Journal of Business, in press.
Pisano, G., 1997. R&D Performance, Collaborative Arrangements, and the Market-for-Know-How: A Test of the 'Lemons' Hypothesis in Biotechnology, mimeo.
Powell, W.W., Brantley, P., 1992. Competitive cooperation in biotechnology: learning through networks? In: Nohria, N., Eccles, R.G. (Eds.), Network and Organizations: Structure, Form and Action. Harvard Business School Press, Boston, pp. 366–394.
Powell, W.W., Koput, K.W., Smith-Doerr, L., 1996. Interorganizational collaboration and the locus of innovation: networks of learning in biotechnology. Administrative Science Quarterly 41, 116–145.
Powell, W.W., Koput, K.W., Smith-Doerr, L., Owen-Smith, J., 1999. Network position and firm performance: organizational returns to collaboration in the biotechnology industry. In: Andrews, S., Knoke, D. (Eds.), Networks in and Around Organizations. JAI Press, Greenich, CT.
Pharmaceutical Research and Manufacturers of America. Pharmaceutical Industry Profile, 2001. PhRMA, Washington, DC. http://www.phrma.org/.

[8]

ORIGINAL RESEARCH ARTICLE

Pharmacoeconomics 2002; 20 Suppl. 3: 11-29
1170-7690/02/0003-0011/$25.00/0

Returns on Research and Development for 1990s New Drug Introductions

Henry Grabowski,[1] *John Vernon*[1] and *Joseph A. DiMasi*[2]

1 Department of Economics, Duke University, Durham, North Carolina, USA
2 Tufts Center for the Study of Drug Development, Tufts University, Boston, USA

Abstract

Background: Previously published research by the authors found that returns on research and development (R&D) for drugs introduced into the US market in the 1970s and 1980s were highly skewed and that the top decile of new drugs accounted for close to half the overall market value. In the 1990s, however, the R&D environment for new medicines underwent a number of changes including the following: the rapid growth of managed-care organisations; indications that R&D costs were rising at a rate faster than that of overall inflation; new market strategies of major firms aimed at simultaneous launches across world markets; and the increased attention focused on the pharmaceutical industry in the political arena.

Objective: The aim of this study was to examine the worldwide returns on R&D for drugs introduced into the US market in the first half of the 1990s, given that there have been significant changes to the R&D environment for new medicines over the past decade or so.

Results: Analysis of new drugs entering the market from 1990 to 1994 resulted in findings similar to those of the earlier research – pharmaceutical R&D is characterised by a highly skewed distribution of returns and a mean industry internal rate of return modestly in excess of the cost of capital.

Conclusions: Although the distribution of returns on R&D for new drugs continues to be highly skewed, the analysis reveals that a number of dynamic forces are currently at work in the industry. In particular, R&D costs as well as new drug introductions, sales and contribution margins increased significantly compared with their 1980s values.

Competition in the research-based pharmaceutical industry centres on the introduction of new drug therapies. In this paper, we examine the returns on research and development (R&D) for new drug entities introduced into the US market in the first half of the 1990s. This research work builds directly on earlier analyses of returns on R&D for the 1970s and 1980s introductions performed by Grabowski and Vernon.[1,2]

Our prior analyses indicate that this industry has exhibited very skewed distributions of returns. In this regard, several significant new classes of drug therapies have been introduced since the late 1970s. Early movers in these classes have obtained the highest returns on R&D. We found that the top decile of new drugs accounted for close to half of the overall market value associated with all the new drug introductions in our 1970s and 1980s' samples.

The results of our prior analysis are also consistent with an economic model of rivalrous R&D competition. In particular, the promise of above-average expected returns produces rapid increases in industry R&D expenditures, as firms compete to exploit these opportunities until the returns become unattractive. From an industry perspective, our results indicate that mean returns on R&D are relatively close in value to the risk-adjusted cost of capital for drug industry investments. This rent-seeking model is also supported by a recent empirical analysis by Scherer, who finds a strong relationship between industry R&D outlays and profits over the period 1962 to 1996.[3]

An investigation into the drug returns in the 1990s is timely on a number of grounds. First, this decade has been characterised by the rapid growth of managed-care organisations on the demand side of the market for pharmaceuticals.[4] This has led to greater access to and utilisation of pharmaceuticals, but also greater generic competition in the post-patent period. Second, a new study of R&D costs by DiMasi and colleagues indicates that the R&D costs for new drugs have continued to rise much faster than the rate of general inflation.[5] This reflects, among other factors, the increased size of clinical trials compared with those for earlier new drug introductions. Third, many firms are changing their market strategies and attempting to launch their products simultaneously across world markets, reflecting the higher R&D investment costs and more intensive competition from new molecules in the same product class.

In addition to these economic developments, the industry continues to be the subject of considerable attention by policy makers. Recent policy initiatives in the US include a Medicare prescription drug benefit, the parallel importation of drugs from Canada and Mexico, and various state programmes affecting drug costs and utilisation by the poor and elderly populations. The potential effects of these policy initiatives on R&D returns remain an important issue for research. Our past work on R&D returns has provided a framework for the Congressional Budget Office and other groups to consider the effects on R&D of the proposed Clinton Health Care Reform Act and the Waxman-Hatch Act of 1984.[6,7]

In the next section of this paper, we describe the data samples and methodology for our analysis of the returns to 1990 to 1994 new chemical entities (NCEs). 'Empirical Results' presents the empirical findings on the distribution of returns and a sensitivity analysis involving the main economic parameters. 'Drug Innovation and Industry Evolution Since 1970' provides a discussion of the results and comparisons with the historical findings from our prior work, which is based on the same methodology. The final section provides a brief summary and conclusions.

Methodology and Data Inputs

Overview

This section explains the methodology and key data inputs used in estimating the returns to 1990 to 1994 NCEs. Our sample includes 'large-molecule' biologics, in addition to traditional 'small molecule' chemical drugs. A detailed discussion of the general methodology is provided in our earlier papers on R&D returns.[1,2] Our focus here is on the similarities and differences of the 1990s sample compared with our analysis of prior NCE cohorts.

The basic sample comprises 118 NCEs introduced into the US between 1990 and 1994. This is a comprehensive sample of the NCEs originating from and developed by the pharmaceutical industry that were introduced into the US in the 1990 to 1994 time period. However, three drugs were omitted from our sample because they failed to appear in any year in the IMS sales data audits. These drugs were distributed outside of normal sales channels and were likely to have nonrepresentative R&D costs because of their special indications.

The number of NCE introductions increased significantly in the early 1990s compared with the 1980s. The corresponding 1980 to 1984 sample was 64 NCEs. This increase in NCEs reflects the increased R&D expenditures for new entities by the traditional pharmaceutical industry as well as the growth of the independent biopharmaceutical industry.[8] The latter industry was in its infancy in the early 1980s, but by the early 1990s it had become a significant source of new drug introductions. There is also a significant increase in the number of new drugs approved for orphan drug indications. As we have discussed elsewhere, there is a high degree of overlap between the biopharmaceutical and orphan drug sub-samples.[8]

Our basic procedure is as follows: for each new drug in our sample, worldwide sales profiles are constructed over the drug's product life cycle. These sales values are converted to after-tax profits and cash-flow values using industry data on profit margins and other economic parameters. These data are combined with R&D investment information, based on the recent analysis by DiMasi et al.[5] Mean net present values (NPVs) and internal rate of return (IRRs) are then computed for this portfolio of new drug introductions. The distribution of returns is another major focus of our analysis.

Cost of Capital

In our earlier analysis of 1980 NCEs, we utilised a 10.5% real cost of capital for the pharmaceutical firms. This was based on an analysis of the industry using the capital asset pricing model (CAPM) that was performed by Myers and Shyum-Sunder.[9] Their study was commissioned by the Office of Technology Assessment as part of a larger study on R&D costs, risk and rewards.[10] They found that the real after-tax cost of capital on equity plus debt varied between 10 and 11% during the 1980s.

For our sample of 1990 to 1994 introductions, the relevant investment period spans the mid-1980s through the late 1990s. In their original article, Myers and Shyum-Sunder provided estimates of the cost of capital for 1985 and 1990. Myers and Howe have subsequently provided a related analysis for 1994.[11] We also performed a comparable CAPM for analysis for January 2000. The results of these CAPM-based studies are summarised in DiMasi et al.[5]

Using these four CAPM-based analyses, occurring at roughly 5-year intervals, we found that the mean cost of capital for pharmaceuticals over this period was just over 11%. Consequently, 11% was selected as the baseline value for the cost of capital in this analysis of 1990 NCEs. This represents a small increase from the 10.5% cost of capital utilised for the 1980 NCEs.

As Myers and Shyum-Sunder indicated in their original article, the CAPM approach provides somewhat conservative cost-of-capital values with respect to investment in new prescription drugs. One reason is that the equity market data on which the CAPM analysis is based pertain to all the different functional areas and commercial activities of drug firms (which can include over-the-counter drugs, animal health, basic chemicals, etc.). Another reason why the cost of capital may be understated is the fact that many pharmaceutical firms carry significant cash balances. Indeed, Myers and Shyum-Sunder found that many pharmaceutical firms have large positive cash balances and are actually net lenders rather than net borrowers. Consequently, these firms have a negative debt ratio. Myers and Shyum-Sunder did a sensitivity analysis to gauge how this factor would affect their 1990 value and they found it causes the nominal (and real cost) of capital to increase by almost a full percentage point.[9]

Several surveys have been performed of the hurdle rates used by US companies. A general finding is that hurdle rates are typically greater than the weighted cost of capital computed by a CAPM analysis.[12] One of the authors undertook an informal survey of six pharmaceutical firms in mid-2001 with respect to the hurdle rates that drug firms utilise in their R&D investment decisions. The survey of these firms yielded (nominal) hurdle rates from 13.5% to over 20%. If one takes 3% as the long-run expected rate of inflation, then an 11% real rate of return corresponds to a nominal rate of 14%. This 14% rate is within the range of hurdle rates utilised by the drug firms in their R&D investment decisions, but it is at the lower end of the range. This is consistent with the view that a CAPM analysis provides conservative estimates on the industry's cost of capital.

Myers and Howe further indicate that the R&D decision process can be modelled as a compound option pricing model.[11] Under this model, at any point in the R&D decision-making process, future R&D serves as a form of leverage, or debt, assuming the firm decides to undertake further development and marketing. Since this 'debt' or leverage declines over the subsequent stages of the R&D process, so will the firm's cost of capital. Implementation of this model requires unobservable informational inputs compared with the standard CAPM approach using a weighted cost of capital. DiMasi et al.[5] performed a sensitivity analysis using this option value approach, and showed that for reasonable values of the forward looking discount rates, the CAPM and option value models yield comparable results.

Research and Development (R&D) Investment Expenditures

To obtain representative R&D investment expenditures for the new drug entities in our sample, we relied on the recently completed study by DiMasi et al.[5] This study obtained R&D cost data for a randomly constructed sample of 68 drugs first tested clinically between 1983 and 1994. The DiMasi study is designed to measure the average cost of a new drug introduction and includes discovery costs as well as the costs associated with failed candidates.

The mean introduction of our sample NCEs is 1992 while the mean introduction of drug candidates analysed in the DiMasi study is 1997. DiMasi and colleagues had previously undertaken an analysis of the costs of 1980s introductions using the same methodology employed in their new study.[13] That study was centred on 1984. Given the availability of these two R&D cost studies centred around 1984 and 1997, we can utilise a linear extrapolation procedure to estimate the mean R&D costs for our sample cohort.[1]

Using this extrapolation procedure, we estimated the mean out-of-pocket R&D expenditures for the drugs in our sample to be $US308.4 million. This is approximately double the estimated R&D expenditures (in $US, 2000 values) for the 1980 to 1984 samples of NCEs. DiMasi also estimated a representative investment period of 12 years from initial drug synthesis to Food and Drug Administration (FDA) approval. We were able to allocate the out-of-pocket R&D costs over this 12-year period using weights derived from the DiMasi et al. study.[5] Capitalising these costs to the date of marketing, at a real cost of capital of 11%, yields $US613 million as the average (pre-tax) capitalised R&D investment per 1990 to 1994 NCE introduction.

Our analysis is performed on an after-tax basis. For the time period under study, we estimated a 30% average effective tax rate for the pharmaceutical industry (see 'Effective Tax Rates'). Since R&D expenditures can be expensed for tax purposes, we multiplied the pre-tax values by 0.7 to get an after-tax value. This is shown in the first row of table I. Utilising the 30% effective tax rate, $US613 million pre-tax capitalised corresponds to an after-tax value of $US429 million.

In addition to these pre-launch R&D expenditures, firms also undertake R&D outlays in the post-approval period for product extensions such as new indications, formulations and dosage levels. Since these activities can be viewed as spillovers from the original NCE introduction, these ongoing R&D investment expenditures, as well as any extra revenues that they generate, are appropriately incorporated into the analysis. On the basis of the DiMasi et al. study,[5] we estimated

Table I. Capitalised research and development (R&D) costs for the mean new chemical entity in the 1990 to 1994 sample

R&D costs ($US millions; 2000 values)[a,b]	Pre-tax	After tax
Discovery and development	$613	$429
Product extensions after launch	$73	$51
Total	**$686**	**$480**

a R&D costs include expenditures on product failures as well as successes.

b R&D costs are capitalised to the first year of marketing using an 11% cost of capital.

1 Since our sample is centred around 1992, we utilise the following linear extrapolation equation to derive R&D costs: $R\&D_{92} = R\&D_{84} + (8/13)\ R\&D_{97}$.

the average post-approval R&D costs per NCE in our sample period to be $US107 million (before tax).[2] We allocated these costs equally over the first 8 years of an NCE's market life, using a discount rate of 11% from the date of marketing. This yields a present value of $US73 million (before tax) and $US51 million dollars (after tax).

When the after-tax values (see column two of table I) are added, the mean capitalised value for both pre- and post-approval R&D for the drugs in our sample is estimated to be $US480 million. This is the baseline value that we compare with the present value of net revenues for the mean NCE in our sample.

Global Sales

In our prior analysis, we obtained US sales data on each NCE in the sample. We then estimated worldwide sales for these compounds using a worldwide sales multiplier common to all NCEs. One limitation of this approach is that the ratio of worldwide sales to domestic sales varies significantly, both over time and across drugs in our sample.

In the current analysis, our approach was to obtain worldwide sales data directly on as large a group of the drugs as possible. We were generally successful in this endeavour, in that we were able to obtain worldwide sales data for a majority of the NCEs in our sample (66 NCEs) using several complementary data sources. These 66 drugs accounted for more than 90% of total US sales realised by our sample of NCEs and presumably a similar, or even larger, share of its realised worldwide sales. With respect to the latter point, there is evidence that the larger selling US drugs diffuse across more countries and have larger sales globally than US compounds with smaller domestic sales.[14]

To obtain worldwide sales data, we collected sales data that firms provide in their annual reports, in the reports of financial analysts, and in publications such as *MedAdNews*. The last-mentioned source has compiled an annual survey of worldwide drug sales, by product, since 1990 on an expanding basis over time. The compilation for 2000 includes information on the 500 top-selling prescription drugs worldwide.[15]

A complementary source of data that we also relied on was IMS data on worldwide sales, which is based on audit data sources from a large number of countries. The IMS data source was available to us (from a prior project) for a sub-sample of drugs consisting of the largest selling global drugs in our sample. It provided a check on the sales information provided by the company sources. In most cases, the IMS sales values were less than the company values. This reflected the fact that the IMS does not capture all the sales channels available across countries, while the company data do include every channel.

In about 25% of the overlapping observations, however, the IMS sales were greater than the company-reported values. An analysis into why this was the case revealed that the sub-sample of drugs with higher IMS sales was marketed internationally under multiple names and by several different companies. Consequently, sources such as *MedAdNews* didn't capture all of the sales that were licensed to different companies for a particular molecule. For the sub-sample of drugs for which this was an issue, we utilised the larger IMS worldwide sales values because they better captured the worldwide market.

Using this approach and these complementary data sources, we assembled worldwide sales data for 66 of the NCEs over the period of 1990 to 2000. For the remaining (very small selling) drugs in our sample, we multiplied their US sales values by a representative global sales multiplier to obtain estimates of their worldwide sales. The value of the global sales multiplier was 2.19. As discussed, this

2 DiMasi et al.[5] obtained data from all the firms participating in his survey on pre-approval and post-approval R&D expenditures. On the basis of an analysis of these data, they estimated that out-of-pocket R&D expenditures for product extensions in the post-approval period were 34.8% of pre-approval R&D expenditures. Applying this percentage to our estimate of $US308.4 million for pre-approval R&D yields an estimate of $US107 million (in $US, 2000 values) as the R&D cost for post-launch product improvements.

latter sub-sample of drugs accounts for a very small share of overall sales for the full sample.

Life-Cycle Sales Profiles

Since data were available for the years 1990 to 2000, 7 to 11 years of worldwide sales values for the NCEs in our sample were provided, depending on their date of introduction into the US market. The next task was to estimate future sales over the complete market life of these products. Twenty years was chosen as the expected market life. This is the same assumption that we utilised for 1980s new drug introductions. We believe this to be a reasonable time horizon for an IRR analysis. Any sales remaining after 20 years of market life are likely to be very small, given the sales erosion experienced by most products from generic competition and product obsolescence. Furthermore, these sales will also be severely discounted by the cost of capital in an IRR analysis.

We utilised a two-step procedure to project future sales values. These steps involve forecasting sales to the point of US patent expiry and then projecting sales in the post-patent period. The two-step approach is illustrated in figure 1 for one of the products in our sample. This product was introduced into the US market in 1992. There are 9 years of sales information and its US patent expires in year 12. By year 9, this product was in the mature portion of its product life cycle. By using a reference life-cycle curve, the product was projected to have relatively stable sales (in constant dollar terms) until year 12. A significant decline is then projected in the period after US patent expiry because of the entry of generic competitors and related economic factors.

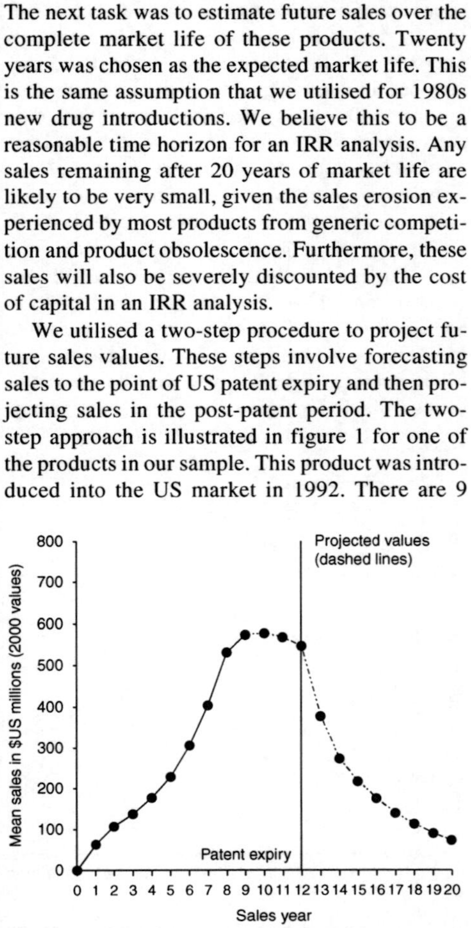

Fig. 1. Actual and projected worldwide sales values for a representative sample product.

The estimated sales decline after patent expiry is based on the experience of major commercial products coming off patent in the 1994 to 1997 period. In particular, we examined worldwide sales losses for a sample of NCEs for a 4-year period following their US patent expiry. The average percentage declines observed were 31, 28, 20 and 20%, respectively. We utilised these percentages to project sales in the first 4 years after patent expiry and, thereafter, a 20% decline until the product's market life is completed in year 20. In our prior work, we found that generic competition is focused on products with significant sales at the time of US patent expiry. Consequently, for the drugs concentrated in the bottom four deciles of our sample (with worldwide sales of less than $US40 million in year 10 of their market life), we assume that the probability of generic competition is very low. For these drugs we assume that sales losses in the mature phase of cycle will proceed at a more moderately declining rate based on the reference curve used for the pre-patent expiry period.

We should note that the percentage declines in sales from generic competition in the US market observed in prior studies are much greater than the worldwide losses in sales for major commercial products observed here.[16] Hence, the decline in worldwide sales in the post-patent period is ameliorated by the lower incidence of generic competition and sales losses outside the US. This may change by the time this cohort actually reaches patent expiry during the current decade, because reference pricing and generic competition are on the rise in many European countries.[17]

Figure 2 provides a plot of the sales life-cycle profile (in $US, 2000 values) for the top two dec-

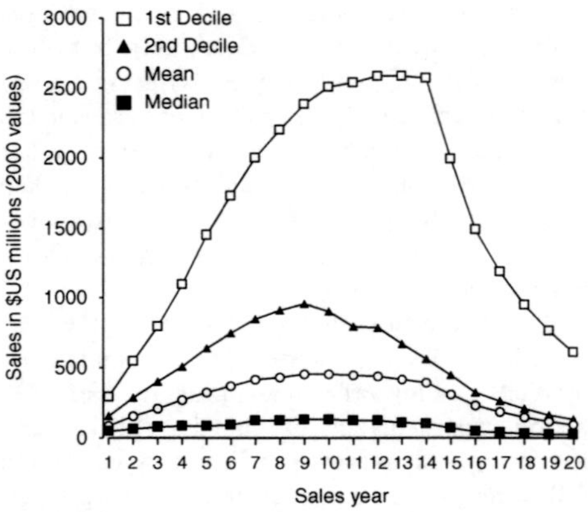

Fig. 2. Worldwide sales profiles of 1990 to 1994 new drug introductions.

iles as well as the mean and median drug compounds in our 1990 to 1994 sample. The sales curves illustrate the highly skewed distribution of sales in pharmaceuticals that was observed for early cohorts. The peak sales of the top decile compounds are several times the peak sales of the second decile compounds. The mean sales curve is also significantly above the median.

Figure 3 provides a plot of mean worldwide sales for the 1990s sample compared with that for the 1980s cohort (in $US, 2000 values). Mean sales have increased significantly in real terms, with peak sales increasing from $US345 million for the 1980s cohort to $US458 million for the 1990s cohort. There is also the suggestion that sales curves have become somewhat steeper in the ascending sales growth stages of the life cycle, with a longer plateau before generic competition and product obsolescence take hold.

Figure 4 shows a corresponding plot of the mean worldwide sales for the top decile compounds in the 1990 to 1994 and 1980 to 1984 periods. This is instructive, given that the prospective returns for top decile compounds are primary drivers of R&D investment activities in pharmaceuticals. For the 1990s cohort, the top decile compounds reached peak sales of more than $US2.5 billion. This may be compared with peak sales of near $US1.8 billion for the 1980s cohort. The peak sales for the 1990s cohort also occur later than for the 1980s cohort.

Pre-Tax Contributions and Other Economic Parameters

The next step in the analysis was to obtain revenues net of production and distribution costs (often categorised in the economic literature as 'quasi-rents'). For this purpose, we analysed pre-tax contribution margins in pharmaceuticals during the 1990s. As in prior work, we utilised data derived from the income statements of the pharmaceutical divisions of a number of major multinational drug companies to obtain representative values on contribution margins over time.[1,2]

Our analysis of the data on these firms indicated that average contribution margins gradually increased from 42% in the early part of the 1980s to approximately 45% at the end of the decade. On the basis of these data, we constructed a linear contribution margin schedule over time. In particular, the contribution margin is 42% in the first year of the product life and grows by increments of 0.3%

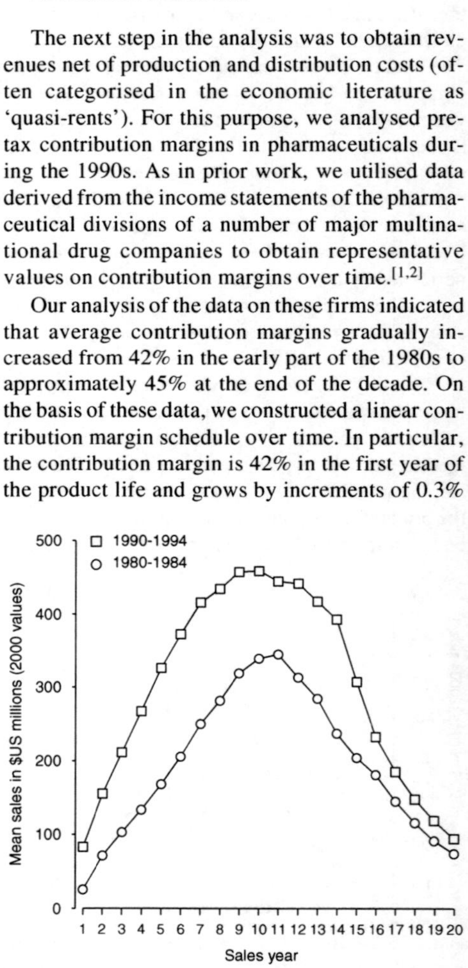

Fig. 3. Comparison of mean worldwide sales curves for new drug introductions in the 1990 to 1994 and 1980 to 1984 samples.

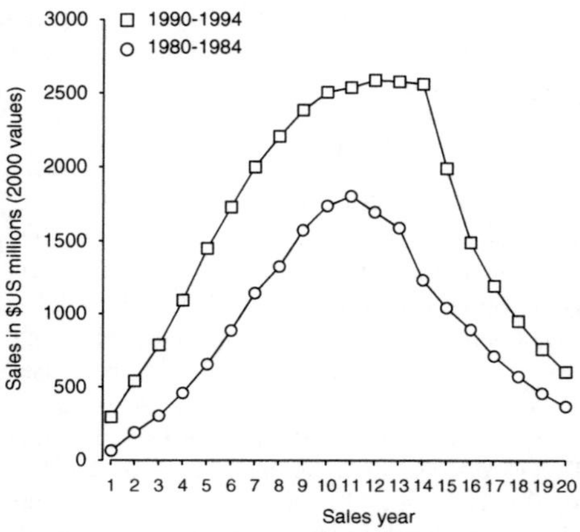

Fig. 4. Comparison of mean worldwide sales curves for top decile drugs in the 1990 to 1994 and 1980 to 1984 samples.

per year. We also assume that contribution margins will continue to rise at this same rate during the current decade. Hence, over the full 20-year life cycle, target contribution margins are expected to rise from 42% in year one, to 48% by year 20, with a mean contribution margin of 45% over the full life cycle.

While we constrained margins to average 45% over the life cycle, we also recognise, as in our earlier analyses, that promotion and marketing expenditures are concentrated in the launch phases of the life cycle. In our prior analysis, we developed the following allocation rule based on a regression analysis of promotional and marketing outlays: promotion and marketing is equal to sales in year 1, declines to 50% in year 2, and falls to 25% in year 3. We retained this assumed pattern on marketing outlays in the present analysis. Interviews with industry participants indicated that the initial post-launch years continue to be the primary focus of marketing and promotion activities.

An analysis performed by Rosenthal et al.[18] indicates that the drug industry's marketing expenses to sales ratios have remained relatively stable around 14% in the 1996 to 2000 period. However, there were some important compositional shifts over this period. The direct-to-consumer advertising to sales ratio increased from 1.2% to 2.2% between 1996 and 2000, at the expense of physician detailing and hospital medical journal advertising.[18]

For the current analysis, we did make one relatively minor change in the allocation and timing of marketing expenditures related to launch. In particular, we estimated pre-marketing launch expenditures in the order of 5 and 10% of first year sales in the 2 years immediately prior to launch. These marketing expenditures are for activities such as pre-launch meetings and symposiums, pricing and focus group studies, and sales force training. Our assumptions concerning the size and timing of these expenditures were guided by a recent survey report on pre-launch marketing expenditures by industry consultants as well as interviews with some of the participating companies.[19]

As indicated above, our model is structured so that margins average 45% over the full product life cycle. Given the assumed pattern of launch expenditures, contribution margins for each product are below representative industry values in the first 3 years of marketing. However, as a product matures, both promotional and administrative costs decline in relative terms, and contribution margins increase over average industry values in the later years of the life cycle.

The model is also structured to provide for capital expenditures on plant and equipment (P&E). As in our model for the 1980s cohort, we assumed overall capital expenditures for P&E to be equal to 40% of tenth year sales. Half of these outlays are assumed to occur in the first 2 years before marketing and the other half during the initial 10 years of the product's market life. These assumptions imply an average capital investment to sales ratio of 3.3% over the full product life cycle. This is generally consistent with data from pharmaceutical industry income statements.

In particular, we checked the reasonableness of our assumptions by comparing this implied 3.3% capital investment to sales ratio with the corresponding ratios observed on industry income statements during the 1990s. We found that the drug industry capital investment to sales ratio averaged about 7.0% during the 1990s. However, the latter value includes investment for R&D as well as production, marketing and administrative facilities. In our model, provisions for capital investment in R&D facilities are included in the cost estimates provided by DiMasi et al.[5] Accordingly, we asked some industry members involved with strategic planning for information on what percentage of their P&E expenditures was devoted to R&D, versus other firm activities. We obtained a range of 40 to 50% of total capital expenditures devoted to R&D. Given this range, the capital investments to sales ratio for non-R&D activities implied by our model is consistent with the observed data from company income statements.

For working capital, it was assumed that accounts receivables are equal to 2 months of annual sales and inventories are 5 months of sales (valued at manufacturing cost). These are also based on the analysis of balance sheet data of major pharmaceutical firms. Working capital is recovered at the end of the final year of product life.

Effective Tax Rates

Our analysis of returns is conducted on an after-tax basis. In our prior studies of returns, we computed average effective tax rates based on analysis of income statement data from eight major pharmaceutical firms. The average effective rate was 35% for the 1970s cohort and 33% for the 1980s cohort. A comparable analysis for the 1990s cohort yielded an effective tax rate of 30%. This is the rate used in our baseline case. The difference between the nominal corporate tax rate (34%) and the average effective tax rate of 30% reflects various credits and deferrals such as the R&D tax credit and manufacturing tax credits for plants in Puerto Rico.[2]

After-tax cash flows are also influenced by the tax treatment of depreciation. In our analysis, cash flow in each year is equal to after-tax profits, plus depreciation charges. Accelerated depreciation, as specified in the US tax code, results in tax deferrals and positive cash flow in the early years of a product's market life. This reverses in the latter years of a product's life.

Summary of Economic Values

Table II provides a summary of the key economic inputs to IRR and NPV analysis for the 1990 to 1994 NCEs cohort compared with the corresponding values for the 1980 to 1984 cohort. R&D investment levels have roughly doubled in real terms, in both uncapitalised as well as capitalised dollar terms. On the revenue side of the equation, sales-life curves have shifted upward significantly. This is reflected in higher peak sales for the 1990 to 1994 cohorts ($US458 million compared with $US345 million for 1980 to 1984 NCEs). While sales have not grown at the same rate as R&D costs, contribution margins have increased in the 1990s, implying higher operational profits from a given level of sales. How all these factors balance out from a returns-on-investment standpoint is a major issue addressed in the analysis that follows. The industry's cost of capital, effective tax rate, and capital investment-to-sales ratio have changed only marginally for the current cohort compared with the 1980s sample.

Table II suggests that R&D investment expenditures are growing over time relative to sales revenues and the other activities of pharmaceutical

Table II. Key economic values for internal rate of return analysis for the 1990 to 1994 versus 1980 to 1984 new chemical entities (NCEs)

Economic parameter	1990 to 1994	1980 to 1984
Average R&D costs[a]		
pre-tax uncapitalised	$US416 mil	$US196 mil
after tax capitalised	$US480 mil	$US251 mil
Peak sales for mean NCE[a]	$US458 mil	$US345 mil
Contribution margin[b]	45%	40%
Cost of capital	11%	10.5%
Effective tax rate	30%	33%
Capital-to-investment sales ratio	3.3%	3.4%

a R&D costs and sales are all expressed in 2000 values.

b Average contribution margins over the full product life cycle; launch costs are concentrated in early phases of life cycle, so margins are lower in initial years and higher in later years.

mil = millions; **R&D** = research and development.

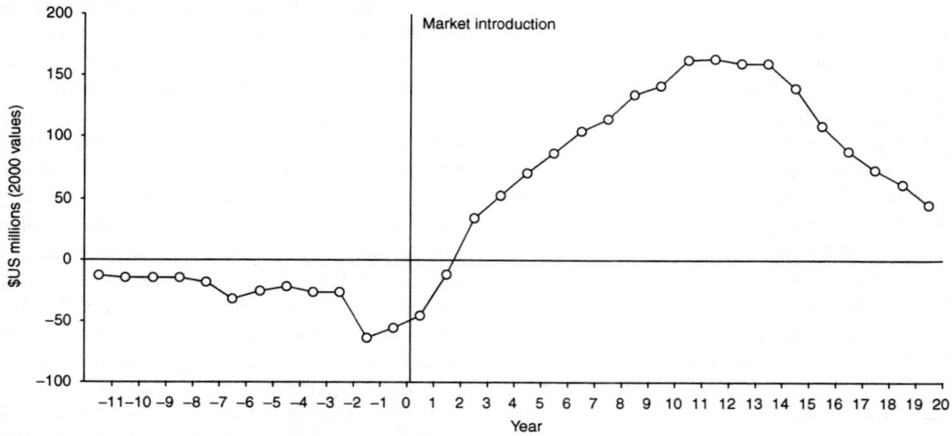

Fig. 5. Cash flows over the product life cycle: baseline case.

firms. This issue is discussed further in 'Drug Innovation and Industry Evolution Since 1970'. This increase in industry research intensity can be interpreted both as a response to increasing profit opportunities from new drug research as well as an equilibrating factor bringing returns in line with the industry cost of capital. This makes the question of industry returns on new drug introduction in the 1990s a particularly interesting question to analyse at the present time.

Empirical Results

The Baseline Case

Using the data and assumptions described above, we constructed the pattern of cash flows for the mean of our sample of 118 NCEs shown in figure 5. The R&D phase lasts for 12 years and results in a stream of negative cash flows. The first years of marketing, years 1 and 2, are also characterised by negative cash flows. This is because of heavy promotion and advertising expenditures during the product launch period. Cash flows rise to a peak in year 12 and then begin to decline. The decline becomes steeper as patent expiry and generic competition begin.

The baseline case results are shown in the first row of table III. The IRR is 11.5% and can be compared with our real cost-of-capital estimate of 11%. Hence, the industry mean performance is positive but only by a small amount. The present value of net revenues at the date of marketing is $US525 million and can be compared with the present value of R&D costs at the same point in time, or $US480 million. This leads to an NPV of $US45 million.

The results for the baseline case for the 1990 to 1994 NCEs are roughly the same as for our earlier 1980 to 1984 sample. In the 1980 to 1984 baseline case, the IRR was 11.1% compared with a cost of capital of 10.5%. The 1990 to 1994 IRR is similarly about a half percentage point above the cost-of-capital estimate.

Sensitivity Analysis

Given the uncertainty surrounding many of the key parameters that affect the IRR and NPV, we have performed a sensitivity analysis for a number of the parameters. These results are reported in table III.

An important parameter is the contribution margin. As discussed earlier, we examined data for a number of firms during the 1990s and found that the average margin increased from 42 to 45%. We then projected a continuing increase in the margin until year 20, i.e. we assumed an increase from 42 to 48% by year 20, yielding an average of 45%. Hence, for the sensitivity analysis, we calculated the IRR and NPV for average margins of 40 and 50% – in both cases the upward trend of the base case was maintained. For example, for the lower margin case we assumed that the margin increased from 37 to 43% by year 20.

The IRR varied significantly from 10.6 to 12.4% as the average margin varied from 40 to 50%. Similarly, the NPV ranged from a negative $US31 million to $US120 million. It should be noted that for the first 10 years or so of product life the margin is based on real data – it is the last 10 years that are more uncertain and difficult to predict. Hence, the range of change in outcomes is perhaps overstated.

The next parameter that we examine in table III is the tax rate. The base case is 30% and we calculate the effect of tax rates of 25% and 35%. Clearly, changing the tax rate results in quite small changes in the IRR and NPV.At 25% the IRR is 11.6% and at 35% it is 11.4% – compared with the base IRR of 11.5%. This relative insensitivity of the IRR to the tax rate reflects the fact that this rate affects the R&D cost and revenue sides of the equation in a parallel fashion.

The effect of generic competition in eroding pioneer brand sales after patent expiry has tended to become greater over time. In the US, generic market shares in terms of pills sold increased from 35% one year after generic entry in the period immediately following the 1984 Hatch-Waxman Act to 64% in the mid-1990s.[6] Europe is also experiencing a rising trend in generic competition.[17] As a result, it is difficult to predict the degree of sales loss in the future. To examine this problem, we assumed two alternative scenarios: that the sales losses of the pioneer brands after patent expiry were 25 and 50% greater than what was assumed in the base case. Figure 6 shows these alternative sales erosion patterns.

Given that the effect of these sales losses occurs in the later stages of the product life cycle, the effect is made smaller when measured in present value terms. The IRR falls modestly from 11.5% in the base case to 11.4% and 11.3% in the 25% and 50% greater erosion cases, respectively. Similarly, the NPV falls from $US45 million in the base case to $US33 million and $US20 million.

Varying the cost-of-capital results in significant changes in the NPVs. A 10% cost of capital would result in an NPV of $US131 million, considerably larger than the base case using the 11% cost of capital of $US45 million. A 12% cost of capital, on the other hand, leads to a negative NPV of

Table III. Returns to 1990 to 1994 new chemical entities

Case	Present value cash flows (after-tax)[a]	Present value R&D costs (after tax)[a]	NPV[a,b]	IRR (%)
Baseline[c]	525.2	480.3	45.0	11.5
At 40% margin	449.8	480.3	(30.5)	10.6
At 50% margin	600.7	480.3	120.4	12.4
At 25% tax rate	571.3	514.6	56.7	11.6
At 35% tax rate	479.2	446.0	33.2	11.4
At 25% greater sales decline after patent life	512.9	480.3	32.7	11.4
At 50% greater sales decline after patent life	500.7	480.3	20.4	11.3
At 10% cost of capital	586.8	455.7	131.1	
At 12% cost of capital	470.0	506.7	(36.8)	
At 1-year reduction in regulatory review time	525.2	437.7	87.5	12.2

a Present value cash flows, present value R&D costs and NPV are shown in $US millions (2000 values).

b Parentheses indicate negative values.

c Baseline case assumes 11% cost of capital, tax rate of 0.30 and margin of 0.45.

IRR = internal rate of return; **NPV** = net present value; **R&D** = research and development.

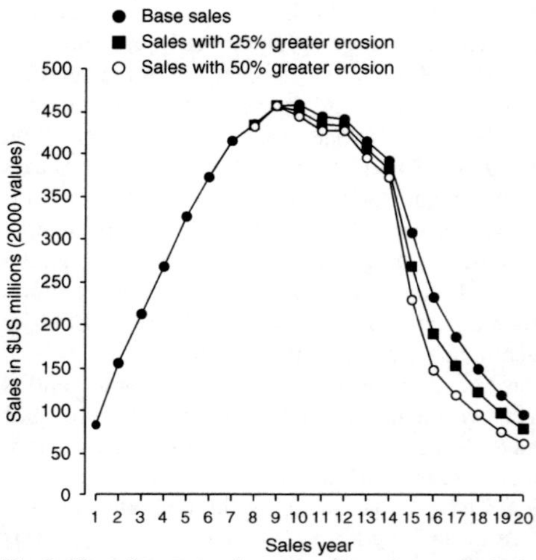

Fig. 6. Alternative assumptions regarding sales erosion in the post-patent period.

$US37 million. These changes are comparable in magnitude to those observed for changes in the contribution margin.

The final sensitivity analysis in table III is the effect of reducing regulatory review time by 1 year. This involves a change in the average regulatory review time from 18 months to 6 months. Our approach is to simply shorten the R&D period by 1 year and compute the lower capitalised value of R&D at the date of marketing. This reduces R&D from $US480 million to $US438 million; hence, the base NPV rises from $US45 million to $US88 million. The IRR increases from 11.5% to 12.2%. These are clearly significant effects.

This sensitivity analysis captures only the direct effects of shorter FDA review times on the capitalised value of R&D costs. We abstracted from any potential benefits associated with a longer effective patent life. As we have explained elsewhere, under the 1984 Hatch-Waxman Act most drugs are eligible for compensatory increases in effective patent life equal to any time lost in regulatory review. Consequently, it is only for a smaller subset of drugs where the patent restoration time is constrained where shorter regulatory review times would increase effective patent life (for example, because there is a maximum of 5 years on the patent life restored under the Act). We abstracted from these potential secondary benefits in the above sensitivity analysis

Distribution of Returns

In figure 7, we show the decile distribution of present values of returns for the 1990 to 1994 samples of NCEs. These returns are gross R&D costs. The deciles are constructed on the basis of the ranking of the 118 NCEs in terms of their individual present values of returns. The average sales of the top decile of NCEs are then used to calculate the present value of returns for the top decile, and so forth.

The graph shows that the distribution is highly skewed. For example, the top decile has an estimated present value of $US2.7 billion. This is almost 6 times the present value of average R&D costs ($US480 million). The top decile alone accounts for about 52% of the total present value generated by all ten deciles. This is comparable to the value of 46% that we found in our 1980 to 1984 study.

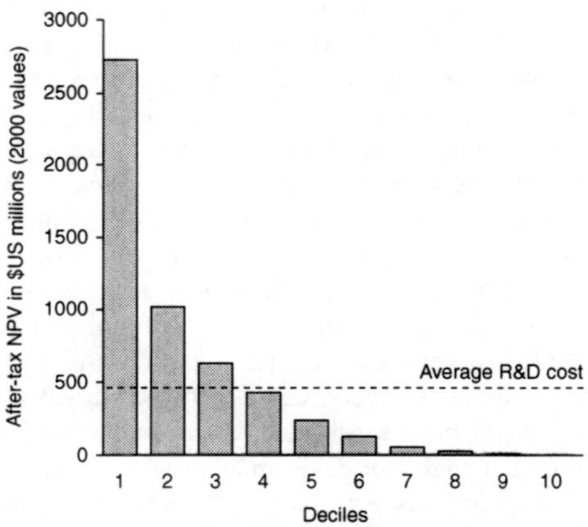

Fig. 7. Present values by decile for 1990 to 1994 new drug introductions. **NPV** = net present value; **R&D** = research and development.

It is also true that the second and third deciles have present values that exceed average R&D costs, or $US1 billion and $US0.6 billion, respectively. However, the fourth decile's present value is only $US433 million in comparison with average R&D costs of $US480 million. A detailed analysis of the present value for the individual NCEs shows that 34% or about one-third of the NCEs have present values in excess of the average R&D cost. By the time one gets to the median drug, present values are significantly below R&D costs.

A further illustration of the importance of top-ranked NCEs to industry returns can be demonstrated by removing the very top-ranked drug from the analysis. That is, we will eliminate Zocor®[3] (simvastatin), thereby reducing the sample from 118 to 117, and re-calculate the mean present value of returns. The result is that the present value falls from $US525 million to $US479 million, and the NPV falls from $US45 million to a negative $US1 million. Hence, if it were not for this one 'blockbuster' drug, the average NCE of the 1990 to 1994 cohort would essentially just break even in terms of an NPV analysis.

We should observe that the fact that most drugs in our sample have present values substantially below the fully allocated R&D cost does not mean that these drugs are not economically important. Since the average R&D cost includes an allocation for drugs that drop out during the development process, an 'unprofitable' drug that more than covers variable costs going forward contributes positively to the firm's bottom line. Many of the uncertainties that exist for a new product (i.e. its clinical profile in terms of risks and benefits, the introduction of substitute products, the size of market demand, etc.), are usually not resolved until late in the R&D process. At this point, most of the R&D costs are sunk. Therefore, it is still worth getting the incremental revenues of these smaller selling drugs, if they can cover their expected variable costs going forward. Over the long run, however, a firm must have its share of products in the top few deciles to have a viable R&D programme.

Figure 8 provides a comparison of the distribution of returns for all four sample cohorts that we have examined to date: 1970 to1974, 1975 to 1979, 1980 to 1984 and 1990 to 1994. The vertical axis in this graph shows the percentage of overall returns that each decile accounts for in its sample cohort. The drug industry has exhibited a high degree of skewness over all four sample cohorts spanning this 25-year period. In this regard, the top decile has accounted for between 46 and 54% of the overall returns over the four sample cohorts that we have analysed. Scherer and colleagues have shown that a high degree of skewness is typical of several different populations of technological innovations, including the outcomes of venture backed start-ups, university licensed patents and venture backed companies in the initial period after their initial public offerings.[20]

Drug Innovation and Industry Evolution Since 1970

As discussed in the introductory section, this is the third study of the industry returns on R&D that we have performed. The three studies employ the same general methodology. Consequently, they provide a convenient window to view the industry's development over the critical period from 1970 through the 1990s.

Trends in Industry Returns and R&D Expenditures

In table IV, we provide a summary of the mean internal return observed for our sample beginning with the 1970 to 1974 cohort and ending with the 1990 to 1994 period. The first column in table IV shows that the IRR has increased steadily from 7% for the 1970 to 1974 sample to 11.5% for 1990 to 1994 introductions. The biggest incremental change occurred during the second half of the 1970s and the first half of the 1980s. Over this time period, the mean return increased from 7.0% to 9.7% and then to 11.1%, respectively.

3 Tradenames are used for identification purposes only and do not imply product endorsement.

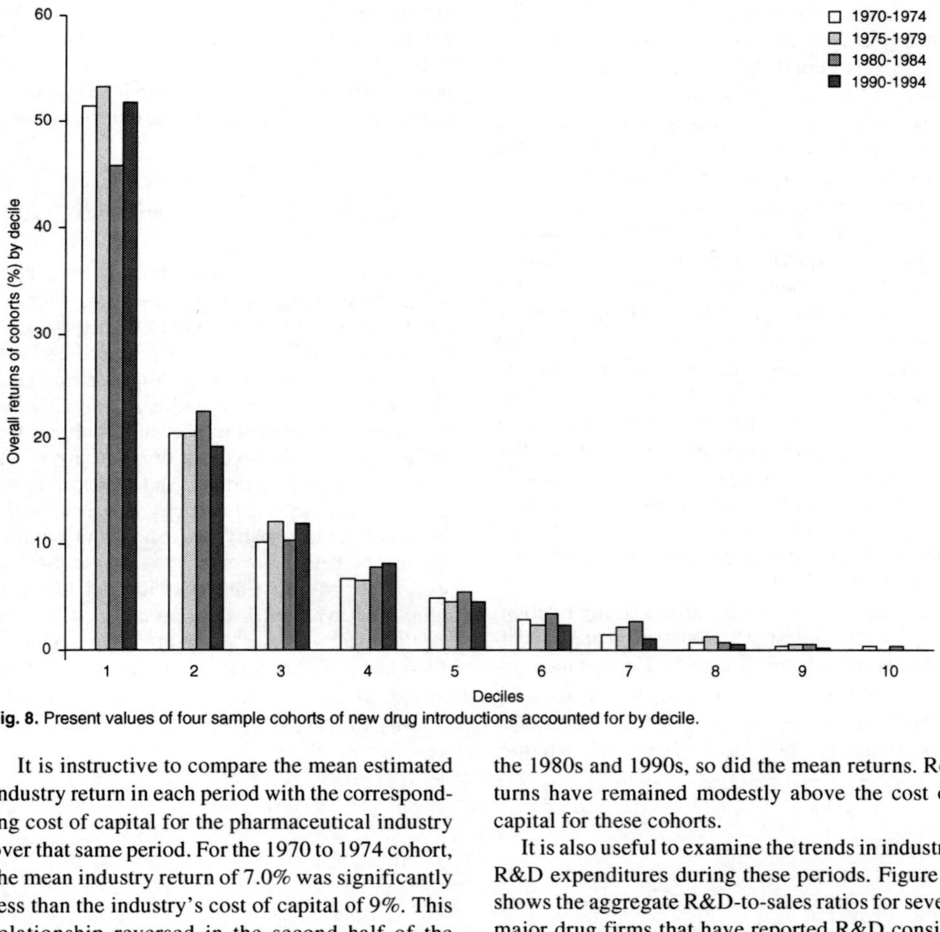

Fig. 8. Present values of four sample cohorts of new drug introductions accounted for by decile.

It is instructive to compare the mean estimated industry return in each period with the corresponding cost of capital for the pharmaceutical industry over that same period. For the 1970 to 1974 cohort, the mean industry return of 7.0% was significantly less than the industry's cost of capital of 9%. This relationship reversed in the second half of the 1970s (with a 9.7% IRR versus a 9% cost of capital). While the industry cost of capital increased in the 1980s and 1990s, so did the mean returns. Returns have remained modestly above the cost of capital for these cohorts.

Table IV. Mean industry returns and cost of capital for different time cohorts of new chemical entities (NCEs)

NCE cohort	Mean IRR	Cost of capital
1970 to 1974	7.0%	9.0%
1975 to 1979	9.7%	9.0%
1980 to 1984	11.1%	10.5%
1990 to 1994	11.5%	11.0%

IRR = internal rate of return.

It is also useful to examine the trends in industry R&D expenditures during these periods. Figure 9 shows the aggregate R&D-to-sales ratios for seven major drug firms that have reported R&D consistently over the complete period 1962 to 1994.[21] This graph shows that the R&D-to-sales ratios for these firms declined in the period 1962 to 1974, stabilised in the second half of the 1970s, and then began a steep increase from 1980 to 1994. The R&D-to-sales ratios for these firms grew from 7% in 1980 to 13% in 1994.

Scherer has recently examined long-term trends in industry R&D expenditures and profit margins for the period 1962 to 1996.[3] He finds a 0.96 rank correlation in the deviations from trends in this industry's expenditures and profit margins over this 35-year period. His results also indicate that R&D expenditures and profit margins in the pharmaceutical industry generally grew at a slower rate relative to the long-run trend until the late 1970s, when they began a steep upward track.

These findings suggest that a beneficial competitive cycle may be at work in the pharmaceutical industry. In particular, R&D investment has not only led to innovation and profits in the form of the highly skewed distribution of returns observed here, but profits, or the expectation of profits, has produced expanding R&D investment. In this latter regard, Grabowski and Vernon also find that industry profit expectations on R&D, as well as internal cash flows, are highly significant explanatory variables of R&D investment outlays.[21] This type of competitive feedback cycle can be viewed as socially beneficial given the extensive literature on the high social returns from pharmaceutical R&D.[22,23]

Scherer has characterised the strong relationship between industry R&D investment and profitability, in conjunction with the fact that mean industry returns are only modestly above the industry cost of capital, as evidence of a 'virtuous rent seeking model'.[3] If this is a correct interpretation of the industry's competitive behaviour, the data on long-term trends suggest that the late 1970s represented a key turning point in terms of both industry returns and the growth in R&D expenditures. This issue is explored further in the next section.

The Pattern of Drug Innovation Since 1970

A number of pharmaceutical industry studies found diminishing returns to R&D characterised the 1960s and 1970s compared with the earlier post-war period.[24,25] The earlier period had witnessed a wave of important drug introductions. This involved many new antibiotic drugs, hydrocortisone and several other corticosteroids, the thiazide diuretics and β-blocker drugs for hypertension, new classes of anxiolytics and antidepressants, and the initial birth control drugs. However, by the early 1970s, the industry was experiencing diminishing returns in many of the drug classes that had seen major advances in the 1950s and 1960s. A number of hypotheses were investigated, including the effects of more stringent FDA regulations, diminishing technological opportunities and increased product liability. Some scholars saw the industry entering a prolonged period of technological maturity.[26]

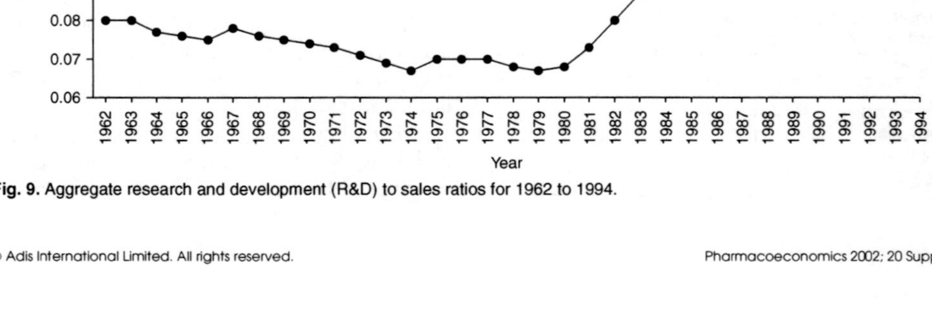

Fig. 9. Aggregate research and development (R&D) to sales ratios for 1962 to 1994.

Finding new drugs that were advances over established drugs had clearly become increasingly costly and more problematical by the early 1970s. Many of the leading firms began to focus their R&D activities on new therapeutic targets and approaches. One important concept that took root during this period was the 'rational drug-design' approach to R&D. This involved the use of x-ray crystallography and other techniques to design specific compounds that could block particular receptor sites and thereby create desired therapeutic responses. The primary approach to discovering new drug therapies prior to this time involved the random screening of compounds against a small number of known targets.

An important milestone for the industry occurred in 1978 with the introduction of Tagamet® (cimetidine) by SmithKline. This drug was not only a significant advance in the treatment of ulcers, but also provided validation of the 'rational drug design' approach to R&D. Tagamet was the first of the histamine H_2 receptor inhibitors. It was specifically designed to block H_2 histamine receptors, which were known to affect the process of acid secretion. Within a few years, it had become the largest selling drug worldwide. This drug by itself had a disproportionate effect on the returns for the full portfolio of 1970s new drug introductions. Indeed, when this one drug was removed from the portfolio of 1970 to 1979 drugs, the average present value for the remaining compounds declined by 14%.[2] Tagamet was eventually replaced by another H_2 blocker, Zantac® (ranitidine), as the largest selling drug worldwide. Zantac® became the top selling drug in our 1980 to 1984 cohort of NCEs.[1]

The 2.5 decades that have elapsed since the introduction of Tagamet® in 1978 have witnessed an impressive renaissance in drug innovation that is reflected in the trends toward higher returns and R&D intensities over this period. Table V provides a list of several important new chemical classes of drugs that were first introduced between 1978 and 1994. These classes all represent a new approach to, or mode of action in, treating particular diseases or indications. The pioneering drugs in these classes are concentrated in the very top deciles of the sample cohorts for which we have analysed returns. Many of these drugs have been the subject of specific cost-benefit and pharmacoeconomic studies.

Table V also provides information on the various indications and disease categories to which these new drug classes are targeted. There are many diseases listed that previously had few or inadequate drug treatments (i.e. herpes, AIDS, ovarian cancer, migraine, schizophrenia, etc.). The list also includes several novel biotech drugs such as erythropoietin (used to treat anaemia in patients undergoing kidney dialysis, and in those with AIDS or cancer) and the α- and β-interferons used in the treatment of cancer and multiple sclerosis. Several of the new classes of drugs listed in table V provide medical and economic benefits in the form of better patient tolerability and adverse-effect profiles in the treatment of widespread medical problems (i.e. hypertension, cholesterol reduction, depression, etc.).

Looking forward, the drug industry is currently confronted with a new wave of technological opportunities. The mapping of the genome and related advances in fields such as bioinformatics have led to an abundance of potential new targets for disease intervention. These advances could have profound effects on the discovery process itself, the size of clinical trials and the nature of demand for pharmaceutical products.[27] However, it remains unclear how quickly these new technologies will result in important new drug therapies and how they will influence industry returns. In this regard, a recent report by Lehman Brothers foresees a negative impact on returns until at least the latter part of this decade, when the substantial required buildup in R&D investments should begin to bear fruit.[28] If this is so, the industry could be facing another crossroads in the immediate future as the transition to new R&D paradigms compounds already existing economic pressures from the healthcare sector, financial markets, and government officials.

Table V. Important new drug classes 1978 to 1994

Year	Class	Early entrants	Indication
1978	H_2 receptor antagonists	Tagamet® (cimetidine), Zantac® (ranitidine)	Ulcers
1981	ACE inhibitors	Capoten® (captopril), Vasotec® (enalapril)	Hypertension
1982	Calcium channel blockers	Procardia® (nifedipine), Calan® (verapamil)	Hypertension
1982	Nucleosides	Zovirax® (acyclovir), Famvir® (famciclovir)	Herpes virus
1983	Interleukin-2 inhibitors	Sandimmune® (cyclosporin A)	Transplantation
1985	Human growth hormones	Protropin®, Humatrope®	Human growth hormone deficiency
1986	Quinolones	Noroxin® (norfloxacin), Cipro® (ciprofloxacin)	Antibiotic
1986	Interferon alphas	Intron A® (interferon α-2b), Roferon A® (interferon α-2a)	Cancer
1987	Statins	Mevacor® (lovastatin), Pravachol® (pravastatin)	Cholesterol reduction
1987	Nucleoside reverse transcriptase inhibitors	Retrovir® (zidovudine), Videx® (didanosine)	AIDS
1988	Serotonin reuptake inhibitors	Prozac® (fluoxetine), Zoloft® (sertraline)	Depression
1989	Proton pump inhibitors	Prilosec® (omeprazole), Prevacid® (lansoprazole)	Ulcers
1990	Erythropoietin	Epogen® (epoetin-α), Procrit® (epoetin-α)	Anaemia
1990	Macrolides (semi-synthetic)	Biaxin® (clarithromycin), Zithromax® (azithromycin)	Antibiotic
1990	Bis-triazoles	Diflucan® (fluconazole)	Antifungal
1991	Serotonin 5-HT_3 antagonists	Zofran® (ondansetron), Kytril® (granisetron)	Antiemetic
1992	Granulocyte colony stimulating factors	Neupogen® (filgrastim)	Cancer adjunct
1993	Taxoids	Taxol® (paclitaxel), Taxotere® (docetaxel)	Ovarian cancer
1993	Interferon-betas	Betaseron® (interferon β-1b), Avonex® (interferon β-1a)	Multiple sclerosis
1993	Serotonin 5-HT_1 antagonists	Imitrex® (sumatriptan), Zomig® (zolmitriptan)	Migraine
1994	D_2/5HT_2 antagonists	Risperdal® (risperidone)	Schizophrenia

a Tradenames are used for identification purposes only and do not imply product endorsement.

Summary and Conclusions

Consistent with our prior studies, a primary finding of the current analysis is that the distribution of returns for 1990 to 1994 new drug introductions is highly skewed. In this regard, only one-third of the new drug introductions had present values in excess of average R&D costs. The top decile of compounds by itself accounted for more than 50% of the present value of post-launch returns generated by the full sample of introductions.

From an industry perspective, the estimated mean return for the 118 new drug introductions in the 1990 to 1994 period was 11.5%. This compares with a real cost of capital of 11% for this sample cohort. At this cost of capital, the mean introduction earned an NPV of $US45 million ($US, 2000 values). A sensitivity analysis showed that returns are robust to changes in the economic parameters and assumptions. Changes in contribution margins and R&D times had the most impact on returns.

The principal results are, therefore, similar in nature to our study of 1980 to 1984 new drug introductions – namely, that R&D in pharmaceuticals is characterised by a highly skewed distribution of returns and a mean industry IRR modestly in excess of the cost of capital. However, the pattern of change on the inputs into our analysis shows a number of dynamic forces at work in this industry. In particular, R&D investments per new drug introduction approximately doubled compared with the 1980 to 1984 period. At the same time, the number of new introductions, the average sales per introduction and industry contribution margins increased significantly in the 1990s compared with the 1980s.

Our studies of industry returns provide support for what has been labelled a 'virtuous rent seeking model' of R&D competition in the pharmaceutical industry. Since the end of the 1970s, the industry has experienced rapid growth in R&D outlays and the introduction of many important new therapeutic classes and blockbuster compounds. At the same time, mean industry returns on R&D over this period have only modestly exceeded the industry's cost of capital. Whether this beneficial cycle of increasing R&D intensities and innovative new product introductions will continue into the future remains to be seen. There are currently a number of promising new developments in the pharmaceutical R&D process, but the benefits from these technologies have an uncertain time horizon and it is likely they will require substantial increases in industry R&D investments. How quickly these evolving new technologies will lead to important new medicines will depend not only on scientific and economic factors, but also on the course of public policy actions.

Acknowledgements

This paper was supported by an unrestricted grant from the Program in Pharmaceuticals and Health Economics at Duke University. We are indebted to a number of individuals who commented on prior versions of this paper, including Mike Scherer, Dennis Mueller, Bill Comanor, Patricia Danzon, Vivian Ho, Mike Morissey, David Grabowski, Robert Helms, Adrian Towse, Paul Meyer, and Steve Propper. Any errors that remain in the manuscript are the responsibility of the authors.

The Program receives support from various foundations, health sector entities and pharmaceuticals firms.

References

1. Grabowski H, Vernon J. Returns to R&D on new drug introductions in the 1980s. J Health Econ 1994; 13: 383-406
2. Grabowski H, Vernon J. A new look at the returns and risks to pharmaceutical R&D. Manage Sci 1990; 36 (7): 167-85
3. Scherer FM. The link between gross profitability and pharmaceutical R&D spending. Health Aff 2001; 20 (5): 136-40
4. Shulman S, Healy EM, Lasagna L, editors. PBMs: reshaping the pharmaceutical distribution network. New York: Haworth Press, 1998
5. DiMasi JA, Hansen RW, Grabowski HG. The price of innovation: new estimates of drug development costs. J Health Econ 2002. In Press
6. Congress of the United States. Congressional Budget Office. How health care reform affects pharmaceutical research and development. Washington: US Government Printing Office, Jun 1994
7. Congress of the United States. Congressional Budget Office. How increased competition from generic drugs has affected prices and returns in the pharmaceutical industry. Washington: US Government Printing Office, Jul 1998
8. Grabowski H, Vernon J. The distribution of sales revenues from pharmaceutical innovation. Pharmacoeconomics 2000; 18 Suppl. 1: 21-32
9. Myers SC, Shyum-Sunder L. Measuring pharmaceutical industry risk and the cost-of-capital. In: Helms RB, editor. Competitive strategies in the pharmaceutical industry. Washington (DC): AEI Press, 1996: 208-37
10. US Congress, Office of Technology Assessment Pharmaceutical R&D. Costs, risks and rewards. Washington (DC): US Government Printing Office, 1993
11. Myers SC, Howe CD. A life-cycle financial model of pharmaceutical R&D: working paper; program on the pharmaceutical industry. Cambridge (MA): MIT, 1997
12. Poterba JM, Summers LH. A CEO survey of US companies time horizons and hurdle rates. Sloan Manage Rev 1995; Fall: 43-53
13. DiMasi J, Hansen R, Grabowski H, et al. The cost of innovation in the pharmaceutical industry. J Health Econ 1991; 10: 107-42
14. Thomas LG. Industrial policy and international competitiveness in the pharmaceutical industry. In: Helms B, editor. Competitive strategies in the pharmaceutical industry. Washington (DC): AEI Press, 1996: 107-129
15. Annual report: the Med Ad News 500: the world's best-selling medicines. Med Ad News 2001; 20 (5)
16. Grabowski H, Vernon J. Effective patent life in pharmaceuticals. Int J Technol Manag 2000; 19: 98-120
17. Burstall ML, Reuben BG, Reuben AJ. Pricing and reimbursement regulation in Europe: an update of the industry perspective. Drug Inf J 1999; 33: 669-88
18. Rosenthal MB, Berndt ER, Donohue JM, et al. Promotion of prescription drugs to consumers. N Engl J Med 2002; 346 (7): 498-505
19. Best Practices LLC. Global marketing launch: an executive summary. Chapel Hill, NC (USA): Best Practices, Feb 2000. Available on the web with associated reports from: URL: http://internet8.eapps.com/bestp/domrep
20. Scherer FM, Harkoff D, Kudies J. Uncertainty and the size distribution of rewards from technological innovation. J Evolut Econ 2000; 10: 175-200
21. Grabowski H, Vernon J. The determinants of pharmaceutical research and development expenditures J. Evolut Econ 2000; 10: 201-15
22. Cutler DM, McClellan M. Is technological change in medicine worth it? Health Aff 2000; 20 (5): 11-29
23. Lichtenberg FR. Are the benefits of newer drugs worth their cost?.: evidence from the 1996 MEPS. Health Aff 2000; 20 (5): 241-51

24. Grabowski H. Drug regulation and innovation. Washington: AEI Press, 1976
25. Baily MN. Research and development costs and returns: the US pharmaceutical industry. J Pol Econ 1972; 80 (1): 70-85
26. Scherer FM. Technological maturity and waning economic growth. Arts and Sciences 1978; 1: 7-11
27. Anderson WH, Fitzgerald CQ, Manasco PK. Current and future applications of pharmacogenomics. New Horiz 1999; 7 (2): 262-29
28. The fruits of genomics: drug pipelines face indigestion until the new biology ripens. New York: Lehman Brothers, Jan 2001

Correspondence and offprints: Dr *Henry Grabowski*, Department of Economics, 314 Social Sciences, Duke University, Box 90097, Durham, NC 27708, USA.
grabow@econ.duke.edu

[9]

American Economic Review 2010, 100:1, 590–607
http://www.aeaweb.org/articles.php?doi=10.1257/aer.100.1.590

The Effect of Medicare Part D on Pharmaceutical Prices and Utilization

By Mark Duggan and Fiona Scott Morton*

Prescription drug expenditures represent the most rapidly growing component of health care spending, increasing from 5 percent of health care spending in 1980 to more than 10 percent by 2005 (Centers for Medicare and Medicaid Services (CMS) 2007a). Further, almost 60 percent of all prescriptions in the United States are filled for beneficiaries of Medicare, Medicaid, and other government programs. Rapid innovation in new pharmaceuticals has contributed substantially to quality of life and longevity in the US (Frank Lichtenberg 1996). These facts, combined, indicate that government procurement schemes are critical both in determining government expenditure on pharmaceuticals and in stimulating innovation of new treatments.

In this paper, we show that the institutions and mechanisms used by the government to purchase prescription drugs can strongly affect market outcomes. By institutions, we have in mind large buyer groups, structured incentives for patients to consume certain products, and the development and use of formularies. A formulary is a mechanism that allows a buyer to identify a therapeutically similar treatment as a viable substitute for a patented treatment, and to create price competition due to the ability to substitute away from the more expensive product. When bargaining with the seller of a patented product, the ability to shift demand to a substitute drug is a powerful negotiating tool.

Our paper provides evidence for what we consider a surprising outcome: in the case of the new prescription drug program for Medicare enrollees, moving consumers from cash-paying status to membership in an insured group *lowers* optimal prices for branded prescription drugs below what they otherwise would be. This is surprising because the standard effect of insurance is to create inelastic demand and therefore elicit higher prices from a seller with market power (Duggan and Scott Morton 2006). However, the insurers that we study bundle insurance with a formulary and other mechanisms to create elastic demand. An individual consumer typically does not know which drugs are acceptable therapeutic substitutes; the consumer's physician typically has poor knowledge of prices, especially negotiated prices; and any one consumer is too small a share of demand to negotiate with a pharmaceutical company. A prescription drug plan can potentially surmount all three hurdles.

Our evidence leads us to conclude that the formulary and other mechanisms perform the special role of allowing buyers to move market share among drugs with patent protection, thereby raising cross-price elasticities and lowering purchase prices (or reducing price increases) for branded drugs. This result contrasts with the common intuition that an uninsured consumer,

* Duggan: Department of Economics, University of Maryland, 3105 Tydings Hall, College Park, MD 20742 (e-mail: duggan@econ.bsos.umd.edu); Scott Morton: Yale School of Management, Box 208200, New Haven, CT 06520-8200 (e-mail: fiona.scottmorton@yale.edu). We thank Abigail Alpert, Tamara Hayford, and Patrick Healy for outstanding research assistance. We are also grateful to the editor and two anonymous referees, as well as Steve Berry, Jay Bhattacharya, Judith Chevalier, Judith Hellerstein, Melissa Kearney, Jeanne Lafortune, and seminar participants at Columbia University, Duke University, University of Maryland, Stanford University, Syracuse University, University of Toulouse, the NBER, and the 2008 AEA meetings for helpful comments. We are grateful to Merck and Co. for providing us IMS data, and to IMS for giving permission for us to use their data. This project was supported by National Science Foundation research grant 0518858, "The Effect of Government Procurement of Pharmaceuticals." The opinions contained herein are those of the authors and not necessarily of any funding agency.

paying at the margin for her own purchases, is the best tool with which to create competition in the market and impose pricing discipline on sellers. Certainly, this reasoning is at least part of the rationale behind many current policies in health care such as tax-free health care savings accounts (R. Glenn Hubbard, John F. Cogan, and Daniel P. Kessler 2005). Our evidence suggests that this picture is incomplete; for maximum effect, the consumer also needs to be part of a group that can substitute one provider for another.

Our setting is the recent significant increase in government intervention in the pharmaceutical industry represented by Medicare Part D. For the first 40 years of its existence after its creation in 1965, the Medicare program provided virtually no coverage for beneficiaries' prescription drug costs outside of treatments such as cancer drugs administered in a doctor's office or hospital. But as prescription drug expenditures increased much more rapidly than other health care spending in recent years, the political pressure built for Medicare to cover prescription drugs. In December 2003, the Medicare Prescription Drug Improvement and Modernization Act created Medicare Part D, which would begin providing coverage for prescription drug costs in January of 2006 for those Medicare recipients who chose to enroll.

Part D is the largest expansion of Medicare since the program's inception and has been projected to cost $780 billion over its first ten years (2006–2015).[1] This feature alone made the program controversial at the outset. Not only is Part D a very large entitlement program, it significantly expands the role of the government as a buyer of prescription pharmaceuticals. Governments outside the United States use their power as large buyers to pay relatively low prices for new, patent-protected medications. In contrast, Part D is set up so that the government does not directly purchase drugs, but rather subsidizes participating private prescription drug plans, which then negotiate with pharmaceutical companies over drug prices.

Part D can also be contrasted to Parts A and B of Medicare, in which the CMS sets prices for each covered service and reimburses providers directly per service.[2] In Part D, CMS pays the participating plan a lump sum per enrollee and has no control over the prices paid to pharmaceutical manufacturers by the plan or the prices charged to enrollees by the plan. Instead, the legislation creates competition among plans for the business of enrollees, which is intended to drive drug prices and premiums to competitive levels. Each Medicare recipient can choose between the plans offered in her area based on the drugs covered, the prices of those drugs, the monthly premium, and other plan parameters.

In the empirical work below, we investigate the effect of Medicare Part D on the price and utilization of branded pharmaceutical treatments. Theoretically, the program could either increase or decrease prices paid to pharmaceutical companies. On the one hand, once enrolled in Part D, enrollees who had previously been uninsured would have a lower elasticity of demand than before, leading to an increase in the manufacturers' profit-maximizing prices for drugs with market power.[3] On the other hand, Part D plans could exclude certain treatments from their formulary or steer their enrollees away from certain treatments in response to the prices of those treatments, which a cash-paying individual could not typically do on her own. This could give these plans a strong lever with which to negotiate price reductions from pharmaceutical manufacturers. We are also interested in the effect of the program on utilization.[4] In addition to any ex-manufacturer price effect, the insurance provided by Part D would lower beneficiaries' out-of-pocket prices, and therefore affect utilization (Teresa Gibson, Ronald Ozminkowski, and Ron Goetzel 2005).

[1] See the "Medicare Trustees Report," http://www.cms.hhs.gov/reportstrustfunds/downloads/tr2006.pdf.

[2] Hospital inpatient reimbursement in Part A depends both on the patient's diagnosis and on the treatment.

[3] See Nina Pavcnik (2002) for evidence on the effect of cost sharing on firms' profit-maximizing prices.

[4] Recent research by Wesley Yin et al. (2008) and Lichtenberg and Shawn Sun (2007) suggests that Part D did increase utilization, although the authors of both studies utilize data from just one pharmacy chain to estimate this.

Our estimation strategy exploits variation across branded drugs in their pre-Part D Medicare market shares to estimate the effects of Part D on pharmaceutical prices and utilization. Our first set of results strongly suggests that Medicare Part D led to a substantial relative decline in average branded pharmaceutical prices. In other words, though branded prescription drug prices trend upward from 2003 to 2006, brands with high sales to consumers eligible for Medicare Part D experienced significantly lower average price increases than other brands.

Additionally, our estimates reveal that the effect is driven by the consumption of drugs by Medicare recipients *without insurance before Part D*. It appears to be the movement of Medicare recipients from cash-paying uninsured status to insured under a plan that causes the relative decline in per unit prices. The most plausible mechanism driving this result is not the insurance per se, but the activities of the insurer.

However, for therapeutic classes with just one or two brands, plans would not be able to move market share to therapeutic substitutes because legislation required them to cover all drugs in small classes. Consistent with this prediction, our analyses show that prices do not decline in relative terms for brands with zero or only one substitute in a class.

Combining our results with the mechanical effect of Part D on out-of-pocket prices, we expect that the average cost of prescription drugs for an uninsured Medicare recipient with average prescription drug spending fell substantially. In light of this, it is not surprising that our results suggest a substantial increase in utilization among Medicare-intensive drugs, although our estimated coefficients for utilization are not precisely estimated.

Our findings come with an important caveat: we analyze only the first year of Part D. This is a complex program in which both regulators and firms are learning over time and coping with moral hazard, adverse selection, technological change, and political pressure. It is plausible, for example, that pharmaceutical manufacturers have not yet fully adjusted to the policy change, and thus more work is clearly warranted to estimate the medium- and-long term effect of the program.

The outline of the paper is as follows. In the next section, we provide background on the Medicare program and on key features of Part D and discuss the effect of Part D on pharmaceutical firms' profit-maximizing prices. Section II describes our data and the construction of our sample of drugs. In the following two sections we specify our empirical framework, summarize our main results, and describe how our estimates vary across therapeutic categories. The final section concludes.

I. Background on, and Incentive Effects of, Medicare Part D

A. *Institutional Background*

While there are several components to the Medicare Prescription Drug Improvement and Modernization Act (MMA), the most important is the creation of Medicare Part D, which provides insurance coverage for prescription drug costs to Medicare recipients who voluntarily enrolled in the program beginning in January of 2006. This legislation also created the Medicare Discount Drug Card Program, which took effect in early 2004 and was designed to help Medicare recipients receive discounts on their prescriptions during the two-year window prior to the commencement of Part D.

In contrast to Parts A and B of the program, Part D benefits are provided through one of two types of private insurance plans.[5] The first type, known as a Prescription Drug Plan (PDP), provides coverage only for prescription drug costs, while Medicare Advantage Plans (MA-PD)

[5] For a detailed discussion, please see Duggan, Patrick Healy, and Scott Morton (2008).

insure all Medicare-covered services, including hospital care, physician services, and prescription drugs.[6]

A plan "sponsor" contracts with CMS to offer a plan in one (or more) of the 34 defined regions of the United States. Plans are allowed to have a formulary that excludes certain drugs from coverage, though they are required to have at least two drugs on the formulary for each therapeutic class.[7] Furthermore, a plan cannot exclude treatments from any of six protected classes (e.g., HIV antiretrovirals, cancer drugs) from the formulary. The actuarial value of the benefits offered by a plan must be at least as generous as those specified in the 2003 MMA legislation. In the 2006 calendar year this included a deductible of $250, a 25 percent co-pay for the next $2,000 in spending, no coverage for the next $2,850 (this is often referred to as the "doughnut hole"), and a 5 percent co-pay once out-of-pocket expenditures reach $3,600. These figures change annually. Plans are financed through a combination of enrollee monthly premiums and subsidies from the federal government.

To enroll in Part D, a Medicare recipient can choose among those plans offered in her region of the country. When making this choice, the recipient would consider the plan's monthly premium, the drugs included on the formulary, the prices of those drugs, and service quality.[8] Dual eligibles, who are Medicare recipients also enrolled in the means-tested Medicaid program, were required to enroll in a Part D plan, although their premiums, co-pays, and deductibles were heavily subsidized by the government. In January of 2007, approximately 36 percent of the 17.3 million PDP enrollees were automatically enrolled in a PDP because they were also on Medicaid (6.3 million) and an additional 13 percent of enrollees (2.2 million) were eligible for low-income subsidies that reduce out-of-pocket costs.

B. *Part D's Impact on Manufacturers' Incentives*

Given the significance of the changes in insurance coverage described above, and the particular structure of drug procurement for this program, it seems plausible that Medicare Part D had an impact on prices and quantities in the pharmaceutical sector. To simplify the theoretical discussion, we assume that the market for Part D plans is perfectly competitive. In every region in the United States there are at least 27 plans competing for local Part D enrollees. While the market is more concentrated than this number would suggest,[9] in this paper we will nevertheless abstract from the issue of whether plans have market power.

If plans are effectively not setting the market price for a patented brand, it is the brand's manufacturer that is choosing prices before and after the Part D program. To fix ideas, suppose that all Medicare enrollees have no coverage prior to Part D and must pay cash for their prescription drugs, but then enroll in Part D when it begins. Notice that when this group paid cash for prescription drugs, its members were not able to create effective price competition between drugs by threatening to switch to a therapeutic substitute. Once in Part D, however, these consumers were represented by a PDP. The result of the change in institutional structure is an increase in the cross-price elasticity of substitution for this group. For a number of common models of demand, as consumers' elasticity of substitution rises, the optimal price for the drug falls.[10] A second

[6] To reduce the likelihood that Part D would crowd out existing prescription drug coverage to retired workers by their former firms, CMS subsidized those firms that continued to provide this insurance.

[7] See Haiden Huskamp et al. (2003) for evidence on the effect of formularies on consumers' utilization of pharmaceutical treatments. The findings suggest that formularies can substantially alter treatment patterns.

[8] See Kosali Simon and Claudio Lucarelli (2006) for an examination of the determinants of plans' monthly premiums.

[9] The top three plans (UHC-Pacificare, Humana Inc., and Wellpoint, Inc.) accounted for 50 percent of Part D enrollment in 2006 (Kaiser Family Foundation 2007).

[10] For a specific model, please see Duggan and Scott Morton (2008).

effect comes from the fact that the group is now subsidized at 75 percent of the cost of the drug in the main coverage region and at 95 percent in the catastrophic region.[11] Sensitivity to price falls and this causes the optimal price to increase. In this setting, we see there are two effects working in opposite directions, and thus it is ultimately an empirical question that dominates.

Consumers with private insurance or those who continue to be uninsured do not experience these changes upon the implementation of Part D.[12] If the average price that we measure in the data comprised sales to consumers who move from uninsured to Part D and consumers who experience no change in demand, we would see a change in the average price of brands that depends on the fraction of that drug purchased by cash-paying but Part D–eligible consumers, as well as the change in price those consumers pay. The empirical strategy of the paper is to use data on average price and the fraction of a drug's sales to Part D–eligible consumers to back out the price changes caused by Part D.

There is one possible spillover between Part D and the private market that might cause private price changes caused by Part D to be nonzero. When dual eligibles move from Medicaid to Medicare, they shift from purchasing through a fairly inelastic purchaser (the state) to a more elastic purchaser (the PDP).[13] Because the inelastic Medicaid demand pays whatever market price is chosen by the manufacturer, a reduction in Medicaid demand might lower the optimal price for the brand in the private market (see Duggan and Scott Morton 2006). If a drug's dual share is zero, this effect will not be present. We investigate this issue in our empirical analyses below.

According to Part D regulations, there are six "protected" therapeutic classes in which each PDP must be less aggressive with their formularies than in other classes.[14] While a PDP cannot exclude any drug in a protected category, it can create financial incentives or administrative hurdles to affect a patient's choice of drug. We do not know whether the restrictions applied to these classes have a measurable impact on the behavior of PDP because in the first year of the program it was not clear how much CMS would oversee formularies. If restrictions are binding, their effect will be to reduce Part D's effect on the substitutability among drugs in these classes and therefore reduce the PDP's ability to extract manufacturer discounts.

Similarly, CMS required that all PDPs include at least two drugs in each therapeutic class and at least one in each Formulary Key Drug Type (FKDT), which is a finer category than class. A class/FKDT with only one or two brands in it will create a challenge for any PDP bargaining for low prices. The CMS regulations limit the PDPs' ability to substitute away from drugs in the class, and presumably the manufacturers of these drugs are aware of their market power. We expect that drugs in these two situations (protected or "small" categories) will have small or negligible changes in cross-price elasticities. We modify our specification to allow for different effects for drugs in this less competitive environment.

Taken together, we predict an ambiguous effect of Medicare Part D on average pharmaceutical prices, with the sign depending on whether the policy-induced reduction in the elasticity of demand more than offsets any plan-induced increase in substitutability across treatments. This latter effect should be less important for brands in one of the six protected therapeutic categories and for those brands that are one of just one or two treatments in a class/FKDT. Furthermore,

[11] The subsidy depends on an enrollee's total prescription drug expenditures. As expenditures rise, an enrollee moves from 100 percent (deductible), to 25 percent, to 100 percent (doughnut hole), to 5 percent (catastrophic region) cost sharing.

[12] Spillovers in negotiation from an insurer's private plans to their Part D plans are prohibited by the legislation.

[13] It is worth noting that many states were negotiating for supplemental rebates based on state-level Medicaid formularies by 2005, so they are not completely unresponsive to price.

[14] All products in the HIV, anticancer, anticonvulsant, immunosuppressant, antipsychotic, and antidepressant categories must be included in all Part D formularies.

to the extent that Part D reduces Medicare recipients' out-of-pocket costs, it should lead to an increase in overall utilization that is increasing in the drug's Medicare market share. We investigate these issues in the empirical analyses below.

II. Data and Constructing the Analysis Sample

A. *IMS Health*

To estimate the impact of Medicare Part D on our outcome variables of interest, we begin by merging data from two sources. The first was obtained from IMS Health and contains data on total sales (excluding those to hospitals and long-term care) for all pharmaceutical products in the United States in each year from 2001 to 2006. The data also contain the number of standardized units of the product that were sold and the average number of units per daily dose in each year. This allows us to calculate the average price per day and the number of daily doses in each year for each product.[15] In calculating both prices and quantities, we aggregate sales for all versions of the same drug in each year.

B. *Medical Expenditure Panel Survey*

Our second main source of data is the Medical Expenditure Panel Survey (MEPS), a publicly available dataset constructed annually by the Agency for Healthcare Research and Quality (AHRQ). In carrying out this survey, AHRQ collects data from a nationally representative sample of the civilian noninstitutionalized population residing in the United States and asks questions about prescriptions filled during the year, as well as demographic characteristics and insurance coverage. We use this dataset to calculate a brand's Medicare Market Share (MMS), which is the proportion of its consumers enrolled in Medicare.

For each reported prescription, the Prescribed Medicines file lists the drug name, the total amount paid, the amount paid out of pocket and the amount paid by each of ten possible sources of insurance, a person-level identifier, and a person-level weight. In the 2003 MEPS data (the same year in which the Medicare Modernization Act was signed into law), there are 304,324 prescriptions reported by 20,475 individuals. To increase our precision in measuring drug-specific Medicare market shares and related explanatory variables of interest, we utilize both the 2002 and 2003 versions of the MEPS Prescribed Medicines file.[16]

Using the person-level identifier, this data on the utilization of prescription drugs can then be linked to the MEPS Full Year Consolidated Data File (CDF), which includes the person's age and information about her health insurance coverage. One question summarized in the CDF portion of the survey asks whether the respondent was ever enrolled in Medicare during the 2003 calendar year. The weighted fraction answering yes to this question is 14.4 percent, which is much greater among those age 65 and older (98.8 percent) than among the nonelderly (2.2 percent). Because Medicare recipients have substantially greater utilization of prescription drugs than their counterparts not in the program, their fraction of prescriptions (40.3 percent) is almost three times greater than their share of the population.

The Prescribed Medicines file also has information on the source of payment for each prescription. The first column of Table 1 summarizes this information for all prescriptions, while

[15] Note that the prices we use in our estimation are not the posted prices at the drugstore, but the revenues of each drug divided by units sold from invoice data.

[16] This approximately doubles the number of prescriptions for the typical drug in our sample. The Medicare shares in 2002 and 2003 are very strongly correlated, with a correlation of 0.92.

TABLE 1—SOURCE OF PAYMENT FOR PRESCRIPTIONS IN THE 2003 MEPS

	All	Medicare	All other
Average total paid per prescription (US$)	69.5	69.9	69.2
Percent paid out of pocket	44.9	50.9	40.5
Percent paid by private insurance	34.5	19.8	45.2
Percent paid by Medicaid	12.4	13.9	11.3
Percent paid by VA	3.3	5.8	1.5
Percent paid by Medicare	3.3	7.8	0.0
Percent paid by TRICARE	1.1	1.2	1.0
Percent paid by other insurance	0.5	0.5	0.5
Total number of prescriptions	298,293	129,990	168,303

columns 2 and 3 differentiate between those with and without Medicare coverage, respectively. In 2003 Medicare recipients paid approximately 51 percent of the cost out of pocket, while those not on Medicare paid substantially less, at 41 percent. The table also reveals that Medicare recipients received much less coverage from private insurers in that year (20 versus 45 percent) but this was partially made up for by greater coverage from public insurance including Medicaid, the Department of Veterans Affairs, and Medicare.[17]

The variation across drugs in the fraction of individuals taking the drug who were eligible for Part D prior to its enactment (and subsequently may have enrolled in it) is critical to the identification strategy of the paper. According to the 2003 MEPS, this variation is substantial. For example, Zoloft, an antidepressant drug that is ranked fifth in terms of sales in the IMS data, has a Medicare market share of 27.1 percent. The corresponding value for Plavix, which is used primarily by those at risk of heart attack or stroke and was ranked sixteenth in terms of sales in that same year, is 72.9 percent.

C. *Constructing the Analysis Sample*

The MMA was signed into law on December 8, 2003. Medicare Part D did not begin operation, however, until more than two years later, in January 2006. During that interim period, the federal government created the Medicare Discount Drug Card Program. One stated goal of this program was to aid Medicare recipients in receiving lower prices for their prescriptions. Thus, MMA may have influenced both pharmaceutical prices and utilization before Part D took effect in 2006. In addition, if the optimal price for a drug was going to change significantly upon the initiation of Part D, a manufacturer may have wanted to adjust the drug's price gradually over time so as to avoid the publicity associated with a sharp price change. We therefore use 2003 as our base year when estimating the effect of the program.

We focus initially on the top 1,000 drugs in the IMS data according to their 2003 sales, which account for 97 percent of the $196 billion in total sales in that same year. We then drop over-the-counter (OTC) drugs and generics,[18] although we later control for the presence of generic competition for the branded drugs in our sample. This exclusion leaves us with a sample of 693 drugs

[17] Recall that Medicare did cover the cost for certain prescription drugs, such as cancer treatments, in this time period.

[18] Of the top 1,000 products, 113 were available over the counter in 2006; these drugs would not be covered by Medicare Part D plans and would also rarely appear in the MEPS Prescribed Medicines file that we use to construct Medicare market shares. We next drop the 194 remaining drugs that are generic, given that there will typically be many manufacturers for each of these drugs and firms would have significantly less pricing power.

that currently or previously enjoyed patent protection, with these treatments accounting for 87 percent of the $196 billion in 2003 spending in our IMS data. We then merge these IMS data on sales and utilization in each year from 2001 to 2006 to the MEPS data on Medicare market shares, with 125 of these 693 treatments dropped from our sample because they do not appear in the MEPS.[19] This leaves us with a sample of 568 drugs that account for 79 percent of total 2003 IMS spending.

One limitation to our focus on the top-selling brand drugs in 2003 is that any drug introduced in 2004 or later or that was not in the top 1,000 sellers in 2003 will not be included in our analyses. Additionally, generic drugs or drugs sold over the counter are not included in our sample. Thus, to the extent that Part D plans influenced the price or utilization of these other products, our main analyses of the top-selling brand drugs will not capture these effects.

D. *Identifying Protected Classes and Therapeutic Substitutes*

Our model predicts a different response to the program from both drugs in the protected classes and drugs without substantial therapeutic competition. To identify the former we rely on IMS drug classifications. To determine which drugs were the only treatments, or one out of just two in the therapeutic class, we consulted a list of top-selling drugs and link it to the US pharmacopoeia and CMS therapeutic classes and FKDT.[20] Recall, PDP are required to "cover" at least two drugs per class and at least one in each FKDT.

III. Empirical Framework and Main Results

The IMS data described above provide us with total sales by product in each year from 2001 to 2006. We can also estimate the number of daily doses for each product by dividing the total quantity (in standardized units) in each year by the corresponding average number of standardized units per daily dose in each year. This allows us to form an estimate of the average price per day for each product. We use these data to estimate specifications of the following type:

$$(1)\qquad \Delta P_{j,2003-6} = \alpha_1 + \beta_1 MMS_{j,2003} + \mu_1 Yrs_{j,2003} + \delta_1 AnyGeneric_{j,2006} + \varepsilon_{1j,2003},$$

$$(2)\qquad \Delta Q_{j,2003-6} = \alpha_2 + \beta_2 MMS_{j,2003} + \mu_2 Yrs_{j,2003} + \delta_2 AnyGeneric_{j,2006} + \varepsilon_{2j,2003},$$

with j indexing drugs and $\Delta P_{j,2003-6}$ ($\Delta Q_{j,2003-6}$) equal to the change in price (quantity) for drug j from 2003 to 2006. As described above, we focus on this three-year change because the legislation that created Part D was enacted in December 2003, but plans did not start enrolling beneficiaries until January 2006.

The explanatory variable of particular interest in this specification is $MMS_{j,2003}$, which represents our estimate of the Medicare market share for drug j using the MEPS Prescribed Medicines files from 2002 and 2003. This is defined to be equal to the fraction of prescriptions filled in 2002 and 2003 for individuals who were ever enrolled in the program during the same year.[21] This specification, which uses one observation per drug, exploits the variation across drugs in their tendency to be used by Medicare recipients. Given that total utilization and average prices

[19] There are two plausible reasons for this. First, MEPS does not include prescriptions that are administered in a physician's office or other institutional setting. Second, MEPS captures approximately 1 out of every 10,000 prescriptions in a typical year and thus some products with small patient populations may not be included.

[20] One version of this can be found at http://www.usp.org/pdf/EN/mmg/drugListTableV3.0.pdf.

[21] In calculating this Medicare market share, we use the person weights in the MEPS.

for the same drug may vary over the life cycle of the drug and can be affected by the presence of generic competition, we also control for the number of years that the drug has been on the market ($Yrs_{j,2003}$) and for whether the drug faces generic competition ($AnyGeneric_{j,2006}$).[22]

It is worth noting that average prices tend to move fairly steadily in our data, and tend to trend up. In contrast, average quantities fluctuate much more due to the entry of therapeutic substitutes, new generations of medicines, clinical news, and other factors we do not observe. Additionally, average quantities in our sample decline from 2003 to 2006, primarily because we restrict attention to drugs that were the top sellers in 2003.

To interpret our estimates for β_1 and β_2 as the causal effects of Medicare Part D on the outcome variable of interest, we are assuming that there are no omitted factors that are correlated with the Medicare market share, and that also influence the change in the outcome variable of interest.[23] Over the short period of this study, that assumption seems reasonable to us. By taking first differences of average prices or total utilization, we remove any unobserved time-invariant differences across drugs.

A. *The Impact on Average Prices*

An examination of the distribution of average price and the change in average prices for the drugs in our analysis sample reveals that they are highly skewed to the right. For example, the change in the average price from 2003 to 2006 for the drugs in our sample has a skewness of more than 12. Thus, following recent research on pharmaceutical prices (Duggan and Scott Morton 2006), we take the log of the average price, which is much more symmetrically distributed and has a skewness of approximately zero.[24] This has intuitive appeal as well, as prices are likely to change proportionally rather than by a fixed dollar amount in response to common factors that affect prices in this sector. With this transformation, we are essentially exploring whether the growth rate of pharmaceutical prices is significantly different on average for Medicare-intensive drugs following the enactment of Part D.

Table 2 summarizes the results from several specifications similar to equation (1) above. In this equation, we exclude 20 of the 568 drugs described above because they either have no sales in 2006 or are missing the year of FDA approval. We weight the observations in each specification by the number of prescriptions in the MEPS to account for the fact that the precision of our estimate for MMS_j will vary across drugs. The estimate of -0.128 for β_1 in the first column, in which no other explanatory variables except a constant are included, suggests that the introduction of Part D reduced the growth rate of pharmaceutical prices by an average of approximately 12 percentage points, with this estimate significant at the 5 percent level. However, because the coefficient on the constant term α_1 is equal to 0.134, this finding suggests that average prices for Medicare Part D recipients remained essentially unchanged, while those for other consumers increased by an average of 13 percent. Our estimates indicate that a drug moving from zero to 100 percent MMS would have price growth drop from 13 percent to 1 percent.

[22] As demonstrated in a previous version of this paper (Duggan and Scott Morton 2008), our results for both price and quantity changes are similar if we control for the preexisting trend for the outcome variable of interest.

[23] In this paper we will not consider insurance-induced changes in practice patterns of physicians, the introduction of new drugs, and similar general equilibrium effects, as is done in Daron Acemoglu et al. (2006), Amy Finkelstein (2007), and Amy Finkelstein and Robin McKnight (2008), in which the authors looks at the effect of the introduction of Medicare. See also David Cutler (1995) and Leemore Dafny (2005) for related research on the effect of other important changes to the Medicare program, or David Card, Carlos Dobkin, and Nicole Maestas (2008) and Ahmed Khwaja (2008) for research on the effect of Medicare coverage.

[24] We inflation-adjust 2003 prices to 2006 dollars using the consumer price index for urban consumers (CPI-U).

TABLE 2—THE IMPACT OF MEDICARE PART D ON THE CHANGE IN AVERAGE PHARMACEUTICAL PRICES FROM 2003–2006

		Dependent variable: Δ log(price per day$_{j,2003-6}$)					
	μ (σ)	(1)	(2)	(3)	(4)	(5)	(6)
Medicare market share$_{2002-03}$	0.348	−0.128**	−0.127**	−0.138**	−0.136**	−0.133**	−0.143***
	(0.264)	(0.057)	(0.057)	(0.056)	(0.056)	(0.056)	(0.054)
Years on the market$_{2003}$	10.95		0.000	0.001	0.001	0.001	0.002
	(7.36)		(0.002)	(0.002)	(0.002)	(0.002)	(0.002)
Any generic competition	0.381		0.005	0.010	0.010	0.011	−0.008
	(0.486)		(0.023)	(0.023)	(0.023)	(0.023)	(0.022)
Constant	—	0.134	0.128	0.127	0.126	0.125	0.127
	—	(0.026)	(0.028)	(0.028)	(0.028)	(0.028)	(0.032)
Observations	548	548	548	538	517	517	200
R^2	—	0.016	0.016	0.024	0.024	0.024	0.049
Outliers excluded?	No	No	No	Yes	Yes	Yes	Yes
Cancer drugs excluded?	No	No	No	No	Yes	Yes	Yes
RX or spending MMS?	RX	RX	RX	RX	RX	Spending	RX
Top 200 only	No	No	No	No	No	No	Yes

Notes: Each column summarizes the results from specifications of the change in the log price per daily dose on the explanatory variables listed in the first column. The unit of observation is the drug, and the sample is constructed as described in Section IIC. Specifications 1 through 4 and specification 6 use the share of a drug's prescriptions purchased by Medicare-enrolled individuals, while specification 5 uses the share of spending for that drug. Specifications 3 through 6 drop those observations with values of the dependent variable in the top 1 percent or the bottom 1 percent of the distribution. Specifications 4 through 6 exclude 21 cancer and immunosuppressant drugs. Specification 6 limits to just the top 200 drugs. Heteroskedasticity-robust standard errors are included in parentheses. The mean and standard deviation of the dependent variable are equal to 0.087 and 0.349, respectively.

***Significant at the 1 percent level.
**Significant at the 5 percent level.
*Significant at the 10 percent level.

The magnitude of our estimate for β_1 is almost identical, at −0.127 in the next specification, in which we add the control variables described above. This estimate increases slightly to −0.138 and remains significant at the 5 percent level in the third specification, in which we exclude outliers that are in the top 1 percent or bottom 1 percent of the log price change (from 2003 to 2006) distribution.

The MEPS Prescribed Medicines files do not include information for drugs administered in a physician's office or clinic. The most common are injectable chemotherapy treatments. One might therefore be concerned that estimates for the Medicare market share for the cancer drugs that are in the sample are inaccurate. In the fourth specification we exclude these 21 treatments and obtain a very similar estimate for β_1.

One potential concern with our estimate for the Medicare market share is that it weights all prescriptions equally. We therefore introduce an alternative measure of the Medicare market share in the fifth specification which represents the fraction of total spending on the drug accounted for by Medicare recipients. The statistically significant estimate of −0.133 for β_1 using this measure is virtually identical to the previous estimates. In the next specification we consider only the top 200 drugs, as we did in our previous work for the Medicaid program, and find that our estimate for β_1 increases to −0.143 and is significant at the 1 percent level.

Taken together, our results indicate that average prices increased by significantly less from 2003 to 2006 for drugs sold differentially to Medicare recipients. When interpreting these estimates, it is important to consider that many Medicare recipients already had insurance for prescription drug costs prior to the enactment of Medicare Part D. To the extent that the price effects were driven only by those enrolling in Part D plans, the estimates for β_1 will understate Part D's average impact on pharmaceutical prices. We explore this issue in more detail below.

B. *The Impact of Part D on the Utilization of Prescription Drugs*

Medicare Part D reduced the out-of-pocket price of pharmaceutical treatments beyond the effects discussed above through an additional channel—the mechanical effect of the insurance coverage. For example, the typical plan in 2006 covered 75 percent of the first $2,000 in prescription drug costs once a person had reached their annual deductible of $250. Additionally, Medicare recipients enrolled in Part D pay just 5 percent of their costs once their out-of-pocket spending reaches $3,600. Because Part D reduced both the gross price of prescription drugs and the share of that price paid by Medicare recipients, one would expect average utilization of these treatments to have increased.

To investigate the effect of Part D on the total utilization of prescription drugs, in this section we estimate quality specifications that are analogous to those in the preceding section for prices. In this case, the dependent variable is equal to the change in the log of the number of daily doses from 2003 to 2006, with the mean and standard deviation of this variable in the sample equal to −0.62 and 1.12, respectively.[25]

The results from these specifications are summarized in Table 3. The estimate of 0.516 for β_2 in the first specification, in which only the Medicare market share and a constant are included, is positive but statistically insignificant, with a p-value of 0.108. In the next specification, we include the number of years that the drug had been on the market as of 2003 and a control for the presence of generic competition. The estimates for the coefficients on the first of these variables is statistically insignificant, while the estimate for δ_2, the coefficient on $AnyGen_{j,2006}$, is significantly negative with a t-statistic of −5.5. This is consistent with previous evidence that use of branded drugs declines substantially once they face generic competition. The estimates of β_2 in the next five columns, which summarize specifications analogous to those for price changes, are similar in magnitude, although in all cases the estimates are statistically insignificant.

The large estimates for δ_2 in specifications two through six of Table 3 suggest that utilization changes among drugs that face generic competition are substantially ditterent from those that do not. To increase the comparability of the drugs included in our sample, in specification 7 we focus on just the 318 drugs in our sample that did not face generic competition by 2006. While smaller in magnitude than the previous estimates, the estimate of 0.265 for β_2 in this specification is significant at the 10 percent level.

To gauge the plausibility of these results, it is instructive to obtain a back-of-the-envelope estimate of the implied elasticity of prescription drug purchases for the 318 drugs in our sample. For a Medicare recipient with average prescription drug spending, the effective co-pay would be 25 percent. Adding to this a 12 percent average reduction in gross prices suggests almost an 80 percent reduction in the out-of-pocket cost *on the margin* for purchases in the coverage area. Combining this with the estimated effect on utilization in column (7), our results suggest an elasticity of approximately −0.38, which falls within the range of drug elasticity estimates from other contexts cited in a recent review article (Gibson et al., 2005).

[25] Utilization is on average declining because we are focusing on top-selling drugs in 2003. Many of these treatments will have seen declines in spending in the subsequent three years.

TABLE 3—THE IMPACT OF MEDICARE PART D ON THE CHANGE IN RX UTILIZATION FROM 2003 TO 2006

		Dependent variable: Δ log(daily doses$_{j,2003-06}$)						
	μ (σ)	(1)	(2)	(3)	(4)	(5)	(6)	(7)
Medicare market share$_{2002-03}$	0.348 (0.264)	0.516 (0.320)	0.434 (0.320)	0.381 (0.313)	0.389 (0.316)	0.321 (0.313)	0.517 (0.470)	0.265* (0.137)
Years on the market	10.95 (7.36)		−0.004 (0.010)	−0.001 (0.011)	−0.001 (0.011)	−0.001 (0.011)	0.007 (0.017)	−0.023*** (0.007)
Any generic competition?	0.381 (0.486)		−1.072*** (0.191)	−1.084*** (0.191)	−1.087*** (0.192)	−1.088*** (0.193)	−1.199*** (0.243)	
Constant	—	−0.826 (0.161)	−0.251 (0.169)	−0.228 (0.164)	−0.235 (0.164)	−0.208 (0.166)	−0.292 (0.246)	0.001 (0.112)
Observations	548	548	548	538	517	517	200	318
R^2	—	0.009	0.262	0.293	0.294	0.293	0.318	0.108
Outliers excluded?	No	No	No	Yes	Yes	Yes	Yes	Yes
Cancer drugs excluded?	No	No	No	No	Yes	Yes	Yes	Yes
RX or spending MMS?	RX	RX	RX	RX	RX	Spending	RX	RX
Top 200 only	No	No	No	No	No	No	Yes	No
Exclude if face gen comp?	No	No	No	No	No	No	No	Yes

Notes: Each column summarizes the results from specifications of the change in the log number of daily doses on the explanatory variables listed in the first column. The unit of observation is the drug. and the sample is constructed as described in Section IIC. Specifications 1 through 4 and specifications 6 and 7 use the share of a drug's prescriptions purchased by Medicare-enrolled individuals, while specification 5 uses the share of spending for that drug. Specifications 3 through 7 drop those observations with values of the dependent variable in the top 1 percent or the bottom 1 percent of the distribution. Specifications 4 through 7 exclude 20 cancer and immunosuppressant drugs. Specification 6 limits to just the top 200 drugs and specification 7 considers only those sample drugs that do not face generic competition. Heteroskedasticity-robust standard errors are included in parentheses. The mean and standard deviation of the dependent variable are equal to −0.56 and 1.13, respectively.

***Significant at the 1 percent level.
**Significant at the 5 percent level.
*Significant at the 10 percent level.

IV. Heterogeneity in Part D's Impact on Pharmaceutical Prices and Utilization

A. *Differentiating between Insured and Uninsured Medicare Recipients*

We begin this section by investigating whether the price effects estimated above also vary with the baseline insurance coverage of Medicare recipients. The shift from being uninsured into a Part D plan may have affected prices by placing individuals paying with cash into a large group that could bargain over prices, increasing their effective sensitivity to price differences. Second, the dual eligibles enrolled in both Medicare and Medicaid were required to switch from Medicaid drug coverage to a Medicare Part D plan. As recent research has demonstrated (Duggan and Scott Morton 2006), the procurement rules used by Medicaid distort prices upward, suggesting that a shift out of Medicaid may have reduced prices.

The specifications summarized in Table 4 shed light on this issue. In column 1, we report the results from our baseline specification that excluded the 21 cancer and 10 outlier treatments and was summarized in the preceding section. Column 2 presents the results from an analogous specification in which we differentiate between the Medicare self-pay and Medicare insured market shares as follows:

TABLE 4—THE IMPACT OF MEDICARE MARKET SHARE: DIFFERENTIATING BETWEEN THOSE WITH AND WITHOUT RX INSURANCE

		Δ log(price per day$_{j,2003-06}$)			Δ log(daily doses$_{j,2003-06}$)			Δ log(total revenues $_{j,2003-06}$)	
	μ (σ)	(1)	(2)	(3)	(4)	(5)	(6)	(7)	(8)
Medicare market share$_{2002-03}$	0.345 (0.262)	−0.136** (0.056)			0.389 (0.316)			0.273 (0.314)	
Medicare self-pay share$_{2002-03}$	0.213 (0.191)		−0.225*** (0.070)	−0.243*** (0.077)		0.461 (0.424)	0.379 (0.449)		0.247 (0.438)
Medicare insured share$_{2002-03}$	0.132 (0.134)		0.059 (0.156)			0.232 (0.881)			0.330 (0.860)
Dual eligible share$_{2002-03}$	0.043 (0.076)			−0.182 (0.274)			−0.914 (1.674)		
Other medicare insured share$_{2002-03}$	0.089 (0.107)			0.190 (0.305)			0.850 (1.216)		
Years on the market	10.9 (7.3)	0.001 (0.002)	0.001 (0.002)	0.001 (0.002)	−0.001 (0.011)	−0.001 (0.011)	−0.001 (0.011)	−0.002 (0.011)	−0.002 (0.011)
Any generic competition	0.385 (0.487)	0.010 (0.023)	0.011 (0.023)	0.010 (0.023)	−1.087*** (0.192)	−1.088*** (0.193)	−1.096*** (0.194)	−1.071*** (0.187)	−1.071*** (0.187)
Constant	— —	0.126 (0.028)	0.115 (0.030)	0.118 (0.028)	−0.235 (0.164)	−0.226 (0.180)	−0.211 (0.179)	−0.107 (0.164)	−0.111 (0.178)
Observations	517	517	517	517	517	517	517	517	517
R^2	—	0.024	0.027	0.033	0.294	0.294	0.297	0.293	0.293

Notes: Specifications 1 through 3, 4 through 6, and 7 through 8 summarize the results from specifications of the change in the log price per daily dose, the log number of daily doses, and the log of product revenues, respectively, that use the explanatory variables listed in the first column. The unit of observation is the drug, and the sample is constructed as described in Section IIC. All eight specifications use the share of a drug's prescriptions purchased by Medicare-enrolled individuals as the measure of Medicare market share, drop those observations with values of the dependent variable in the top 1 percent or the bottom 1 percent of the distribution, and exclude the 20 cancer and immunosuppressant drugs. Heteroskedasticity-robust standard errors are included in parentheses.

*** Significant at the 1 percent level.
** Significant at the 5 percent level.
* Significant at the 10 percent level.

$$\Delta Y_{j,2003-6} = \alpha + \beta_1 MMS\_Self_{j,2003} + \beta_2 MMS\_Ins_{j,2003} + \mu Yrs_{j,2003} + \delta_1 AnyGeneric_{j,2006} + \varepsilon_{j,2003}, \quad (3)$$

in which Y is the outcome variable, price, or quantity. The average values for the two Medicare explanatory variables in our sample of 517 drugs are 0.217 and 0.135, respectively, and the latter share variable includes both private and public insurance.

The estimates for β_1 and β_2 displayed in column 2 suggest that the price effects of Medicare Part D do vary with a particular drug's level of pre–Part D insurance coverage on the part of Medicare recipients. More specifically, the estimate of −0.225 for β_1 implies that the average (gross) price of prescription drugs consumed by uninsured Medicare recipients fell by more than 20 percent from 2003 to 2006 relative to other drugs, and this estimate is significant at the 1 percent level. The magnitude of the corresponding estimate for β_2 has the opposite sign and is statistically insignificant. This suggests that the relative price declines observed for Medicare-intensive drugs were driven by declines for drugs consumed disproportionately by beneficiaries previously without prescription drug coverage. Additionally, because the estimate of 0.115 for the constant α_1 is smaller in magnitude than our estimate of −0.225 for β_1, our results suggest that Medicare recipients' average prices declined by approximately 10 percent in real terms while those for other consumers increased by 12 percent.

In the next specification summarized in column 3, we differentiate between Medicare recipients also enrolled in Medicaid and those with an alternative source of insurance. Given the price distortions created by Medicaid's procurement rules, one might expect the movement of duals into Part D to cause a reduction in private market prices. If so, we will see price reduction associated with a drug's dual share, rather than its MMS. The estimate of -0.182 for the coefficient on the dual eligible share is consistent with this hypothesis, although it is not statistically significant. Furthermore, the estimate of -0.243 for β_1 remains of similar magnitude and is statistically significant at the 1 percent level. We thus conclude that the movement of duals is not responsible for the effect we measure.

In the next three columns of this table, we summarize the results from an analogous set of specifications for the utilization (in terms of the log of the number of daily doses) of the 517 drugs in our sample. To the extent that the enactment of Part D reduced the net cost of prescription drugs by more for uninsured Medicare recipients than for their counterparts who already had insurance, one would expect a larger increase in utilization for drugs consumed by this group. Consistent with this, the estimate of 0.461 for β_1 in specification 5 is almost twice as large as the corresponding estimate for β_2, though given the large standard errors the difference is not statistically significant.

The results in the final columns investigate the effect of Part D on total US revenues. Given that Part D reduced pharmaceutical prices below what they otherwise would have been while increasing the quantity consumed, it is theoretically ambiguous whether the revenues of pharmaceutical products increased or declined as a result of this legislation. The estimate of 0.273 for β_1 in column 7 suggests an increase in revenues for Medicare-intensive drugs, though it is not statistically significant.

Taken together, the results presented in this section suggest that Medicare Part D led to smaller price increases than would otherwise have occurred for Medicare recipients who lacked insurance coverage for prescription drug costs, which is the group most likely to have enrolled in Part D plans. We find little evidence to suggest that there was a corresponding effect on the price of drugs sold differentially to Medicare recipients who already had prescription drug coverage.

B. *Protected Therapeutic Categories*

While private firms providing Part D benefits had considerable latitude in designing their formularies, they were required to cover at least two treatments in each eligible therapeutic category. This requirement was introduced to reduce plans' ability to "cream skim" the least costly patients by excluding treatments for certain conditions. However, the ability to exclude certain treatments from the formulary provides plans with potentially important leverage when negotiating prices with pharmaceutical manufacturers.

The Part D requirements were substantially more stringent for a small subset of the 146 therapeutic categories defined by CMS. Specifically, plans were required to cover "substantially all" drugs in the following six therapeutic categories: antiretrovirals, antidepressants, antipsychotics, anticonvulsants, immunosuppressants, and antineoplastics. Part D plans could still try to steer patients toward certain treatments within these categories through differential co-pays, prior authorization requirements, or step therapy. However, plans were restricted in their use of utilization tools in the protected classes.

Thus, all else equal, a plan's leverage in negotiating low prices for drugs in these six protected categories would be less than if it could exclude the drug altogether. The same would be true for categories with just one or two available treatments. Note that this group of drugs is therefore missing one of the two effects we discussed above: while the impact of insurance increasing optimal prices is present, the offsetting effect of therapeutic competition among substitutes is likely to be very weak.

To investigate whether the price effects of Medicare Part D were different for protected classes or for classes with just one or two treatments, we estimate specifications of the following type:

$$(4) \qquad \Delta Y_{j,2003-6} = \alpha + \beta MMS_{j,2003} + \lambda Prot_j + \sigma MMS_{j,2003}\, Prot_j + \mu Small + \rho MMS_{j,2003}\, Small_j + \varepsilon_{j,2003}.$$

In this equation, $Prot_j$ is set equal to one if drug j is in one of the protected categories, and is otherwise set equal to zero. Similarly, $Small_j$ is set equal to one if drug j is in a therapeutic category with just one or two available treatments. Both variables are interacted with the Medicare market share to explore whether the average price effects differ for drugs in this category. To the extent that Part D plans were less successful at negotiating price reductions in these two categories, one would expect positive estimates for σ and ρ.

The results summarized in Table 5 shed light on this prediction. In the first three columns we include all 517 drugs in the sample, with 48 of these treatments falling into one of the six protected classes, and 22 of them belonging to a category with just one or two available treatments. In the first specification we add only the $Prot_j$ indicator and its interaction with MMS_j to our baseline specification. Consistent with our prediction, our estimate for σ is positive and at 0.175 is larger in magnitude than the estimate of −0.141 for β. However, this estimate for σ is not statistically significant. Standard errors are clustered by therapeutic subcategory given that the protected class indicator varies at this level.

In the specification summarized in the next column, we add the indicator for being in a "small" therapeutic category and its interaction with the Medicare market share to our baseline specification. Consistent with our theoretical predictions, the estimate for the coefficient on the interaction variable is positive and statistically significant at the 10 percent level. The magnitude of this estimate of 0.304 is more than twice as large as the main effect estimate of −0.142, suggesting that, if anything, Medicare-intensive treatments in the "small" categories experienced average price increases relative to other drugs.

These findings for price effects are similar when we include both indicators and their interactions with the Medicare market share in specification three, and becomes significant at the five percent level when we focus only on treatments without generic competition (column 4). Taken together, our results suggest that Medicare Part D did not lead to lower price increases for treatments in the "small" therapeutic categories.

The next four columns report the results from an analogous set of specifications for the utilization measure defined above. In specifications five, six, and seven, the estimate for both σ and ρ are significantly negative, suggesting that Medicare-intensive drugs in protected classes and in classes with just one or two treatments experienced *decreases* in utilization following the enactment of Part D. The first of these two estimates becomes small in magnitude and statistically insignificant in specification eight, where we focus on just treatments that do not face generic competition. However, the significant negative estimate for ρ remains, suggesting that perhaps Part D plans shifted recipients away from treatments in these "small" categories. While the CMS formulary discourages such shifting, plans are permitted to develop differentiated formularies, provided they can justify their choices to CMS as both providing sufficient quality, and not attempting to cream-skim. The combination of results suggests that brands given market power by the CMS formulary raised their prices and saw some market share losses due to Part D formulary design. However, because our quantity results are generally imprecise, we do not put emphasis on this explanation.

TABLE 5—THE IMPACT OF MEDICARE MARKET SHARE: VARIATION ACROSS THERAPEUTIC CATEGORIES

	Δ log(price per day$_{j,2003-06}$)				Δ log(Daily Doses$_{j,2003-06}$)			
	(1)	(2)	(3)	(4)	(5)	(6)	(7)	(8)
Medicare market share$_{j,2002-03}$	−0.141**	−0.142**	−0.147**	−0.173**	0.527*	0.429	0.572*	0.345**
	(0.059)	(0.057)	(0.061)	(0.080)	(0.299)	(0.315)	(0.310)	(0.147)
Protected	−0.042		−0.043	−0.029	1.027*		1.048**	0.102
	(0.071)		(0.055)	(0.073)	(0.497)		(0.498)	(0.156)
Protected × $MMS_{j,2002-03}$	0.175		0.174	0.173	−3.610**		−3.655**	−0.030
	(0.192)		(0.200)	(0.151)	(1.662)		(1.669)	(0.355)
Small category		−0.083	−0.083	−0.103*		0.712***	0.740***	0.631***
		(0.058)	(0.058)	(0.058)		(0.212)	(0.212)	(0.171)
Small category × $MMS_{j,2002-03}$		0.304*	0.303*	0.366**		−1.252**	−1.272**	−1.151**
		(0.155)	(0.154)	(0.163)		(0.542)	(0.577)	(0.454)
Years on the market	0.001	0.001	0.001	0.003	−0.001	−0.001	−0.001	−0.023***
	(0.002)	(0.002)	(0.002)	(0.003)	(0.008)	(0.008)	(0.008)	(0.007)
Any generic competition	0.010	0.012	0.011		−1.095***	−1.074***	−1.082***	
	(0.024)	(0.023)	(0.024)		(0.248)	(0.232)	(0.249)	
Constant	0.127	0.127	0.128	0.119	−0.278	−0.270	−0.317	−0.054
	(0.029)	(0.031)	(0.032)	(0.042)	(0.140)	(0.146)	(0.144)	(0.117)
Observations	517	517	517	318	517	517	517	318
R^2	0.025	0.026	0.028	0.059	0.315	0.297	0.319	0.131
Exclude if face gen comp?	No	No	No	Yes	No	No	No	Yes

Notes: Specifications 1 through 4 and 5 through 8 summarize the results from specifications of the change in the log price per daily dose and in the log number of daily doses, respectively, that use the explanatory variables listed in the first column. The unit of observation is the drug, and the sample is constructed as described in Section IIC. All eight specifications use the share of a drug's prescriptions purchased by Medicare-enrolled individuals as the measure of Medicare market share. All eight specifications drop those observations with values of the dependent variable in the top 1 percent or the bottom 1 percent of the distribution and exclude the 20 cancer and immunosuppressant drugs. Specifications 4 and 8 drop those treatments that face generic competition in 2006 or earlier. Heteroskedasticity-robust standard errors are included in parentheses.

***Significant at the 1 percent level.

**Significant at the 5 percent level.

*Significant at the 10 percent level.

V. Discussion

The introduction of Medicare Part D is arguably the most significant change to the Medicare program since its inception more than 40 years ago. The procurement rules that are used by Part D differ substantially from those used by Medicare for other health care services, by the federal-state Medicaid program, or by the US Department of Veterans Affairs for prescription drugs. One of the central criticisms of Part D was that it would lead to significant increases in pharmaceutical prices, to some extent offsetting the benefit of the additional insurance coverage.

In this paper, we investigate this issue using price, quantity, and sales data for the top-selling branded pharmaceutical treatments in the United States for the period before the enactment of Medicare Part D and in the one year immediately following. We combine this with information on the insurance coverage of each brand's consumers, which allows us to compare price and utilization changes as a function of each treatment's baseline Medicare market share. Our findings strongly suggest that Part D plans have succeeded in negotiating lower price increases for Part D enrollees —approximately 20 percent lower than they otherwise would have been—with this effect augmenting the mechanical effect of the program in reducing out-of-pocket prices. Our findings also suggest, consistent with recent research (e.g., Lichtenberg and Sun 2007), that Part D has increased the utilization of pharmaceutical treatments.

In contrast to the usual intuition that the uninsured customer is the most price-sensitive, we find that the insured customer is more price-elastic. The most plausible explanation is that in Part D, insurance is bundled with group purchasing and the implementation of a formulary. The

PDP's ability to obtain lower prices indicates that a significant benefit of the program is the way it is organized, regardless of the subsidy level. Our evidence indicates that the PDP's ability to encourage the use of therapeutic substitutes by a large group outweighs the classic insurance-induced increases in pharmaceutical prices, and therefore leads to relative price declines for brands. It is perhaps partly because of the price effects estimated in this paper that Part D expenditures by the federal government have been substantially lower than the most widely cited estimates suggested (CMS 2007b). Furthermore, our results provide an example of the more general point that including the uninsured in a large group with the ability to select providers may greatly reduce costs even in the absence of a government subsidy.

When interpreting the results in this paper, a number of caveats should be mentioned. First and most important, given the available data, we can investigate the effect of Part D only in its first year. To the extent that plans become more or less successful at negotiating prices in future years, the results may of course change. Second, we are unable to measure any ex post rebates that PDPs may have been able to negotiate and that affect net prices to PDPs. Such rebates do not appear on the invoice, which is the source of IMS data, and might be causing prices to be even lower than those measured here. The other rebates that we do not measure are Medicaid rebates paid by manufacturers to the Medicaid program. Dual eligibles' pharmaceutical purchases under Medicaid automatically generated this rebate. Once dual eligibles move into Medicare Part D plans, their pharmaceutical purchases occur at different prices, which is what we document here, but they no longer trigger automatic rebates. Any study of the total cost of Part D to the government would want to consider both sets of rebates. Third, our results do not shed light on the effect of the program on the health of enrollees nor on their ability to smooth consumption in response to adverse health shocks. And, finally, we have not considered the effect of Part D on innovation, as this is a long-run outcome. However, to the extent that Part D reduces prices for drugs that have close substitutes rather than for drugs that do not have substitutes, we would conjecture that Part D increases the incentives for firms to invent novel treatments. All of these issues remain important areas for future research.

REFERENCES

Acemoglu, Daron, David Cutler, Amy Finkelstein, and Joshua Linn. 2006. "Did Medicare Induce Pharmaceutical Innovation?" *American Economic Review*, 96(2): 103–07.

Card, David, Carlos Dobkin, and Nicole Maestas. 2008. "The Impact of Nearly Universal Insurance Coverage on Health Care Utilization: Evidence from Medicare." *American Economic Review*, 98(5): 2242–58.

Centers for Medicare and Medicaid Services. 2007a. *Medicare and Medicaid Statistical Supplement.*

Centers for Medicare and Medicaid Services. 2007b. "Strong Competition and Beneficiary Choices Contribute to Medicare Drug Coverage with Lower Costs than Predicted." Washington, DC: US Department of Health and Human Services.

Cutler, David M. 1995. "The Incidence of Adverse Medical Outcomes under Prospective Payment." *Econometrica*, 63(1): 29–50.

Cutler, David M., and Jonathan Gruber. 1996. "Does Public Insurance Crowd Out Private Insurance?" *Quarterly Journal of Economics*, 111(2): 391–430.

Dafny, Leemore S. 2005. "How Do Hospitals Respond to Price Changes?" *American Economic Review*, 95(5): 1525–47.

Duggan, Mark, and Fiona Scott Morton. 2006. "The Distortionary Effects of Government Procurement: Evidence from Medicaid Prescription Drug Purchasing." *Quarterly Journal of Economics*, 121(1): 1–30.

Duggan, Mark, and Fiona Scott Morton. 2008. "The Effect of Medicare Part D on Pharmaceutical Prices and Utilization." National Bureau of Economic Research Working Paper 13917.

Duggan, Mark, Patrick Healy, and Fiona Scott Morton. 2008. "Symposium: Health Care: Providing Prescription Drug Coverage to the Elderly: America's Experiment with Medicare Part D." *Journal of Economic Perspectives*, 22(4): 69–92.

Finkelstein, Amy. 2007. "The Aggregate Effects of Health Insurance: Evidence from the Introduction of Medicare." *Quarterly Journal of Economics*, 122(1): 1–37.

Finkelstein, Amy, and Robin McKnight. 2008. "What Did Medicare Do? The Initial Impact of Medicare on Mortality and Out of Pocket Medical Spending." *Journal of Public Economics*, 92(7): 1644–68.

Gibson, Teresa, Ronald Ozminkowski, and Ron Goetzel. 2005. "The Effects of Prescription Drug Cost Sharing: A Review of the Evidence." *The American Journal of Managed Care*, 11(11): 730–40.

Hubbard, R. Glenn, John F. Cogan, and Daniel P. Kessler. 2005. *Healthy, Wealthy, and Wise.* Washington, DC: AEI Press/Hoover Institution.

Huskamp, Haiden A., Patricia A. Deverka, Arnold M. Epstein, Robert S. Epstein, Kimberly A. McGuigan, and Richard G. Frank. 2003. "The Effect of Incentive-Based Formularies on Prescription Drug Utilization and Spending." *New England Journal of Medicine*, 349(23): 2224–32.

Kaiser Family Foundation. 2007. "Overview of Medicare Part D Organizations, Plans and Benefits By Enrollment in 2006 and 2007." http://www.kff.org/medicare/upload/7710.pdf.

Khwaja, Ahmed. 2008. "A Life Cycle Analysis of the Effects of Medicare on Individual Health Incentives and Health Outcomes." Unpublished.

Lichtenberg, Frank R. 1996. "Do (More and Better) Drugs Keep People Out of Hospitals?" *American Economic Review*, 86(2): 384–88.

Lichtenberg, Frank R., and Shawn Sun. 2007. "The Impact of Part D on Prescription Drug Use by the Elderly." *Health Affairs*, 26(6): 1735–44.

Pavcnik, Nina. 2002. "Do Pharmaceutical Prices Respond to Potential Patient Out-of-Pocket Expenses?" *RAND Journal of Economics*, 33(3): 469–87.

Simon, Kosali I., and Claudio Lucarelli. 2006. "What Drove First Year Premiums in Stand-Alone Medicare Drug Plans?" National Bureau of Economic Research Working Paper 12595.

Yin, Wesley, Anirban Basu, James Zhang, Atonu Rabbani, David Meltzer, and Caleb Alexander. 2008. "The Effect of the Medicare Part D Prescription Benefit on Drug Utilization and Expenditures." *Annals of Internal Medicine*, 148(3): 169–77.

[10]

Pharmaceutical Innovation, Mortality Reduction, and Economic Growth

Frank R. Lichtenberg

I. Introduction

The explanation of long-run growth in the value of per-capita output is a central issue in economics. In recent years, economists have increasingly recognized that traditional, official measures of growth in real per-capita output significantly understate true economic growth. One reason for this shortcoming is that the price indexes that are used to deflate nominal output tend to overestimate inflation, by approximately 1–1.5 percentage points per year (Advisory Commission to Study the Consumer Price Index, 1996).

A second reason is that gross domestic product (GDP) does not fully account for several important, highly valued "commodities," such as leisure, health, and longevity. The average person born in 1995 expects to live 22 years (41 percent) longer than the average person born in 1920. Although the rate of increase of longevity appears to be declining, as table 3.1 indicates, between 1970 and 1991 mean age at death still increased 5.4 years. In a recent paper, Nordhaus (this volume) argues that the underestimation of economic growth resulting from failure to account for increased longevity is substantial: he estimates that, "to a first approximation, the economic value of increases in longevity over the twentieth century is about as large as the value of measured growth in non-health goods and services" (p. 17). In other words, economic growth adjusted for longevity increase is twice as large as unadjusted economic growth.

Frank R. Lichtenberg is the Courtney C. Brown Professor of Business at Columbia University and a research associate of the National Bureau of Economic Research.

I am grateful to Judith Jones, Richard Levy, Richard Manning, and Gary Persinger for helpful comments and discussions, and to conference and seminar participants at Columbia University, NBER, NYU, the University of Chicago, Ohio State University, Purdue University, Georgia State University, and the International Schumpeter Society for their comments. I am responsible for any errors.

Pharmaceutical Innovation, Mortality Reduction, and Economic Growth

TABLE 3.1 Mean Life Expectancy and Statistics of Age Distribution of Deaths, 1970, 1980, and 1991

	1970	1980	1991
Life expectancy at birth (years)[a]	70.8	73.7	75.5
Age at death (years)[b]			
Mean	64.6	67.7	70.0
Standard deviation	21.8	20.4	19.8
Coefficient of variation	.337	.302	.283
Median	70	72	74
25%	57	60	63
10%	35	41	43
5%	10	22	28

[a]SOURCE: Health, United States, 1994, table 30.
[b]SOURCE: Author's calculations based on 1970, 1980, and 1991 Vital Statistics—Mortality Detail files.

The Solow model, which is perhaps the most widely accepted theory of economic growth, implies that technological progress is the fundamental source of growth in per-capita income. While early models of growth treated the rate of technological progress as an exogenous variable, more recent ("endogenous growth") models recognize that technological progress depends on investment in research and development (R&D) and on the creation of new products and processes. There is abundant empirical evidence supporting the hypothesis that the growth in conventionally defined per-capita output (or total-factor productivity) is positively related to previous investments in research and development. Griliches and Lichtenberg (1984), for example, found that the most R&D intensive manufacturing industries tend to have the highest rates of growth of output per worker.

In this chapter, we investigate econometrically whether the "other" (unmeasured) half of economic growth—the increase in longevity—can also be explained by a certain kind of technological progress: the development and diffusion of new drugs. Since Nordhaus argues that increased longevity accounts for half the total U.S. economic progress, and Bresnahan and Gordon claim that, in general, "new goods are at the heart of economic progress" (1997: 1), the hypothesis that new drugs deserve a substantial amount of credit for increased longevity seems quite plausible.

Econometric investigations of the impact of technological change are usually hampered by lack of reliable data. In the case of pharmaceuticals, however, it is possible to identify, date, and classify every major and minor innovation since 1939 (because the industry has been strictly regulated by the FDA since then), and to measure the consumption (utilization) of

Frank R. Lichtenberg

TABLE 3.2 Number of New Molecular Entities Approved by FDA

Period	Frequency	Percentage	Cumulative Frequency	Cumulative Percentage
1940–44	2	0.2	2	0.2
1945–49	11	1.1	13	1.3
1950–54	116	11.2	129	12.5
1955–59	142	13.7	271	26.2
1960–64	100	9.7	371	35.8
1965–69	53	5.1	424	41.0
1970–74	81	7.8	505	48.8
1975–79	92	8.9	597	57.7
1980–84	98	9.5	695	67.1
1985–89	106	10.2	801	77.4
1990–94	114	11.0	915	88.4
1995–97	120	11.6	1035	100.0

SOURCE: Author's calculations based on unpublished FDA data.
NOTE: Year of approval unknown for 15 NMEs.

about 900 distinct drugs (molecules) since 1980. We obtained from the Food and Drug Administration (by submitting a Freedom of Information Act request) a computerized list of all New Drug Approvals (NDAs) and Abbreviated New Drug Approvals (ANDAs) since 1939. The list includes the NDA or ANDA number, the approval date, the generic and trade names of the drug, the dosage form, route of administration, strength, applicant name, "therapeutic potential" (priority or standard), and "chemical type" (new molecular entity, new formulation, new manufacturer, etc.). This enables us to reconstruct the precise history of pharmaceutical innovation during the last almost 60 years.

We obtain data on the utilization (market shares) of various drugs from the 1980 and 1991 National Ambulatory Medical Care Surveys (NAMCS), which survey doctor-office visits, and the 1993 National Hospital Ambulatory Medical Care Survey (NHAMCS), which surveys visits to hospital outpatient departments and emergency departments.[1] These surveys enable us to estimate the number of drug "mentions" (prescriptions), by molecule, in 1980 and subsequent years.

Time-series data on the number of new molecular entities (NMEs) approved by the FDA are shown in table 3.2. More than half of the 1,035 NMEs that the FDA has approved since its inception were approved after 1974. It is therefore not surprising that, as table 3.2 shows, the distribution of drugs prescribed by physicians changed considerably between 1980 and 1994. Ten of the drugs that were among the top 20 prescribed in 1980 lost that standing by 1994 (see table 3.3). Similarly, ten of the top 20 drugs in 1994 were not in the top 20 in 1980. Some of them, such as albuterol (for which

TABLE 3.3 Top 20 Drugs Prescribed in Doctor-Office Visits in 1980 and 1994

Rank in 1980	Percentage of 1980 Prescriptions	Percentage of 1994 Prescriptions	Drug	Class
1	2.9	1.4	Hydrochlorothiazide	Diuretics
2	2.3	1.5	Aspirin	General analgesics
3	1.9	x	Penicillin	Penicillins
4	1.8	1.0	Phenylpropanolamine	Nasal decongestants
5	1.8	x	Alcohol	Antitussives, expectorants, mucolytics
6	1.7	1.2	Erythromycin	Erythromycins and lincosamides
7	1.7	1.0	Phenylephrine	Nasal decongestants
8	1.7	3.0	Acetaminophen	General analgesics
9	1.5	0.9	Codeine	Antitussives, expectorants, mucolytics
10	1.4	x	Tetracycline	Tetracyclines
11	1.4	x	Pseudoephedrine	Nasal decongestants
12	1.3	x	Riboflavin	Vitamins, minerals
13	1.3	1.1	Digoxin	Cardiac glycosides
14	1.3	x	Chlorpheniramine	Nasal decongestants
15	1.3	x	Ampicillin	Penicillins
16	1.2	3.8	Amoxicillin	Penicillins
17	1.2	x	Propranolol	Antihypertensive agents
18	1.1	1.2	Furosemide	Diuretics
19	1.1	x	Ergocalciferol	Vitamins, minerals
20	1.1	x	Neomycin	Ocular anti-infective and anti-inflammatory agents
	31		SUM OF TOP 20 DRUGS	

continued

TABLE 3.3 *continued*

Rank in 1994	Percentage of 1994 Prescriptions	Percentage of 1980 Prescriptions	Drug	Class
1	3.8	1.2	Amoxicillin	Penicillins
2	3.0	1.7	Acetaminophen	General analgesics
3	1.6	x	Albuterol	Bronchodilators, antiasthmatics
4	1.5	2.3	Aspirin	General analgesics
5	1.4	x	Ibuprofen	Antiarthritics
6	1.4	2.9	Hydrochlorothiazide	Diuretics
7	1.3	x	Multivitamins General	Vitamins, minerals
8	1.2	1.1	Furosemide	Diuretics
9	1.2	1.7	Erythromycin	Erythromycins and lincosamides
10	1.2	x	Guaifenesin	Antitussives, expectorants, mucolytics
11	1.1	x	Estrogens	Estrogens and progestins
12	1.1	1.3	Digoxin	Cardiac glycosides
13	1.1	x	Prednisone	Adrenal corticosteroids
14	1.0	x	Diltiazem	Antianginal agents
15	1.0	x	Beclomethasone	Unclassified
16	1.0	1.7	Phenylephrine	Nasal decongestants
17	1.0	1.8	Phenylpropanolamine	Nasal decongestants
18	0.9	x	Triamcinolone	Adrenal corticosteroids
19	0.9	1.5	Codeine	Antitussives, expectorants, mucolytics
20	0.9	x	Levothyroxine	Agents used to treat thyroid disease
	27.6		SUM OF TOP 20 DRUGS	

NOTE: x denotes not in top 20 in that year. Total estimated number of prescriptions was 899 million in 1980 and 921 million in 1994.

Schering received FDA approval in 1981), had not yet been approved by the FDA in 1980.

We analyze the relationship *across diseases* between the long-term reduction in life-years lost before age 75 and the relative utilization of new pharmaceutical products. In other words, we investigate whether there were *above-average* reductions in mortality from diseases for which there were above-average utilization rates of new drugs. By combining the FDA and NAMCS data, we can calculate (subject to some measurement problems) *disease-specific* measures of pharmaceutical innovation—that is, quantify the amount of innovation relevant to each disease, since NAMCS reveals the relative frequency with which each drug is used for each disease.

This methodology controls for the effects of any general economic and social trends (such as changes in wealth, nutrition, smoking, or sanitation) that affect *average* mortality. The analysis of mortality change in a cross section of diseases seems quite analogous to the analysis of output or productivity growth in a cross section of industries. Industries produce goods; diseases may be considered "bads," or negative goods. The extent of innovation varies across both industries and diseases, due, in part, to variation in the extent of "technological opportunity."

We estimate this relationship for the entire period 1970–91 and for two subperiods (1970–80 and 1980–91), and for different categories of disease (based on the average age at which people die from the disease). We also distinguish between "drugs that appear (to the Food and Drug Administration) to represent an advance over available therapy" ("priority drugs") and "drugs that appear to have therapeutic qualities similar to those of already marketed drugs" ("standard drugs"). The data we analyze cover all diseases and all (outpatient) drugs, thus allowing us (assuming that our model is correctly specified) to draw general conclusions about the impact of new drugs on longevity, something that cannot be accomplished using existing studies, which are about specific diseases and/or drugs.

In the next section we briefly review some of the previous evidence on the impact of drugs on life expectancy, including anecdotal evidence, a case study of a specific disease (heart attacks), and data from a few clinical studies of specific drugs. In section III we present a simple econometric model for estimating this impact, describe our procedures for constructing the variables included in this model, and discuss issues pertaining to estimation and interpretation of parameter estimates. Estimates of the model and their economic implications are discussed in section IV. The effects of controlling for physician counseling, vaccine availability, and surgical innovation are presented in section V. An estimate of the social rate of return to pharmaceutical innovation is derived in section VI. The final section contains a summary and conclusions.

II. Previous Evidence

Pharmaceutical Research and Manufacturers of America (2001) provides an informal, anecdotal account of the contribution of drug innovation to medical progress in this century. We simply quote their account here:

> Antibiotics and vaccines played a major role in the near eradication of major diseases of the 1920s, including syphilis, diphtheria, whooping cough, measles, and polio. Since 1920, the combined death rate from influenza and pneumonia has been reduced by 85 percent. Despite a recent resurgence of tuberculosis (TB) among the homeless and immuno-suppressed populations, antibiotics have reduced the number of TB deaths to one tenth the levels experienced in the 1960s. Before antibiotics, the typical TB patient was forced to spend three to four years in a sanitarium and faced a 30 to 50 percent chance of death. Today most patients can recover in 6 to 12 months given the full and proper course of antibiotics.
>
> Pharmaceutical discoveries since the 1950s have revolutionized therapy for chronic as well as acute conditions. From 1965 to 1995 cardiovascular drugs such as antihypertensives, diuretics, beta-blockers, and ACE inhibitors drastically reduced deaths from hypertension, hypertensive heart disease, and ischemic heart disease.[2]
>
> Similarly, H2 blockers, proton pump inhibitors and combination therapies cut deaths from ulcers by more than 60 percent. Anti-inflammatory therapies and bronchodilators reduced deaths from emphysema by 31 percent and provided relief for those with asthma. Had no progress been made against disease between 1960 and 1990, roughly 335,000 more people would have died in 1990 alone.
>
> Since 1960, vaccines have greatly reduced the incidence of childhood diseases—many of which once killed or disabled thousands of American children. Likewise, vaccines for Hepatitis B introduced during the 1980s now protect a new generation of American children from a leading cause of liver disease. (chap. 1, pp. 2–4)

Brand-new evidence indicates that new drug therapies have sharply reduced fatalities from AIDS:

> AIDS deaths in New York City plummeted by 48 percent last year, accelerating earlier gains attributed to improved drug therapies.... [T]he declines crossed sex and racial lines, suggesting that the new therapies were reaching all segments of the AIDS population. National figures for the first six months of 1997 also showed a similar sharp decline, 44 percent, from

> the corresponding period of 1996. . . . Theoretically, the decline in AIDS deaths could have resulted from prevention efforts or some unknown factor. . . . But the likeliest explanation is expanded use of combinations of newer and older drugs that began to be introduced in recent years, New York City and Federal health officials said.[3]

The anecdotal evidence about the impact of new drugs on mortality is in stark contrast to econometric evidence presented by Skinner and Wennberg (2000) about the relationship between total medical expenditure in the last six months of life and outcomes.[4] They analyzed this relationship using both a 20 percent sample of all Medicare enrollees and a 5 percent sample of very ill Medicare patients hospitalized with heart attack (acute myocardial infarction, or AMI), stroke, gastrointestinal bleeding, and lung cancer. Per-capita medical expenditures vary considerably across regions. For example, average Medicare expenditures on elderly patients in the last six months of life are twice as high in Miami as they are in Minneapolis, and the average number of visits to specialists is five times as high. However, intensive econometric analysis provided "no evidence that higher levels of spending translates into extended survival" (p. 188).[5]

Cutler, McClellan, and Newhouse (1998) performed a case study of a single but important disease—heart attacks—by compiling results about the effect of various treatments on mortality from the universe of clinical studies published in the medical literature. They found that changes in the medical treatments used in the acute management of AMI account for approximately 55 percent of the reduction in mortality that has occurred in AMI cases between 1975 and 1995, with the bulk of this improvement (50 percent) coming from pharmaceuticals. Three drug therapies—aspirin, thrombolytics, and beta-blockers—resulted in the largest improvements in heart attack mortality. They also noted that "the long-term improvement in mortality may be even more substantial than the acute improvements" (p. 17). Many innovations have occurred in the treatment of patients whose heart sustained substantial damage from the attack, including drug therapies such as ACE inhibitors and anticoagulation therapy, but limited quantitative evidence makes it difficult to quantify these important effects. Cutler, McClellan, and Newhouse's findings are extremely interesting; as they observe, "the important question is whether [their] results generalize to other types of medical care" (p. 34).

Frech and Miller (1999) examined the relationship between pharmaceutical expenditures per capita (in 1990 U.S. dollars) and life expectancy at different ages (birth, 40 years, and 60 years), controlling for a number of other variables and using longitudinal country-level data for 21 Organisation for Economic Co-Operation and Development (OECD) countries. They found a significant positive relationship between pharmaceutical expenditure and life expectancy at age 40, and a stronger one at age 60. But because older people tend to consume more drugs, this correlation may reflect the effect of life expectancy on pharmaceutical expenditure as well as the effect of pharmaceutical expenditure on life expectancy. The following table shows the mean number of medications ordered by physicians in office visits, by patient age:[6]

Patient Age	Mean Number of Medications Ordered
0–17 years	0.986
18–44	0.948
45–64	1.332
65+	1.652

45- to 64-year-old patients receive 37 percent more medications per visit, and patients over the age of 65 receive 70 percent more, than patients under age 45. (Moreover, older patients probably visit doctors more frequently.) Hence, the coefficient on pharmaceutical expenditure in Frech and Miller's life expectancy equation overstates the effect of the former on life expectancy.[7]

Clinical trials, of which there have undoubtedly been thousands, have provided a great deal of evidence about the impact on mortality of new drugs. One such study was the West of Scotland Coronary Prevention Study of 6,595 ostensibly healthy men aged 45 through 64 years. The results of the study indicated that

> [the cholesterol-lowering drug] pravastatin reduces the risk of heart attack and death in a broad range of people, not just those with established heart disease, but also among those who are at risk for their first heart attack.... Over five years, those [healthy individuals] treated with ... pravastatin suffered 31 percent fewer nonfatal heart attacks and at least 28 percent fewer deaths from heart disease than a comparable group of men who received a placebo.... In previous studies, pravastatin had been shown to reduce the risk of heart attack by 62 percent in patients with high cholesterol who already had heart disease.[8]

Evidence from clinical trials is extremely useful and of great scientific value, but some public health experts argue that clinical-trial results cannot simply be extrapolated to real-world experience. Also, there does not appear to be any way to summarize or combine all the clinical-trial evidence to shed light on the average or aggregate contribution of pharmaceutical innovation to mortality reduction and economic growth, which is our goal.

III. Model Specification and Estimation

To assess the contribution of pharmaceutical innovation to the reduction in ("premature") mortality of Americans, I will perform several different analyses of the relationship, across diseases, between the relative utilization of new drugs and the reduction in life-years lost, including estimation of models of the form

$$(1)\quad \ln(LYL_{t-k}/LYL_t) = \alpha + \beta(DRUGS_{t-k,t}/DRUGS_{.t}) + \varepsilon$$

using data on a cross-section of diseases, where LYL_t = aggregate life-years lost before age 75 divided by population in year t (defined below); $DRUGS_{t-k,t}$ = the number of drugs prescribed in year t that received FDA approval in year $t-k$ or later; and $DRUGS_{.t} = \Sigma_k DRUGS_{t-k,t}$ = the total number of drugs prescribed in year t. For example, if $t = 1991$ and $k = 21$, the equation becomes

$$\ln(LYL_{1970}/LYL_{1991}) = \alpha + \beta(DRUGS_{1970,1991}/DRUGS_{.1991}) + \varepsilon.$$

The dependent variable is the percentage reduction in life-years lost between 1970 and 1991. As Murray and Lopez (1996: 6–7) observe, "since the late 1940s, researchers have generally agreed that . . . time (in years) lost through premature death" is the appropriate way to measure the burden of premature mortality. However, "in order to measure burden, a society has to decide what the ideal or reference status should be. This involves [deciding], how long 'should' people live? If health researchers are to estimate how many years of life are lost through death at any given age, they must decide on the number of years for which a person at that age should expect to survive in the ideal, or reference, population. That could be, for example, 60, 80, or 90 years from birth." The "reference age" used by the National Center for Health Statistics and the World Health Organization is 65 years. For making international comparisons, Murray and Lopez use reference ages of 82.5 years for women and 80 years for men—life expectancy in the world's longest-surviving population, the Japanese.[9] I will use an intermediate value of the reference age: 75 years. (Our main findings are essentially unchanged when a reference age of 65 years is used instead.) The mortality measure that we will analyze is life-years lost before age 75 per population (LYL). This measure is defined as follows:

$$LYL = \left\{\sum_i \max(0, 75 - \text{age\_death}_i)\right\}/POP,$$

where age_death$_i$ is the age of death of the ith decedent, and POP is the population. For example, in a population of 1,000, if in a given year 2 people die at age 60, 3 people die at age 70, and 5 people die at age 75 or later, LYL = [2(75 − 50) + 3(75 − 60) + 5(0)]/1000 = 95/1000 = .095. This measure gives a great deal of weight to deaths that occur at early ages (especially infant mortality), and no weight at all to deaths beyond age 75.

Data on LYL, by disease, were computed from the 1970, 1980, and 1991 Vital Statistics-Mortality Detail Files. Each record in the file includes a single *International Classification of Diseases, Ninth Revision (ICD-9)* code to indicate the cause of death.[10] We used this code to calculate the various mortality statistics by *ICD-9* disease, by year.[11]

The independent variable in equation (1) is the fraction of drugs prescribed in 1991 that were approved in 1970 or later. We hypothesize that the greater the percentage of drugs prescribed in 1991 that were not yet available in the "baseline" year (1970), the greater the reduction in mortality since the baseline year.[12] We recognize that, due to a heterogeneous rate of obsolescence of drugs across diseases, a given value of the new-drug share may reflect varying degrees of drug improvement. Suppose that for disease *A*, there is only one drug approved after 1970, and this has a 50 percent market share in 1991. For disease *B*, one new drug is approved in 1975, and it captures 50 percent of the market; another drug is approved in 1985, and all patients on the first drug (and only those patients) switch to the second drug. Disease *B* has the same new-drug share in 1991 as disease *A*, even though it has benefited from two waves of innovation rather than one. Although diseases with a given new-drug share may have different rates of drug improvement, we postulate that, on average, diseases having higher new-drug shares have higher rates of drug improvement.

This specification is very consistent with the most widely accepted theory of economic growth, the Solow model. As Mankiw (1992: 102) observes, the Solow model implies that "once the economy is in a steady state, the rate of growth of output per worker depends only on the rate of technological progress." We argued above that mortality reduction may be interpreted as a component or form of per-capita income (or output) growth. As Bresnahan and Gordon (1997: 1) observe, "new goods are at the heart of economic progress," so the fraction of all goods (drugs) consumed that are new appears to be a very appropriate measure of the rate of technological progress.

Although there is only one variable on the right-hand side of equation (1), the validity of our analysis is *not* based on the assumption that pharmaceutical innovation is the *only* source of mortality reduction. Changes in mortality are likely to depend upon a number of factors, such as changes in wealth, changes in environmental quality, and changes in the prevalence of smoking. If the changes in these other factors were "across the board" changes—they did not vary across diseases—then their effect would be captured by the intercept term (α), which reflects the mean reduction in mortality not explained by pharmaceutical innovation (α = mean (Y) – β mean(X)).[13] Our estimates of, and hypothesis tests about, the effect of pharmaceutical innovation on mortality reduction (β) depend entirely on diseases' *deviations from sample means* and not at all on the mean values of Y and X.

It is likely, of course, that changes in these other factors vary to some extent across diseases. If determinants of mortality change other than pharmaceutical innovation are uncorrelated across diseases with pharmaceutical innovation, then equation (1) still yields unbiased estimates of β.[14] There does not appear to be good reason to expect changes in most determinants of mortality other than drug innovation to be correlated across diseases with drug innovation. It is not obvious, for example, why diseases for which many new drugs were developed should be the ones whose sufferers reduced smoking the most or whose wealth increased the most.[15] Ideally, one might estimate an expanded version of equation (1) that includes a large number of other potential determinants of mortality change. Many of these are difficult or impossible to measure at the disease level. But there are several potentially relevant covariates that we can measure, and will include in a more elaborate model of mortality reduction (presented in section V), to check the robustness of our estimates. These are (1) the probability that the physician provides nonmedication therapy—primarily counseling and education—to the patient; (2) a dummy variable indicating whether a vaccine is available for a disease; and (3) the rate of introduction of new surgical procedures.

The *ICD-9* classification includes three kinds of codes: disease (or natural causes of death) codes (000–799), nature of injury codes (800–999), and external causes of death codes (E800–E999).[16] In the mortality files, only the first and last sets of codes are used, whereas in the ambulatory care surveys, only the first and second sets of codes are used. We therefore confine our analysis to diseases (natural causes of death).

Equation (1) can be estimated using data at different levels of aggregation, such as either *ICD-9* two-digit- or three-digit-level disease data (at which there are approximately 80 and 1,000 diseases, respectively). There is no theoretical reason to believe that the parameter estimates should depend in any particular way on the level of aggregation. As a practical matter, greater disaggregation has both advantages and disadvantages.[17] The advantages are that the number of observations (and statistical degrees of freedom) increases, and that each observation is less heterogeneous (covers a less diverse group of diseases). The disadvantages are that both measurement or classification error (in the dependent variable) and sampling error (in the independent variable) are amplified. Murray and Lopez (1996: 16) note that "miscoding of deaths—that is, assigning the death to the 'wrong' cause in *ICD-9*, occurs regularly in all countries with registration systems. For example, the choice of codes for cardiovascular diseases is notoriously variable between industrialized countries, with a significant proportion of ischaemic heart disease deaths being attributed to ill-defined codes such as heart failure." Since we are analyzing *changes* in mortality, by disease, our estimates would not be affected by systematic (permanent) miscoding of deaths, for example if ischaemic heart disease deaths were always underestimated by 25 percent. But the miscoding of cause of death is likely to have a random component as well, and the probability that a three-digit diagnosis is wrong is undoubtedly much greater than the probability that a two-digit diagnosis is wrong. The greater the extent of miscoding, the lower the precision of our parameter estimates. As we will describe below, the data we use on the new-drug share are *estimates* based on random 1 in 10,000 or 1 in 16,000 samples of doctor-office visits. The greater the extent of disaggregation by disease, the smaller the number of visits in each disease category, and the larger the sampling error associated with each observation. Amplification of sampling error biases the coefficient on the new-drug share toward 0; it increases the probability of finding no relationship between pharmaceutical innovation and mortality reduction when there really is a relationship. Since the statistically optimal level of disease aggregation is not obvious a priori, we tried performing the analysis at both the two-digit and the three-digit level. The two-digit-level estimates were more significant and robust, so these are the ones that we will present.

Estimates of $\text{DRUGS}_{t-k,t}$—the number of drugs prescribed in year t that received FDA approval in year $t - k$ or later—were obtained by combining data from several sources. The first data source was the NAMCS, which contains records of 46,081 doctor-office visits in 1980 and of 33,795 visits in 1991. Each record lists the drugs (if any) prescribed by the physician. Up to five drugs may be coded. If a drug is a combination drug, its ingredients (up to five) are coded, so that as many as 25 ingredients (molecular entities) could be coded in a single record. The record also lists up to three diagnoses (*ICD-9* codes) along with a "drug weight," which is used to compute population-level estimates of drug utilization from the sample data. Because multiple diagnoses may be cited in a given record, we sometimes confront the problem of "allocating" the mention of a drug across diagnoses. We adopted the simple, feasible approach of *equal* allocation of the drug mention across the several diagnoses. For example, if two diagnoses were cited and the drug weight was 10,000, we replaced the mention of that drug by two mentions of the same drug, one for each diagnosis, each with a drug weight of 5,000; this procedure does not change the population estimates of drug mentions by molecule. We then calculated estimates of the aggregate number of prescriptions by molecule and patient diagnosis.

To calculate the fraction of drugs that were approved by the FDA after a certain date, we linked these data to a list of all New Drug Applications since 1939 provided by the administration. Both files included the scientific name of the drug, and the FDA file included the date the drug was first approved as a new molecular entity (NME).[18]

Figure 3.1 shows the distribution of drugs prescribed in 1994 by year of FDA approval. Almost half the drugs prescribed in 1994 were approved after 1979; about a quarter were approved after 1984.

Only patient visits to doctors' offices are covered by NAMCS. In 1992 the National Center for Health Statistics began conducting a similar survey (NHAMCS) of visits to hospital outpatient departments and emergency rooms, the number of which is believed to have grown much more rapidly during the last 10 to 15 years than the number of doctor-office visits. Doctor-office visits still accounted for more than 80 percent of total visits in the 1990s,[19] but we sought to improve the precision of our estimates of the new-drug proportion by combining information from the NAMCS and NHAMCS surveys. We calculated the share of new drugs in total drugs prescribed in the consolidated sample as well as separately for each of the three outpatient "sectors."[20]

In the course of the approval process, the FDA classifies drugs into two categories: "priority review drugs"—drugs that appear to represent an advance over available therapy—and "standard review drugs"—drugs that appear to have therapeutic qualities similar to those of already marketed drugs.[21] One might reasonably hypothesize that new priority drugs have a larger impact on mortality than new standard drugs. Indeed, whether a new drug is expected to reduce mortality may be one of the FDA's classification criteria.[22] We will test this hypothesis by estimating versions of equation (1) in which the new-drug share is disaggregated into two components: the shares of new priority drugs and new standard drugs in total drugs prescribed at the end of the period.

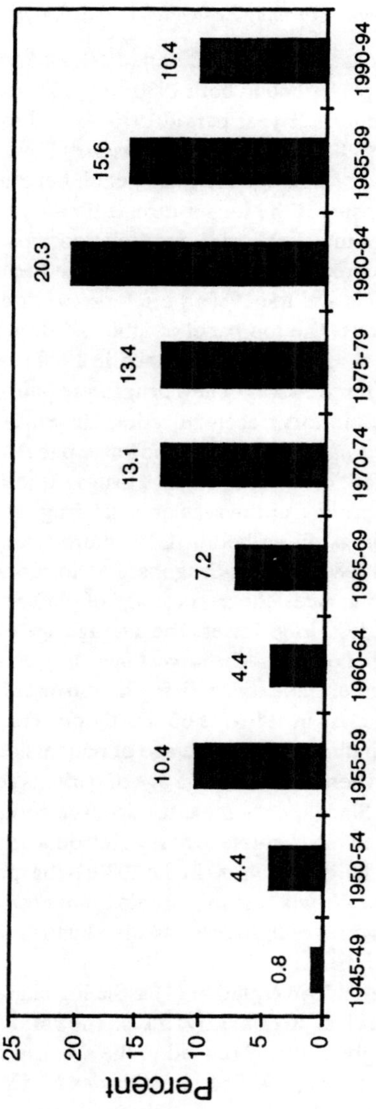

FIGURE 3.1: Distribution of drugs prescribed in 1994, by year of FDA approval

Pharmaceutical Innovation, Mortality Reduction, and Economic Growth

We have mortality data for 1970, 1980, and 1991, and data on the vintage distribution of drugs prescribed in both 1980 and 1991, so we can estimate equation (1) for the entire 21-year period 1970–91 and for the two subperiods, 1970–80 and 1980–91. Since some drugs may have to be consumed for a sustained period of time for their full health benefits to be realized, it would not be surprising if the longer-term estimated relationship were stronger than either of the two shorter-term relationships.[23] Moreover, the data indicate that the important (in terms of market demand) new drugs introduced in the 1970s and the 1980s were targeted at different diseases and patient populations. The top panel of table 3.4 shows the percentage distribution by drug class of drugs prescribed in 1980 that were less than 10 years old. The top three classes of new drugs were pain relievers, antimicrobial agents, and respiratory tract medications; together these accounted for about half of new drug prescriptions. The lower panel of the table shows the percentage distribution by drug class of drugs prescribed in 1991 that were less than 11 years old. Cardiovascular-renal drugs accounted for over a third of the new drugs prescribed in 1991, more than four times their share of new drugs in 1980; the new-drug share of hormones also increased sharply. As table 3.5 indicates, the average age of patients receiving drugs varies significantly across drug classes. The average age of patients receiving drugs used for relief of pain—the largest new drug class in 1980—is 48, while the average age of patients receiving cardiovascular-renal drugs—the largest new drug class in 1991—is 66. Further calculations show that, consistent with this finding, the average age of patients receiving any new drug in 1980 was 44, whereas the average age of patients receiving any new drug in 1991 was 52. Since the clientele for drugs introduced in the 1980s tended to be older than the clientele for drugs introduced in the 1970s, one would expect the mortality reductions in the 1980s to be more concentrated among older patients. We will test this prediction by estimating equation (1) for different categories of diseases, classified by the mean age at which people die from the disease.

The dependent variable in equation (1) is the log-change (growth rate) of per-capita life-years lost, $\ln(LYL_{t-k}/LYL_t)$. The variance of the dependent variable is strongly inversely related to the average size or burden of the disease, $(LYL_{t-k} + LYL_t)/2$. The growth rates of diseases affecting a relatively small number of people are likely to be much farther away (in both directions) from the mean than those of major diseases.[24] To correct for heteroskedasticity, the equation is estimated via weighted least squares, where the weight is $(LYL_{t-k} + LYL_t)/2$. Diseases that are responsible for larger average numbers of life-years lost are given more weight.

TABLE 3.4 Percentage Distribution of Drugs Prescribed in 1980 That Were less than 10 Years Old, by Drug Class

Drugs used for relief of pain	19.7
Antimicrobial agents	17.1
Respiratory tract drugs	11.2
Psychopharmacologic drugs	9.5
Skin/mucous membrane	8.7
Cardiovascular-renal drugs	8.6
Metabolic and nutrient agents	8.0
Gastrointestinal agents	6.7
Ophthalmic drugs	4.0
Anesthetic drugs	2.3
Neurologic drugs	1.7
Unclassified/miscellaneous	1.2
Oncolytics	0.7
Antidotes	0.2
Hormones and agents affecting hormonal mechanisms	0.2
Antiparasitic agents	0.1

Percentage Distribution of Drugs Prescribed in 1991 That Were less than 11 Years Old, by Drug Class

Cardiovascular-renal drugs	36.5
Respiratory tract drugs	12.6
Hormones and agents affecting hormonal mechanisms	10.8
Psychopharmacologic drugs	9.9
Antimicrobial agents	7.3
Drugs used for relief of pain	5.9
Gastrointestinal agents	5.1
Skin/mucous membrane	4.7
Metabolic and nutrient agents	4.5
Ophthalmic drugs	2.5
Oncolytics	0.2
Neurologic drugs	0.0
Otologic drugs	0.0

There are a number of reasons why estimates of the parameters of equation (1) might be biased. Several considerations imply that estimates of β will be biased toward 0, and therefore that our hypothesis tests will be strong tests. Measurement error in the new-drug proportion is perhaps the main reason to suspect downward bias.[25] The variable we calculate $(DRUGS_{t-k,t}/DRUGS_{.t})$ may be a noisy measure of the true share of new drugs for a number of reasons.

- Sampling error: the NAMCS survey is a random 1 in 10,000 or 1 in 16,000 sample of doctor-office visits;

Pharmaceutical Innovation, Mortality Reduction, and Economic Growth

TABLE 3.5 Average Age (in 1991) of Patients Receiving Drugs, by Drug Class

Cardiovascular-renal drugs	66.4
Ophthalmic drugs	60.9
Hematologic agents	57.6
Oncolytics	57.0
Gastrointestinal agents	53.3
Anesthetic drugs	52.2
Psychopharmacologic drugs	50.9
Hormones and agents affecting hormonal mechanisms	49.5
Antiparasitic agents	48.3
Drugs used for relief of pain	48.2
Neurologic drugs	46.4
Unclassified/miscellaneous	43.6
Otologic drugs	40.7
Metabolic and nutrient agents	39.1
Antidotes	36.8
Skin/mucous membrane	36.2
Respiratory tract drugs	32.0
Antimicrobial agents	29.6
Radiopharmaceutical/contrast media	20.4
Immunologic agent	12.4

SOURCE: Author's calculations based on 1991 NAMCS file.

- Coverage: our drug data refer only to doctor-office visits in 1980, and to outpatient visits in 1991 (no inpatient data), and primarily refer to prescription rather than over-the-counter drugs;[26]
- Misallocation: drugs assigned to the wrong diseases because of errors in allocation procedure described above (when there are multiple diagnoses); and
- Noncompliance: Our data refer to drugs prescribed by physicians, not drugs consumed by patients. It is estimated that only about half the medicine prescribed is taken correctly. The National Council on Patient Information & Education divides the problem of noncompliance into two categories: acts of omission and acts of commission. Acts of omission include never filling a prescription; taking less than the prescribed dosage; taking the drug less frequently than prescribed; taking medicine "holidays"; and stopping the regime too soon. Acts of commission include overuse, sharing medicines, and consuming food, drink, or other medicines that can interact with the prescribed drug.[27]

It is plausible that reverse causality (endogenous innovation), as well as measurement error in the independent variable, could bias estimates of

β toward 0. Suppose that there is a significant anticipated increase in fatalities from a certain disease (such as AIDS), and that this prospect stimulates a high rate of development and diffusion of new drugs targeted at that disease. Behavior of this sort would reduce the probability of observing a positive relationship across diseases between mortality reduction and new drug utilization.

We can also think of one possible reason for the least-squares estimate of β to be biased upward, in other words, to overestimate the average contribution of pharmaceutical innovation to medical progress. Suppose that the rate of progress (P) against a disease is a deterministic, concave function of research expenditure on the disease (X) and research productivity (π): $P_i = \pi_i X_i^{\theta}$, where i denotes disease i and $0 < \theta < 1$. Taking logarithms of the progress function, $\ln P_i = \ln \pi_i + \theta \ln X_i$. Suppose that disease-specific research productivity (π_i) is unobservable. If π_i were uncorrelated with research expenditure X_i, the least-squares estimate of the elasticity of progress with respect to spending θ would be unbiased. However, as argued in Lichtenberg (2001a), if decision makers are efficiently allocating the research budget across diseases (i.e. to maximize the total number of people cured of all diseases), they should devote more research funds to diseases where research productivity is high. Therefore π_i and X_i are likely to be positively correlated, and the slope coefficient from the simple regression of $\ln P_i$ on $\ln X_i$ would overestimate θ. More progress tends to be made on diseases with high research funding in part because those are the diseases where research productivity is highest. We are examining the relationship between progress and the new drug proportion, not research expenditure, but the latter two variables are likely to be positively correlated.[28]

IV. Empirical Results

Descriptive statistics for the dependent and independent variables for two-digit *ICD-9* diseases over the 1970–91 period and the two subperiods are shown in table 3.6.

The weighted-average decline in per-capita LYL during the period 1970–91 was 42.9 percent [$= 1 - \exp(-.561)$]; 5 percent of diseases exhibited a decline of more than 85 percent; however, 5 percent of diseases exhibited an increase of at least 117.3 percent.

As table 3.7 indicates, the mean shares of drugs prescribed in 1991 that were approved after 1970 and 1980, computed from NAMCS data, are quite close to the shares of drugs approved by the beginning of 1991 that were approved after 1970 and 1980, computed from FDA data.

Pharmaceutical Innovation, Mortality Reduction, and Economic Growth

TABLE 3.6

Variable	N	Mean (wtd)	5%	25%	Median	75%	95%
ln (LYL_{1970}/LYL_{1991})	75	.561	−.776	.101	.563	1.267	1.955
ln (LYL_{1970}/LYL_{1980})	75	.339	−.704	−.026	.432	.979	1.970
ln (LYL_{1980}/LYL_{1991})	78	.204	−.357	.025	.185	.419	.786
($DRUGS_{1970,1991}/DRUGS_{.1991}$)	75	.627	.337	.490	.584	.693	.904
($DRUGS_{1970,1980}/DRUGS_{.1980}$)	75	.225	.046	.106	.190	.284	.564
($DRUGS_{1980,1991}/DRUGS_{.1991}$)	78	.365	.084	.241	.317	.441	.637

TABLE 3.7

Period	% of Drugs Prescribed at the End of the Period That Were Approved since the Beginning of the Period	% of Drugs Approved by the End of the Period That Were Approved since the Beginning of the Period
1970–91	62.7	65.7
1970–80	22.5	43.0
1980–91	36.5	39.7

While these shares need not be close to one another, their proximity is reassuring. However, the mean share of drugs prescribed in 1980 that were approved after 1970 is much smaller than (about half) the share of drugs approved by the beginning of 1980 that were approved after 1970. This suggests that (for unknown reasons) the new-drug share data may be understated, by a factor of about 2, for the 1970–80 period. If this were the case, it would not affect the level of significance of our test of the null hypothesis of no relationship between the new-drug share and mortality reduction.[29] However, it would cause the point estimate of β to be twice as large as it would be in the absence of understatement. Since the 1970–91 and 1980–91 new-drug share data do not appear to be understated, the *ratio* of the estimate of β for 1970–80 to the estimate in 1980–91 (or 1970–91) would be overstated by a factor of 2.

Table 3.8 presents illustrative data for two diseases—*ICD-9* codes 20 (malignant neoplasm of lymphatic and hematopoietic tissue) and 48 (pneumonia and influenza)—which exhibited very different patterns of mortality reduction and new drug utilization during the period 1970–91. The table shows the five drugs most frequently prescribed in 1991 to patients diagnosed as having each of the diseases.[30] Only one of the top five drugs prescribed in 1991 for *ICD-9* code 20 was approved after 1970, and the decline in per-capita life-years lost (28 percent) was below the average for all diseases (43 percent).[31] In contrast, *all* of the top five drugs prescribed to patients diagnosed as having pneumonia and influenza were new drugs,

Frank R. Lichtenberg

TABLE 3.8 Five Drugs Most Frequently Prescribed in 1991 to Patients with Two Different Diagnoses

Percentage of Total Prescriptions in 1991	Drug	Drug Class	1 = Post-1970 Approval 0 = 1970 or Earlier Approval	FDA Approval Date	P = Priority Status Drug S = Standard Drug
Diagnosis = Pneumonia and influenza (ICD-9 code 48) (74% reduction in per-capita life-years lost, 1970–91)					
13.34	Amoxicillin	Antibacterial	1	01/18/74	P
10.35	Albuterol	Bronchodilator	1	05/01/81	P
6.75	Ibuprofen	Anti-inflammatory	1	09/19/74	P
6.13	Cefaclor	Antibacterial	1	04/04/79	S
5.34	Ceftriaxone	Antibacterial	1	12/21/84	P
Diagnosis = Malignant neoplasm of lymphatic and hematopoietic tissue (ICD-9 code 20) (28% reduction in per-capita life-years lost, 1970–91)					
8.16	Cyclophosphamide	Antineoplastic	0	11/16/59	P
7.66	Prednisone	Glutocorticoid	0	09/15/55	P
5.65	Vincristine	Antineoplastic	1	03/07/84	P
5.13	Digoxin	Cardiotonic	0	11/16/54	P
4.70	Allopurinol	Xanthine Oxidase Inhibitor	0	08/19/66	P

and the decline in per-capita life-years lost (74 percent) was well above average. The data for these two diseases are consistent with the hypothesis that utilization of new drugs reduces mortality, but we need to analyze data on the full cross section of diseases in order to have meaningful, general tests of this hypothesis.

Key econometric results are summarized in table 3.9. The first part of the table reports estimates of our basic model (equation [1]) by period. The second part reports estimates of models in which we allow priority and standard drugs to have different effects on mortality. The third part reports the results of estimating the basic model separately for three different groups of diseases, classified by the mean age at which people die from the disease.

Part I of the table indicates a highly significant positive relationship between the new-drug share and mortality reduction in all three periods. The magnitude and significance of the effect of the new-drug share on mortality reduction is much higher in 1970–80 than it is in 1980–91. As noted above, the ratio of the 1970–80 point estimate of β to the 1980–91 estimate may be overstated by a factor of about 2 due to apparent systematic underestimation of the new-drug share in the first period. But even in the second

Pharmaceutical Innovation, Mortality Reduction, and Economic Growth

TABLE 3.9 Estimates of the Relationship across Diseases between Relative Utilization of New Drugs and Reduction in Life-Years Lost, by Period

Period:	1970–80	1980–91	1970–91
		I. Basic Model	
β	2.069	0.378	2.866
	(3.85)	(2.34)	(7.06)
Weighted R^2	.1687	.0670	.4058
		II. Priority vs. Standard Drugs	
Priority	3.306	0.429	2.840
	(5.81)	(1.88)	(7.13)
Standard	−0.245	0.351	1.965
	(0.33)	(1.53)	(2.72)
Prob>F:	0.0001	0.8082	0.1287
		III. Estimates by Disease Group, Classified by Mean Age at which People Die from the Disease	
Low age	6.577	−0.077	2.796
	(7.89)	(0.33)	(5.66)
Middle age	2.920	0.573	1.451
	(2.86)	(1.08)	(1.09)
High age	−0.436	1.024	2.910
	(0.79)	(3.49)	(2.85)

NOTE: *t*-statistics are in parentheses.

period, we can reject the null hypothesis of no relationship between these two variables at about the 2 percent level. The magnitude and significance of β is larger over the entire 21-year period than it is in either of the two subperiods. This is consistent with the view that the long-run effects of new drugs on mortality are larger than the short-run effects. Over 40 percent of the variation across diseases in the 1970–91 reduction in mortality is explained by the new-drug share.

We wanted to ensure that our estimates were not unduly affected by a small number of highly influential observations. Following Belsley, Kuh, and Welsch (1980), we used the studentized residual with the current observation deleted (RSTUDENT) as the measure of that observation's influence. This statistic is approximately distributed as standard normal,[32] so that if RSTUDENT is greater than 2, "the particular observation may deserve scrutiny as perhaps not conforming to the model" (Greene, 1997: 445). Estimating the 1970–91 model excluding 7 observations for which the absolute value of RSTUDENT exceeds 2[33] reduces β, but not dramatically—by about 25 percent, from 2.87 to 2.14. The coefficient remains highly

Frank R. Lichtenberg

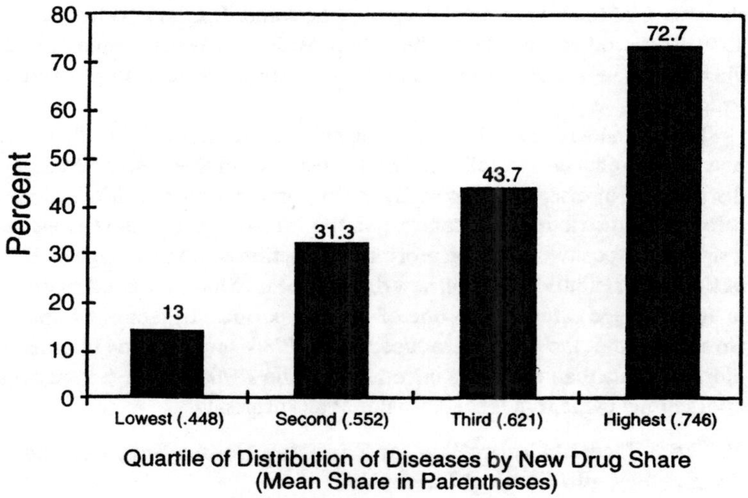

FIGURE 3.2: Mean 1970–91 reduction in life-years lost, by diseases grouped by new drug share

significant ($t = 4.26$). Moreover, Greene (p. 411) states that there is a "general principle that allowing the data and the values of sample test statistics to dictate the form of the model can lead to estimators with demonstrably poor statistical properties," and that "there is a certain danger in singling out particular observations for scrutiny or even elimination from the sample on the basis of statistical results that are based on those data. At the extreme, this may invalidate the usual inference procedures" (p. 415).

An alternative way of analyzing this relationship is to group diseases into a number of categories on the basis of the new-drug share, and to calculate the mean reduction in mortality for each group of diseases. The results from performing this procedure on the 1970–91 data with the number of groups equal to 4 are summarized in figure 3.2. The mean percentage reduction in life-years lost for the 19 diseases with the highest relative utilization of new drugs (whose mean new-drug share was 74.6 percent) was over five times as great—72.7 percent versus 13.0 percent—as the mean percentage reduction in life-years lost for the 19 diseases with the lowest relative utilization of new drugs (whose mean new-drug share was 44.8 percent).

The estimates in part II of table 3.9 indicate that in the 1970–80 period, only priority drugs had a statistically significant effect on mortality reduction. In the 1980–91 period, the coefficient on priority drugs is larger than the coefficient on standard drugs, but we cannot reject the hypothesis that

Pharmaceutical Innovation, Mortality Reduction, and Economic Growth

the effects of the two types of drugs are the same. The same is true for the 1970–91 period as a whole, so the data provide only weak support for the view that new priority drugs reduce mortality more than new standard drugs.

The estimates in part III of the table indicate that in the 1970–80 period, new drugs reduced mortality in the lowest and middle thirds of the age distribution of diseases—especially in the former—but not in the highest third of the distribution. In contrast, in the 1980–91 period, new drugs had a significant positive effect on mortality reduction only in the highest third of the age distribution. Hence, new drugs appear to have reduced mortality in all three age categories in one of the two periods. In tables 3.4 and 3.5 we showed that the drugs introduced in the 1980s tended to be targeted at older patients than the drugs introduced in the 1970s, so the "vintage-age interaction" evident in table 3.9 is not at all surprising.

V. The Effects of Controlling for Physician Counseling, Vaccine Availability, and Surgical Innovation

As discussed earlier, the (simple regression) coefficients on pharmaceutical innovation presented in table 3.9 could be biased due to failure to control for other determinants of mortality reduction. Improved patient knowledge about the impact of behavior on health is a potentially important source of mortality reduction. Although this knowledge can be acquired in a number of ways (e.g. via the mass media), counseling by physicians is likely to be a major means of its acquisition. According to 1991 NAMCS data, physicians provide therapeutic services other than medication in about one-third of office visits (they prescribe medications in about two-thirds of visits). Most of these nonmedication therapeutic services are in the form of counseling and education; the kinds of counseling and education offered are as follows:

Type of Counseling/Education	Percentage of Office Visits in which Provided
Diet	11.4%
Exercise	8.2
Cholesterol reduction	3.1
Weight reduction	3.8
Drug abuse	0.2
Alcohol abuse	0.5
Smoking cessation	1.9
Family/Social	1.9
Growth/Development	3.1
Family planning	0.8
Other counseling	8.3

Frank R. Lichtenberg

The probability that nonmedication therapeutic services are offered varies according to patient diagnosis. For example, some kind of nonmedication therapy is provided to almost half of patients with hypertension, but to only 10 percent of patients with upper respiratory tract diseases. We will attempt to control for the effect of improved patient knowledge by including as a covariate the fraction of 1991 patients receiving nonmedication therapeutic services (denoted NON_MED%).

There is good reason to believe that the development and diffusion of *vaccines*, as well as drugs, contributes to mortality reduction. The NAMCS file includes data on vaccine utilization; the vaccines cited in the 1991 file are as follows:

Vaccine	Estimated Number of Vaccinations in 1991
Influenza virus	2,725,489
Diph Pertussis Tetanus	943,313
Polio	683,140
Haemophilus B	525,842
Pneumococcal	214,401
Measles Virus	48,484
Mumps Virus	34,335
Rabies	22,252
Bcg	14,966

Unlike a drug, it would not make sense to link a vaccine with the patient's *current* diagnosis, since a vaccine is administered to *prevent* the person from receiving that diagnosis. Vaccines are therefore excluded from the pharmaceutical variable ($DRUGS_{t-k,t}/DRUGS_{.t}$) in equation (1). In order to control (admittedly imperfectly) for the effect of vaccine availability on mortality reduction, we included a dummy variable (denoted VACCINE) equal to 1 for diseases for which a vaccine was available in 1991, and equal to 0 for other diseases.[34]

The third potential nonpharmaceutical source of mortality reduction we can account for is the rate of introduction of new surgical procedures. Using data from the 1980 and 1991 National Hospital Discharge Surveys, we construct an index (denoted NEWSURG), by disease, of the rate at which new surgical procedures were introduced during the period 1980–91.[35] Let N_{ijt} represent the number of times surgical procedure i was performed on patients with two-digit diagnosis j in year t ($t = 1980, 1991$). Then $N_{.jt} = \Sigma_i N_{ijt}$ denotes the total number of surgical procedures performed on patients with diagnosis j in year t, and $n_{ijt} = N_{ijt}/N_{.jt}$ denotes

Pharmaceutical Innovation, Mortality Reduction, and Economic Growth

TABLE 3.10 Effect of Controlling for Counseling /Education and Vaccine Availability in 1991 on 1970–91 Mortality Reduction

Column:	(1)	(2)	(3)	(4)
($DRUGS_{1970,1991}/DRUGS_{.1991}$)	2.87			2.43
	(7.06)			(5.21)
NON_MED%		1.85		0.95
		(3.41)		(1.81)
VACCINE			0.52	0.37
			(1.39)	(1.13)
Weighted R^2	.4058	.1393	.0261	.4343

NOTE: *t*-statistics are in parentheses. NON_MED% denotes the fraction of 1991 patients receiving non-medication therapeutic services. VACCINE equals 1 for diseases for which a vaccine was available in 1991, and 0 for other diseases.

procedure *i*'s share in total procedures performed on patients with diagnosis *j* in year *t*. We computed NEWSURG as follows:

$$NEWSURG_j = 1 - \frac{\sum_i n_{ij,80}\, n_{ij,91}}{[(\sum_i n_{ij,80}^2)(\sum_i n_{ij,91}^2)]^{1/2}}$$

This index measures the degree of similarity (or dissimilarity) of disease *j*'s 1980 and 1991 percentage distributions of surgical procedures.[36] It is bounded between 0 and 1; a value of 0 indicates no novelty, that is, perfect similarity of the two distributions; and a value of 1 indicates complete novelty, or zero similarity.

Table 3.10 presents 1970–91 mortality-reduction regressions that include the counseling and vaccine variables, NON_MED% and VACCINE. Because the surgical innovation variable NEWSURG pertains to the 1980–91 period, we will analyze the effect of that variable separately below. Column 2 of table 3.10 indicates that diseases for which there was a higher probability of physician counseling in 1991 had greater declines in life-years lost between 1970 and 1991; this is consistent with the hypothesis that improved patient knowledge reduces mortality. Column 3 reveals that diseases for which a vaccine was available in 1991 exhibited greater reductions in mortality than nonvaccine diseases. The relationship is not very significant (*p*-value = .17), however, perhaps due to the crudeness of this measure. When both of these variables and the new drug variable are included in the model (column 4), the coefficient on the latter is reduced by only 15 percent, and it remains highly significant. Neither of the other two coefficients is significant at the 5 percent level. This suggests that failure to account for counseling/education and vaccine availability produces little, if any, upward bias in our estimate of the impact of pharmaceutical innovation on mortality reduction.[37]

Frank R. Lichtenberg

When NEWSURG is included in the 1980–91 mortality reduction model, the results are as follows (*t*-statistics in parentheses):

$$\ln(LYL_{1980}/LYL_{1991}) = \underset{(0.89)}{.080} + \underset{(2.21)}{.359}\ (DRUGS_{1970,1980}/DRUGS_{.1980}) + \underset{(1.31)}{.158}\ NEWSURG$$

$N = 78$; weighted $R^2 = .0880$

As might be expected, the coefficient on NEWSURG is positive—consistent with the view that surgical innovation as well as pharmaceutical innovation contribute to mortality reduction—but it is only significant at the 20 percent level. Moreover, both the point estimate of the drug coefficient and its *t*-statistic are virtually identical to their values when NEWSURG is excluded from the model.[38] Controlling for a potentially important other form of medical innovation has no effect on the estimate of the impact of pharmaceutical innovation.

VI. Estimation of the Social Rate of Return

Our data can be used to obtain approximate measures of the economic benefits (in terms of reduced mortality) of, and social rate of return to, pharmaceutical innovation. Estimates of equation (1) provide one possible way to do this. Note that the intercept of this equation, α, is the expected or predicted value of mortality reduction under no innovation, in other words, $E[\ln(LYL_{1970}/LYL_{1991}) | (DRUGS_{1970,1991}/DRUGS_{.1991}) = 0] = \alpha$. The total benefit of innovation could be measured by the difference between actual mortality reduction and predicted mortality reduction under no innovation. The problem with this approach is that, because there are very few diseases with low values of NEWDRUG%—there is only 1 disease for which NEWDRUG% = 0, and 2 for which NEWDRUG% < 1/3—predicting mortality reduction under no innovation requires extrapolating far from the sample mean and is therefore subject to high forecast error variance.

A second approach, and the one we will adopt because it does not entail extrapolation far from the sample mean, is based on a slightly different functional form of the relationship between the new-drug share and mortality reduction. Suppose that there is a log-linear relationship between the ratio of beginning-of-period to end-of-period LYL and the number of drugs approved during the period (APPS):

(2) $\ln(LYL_{1970}/LYL_{1991}) = \alpha + \beta \ln(APPS_{1970,1991}) + \varepsilon.$

Pharmaceutical Innovation, Mortality Reduction, and Economic Growth

If $0 < \beta < 1$, there are positive but diminishing marginal benefits to approvals. $-\beta$ is the elasticity of LYL_{1991} to $APPS_{1970,1991}$, conditional on LYL_{1970}:

$$-\beta = \frac{d \ln (LYL_{1991})}{d \ln (APPS_{1970,1991})} = \frac{d (LYL_{1991})}{d (APPS_{1970,1991})} \frac{(APPS_{1970,1991})}{(LYL_{1991})}$$

The marginal effect of the number of drugs approved on LYL_{1991} is

$$\frac{d (LYL_{1991})}{d (APPS_{1970,1991})} = -\beta \frac{LYL_{1991}}{APPS_{1970,1991}}$$

At the beginning of 1970, 424 drugs had already been approved by the FDA. Hence the percentage of drugs approved by the beginning of 1991 that were approved after 1970 (%APP7091) is

$$\%APP7091 = APPS_{1970,1991}/(424 + APPS_{1970,1991}).$$

Solving this expression for $APPS_{1970,1991}$,

$$APPS_{1970,1991} = 424 [\%APP7091/(1 - \%APP7091)]$$

and

$$\ln APPS_{1970,1991} = \ln 424 + \ln [\%APP7091/(1 - \%APP7091)].$$

Substituting this expression into equation (2),

(3) $\ln (LYL_{1970}/LYL_{1991}) = \alpha' + \beta \ln [\%APP7091/(1 - \%APP7091)] + \varepsilon,$

where $\alpha' = \alpha + \beta \ln (424)$. Thus, one can estimate the parameter β by regressing $\ln (LYL_{1970}/LYL_{1991})$ on $\ln [\%APP7091/(1 - \%APP7091)]$, where %APP7091 is the percentage of drugs *approved by the beginning of 1991* that were approved after 1970. The latter variable cannot be measured on a disease-by-disease basis. However, a closely related variable, the percentage of drugs *prescribed in 1991* that were approved after 1970, whose average value is fairly similar to that of %APP7091,[39] *can* be measured on a disease-by-disease basis. We therefore estimated the following equation (*t*-statistics in parentheses):

$$\ln (LYL_{1970}/LYL_{1991}) = \underset{(4.329)}{0.304} + \underset{(7.652)}{0.507} \ln [(DRUGS_{1970,1991}/DRUGS_{.1991})/(1 - (DRUGS_{1970,1991}/DRUGS_{.1991}))]$$

$N = 73$, weighted $R^2 = .4519$.

The estimated elasticity of mortality with respect to the number of new drug approvals is about one-half: a 10 percent increase in new drug approvals is estimated to reduce mortality by 5 percent. This functional form fits the data slightly better than equation (1) does; the weighted R^2 has increased from .4058 to .4519.

We can use this estimate of β and sample aggregate values of LYL_{1991} and $APPS_{1970,1991}$ to calculate the number of life-years *saved* by the average new drug approval:

$$\frac{-d\,(LYL_{1991})}{d\,(APPS_{1970,1991})} = \beta\frac{LYL_{1991}}{APPS_{1970,1991}} = \frac{0.507\ (14.8\ \text{million})}{399} = .0188\ \text{million} = 18{,}800.$$

On average, each new drug approved during the period 1970–91 saved 18,800 life-years in 1991 (and presumably will do so in all future years). This is the "marginal physical product" of new drug approvals. By attaching "prices" to new drug approvals and to life-years, we can calculate the social rate of return to investment in pharmaceutical innovation. Myers and Howe (1997) estimate the cost of a new drug approval to be $697 million with program costs allocated and $429 without program costs. Cutler et al. (1996), citing Viscusi (1993), use a "benchmark estimate" of the value of a life-year of $25,000, and upper and lower bounds of $50,000 and $10,000. The aggregate value of 18,800 life-years, each valued at $25,000, is $470 million. If the cost of a new drug approval is $697 million, the social rate of return to pharmaceutical innovation is ($470 m./$697 m.) = 67.5 percent.[40]

This should be regarded as a very rough estimate; for a number of reasons it may be either too high or too low. Industry R&D expenditure may understate the true social cost of drug development. Toole (1998) presents evidence consistent with the view that the number of new molecular entities approved in a given year is positively related to *government*-funded biomedical research expenditure many (e.g. 25) years earlier, as well as to industry-funded R&D. It may therefore be appropriate to include some government-funded R&D in our cost estimate.[41] On the other hand, pharmaceutical innovation probably confers benefits other than reduced mortality, such as reduced hospitalization and surgical expenditures (see Lichtenberg 1996, 2001b), reduced workdays and schooldays lost, and improved quality of life; the above calculation does not account for these.

A rate of return of 68 percent is very high. However, many previous econometric and case studies (see Griliches [1998]) have indicated that the rate of return to R&D investment in general is high—much higher than the rate of return to ordinary investment. Moreover, Cutler, McClellan, and Newhouse (1998: 34) argue that "medical care is a more productive investment than the average use of our funds outside the medical sector," and Nordhaus (this volume) concluded that "the social productivity of health care spending might be many times that of other spending."

VII. Summary and Conclusions

We have analyzed the relationship *across diseases* between the long-term reduction in life-years lost before age 75 and the relative utilization of new pharmaceutical products. This methodology controls for the effects of any general economic and social trends (such as changes in wealth, nutrition, or sanitation) that affect *average* mortality. The data we analyzed cover all diseases and all (outpatient) drugs, thus allowing us (assuming that our model is correctly specified) to draw general conclusions about the impact of new drugs on longevity—a conclusion that cannot be drawn from existing studies, which are about specific diseases and/or drugs.

Previous investigators have argued that increased longevity should be considered an important part of economic growth, and the model we estimated is very consistent with the most widely accepted theory of growth, which implies that the rate of growth of per-capita output depends only on the rate of technological progress. The fraction of drugs prescribed by physicians that are new is, we believe, an excellent indicator of the rate of technical progress in the health care sector of the economy.

We found a highly significant positive relationship between the new-drug share and mortality reduction in all three periods we analyzed. Over 45 percent of the variation across diseases in the 1970–91 reduction in mortality is explained by the new-drug share. The mean percentage reduction in life-years lost for the 19 diseases with the highest relative utilization of new drugs (whose mean new-drug share was 74.6 percent) was over five times as great—72.7 percent vs. 13.0 percent—as the mean percentage reduction in life-years lost for the 19 diseases with the lowest relative utilization of new drugs (whose mean new-drug share was 44.8 percent).

Cutler, McClellan, and Newhouse (1998) found that drug therapies resulted in substantial improvements in heart attack mortality during the period 1975–95, and wondered whether their results "generalize to other types of medical care"(p. 34). Our econometric results strongly suggest that they *do* generalize.

The effect of the new-drug share on mortality reduction appears to have been much higher in 1970–80 than it was in 1980–91. Also, the magnitude and significance of this effect is larger over the entire 21-year period than it is in either of the two subperiods, which is consistent with the view that the long-run effects of new drugs on mortality are larger than the short-run effects. The data provide only weak support for the view that new priority drugs reduce mortality more than new standard drugs.

New drugs appear to have reduced mortality among all broad age groups in one of the two periods. In the 1970–80 period, new drugs reduced mortality only in the lowest and middle thirds of the age distribution of diseases—especially in the former—while in the 1980–91 period, new drugs had a significant positive effect on mortality reduction only in the highest third of the age distribution. Since the drugs introduced in the 1980s tended to be targeted at older patients than the drugs introduced in the 1970s, this "vintage-age interaction" is not surprising.

Pharmaceutical innovation, like most other economic activities, appears to be subject to the law of diminishing marginal productivity: the estimated elasticity of mortality with respect to the number of new drug approvals is about one-half (e.g., a 10 percent increase in new drug approvals is estimated to reduce mortality by 5 percent).

In principle, our initial estimates of the effect of pharmaceutical innovation on mortality reduction could be biased due to failure to control for other determinants of mortality reduction. But further investigation indicated that controlling for counseling/education and vaccine availability has only a small effect on our estimate of the impact of pharmaceutical innovation on mortality reduction. Controlling for the rate of introduction of new surgical procedures had no effect.

We used the data to obtain approximate measures of the economic benefits (in terms of reduced mortality) of, and social rate of return to, pharmaceutical innovation. On average, each new drug approved during the period 1970–91 is estimated to have saved 18,800 life-years in 1991 (and presumably continued to do so in subsequent years). If, as previous researchers have argued, the value of a life-year is about $25,000, and the average cost of a new drug approval is $697 million, then to a first approximation, the social rate of return to pharmaceutical innovation is about 68 percent. This is a very high rate of return, but previous studies have also found high social returns to innovation, and have suggested that "the social productivity of health care spending might be many times that of other spending." This estimate only accounts for the mortality-reduction benefits of new drugs; it does not account for possible morbidity reduction or quality-of-life enhancement. We plan to assess these in future research.

Pharmaceutical Innovation, Mortality Reduction, and Economic Growth

Notes

1. The National Center for Health Statistics first administered the NHAMCS in 1992. Unfortunately, there are no publicly-available data on pharmaceutical utilization in an inpatient setting.

2. Dustan et al. (1996: 1926) arrive at a similar conclusion: "In the past 2 decades, deaths from stroke have decreased by 59% and deaths from heart attack by 53%. An important component of this dramatic change has been the increased use of antihypertensive drugs."

3. "AIDS Deaths Drop 48% in New York," *New York Times*, 3 February 1998, p. A1.

4. Pharmaceutical expenditure accounts for about 10 percent of total U.S. health expenditure.

5. Lichtenberg's (2000) analysis of longitudinal quinquennial country-level data for a sample of 17 member countries of the Organisation for Economic Co-Operation and Development during the period 1960–90 also found no significant effect of either inpatient or ambulatory expenditure on mortality. I did, however, find significant effects of pharmaceutical consumption on both life expectancy at age 40 and life-years lost.

6. Source: author's calculations based on 1991 NAMCS file.

7. It might be possible to eliminate or at least reduce this overstatement by using data similar to those shown above to calculate *age-adjusted* pharmaceutical expenditure.

8. "Benefit to Healthy Men Is Seen from Cholesterol-Cutting Drug," *New York Times*, 16 November 1995, p. A1.

9. Of course, these mean life expectancies are affected by premature mortality.

10. As Murray and Lopez (1996: 16) observe, "Under the rules of the International Classification of Diseases, deaths must be assigned to one cause only, and this must be the underlying cause: for example, if someone has a heart attack and later dies of pneumonia in hospital, the cause of death must be recorded as ischaemic heart disease."

11. The calculated distribution of the log change between 1980 and 1991 of life-years lost included two extreme outliers. The mean, median, and highest and lowest five values of this distribution (N = 79) were as follows: mean = .079; median = .093; lowest = (−4.31, −1.21, −1.07, −0.61, −0.50); highest = (0.66, 0.70, 0.81, 0.86, 3.51). The lowest value was for poliomye . . . ; the highest was for Disorder . . . A log change of −4.31 corresponds to a 75-fold increase in life-years lost, and a log change of 3.51 corresponds to a 33-fold decrease. We were suspicious of such extreme magnitudes, and these observations were statistically quite influential, so we excluded them from the sample.

12. This model embodies the assumption of diminishing marginal returns to innovation. Suppose that there were 100 old drugs. If 25 new drugs were introduced, the "new-drug share" (the share of new drugs in total end-of-period drugs) would be 20 percent [= 25/(100 + 25)]. If twice as many new drugs (50) were introduced, the new-drug share would be less than twice as high, 33 percent [= 50/(100 + 50)]. If mortality reduction is a linear function of the new-drug share (as in equation [1]), the first 25 new drugs reduce mortality more than the second 25 new drugs.

13. Some general societal trends, such as the increase in the fraction of the population that is obese, may be mortality-increasing rather than mortality-reducing.

14. In aggregate time-series analyses of overall trends in mortality (e.g. Frech and Miller [1999]), to obtain unbiased estimates of the impact of drugs, it is crucial to control for trends in nondrug determinants of mortality. In contrast, in our longitudinal, disease-level analysis, it is necessary to control only for those determinants that are correlated across diseases with pharmaceutical innovation.

15. The extent of drug innovation seems more likely to depend on the *level* of average wealth than on its growth rate.

16. There is no direct correspondence between the nature of injury codes and the external cause of death codes, e.g. 821 does not correspond to E821.

Frank R. Lichtenberg

17. For a discussion of the statistical tradeoffs associated with aggregation, see Grunfeld and Griliches (1960).

18. The FDA data enable us to identify the dates of "minor" innovations—new formulations of existing molecules—as well as the dates of "major" innovations—new molecules. For example, approval dates of different dosage forms of the molecule aminophylline are as follows:

1940 tablet
1979 tablet, sustained action
1982 solution
1983 suppository
1991 injection

Minor as well as major innovations may confer health benefits. Unfortunately, we are unable to monitor the diffusion of minor innovations, since the drug information provided in NAMCS does not include the dosage form or route of administration of the drug prescribed, only the name of the compound.

19. Estimated annual number of outpatient visits, by venue, are as follows.
Doctors' offices : 670 million
Hospital outpatient departments: 63 million
Emergency rooms: 90 million

20. Unfortunately, there is a slight temporal misalignment between the two surveys: the NAMCS data are for 1991 (the same year as the mortality data), but the NHAMCS data are for 1993.

21. The FDA's stated goal is to review and act on complete applications for "priority" drugs within 6 months of an NDA's submission date, and to review and act on NDAs for "standard" drugs within 12 months. However, until the recent prescription drug fee legislation, few drugs were approved within 6 months. All AIDS drugs are classified as priority drugs.

22. Of course, new drugs may confer health and economic benefits to patients other than mortality reduction. In future research, we plan to investigate the effect of pharmaceutical innovation on morbidity and "quality of life" using data from National Health Interview Surveys. (If, as we argue in this paper, new drugs tend to reduce mortality, one should examine the impact of pharmaceutical innovation on morbidity reduction *controlling for mortality reduction*, since new drugs are likely to keep less healthy people alive.) The introduction of a new, standard drug is likely to make the market for drugs in that class more competitive, and to lower prices to consumers.

23. Many economic relationships are stronger in the long run than they are in the short. For example, as Hall and Taylor (1997: 265–67) observe, the relationship between consumption expenditure and disposable income is stronger in the long run than it is in the short run.

24. To illustrate this, we estimated the unweighted regression of the log change between 1980 and 1991 in LYL on the share of new, priority drugs in 1991, and computed the absolute value of the residuals from this regression. We then divided the diseases into three size categories, based on the average number of LYL in 1980 and 1991. The means of the absolute residuals in each of the three size groups were

smallest: 0.322
middle: 0.288
largest: 0.137.

Also, there is a highly significant (p-value $< .01$) inverse correlation between the absolute residual and the logarithm of mean LYL.

25. The consequences of random measurement error in the independent variable are well known to econometricians. Suppose the true model is $y = \beta x^* + u$, but x^* is not observed; instead we observe $x = x^* + e$, where e is a random error term, with mean 0 and variance σ_e^2.

Then $E(b) = \beta\,(\sigma_*^2/(\sigma_*^2 + \sigma_e^2))$, where b is the OLS slope coefficient, and σ_*^2 is the variance of x^*. The larger the "noise-to-signal ratio" (σ_e^2/σ_*^2), the greater the bias toward 0 of b.

26. 9.8 percent of the medications whose prescription status could be determined in 1991 were nonprescription drugs.

27. Compliance rates vary with the disease and setting of the patient group. According to data reported in the *Journal of Clinical Pharmacy and Therapeutics*, patients in homes for the aged had relatively high rates of compliance, as did patients in the first year of antihypertensive treatment. In contrast, patients taking penicillin for rheumatic fever had relatively low rates of compliance.

28. We attempted to explore the relationship across drug classes between unpublished PhRMA data on R&D intensity (the ratio of R&D expenditure to sales) and our data on the share of new drugs in total prescriptions. Unfortunately, the PhRMA data are available for only eight highly aggregated drug classes (e.g. cardiovascular drugs), and we failed to find a statistically significant relationship based on such a small sample.

29. If the coefficient from the regression of Y on X is b, the coefficient from the regression of Y on $(X/2)$ is $2b$. The t-statistic on b and the R^2 of the two regressions are the same.

30. Since, as noted above, patients may have multiple diagnoses, the drugs are not necessarily prescribed *for* these diseases.

31. Fortunately, however, at the present time many people expect that there will soon be a number of highly effective drugs to fight cancer.

32. In our sample, we can't reject the null hypothesis that the studentized residuals are a random sample from a normal distribution (p-value = .24).

33. The studentized residuals for these observations are −2.89 (Other forms of heart disease [420–29]), −2.56 (Chronic obstructive pulmonary disease and allied conditions), −2.43 (Malignant neoplasm of respiratory and intrathoracic organs), −2.23 (Nonspecific abnormal findings, Ill-defined and unknown causes), 2.21 (Acute rheumatic fever [390–92] and chronic rheumatic heart disease), 2.60 (congenital anomalies), and 2.83 (Other conditions originating in the perinatal period [764–77]).

34. VACCINE = 1 for *ICD-9* codes 03-07 and 48. Unfortunately, we lack data on the date of FDA approval of these vaccines.

35. Unfortunately, it does not appear to be feasible to measure the fraction of surgical procedures performed that are new, analogous to the fraction of drugs prescribed that are new, since comprehensive data on the date of introduction of all surgical procedures are not available. Unlike drugs, the introduction of new surgical procedures is not subject to government regulation.

36. Jaffe (1986) used the cosine of firms' distributions of patents by patent class to measure their technological proximity.

37. Since new vaccines, as well as new drugs, are the fruits of innovative activity, the total effect on mortality of drug-cum-vaccine innovation is the *sum* of the drug and vaccine coefficients.

38. We also estimated the model including an interaction term between the two regressors, to allow for the possibility of complementarity between pharmaceutical and surgical innovation. In this model, the main effect of NEWSURG is positive and significant and the interaction term is negative and significant. However, the marginal effect of surgical novelty, evaluated at the sample mean value of NEWDRUG, is not significantly different from 0 (p-value = .49). The significance of the NEWDRUG effect (evaluated at the sample mean value of NEWSURG), increases slightly (the p-value falls from .022 to .004).

39. FDA data indicate that 46.4% (= 1 − (442/824)) of the drugs approved by the beginning of 1991 were approved after 1970; NAMCS data reveal that 62.7 percent of the drugs prescribed in 1991 were approved after 1970.

40. If life-years are valued at $10,000, the social rate of return is 27 percent.

Frank R. Lichtenberg

41. In 1992, about half the total health R&D expenditure in the United States was publicly supported, but during the last few decades, private funding has grown much more rapidly than public funding. In 1980, government R&D accounted for almost 80 percent of U.S. health R&D. Source: National Science Board (1993: 365).

References

Advisory Commission to Study the Consumer Price Index. 1996. "Toward a More Accurate Measure of the Cost of Living." Final report to the Senate Finance Committee, 4 December. <http://www.ssa.gov/history/reports/boskinrpt.html>

Belsley, D. A., E. Kuh, and R. E. Welsch. 1980. *Regression Diagnostics*. New York: John Wiley & Sons.

Bresnahan, Timothy, and Robert J. Gordon. 1997. *The Economics of New Goods.* Chicago: University of Chicago Press.

Cutler, David, Mark McClellan, and Joseph Newhouse. 1998. "The Costs and Benefits of Intensive Treatment for Cardiovascular Disease." National Bureau of Economic Research Working Paper no. 6514, April.

Cutler, David, Mark McClellan, Joseph Newhouse, and Dahlia Remler. 1996. "Are Medical Prices Declining?" NBER Working Paper no. 5750, September.

Dustan, Harriet, et al. 1996. "Controlling Hypertension: A Research Success Story." *Archives of Internal Medicine* 56 (23 September): 1926–35.

Frech, H. E., and Richard D. Miller Jr. 1999. *The Productivity of Health Care and Pharmaceuticals: An International Comparison.* Washington, D.C.: AEI Press.

Greene, William H. 1997. *Econometric Analysis.* Upper Saddle River, N.J.: Prentice Hall.

Griliches, Zvi. 1998. *R&D and Productivity: The Econometric Evidence.* Chicago: University of Chicago Press.

Griliches, Zvi, and Frank Lichtenberg. 1984. "R&D and Productivity at the Industry Level: Is There Still a Relationship?" In *R&D, Patents, and Productivity,* edited by Zvi Griliches. Chicago: University of Chicago Press.

Grunfeld, Yehuda, and Zvi Griliches. 1960. "Is Aggregation Necessarily Bad?" *Review of Economics and Statistics* (February): 1–13.

Hall, Robert, and John Taylor. 1997. *Macroeconomics,* 5th ed. New York: Norton.

Jaffe, Adam B. 1986. "Technological Opportunity and Spillovers of R&D: Evidence from Firms' Patents, Profits and Market Value." *American Economic Review* 76 (December): 984–1001.

Lichtenberg, Frank. 1996. "Do (More and Better) Drugs Keep People Out of Hospitals?" *American Economic Review* 86 (May): 384–88.

———. 2000. Comment on papers by Richard Frank and David Salkever and by Jonathan Skinner and John Wennberg in *The Changing Hospital Industry: Comparing Not-for-Profit and For-Profit Institutions,* edited by David M. Cutler, pp. 221–26. Chicago: University of Chicago Press.

———. 2001a. "The Allocation of Publicly Funded Biomedical Research." In *Medical Care Output and Productivity,* 565–89, edited by Ernst Berndt and David Cutler. Studies in Income and Wealth, vol. 62. Chicago: University of Chicago Press.

———. 2001b. "Are the Benefits of Newer Drugs Worth Their Cost? Evidence from the 1996 MEPS." *Health Affairs* 20, no. 5 (September/October): 241–51.

Pharmaceutical Innovation, Mortality Reduction, and Economic Growth

Mankiw, N. Gregory. 1992. *Macroeconomics.* New York: Worth Publishers.

Myers, Stewart C., and Christopher D. Howe. 1997. "A Life-Cycle Financial Model of Pharmaceutical R&D." MIT Sloan School of Management Program on the Pharmaceutical Industry Working Paper no. 41–97, April.

Murray, Christopher, and Alan Lopez. 1996. *The Global Burden of Disease: Summary* Cambridge, Mass.: Harvard School of Public Health.

National Science Board. 1993. *Science and Engineering Indicators—1993.* Washington, D.C.: GPO.

Pharmaceutical Research and Manufacturers of America (PhRMA). 2001. *Pharmaceutical Industry Profile 2000.* Washington, D.C.

Skinner, J., and J. E. Wennberg. 2000. "How Much Is Enough? Efficiency and Medicare Spending in the Last Six Months of Life." In *The Changing Hospital Industry: Comparing Not-for-Profit and For-Profit Institutions,* 169–93, edited by David Cutler. Chicago: University of Chicago Press.

Toole, Andrew. 1998. "The Impact of Federally Funded Basic Research on Industrial Innovation: Evidence From the Pharmaceutical Industry." Unpublished paper, Laurits R. Christensen Associates, Madison, Wis., 22 February.

Viscusi, W. Kip. 1993. "The Value of Risks to Life and Health." *Journal of Economic Literature* 31: 1912–46.

[11]

Lessons from 60 years of pharmaceutical innovation

Bernard Munos

Abstract | Despite unprecedented investment in pharmaceutical research and development (R&D), the number of new drugs approved by the US Food and Drug Administration (FDA) remains low. To help understand this conundrum, this article investigates the record of pharmaceutical innovation by analysing data on the companies that introduced the ~1,200 new drugs that have been approved by the FDA since 1950. This analysis shows that the new-drug output from pharmaceutical companies in this period has essentially been constant, and remains so despite the attempts to increase it. This suggests that, contrary to common perception, the new-drug output is not depressed, but may simply reflect the limitations of the current R&D model. The implications of these findings and options to achieve sustainability for the pharmaceutical industry are discussed.

New molecular entity (NME). A medication containing an active ingredient that has not been previously approved for marketing in any form in the United States. NME is conventionally used to refer only to small-molecule drugs, but in this article the term includes biologics as a shorthand for both types of new drug.

Prescription Drug User Fee Act A US law passed in 1992 that allows the US Food and Drug Administration to collect fees from drug manufacturers to fund the new-drug approval process.

From 1950 to 2008, the US Food and Drug Administration (FDA) approved 1,222 new drugs (new molecular entities (NMEs) or new biologics). However, although the level of investment in pharmaceutical research and development (R&D) has increased dramatically during this period — to US$50 billion per year at present[1] — the number of new drugs that are approved annually is no greater now than it was 50 years ago. Indeed, in 2008, only 21 new drugs were approved for marketing in the United States, which is well below the level required to secure the future of the pharmaceutical industry.

With the aim of investigating this issue, this article analyses the output of new drugs — NMEs or new biologics approved by the FDA — from the companies responsible during the past 60 years (see BOX 1 for details of the methodology). This analysis shows that the rate of production of new drugs by these companies has been constant (although the rates differ for each company) since they began producing drugs. Surprisingly, nothing that companies have done in the past 60 years has affected their rates of new-drug production: whether large or small, focused on small molecules or biologics, operating in the twenty-first century or in the 1950s, companies have produced NMEs at steady rates, usually well below one per year. This characteristic raises questions about the sustainability of the industry's R&D model, as costs per NME have soared into billions of dollars. It also challenges the rationale for major mergers and acquisitions (M&A), as none has had a detectable effect on new-drug output. Finally, it suggests that drug companies need to be bolder in redesigning their research organizations if they are to escape the increasing pressures created by linear new-drug output and rapidly rising R&D costs.

Rate of new drug introduction

Of the 1,222 NMEs that have been approved since 1950, 1,103 are small molecules and 119 are biologics. FIGURE 1a shows the timeline of these approvals. Although at first glance there are no obvious patterns, on closer observation subtle trends emerge. For the 30 years between 1950 and 1980, the trend line is basically flat. Then for the next 15 years, the curve slopes gently upwards, culminating in 51 approvals in 1996, 4 years after the enactment of the Prescription Drug User Fee Act (PDUFA). Since 1996, approvals have returned to their historical range. There has been speculation that the peak in 1996 was caused by the FDA processing a backlog of applications with the help of the recently approved user fees. Although this may have played a part, other factors were involved, as discussed below. A second trend is that approvals of biologics are not taking off as might be expected from a new technology.

Many players, but few winners

At present, there are more than 4,300 companies that are engaged in drug innovation[2], yet only 261 organizations (6%) have registered at least one NME since 1950. Of these, only 32 (12%) have been in existence for the entire 59-year period. The remaining 229 (88%) organizations have failed, merged, been acquired, or were created by such M&A deals, resulting in substantial turnover in the

Lilly Corporate Center, Indianapolis, Indiana 46285, USA.
e-mails: b.munos@lilly.com; bhmunos@stanfordalumni.org
doi:10.1038/nrd2961

Box 1 | Data collection and analysis

Definitions

- For the purpose of this study, an innovation is a new molecular entity (NME) or a new biologic approved by the US Food and Drug Administration (FDA), and excludes non-drug compounds such as imaging agents and cosmetics. This article uses NME as shorthand for both types of drugs.
- Biologics are all therapeutic proteins, regardless of their approval route.
- A blockbuster is defined here as an NME the peak sales of which exceed $1 billion, expressed in year-2000 dollars equivalent. Figures have been adjusted for inflation using the US Bureau of Labor Statistics' Drug Inflation Index.
- A large pharmaceutical company is one of the top 15 drug companies, or their predecessors and joint ventures (for example, Ciba, SmithKline and DuPont–Merck). All other companies, including biotechnology companies, are categorized as small pharmaceutical companies.

Data sources

- NME data were obtained from the FDA under a freedom-of-information request, and were cross-checked against Lilly's own record, as well as lists of FDA approvals that are routinely published in the press. When several companies have collaborated on the development of a drug, or the ownership of the compound has changed before approval, the company receiving FDA approval has been credited with the innovation.
- Sales and patent data were obtained from the EvaluatePharma Database (see Further information).
- Inflation data were obtained from the US Bureau of Labor Statistics.

Tools

- All statistical calculations were done with the JMP software, version 5.1.1, or Excel 2007.

Exclusions

- 11 organizations out of 261 (accounting for 13 NMEs out of 1,222) are non-commercial entities (non-profit and governmental organizations) or companies that no longer exist and have been omitted from most of the analysis. Of the remaining 250 companies, 26 (accounting for 63 NMEs) had fewer than 10 data points and were also excluded from most of the analysis.

Potential limitations

- It could be argued that defining innovation as NMEs approved by the FDA does not give due credit to innovation originating outside the United States. However, because the pharmaceutical industry is global, and the United States is by far its largest market, most NMEs are eventually submitted to the FDA for approval.
- There is some debate about the number of NMEs that were approved prior to the US Kefauver–Harris amendment of 1962, which requires proof of effectiveness and safety before a drug can be registered. Data that were compiled at the time by de Haen and used in a congressional testimony by FDA Commissioner Alexander Schmidt in 1974 show that 360 NMEs were approved between 1951 and 1962, or ~30 per year. It seems that this figure was subsequently revised by the FDA, and reduced to 227. As this occurred a long time ago, it is difficult to reconstruct what happened. However, the editing seems to have been careful, as the data provided by the FDA meticulously listed each drug by its brand name and active ingredient, as well as its dosage form, sponsor and exact date of approval. The 133 missing potential NMEs were evidently excluded for a reason and, lacking evidence to challenge it, the data were used as provided.
- It might be argued that NMEs are an inappropriate measure of innovation because a molecule with little therapeutic value can conceivably be approved, provided it meets FDA requirements. However, given the costs of drug research and development, this is unlikely to occur in practice. A drug that is innovative may nevertheless fail to generate substantial sales revenues, raising questions about the value of its innovation (for example, as with Pfizer's inhaled insulin product Exubera). This article considers that these molecules represent genuine advances and should count as innovation, as their market failure can be explained by several factors that are unrelated to innovation, such as mispricing, reluctance on the part of physicians or patients to change from established drugs, and competition.
- The decision to credit the company that secures a drug approval with the corresponding innovation could be questioned, because that molecule may have been licensed from another company that receives no credit. As licensees are often thought to be large companies, and licensors smaller ones, this could potentially bias the analysis by giving certain companies more, or less, credit than warranted. However, this concern does not seem to be justified. Over the past 20 years, a thriving market for innovation has developed, involving thousands of collaborations each year — including licensing, cross-licensing, sublicensing, joint discovery, co-development, buy-back options, loans, equity stakes, outsourcing, warrants and joint ventures — which often makes it impossible to assess the precise contribution made by a company to the approval of a new drug. In addition, small companies are eager participants in this market, in which they collaborate with other small companies more frequently than with large ones. Between 1980 and 2004, small companies had a slightly greater share of discovery projects than did larger companies (47% versus 38%), but both shared equally in the number of development projects (45% versus 46%)[42]. The view that the division of labour might allow large companies to capture a greater share of development projects and FDA approvals is therefore not supported by the data. In addition, as innovation networks spread, the locus of innovation tends to shift from individual companies to the network[43]. So, the decision to credit the company at the centre of that network with the innovation that it creates seems to be justified, especially given that, by organizing and managing the network to gain FDA approval, that company often makes the greatest contribution to the process.

industry (FIG. 1b). Of the 261 organizations, only 105 exist today, whereas 137 have disappeared through M&A and 19 were liquidated.

Despite this intense turnover, the fact that 32 companies have survived the entire period suggests that there are ways to innovate that are sustainable. This group includes 23 companies that have found unique ways to thrive despite their smaller size. Some are highly focused on a particular disease area or therapeutic strategy (Novo Nordisk, Ferring, Grifols, UCB, Endo and Purdue); some sell products and services in addition to drugs (Bausch and Lomb, and Allergan); some are entrenched in their home-country market (Takeda, Santen, Eisai, Angelini and Orion); some are conglomerates (Boehringer–Ingelheim, Solvay, Baxter and Carter–Wallace); and some concentrate on generics (Teva and Mission Pharmacal).

At the high end of the innovation scale, 21 companies have produced half of all the NMEs that have been approved since 1950, but half of these companies no longer exist. FIGURE 1c shows that Merck has been the most productive firm, with 56 approvals, closely followed by Lilly and Roche, with 51 and 50 approvals, respectively. Given that many large pharmaceutical companies estimate they need to produce an average of 2–3 NMEs per year to meet their growth objectives, the fact that none of them has ever approached this level of output is concerning.

The dynamics of drug innovation

The timelines of cumulative NME approvals for the three most productive companies in the industry are shown in FIG. 2a. Surprisingly, the plots are almost straight lines, indicating that these companies have delivered innovation at a constant rate for almost 60 years. The outputs from less productive companies, some of which are plotted in FIG. 2b, show a similar linear pattern, although it is more erratic and with smaller slopes. The stable rates of output that are apparent in FIGS 2a,b suggest that NME production at a pharmaceutical company follows a Poisson distribution. This hypothesis is confirmed by the statistical analysis described in Supplementary information S1 (box)).

Importantly, as Poisson distributions are characterized by a constant but stochastically variable rate of occurrence, this implies that the average annual NME output of drug companies is constant, and has been so for nearly 60 years. This is consistent with the fact that the drug industry produces no more NMEs today than 60 years ago, which has important implications. If nothing that drug companies have done in the past 60 years has succeeded in raising their mean annual NME output, there is not a high probability that established strategies will change this now. FIGURE 2c shows that the industry's NME output has tracked its expected values. This suggests that the output may not be depressed, as commonly thought, but may simply reflect the innovative capacity of the established R&D model. As the integrated corporate laboratory is one of the few features shared by companies during the 60-year period, it is possible that the constant NME output is a fixture of that model. If this is true, the industry's efforts to embrace new approaches to innovation, such as open innovation[3], are of particular importance.

Another surprising finding is that companies that do essentially the same thing can have rates of NME output that differ widely. This suggests there are substantial differences in the ability of different companies to foster innovation. In this respect, the fact that the companies that have relied heavily on M&A (FIG. 2b) tend to lag behind those that have not (FIG. 2a) suggests that M&A are not an effective way to promote an innovation culture or remedy a deficit of innovation.

If the NME output of drug companies is constant, the only way to increase the overall industry output is to increase the number of companies, which runs counter to the surge of M&A activity of the past 12 years. Indeed, FIG. 2c suggests that there may be a correlation between the expected NME output for the industry (on the basis of the analysis described in Supplementary information S1 (box)) and the number of companies involved. A closer examination of this relationship (FIG. 2d) confirms that the expected NME output and the number of companies are closely correlated in a nonlinear relationship that explains 95% of the changes in expected NME output by changes in the number of companies. As the number of companies increases, the expected NME output increases more than proportionally. One possible interpretation is that a larger number of companies accelerates the acquisition of knowledge, creating what economists call a spillover — an industry-wide benefit that enables all companies to be more productive. This has important implications for the design of new R&D models.

As can be seen in FIG. 2c, actual NME output for 1996–1997 clearly lies outside the 95% confidence band of its expected value, suggesting that an external factor temporarily boosted the number of NMEs that were approved. Several explanations have been offered, most of which centre on the impact of the PDUFA of 1992. They include a clearing of the backlog of new drug applications that were submitted before 1992; the setting of performance goals that required swift action on post-1992 submissions; a surge of post-1992 submissions to take advantage of PDUFA before it might expire; and a temporary acceleration of drug R&D across the industry to try to increase NME output. These hypotheses are not amenable to statistical testing, but the last two can be readily dismissed, as they are not consistent with the way the industry works. The factor relating to performance goals may have played a part, but much of the surge can probably be ascribed to the clearing of the backlog of new drug applications.

As the output of new biologics also follows a Poisson distribution, its pattern is similar to that for NMEs, in which approvals fluctuate around a constant, low level (FIG. 1a). This has led to the suggestion that biotechnology is not delivering on its promise to increase the rate of innovation because it has co-opted the pharmaceutical industry's ageing business model instead of crafting its own[4].

Lastly, further statistical analysis (see Supplementary information S2 (box)) can be used to calculate the probability that a company's NME output will exceed 2 or

ANALYSIS

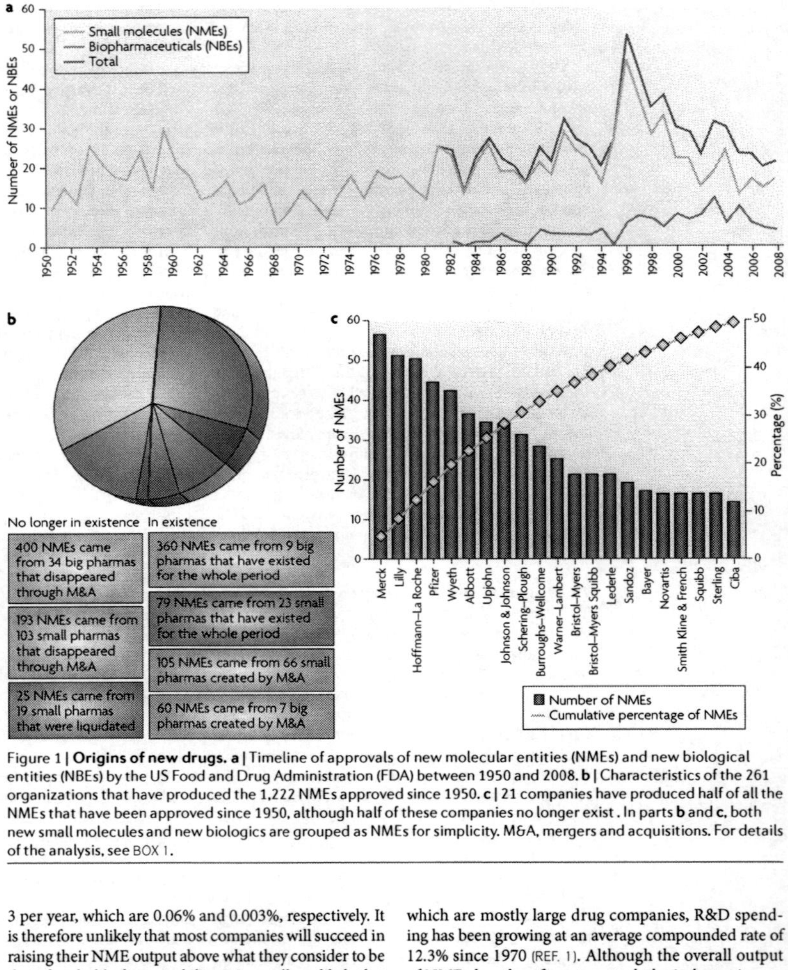

Figure 1 | **Origins of new drugs. a** | Timeline of approvals of new molecular entities (NMEs) and new biological entities (NBEs) by the US Food and Drug Administration (FDA) between 1950 and 2008. **b** | Characteristics of the 261 organizations that have produced the 1,222 NMEs approved since 1950. **c** | 21 companies have produced half of all the NMEs that have been approved since 1950, although half of these companies no longer exist. In parts **b** and **c**, both new small molecules and new biologics are grouped as NMEs for simplicity. M&A, mergers and acquisitions. For details of the analysis, see BOX 1.

3 per year, which are 0.06% and 0.003%, respectively. It is therefore unlikely that most companies will succeed in raising their NME output above what they consider to be their threshold of sustainability. It is equally unlikely that the industry will achieve an overall output that is much greater than the current one.

The cost of NMEs

The cost per NME has been increasing for decades. FIGURE 3a displays 12 independent NME cost estimates[5–14] spanning 48 years, and FIG. 3b plots the same data on a logarithmic scale. Both charts show that NME costs have been growing exponentially at an annual rate of 13.4% since the 1950s.

According to the Pharmaceutical Research and Manufacturers of America (PhRMA), the members of which are mostly large drug companies, R&D spending has been growing at an average compounded rate of 12.3% since 1970 (REF. 1). Although the overall output of NMEs has therefore stagnated, the industry is producing them more efficiently as it has been able to meet the increase in the cost per NME with a less than commensurate increase in R&D spending. In other words, the industry is better at what it does than it was previously, much of which is to generate data to meet FDA requirements. However, this increased efficiency has not translated into a sustained increase in the discovery of new treatments.

DiMasi has estimated that the average cost per NME was $802 million in 2000 for small molecules[8], and $1,318 million in 2005 for biologics[11]. These averages, however, do not include post-approval costs for Phase IV

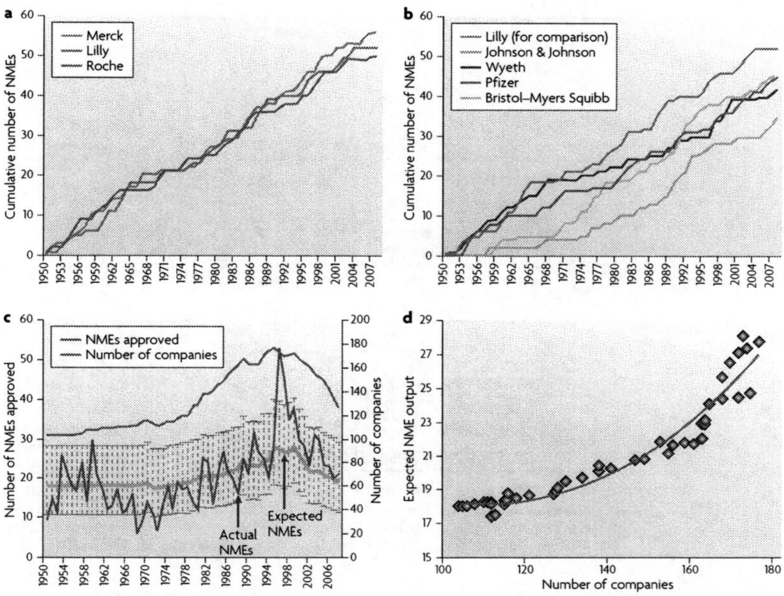

Figure 2 | **The dynamics of drug innovation. a** | The cumulative number of new molecular entities (NMEs) originating from the three most productive companies over the period studied: Merck, Lilly and Roche. **b** | The cumulative number of NMEs from selected companies that have been heavily involved in mergers and acquisitions, with Lilly included for comparison. **c** | The NME output of the industry closely tracks the expected value on the basis of the analysis described in Supplementary information S1 (box), suggesting that output is not depressed at present, but simply reflects the innovative capacity of the established research and development model. **d** | The expected NME output and the number of companies are closely correlated in a nonlinear relationship that explains 95% of the changes in expected NME output by changes in the number of companies.

studies that might be required by the FDA; they also omit costs to gain regulatory approval in non-US markets or obtain additional label claims for new indications. Most importantly, they assume that the probability that a molecule will successfully emerge from clinical trials is about 21.5%, whereas recent industry data suggest that this value is 11.5%. When DiMasi's figures are adjusted for these items as well as for inflation and other cost increases (for example, owing to more stringent regulatory requirements), the cost per NME increases considerably, as summarized in FIG. 3c. These averages also conceal potentially large differences between companies. For example, between 2000 and 2008, Pfizer spent a total of $60 billion on R&D, and received FDA approval for nine NMEs. By contrast, Progenics, which received FDA approval for methylnaltrexone bromide (Relistor) in 2008, spent $400 million on R&D over the same period, suggesting a cost per NME that is substantially lower than Pfizer's.

Estimating the cost of NMEs is complex because the money spent on R&D is returned in revenue over several years. R&D expenses should therefore be depreciated over that period. However, the duration of this period is unclear, and has probably changed over time, as science and regulations have transformed drug research. Practically, there is little consensus among experts on how to capitalize and depreciate drug R&D. Published studies have used periods ranging from 4 to 12 years.

However, the finding that drug companies produce NMEs at a constant rate makes it possible to develop simple estimates of NME costs at a company level by dividing each company's annual R&D spending by its rate of NME production. FIGURE 3d shows the distribution of NME costs across the industry for 2008. Only 27% of companies have costs per NME below $1.0 billion. The magnitude of these figures is worrying and calls for more research to fully understand the implications.

Does regulation hinder innovation?

The growth in R&D spending is needed to offset inflation and the increasing burden of regulation, as well as other factors that could be contributing to greater costs, such as higher failure rates. As inflation has been ~3.7% since 1950 and the annual growth in R&D spending has

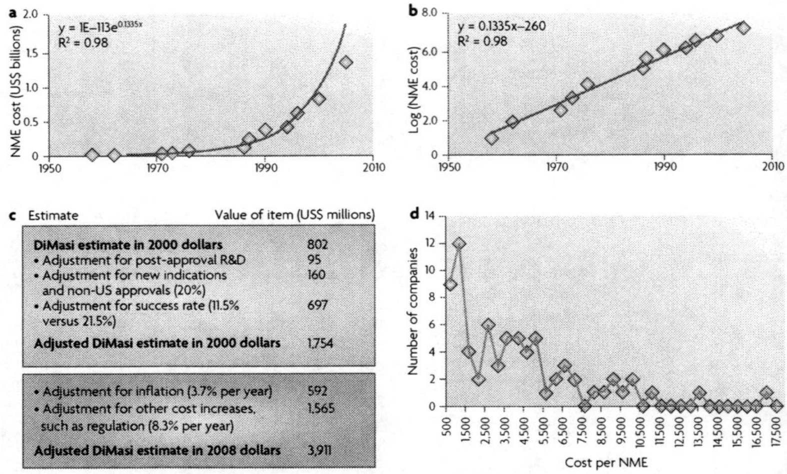

Figure 3 | **The cost of new drugs. a** | A plot of twelve independent estimates of the cost of a new molecular entity (NME) spanning 48 years[5–14]. **b** | The same data plotted on a logarithmic scale. The exponent in the line equation in part **a** and the gradient of the line in part **b** show that the cost per NME has grown at an annual compound rate of 13.35% since the late 1950s. **c** | Adjusted costs per NME: 2000 versus 2008. **d** | Distribution of costs per NME for the industry in 2008.

been 12.3%, one can infer that regulatory and other costs have been growing at ~8.3% annually, which translates into a doubling every 8.5 years. This increase has often been attributed to the increasing prudence of regulatory bodies following the high-profile withdrawals of drugs such as rofecoxib (Vioxx; Merck), cerivastatin (Baycol; Bayer), troglitazone (Rezulin; Warner-Lambert) and cisapride (Propulsid; Janssen Pharmaceutica).

The evidence available on the effect of regulation on innovation is more nuanced. It is interesting that a 1983 study of the drug industry by the National Academy of Engineering[15] had already noted the increasing regulatory burden, and voiced concern that the resulting higher cost of innovation in the United States was undermining the competitiveness of the US drug industry and putting it at a disadvantage compared with its European and Japanese competitors. In fact, the opposite happened: since that report was published, US pharmaceutical companies have outperformed their international competitors and emerged as the dominant force in the industry.

A possible reason for this paradox can be found in other research published at about the same time[16]. It shows that countries with a more demanding regulatory apparatus, such as the United States and the UK, have fostered a more innovative and competitive pharmaceutical industry. This is because exacting regulatory requirements force companies to be more selective in the compounds that they aim to bring to market. Conversely, countries with more permissive systems tend to produce drugs that may be successful in their home market, but are generally not sufficiently innovative to gain widespread approval and market acceptance elsewhere. This is consistent with studies indicating that, by making research more risky, stringent regulatory requirements actually stimulate R&D investment and promote the emergence of an industry that is research intensive, innovative, dominated by few companies and profitable[17,18].

Is bigger better?

A puzzling trend of recent years has been the gradual erosion in the share of innovation that is captured by NMEs sponsored by large pharmaceutical companies (see BOX 1 for definitions). Since the early 1980s, their share of NMEs has declined from ~75%, a level that had been constant since 1950, to ~35% (FIG. 4a). At the same time, the share of NMEs that is attributable to small biotechnology and pharmaceutical companies has almost trebled, from ~23% to nearly 70%. Since 2004, small companies have consistently matched or outperformed their larger competitors. The expected share of NMEs generally follows these trends until 2004, when they stabilize at about 50% each.

The increase in the NME output from small companies has been driven by two factors. The first is a rise in the number of small companies that have produced an NME, which nearly doubled from 78 to 145 during the 1980s and 1990s. This was facilitated by the growth of venture capital that has funded much of the 'biotech boom'. Second, the mean annual NME output of small companies

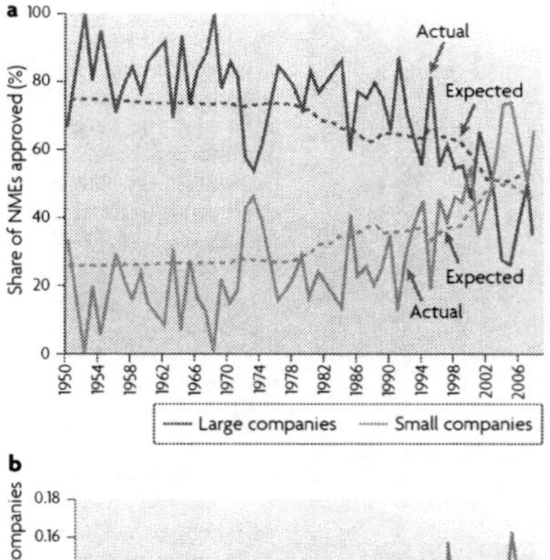

Figure 4 | **Is bigger better? a** | Actual versus expected shares of new molecular entities (NMEs) for large and small pharmaceutical companies. **b** | Mean annual NME output for small companies. See BOX 1 for definitions.

has increased from ~0.04 to ~0.12 since 1995, owing to the emergence of new, more productive companies (FIG. 4b). Conversely, the decline in the output of large companies has been driven by the dwindling number of large pharmaceutical companies, which has decreased by 50% over the past 20 years.

It is too early to tell whether the trends of the past 10 years are artefacts or evidence of a more fundamental transformation of the drug innovation dynamics that have prevailed since 1950. Hypotheses to explain these trends, which could be tested in the future, include: first, that the NME output of small companies has increased as they have become more enmeshed in innovation networks; second, that large companies are making more detailed investigations into fundamental science, which stretch research and regulatory timelines; and third, that the heightened safety concerns of regulators affect large and small companies differently, perhaps because a substantial number of small firms are developing orphan drugs and/or drugs that are likely to gain priority review from the FDA owing to unmet medical needs.

Orphan drug
A drug that is specifically developed for a disease that affects a patient population of fewer than 200,000 people in the United States. The Orphan Drug Act provides financial incentives to develop such drugs, including marketing exclusivity for that indication for 7 years after approval.

According to a recent report[2], the 4,300 biotechnology companies spend ~$28 billion annually on R&D, compared with $50 billion for large pharmaceutical companies[1]. By virtue of their number, small firms collectively can explore far more directions, and investigate areas that their larger, more conservative competitors avoid. However, only a small fraction of these small companies will be rewarded with an FDA approval. Individually, they are a much less reliable source of NMEs than large companies, but collectively, they produce more, for less. In this strange equation lies perhaps one potential avenue for renewing the pharmaceutical R&D model. The innovation crisis of the pharmaceutical industry is occurring in the midst of a new golden age of scientific discovery. If large companies could organize innovation networks to harness the scientific diversity of biotechnology companies and academic institutions, and combine it with their own development expertise, they might be able to reverse the forces that are undermining their research model; that is, they might be able to lower their costs and increase their output.

Is consolidation good for innovation?

M&A activity is often seen as a strategy to tackle a thinning pipeline. Using the data collected for this study, this strategy can be tested by measuring the 'before and after' Poisson parameters of companies that have engaged in these transactions (as the expected NME output of a group of companies is equal to the sum of their Poisson parameters). The population in this study has 24 acquisitions and 6 mergers with a minimum of 10 years of data before and after each transaction. FIGURE 5a summarizes the collective expected annual NME output of the companies involved. Only small companies show a slight, but significant, increase in NME output at the 95% confidence level. For large companies, M&A do not seem to create or destroy value. In fact, one can summarize the impact of M&A in the pharmaceutical industry on R&D as '1+1=1'. This is consistent with a recent analysis[19].

A more detailed analysis adds interesting nuances. FIGURE 5b looks separately at M&A involving large and small companies. For large companies, half of the six mergers analysed increased NME output (by 44%), whereas the other half reduced NME output (by 36%). For small companies, nearly 80% of acquisitions increased NME output (by 118%), whereas the rest reduced NME output (by 33%). For large companies, the proportions were reversed: 70% of acquisitions reduced NME output (by 20%), whereas 30% of acquisitions increased NME output (by 41%). Caution should be taken in interpreting these numbers because of the small sample size. In addition, many companies involved in M&A since 2000 were not included in the analysis because they did not meet the inclusion criteria of 20 years of data. This analysis will need to be repeated as more data become available. For now, the evidence suggests that M&A can help small companies, but are not an effective means to boost NME output among larger companies.

What next?

Scaling patent cliffs. Not only is the discovery of NMEs elusive, but their sales prospects are highly skewed towards zero, further reducing the likelihood of obtaining

ANALYSIS

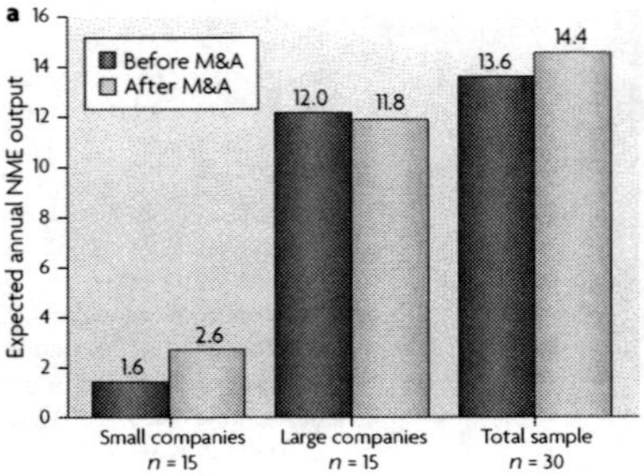

b

	Mergers (large companies)	Acquisition involving Small companies	Acquisition involving Large companies
Number of companies	6	14	10
Resulted in greater NME output	50%	79%	30%
NME increase (%)	44%	118%	41%
Resulted in lower NME output	50%	21%	70%
NME decrease (%)	−36%	−33%	−20%

Figure 5 | **Impact of industry consolidation. a** | Impact of mergers and acquisitions (M&A) on new molecular entity (NME) output. For small companies, there is a 95% probability that M&A has increased NME output slightly. However, for large companies, and for the total sample, there is a 95% probability that M&A did not increase NME output. **b** | Value created by M&A. See BOX 1 for definitions.

a return on investment in R&D. FIGURE 6a plots the frequency distribution of peak sales for NMEs. It is based on 329 of the more recent NMEs for which such data are available. The underlying data show that the probability that an NME will achieve blockbuster status is ~21%, a success rate that has not changed in 20 years despite considerable investment to improve the chances of success. This low probability is seen even though large pharmaceutical companies and venture capitalists will seldom proceed with the development of a molecule unless it has blockbuster potential, supported by sophisticated forecasts and reviews by experienced executives.

More worryingly, it also suggests that the industry's most hallowed competencies — customer knowledge, disease expertise and decades of experience — do not seem to be of much help in predicting success[20]. This forces the industry to navigate without a reliable road map, which is a challenge it shares with other blockbuster-dominated businesses such as motion pictures or oil and gas exploration. This has important implications for the management of innovation, which is discussed in the next section.

It is now possible to combine knowledge of drug innovation and new-product sales with patent expirations to model how drug companies might survive the large upcoming revenue losses caused by the expiration of patents on key blockbuster drugs, something often referred to as 'patent cliffs' (see Supplementary information S3 (box) for a description of this simulation tool). FIGURES 6b,c summarize the results for the 13 largest pharmaceutical companies, created by using this tool to generate probability distributions for sales and net income that reflect the stochastic nature of drug innovation at the company level. The results indicate that continuing with the current business model may result in a reduction of 5–10% in sales and 20–30% in net income in 2012–2015. Sales should subsequently recover to their 2011 peak, but net income may remain down by 15% — a performance that is unlikely to please stakeholders.

Choosing a course. If the performance of the current business model cannot satisfy stakeholders, M&A are not a solution, and the process improvements and cost-cutting measures that are commonly used cannot make a sufficient difference, perhaps the industry ought to embrace more radical change and seize the opportunity to redesign the model. Four points to consider in discussions on such a redesign can be put forward on the basis of the analysis in this article.

First, the industry needs to change its innovation dynamics to move beyond constant NME output. This is a daunting task. As nothing that the industry has done in the past 60 years has substantially affected mean output, it must venture further away from its comfort zone as it rebuilds its R&D model. As was noted by the previous Chief Executive Officer of GlaxoSmithKline, Jean-Pierre Garnier[21]: "R&D productivity is the number one issue". If it is not fixed, nothing else can work.

Second, there are radical and successful experiments that can be used as building blocks or for inspiration; for example, Innocentive[22,23], Chorus[24], public–private partnerships[25–27], open-source R&D[28–30], X Prize[31], innovation networks[32], FIPNet[33], consortia and various combinations of these and other initiatives[34]. These efforts aim to harness the 'global brain' to access the best science and ideas wherever they may be. Such open architecture for R&D has key advantages: it heightens competition, reduces costs and increases agility by making it easier to initiate and terminate projects. More importantly, it makes it easier to manage 'disruptive innovation' by locating it outside the corporate walls, where it can thrive unencumbered.

Third, in many organizations, short-term priorities encourage marginal innovation, which provides more reliable returns on investment, at the expense of major change. Therefore, organizations that depend on breakthrough discoveries need a separate, protected area the sole purpose of which is disruptive innovation. In the past, this was provided by independent laboratories, such as Bristol–Myers Squibb's Pharmaceutical Research Institute or Merck Research Labs. However, these units were never quite able to free themselves from corporate attempts to increase the number of blockbusters by making scientists more responsive to market needs. The result has usually been a greater emphasis on imitative research, fewer breakthroughs and drugs that miss the blockbuster mark 80% of the time.

Open-source R&D
A broad-based participatory research model in which a virtual network of volunteers use online tools to address a problem in which they share an interest.

Disruptive innovation
A process to turn cutting-edge science into novel products with such superior features that they create vast new markets, which unsettles established products and technology.

Black swan
A metaphor that designates rare random events of key importance that reshape markets, industries and societies.

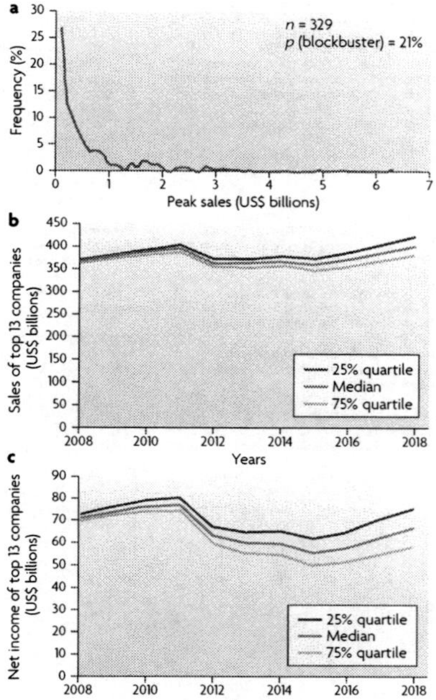

Figure 6 | **Sales of new molecular entities (NMEs).** **a** | Frequency distribution of peak sales for NMEs. **b** | Predicted sales for the top 13 pharmaceutical companies from 2009–2018. **c** | Predicted net income for the top 13 pharmaceutical companies from 2009–2018.

Fourth, the industry must rethink its process culture. Success in the pharmaceutical industry depends on the random occurrence of a few 'black swan'[35] products. Common processes that are standard practice in most companies create little value in an industry dominated by blockbusters[36]. These include developing sales forecasts for new products, which are inaccurate nearly 80% of the time. Another example is portfolio management, which has been widely adopted by the industry as a risk management tool, but has failed to protect it from patent cliffs. During the past couple of decades, there has been a methodical attempt to codify every facet of the drug business into sophisticated processes, in an effort to reduce the variances and increase the predictability. This has produced a false sense of control over all aspects of the pharmaceutical enterprise, including innovation. As Jean-Pierre Garnier puts it: "The leaders of major corporations including pharmaceuticals have incorrectly assumed that R&D was scalable, could be industrialized and could be driven by detailed metrics and automation. The grand result: a loss of personal accountability, transparency and the passion of scientists in discovery and development"[37].

Conclusion

In the past 60 years, the pharmaceutical industry has delivered over 1,220 new drugs that have played an important part in improving public health and extending life expectancy by an average of 2 months each year[38]. The R&D model that has powered that success, however, is showing signs of fatigue: costs are skyrocketing, breakthrough innovation is ebbing, competition is intense and sales growth is flattening. This cluster of symptoms has often foretold major disruption in other industries[39,40]. Their experiences show that industries can survive such upheavals; someone always finds a way to redesign the business model, but that someone, ominously, has seldom been an incumbent[41].

Could pharmaceuticals be different? Drug research today is the locus of many interesting experiments that have the potential to rejuvenate the R&D model. Many of them are taking place in areas that have traditionally been overlooked by the large companies, such as neglected diseases and biodefence, which is consistent with the predictions of Clayton Christensen[41]. Nevertheless, large companies have also sponsored some highly innovative concepts, some of which are highlighted in the previous section. However, although these experiments are proceeding, the industry is increasingly caught in a pincer between an NME output that is essentially linear, and likely to remain so, and a cost of producing NMEs that is increasing exponentially. At some point, the situation will become untenable. This could tempt investors to force wholesale change onto the industry, unless the industry pre-empts them with radical initiatives.

1. PhRMA. Pharmaceutical Industry Profile 2009. *PhRMA website* [online] <http://www.phrma.org/files/PhRMA%202009%20Profile%20FINAL.pdf> (2009).
2. Burrill & Company. Biotech 2008: a 20/20 vision to 2020. Available from the *BayBio website* [online] <http://www.baybio.org/pdf/Breakfast_Plenary_2020.pdf> (2008).
3. Stoeffels, P. Collaborative innovation for the post-crisis world. *Boston Globe* (2 Feb 2009).
4. Pisano, G. *Science Business: The Promise, The Reality, and The Future of Biotech* (Harvard Business School Press, Boston, Massachusetts, 2006).
5. Hansen, R. W. in *Issues in Pharmaceutical Economics* (ed. Chien, R. I.) 151–187 (Lexington Books, Lexington, 1979).
6. DiMasi, J. A., Hansen, R. W., Grabowski, H. G. & Lasagna, L. Cost of innovation in the pharmaceutical industry. *J. Health Econ.* **10**, 107–142 (1991).
7. Wiggins, S. N. *The Cost of Developing a New Drug* (Pharmaceutical Manufacturers Association, Washington, 1987).
8. DiMasi, J. A., Hansen, R. W. & Grabowski, H. G. The price of innovation: new estimates of drug development costs. *J. Health Econ.* **22**, 151–185 (2003).
9. US Congress, Office of Technology Assessment. *Pharmaceutical R&D: Costs, Risks, and Rewards, OTA-H-522* (US Government Printing Office, Washington, 1993).
10. Lehman Brothers. Drug R&D Costs, Success Rates, and Emerging Technologies (1997) in *PAREXEL's Pharmaceutical R&D Statistical Sourcebook 2000* (Parexel International Corp, Waltham, 2000).
This document also includes another estimate of NME costs from the US Office of Technology Assessment for the year 1990.
11. DiMasi, J. A., Grabowski, H. G. The cost of biopharmaceutical R&D. *Manage. Decis. Econ.* **28**, 469–479 (2007).
12. Schwartzman, D. *Innovations in the Pharmaceutical Industry* (Johns Hopkins University Press, Baltimore, 1976).
13. Clymer, H. A. in *The Economics of Drug Innovation* (ed. Cooper, J. D.) 109–124 (The American University, Washington, 1970).
14. Bailey, M. Research and development costs and returns: the U. S. pharmaceutical industry. *J. Polit. Econ.* **80**, 70–85 (1972).
This article contains estimates of NME costs before and after the 1962 Kefauver–Harris amendment.
15. National Academy of Engineering. *The Competitive Status of the U.S. Pharmaceutical Industry* (National Academies Press, Washington, 1983).

ANALYSIS

16. Grabowski, H. G., Vernon, J. M. & Thomas, L. G. Estimating the effects of regulation on international innovation. *J. Law Econ.* **21**, 133–163 (1978).
17. Scherer, F. M. *Pharmaceutical Innovation* (John F. Kennedy School of Government, Harvard University, Cambridge, Massachusetts, 2007).
18. Scherer, F. M. Time-cost trade-offs in uncertain empirical research projects. *Nav. Res. Logistics Q.* **13**, 71–82 (1966).
19. Grabowski, H. G. & Kyle, M. in *The Economics of Corporate Governance and Mergers* (eds Gugler, K. & Yurtoglu, B.) 262–287 (Edward Elgar, Cheltenham, 2008).
20. Jack, A. An acute talent for innovation. *Financial Times* (2 Feb 2009).
21. Iglehart, J. K. Good science and the marketplace for drugs: a conversation with Jean-Pierre Garnier. *Health Aff.* **22**, 119–127 (2003).
22. Wilan, K. Profile: Alpheus Bingham. *Nature Biotech.* **25**, 1072 (2007).
23. Travis, J. Science by the masses. *Science* **319**, 1750–1752 (2008).
24. Bonabeau, E., Bodick, N. & Armstrong R. A more rational approach to new product development. *Harvard Bus. Rev.* (March 2008).
25. Moran, M. *et al. The new landscape of neglected disease drug development* (The Wellcome Trust, London, 2006).
26. Moran, M. *et al. The malaria product pipeline* (The George Institute for International Health, Sydney, 2007).
27. Berkley S. Ending an epidemic: the international AIDS vaccine initiative pioneers a public–private partnership. *Innovations* **1**, 52–66 (2006).
28. Munos, B. Can open-source R&D reinvigorate drug research? *Nature Rev. Drug Discov.* **5**, 723–729 (2006).
29. Singh, S. India takes an open source approach to drug discovery. *Cell* **133**, 201–203 (2008).
30. Scott, W. & O'Donnell, M. Distributed drug discovery, Part 1: linking academia and combinatorial chemistry to find drug leads for developing world diseases. *J. Comb. Chem.* **11**, 3–13 (2009).
31. Singer, E. The X Prize's new frontier: genomics. *Technology Review* (5 Oct 2006).
32. Huston, L. (interview) Innovation networks: looking for ideas outside the company. *Knowledge@Wharton* (14 Nov 2007).
33. Maurer, S. Choosing the right incentive strategy for research and development in neglected diseases. *Bull. World Health Organ.* **84**, 376–381 (2006).
34. Hughes, B. An audience with Steven Paul. *Nature Rev. Drug Discov.* **8**, 14 (2009).
35. Taleb, N. *The Black Swan: The Impact of the Highly Improbable* (Random House, London, 2007).
36. De Vany, A. *Hollywood Economics: How Extreme Uncertainty Shapes the Film Industry* (Routledge, London, 2003).
An important book about the dynamics of blockbuster economics, and its first rigorous mathematical treatment.
37. Garnier, J.-P. Rebuilding the R&D engine in big pharma. *Harvard Bus. Rev.* **86**, 68–76 (2008).
A candid assessment by the former CEO of GSK of the process culture that dominates pharmaceutical R&D.
38. Arias, E. United States Life Tables, 2004. *National Center for Health Statistics website* [online] <http://www.cdc.gov/nchs/data/nvsr/nvsr56/nvsr56_09.pdf> (2004).
39. Hartung, A. *Create Marketplace Disruption* (FT Press, Upper Saddle River, 2008).
40. Anthony, S. D. Can you spot the early warnings? *Strategy & Innovation* **3**, no. 2 (March/April 2005).
41. Christensen, C. *Seeing What's Next: Using Theories of Innovation to Predict Industry Change* (Harvard Business School Press, Boston, Massachusetts, 2004).
42. Pammolli, F. & Riccaboni, M. *Innovation and Industrial Leadership: Lessons from Pharmaceuticals* (Center for Transatlantic Relations, Washington, 2008).
43. Powell, W. W., Koput, K. W. & Smith-Doerr, L. Interorganizational collaboration and the locus of innovation. *Admin. Sci. Q.* **41**, 116–145 (1996).

Acknowledgements
I thank the late Armen Tashjian (Harvard School of Public Health and Harvard Medical School) for his unrelenting support, and M. Munos (Johns Hopkins School of Public Health) for her extensive feedback on previous versions of the manuscript.

Competing interests statement
The author declares competing financial interests: see web version for details.

FURTHER INFORMATION
EvaluatePharma database:
http://www.evaluatepharma.com/Default.aspx

SUPPLEMENTARY INFORMATION
See online article: S1 (box) | S2 (box) | S3 (box)
ALL LINKS ARE ACTIVE IN THE ONLINE PDF

C
The Generic Drug Industry

[12]

RICHARD E. CAVES
Harvard University

MICHAEL D. WHINSTON
Harvard University and National Bureau of Economic Research

MARK A. HURWITZ
Columbia Law School

Patent Expiration, Entry, and Competition in the U.S. Pharmaceutical Industry

THE ETHICAL PHARMACEUTICAL industry is an important one, not so much for its economic size as for the benefits that it delivers to users of its products. The industry has been transformed structurally since the 1940s from a producer of selected chemicals to a research-oriented sector that makes a major contribution to the technology of health care.[1] Its very success in generating a stream of new drugs with important therapeutic benefits has involved the industry in intense public policy debates over the financing of the cost of its research, the veracity of claims for its products, the prices charged for them (not to mention who pays those charges), and the socially optimal degree of patent protection.

The policies and policy debates bearing on competition in the pharmaceutical industry revolve around two interrelated issues of welfare economics. The first is the trade-off between promoting innovative effort and securing competitive market outcomes. The research-oriented

We would like to thank Joshua Angrist, Zvi Griliches, Andrea Shepard, and members of the National Bureau of Economic Research productivity group for helpful comments and discussion; numerous individuals in the industry who generously gave their time to provide us with background information; Denise Neumann for research assistance; and Ann Flack and Claudia Napolilli for their help in preparing this manuscript. Whinston thanks the National Science Foundation for financial support (SES-8921996).

1. Temin (1980, chaps. 1–4).

sector of the industry relies heavily on the patent system. In principle, the expected monopoly profits from sales during the patent's life warrant the innovator's risky investment, while the onset of competition after the patent expires limits society's cost to the deadweight losses stemming from monopoly pricing under patent.[2] Because regulation has had important effects on the cost of innovation in the pharmaceutical industry, a great deal of research has been done on the innovation end of this trade-off between innovation and competition. The costs of innovation, the effect of regulation on cost and innovative output, and the dependence of pharmaceutical manufacturers' rents on innovation have been much studied. Little is known, however, about the postpatent competitive process: the speed and fullness with which competitive entry then erodes patent-protected monopoly rents and eliminates the associated deadweight losses.[3] Although the patent on an innovative drug expires on a specific date, the drug's trademark lives on as the vehicle for maintaining the innovator's goodwill and possibly delaying or impeding subsequent competition. That possibility, however, touches on the other issue of welfare economics, the information structure of the drug market.

Promotional activities in the ethical segment of the pharmaceutical industry raise important questions of "information vs. persuasion." The dissemination of information by the drug's innovator may serve to inform physicians and pharmacists efficiently about the therapeutic effects of a particular chemical entity and the indications for its use. On the other hand, because the health care professionals who choose the prescription drugs that patients consume may have only attenuated incentives to minimize the cost of drugs to the users (or their insurers), sales promotion by pharmaceutical firms may also exploit rent-seeking opportunities that stem from the imperfect alignment of the incentives of these providers with the interests of their patients. This second policy

2. As Nordhaus (1969) showed, the patent's life can then be set to optimize the trade-off between surplus from consuming the innovative good and deadweight losses due to monopoly pricing.

3. As Comanor (1986) pointed out, most modern research on the industry was motivated by the 1962 amendments to the Pure Food Act (requiring drug innovators to demonstrate effectiveness as well as safety) and the extensive congressional hearings that preceded them. Dominated by efforts to measure and evaluate the rate of new-drug introduction, this research consequently slighted the market behavior of patent recipients.

issue is not without link to the first, because the nature of the promotional process in these markets may strongly influence the course of events expected once a patent expires and generic competitors enter the market. To the extent that an innovative company's promotion merely disseminates information about the benefits of the chemical entity, generic entrants are unlikely to be particularly disadvantaged. In contrast, persuasion activities that incline providers toward prescribing the brand of the innovating company may serve to attenuate the welfare gains arising from postpatent generic competition.

In addition to these important issues for public policy, the pharmaceutical industry offers an excellent site for examining some general issues in industrial organization. Because a legal monopoly of an innovative product in this industry commonly depends on a single patent (that on the chemical entity itself), the industry provides a setting in which the conditions of entry and competition change radically on a given date set by the terms of the patent law. This natural experiment offers a unique opportunity to study both the process and effects of entry.

In this paper we report on an exploratory analysis of the patterns of competition surrounding patent expiration and subsequent generic entry in ethical pharmaceutical markets.[4] We identify the patterns displayed by branded and generic drugs' prices, market shares, and quantities sold as well as branded drugs' advertising over the years 1976–87 for a panel of thirty drugs that lost patent protection during this period. The use of a panel data set permits us to follow these variables over time and to employ controls for changes in these variables that would occur with the natural unfolding of a drug's life cycle and with changes in market conditions in either its therapeutic class or the industry in general.

Given the exploratory nature of our investigation, our approach here is nonstructural, focusing on the ''semireduced'' form relationship between the occurrence of patent expiration and generic entry and these various endogenous variables. Such an approach is responsive to the difficulty of imposing any single a priori theoretical model on the process of generic entry and postentry competition. The literature of in-

4. A few previous researchers have also addressed parts of this issue. We discuss this work and its relation to our own in our review of market structure.

dustrial organization is, of course, awash with models of entry, entry deterrence, and postentry competition. Our approach is designed to reveal the basic characteristics of these aspects of pharmaceutical competition within a broad range. The patterns observed in this manner are not only directly informative about the competitive process in the industry, but also, by suggesting the relative importance of particular mechanisms of strategic behavior, will serve, we hope, as a useful step toward development of more complete structural models of competitive interaction in this industry.

In the next section of this paper we survey the structure of markets for ethical pharmaceuticals and review past research on behavior of the various types of decisionmakers that may affect postpatent competition. The third section describes the sources and construction of the data base and provides descriptive statistics. The fourth explains the statistical procedure in detail and presents our empirical results concerning the effects of generic entry and competition. The concluding section summarizes our findings, discusses the light they shed on behavior and structure in the industry as well as their implications for public policy, and indicates desirable avenues for future research.

Structure of the Market

As background to our study, here we summarize structural characteristics of the pharmaceutical industry relevant to the rivalry that stems from patent expiration and subsequent entry by generic competitors. The prescription and use of ethical pharmaceuticals as well as their production and marketing are closely regulated, so we also refer to the major government regulations that shape market structure and behavior.

Demand Side Influences

Unlike most markets, the realized demands for pharmaceuticals depend not only on ultimate consumers' tastes but also on the behavior of physicians who prescribe these drugs and the retail and hospital pharmacists who dispense the prescriptions. Since 1938 the decision about the patient's consumption of any drug with substantial therapeutic effect has been in the hands of the physician. The physician's primary choice is what drug (that is, chemical entity) to prescribe. The physician then can designate that drug by either a brand or its generic name. The trademarked brand name attached to a pioneering drug by the innovator is short and easier to remember than its generic name, which in turn is a shorter, simpler version of the chemical name that describes the molecular structure of the active chemical entity to scientists.

Physicians may not be well positioned to choose drug therapies that maximize value for their patients. Evidence on this point pertains to choices among similar but distinct drugs as well as to choices between branded and generic versions of the same drug. As Temin showed, the physician lacks ready and well-organized information on the comparative effectiveness and riskiness of substitute chemical entities, and the choice is based strongly on custom as evolved in the peer community of prescribers.[5] Customary prescribing behavior not only minimizes effort but also provides a legal defense.

When the choice lies between a branded pioneer drug and its generic competitors, the physician may not be sensitive to price differences. Physicians do not ordinarily have information on the drug prices charged by pharmacists, and that information is certainly not pressed upon them in the promotional information supplied by makers of branded drugs. Surveys accordingly have found physicians ill-informed about the prices of competing drugs.[6] Furthermore, except possibly in the treatment of chronic conditions, prescribing a drug therapy in the most cost-effective way is a relatively minor aspect in the overall performance of the physician's function. Correspondingly, patients seem unlikely to select or change physicians simply because they do not prescribe the lowest-cost drugs. In addition, physicians may be concerned about the quality or therapeutic equivalence of generic drugs (evidence on this point is noted below). Confirming the low priority that minimizing prescription costs holds for physicians, Masson and Steiner found that the incidence of generic prescribing depends strongly on a seemingly trivial factor:

5. Temin (1980, chap. 5). Temin pointed out that the individual physician typically does not obtain a great deal of experience with the effects of any particular drug and that the available published research on competing drugs tends to deal with bioavailability rather than actual effects.

6. Temin (1980, pp. 102–06).

whether the form of the prescription pad makes permitting or precluding generic substitution the easier course of action.[7] In 1989 physicians prohibited substitution in 23 percent of prescriptions overall, 41 percent of prescriptions where physicians could easily prohibit substitutions by signing on one rather than another line of the form and only 11 percent in jurisdictions where a specific notation had to be written.[8]

The potential importance of physicians' prescribing behavior for generic drug use can be seen in the distribution of new prescriptions by number (from IMS America, *National Prescription Audit*):

	1980	*1989*
Single source drugs	31.0%	28.8%
Multisource drugs:		
Written by brand name	54.5	57.8
Written generically	14.5	13.5

Somewhat surprisingly, the proportion of prescriptions for multisource drugs that were written generically actually fell from 21 percent in 1980 to 19 percent in 1989.

Once the physician has chosen to prescribe a drug that is available generically, the pharmacist and the consumer may play a role in deciding whether the original brand or a generic equivalent is dispensed. At one time laws in most states required the pharmacist to fill a prescription as written, precluding generic dispensing when the physician had written the brand name, but the last of these antisubstitution laws was repealed in 1984 (most were repealed in the mid- to late-1970s). They were replaced by legislation that in some cases requires substitution in the absence of contraindication by the physician but generally leaves the choice with the pharmacist and the consumer. Masson and Steiner provided evidence that generic products not only carry lower prices than branded drugs, but also tend to yield higher gross margins to pharmacists, so that both pharmacist and consumer share an interest in substituting generic products where possible.

Aggregate statistics on ways in which prescriptions for multisource drugs are written and dispensed reveal two basic facts about the process.

7. Masson and Steiner (1985, pp. 89, 101). See also Grabowski and Vernon (1979).

8. "National Audit Finds Drug Substitution Rate Steady," *Drug Topics*, June 4, 1990, pp. 12–14.

First, generic substitution for brand-written multisource prescriptions is relatively infrequent, confined to 29 percent of these prescriptions in 1989. Interestingly, nearly all generically written prescriptions are filled generically, suggesting that pharmacists and/or consumers place significant faith in the physician's choice.[9] Second, generic substitution has nonetheless increased substantially over time, for generics were substituted for only 5 percent of brand-written multisource prescriptions in 1980.[10] One factor behind the increase is intensified pressure from some third-party payers for the minimization of drug prices. Masson and Steiner observed a strong effect of federal and state reimbursement limits for medicaid prescriptions; the substitution rates on these prescriptions are more than double those on prescriptions subject to reimbursement by private insurers.[11] Those results were confirmed by another study, which found also that substitution decreases as the intrinsic risk associated with the drug's use increases.[12]

This review of the demand for prescription drugs has so far concentrated on prescriptions written by independent physicians and filled by pharmacists. In 1989 the pharmacy market accounted for 82 percent of the total value of drugs distributed through pharmacies and hospitals together. When drugs are prescribed and dispensed in hospitals, the incentives and information capabilities of the actors may be rather different. The hospital's formulary system rests on a contract under which the hospital may fill generically prescriptions written by brand name unless the physician indicates otherwise. The physician is encouraged to prescribe those products listed on the hospital's formulary, which is a continuously revised list of drug products approved by a therapeutic committee consisting of pharmacy, clinical, and nursing staff members.

9. Combined with the prescription distribution data presented above, these substitution figures imply that the generic market share for multisource drugs in 1989 was approximately 42 percent (based on the number of new prescriptions filled).

10. Tabulation provided by IMS America (from *National Prescription Audit*). Masson and Steiner (1985, pp. 41–47) placed significant weight on drug consumers' own resistance to generic substitution as a reason why it had not proceeded farther. Note also that the increased ease of generic substitution may possibly have contributed to the decrease in generic prescribing observed above.

11. Masson and Steiner (1985, chap. 4). Private insurers have stepped up their efforts to contain drug costs (Milt Freudenheim, "Insurers Press Use of Cheaper Drugs," *New York Times*, November 18, 1990, sec. 1, p. 1).

12. Carroll, Siridhara, and Fincham (1987, pp. 11–18).

This system serves to pool information on the cost and effectiveness of different drugs and assists cost minimization, an objective increasingly pressed upon the hospitals by the public and third-party payers, who together cover 82 percent of hospitals' drug expenditures.[13]

The proposition that the choice between generic and branded drugs is more price-sensitive for drugs dispensed in hospitals than through retail pharmacies implies less payout for advertising to the hospital sector. Leffler noted the low levels of sales promotion by pharmaceutical manufacturers for drugs sold mainly through hospitals. Hurwitz and Caves (weakly) confirmed this observation and also showed that the shares retained by branded producers against their generic competitors in the hospital market are significantly less sensitive than in the pharmacy market to both their current sales promotion and accumulated goodwill.[14]

Supply Side Influences

The pharmaceutical industry consists of a large number of firms (584 in the 1982 Census of Manufactures) that produce many different (and mainly nonsubstitutable) drug products, ethical and over-the-counter, branded and generic. As Temin showed, the industry assumed its modern research-oriented form after World War II, when a number of firms emerged that both carried out extensive research and maintained extensive sales forces to promote their innovations.[15] Their rise, however, was not accompanied by a decline in the number of small firms, and even among the research-oriented firms, concentration is low.[16] In 1989 approximately 400 companies had approved New Drug Applications (NDAs) with the Food and Drug Administration (FDA).[17]

Of course, the number of firms producing any given (off-patent) drug or drugs that are close substitutes within a therapeutic class is commonly much smaller. Scale economies in production are not important. The fermentation technologies extensively used to produce the active chem-

13. For more detail and sources, see Hurwitz and Caves (1988, pp. 306–7).

14. Leffler (1981, pp. 53–54); and Hurwitz and Caves (1988, pp. 316–17).

15. Temin (1979). See also Grabowski and Vernon (1976).

16. According to data from IMS America, the largest firm's sales in 1989 accounted for 7.4 percent of total sales, the largest four firms 23.8 percent.

17. U.S. Food and Drug Administration (annual).

ical entities are batch processes carried out on small scales. Both quality-control considerations and the small absolute quantities of active ingredients produced discourage large-scale continuous-process technologies.[18] Production capacity for assembling active and inert ingredients into pills or capsules is largely fungible. Thus, although actual competitors for a given drug or therapy may be few, potential entrants are numerous.

Although manufacturing and distribution are not generally integrated, the research-oriented drugmakers are partly integrated forward. These firms (members of the Pharmaceutical Manufacturers Association) make 68 percent of their sales to wholesalers, 32 percent directly to hospitals, health maintenance organizations (HMOs), and pharmacy chains. The wholesale percentage has increased from 45 percent in 1972.[19] Because the major drug manufacturers vary greatly in their reliance on arm's-length wholesalers, the choice of integration is apparently a close call. The increased role of independent wholesalers stems from computerization that allows specialist wholesalers to provide extensive services for pharmacies (including hospital pharmacies) that they supply exclusively. While the largest wholesaler accounts for one-fourth of the U.S. wholesale market, many small firms also exist.[20] The generic producers depend entirely on full-line marketing and wholesaling firms, some of which are large and themselves take an active role in postpatent entry into the markets of innovative drugs.[21]

The innovation process has been studied intensively since the 1962 amendments to the Pure Food Act (also known as the Kefauver amendments) required that effectiveness as well as safety be demonstrated for approval by the FDA. Each of the twenty or so new molecular entities introduced each year was estimated in 1987 to incur total development costs of $125 million.[22] The profitability of pharmaceutical innovation may have been reduced by the 1962 legislation, not only because of the cost of compliance to the manufacturer but also because of the delay that the approval process causes between the time patent protection is granted and the time the new drug can be placed on the market. For the typical

18. Walker (1971, pp. 36–37).
19. Pharmaceutical Manufacturers Association (1988, p. 5).
20. Smith (1985, pp. 249–63).
21. Smith (1985, pp. 201–2).
22. Wiggins (1987).

patented drug the period of exclusive marketing contracted substantially after 1962; Grabowski and Vernon reported a decline from 13.6 years for patents expiring in 1966 to 9.5 years in 1979.[23] A considerable controversy ensued over the extent of the decline in pharmaceutical innovation attributable to this regulation and the degree to which it pushed pharmaceutical innovation and initial availability of new drugs overseas.[24]

If regulations based on the 1962 legislation cut into the profitability of drug innovations, they also imposed a barrier to entry by generic competitors once the patent expired. That barrier stemmed from the requirement that subsequent entrants duplicate the testing for safety and efficacy undertaken by the innovator. The Waxman-Hatch Act of 1984 eliminated the requirement of socially wasteful duplicative testing by generic entrants and granted drug innovators some restoration of the effective lives of their patents. The act allows a generic entrant to submit an Abbreviated New Drug Application (ANDA) that demonstrates only the bioequivalence of its drug to the original. At the same time, the 1984 law permits the innovator to recoup part of the interval of patent protection lost due to regulatory delay and allows a period of exclusive marketing for new drugs regardless of their patent protection.[25]

Apart from the cost of obtaining FDA approval, generic entrants apparently face only minor barriers to entry on the cost side. They may encounter technical difficulty in producing the active chemical ingredient for some drugs. The evidence does not, however, suggest any substantial scale-economy barriers in production or distribution.[26] The primary im-

23. Grabowski and Vernon (1983, p. 50). On the other hand, drug innovators have sometimes forestalled this costly shortening of their period of monopoly by using amended applications to stretch out the process of the patent's consideration and delay approval, or by securing patent protection with broad claims for therapeutic usefulness that are focused by subsequent applications making narrower and more specific claims. A study prepared by the generic drug producers claimed that the effective patent life for the leading twelve products in 1980 was 18.5 years, more than the statutory life of a patent. For the next thirteen products the mean was 15.1 years, suggesting that innovators invest in prolonging patent lives in proportion to the expected value of potential rents. The tactics employed by drug innovators are apparently no different from those used by other inventors. See U.S. House of Representatives, Committee on Science and Technology (1982, pp. 206–21, 236–49).

24. See, for example, Peltzman (1974); Grabowski (1980); Temin (1980); and Wiggins (1981).

25. Grabowski and Vernon (1986).

26. Schwartzman (1976, pp. 260–64).

pediments appear to come on the demand side from the accumulated goodwill assets of branded producers and any concerns about quality differences between branded and generic drugs.[27]

The potential generic competitors with an off-patent drug include the large research-intensive firms other than its innovator. Thus, a distinction can be made between ''branded generics,'' emanating from research-oriented firms whose company names enjoy goodwill value, and generic drugs from other (small) producers. We do not pursue this distinction in the analysis that follows, although some evidence suggests that prescribers regard branded generics as closer substitutes for the innovator's drug, increasing the likelihood that the innovator will lower its prices in response to a reduction in generic prices.[28]

Decision Variables of Innovators

Pharmaceutical innovators have two principal instruments, price and sales-promotion outlays, for maximizing the value of their innovations, both during the period of exclusive marketing and in the postentry game.

Sales promotion takes several forms. The most important is detailing, visits to health-care professionals by the manufacturer's representatives who provide information on new drugs and their administration and answer questions from the physician.[29] The large staffs of detailers employed by the big, research-oriented drug firms represent a substantial fixed cost and an incentive for these firms to maintain a steady flow of innovations over time so that the sales representatives are fully utilized. Temin showed that detailing forces evolved as the industry assumed its modern shape, serving as a strong com-

27. Two specific quality issues arise. One is that of bioequivalence, which prevails when different producers' versions of the drug have the same bioavailability at the site of therapeutic effect. Information disseminated by the Food and Drug Administration now seems adequate to establish where bioequivalence does and does not prevail. In any case differences in bioavailability where found do not appear to be therapeutically significant (Temin, 1980, pp. 96–102). The second issue is that of quality control. Schwartzman (1976, pp. 215–23, 226–50) noted that small generic producers may have less to lose in reputational assets than large producers from suboptimal quality control. However, the evidence does not seem to indicate any therapeutically significant differences in quality control between branded and generic producers.

28. See the case studies by Schwartzman (1976, pp. 273–92) of pricing behavior in antibiotics and some other drugs.

29. The term ''detailing'' has apparently fallen out of use in the industry but is retained here because of its prevalence in the academic research literature.

plement to the innovation process itself.[30] Detailing certainly disseminates valuable information to physicians and thereby expands demand for the drugs thus promoted, but it is also widely regarded as an instrument for inducing brand loyalty.[31]

In 1989 detailing accounted for 74 percent of total promotion outlays, advertisements in medical journals accounted for 23 percent, and direct-mail advertising the remaining 3 percent.[32] Journal and direct-mail advertising conveys information and for new drugs is regarded as complementary to visits by the detailers, but such advertising also evidently seeks to maintain the general goodwill of the company.

Leffler and Hurwitz and Caves concluded that sales promotion outlays represent a mixture of information and persuasion. Spending in a therapeutic class increases with the number of new products entering the class and the extent of their therapeutic benefit, and may be lower for "maintenance" drugs that serve to treat chronic rather than acute and sporadic conditions. Promotion outlays increase strongly with the extent to which a drug is sold through the pharmacy market rather than to hospitals, consistent with the difference in information sets and incentives noted above.

Promotion may also serve as a competitive weapon and therefore possibly as a vehicle for strategic behavior. The large overall volume of advertised information aimed at each physician by the major drug producers has been suspected to exert a signal-jamming effect on the promotions mounted by generic entrants or firms introducing substitute therapies. Hurwitz and Caves found that the shares attained by generic entrants and the numbers of generic entrants decrease as both the current promotion outlays and the goodwill stocks of innovators' brands increases.[33] The degree to which promotion can be used in this manner should affect rates of expenditure over time on promotion of a given drug—examined below—but previous research yields no evidence on this point.

30. Temin (1979). During this period the previously common practice of licensing new chemical entities to other producers dried up as the innovators sought to capture for themselves all rents generated by the information disseminated by their detailing forces.

31. Observers taking these positions are cited by Comanor (1986).

32. Promotional audits by IMS America.

33. Walker (1971, p. 47); Hurwitz and Caves (1988, pp. 313, 316); see also Temin (1980, pp. 115–18). Leffler (1981) found no reactions of incumbents' advertising levels to new entry, but his analysis pertained to members of a therapeutic class and not to producers of the same chemical entity.

Richard E. Caves, Michael D. Whinston, and Mark A. Hurwitz 13

Previous research on pricing behavior gives only a little indication how drug pioneers react to either substitute products or generic entry. Isolated data quoted from the 1960–62 Kefauver Committee hearings suggest that variable costs may be as low as 5 percent of price.[34] Statman's analysis of twelve drugs that lost patent protection between 1970 and 1976 showed that in 1978 only four charged real prices lower than those prevailing three years before the patent's expiration. Schwartzman's case study of antibiotics in the 1960s revealed diverse behavior, with most innovators holding their prices constant while losing varying amounts of market share and a minority meeting the prices of imitators and generic competitors.[35] In none of these studies did the authors control for what would have happened to innovaters' prices, absent competition, due to either general shifts in market conditions or the normal pattern traced by a drug's price over its life cycle, nor were the precise responses to the level of entry quantified.

As background for analyzing the movement of these decision variables over the years 1976–87, we examined aggregate data on drug prices and costs during this period. Figure 1 plots an index of unit labor costs and an index of prices of bulk pharmaceutical prices as well as an output price index for the pharmaceutical industry overall.[36] The pattern is clearly peculiar after 1982. The rise in unit labor costs came to a halt, and the cost of bulk pharmaceutical inputs fell, yet the prices of outputs rose quite sharply.[37] Although the causes of this price rise are not our focus, its

34. Data from the Senate Judiciary Antitrust and Monopoly Subcommittee (known as the Kefauver Committee) hearings are quoted by Steele (1962, pp. 159–60).

35. Statman (1981); and Schwartzman (1976, pp. 257, 273–92). Diversity in pricing competition was also suggested by Cocks and Virts (1974).

36. Employment and employee-compensation information for Standard Industrial Classification (SIC) industry 2834 was taken from U.S. Bureau of the Census, *1982 Census of Manufacturers, Industry Statistics*, section 28C, tables 1B and 7, and U.S. Bureau of the Census, *Annual Survey of Manufactures*, various years. A weighted index of employment costs based on data for production and nonproduction workers was then converted to an index of unit labor costs using information on productivity growth from U.S. Bureau of Labor Statistics, *Productivity Measures for Selected Industries, 1958–84*, Bulletin No. 2256, extrapolated to later years. The index of pharmaceutical input costs is simply the output price index for SIC 2833, taken from U.S. Bureau of Labor Statistics, *Producer Prices and Price Indexes*. In 1982 inputs purchased from SIC 2833 made up 42.5 percent of the costs of material inputs purchased by SIC 2834. The output price index for SIC 2834 is also taken from *Producer Prices and Price Indexes*.

37. For a recent work investigating the accuracy of the pharmaceutical price index, see Berndt, Griliches, and Rosett (1990).

Figure 1. Pharmaceutical Prices, Labor Costs, and Material Input Costs, 1976–87

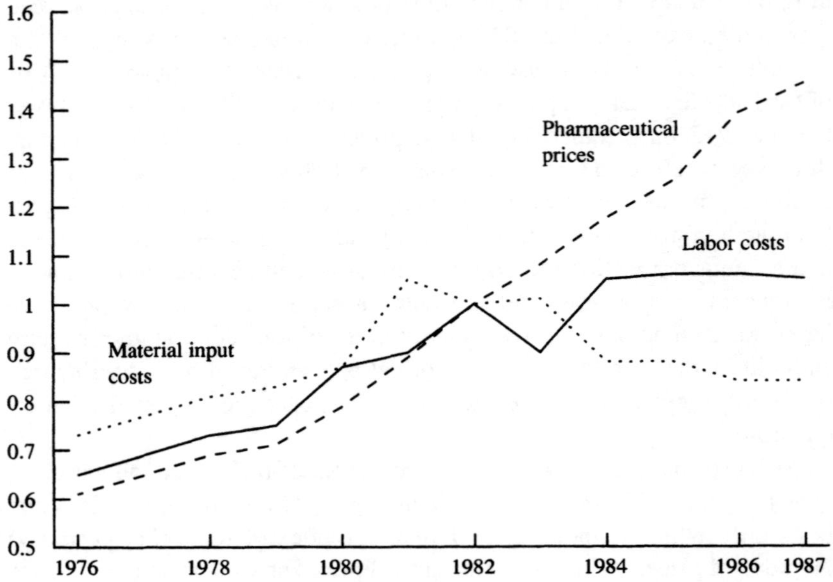

Source: See text, note 36.

occurrence has important implications for the empirical strategy that we use below to uncover the effects of patent expiration and entry.

Data

Our data base covers thirty pharmaceuticals that had enjoyed patent protection as new chemical entities but went off-patent during the period 1976–87. We constructed our sample by identifying therapeutic classes known to contain important drugs that had lost patent protection.[38] Then we examined the other drugs in these classes, picking up all drugs that were marketed by a single innovating firm and experienced a loss of

38. Our data source (a leading pharmaceutical company) and the fact that we had to work from original hard copies required that we confine our data collection to a limited number of therapeutic classes.

patent protection during our period of observation.[39] The drugs (and their number) belong to the following therapeutic classes: cardiovascular (11), psychotherapeutic (7), systemic anti-infectives (4), diabetes therapy (4), antiarthritics (2), diuretics (1), and antispasmodics (1).[40]

Because of our focus on generic entry, it was important that drugs included in the sample have unambiguous dates of patent expiration. We determined these by consulting lists compiled by various sources within the trade, including the Merck Drug Index and the U.S. Patent and Trademark Register as well as data from IMS America. In most cases we also contacted the innovating company itself to verify the month and year of patent expiration. We believe that each drug retained in the sample relied on a single key patent.[41]

Data on sales revenue, quantities sold, and sales-promotion expenditures were obtained from the Drugstore, Hospital, Detailing, and Journal Audits compiled by IMS America. The information on sales revenue and quantity reflects transactions at the wholesale level (that is, purchases by pharmacies and hospitals) and is obtained from two sources: warehouse withdrawal information from wholesalers and the actual invoices of a panel of pharmacy and hospital purchasers.[42] The data obtained from these sources are then extrapolated to the national market. The information on sales revenue and quantity permit average transaction prices to be calculated directly. These prices reflect actual wholesale transaction prices subject to two qualifications. First, the invoiced price is the price indicated for the specific drug in question.

39. Occasionally, new drugs are sold by more than one firm, due either to licensing by a foreign innovator or to simultaneous discovery combined with a cross-licensing agreement.

40. The therapeutic classes used to obtain the sample were not these broad, two-digit classes but finer, five-digit classes. The specific drugs included are: Aldomet, Apresazide, Catapres, Combipres, Diutensen, Harmonyl, Inderal, Ismelin, Minipress, Norpace, and Salutensin (cardiovasculars); Ativan, Haldol, Mellaril, Serax, Transxene, Valium, and Vesprin (psychotherapeutics); Declomycin, Keflex, Keflin, and Minocin (anti-infectives); Diabinese, Dymelor, Orinase, and Tolinase (diabetes therapy); Indocin and Meclomen (antiarthritics); Hygroton (diuretic); and Reglan (antispasmodic).

41. None of our drugs were affected by the patent extension or exclusive marketing provisions of the Waxman-Hatch Act.

42. For most products the information on warehouse withdrawals comes from a virtually complete sample of warehouses; for the remainder we rely on a sample of twenty-four warehouses that is then used to provide population estimates. The panels of pharmacy and hospital purchasers are used to capture direct sales that do not go through wholesalers.

Thus, if volume discounts are applied to a total order rather than to the purchase of an individual drug or if manufacturers offer rebates directly to purchasers, these discounts are missed. Second, for pharmacy chains that utilize their own warehouses, the recorded price is an intrafirm transfer price. Because of our study's focus on the *change* in prices over time and with respect to patent expiration, these issues will present problems for our conclusions only to the extent that the biases involved vary in a manner related to these variables.

This information on sales revenues and quantities is reported in each year for each seller of a given drug, both branded and generic, and by individual dosage. Following most previous researchers, we chose to work with the most popular dosage of each drug for the purpose of measuring prices, sales volumes, and market shares.[43]

The data from IMS America also distinguish between sales to pharmacies and sales to hospitals. We retained this distinction because of the bases, indicated above, for expecting that the willingness of prescribers and consumers to switch to lower-priced generics might differ between the sectors. Finally, the IMS data provide the month and year that each innovative drug was first marketed.

The generic sellers of record in the IMS data are commonly generic drug *distributors* rather than the actual manufacturers. The number of recorded distributors for a given drug may not be the best measure of the degree of generic threat to a drug innovator, because a typical generic manufacturer may supply several generic distributors whose number is relatively independent of the conditions of competition in any one drug.[44] We therefore obtained information on entry into generic manufacturing of each drug by looking at the dates of approval by the FDA of all pertinent NDAs and ANDAs.[45]

Sales-promotion information was also taken from IMS America tabulations, which are in turn obtained from a survey of the medical jour-

43. Occasionally, minor generic sales are recorded before the date of patent expiration and regulatory approval of any generic competitor's New Drug Application. We ignored these sales, concluding that they must have been made, probably indirectly, by the innovator.

44. An additional problem with using the information on distributors arises because different divisions of a single generic distributor may be recorded with different names.

45. Approval dates after 1982 were taken from U.S. Food and Drug Administration (annual); approval dates prior to 1982 were obtained through a Freedom of Information Act request.

Table 1. Average Characteristics (and Standard Deviations) of Sample Drugs

Characteristic	All drugs	Drugs with patents expiring 1976–81	Drugs with patents expiring 1982–87
Number of drugs	30	9	21
Market size, year before expiration, in millions of 1982 dollars	67.3 (76.1)	28.7 (33.3)	83.9 (83.7)
Mean annual growth rate under patent of quantity sold[a]	0.068 (0.194)	0.024 (0.198)	0.086 (0.194)
Proportion of sales through pharmacies[b]	0.87 (0.20)	0.87 (0.16)	0.87 (0.21)
Sales promotion fraction of sales[b]	0.062 (0.066)	0.056 (0.052)	0.065 (0.072)
Detailing proportion of sales promotion[b]	0.62 (0.27)	0.74 (0.21)	0.58 (0.28)
Years of exclusive marketing	14.7 (6.4)	16.4 (4.8)	14.0 (7.0)

Source: See text.
a. Annualized proportional change in quantity sold between 1976 and year patent expired.
b. Measured in year of patent's expiration.

nals for journal advertising and a panel of physicians for time spent by detailers in the direct promotion of individual drugs. This information is converted by IMS to estimated expenditures on the basis of quoted advertising rates of the publications and dollar conversions of minutes spent by sales representatives.

Table 1 reports a number of descriptive statistics about our sample of drugs. The total size of the market for the pioneering drug was observed in the year before expiration of its patent, as was the proportion of units sold in that year in the pharmacy market (out of the total of hospital and pharmacy sales). On average, a drug in our sample had sales revenues of $67.3 million (1982 dollars) in the year before its patent expired. The dispersion in market sizes is large: the standard deviation is $76.1 million, and the drug sales range in size from a minimum of $0.3 million to a maximum of $268.5 million. Consistent with the overall distribution of drug sales, our sample was marketed chiefly through pharmacies, with the average drug making 87 percent of sales through pharmacies. Indeed, twenty-five of the thirty drugs had pharmacy shares over 80 percent, four had shares between 50 and 80 percent, and one had a pharmacy share of only 2 percent. Sales-promotion outlays as a fraction of sales are not particularly large by the year of patent expiration, about 6 percent, although they are typically higher in the early years of a drug's market life. The bulk of outlays are for detailing. The mean annual growth rate of quantity sold over the drug's period of exclusive marketing was 7 percent, but declines are not uncommon and indeed become common as the patent's expiration approaches. The mean period of exclusive marketing, 14.7 years, was close to the full patent term (17 years), and the range was between 4 and 26 years. Our sample does not display the shortened lifespans of exclusive marketing noted in aggregate data by Grabowski and Vernon (but see footnote 23). Table 1 also distinguishes between drugs that went off-patent in 1976–81 and those whose patents expired in 1982–87. The latter group was not only more numerous but also tended to have larger markets as measured by real sales revenue in the year before patent expiration.

In table 2 information on the patent expiration and generic entry process is summarized for the thirty drugs. The distribution of drugs by year of patent expiration can be seen in the left two columns of the table. Of the thirty drugs, the patents of seven expired before 1980, sixteen between 1980 and 1984, and seven after 1984 (the Waxman-Hatch Act was passed at the end of 1984). The remaining columns of table 2 provide, for the drugs whose patents expired in any given year, a count of the average cumulative number of generic NDAs and ANDAs approved a given number of years after the year of patent expiration.[46]

At least two points are notable about this information. First, the generics that enter a given drug market do not all enter on the date the drug's patent expires but rather flow into the market over time. Several factors might lie behind this observation. First, even if all entrants begin their attempts to enter at the same time, the time needed to gain approval (starting from the date of initial investment) is no doubt random, particularly before the Waxman-Hatch Act eliminated clinical

46. Thus, for each of the seven drugs whose patents expired in 1984, the average number of generics active in 1985 (averaged across the seven drugs) is 2.9. The number of active generics for a given drug in a given year is calculated by attributing to each approved generic producer of that chemical entity the number of months remaining in the year from the time of approval.

Table 2. Average Cumulative Number of Approved Generic Producers by Year Patent Expired and Number of Years after Patent Expiration

Year patent expired	*Number of drugs whose patents expired*	*Number of years after year of patent expiration*											
		0	*1*	*2*	*3*	*4*	*5*	*6*	*7*	*8*	*9*	*10*	*11*
1976	1	0	0	0	0	0	0	0	0	0	0	0	0
1977	2	0	0	0	0	0	0	0	0	0.4	0.5	0.5	...
1978	2	0.5	1.6	3.6	4.9	5.4	5.9	6.1	6.8	7.0	7.3	...	...
1979	2	0	0	3.6	5.4	7.6	8.1	9.0	13.6	15.6	...	...	...
1980	0	...	...	...	...	...	...	...	...	...	...	...	...
1981	2	0	0	0	1.6	3.6	5.6	8.5	...	...	...	...	...
1982	4	0	0.1	0.2	1.3	4.4	7.3	...	...	...	...	...	...
1983	3	2.0	4.4	5.6	6.5	6.7	...	...	...	...	...	...	...
1984	7	1.2	2.9	5.7	9.3	...	...	...	...	...	...	...	...
1985	1	2.7	15.1	19.7	...	...	...	...	...	...	...	...	...
1986	3	2.4	7.7	...	...	...	...	...	...	...	...	...	...
1987	3	2.7	...	...	...	...	...	...	...	...	...	...	...
Average cumulative number of entrants across all drugs[a]		1.1	2.8	3.8	4.9	4.4	5.3	5.3	5.8	6.6	3.1	0.3	0
Proportion of drugs with some entrants		0.4	0.5	0.5	0.7	0.6	0.5	0.4	0.4	0.6	0.4	0.3	0

a. An entrant is counted as present in the year of its approval for only the fraction of the year's months that follow approval. The average cumulative number of approved generic producers for a given cohort (for example, drugs with patent expirations in 1984) in a given year (for example, two years after the year of patent expiration) is computed by averaging the numbers for the drugs in the cohort in that year.

trials for generics. In addition, for a variety of reasons, the equilibrium sequencing of investment by various entrants may be staggered.[47] A

47. This could be true for several reasons. First, the marginal value of an entrant investing a little earlier is the expected incremental profits achieved by doing so (the marginal cost is the time value of the investment funds). This marginal benefit depends, however, on how many other entrants are already in the market. Hence, in some circumstances, investment may be staggered since the marginal value is higher for a first entrant than for subsequent ones. Second, if information about market opportunities for generics is uncertain, some potential entrants may wait to see how early entrants fare. Third, if the overall market for a drug evolves stochastically, then entrants may enter over time when there turns out to be an unanticipated growth in the market's size.

second point of interest is the marked shift in the rate of entry in the three years (1985–87) following the passage of the Waxman-Hatch Act. While one explanation for this change is surely the change in regulations governing generic entry that accompanied passage of the act, the fact that large drug markets were losing protection during this period (recall table 1) is likely also to have been important.

The bottom of table 2 reports two additional pieces of information regarding the flow of entrants into these markets. First, the average number of approved generics by years after the year of patent expiration is averaged over all cohorts. This cumulative total rises until roughly eight years after expiration and then declines; the decline is explained by the fact that only drugs whose patents expired in the 1970s have postpatent experiences of more than eight years in our sample, and overall these drugs attracted fairly little competition from generics entering the market, which is why it is important to look at entry by cohort. Second, the last row in table 2 reports on the proportion of drugs for which one or more generics entered the market by any number of years after the year of the patent expiration. For similar reasons, this proportion first rises and then declines. Overall, for six of the thirty drugs no generic competition entered the market during our sample period.

Finally, for our sample of drugs, the average number of approved generic producers across postpatent expiration observations is 3.66. Restricting attention to those drugs and years in which entry actually occurred (that is, conditional on entry), the average number of entrants is 7.28. By the end of the sample period, of course, the average cumulative number of entrants is larger, equal in 1987 to 7.63 over all of the drugs and to 9.54 for those drugs that actually experienced generic entry.

One omission from the data is any measure of the closeness of substitution between the sampled drugs and others in their therapeutic classes. Although we sought to develop controls for this important factor influencing the elasticity of demand for a drug, we found the problem of quantifying the closeness of substitutes a daunting one. The familiar relevant concepts are not easily applied to the available information on medical practice. A given pharmaceutical might represent the therapy of choice for certain symptoms, although not in the face of side conditions that occur in unknown proportions of patients. A drug may be one of several used to treat a given condition, with the selection resting on trial-and-error with individual patients or local preferences among prescribers. A drug used for several conditions might face different substitutes in each use. Furthermore, these patterns change continually as competing drugs enter a therapeutic class, large shifts occur in their relative prices, and accumulations of evidence shift prescribers' preferences. Reluctantly, we abandoned our effort to reduce this information to some summary measure of closeness of substitution in the therapeutic class.

Entry and Competitive Patterns

The investigation turns next to the general patterns of competitive behavior that accompany patent expiration and the subsequent entry of generic competitors for our sample of drugs. We begin with an examination of branded drugs' prices, and then investigate, in turn, generics' prices and market shares, branded drugs' advertising, and quantities of each drug sold.

Prices of Branded Drugs

To examine the general price movements induced by patent expiration and entry, we estimate several simple "semireduced" form equations. Although we do not formally derive these equations from any fully specified structural model of competition between branded and generic producers, they can probably best be understood with reference to a simple constant-elasticity pricing formula. This pricing rule relates the price of branded drug i in period t, P_{it}, to marginal cost for that drug in period t, $C(i, t)$, and a markup term, $\Theta(i, t)$, that is a function of the elasticity of demand faced by the producer of branded drug i in period t:

$$P_{it} = \Theta(i,t)\cdot C(i,t). \tag{1}$$

Because we do not have any information on costs of specific drugs, we first decompose the marginal cost term $C(i,t)$ into the product of a drug-specific effect Λ_i and an industry aggregate effect MC_t:

$$P_{it} = \Theta(i,t)\cdot\Lambda_i\cdot MC_t. \tag{2}$$

Taking logarithms of equation 2, we then have

$$p_{it} = \theta(i,t) + \lambda_i + mc_t, \tag{3}$$

where lowercase letters now refer to natural logarithms of the respective variables.

We now take the markup term, $\theta(i,t)$, to depend potentially on three types of variables: effects of drug "age" (time since initial introduction), effects due to patient expiration, and a drug-specific effect. That is, we represent $\theta(i,t)$ as

$$\theta(i, t) = \alpha_i + h(A_{it}|\boldsymbol{\beta}) + f(E_{it}|\boldsymbol{\gamma}), \tag{4}$$

where A_{it} are variables related to the drug's age, E_{it} are variables related to the expiration of the drug's patents (such as the number of generic producers), α_i is a drug-specific fixed effect capturing differences in fundamental demand elasticities among drugs, and $(\boldsymbol{\beta}, \boldsymbol{\gamma})$ are parameter vectors to be estimated.

The age variables A_{it} in equation 4 are included to capture various life-cycle effects on an innovative drug's optimal price. Physicians' and consumers' experience with the drug, information about it, and advertising effects all accumulate over its life. In addition, with the passage of time, new innovative chemical entities that serve as potentially superior substitutes are likely to be introduced into the marketplace. In the absence of good information on the extent of entry by alternative chemical entities, we rely in part on general life-cycle variables to control for the typical pattern of such competition.[48] As an example of how the entry variables E_{it} in equation 4 might be used to capture the effect of patent expiration, consider a simple dominant-firm/competitive-fringe model with differentiated products as in Suslow.[49] In such a model, increases in the number of generic producers shift a competitive generic supply curve outward and thereby lower the elasticity of the branded producer's residual demand curve.

Substituting equation 4 into equation 3, we have

$$p_{it} = \phi_i + mc_t + h(A_{it}|\boldsymbol{\beta}) + f(E_{it}|\boldsymbol{\gamma}), \tag{5}$$

48. We introduce some further controls for changes in the competitive environment shortly. Subsequently we discuss the possible biases that may be introduced by imprecise controls for these events.

49. Suslow (1986).

where $\phi_i \equiv (\alpha_i + \lambda_i)$.

In principle, we might consider estimating equations based on equation 5 using some industrywide cost index for mc_t. As figure 1 suggests, however, this approach is unlikely to prove very fruitful, as industry price movements during the 1982–87 period seem to bear little relation to any such measure of costs. Instead, we decided to make use of the panel structure of our data set to estimate the mc_t term for our drugs. That is, we replace equation 5 with

$$(6) \qquad p_{it} = \phi_i + \mu_t + h(A_{it}|\beta) + f(E_{it}|\gamma),$$

where μ_t is a parameter to be estimated.[50] Note that the μ_t term in equation 6 can capture not only changes in marginal cost but also any industrywide changes in demand elasticities that may have contributed to the general increase in prices during the sample period. In particular, if we introduce a demand elasticity effect ψ_t into equation 4 we still end up with equation 6. These changes in demand elasticities facing individual drugs could arise either from changes to underlying demand conditions or from changes in general competitive conditions, such as the number of new chemical entities coming to market.

Finally, inspection of the disaggregated price indices of our therapeutic classes revealed a significant dissimilarity in their price movements over the period 1976 to 1987. This fact led us to estimate equation 6 replacing μ_t with μ_t^c, year effects that are specific to drug i's two-digit therapeutic class.[51] Note that these therapeutic class-specific time effects, μ_t^c, provide a significant additional control for changes in the level of competition from substitute chemical entities (in addition to the age effects mentioned above), at least for changes that affect the therapeutic class as a whole. Replacing μ_t with μ_t^c and adding error ϵ_{it}, we have

$$(7) \qquad p_{it} = \phi_i + \mu_t^c + h(A_{it}|\beta) + f(E_{it}|\gamma) + \epsilon_{it}.$$

50. In fact, the overall prices for our sample of drugs seem to have been rising at a rate even *faster* than the price index for SIC 2834: the price index implied by a simple regression of p_{it} on drug and year dummy variables yields year effects of 0.54 in 1976 and 1.71 in 1987 (1982 = 1.0).

51. Doing so causes us to effectively lose the two drugs that are "orphans" in their therapeutic classes (Hygroton and Reglan). Nonetheless, the step is unavoidable, because a test called strongly for rejecting the hypothesis that year effects are the same for each therapeutic class.

Expressing equation 7 in first-differences leads to our basic estimating equation:[52]

$$(8) \qquad \Delta p_{it} = \eta_t^c + \Delta h(A_{it}|\boldsymbol{\beta}) + \Delta f(E_{it}|\boldsymbol{\gamma}) + u_{it},$$

where $\eta_t^c \equiv \mu_t^c - \mu_{t-1}^c$ and $u_{it} \equiv \epsilon_{it} - \epsilon_{it-1}$.

Each observation used to estimate equation 8 is a drug-year combination. The data for various drugs are stacked and the η_t^c parameters are estimated by including class-specific year dummies in addition to the variables in $\Delta h(\cdot)$ and $\Delta f(\cdot)$.[53] In all of our reported estimations we employ a weighted regression technique to control for drug-specific differences in the variance of u_{it}. In this procedure equation 8 is first estimated, consistent estimates of the variance of u_{it} are then computed from the residuals for each drug over time, and then Generalized Least Squares estimates are computed using these weights.

ESTIMATES FOR COMBINED DRUG AND HOSPITAL MARKETS. Table 3 presents our basic results for the prices of branded drugs in the drugstore and hospital submarkets combined (that is, total revenue in the most popular dosage divided by total sales). Specification 1 in the table represents a very simple form for the functions $h(\cdot)$ and $f(\cdot)$ introduced above. In this equation, the effect of a drug's age on its price is effectively captured through three variables: $TAFS_{it}$, the time (in year t) since first sale of drug i; $TAFS2_{it}$, its square; and FS_{it}, a dummy variable for drug i that is "on" during the first two years of the drug's sales.[54] We say "effectively" because the class-specific year effects (estimates omitted from table 3) implicitly incorporate the linear time effect $TAFS_{it}$. The effect of generic entry, on the other hand, is captured through the variable *NN*. *NN* is constructed as follows: if drug i in year t has a positive level of generic sales, then *NN* is equal to the average number of approved generic NDAs (or ANDAs) in existence over years t and $t-1$ (measured

52. In addition to the first-difference form in equation 8 being computationally simpler, estimates using the "levels" form in equation 7 display an extremely high level of positive serial correlation; the first-difference form equation in 8 does not have this problem.

53. That is, a set of class-specific year dummies, say $\{D_{it}^c\}$, was included, with dummy variable D_{it}^c taking the value of 1 for drug i in year t if and only if drug i is in therapeutic class c, and it is year t.

54. Variable definitions are also summarized in the addendum to table 3. This form for $h(\cdot)$ can be thought of as a simple second-order approximation with a separate effect added for introductory sales.

Table 3. Branded Price Regressions: Total Market

	Specifications				
Variable[a]	*1*	*2*	*3*	*4*	*5*
ΔFS[b]	−0.0086 (0.0211)	−0.0071 (0.0214)	−0.0102 (0.0214)	−0.0038 (0.0216)	−0.0053 (0.0228)
$\Delta TAFS2$[c]	0.2 E-3 (0.3 E-3)	0.2 E-3 (0.3 E-3)	0.2 E-3 (0.3 E-3)	0.3 E-3 (0.3 E-3)	0.6 E-4 (0.3 E-3)
ΔNN[d]	−0.0078 (0.0038)	−0.0266 (0.0107)	−0.0151 (0.0104)	−0.0193 (0.0061)	−0.0184 (0.0061)
$\Delta NNHS$[e]	. . .	0.2180 (0.0964)	0.1014 (0.0975)	. . .	. . .
$\Delta NNHS2$[f]	. . .	−0.5884 (0.2093)	−0.3453 (0.2187)	. . .	. . .
$\Delta NN2$[g]	. . .	. . .	. . .	0.41 E-3 (0.31 E-3)	0.48 E-3 (0.32 E-3)
ΔBPE[h]	. . .	. . .	. . .	. . .	0.0023 (0.0149)
ΔAPE[i]	. . .	. . .	. . .	. . .	0.0096 (0.0242)
$\Delta TAPTR$[j]	. . .	. . .	. . .	. . .	0.0343 (0.0132)
R^2 (weighted)	0.40	0.43	0.43	0.47	0.47
R^2 (unweighted)	0.22	0.29	0.34	0.36	0.39
Sample		Full	Keflin out	Hospital share ≤ 0.20	
Number of observations		301	291	258	

Source: Authors' calculations.

a. Dependent variable: Δ log (price); weighted IV estimates with class-specific year dummies. Variable indexed by (*i*, *t*).

b. First sale dummy. Equals fraction of year *t* falling within first two years of drug *i*'s sales.

c. Time after first sale squared. Equals the number of years drug *i* has been on the market at the end of year *t*, squared.

d. Number of NDAs. For years with generic sales, equals the average of year *t* and year (*t* − 1)'s number of NDA-years for drug *i*; equals zero in other years.

e. Product of *NN* and *HS*, the hospital share of drug *i*'s revenue in the year before entry.

f. Same as NNHS, but hospital share is squared.

g. Square of *NN*.

h. Before patent expiration dummy. Equal to fraction of year *t* falling within two years prior to patent expiration of drug *i*.

i. After patent expiration dummy. Equal to fraction of year *t* falling after patent expiration of drug *i*.

j. Time after patent expiration truncated. Equal to maximum of zero and number of years after patent expiration of drug *i* if year *t* is prior to generic entry, equal to maximum of zero and number of years after expiration at time of first generic entry otherwise (adjusted to give average within year *t*).

in NDA-years) for that drug.[55] We employ this averaging procedure because some delay typically occurs between the awarding of an NDA or ANDA and initial sales by a generic entrant. Thus, specification 1 involves taking $\Delta h(\cdot)$ and $\Delta f(\cdot)$ in equation 8 to be $\Delta h(\cdot) = \boldsymbol{\beta}_1 \cdot \Delta FS_{it} + \boldsymbol{\beta}_2 \Delta TAFS2_{it}$ and $\Delta f(\cdot) = \boldsymbol{\gamma}_1 \cdot \Delta NN_{it}$.

Specification 1 is estimated by means of an instrumental-variables technique that instruments for the endogenous variable ΔNN. Natural choices for instruments (and the ones we employ) are combinations of variables representing the amount of time that has passed since patent expiration, a time trend, a dummy indicating passage of the Waxman-Hatch Act, and measures of the drug's general level of demand. Lacking more directly exogenous measures for the last of these instruments, we used the drug's level of (real) sales revenue in the year prior to patent expiration. While not as fully exogenous as our other instruments, the dramatic range displayed by this variable across our sample of drugs (discussed above) relative to the variation in sales revenue for any drug over time, and our use of market size before expiration, lead us to believe that the bias introduced by the use of this instrument is slight relative to the increase in precision it affords.[56]

The results for specification 1 reported in table 3 reveal a statistically significant, but small, effect of entry on branded drugs' prices: each generic NDA leads to a fall of 0.8 percent in the branded drug's price. At the mean number of generic entrants for our sample of 2.46 (that is, the mean of *NN* computed over all postpatent expiration observations), this coefficient implies a postentry price decline of roughly 2 percent. Even conditional on a drug facing generic competition in a given year, for which the conditional mean level of *NN* is 5.67, the decline in branded price due to generic entry is only 4.5 percent. The age-related variables *FS* and *TAFS*2, on the other hand, are both insignificant.

For reasons discussed above, it is natural to wonder whether the share of the market accounted for by hospital sales has important effects on the responses of branded drugs' prices to generic entry. In specification 2 of table 3 we investigate this possibility, expanding the function $f(\cdot)$ by introducing interactions of NN_{it} with HS_i, the hospital share of drug i in the year before patent expiration, and with its square, $HS2_i$, yielding variables $NNHS_{it}$ and $NNHS2_{it}$ respectively. We now need to instrument

55. We use the numbers of NDAs and ANDAs in existence over *all* dosage forms for a drug.

56. Unfortunately, estimates without this instrument are fairly imprecise.

Table 4. ΔNN Coefficients for Various Hospital Share Levels

	From regression			
Hospital share	*2*	*3*	*2D*	*2H*
0.00	−0.027	−0.015	−0.023	−0.051
	(0.011)	(0.010)	(0.011)	(0.014)
0.05	−0.017	−0.011	−0.016	−0.034
	(0.007)	(0.006)	(0.007)	(0.008)
0.10	−0.011	−0.008	−0.011	−0.022
	(0.004)	(0.004)	(0.004)	(0.005)
0.15	−0.007	−0.008	−0.008	−0.014
	(0.003)	(0.003)	(0.003)	(0.006)
0.20	−0.007	−0.009	−0.008	−0.010
	(0.004)	(0.004)	(0.004)	(0.008)
0.30	−0.014	−0.016	−0.014	−0.015
	(0.006)	(0.006)	(0.007)	(0.010)
0.40	−0.034	−0.030	−0.030	−0.037
	(0.012)	(0.012)	(0.012)	(0.011)
0.50	−0.065	−0.051	−0.055	−0.075
	(0.021)	(0.022)	(0.021)	(0.017)
0.75	−0.194		−0.160	−0.246
	(0.064)	. . .	(0.063)	(0.062)
1.00	−0.397		−0.324	−0.523
	(0.133)	. . .	(0.132)	(0.144)

Source: Authors' calculations.

for ΔNN_{it}, $\Delta NNHS_{it}$, and $\Delta NNHS2_{it}$ and we expand the instrument set here (and in all subsequent specifications in table 3) to include interactions of our previous instruments with HS_i and $HS2_i$.[57]

The results from specification 2 reveal a strong effect of hospital share on the price response of branded producers to generic entry. The implied coefficients for ΔNN (along with their standard errors) for various levels of the hospital share are depicted in table 4. The effect of entry increases dramatically for hospital shares that exceed 0.40, with a coefficient of −0.397 arising as this share approaches 1.

57. The same comments with regard to exogeneity apply here as in our discussion of the use of market size as an instrument.

Because of our sample's uneven distribution of markets by hospital share, we had some concern that the presence of just one drug sold primarily to hospitals (Keflin, with a hospital ratio of 0.98) might distort the estimates for the remainder of the sample. Specification 3 in table 3 drops Keflin from the sample. Table 4 depicts the implied coefficient of ΔNN for various levels of hospital share (the sample now includes only drugs with hospital shares less than 0.50). Although the results have a flavor similar to those of specification 2 (the effect of entry still tends to increase as hospital shares exceed 0.30), the magnitude of the hospital share's effect is somewhat smaller, and a quasi-likelihood ratio test for the significance of the $\Delta NNHS$ and $\Delta NNHS2$ terms can now only reject the hypothesis of no effect at a critical value of around 0.30. Finally, note that both here and in specification 2, the implied coefficient on ΔNN is larger than that in specification 1 at almost every hospital share level; the unmodeled heterogeneity of hospital shares in specification 1 must have distorted the estimates of the drug, class-year, or age effects in a way that lowered the estimated effect of ΔNN.

Given these results, in examining two further specifications we focused our attention on the relatively homogeneous majority of our sample that had hospital shares below 20 percent (twenty-five of the thirty drugs). First, it is natural to think that the effect of generic entry on the prices of branded drugs would be largest for the first few entrants and would decline after that (this pattern is predicted by most models of oligopolistic interaction in which branded price converges on some minimum point as generic prices approach marginal cost). To investigate this possibility, we included the square of NN, $NN2$, in the function $f(\cdot)$.

The results depicted in specification 4 of table 3 support this view somewhat, although the t-statistic on $\Delta NN2$ is only 1.32. The inclusion of $\Delta NN2$ raises the estimated coefficient on ΔNN (compare with values in the 0.00–0.20 range in table 4).[58] Now the branded drug's price falls roughly 2 percent with the entry of the first generic competitor, 8.5 percent with five generic competitors, 15 percent with ten generic competitors, and 22 percent with twenty generic producers.[59]

58. A regression for the restricted sample using only ΔNN yields a coefficient on ΔNN of 0.013 (0.003).

59. To calculate the total price decline for any given level of NN, we take $\exp(\Delta)$ where Δ is the value attained by the estimated effects for that level of NN.

Second, we wondered whether patent expiration might exert any effects not tied to entry per se. These effects could arise for two basic reasons. First, pricing decisions could have dynamic aspects. For example, producers of branded drugs could conceivably practice some kind of limit pricing during this interval, or, alternatively, the lags in doctors' information about prices might cause pricing in any year to affect primarily *future* demand. In the latter case, prices might rise in the period prior to entry, because the likelihood of future entry reduces the loss in future sales revenue caused by a price increase today. Second, the anticipation of entry could lead to changes in other variables, notably advertising, that indirectly affect the optimal choice of price by the branded drug's producer. In principle, a change in advertising could either increase or decrease price. Decreases in advertising might at first be thought to lower the demand for the drug and hence the optimal price. However, if advertising is primarily aimed at increasing sales of the drug for uses in which close substitutes exist, a reduction in advertising might reduce demand to only those users for whom the drug lacks good alternatives and might therefore lead to an increase in the branded producer's optimal price.[60] To capture this effect we added three variables to the function $f(\cdot)$: BPE_{it}, a dummy variable equal to 1 in the two years preceding drug i's patent expiration; APE_{it}, a dummy variable equal to 1 after drug i's patent expiration, and $TAPTR_{it}$, a variable equal to the number of years after patent expiration in period t if drug i has not yet had any generic entrants and equal to the number of years after expiration that entry occurred if drug i does face generic competition by year t (that is, it is a *TR*uncated version of the *T*ime *A*fter *P*atent expiration).[61]

The results of this specification (number 5 in table 3) suggest that the prices of branded drugs tend to *increase* in the period between

60. This could occur if doctors become price-sensitive in their prescribing patterns only when they can choose among several roughly equivalent drugs. A related point is that doctors may be hesitant to switch patients who are already successfully using the branded drug. If advertising largely serves to stimulate demand for new prescriptions, for which there is greater price sensitivity, more advertising may lead to lower prices.

61. Thus, *TAPTR* captures any effects that accumulate during the period between patent expiration and generic entry. The truncation casues the entry variables (*NN* and *NN*2) to measure the effect of entry from the price level in existence at the time of first generic entry. Note that *TAPTR* is a function of the endogenous variable *NN*, so it too is instrumented.

patent expiration and entry. Although the coefficients on ΔBPE and ΔAPE are insignificant, that on $\Delta TAPTR$ is significant and indicates that branded prices tend to increase at a rate of roughly 3.5 percent a year in this interval. Although specification 5 does not directly reveal the reasons for this price increase, below we investigate the pattern of advertising expenditures for clues. Finally, the estimates of the effects of entry on branded prices are similar to those seen in specification 4, although slightly smaller.

ESTIMATES FOR DRUGSTORE AND HOSPITAL SUBMARKETS. We also examined pricing patterns of branded drugs in the drugstore and hospital submarkets separately. Given the results from table 3, we expected to see dramatically larger price reductions in the hospital market than in the drugstore market. Surprisingly, that is *not* what we encountered. Table 5 reproduces specification 2 for the drugstore and hospital submarkets (labeled 2D and 2H) and table 4 depicts the implied coefficients for ΔNN at various levels of hospital share. As can be seen, the drugstore and hospital markets both resemble the aggregate results discussed above. That is, while prices decline more in the hospital than in the drugstore market for any given level of hospital share, for the full sample examined in specifications 2D and 2H this difference is swamped by the difference caused in *both* submarkets as the hospital share grows large.

For the subset of the sample with hospital shares under 0.20, specifications 4D, 4H, 5D, and 5H in table 5 confirm that reactions to entry do differ in the two submarkets. The price response to entry is about 70 percent larger in the hospital submarket, both for the first entrant and at all levels of *NN* (see table 6, which depicts the total price effect for various levels of *NN*).[62] At the same time, though, the response in either submarket is fairly small in absolute terms, corresponding to approximately 8 percent in the drugstore market and 13 percent in the hospital market at the restricted sample mean of *NN* of 5.37 (conditional on the existence of some generic competition).[63]

Given the bases for expecting greater price sensitivity in the hospital segment of the market, it is worthwhile recalling that we may possibly

62. Overall, in our sample, the mean ratio of branded hospital to drugstore prices is 0.93.

63. Interestingly, prices in the hospital market do seem to have a somewhat different age profile than do prices in the drugstore market.

Table 5. Branded Price Regressions: Drugstore and Hospital Submarkets

Variable[a]	*2D*	*2H*	*4D*	*4H*	*5D*	*5H*
△*FS*	−0.0139 (0.0217)	−0.0273 (0.0251)	−0.0006 (0.0220)	−0.0252 (0.0246)	−0.0176 (0.0232)	−0.0315 (0.0258)
△*TAFS*2	0.2 E-3 (0.3 E-3)	0.2 E-2 (0.3 E-3)	0.1 E-3 (0.3 E-3)	0.18 E-2 (0.4 E-3)	−0.5 E-4 (0.3 E-3)	0.16 E-2 (0.4 E-3)
△*NN*	−0.0231 (0.0114)	−0.0506 (0.0137)	−0.0189 (0.0059)	−0.0293 (0.0074)	−0.0183 (0.0060)	−0.0304 (0.0081)
△*NNHS*	0.1730 (0.1017)	0.3734 (0.1469)	. . .	. . .	. . .	. . .
△*NNHS*2	−0.4740 (0.2119)	−0.8458 (0.2702)	. . .	. . .	. . .	. . .
△*NN*2	. . .	. . .	0.43 E-3 (0.31 E-3)	0.55 E-3 (0.44 E-3)	0.49 E-3 (0.31 E-3)	0.70 E-3 (0.49 E-3)
△*BPE*	. . .	. . .	. . .	. . .	0.0024 (0.0145)	−0.0206 (0.0219)
△*APE*	. . .	. . .	. . .	. . .	0.0097 (0.0237)	−0.0182 (0.0323)
△*TAPTR*	. . .	. . .	. . .	. . .	0.0325 (0.0132)	0.0298 (0.0164)
R^2 (weighted)	0.38	0.46	0.47	0.52	0.46	0.52
R^2 (unweighted)	0.20	0.27	0.35	0.28	0.38	0.28
Sample	Full		Hospital share ≤0.20		Hospital share ≤0.20	
Number of observations	299	289	258	246	258	246

Source: Authors' calculations.
a. Dependent variable: △ log (price); weighted IV estimates with class-specific year effects.

be missing some discounting behavior in our data. Though we do not have any hard information about the extent of this problem, our sense from talking to individuals in the industry is that such discounts are more prevalent in the hospital segment of the market.[64] For example, if the

64. Some preliminary work by Berndt, Griliches, and Rosett (1991) suggests a close correspondence in average price movements between IMS data and data received directly from some leading pharmaceutical manufacturers for a sample of drugs produced by these companies. Their comparison, however, averages over pharmacy and hospital sales and so

Table 6. Implied Percentage Branded Price Reductions from Specifications 5D and 5H

	Submarket	
Number of generics	*Drugstores*	*Hospitals*
1	−0.018	−0.030
2	−0.034	−0.056
3	−0.049	−0.081
5	−0.076	−0.126
10	−0.125	−0.209
15	−0.151	−0.258
20	−0.156	−0.280
Minimum attained at:	18.7	21.7
Value at minimum:	−0.157	−0.281

Source: Authors' calculations.

optimal price of a branded drug to final users in the hospital segment is lower than in the pharmacy market and if the branded drug producer is unable to directly control the prices charged by the wholesaler to these two sets of users, the branded producer may decide to pay direct discounts to hospital purchasers. Indeed, such a scenario coincides with that described to us by these individuals: sales to hospitals are largely channeled through the same wholesalers that sell to the pharmacy market, while hospitals and hospital buying groups solicit bids from manufacturers on the level of "charge-backs" the manufacturers will provide for purchases of their products (these rebate levels are not observed by the wholesalers). While discounts present a problem for our estimates only if their extent is related to patent expiration, in this case these hospital discounts could increase in response to generic entry if the required price differential grows. We shall return to this issue below after considering the responses of several other variables across the two markets.

STRUCTURAL SHIFTS OVER TIME. Finally, as we have noted, a number of structural changes were occurring in the industry over the course of our sample period that might be thought to alter various actors' elasticities of substitution between branded and generic drugs (for example, repeal of the state antisubstitution laws and changes in insurers' and

is likely to be more informative about the accuracy of the data from the much larger pharmacy submarket.

Table 7. Branded Price Regressions: Time Effects by Submarket

Variable[a]	*Drugstores*	*Hospitals*
Δ*FS*	−0.0030	−0.0315
	(0.0233)	(0.0248)
Δ*TAFS*2	−0.4 E-4	0.16 E-2
	(0.3 E-3)	(0.4 E-3)
Δ*NN*	−0.0210	−0.0470
	(0.0088)	(0.0113)
Δ[*NN**(1987-Year)]	0.0016	0.0074
	(0.0034)	(0.0041)
Δ*NN*2	0.65 E-3	0.16 E-2
	(0.47 E-3)	(0.67 E-3)
Δ*BPE*	0.0019	−0.0218
	(0.0147)	(0.0214)
Δ*APE*	0.0063	−0.0247
	(0.0244)	(0.0320)
Δ*TAPTR*	0.0316	0.0263
	(0.0134)	(0.0161)
R^2 (weighted)	0.46	0.55
R^2 (unweighted)	0.38	0.30
Sample	Hospital share ≤ 0.20	
Number of observations	258	246

Source: Authors' calculations.
a. Dependent variable: Δ log (price); weighted IV estimates with class-specific year dummies.

hospitals' behavior). We wondered whether the price reaction of branded drugs to generic entry might have increased. To investigate this issue we reestimated specifications 5D and 5H from table 5, including a variable in the function $f(\cdot)$ interacting NN_{it} with (1987-t). Unfortunately, for this subsample (those with hospital shares less than 0.20), there is no generic entry before 1982, so we can at best pick up the effects of structural shifts in the latter part of our sample.[65] Table 7 reports the results. The coefficient of this new variable is positive in

65. This problem would not be solved by looking at the entire sample; for the full sample we have only four drug-years with generic entrants before 1982 (out of a total of sixty-five over all years).

both submarkets although significant only in the hospital submarket. This finding is consistent with the view that many of the structural changes affecting the pharmacy market occurred before 1981, while the primary changes affecting hospital behavior occurred largely in the 1980s.

Generic Prices and Market Shares

We examined the effects of generic entry on the prices of generic as well as branded drugs. This inquiry is of interest for several reasons. First, under the reasonable assumption that the marginal costs of generic production are similar to those of the original innovator, generic prices provide an upper bound on the level of marginal costs. Thus, the level of generic prices can give us information on the level of price-cost margins existing during the period when a drug's sales are protected by patents. The level of generic prices also allows us to gauge the extent of reductions in the price of branded drugs caused by generic entry relative to the preentry price-cost margin. Another issue of interest concerns the degree of product differentiation present in these markets. Clearly the price differential between branded and generic drugs can provide information on the level of differentiation between the innovator's and generic producers' products. It is also of interest to assess the differentiation between generic producers (relative to that existing between the original innovator and generic producers overall). One way to gain some insight into this second issue is to examine the degree to which an increase in the number of generic producers lowers *generic* prices more than it lowers *branded* prices.

To address these issues we assumed that generic drug prices satisfy a condition parallel to equation 7 for any drug i; thus,

$$(9) \qquad p_{it} = (\phi_i + \delta_i) + \mu_i^c + h(A_{it}|\boldsymbol{\beta}) + g(E_{it}|\boldsymbol{\gamma}^G) + \eta_{it},$$

where δ_i is the generic "quality" discount and $g(\cdot)$ reflects the fact that entry of a generic drug may affect existing generics and the branded drug differently. Subtracting equation 7 from equation 9, we get an equation for the log of the ratio of generic to branded drug prices:

$$(10) \qquad \log\left(\frac{P_{it}^G}{P_{it}^B}\right) = \delta_i + [g(E_{it}|\boldsymbol{\gamma}^G) - f(E_{it}|\boldsymbol{\gamma}^B)] + u_{it},$$

where $u_{it} \equiv (\eta_{it} - \epsilon_{it})$.

We estimated this equation for the sample of drugs with hospital shares less than 0.20 using specification 5 for $f(\cdot)$ and $g(\cdot)$; that is, taking $f(\cdot) = \gamma_1^B \cdot NN + \gamma_2^B \cdot NN2$ and $g(\cdot) = \gamma_1^G \cdot NN + \gamma_2^G \cdot NN2$. For this specification, equation 10 becomes

$$(11) \quad \log\left(\frac{P_{it}^G}{P_{it}^B}\right) = \delta_i + (\gamma_1^G - \gamma_1^B) \cdot NN_{it} + (\gamma_2^G - \gamma_2^B) \cdot NN2_{it} + \eta_{it}.$$

We estimated equation 11 over the subset of those branded drugs that had at least two years of competition from generic drug sales, once again instrumenting for the number of entrants.[66]

The results of this estimation, presented in table 8, reveal three basic facts. First, generic drugs sell for a substantial discount from the price of the branded drug; the estimates suggest that with a single generic entrant, the generic price is roughly 60 percent of the branded drug price. Tabulations of this ratio for various levels of *NN* are presented in the first column of table 9. For this sample of drugs, the average value of *NN*, conditional on there being some generic sales in a year, is 5.8, which corresponds to a generic/branded price ratio of 0.43 (the actual sample average for these drugs is 0.48).

Second, the entry of additional generic producers depresses the prices

66. It should be pointed out, however, that even with this instrumental variables procedure, a potential selection bias still exists here since equation 11 can only be estimated for periods in which we observe generic entry. Put differently, *conditional on observing generic sales in period* t, η_{it} will potentially be correlated with our instruments for *NN*. This selection problem may not be too severe in the present instance, however, because of the delay between the decision to invest in regulatory permission to enter and the actual event of entry. Indeed, the desire to eliminate any persistent component of η is one of the reasons for γ_i, the generic "discount" for drug *i*, to be drug-specific even though it costs us several observations on drugs with only one year of generic sales in our sample.

For this estimation we actually altered the definition of *NN* somewhat. In particular, we altered any observation in which *NN* was less than one to set it equal to one. The reason we did this is that the average generic price recorded in a year in which one generic producer was active but only entered in, say, October will be the generic price associated with the presence of one generic, not 0.25 generics. Given the small extent of branded price movements in response to generic entry, this alteration is unlikely to cause much of a misspecification in terms of the branded price.

Finally, we estimated equation 11 in levels because in this case we are interested in the drug-specific constants δ_i, which are needed to measure the extent of the generic discount. For this equation, whose dependent variable is a ratio of prices rather than a price level as in equation 7, no significant serial correlation is present.

Table 8. Generic Prices and Market Shares: Total Market

Variable[a]	Dependent variable: $Log\left(\frac{P_G}{P_B}\right)$	Dependent variable: $Log\left(\frac{Q_B}{Q_B+Q_G}\right)$
Mean of estimated drug-specific constants	−0.441	0.048
	(0.032)	(0.025)
NN	−0.0722	−0.0825
	(0.0151)	(0.0081)
*NN*2	0.70 E-3	0.30 E-2
	(0.66 E-3)	(0.49 E-3)
R^2 (weighted)	0.98	0.97
R^2 (unweighted)	0.94	0.80
Number of observations	45	45

Source: Authors' calculations.
a. Weighted IV estimates with drug-specific dummies.

Table 9. Implied Ratios from Results in Table 8

NN	$\left(\frac{P_G}{P_B}\right)$	$\left(\frac{P_G}{P_B \text{ absent entry}}\right)$	$\left(\frac{Q_B}{Q_B+Q_G}\right)$
1	0.599	0.588	0.969
2	0.558	0.540	0.900
3	0.521	0.496	0.841
5	0.456	0.422	0.748
10	0.335	0.294	0.618
15	0.255	0.217	0.594
20	0.201	0.171	0.661

Source: Authors' calculations.

of existing generic producers much more severely than the price of the original innovator. The ratio of generic drug prices to the branded drug's price that would have prevailed absent any reaction to entry can be obtained by adding the estimated coefficients from table 8 and the estimated coefficients from specification 5 of table 3 to calculate β_1^G and β_2^G. The implied ratios as a function of *NN* are given in the second column of table 9. With one entrant this ratio is 0.588, and with three it drops to 0.496; by the time ten generic drug producers are in the market, this ratio falls to 0.294, and with twenty it is 0.171. The decline shown is consistent with one point that industry experts have repeatedly made to us: generic drug companies make money by being the first to enter after patent expiration.[67] Yet, at the same time, this pattern is still far from what would arise with Bertrand pricing. The third fact is clear from these figures: preentry price-cost margins of branded drugs are very large, and the decline in branded prices caused by entry of generics represents a very small fraction of this margin.

Given these striking differences between branded and generic drug prices, it is of some interest to examine the effects of generic entry on the sales of the branded producer. The second column of table 8 reports a regression in the same form as that for the generic/branded price ratio, but with the log of the branded producer's market share (of quantity sold) as the dependent variable. It is estimated over the same set of observations as the generic/branded price regression; the implied market shares as a function of *NN* are depicted in the third column of table 9. This tabulation shows that although branded drug producers do sacrifice significant market shares to low-priced generic substitutes, these reductions are fairly small given the size of the price differentials. For example, with five generic competitors the generic/branded price ratio is 0.456, but the branded drug's share falls only to 0.748.[68] These estimates are also fairly consistent with the aggregate data on the generic share of multisource drug markets cited above for 1989. The average level of *NN* in 1987 for those branded drugs in our sample facing generic competition, for example, is 8.61.[69] Our estimates would then imply a generic market share of 36 percent, a number fairly close to the

67. This fact seemed to have played an interesting role in the recent generic drug scandal in which generic producers attempted not only to advance their own drug applications but also to slow down those of rivals. See, for example, U.S. House of Representatives, Committee on Energy and Commerce (1989).

68. One point worth noting is that there is a fair amount of variation across our drugs in the level of their estimated fixed effects. In the generic price/branded price regression, the standard deviation of the estimated fixed effects is 0.283, while it is 0.091 in the branded market share equation. We made some attempt to explain this variance but were not very successful with the limited number of drug-specific characteristics that we possessed. We did detect some tendency for branded share to decline less the longer the drug was on the market and if it was used for "chronic" conditions. Given more data and better measures of drug characteristics, further exploration of the possibility of differing effects of entry across drugs would seem desirable.

69. This average is slightly lower than the 9.54 reported in the data section for 1987 because here we are using *NN*, which for any year t is an average of the number of approved generic producers for years t and $t - 1$.

aggregate generic share, reported earlier, of 42 percent in 1989.[70] All of this, of course, reiterates the point that for at least some of the actors affecting demand, the branded and generic products are strongly differentiated.

Finally, we also were curious about the existence of any differential responses across the hospital and drugstore submarkets. The subset of the sample in table 8 with positive generic drug sales in the hospital submarket involves only thirty-one observations. Though we did not run any regressions for this small sample, we did examine the means of the generic/branded price ratio and the branded market share. For the pharmacy submarket the average ratio (and standard deviation) of generic to branded prices in this sample was 0.413 (0.146) and the average branded market share was 0.763 (0.153). For the hospital market, on the other hand, the corresponding means were 0.473 (0.228) and 0.725 (0.217). Thus, we again see a difference in outcomes that is in the direction we would expect, but one that is also fairly small. Notably, this now holds true for quantity responses (for which there is no potential data problem) as well as for price responses.[71]

70. At least two factors may explain this slightly lower share figure. First, aggregate generic market shares were likely to be lower in 1987 than in 1989 (indeed, for 1988 the aggregate generic share was roughly 38 percent), and second, the 42 percent figure is the generic share of *new* prescriptions, which are likely to show a higher generic share than do refill prescription sales (if experienced users of branded drugs are less likely to be switched). In addition, note that our sampling procedure excluded multisource drugs whose patents expired before 1976. This selection could also lead to a difference between generic shares in our sample and in the market as a whole: entrants may have been less willing to enter markets for drugs expiring in those years when entry costs were high. At the same time, the selection excludes some drugs (for example, antibiotics such as penicillin) with traditionally high generic shares.

71. We also explored (for the total market) whether there seemed to be any effect of generic entry that accumulates over time independent of whether additional generic entry occurs. Such effects could arise because physicians or consumers become more familiar with the possibility of prescribing or purchasing the generic version of the drug or, alternatively, because generic entrants increase their productive capacity over time. We did find some evidence for this type of effect. Introducing a constant into the first-differenced form for the generic/branded price equation yields a parameter value of -0.11 (0.03) and lowers the coefficient of NN to -0.048 (0.020). For a similar change to the branded share equation the estimated constant is -0.059 (0.023), while the estimate of NN is essentially unchanged (without the constant, these first-differenced forms yield estimates almost identical to those in table 8). With more data and longer postentry time series, a more thorough examination of this type of effect would seem desirable.

Advertising

We now consider the effects of patent expiration and generic drug entry on drug innovators' advertising expenditures, the second of their decision variables. Correct modeling of this strategic decision variable is more difficult than was modeling branded prices because of the durable intertemporal effects advertising may have. Our fairly crude strategy here aims to uncover the broad facts about advertising's dynamic trajectory and its response to the entry of generic competition.

Table 10 reports the results of a specification for real advertising expenditures parallel to that of specification 5 in table 3 on branded price. We use the same sample as in this earlier estimation: those drugs with hospital shares below 0.20. Only two changes are made. First, because advertising expenditures might reasonably be thought to decline smoothly as a drug's stock of goodwill increases, we add to the function $h(\cdot)$ an additional variable called *AFS*, which takes the value 1/*TAFS* (except in the first year of sale where we set it equal to 1 regardless of the value of *TAFS*). Second, we omit the (class-specific) year dummies that the general industry price rise necessitated in our analysis of price movements. Thus, in the results shown in table 10, the coefficient on $\Delta TAFS$ is reported (recall that previously the year dummy variables implicitly included the *TAFS* effect).[72]

The results reported in the first column of table 10 provide two basic, and complementary, facts about the effects of patent expiration and generics entry on drug innovators' advertising expenditures. First, generic entry significantly depresses the innovator's advertising expenditures; branded advertising falls roughly 20 percent with the entry of the first generic drug, another 40 percent when the number of generic entrants reaches five, and still another 20 percent when the number of entrants reaches ten. Second, branded advertising begins its decline before generic entry occurs, falling roughly 10 percent in the two years before patent expiration and then declining at a rate of roughly 25 percent a year between patent expiration and entry of the first generic competitor.

72. The quasi-likelihood ratio test for inclusion of year dummies in the estimations reported in table 10 comes nowhere near rejecting the hypothesis of no year effects (we could reject the hypothesis only at a significance level of roughly 0.50).

Table 10. Advertising Regressions

	Subsample of hospital share ≤ 0.20 drugs		
Variable[a]	Full	Small markets (<$65M)	Large markets (>$65M)
ΔAFS	0.7909	0.5368	1.724
	(0.3545)	(0.3459)	(0.428)
ΔFS	−0.3425	−0.4669	−0.4572
	(0.2211)	(0.2851)	(0.2619)
ΔTAFS	0.0130	−0.1849	0.1898
	(0.0553)	(0.1048)	(0.0637)
ΔTAFS2	0.16 E-3	0.30 E-2	−0.45 E-2
	(0.19 E-2)	(0.42 E-2)	(0.28 E-2)
ΔNN	−0.1947	−0.0134	−0.1875
	(0.0387)	(0.1664)	(0.0528)
ΔNN2	0.34 E-2	−0.0213	0.0021
	(0.23 E-2)	(0.0160)	(0.0030)
ΔBPE	−0.1145	−0.0375	−0.1893
	(0.0888)	(0.1588)	(0.1113)
ΔAPE	−0.0088	0.1101	−0.2738
	(0.1370)	(0.2396)	(0.1822)
ΔTAPTR	−0.2489	−0.2539	−0.0158
	(0.0990)	(0.1786)	(0.2350)
R^2 (weighted)	0.27	0.17	0.58
R^2 (unweighted)	0.02	0.02	0.24
Number of observations	258	149	109

Source: Authors' calculations.
a. Dependent variable: Δ log (real advertising expenditures); weighted IV estimates. Real advertising expenditures are deflated by GNP deflator.

These findings reveal two points about advertising for branded drugs. First, the significant declines in advertising levels due to impending and actual entry of generic drugs strongly suggest that expanding the overall market for the chemical entity is a significant function of branded drug advertising; the arrival of generic entrants reduces the payout to the innovator's investments in market expansion because benefits will now be shared with these entrants. While this finding does not bear directly on the degree to which the advertising of branded drugs is ''informative'' or ''persuasive'' (messages that increase demand for the chemical entity may be of either kind), it does reduce the degree to which branded drug advertising can be viewed as limiting generic competition after expiration of the drug's patent.[73] Second, the declines in advertising expenditures before actual generic entry seem to confirm the durability of advertising's effects because they imply that drug innovators expect lower returns from advertising expenditures once the patent expires and generic entry grows likely.[74]

To gain a bit more insight into the dependence of these advertising declines on the drug innovator's expectations about entry, we divided the sample between those branded drugs with sales revenue above $65 million in the year before expiration and those below $65 million (roughly the mean of the sample: fourteen of this sample's twenty-four drugs fell into the lower revenue group). We expect drugs in the higher revenue group to face a greater likelihood of rapid entry of generic competition, so the pattern of advertising reductions should differ between these two subsamples if they depend on anticipation of entry. As the second and third columns of table 10 reveal, these patterns do differ exactly as the hypothesis predicts: following patent expiration, advertising of branded drugs declines quickly in large markets (through the *BPE* and *APE* variables) but more gradually in small markets (through the *TAPTR* variable).[75]

Admittedly, these findings are at best suggestive of the effects at work. A proper model would explicitly incorporate the expected level of future entry at any given time *t*, conditional on the information set at that time, and would more fully address the durable stock aspects of advertising.[76]

73. Of course, this finding does not preclude such market-share shifting aspects to branded drugs' advertising. Indeed, the content of the remaining advertising expenditures may well shift toward loyalty-inducing messages (''Isn't quality important?'') and away from messages designed to expand the overall use of the chemical entity. This finding does, however, limit the degree of the market-share shifting aspects.

74. The results also reveal another point: some branded drugs' advertising levels are quite noisy. That can be seen from the low levels of R^2 and the sizable difference between its weighted and unweighted levels. In the regressions that distinguish between large and small markets, discussed below and reported in table 10, we shall see that this noise is due mostly to the drugs that supply small markets.

75. Note that the effect of actual entry is very imprecisely estimated for the small markets because so few generics entered these markets compared with the large ones.

76. Note, in particular, that the interaction of the ''anticipation effects,'' *BPE*, *APE*, and *TAPTR*, with variables that affect entry rates (such as market size) cannot ultimately be a viable modeling strategy (despite our use of this strategy here to get a crude look at

Nonetheless, the occurrence of a strong decline in advertising due to anticipated and actual generic entry seems evident in the data and may in part explain the pattern of preentry increases of branded prices reported above.

Total Quantity

Finally, we examined the effects of patent expiration and generic entry on the total quantities sold of drugs in our sample. We pursue two objectives. First, one might, as a first approximation, ignore product differentiation (or take the paternalistic view that generic and branded drugs really are the same) and use the increase in quantity sold as an indicator of overall welfare effects of generic entry. Second, examination of this variable can prove important for tying together the story that emerged from the results presented so far. Table 11 reports the results of a specification parallel to that in table 10 except for the exclusion of the *AFS* variable.[77]

The basic picture revealed in table 11 is striking in light of our earlier results. First, the quantity of the branded drug sold declines significantly before generic drugs enter the market: it falls roughly 20 percent in the year of patent expiration and continues to decline at roughly 12 percent a year thereafter until entry occurs. Obviously, this finding is strongly consistent with the steep decline in advertising revealed above (as well as with the small price increase). Second, entry of generic competition exerts little overall effect on the total quantity of the drug sold: the point estimates (which are statistically insignificant) indicate that total quantity sold initially rises slightly (reaching a maximum 3 percent increase with 4.6 entrants) and then declines.

The lack of any significant increase in total quantity sold due to generic entry may at first be surprising, but this finding is consistent with the basic facts developed above. Generic entry brings with it two

---

the anticipation issue), because as we include these interactions we lose the ability to identify the effect of actual entry (such interaction terms are exactly our instruments for *NN*). In principle, the correct procedure is to include explicit terms for expected entry that we then instrument. However, incorporation of anything beyond very short anticipations would dramatically reduce our sample.

77. As in table 10, we omit year dummies. A quasi-likelihood ratio test of the hypothesis that they are not needed overwhelmingly supports this hypothesis: we only could reject at a significance level of 0.95.

Table 11. Total Quantity Regression

Variable[a]	*Estimate*
ΔFS	−0.3476 (0.1067)
$\Delta TAFS$	0.1734 (0.0236)
$\Delta TAFS2$	−0.58 E-2 (0.81 E-3)
ΔNN	0.0130 (0.0193)
$\Delta NN2$	−0.14 E-2 (0.12 E-2)
ΔBPE	0.0024 (0.0384)
ΔAPE	−0.0993 (0.0609)
$\Delta TAPTR$	−0.1280 (0.0282)
R^2 (weighted)	0.40
R^2 (unweighted)	0.28
Sample	Hospital share ≤ 0.20
Number of observations	258

Source: Authors' calculations.
a. Dependent variable: $\Delta \log (Q_B + Q_G)$; weighted IV estimates.

offsetting effects: first, generic entrants offer significantly lower prices, which tend to expand overall sales of the drug, but their arrival also leads to a significant reduction in the level of advertising for the drug, which acts to counterbalance this price effect. To the extent that the price elasticity of overall demand for a drug is low and the advertising reduction by the branded drug producer is large, the former effect will dominate and total quantity sold will fall as a result of patent expiration and subsequent generic entry. It should be stressed that the demand declines that we attribute here to patent expiration and generic entry are those arising after controlling for both life-cycle and therapeutic class-specific year effects (although the latter are insignificant, as noted above). Thus, to the extent that these measures adequately control for changes in competition from alternative chemical entities, these quantity reductions are solely attributable to patent expiration and generic entry (note that our estimates reveal a life-cycle effect with a peak in sales at around fourteen years, presumably due to the introduction of alternative, therapeutically superior substitutes). Furthermore, it seems likely that, if anything, our inability to control for this factor directly would bias our results toward attributing too *little* of a decline in demand to patent expiration and generic entry since we would generally expect the introduction of substitute chemical entities by other producers to be negatively correlated with the expiration of a given drug's patent. One possible counterbalancing effect, though, could arise if generic entry into an innovative branded producer's drug made *that* producer more likely to introduce a new superior product. This decrease in quantity sold raises important—and difficult—questions about the welfare impact of generic entry, an issue that we discuss further in the concluding section.

Summary and Conclusions

We undertook a simple exploratory analysis of the effects of patent expiration and subsequent entry of generic drugs into markets for innovative pharmaceuticals that lost their patent protection during 1976–87. We found considerable regularity in the behavior of the drug innovators who face the arrival of competitors and in the effects of the competitors on market prices and quantities. The innovator's price declines with the number of generic entrants, but the rate of decline is small, with the branded drug's price depressed only 4.5 percent for the mean number of generic drugs that entered contested markets. The sensitivity of the innovator's price to entry decreases with successive entrants, falling roughly 2 percent after the first entry but only 22 percent with twenty generic competitors. Some evidence was found that innovators' prices grew more sensitive to entry during the 1980s. There is no evidence of limit pricing: after the patent expires, the innovator's price actually rises until a generic competitor enters the market.

Generic producers enter the market quoting prices much lower than those of their branded competitors, and these prices also decline as the number of generic competitors increases, potentially falling to roughly 17 percent of the branded producer's preentry price. The effect of additional generic competitors is also noticeably stronger on generic prices than on branded ones. The share commanded by generic producers increases with their number, but the striking fact is the relatively small shares generics gain in light of the discounts they offer from branded firms' prices: when the ratio of generic to branded price is 0.456, we estimate that the generics capture a share of only 25.2 percent.

Besides price, the main decision variable of the drug innovator is the level of sales-promotion outlays. Although innovators' promotional patterns for individual drugs are more diverse than their pricing decisions, it is clear that both anticipated and actual entry of generic drugs lead to substantial declines in the innovators' sales promotion activities.

To check implications of the changes in innovators' prices and sales promotion, we undertook a parallel analysis of changes in total quantity sold in each drug market. We found that quantity sold falls after the patent's expiration and before generics enter the market, with the lower prices offered by generic entrants failing to compensate for the demand contraction apparently caused by the branded producer's reduction in advertising expenditures.

Less clear is the interpretation of our findings regarding the differences between the pharmacy and hospital submarkets. In all of our results, the hospital market seems more susceptible to generic competition: branded drug price reductions are larger, the generic price discount is smaller, and the market share of the branded drug falls more in the hospital than in the pharmacy segment of the market. At the same time, however, these differences are smaller than we might have expected. The difficulty in interpreting these findings arises because we may be missing price discounts that serve as an important means by which producers of branded drugs respond to generic entry in the hospital segment. The small difference in branded market shares between the two segments (which have no corresponding data problem) suggests two possibilities. Either, on average, the differences between these two segments are smaller than is commonly believed or, alternatively, significant enough unobserved discounts are being offered to keep the branded drug share reasonably close across the two segments. In this light, our finding concerning the effects of the overall hospital share of the market on branded price response may be suggestive of the latter possibility, since the use of selective direct discounts may be lower for drugs sold primarily to hospitals. Examination of a sample with a larger set of drugs primarily sold to hospitals might prove helpful in sorting out these hypotheses more definitely.

Implications for Market Behavior and Structure

The research design that yielded these conclusions does not embody any particular model of competitive interaction between producers of branded and generic drugs. Nevertheless, it does seem to suggest a number of preliminary conclusions regarding structure and behavior in these markets. First, the goodwill stock that the drug innovator develops over the course of the period of exclusive marketing clearly seems to provide a significant degree of differentiation from later generic entrants. The extent of this differentiation can be seen in the relatively small share that generic drug firms achieve despite their significant price discounts, the relatively muted price response of the branded producer to generic entry, and the quite different effects that successive generic entries have on branded and generic prices.

Second, while the branded producer does accumulate loyalty-inducing goodwill during the period of patent protection, the marked decline in promotional activity caused by patent expiration and generic entry, as well as the accompanying decline in quantities sold, suggests that a significant component of sales promotion activity for branded drugs is of the "market expansion" variety. While this fact does not lead to any direct conclusions regarding the relative share of "informative" and "persuasive" messages in sales promotion activities for branded drugs, it does reduce the extent to which those activities can be viewed as limiting the opportunities faced by generic competitors. One possible reading of these two findings is that the advantage achieved by the innovative drug relative to later generic entrants is in large part tied to doctors' habitual use of the brand name; after generic entry, however, a large share of possible promotional activities by the branded producer would have positive spillovers to generic producers, not only by increasing prescriptions written for generics, but also through generic substitution of brand-written prescriptions.

Third, we see little in this evidence that suggests any very active attempt by producers of branded drugs to deter the entry of rivals. Although such concerns about deterrence may still affect branded producers' prices and advertising levels on the margin, the overall response seems to be one that takes the likely extent of entry as given and optimizes accordingly.

Implications for Public Policy

In undertaking this analysis, we sought to contribute to the debate on "innovation vs. competition" by providing additional evidence on the effects of postpatent competition. One of the aspects of our results that perhaps most surprises us is the ultimate ambiguity they yield regarding the welfare effects of this competition. As we expected when we began our study, generic entry makes a drug available at much lower prices than prevailed during its period of patent protection. Yet it does not significantly lower the prices of branded drugs and, even more importantly, it does not lead to increases in the quantities of the contested drug that are sold. Indeed, quantities may decrease relative to those sold before patent expiration. While this fact may be in part related to the presence of low demand elasticities for these drugs, we suspect that the decline in advertising expenditures on branded drugs is an important factor in this finding. Thus, in the end, it appears that any evaluation of the welfare impact of generic entry must inevitably address the difficult question of the welfare properties of advertising for branded drugs. In particular, it seems that the welfare consequences of generic entry are ultimately closely tied to the degree to which promotion by innovative pharmaceutical manufacturers is informative rather than persuasive.[78]

Directions for Further Research

Like most studies, ours fails to preempt opportunities for further research. We see at least three desirable directions for further study.

78. This discussion has focused only on the welfare impact of generic entry *gross* of any fixed entry costs. A second welfare concern surrounds the issue of whether there is excess entry of generics relative to these fixed costs. See, for example, Mankiw and Whinston (1986). The relatively small increases in overall generic market share achieved as the number of generic competitors increases might suggest some concern in this regard. The lowering of these fixed entry costs that accompanied the passage of the Waxman-Hatch Act, however, seems likely to have lowered the extent of any welfare losses arising from this problem, as discussed in Mankiw and Whinston (1986).

The first is a more structural empirical modeling of the competitive interaction in these drug markets. Clearly, a number of questions whose answers we desire can be addressed only through such an approach. (For example, what is the elasticity of demand for these drugs? What is the cross-elasticity between branded and generic drugs? What model of competitive interaction best describes behavior here?) We hope the results we have described can serve as a useful guide to such efforts by narrowing down the set of reasonable structural models.

Second, in all of the preceding analysis we took a drug "market" to consist of the demand for a single chemical entity. As we noted earlier, however, various chemical entities are in fact substitutes for other chemical entities for a variety of conditions and in varying degrees. While our study employs a number of direct controls for such changes in competitive conditions, explicit consideration of the effects of this differentiated product structure on competition in the pharmaceutical industry seems desirable.

Finally, in this paper we have addressed the competition that arises as patents expire and generic entry occurs without any explicit examination of the process of entry itself. As in the work of Bresnahan and Reiss, and Berry, such an examination can provide another source of information about the market opportunities of generic firms.[79] Of additional interest is the assessment it could provide of the impact that the Waxman-Hatch Act has had on the extent of generic entry, an impact that is difficult to discern directly from table 2 because of the generally larger sizes of the markets whose patents expired in the latter part of our sample. In contrast to the work of Bresnahan and Reiss, and Berry, however, here a proper model of this phenomenon will need to take account of the explicitly dynamic process by which entrants flow into a drug market after the drug's patent has expired.

79. Bresnahan and Reiss (1990); and Berry (1990).

References

Berndt, Ernst R., Zvi Griliches, and Joshua G. Rosett. 1990. "On the Accuracy of Producer Price Indexes for Pharmaceutical Preparations: An Audit Based on Detailed Firm-Specific Data." Working Paper 3490. Cambridge, Mass.: National Bureau of Economic Research (NBER).

———. 1991. "Price Indices for Pharmaceutical Preparations: Additional Findings." Presentation at NBER Productivity Program Meeting.

Berry, Steven. 1990. "Estimation of a Model of Entry in the Airline Industry." Mimeo, Yale University. (July).

———. 1990. "Discrete Choice Models of Oligopoly Product Differentiation." Mimeo, Yale University (February).

Berry Steven, Jim Levinsohn, and Ariel Pakes. 1990. "Automobile Prices in Market Equilibrium." Mimeo, Yale University (December).

Berry, S., and Lutz, N., 1989. "A Proposal for Research on Pharmaceutical Markets Pricing and Promotion." Mimeo, Yale University (September).

Bond, Ronald S., and David F. Lean. 1977. *Sales, Promotion, and Product Differentiation in Two Prescription Drug Markets*. Staff Report to the Federal Trade Commission. Washington: Federal Trade Commission.

Bresnahan, Timothy F., and Peter C. Reiss. 1990. "Entry in Monopoly Markets." *Review of Economic Studies* 57 (October):531–53.

Caplin, A., and Nalebuff B. 1991. "Aggregation and Imperfect Competition: On the Existence of Equilibrium." *Econometrica*, forthcoming.

Carroll, Norman V., Chanaporn Siridhara, and Jack E. Fincham. 1987. "Factors Affecting Market Acceptance of Generic Drug Products: An Examination of Inherent Risk, Price, and Maximum Allowable Cost Coverage." *Akron Business and Economic Review* 18 (Spring):11–18.

Cocks, Douglas L., and John R. Virts. 1974. "Pricing Behavior of the Ethical Pharmaceutical Industry." *Journal of Business* 47 (July):349–62.

Comanor, William S. 1986. "The Political Economy of the Pharmaceutical Industry." *Journal of Economic Literature* 24 (September):1178–1217.

Communications Workers of America. 1990. *CWA Information Industry Report*. Washington (November).

Ericson, Richard, and Ariel Pakes. 1989. "An Alternative Model of Firm and Industry Dynamics." Mimeo, Columbia University (September).

Richard E. Caves, Michael D. Whinston, and Mark A. Hurwitz 65

Grabowski, Henry G. 1980. ''Regulation and the International Diffusion of Pharmaceuticals.'' In *The International Supply of Medicines: Implications of U.S. Regulatory Reform*, edited by Robert B. Helms. American Enterprise Institute.

Grabowski, Henry G., and John M. Vernon. 1976. ''Structural Effects of Regulation on Innovation in the Ethical Drug Industry.'' In *Essays on Industrial Organization in Honor of Joe S. Bain*, edited by Robert J. Masson and P. David Qualls. Ballinger.

———. 1979. ''Substitution Laws and Innovation in the Pharmaceutical Industry.'' *Law and Contemporary Problems* 43 (Winter–Spring):43–66.

———. 1983. *The Regulation of Pharmaceuticals: Balancing the Benefits and Risks*. American Enterprise Institute.

———. 1986. ''Longer Patents for Lower Imitation Barriers: The 1984 Drug Act.'' *American Economic Review, Papers and Proceedings, 1985* 76 (May):195–98.

Hurwitz, Mark A., and Richard E. Caves. 1988. ''Persuasion or Information? Promotion and the Shares of Brand Name and Generic Pharmaceuticals.'' *Journal of Law and Economics* 31 (October):299–320.

Leffler, Keith B. 1981. ''Persuasion or Information? The Economics of Prescription Drug Advertising.'' *Journal of Law and Economics* 24 (April):45–74.

Mankiw, N. Gregory, and Michael D. Whinston. 1986. ''Free Entry and Social Inefficiency.'' *Rand Journal of Economics* 17 (Spring):48–58.

Masson, Alison, and Robert L. Steiner. 1985. *Generic Subsitution and Prescription Drug Prices: Economic Effects of State Drug Product Selection Laws*. Washington: Federal Trade Commission.

Nordhaus, William D. 1969. *Invention, Growth and Welfare: A Theoretical Treatment of Technological Change*. MIT Press.

Pakes, Ariel, 1991. ''Structural Econometric Modeling; Problems and Prospects—Part II: Mixed Continuous Discrete Control Models and Market Interactions.'' In *Advances in Econometrics*, proceedings of the Sixth World Congress of the Econometric Society, edited by C. Sims, forthcoming.

Pakes, Ariel, and Paul McGuire. 1991. ''Computation of Markov Perfect Equilibria: A Dynamic Differentiated Product Model.'' Mimeo, Yale University (February).

Peltzman, Sam. 1974. *Regulation of Pharmaceutical Innovation: The 1962 Amendments*. American Enterprise Institute.

Pharmaceutical Manufacturers Association. 1988. *PMA Statistical Fact Book*. Washington.

Schwartzman, David. 1976. *Innovation in the Pharmaceutical Industry*. Johns Hopkins University Press.

Smith, Mickey C. 1983. *Principles of Pharmaceutical Marketing*. 3d ed. Lea & Febinger.

Statman, Meir. 1981. "The Effect of Patent Expiration on the Market Position of Drugs." In *Drugs and Health: Economic Issues and Policy Objectives*, edited by Robert B. Helms. American Enterprise Institute.

Steele, Henry. 1962. "Monopoly and Competition in the Ethical Drugs Market." *Journal of Law and Economics* 5 (October):131–63.

Suslow, Valerie Y. 1986. "Estimating Monopoly Behavior with Competitive Recycling: An Application to Alcoa." *Rand Journal of Economics* 17 (Autumn):389–403.

Temin, Peter. 1979. "Technology, Regulation, and Market Structure in the Modern Pharmaceutical Industry." *Bell Journal of Economics* 10 (Autumn):429–46.

———. 1980. *Taking Your Medicine: Drug Regulation in the United States*. Harvard University Press.

U.S. Food and Drug Administration, Center for Drug Evaluation and Research. Annual. *Approved Drug Products with Therapeutic Equivalence Evaluations* (titles vary). Washington.

U.S. House of Representatives. Committee on Energy and Commerce. Subcommittee on Oversight and Investigation. 1989. *FDA's Generic Drug Approval Process*, Part 2. Hearings. 101 Cong. 1 sess. Government Printing Office.

U.S. House of Representatives. Committee on Science and Technology. Subcommittee on Investigations and Oversight. 1982. *Patent Term Extension and Pharmaceutical Innovation*. Hearings. 97 Cong. 2 sess. Government Printing Office.

Walker, Hugh D. 1971. *Market Power and Price Levels in the Ethical Drug Industry*. Indiana University Press.

Wiggins, Steven N. 1981. "Product Quality Regulation and New Drug Introductions: Some New Evidence from the 1970s." *Review of Economics and Statistics* 58 (November):615–19.

———. 1984. "The Effect of U.S. Pharmaceutical Regulation on New Introductions." In *Pharmaceutical Economics: Papers Presented at the 6th Arne Ryde Symposium, Helsingborg, Sweden, 1982*, edited by Bjorn Lindgren. Stockholm: Swedish Institute for Health Economics and Liber Forlag.

———. 1987. *The Cost of Developing a New Drug*. Washington: Pharmaceutical Manufacturers Association.

[13]

Competition between Generic and Branded Drugs

Henry Grabowski

I. Introduction

The United States is the country for which generic competition is the most highly developed. It is a key location of drug price competition, and there are many institutional mechanisms to encourage the utilization of generics. The Hatch-Waxman Act of 1984 was enacted with the dual objectives of facilitating entry of generic competition while preserving sufficient patent exclusivity time to incentivize drug innovation. In this chapter's next section, I discuss the provisions of the 1984 Act in some detail and review how managed care organizations encourage generic competition. Sections III through V examine findings of several economic analyses of generic competition. Section VI examines studies of effective patent life and how the 1984 Act has affected the incentives for drug innovation. Section VII focuses on the strategic responses of branded and generic firms to the 1984 Act. Section VIII provides a brief summary and discusses issues for further research.

II. Drivers of Generic Industry Growth

The Hatch-Waxman Act

The generic industry has evolved rapidly since the mid-1980s. A key event fostering the development of this industry was the passage of the Drug Price Competition and Patent Term Restoration Act of 1984, also known as the Hatch-Waxman Act. This Act changed the regulatory criteria for U.S. Food and Drug Administration (FDA) approval of generics, thereby significantly reducing the costs and time delays of generic entry. The Act also provided benefits to innovative firms by restoring some of the patent life lost during the long regulatory period for new drugs. However, the primary impact of the Act has been to foster greater generic competition, since the patent term extension benefits to innovators were more than offset by the increased generic competition after patent expiration that was facilitated by the law (U.S. Congressional Budget Office [CBO] 1998).

Prior to passage of the Hatch-Waxman Act, generic firms could not rely on branded drugs' safety and efficacy data for all the drugs introduced after 1962 unless this information was published in the scientific literature. In effect, these safety and efficacy data were given "trade secret" status. Hence a generic imitator had to undertake many of the same safety and efficacy tests as the innovator to gain FDA approval.[1] A few drug entities were able to avoid new clinical trials on safety and efficacy by relying on established studies published in the scientific literature. This procedure was called a "paper NDA" (new drug application). However, according to a 1984 House Congressional report, only about 14% of drug introductions after 1962 had sufficient published information to support a paper NDA.[2]

In the pre-1984 period, generic competition was mainly concentrated in the antibiotic class, which was regulated by separate monograph procedures. According to the IMS New Prescription Audit data survey, generic drugs accounted for only 19% of all prescriptions in 1984 (Pharmaceutical Research and Manufacturers of America [PhRMA] 2000, p. 69). Moreover, many large selling off-patent drugs had no generic competitors. In a study of the top 200 off-patent drugs in the early 1980s (excluding antibiotics) John Vernon and I (1986) found that only about one-third of these drugs had any generic competition at all. Moreover, those brands with generic competition typically experienced small losses in market shares to the generic brands.

The Hatch-Waxman Act dramatically altered the nature and terms of generic competition after 1984. First, the Act established an Abbreviated New Drug Application (ANDA), which substantially reduced the cost of generic entry. Second, the Act allowed generic manufacturers to conduct their testing prior to patent expiration. This allowed generics to enter the market much more quickly after patent expiration than previously.

Under the ANDA procedure established by the Act, the primary requirement for generic manufacturers is that they need to demonstrate that their drug is bioequivalent to the innovator's product.[3] The ANDA procedure essentially allows generics to rely on the safety and efficacy clinical trial data submitted by the manufacturer of the branded product part of the original NDA. Generic drugs must meet the same reference standards on strength, quality, purity, and identity, but they may differ in such characteristics as shape, color, and packaging.

Once a generic product meets the FDA bioequivalence requirements and other reference standards, it is assigned an AB therapeutic code, indicating that the FDA considers the generic product as therapeutically equivalent to branded product. In particular, according to the FDA, "Drug products are considered to be therapeutically equivalent only if they are pharmaceutical equivalent and if they can be expected to have the same clinical effect and safety profile when administered to patients under the conditions specified in the label."[4] All therapeutically equivalent products are listed in the FDA's "Orange Book" (see note 3). Once a product is listed in the Orange Book with an AB equivalence rating, this means the product can be freely substituted by pharmacists for the corresponding branded product unless physicians take specific actions to prohibit such substitutions.

By establishing an ANDA process for generic approval and obviating the need to do expensive clinical trials on safety and efficacy, the 1984 Act dramatically lowered the cost of generic entry. Reiffen and Ward (2005) found that the cost of obtaining an ANDA approval in the first half of the 1990s was on the order of one million dollars. This compares to an average out-of-pocket research and development (R&D cost for new brand drug approval in the 1990s of over $400 million (DiMasi, Hansen, and Grabowski 2003).

Another effect of the 1984 Act was to drastically shorten the time lag between patent expiration and initial generic entry. In an analysis of several drugs that experienced generic competition between 1989 and 1993, the U.S. Congressional Budget Office (1998) found the typical time period between expiration and generic entry was one to three months. This compares to an average of three to four years for generic entry in the period prior to the 1984 Act.

Managed Care, PBMs, and Demand-Side Factors

In the United States the substitution of a generic drug for a branded drug is well known and generally predictable. Generic substitution is regulated by state law, and all states have passed substitution laws that allow pharmacists to substitute AB-rated generics for branded counterparts, unless the prescribing physician takes specific steps to prohibit substitution, such as specifically ordering that the pharmacists "dispense as written." Strong incentives exist at present for physicians, pharmacists, and patients to utilize generic products where these products are available.

States generally have one of two types of substitution laws: permissive substitution laws and mandatory substitution laws. Mandatory substitution states require that pharmacists substitute generic drugs for branded drugs where a generic is available and other requirements are fulfilled. Permissive substitution states allow pharmacists to substitute generic drugs for branded drugs. According to the 2003–2004 National Association of Boards of Pharmacy's *Survey of Pharmacy Law* (2004), 11 states and Puerto Rico had mandatory generic substitution laws.[5] In 38 other states plus the District of Columbia and Guam, pharmacists were permitted, but not mandated, to substitute generic drugs for brand name drug products. In either case, payers, physicians, and pharmacists had a strong economic incentive to substitute generic drugs for branded drugs.

According to a 2000 report of IMS Health, 82% of pharmaceutical prescriptions were reimbursed at least in part through third-party payers. Of that 82%, 13% are reimbursed by state-run Medicaid programs. Of the remaining 69%, most were reimbursed through a managed care organization, such as Health Maintenance Organizations (HMOs), Preferred Provider Organizations (PPOs), or point-of-service plans.[6] The U.S. Center for Medicaid and Medicare Services (2003) estimated that for the private sector, insurance covered 69.3% of prescription drug costs and 30.7% of these costs were paid out of pocket in 2001.

The government, employers, and managed care organizations have hired specialized companies called Pharmacy Benefit Managers (PBMs) to manage their drug benefit programs. PBMs now provide these benefits for more than half of the insured population in the United States (PhRMA 2000, p. 66). At the most basic level, PBMs perform electronic claims processing, provide a network of retail pharmacies and mail order pharmacy service, and offer pharmacy benefit plan design with patient cost sharing and other incentives. These activities generate costs savings to plan sponsors by reducing prescription claims-processing charges, lowering ingredient and dispensing fees, and increasing patient copayments.

Beyond those basic services, PBMs also engage in various activities designed to influence drug prescribing and dispensing (Grabowski and Mullins 1997). These activities influence the decision making process from the economic standpoint of patients, physicians, and payers. The practical effect of many of those programs is to provide strong incentives to utilize generics where available.

One of the strongest PBM approaches to encourage generic utilization involves adjusting the patient copayments so that patients will request generic prescribing and substitution. A common form of that program is the three-tiered formulary system employed by most PBMs. Under that system, generics occupy tier one and require the lowest copayment from the patient (usually on the order of $5.00 per prescription). Branded drugs categorized as preferred by the PBMs are in tier two and require a higher copayment than generics. Tier three mainly consists of branded drugs for which less expensive generic drugs or therapeutic substitutes are available. That is, once a generic drug enters the market, most PBM formularies automatically relegate the branded counterpart to tier three. Those drugs pay the highest copayment. As of 2002, tier three copayments could be $30 or higher (Berndt 2002).

More stringent forms of the copayment approach are maximum allowable cost programs. Those programs require that the patient pay the full difference between the branded prescription and the normal prescription copayment. In the extreme case, mandatory generic substitution programs require that generics be dispensed or the patient receive no reimbursement at all.

PBMs also provide strong incentives for physicians to prescribe generic drugs. One such incentive arises from the PBMs' use of physician profiling and retrospective drug utilization review databases to identify "outlier" physicians; such physicians include those that more frequently prohibit generic substitution by the pharmacists (Grabowski and Mullins 1997, p. 539). Under this approach, physicians who fall outside prescribing norms are subject to "alert letters," visits from PBM personnel, and possible financial penalties. Some PBMs have capitated physicians for drug costs or instituted "withholds" based on formulary compliance.[7] According to PBMs, the assumption of risk for pharmacy utilization is a powerful incentive enhancing physicians' willingness to comply with formularies (Kreling et al. 1996).

PBMs also typically pay higher dispensing fees to pharmacists to dispense generics over their branded counterparts (Rubin, Hawk, and Cascade 1998). Moreover, several studies have demonstrated that pharmacists earn higher absolute margins when generics are substituted.[8] Hence, pharmacists also have strong incentives to dispense generics regardless of whether the drug prescription is paid for by a third party or is paid out of pocket by the patient.

Like managed care organizations, state and federal governments in the United States employ PBMs to manage pharmacy benefit programs. U.S. government agencies (e.g., Veterans' Administration, Medicaid) are among the most price-sensitive buyers of pharmaceuticals. The Medicaid program, which is jointly funded by the federal government and the states, was the first payer to adopt the maximum allowable cost program with respect to generics. In addition, many state Medicaid programs have automatic generic substitution requirements.[9]

The programs designed to encourage generic utilization by payers have been very effective. In terms of the overall pharmaceutical market, generic products accounted for only 19% of all prescriptions in 1984, but this share increased to 51% in 2002.[10] Saha et al. (2006) found evidence for the proposition that the growth of managed care has been a key factor in the increased utilization of generic products, after controlling for various other factors affecting the demand and supply of generics.

III. Economic Analyses of Generic Competition

A number of studies have investigated characteristics and intensity of generic competition in the United States since 1984. A distinctive pattern of generic competition has been observed (Grabowski and Vernon 1992, 2000). First, commercially significant products have experienced a large number of generic entrants within a short period after patent expiration. Second, there is a strong positive relationship between the size of the branded drug's market sales in the preexpiration period, the number of generic entrants, and the intensity of generic price competition after patent expiration.[11] Third, the more entrants and more intense the degree of price competition, the more rapid the erosion in the brand product market share in units to the generic firms. Fourth, an increasing number of products now are subject to patent challenges early in their product life cycle as a result of the 180-day exclusivity awarded to the generic firm that is first to file for an ANDA and successfully challenge the product in court (Grabowski 2004).

Figure 8.1, which provides some illustrative values for these trends, is based on an analysis of a representative sample of 40 oral prescription drug products that experienced first generic entry during the 1990s (Saha et al. 2006). Figure 8.1A shows there is a rapid build-up of generic competitors in the months after first entry, with an average of eight generic competitors experienced by these 40 products after 12 months' time. Correspondingly, Figure 8.1B and 8.1C show average generic prices are discounted approximately 50% below branded prices, and average generic unit shares are more than half of the unit sales (in grams) for the molecule after 12 months. The number of generics, generic discounts, and generic shares continue to increase as markets tend toward commodity status over the three-year time frame shown in Figure 8.1. A simultaneous regression model of these three variables demonstrates that the preentry market sale of the molecule is a key variable in how rapidly markets converge to their long-term equilibrium values. In addition, as discussed, the growth of third-party insurance for pharmaceuticals is an important factor in increasing the overall speed of generic penetration during the 1990s (Saha et al. 2006).

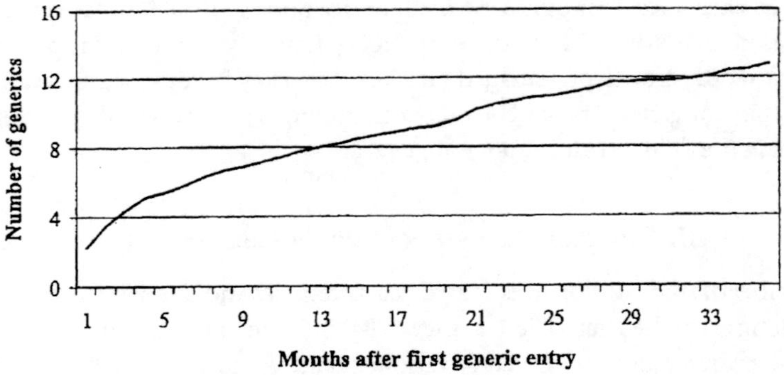

Figure 8.1A. Average number of generic drug manufacturers.

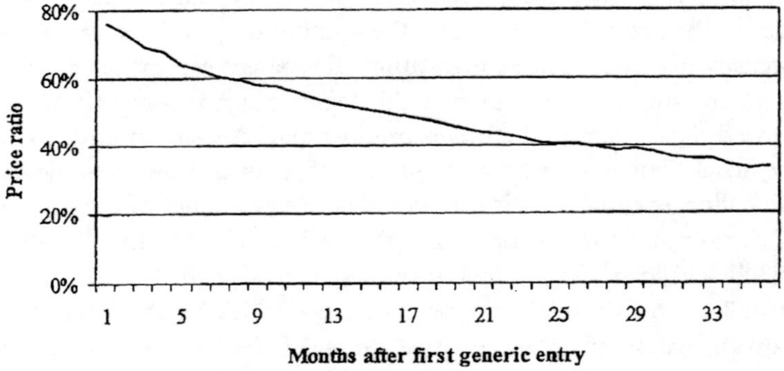

Figure 8.1B. Average generic-to-brand price ratio.

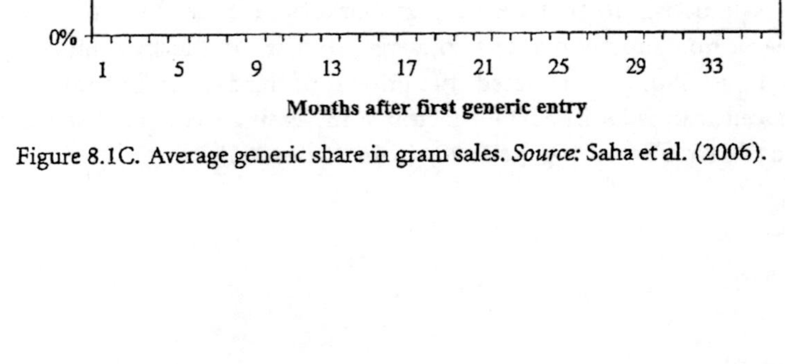

Figure 8.1C. Average generic share in gram sales. *Source:* Saha et al. (2006).

Data from the most recent launches show that, in the case of the top-selling drugs, generics are capturing most of the market within weeks of their launch. In this regard, I have examined data on the three top-selling drug products experiencing their first generic competition in 2000 and 2001 (Grabowski 2004). These products are Vasotec (enalapril), Zestril/Prinivil (lisinopril), and Prozac (fluoxetine), all of which had annual sales greater than $1 billion. These data show that the launch of generic enalapril in August 2000 resulted in the generics obtaining 66.4% of new prescriptions just four weeks after generic launch. Generic lisinopril, launched in May 2001, acquired 84.0% of new prescriptions in four weeks. Generic fluoxetine, launched in August 2001, acquired 74.9% of new prescriptions in four weeks.

Scott Morton (1999) examined the entry decisions of generic firms. She showed that firms are more likely to enter markets in which they have some experience, for example, in form, therapy, or ingredient, and to enter markets for chronic conditions with large sales. Scott Morton (2000) found that generic entry is positively related to brand revenue and price elasticity, and negatively affected by FDA regulations. She found no evidence that brand advertising is a deterrent to generic entry.

A number of investigators dating back to Caves, Whinston, and Hurwitz (1991) have considered the response of brand firms to generic entry, and whether branded firms have pursued entry-deterring strategies. There is little evidence to support the hypothesis of entry deterrence utilizing pricing or promotional strategies. First, with respect to promotional activities, the prevalent strategy is for branded firms to curtail most of their expenditures, usually beginning in the preentry period (Ellison and Ellison 2000). Second, evidence is scant on the brand firms matching generic prices, except for selective discounts to their large institutional customers (U.S. Congressional Budget Office 1998, p. 38). Most studies have found that brand firms continue to raise their prices after generic entry, but there is some disagreement in the literature about whether the impact of generics on the rate of change in prices is positive or negative.[12]

As the rate of sales losses for branded firms has intensified after generic entry, many brand firms have turned to the "authorized generic" strategy. This strategy authorizes a generic partner or subsidiary to rely on the branded firm's approved new drug application, and to enter at a point in time prior to or simultaneous with the first "outside" generic entrant. This strategy is particularly prevalent where the rival generic firm enjoys a 180-day exclusivity period as the result of a successful patent challenge (Siegel 2004). There are first-mover advantages to being an early entrant in the generic market (Grabowski and Vernon 1992). The authorization of a generic entrant allows branded firms to capture some of the short-term rents associated with early entry into the market, usually in partnership with a leading generic firm.

During the 180-day exclusivity period, the presence of an authorized generic as a second generic entrant works to intensify price competition. However, an interesting policy issue is whether there are situations where an authorized generic from the branded manufacturer adversely affects the total number of generic competitors in equilibrium. (Reiffen and Ward 2006). This is an issue currently under consideration at the U.S. Federal Trade Commission.

Branded firms have employed a variety of "life cycle management" strategies, such as the introduction of new formulations and combination products and shifting a prescription product to over-the-counter (OTC) status as a means of retaining patients and preserving sales revenues in the face of patent expiration and imminent generic entry. Some firms have also tried to use provisions of the 1984 Act in patent challenges to erect legal or regulatory barriers to entry. The strategic uses of provisions of the 1984 Act by brand and generic firms are considered in the last section of the chapter.

IV. Effects of Generic Competition on Total Expenditures for Prescription Drugs

As the number of generic competitors increase for a particular prescription drug, several studies show that prices fall toward marginal cost (Reiffen and Ward 2005). In particular, generic prices can drop to less than one-third of the brand prices with 20 or more generic competitors in the market. Even for cases with significantly fewer generic competitors, generic prices typically decline to less than half the brand price within a year or more of initial generic entry (Saha et al. 2006).

Given these lower prices of generic products and the rising share of overall prescriptions, they are a source of significant savings. In this regard, the U.S. Congressional Budget Office (CBO 1998) estimated that purchasers of prescription drugs saved between $8 billion and $10 billion dollars in the mid-1990s. The CBO utilized a straightforward approach in computing these cost savings. In particular, it multiplied the price difference between brand and generic drugs times the number of units dispensed generically. It utilized a representative sample of multiple source pharmaceuticals, and projected their estimates to the overall market. While this approach is subject to various qualifications, it demonstrates that the overall savings from generic products are substantial.[13] Furthermore, the share of prescriptions dispensed generically has grown significantly since the mid-1990s; thus more recent estimates of savings would be much greater.

The beneficiaries of these large cost savings, at least in the first instance, are the payers for prescription drugs. Since most drugs are covered by third parties, this list includes health insurers, PBMs, employers, and the government, along with some consumers who pay out of pocket. Most employer-based prescription drug plans have a tiered system of copayments. Given the fact that almost all plans have generics in the lowest tier of copayments with a nominal copayment, some of the savings are passed on directly to plan participants when they purchase pharmaceuticals. Furthermore, to the extent that the overall health insurance market is competitive and health care costs are ultimately borne by employees, economists argue that the cost savings will also be reflected in lower premiums and higher wages to the plan participants (Pauly 1998). Because most privately insured employer-based plans integrate drug coverage with other forms of health care services, it is difficult, however, to isolate the distributional effects of generic savings.

V. Generic Competition from an International Perspective

Danzon and Chao (2000) examined the effects of generic competition on pharmaceutical prices in countries with alternative regulatory regimes. In particular, to analyze this issue, they utilize comprehensive data on outpatient drug sales in 1992 for seven countries (Canada, France, Germany, Italy, Japan, the United Kingdom, and the United States). These countries were selected to provide a spectrum of price regulation and competition. In particular, the United States had virtually free pricing of prescription drug products. By contrast, France, Italy, and Japan were characterized by strong systems of price regulation on a product-by-product basis (as well as sharply declining trends in overall drug prices). The United Kingdom, Germany, and Canada were intermediate cases with considerable discretion to price new drug products, but they were also subject to either profit constraints (the United Kingdom), price caps adjusted for inflation (Canada), or a reference pricing reimbursement system (Germany).

A key finding was that the price sensitivity with respect to the number of generic competitors was greatest in the case of the United States (with a price elasticity of −0.50).[14] Danzon and Chao also found that the United States had more generic entrants, more generic price competition, and higher returns to later entrants than in the more regulated price environments.[15] Germany, the United Kingdom, and Canada also exhibited significant price sensitivities to generic competitors. Germany, in particular, with its reference price system had an effect on prices of generic competition that was most similar to that of the United States.

Little association was found between drug prices and the number of generic competitors in Japan, France, or Italy. Their price regulatory plans apparently undermined generic competition. In the case of France and Italy, products were typically introduced with prices well below those of other major pharmaceutical markets. There was also little possibility for inflation adjustments, so real product prices exhibited a down spiral over time. Consequently, firms have little incentive to introduce multisource drugs, and when they do, they are frequently new forms of old molecules to obtain a higher regulated price. Generic competition was also undermined in France and Italy by the regulation of retail pharmacy. Pharmacists were paid a regulated dispensing margin based on product price, and the requirement to dispense unit packs reduced the potential for volume discounts. In the case of Japan, physicians dispensed drugs directly and were strongly motivated to prescribe drugs with the highest margin between the reimbursed price and the acquisition price.

A relevant issue is whether the regulatory pressures on prices over the product life cycle in countries with stringent price regulation like Japan, France, and Italy achieve similar effects to generic competition in less regulated markets like the United States, the United Kingdom, or Germany. The net welfare effects are not comparable in the two contexts. First, the stringent price regulatory policies followed in countries such as Italy, France, and Japan have had a deleterious effect on drug innovation incentives in these countries (Grabowski and Wang 2006). Second, the lack of a competitive retail pharmacy system in France and Italy means that pharmacists and wholesalers capture part of the potential savings from lower prices in these countries (as do physicians in Japan from dispensing drugs with the highest margins).

One lesson from this multicountry study is that a reference-based price system of reimbursement can produce powerful incentives for generic competition and lower drug prices for a particular molecule. This is significant because several other countries such as Denmark, Norway, and the Netherlands have adopted reference pricing and have experienced rising levels of generic competition in recent periods. In the case of the United Kingdom, the incentives for generic usage have emanated from physicians. In particular, the British National Health Service (NHS) allows holding general practioners who underspend their budgets to reinvest the savings in their practice. Baines, Tally, and Whynes (1997) found the main impact of the fund-holding program was to encourage more generic prescribing.

VI. Effective Patent Life and Drug Innovation

In designing a patent system or set of intellectual property rights, the key policy challenge is setting the optimal balance between short-term benefits from greater price competition and longer-term benefits from greater incentives for innovation. This balance is particularly important in the case of an innovative industry like pharmaceuticals in which there are high social returns to innovation (see, e.g., Cutler and McClellan 2001a; Murphy and Topel 2003; Hsieh et al., Chapter 13).

Patents are considered critically important to research-oriented pharmaceutical firms in obtaining positive returns from innovations. This has been demonstrated in several economic studies.[16] In cross-industry analyses, Levin et al. (1987) and Cohen, Nelson, and Walsh (2002) found that the pharmaceutical industry placed the highest importance on patents. By contrast, many other research-intensive industries, such as computers and semiconductors, placed greater stress on factors like lead time and efficiencies in the production of new products accruing to first movers.

The critical importance of patents to research-intensive pharmaceutical firms follows directly from the characteristics of the drug innovation process. In essence, imitation costs in pharmaceuticals are extremely low compared to the innovators' costs of discovery and development. Pharmaceutical R&D is a complex, costly, risky, and time-consuming process. It has been estimated that the mean out-of-pocket R&D costs incurred by firms for a U.S. new drug approval is in excess of $400 million (DiMasi, Hansen, and Grabowski 2003). By contrast, the cost of a generic firm to obtain an ANDA has been estimated to be only about $1 million. Hence, absent patent protection or some equivalent barrier to entry, imitators could free ride on the innovators' FDA approval and duplicate the compound for a small fraction of the innovator's cost of discovering and developing a new drug.

Given the high costs of drug innovation relative to imitation, effective patent life (EPL), defined as the patent life remaining after a product is approved by the FDA, is an important factor in drug company decisions to undertake an R&D project. Companies typically file their key patent application prior to the start of clinical testing. Because of the long clinical trial period and regulatory review periods that occur in pharmaceuticals, much of the nominal patent life of 20 years is lost prior to FDA approval. At the time of the passage of the Hatch-Waxman Act in 1984, effective patent life for the representative new drug compound was less than 10 years and exhibited a declining trend (Grabowski and Vernon 2000).

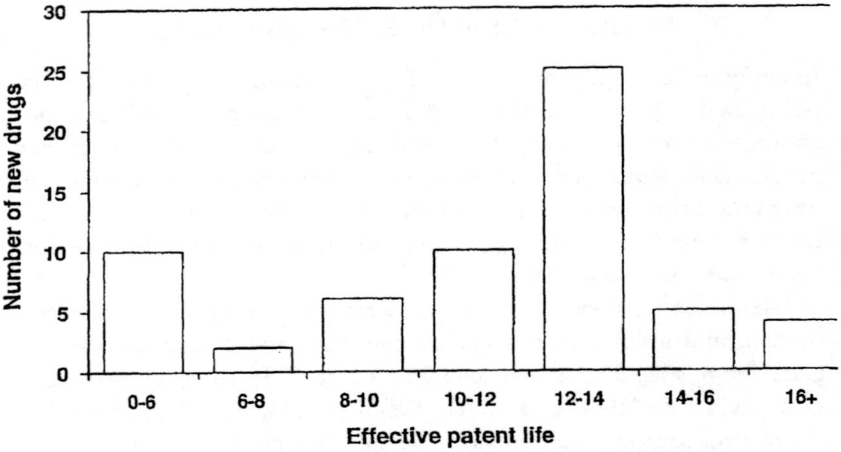

Figure 8.2. Frequency distribution of EPL 1993–1995 introductions.

In the Hatch-Waxman Act, Congress attempted to balance the incentives for innovative and imitative competition. Title II of the law provided for partial restoration of the patent time lost during the clinical and regulatory periods. In particular, new drugs were eligible for a Hatch-Waxman extension in patent life equal to the sum of the NDA regulatory review time plus one-half of the IND testing time. The law also constrained extensions to a maximum effective patent lifetime of 14 years and capped extensions at five years. In addition, Title I of the law involving ANDAs and generic competition provided for a five-year data exclusivity period. In essence, no generic firm could submit an ANDA and rely on the safety and efficacy data of the innovating firm until five years after FDA approval.

John Vernon and I (2000) examined the effect of Hatch-Waxman Act on effective patent life for 1990–1995 new chemical entities (NCEs). We found that the mean effective patent life was 11.7 years, with patent term extension contributing 2.3 years to this EPL. This EPL also included a 0.4-year average extension from the passage of GATT, which harmonized global IP rules. Subsequently, some of these NCEs also earned additional six-month exclusivity for doing further clinical trials to establish a pediatric dose under the Prescription Drug User Fee Act of 1994.

While the average effective patent life for new drugs was about 12 years, there was also considerable heterogeneity in the effective patent life across NCEs. Figure 8.2 shows the frequency distribution for the 62 NCEs approved over the last three years of our sample (1993–1995). The mode of the distribution is the 12–14 year EPL interval. A little over 70% of the NCEs in the sample had EPLs in excess of 10 years. At the bottom of the spectrum, 15% of the NCEs in the sample were relying on the five-year data exclusivity as their main form of IP protection (Grabowski and Vernon 2000, p. 110). A new paper by Grabowski and Kyle (2006) found that actual market exclusivity times, defined as the period between brand launch and the entry of the first generic, exhibit a similar distribution. This analysis focused on the sample of new molecular entities that experienced their first generic entry between 1995 and 2005. One interesting finding is the large number of drugs with small market size (i.e., below $100 million in the preentry period) that now have generic competitors. Generic firms appear to be broadening their portfolios to include even niche products with small sales in more recent time periods.

The U.S. Congressional Budget Office (1998) has conducted an analysis of the economic effects of the Act. As discussed in Section IV, they estimated the increased generic competition fostered by the Act has resulted in annual savings of $8–10 billion to consumers by the mid-1990s. From the perspective of R&D returns, however, the CBO (1998, p. 38) estimated a negative effect in the after-tax profits to innovators. The framework the CBO utilized is illustrated in Figure 8.3.[17] Utilizing data from an analysis of R&D returns on pharmaceuticals in the 1980s combined with other information, the CBO estimated that the present value of cash flows from a representative new drug introduction declined by an average of 12% as a result of increased generic competition facilitated by the 1984 Act. In essence, the much more rapid loss of sales after generic entry (Fig. 8.3) has outweighed any patent term extensions provided by the Act. This can result in particularly adverse consequences for compounds of above-average riskiness, or those with shorter-than-average effective life.

Despite these negative estimated effects of the Act on innovative returns, pharmaceutical R&D has continued to grow at a substantial rate since the passage of the 1984 Act (Scherer 2001). Grabowski and Wang (2006) also have found an upward trend since 1983 in the number of high-quality or important drug introductions (as measured by the number of first-in-class and new drugs introduced in a majority of leading drug markets). This underscores the importance of examining both partial equilibrium effects as well as system-wide performance influences in considering the impact of new policy measures. This is especially important given the fact that the pharmaceutical industry now appears to have entered a more difficult period in terms of its R&D costs and returns and is experiencing generic challenges to innovators' patents much earlier in the product life cycle than

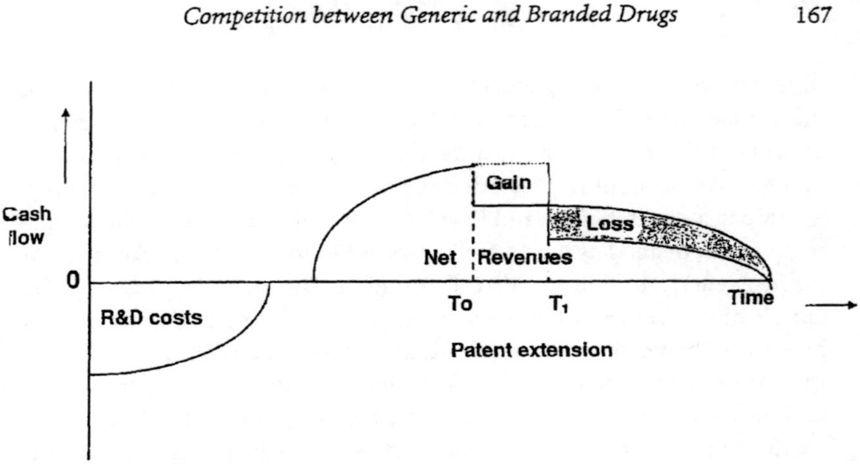

Figure 8.3. Conceptual framework for evaluating effects of the 1984 Act on R&D returns.

was previously the case (Grabowski 2004; Scherer 2001). Hence, effects of generic competition on drug innovation now may reinforce rather than counter other industry developments and be more pronounced in nature. This issue is considered in the next section of the paper, along with various policy options.

VII. Strategic Responses of Brand and Generic Firms to the 1984 Act

Life Cycle Management Strategies of Brand Firms

Given the large decline in expected sales that typically occur where generics enter the market, brand firms begin planning a strategic response to this entry well in advance of the patent expiration of a commercially important product. These responses are typically referred to as life cycle management strategies. Among the options available to brand firms are (1) the introduction of a new class of therapeutics for the same indication; (2) the introduction of a new formulation (e.g., a new delivery system or a combination product) that has improved therapeutic benefits in terms of patient tolerance, compliance, safety or efficacy; and (3) the introduction of an over-the-counter version of the product. Each of these strategies has been employed on a selective basis with some success by brand firms.

Arguably, the most effective life cycle management strategy is the introduction of a new class of therapies. Competition evolves in pharmaceuticals by the introduction of new classes of entities with superior therapeutic properties to prior generations of products. Firms that have a commercially important product subject to patent expiration will frequently be conducting R&D on new therapeutic approaches for the same indication. However, there are no guarantees in this regard because the candidates for the next advance in therapeutics often span a large spectrum. Furthermore, the R&D process is subject to many technical, regulatory, and competitive uncertainties with long time durations.

Another life cycle management option for the brand firm is the introduction of a product line extension such as a new delivery system. Under the Hatch-Waxman Act, a new formulation involving additional clinical trials is eligible for a three-year exclusivity period. Moreover, a new delivery mechanism or formulation may be covered by a new patent. One of the most successful cases in this regard was the introduction by Pfizer of Procardia XL, a once-a-day formulation of a leading calcium channel blocker for hypertension. The extended release version of Procardia improved the tolerability and the side-effects profile associated with the active ingredient. As a consequence, Procardia XL turned out to be a much larger commercial success than the earlier formulation of Procardia. This life cycle management strategy has been employed in several other situations with somewhat mixed success. The weekly formulation of Prozac, for example, has enjoyed only very limited success. The degree of therapeutic improvement is a key factor in the success of this life cycle management strategy.[18]

A third basic option available in the case of some therapeutic categories is to develop an over-the-counter version of a product subject to patent expiration. The strategy has been employed for example for anti-inflammatory pain relievers such as Motrin and Naprosyn, anti-ulcer therapies such as the H_2 blockers Tagamet and Zantac, proton pump inhibitors such as Prilosec, and in several other therapeutic categories. However, a shift to OTC status requires approval by the FDA that the drug is safe for self-medication (Juhl 2000; McCarran 1991; Schweitzer 1997). A company will normally need to submit new clinical trial evidence to that effect. If approved by the FDA, the company receives a three-year exclusivity period for its OTC product in recognition for the new clinical trial work.

A key driver of success in the OTC market is the ability to capitalize on the brand loyalty enjoyed by the prescription product. The number of category shifts to OTC status approved by the FDA has grown over time. At the same time, there are many therapeutic categories where this is not as viable strategy because they would not meet the FDA's requirement on safety for self-medication (e.g., mental health and cancer drugs). The FDA has also declined several product requests for shifts to OTC status, such as anticholesterol drug agents.

Patent Challenges and the Strategic Use of the Hatch-Waxman Act by Brand Firms

The Hatch-Waxman Act includes a marketing exclusivity provision that rewards generic firms for successfully challenging a patent in court on the basis of invalidity or noninfringement. To initiate the process, the generic firm files an ANDA with the FDA asserting the patent is invalid or noninfringed (a so-called Paragraph IV filing). The branded firm has 45 days to file an infringement suit. The law also provides for a stay of up to 30 months on approval of the ANDA while the patent infringement suit is ongoing. The first generic to file and prevail on a patent challenge obtains a 180-day marketing exclusivity.

Some practices utilized by brand firms to delay generic competition have been the target of recent FTC and legislative actions. One concern was the practice of listing several new patents late in the product life cycle in an apparent effort to trigger successive 30-month stays to delay generic competition. To prevent this practice, the Medicare Prescription Drug, Improvement, and Modernization Act of 2003 limited each branded product to one 30-month stay (Padden and Jenkins 2004).

The generic entrant with first-to-file exclusivity rights and the brand manufacturer has sometimes entered into an agreement whereby the generic firm receives compensation from the branded firm for not entering the market. Where there is uncertainty about the outcome of the patent case, this may be an attractive economic outcome to both parties. However, payers and consumers generally lose when price competition is delayed through such agreements. This practice has been subject to successful antitrust prosecution and class action suits, and is also further constrained under the Medicare Prescription Drug Act.[19]

Patent Challenges and Strategic Uses of the 1984 Act by Generic Firms

While potential anticompetitive abuses of the 30-month stay have been addressed by recent litigation, the 180-day exclusivity provision for successful generic challenges remains in effect. In effect, this provision is an invitation to the generic firms to trigger a lawsuit. Even if the odds of winning are low, the payoff to successfully challenging a blockbuster patent is large. Since the 180-day exclusivity goes to the first firm filing and successfully challenging the patent, there is now a race to obtain exclusivity status of commercially significant projects. The FDA accepts a Paragraph IV ANDA

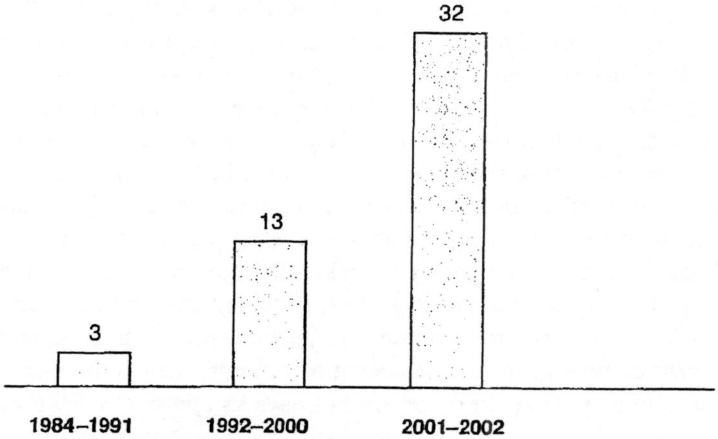

Figure 8.4. Average number of Paragraph IV ANDA filings per year. *Source:* U.S. Federal Trade Commission, Bear Stearns.

filing four years after approval of the pioneering product in recognition of the five-year data exclusivity. Generic marketing can begin as soon as the courts have resolved the suits or the 30-month stay has expired. This creates a range on exclusivity times of between five and seven and a half years.

Multiple lawsuits involving infringement have become the rule for the commercially important drugs early in the brand product's life cycle. The number of Paragraph IV ANDA filings has increased from three per year in the years 1984–1991 to 13 per year in 1992–2000 to 32 per year in 2001–2002 (Fig. 8.4). If a substantial fraction of these early-stage patent challenges are overturned by the courts, this would likely have significant adverse effects on the long-term expectations regarding R&D returns in this industry. As of June 2002, generic firms had won the vast majority of the suits, but most of these cases with outcomes to date involve late-stage patent challenges (Bear Stearns 2002; U.S. Federal Trade Commission 2002).

A patent can be challenged on the grounds of obviousness, prior art, or double patenting. A court may determine, for example, that a drug invention was "obvious," allowing the generic challenger to enter if the five-year data exclusivity period has expired. The issue of patent type is also relevant from a policy standpoint. Process, method-of-use, and formulation patents have less breadth than product patents and may be more vulnerable to challenge, although each situation must be evaluated on a case-by-case basis. It is worth noting that many important drug products such as the first AIDS therapy AZT (Zidovudine) relied on formulation or method-of-use patents because their product patents had already expired.[20]

From a strategic perspective, generic firms are prospecting in patent suits. They are spending millions of dollars in filing and litigation fees with their portfolio of patent challenges for the rights to obtain a very large payoff from the 180-day exclusivity period if they win a few of these suits. However, this wave of lawsuits crowds the courts and creates uncertainty around the commercial viability of the innovator's product. Furthermore, this uncertainty adversely affects market valuations of research-oriented pharmaceutical firms. It can cause firms to abandon R&D projects on future drug candidates with uncertain patent prospects. In addition, early patent challenges with uncertain outcomes can have a chilling effect on development of new indications and formulations. In particular, there may be no way to prevent cheaper generics from being used for the new indication after they enter the market even if they do not have an approved label for that indication.[21]

The five-year NCE data exclusivity was put into the Hatch-Waxman Act to incentivize innovators faced with little or no patent exclusivity time. However, this exclusivity period as currently constituted in the United States is not sufficient to sustain a high level of R&D activity. Since the 1984 Act was enacted, R&D costs have more than doubled in real terms (DiMasi, Hansen, and Grabowski 2003). At the same time, generic competition has become more intense. As discussed, generic patent challenges are occurring very early in the product life cycle. The NCE data exclusivity affords branded products a floor of effective exclusivity, depending on how long courts take to resolve in infringement suits. This is insufficient time for most new drugs to recoup the upfront R&D costs and earn a positive return on this investment.

In the European Union, new drugs receiving approval by the European Agency for the Evaluation of Medicinal Products (EMEA) or by individual EU countries receive a 10-year data exclusivity period. In particular, generic firms can file an abridged market application after eight years from the date of first EU authorization and begin the process of development and license application. However, the license may not be effective until 10 years of exclusivity from licensing has expired. This is commonly called the "eight plus two" policy.[22]

This is a policy option that U.S. policy makers should consider as a means for preserving R&D incentives under the Hatch-Waxman Act. A 10-year NCE data exclusivity period recognizes the high R&D costs of drug innovation and operates to discourage patent challenges early in the product life cycle. This would defer early patent challenges because few imitators are likely to incur the high cost of a new drug application (i.e., repeating safety and efficacy trials, a process that also raises ethical issues) that would be necessary to enter before the expiration of the 10-year data exclusivity period.

In terms of the objective of the 1984 Act to encourage innovation, a 10-year data exclusivity is more closely aligned with the minimum time necessary for the typical new chemical entity to earn a positive return on the large, upfront R&D investment now required for FDA approval (Grabowski and Vernon 2000). On these grounds, it would be a reasonable reform policy for policy makers to consider in the face of the explosion in patent challenges that has occurred in recent years. These challenges have led to higher litigation expenses and potential disincentives for R&D investments in new drugs and new indications for recently launched drugs.

VIII. Summary and Conclusions

The 1984 Hatch-Waxman Act has maintained a reasonable balance between generic competition and innovation incentives. Under the patent restoration provisions of the Act, branded products typically enjoy an exclusivity period of 10–14 years. After patents expire and generic entry occurs, prices for the molecule typically decline markedly. Prices approach marginal costs when a large number of generics are present in the market. Generics now account for over 50% of U.S. prescriptions; thus the savings to the payers and consumers of drug products have been substantial (U.S. Congressional Budget Office 1998).

Both brand and generic firms have responded to the law with strategies designed to create competitive advantages. Brand firms have utilized a variety of life cycle management strategies. These include new product formulations, shifts of the brand to OTC status, and authorized generics. These strategies are all legal and generally procompetitive, although they are limited in applicability to particular situations and therapeutic classes. At the same time, the U.S. Congress has recently acted to prohibit some life cycle management strategies that are not typically procompetitive such as agreements between generics and branded firms or the use of multiple 30-month stays to deter entry.

One aspect of the law that needs further scrutiny by policy makers is the 180-day exclusivity period that is awarded to the first generic firm that successfully challenges a patent. As generic competition has intensified, the strategic advantage to generic firms of the 180-day exclusivity period has become more valuable. Accordingly, they are devoting increasing resources to gaining core competencies in the art of patent challenges. This has led to a race to litigate as generics file challenges to the patents of commercially important products as soon as legally possible. Left unchecked, this wave of litigation early in the product life cycle could upset the delicate balance between price competition and innovation that has existed in the two decades since the 1984 Act was passed.

Another issue that warrants policy consideration is the question of generic or follow-on biologicals. New biological entities are regulated by a different division of the FDA. Follow-on biologicals are not covered by the Hatch-Waxman Act. A few of the older biologicals, such as human growth hormone, have multiple suppliers, but they are branded products that have performed additional safety and efficacy trials to gain FDA approval. The process for developing and manufacturing a new biological is more complex than in the case of new chemical entities. There are scientific, regulatory, and economic issues that need to be examined in the case of follow-on biologicals (Grabowski, Cockburn, and Long 2006). Congress and the FDA are currently considering whether regulatory procedures for follow-on biologicals should be changed. Given that a number of commercially important biologicals are scheduled to experience patent expiration in the next five years, this will also continue to be an important issue for further research and attention by policy makers.

Outside the United States, generic competition has had a significant effect on prices in countries that encourage generics through reference pricing-based reimbursement systems (e.g., Germany) as well as countries that create significant incentive programs for physicians to prescribe generically (the United Kingdom). By contrast, countries like France and Italy, which have stringent price regulation of new product launches and declining prices over time, along with competitive barriers in their pharmacy distribution system, have experienced negligible benefits or savings from generic competition.

Notes

1. One notable exception to this situation involved antibiotic drugs. These drugs did not have to conduct any new safety and efficacy trials because FDA approval of generic antibiotics was governed by the reference monograph approach.
2. H.R. 98–857 (I) at 16 (1984), reprinted in 1984 U.S.C.CAN. 2647, 2649.
3. Preface to the 22nd edition of FDA's *Approved Drug Products with Therapeutic Equivalence Evaluations*, commonly known as the "Orange Book."
4. Orange Book, preface.
5. This list is also available on line at www.express-scripts.com/ourcompany/pressroom/mediakit/generics/docs/laws.pdf, accessed June 27, 2006.
6. PhRMA (2000), p. 66, based on original data from IMS® Health 2000.
7. Capitation is a method of payment in which a physician receives a fixed amount for each person eligible to receive services (dollar/participant/month).
8. See, e.g., Grabowski and Vernon (1996), Masson and Steiner (1985), and Bloom, Wiertz, and Pauly (1986).
9. Ironically, this can lead to the government's paying a higher price for the generic product compared to its branded version when generics first enter the market. This can occur because brand manufacturers are required to give Medicaid discounts based on their "best price" to any buyer and, in any case, a minimum discount of 15.1%. The comparable requirement for generics is 11%. For example, the state of Maine, in 2001, initially paid 17% more for the generic fluoxetine than it had been paying for Prozac prior to automatically switching Medicaid users to the generic (Caffrey 2002).
10. Data audits of IMS Health as reported in PhRMA 2000 *Pharmaceutical Industry Profile* and subsequent IMS news releases.
11. For a simultaneous equation analysis of these various market variables, see Saha et al. (2006).
12. Richard Frank and David Salkever (1992, 1997) find the impact was positive, consistent with specific conditions on a brand firm's demand curve becoming more inelastic after generic entry. More recently, Saha et al. (2006), focusing on the 1990s, found that the net impact of generics on the rate of change in prices was negative, but relatively small in magnitude. In particular, they found that it takes 16 or more generic entrants to cause brand prices to actually decline in value in the first full year after generic entry.
13. One key assumption is that total sales of the molecule remain constant in terms of units in the face of generic competition (zero elasticity of demand). This can lead to an overstatement of savings, but studies of the effect of generic competition on the sales of the molecule indicate this is a reasonable first approximation (IMS generic spectra product summaries in 2002).
14. The sample involves a regression analysis framework that estimates the effect on price of the number of generic products of the same molecules. Danzon and Chao (2000) also control for the number of therapeutic substitutes, first-mover advantages, molecule age, and several other factors.
15. In a related approach involving a multicountry study, Hudson (2000) found that the impact on brand sales from generic entry is much greater in the case of the United States compared to the United Kingdom, Germany, or France.
16. For example, Edwin Masefield (1986) surveyed the chief research officers of 100 U.S. corporations and found that 60% of the innovations commericalized in 1981–1983 by the pharmaceutical firms would not have been developed without patent protection. The mean for all industry was 14%.
17. This framework was originally employed by Grabowski and Vernon (1986) to simulate the potential effects of the Act on R&D returns when the Act was first passed.

18. Another formulation strategy for the life cycle management is to combine a drug product subject to patent expiration with a newer product that has a much longer effective patent. In this case one needs to demonstrate to the FDA that the product, in combination, has a synergistic effect. According to IMS (2004), fixed combinations have become an important life cycle management approach in recent years.
19. Any agreements among ANDA applicants and brand name companies, or involving other ANDA applicants, must be filed with the Federal Trade Commission and the Department of Justice within 10 days of execution (Padden and Jenkins 2004).
20. AZT was originally developed unsuccessfully as a cancer remedy and remained as an unapproved drug candidate until its antiviral activity was discovered in the mid-1980s. For a case history, see Emmons and Nimgade (1991).
21. When a new indication is approved, only that indication receives three years of additional exclusivity under the Act. However, there is no effective way to prevent a less expensive generic firm from being used for all indications during this three-year exclusivity period, since physicians do not specify an indication when they write a prescription. This will be the case unless the brand firm utilizes an alternative delivery system or formulation that has exclusivity or patent protection.
22. In addition the EU law also allows for one year of additional data exclusivity for the whole compound if additional indications of significant overall therapeutic value are approved within the eight-year period (Towse 2004).

References

Baines, Darrin L., Keith H. Tally, and David K. Whynes. 1997. *Prescribing Budgets and Fundholding in General Practice*. London: Office of Health Economics.

Bear Stearns. 2002. "Attack of the Clones: 18 Years past Waxman–Hatch." October 2. New York: Bear Stearns.

Berndt, E. R. 2002. "Pharmaceuticals in U.S. Health Care: Determinants of Quality and Price." *Journal of Economic Perspectives* 16(4): 45–66.

Bloom, B. D. J., J. Wiertz, and M. Pauly. 1986. "Cost and Price of Comparable Branded and Generic Pharmaceuticals." *Journal of the American Medical Association* 256(18): 2523–2530.

Caffrey, Andrew. 2002. "Why Generics Can Cost States More Money." *Wall Street Journal*, February 13.

Caves, R. E., M. D. Whinston, and M. Hurwitz. 1999. "Patent Expiration, Entry, and Competition in the U.S. Pharmaceutical Industry." *Brookings Papers on Economic Activity Microeconomics* (1991): 1–66.

Cohen, Wesley M., Richard R. Nelson, and John P. Walsh. 2002. "Protecting Their Intellectual Assets: Appropriability Conditions and Why U.S. Manufacturing Firms Patent (Or Not)." National Bureau of Economic Research Working Paper 7552.

Cutler, David M. and Mark McClellan. 2001a. "Is Technological Change in Medicine Worth It?" *Health Affairs* 20(5): 11–29.

Danzon, Patricia M. and Li-Wei Chao. 2000. "Cross-national Price Differences for Pharmaceuticals: How Large, and Why?" *Journal of Health Economics* 19(2), March: 159–95.

DiMasi, Joseph A., Ronald W. Hansen, and Henry G. Grabowski. 2003. "The Price of Innovation: New Estimates of Drug Development Costs." *Journal of Health Economics* 22(2) 151–85.

Ellison, G. S. and F. Ellison. 2000. "Strategic Entry Deterrence and the Behavior of

Pharmaceutical Incumbents Prior to Patent Expiration." Working paper, MIT, Cambridge, MA.

Emmons, Willis A. and Ashok Nimgade. 1991. "Burroughs Welcome and AZT." Harvard Business School Case No. 9-792-004, Cambridge, MA.

Frank, Richard and David Salkever. 1992. "Pricing, Patent Loss and the Market for Pharmaceuticals." *Southern Economic Journal* 59: 165–179.

Frank, Richard and David Salkever. 1997. "Generic Entry and the Pricing of Pharmaceuticals." *Journal of Economics and Management Strategy* 6(1), Spring: 75–90.

Grabowski, Henry. 2004. "Are the Economics of Pharmaceutical R&D Changing? Productivity, Patent and Political Pressures." *PharmacoEconomics* 22(Suppl. 2): 15–24.

Grabowski, Henry, Iain Cockburn, and Genia Long. 2006. "The Market for Follow-on Biologics: How Will It Evolve?" *Health Affairs* 25(5): 1291–1301.

Grabowski, Henry and Margaret Kyle. 2006. "Generic Competition and Market Exclusivity Periods in Pharmaceuticals." *Managerial and Decision Economics*, forthcoming.

Grabowski, Henry and C. Daniel Mullins. 1997. "Pharmacy Benefit Management Cost-Effectiveness Analysis and Drug Formulary Decisions." *Social Science and Medicine* 45(4): 535–544.

Grabowski, Henry and John M. Vernon. 1992. "Brand Loyalty Entry and Price Competition in Pharmaceuticals after the 1984 Act." *Journal of Law and Economics* 35(2) 331–350.

Grabowski, Henry and John M. Vernon. 1996. "Longer Patents for Increased Generic Competition: The Waxman–Hatch Act after One Decade." *PharmacoEconomics* 10 (Suppl. 2): 110–123.

Grabowski, Henry and John M. Vernon. 2000. "Effective Patent Life in Pharmaceuticals." *International Journal of Technology Management* 19(1–2): 98–120.

Grabowski, Henry and Richard Wang. 2006. "The Quantity and Quality of Worldwide New Drug Introductions: 1982–2003." *Health Affairs* 25(2): 452–460.

Hudson, John. 2000. "Generic Take-up in the Pharmaceutical Market Following Patent Expiry: A Multi-Country Study." *International Review of Law and Economics* 20: 205–221.

IMS. 2004. *Global Pharmaceutical Review*. October. London.

Juhl, R. P. 2000. "Prescription to Over-the-Counter Switch: A Regulatory Perspective." *Clinical Therapeutics* 20(Supp. C): 111–117.

Kreling, D. H., T. Collins, H. Lipton, and K. C. Hertz. 1996. "Assessing the Impact of Pharmacy Benefit Managers." HCFA Contract Report, HCFA 95-023/PW, September 30.

Levin, Richard C., Alvin K. Klevorick, Richard R. Nelson, and Sidney G. Winter. 1987. "Appropriating the Returns from Industrial Research and Development." *Brookings Papers on Economic Activity* 3: 783–820.

Mansfield, Edwin. 1986. "Patents and Innovation: An Empirical Study." *Management Science* 32(2): 173–181.

Masson, A. and R. Steiner. 1985. "Generic Substitution and Prescription Drug Prices: Economic Effects of State Drug Product Selection Laws." Staff Report of the Bureau of Economics, FTC, Washington, DC, October.

McCarran, E. 1991. "Rx to OTC Switches: Promises and Pitfalls." *Medical Marketing and Media* 13–26.

Murphy, Kevin and Robert H. Topel. 2003a. "The Economic Value of Medical Research," in *Measuring the Gains from Medical Research: An Economic Approach*, ed. Kevin M. Murphy and Robert H. Topel, 41–73. Chicago, University of Chicago Press.

National Association of Boards of Pharmacy. 2004. *Survey of Pharmacy Law for 2003–2004*. Park Ridge, IL: NABC.

Padden, Michael and Thomas Jenkins. 2004. "Hatch–Waxman Changes." *National Law Journal* February 23, p. 13.

Pauly, M. V. 1998. *Health Benefits at Work: An Economic and Political Analysis of Employment-Based Health Insurance*. Ann Arbor: University of Michigan Press.

Pharmaceutical Research and Manufacturers of America. 2000. *Pharmaceutical Industry Profile*. Washington, DC: Pharmaceutical Research and Manufacturing Association.

Reiffen, David and Michael R. Ward. 2005. "Generic Drug Industry Dynamics." *Review of Economics and Statistics* 87(1): 37–49.

Reiffen, David and Michael R. Ward. 2006. "Branded Generics as a Strategy to Limit Cannibalization of Pharmaceutical Markets." *Managerial and Decision Economics*, forthcoming.

Rubin, Robert, Ann Hawk, and Elisa Cascade. 1998. "PBMs: A Purchaser's Perspective," in *PBMs: Reshaping the Pharmaceutical Distribution Network*, ed. by Sheila Shulman, Elaine Healy, and Louis Lasagna, 30. Binghamton, NY: Pharmaceutical Products Press.

Saha, Atanu, Henry Grabowski, Howard Birnbaum, Paul Greenberg, and Oded Bizan. 2006. "Generic Competition in the U.S. Pharmaceutical Industry." *International Journal of the Economics of Business* 13(1): 15–38.

Scherer, F. M. 2001. "The Link Between Gross Profitability and Pharmaceutical R&D Spending." *Health Affairs* 20: 216–220.

Schweitzer, Stuart. 1997. *Pharmaceuticals, Economics, and Policy*. New York: Oxford University Press.

Scott Morton, F. M. 1999. "Entry Decisions in the Generic Pharmaceutical Industry." *RAND Journal of Economics* 30(3): 421–440.

Scott Morton, F. M. 2000. "Barriers to Entry Brand Advertising, and Generic Entry in the U.S. Pharmaceutical Industry." *International Journal of Industrial Organization* 18(7): 1085–1104.

Siegel, Jonathan B. 2004. "Financial Aspects of 180-Day Generic Exclusivity." Presentation to the Food and Drug Law Institute Conference on Two Decades of Hatch–Waxman, December 1–2, Washington, DC.

Towse, A. 2004. "Developing the Idea of Transferable Intellectual Property Rights (TIPP) to Incentivize R&D in Drugs and Vaccines for Neglected Diseases." Office of Health Economics, London, March 2, Appendix I, 22–24.

U.S. Centers for Medicaid and Medicare Services. 2003. "The Nation's Health Care Dollar: 2001." Washington, DC: Government Printing Office.

U.S. Congressional Budget Office. 1998. "How Increased Competition Has Affected Prices and Returns in the Pharmaceutical Industry." July, 38. Washington, DC: Government Printing Office.

[14]

RAND Journal of Economics
Vol. 30, No. 3, Autumn 1999
pp. 421–440

Entry decisions in the generic pharmaceutical industry

Fiona M. Scott Morton*

Data on all generic drug entries in the period 1984–1994 are used to estimate which markets heterogeneous potential entrants will decide to enter. I find that organizational experience predicts entry. Firms tend to enter markets with supply and demand characteristics similar to the firm's existing drugs. Larger revenue markets, markets with more hospital sales, and products that treat chronic conditions attract more entry. The simultaneous nature of entry leads to an additional interpretation: specialization is profitable because of the severe risk to profits when a market is "overentered." However, I am unable to make any conclusions about the efficiency of entry decisions.

1. Introduction

■ A firm's decision to enter a particular market is one of the most important actions in the economy. I examine the entry choices of generic pharmaceutical firms. Generic pharmaceutical products are copies of branded pharmaceuticals, made after the original patent has expired. Producers enter by applying to the Food and Drug Administration (FDA) and being approved. I use data from the FDA on all generic drug entry from 1984 to 1994. I account for heterogeneity among potential entrants to predict which firms are likely to enter specific markets. I find that a firm's history and experience lead it to specialize along scientific and marketing dimensions. These can be thought of as "capabilities," as that word is used in the business press. I also analyze the generic scandal that caused substantial upheaval at the FDA and find that firms subsequently entered markets that differed from those they were already in.

Unfortunately, the institutional setting and available data prevent me from making any inferences about efficiency. I cannot say whether too many firms entered a particular market. However, I can describe *which* firms choose to enter particular markets. I explore whether generic entrants are choosing markets based on past experience as measured by characteristics of their portfolios. I find that previous experience with a drug or therapy increases the probability of entry. The experience of the parent firm

---

* University of Chicago and NBER; fionasm@gsb.uchicago.edu.

Thanks are due to Judy Chevalier, Peter Reiss, John Roberts, Garth Saloner, Andrea Shepard, Dimitri Vayanos, Matthew White, seminar participants at University of British Columbia, Northwestern, University of Chicago, University of Michigan, and the NBER IO Winter conference. I also thank the Editor and two referees for providing helpful comments and substantially improving the exposition of the article. Merck and Co. very kindly allowed me to gather data from its library. Research support from the National Science Foundation, grant no. SBR-9810178, is gratefully acknowledged. All errors are the responsibility of the author.

does not help predict entry, above and beyond the subsidiary's experience. Specialization across firms and within a corporation is consistent with the organizational design literature such as Rotemberg and Saloner (1994), where a firm incurs the cost of conflict between divisions if it tries to be a generalist.

I also find that marketing similarities between the entry opportunity and characteristics of the firm's portfolio such as market revenue and hospital share—demand-side factors—are important in explaining entry. This illustrates branding strategies discussed in the marketing literature (e.g., Keller, 1998), that a firm should group similar products to take advantage of a common brand. It also supports the notion that there are economies of scope in distribution channels and sales relationships. The generic industry appears to be heterogeneous, and measures of market concentration and competition should be carefully constructed. I also show that larger prepatent expiration brand revenue, larger sales to hospitals, and drugs that treat chronic conditions attract more generic entry.

The generic pharmaceutical entry decision is complex because evidence suggests that payoffs depend on the number of firms in a market, which affects the margin and quantity per firm. The profits of an entrant therefore depend on others' entry decisions. In addition, entrants sink entry costs simultaneously because entry information is kept secret by the FDA. These two facts suggest that there are many possible equilibria of the entry game. The question of which firms are expected to enter which markets—as well as which actually enter—in a simultaneous game has important financial repercussions. I discuss how a firm might make these decisions and examine the characteristics of the realized equilibrium.

I find that the amount of entry as a function of market revenue is positive but concave, as in Bresnahan and Reiss (1987), providing evidence that additional entrants erode price-cost margins. There is a risk to profits from excessive entry. I examine the effect of a firm's estimate of its own rank order of entry cost and find that beliefs about *relative*, rather than absolute, levels of cost may be playing a role in entry decisions. I also find that a bribery scandal in 1989 caused firms to branch into different types of markets, while fewer firms entered a market of any given size. These results are consistent with the breakdown of entry expectations during the scandal and increased regulatory delay and risk.

2. Institutional environment and timing

■ **Entry rules.** The Waxman-Hatch Act of 1984, among other things, allowed generic firms to submit Abbreviated New Drug Applications (ANDAs) for drugs approved since 1962. A flood of new ANDAs was filed in response. The application was called "abbreviated" because the generic manufacturer was no longer required to repeat the tests showing the substance to be safe and effective, since the innovator had already done so. Instead, the generic manufacturer had to prove that its product was identical in strength, dosage form, and route and that the product was bioequivalent. Additionally, the ANDA approval process included an evaluation of the firm's facilities and manufacturing processes. Although the new approval process took time and had several parts, it represented a large drop in the cost of entry relative to the previous regime, and therefore it caused more entry into existing and new markets. The generic industry also grew due to earlier relaxation of state substitution laws and the rise of managed care.

Researching how to manufacture a drug and performing the bioequivalency studies required for the ANDA can take months to years, depending on the formulation of the drug, the effort and skill of the firm, and the availability of good suppliers. The application process requires factory inspections from the FDA and independent laboratory tests of several preliminary batches of the product. A firm must therefore be ready to make the product—new equipment must be purchased and operational, for example—months before it is legally permitted to begin selling it. These expenditures therefore form a sunk cost that the firm must pay before it can attempt to enter the market. The FDA imposes no requirement to produce once an ANDA is granted.[1] An ANDA can be sold or transferred easily with the physical production site. However, buying an ANDA without its factory means that new tests and inspections must be carried out to the FDA's satisfaction; this is not necessarily faster or cheaper than starting from scratch. Thus, entry by a particular firm is a fairly irreversible decision; the costs that can be recovered upon exit from one drug (and not a factory) are close to zero.

Although creating and filing an ANDA is much less costly than inventing a new drug, entry costs are nevertheless significant when there is likely to be vigorous price competition. The average size of brand markets in the sample that later attract one generic entrant is $22 million in annual revenue. Generic products usually capture about half of molecule volume, although at prices 30–50% lower than the brand price. Thus generic revenues in one-firm markets are likely to be less than $10 million per year. Interviews with FDA officials and several generic pharmaceutical managers generated estimated costs of filing an ANDA from $250,000 to $20 million. The variability is due to substantial heterogeneity of entry costs across drugs and firm-drug combinations. However, costs of this order of magnitude are consistent with a one-entrant market size.

□ **Information.** The FDA does not reveal when it receives applications or who they are from; in this sense the entry process is simultaneous. However, managers might announce their entry plans in order to deter competitors from entering the market. An examination of available annual reports from the early 1990s and several telephone interviews with managers in the generic pharmaceutical industry uncovered only one case of announced entry. The managers said that generic manufacturers do not announce because they do not want to reveal that they think a particular market is a good one to enter. Other firms' opinions may signal a common market value. Additionally, although a firm might announce it has applied for a particular drug, there is no guarantee that approval will be granted in the time frame anticipated by the applicant. A sample or a factory might fail an FDA test. A year's delay can cause an application that was submitted and announced to be approved *after* that of a competitor responding to the announcement. A firm therefore cannot commit to a market with an application announcement. As a result, generic firms effectively sink entry costs simultaneously.[2]

Some entrants are "late" in applying; when a rival is approved they may be able to withdraw and save a significant part of the entry cost. FDA officials confirmed that firms do withdraw applications in response to rivals' approvals. No information can be obtained on applicants who were never approved (dropped out). However, in a later section I discuss the motivations of late entrants who drop out and those who stay in.

[1] An unused but approved ANDA is an option, available to be used if prices rise, rivals exit, or the market becomes more attractive for any reason. Exit—formal withdrawal of the ANDA—is not an attractive alternative under these conditions.

[2] Of course, credible commitment can be achieved by winning approval of an ANDA before competitors submit applications. To be effective, a deterring firm would want its application to be approved about two years before patent expiration. In the dataset, there is only one case of such an early approval.

The important actors in the entry game are the early movers who play a simultaneous game; I do not focus on the few late sequential movers.

The generic drug industry participants also stated concern about the business risk posed by unanticipated entry by competitors and its effect on prices. Commonly, such a statement of concern would be followed by an example of a product that unexpectedly failed (to be profitable) due to the entry of many competitors and vigorous price competition. These examples are consistent with an obvious feature of the approval process—winning regulatory approval constitutes a fixed and sunk cost. Thus, an entry decision has important financial consequences for the firm.

□ **Scandal.** In 1989 the "generic scandal" broke out. Four reviewers at the FDA were found to have been taking bribes in return for speeding approval of ANDAs.[3] Additionally, some firms submitted the original branded product as their own for official FDA tests. Violations of manufacturing rules were also uncovered. The fallout from these discoveries affected approvals and manufacturing in the following years. The FDA's Generic Drug Division fired many reviewers, the remaining reviewers proceeded cautiously, ethics standards were promulgated, and the division was reorganized. ANDAs granted from 1990 to 1993 took longer to be approved than those submitted in previous years.

The discovery of irregularities in the approval process led to a review of "good manufacturing practices." Many more, and stricter, inspections of manufacturing facilities were carried out. Many firms were forced to withdraw products from the market for a period of months—years, in some cases—until their manufacturing process, suppliers, and training satisfied the FDA. Overall, the period from 1988 to at least 1992 was a time of upheaval and uncertainty in the generic drug industry.

3. Model

■ This section lays out a basic model of an entry game in the presence of competition, sunk costs, and heterogeneous potential entrants.[4] Berry's (1992) article on the airline industry examines firm heterogeneity; it asks which and how many firms enter a market. Christensen and Caves (1997) analyze capacity expansions in the pulp and paper industry. Although not a simultaneous game, their setting also features indeterminacy about which firm will build what amount of capacity. Berry (1992) is most closely related to my research, and I adopt his basic structure. A key difference between the airline industry and generic pharmaceuticals is the timing of the entry decision, simultaneous rather than sequential. Therefore, an important difference is that the current number of firms in the market cannot be used to predict generic pharmaceutical entry patterns.

Firms simultaneously choose whether or not to enter specific markets by sinking their fixed costs. Given the entry decisions, production and prices determine net profits. The entry decision is assumed to be independent of decisions in other markets, although error terms are correlated in the empirical work. A firm's existing portfolio is taken as given. Staying out yields zero payoff to the firm, and entry occurs when expected postentry profits are positive. However, profits depend on the actions of rival firms.

[3] The investigation was launched because Mylan became suspicious that its drugs were not getting approval as quickly as competitors' and found incriminating evidence in the garbage can of its FDA reviewer. (*Chicago Tribune*, November 22, 1992).

[4] Sherman and Willett (1967) and Bresnahan and Reiss (1987, 1991) discuss entry games with sunk costs.

Although the product appears homogeneous and the industry should then exhibit Bertrand pricing, several studies have documented that generic prices fall steadily with the number of generic firms (Caves, Whinston, and Hurwitz, 1991; Frank and Salkever, 1997; and Wiggins and Maness, 1995). Total profits in a particular market therefore strictly decline in the number of entrants that decide to enter.

The identities of potential entrants are known, and they have heterogeneous costs of entry. All cost differences are assumed to be in fixed costs. The empirical work investigates which characteristics of potential entrants affect the cost of entry. I assume marginal costs are identical and information is symmetric across firms.[5] In particular, they know each other's costs. The identity of individual entrants does not affect variable profits or conduct. Drugs vary in difficulty of formulation and testing, and therefore average entry costs vary across markets. However, for any given market (k), I assume that potential entrants (i) can be ranked in order of fixed cost of entry, ϕ_{ik}. Berry (1992) shows that the number of entrants is unique under these assumptions, although one cannot necessarily predict which potential entrants will enter.

Profits for a particular generic firm i in market k can be represented as

$$\Pi_{ik} = v_k(N) + \phi_{ik}, \tag{1}$$

where Π is total profits, v is variable profits, ϕ is fixed cost, and N is the number of entrants in the market. A pure-strategy Nash equilibrium exists when all entrants earn positive profit and all nonentrants would not earn positive profit if they entered, holding the strategies of the other potential entrants fixed. One Nash equilibrium assumes that the most profitable N^* entrants enter, where firm $(N^* + 1)$ would earn negative profit from entry, given that N^* have entered.[6] This equilibrium maximizes social welfare, and it imitates the outcome that would occur if entrants bid for an entry slot. Dixit and Shapiro (1986) describe a case of N identical potential entrants vying for spots in a market that "holds" only M firms. They point out that choosing a pure-strategy equilibrium in which only M firms play "enter" is artificial unless the reason for choosing those M firms is incorporated into the game. Here that reason is entry cost. To predict the entry decisions of firms one must measure fixed entry costs, since those with the lowest costs enter.[7] Denote F_k^* as the cutoff value for market k, such that all those with entry cost at or below F_k^* will enter and those with entry costs above F_k^* will stay out. Then the probability the firm enters is

$$\text{pr}(enter_{ik}) = \text{pr}(\phi_{ik} \leq F_k^*), \tag{2}$$

when F_k^* satisfies $\phi_{N^*,k} \leq F_k^* < \phi_{N^*+1,k}$. F_k^* varies across markets for two reasons. The mean and the distribution of entry costs may differ across markets. Secondly, different markets may support different numbers of firms in equilibrium.

[5] The model will produce the same entry rule whether firms differ in marginal or fixed cost. The true marginal cost of a batch includes the opportunity cost of capital. The outside option for a piece of capital is the value of producing one of its other drugs, which will vary across firms and over time. Since I lack the data, I ignore this source of cost variation.

[6] See Berry (1992) for a proof that this equilibrium exists.

[7] Bolton and Farrell (1990) compare welfare under a central planner and a decentralized case, when the randomness inherent in not coordinating entry into a natural monopoly results in "mistakes." Planning increases social welfare by reducing "duplication" (both firms enter) and "delay" (both firms wait for the other to enter).

4. Data

■ I use data on ANDA approvals granted from 1984 to 1994. After dropping unnecessary observations, the dataset contains 1,233 ANDAs; each is a unique combination of applicant, drug, form, and patent expiration. See the Appendix for a detailed description of data preparation. The total number of entry-opportunities, or markets, is 363. For each ANDA, the FDA provided the submission date, the approval date, and the applicant name, as well as characteristics of the drug such as ingredients, form, route (into the body), and strength. Note that the dataset is not a sample, but the complete set of ANDAs approved in the United States during this period.

The dataset includes additional characteristics of the drug markets and firms. I used information from the 1993 volume of *Physician's GenRx,* a comprehensive pharmaceutical reference, to assign a drug's therapeutic class. I also include the date that legal restrictions on entry into the drug market expire. The revenue of the brand in the year before patent expiration comes from IMS Drugstore and Hospital Audits of the appropriate year. Total revenue includes 1984 sales of both brand and generic products in markets that experienced their first generic entry before the Waxman-Hatch Act passed.

In most markets it is difficult to find any information on the existence, number, or characteristics of potential entrants who do not enter. I employ the following methodology to deal with this problem. The unit of analysis for *potential* cases of entry will be the firm-opportunity, defined by a firm name and a drug about to lose patent protection. Potential entrants are assumed to decide if they want to enter at the time of the first entrant's ANDA submission date.[8] I define the set of potential entrants as the product of all firms (123) and all drug markets (363) that are in the sample; this interaction forms a dataset of all possible firm*drug combinations. Those combinations that did not see actual entry are assigned a zero as the value of the dependent variable, whereas those that did get a one. I employ this methodology a second time by using the parent company as the firm unit rather than the subsidiary.

The vast majority of observations in the dataset do not experience entry (98%). The second potential entrant dataset limits firms to considering entry into markets that open *after* the firm has submitted an ANDA for another product; a firm may not be a potential entrant until it has been a real entrant, which reduces the number of nonentries for each firm. The final, and most restrictive, method of constructing potential entrants allows only firms with form experience to be potential entrants. The idea is that only a particular type, a "pill firm" for example, will enter pill markets. Those firms that have a pill in their portfolio, or will by the end of 1994, can be considered potential entrants for a pill market.

I record the stock of drugs approved before 1984 for all firms. These portfolios are added to the 1984–1994 flow of entries (and potential entries) to form the complete dataset. Some observations cannot be used in the estimation because of irregular regulatory or restriction information, but I keep them in the dataset so that portfolios are complete. Other unused observations are those where the applicant primarily manufactures branded drugs but has also applied for one or more ANDAs; such a manufacturer could have many reasons to enter a market that are beyond the scope of this article. Applications received before November 1984 are not used for estimation, since the new regulatory regime had not yet started. Means of the variables and counts in the different datasets are reported in Tables 1 and 2.

[8] Using the time of the second ANDA to be submitted does not affect the results.

TABLE 1 Summary Statistics
Categories of Observations and Market Size Regressors

Generic entries post-Waxman-Hatch	1,233
Complete observations	1,178
On time or slightly late entries	936
Very late entries	242
Number entering post-Waxman-Hatch markets	768
Unique product markets	363
Unique firms	123
Total entry opportunities	44,649
Observation in portfolios before Waxman-Hatch (11/84)	3,567
Observations in final dataset (with potential entry cases)	48,216
Observations where probability of entry estimated (not portfolio or very late or irregular and no missing revenue data)	42,059
Observations if potential entrants must previously exist	33,979
Observations if must exist and no pre-Waxman-Hatch markets	23,811
Observations if no pre-Waxman-Hatch markets	29,052

Generic Entries: Not very late, complete observations = 936

	Mean	Standard Deviation	Minimum	Maximum
Total revenue[a]	75,793	109,934	72	619,645
LnRevenue	10.33	1.53	4.28	13.34
Squared LnRevenue	108.9	30.3	18.3	177.9
LnHospital Revenue	8.16	1.54	2.40	12.15
Hospital revenue share	.267	.346	.009	1
Chronic drug	.482	.500	0	1
Single strength market	.046	.209	0	1
Firms indicted in scandal	.239	.427	0	1
Approval time (in days)	564.7	374.5	60.8	2,585.4
Number incumbent brands	1.18	.912	0	18
Pre-Waxman-Hatch generic entry	1.26	4.46	0	47
Patent year	85.97	2.85	84	97
Applications per firm	27.8	17.6	1	60
Applications per drug	6.77	4.69	1	18

Note: The maximum patent expiration year is 1997 because the dataset contains one tentative ANDA approval that was granted three years before patent expiration; the firm could be trying to credibly commit to the market to deter additional entry.
[a] Revenue is expressed in thousands.

If a firm submits an application six months or more after the first approval for the drug has been granted, I define its entry decision to be "late," rather than a decision made simultaneously with other firms. There are three main reasons for submitting an ANDA after other firm(s) have been approved. First, if demand is more positive than expected, additional, higher-cost firms will want to enter. Second, a firm might have experienced delays in preparing an application but enters because in equilibrium it is expected to enter. Third, a firm could receive information indicating that there has been

TABLE 2 **Cost of Entry Regressors**

Match variable N = 42,059	Mean	Standard Deviation	Minimum	Maximum	Mean Enter = 0	Mean Enter = 1
Firm form	6.73	17.85	0	121	6.01	38.3
Parent form	3.65	13.54	0	122	3.66	3.28
Firm therapy	.994	2.54	0	26	.936	3.58
Parent therapy	.620	2.33	0	28	.615	.850
Firm family	.023	.204	0	7	.021	.099
Parent family	.017	.210	0	9	.017	.022
Firm ingredient	.084	.487	0	17	.077	.377
Parent ingredient	.059	.490	0	20	.057	.112
Absolute difference from revenue in portfolio	50,360	87,749	0	619,645	50,067	63,250
Absolute difference from hospital share in portfolio	.327	.352	0	1	.330	.166
Form of drug						
Pill			19,233			
Extended release pill			1,100			
Inject			11,357			
Topical			2,299			
Oral liquid			5,382			
Eye			2,565			
Other			123			

a "mistake" in the entry process; perhaps an expected entrant is absent.[9] Late observations fit the model if explanations one or two hold. I assume explanation three cannot hold when the entrant applies early enough to have incomplete information about other entrants.[10] Results including these "not too late" late observations are very similar to those without any late observations.

□ **Entry cost.** The variables I use to measure the entry cost of a generic manufacturer indicate the amount of experience the firm has with some aspect of the current entry opportunity. The premise is that it is much cheaper to prepare an ANDA requiring equipment or procedures a firm already has in place. For example, a firm making its first topical drug has to purchase a "cream line" years before it can be used regularly, and the firm's chemists have to work with tests and FDA standards that are new and unfamiliar. A firm that already makes creams will have a lower cost of preparing the same ANDA. An application that includes an ingredient the firm has used before in another product lowers the cost of preparing the ANDA because the firm already has FDA-certified suppliers and its research team is familiar with the properties of that supplier's product. The cost of preparing the ANDA may also be lower if the research team has experience with the therapeutic class; FDA standards for absorption into the body vary according to the therapeutic goal of the drug. These are supply-side reasons for entry. There may also be demand-side reasons for a firm to specialize in a particular area: A therapy or a product that is part of a drug family may create distribution or

[9] A firm will withdraw its late application when it gets new information about any of these market features, such as demand (substitute technology) or supply (approvals) shocks.

[10] See the Appendix for a definition of "very late."

reputation economies of scope if the firm manufactures related products. Retail establishments may prefer to purchase a complete line of products from one manufacturer; purchasing agents for chain drugstores and hospitals or for large distributors are likely to be familiar with the manufacturer already.

I would like to know how similar the current entry opportunity is to the firm's portfolio. I compare the past experience of the firm to the current application opportunity by matching values for the current opportunity's therapeutic class, specific ingredients, drug family, and manufacturing form with the characteristics of drugs in the firm's portfolio. (I define a drug "family" to consist of closely related drugs that cannot be classified as the same—two iron compounds, for example.) I create match variables for each of the characteristics listed above that simply count the number of times a firm has had experience with that feature of the new entry opportunity.[11] The components that make up the cost of preparing an ANDA are listed in Figure 1. Below each category is an estimate of the effect of firm experience on cost.

An important decision is whether the unit of analysis should be the subsidiary or the parent firm. Subsidiaries of a firm might have their own research labs and be fairly freestanding, or the firm might be centralized. To allow for either case, I create variables based on both the applicant name and the parent firm. If the parent is outside the pharmaceutical industry, there is no relevant information to include. I subtract the number of firm matches from the total number of parent matches to create a variable that measures the net impact of parents. The coefficients on the parent variables therefore represent the impact of parent experience above and beyond firm experience. In the same way, the family match variable is created by subtracting ingredient matches from total family matches.

Three other variables measure firm characteristics. One is a dummy variable indicating the firm was later indicted in the generic scandal. These firms would submit more applications if the probability of quick and smooth approval was higher due to bribes. The final two variables measure how closely the market characteristics of the current entry opportunity match those of the firm's portfolio. *Difference from Hospital Share* is the absolute value of the difference between the current opportunity's share of revenues from hospitals and the equal-weighted average of that variable in the firm's recent portfolio. I do not have the hospital share information for older portfolio drugs, so they are not included in the measure. *Difference in Revenue* is defined analogously: the absolute value of the difference between the current entry opportunity's revenue and that of the firm's recent portfolio.

Specialization is clear in the data. Summary statistics for the firm-characteristic variables are listed in Table 2. There is a strong correlation between the outcome of the entry decision and the match variables. For example, the mean form match for firms that enter as opposed to potential entrants that did not is 38 versus 6. Those firms that entered had a therapy match level of 3.6 as opposed to .9.

5. Analysis and results

■ The estimation technique used here is a probit: enter or not enter, using the decision rule discussed above:

[11] Firms have an incentive to enter several related markets at one time to spread the cost of learning about a new form or therapeutic area over several projects. Seventeen out of fifty-two cases of firms entering a new form show signs of economies of scope; the firm enters a second market in the same form within six months of the first.

FIGURE 1

FIXED COST OF ENTRY DECLINES WITH EXPERIENCE

Component of fixed cost	Ingredient	Recipe and testing	Capital	Distribution
Large effect?	Large	Medium	Large	Medium
Reason	Suppliers located and certified; compound properties known	Experience with form, family, and ingredient reduces research resource expenditure	Experience with form reduces cost to opportunity cost of a few batches rather than purchase price for one to two years	If distributing therapy already, reduces effort to find customers

$$\text{pr}(enter_{ik}) = \text{pr}(\phi_{ik} \leq F_k^*).$$

Both ϕ_{ik} and F_k^* are estimated with linear models. Z_k is a matrix of characteristics of market k that determine market size, while X_{ik} is a matrix of firm characteristics that predict the fixed cost of entry for firm i into market k. A further econometric issue is that a firm's actions may be correlated across markets. Suppose, for example, that a firm's manager wanted to expand its product line. That firm would be more likely to enter any given market than the model would predict. The error term ϵ_{ik} is therefore composed of a component that is idiosyncratic and independently distributed across observations, ξ_{ik}, and a component v_i that captures unobserved firm-specific factors.

$$\text{pr}(enter_{ik}) = \text{pr}(\xi_{ik} + v_i \geq Z_k\delta - X_i\,\beta). \tag{3}$$

The components of the error term, ξ_{ik} and v_i, are assumed to be normally distributed and independent of one another. The estimation method is a probit with a variance-covariance matrix of the block-diagonal form described above.

The variables discussed in the preceding section are used to form an estimate of entry cost (X) for each firm opportunity. Each match variable is labelled with either "firm" or "parent," depending on how the match was calculated, and a variable name, e.g., "therapy," to indicate the variable matched over. I use a reduced-form linear model to predict market size, or the expected number of entrants that can earn positive profits in a market. Since the revenue of the drug market before entry is the single most important predictor of the number of generic entrants, I use *LnRevenue* and *SquaredLnRevenue* as explanatory variables. This allows the number of entrants to be convex or concave (Bresnahan and Reiss, 1987) in market revenue. Expected future molecule revenue would be preferable for predicting entry but is difficult to measure.[12] Sometimes a patent or exclusivity restriction applies only to one strength of a drug out of several—usually a strength appearing on the market after the initial products. Revenue from the second strength will have a negative coefficient if the delayed revenues make the market less attractive.

Scott Morton (forthcoming) finds that if a drug treats a chronic condition, it attracts more generic entry. The dummy variable *Chronic* and its interaction with *LnRevenue*

[12] An important omitted determinant of the expected future size of the market is the amount of new innovation in the therapeutic class. Without innovation, generic products will capture a larger share of the class. I assume all potential entrants have the same information, so there should not be bias across entrants due to omitting future market size.

are included. Lastly, the amount of the drug's revenues coming from hospitals might affect the penetration of generics relative to the incumbent brand, so the variable *LnHospRevenue* is in the specification.

The results of the estimation are reported in Table 3. The cost variables perform as predicted. *Firm form* has a precisely estimated coefficient; previous experience with a particular form reduces the cost of entry and increases its likelihood. I include the squares of the *Firm form* and *Firm therapy* match variables to reflect nonlinearity in their impact. As one might predict, the coefficient on the quadratic term is negative, indicating that an additional match increases the probability of entry less as the number of matches grows. The last line of Table 3 contains the standard normal probability density function value of the mean of the estimated index, which, when multiplied by a coefficient, creates a marginal effect. For the first match in the firm's portfolio, the probability of entry increases by about .04%; a firm with one hundred form matches increases its probability of entry by 1%.[13] *Parent form's* coefficient is negative owing to specialization of subsidiaries by form. The injectable subsidiary is less likely to enter a pill market than the parent as a whole, which has experience from the pill division.[14] *Firm therapy* also has a significantly positive coefficient, slightly bigger but less precisely estimated than the form coefficient. The coefficient on squared firm therapy is an order of magnitude larger than the squared form coefficient because therapy matches are rarer than form matches (mean value 1 instead of 6.7). The total effect of firm therapy matches is positive for all observations in the sample. It appears that a firm's R&D and distribution costs are lower for familiar therapies and lead to a greater probability of entry. The coefficient on *Parent therapy* is insignificant, perhaps again owing to specialization by subsidiaries.

The ingredient variables both have positive coefficients, as expected; having established suppliers and R&D experience with a particular compound lowers the cost of entry. The *Parent ingredient* coefficient may be driven by the importance of transfers of branded products from parents to generic subsidiaries. The *Firm family* coefficient is positive, large, and significant, in contrast to the *Parent family* coefficient, which is not significantly different from zero. Moving from zero to seven *Firm family* matches increases the probability of entry by 1.3%. It may be that a parent can transfer specific knowledge of a drug or ingredient to its generic subsidiary, whereas less well-defined information (family matches) is harder to transfer between subsidiaries.

Firms enter the types of markets, as well as products, with which they already have experience. Absolute differences between the current entry opportunity and the characteristics of the firm's portfolio negatively affect the probability of entry. A revenue difference of $75 million (mean revenue), reduces the probability of entry by about .1%. The share of a drug's revenues from hospitals is also an important portfolio characteristic. A difference of .33 between a firm's portfolio hospital share and current opportunity reduces the probability of entry by .3%. A simple dummy variable indicating whether the firm was later indicted in the generic scandal has an insignificant coefficient. This is because indicted firms had no success entering markets after the scandal which counter-balanced high early entry rates.

[13] Though not called for by the model, including firm size (positive and significant coefficient) in the regression does not alter the magnitude or significance of any other coefficient. Number of matches does not proxy for bigger firms entering with greater probability.

[14] Subsidiaries sometimes specialize by form (therapy). In such a case, there is no chance that a pill subsidiary, for example, will enter the injectable market. This creates a negative parent form coefficient. If subsidiaries specialized by form (therapy) are defined to be one firm, the coefficient on parent form (therapy) match is positive.

TABLE 3 Basic Entry Results
Dependent Variable: *Enter*

	Market Size Estimation	Market Dummies
Firm form match	.040	.047
	(.002)	(.002)
Firm form match squared	−.00029	−.00033
	(.00002)	(.00002)
Parent form match	−.006	−.003
	(.002)	(.002)
Firm therapy match	.064	.093
	(.012)	(.014)
Firm therapy match squared	−.0020	−.0027
	(.0006)	(.0007)
Parent therapy match	−.006	.087
	(.008)	(.009)
Firm ingredient match	.047	.075
	(.018)	(.026)
Parent ingredient match	.066	.073
	(.025)	(.031)
Firm family match	.214	.270
	(.045)	(.054)
Parent family match	.034	.028
	(.076)	(.089)
Difference from recent portfolio revenue	−1.59E-06	−4.45E-06
	(3.50E-07)	
		(7.11E-07)
Difference from recent hospital share	−.924	−1.59
	(.096)	(.126)
Firm implicated in scandal	.103	.097
	(.071)	(.063)
LnRevenue	−.442	—
	(.105)	
Squared LnRevenue	.018	—
	(.006)	
LnRevenueWH	−.025	—
	(.004)	
LnHospitalRevenue	.243	—
	(.023)	
*LnRev*Chronic*	.050	—
	(.023)	
Second Strength Revenue	−9.63E-07	—
	(9.39E-07)	
Chronic	−.417	—
	(.241)	
Constant	−1.54	−2.74
	(.452)	(.311)
Observations	42,059	42,059
$\phi(\text{mean}X*\beta)$	.009	.004

Market dummy variables are included but not reported in column 2.

Thirty percent of markets already have entry by 1984 and also experience entry during the sample period. Revenue in these markets is not comparable to revenue in markets with only brand sales, as is clear from the negative coefficient on *LnRevenueWH*. This variable is an interaction between revenue and a dummy for pre-Waxman-Hatch entry.[15] However, as expected, I find that the probability of entry increases as market size grows; the total effect of all the revenue variables is increasing in revenue. The coefficient on *LnHospitalRev* is positive and significant, as predicted; generic producers sell to hospitals disproportionately, so hospital revenue is important. The coefficient on the *Chronic* variable is negative but is overwhelmed by the revenue interaction; chronic markets appear to be more attractive than nonchronic markets, indicating that patient switching costs are not blocking generic entry. *Second Strength Revenue* has a negative coefficient, as expected, but it is insignificant.

The revenue coefficients show that there is more entry as the brand pre-expiration sales grow; more entrants can "fit" in larger markets. However, it appears that entry is driving down the price-cost margin faced by all entrants. By setting *Chronic, Bad, Second Strength,* and *Waxman-Hatch* to zero, using the means of the firm-specific variables and the coefficients in the first column of Table 3, and fixing hospital share at .05, I calculate revenue per expected entrant. With 123 potential entrants, the revenue size that generates one entrant in expectation is $47 million. The market size required for two (three) entrants is $164 million ($325 million), clearly more than double the one-firm market size, and consistent with the finding in Bresnahan and Reiss (1987).[16]

The market size specification may not include all relevant characteristics, so I also use market fixed effects. In this method, market size does not rely on a specific functional form or market characteristics. The results of the dummy variable specification are in the second column of Table 3. Model fit is improved somewhat, and the cost variable coefficients follow the same pattern as in the first two columns. Most coefficients are larger in magnitude, but the normal probability density function value of the average index declines by half, so that overall, the marginal effects of the variables decline somewhat. The only marginal effect that increases slightly is the effect of market revenue differences. The market fixed-effect coefficients are not reported in the table because there are several hundred of them.

Subsidiaries of the same parent have the option to all enter the same market. The parent might let each subsidiary make its own decision, or corporate headquarters might prevent duplication within the firm by coordinating the entry decision across subsidiaries. In such a case, entry is determined simultaneously for several observations. This situation can be addressed in the estimation by using variables and entry opportunities defined at the parent level. Instead of creating firm-drug entry opportunities, the entry opportunities are created at the parent-drug level. The coefficients on the parent match variables (now the only match variables) using a sample without Waxman-Hatch entry are reported in Table 4. Since parent experience was not generally significant in Table 3, the combination of firm and parent variables produces coefficients slightly smaller than the firm coefficients from Table 3. The marginal effects are stable since the coefficients decline slightly, but the probability density function of the mean index rises. Marginal effects fall in column 2 when market dummies are used, as they do in Table 3.

[15] Since markets with pre-Waxman-Hatch entry may exhibit a different entry game, I reestimated the regression without those observations. The significant coefficients are almost identical in size and the normal probability density function value of the average index hardly changes between the two samples.

[16] Plus or minus one (bootstrap) standard deviation of estimated market size is $35–63 million for one expected entrant, $108–251 million for two, and $191–552 million for three. I redrew the sample 100 times, estimated and saved the coefficients, calculated market size, and took the standard deviation of the 100 market size estimates.

TABLE 4 Parent Results: Entry Opportunities Formed Using Parents Cost Variables Based on Parent Portfolios Dependent Variable: *Enter*

	No Market with Entry Before Waxman-Hatch	
Restriction	Market Size Estimation	Market Dummies
Parent form match	.033 (.002)	.037 (.002)
Parent form match squared	−.00018 (.00002)	−.0002 (.00002)
Parent therapy match	.041 (.011)	.077 (.013)
Parent therapy match squared	−.0010 (.0005)	−.0018 (.0006)
Parent ingredient match	.073 (.017)	.108 (.026)
Parent family match	.197 (.049)	.209 (.059)
Difference from recent parent portfolio revenue	−1.65E-06 (3.92E-07)	−3.48E-06 (6.24E-07)
Difference from recent parent hospital share	−1.11 (.119)	−1.91 (.154)
Firm implicated in scandal	−.250 (.094)	−.006 (.066)
LnRevenue	−.435 (.123)	—
Squared LnRevenue	.016 (.007)	—
LnHospitalRevenue	.2979 (.029)	—
*LnRev*Chronic*	.050 (.027)	—
Second Strength Revenue	−9.08E-07 (9.75E-07)	—
Chronic	−.403 (.285)	—
Constant	−1.76 (.531)	−2.25 (.219)
Observations	26,828	26,828
$\phi(\text{mean}X*\beta)$	.011	.004

Market dummy variables are included by not reported in column 2.

Overall however, one can conclude that the choice of organization level from which to analyze entry does not drive the results.

One potential problem is that many zeroes are created where they might not belong because we do not actually know which firms were valid potential entrants. I also estimate the specifications in Table 3 using the second definition of a potential entrant. This restriction on potential entry increases the percentage of ones to about 3.5, but it does not change the results at all. I also use the third definition of potential entrant, those that have experience with the form already. I reestimate the regressions above on the "pill" subsample of the data, which has 7% ones. I find results that are more specific to the pill class and larger marginal effects, but otherwise the results are similar to those in Table 3.[17]

I create estimates of a firm's guess at its own cost position and of the size of the market that can be compared to each other and the realized entry decision. Each firm has a rank order in each market according to its index value. I use the estimated coefficients from the specification in Table 3, column 1, omitting markets with pre-Waxman-Hatch entry. The lowest-cost firm—with the highest index value—is ranked one, the second, two, etc. I then estimate the size of each market where the dependent variable is the total number of firms entering.[18] This produces a predicted number of entrants for each market. A firm will expect itself to enter a market and others to stay out if its rank order is equal to or less than the expected number of entrants. ***Below*** is a dummy variable that takes a value of one when this condition is true. ***Below*** is in some ways an interaction between the firm being low cost and the market being large. ***Below*** has a significant coefficient of .4 (.06) if included in the regression, while the other coefficients remain stable; it is a strong predictor of entry into a market.[19] Entry appears to be positively affected by more than just having low absolute costs: being a low ***relative*** cost potential entrant is important.

□ **Regime shift.** The generic scandal was a large disruption that should have radically altered market players' beliefs about which firms would enter which markets. After the scandal broke, the FDA virtually stopped approving ANDAs and the industry was thrown into chaos for several years. Firms were operating in an environment of great uncertainty, which has three effects on the model. First, the additional uncertainty creates more risk, thereby reducing the equilibrium number of entrants in a market. Second, the change in FDA priorities meant firms needed a new model of the cost of constructing an ANDA. Third, the inability of some firms to enter new markets due to FDA disciplinary actions created entry opportunities for other firms. The result of these changes to the model will be that fewer firms enter, the regressors do not predict entry as well after the regime change, and firms enter areas they had not formerly specialized in. I divide the sample into two parts, ANDAs submitted before 1989 and 1990 onward. The prescandal results differ somewhat from the full-sample ones. The scandal dummy is now positive and significant, as predicted. The indicted firms entered at above-average rates before the scandal and did not enter at all afterward. Also, the coefficients on the chronic variables change so that nonchronic markets are slightly more attractive than chronic markets.

The reorganization at the FDA caused application times to rise significantly. This change combined with additional risk should certainly reduce the number of entrants in any given market after the scandal. Looking at the effect of all the revenue coefficients together (and holding hospital share at .25) reveals that all but the smallest markets attract fewer entrants in the postscandal period than before.[20]

---

[17] Did the correct number of firms enter each market? Testing the efficiency of entry is impossible without postentry prices and quantities. Markets with unobserved positive characteristics attract more entrants than expected, both on-time and late. Thus, counts of very late entry cannot be used to identify *ex post* correction of mistakes.

[18] The results of this ordered probit regression are not reported in the interests of brevity. They may be obtained from the author on request.

[19] The estimated standard errors reported here are incorrect because they do not take into account the first-stage estimation.

[20] However, during the postscandal sample period there may have been entrants that submitted applications for these markets and were still waiting for approval at the time I collected my data. The analysis omits markets that opened up in the final eighteen months of the sample, but some bias likely remains.

Using the estimated coefficients from the prescandal period to construct an index for postscandal observations yields a correlation between the index and actual entry of only .19, as opposed to a correlation of .33 between the index and prescandal entry. The percentage of correctly predicted entry in the two regimes using coefficients from the prescandal era is 55% and 38% (correctly predicted nonentry is 96% and 94%, before and after the scandal, respectively).[21] The prescandal model loses some of its ability to predict entry, as hypothesized, when firms begin to enter unexpected markets after 1989.

The coefficients reported in Table 5 also show that firms choose to enter different markets. Coefficients on market revenue differences and hospital share differences fall in magnitude in the postscandal period. The *Difference in Revenue* coefficient becomes insignificantly different from zero. These variables measure cost savings in distribution and marketing that did not change in value due to the scandal. The drop in the magnitude of the coefficients suggests that after the scandal, firms entered markets where they lacked previous experience and a cost advantage.

6. Conclusions

■ The preceding empirical work demonstrates that heterogeneity among potential entrants is useful in predicting entry into markets with differing characteristics. The technical and demand-side characteristics of drugs in a generic pharmaceutical firm's portfolio determine which markets it is most likely to enter. The more experience a firm has with the form, therapy, or ingredient that characterizes an entry opportunity, the more likely it is to enter that market. Lower costs due to organizational experience are an example of "capabilities" or "position," commonly used concepts in the strategy literature. I do not find evidence that low costs, or capabilities, transfer across subsidiaries within the corporation. Firms later indicted in the generic scandal have above-normal entry rates during the time they were allegedly bribing FDA officials. Several methods for creating a set of potential entrants are introduced, but the results are robust to methodological variation.

The specialization findings are consistent with the organizational design literature, where there are costs to a generalist strategy (Rotemberg and Saloner, 1994). Supply-side benefits to specialization arise in manufacturing and regulatory cost reductions; demand-side benefits are due to economies of scope in distribution or optimal product-line design. Entrant specialization implies that the generic market is strongly segmented. Standard measures of market share and concentration will miss the more intense interaction some firms have by being specialized in particular types of markets.

I find that markets with more prepatent expiration revenue attract more entry by generic firms, as do markets with more sales to hospitals and those in which the drug treats a chronic condition. The estimated coefficients support the notion that profits per firm decline in the number of entrants. Bresnahan and Reiss's (1987) result that duopoly markets are more than twice as big as monopoly markets is confirmed for this industry, where sunk costs are also present. The simultaneous nature of entry in the industry leads to an additional interpretation of the entry coefficients: specialization is profitable for firms because of the severe risk of low profits in the case of overentry. An examination of the effect of a firm's rank order of entry cost indicates that beliefs about *relative*, rather than absolute, levels of cost may be important in entry decisions.

[21] The vast majority of observations are not entries, so very few observations have estimated index values greater than zero. For the purposes of forming a useful statistic, I define "correctly predicted" observations to be those with an estimated index greater than negative one. The mean index is approximately −2.5.

TABLE 5 Before and After the Generic Scandal
Dependent Variable: *Enter*

	Market Size Estimation No Market with Entry Before Waxman-Hatch	
	Before	After
Firm form match	.0469	.0337
	(.0025)	(.0052)
Firm form match squared	−.00033	−.00022
	(.00003)	(.00005)
Parent form match	−.0049	−.0029
	(.0027)	(.0044)
Firm therapy match	.0649	.0508
	(.0156)	(.0305)
Firm therapy match squared	−.0019	−.0014
	(.0009)	(.0015)
Parent therapy match	−.0004	.0374
	(.0114)	(.0160)
Firm ingredient match	.0673	.0388
	(.0227)	(.1668)
Parent ingredient match	.0532	−.2942
	(.0303)	(.2385)
Firm family match	.2153	1.323
	(.0688)	(.3824)
Parent family match	.0585	1.793
	(.1098)	(.6719)
Difference from recent portfolio revenue	−3.97E-06	−4.52E-07
	(6.38E-07)	(5.87E-07)
Difference from recent hospital share	−1.10	−.6989
	(.134)	(2.811)
Firm implicated in scandal	.168	—
	(.078)	
LnRevenue	−.8821	−.4635
	(.1519)	(.3586)
Squared LnRevenue	.0425	.0217
	(.0088)	(.0189)
LnHospitalRevenue	.3232	.1188
	(.0320)	(.0648)
Chronic	−.6354	−.6225
	(.3416)	(.8677)
*LnRev*Chronic*	−.0697	.0642
	(.0332)	(.0744)
Second Strength Revenue	−4.70E-07	2.08E-06
	(1.14E-06)	(1.22E-05)
Constant	−.2112	−.9474
	(.6383)	(1.671)
Observations	23,623	4,568
$\phi(\text{mean}X*\beta)$	.008	.009

I am unable to make any conclusions about the efficiency of entry decisions in this industry. Because generic firms have no incentive to exit when there is overentry, there is no method for a researcher to identify out-of-equilibrium outcomes. Production data for each generic manufacturer would be necessary to determine which firms are participating in the market, and this is not commonly available.

The generic scandal caused fewer firms to enter a market of any given size due to regulatory delay and increased risk. The priorities of the FDA changed, so the prescandal model fits the postscandal data less well. Secondly, the drop in the coefficients on revenue differences and hospital market share differences suggests that firm strategies changed; firms began branching into markets that differed from their previous products. These results are consistent with the breakdown of entry expectations because of legal and regulatory upheaval.

Appendix

■ This Appendix contains additional details of how the data in this article were constructed. I use ANDA approvals granted from 1984–1994 provided by the FDA under the Freedom of Information Act. I do not include ANDAs filed for a "bulk" product, an intermediate step en route to the final pharmaceutical product. Also, a separate ANDA is required for each concentration, for each packaging type in the case of injectables, and sometimes for different manufacturing plants. I compare observations to locate and remove the duplicate ANDAs in my dataset, keeping the application with the earliest submission date. Eighteen markets are missing revenue data, so there are 345 markets in most regressions. I recode the FDA's detailed form and route descriptions into five basic categories according to the type of machinery needed to manufacture a drug with certain characteristics and the cleanliness standards required in the manufacturing facility. The first category is oral solid, which forms the bulk of the observations in the data. The second group is injectable drugs, the third is topical preparations, the fourth is oral liquids, and the fifth is ocular drugs. The sixth category is "other," which only contains an aerosol preparation.

I add information on the firm's primary type of product (brand or generic) and the parent of the applicant (if it exists). A drug's therapeutic class is assigned according to the "indications" in the 1993 volume of *Physician's GenRx*. There are approximately thirty therapeutic categories in the dataset. I also include the date that legal restrictions on entry into the drug expire. Simply including the last patent expiration date is not a good method because, first of all, there are usually several patents in force and it is not obvious to the uninformed observer which is the binding patent. Also, the FDA may have extended exclusivity rights due to excessive approval times, or it may have granted an exclusivity period for a new route or dosage form, among other innovations. I resolved cases where the published dates for these restrictions did not match the entry pattern by telephoning patent lawyers at the firm in question.

A few products have multiple concentrations with different patent expiration dates; those products appear more than once in the dataset because the concentrations are effectively separate markets. In one case, the additional strength was not approved until years after generic entry, so when applying, generic firms might not have known of its existence. In all other cases, the brand's version of the late concentration was approved before the first patent expired, so potential entrants were aware of total future market size. IMS (a large pharmaceutical data-collection firm) Drugstore and Hospital Audits of the appropriate year provided the revenue data. Some approved ANDAs are for drugs that had their first generic entry before the Waxman-Hatch Act passed. For these drugs I record total revenue in 1984, both brand and generic.

The unit of analysis for *potential* cases of entry is the firm-opportunity, defined by a firm name and a drug about to experience patent expiration. For all the methods described below, potential entrants are assumed to decide if they want to enter or not at the time of the first entrant's ANDA submission date. All firms (123) and drugs (363) that show up in any ANDA approved from 1984–1994 are interacted (once each) to form a large dataset of all possible firm*drug combinations. I employ this methodology a second time by using the parent company as the firm unit rather than using the subsidiary.

The datasets created by the first method include "firm-opportunities" in years when the firm has not yet come into existence. Of the firms active at the beginning of the sample, only about half are active at the end. Some of the lack of approvals is due to the scandal, but there seems to have been substantial creation and destruction of generic manufacturing firms over the period. Therefore, a generous definition of potential entrant, such as the one above, may be appropriate.

The second potential entrant dataset I experiment with limits firms to considering entry into markets that open *after* they have submitted an ANDA for something else. The final, and most restrictive, method of constructing potential entrants allows only firms with experience with the particular form in question to be potential entrants. For all methods of constructing potential entrants, information about NDAs and ANDAs approved before 1984 must be matched to existing firms; this is the stock of products. I record the portfolios of all generic firms in the dataset and the portfolios of all "brand" firms in the same corporate entity as a generic firm in the dataset. These observations are added to the 1984–1994 flow of entries (and potential entries).

Some observations cannot be used in the estimation, but they are kept in the dataset so that the portfolios are complete. These observations mostly have irregular regulatory or restriction information. For example, there are a few ANDAs that have a reported application date *later* in time than the approval date. According to the FDA, this happened because a firm had to withdraw an ANDA to meet a new standard and the official resubmission date then ended up being after the approval to make the drug had been granted. Other unused observations are those where the applicant primarily manufactures branded drugs but has also applied for one or more ANDAs; such a manufacturer could have many reasons to enter a market that are beyond the scope of this article. Applications received before November 1984 are not used for estimation, since the new regulatory regime had not yet started.

If a firm submits an application six months or more after the first approval for the drug has been granted, I define its entry decision to be "late," rather than a decision made simultaneously with other firms. Approximately 400 entries in the dataset are "late." If the late entrant does not submit its application after more than three-quarters of all final applicants enter and not more than two years after the first entrant, I add it to the set of on-time entrants. The results use data excluding only very late observations.

The past experience of the firm is compared to the current application opportunity by matching values for the current opportunity's therapeutic class, specific ingredients, drug family, and manufacturing form with those same characteristics of drugs in the firm's portfolio. I define a drug "family" to be closely related drugs that cannot be classified as the same thing—two iron compounds, for example, or the five or six different kinds of erythromycin. A family match is a slightly weaker version of an ingredient match. The match variables are simple counts of the number of different drugs in a firm's portfolio that share a characteristic with the current entry opportunity. For example, if a firm has the option to make a pill and it has made 25 pills before (according to its portfolio data), then the value of the "form match" variable will be 25.

A particular problem is keeping track of the changes in firm names and ownership of an ANDA over the 12-year sample period. Simple name changes were easily tracked and accounted for. The portfolios of firms that merged were adjusted to create a combined postmerger portfolio. The remaining changes in ownership appear to be genuine transfers of an ANDA from one firm to another. There are about 50 of these observations in the dataset.

To allow the subsidiary or the parent firm to make decisions, I create variables based on both the applicant name and the parent firm. A parent match variable is clearly one each time the equivalent variable for the subsidiary is one; if subsidiary B has made a particular form before, then, in looking across all drugs belonging to parent B, we will find a match on form also. Ideally, one wants the parent match variable to take the value one only if, for example, a particular form is *not* made at the firm level but *is* made somewhere else in the corporate organization. I subtract the number of firm matches from the number of parent matches to find the net impact of parent organizations. In the same way, family matches are corrected by subtracting ingredient matches, since the latter is a subset of the former.

None of the firms indicted in the scandal has an approval after the scandal breaks. *Difference from Hospital Share* is the absolute value of the difference between the current opportunity's share of revenues from hospitals and the equal-weighted average of that variable in the firm's recent portfolio. I do not have the hospital share information for older portfolio drugs, so they are not included in the measure. The earliest entry opportunity has no portfolio characteristic to be compared to; the variable is given a zero value for these observations. *Difference in Revenue* is defined analogously: the absolute value of the difference between the current entry opportunity's revenue and that of the firm's recent portfolio.

I also construct Herfindahl indices for all the firms in the dataset over therapeutic classes and the FDA's definition of form. All a firm's products (portfolio and new entry) are included with equal weights. There are 12 main FDA form categories and 37 main therapeutic categories. I bias the statistic against my hypothesis by excluding form and therapy categories that have very few observations. The Herfindahl one would expect to see if a firm's products were evenly distributed in every category is .083 and .027 respectively. Instead, we find that even a firm with more than 100 products in its portfolio has Herfindahl values of, on average, .75 and .07 ($N = 8$). Firms with more than 12 products have average Herfindahls of .60 and .14 ($N = 91$), which are much higher than the evenly distributed statistic.

References

BERRY, S.T. "Estimation of a Model of Entry in the Airline Industry." *Econometrica*, Vol. 60 (1992), pp. 889–917.

BOLTON, P. AND FARRELL, J. "Decentralization, Duplication, and Delay." *Journal of Political Economy*, Vol. 98 (1990), pp. 803–826.

BRESNAHAN, T.F. AND REISS, P.C. "Do Entry Conditions Vary Across Markets?" *Brookings Papers in Economic Activity* (1987), pp. 833–871.

——— AND ———. "Empirical Models of Discrete Games." *Journal of Econometrics*, Vol. 48 (1991), pp. 57–81.

CAVES, R.E., WHINSTON, M.D., AND HURWITZ, M.A. "Patent Expiration, Entry, and Competition in the U.S. Pharmaceutical Industry." *Brookings Papers on Economic Activity* (1991), pp. 1–48.

CHRISTENSEN, L.R. AND CAVES, R.E. "Cheap Talk and Investment Rivalry in the Pulp and Paper Industry." *Journal of Industrial Economics*, Vol. 45 (1997), pp. 47–73.

DIXIT, A. AND SHAPIRO, C. "Entry Dynamics with Mixed Strategies." In L.G. Thomas, ed., *The Economics of Strategic Planning*. Lexington, Mass: Lexington Books, 1986.

FRANK, R.G. AND SALKEVER, D.S. "Generic Entry and the Pricing of Pharmaceuticals." *Journal of Economics and Management Strategy*, Vol. 6 (1997), pp. 75–90.

KELLER, K.L. *Strategic Brand Management: Building, Measuring, and Managing Brand Equity*. Upper Saddle River, N.J.: Prentice-Hall, 1998.

ROTEMBERG, J.J. AND SALONER, G. "Benefits of Narrow Business Strategies." *American Economic Review*, Vol. 84 (1994), pp. 1330–1149.

SCOTT MORTON, F. "Brand Advertising, Barriers to Entry, and Generic Entry in the U.S. Pharmaceutical Market." *International Journal of Industrial Organization*, forthcoming.

SHERMAN, R. AND WILLETT, T. "Potential Entrants Discourage Entry." *Journal of Political Economy*, Vol. 75 (1967), pp. 400–403.

WIGGENS, S. AND MANESS, R. "Price Competition in Pharmaceuticals: The Case of Antiinfectives." Mimeo, Texas A&M, 1995.

[15]

Generic Entry and the Pricing of Pharmaceuticals

Richard G. Frank
Harvard University
Boston, MA 02115

David S. Salkever
Johns Hopkins University
Baltimore, MD 21205

During the 1980s the share of prescriptions sold by retail pharmacies that was accounted for by generic products roughly doubled. The price response to generic entry of brand-name products has been a source of controversy. In this paper we estimate models of price responses to generic entry in the market for brand-name and generic drugs. We study a sample of 32 drugs that lost patent protection during the early to mid-1980s. Our results provide evidence that brand-name prices increase after generic entry and are accompanied by large decreases in the price of generic drugs.

1. Introduction

Since the passage of the Waxman-Hatch Act in 1984 there has been a dramatic increase in entry of generic drugs into markets for pharmaceutical products. The Waxman-Hatch Act eased the testing requirements for entry by generic drugs. This legislation, accompanied by the expiration of patents on a large number of high-sales-volume brand-name drugs, is altering the competitive dynamics of the pharmaceutical marketplace. During the 1980s the share of prescriptions sold by retail pharmacies that were accounted for by generics roughly doubled. The price response of brand-name drugs was surprising and remains con-

The authors are grateful to Ernie Berndt and Judy Wagner for providing data and advice for this analysis. Marissa Domino provided expert research assistance. Dr. Albert Wu assisted us in classifying clinical conditions, and we thank him for that help. Useful comments were received from Zvi Griliches, Alison Keith, Alan Garber, two anonymous referees, and participants in seminars at the NBER Summer Institute, the 2nd D.V.A. Industrial Organization and Health Conference, the NBER Productivity Workshop, the Department of Statistics, and the Department of Health Care Policy at Harvard University.

Journal of Economics & Management Strategy, Volume 6, Number 1, Spring 1997, 75–90

troversial (Office of Technology Assessment, 1993). Prices for drugs were observed to rise in response to generic entry (see for example Grabowski and Vernon, 1992). At the same time, these conclusions were questioned by recent empirical analyses (Wiggins and Maness, 1994). In their analysis of the market for antiinfective drugs they found a response to entry that is consistent with the predictions of traditional market models: pioneer (or brand-name) price declines as entry expands. In this paper we estimate models of price responses to generic entry in the markets for generic and brand-name drugs for a broad sample of drugs that lost patent protection between the years 1979 and 1987.

The price models estimated below examine the experiences of 32 drugs that faced generic competition for the first time during the mid 1980s. We make use of information on transactions prices paid by retail pharmacies. All the drugs studied experienced significant entry by generics during the first few years off patent. Our results provide evidence that brand-name prices increase after entry but are accompanied by large decreases in the price of generic products. The net effect is a reduction in the average price of a prescription for an off-patent drug.

The paper is organized into five sections. The second section takes up some theoretical considerations for the empirical model of prices and examines existing evidence on price responses to entry from the literature. The empirical implementation of the pricing models is described in the third section. The fourth section presents estimation results. A discussion of the implications of the findings appears in the fifth and final section of the paper.

2. Background

2.1 Theoretical Considerations

The theoretical point of departure for the empirical models estimated below is the model of Frank and Salkever (1992). Their model was developed to explain the positive correlation between generic entry and brand-name price levels. In that analysis the demand side of the market for a particular drug is conceived as consisting of two major segments, one that is price-insensitive and a second that is price-sensitive. The insensitive component might consist of the patients of physicians in fee-for-service practice, and the sensitive component of prescriptions filled on behalf of enrollees in HMOs and patients in hospitals. Entry of generics leads price-sensitive buyers to shift to generics, leaving only price-insensitive buyers to purchase brand-name products. This causes the brand-name producers' demand function to shift inward and to become less elastic, allowing the profit-maximizing brand-name firm to raise its price.

The model posits that brand-name drug manufacturers behave as von Stackelberg price leaders. That is, a brand-name drug producer is a dominant firm that makes its profit-maximizing pricing decisions taking account of the reaction to its pricing choices in the generic market. Producers of generic versions of brand-name products are viewed as fringe firms playing a Nash-Cournot noncooperative game. Each firm takes the brand-name producer's price and the behavior of rival generic producers as given in making its profit-maximizing pricing decision. The implications of this model for empirical analyses are several:

1. The price equation for generic product price can be written as

$$P_g^* = P_g^*(n, P_b), \tag{1}$$

where P_g^* is the equilibrium price of a generic product, n is the number of generic producers, and P_b is the brand-name producer's price.

2. The price equation for brand-name price can be written as

$$P_b = P_b(n, w), \tag{2}$$

where w is a vector of input prices. The reduced-form brand-name price equation suggests that generic entry affects price through the effect of generic price on brand-name demand. Frank and Salkever (1992) show that $dP_b/dn < 0$ unless entry increases brand-name demand, marginal costs are decreasing, or entry makes the demand curve less elastic (steeper). There is little support for the first two conditions in the empirical literature (OTA, 1993; Comanor, 1986; Scherer, 1993). Thus, we posit that a positive partial correlation between n and P_b would primarily reflect the impact of generic entry on the brand-name demand curve.

2.2 Evidence from the Literature

Three recent empirical analyses have estimated dP_b/dn and have arrived at substantially different conclusions. Grabowski and Vernon (1992) examined the effect of generic entry on prices for 18 high-sales-volume pharmaceutical products that were first exposed to generic competition during the years 1983 through 1987. For each drug the authors examined prices prior to entry and prices 1 year following generic entry. They specified regression models that had as the dependent variable the ratio of generic to brand-name price and three independent variables: (1) the number of generic-product sellers, (2) the total dollar volume of sales in the market for the chemical, and (3) a time dummy variable. The estimated coefficient for the effect of the number of generics on the ratio of generic to brand-name price was negative and significantly different from zero. This result is consistent with the descriptive information reported by Grabowski and Vernon (1992) showing brand-name prices rising relative to generic prices subsequent to generic entry.

Caves et al. (1991) are concerned that simple pre–post-entry brand-name price comparisons or simple regression of price on number of generic entrants may lead to underestimates of the downward impact on prices that generic entry may really have. They suggest that other omitted factors may have caused brand-name prices to rise over time. Specifically, they argue that after 1982 the producer price index (PPI) for pharmaceutical rose sharply relative to indices of labor and material costs.[1] The authors therefore take great pains to minimize the effect from unobservable time-varying factors that might be responsible for the types of results reported by Grabowski and Vernon (1992).

Caves et al. (1991) studied the experience of 30 drugs that went off patent between 1976 and 1987. The drugs studied represent all drugs in therapeutic classes where "important" drugs lost their patent protection. In the regression models of brand-name prices reported by Caves et al., more than 50 individual intercepts were included to account for each of the year–therapeutic-category combinations in their data. The regression results therefore represent an analysis of deviations in individual drug prices from the therapeutic-category–year-group average changes in each year. The regression model also included time-related dummy variables, a linear time trend, and a quadratic time trend in order to capture discontinuities in price behavior around the time of patent expiration.

The measure of generic entry used in the model was the number of amended new-drug applications for marketing of a new chemical entity; actual entry was not directly measured. In some specifications entry was treated as endogenous. The estimated regressions found that initial entry by generic products led to reductions in brand-name price of about 2%. Entry by 20 generics results in price decreases of 17%. These were viewed as very small price responses to entry. The responses were somewhat larger in markets where the hospital share of sales was larger. Caves et al. (1991) also estimate a regression model

1. Berndt et al. (1990) point out that the PPI was substantially biased in an upward direction. They argue that the reason for this bias is that there were important differences between the PPI sample and the universe of pharmaceutical products.

that was quite similar to the one estimated by Grabowski and Vernon (1992) and obtained very similar results. In view of the enormous complexity of the models estimated by Caves et al., it would be important to understand the sensitivity of their results to the specific model chosen by the authors.

Wiggins and Maness (1994) have recently studied price competition in the market for antiinfectives over the period 1984 to 1990. The antiinfectives studied include 98 compounds. Some of the drugs studied had been off patent for many years (e.g. penicillin), while others more recently became prone to generic competition. Following Caves et al. (1991), Wiggins and Maness include a number of fixed effects to control for unobserved factors that might influence price. The specific fixed effects specified include one set for type of antiinfective, a second set indicating if the product was introduced in a given year, and a third set that was a vector of year-specific dummy variables. The specification used for estimating the model of pioneer brand prices reflected a Cournot formulation and allowed for a nonlinear effect of exogenous entry.

The model was estimated using data on brand-name prices only. The estimated coefficients showed that market entry by generics results in significant reductions in the price of antiinfective products. The entry by other brand-name products was estimated to lower price, but was significant only at the 10% level. Descriptive information reported by Wiggins and Maness (1994) suggests that there are three observations in the data where there are few (or zero) entrants accompanied by high prices (Panel C, Fig. 2). They speculate as to why their results differ from other studies; they offer sample size and use of fixed effects as two explanations. They also suggest, as do other students of the pharmaceutical industry, that antiinfectives have followed a different pattern from the larger universe of pharmaceutical products (Scherer, 1993; OTA, 1993). It is therefore important to use a large sample with careful attention to unmeasured factors to determine the extent to which analyses based solely on data from the antiinfective market generalizes to the industry.

3. Empirical Implementation

The empirical analysis of pharmaceutical pricing reported below estimates parameters for models of both brand-name and generic products. These empirical models correspond to equations (1) and (2) discussed above. The unit of observation in these models is either the brand-name compound-year or the generic compound-year. We make use of a data set that consists of drugs that first faced competition during the period 1984–1987. The econometric models estimated include both single-equation models where the number of competitors is treated as exogenous [such as in the work of Grabowski and Vernon (1992) and Wiggins and Maness (1994)] and two-stage least-squares models where the number of competitors is endogenous.

3.1 Data

Between 1984 and 1987, 83 compounds faced generic competition for the first time. All these drugs lost patent protection between 1979 and 1987. From this group of products, drugs were eliminated if (1) they became over-the-counter products that no longer required a prescription for purchase (e.g. ibuprofen), (2) they were combination products, or (3) they were not sold to drugstores in quantity (these include injectibles and infusibles, which account for a very small part of the outpatient market). After applying the above exclusion criteria, 45 drugs remained in the sample.[2]

Several of the drugs reported zero sales during the 1980s and were thus eliminated from the data base, reducing the sample to 41 compounds. Antibiotics were eliminated from the sample due to the complicated licensing arrangements that exist in this area, which made defining entry and patent loss hazardous. The resulting sample of drugs for analysis was 32.[3] Because generic entry occurred unevenly during the 1984–1987 period, the panel data set is unbalanced. It also means that some chemical entities were counted more often than others. These features of the data set support the adoption of the fixed-effects estimator for the price equations discussed below.

Information on dollar sales volume, unit sales volume, and generic market share were obtained from IMS America Inc.'s MIDAS system using the United States Drugstore and Hospital data base for the years 1980 through 1991. According to IMS, in 1986 these data covered 98% of pharmaceutical sales in the U.S. data on years for which a name brand was sold prior to patent loss; they included the market entry date for generics, number of nonoriginator firms, and whether drugs are used primarily to treat chronic, acute, or subacute conditions. The definitions of key variables and their data sources are listed on

2. The data on volume and prices of drugs were originally collected by Stephen Schondelmeyer on behalf of the U.S. Office of Technology Assessment. We are grateful to Judy Wagner for making these data available to us.

3. The drugs included in the analysis had average sales of $80 million in the year prior to patent loss.

TABLE I.
DESCRIPTION OF VARIABLES

Variable	Definition	Mean (SD)
NMFT	Number of generic entrants (source: USP DI and Orange Book)	3.62 (5.29)
Mkt Age	Age of market in terms of time the brand-name product was sold (source: Paul deHaen International)	13.78 (7.73)
Yrs Off	Years since the patent expired (source: FDA and telephone contact with originator firm)	1.35 (2.01)
P_G	Average revenue per generic extended unit (source: IMS)	0.15 (0.15)
P_B	Average revenue per brand name extended unit (source: IMS)	0.29 (0.21)
QPre	Number of extended units sold before patent loss	0.36×10^6 (0.55×10^6)

Table I. All data were aggregated to the year level from quarterly reports of sales.

The main dependent variables in the analyses reported here are the average transactions revenue per extended unit of a drug. An extended unit is defined as the most basic unit measure of volume for a given product, such as a capsule, or a gram for drugs sold by weight. The extended unit varies by product. Thus, the dependent variable is the manufacturer dollar sales based on transactions data divided by the number of extended units.[4] For generics the dependent variable is the sum of generic sales (across producers) divided by the sum of extended units sold. The main right-hand-side variable of interest in this analysis is the number of generic sellers in the market (NMFT). This variable was constructed by using information from the USP DI (or Orange Book) for 1987, 1990, and 1991. The variable NMFT is the number of nonoriginator drug sellers in the market in each year after patent expiration.

3.2 ESTIMATION

In order to estimate the impact of generic entry on market prices, three sets of models were estimated for the prices of brand-name and generic drugs. We first estimate single-equation fixed-effects models where

4. All dollar sales figures were deflated by the CPI All-Items Index.

NMFT is treated as exogenous.[5] In this model we make use of time and compound specific fixed effects to control for unobserved secular trends (e.g. input prices) and time invariant (compound specific) unobservables. The second specification relaxes the assumption that NMFT is exogenous. Following Caves et al. (1991), we use the amount of time off patent as one instrument. A two-stage least-squares fixed-effects estimator is used for this model.

The identifying assumption in our fixed-effects models with NMFT endogenous is that the number of generic competitors is influenced by the passage of time but there is no systematic time trend in demand for the drug. Since the coefficient NMFTHAT in the second-stage price regression is exactly identified in this case, we cannot test this identifying restriction. Previous research suggests, however, that this assumption may be reasonable, at least for a small number of years following initial generic entry. In particular, earlier research suggests that when advertising stock is held constant, market age increases demand for the drug; but it also suggests that advertising stock declines with time as generic entry continues (Caves et al., 1991). The offsetting impact of these two time-trend effects on demand lends supports to our identifying assumption.

The third model also makes use of a two-stage estimator. In this specification we include an indicator of market size and the age of the market as well as the time off patent as an instrument in the first stage. Market size is measured as the sales in the year prior to patent expiration. Market size per se should not be related to price, but may make entry more or less attractive. The age of the market is another instrument. Since these two variables are time-invariant, we used a random-effects estimator instead of the fixed-effects model. In the second stage a fixed-effects estimator is used.[6] The Hausman test led to a rejection of the consistency of the random-effects estimator in the second stage in all specifications.

4. Results

4.1 Descriptive Findings

Figure 1 shows the behavior of brand-name prices subsequent to market entry by generic producers. The vertical axis measures the current brand-name price relative to the prepatent price. The horizontal axis

5. Of particular concern are trends in shifting market composition. For example, enrollment in managed care plans grew during the period. The time fixed effects were introduced to allow for these trends.

6. It is worth noting that we estimate two versions of the first-stage random-effects model.

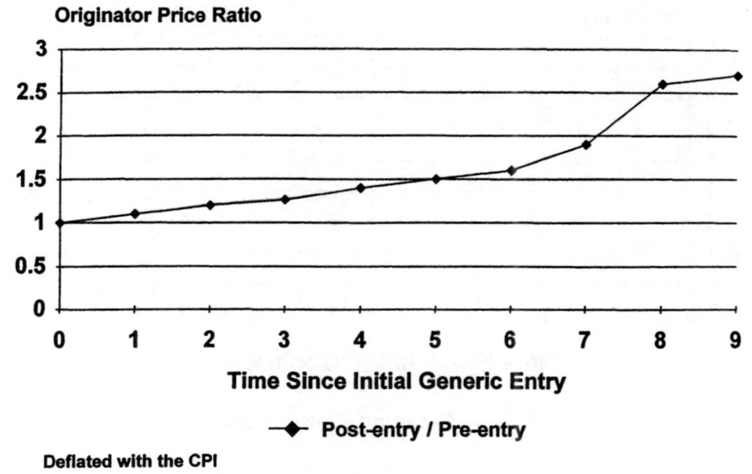

FIGURE 1.

measures the time, in years, since the initial entry into the market by generics. Note that the data suggest an upward drift in real brand-name prices. These data are consistent with the observations made by Grabowski and Vernon (1992). The figure shows a 50% rise in brand-name price five years after generic entry. The trend runs counter to the notion that brand-name producers engage in vigorous price competition with generic entrants. Figure 2 offers a analogous view of the behavior of generic prices during the period following initial market penetration. Note that three years after generic entry generic prices are less than 50% of the brand-name price. These data are supportive of the view that the generic market represents a highly competitive fringe to the brand-name drug market.

Figure 3 presents information on the behavior of generic prices relative to brand-name prices as the number of firms selling a compound increases. The graph in Figure 3 suggests that expanded entry is consistent with a downward drift in the ratio of generic to brand-name price. The relationship is not monotonic as the time path of prices was. This indicates that the timing of entry by generics does not occur continuously over time. Figure 4 shows the number of generic entrants in relation to the years since patent protection was lost. The graph reflects the fact that on average about five generic producers enter a market during the first postpatent year of the brand-name product.

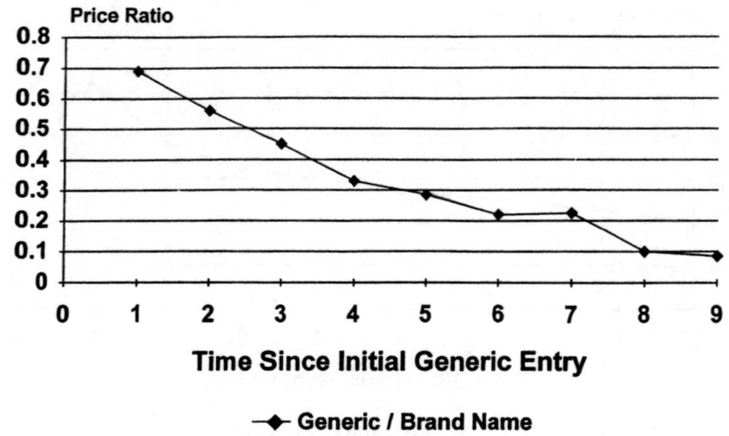

FIGURE 2.

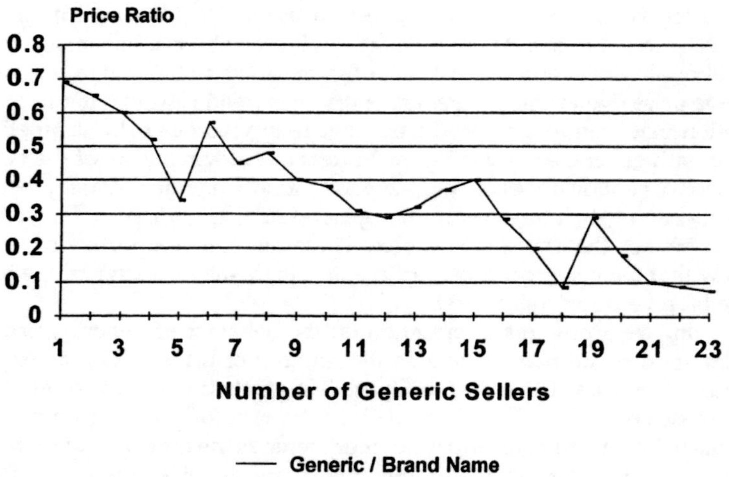

FIGURE 3.

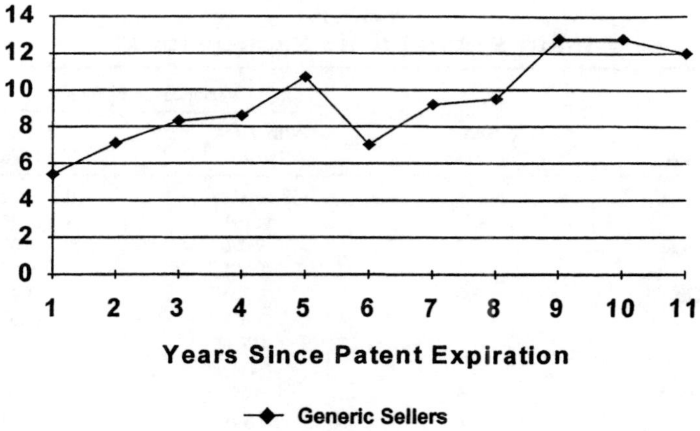

FIGURE 4.

During the subsequent three years entry is considerably slower, with three additional generic producers entering on average. These data are consistent with robust competition in the market for generic products.

4.2 Econometric Estimates

In this section we present the results from our econometric models of pharmaceutical prices. We begin by examining the estimates for our reduced-form model of the number of generic entrants into the market for specific compounds subsequent to loss of patent protection. Table II reports one fixed-effects and two variance-components regressions for the number of generic entrants (NMFT). The first column reports the fixed-effects estimates. The likelihood-ratio tests indicate that both the time and compound specific fixed effects are significantly different from zero (240.69 and 338.62 respectively). The coefficient estimate for the variable Yrs Off is significantly different from zero. The magnitude of the coefficient implies that for each year after patent loss there is about one additional entrant into the market for a particular drug.

The random-effects regressions are presented in the second and third columns of Table II. Two specifications are presented, with and without a linear time trend. The pre-patent-loss brand-name level of sales of the drug is included as a proxy for the size of the market for the compound. The results reported in the second column suggest that the pre-patent-loss sales are significantly associated with higher levels

TABLE II.
FIRST-STAGE ENTRY REGRESSIONS[a]

		Variance Components	
Variable	Fixed Effects	With Time Trend	Without Time Trend
QPre	—	0.53×10^{-5}	0.51×10^{-5}
	—	(4.09)	(4.05)
Mkt Age	—	0.020	0.026
		(0.20)	(0.27)
Yrs Off	0.900	0.734	1.475
	(5.13)	(1.80)	(9.62)
Time	—	0.750	—
	—	(1.85)	—
Constant	4.588	−3.693	1.041
	(9.40)	(1.23)	(0.68)
N	179	179	179

[a] Dependent variable: NMFT (*t* statistic in parentheses).

of subsequent generic entry. The number of years for which the brand-name drug was sold had no significant relation to entry.[7] The measure of years off patent shows that for each year off patent there is on average one new entrant.

The results reported in the third column are qualitatively similar. The estimated coefficient for years off patent varies across the models from 0.734 to 1.45. The fixed-effects result lies between the other two specifications. The rather strong estimates for the time-trend effect in Table II suggest that the entry process has become substantially easier over the time period studied. This is consistent with the objectives of the Waxman-Hatch Act.

Table III reports the estimates for the brand-name price regressions. Recall that these estimates are all based on fixed-effects models that include separate intercepts for each compound and each year. The first column of Table III reports regression results for a model where the number of generic competitors is assumed to be exogenous. Unobserved factors that affect both entry and brand-name price are posited to be accounted for by the fixed effects. In that model the brand-name price is estimated to be positively and significantly associated with the

7. Recall that this variable is time-invariant, so that it is excluded from the first-stage fixed-effects model.

TABLE III.
BRAND-NAME PRICE REGRESSION[a]

Variable	Fixed Effects	TS Fixed Effects[b]	TS Fixed Effects[c]
NMFT	0.007	—	—
	(2.25)	—	—
NMFTHAT	—	0.011	0.016
	—	(2.97)	(3.96)
Constant	−1.487	−1.479	−1.486
	(101.97)	(95.12)	(101.38)
N	343	179	179

[a] Dependent variable: P_B (*t* statistics in parentheses).
[b] First-stage fixed-effects model (column 1 of Table II)
[c] First-stage variance components with time trend (column 2 of Table II)

number of competitors. The parameter estimate suggests that each new entrant is associated with roughly a 0.7% rise in the brand-name price.

The estimated models reported in the second and third columns of Table III each treat the number of competitors as endogenous. Recall that our two-stage estimators rely on rather strong assumptions about the information accounted for by the time trend measured by the time since patent expiration and the demand for brand-name drugs. For this reason the results reported below should be interpreted cautiously. The model in the second column uses a first-stage model that corresponds to the first column of Table II. The third column uses a first-stage model that corresponds to the second column of Table II. The results for the two-stage models indicate considerable stability in the coefficient estimates for the number of competitors. The estimates for both two-stage models of generic entry are significantly different from zero at conventional levels. The range of the estimates is quite small (0.007 to 0.016). It should be noted that the estimates 0.007 and 0.016 are significantly different from one another at close to the 0.05 level. The evidence is therefore consistent with the view that generic entry is linked to an upward drift in brand-name price.[8]

8. We also examined the possibility that drugs used regularly for chronic conditions may display different price dynamics. We therefore interacted a dummy variable representing chronic use with the level of generic competition in our pricing models. In all cases we failed to reject the hypothesis that drugs used for different types of illnesses had different price responses to competition.

TABLE IV.
GENERIC PRICE REGRESSIONS[a]

Variable	TS Fixed Effects[b]	TS Fixed Effects[c]	TS Fixed Effects[d]
NMFTHAT	−0.073	−0.097	−0.102
	(3.83)	(2.58)	(2.49)
P_B	0.074	0.089	0.082
	(0.41)	(0.30)	(0.02)
Constant	−1.480	−1.337	−1.510
	(5.06)	(2.65)	(2.97)
N	154	154	154

[a] Dependent variable: P_G (t statistics in parentheses).
[b] First-stage fixed-effects model.
[c] First-stage variance components with time trend.
[d] First-stage variance components with no time trend.

Table IV reports two-stage fixed-effects generic price regression results. All three specifications treat the number of competitors as endogenous. The coefficient estimates for the variable NMFTHAT are quite consistent across the three specifications. In all cases the coefficient estimates are negative and significantly different from zero at conventional levels. The parameter estimates indicate that with each additional entrant there is a fall in the average price of a generic product of between 5.6% and 7.2%. Thus on moving from the sample mean of about 3 competitors to 6 competitors there is a reduction in prices of between 17% and 22%. The coefficient estimate for the brand-name price was estimated to be consistently positive but was never significantly different from zero.[9] This is probably due to the fact that the between-compound variation in brand-name price is considerably greater than the within-variation. Thus, the inclusion of compound-specific fixed effects may lead to the imprecision in the coefficient estimate for the brand-name price variable.[10]

9. We tested the exogeneity of the brand-name price variable using a Hausman test and were unable to reject exogeneity of the variable.

10. We recognize the possibility of endogeneity of brand-name price from unique characteristics of markets for specific compounds that are observable to the firm but not the researcher. However, if these features are stable over time, the fixed-effects model should control for them. We also estimated a model where brand-name price was dropped from the models in Table IV. Virtually no change occurred in the NMFTHAT estimates from the specification change.

5. Implications and Conclusions

Pricing in the pharmaceutical industry has often received a great deal of attention from policy makers (U.S. Senate, 1961). Recently questions concerning the competitive dynamics in the industry have resurfaced because of the renaissance in the generic drug industry (Scherer, 1994). In particular, the puzzling rise in the prices of brand-name products subject to generic competition ran counter to simple explanations based on traditional conceptions of competition. These observations have led to a series of theoretical and empirical analyses of pricing in markets for pharmaceuticals. These analyses have reached different conclusions. In the work reported here we examined a sample of drugs with relatively large sales that have recently lost patent protection and faced competition from generics for the first time during the mid-1980s. Our data set represents the experience of drugs in a variety of therapeutic categories (except antibiotics) and reflects drugs that lost patent during the time period where the Waxman-Hatch Act changed the rules governing generic entry.

Our econometric analysis leads us to make several observations regarding price behavior in this market. First, it appears that more competition among generic drug producers is linked to price reductions for those drugs. Second, increased competition from generics is not accompanied by lower prices for brand-name drugs. We found no evidence of brand-name price reductions being associated with entry by generic producers. In fact, the evidence we did uncover is consistent with small price rises being tied to expanded competition. The substantial shift in market share from brand-name to generic producers (40%–50%) along with the significantly reduced price of generic substitutes (25%–30% lower) means that the average price of a prescription for a compound subject to generic competition has fallen.

Two sets of important limitations to our analysis should be noted. First, while a reasonable case can be made for our identification strategy, legitimate challenges to our approach can be made. Therefore the regression results presented on Tables III and IV must be interpreted cautiously. In particular, if the time trend measured by time off patent contains significant demand-side forces, then interpretation of the coefficient NMFTHAT as a pure entry indicator would not be appropriate and thus the positive association of number of competitors and price might be due to shifting demand. It is worth noting that we do not observe large increases in demand for most of the chemicals studied here. A second important limitation is that this study focused on competition at the level of the compound. That is, generics were assumed to compete with brand-name drugs and generic products that were the same chemical compound. Competition among drugs is more complicated than this. HMOs, managed-care organizations, and some physicians make choices among drugs within a therapeutic class. We have not allowed for therapeutic competition in this analysis. Wiggins and Maness did, and that may explain some differences in results between the studies.

In sum, our results are consistent with notions of market segmentation on the demand side between classes of buyers with differing sensitivity to price. The absence of brand-name price reductions accompanying generic competition, alongside large decreases in generic prices associated with increased competition, lends support to these ideas. The stylized facts and the consistency of findings across various econometric specifications suggest that simple market models do not capture price dynamics in this industry. The complexity of competition between brand-name drugs and generics needs to be taken into account with more complex formulations of pricing models in this market and use of more disaggregated data.

References

Berndt, E.R., Z. Griliches, and R.G. Rosett, 1990, "On the Accuracy of Producer Price Indexes for Pharmaceutical Preparations: An Audit Based on Detailed Firm Specific Data," NBER Working Paper 3490, October.

Caves, R.E., M.D. Whinston, and M.A. Hurwitz, 1991, "Patent Expiration, Entry and Competition in the U.S. Pharmaceutical Industry: An Exploratory Analysis," *Brookings Papers on Economic Activity*.

Comanor, W.S., 1986, "The Political Economy of the Pharmaceutical Industry," *Journal of Economic Literature*, September.

Frank, R.G., and D.S. Salkever, 1992, "Pricing Patent Loss and the Market for Pharmaceuticals," *Southern Economic Journal*, October.

Grabowski, H. and J. Vernon, 1992, "Brand Loyalty, Entry and Price Competition in Pharmaceuticals after the 1984 Drug Act," *Journal of Law and Economics*, October.

Office of Technology Assessment, 1993, *Pharmaceutical R&D Costs, Risks and Rewards*, U.S. G.P.O.

Scherer, F.M., 1993, "Pricing, Profits and Technological Progress in the Pharmaceutical Industry," *Journal of Economic Perspectives*, Summer.

Scherer, F.M., 1994, "The Pharmaceutical Industry," Unpublished Manuscript, Harvard University.

U.S. Senate, Subcommittee on Antitrust and Monopoly, 1961, Hearings on the Drug Industry.

Wiggins, S.N. and R. Maness, 1994, "Price Competition in Pharmaceutical Markets," Unpublished Manuscript, Department of Economics, Texas A&M University.

D
Biologics

[16]

The NEW ENGLAND JOURNAL of MEDICINE

Perspective
AUGUST 4, 2011

Developing the Nation's Biosimilars Program

Steven Kozlowski, M.D., Janet Woodcock, M.D., Karen Midthun, M.D., and Rachel Behrman Sherman, M.D., M.P.H.

Biologic products developed over the past three decades and approved by the Food and Drug Administration (FDA) now provide important therapeutic options for a variety of serious clinical conditions (see graph). Therapeutic biologics such as genetically engineered recombinant proteins and monoclonal antibodies represent a large portion of newly approved therapies for conditions such as chronic inflammatory diseases and cancer. Biologic enzyme-replacement therapies provide clinical benefits in previously untreatable genetic disorders. Although typically more structurally complex than the small-molecule drugs more prevalent in today's market, biologics vary in complexity from cellular therapies to small, highly purified proteins. Unfortunately, access to such products may be limited, not infrequently because of their cost.

To improve access, Congress passed the Biologics Price Competition and Innovation (BPCI) Act of 2009, authorizing the FDA to oversee an "abbreviated pathway" for approval of biologics that are "biosimilar" to already-approved products.[1] Utilizing knowledge from the reference products, the abbreviated pathway will eliminate unnecessary (and therefore unethical) testing of biosimilars in animals and humans.

Since 1984, U.S. laws regulating nonbiologic products have allowed an abbreviated approval pathway, permitting the rapid approval of thousands of less expensive generic drugs based on comparisons to reference drugs and dramatically increasing medicines' affordability. In 2009, almost 75% of small-molecule prescriptions dispensed in the United States were for generics, and the approval of a generic drug resulted in average savings of 77% of the product's cost within 1 year. Although cost reductions for biosimilars probably won't be as large, the Federal Trade Commission predicts that their availability will significantly reduce biologics' cost and increase their accessibility.[2]

Reconciling the science of biosimilar development with the new regulatory framework required by the BPCI Act presents the FDA with numerous challenges. First and foremost, the agency must establish scientific criteria that address the key question: how similar is similar enough when it comes to the substitution of complex biologic drug products in clinical practice? The complex structures of biologic products

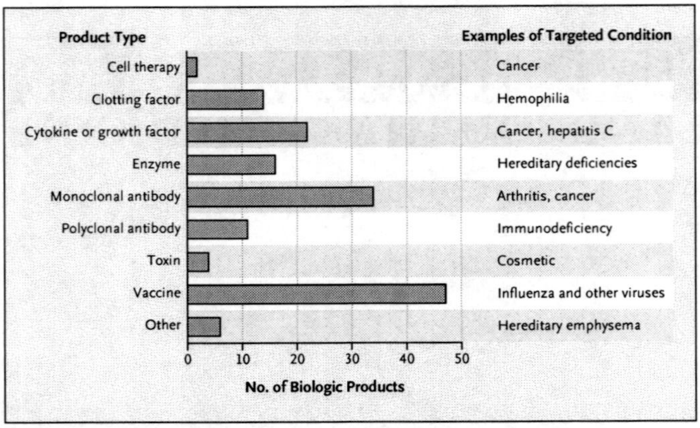

Numbers of FDA-Approved Biologic Products of Various Types Available for Treating or Preventing Various Conditions.

The numbers are based on proper names for therapeutics from the Drugs@FDA Web site and the Center for Biologics Evaluation and Research list of biologics (www.fda.gov). The examples of targeted conditions are general, and specific product indications should be based on product labels.

are usually not easily characterized (see diagram). Generally, therapeutic proteins must have a specific set of structural features (e.g., amino acid sequence, glycosylation, protein folding) essential to their intended effect, and slight modifications can affect their performance in humans. In addition, inadvertent chemical modifications can affect their immunogenicity.

Fortunately, progress in the characterization and understanding of biologics now permits demonstration that some products are highly similar to a reference product. Furthermore, the FDA's experience with biologics provides important relevant knowledge. Since the mid-1990s, for example, physicochemical and functional assays have been used to characterize changes in manufacturing processes for some biologics, and then animal or clinical studies are used to resolve any remaining uncertainties about the comparability of the products created before and after such changes and to provide sufficient confidence that safety and efficacy are not diminished. The FDA also has extensive experience with abbreviated applications for proteins that are regulated as drugs.[3] Moreover, the agency is carefully scrutinizing lessons from the European Medicines Agency (EMA), which published general guidelines on biosimilars in 2005[4] and approved its first biosimilar in 2006. Initial EMA guidance has suggested product-specific requirements for structural, animal, and clinical studies. Given the complex nature of biologics, it's unlikely that a "one size fits all" systematic assessment of biosimilarity can be developed. Instead, FDA scientists will need to integrate various types of information to provide an overall assessment that a biologic is biosimilar to an approved reference product.

The FDA has traditionally relied on integrating various kinds of evidence in making regulatory decisions. Such a "totality of the evidence" approach can also be applied to assessing biosimilars, since it seems possible to exceed a current state-of-the-art analytic characterization by evaluating more attributes and combinations of attributes at greater sensitivities with multiple complementary methods. There may be strategies that allow a "fingerprint"-like identification of very similar patterns in two different products. Such strategies were used in supporting the approval of a generic low-molecular-weight heparin product, enoxaparin — which, though it differs from proteins in important ways, is structurally complex. Although additional animal and clinical studies will generally be needed for protein biosimilars for the foreseeable future, the scope and extent of such studies may be reduced further if more extensive fingerprint-like characterization is used.

The totality-of-the-evidence approach faces several challenges. Developers of biosimilars who intend to match reference products more closely will, for example, need to select appropriate source materials and tune their processes carefully. Current approaches to manufacturing process design and improvements in process analytics may be useful.

To help ensure that any additional animal and human testing is appropriately targeted and that biosimilar development plans are optimally streamlined, studies assessing biosimilarity must be carefully tailored to address residual uncertainty. The recent EMA draft guideline on biosimilar monoclonal antibodies[5] introduces concepts relevant to the design of biosimilarity studies, including the use of populations,

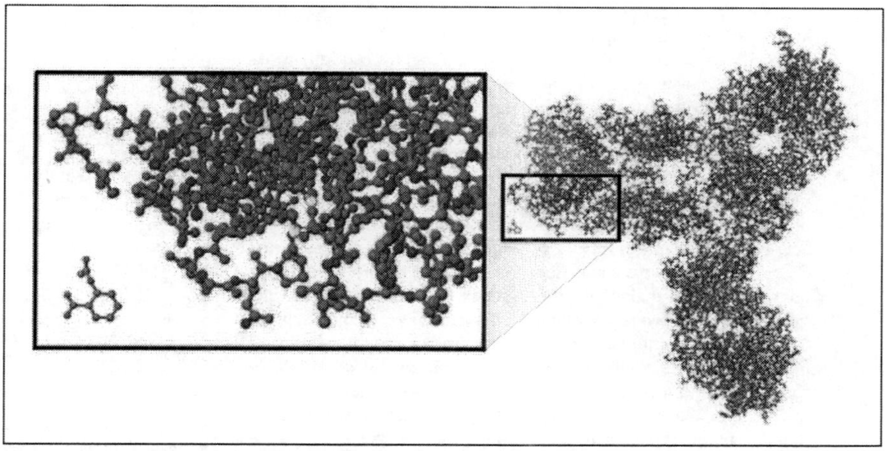

Comparison between a Biologic Monoclonal Antibody and an Aspirin Molecule.
An approximately 800-fold difference in size necessitates magnifying the boxed area to clearly identify the aspirin molecule on the lower left. The antibody structure was taken from the RCSB Protein Data Bank and has the identifier 1HZH.

pharmacodynamic markers, and end points that are sensitive to the potential differences between products. The guideline thus suggests an increasing alignment with the totality-of-the-evidence approach favored by the FDA. This approach, along with the FDA's experience with fingerprint-like characterization of complex products, will be essential in designing a U.S. biosimilars policy that encourages development of biosimilars, emphasizing the use of innovative technologies.

The new pathway will require a new paradigm for sponsor–FDA interactions. To provide the best advice on the scope of any required animal and human studies, the FDA should already have completed an in-depth review of comparative analytic characterization and in vitro data. Although the agency frequently meets with sponsors before they submit investigational new drug applications, a more extensive product review will be required to determine how much additional data are needed for a biosimilar. The FDA is currently considering how such interactions might be structured and how they will affect the user-fee program that Congress has mandated for biosimilars.

The FDA evaluation of biosimilarity must consider the product's complexity, its formulation, its stability, and the usefulness of biochemical and functional characterizations and incorporate these factors into a risk-based approach. The mechanistic understanding of the clinical effect of a biologic and the level of clinical information available about it will also affect the evaluation of risk, and the manufacturing processes may introduce potential variants or impurities that could affect risk. Evaluating biosimilarity with a risk-based approach is scientifically appropriate and familiar to the FDA, whose decisions are commonly based on reducing residual uncertainty to an acceptable level in any given clinical setting.

Immunogenicity remains a critical factor when assessing biosimilarity, and the FDA will evaluate immunogenicity in a risk-based manner. For example, aggregation of proteins may be associated with higher risks of immunogenicity, and the risks related to an immune response are greater with products that stimulate immunity to nonredundant self-proteins, such as erythropoietin.

The FDA process for biosimilars must include product-specific safety monitoring. History suggests that pharmaceutical companies will make manufacturing-related changes to biologics periodically throughout their lifecycles, and even small changes could affect safety or efficacy. Tracking adverse events associated with the use of reference and biosimilar products will be difficult if the specific product or manufacturer cannot be readily identified, and appropriate strategies must be developed to ensure the implementation of robust, modern pharmacovigilance programs for biologics.

Under the BPCI Act, biosimilars will also have the opportunity to meet a higher standard of similarity to a reference product — "interchangeability," reflecting an FDA assessment that pharmacists can make substitutions between biologics without the prescriber's intervention. A biologic will be considered interchangeable with a reference product if the developer demonstrates that it can be expected to produce the same clinical result in any given patient and that the risk associated with alternating or switching between the two products is not greater than that involved in continuing to use the reference product.

The FDA will carefully consider what data will be necessary for this purpose and translate that assessment into effective regulatory standards. The agency will also develop standards to ensure that products not deemed interchangeable are not inadvertently substituted for a reference product without the prescriber's consent. But even without interchangeability, recognition that two products are biosimilar will give clinicians far more information than the mere knowledge that they were developed for the same indication.

Disclosure forms provided by the authors are available with the full text of this article at NEJM.org.

From the U.S. Food and Drug Administration Center for Drug Evaluation and Research (S.K., J.W., R.B.S) and Center for Biologics Evaluation and Research (K.M.), Silver Spring, MD.

1. Biologics Price Competition and Innovation Act, 2009. (http://www.fda.gov/downloads/Drugs/GuidanceComplianceRegulatoryInformation/UCM216146.pdf.)
2. Emerging health care issues: follow-on biologic drug competition. Washington, DC: Federal Trade Commission, 2009. (http://www.ftc.gov/os/2009/06/P083901biologicsreport.pdf.)
3. Woodcock J, Griffin J, Behrman R, et al. The FDA's assessment of follow-on protein products: a historical perspective. Nat Rev Drug Discov 2007;6:437-42.
4. Guideline on similar biological medicinal products. London: European Medicines Agency, 2005. (http://www.emea.europa.eu/pdfs/human/biosimilar/043704en.pdf.)
5. Draft: guideline on similar biological medicinal products containing monoclonal antibodies. London: European Medicines Agency, 2010. (http://www.ema.europa.eu/docs/en_GB/document_library/Scientific_guideline/2010/11/WC500099361.pdf.)

Biosimilars: Policy, clinical, and regulatory considerations

SCOTT GOTTLIEB

Purpose. The regulatory background surrounding biosimilars (biopharmaceuticals that are considered similar in composition to an innovator product, but not necessarily clinically interchangeable); equivalence, interchangeability, and unique considerations associated with biopharmaceuticals; the biopharmaceutical protein production process; scientific facts for use in the policy discussion about biosimilars; the European Union system for biosimilars; and the current status of biosimilars legislation in the United States are described.

Summary. An abbreviated regulatory pathway for the approval of biosimilars, and a process for safely demonstrating the therapeutic interchangeability of these proteins, has the potential to provide meaningful cost savings. This economic advantage to patients can translate into important public health benefits. But to date, no formal regulatory process exists in the United States for bringing these drugs to market. In addition, the current tools for fully characterizing biopharmaceuticals are not—in certain cases—well developed, especially for proteins that have complex structures or are heavily glycosylated. In addition, using "similar" but not completely "identical" proteins interchangeably raises concerns about potentiating immunogenicity. The bottom line is that demonstrating therapeutic equivalence and interchangeability for biosimilars is not a straightforward matter—it cannot be based on the same criteria as for conventional small-molecule drugs. The science, while obtainable, is more complex. For example, it is assumed that showing that a biosimilar protein can be safely used interchangeably with an innovator protein would require, at the least, some limited clinical data and interchangeability studies. Notwithstanding the more complex scientific and clinical issues particular to protein products, most believe that a process for enabling the approval of safe and effective biosimilar proteins is not only possible, but an important public health goal. The European Union system for biosimilars may provide a model for anticipating and resolving the scientific and policy issues related to biosimilars in the U.S. However, biosimilars legislation is unlikely to be passed before the 2008 presidential election.

Conclusion. The legal and regulatory status of biosimilars remains to be resolved in the United States as policymakers address the scientific and policy issues surrounding product manufacturing, patent terms, and clinical use.

Index terms: Biologicals; Economics; Equivalency, therapeutic; European Union; Immunogenicity; Regulations; United States

Am J Health-Syst Pharm. 2008; 65(Suppl 6):S2-8

The legal and regulatory status of biosimilars (biopharmaceuticals that are considered similar in composition to an innovator product, but not necessarily clinically interchangeable) is a health policy issue currently under consideration by the Food and Drug Administration (FDA) and U.S. legislators on Capitol Hill. The establishment of a pathway for enabling the approval of biosimilars through an abbreviated regulatory process, and, in certain cases, for demonstrating their therapeutic equivalence and interchangeability with innovator products (i.e., originator), has the potential to provide meaningful cost savings to healthcare consumers and the government that could translate into public health benefits from improved access.[1] To wit, enabling the approval of follow-on proteins through an abbreviated regulatory process, after the intellectual property on the originator protein has lapsed, could enable price competition between similar products. In addition, the follow-on product could presumably be priced lower than the originator as a consequence of the follow-on product's lower development costs. The ensuing

SCOTT GOTTLIEB, M.D., is Resident Fellow, American Enterprise Institute for Public Policy Research, 1150 17th Street, Washington, DC 20036 (scott.gottlieb@mssm.edu).

Based on the proceedings of a symposium held December 3, 2007, during the 42nd ASHP Midyear Clinical Meeting and Exhibition in Las Vegas, NV, and supported by an unrestricted education grant from Allergan, Inc. Dr. Gottlieb received an honorarium for his participation in the symposium and for the preparation of this article. Dr. Gottlieb reports that he has no relationships pertinent to this activity.

 1079-2082/08/0702-00S2$06.00.
DOI 10.2146/ajhp080210

competition among multiple manufacturers, and additional incentives this will generate for innovators to develop improved versions of existing proteins, could generate still more public health benefits.[1] However, the cost savings probably are not as large as some have estimated. Some current estimates, which envision substantial cost savings, extrapolate from experience with small-molecule generic drugs. This is not an appropriate economic comparison given the scientific and clinical differences between protein and small-molecule drugs. But even smaller cost savings, perhaps on the order of 15–30% off of the cost of an originator protein, could be meaningful. This magnitude of savings mirrors the experience seen in protein drug categories that have benefited from multiple product introductions. As such, it may be a more realistic estimate of the potential savings from biosimilars. This more conservative estimate should not dampen enthusiasm for a thoughtful process for enabling the approval of safe and effective biosimilars proteins. Proponents of the creation of an abbreviated regulatory pathway for FDA approval of biosimilars have every reason to view such a process, and the potential for cost savings, as an important public health goal.

Despite these opportunities, legislation is still needed to create a transparent and predictable pathway for the regulatory approval and marketing of biosimilars. Legislative measures are unlikely to be passed before the 2008 presidential election. This owes to the complexity of the issue as well as continued political debate around key questions among other issues—the appropriate patent terms for innovator products, clinical testing requirements for demonstrating interchangeability, and the regulatory process that should be required before biosimilars products are approved. In particular, there is debate as to whether FDA should be required to delineate up front, presumably in guidance, the agency's requirements for approval of a particular class of biosimilars before approval of the first product. This guidance development process would presumably be modeled after a similar approach currently used in the European Union. Notwithstanding these ongoing policy discussions, the issue of biosimilars is likely to become a priority after the presidential election and could see quick resolution in the form of new legislation creating an approval pathway.

First and foremost, new legislation must balance the need to protect the public health and to provide innovator manufacturers with incentives for product innovation, against the desire for a risk-based regulatory process that does not impose unnecessarily requirements that add substantially to costs while doing little to promote product safety. Most agree that these competing and sometimes overlapping goals can be resolved in carefully planned legislation that has important implications for access, incentives for innovation, and future research and development efforts.[2]

Regulatory background

Legislation is required because currently no regulatory pathway exists for the approval of biosimilars proteins through an abbreviated regulatory process. This stands in contrast to the situation surrounding small-molecule drugs, where the Hatch–Waxman Act creates an abbreviated pathway for the approval of generic chemical drugs. Hatch–Waxman represented a compromise between the need to establish a minimum period of exclusivity for brand name innovator products in order to provide appropriate incentives for innovation and the need to eliminate a backlog of applications for generic drugs after expiration of the patents for innovator products. The law requires generic drug manufacturers to demonstrate bioequivalence to brand name products in healthy subjects, according to well-established FDA regulations and scientific principles, but it allows generic manufacturers to rely on an innovator's clinical efficacy and safety data. The approval process requires that the active ingredients in generic and brand name products are "the same," but the demonstration of therapeutic equivalence and interchangeability through clinical studies is not required. Under Hatch–Waxman, generic products are approved by an Abbreviated New Drug Application (ANDA) and are automatically deemed to be interchangeable with the innovator product unless the FDA specifically states why the newly approved generic product should not be given an AB rating and thus be deemed to be interchangeable.

But Hatch–Waxman legislation does not apply when it comes to protein drugs. For one thing, the relevance of the Hatch–Waxman Act to biopharmaceuticals is limited because it simply does not take into consideration the issues unique to protein drugs. There were no FDA-approved biotechnology drug products approved at the time the Hatch–Waxman legislation was passed. Moreover, no formal scientific framework for evaluating and approving biosimilars has been established to date. From a policy and legal standpoint, Hatch–Waxman is also simply not germane to the vast majority of protein drugs. The FDA approval process for biopharmaceuticals is governed by two different laws and associated pathways, each with different legal standards for approval. A vast majority of biopharmaceuticals are approved through Public Health Service Act (PHS) section 351 and a biologicals license application, although a few biological products (e.g., insulin, some versions interferon, imiglucerase, human growth hormone) are regulated under the Federal Food, Drug, and Cosmetic

Act (FDCA) as a result of historical precedent.[3,4] Hatch–Waxman only applies to drugs approved and regulated under the FDCA, which includes all of the small-molecule drugs. Because some protein drugs like insulin and human growth hormone are regulated under the FDCA, a special provision—called Section 505(b)(2)—has enabled FDA to approve follow-on versions of these proteins through an abbreviated regulatory process. Specifically, Section 505(b)(2) of the FDCA allows FDA to approve a follow-on version of an established drug, after patent expiration, on the basis of efficacy and safety findings for the innovator product, although these products are not considered interchangeable or substitutable. However, there is no analogous process under the Public Health Services Act. For that reason, to enable the approval of biosimilars for the vast majority of protein drugs, new legislation would need to be created that would apply a provision, perhaps similar to the 505(b)(2) process, to drugs regulated under the PHS.

Some point to precedents for how this process might work as a matter of science, as well as policy. Omnitrope (somatropin [rDNA origin]) was approved by FDA through section 505(b)(2) of the FDCA through an expedited process that relied on the finding of efficacy and safety for the innovator product (Genotropin), although the manufacturer of Omnitrope (Sandoz) was required to produce some of its own clinical efficacy and safety data. Nevertheless, Omnitrope is not rated therapeutically equivalent to and therefore is not substitutable for any other FDA-approved human growth hormone product.[5]

While section 505(b)(2) of the FDCA provides some regulatory foundation for how an abbreviated regulatory process for biosimilars could be developed as part of the PHS, the Hatch–Waxman Act (known more formally as the Drug Price Competition and Patent Term Restoration Act of 1984) provides no such insight. As a matter of science and policy, protein drugs are sufficiently dissimilar from small-molecule drugs and require a fundamentally new approach than the pathway contemplated under Hatch–Waxman. In spite of this, there continue to be comparisons made between the Hatch–Waxman process and the desire for a similar "generic" pathway for protein products.[1,6] Biosimilars are unique in many respects, but fundamentally, they contain large, complex, or long-chain proteins, and FDA has limited experience using standard laboratory equipment like mass spectrometry for comparing similar biopharmaceutical products produced through different manufacturing processes, and by different sponsors.[7] For these reasons, and others, the agency has consistently maintained that there are no generic biological products. Even under section 505(b)(2), some formal clinical efficacy and safety studies are typically needed for approval of each product. A new process is needed, one that is uniquely specific to the clinical and scientific attributes of proteins. Such a framework probably will be developed in conjunction with legislation for biosimilars.

Unique considerations around proteins

Biopharmaceuticals present unique clinical and scientific concerns compared with conventional drugs (i.e., small-molecule chemicals) because the active ingredients typically are much larger and more complex. Conventional drugs have fewer molecular ingredients, and most small molecules can be completely characterized on the basis of their chemical structures. By contrast, biotechnology products have many molecular ingredients and often are not fully characterized using evaluative tools alone.[8]

Biologics comprise a wide spectrum of complexity, and so these considerations do not apply equally to all products. Simple and short-chain proteins as well as peptides are relatively easy to compare through laboratory assays, without clinical data. But clinical data may be required for prediction of the therapeutic response to long-chain or heavily glycosylated proteins or those with considerable folding. Along this continuum of complexity of proteins, heavily glycosylated proteins and monoclonal antibodies are among the most difficult products to copy. The need for clinical data to fully characterize the clinical performance of a biosimilar will increase as the complexity of the underlying protein products increases.

Another aspect of a protein drug's complexity emanates from how it is manufactured. Unlike small-molecule drugs, the manufacturing process for protein drugs is inextricably linked to the characteristics and performance of the resulting medicine. Biopharmaceuticals are manufactured in living systems, with the potential for variability in product composition and structure.[2] Small differences in starting materials and production processes can affect the final product. Modification of even one small part of a protein can make it ineffective or unsafe. Rare but serious immunologic effects could occur that are not detected in preapproval testing with existing tools (in the absence of clinical data). Indeed, there is precedent for circumstances in which undetected changes in the manufacturing of an established protein had serious clinical consequences. This experience underscores the complexity of the manufacturing process and its correlation to the clinical behavior of the final protein product. For these reasons, evidence of the integrity and consistency of manufacturing processes is among the significant factors FDA considers in evaluating protein products.[2]

Among the unique safety issues that must be considered, immunogenicity is a major concern with biopharmaceuticals because these products are manufactured in living cells (e.g., hamster, rabbit, or bacterial cells) that are considered foreign by the human body. Administration of biopharmaceuticals bypasses some of the body's natural defenses (e.g., injection directly into a vein traverses the skin) and can therefore result in an immune response and the formation of neutralizing antibodies. The use of scientific tools to evaluate immunogenicity is feasible, but these tools are not available for the full range of biopharmaceuticals. Instead, in many cases, it may be necessary to look at clinical data from switching studies to give assurances against formation of immune reactions. In a switching study, patients are switched between the innovator and the biosimilar protein. Such studies involve the use of assays for detection of neutralizing antibodies and the collection of clinical efficacy and safety data, to make sure subjects had a similar therapeutic outcome to what they would have achieved if they had been continued on just one protein drug and not switched between the innovator and biosimilars product. The data are used to determine whether an immunologic response is generated, whether efficacy and safety are affected by the change in products, and if a biosimilar can be given a labeling claim for interchangeable use with the branded comparator product.

Major unresolved issues of policy

In developing biosimilars legislation, the U.S. Congress and FDA will need to address three major issues: (1) product interchangeability, (2) whether there is a need for formal guidance to delineate the regulatory process for each category of protein drugs prior to the approval of the first biosimilars (this is framed as an issue of regulatory transparency and well as the benefits and rigor of subjecting approval standards to external scrutiny), and (3) data protection (i.e., patent exclusivity).

Decisions about data protection are probably the most contentious of the three issues. Resolution will require a compromise between manufacturers of innovator products, who seek the longest possible patent exclusivity in order to preserve maximum incentives for development and investment, and manufacturers of biosimilars, who seek the shortest possible patent exclusivity in order to enable early competition.

Regarding product interchangeability, therapeutic equivalence and interchangeability for biosimilars cannot be based on the same criteria used for conventional small-molecule chemicals. According to FDA, different large protein products with a similar molecular composition may behave differently in different individuals, and substitution of one product for another could result in serious health outcomes (e.g., a pathologic immune response).[9] To date, the means by which interchangeability can be established for complex protein products has not been determined by FDA, although it is presumed that FDA would articulate a process in guidance or regulation after the passage of legislation addressing the broader issues.[9]

The issue of regulatory transparency deserves greater discussion. Guidance documents will be developed in the future by FDA to address other issues pertaining to not only interchangeability, but also approval standards in specific categories of proteins. The question is whether Congress will direct the agency to develop these guidance documents in advance of biosimilars product approvals, or whether FDA will be given discretion to work internally to design the appropriate regulatory process, and not have to subject these decisions about regulatory architecture to external scrutiny in each instance. Critics of greater transparency worry that an extensive process of guidance development—similar to the process developed in Europe—would slow the introduction of biosimilar proteins in the U.S. since it could take FDA months to years to develop each guidance document. These arguments have some merit, but may also betray some more complicated motives. For example, it is worth noting that the absence of product-specific guidance will inevitably favor large generic drug manufacturers over smaller rivals, since the large firms are more likely to have the resources and relationships to navigate FDA's regulatory requirements in the absence of specific product guidance that explains the agency's requirements. In this regard, the absence of guidance may serve as a barrier to entry for some low cost producers. To these ends, it should be considered whether excluding a requirement for product-specific guidance is a way for large generic firms that have sophistication in dealing with FDA to freeze out of the process some of their smaller, but perhaps lower-cost competitors.

Special considerations around manufacturing

The typical process used to create protein drugs is standardized, but it is sensitive to change. A gene sequence is designed, and the sequence is inserted into a plasmid or viral vector (Figure 1). The vector is then inserted into a specific type of host cell that produces the protein through a process of fermentation. These host cells are grown in a culture and then transferred to large vessels containing culture medium. Nutrients and oxygen are supplied to keep the host cells alive, and temperature, humidity, and pressure are carefully controlled to produce the desired protein at maximum yield. The protein is separated from the culture medium and cellular proteins, and

Figure 1. Typical protein production process.

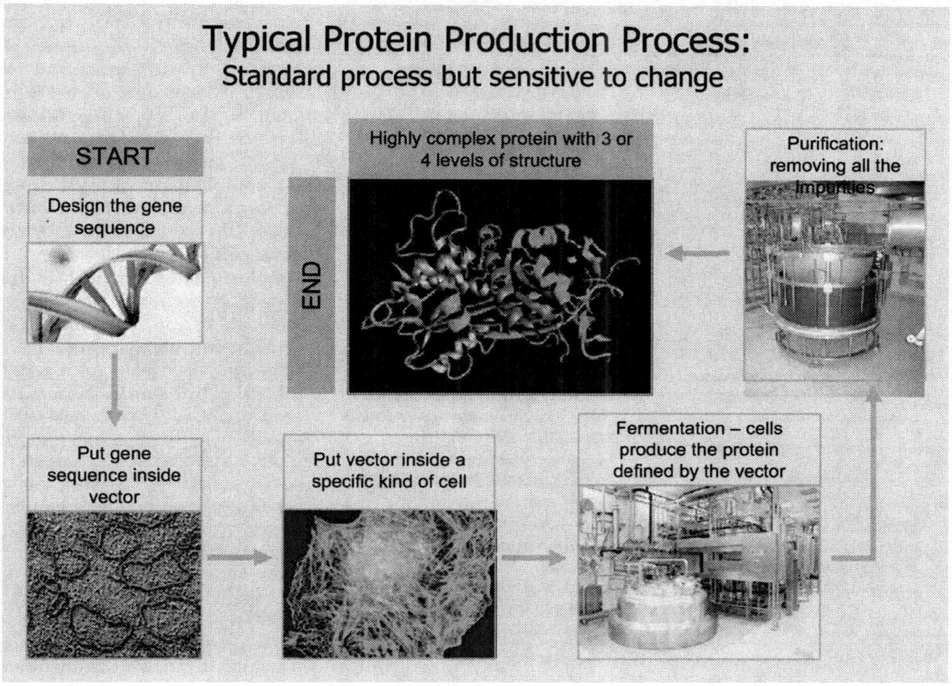

impurities are removed during purification, yielding a highly complex protein. This manufacturing process is elaborate and sophisticated, and it is considered intellectual property.[7] For these reasons, attempts to draft legislation that allows manufacturers of biosimilars to expedite the FDA approval process by engineering around the innovator's manufacturing process have been contentious for manufacturers of innovator products. In addition to the issues of intellectual property, innovator companies argue that the manufacturing process is inextricably linked to the therapeutic qualities of the resulting protein (Table 1).

European Union system as a model

Some believe the European Union system for biosimilars provides a model for anticipating and resolving issues related to biosimilars in the United States. In 1986, the European Union enacted legislation that created a legal basis for approval of "generic" biologicals applications that was similar to the traditional system used in the United States for small-molecule chemical drugs. European authorities realized that the arrangement was inappropriate for biological products. Among other things, there was concern that it provided no assurance that the active substances were the same in biosimilars and innovators. There was also no assurance that published scientific literature relating to innovator products was relevant to biosimilars. The system was abandoned because of concerns about public safety.

The European Union reworked its system for approval of biosimilars, with basic provisions for governing "similar biological medicinal products (biosimilars)" that went into effect in 2003 and remain in place today.[12] Data protection is provided for 10 to 11 years, and a process for making determinations about interchangeability and supporting clinical data

Table 1.
Scientific Facts for Use in the Political Debate about Biosimilars[2,7,10,11,a]

Political Statement	Scientific Facts
Biosimilars are identical to the innovator product that they are designed to match.	Biosimilars may be similar to the innovator, but they are not identical. "It is not expected that the quality attributes ... will be identical," per EMEA guidelines.
Innovator product composition varies from one batch or lot to another.	Batch-to-batch variability is a characteristic of all biological products, including innovators and biosimilars. Variability is unique to each product and carefully restricted by FDA. Limits of acceptable variability are defined by clinical experience.
Laboratory data can predict what will happen in the clinical setting, so clinical data are not needed for biosimilars.	Laboratory tests are not sufficiently sensitive to predict clinical response to biosimilar or innovator products. Clinical data are needed to ensure that the efficacy, safety, and immunogenicity are similar (neither worse nor better) for biosimilars and the innovator.
Manufacturing process changes are made frequently for innovator products without supporting clinical studies.	FDA requires clinical data to support certain manufacturing process changes. Significant manufacturing process changes are supported by clinical study data.

[a]FDA = Food and Drug Administration; EMEA = European Medicines Agency.

requirements was established. The process is different from that used for the approval of generic small-molecule chemical drugs. The European Union system for approval of biosimilars involves a combination of primary and secondary legislation and requirements for a guidance process. Guidance documents with detailed product-specific requirements must be issued through an open public process, with participation by expert committees, national authorities, the scientific community, and industry. Preclinical and clinical research is required for all biological products in Europe. The European Union system for biosimilar approval devotes special attention to immunogenicity concerns and to post-marketing testing and surveillance for safety problems. Biosimilars are not considered "generic" equivalents of innovator products—in other words, they are not assumed to be fully interchangeable. To date, two biosimilars (both human growth hormone products) have been approved and one product (interferon alfa) has been rejected in Europe.[13]

The European experience with biosimilars is of great interest to American policymakers because patents for drugs tend to expire earlier in Europe than in the United States. European manufacturers with expertise in biopharmaceuticals already have begun to seek approval for biosimilars, and the collective experience with biosimilars drugs in Europe could provide a basis for understanding their use in the U.S.

What's next

Multiple bills to address a pathway for approval of biosimilars currently are under consideration in the U.S. House of Representatives and the Senate, although none of these legislative measures appear likely to come up for a final vote and passage before the 2008 presidential election. While the need for biosimilars legislation has been largely accepted by members of the Republican and Democratic parties, several sticking points remain to be resolved, including data protection, interchangeability, and clinical research requirements. Some of these unresolved issues turn on matters of science, but it is data protection that remains perhaps the most profound point of policy disagreement. At one point, members of both parties agreed on 12 years of patent exclusivity. However, lobbyists from the generic drug industry balked at that time frame, hoping that a unified Democratic government after 2008 might be able to shorten the duration of patent exclusivity to 10 or 8 years, thus enabling faster entry of biosimilar products after initial approval of the innovator protein.

As for the FDA's handling of biosimilars products, concerns about safety will remain their primary focus. The agency is likely to take a conservative approach and in some cases, ask for a substantial amount of clinical safety and efficacy data before approving biosimilars, especially for the most complex proteins. Policymakers and clinicians in the United States have the advantage of time in deciding how to best address these issues. There are few biopharmaceutical patents set to expire and few biosimilar products for which approval might be sought in the near future. Scientific information for use in guiding decisions about the approval of biosimilars will continue to evolve in the coming years and might help resolve current issues and better inform our decisions.

Conclusion

The complexities of biopharmaceuticals present U.S. policymakers with a challenge in developing legislation to address the legal and regulatory status of biosimilars. Experience in Europe can provide lessons to guide decision-making.

References

1. Frank RG. Regulation of follow-on biologics. *N Engl J Med.* 2007; 357:841-3.
2. Woodcock J, Griffin J, Behrman R et al. The FDA's assessment of follow-on protein products: a historical perspective. *Nat Rev Drug Discov.* 2007; 6:437-42.
3. Federal Food, Drug, and Cosmetic Act. New drugs. Sec. 505 [21 U.S.C. 355]. www.fda.gov/opacom/laws/fdcact/fdcact5a.htm#sec505 (accessed 2007 Dec 8).
4. Food and Drug Administration. Biological products regulated under section 351 of the Public Health Service Act; implementation of biologics license; elimination of establishment license and product license. www.fda.gov/cber/rules/elapla.pdf (accessed 2007 Dec 8).
5. U.S. Food and Drug Administration. Omnitrope (somatropin [rDNA origin]) questions and answers. www.fda.gov/cder/drug/infopage/somatropin/qa.htm (accessed 2007 Dec 8).
6. Frank RG. The ongoing regulation of generic drugs. *N Engl J Med.* 2007; 357:1993-6.
7. Kuhlman M, Covic A. The protein science of biosimilars. *Nephrol Dial Transplant.* 2006; 21(Suppl 5):v4-8.
8. Crommelin DJ, Storm G, Verrijk R et al. Shifting paradigms: biopharmaceuticals versus low molecular weight drugs. *Int J Pharm.* 2003; 266:3-16.
9. U.S. Food and Drug Administration. U.S. FDA considerations: discussion by national regulatory authorities with World Health Organization (WHO) on possible international non-proprietary name (INN) policies for biosimilars. September 1, 2006. www.fda.gov/cder/news/biosimilars.htm (accessed 2007 Dec 8).
10. European Medicines Agency Committee for Medicinal Products for Human Use. Guideline on similar biological medicinal products containing biotechnology-derived proteins as active substance: quality issues. www.emea.europa.eu/pdfs/human/biosimilar/4934805en.pdf (accessed 2007 Dec 8).
11. Biotechnology Industry Organization (BIO). Follow on biologics (FOB). http://bio.org/healthcare/followonbkg/ (accessed 2008 May 30).
12. Wiecek A, Mikhail A. European regulatory guidelines for biosimilars. *Nephrol Dial Transplant.* 2006; 21(Suppl 5):v17-20.
13. Nowicki M. Basic facts about biosimilars. *Kidney Blood Press Res.* 2007; 30:267-72.

Part II
The Demand for Pharmaceuticals: Demand and Incentives

[18]

Health Insurance and the Demand for Medical Care: Evidence from a Randomized Experiment

By WILLARD G. MANNING, JOSEPH P. NEWHOUSE, NAIHUA DUAN, EMMETT B. KEELER, ARLEEN LEIBOWITZ, AND M. SUSAN MARQUIS*

We estimate how cost sharing, the portion of the bill the patient pays, affects the demand for medical services. The data come from a randomized experiment. A catastrophic insurance plan reduces expenditures 31 percent relative to zero out-of-pocket price. The price elasticity is approximately −0.2. We reject the hypothesis that less favorable coverage of outpatient services increases total expenditure (for example, by deterring preventive care or inducing hospitalization).

Over the past four decades medical care costs have grown about 4 percent per year in real terms, and the share of GNP devoted to medical care has increased from 4.4 percent in 1950 to 10.7 percent in 1985 (Daniel Waldo, Katherine Levit, and Helen Lazenby, 1986). A prominent explanation of this rapid increase has emphasized the spread of health insurance, which has generated demand for both a higher quality and an increased quantity of medical services (Martin Feldstein, 1971, 1977). In turn, the spread of health insurance has been linked to the exemption of employer-paid health insurance premiums from the individual income tax (Feldstein and Elizabeth Allison, 1974; Feldstein and Bernard Friedman, 1977; Mark Pauly, 1986). Thus, the increase in expenditure is often portrayed as a type of market failure induced by public policy, although such an argument is not universally accepted (Morris Barer, Robert Evans, and Gregory Stoddart, 1979; Robert Evans, 1984; John Goddeeris and Burton Weisbrod, 1985).

No one has shown, however, that the spread of health insurance can quantitatively account for most of the sustained rise in health expenditure (Pauly, 1986). If it cannot, the widespread presumption that distorted prices (because of insurance) are inducing excess resources in medical care is not necessarily correct. Central to appraising the quantitative role of insurance, of course, is the magnitude of the demand response to changes in insurance. The literature exhibits substantial disagreement, by a factor of 10 or more, about the price elasticity, or coinsurance elasticity, of demand (Richard Rosett and Lien Fu Huang, 1973; Karen Davis and Louise Russell, 1972; Charles Phelps and Newhouse, 1974; Fred Goldman and Michael Grossman, 1978; Ann Colle and Grossman, 1978; Newhouse and Phelps, 1974, 1976).[1]

Such disagreement is not surprising in light of the problems of using nonexperimental data to estimate elasticities (Newhouse,

*The Rand Corporation, 1700 Main Street, Santa Monica, CA 90406. This research was conducted under grant 016B80 from the Department of Health and Human Services. Neither the Department nor the Rand Corporation necessarily agrees with the conclusions presented here. We acknowledge the comments of three very detailed anonymous referee reports. We, of course, are responsible for any remaining errors. Bernadette Benjamin and Jack Zwanziger provided invaluable programming support and assistance throughout the analysis underlying this paper. Individuals too numerous to mention provided advice, assistance, and support throughout the project; however, two of our government project officers, Larry Orr and James Schuttinga, deserve special mention; so too do our former colleagues Charles Phelps and Carl Morris.

[1]The elasticity estimates at the mean vary from around −0.1 to −2.1.

Phelps, and Marquis, 1980). In cross-sectional data, insurance is endogenous; those who expect to demand more services have a clear incentive to obtain more complete insurance, either by selecting a more generous option at the place of employment, by working for an employer with a generous insurance plan, or by purchasing privately more generous coverage.

Ignoring this selection issue (i.e., treating insurance as exogenous) has generally produced results showing that demand for medical care responds to insurance-induced variation in price. Treating insurance as endogenous, however, has generally led to coefficients with confidence intervals that are insignificantly different from zero at conventional levels (Newhouse and Phelps, 1976).[2]

That upward bias may be present is suggested by results from several natural experiments that compared demands of the same individuals before and after their group insurance changed (Anne Scitovsky and Nelda Snyder, 1972; Scitovsky and Nelda McCall, 1977; Phelps and Newhouse, 1972; R. G. Beck, 1974). In these cases the change in insurance is presumptively exogenous, and the elasticity estimates cluster near the low end of those cited above. But natural experiments have no control group, so that any other factor that changed over time is perfectly confounded with the insurance change. Moreover, the samples available in such studies are not necessarily representative of the general population, and the changes in insurance that could be studied were limited to those that occurred in the natural experiment. Hence, these results too have been suspect.[3]

In light of the uncertainty about how demand responds to insurance-induced changes in price, and the importance for both public and private decisions of quantifying that response, the federal government initiated the Rand Health Insurance Experiment (HIE) in 1974, one aim of which was to narrow uncertainty about this issue (Newhouse, 1974). In this article we report the results of that experiment. Our findings have implications for the role of insurance in explaining the postwar increase in medical expenditure, as well as for the magnitude of the welfare loss from health insurance.

The HIE had several objectives other than improved estimates of how demand responds to insurance. Four such objectives merit mention here:

1) Many poor individuals are insured through public programs; whether the demand response differs for the poor is therefore an issue in decisions on the scope of these programs.

2) Insurance need not be uniform across various medical services. In fact, second-best pricing implies that coverage should be more generous for less price elastic (or less insurance elastic) services (Frank Ramsey, 1927; Richard Zeckhauser, 1970; William Baumol and David Bradford, 1970). We therefore wished to learn if insurance elasticities differed for various types of medical services. In particular, are demand elasticities greater for outpatient physician services, psychotherapy, and preventive services, which would accord with the observed lesser coverage of these services?[4]

3) The public financing of medical care has been justified by its status as a merit good (Richard Musgrave, 1959) and in particular the claim that the consumption of medical services leads to improved health, which can generate externalities (Cotton Lindsay, 1969; Anthony Culyer, 1971, 1976, 1978; Pauly, 1971; Evans, 1984). Thus, we

[2]Although many believe this failure to reject the null hypothesis when insurance is treated as endogenous occurs because the insurance variable is only weakly identified, the magnitude of any upward bias in elasticity estimates from treating insurance as exogenous remains unknown. Hausman (or Wu) type tests have not been used to test for endogeneity, but if they failed to reject the null hypothesis of exogeneity, it could be for lack of power because of a lack of a useful set of instruments.

[3]For reviews of the nonexperimental demand literature and a discussion of its methodological problems, see Newhouse (1978; 1981).

[4]Other explanations, not mutually exclusive, for the lower coverage of these services include greater loading charges and asymmetric information between insurer and insured.

sought to quantify how the change in the consumption of medical services at the margin might affect health. The answer to this question would inform the political debate about the benefits of public financing of medical care services for the indigent and would also inform the insurance decisions of private agents such as employers and unions.

4) For the past decade, public policy has promoted Health Maintenance Organizations (HMOs) on the groups that such organizations were more efficient in the delivery of services. Almost all evidence of lower cost, however, came from uncontrolled settings, leaving unresolved the question of whether selection of healthier members or more efficient treatment was responsible for lower costs in HMOs (Harold Luft, 1981). Also unresolved was the question of whether any true reduction in services at HMOs might adversely affect health status. Therefore, we sought to decompose the observed lower use of services at one HMO into the pure effect of the HMO, on the one hand, and treating a possibly less sickly group of enrollees on the other. Moreover, we sought to determine whether any reduced use of services affected health status and satisfaction.

This article considers the first two questions in some detail and summarizes the findings on the latter two.

I. Data and Sample

A. *The Design of the Rand Health Insurance Experiment*[5]

Between November 1974 and February 1977, the HIE enrolled families in six sites: Dayton, Ohio; Seattle, Washington; Fitchburg, Massachusetts; Franklin County, Massachusetts; Charleston, South Carolina; and Georgetown County, South Carolina.[6]

Families participating in the experiment were assigned to one of 14 different fee-for-service insurance plans or to a prepaid group practice; additionally, some members already enrolled in the prepaid group practice were enrolled as a separate group. The fee-for-service insurance plans, the main focus of this article, had different levels of cost sharing, which varied over two dimensions: the coinsurance rate (percentage paid out-of-pocket) and an upper limit on annual out-of-pocket expenses. The coinsurance rates were 0, 25, 50, or 95 percent. Each plan had an upper limit (the Maximum Dollar Expenditure or MDE) on annual out-of-pocket expenses of 5, 10, or 15 percent of family income, up to a maximum of $1,000.[7] Beyond the MDE, the insurance plan reimbursed all covered expenses in full.

Covered expenses included virtually all medical services.[8] One plan had different coinsurance rates for inpatient and ambulatory medical services (25 percent) than for dental and ambulatory mental health services (50 percent). And on one plan, the families faced a 95 percent coinsurance rate for outpatient services, subject to a $150 annual limit on out-of-pocket expenses per person ($450 per family). In this plan, all inpatient services were free; in effect, this plan had approximately an outpatient individual deductible.[9]

[5]Newhouse (1974) and Robert Brook et al. (1979), provide fuller descriptions of the design. Newhouse et al. (1979) discuss the measurement issues for the second generation of social experiments, to which the HIE belongs. John Ware et al. (1980) discuss many aspects of data collection and measurement for health status.

[6]The sites were selected to represent the four census regions; to represent the range of city sizes (a proxy for the complexity of the medical delivery system); to cover a range of waiting times to appointment and physician per capita ratios (to test for the sensitivity of demand elasticities to nonprice rationing); and to include both urban and rural sites in the North and the South.

[7]The maximum was $750 in some site-years for the 25 percent coinsurance plans. The $1000 was kept fixed in nominal dollars from 1974 to 1981. During this time the medical care component of the CPI rose by 96 percent.

[8]See Lorraine Clasquin (1973) for a discussion of the rationale for the HIE structure of benefits. Nonpreventive orthodontia and cosmetic surgery (related to preexisting conditions) were not covered. Also excluded were outpatient psychotherapy services in excess of 52 visits per year per person. In the case of each exclusion, it is questionable whether anything could have been learned about steady-state demand during the 3- to 5-year lifetime of the experiment.

[9]The coinsurance rate for the 95 percent and individual deductible plans was actually 100 percent in the first

Families were assigned to these insurance plans using the Finite Selection Model (Carl Morris, 1979). This model was used to achieve as much balance across plans as possible while retaining randomization; that is, it minimizes the correlation between the experimental treatments and health, demographic, and economic covariates.

To study methods effects, the HIE employed four randomized subexperiments (Newhouse et al., 1979). We describe two here. To test for transitory demand effects (Charles Metcalf, 1973; Kenneth Arrow, 1975), 70 percent of the households were enrolled for three years; the remainder for five years. Also, to ensure that no one was worse off financially from participating in the study, families were paid a lump sum payment.[10] To test for a possible stimulus to utilization, 40 percent of the families were given an unanticipated increase in their lump sum payment during the next to the last year of the study.

B. *The Sample*

The enrolled sample is for the most part a random sample of each site's nonaged population, but some groups were not eligible.[11] Table 1 gives the sample by plan and site; it excludes the 1,982 persons in the HMO experiment. Note that plans are not perfectly balanced by site; in particular, no one was enrolled in the 50 percent plan in Seattle, and about half of those in the 50 percent plan are in Dayton, whereas only 20 percent of all participants are in Dayton.[12]

1. *Dependent Variables*. In the interest of brevity, we focus primarily on the use of medical services other than outpatient psychotherapy and dental services.[13] We do, however, summarize results for dental services below.

---

year of Dayton, the first site. The rate was changed to 95 percent for all other site-years of the experiment, in order to increase the incentive to file claims, although there was no statistical evidence at that time of underfiling. Subsequent analysis has shown that the mean outpatient physician expenditure on the 95 percent coinsurance plans relative to the free-care plan is understated by about 5 to 10 percent because of a lower propensity to file claims (William Rogers and Newhouse, 1985).

[10]Because of size of the lump sum payment, there is a theoretical presumption of no bias from refusal or attrition. Although refusal and attrition occurred at higher rates on higher coinsurance plans, refusal and attrition appear to have been random within plan. More precisely, we detect no differences by plan at enrollment in pre-experimental use or health status, nor do we detect differences in the rate of spending between those who withdrew from the experiment and those who did not. More detailed data on issues of refusal and attrition can be found in Brook et al. (1983, 1984); Kevin O'Grady et al. (1985); Newhouse et al. (1987). The details of the lump sum payment rules can be found in Clasquin and Marie Brown (1977).

[11]The ineligible groups include: 1) those 62 years of age and older at the time of enrollment; 2) those with incomes in excess of $25,000 in 1973 dollars or $58,000 in 1984 dollars); this excluded 3 percent of the families contacted; 3) those eligible for the Medicare disability program, 4) those in jails or institutionalized for indefinite periods; 5) those in the military or their dependents; and 6) veterans with service-connected disabilities.

[12]About 3 percent of the actual participant-years are truncated because the participant withdrew partway through an accounting year. With the exception of deaths, we do not use such participants in the estimation sample because the 4-part model (see below) requires equal time periods for each observation. If a person is only observed for one quarter and the expenditure distribution is lognormal, the annual distribution is not simply the quarterly distribution scaled up by a factor of 4; i.e., the lognormal distribution does not convolute. The sample used in this analysis more specifically includes enrollees during each full year that they participated, and the last accounting year in the study for those who died. We excluded data on partial years of participation by newborns. (Their expenses in the hospital at the time of birth, however, are attributed to the mother.) We tested the legitimacy of excluding those with partial years by comparing expenditure rates of part-year persons, adjusted for time at risk, with what they would have spent if they behaved like full-year people. Specifically we regressed actual expenditure minus (time at risk times the 4-part model prediction) on plan dummy variables. We could not reject the null hypothesis of no difference by plan ($\chi^2(4) = 2.67$, $p > .50$). The estimated effect of including part-year participants is to negligibly increase the estimated response to plan.

[13]See Manning et al. (1984b, 1986b) and Kenneth Wells et al. (1982) for additional results on the use of mental health care, and Manning et al. (1985) for additional results on dental use. Mental health care use is on the order of 4 percent of the expenditures discussed here.

TABLE 1—NUMBER OF PERSONS AT ENROLLMENT AND NUMBER OF PERSON-YEARS IN ESTIMATION SAMPLE

Plan	Site							
	Dayton	Seattle	Fitchburg	Franklin County	Charleston	Georgetown	Enrollment Total[a]	Estimation Sample Total[b]
Free	301	431	241	297	264	359	1893	6822
25 Percent[c]	260	253	125	152	146	201	1137	4065
50 Percent	191	0	56	58	26	52	383	1401
95 Percent	280	253	113	162	146	166	1120	3727
Individual Deductible	105	285	188	220	196	282	1276	4175
Total	1137	1222	723	889	778	1060	5809	20190

[a] Persons.
[b] Person-years.
[c] Includes those with 50 percent coinsurance for dental and mental health and 25 precent coinsurance for all other services.

2. *Independent Variables*. Although we present sample means by plan, we also present results controlling for site, health status, sociodemographic, and economic variables.

Insurance Plan Variables. Rather than impose a functional form, we have conservatively used dummy variables for insurance plans. We have grouped the insurance plans into five groups: 1) the free plan (no out-of-pocket cost to the family); 2) 25 percent coinsurance rate plans for medical services; 3) 50 percent coinsurance rate plans for medical services; 4) 95 percent coinsurance rate plans for medical services; and 5) the plan with a 95 percent coinsurance rate for outpatient services (subject to a limit of $150 per person or $450 per family per year) and free inpatient care.[14] The middle three groups we call the family-pay plans.

Other Covariates. In addition to dummy variables for each plan group, we also included covariates for age, sex, race, family income, health status, family size, and site (Manning et al., 1987). With the exception of family size and income, the data were collected before or at enrollment in the study. The value for family size varies by year. Family income data are from 1975 in Dayton, 1978 for the three-year group in South Carolina, and 1976 for all other participants.[15] Health status measures are described more fully in Brook et al. (1983, 1984), R. Burciaga Valdez et al. (1985), and Valdez (1986).

Although we have not tested for all possible interactions among covariates, we did examine some that are important for policy purposes (for example, income and plan). As a result, we have included interactions between being a child and plan in the inpatient and outpatient use equations (see below), between plan and income in the probabilities of any use of medical and of any inpatient use (see below), and between sex and age in all equations. The remaining interactions

[14] Differences among plans with 5, 10, and 15 percent upper limits are too small to detect at the level of annual expenditure. Hence, we have pooled across these different expenditure ceilings. See Keeler et al. (1987) for further discussion of how a varying ceiling affects demand.

[15] The first year of participation was 1975 for the Dayton participants; the South Carolina 3-year group began participation in late 1978 (about a quarter participated for two months and another quarter for one month of 1978); and the remainder of the sample enrolled in 1976 or early 1977. Most of the enrollment was in the latter half of 1976. We used these data because we believed the income measure was more reliable than the data on pre-experimental income. The data we used were collected on forms keyed to income tax returns, whereas data on pre-experimental income were responses to a personal interview.

were neither significant nor appreciable, and have been omitted.

C. *Unit of Analysis*

The unit of analysis is a person-year. We use the year as the time frame for ease of interpretation and because the upper limit on out-of-pocket expenses is an annual limit. We use the person as the unit of observation because most major determinants of the use of services are individual (for example, age, sex, and health status) rather than family (for example, insurance coverage, and family income).

II. Statistical Methods

We estimated two types of models. In addition to simple means (ANOVA), we present more robust estimates based on a four-equation model developed by Duan et al. (1982 and 1983). This model gains over ANOVA (and ANOCOVA) by exploiting three characteristics of the distribution of medical expenses. First, a large proportion of the participants use no medical services during the year. Second, the distribution of expenses among users is highly skewed. Third, the distribution of medical expenses is different for individuals with only outpatient use than for individuals with inpatient use.

Because of these three characteristics, ANOVA (and ANOCOVA) yields imprecise, though consistent, estimates of the effects of health insurance, health status, and socioeconomic status on the use of medical services, even for a sample size on the order of 20,000 (not all independent) observations. As Duan et al. (1982 and 1983) and Manning et al. (1987) show, a four-equation model that exploits the characteristics of the medical expense distribution yields consistent estimates with lower mean square error than ANOVA.

A. *The Four-Equation Model*

We partition the participants into three groups: nonusers, users of only outpatient services, and users of any inpatient services. We examine the expenses of the last two groups of users separately.

The first equation of the model is a probit equation for the probability that a person will receive any medical service during the year—from either inpatient or outpatient sources. Thus, this equation separates users from nonusers, and addresses the first characteristic described above, a large proportion of the population does not use medical services during the year. The second equation is a probit equation for the conditional probability that a user will have at least one inpatient stay, given that he has some medical use. This equation separates the two user groups, and thus addresses the third characteristic noted above, different distributions of medical expenses for inpatient and outpatient users.

The third equation is a linear regression for the logarithm of total annual medical expenses of the outpatient-only users. The fourth equation is a linear regression for the logarithm of total annual medical expenses for the users of any inpatient service. This last equation includes both outpatient and inpatient expenses for users of any inpatient services.[16]

The logarithmic transformation of annual expenses practically eliminates the undesirable skewness in the distribution of expenses among users, the second characteristic noted above. In particular, the logarithmic transform yields nearly symmetric and roughly normal error distributions. Further details are available in Duan et al. (1982 and 1983) and Manning et al. (1987).

While our use of the four-equation model is motivated by our desire to have the stochastic term approximate the normal assumption as closely as possible (to obtain robust estimates), the error distributions for the two levels of expense equations still deviate from the normal assumption. As a re-

[16]Grouping expenses by person rather than the more natural all-inpatient and all-outpatient expenditure eliminates the need to account for across-equation correlation in calculating standard errors of total expenditure.

sult, if we were to use the normal theory retransformation from the logarithmic scale to the raw dollar scale ($\exp(\sigma^2/2)$), the predictions would be inconsistent. Instead we use a nonparametric estimate of the retransformation factors, the smearing estimate, developed by Duan (1983), which in this application is the sample average of the exponentiated least squares residuals:

$$(1) \quad \hat{\phi}_j = \sum_i \exp(\hat{\varepsilon}_{ij})/n_j, \quad j = 3,4,$$

where n_j = sample size for equation j,

$\hat{\varepsilon}_{ij} = \ln(y_{ij}) - x_{ij}\hat{\beta}_j$,

$\hat{\beta}_j$ = OLS estimate of β_j,

and i indexes the person. The smearing estimate is weakly consistent (asymptotically unbiased) for the retransformation factor if the error distribution does not depend on the characteristics x_i.[17]

A consistent estimate of the expected medical expense for person i based on the four-equation model is given by

$$(2) \quad E(\textit{Medical Expenditure}_i)$$
$$= \hat{p}_i\left[(1-\hat{\pi}_i)\exp(x_i\hat{\beta}_3)\hat{\phi}_3 + \hat{\pi}_i\exp(x_i\hat{\beta}_4)\hat{\phi}_4\right]$$

where $\hat{p}_i = \Phi(x_i\hat{\beta}_1)$ = estimated probability of any medical use,

$\hat{\pi}_i = \Phi(x_i\hat{\beta}_2)$ = estimated conditional probability for a medical user to have any inpatient use,

$\exp(x_i\hat{\beta}_3)\hat{\phi}_3$) = estimate of the conditional expense for medical services if outpatient only,

$\exp(x_i\hat{\beta}_4)\hat{\phi}_4$) = estimate of the conditional expense for medical services if any inpatient,

$\hat{\phi}_3, \hat{\phi}_4$ = estimated retransformation ("smearing") factors of the error terms for level of outpatient only and any inpatient expenditure equations.

Our estimates of predicted expenditure presented below are based on equation (2). We use equation (2) to predict medical expenditure for each person we enrolled, alternatively placing that person on each plan (by successively turning on plan dummy variables). We then average within plans over each predicted value to obtain a mean value for each plan. Standard errors of the predicted values are obtained by the delta method (see Duan et al., 1983, pp. 40, 48). The regression equations underlying our predicted values are presented in Manning et al. (1987).

B. *Correlation in the Error Terms*

Although we have over 20,000 observations, we do not have the same number of independent observations, because of substantial positive correlations in the error terms among family members and over time among observations on the same person. These correlations exist in all four equations. Failure to account for them in the analysis would yield inefficient estimates of the coefficients and inconsistent estimates of the standard errors. In the results presented below we have corrected the inference statistics (t, F, and χ^2) for this positive correlation using a nonparametric approach.[18]

C. *Selection Modes*

The econometric literature provides an additional class of models for continuous but limited dependent variables such as medical

[17] Moreover, when the normal assumption does hold, the smearing factor has high efficiency (90 percent or more) relative to the normal retransformation for a wide range of parameter values, including those in this analysis (see Duan, 1983, Section 5; and F. Mehran, 1973). In the results presented below, the smearing factors for the log level of expense for outpatient only users are estimated separately by plan and year to allow for heteroscedasticity. For the log level of expenses for users of any inpatient services, the smearing factor is a constant. See Duan et al. (1983) and Appendix C of Manning et al. (1987) for a comparison of normal theory and nonparametric retransformations.

[18] The correction is similar to that for the random effects least squares model, or equivalently the intracluster correlation model (S. R. Searle, 1971). The model is described in Brook et al. (1984), based on prior work by P. J. Huber (1967) on the variance of a robust regression.

expenditure. These models include the Tobit model (James Tobin, 1958), the Adjusted Tobit model (Wynand van de Ven and Bernard van Praag, 1981a,b), and sample selection models (G. S. Maddala, 1983). Like our four-equation model, these are multi-equation models, with an equation (often a probit) for whether there is a positive amount, and another equation for the level of the positive amount. These models differ from ours in that they explicitly model the correlation between the probability of any use and the level of use. Although they may appear to be more general, in fact for this problem they are not (Duan et al., 1984). In particular, the four-equation model just described is not nested within the sample selection model. Manning et al. (1987) provides a fuller discussion of these models and, using a split-sample validation, show that the four-equation model has significantly less bias than the sample selection model and is statistically indistinguishable on the basis of mean square error.[19] In a separate Monte Carlo study, Manning, Duan, and William Rogers (forthcoming) show that models such as the four-equation model can be more robust, and are no worse than selection models when the data are truly generated by a selection model.

III. Empirical Results

A. *Main Effects of Insurance Plan: ANOVA Estimates*

The data from the Health Insurance Experiment (HIE) clearly show that the use of medical services responds to changes in the amount paid out-of-pocket. Table 2 provides the sample means and standard errors by plan for several measures of use of services —the probability of being treated, visit and admission rates, and total expenses. The per capita expenses on the free plan (no out-of-pocket costs) are 45 percent higher than those on the plan with a 95 percent coinsurance rate, subject to an upper limit on out-of-pocket expenses. Spending rates on plans with an intermediate level of cost sharing lie between these two extremes. The right-most column shows that adjusting for the site imbalance in plan assignments (see Table 1) makes little difference.

Cost sharing affects primarily the number of medical contacts, rather than the intensity of each of those contacts. In other words, the differences in expenditures across plans reflect real variation in the number of contacts rather than an increase in the intensity or charge per service.[20] For example, outpatient expenses on the free plan are 67 percent higher than those on the 95 percent plan, while outpatient visit rates are 66 percent higher.

The largest decreases in the use of outpatient services occurs between the free and 25 percent plans, with smaller but statistically significant differences between the 25 percent and other family coinsurance (pay) plans ($\chi^2(2) = 9.48$, $p < .01$).

There are no significant differences among the family coinsurance (25, 50, and 95 percent) plans in the use of inpatient services. For the probability of any inpatient use, total admission rates, and inpatient expenses, the contrasts between the 25, 50, and 95 percent plans have p values greater than 0.50. As noted above, this lack of a significant difference is probably due to the effect of the upper limit on out-of-pocket expenses. Seventy percent of people with inpatient care exceeded their upper limit. Hence, the out-of-pocket cost of a hospitalization was at most $1000 (in current dollars), and did not vary much among the pay plans (other than the individual deductible).[21]

[19] The bias in the selection models in the forecast sample was appreciable, on the order of 10–25 percent of the mean in the two replications we made ($p < .10$). In contrast, the bias for the 4-part model was 2 percent ($t = .50$).

[20] Keeler and John Rolph (1982) found that cost sharing affected the number of episodes of treatment, rather than the size of the episode. They used data from the first three years of the Dayton site. Kathleen Lohr et al. (1986) found a similar result for diagnosis-specific episodes.

[21] This is a good example of the difference between the response to a marginal price or coinsurance and the response to plan.

TABLE 2—SAMPLE MEANS FOR ANNUAL USE OF MEDICAL SERVICES PER CAPITA

Plan	Face-to-Face Visits	Outpatient Expenses (1984 $)	Admissions	Inpatient Dollars (1984 $)	Prob. Any Medical (%)	Prob. Any Inpatient (%)	Total Expenses (1984 $)	Adjusted Total Expenses (1984 $)[a]
Free	4.55	340	.128	409	86.8	10.3	749	750
	(.168)	(10.9)	(.0070)	(32.0)	(.817)	(.45)	(39)	(39)
25 Percent	3.33	260	.105	373	78.8	8.4	634	617
	(.190)	(14.70)	(.0090)	(43.1)	(1.38)	(0.61)	(53)	(49)
50 Percent	3.03	224	.092	450	77.2	7.2	674	573
	(.221)	(16.8)	(.0116)	(139)	(2.26)	(0.77)	(144)	(100)
95 Percent	2.73	203	.099	315	67.7	7.9	518	540
	(.177)	(12.0)	(.0078)	(36.7)	(1.76)	(0.55)	(44.8)	(47)
Individual Deductible	3.02	235	.115	373	72.3	9.6	608	630
	(.171)	(11.9)	(.0076)	(41.5)	(1.54)	(0.55)	(46)	(56)
Chi-Squared (4)[b]	68.8	85.3	11.7	4.1	144.7	19.5	15.9	17.0
P Value for *chi*-Squared (4)	<.0001	<.0001	.02	n.s.	<.0001	.0006	.003	.002

Note: All standard errors (shown in parentheses) are corrected for intertemporal and intrafamily correlations. Dollars are expressed in June 1984 dollars. Visits are face-to-face contacts with MD, DO, or other health providers; excludes visits for only radiology, anesthesiology or pathology services. Visits and expenses exclude dental care and outpatient psychotherapy.

[a] The figures in this column are adjusted for the imbalance of plans across sites as follows: the site-specific responses on each plan (simple means by site) are weighted by the fraction of the sample in each site and summed across sites. In the case of the 50 percent plan, which has no observations in Seattle, the weights are renormalized excluding Seattle.

[b] The *chi*-square statistic with 4 d.f. tests the null hypothesis of no difference among the five plan means. The *chi*-square statistic is a Wald test from the robust estimate of the information matrix (see Brook et al., 1984, for further details). It is used in lieu of the usual *F*-statistic because of the difficulty of computing such a statistic while allowing for intertemporal and interfamily correlation.

The Individual Deductible plan exhibits a somewhat different pattern from the other cost sharing plans. Recall that this plan has free inpatient care, but a 95 percent coinsurance rate (up to a $150 per person, or $450 per family annual maximum) for outpatient services. Total expenditures on this plan are significantly less than the free plan ($t = -2.34$, $p < .02$). This overall response is the sum of a one-third reduction in outpatient expenses ($t = -6.67$), and a less than one-tenth reduction in inpatient expenses ($t = -0.68$). Thus, this plan looks like a combination of the 50 or 95 percent plans for outpatient care and the free of 25 percent plan for inpatient care. The admission rate for the Individual Deductible plan lies roughly midway between the free plan and family coinsurance plan rates, suggesting a nontrivial cross-price elasticity between inpatient and outpatient services.

B. *Main Effects of Insurance Plan: Four-Equation Estimates*

Because sample means are quite sensitive to the presence of catastrophic cases, we used the four-equation model to provide more robust estimates of the plan responses.[22] The use of covariates in these equations further enhances precision and re-

[22] For example, the ANOVA estimates of the response to cost sharing for total expenses (not adjusted for site) show a statistically insignificant reversal between the 50 and 25 percent plans. Although such a reversal is compatible with theory (due to the MDE) the reversal is almost certainly due to chance. One participant on the 50 percent plan had a very expensive hospitalization (total medical expenses of $148,000 in one year); that single observation, which was the largest observation in the entire sample, adds $106 dollars to the 50 percent plan mean (16 percent of that plan's mean).

TABLE 3—VARIOUS MEASURES OF PREDICTED MEAN ANNUAL USE OF MEDICAL SERVICES, BY PLAN

Plan	Likelihood of Any Use (%)	One or More Admissions (%)	Medical Expenses (1984 $)
Free	86.7	10.37	777
	(0.67)	(0.420)	(32.8)
Family Pay			
25 Percent	78.8	8.83	630
	(0.99)	(0.379)	(29.0)
50 Percent	74.3	8.31	583
	(1.86)	(0.400)	(32.6)
95 Percent	68.0	7.75	534
	(1.48)	(0.354)	(27.4)
Individual Deductible	72.6	9.52	623
	(1.14)	(0.529)	(34.6)

Note: Standard errors are shown in parentheses. Medical services exclude dental and outpatient psychotherapy. The predictions are for the enrollment population carried forward through each year of the study. The standard errors are corrected for intertemporal and intrafamily correlation. The t-statistics for the contrasts with the free plan are -6.69, -6.33, -11.57, and -10.69 for the last four rows of the first col., respectively; -2.74, -3.57, -4.80, and -1.28 for the last four rows of the second col., respectively, and -4.05, -4.91, -6.74, and -3.78 for the last four rows of the third col., respectively. These t-statistics are larger than those one would compute from the standard errors shown in the table because use of the standard errors ignores the positive covariance between the two predicted plan means from the shared $X\beta$ terms. The differences in expenses between the 25 and 50 percent plans are significant at the 5 percent level ($t = 1.97$), and between the 50 and 95 percent plans are significant at the 6 percent level ($t = 1.93$). The parameter estimates underlying these predictions are available in Manning et al. (1987).

moves the relatively minor imbalances across plan, including the site imbalance. Table 3 presents estimates from this model of plan response for the probability of any use of medical services, the unconditional probability of any inpatient use, and total medical expenses. Figure 1 displays the expenditure results.

Mean predicted expenditure in the free care plan is 46 percent higher than in the 95 percent plan ($p < .001$), almost exactly the difference found in the sample means.[23] Like

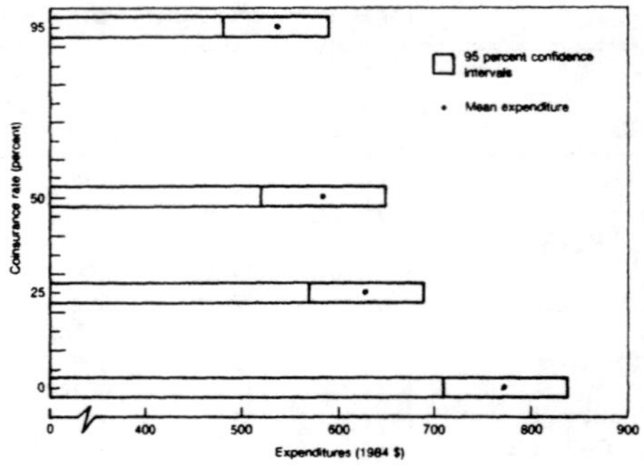

FIGURE 1. DEMAND AND 95 PERCENT CONFIDENCE INTERVALS BY COINSURANCE RATE

the sample means, these more robust estimates also indicate that the largest response to plan occurs between free care and the 25 percent plan, with smaller decreases thereafter.

Not surprisingly, given the approximate orthogonality of plan and covariates, adding covariates does not change the estimated probability of any use of medical services—87 percent of the free plan participants are predicted to use any service during the course of the year, while only 68 percent of the 95 percent plan participants are. These differences in the likelihood of receiving any care account for over three-fifths of the overall response to cost sharing. Virtually all the remaining response is attributable to the effect of cost sharing on hospital admissions.

Cost sharing for outpatient services only (the individual deductible plan) produces a different pattern of utilization than cost sharing for all services. Outpatient-only cost sharing reduces total expenditures relative to free care ($p < .0001$), largely by reducing the likelihood of any use ($p < .0001$). Outpatient-only cost sharing also reduces inpatient use, but by an insignificant amount ($p = .20$ for the probability of any inpatient use). This last result is the only important change

[23] It may seem that this is a trivial result that follows from the orthogonality of plan and covariates. Such is not the case because of the nonlinear transformations in the 4-part model. Using the logarithm of expenditure plus $5, for example, as a dependent variable instead of the 4-part model would lead to a much larger estimate of plan response, one that would be biased upward. (See Duan et al., 1983; Manning et al., 1987.)

TABLE 4—VARIOUS MEASURES OF PREDICTED ANNUAL USE OF MEDICAL SERVICES, BY INCOME GROUP

	Income			Significance Tests t on Contrast of:	
Plan	Lowest Third Mean	Middle Third Mean	Highest Third Mean	Middle vs. Lowest Thirds[a]	Highest vs. Lowest Thirds[a]
Likelihood of Any Use (Percent)					
Free	82.8	87.4	90.1	4.91	5.90
Family Pay					
25 Percent	71.8	80.1	84.8	5.45	6.28
50 Percent	64.7	76.2	82.3	4.35	4.86
95 Percent	61.7	68.9	73.8	3.96	4.64
Individual Deductible	65.3	73.9	79.1	6.09	7.09
Likelihood of One or More Admissions (Percent)					
Free	10.63	10.14	10.35	−0.91	−0.35
Family Pay					
25 Percent	10.03	8.44	7.97	−2.95	−2.75
50 Percent	9.08	8.06	7.77	−1.78	−1.66
95 Percent	8.77	7.38	7.07	−2.79	−2.46
Individual Deductible	9.26	9.44	9.88	0.31	0.68
Expenses (1984 $)					
Free	788	736	809	−1.78	0.53
Family Pay					
25 Percent	680	588	623	−3.17	−1.47
50 Percent	610	550	590	−1.89	−0.49
95 Percent	581	494	527	−3.09	−1.41
Individual Deductible	609	594	670	−0.57	1.38

Note: Excludes dental and outpatient psychotherapy. Predictions for enrollment population carried forward for all years of the study.

[a] The t-statistics are corrected for intertemporal and intrafamily correlation. The statistics test the null hypothesis that the mean of middle (highest) third equals the mean of the lowest third; for example, the 4.91 figure implies we can reject at the .001 level the hypothesis that in the free plan the likelihood of any use for the lowest and middle thirds of the income distribution are equal.

from the previously published analysis of the first 40 percent of the data (Newhouse et al., 1981). In that analysis, inpatient use was less on the deductible plan, and one could reject at the 5 percent level the hypothesis that the free plan and individual deductible plan means for inpatient use were the same. This difference may have occurred because inflation in the late 1970's reduced the real value of the deductible, which was kept fixed at $150 (i.e., in nominal dollars), or may have simply been due to chance.

C. *Use by Subgroups*

An important goal of the HIE was to study how the response to cost sharing varied across subgroups. These included differences in responses across income groups, differences between adults and children, differences between the sickly and healthy, as well as differences across time (for example, any transitory surges in use as insurance changed), and differences across medical markets (for example, urban vs. rural).

1. *Across Income Groups*. Different aspects of the use of medical services exhibit different responses to income (Table 4).[24] In Ta-

[24] Recall that the income measure comes from the first partial year of enrollment.) The division into thirds is site specific (for example, the lowest third is the lowest third of each site's income distribution), because

ble 4 we observe differences in use that are due to both income directly and the effects of variables correlated with income; that is, these are not partial effects.

Within each of the five plans the probability of any use of medical services increases with income, with larger increases for the family pay (25, 50, and 95 percent) and individual deductible plans than the free plan.[25] In contrast, the (unconditional) probability of any use of inpatient services declines with income for the family pay plans, but is not significantly different across income groups for the two plans with free inpatient care (the free and individual deductible plans). Because of these two conflicting effects of income—positive on outpatient use but negative on inpatient use—the net result on total expenditure is a shallow U-shaped response.

Our estimate of the differences by income group within the family-pay plans is influenced by the income-related upper limit in out-of-pocket expenses. The observed response in a combination of the direct response to income, and the fact that families with lower incomes are more likely to exceed their (lower) limit and receive free care for part of the year.[26] If medical care is a normal good, then any positive direct effect of greater income would be reduced by the decreased likelihood of going over the limit. In the case of the positive effect of income on the probability of any use, the direct income effect is probably more important, and in the case of the negative effect on the probability of any inpatient use, the limit has relatively more influence.[27]

The Individual Deductible plan provides a cleaner test of the differences by income group of use of medical services, because the deductible in that plan is not income related. We observe an insignificant 10 percent increase in medical expenses between the bottom and top third of the income distribution. The effect of income is limited to an increased likelihood of using outpatient services, probably because inpatient services are free on this plan.

Thus far we have compared response among income groups rather than examining the partial effect of income. Although income has a statistically significant positive partial effect on use of service, the magnitude is small enough to be swamped by other factors correlated with income (for details see Manning et al., 1987, Appendix A, Tables 2–4 and 6).[28]

2. *Across Age Groups*. We found about the same outpatient response to insurance plans for children (ages less than 18) as for adults, but children are less plan responsive for inpatient care (Table 5).[29] As we observed with a subset of these data (see Newhouse et al., 1981 and 1982; Leibowitz et al., 1985), we cannot reject the hypothesis that admission rates for children show no response to insurance coverage.[30] By contrast, adults

1) expenses are not corrected for cross-sectional differences in prices, and 2) we did not want to confound income and site; the sites were chosen to represent a spectrum of medical market characteristics. See Manning et al. (1987, Table 1, Appendix D) for the ANOVA estimates by plan income group (as well as by other subgroups).

[25] Note that this is not a *ceteris paribus* statement, so there is no contradiction with standard theory, which would suggest no income effect in the free plan.

[26] See Manning et al. (1987, Appendix B) for data on the proportion exceeding the upper limit on out-of-pocket expenses.

[27] Some may argue that income is endogenous with respect to inpatient expenditure. This may well be true, but is not likely to account for our result because only a few months of data are "tainted."

[28] Income has a moderately significant (at $p < .10$) and positive partial effect on use in all but the inpatient expenditure equation; in the level of outpatient-only expenditures, however, the income coefficients are of mixed sign. The probabilities with which we can reject the null hypothesis that the income coefficients are zero are: $p < .001$ for any use of medical services, $p < .10$ for the probability of any inpatient use given any medical use, $p < .001$ for the (log) level of outpatient-only use, and $p > .10$ for (log) level of medical expenditure if any inpatient use. The test statistics include plan income interactions and missing value replacement dummy variables.

[29] Recall that children are overrepresented in the study relative to the population of our sites. Hence, our estimates understate (modestly) the population responsiveness in our sites.

[30] $\chi^2(4) = 5.19$ using ANOVA estimates for the probability of any inpatient use, and $\chi^2(4) = 5.36$ for the admission rate. Another possible hypothesis is no differential plan response for children relative to adults.

TABLE 5—VARIOUS MEASURES OF PREDICTED ANNUAL USE OF MEDICAL SERVICES, BY AGE GROUP AND PLAN

Plan	Likelihood of Any Use (%) Mean	One or More Admissions (%) Mean	Medical Expenses (1984 $) Mean
Children			
Free	84.0	5.33	346
Family Pay			
25 Percent	75.1	4.98	287
50 Percent	70.3	4.62	279
95 Percent	63.5	4.23	236
Individual Deductible	68.5	5.86	299
Adults			
Free	88.6	13.9	1080
Family Pay			
25 Percent	81.4	11.5	872
50 Percent	77.1	10.9	797
95 Percent	71.2	10.2	744
Individual Deductible	75.6	12.1	852

Note: Excludes dental and outpatient psychotherapy services. The eight *t*-statistics for the contrasts between the free plan and the pay plans for the likelihood of any use all exceed 6. For one or more admissions, the *t*-statistics for children for contrasts with the free plan (rows 2–5) are 0.55, 1.13, 1.81, and −0.63, respectively, and for adults are 2.92, 3.64, 4.69, and 1.89, respectively (for example, the *t*-statistic on the difference between 13.9 and 12.1 is 1.89). For medical expenses the *t*-statistics on contrasts with the free plan for children are 2.16, 2.20, 4.10, and 1.42, respectively, and for adults are 3.70, 4.80, 6.07, and 3.63, respectively.

have significantly lower use of inpatient services on the family-pay plans than they do on the free plan.[31] For outpatient services, we observe a very similar pattern of plan responses for children and adults.

D. *Other Subgroups*

1. *Health Status.* Although health status was a strong predictor of expenditure levels, we observed no differential response to health insurance coverage between the healthy and the sickly (Manning et al., 1987). This null result is striking because of the upper limit feature. If anything, the presence of an upper limit on out-of-pocket expenses would lead to less plan response for the sickly; all other things equal, sicker individuals are more likely to exceed their upper limit and receive some free care—especially on the 95 percent plan, where care is free after gross expenditures of $1050 or more. Furthermore, some might expect the sickly to be less responsive to insurance coverage than the healthy, on the supposition that their use of services is less discretionary. If, in fact, there is no interaction between plan and health status, one can infer that the opposite is true at the margin; that is, at the margin the sickly exhibit more discretion.

2. *Sites.* The six sites in the HIE were selected to reflect a spectrum of city sizes, waiting times to appointment, and physician to

We can reject this hypothesis; the test statistics are $\chi^2(4) = 16.49$ for the probability of any inpatient use and $\chi^2(4) = 14.08$ for total admissions. Hence, it appears that children and adults respond differently and that children do not respond to cost sharing for inpatient care.

[31] $\chi^2(3) = 24.22$ for the probability of any inpatient use and 16.31 for the admission rate. By contrast, there are no significant differences among the family pay plans for adults. $\chi^2(2) = 1.69$ for expenditures, 0.73 for total admissions, and 1.39 for the probability of any inpatient use, again based on ANOVA (see Manning et al., 1987, Table 2, Appendix D for the ANOVA estimates).

TABLE 6—USE OF DENTAL SERVICES BY DENTAL PLAN: SAMPLE MEANS

	Year 1 of Dental Coverage			Year 2 of Dental Coverage		
Dental Insurance Plan	Probability (%)	Visits	Expenses per Enrollee ($)	Probability (%)	Visits	Expenses per Enrollee ($)
Free	68.7 (1.19)	2.50 (.065)	380 (18.0)	66.8 (1.18)	1.93 (.049)	261 (12.5)
25 Percent	53.6 (3.39)	1.73 (.138)	224 (32.8)	52.6 (3.34)	1.51 (.111)	190 (28.0)
50 Percent	54.1 (2.41)	1.80 (.118)	219 (31.3)	53.0 (2.55)	1.50 (.103)	177 (32.3)
95 Percent	47.1 (2.59)	1.39 (.098)	147 (18.7)	48.3 (2.62)	1.44 (.099)	179 (24.9)
Individual Deductible	48.9 (2.12)	1.70 (.104)	242 (24.1)	48.1 (2.12)	1.33 (0.080)	158 (20.4)

Note: Expenses were converted to January 1984 dollars using the dental fee component of the Consumer Price Index. There has been no adjustment for regional differences in prices, or differences in population characteristics across plans and years. Standard errors (shown in parentheses) are corrected for intrafamily correlations.

population ratios (Newhouse, 1974).[32] Our concern was that the response to insurance coverage could vary according to the complexity of the medical market or to the excess demand in the medical delivery system. Yet we found no differences among the sites in the response to insurance coverage, $\chi^2(19) = 14.96$ ($p > .50$). The uniformity of response across the sites gives some reason to believe the results may be representative of the United States, and we have so used them below.

Interestingly, the site with the longest delay to appointment and lowest physician to population ratio (Fitchburg) had the second highest probability of any use, the second highest expenditures per enrollee, and the highest probability of any inpatient use. The latter two phenomena may represent substitution of inpatient for outpatient care (Jeffrey McCombs, 1984), and the first may indicate that the presence of emergency rooms removes the constraint of the queue (Stephen Long, Russell Settle, and Bruce Stuart, 1986).[33]

2. *Period of Enrollment*. As noted above, we enrolled families for three or five years to see if the response to insurance changed over time and if the duration of enrollment mattered. The free plan might generate transitorily high demand; the 95 percent plan might generate postponement of demand at the end of the experiment (Arrow, 1975; Metcalf, 1973). Neither effect was found; see Manning et al. (1987) for further details.[34] Nor did duration of enrollment matter to either the absolute level of spending or the responsiveness to plan.

3. *Subexperiments*. As described above, the Health Insurance Experiment contained a number of subexperiments to study methods effects. None of the subexperiments had a measurable effect on expenditure (Manning et al., 1987).

[32] For example, city sizes in 1970 ranged from 34,000 (Georgetown County) to 1.2 million (Seattle), waiting times for nonemergent care in 1973–74 ranged from 4.1 days (Seattle) to 25.0 days (Fitchburg), and physicians per capita in 1972 ranged from 30 per 100,000 (Fitchburg) to 59 per 100,000 (Seattle).

[33] Length of waiting time to an appointment with a primary care physician is associated positively with the use of emergency rooms (O'Grady et al.).

[34] A transitory effect was found for dental services; see Manning et al. (1985, 1986a) for details.

E. *Dental Results*

These results are reported in greater detail elsewhere (Manning et al., 1985, 1986a). Dental services do show greater responsiveness to plan in Year 1 than in subsequent years ($p < .001$) (Table 6). This would be expected if dental services were more durable than other medical services, as is plausible. The responsiveness of demand by plan in Year 2, which is typical of the middle years, is of the same general magnitude as that for other medical services.

F. *Health Status Outcome Results*

These results also are reported in greater detail elsewhere (Brook et al., 1983, 1984; Valdez et al.; Valdez; Howard Bailit et al., 1985). For the person with mean characteristics, we can rule out clinically significant benefits from the additional services in the free fee-for-service plan relative to either the cost-sharing plans or the HMO experimental group. For poor adults (the lowest 20 percent of the income distribution) who began the experiment with high blood pressure (specifically, who were in the upper 20 percent of the diastolic blood pressure distribution) there was a clinically significant reduction in blood pressure in the free fee-for-service plan compared to the plans with cost sharing. Epidemiologic data imply that the magnitude of this reduction would lower mortality about 10 percent each year among this group, about 6 percent of the population. (The sample size is much too small to test this prediction with actual mortality among the experimental population.) For poor adults who began the experiment with vision problems that were correctable with eyeglasses, there was a modest improvement in corrected vision. Individuals on the free care plan between the ages of 12 and 35 showed a modest improvement in the health of the gums; caries (decayed teeth) were also more likely to be filled on the free care plan.

The specific gains in health just described, for high blood pressure, myopia, and dental care, were all for relatively prevalent chronic problems (of course, we had difficulty detecting effects for rare problems) that are relatively inexpensive to diagnose and remedy. One can infer that programs targeted at these problems would be much more cost effective in achieving these gains in health than free care for all services. For example, more than half the benefit of free care for high blood pressure (and presumably for risk of dying) was available from a one-time screening examination, whose cost is a small fraction of free care for all services (Keeler et al., 1985).

G. *Health Maintenance Organization Results*

We also randomized a group of participants into an HMO, the Group Health Cooperative of Puget Sound in Seattle.[35] This group, whom we call the HMO Experimentals, was given a plan of benefits identical to the free fee-for-service (FFS) plan. In addition, we enrolled a random sample of existing HMO enrollees, the HMO Controls. Thus, a comparison of the experimentals and the free fee-for-service plan establishes the "pure" HMO effect on use; a comparison of the experimentals and controls establishes the extent, if any, of selection with respect to the HMO.[36]

Our results (Table 7) show no evidence of selection in the single HMO that we studied; those previously enrolled at the HMO (the Controls) used services at approximately the same rate as those who were not previously enrolled (the Experimentals). By contrast, the percentage of Experimental plan participants with one or more hospital admissions was only two-thirds as great as the percentage on the free fee-for-service plan. Because outpatient use was approximately similar on the two plans, the expenditure difference between the HMO Experimentals and free fee-for-service participants was

[35] An HMO is reimbursed a fixed amount per month, in return for which it agrees to provide medical care. Thus, unlike fee-for-service medicine, the approximate marginal revenue from delivering additional services is zero. Of course, there are market constraints on the HMO's behavior because is competes with fee-for-service medicine for patients.

[36] The fee-for-service sample in this comparison is from Seattle, in order to keep the population sampled the same between the two groups.

TABLE 7—ANNUAL USE OF MEDICAL SERVICES PER CAPITA, SEATTLE SAMPLE, BY HMO AND FFS STATUS[a]

Plan	Likelihood of Any Use (%)	One or More Admissions (%)	Imputed Expenditures ANOVA[b] (1983 $)	Imputed Expenditures with Age-Sex Covariates[b] (1983 $)	Person Years
HMO Experimental	87.0	7.1	434	426	3687
	(1.0)	(0.50)	(28)	(23)	
HMO Control	91.1	6.4	432	465	2596
	(0.8)	(0.55)	(34)	(47)	
Free Fee-for-Service	85.3	11.2	640	612	1221
	(1.6)	(1.17)	(81)	(66)	
t-Statistic on Free-Experimental Difference[c]	−0.88	3.24	2.44	2.69	
p Value for t-Statistic, 2 tail	n.s.	.0012	.016	.007	

[a]Standard errors are shown in parentheses. The sample includes participants while they remained in the Seattle area. The sample excludes children born into the study and excludes partial years except for deaths, similar to Tables 1 and 2 above. For HMO Controls and Experimentals, the data include both in- and out-of-plan use. The standard errors are corrected for intertemporal and intrafamily correlation using an approach due to Huber in a similar fashion to Tables 1 and 2 above. The numbers differ slightly from those in Manning et al. (1984), because of minor corrections in the data, as well as the use of a less precise, but more robust method of calculating standard errors. The method is the same as that described in Table 2.

[b]See Manning et al. (1984) for details of imputation method.

[c]Testing null hypothesis of no difference between HMO Experimental and Free Fee-for-Service plan.

somewhat narrower; expenditures per person among the HMO Experimentals were only 72 percent of expenditures on the free fee-for-service plan.

These findings demonstrate that a markedly less hospital-intensive style of medicine than is commonly practiced in the fee-for-service system is technically feasible. Whether the technical style will be attractive to consumers, and, if it is, whether a market of competing HMOs is economically feasible —or whether adverse selection problems will prove insurmountable (Michael Rothschild and Joseph Stiglitz, 1976)—are still somewhat open questions, although the size and history of large HMOs such as Group Health Cooperative of Puget Sound suggest that the style is attractive to some consumers.

In projecting the effect of the growing HMO market share on hospital admissions and medical expenditure, one must keep in mind that the above comparisons have been made against the free care plan. Because virtually all private fee-for-service health insurance plans include some cost sharing, one should compare the reduction in hospital admissions at the HMO, some 35 percent, with the reduction caused by cost sharing, some 15 to 25 percent depending on plan. The values presented above, however, do represent the *ceteris paribus* HMO effect; if an HMO were to use cost sharing, its observed rates of use might be even lower.

Consumers contemplating enrollment in an HMO will weigh the cost savings against any effect of the reduction in services upon health status and consumer satisfaction. Our findings on health status of the HMO are analogous to those in the free fee-for-service system; the mean person in the fee-for-service plan appeared to derive few or no benefits from the additional hospital services (Ware et al., 1986; Elizabeth Sloss et al. 1987). Those who are both in poor health and of low income who were in the HMO exhibited a higher rate of bed-days and serious symptoms (relative to those in the free fee-for-service plan). There is thus some suggestive evidence that special programs to facilitate access for Medicaid enrollees in HMOs may be worthwhile, but we caution that this result comes only from one HMO (albeit a well-established and well-regarded HMO) and that the precision with which we could measure results among the poor, sick group makes this result less than definitive, even in the case of this HMO.

Those who had self-selected the HMO (the Controls) were on average as satisfied with their care as those in the fee-for-service system (Allyson Davies et al., 1986). Theory would suggest the marginal person would be equally satisfied in both systems, and it is not surprising that we detected no difference for the average person. By contrast, the HMO Experimentals were less satisfied overall with their care than those in the fee-for-service system, although on certain dimensions they were as satisfied or even more satisfied.

IV. Conclusions

A. *On Comparing our Estimates of Demand with those in the Literature*

Our results leave little doubt that demand elasticities for medical care are nonzero and indeed that the response to cost sharing is nontrivial. How do our estimates compare with those in the nonexperimental literature?

This question is difficult to answer, because most prior empirical work has parameterized cost sharing as a constant coinsurance rate (for example, Feldstein, 1971, 1977) or has examined particular changes in insurance plans (for example, an imposition of a $3 per visit copayment: Scitovsky and Snyder; Phelps and Newhouse, 1972; Scitovsky and McCall). By contrast, experimental policies were from a two-parameter family (coinsurance rate and maximum dollar expenditure). We make no apologies for this intentional noncomparability; a constant coinsurance rate, while convenient for obtaining comparative statics results, is not an insurance policy that theory suggests would be optimal, assuming risk aversion (Arrow, 1963, 1971, 1973, 1975). Indeed, an optimal policy would almost certainly contain a stop-loss feature, exactly as the experimental plans did.[37]

One could, of course, attempt to estimate the functional response of demand to variation in the two parameters; one can view the values presented above as selected points in the response surface generated by varying coinsurance at given maximum dollar expenditure levels. In order to compare our results with those in the literature, however, we must extrapolate to another part of the response surface, namely, the response to coinsurance variation when there is no maximum dollar expenditure. Although any such extrapolation is hazardous (and of little practical relevance given the considerable departure from optimality of such an insurance policy), we have undertaken such an extrapolation rather than forego entirely any comparison with the literature. Specifically, we have used three different methods to estimate a price elasticity comparable to the estimates in the literature:

1) One can estimate a pure coinsurance elasticity by analyzing variation in the demand for episodes of care rather than annual expenditure per person (Keeler and John Rolph, 1982; Keeler et al., 1987). The theory of demand suggests that individuals who have not yet exceeded the upper limit on out-of-pocket expenses, when making a marginal medical consumption decision, will discount the nominal price by the probability of exceeding the limit (because with that probability the true price is zero) (Keeler, Newhouse, and Phelps, 1977; Randall Ellis, 1986).[38] We therefore examine demand for episodes of treatment by individuals who are more than $400 from their limit. This gives an approximation of the pure price effect if such people treat the true probability of exceeding their limit as nearly zero.[39] The

[37]A stop-loss feature means there is a maximum out-of-pocket loss that the insured can sustain. In addition to its risk-reduction properties, no worst-case payment would have been possible without a stop-loss feature, and hence selection effects might have been introduced into the experiment.

[38]The specific result requires risk neutrality and separability of the utility function in health and money, but the qualitative results does not.

[39]Because there was no appreciable difference between demand for outpatient episodes when the MDE remaining was between $1 and $400 and when it was more than $400, this assumption seems reasonable for

TABLE 8—ARC ELASTICITIES FOR VARIOUS TYPES OF CARE CALCULATED FROM EPISODES[a]

Range of Nominal Coinsurance Variation	Type of Care					
	Outpatient[b]					
	Acute	Chronic	Well	All[c]	Hospital	All Care[c]
0–25 Percent	.16	.20	.14	.17	.17	.17
	(.02)	(.04)	(.02)	(.02)	(.04)	(.02)
25–95 Percent	.32	.23	.43	.31	.14	.22
	(.05)	(.07)	(.05)	(.04)	(.10)	(.06)

[a] The method of calculating standard errors (shown in parentheses) is described in Keeler et al. (1987).

[b] Acute conditions are unforeseen and treatment opportunities are nondeferrable. Chronic episodes comprise foreseen and continuing expenditure; treatment is designed to ameliorate the consequences of the disease rather than cure. Flare-up of chronic conditions, which are unforeseen, we treat as acute. Well care episodes are medically deferrable without great loss and can occur when the patient is not considered sick.

[c] Estimate derived by weighting elasticities for various types of care by budget shares.

estimation method controls for unobserved propensities to have episodes, as well as other observed covariates by looking at experience before and after the MDE is exceeded; see Keeler and Rolph for a description of the methodology. We have computed arc elasticities for the 0–25 and 25–95 percent ranges of coinsurance; those elasticities are shown in Table 8.

2) A second estimate comes from using an indirect utility function and applying it to total expenditure in the 25–95 percent range. This estimate is very close to the first, −0.18 (Manning, 1986).

3) A third estimate comes from a similar calculation to those in the literature, that is, it uses average coinsurance rates (Table 9). The usual proof of an upward bias in the elasticity estimate from using the average coinsurance rate (Newhouse, Phelps, and Marquis) does not apply here because of the balance across plans. The amount of bias, if any, depends on two effects that work in opposite directions. For small expenditures the experimental plans will exhibit smaller expenditure than would a pure coinsurance rate plan of 16 or 31 percent (because the effective coinsurance rate is likely to be higher); for large expenditures exceeding the MDE the opposite will be true (because the marginal coinsurance rate will be zero, not positive). Which effect predominates is an empirical question the experimental data cannot resolve; empirically, this method yields values that are somewhat lower but still close to those of the other two methods. (The lower value suggests the first bias predominates.)

In sum, these three methods suggest that price elasticities for a constant coinsurance policy are in the −0.1 to −0.2 range, values that are consistent with those in the lower range of the nonexperimental literature.

TABLE 9—ARC ELASTICITIES FOR VARIOUS TYPES OF CARE CALCULATED FROM AVERAGE COINSURANCE RATES

Range of Nominal Coinsurance Variation	Range of Average Coinsurance Variation	All Care	Outpatient Care
0–25 Percent	0–16	.10	.13
25–95 Percent	16–31	.14	.21

Source: Calculated from data in Table 2 (outpatient) and Table 3 (total). For those who wish to calculate arc elasticities with the 50 percent plan, from the data in Tables 2 or 3, the average coinsurance rate in the 50 percent plan is 24 percent.

outpatient episodes. It may cause some bias in the estimated hospital elasticity; if the true MDE were, say $10,000 rather than $1000, we might observe fewer hospitalizations.

B. *On the Explanation of the Sustained Rise in Medical Expenditure*

At first blush, our estimates of demand response imply that the spread of health insurance can account for only a modest portion of the postwar rise in medical expenditure, contrary to the commonly held view described in the introduction. Between 1950 and 1984, real medical expenditure rose by a factor of 7,[40] but our estimates of insurance elasticity do not begin to imply this degree of increase. To demonstrate this point, we use the average coinsurance rate. Despite its imperfect measure of the generosity of insurance, it is a gross measure of how much insurance changed over the post-1950 period and therefore indicative of the role insurance might have played in this increase. Table 10 shows the average coinsurance rate by type of service (see Table 9 for comparable values from the 25, 50, and 95 percent plans). Although the figures by service are based on an arbitrary accounting convention, they suggest that the change in insurance in the postwar period was of roughly the same absolute magnitude as the difference between the 95 percent coinsurance and free care plans.[41]

Because the free plan demand was only around 1.5 times that of the 95 percent plan, it appears that the change in insurance can explain only a small part, perhaps a tenth, of the factor of 7 change in health expenditure in the post-World War II period.

Nor can changes in real income (around a factor of 3 during this period) directly account for much of the rise. Income elasticities estimated from the experimental data (the partial response, not the one shown in Table 5) are at most 0.2—much too small to account for anything like a factor of 7 change.[42]

TABLE 10—CHANGE IN AVERAGE COINSURANCE RATE, 1950–84, BY TYPE OF SERVICE

Year	Hospital	Physician	Other	Total
1950	.30	.83	.86	.66
1984	.09	.28	.56	.28

Source: Levit et al. (1985).

Thus, we still must account for the bulk of the expenditure increase. The rather obvious "accounting" explanation of the expenditure increase is technological change; there are a host of new medical products and procedures today that did not exist in 1950. For example, those with kidney failure are now treated with renal dialysis or kidney transplantation; in 1950 these individuals died rather quickly. This merely pushes the puzzle back one stage, however; what role, if any, did insurance (and income growth) play in inducing the technological change? Unfortunately that question cannot be answered from experimental data.[43]

Thus, if insurance is playing a role in inducing a welfare loss, given the rate of increase in medical expenditure, the bulk of that loss must come from its having induced innovation for which unsubsidized consumers would not be willing to pay.[44] Given that most countries in the world have also experienced a long-term sustained increase in expenditure despite widely varying institutional arrangements, it is at least arguable that consumers would be willing to pay for much of the increase, but there clearly

[40] Nominal expenditure data from Katherine Levit et al. (1985) deflated by the GNP deflator.

[41] The accounting convention used by the Health Care Financing Administration allocates a common deductible to services in proportion to gross expenditure. We have followed the same convention in calculating comparable figures from the experimental data.

[42] Real GNP increased between 1950 and 1983 by a factor of 2.9. Even allowing for the usual downward bias from using measured income to estimate income elasticities, it is clear that changes in income can only explain a modest portion of the expenditure increase.

[43] Because most consumers have been insured for inpatient services throughout the relevant time period, it is an extremely difficult question to answer from non-experimental data. Moreover, one does not observe insurance policies that do and do not cover new procedures, so there is no straightforward test of willingness to pay for new technology. Although virtually all policies do not cover "experimental" procedures, once efficacy and "safety" are demonstrated, insurance plans tend to cover all procedures.

[44] The willingness-to-pay calculation should include any willingness to pay for others' care.

has been no pure market test (Newhouse, 1977, 1984).

C. *On the Magnitude of Welfare Loss from Health Insurance*

Setting aside the issue of possible welfare loss from induced technological change, one can estimate the welfare loss in the usual static framework. Under a number of strong assumptions (including that gross medical care prices are competitive and there are no externalities), our estimates imply a nontrivial welfare loss from first-dollar health insurance coverage. An approximation to the loss from moving from a universal 95 percent plan (with a $1000 MDE) to the free care plan is $37 to $60 billion, as against an expenditure around $200 billion on these services in 1984 by the under 65 population.[45] From the $37–60 billion figure must be deducted some amount for the reduced risk in the free plan relative to the 95 percent plan. Usual values for risk aversion, however, would suggest the deduction is small in the presence of a $1000 cap (Feldstein, 1973; Keeler, Morrow, and Newhouse, 1977). Although the $37–60 billion figure is probably overstated by ignoring externalities and assuming medical care prices are competitive, it ignores any welfare loss from induced technological change.[46]

D. *On the Existing Insurance Coverage of Various Medical Services*

One can find several economic reasons for the traditionally more generous coverage of inpatient services relative to outpatient services (Table 10). Loading charges (as a per-

[45] The $37 and $60 billion figures are calculated in the usual Harberger fashion by taking the $325 per capita difference in spending between the 95 percent and free plans from Tables 3 and 6 (Year 2 values) and adding $19 for mental health services (Wells et al., inflated by the change in the CPI Medical Services prices index between 1977 and 1984). We then multiply by 207 million, the number of resident civilians under 65. This yields a figure of $71 billion. One then multiplies by 0.525 or 0.845. Both fractions are larger than the usual 0.5 because we do not start at an unsubsidized point. Our 95 percent $1000 MDE plan had an average coinsurance rate of 0.31. An upper bound on the welfare loss comes from assuming that individuals valued the last dollar at 0.31. A lower bound on the welfare loss comes from assuming that the extra spending is all from individuals who valued the last dollar of spending at 0.95, the nominal coinsurance rate. The 0.525 figure equals $1-.95/2$, and the 0.845 figure equals $1-.31/2$.

The $200 billion figure can be estimated in two ways: 1) Data from Levit et al. show expenditure on personal health care services of $342 billion in 1984. Waldo and Lazenby (1984, Table 11) estimate that $120 billion of this is for the over 65, leaving $222 billion for the under 65. Some of this, however, is for noncovered services, such as nonprescription drugs, and some other part is for ineligible populations, such as the institutionalized. Adjusting for these noncomparabilities is necessarily somewhat imprecise, but would probably leave a final figure around $200 billion. 2) Data from Tables 3 and 6 (Year 2 values) plus data on outpatient mental health spending from Wells et al. inflated to 1984 and scaled up by 207 million population imply an expenditure of $224 billion on the free care plan in our sites and $178 billion on the 25 percent coinsurance plans. Adjusting for price and usage levels in our sites relative to the nation is necessarily imprecise, but these two values probably bracket the true national figure.

[46] The induced technological change is clearly only a welfare loss if patent protection is at the level to induce the appropriate investment in new products in an unsubsidized market. If there is not enough patent protection, there is no necessary welfare loss from insurance's inducing a too rapid rate of innovation. There appears to be one estimate in the literature of the welfare loss from induced change; Feldstein (1973) attempted to adjust for the willingness of consumers to pay for "higher quality care." There is no empirical way to do this, however, so the magnitude of the true welfare loss is highly problematic. Feldstein's method, although not explicit on the point, in effect ignores true technological change. He implicitly assumes that consumers in earlier years could have purchased "higher quality" medical care, but they chose not to because they faced a higher coinsurance rate and/or had lower incomes. (Alternatively, physician "norms of care" were lower because of the higher coinsurance rate and lower income.) As the renal dialysis example makes clear, however, consumers were simply unable to purchase some medical services in earlier years because they did not exist. In many cases their subsequent existence depended on fundamental scientific advance such as the discovery of DNA and would not have occurred without that advance, despite lower coinsurance or higher incomes. Whether consumers in the 1950's and early 1960's would have purchased such services if they had existed then obviously cannot be answered from actual expenditure data. Feldstein's method also yields an upper bound for the same reason our $60 billion estimate is an upper bound.

centage of premium) are less, and the risk of a large loss is greater. For children, price elasticities for inpatient services are not measurably different from zero, and hence for them there is no measurable moral hazard.

This structure of more extensive insurance for inpatient services has been attacked as misguided, however (Milton Roemer et al., 1975), on the grounds that lack of insurance for outpatient services deters ignorant individuals from seeking care at a time in their illness when they can be treated relatively cheaply. Others have also asserted that the more generous coverage of inpatient services leads physicians to hospitalize patients who could be treated on an outpatient basis, thereby minimizing private but increasing social expenditure.

Analysis of a natural (not randomized) experiment supported the claim that more complete coverage of outpatient expenditure reduced total expenditure (Roemer et al.; L. Jay Helms, Newhouse, and Phelps, 1978), but a prior controlled experimental study testing this hypothesis rejected it (Charles Lewis and Harold Keairnes, 1970; D. B. Hill and James Veney, 1980). At issue is whether outpatient and inpatient services are substitutes or complements.

Our findings decisively reject the hypothesis that increased coverage of outpatient services, holding constant the coverage of inpatient services, will reduce expenditure. As Table 3 shows, the mean expenditure on the individual deductive plan (free inpatient, costly outpatient care) is 20 percent less than the mean on the free care plan (free inpatient, free outpatient care), and the difference is statistically significant ($p < .001$).[47] Disaggregation shows that the outpatient deductible not only reduces outpatient expenditure (Table 2) but, if anything, decreases hospital admissions for adults as well (Table 5). The (possibly) decreased admissions for adults suggests that outpatient and inpatient services are, if anything, complements not substitutes.

In the interests of brevity we summarize four other implications for health insurance coverage (these are discussed at greater length in Manning et al., 1987):

There appears to be little justification for the common practice of group insurance policies' treating emergency room services more generously than physician office visits, because emergency room services are as responsive to plan as physician office visits.[48]

There is no support for the so-called offset hypothesis, namely that more complete coverage of psychotherapy services will reduce total medical costs (or at least not increase them) (W. Follette and Nicholas Cummings, 1967, 1968). The experimental data, however, are not very precise on this question.

The observed lesser coverage of outpatient mental health care relative to all outpatient care would be consistent with a greater plan response for mental health care. Although the estimated plan response is in fact substantially larger for mental health care, the difference with all outpatient care is statistically insignificant.[49]

Well-care services are about as price responsive as other medical services. Although there are other reasons for the common practice of not covering well-care

[47] In the ANOVA results (Table 2), the estimated reduction is 19 percent and the t-statistic is 2.34 ($p < .02$, two-tailed test).

[48] We assume that a presumed lower response to insurance is the reason for greater coverage of emergency room services. The alternative explanations, differential loading charges or asymmetric information, are not particularly plausible as explanations of the better coverage of emergency room services. Asymmetric information (differential knowledge of insurer and insured) is not very relevant to a single insurance plan offered in a group setting unless the service is costly enough to motivate an employment change (which might apply to psychotherapy or certainly costly dental services such as orthodontia). Routine office visits do not match this description. Moreover, asymmetric information may apply to both office and emergency room services. An individual may know that his use of office visits differs from average (whereas the insurer does not) but may also know that his likelihood of an accident differs from average, and the insurer may not.

[49] The estimated ratio of the free to 95 plan expenditures is 233 percent, compared with a 169 percent estimate for medical outpatient care (Manning et al., 1986b).

services as generously as other outpatient services (primarily there is little or no uncertainty and loadings are relatively high), greater price responsiveness is not a reason.

E. *Was It Worth It?*

One question frequently raised about social experimentation is whether its benefits are worth its costs (for example, Orley Ashenfelter, 1986; Robert Haveman, 1986). Because the question concerns the value of information, and because the links from this type of information to actual behavior are generally impossible to establish with any rigor, the question admits of no easy answer (save for the trivial case in which the experiment was so poorly designed or conducted that it produced no information). In other words, any attempt to justify the cost of an experiment is necessarily speculative.

Despite the circumstantial nature of the evidence, we believe that the benefits of this particular experiment greatly exceeded the (current dollar, undiscounted) costs of a little over $80 million ($136 million if put in 1984 dollars, and brought forward to 1984 using a 3 percent real discount rate.[50] Between 1982 and 1984, there was a remarkable increase in initial cost sharing in the United States, at least for hospital services. For example, the number of major companies with first-dollar charges for hospital care rose from 30 to 63 percent in those two years, and the number of such firms with an annual deductible of $200 per person or more rose from 4 percent to 21 percent (Jeff Goldsmith, 1984). Although it is impossible to know how much of this change can be attributed to the experimental results, the initial findings of the experiment were published in December 1981 (Newhouse et al., 1981) and December 1983 (Brook et al., 1983) and given wide publicity in both the general and trade press. In certain instances a direct link between changes in cost sharing and the experimental results can be made.[51]

According to the experimental results, this increase in cost sharing should have decreased demand. Hospital days (excluding deliveries) among the under 65 decreased by 19 million days, or 13 percent, discharges decreased by 8 percent (USDHHS, Series 13, 1984; 1986). We estimate the cost saving from this reduced use to be around $7 billion.[52] Physician office and hospital visits among the under 65 fell 27 million during these two years, but to be conservative we have not taken account of this change in estimating the cost savings.[53]

[50] We have used the GNP deflators to inflate costs.

[51] For example, the Xerox Corporation in 1983 announced an increase in its deductible from $100 per person or $200 per family to 1 percent of earnings per family. It raised coinsurance on hospital and surgical services from 0 to 20 percent. Additionally, it lowered its cap on out-of-pocket expenditures (analogous to the MDE) from 6 percent of earnings to 4 percent of earnings. In a brochure distributed to its employees it said: "According to a study by the Rand Corporation, when consumers are required to increase their share of medical costs, there is a significant decrease in the total amount spent for these services. Furthermore, this study —and other similar studies—does not indicate that the health of the employees was affected adversely by the decrease in costs." Despite the large increase in initial cost sharing, the average coinsurance rate for hospital services nationally only rose from 7.6 to 8.7 percent between 1982 and 1984. This modest change in the average rate may reflect both the lowering of ceilings on out-of-pocket expenditure, as in the Xerox case and the highly skewed distribution of hospital expenditure, which means most expenditure exceeds the initial cost sharing.

[52] The average cost per hospital day in 1984 was $417. This uses the 1983 $368 figure from the American Hospital Association (1984) inflated by 13.3 percent, the change in per day inpatient costs from 1983 to 1984 (American Hospital Association, 1985). Bernard Friedman and Pauly (1981, 1983) have argued that the marginal cost/average cost ratio for hospital services is near one. Hence, a *ceteris paribus* estimate of the savings from decreased use, assuming a marginal cost/average cost ratio of 0.9, is around $7 billion (19 million × 417 × 0.9). The American Hospital Association cost per day figure includes the over 65; however, cost per day is not very different for the over 65.

[53] In part, we do not account for such a change because the physician visit rate rose in 1985 to its 1982 value. Thus, the decrease from 1982 to 1984 could have been attributable to chance; alternatively the continued decrease in hospital care in 1985 (another 7.1 percent decrease in patient-days, USDHHS, 1987) may have led to a substitution of outpatient use. Data on physician visits are from the *National Health Interview Survey* (USDHHS, Series 10, 1985; 1986).

If all the changes in patient-days were attributable to the increased cost sharing, and if all the increase in cost sharing is due to the publication of experimental results, and if the benefits of the foregone use were negligible, as our results suggest, the experiment paid for itself in about a week (.136/7)(52)![54] It is clear that these assumptions overstate the benefits of the experiment, yet it is equally clear that the assumptions can be greatly relaxed and still yield the result that the experiment was worth it. Moreover, we have ignored any benefits to countries other than the United States, and any benefits from the decrease in physician visits or changes in dental or mental health coverage or emergency room coverage. We have also ignored any benefits from the results of the HMO portion of the experiment, although HMO's market share has been expanding rapidly from a period just before and subsequent to our first article describing the HMO results (Manning et al., 1984a). Finally, we have ignored the value of the public use files to future research efforts.[55]

Implicit in our conclusions is the assumption that one could not reduce uncertainty with nonexperimental data to the satisfaction of those making decisions about cost sharing. We believe this is likely to be true, because of the wide range of nonexperimental estimates of insurance elasticity cited in the introduction, the difficulty of inferring health status effects from nonexperimental data, and the temporal proximity of the changes in cost sharing to the publication of the experimental results (many of the nonexperimental results had been in the literature for a decade, during which time cost sharing had, if anything, decreased). Thus, we think it highly plausible that the benefits of this endeavor were indeed worth its costs.

[54] The negligible benefits assumption relies on the observation that cost sharing for hospital services was near zero in 1982 and that there were no measurable health benefits outside the dental area for the middle-class employees who would have been the dominant group for whom the cost sharing changed.

[55] The public use files can be ordered from Publications Department, The Rand Corporation, 1700 Main Street, Santa Monica, CA 90406-2138.

F. *On Experimentation in Economics*

Econometric and economics texts often have a statement near the beginning that experimentation is not nearly as possible in economics as it is in the physical sciences. Perhaps the degree of difference is not as great as many think. Well-designed and executed field and laboratory experiments are feasible and can add substantially to the body of knowledge (Walter Heller, 1975; Charles Plott, 1982).[56] We hope this example will encourage others to ask whether an experiment is practical or feasible when approaching empirical questions.

[56] For other views of field experiments see Jerry Hausman and David Wise (1985) and Robert Ferber and Werner Hirsch (1978).

REFERENCES

Arrow, Kenneth J., "Uncertainty and the Welfare Economics of Medical Care," *American Economic Review*, December 1963, *53*, 941–73.

______, *Essays in the Theory of Risk-Bearing*, Chicago: Markham, 1971.

______, *Optimal Insurance and Generalized Deductibles*, Publ. No. R-1108-OEO, Santa Monica: Rand Corporation, 1973.

______, "Two Notes on Inferring Long Run Behavior from Social Experiments," Publ. No. P-5546, Rand Corporation, 1975.

Ashenfelter, Orley, "Book Review of *The National Supported Work Demonstration*," *Journal of Economic Literature*, September 1986, *24*, 1268–1270.

Bailit, Howard et al., "Does More Generous Dental Insurance Coverage Improve Oral Health?," *Journal of the American Dental Association*, May 1985, *110*, 701–07.

Barer, Morris L., Evans, Robert G. and Stoddart, Gregory L., "Controlling Health Care Costs by Direct Charges to Patients: Snare or Delusion?," Occasional Paper No. 10, Toronto: Ontario Economic Council, 1979.

Baumol, William J. and Bradford, David F., "Optimal Departures from Marginal Cost Pricing," *American Economic Review*, June 1970, *60*, 263–83.

Beck, R. G., "The Effects of Co-Payment on the Poor," *Journal of Human Resources*, Winter 1974, *9*, 129–42.

Brook, Robert H. et al., "Overview of Adult Health Status Measures Fielded in Rand's Health Insurance Study," *Medical Care*, 1979, Suppl., *17*, 1–131.

______ **et al.**, "Does Free Care Improve Adults' Health? Results from a Randomized Controlled Trial," *New England Journal of Medicine*, December 8, 1983, *309*, 1426–34.

______ **et al.**, *The Effect of Coinsurance on the Health of Adults*, Publ. No. R-3055-HHS, Santa Monica: Rand Corporation, 1984.

Clasquin, Lorraine A., *Mental Health, Dental Services, and Other Coverage in the Health Insurance Study*, Publ. No. R-1216-OEO, Santa Monica: Rand Corporation, 1973.

______ **and Brown, Marie E.**, *Rules of Operation for the Rand Health Insurance Study*, Publ. No. R-1602-HEW, Santa Monica: Rand Corporation, 1977.

Colle, Ann D. and Grossman, Michael, "Determinants of Pediatric Care Utilization," *Journal of Human Resources*, 1978, Suppl., *13*, 115–58.

Culyer, Anthony J., "The Nature of the Commodity 'Health Care' and Its Efficient Allocation," *Oxford Economic Papers*, July 1971, *23*, 189–211.

______, *Need and the National Health Service* Totowa: Rowman and Littlefield, 1976.

______, "Measuring Health: Lessons for Ontario," Ontario Economic Council Research Studies No. 14, University of Toronto, 1978.

Davies, Allyson et al. "Consumer Acceptance of Prepaid and Fee-for-Service Medical Care: Results from a Randomized Trial," *Health Services Research*, August 1986, *21*, 429–52.

Davis, Karen and Russell, Louise B., "The Substitution of Hospital Outpatient Care for Inpatient Care," *Review of Economics and Statistics*, May 1972, *54*, 109–20.

Duan, Naihua, "Smearing Estimate: A Nonparametric Retransformation Method," *Journal of the American Statistical Association*, September 1983, *78*, 605–10.

______ **et al.**, "A Comparison of Alternative Models for the Demand for Medical Care," *Journal of Economic and Business Statistics*, April 1983, *1*, 115–26 [also R-2754-HHS, Rand Corporation, 1982].

______ **et al.**, "Choosing Between the Sample-Selection Model and the Multi-Part Model," *Journal of Business and Economic Statistics*, July 1984, *2*, 283–89.

Ellis, Randall P., "Rational Behavior in the Presence of Coverage Ceilings and Deductibles," *Rand Journal of Economics*, Summer 1986, *17*, 158–75.

Evans, Robert G., *Strained Mercy: The Economics of Canadian Health Care*, Toronto: Butterworths, 1984.

Feldstein, Martin S., "Hospital Cost Inflation: A Study of Nonprofit Price Dynamics," *American Economic Review*, December 1971, *61*, 853–72.

______, "The Welfare Loss of Excess Health Insurance," *Journal of Political Economy*, March/April 1973, *81*, 251–80.

______, "Quality Change and the Demand for Hospital Care," *Econometrica*, October 1977, *45*, 1681–702.

______ **and Allison, Elizabeth**, "Tax Subsidies of Private Health Insurance," in *The Economics of Federal Subsidy Programs*, Pt. 8, papers submitted to the Subcommittee on Priorities and Economy in Government of the Joint Economic Committee, 93rd Congress, 2nd session, July 1974.

______ **and Friedman, Bernard**, "Tax Subsidies, the Rational Demand for Insurance, and the Health Care Crisis," *Journal of Public Economics*, April 1977, *7*, 155–78.

Ferber, Robert and Hirsch, Werner, "Social Experimentation and Economic Policy: A Survey," *Journal of Economic Literature*, December 1978, *16*, 1379–404.

Follette, W. and Cummings, Nicholas A., "Psychiatric Services and Medical Utilization in a Prepaid Health Plan Setting," *Medical Care*, January 1967, *5*, 26–35.

______ **and** ______, "Psychiatric Services and Medical Utilization in a Prepaid Health Plan Setting, Part 2," *Medical Care*, January 1968, *6*, 31–41.

Friedman, Bernard and Pauly, Mark, "Cost Functions for a Service Firm with Variable Quality and Stochastic Demand," *Review of Economics and Statistics*, November 1981, *63*, 610–24.

______ **and** ______, "A New Approach to Hospital Cost Functions and Some Issues in Revenue Regulation," *Health Care Financing Review*, March 1983, *4*, 105–14.

Goddeeris, John and Weisbrod, Burton, "What We Don't Know about Why Health Expenditures Have Soared: Interaction of Insurance and Technology," *Mount Sinai Journal of Medicine*, November 1985, *52*, 685–91.

Goldman, Fred and Grossman, Michael, "The Demand for Pediatric Care: An Hedonic Approach," *Journal of Political Economy*, April 1978, *86*, 259–80.

Goldsmith, Jeff, "Death of a Paradigm: The Challenge of Competition," *Health Affairs*, Fall 1984, *3*, 5–19.

Hausman, Jerry and Wise, David, *Social Experimentation*, Chicago: University of Chicago Press, 1985.

Haveman, Robert, "Social Experimentation and *Social Experimentation*," *Journal of Human Resources*, Fall 1986, *21*, 586–605.

Helms, L. Jay, Newhouse, Joseph, P. and Phelps, Charles E., "Copayments and the Demand for Medical Care: The California Medicaid Experience," *Bell Journal of Economics*, Spring 1978, *9*, 192–208.

Heller, Walter, W., "What's Right with Economics," *American Economic Review*, March 1975, *65*, 1–26.

Hill, D. B. and Veney, James E., "Kansas Blue Cross/Blue Shield Outpatient Benefits Experiment," *Medical Care*, March-April 1980, *8*, 143–58.

Huber, P. J., "The Behavior of Maximum Likelihood Estimates Under Nonstandard Conditions," *Fifth Berkeley Symposium on Mathematical Statistics and Probability*, Vol. 1, 1967, 221–33.

Keeler, Emmett B. and Rolph, John E., *The Demand for Episodes of Medical Services: Interim Results from the Health Insurance Experiment*, R-2829-HHS, Santa Monica: Rand Corporation, December 1982.

______, Morrow, Daniel and Newhouse, Joseph P., "The Demand for Supplementary Health Insurance, or Do Deductibles Matter?," *Journal of Political Economy*, August 1977, *85*, 789–802.

______, Newhouse, Joseph, P. and Phelps, Charles E., "Deductibles and the Demand for Medical Care Services: The Theory of a Consumer Facing a Variable Price Schedule under Uncertainty," *Econometrica*, April 1977, *45*, 641–56.

______ et al., "How Free Care Reduced Hypertension of Participants in the Rand Health Insurance Experiment," *Journal of the American Medical Association*, October 11, 1985, *154*, 1926–31.

______ et al., *The Demand for Episodes of Medical Treatment*, Publ. No. R-3454-HHS, Santa Monica: Rand Corporation, 1987.

Leibowitz, Arleen et al., "Effect of Cost Sharing on the Use of Medical Services by Children: Interim Results from a Randomized Controlled Trial," *Pediatrics*, May 1985, *75*, 942–51.

Levit, Katherine R. et al., "National Health Expenditures, 1984," *Health Care Financing Review*, Fall 1985, *7*, 1–35.

Lewis, Charles E. and Keairnes, Harold, "Controlling Costs of Medical Care by Expending Insurance Coverage," *New England Journal of Medicine*, June 18, 1970, *292*, 1405–12.

Lindsay, Cotton M., "Medical Care and the Economics of Sharing," *Economica*, November 1969, *36*, 351–62.

Lohr, Kathleen N. et al., "Use of Medical Care in the Rand Care in the Rand Health Insurance Experiment: Diagnosis- and Service-Specific Analyses," *Medical Care*, September 1986, Suppl.

Long, Stephen H., Settle, Russell F. and Stuart, Bruce C., "Reimbursement and Access to Physicians' Services under Medicaid," *Journal of Health Economics*, September 1986, *5*, 235–52.

Luft, Harold S., *Health Maintenance Organizations*, New York: Wiley & Sons, 1981.

McCombs, Jeffrey S., "Physician Treatment Decisions in a Multiple Treatment Model: The Effects of Physician Supply," *Journal of Health Economics*, August 1984, *3*, 155–71.

Maddala, G. S., *Limited-Dependent and Qualitative Variables in Econometrics*, Cambridge: Cambridge University Press, 1983.

Manning, Willard G., "Estimating Demand Functions with Data from Declining Block Tariffs," draft, June 1986.

______, Duan, Naihua and Rogers, William H., *Monte Carlo Evidence on the Choice between Sample Selection and Two-Part Models*, Santa Monica: Rand Corporation, forthcoming.

______ **et al.**, (1984a) "A Controlled Trial of the Effect of a Prepaid Group Practice on Use of Services," *New England Journal of Medicine*, June 7, 1984, *310*, 1505–10 [also R-3029-HHS, Rand Corporation, December 1985].

______ **et al.**, (1984b) "Cost Sharing and the Demand for Ambulatory Mental Health Services," *American Psychologist*, October 1984, *39*, 1090–100.

______ **et al.**, "The Demand for Dental Care: Evidence from a Randomized Trial in Health Insurance," *Journal of the American Dental Association*, June 1985, *110*, 895–902.

______ **et al.**, (1986a) *Health Insurance and the Demand for Dental Care: Evidence from a Randomized Experiment*, Publ. No. R-3225-HHS, Santa Monica: Rand Corporation, 1986.

______ **et al.**, (1986b) "How Cost Sharing Affects the Use of Ambulatory Mental Health Services," *Journal of the American Medical Association*, 1986, *256*, 1930–34.

______ **et al.**, *Health Insurance and the Demand for Medical Care: Evidence from a Randomized Experiment*, Publ. No. R-3476-HHS, Santa Monica: Rand Corporation, 1987.

Mehran, F., "Variance of the MVUE for the Log Normal Mean," *Journal of the American Statistical Association*, 1973, *68*, 726–27.

Metcalf, Charles E., "Making Inferences from Controlled Income Maintenance Experiments," *American Economic Review*, June 1973, *63*, 478–483.

Morris, Carl N., "A Finite Selection Model for Experimental Design of the Health Insurance Study," *Journal of Econometrics*, September 1979, *11*, 43–61.

Musgrave, Richard, *The Theory of Public Finance*, New York: McGraw-Hill, 1959.

Newhouse, Joseph P., "A Design for a Health Insurance Experiment," *Inquiry*, March 1974, *11*, 5–27.

______, "Medical Care Expenditure: A Cross-National Survey," *Journal of Human Resources*, Winter 1977, *12*, 115–25.

______, "Insurance Benefits, Out-of-Pocket Payments, and the Demand for Medical Care: A Review of the Literature," *Health and Medical Care Services Review*, July-August 1978, *1*, 3–15.

______, "The Demand for Medical Care Services: A Retrospect and Prospect," in J. van der Gaag and M. Perlman, eds., *Health, Economics, and Health Economics*, Amsterdam: North-Holland, 1981.

______, "Are Medical Care Costs Too High?," *Journal of Dental Education*, November 1984, *48*, 587–90.

______ **and Phelps, Charles E.**, "Price and Income Elasticities for Medical Care Services," in M. Perlman, ed., *The Economics of Health and Medical Care*, New York: Wiley & Sons, 1974.

______ **and** ______, "New Estimates of Price and Income Elasticities of Medical Care Services," in R. N. Rosett, ed., *The Role of Health Insurance in the Health Services Sector*, Universities-National Bureau Conference Series No. 27, New York, 1976.

______, ______, **and Marquis, M. Susan,** "On Having Your Cake and Eating It Too: Econometric Problems in Estimating the Demand for Health Services," *Journal of Econometrics*, August 1980, *13*, 365–90.

______ **et al.**, "Design Improvements in the Second Generation of Social Experiments: The Health Insurance Study," *Journal of Econometrics*, September 1979, *11*, 117–29.

______ **et al.**, "Some Interim Results from a Controlled Trial of Cost Sharing in Health Insurance," *New England Journal of Medicine*, December 17, 1981, *305*, 1501–07 [see R-2847-HHS, Rand Corporation, 1982].

______ **et al.**, "The Findings of the Rand Health Insurance Experiment: A Response to Welch et al.," *Medical Care*, February 1987, *25*, 157–79.

O'Grady, Kevin F. et al., "The Impact of Cost Sharing on Emergency Department Use," *New England Journal of Medicine*, August 22, 1985, *313*, 484–90.

Pauly, Mark V., *Medical Care at Public Expense*, New York: Prager, 1971.

______, "Taxation, Health Insurance, and Market Failure," *Journal of Economic Literature*, June 1986, *24*, 629–75.

Phelps, Charles E. and Newhouse, Joseph P., "Effects of Coinsurance: A Multivariate Analysis," *Social Security Bulletin*, June 1972, *35*, 20–29.

______ **and** ______, "Coinsurance, the Price of Time, and the Demand for Medical Services," *Review of Economics and Statistics*, August 1974, *56*, 334–42.

Plott, Charles R., "Industrial Organization Theory and Experimental Economics," *Journal of Economic Literature*, December 1982, *20*, 1435–527.

Ramsey, Frank, "A Contribution to the Theory of Taxation," *Economic Journal*, March 1927, *37*, 47–61.

Roemer, Milton J. et al., "Copayments for Ambulatory Care: Penny-wise and Pound-foolish," *Medical Care*, 1975, *13*, 475–66.

Rogers, William H., and Newhouse, Joseph P., "Measuring Unfiled Claims in the Health Insurance Experiment," in L. Burstein et al., eds., *Collecting Evaluation Data: Problems and Solutions*, Beverly Hills: Sage, 1985, 121–33.

Rosett, Richard N. and Huang, Lien Fu, "The Effect of Health Insurance on the Demand for Medical Care," *Journal of Political Economy*, March/April 1973, *81*, 281–305.

Rothschild, Michael and Stiglitz, Joseph, "Equilibrium in Competitive Insurance Markets: An Essay on the Economics of Imperfect Information," *Quarterly Journal of Economics*, November 1976, *90*, 629–50.

Scitovsky, Anne A. and McCall, Nelda M., "Coinsurance and the Demand for Physician Services: Four Years Later," *Social Security Bulletin*, May 1977, *40*, 19–27.

______ **and Snyder, Nelda M.**, "Effect of Coinsurance on Use of Physician Services," *Social Security Bulletin*, June 1972, *35*, 3–19.

Searle, S. R., *Linear Models*, New York: Wiley & Sons, 1971.

Sloss, Elizabeth M. et al., "Effect of a Health Maintenance Organization on Physiologic Health: Results from a Randomized Trial," *Annals of Internal Medicine*, January 1987, *106*, 130–38.

Tobin, James, "Estimation of Relationships for Limited Dependent Variables," *Econometrica*, January 1958, *26*, 24–36.

Valdez, R. Burciaga, *The Effects of Cost Sharing on the Health of Children*, Publ. No. R-3270, Santa Monica: Rand Corporation, 1986.

______ **et al.**, "The Consequences of Cost Sharing for Children's Health," *Pediatrics*, May 1985, *75*, 957–61.

Van de Ven, Wynand P. and van Praag, Bernard M., (1981a) "The Demand for Deductibles in Private Health Insurance: A Probit Model with Sample Selection," *Journal of Economics*, November 1981, *17*, 229–52.

______ **and** ______, (1981b) "Risk Aversion of Deductibles in Private Health Insurance," in J. van der Gaag and M. Perlman, eds., *Health, Economics, and Health Economics*, Amsterdam: North-Holland, 1981.

Waldo, Daniel and Lazenby, Helen C., "Demographic Characteristics and Health Care Use and Expenditures by the Aged in the United States, 1977–1984," *Health Care Financing Review*, Fall 1984, *6*, 1–29.

______**, Levit, Katherine R. and Lazenby, Helen C.**, "National Health Expenditures, 1985," *Health Care Financing Review*, Fall 1986, *8*, 1–21.

Ware, John E. et al., *Conceptualization and Measurement of Health*, Vol. I, R-1987/1-HEW, Santa Monica: Rand Corporation, May 1980.

______ **et al.**, "Comparison of Health Outcomes at a Health Maintenance Organization with Those of Fee-for-Service Care," *The Lancet*, May 3, 1986, *848*, 1017–22.

Wells, Kenneth B. et al., *Cost Sharing and the Demand for Ambulatory Mental Health Services*, Publ. No. R-2960-HHS, Santa Monica: Rand Corporation, 1982.

Zeckhauser, Richard J., "Medical Insurance: A Case Study of the Trade-Off between Risk Spreading and Appropriate Incentives," *Journal of Economic Theory*, March 1970, *2*, 10–26.

American Hospital Association, "1984 Hospital Cost and Utilization Trends," *Economic Trends*, Spring 1985, 1.

______, *Hospital Statistics*, 1984 Edition, Chicago: AH Association, 1984.

U.S. Department of Health and Human Services, "Current Estimates from the *National Interview Health Survey*," Series 10: 150, 1985; 156, 1986, Washington: USDHHS.

______, "Utilization of Short Stay Hospitals," Series 13: 78, 1984; 84, 1986; 90, 1987; Washington: USDHHS.

[19]

The Impact Of Medicare Part D On Prescription Drug Use By The Elderly

Evidence from a large retail pharmacy chain suggests that Medicare Part D increased the number of prescriptions used by the elderly and reduced their out-of-pocket drug spending.

by Frank R. Lichtenberg and Shawn X. Sun

ABSTRACT: This study investigates the effect of Medicare Part D on the elderly's prescription drug use and out-of-pocket costs using a difference-in-differences research design. We estimate that Medicare Part D reduced user cost among the elderly by 18.4 percent, increased their use of prescription drugs by about 12.8 percent, and increased total U.S. usage by 4.5 percent in 2006. The estimated crowd-out rate was about 72 percent: Every seven prescriptions paid for by the government crowded out five other prescriptions and resulted in only two additional prescriptions used. This does not necessarily mean that Medicare Part D is an economically inefficient program. [*Health Affairs* 26, no. 6 (2007): 1735–1744; 10.1377/hlthaff.26.6.1735]

THE MEDICARE PRESCRIPTION DRUG, IMPROVEMENT, and Modernization Act (MMA), enacted in 2003, produced the largest overhaul of Medicare in its thirty-eight-year history. MMA's most important provision was the establishment on 1 January 2006 of a federal entitlement benefit for prescription drugs for Medicare beneficiaries (Medicare Part D), through tax breaks and subsidies. The Congressional Budget Office (CBO) estimates that net Medicare Part D outlays were $32 billion in 2006, and it projects that cumulative outlays through 2015 will be $797 billion.[1]

As of 1 January 2006, all forty-three million Medicare beneficiaries had access to the new Part D prescription drug benefit offered by stand-alone prescription drug plans (PDPs) or Medicare Advantage prescription drug (MA-PD) plans. The Medicare drug benefit is voluntary; people may choose whether or not to enroll in a Part D plan. For beneficiaries who previously had no drug coverage, Part D represented a new opportunity to get help with their drug costs. For many beneficia-

Frank Lichtenberg (frl1@columbia.edu) is the Courtney C. Brown Professor of Business at Columbia University in New York City and a research associate of the National Bureau of Economic Research in Cambridge, Massachusetts. Shawn Sun is manager of Health Outcomes Collaborative Research, Health Outcomes Department, Walgreens Health Services, in Deerfield, Illinois.

DOI 10.1377/hlthaff.26.6.1735

ries, Part D replaced the drug coverage they had under Medicare health maintenance organizations (HMOs), Medigap, or Medicaid. Others could keep the drug coverage they had from an alternative source, such as an employer or the Department of Veterans Affairs (VA), provided it was "creditable"—that is, at least as generous as standard Part D coverage. Still others elected to go without any creditable source of drug coverage, although those without creditable coverage could be subject to late enrollment penalties.

The 2006 enrollment period ended 15 May 2006. The U.S. Department of Health and Human Services (HHS) reported that as of 11 June 2006, 22.5 million Medicare beneficiaries had prescription drug coverage from a Medicare Part D plan. Another 10.4 million had creditable drug coverage from an employer plan. HHS also estimated that 5.4 million beneficiaries had creditable drug coverage from an alternative source, such as the VA. Altogether, the Bush administration reports that by June 2006 about 90 percent of Medicare's forty-three million beneficiaries had creditable drug coverage.

There is debate about the magnitude of Medicare Part D's impact on prescription drug use by, and the health of, the Medicare population. The Centers for Medicare and Medicaid Services (CMS) claims that "the MMA legislation provides seniors and people with disabilities with the first comprehensive prescription drug benefit ever offered under the Medicare program, the most significant improvement to senior health care in nearly 40 years."[2] But in a 2004 paper, Mark Pauly argued that "from the viewpoint of improvements in health, national spending on drugs, or pharmaceutical firm revenues, effects [of Medicare drug coverage improvement] are small."[3] Pauly predicted that Medicare drug coverage improvement would increase the elderly's use of drugs by only about 6 percent. This prediction was based on the following reasoning. Medicare drug coverage improvement affects drug usage via its effect on the out-of-pocket cost (or "user cost") of prescription drugs. Pauly estimated that for people with no previous drug coverage, Medicare drug coverage improvement would reduce user cost by almost 50 percent. However, almost three-fourths of elderly Americans already had some kind of drug coverage; Medicare drug coverage improvement would have almost no effect on their user cost. He estimated that overall, Medicare drug coverage improvement would reduce user cost by 14 percent. Previous studies indicated that the price elasticity of demand for prescription drugs is about 0.4. The implied impact of Medicare drug coverage improvement on drug utilization by the elderly is about 6 percent (0.4×14 percent).

The standard way to evaluate the impact of public insurance expansions is to compare the behavior of individuals or groups made eligible and not made eligible by expansions, even when these individuals and groups had some coverage (including private coverage) prior to the expansion. David Cutler and Jonathan Gruber estimated regressions of insurance coverage on eligibility for insurance and other variables.[4] David Card and Lara Shore-Sheppard compared changes in insurance coverage in populations made eligible and not made eligible by expansions.[5] Almost all (97.4 percent of) elderly people (age sixty-five and older), and relatively few (2.4 percent of) nonelderly people, are enrolled in Medicare, hence eligible for Medicare Part D. Comparing the behavior of the elderly and nonelderly is therefore almost equivalent to comparing the behavior of people eligible and not eligible for Medicare Part D.[6]

In this paper we used a difference-in-differences (DD) research design to evaluate the impact of Medicare Part D: We calculated changes in the ratio of elderly to nonelderly mean user cost and utilization before and after 1 January 2006. The DD approach controlled for the effects of all time-varying determinants of prescription drug use and cost that are common to elderly and nonelderly people. One of us (Frank Lichtenberg) used a similar approach to evaluate the effects of launching Medicare Parts A and B in the 1960s.[7]

Study Data And Methods

We used data on prescriptions filled by one of the nation's largest retail pharmacy chains during the period September 2004–December 2006.[8] The pharmacy chain fills about 1.4 million prescriptions per day, on average—about 18 percent of all prescriptions filled in the United States. To reduce computing burden, we drew a 50 percent sample (essentially, every other week) of the prescription drug claims. Each claim includes the following information: the date the prescription was filled, the patient's age, the number of days of therapy dispensed, the amount paid by the patient (for example, copayment), the amount paid by third parties, and whether the prescription was retail or mail order. Hence, we could compute the total amount paid for the prescription (amount paid by the patient plus amount paid by third parties). By aggregating the data, we calculated the number of prescriptions, the number of days of therapy dispensed, mean amount paid by the patient, and mean total amount paid, by date and patient age.

Prescriptions dispensed by the pharmacy chain differ from all U.S. prescriptions in two respects. First, the pharmacy chain's drug customers tend to be younger than U.S. drug customers in general. One-fifth (21 percent) of the pharmacy's prescriptions were dispensed to elderly customers. Data from the Medical Expenditure Panel Survey (MEPS) indicate that during the period 1996–2003, 33–35 percent of U.S. prescriptions were dispensed to elderly patients.[9] If the difference between the age distribution of the pharmacy chain's customers and other drug customers was fairly stable over time, this discrepancy will not bias our estimate of the impact of Medicare Part D on prescription drug use.

Second, the mail-order share of the pharmacy chain's prescriptions is lower than the mail-order share of all U.S. prescriptions. In December 2006, 4.5 percent of spending on the pharmacy chain's prescriptions was on mail-order prescriptions. Mail order accounted for 14 percent of retail prescription drug sales nationwide in 1999, up from 13 percent in 1998.[10]

Study Results

Exhibit 1 shows summary statistics for the approximately 50 percent sample of the pharmacy chain's prescription drug claims during the period September 2004–December 2006. The data set contains information about fifteen billion days of therapy, whose total cost was $33 billion.

Exhibit 2 shows monthly data on the amount paid by the patient per day of therapy, by age group. From September 2004 to December 2005, the amounts paid by elderly and nonelderly patients per day of therapy were quite similar; in December 2005 they differed by less than 1 percent.[11] But from December 2005 to June 2006, the amount paid by elderly patients per day of therapy fell, while the amount paid by nonelderly patients per day of therapy remained essentially unchanged. In June 2006 the amount paid by elderly patients per day of therapy was about 24 percent lower than the amount paid by nonelderly patients. The fact that relative user cost fell gradually, rather than suddenly, is consistent with the gradual enrollment of seniors in Medicare Part D. According to the CMS, the number of Medicare beneficiaries with prescription drug coverage increased from twenty-four million on 1 January 2006 to thirty-eight million on 11 June 2006.[12]

The user-cost differential narrowed slightly in the last six months of 2006; it was 21 percent in December 2006. This may be attributable to an increasing number of Medicare patients' falling into the Part D coverage gap ("doughnut hole") in the second half of the year.

Exhibit 3 shows monthly data on the relative user cost (mean amount paid by the patient per day of therapy) and relative utilization (number of days of therapy) of elderly and nonelderly patients. The exhibit shows log-differences between elderly and non-elderly patients. For example, relative user cost is $(\log(USER_E) - \log(USER_N))$, where $USER_E$ = mean amount paid by elderly patients per day of therapy, and $USER_N$ = mean amount paid by nonelderly patients per day of ther-

EXHIBIT 1
Summary Statistics For The Approximately 50 Percent Sample Of Prescription Drug Claims From The Major Retail Pharmacy Chain, September 2004–December 2006

	Elderly	Nonelderly	Total
Number of prescriptions	125,168,312	459,341,225	584,509,537
Number of days of therapy	3,970,483,265	11,030,571,174	15,001,054,439
Total amount paid	$7,032,500,017	$26,395,283,980	$33,427,783,997
Amount paid by patient	$2,422,995,529	$7,431,808,189	$9,854,803,718
Amount paid by third parties	$4,609,504,488	$18,963,475,792	$23,572,980,280
Total amount paid per day of therapy	$1.77	$2.39	$2.23
Amount paid by patient per day of therapy	$0.61	$0.67	$0.66
Amount paid by third parties per day of therapy	$1.16	$1.72	$1.57
Amount paid by patient/total amount paid	34%	28%	29%

SOURCE: Authors' calculations.

EXHIBIT 2
Amount Paid For Prescription Drugs By The Patient Per Day Of Therapy, Elderly And Nonelderly In Sample, September 2004–December 2006

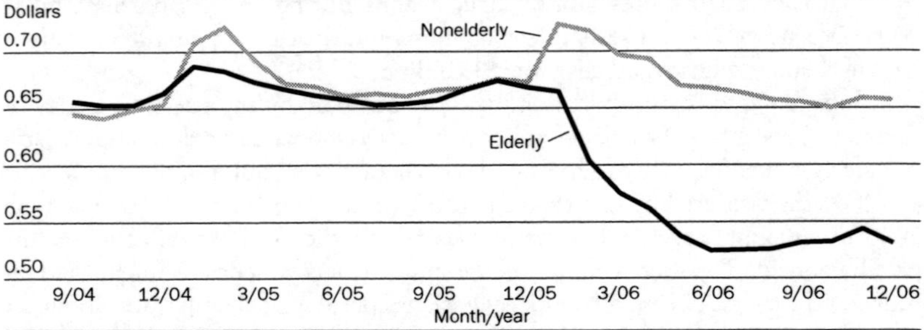

SOURCE: Authors' calculations based on data from major retail pharmacy chain, September 2004–December 2006.

apy. Relative utilization is shown on an inverted scale.

There was a gradual but substantial increase in relative utilization by the elderly between December 2005 and June 2006; it increased almost 19 percent. In the second half of 2006, as relative user cost increased, relative utilization declined by about 6 percent. The increase in relative utilization from December 2005 to July 2006, and the smaller decline in relative utilization from July 2006 to December 2006, could have been attributable to factors other than changes in relative user cost, but it is not apparent what those factors might be.

EXHIBIT 3
Relative Utilization (Number Of Days Of Therapy) And Relative User Cost (Mean Amount Paid By The Patient Per Day Of Therapy), Elderly And Nonelderly Patients, September 2004–December 2006

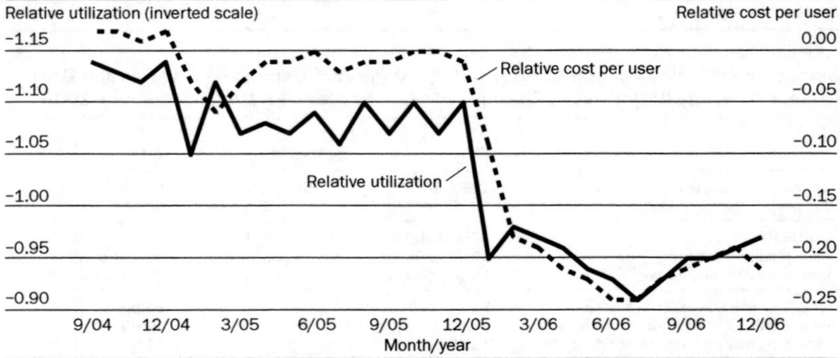

SOURCE: Authors' calculations based on data from major retail pharmacy chain, September 2004–December 2006.
NOTES: Relative utilization (solid line) relates to the left-hand *y* axis. Relative cost per user (dotted line) relates to the right-hand *y* axis.

Under certain assumptions, the slope of the simple regression of relative utilization on relative user cost is an estimate of the elasticity of demand for prescription drugs.[13] The estimate of this elasticity, based on twenty-eight monthly observations, is 0.72 (t-stat = 14.1, $p < 0.0001$). This is considerably larger than the estimate (0.4) that Pauly used to make his forecast of the utilization impact of Medicare drug coverage improvement. An alternative estimation approach, based on data aggregated by drug and month rather than by age group and month, also indicates a demand elasticity well above 0.4, albeit not as high as 0.72.[14]

A simple way to assess the impact of Medicare Part D is to compute the difference in the 2005–2006 growth rates of key variables for the elderly versus the nonelderly. These calculations are shown in Exhibit 4.[15] The mean amount paid by nonelderly patients per day of therapy declined 0.4 percent, while the mean amount paid by elderly patients declined 18.8 percent. The number of days of therapy for the nonelderly increased 6.8 percent, while the number of days of therapy for the elderly increased 19.5 percent. This suggests that Medicare Part D reduced user cost among the elderly by 18.4 percent and increased utilization among them by about 12.7 percent. The ratio of the latter to the former is 0.70—virtually the same as the estimate of the demand elasticity reported above.

Because of the increase in utilization, Medicare Part D reduced the total amount paid by patients by only 5.6 percent. It increased the amount paid by third parties by 22.3 percent. Medicare Part D seems to have had a negligible impact on the overall price of prescription drugs (expenditure per day of therapy); the elderly and nonelderly growth rates differ by just 0.3 percent.

The preceding calculations were based on partitioning the pharmacy customers into just two age groups: elderly (age sixty-five and older) and nonelderly (under age sixty-five). We also calculated the percentage increase between 2005 and

EXHIBIT 4
Elderly Versus Nonelderly Difference In The 2005–06 Growth Rates Of Key Variables

	Percent change from 2005 to 2006		
Variable	**Elderly**	**Nonelderly**	**Difference**
Amount paid by patient per Rx	−13.7	1.9	−15.6
Amount paid by patient per day of therapy	−18.8	−0.4	−18.4
Spending per Rx	7.1	4.6	2.5
Spending per day of therapy	2.0	2.3	−0.3
Number of Rx	14.4	4.5	10.0
Number of days of therapy	19.5	6.8	12.8
Days of therapy per Rx	5.1	2.3	2.8
Total amount paid by patients	0.8	6.4	−5.6
Total payments by third parties	32.4	10.1	22.3
Total spending	21.5	9.0	12.5

SOURCE: Authors' calculations based on data from major retail pharmacy chain, September 2004–December 2006.

2006 in utilization (number of days of therapy) by single year of age for people ages 45–84.[16] Three below-sixty-five ages (fifty-nine, sixty, and sixty-four) exhibit large (more than 19 percent) growth, which is a bit puzzling. However, all but three of the top twenty ages, ranked by 2005–06 utilization growth, are sixty-five or older. This supports the view that the elderly versus nonelderly differences we have documented are primarily due to Medicare Part D.

We next used our estimate of the impact of Medicare Part D on the elderly's use of drugs to calculate the market value of the increase in prescriptions among the elderly in 2006 attributable to Medicare Part D and the extent of crowding out of prescription drug use (Exhibit 5).

Line 1 shows that the elderly versus nonelderly difference in the 2005–06 percentage change in the number of days of therapy was 12.8 percent. Since a small fraction of elderly Americans are not enrolled in Medicare, and a small fraction of nonelderly Americans are enrolled in Medicare, the Medicare versus non-Medicare difference is likely to be a little larger than the elderly versus nonelderly difference. Lines 2 and 3 make an adjustment for this. Line 3 indicates that Medicare Part D is estimated to have raised the Medicare population's use of drugs by 13.5 percent in 2006. Since this population uses about one-third of prescription drugs, this implies that Medicare Part D increased total U.S. drug utilization by 4.5 percent (one-third of 13.5 percent) in 2006.

To calculate the absolute increase in drug utilization resulting from Medicare Part D, we need to know the number of prescriptions used by the Medicare popu-

EXHIBIT 5
Calculation Of The Market Value Of The Increase In Prescriptions For The Elderly In 2006 Attributable To Medicare Part D

Line	Description	Estimate	Source
1	Elderly versus nonelderly difference in percent change, 2005–06, in number of days of therapy	12.8%	Exhibit 4
2	Estimated ratio of (Medicare versus non-Medicare difference) to (elderly versus nonelderly difference)	105.3%	Note 6 in text
3	Medicare versus non-Medicare difference in percent change, 2005–06, in number of days of therapy	13.5%	Line 1 times line 2
4	Projected number of elderly prescriptions in 2006, based on 1996–2003 trend	1.172 billion	Authors' calculations based on data from MEPS
5	Estimated absolute increase in elderly prescriptions in 2006 due to Medicare Part D	158 million	Line 3 times line 4
6	Mean cost of Rx	$57.19	Exhibit 1
7	Estimated market value of increase in elderly prescriptions in 2006 due to Medicare Part D	$9.034 billion	Line 5 times line 6
8	Cost of Medicare Part D in 2006	$32 billion	CBO

SOURCES: See above.
NOTES: MEPS is Medical Expenditure Panel Survey. CBO is Congressional Budget Office.

lation in 2006, or what usage would have been in the absence of Medicare Part D. We approximated the latter by calculating the growth rate of the MEPS estimate of the number of prescriptions dispensed to elderly patients during 1996–2003 and extrapolating to 2006. The average annual growth rate is 6.4 percent, so the projected number of prescriptions for the elderly in 2006, without Medicare Part D, is 1.172 billion. Therefore, as shown in line 5 of Exhibit 5, Medicare Part D is estimated to have raised the number of prescriptions by 158 million in 2006.

The average cost of a prescription was $57.19 in 2006, so the market value of the 158 million additional prescriptions was $9.0 billion. The CBO estimates that net Medicare Part D outlays were $32 billion in 2006. The cost to the federal government of increasing drug usage was 3.5 times as great as the market value of the additional prescriptions. In other words, every seven prescriptions paid for by the government crowded out five other prescriptions and resulted in only two additional prescriptions used. The crowd-out rate was about 72 percent (1 – [$9 billion/$32 billion]).

Discussion And Policy Implications

To evaluate the health and economic impact of increased public insurance coverage or spending, one thing we need to know is how much these policies reduce private insurance coverage or spending. A number of previous studies have attempted to estimate the rate of crowd-out from other public insurance expansions. The most commonly used measure of this is the decline in private coverage among those newly eligible relative to the increase in public coverage among the newly eligible.[17] Gruber and Kosali Simon estimate that the crowd-out rate of public insurance expansions during 1996–2002 was about 60 percent.[18] They also found that anti-crowd-out efforts (such as waiting periods and especially cost sharing) that have accompanied the State Children's Health Insurance Program (SCHIP) have probably raised crowd-out more than they have lowered it: They have reduced take-up by the uninsured faster than they have deterred crowd-out from private insurance.

Our estimate of the Medicare Part D crowd-out rate is higher, but not much higher.[19] A high crowd-out rate implies that large increases in public spending are required to obtain relatively small increases in prescription drug use by the elderly. We estimate that the federal government spent about $203 ($32 billion/158 million) for each additional prescription consumed by the elderly—3.5 times as much as the average price of a prescription ($57).

This does not necessarily mean that Medicare Part D is an economically inefficient program. First, the cost to society per additional prescription is probably well below $203. The cost to society of an additional prescription is the cost of producing and marketing it, which is likely to be much lower than $57, plus the "excess burden of taxation" required to finance the Medicare drug benefit.[20] Arye Hillman notes that estimates of the excess burden of taxation have ranged from high to low values.[21]

Second, there is evidence that although reducing the user cost of prescription drugs increases drug spending, it reduces other medical spending, because it increases compliance with drug therapy. Dana Goldman and colleagues examined the relationship between copayments for cholesterol-lowering drugs and compliance in the year after initiation of therapy, using claims data from eighty-eight health plans during 1997–2001. They also examined the association between compliance and subsequent hospital and emergency department (ED) use for up to four years after initiation. They found a large inverse relationship between copayments and compliance in all risk groups: For each $10 rise in copayments, average compliance in a plan-year fell by five percentage points. They estimated that if the health plans had reduced high- and medium-risk patients' copayments on cholesterol-lowering medications from $10 to $0, their pharmacy payments would have increased by $486 million, but their inpatient hospital spending would have declined by $839 million.[22] Their spending on ED visits would also have declined. The 18.4 percent decline in the amount paid by patient per day of therapy attributable to Medicare Part D has probably reduced Parts A and B spending, but the magnitude of the decrease is not yet known.

To perform a comprehensive difference-in-differences assessment of Medicare Part D, we would also like to have data on the relative health outcomes (mortality and morbidity) of elderly and nonelderly Americans before and after the program began. Because of lags in availability of public-use data, this won't be feasible for another year or two. The most recent published government data on mortality are for 2004, and available data on health status and hospital use are for 2005.

The authors did not receive any financial support for the preparation of this paper.

NOTES

1. For details, see Appendix Exhibit 1, online at http://content.healthaffairs.org/cgi/content/full/26/6/1735/DC1. Also see Congressional Budget Office, "Projection of Spending for the Medicare Part D Benefit," 9 February 2005, http://www.cbo.gov/showdoc.cfm?index=6076&sequence=0 (accessed 28 January 2007).
2. Centers for Medicare and Medicaid Services, "Prescription Drug Coverage—General Information: Overview," 23 May 2007, http://www.cms.hhs.gov/PrescriptionDrugCovGenIn/01_Overview.asp (accessed 13 August 2007).
3. M.V. Pauly, "Medicare Drug Coverage and Moral Hazard," *Health Affairs* 23, no. 1 (2004): 113–122. Others have made predictions about the impact of Part D. For example, Bruce Stuart and colleagues predicted that Part D would cover less than half of the annual drug bills for enrollees with high or catastrophic costs in 2006–2008. However, only Pauly made predictions about the effects of Part D on overall user costs and use. B. Stuart et al., "Riding the Rollercoaster: The Ups and Downs in Out-of-Pocket Spending under the Standard Medicare Drug Benefit," *Health Affairs* 24, no. 4 (2005): 1022–1031.
4. D. Cutler and J. Gruber, "Does Public Health Insurance Crowd Out Private Insurance?" *Quarterly Journal of Economics* 111, no. 2 (1996): 391–430.
5. D. Card and L. Shore-Sheppard, "Using Discontinuous Eligibility Rules to Identify the Effects of the Federal Medicaid Expansions on Low Income Children," *Review of Economics and Statistics* 86, no. 3 (2004): 752–766.
6. Medicare versus non-Medicare differences are about 5.3 percent ([1/(97.4 percent – 2.4 percent)] – 1) larger than elderly versus nonelderly differences.

7. F.R. Lichtenberg, "The Effects of Medicare on Health Care Utilization and Outcomes," *Forum for Health Economics and Policy*, Frontiers in Health Policy Research 5, Article 3, 2002, http://www.bepress.com/fhep/5/3 (accessed 28 January 2007).
8. The pharmacy chain is Walgreens, operated by Walgreen Co., Deerfield, Illinois. As of 30 November 2006, Walgreens had 5,580 retail pharmacies throughout the United States.
9. See Appendix Exhibit 2, online as in Note 1.
10. Maryland Health Care Commission, "Prescription Drug Spending," Spotlight on Maryland, December 2000, http://mhcc.maryland.gov/spotlight/drug.pdf (accessed 3 May 2007). More recent data are not available.
11. Total amount paid per day of therapy was lower for elderly patients; the elderly paid for a larger fraction of their prescription drug costs.
12. U.S. Department of Health and Human Services, "Nearly Twenty-four Million Medicare Beneficiaries Now Have Prescription Drug Coverage," Press Release, 17 January 2006, http://www.hhs.gov/news/press/2006pres/20060117.html (accessed 13 August 2007); and HHS, "Thirty-seven Million Medicare Beneficiaries Now Receiving Prescription Drug Coverage," Press Release, 10 May 2006, http://www.hhs.gov/news/press/2006pres/20060510.html (accessed 13 August 2007). The CMS figure implies that about 57 percent (24 million out of 42.4 million) of Medicare beneficiaries had prescription drug coverage in January 2006. However, Stuart and colleagues estimated that in 1998, 75.3 percent of all community-dwelling Medicare beneficiaries had prescription drug coverage, and the CBO estimated that in 2000, 73 percent of beneficiaries (including institutionalized beneficiaries) had coverage. CBO data, as reported in Douglas Holtz-Eakin, director, Congressional Budget Office, "Prescription Drug Coverage and Medicare's Fiscal Challenges," Statement before the House Committee on Ways and Means, U.S. House of Representatives, 9 April 2003.
13. See Section I of the Technical Appendix, online as in Note 1.
14. See Section II of the Technical Appendix; ibid.
15. Estimates based on data just for the second halves of 2005 and 2006 are very similar.
16. See Appendix Exhibit 3, online as in Note 1.
17. Robert Wood Johnson Foundation, "Public Program Crowd-Out of Private Coverage: What Are the Issues?" Research Synthesis Report no. 5, http://www.rwjf.org/pr/synthesis/reports_and_briefs/issue5.html (accessed 13 August 2007).
18. J. Gruber and K. Simon, "Crowd-Out Ten Years Later: Have Recent Public Insurance Expansions Crowded Out Private Health Insurance?" NBER Working Paper no. 12858 (Cambridge, Mass.: National Bureau of Economic Research, January 2007).
19. The general definition of the crowd-out rate is 1 minus the ratio of change in total insurance coverage or spending to change in public insurance coverage or spending. Estimates of Medicaid expansion crowd-out have generally been based on changes in insurance coverage: 1 minus the ratio of change in total insurance coverage to change in public insurance coverage (where total insurance coverage includes both public and private). Our estimate of Medicare Part D crowd-out is based on changes in spending: 1 minus the ratio of change in total drug spending to change in public drug spending—in this case, 1 – ($9 billion/$32 billion), or 72 percent.
20. The excess burden of taxation, also known as the distortionary cost or deadweight loss of taxation, is the economic loss society suffers as the result of a tax, over and above the revenue it collects. See the Wikipedia entry on "Excess Burden of Taxation," http://en.wikipedia.org/wiki/Excess_burden_of_taxation (accessed 13 August 2007). To the extent that Medicare Part D was financed by government borrowing, rather than current taxation, the excess burden may fall on future taxpayers.
21. "Estimating the size of the excess burden of taxation is an empirical task that requires us to look at how people respond in their labor supply or effort decisions to increased taxes. ...Empirical measurement of the excess burden of taxation has provided different answers." A.L. Hillman, *Public Finance and Public Policy: Responsibilities and Limitations of Government* (Cambridge: Cambridge University Press, 2003), 136.
22. D.P. Goldman, G.F. Joyce, and P. Karaca-Mandic, "Varying Pharmacy Benefits with Clinical Status: The Case of Cholesterol-Lowering Therapy," *American Journal of Managed Care* 12, no. 1 (2006): 21–28.

[20]

Demand Effects of Recent Changes in Prescription Drug Promotion

"Advertisements contain the only truth to be relied on in a newspaper."
Thomas Jefferson

"Advertising is a racket . . . its constructive contribution to humanity is exactly minus zero."
F. Scott Fitzgerald[1]

"I think I was wrong . . . . On the whole, I think there is a lot of educational benefit" (to direct-to-consumer prescription drug advertising).
David A. Kessler, M.D., former FDA Commissioner [2]

Since 1994, total spending on consumer-directed promotion for prescription drugs has grown nearly tenfold [Henry J. Kaiser Family Foundation 2000]. Consumers and their physicians report that prescription drug advertisements are increasingly influential. In surveys of consumers, the share of people reporting they have seen an advertisement on television or heard an advertisement on the radio for a prescription drug more than doubled between 1993 and 2000, reaching 81% by 2002 [Alperstein and Peyrot 1993; NewsHour/Kaiser/HSPH 2000; Aikin 2002]. Some estimates indicate that as many as 25% of Americans have asked their doctors about a medication as a result of seeing an advertisement [Prevention Magazine, 2001]. Similarly, many physicians report that their patients have asked them about drugs as a direct consequence of consumer advertising [Borzo 1997; Kaufman and Hoffman 1997].

The rise of direct-to-consumer advertising (DTCA) of prescription drugs represents a departure from the industry's historical concentration on promotion to physicians, hospitals, and other health care organizations.[3] This phenomenon is highly targeted towards a minority of products. In one recent study of 391 major branded drugs in 1999, only 18% had positive DTCA expenditures, whereas 95% of brands sent "detailers" to visit physicians' offices [Neslin, 2001]. Traditional physician-oriented forms of promotion remain important. Even among those products that employ DTCA, professional promotion continues to command a larger share of marketing budgets [Table 2].

The change in marketing mix by pharmaceutical manufacturers is likely a response to recent changes in market and regulatory conditions.[4] Consumers are increasingly seeking active participation in their own health care, aided in part by the wealth of information available on the Internet. At the same time, physicians may have less discretion over choice of brand name drugs than they once did as a result of direct and indirect constraints placed on their prescribing behavior by managed care. In addition, in 1997 the FDA released tentative guidelines (finalized in 1999) regarding advertising to consumers via electronic media such as radio and TV. These guidelines may have facilitated more widespread use of these media. In particular, the new FDA guidelines clarified the requirements for adequate disclosure of information concerning indications, risks and effects of a drug, thus removing a major barrier to television and radio advertising [Rosenthal et al. 2002].

The release of updated FDA guidelines and independent changes in consumer behavior provide an opportunity to study the effects of DTCA in the prescription drug market as well as the effects of various physician-oriented promotions. In this paper, we examine the effects of two types of promotional spending for brands in five therapeutic classes of drugs, using monthly aggregate U.S. data from August 1996 through December 1999. Specifically, we provide evidence on two issues: (i) Do increases in DTCA increase the market size of an entire therapeutic class? (ii) Does relative DTCA within a given therapeutic class affect market shares within that therapeutic class? In both cases, we examine these impacts relative to traditional physician-oriented promotional efforts.

I. Review of Related Literature

Our research builds on and relates to a number of other studies. Early economic studies of physician-oriented marketing of prescription drugs by Bond and Lean [1977], Hurwitz and Caves [1988], Leffler [1981], and Vernon [1981] considered evidence that this marketing was more "persuasive" than "informative", although the distinction between the two was ambiguous. This distinction reflects a more general literature that viewed advertising alternatively as changing consumers' preferences [Kaldor 1950], creating or exaggerating product differentiation and thereby increasing barriers to entry [Bain 1956], or as providing information about a product's characteristics and its price [Stigler 1961]. A common finding from the empirical literature was that professional promotion of prescription drugs increased entry costs and decreased price competition by increasing perceived product differentiation. A related medical study on physician detailing is by Avorn, Chen and Hartley [1982], who advocated counter-detailing to offset the unbalanced information provided by prescription drug detailers.[5]

More recent research by King [2000] on anti-ulcer medications finds that own marketing reduces (in absolute value) a brand's own price elasticities of demand, but that total industry marketing reduces the extent of product differentiation. Berndt et al. [1997] distinguish between "industry expanding" and "rivalrous" marketing efforts, and find that for antiulcer medications cumulative spending on both medical journal and physician detailing increases own-brand sales. They also report that the impact of total class marketing efforts on total class sales is positive, and generally (but not always) declines with the number of products on the market. Rizzo [1999] reports that for antihypertensive drugs, both stocks and flows of detailing expenditures decrease the price elasticity through the development of greater brand loyalty.

Using a proprietary data set from a pharmaceutical manufacturer that incorporates physician-specific marketing measures for one of its brands, Manchanda, Chintagunta and

Gertzis [2000] find that detailing has a significant positive impact on the number of prescriptions written for that drug by the physician, that this marginal impact increases when free product samples are also provided to the physician, and that for the majority of physicians in their sample, diminishing (though still positive) returns to detailing had already set in. Gonul et al. [2001] report similar diminishing returns to physician detailing, but find that detailing and free samples increase price sensitivity, where price is measured as the average retail price for the drug.

The empirical studies cited above focused on physician detailing, and in some cases, medical journal advertising, but did not examine DTCA.[6] Unlike physician-oriented promotions, to the extent that DTCA raises awareness among previously untreated consumers of the existence of potentially effective treatments, DTCA could bring more patients into physician offices. Whether the effect of such increased "physician office foot traffic" is greater on overall therapeutic class sales, or on the share of sales for the specific brand named in the advertisement, is unclear a priori and is an empirical question addressed in this study.

Prior to 1997, DTCA was permitted if a medical condition was mentioned but the brand was not, or if the brand was mentioned, no mention was made of the medical condition for which it was intended, and instead the ad encouraged the individual to see her/his physician regarding the brand. Berndt et al. [1995] obtained ad agency DTCA data for branded antiulcer (H_2-antagonist) prescription drugs up through May 1994, along with detailing and medical journal advertising data from other sources. For the entire H_2 therapeutic class, advertising demand elasticities were 0.55 for detailing, 0.20 for medical journal advertising, and 0.01 for this type of DTCA; the sum of these elasticities is 0.76, suggesting decreasing returns to scale to overall advertising. Within this therapeutic class, although own-detailing and own-medical journal advertising stocks positively affected own-market shares, own DTCA had no significant impact on own-market share.

Two recent studies of DTCA by Wosinska [2001] and Ling, Berndt and Kyle [2002] incorporate data after the FDA's 1997 clarification of DTCA guidelines. Wosinska uses 1996-

1999 prescription drug claims data for 4,728 patients who filled a total of 11,529 new prescriptions for cholesterol reducing drugs in the Blue Shield of California medical plans, along with national data on physician detailing, samples and DTCA. She finds that DTCA positively impacts total therapeutic class sales, but only impacts an individual brand positively if that brand has a preferred status on the third party payer's formulary.

Unlike the cholesterol-reducing drugs, the H_2-antagonist drugs are sold not only in prescription (Rx) form, but since 1995-96 also as over-the-counter (OTC) drugs. Both OTC and Rx versions of these brands have utilized DTCA, and thus various spillovers between Rx and OTC DTCA can be assessed, both between and within brands. Ling, Berndt and Kyle find that DTCA marketing of OTC brands has no spillover to the same brand in the Rx market. Within the Rx market, own-brand physician-oriented detailing and medical journal advertising efforts have positive and long-lived impacts on own Rx market share, while DTCA of the Rx brand has no significant impact on own Rx market share. Within the OTC market, not only are own-brand impacts of DTCA on the OTC brand significantly positive and long-lived, but physician-oriented Rx marketing efforts have positive own-brand spillovers to the OTC share. DTCA efforts for Rx brands have no significant impact on same-brand OTC shares.

II. Theoretical Considerations

The codfish lays ten thousand eggs,
The homely hen lays one.
The codfish never cackles
To tell you what she's done.
And so we scorn the codfish,
While the humble hen we prize,
Which only goes to show you
That it pays to advertise.[7]

The theoretical foundations underlying the economics of advertising rely in large part on Dorfman and Steiner [1954], who showed that for a profit-maximizing monopolist facing a downward-sloping linear demand curve, the optimal advertising expenditure to dollar sales ratio equaled the ratio of two-elasticities, ε_{QA} -- the elasticity of quantity demanded with respect to advertising efforts, and ε_{QP} -- the elasticity of quantity demanded with respect to price (in absolute value), i.e.,

$$\$ \text{ Advertising}/\$ \text{ Sales} = \varepsilon_{QA}/ \varepsilon_{QP}. \quad (1)$$

The Dorfman-Steiner theorem is static in that it assumes that advertising efforts last only one time period, but it can readily be generalized to a dynamic case in which the effects of advertising efforts persist several periods into the future -- so-called "carryover" effects [Schmalensee 1972]. When there are several marketing instruments (and constant unit marketing media costs), under reasonable conditions the optimal ratio of expenditures for any two media equals the ratio of their marketing elasticities [Palda 1969].

In terms of demand marketing elasticities and advertising-sales ratios, it is useful to consider the taxonomy of Nelson [1970,1974], who has distinguished as polar opposites search and experience goods. If a consumer can determine a product's quality and impact prior to purchase merely by visual, tactile or analytical inspection, the product is said to have search qualities. Examples of search goods are many electronic goods, tools, and credit cards. If a customer must consume the product to predict its quality and impact, the good is said to have experience qualities. Examples of experience goods include cosmetics, restaurants and cereals. Although in practice precise demarcation of goods into search vs. experience is not possible, particularly when multi-attribute goods have both search and experience qualities, in general goods with dominant experience attributes have greater advertising-sales ratios than do goods with dominant search qualities. To the extent prescription pharmaceuticals have idiosyncratic and unpredictable impacts (differential efficacy, side effects and adverse interactions with other drugs), pharmaceuticals would appear to have more experience than search qualities. However, for those pharmaceuticals having highly predictable outcomes, search qualities may dominate.

Carlton-Perloff [1994] suggest that producers of search goods are more likely to use informational advertising, while experience goods producers are more likely to use persuasive advertising, although they note that the division is not perfect, nor is there unanimity in what constitutes information vs. persuasion. They interpret the greater advertising-sales ratios of experience goods as possibly reflecting the fact that "images (used in persuasive advertising) are forgotten more quickly than facts (used in informative advertising). Thus, consumers may learn and remember that a particular good has fewer calories (is "less filling") in one or a few exposures to an advertisement, but need to be bombarded with repeated exposures to be convinced that a product "tastes great"."[8]

The effects of advertising on the welfare of individuals have long been analyzed and debated. Carlton-Perloff summarize this literature by stating that "the welfare effects of advertising are complex and depend on the type of product and type of advertising", and therefore "are generally ambiguous".[9] Brand loyalty, for example, may reduce price responsiveness of demand, but can also reduce consumers' search costs.[10] Bagwell [2001] provides a useful collection of economics articles dealing with the theoretical foundations and empirical analyses of advertising as information vs. persuasion, search vs. experience, and the relationships among advertising, product quality and market structure.[11]

Finally, in addition to affecting demand, advertising can be used as a strategic tool to affect possible entry into a product market. Ellison and Ellison [2000] hypothesize and empirically assess branded pharmaceutical firms' advertising strategies in the context of affecting potential generic entry as the brand's patent protection expires. They find empirical evidence supporting their theoretical prediction that branded drugs with medium size markets reduce their advertising intensities to a greater extent prior to patent expiration than do drugs with either very small or very large markets.

III. The Marketing of Prescription Pharmaceuticals: Descriptive Data

Pharmaceutical companies currently employ a number of promotional strategies for prescription drugs designed to target professionals and consumers, respectively (Table 1). Because physicians have long been the key decision makers when it comes to choosing a prescription drug, pharmaceutical companies traditionally have concentrated most of their marketing efforts on physicians, and still do so today. These physician-oriented marketing efforts include visits or phone calls by pharmaceutical sales representatives to physicians (detailing), free samples, print advertising, and sponsorship of medical education events. In 2000, the vast majority of spending on professional promotion (about 81%) was concentrated on detailing (30.6%) and samples (50.6%).

Consumer-oriented promotion, which includes advertising in both print and electronic media, was nearly non-existent as an approach to promotion of pharmaceuticals in the U.S. as of 1980. Beginning in the 1980s and early 1990s a limited amount of DTCA began appearing. By 1994 a rapidly increasing trend in DTCA spending became apparent (Figure 1). The release of the clarified FDA guidelines in 1997 occurred in the midst of this trend and may have accelerated it. By 2000, DTCA comprised 15.7% of total promotion expenditures.[12]

As shown in Table 2, there is very substantial heterogeneity in DTCA and physician-oriented promotion to sales ratios. For new products, this ratio can be as high as 2.05 (Aciphex, a proton pump inhibitor), and as low as 0.0 (Mevacor, a cholesterol reducing drug). Within classes, there is also substantial heterogeneity in DTCA, detailing and sampling to dollar sales ratios (e.g., the antidepressants and nasal spray classes in Table 2).

IV. Empirical Implementation

Our aim is to estimate the impact of DTCA on consumer demand for prescription drugs. The literature on the demand for prescription drug products makes use of a number of approaches to model specification. These include implementation of Almost Ideal Demand System (AIDS), Cobb-Douglas specifications and logit models [Ellison et al. 1997; Rizzo 1999; King 2000; Ling, Berndt and Kyle 2002; Frank and Hartman 2002]. Each specification has its advocates in the literature. None has yet been shown to be superior in estimating demand models in markets for prescription drugs.

Following others, in the demand analysis pursued here we estimate the demand for prescription drug products in the context of multi-stage budgeting. That is, we estimate models of the impact of promotional spending (DTCA and detailing) at the level of the entire therapeutic class (e.g., Selective Serotonin Reuptake Inhibitors (SSRI) antidepressants) and at the level of the individual product within the class (e.g., Prozac among the SSRIs).[13] This multi-stage structure is illustrated in Figure 2. At the top level of the tree, which represents the therapeutic class of drugs, we estimate the impact of DTCA spending and detailing in the context of a Cobb-Douglas demand specification (double logarithmic). In the analysis of competition at the individual product level within each class we specify and estimate three alternative models: 1) an AIDS type specification; 2) a logit model with log of quantity share divided by (1- quantity share) on the left hand side, and prices and promotional spending on the -right hand side; and 3) a Cobb-Douglas model in log levels.

A. Data Sources

We examine monthly data from August 1996 to December 1999 for five therapeutic classes of drugs: recent vintage anti-depressants (SSRIs plus serotonin/norepinephrine reuptake inhibitors (SNRIs)), antihyperlipidemics, proton pump inhibitors, nasal sprays, and antihistamines (Table 2). These classes were selected on the basis of the following criteria: (1) presence of at least one product with high DTCA expenditures during the time period, (2) within class variation in DTCA, and (3) within class variation in the life cycles of the drugs. The classes treat a wide variety of ailments, are indicated for different patient populations and are prescribed by a number of different clinical specialties. Data were collected on all of the drugs in each of these five classes.

Sales and promotion data for selected products were obtained from marketing research firms. Data on DTCA spending were obtained from Competitive Media Reporting (formerly known as Leading National Advertisers), which tracks local and national advertising campaigns in major media such as television and radio for brands with at least $25,000 in annual advertising expenditures. Three major components of professional promotional spending are reported here: detailing to office-based physicians, detailing to hospital-based physicians, and the value of free samples left with physicians. Drug-specific data on professional journal advertising, which represents a small percentage of overall promotional expenditures for products in the six drug classes, was not included.

Spending data on detailing was obtained from Scott-Levin Inc., a pharmaceutical market research firm. Scott-Levin imputes spending on detailing from a panel of roughly 12,000 office- and hospital-based physicians, which comprises roughly two percent of the U.S. physician population. The physicians track their contacts with pharmaceutical sales representatives. Data on the retail value of free samples provided by pharmaceutical companies were obtained from IMS Health, which uses a panel of 1,265 front office staff in medical practices to monitor the volume of samples dropped off by sales representatives. We used the retail value of samples to approximate the opportunity cost to the pharmaceutical companies of giving away free samples. Because samples presumably crowd out at least some sales, production costs would understate the cost of samples to the manufacturers. Using the retail price to value all free samples probably overstates the opportunity cost to the manufacturer, however, so that our marketing elasticity for professional promotion may be underestimated. Sales data were obtained from Scott-Levin, which audits over 35,000 retail pharmacies and projects total sales based on an independent estimate of total U.S. retail sales of prescription drugs.

Market shares were constructed from product-level data on sales for the drugs in each of the six classes. Price data were constructed by Scott-Levin using their sales data. We then created a quantity sold variable based on dividing sales by price for a particular month. Note that this price variable is not the average consumer copayment for that drug, but instead is the average price received by wholesalers from their customers.

Patent information was collected from the Food and Drug Administration's *Orange Book*. A variable was created to indicate the number of months left on a product's patent. Order of entry within a class was determined based on the FDA approval date available through the *Orange Book*.

Table 2 identifies the therapeutic class and individual product combinations that are analyzed below. Together these five classes accounted for 30% of all DTCA in 1999. Table 2 also reports the year each drug was approved, the three-year average promotion to sales ratio for detailing, sampling and for DTCA.

B. Basic Models

We now set out the basic estimation models used in the analysis. As noted above, the Cobb-Douglas formulation is used for both the class level demand model as well as the individual product demand model. Equation (2) is the Cobb-Douglas specification for the product specific analyses:

$$\ln q = \alpha + \beta_1 \ln DTCA + \beta_2 \ln Det + \sum_j \delta_j X_j \qquad (2)$$

where Det is detailing and the X_j 's are other explanatory variables.

Equation (3) represents the general specification of the modified AIDS model.

$$S_i = \alpha + \beta_i \ln\left(\frac{P_i}{P_j}\right) + \phi_i \ln DTCA + \phi_2 \ln Det + \sum_{ix} \sigma_{ix} X_{ix} \ , \qquad (3)$$

where S_i is the dollar revenue share of the ith drug within a therapeutic class, and P_i and Pj are prices of drugs i and j (in our model, P_j is actually the share-weighted price index for other competitors in the class because there are more than two drugs in every class). Finally, we use the same right hand side variable in estimating model specifications where the dependent variable is specified as the logit of quantity shares for the individual drug products. Several variants of these specifications are also estimated as discussed below.

C. Specification and Measurement of Key Variables

There are two important sets of measurement and specification issues with our demand models of prescription drug promotion. They are: 1) the measurement and specification of the price variables, and 2) the specification of promotional spending. The appropriate price to measure in a traditional consumer demand model is the out-of pocket cost of the drug to the consumer. For a variety of reasons this desired measure is not available. The Scott-Levin data we analyze measures price as the payment made by drug stores to wholesalers for each drug. Because this measure takes into account discounts and charge-backs to pharmaceutical manufacturers, these prices are not simple list prices. Nevertheless, these observed prices do not take account of the rebates that are given to health plans and other third party payers for prescription drugs, nor the structure of beneficiary cost sharing for prescription drugs by health plans. Both the level of rebates obtained by different payers and the structure of co-payments are quite heterogeneous, even within the customers of a single drug store [Frank 2001]. Thus, the observed prices are measured with error and are probably not closely correlated with the desired consumer out of pocket price. For these reasons we take two approaches in empirical implementation. In one set of models we include the mismeasured price variables. In another set of models we omit the price variables and instead include a more extensive set of indicator variables to account for time trends and unobserved cross sectional effects.

The specification of measures of promotional spending has generally taken one of the three forms in the literature. Promotion has been treated as a simple flow variable that is measured by current levels of promotional spending [Wosinska 2001]. That approach assumes that current buying behavior depends largely on current exposure to promotional activities. A second approach specifies promotional activity as affecting consumer choice in terms of a lag structure [Rizzo 1999, Wosinka 2001]. The assumption here is that the appropriate measure is still viewed as a flow, only there is a lagged response to the promotional activities. The third approach is to treat promotional activity as a stock that depreciates at a constant rate over time [Berndt et al., 1995, 1997].

Our point of departure is to treat promotional spending as a simple flow. We also explored creating a stock. Our historical data on DTCA and detailing is, however, quite limited. We therefore experimented with a variable based on three-month cumulative spending. When we used this variable in the specifications, our time series was shortened, and the resulting parameter estimates did not differ markedly from those assuming a simple flow. We therefore chose to focus on the results that are based on treating promotional spending as a simple flow.

We take account of the possibility that spending on DTCA and physician promotion and product sales are jointly determined by estimating instrumental variables (IV) models where all three variables are assumed to be endogenous. Three sets of variables serve as the basis for our exclusion restrictions in the IV specifications for the product specific demand equations. The first is the time left on patent for each drug (and its square). This is based on the notion that for products reaching the end of their patent protection period there is little incentive to invest in promotion [Frank and Salkever 1992; Berndt, Kyle and Ling 2002]. The length of the patent life remaining is determined far in advance of current sales decisions, and there is no direct effect on sales because there is no generic competition for these drugs yet in place. The second instrument reflects the timing of the FDA's clarification of the conditions governing direct-to-consumer advertising on television (and the interaction of that indicator with time). In 1997 the FDA clarified that television advertisements could refer consumers to a physician, a 1-800 number, a manufacturer web site and a magazine article that provides the full description of the drugs as required by labeling regulations. This clarification served to reduce the cost of airing a television promotional spot but should not have had a direct impact on sales. The third instrument is the interpolated monthly value of television advertising costs per minute, based on annual data from Robert M. Coen Associates.

The IV model for DTCA is estimated using a two-part model where the first stage is a logit of whether there was any spending on DTCA in a given month and the second stage is a regression model on the natural log of DTCA conditional on any spending (Cragg 1971; Duan et al. 1983). For detailing a simple two-stage IV was estimated because all drugs in the sample were promoted via detailing.

Finally, we experiment with several specifications of a time effect. We use a combination of quarterly dummy variables to capture seasonal effects, and a quadratic time trend to account for secular trends in the pharmaceutical marketplace. All models estimate standard errors robust to heteroskedasticity and clustering.

VI. Econometric Results

We begin by presenting results in Table 3 for the top of the tree structure in Figure 2, the class level quantity equations. Three specifications of the Cobb-Douglas functional form are reported. They differ according to whether a monthly time trend was included in the model (only in column 3) and whether interaction effects between drug class and quarter were included (only in column 3). Overall the models fit the data well with R^2 statistics of 0.60 to 0.95.

The estimated elasticities of DTCA and detailing are quite stable across model specifications. For spending on DTCA the estimated elasticity ranges from 0.096 to 0.114. All estimates are very precise with t-statistics of about 10. The results suggest that a 10% increase in DTC spending would result in an approximately 1% increase in sales, other things equal.

The case of proton pump inhibitors (PPIs) offers insights into the implications of this result. Between 1998 and 1999 PPI class sales grew from \$4.2 billion to \$5.7 billion, a change of nearly 36%. During the same period DTCA spending for PPI products grew from \$49.7 million to \$80.1 million, an increase of 60%. Using an elasticity of 0.10 based on the results reported above suggests that about 6 percentage points of the growth in PPI spending is directly attributable to DTCA. That translates into \$252 million in sales or about 17% of the sales increase from 1998 to 1999. Note that the increase in PPI sales directly attributable to increased DTCA is about 8.3 times the increase in DTCA ($252 vs. $30.4 million).

For the case of nasal sprays DTC spending grew by 37% between 1998 and 1999 (from $83 to $115.2 million). The corresponding growth in sales was from $726 million to $990 million or 36%. The elasticity estimate suggests that the growth in DTC spending was responsible for a 3.7% growth in sales, or 10.3% of the total growth in sales. That amounts to about $26 million. Here the sales increase directly attributable to increased DTCA spending is only 0.8 times the DTCA increase ($26 vs. $32.2 million). Industry officials have suggested to us that their targeted changes in sales are in the range of four to five times the change in DTCA spending at the brand level (increased sales are also associated with increased production costs, sales commissions, licensing fees and general administrative costs).

The coefficient estimates for the impact of detailing on sales imply elasticity estimates of between 0.017 and 0.034. Again all three estimates are quite precisely estimated with t-statistics ranging from 4.25 to about 10. Because changes in detailing were on the order of 7% to 15% in the late 1990s and early 2000s, the impact of growth in detailing on class sales is considerably smaller than it was for drugs using DTCA as a key promotional strategy. Thus, at the entire class level, for these therapeutic classes DTCA has a larger marketing elasticity than does detailing.

Tables 4 and 5 present the product specific demand models. All product-specific models include class fixed effects. Table 4 presents results for models where a relative price measure is included as a right hand side regressor. Table 5 omits the relative price measure and instead includes quarterly dummy variables and interactions between quarter and class. The quarters are meant to account for seasonal effects and the fact that these might vary for different classes (antihistamines vs. antidepressants). All six sets of estimates presented treat detailing and DTCA as endogenous.[14] Incidentally, one finding worthy of note in the first stage regressions is that the impact of the 1997 FDA clarification on regulations governing DTCA had no significant effect on DTCA spending levels

IV estimates of the coefficient on the price variable in Table 4 are positive, significant in two of the three models, and of the wrong sign. As noted earlier, we believe the price variable is measured with error, and has no close relationship to patient copayments.

The various models in Tables 4 and 5 yield relatively consistent findings with respect to the estimates for the effect of DTCA and detailing on individual product sales. The coefficient estimates for the log of DTCA are consistently positive and quite imprecisely estimated. In five of six specifications the standard errors are larger than the estimated coefficient. In the first column of Table 5 the estimated coefficient has a t-statistic of 1.92 that is not quite significantly different from zero at conventional levels. The estimated DTCA elasticities are not consistent in magnitude across the estimated models, nor in levels vs. shares. To the extent DTCA affects class sales, one would expect a larger level elasticity (column 3) than a share elasticity (columns 1 and 2). This is not always the case. However, the Cobb Douglas model on Table 5 yields an elasticity of about 0.22, larger than the share elasticity.

The results for the impact of detailing on sales for individual drugs show coefficient estimates that are typically positive and imprecisely estimated. The first column of Table 5 reports a negative coefficient estimate for the log of detailing variable, but this coefficient is not significantly different from zero at conventional levels. Although the detailing elasticity estimates are all larger than those for DTCA, the detailing elasticity estimates never approach statistical significance.

Order of entry and its square were never found to be significantly different from zero in any of the estimated models. The magnitudes of the DTCA and detailing coefficients in the product-level models are quite sensitive to the form of the dependent variable and to the manner in which time dummies are specified. Finally, we also estimated a variant of the Cobb-Douglas model where both own DTCA and competitor DTCA levels were specified as right hand side variables. The results were not materially different from those reported in Tables 4 and 5. The time trend results for the share regressions reflect therapeutic competition in that they tend to be negative for most of the observed period as the number of competitors increases. The quantity regression reflects the growth in the class over time and this a generally positive time trend.

VII. Comments on Results

The DTCA parameter estimates we obtained at the therapeutic class level are both robust and precisely estimated. Estimates of the detailing elasticities at the therapeutic class level are also positive and significantly different from zero. They are generally smaller than the DTCA elasticities, and not as robust. In contrast, both DTCA and detailing parameter estimates for the individual product demand models are neither robust nor precisely estimated.

To simulate the overall impact of changes in DTC advertising on drug spending growth, our estimates were applied to changes in spending from 1999 to 2000 for the 25 drug classes with the highest retail sales. Drugs in these classes accounted for about 60% of the DTC advertising and about 75% of retail sales over that period. We applied our 0.10 elasticity to total DTCA spending growth for those classes that advertise and multiplied this figure by 1999 sales for those classes.[15] The absolute change in sales attributable to DTCA was then compared to the actual growth in prescription drug sales. Using this approach, we estimate that $2.6 billion or 12% of the growth in total prescription drug spending between 1999 and 2000 was attributable to DTCA. This effect translates into a yield of an additional $4.20 in sales for every dollar spent on

DTC advertising. Thus, our estimates indicate that DTCA is important, but not the primary driver of recent growth.

Despite these results, we believe it is premature to conclude that DTCA only affects class level sales, and not individual product sales. The stability of both DTCA and detailing spending is far greater at the class than at the individual product level, and thus the product level demand models may not be properly capturing the complex timing relationships between marketing efforts and measured sales, particularly because the latter involve sales to drug stores, not from drug stores to patients. However, the three-month cumulative log formulation gave similar results, even though it was less volatile than the current flow measure. The greater stability at the class level gives us some confidence in the class level results.

One potential reason for the instability of results at the product level is experimentation with DTCA by drug manufacturers. An implication is that such trial and error spending creates noise at the individual product level while there is relative stability at the class level. In addition, some of this experimentation may have failed to increase own brand sales, but still increased class demand. As a result, we view the question of the impact of DTCA spending at the individual product level as still remaining quite uncertain, and meriting further research. If our results suggesting larger class effects stand up after further research, they are consistent with the notion that DTCA leads previously untreated patients to talk to their doctors about advertised treatments and that these discussions sometimes lead to a prescription. How physicians balance their own product preferences and those of consumers is less certain.

This interpretation of our DTCA findings fits with the microeconomic evidence reported by Wosinska [2001] for cholesterol-reducing medications. She finds that DTCA, unlike detailing, affects individual drug market share only if that brand happens to have preferred status on the third party payer's formulary. It is also consistent with evidence from Ling, Berndt and Kyle [2002], who find that for the H_2-antagonists DTCA on over-the-counter (OTC) brands has a positive impact on own-brand OTC market share, but there is no significant spillover impact on same-brand Rx market share, nor does DTCA on the Rx brand impact Rx market share.

If health care were like any other commodity, we could presume that increasing utilization of pharmaceutical treatments is unequivocally beneficial. Due to the presence of insurance and asymmetric information, however, the welfare effects of DTCA are uncertain. For conditions such as depression and high cholesterol, which are believed to be under-treated in the population, increases in prescription drug treatment may have substantial benefits. There are also reasons to question, however, the appropriateness and cost-effectiveness of the treatment that results from DTCA. Further exploration of the characteristics of the patients, doctors, and treatment episodes that are influenced by DTCA is clearly needed.

Table 1: Spending on Physician-Directed Promotion and Promotion to Sales Ratios, 1996-2000

Dollars (millions)	1996	1997	1998	1999	200
Detailing	3,010	3,365	4,057	4,320	4,80
Journal Advertising	459	510	498	470	48
Retail Value of Samples	4,904	6,047	6,602	7,230	7,95
Total Physician Promotion	8,373	9,922	11,157	12,020	13,24
Direct-to-Consumer Promotion	791	1,069	1,317	1,848	2,46
Total Promotion	9,164	10,991	12,474	13,868	15,70

Promotion to Sales Ratios	1996	1997	1998	1999	200
Detailing	0.046	0.047	0.050	0.043	0.04
Journal Advertising	0.007	0.007	0.006	0.005	0.00
Retail Value of Samples	0.076	0.084	0.081	0.071	0.07
Total Physician Promotion	0.129	0.138	0.137	0.118	0.11
Direct-to-Consumer Promotion	0.012	0.015	0.016	0.018	0.02
Total Promotion	0.141	0.153	0.153	0.136	0.14

Sources: Physician Promotion spending data are from IMS Health, *Integrated Promotion Service,* June 2001; Sales data are from Pharmaceutical Research and Manufacturers of America, Annual Survey, 2001; Direct-to-Consumer Promotion spending data are from IMS Health and Competitive Media Reporting, June 2001.

Table 2: Manufacturer, Approval Date and Promotion to Sales Ratios for Five Therapeutic Classes, 1997-1999

	Manufacturer	FDA Approval Date	3-year Detailing to Sales Ratio	3-year Sampling to Sales Ratio	Total Physician Promotion to Sales Ratio*	3-year DTC to Sales Ratio
Antidepressants						
CELEXA	Forest Labs	1998	0.31	0.21	0.52	0.00
SERZONE	Bristol Myers Squibb	1994	0.21	0.15	0.35	0.01
EFFEXOR XR	Wyeth Ayerst	1993	0.12	0.09	0.21	0.00
PAXIL	GlaxoSmithKline	1992	0.05	0.10	0.16	0.01
ZOLOFT	Pfizer	1991	0.05	0.10	0.14	0.00
PROZAC	Eli Lilly	1987	0.03	0.06	0.09	0.01
PPIs						
ACIPHEX	Eisai	1999	1.21	0.84	2.05	0.00
PREVACID	Tap Pharm	1995	0.05	0.10	0.15	0.00
PRILOSEC	Astrazeneca	1989	0.02	0.06	0.08	0.02
Antihistamines						
ASTELIN	Wallace	1996	0.49	0.19	0.68	0.00
SEMPREX-D	Celltech Pharms	1994	0.26	0.18	0.44	0.00
ALLEGRA	Aventis	1996	0.17	0.09	0.26	0.11
ZYRTEC	Pfizer	1995	0.14	0.17	0.30	0.15
CLARITIN	Schering Plough	1993	0.04	0.04	0.08	0.06
Cholesterol						
LESCOL	Novartis	1993	0.11	0.07	0.18	0.00
PRAVACHOL	Bristol Myers Squibb	1991	0.06	0.07	0.13	0.05
LIPITOR	Pfizer	1996	0.05	0.07	0.12	0.01
ZOCOR	Merck	1991	0.04	0.07	0.11	0.03
MEVACOR	Merck	1991	0.00	0.02	0.02	0.00
Nasal Sprays						
NASONEX	Schering Plough	1997	0.22	0.26	0.48	0.23
RHINOCORT	Astrazeneca	1994	0.12	0.20	0.32	0.00
NASACORT	Aventis	1991	0.11	0.37	0.47	0.09
FLONASE	GlaxoSmithKline	1994	0.06	0.14	0.20	0.12
VANCENASE	Schering Plough	Prior to 1982	0.03	0.37	0.40	0.00
BECONASE	GlaxoSmithKline	Prior to 1982	0.00	0.00	0.00	0.00

Sources: Detailing data from Scott-Levin Personal Selling Audit, 2001; Sales data from Scott-Levin, Source Prescription Audit, 2001; Sampling data from IMS Health, 2001; DTCA data from Competitive Media Reporting, Strategy Report, 2001; Manufacturer and FDA Approval Date obtained from the Food and Drug Administration's *Orange Book.*

* Total Physician Promotion includes detailing and retail value of free samples. It does not include journal advertising.

Figure 1: Trend in Direct-to-Consumer Advertising Spending, 1994-2000

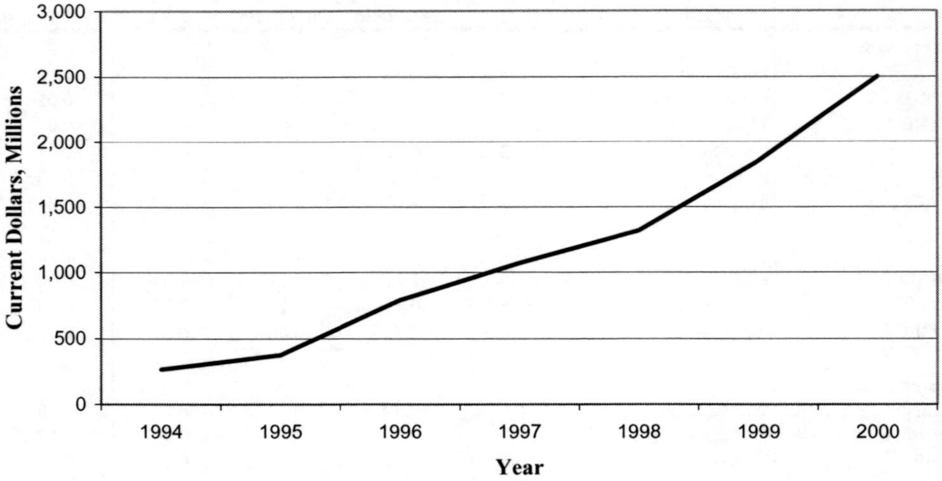

Source: IMS Health and Competitive Media Reporting, Inc.

Figure 2: Multi-Tier Demand Structure

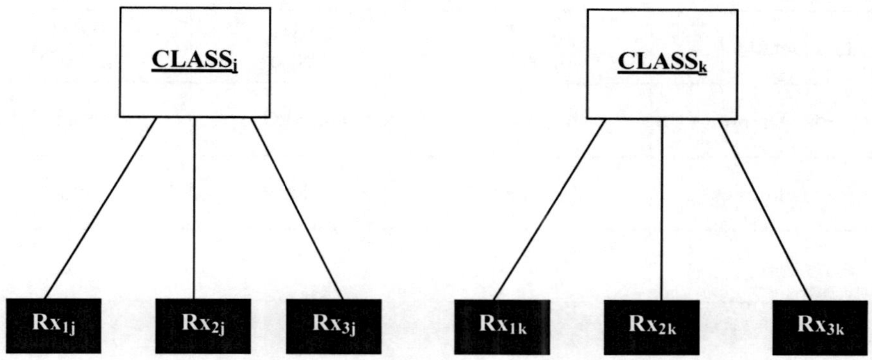

Table 3: Drug Class Demand Models

	Dependent Variables		
	ln Q	ln Q	ln Q
Class DTC*	0.114 (0.01)	0.099 (0.01)	0.096 (0.009)
Class Detail*	0.017 (0.004)	0.034 (0.003)	0.031 (0.003)
Quarter Dummies	Included	Included	Included
Class Dummies	Included	No	No
Interaction	Included	No	No
Month	No	No	Included
$Month^2$	No	No	Included
Constant	10.02 (0.18)	9.92 (0.19)	9.89 (0.20)
R^2	0.95	0.60	0.62
Equation F	280.0	56.0	48.87

*Endogenous, IV estimated

Note: Robust SE in parentheses

Table 4: Individual Product Demand Models With Prices

	Dependent Variables		
	Dollar Share	Ln [(Q Share)/(1-Q Share)]	ln Q
Constant	-0.281 (0.88)	-9.971 (4.66)	1.544 (4.23)
ln DTCA*	0.025 (0.03)	0.091 (0.11)	0.071 (0.11)
ln Det*	0.004 (0.14)	0.690 (0.698)	0.730 (0.63)
Order entry	0.127 (0.69)	0.619 (0.49)	0.615 (0.49)
$(\text{Order entry})^2$	-0.017 (0.009)	-0.087 (0.09)	-0.089 (0.09)
$\ln (P_i/P_{others})$	0.129 (0.07)	1.120 (0.41)	1.108 (0.39)
Class dummies	Included	Included	Included
Month	-0.0004 (0.03)	-0.171 (0.01)	0.042 (0.02)
Month^2	0.720 (0.88)	0.0022 (0.0003)	-0.0007 (0.0004)
R^2	0.54	0.65	0.69
Equation F	16.51	54.99	34.97

*Endogenous, IV estimated

Note: Robust SE in parentheses

Table 5: Individual Product Demand Models With Price Excluded As Regressor

	Dependent Variables		
	Dollar Share	ln [(Q Share)/(1-Q Share)]	ln Q
Constant	1.746 (1.29)	-9.771 (10.58)	4.413 (10.79)
ln DTCA*	0.077 (0.04)	0.167 (0.23)	0.216 (0.24)
ln Det*	-0.254 (0.18)	0.77 (1.43)	0.443 (1.46)
Order entry	0.100 (0.06)	0.269 (0.62)	0.313 (0.61)
$(\text{Order entry})^2$	-0.011 (0.01)	-0.067 (0.10)	-0.071 (0.10)
Class dummies	Included	Included	Included
Quarter dummies	Included	Included	Included
Interaction	Included	Included	Included
Month	-0.007 (0.004)	-0.181 (0.04)	0.026 (0.03)
Month^2	0.0001 (0.0001)	0.002 (0.0009)	-0.0003 (0.001)
R^2	0.37	0.47	0.52
Equation F	24.42	51.86	17.96

*Endogenous, IV estimated

Note: Robust SE in parentheses

REFERENCES

Aikin, Kathryn J., "Direct-to-Consumer Advertising of Prescription Drugs: Preliminary Patient Survey Results," PowerPoint presentation given at Second Annual DTC National Conference and Exposition, Boston, MA, April 18, 2002.

Alperstein, N. and M. Peyrot, "Consumer Awareness of Prescription Drug Advertising," Journal of Advertising Research, July/August 1993, vol. 33, #4 pp. 50-56.

Avorn, Jerry, Milton Chen and Robert Hartley, "Scientific versus Commercial Sources of Influence on the Prescribing Behavior of Physicians," The American Journal of Medicine, 73, July 1982, pp. 4-8.

Bagwell, Kyle, ed., The Economics of Advertising, The International Library of Critical Writings in Economics, Vol. 136, Cheltenham UK: Edward Elgar Publishing Ltd., 669 pp., 2001.

Bain, Joe S., Barriers to New Competition, Cambridge, MA: Harvard University Press, 1956.

Berndt, Ernst R., Linda T. Bui, David H. Reiley and Glen L. Urban, "The Roles of Marketing, Product Quality and Price Competition in the Growth and Composition of the U.S. Anti-Ulcer Drug Industry," chapter 7 in Timothy F. Bresnahan and Robert J. Gordon, eds., The Economics of New Products, Studies in Income and Wealth, Volume 58, Chicago: University of Chicago Press for the National Bureau of Economic Research, 1997, pp. 277-322.

Berndt, Ernst R., Linda T. Bui, David H. Reiley and Glen L. Urban, "Information, Marketing and Pricing in the U.S. Anti-Ulcer Drug Market," American Economic Review, Vol. 85, No. 2, May 1995, pp. 100-105.

Berndt, Ernst R., Margaret Kyle and Davina Ling, "The Long Shadow of Patent Expiration: Generic Entry and Rx to OTC Switches," MIT Program on the Pharmaceutical Industry, September 2000. Revised January 2002. Forthcoming in Robert C. Feenstra and Matthew D. Shapiro, eds., Scanner Data and Price Indexes, NBER Series on the Conference on Research in Income and Wealth, Chicago: University of Chicago Press for the National Bureau of Economic Research, 2002.

Bond, Ronald S. and David F. Lean, Sales, Promotion and Product Differentiation in Two Prescription Drug Markets, Washington DC: Staff Report of the Bureau of Economics of the Federal Trade Commission, February 1997.

Borzo, G., "Consumer Drug Ads Booming: FDA Reviews Restrictions," American Medical News, 40(6):1,37, February 10, 1997.

Butters, Gerard R., "Equilibrium Distributions of Sales and Advertising Prices," Review of Economic Studies, 64:3, October 1977, pp. 465-491.

Carlton, Dennis W. and Jeffrey M. Perloff, Modern Industrial Organization, Second Edition, New York: HarperCollins College Publishers, 1994.

Cragg, John G., "Some Statistical Models for Limited Dependent Variables with Application to the Demand for Durable Goods," Econometrica, 39:5, September 1971, pp. 829-844.

Dorfman, Robert and Peter O. Steiner, "Optimal Advertising and Optimal Quality," American Economic Review, 44:5, December 1954, pp. 826-836.

Duan, Naihua, Willard G. Manning, Jr., Carl N. Norris and Joseph P. Newhouse, "A Comparison of Alternative Models for the Demand for Medical Care," Journal of Business and Economic Statistics, 1:2, April 1983, pp. 115-126.

Ellison, Glenn and Sara Fisher Ellison, "Strategic Entry Deterrence and the Behavior of Pharmaceutical Incumbents Prior to Patent Expiration," unpublished manuscript, Cambridge, MA: Massachusetts Institute of Technology, Department of Economics, 2000. Downloaded from web.mit.edu/gellison/www/drugs20.pdf.

Ellison, Sara Fisher, Iain Cockburn, Zvi Griliches and Jerry Hausman, "Characteristics of Demand for Pharmaceutical Products: An Examination of Four Cephalosporins," RAND Journal of Economics, 28:3, Autumn 1997, pp. 446-466.

Frank, Richard G., "Prescription Drug Prices: Why Do Some Pay More Than Others Do?," Health Affairs, 2001, March/April 20:2, pp. 115-128.

Frank, Richard G. and Raymond S. Hartman. "Competition Between Brands and Generic Drugs and the Merger Guidelines," Boston, MA: Harvard Medical School Working Paper April 2002.

Gonul, Fusun, Franklin Carter, Elina Petrova and Kannan Srinivasan, "Promotion of Prescription Drugs and Its Impact on Physician Choice Behavior," Journal of Marketing, 65:3, 2001, pp. 79-90.

Gonul, Fusun, Franklin Carter and Jerry Wind, "What Kind of Patients and Physicians Value Direct-to-Consumer Advertising of Prescription Drugs," Health Care Management Science, Vol. 3, 2000, pp. 215-226.

Grossman, Gene M. and Carl Shapiro, "Informative Advertising with Differentiated Products," Review of Economic Studies, 51:1, January 1984, pp. 63-81.

Henry J. Kaiser Family Foundation, Prescription Drug Trends: A Chartbook, Menlo Park, CA, July 2000.

Hurwitz, Mark A. and Richard E. Caves, "Persuasion or Information? Promotion and the Shares of Brand Name and Generic Pharmaceuticals," Journal of Law and Economics, 31:5, October 1988, pp. 299-320.

Kaldor, Nicholas, "The Economic Aspects of Advertising," Review of Economic Studies, Vol. 18, 1950, pp. 1-27.

Kaufman-Sherr, M. and D. Hoffman, "Physicians -- Gatekeepers to DTC Success," Pharmaceutical Executive, 17:10, Oct 1997, pg. 56.

King, Charles III, "Marketing, Product Differentiation and Competition in the Market for Antiulcer Drugs," Boston MA: Harvard Business School Working Paper No. 01-014, 2000.

Leffler, Keith B., "Promotion or Information? The Economics of Prescription Drug Advertising," Journal of Law and Economics, 24:2, April 1981, pp. 45-74.

Ling, Davina C. Y., Ernst R. Berndt and Margaret K. Kyle, "Deregulating Direct to Consumer Marketing of Drugs: Effects on Prescription and Over-the-Counter Product Sales," paper presented at the University of Chicago Law School - Medical School Conference, The Regulation of Medical Innovation and Pharmaceutical Markets, Chicago, IL, April 20-21, 2001. Revised version, March 2002.

Lodish, Leonard M., Ellen Curtis, Michael Ness and M. Kerry Simpson, "Sales Force Sizing and Deployment Using a Decision Calculus Model at Syntex Laboratories, Interfaces, 18:1, January-February 1988, pp. 5-20.

Manchanda, Puneet, Pradeep Chintagunta and Susan Gertzis, "Responsiveness of Physician Prescription Behavior to Salesforce Effort: An Individual Level Analysis," Chicago: University of Chicago, Graduate School of Business, unpublished manuscript, May 2000. Downloaded from puneet.manchanda@gsb.uchicago.edu.

Masson, Alison, "Direct-to-Consumer Advertising: A Continuing Controversy," in Robert N. Mayer, ed., Enhancing Consumer Choice, Proceedings of the Second International Conference on Research in the Consumer Interest, Columbia, MO: American Council on Consumer Interests, 1991, pp. 159-168.

Mishra, Raja, "Ex-FDA chief recants on drug advertising," Boston Globe, April 17, 2002, p. A2.

Nelson, Phillip K., "Advertising as Information," Journal of Political Economy, 82:4, July/August 1974, pp. 729-754.

Nelson, Phillip K., "Information and Consumer Behavior," Journal of Political Economy, 78:2, March/April 1970, pp. 311-329.

Neslin, Scott, ROI Analysis of Pharmaceutical Promotion: An Independent Study. Hanover NH: Dartmouth College, Amos Tuck School of Business, unpublished PowerPoint presentation, May 22, 2001.

NewsHour with Jim Lehrer/Henry J. Kaiser Family Foundation/Harvard School of Public Health Survey, September 2000.

Palda, Kristian, Economic Analysis for Marketing Decisions, New York: Prentice-Hall, 1969.

Prevention Magazine, "International Survey on Wellness and Consumer Reaction to DTC Advertising of Prescription Drugs," Vol. 1, 2000/2001, Emmaus PA: Rodale, 2001.

Rizzo, John A., "Advertising and Competition in the Ethical Pharmaceutical Industry: The Case of Antihypertensive Drugs," Journal of Law and Economics, 42:1, 1999, pp. 89-116.

Rosenthal, Meredith B., Ernst R. Berndt, Julie M. Donohue, Richard G. Frank and Arnold M. Epstein, "Promotion of Prescription Drugs to Consumers," New England Journal of Medicine, 346:7, February 14, 2002, pp. 498-505.

Scherer, F. Michael, "The Pharmaceutical Industry," chapter x in Anthony J. Culyer and Joseph P. Newhouse, editors, Handbook of Health Economics, Amsterdam: Elsevier Publishers, Vol. 1B, 2000, pp. 1297-1336.

Schmalensee, Richard, The Economics of Advertising, Amsterdam: North-Holland, 1972.

Sinha, Prabhakant and Andris A. Zoltners, "Sales-Force Decision Models: Insights from 25 Years of Implementation," Interfaces, 31:3, Part 2 of 2, May-June 2001, pp. S8-S44.

Sorenson, Alan T., "Equilibrium Price Dispersion in Retail Markets for Prescription Drugs," Journal of Political Economy, 4:108, August 2000, pp. 833-850.

Stigler, George J., "The Economics of Information," Journal of Political Economy, 69:3, June 1961, pp. 213-225.

Temin, Peter, Taking Your Medicine: Drug Regulation in the United States, Cambridge, MA: Harvard University Press, 1980.

Vernon, John, "Concentration, Promotion, and Market Share Stability in the Pharmaceutical Industry," Journal of Industrial Economics, 19:3, 1981, pp. 246-266.

Wosinska, Marta, "Promoting to Multiple Agents: The Case of Direct-to-Consumer Drug Advertising," chapter in unpublished Ph.D. dissertation, Berkeley, CA: University of California-Berkeley, Department of Economics, October 2001. Downloaded from wosinska@econ.berkeley.edu.

Ziegler, M.G., P. Lew and B.C. Singer, "The Accuracy of Drug Information from Pharmaceutical Sales Representatives," Journal of the American Medical Association, 273, 1995, pp. 1296-1298.

ENDNOTES

[1] These and other quotes are shamelessly lifted from Carlton-Perloff [1994], chapter 15, Advertising and Disclosure, pp. 596-629.

[2] As quoted in the Boston Globe (Mishra [2002]). Words in parentheses added for clarification.

[3] However, prior to the 1938 FDA prescription-only legislation and the 1951 Humphrey-Durham Amendment to the Federal Food, Drug and Cosmetic Act that established physicians as "learned intermediaries" and made many drugs available only with a physician's prescription, DTCA dominated drug advertising. Temin [1980, pp. 82-87] estimates that in 1930, 90% of drug advertising expenditures occurred in newspapers and popular magazines, only 2% in technical journals, and only 3% involved detailing, samples and other.

[4] For an historical account of DTCA controversies, see Masson [1991].

[5] On this, also see Ziegler, Lew and Singer [1995].

[6] Twenty-five years of experience in modeling the impacts of detailing on sales, and on optimizing sales force size and targets, is summarized in Sinha and Zoltners [2001]. A classic study of detailing is that by Lodish et al. [1988].

[7] These and other quotes are shamelessly lifted from Carlton-Perloff [1994], chapter 15, Advertising and Disclosure, pp. 596-629.

[8] Carlton-Perloff [1994], p. 603.

[9] Carlton-Perloff [1994], p. 625.

[10] For empirical evidence on consumers' search costs for acute vs. chronic medications, and impacts on retail pricing of drugs, see Sorenson [2000].

[11] Also see Scherer [2000].

[12] Industry officials tell us that absolute levels of DTCA spending are likely overstated because CMR estimates DTCA spending using "list" rather than actual transaction prices. Because of the large amount of advertising services pharmaceutical firms purchase, they typically obtain substantial discounts off list prices. These industry officials suggest that the DTCA estimates by CMR are reasonably reliable estimates of relative DTCA across drugs.

[13] We also estimate a variant of the strict two stage budgeting model where we allow both class level DTCA and own DTCA to affect the demand for a particular drug.

[14] First stage estimates are available from the authors upon request.

[15] We also attempted to simulate the impact of DTC advertising class by class as would be appropriate given the underlying economic model, but were forced by this method to exclude a number of classes with positive DTC spending because of sales or DTC spending reductions from 1999 to 2000, or because DTC spending was zero in either 1999 or 2000. Such exclusions inflated our simulated result, yielding an estimate that 22% of prescription drug sales growth was attributable to DTC spending increases. The simulation we report in the text (a 12% growth in sales attributable to DTC) aggregates sales and DTC advertising across classes to smooth out these anomalies. While this approach may have some downward bias due to the way DTC spending is distributed across classes with different levels of dollar sales, we believe that this estimate is more defensible because it includes all of our data from the 25 classes studied.

[21]

DEREGULATING DIRECT-TO-CONSUMER MARKETING OF PRESCRIPTION DRUGS: EFFECTS ON PRESCRIPTION AND OVER-THE-COUNTER PRODUCT SALES*

DAVINA C. LING,
Harvard University

ERNST R. BERNDT,
Massachusetts Institute of Technology

and

MARGARET K. KYLE
Carnegie Mellon University

ABSTRACT

This paper examines the impact and interrelationships between direct-to-consumer (DTC) and physician-oriented marketing on the sales composition of the prescription (Rx) and over-the-counter (OTC) versions of antiulcer and heartburn medications. To understand better the implications for competition of the 1997 Food and Drug Administration's policies regarding DTC marketing, as well as recent Rx-to-OTC switch approvals, we also examine the relationship between order-of-entry effects and marketing intensities. We find spillover effects of marketing for Rx drugs on same-brand OTC versions of the drugs. We also find that the ratio of cumulative marketing intensity (cumulative marketing efforts divided by cumulative sales) in the OTC segment increases monotonically with order of entry. Our regression results show that various marketing demand elasticities depend on order of entry. Our findings document the importance of nonprice competition in the OTC drug market and suggest that the recent deregulation of Rx DTC marketing enhances rivalry and facilitates competition.

* This paper was presented at the University of Chicago Law School–Medical School conference Regulation of Medical Innovation and Pharmaceutical Markets, April 20–21, 2001. Research support from the National Science Foundation (to E.R.B.) and the Massachusetts Institute of Technology Program on the Pharmaceutical Industry (to E.R.B. and M.K.K.) is gratefully acknowledged, as is data support from Information Resources, Inc., J&J Merck Consumer Products, IMS Health, and Merck & Co. We have benefited from discussions with Richard Frank, Richard Manning, and Will Manning and from the comments of anonymous referees and the editor, Sam Peltzman. The views expressed in this paper are those of the authors only and do not necessarily reflect those of any institutions with which they are related or of any research sponsor.

[*Journal of Law and Economics*, vol. XLV (October 2002)]

I. Introduction

THE effects of marketing efforts on consumer choice and well-being have long been controversial among economists, marketing analysts, and public policy makers. Classic debates include the following: Do marketing efforts generate informational and educational value for consumers, which enables them to make more informed choices? Do marketing efforts exploit informational asymmetry between producers and consumers, increase perceived product differentiation, and induce inefficient rent-seeking behavior by producers? Or do both of these effects hold, varying by product and stage in the product life cycle?[1] These issues are at the heart of current debates concerning the welfare effects of recent regulatory changes at the U.S. Food and Drug Administration (FDA) regarding direct-to-consumer (DTC) marketing for prescription (Rx) drugs.[2]

In 1997, the FDA clarified guidelines on DTC marketing of Rx drugs that allow manufacturers to place both the drug's name and the condition that the drug treats in an advertisement without requiring manufacturers to include all the additional safety and efficacy information that are traditionally found in the product insert.[3] Prior to this change, whenever a drug's brand name appeared in an advertisement, such detailed product insert information was required as well.

Recent years have also seen an acceleration in the number of Rx-only to over-the-counter (OTC) (Rx-to-OTC) switches that have been approved by the FDA.[4] In the 14-year period between 1976 and 1989, the FDA approved 39 Rx-to-OTC switches (about 2.8 per year), but between 1990 and 1996,

[1] See, for example, Federal Trade Commission, Advertising for Over-the-Counter Antacids: Final Staff Report and Recommendations (1983); Mark A. Hurwitz & Richard E. Caves, Persuasion or Information? Promotion and the Shares of Brand Name and Generic Pharmaceuticals, 31 J. Law & Econ. 299 (1988); Keith B. Leffler, Persuasion or Information? The Economics of Prescription Drug Advertising, 24 J. Law & Econ. 45 (1981); Richard L. Schmalensee, The Economics of Advertising (1972); and Richard L. Schmalensee, Product Differentiation Advantages of Pioneering Brands, 72 Am. Econ. Rev. 349 (1982).

[2] See, for example, Ronald S. Bond & David F. Lean, Sales, Promotion, and Product Differentiation in Two Prescription Drug Markets: Staff Report of the Bureau of Economics of the Federal Trade Commission (1977); Marcel P. Gemperli, Rethinking the Role of the Learned Intermediary: The Effect of Direct-to-Consumer Advertising on Litigation, 284 JAMA 2241 (2000); Jane E. Henney, Challenges in Regulating Direct-to-Consumer Advertising, 284 JAMA 2242 (2000); Alison J. Huang, The Rise of Direct-to-Consumer Advertising of Prescription Drugs in the United States, 284 JAMA 2240 (2000); National Survey of Consumer Reactions to Direct-to-Consumer Advertising, Prevention Mag. 8 (1999); Meredith Rosenthal *et al.*, Demand Effects of Recent Changes in Prescription Drug Promotion, in 6 Frontiers in Health Policy Research (Alan M. Garber & David M. Cutler eds. 2003); and Michael S. Wilkes, Robert A. Bell, & Richard L. Kravitz, Direct-to-Consumer Prescription Drug Advertising: Trends, Impact and Implications, 19 Health Aff. 110 (2000).

[3] Manufacturers are required to direct the audience to another source (for example, a toll-free number or a Web site) to obtain additional safety and efficacy information.

[4] For FDA comments on switches, see Tamar Nordenberg, Now Available without a Prescription, FDA Consumer Magazine (1996) (http://www.fda.gov/fdac/features/996_otc.html).

20 switches occurred (about 3.3 per year). Between 1994 and 1996 alone, the FDA approved 10 Rx-to-OTC switches, including Children's Advil, Children's Motrin, Orudis KT, and Actron for pain relief; Femstat 3 for treating vaginal yeast infection; Pepcid AC, Tagamet HB, Zantac 75, and Axid AR for heartburn; and Rogaine for promoting hair growth. Many of today's leading selling OTC products had an Rx heritage. For example, OTC medications such as Advil, Motrin IB, Benadryl, and NyQuil were originally Rx-only drugs that switched to OTC status in the 1980s.[5] The increase in approvals of Rx-to-OTC switches reflects in part the impact of those advocating greater consumer choice, self-medication, and consumer empowerment. It also likely reflects manufacturer incentives as embodied in the Waxman-Hatch Act of 1984, which in some cases permits an additional 3 years of marketing exclusivity for previously Rx-only products whose new approved efficacy indications involve an OTC formulation.

The clarified DTC advertising guidelines provide manufacturers even greater inducements for Rx-to-OTC switches. Specifically, by marketing the Rx version of a drug directly to consumers while it is still under patent protection, a producer may be able to exploit spillovers to its subsequent OTC version, particularly when marketing signals quality and translates into long-lived brand-name equity. Hence, DTC marketing of a branded Rx product may have long-term effects on the subsequent success of Rx-to-OTC switches.

In this paper, we examine recent DTC marketing efforts and Rx-to-OTC switches involving the H_2-antagonist class of drugs, which treats a wide variety of gastrointestinal disorders including duodenal and gastric ulcers, hypersecretory conditions, acid indigestion, and heartburn. These top-selling Rx medications all switched from Rx to OTC in 1995–96—Pepcid to Pepcid AC, Tagamet to Tagamet HB, Zantac to Zantac 75, and Axid to Axid AR. The Rx version of Tagamet lost patent protection in 1994, as did Rx Zantac in 1997, Rx Pepcid in 2001, and Rx Axid in 2002. For some of these drugs, DTC advertising has been used for both the Rx and OTC formulations.

In this paper, we first assess whether order-of-entry effects, documented to be strong in the H_2 Rx market, are also present in the H_2 OTC segment and examine whether there is any carryover of order of entry from the Rx

[5] For further discussion, see Davina C. Ling, Advertising, Competition, and Prescription-to-Nonprescription Drug Switches in the US Antacid Market (unpublished Ph.D. dissertation, Massachusetts Inst. Tech., June 1999); Barbara Hesselgrave, Will Managed Care Embrace Rx-to-OTC Switches? Drug Topics, June 2, 1997, at 13; Robert McCarthy, OTCs: The Wild Card in Cost-Effectiveness, 17 Bus. Health 33 (1999); Mickey C. Smith, Rx-to-OTC Switches: Reflections and Projections, Drug Topics, July 20, 1998, at 70; Bruce Stuart & James Grana, Are Prescribed and Over-the-Counter Medicines Economic Substitutes? A Study of the Effects of Health Insurance and Medicine Choices by the Elderly, 33 Med. Care 487 (1995); and Elyse Tanou & Thomas M. Burton, More Firms "Switch" Prescription Drugs to Give Them Over-the-Counter Status, Wall St. J., July 29, 1993, at B1.

to the OTC markets.[6] Next we consider the role of DTC marketing, as well as traditional physician-oriented "detailing" marketing, on the sales composition of the OTC H_2s and of the Rx H_2s. Finally, we assess whether there are any significant interactions between the Rx and OTC DTC marketing efforts for a brand.

As best we can determine, the research we report here is the first systematic empirical examination of the impact and interrelationships between DTC marketing on Rx and OTC versions of "sunset" branded pharmaceuticals facing Rx patent expiration.[7] Our research integrates data from various sources, such as Rx drug sales and marketing data from IMS Health, scanner OTC data from Information Resources, Incorporated (IRI), as well as DTC marketing data from Leading National Advertisers. We begin with a historical overview of regulatory and other factors affecting the Rx and OTC H_2-antagonist products.

II. Background

As early as the 1800s, patent medicine advertisers were the largest patrons of newspaper advertising.[8] The modern distinction between Rx and OTC drugs began with the 1938 Federal Food, Drug, and Cosmetic Act, which defined different labeling guidelines for Rx and OTC drugs. Under the 1938 act, even though the authority over the labeling of both Rx and OTC drugs was given to the FDA, control over drug marketing remained with the Federal Trade Commission. The 1962 Kefauver-Harris amendments to the Federal Food, Drug, and Cosmetic Act gave the FDA its current responsibility for monitoring Rx drug promotional materials. The 1962 amendments outlined basic requirements for Rx marketing: Rx promotional materials cannot be false or misleading; they must provide a "fair-balance" coverage of risks and benefits of using the drug; they must provide a summary of contraindications, side effects, and effectiveness; and they must also meet specific guidelines for readability and size of print.

[6] See Ernst Berndt *et al.*, Information, Marketing and Pricing in the U.S. Anti-ulcer Drug Market, 85 Am. Econ. Rev. 100 (1995); Ernst Berndt *et al.*, The Roles of Marketing, Product Quality and Price Competition in the Growth and Composition of the U.S. Anti-ulcer Drug Industry, in The Economics of New Goods 277 (Timothy F. Bresnahan & Robert J. Gordon eds. 1997).

[7] For related empirical research on Rx-to-OTC switches, see Peter Temin, Costs and Benefits in Switching Drugs from Rx to OTC, 2 J. Health Econ. 187 (1983); Peter Temin, Realized Benefits in Switching Drugs, 35 J. Law & Econ. 351 (1992); and Ernst R. Berndt, Margaret K. Kyle, & Davina Ling, The Long Shadow of Patent Expiration: Generic Entry and Rx-to-OTC Switches, in Scanner Data and Price Indexes 229 (Robert C. Feenstra & Matthew D. Shapiro eds. 2002). Additional research on order-of-entry effects in Rx pharmaceutical markets is Ernst Berndt *et al.*, An Analysis of the Diffusion of New Antidepressants: Variety, Quality and Marketing Efforts, 5 J. Mental Health & Pol. Econ. 3 (2002).

[8] James Harvey Young, The Medical Messiahs: A Social History of Health Quackery in Twentieth Century America (1967), as cited in Wilkes, Bell, & Kravitz, *supra* note 2.

Since then, Rx drugs have been marketed not only to physicians, but also more directly to consumers. As noted by Ernst Berndt and coauthors,[9] for example, in March 1988 Tagamet Rx launched "Tommy Tummy" and "stomach TLC" DTC marketing campaigns, and soon after Glaxo initiated an extensive television and print DTC effort for Zantac. Under the interpretation of FDA regulations regarding DTC marketing at that time, the marketing was quite restrictive in that if a brand name was mentioned in the advertisement, extensive product-labeling information was required to accompany the advertisement.

These restrictions on DTC marketing were relaxed and clarified in 1997 when the FDA issued new draft guidelines. A manufacturer is now permitted to advertise an Rx drug's name and the condition for which it is indicated without needing to issue as fully detailed a summary regarding the product's side effects and other risks. The FDA requirements for risk disclosure in advertisements may be met if the advertisements contain information on the product's main risks and refer to other sources from which consumers may obtain additional product information and full product labeling. For instance, a prominently positioned toll-free phone number (or Web address) must now be found on the advertisement, which the consumer can use to obtain further information. Usually, there is explicit encouragement for readers and viewers of DTC advertisements to discuss the product with their physicians.

While relatively little is known to date regarding the ultimate impacts of DTC marketing of Rx products on consumer utilization and health status,[10] there is little doubt that relaxation of the DTC restrictions by the FDA has been associated with a very substantial increase in DTC marketing of Rx products. In particular, according to IMS Health, DTC marketing expenditures for Rx medications increased from $1.1 to $2.5 billion between 1997 and 2000.[11]

Both the shift in regulatory regime for DTC advertising and the more favorable regulatory environment for Rx-to-OTC switches are important in explaining recent developments in the H_2-antagonist market. The first H_2-antagonist, Tagamet (chemical name, cimetidine), was introduced in 1977. It revolutionized the treatment of ulcers by allowing pharmacological treatment on an outpatient basis, rather than with expensive inpatient care such as hospital stays and surgeries. Three other H_2-antagonists were launched between 1983 and 1988: Zantac (ranitidine), Pepcid (famotidine), and Axid (nizatidine). The benefits of patent protection, together with successful marketing and the resulting widespread utilization, led to spectacular revenue

[9] Berndt *et al.*, The Roles of Marketing, *supra* note 6.

[10] For an initial and preliminary analysis, see Prevention Mag., *supra* note 2. Also see Wilkes, Bell, & Kravitz, *supra* note 2; and Meredith Rosenthal *et al.*, Promotion of Prescription Drugs to Consumers, 346 New Eng. J. Med. 498 (2002).

[11] IMS Health data can be obtained at http://www.imshealth.com. Also see Rosenthal *et al.*, *supra* note 2.

sales growth for the Rx-only H_2s. In the early to mid-1990s, Zantac was the most widely prescribed and the highest-sales-volume Rx drug in the United States, and Tagamet was among the top 10 best-selling Rx medications.

Although the introductions of the Rx H_2s marked the beginning of new medical treatments for gastrointestinal disorders, the H_2s were not spared from the forces of creative destruction. In 1989, new and more potent drugs for the treatment of ulcers and gastroesophageal reflux disease (GERD), namely, the proton pump inhibitors (PPIs), were introduced. This latest generation of drugs has a convenient once-a-day dosing regimen and very few side effects. Even at the time of its initial approval in May 1995, the manufacturer of one of the PPIs (Prevacid) was able to claim superiority in its labeling and promotion over ranitidine (then the best-selling and most prescribed H_2) for the treatment of heartburn. By 1997, the PPIs had overtaken the H_2s as the largest-revenue-generating Rx drugs in the United States (and the world).

Besides confronting intense competition from the PPIs in the 1990s, the H_2s also faced the threat of Rx patent expiration and imminent generic entry. Tagamet's patent expired on May 17, 1994, followed by the loss of Zantac's market exclusivity in late July 1997.[12] Drug manufacturers may benefit from Rx-to-OTC switches because in certain cases they can gain the limited additional market exclusivity granted by the Waxman-Hatch Act of 1984. This provision allows pioneer manufacturers an extra 3 years of market exclusivity provided that the manufacturer obtains FDA approval for a new presentation and indication for a chemical entity.[13] Expecting loss of patent protection in the mid-1990s, for example, beginning as early as 1985, SmithKline discussed with the FDA the possibility of seeking and gaining approval for an OTC version of Tagamet to treat heartburn.[14]

With this as background, we proceed with the remainder of this paper as follows. In Section III, we provide a brief literature review and examine important concepts for the Rx and OTC markets. In Section IV, we discuss data sources and the construction and interpretation of various price, quantity, and marketing measures, first for Rx drugs and then for OTCs. In Section

[12] See Berndt, Kyle, & Ling, *supra* note 7; Berndt *et al.*, Information, Marketing and Pricing, *supra* note 6; and Berndt *et al.*, Roles of Marketing, *supra* note 6, for a more detailed discussion of the historical development in the H_2-antagonist market.

[13] Empirical analyses of the effect of the Waxman-Hatch Act include those by Henry G. Grabowski & John M. Vernon, Brand Loyalty, Entry, and Price Competition in Pharmaceuticals after the 1984 Drug Act, 35 J. Law & Econ. 331 (1992); Richard E. Caves, Michael D. Whinston, & Mark A. Hurwitz, Patent Expiration, Entry, and Competition in the U.S. Pharmaceutical Industry, Brookings Papers on Economic Activity: Microeconomics 1 (1991); and Richard G. Frank & David S. Salkever, Generic Entry and the Pricing of Pharmaceuticals, 6 J. Econ. Mgmt. 75 (1997). For a historical overview of FDA regulation of the drug industry prior to 1980, see Peter Temin, Taking Your Medicine: Drug Regulation in the United States (1980).

[14] For a Harvard Business School case study discussion of the race to develop and launch the first OTC H_2-antagonist in the United States, see Charles King III *et al.*, Pepcid AC(A): Racing to the OTC Market (2000).

V, we present evidence on the importance of order-of-entry effects in the OTC market for H_2-antagonists and assess the extent of order-of-entry spillovers from the Rx heritage to the OTC market. In Section VI, we formulate, and then provide empirical evidence for, a relatively simple set of econometric models quantifying the effects of DTC and traditional detailing on shares among the Rx and OTC H_2-antagonists. Finally, in Section VII we summarize and conclude.

III. Literature Review and Conceptual Considerations

The market for Rx drugs involves complex interactions among pharmaceutical companies and regulators as well as among patients, physicians, pharmacists, third-party payers, and policy makers. Physicians act as agents for their patients and in that capacity prescribe drugs for them. Since physicians choose among competing drugs, and because of historical restrictions on advertising to patients, until recently most marketing efforts for Rx drugs have been directed at physicians, both in the form of visits by sales representatives to physicians (detailing) and by print advertising in medical journals. Previous studies, such as those by Berndt and coauthors,[15] have shown that along with other factors, such physician-directed marketing efforts in the Rx market have had a substantial sales impact and are long-lived.

Moral hazard likely affects sales in the Rx market, for patients with Rx drug coverage typically make copayments that are considerably less than the total payment for the Rx, with the third-party insurers responsible for most of the cost. Other things equal, this insurance-induced wedge between patient copayments and total payments for a Rx undoubtedly increases demand for Rx drugs.[16]

The roles of principal-agent issues and moral hazard are likely to be much smaller in the OTC than in the Rx market. Over-the-counter drugs are typically inexpensive relative to brand-name Rx drugs, although consumers usually bear the total costs out-of-pocket because third-party insurance rarely reimburses for OTC drugs. Since many OTC (and, for that matter, Rx) products are primarily "experience" rather than "search" goods, brand loyalty is strong, which perhaps reflects consumers' idiosyncratic responses to medications, risk aversion, and/or imperfect information. Thus, even for OTC products, perceived switching costs may be high despite their relatively low cost.[17] Once consumers experience benefits from use of a particular OTC

[15] Berndt *et al.*, Information, Marketing and Pricing, *supra* note 6; and Berndt *et al.*, Roles of Marketing, Product Quality and Price Competition, *supra* note 6.

[16] For more discussion of this point, see Ernst R. Berndt, The U.S. Pharmaceutical Industry: Why Major Growth in Times of Cost Containment? 20 Health Aff. 100 (2001).

[17] For a classic discussion of search and experience goods and the importance of their distinction in understanding marketing efforts, see Philip K. Nelson, Advertising as Information, 82 J Pol. Econ. 729 (1974). Additional discussion of decision making in the OTC market is found in Ling, *supra* note 5.

medication, they may be reluctant to experiment with alternative OTC products. Consumers may be less informed than medical professionals regarding the efficacy and appropriate uses of various OTC medications. In such ways, risk aversion and imperfect information may raise switching costs and confer important roles on brand names, which signal quality. As noted by Richard Schmalensee[18] and others, high switching costs and imperfect information can lead to first-mover, or at least order-of-entry, advantages to incumbents.

Ronald Bond and David Lean,[19] Berndt and coauthors,[20] and Charles King and coauthors[21] have documented strong order-of-entry effects in the branded Rx H_2-antagonist market. Within OTC and other nonmedication consumer markets, there is a large literature documenting the importance of order of entry for pioneering brands; surveys are given by Glen Urban and coauthors[22] and William Robinson and coauthors.[23]

To date, there is no empirical evidence on the spillover of order of entry in Rx markets onto the OTC market. In the current context, it is worth emphasizing that Zantac was able to overcome Tagamet's first-mover advantage in the Rx market in part by employing aggressive marketing efforts that conveyed information on Zantac's claimed advantages—more convenient daily dosing, fewer side effects, and fewer adverse interactions with other drugs than Tagamet. Although their product profiles were more like Zantac than Tagamet, third Rx entrant Pepcid and fourth Rx entrant Axid were not able to overcome their late-entrant disadvantages. As we discuss in more detail in Section V, order of entry in the OTC market differed from that in the Rx segment; in the OTC segment, Pepcid AC was first entrant, then Tagamet HB, Zantac 75, and finally Axid AR. While the time gap between first and second entrants was only about 2 months in the OTC market, in the Rx market it was 6 years.

Davina Ling[24] notes that unlike in the Rx market, most private labels, minor brands, and other drugs in the OTC market do not need to seek specific approvals from the FDA before marketing, so long as they meet good manufacturing practice and other drug regulatory standards. For off-patent products having approved active ingredients, OTC drugs encounter relatively minor barriers to entry. In spite of this, OTC markets for, say, gastrointestinal (GI) and pain remedies are relatively concentrated, with old brand names

[18] Schmalensee, Product Differentiation Advantages, *supra* note 1.

[19] Bond & Lean, *supra* note 2.

[20] Berndt *et al.*, Information, Marketing and Pricing, *supra* note 6; and Berndt *et al.*, Roles of Marketing, *supra* note 6.

[21] King *et al.*, *supra* note 14.

[22] Glen Urban *et al.*, Market Share Rewards to Pioneering Brands: An Empirical Analysis and Strategic Implications, 32 Mgmt. Sci. 645 (1986).

[23] William T. Robinson, Gurumurthy Kalyanaram, & Glen L. Urban, First-Mover Advantages from Pioneering New Markets: A Survey of Empirical Evidence, 9 Rev. Indus. Org. 1(1994).

[24] Ling, *supra* note 5.

still dominating sales. For example, as early as the 1970s, the OTC GI remedies market was already dominated by eight major brands, which accounted for approximately 80 percent of the market revenue share. Similarly in 1995, OTC drugs such as Tylenol and Advil, more than 20 years old, still achieved combined sales of more than $1.2 billion.

Consistent with the endogenous sunk-cost theory proposed by Sutton,[25] the OTC drug market has traditionally been dominated by a few major brands that invested heavily in marketing and a small competitive fringe with numerous firms and low marketing investments. In particular, in 1977, the average advertising/retail sales ratio for the eight major brands in the OTC GI remedies market was approximately 21 percent.[26] Direct-to-consumer marketing has continued to play an important role in the more recent OTC GI remedies market. For the seven largest-selling antacid OTC products, between 1990 and 1996 the median advertising/retail sales ratio was approximately 34 percent.[27]

While first-mover advantages are considerable, they may not be insurmountable. Entrants who invest heavily in marketing and who can differentiate their products from the pioneer may overcome the incumbent's edge. In such cases, the information content of marketing efforts reduces switching costs by informing consumers of other, possibly more effective, alternative medications. In this context, deregulation of DTC marketing of Rx products can play an important role in reducing order-of-entry advantages to pioneers, thereby increasing nonprice competition among early and later entrants. How such deregulation of DTC marketing of Rx products spills over into same-brand advantages in the subsequent OTC market is not clear, however. Our modest goal in this paper is to identify and quantify such impacts, if they exist.

In evaluating the impacts of DTC marketing on Rx and OTC versions of H_2-antagonists, we expect the marginal product of marketing to vary over the product life cycle. For example, for new products, marketing may convey important incremental information, attracting new users and raising consumer awareness of the product and its uses (particularly when the medical condition is underdiagnosed and undertreated), thereby increasing the size of the market being served. However, for mature products for which consumers have already developed strong preferences and high levels of brand loyalty, and particularly when the market has been saturated, the social marginal product of additional marketing may be much smaller, even though the private mar-

[25] John Sutton, Sunk Costs and Market Structure (1991).

[26] Federal Trade Commission, *supra* note 1.

[27] Ling, *supra* note 5. The seven brands are Tums, Mylanta, Gaviscon, Maalox, Alka Seltzer, Rolaids, and Pepto Bismol.

ginal product for each participant may be positive. This is consistent with the market expansion and "market-stealing" effects of marketing.[28]

IV. Data Sources, Descriptions, and Interpretations

Empirical research on interactions among Rx drug and OTC markets at the time of patent expiration requires integrating data from a number of diverse sources. We now briefly summarize our data sources. We begin with Rx drugs and then move on to the OTCs.

A. *Prescription Drug Markets*

Price, quantity, revenue, and marketing data for antiulcer and heartburn Rx drugs are taken from IMS Health, monthly from January 1988 through June 1999. IMS's Retail Perspective tracks monthly shipments from manufacturers and wholesalers to retail warehouses and outlets. The revenue data are those to manufacturers and wholesalers, and not to the retail outlets (who add retail margins). Although revenues are net of charge backs (discounts given to purchasers and channeled through wholesalers), rebates (payments made to providers who often do not take title to the pharmaceuticals, for example, managed care organizations) are not included in the IMS revenue data, and neither are prompt payment discounts. The exclusion of rebates from the revenue data implies an overstatement of Rx revenues and prices, but the extent of this overstatement is unknown, for data on rebates tend to be highly proprietary. In spite of this drawback in the IMS data, however, many branded and generic pharmaceutical companies purchase and utilize the IMS data for their internal research.

The level of aggregation of the IMS retail purchase data is at the presentational form, for instance, bottles of 30 tablets each having a 150-mg strength. We convert these various presentational sales measures into quantity or unit data by using the recommended daily dosage for active duodenal ulcer treatment as the transformation factor. The resulting quantity data can then be interpreted as the hypothetical patient-days of therapy per month if all patients were taking the recommended active duodenal ulcer daily dosage.[29] Data on recommended daily dosages are taken from the *Physicians' Desk Reference*.[30] Price per day of therapy is then computed as revenues divided by the quantity of therapy days in that month. Further details on

[28] Also see Berndt *et al*., Information, Marketing and Pricing, *supra* note 6; and Berndt *et al*., Roles of Marketing, *supra* note 6, for an analysis of market expansion versus competitive effects of marketing in the Rx H_2 market.

[29] The transformation factors are Tagamet (cimetidine), 800 mg/day; Zantac (ranitidine), 300 mg/day; Pepcid, 40 mg/day; and Axid, 300 mg/day.

[30] Physicians' Desk Reference (2000).

price, quantity, and revenue measurement are found in the data appendix of Berndt and coauthors.[31]

The price, quantity, and revenue data we employ cover only sales into drugstores. While drugstore sales constitute on average about 70–80 percent of sales in all outlets, the data exclude sales to hospitals, long-term care facilities, and mail order distributors.[32] Since hospital usage and marketing differs considerably from the outpatient environment, we confine our attention here to the traditional retail sector.

To measure marketing efforts involving pharmaceutical sales representatives' (detailers') physician office visits, we employ IMS Health data from their Office Contact Report. On the basis of a panel of about 3,800 physicians who report the number of visits and minutes spent with detailers discussing particular products, IMS extrapolates monthly detailing efforts by drug to the national level. Using an estimated cost per detailing visit, IMS also estimates total detailing expenditures.

Medical journal advertising pages and expenditures are estimated by IMS in their National Journal Audit. The universe measured by this audit includes journal pharmaceutical advertising directed to those in all types of medical practice, including pharmacists, nurses, podiatrists, and dentists as well as medical and osteopathic practitioners. On the basis of circulation, the number of square inches and pages of advertisements, and the copy characteristics such as premium positioning and the number of colors in each advertisement, IMS uses standard rate sheets from over 300 major medical journals to estimate total dollars of journal advertising by drug on a monthly basis. Further details on these marketing measures can be found in the data appendix of Berndt and coauthors[33] and in IMS Health's *Information Services Manual*.[34]

Data on DTC marketing of Rx brands from Leading National Advertisers (LNA)/Media Watch Multi-Media Service is published on a quarterly basis by Competitive Media Reporting.[35] This service reports Rx brand advertising expenditure estimates in 10 major media: consumer magazines, Sunday magazines, newspapers, outdoor, network television, spot television, syndicated television, cable television, network radio, and national spot radio. The LNA/Media Watch Multi-Media Service includes only brands of companies spending a total of $25,000 or more year-to-date in the 10 media measured. The data we employ report advertising expenditures by company and then list brands for each company. Currently, our DTC data are available through the second quarter of 2000. We gathered quarterly Rx brand advertising data for the companies selling the branded H_2s. To transform the quarterly data into

[31] Berndt *et al.*, The Roles of Marketing, *supra* note 6.

[32] IMS Health, Information Services Manual (1998).

[33] Berndt *et al.*, The Roles of Marketing, *supra* note 6.

[34] IMS Health, *supra* note 32.

[35] Now called TNS Media Intelligence/CMR. See http://www.tnsmi-cmr.com.

monthly periodicity, we employed the STATA command ipolate.[36] The monthly expenditure data were then deflated by the Bureau of Labor Statistics (BLS) Advertising Agency Producer Price Index to convert them into constant-dollar figures.[37]

B. *Over-the-Counter Drug Markets*

The quantity, price, and revenue data used to analyze the OTC H_2 market are taken from InfoScan and are based on store-level optical scanner data that are purchased and collected from multiple retail outlets by IRI.[38] These scanner data are collected weekly from more than 29,000 chain drugstores, mass merchandisers, food stores, and chain convenience stores located in major metropolitan areas and rural areas. They are then projected to national levels for these chains. The IRI data provide detailed information on sales, pricing, and promotion on a stock-keeping unit basis. The volume of sales is recorded for each package size of each brand on an average weekly basis. The weekly data are aggregated to the monthly level.

Since our research goal is to examine interactions between the Rx and OTC markets, we need to establish comparable units of consumption. For each OTC brand, we aggregate the data across presentations and regional outlets so that the quantity measure reflects the total milligrams sold each month nationally. For instance, if 5,000 packages of Tagamet HB each having 25 tablets of 200 mg cimetidine are sold, we compute the total number of milligrams of Tagamet HB sold that month as $5{,}000 \times 25 \times 200$ mg $= 25 \times 10^6$ mg. The IRI data record sales from drugstores, mass merchandisers, and food stores to consumers and therefore include both wholesale and retail margins, unlike the IMS Health data for Rx sales. Another important distinction between these data sources is that the IMS data reflect inventory-stocking behavior by, for example, chain drugstore warehouses, while the IRI data include only actual sales to final consumers.

To make the quantity units of the various OTC H_2 brands comparable to each other and comparable to the Rx H_2 brands, we normalize the total number of milligrams per brand sold each month by the Rx daily dosage recom-

36 See STATA Reference Manual, STATA Reference Manual Release 6 (1999).

37 For July 1995 onward (when the deflators first became available), we constructed this deflator as the arithmetic average of the Bureau of Labor Statistics, Producer Price Index for "Advertising agencies, ad creation, billed separately," and "Advertising agencies, media placement, including ad creation not billed" (http://www.bls.gov). For months prior to July 1995, we employed the Producer Price Index for "All finished goods."

38 See Information Resources, Inc., Store Data Measures (1997); Peter M. Guadagni & John D. C. Little, A Logit Model of Brand Choice Calibrated on Scanner Data, 2 Marketing Sci. 203 (1983); and Randolph E. Bucklin & Sunil Gupta, Commercial Use of UPC Scanner Data: Industry and Academic Perspectives, 18 Marketing Sci. 247 (1999). The IRI Web address is http://www.infores.com.

mended to treat active duodenal ulcers.[39] Although we describe our quantity measure as patient-days of therapy, in fact this is not literally true.[40] Rather, the quantity measures should be interpreted as the number of patient-days of therapy that would be consumed hypothetically if all the OTC H_2s were used for the treatment of active duodenal ulcers at recommended Rx dosages. It is worth emphasizing here that this is a theoretical construct, and we do not wish to imply or suggest that any or all patients actually (mis)use the OTC H_2s to treat active duodenal ulcers.[41] We make this transformation solely for the purpose of standardizing units of active ingredient.

Once quantity units are calculated, we divide total revenues by quantity, thereby obtaining a price per patient-day of therapy. It is useful to note that both the revenue and price OTC data reflect the impacts of periodic "sales" and discounts, as well as the effects of coupons redeemed by consumers at the time of the retail transaction.

To obtain measures of monthly advertising of OTC H_2s, we again employ data from LNA/Media Watch Multi-Media Service. LNA distinguishes consumer-oriented OTC brand advertising from that for Rx brands. Quarterly data on media advertising over the 10 media mentioned earlier for the H_2 OTC brands are taken from Class D213, Over-the-Counter Digestive Aids and Antacids. The ipolate command in STATA is again employed to convert expenditure data from quarterly to monthly. Monthly advertising expenditures in current dollars are then deflated by the BLS's Producer Price Index for Advertising Agencies, as discussed above.

V. Order of Entry, Marketing Efforts, and Market Shares in the Over-the-Counter H_2 Market

The four branded H_2s all entered the OTC market within 13 months of one another—first Pepcid AC in June 1995, followed by Tagamet HB in August 1995, Zantac in April 1996, and, finally, Axid AR in July 1996. Would Pepcid AC be able to fully exploit the potential first-mover advantages it had achieved? How would subsequent entrants fare? What would be the impact of Rx order of entry on the OTC market? Here we report results of an initial analysis of order-of-entry effects. We first analyze the relationship between the advertising/sales ratio and order-of-entry effects. We then describe sales developments for the OTC H_2s by examining factors affecting the monthly revenue sales and revenue shares among the four OTC H_2s.

[39] This follows procedures utilized by Ling, *supra* note 5.

[40] Recommended dosages vary by indication. For example, while the recommended dosage of Zantac for treating active duodenal ulcers, active gastric ulcers, and gastroesophageal reflux disease is 300 mg per day (either 300 mg once daily or 150 mg twice daily), the recommended dosage for duodenal ulcer maintenance therapy is only 150 mg per day.

[41] For each of the four OTC H_2s, the transformation of OTC to Rx involves using twice the maximum daily recommended OTC dosages.

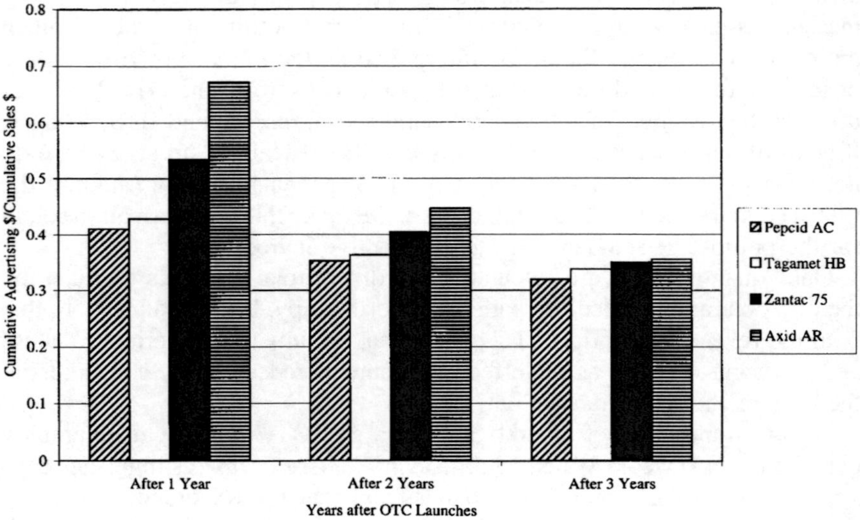

FIGURE 1.—Cumulative detailing/sales ratios by over-the-counter (OTC) drug

Order-of-entry effects can manifest themselves in a number of ways, one of which involves advertising intensity. In the Rx H_2 market, for example, 1, 2, and 3 years after initial launch, marketing/sales ratios (cumulative detailing minutes divided by cumulative units sold) were smallest for the pioneer and were successively higher for each subsequent Rx H_2 entrant.[42] This finding is consistent with the theory of first-mover advantage and consumer switching costs in the Rx market.

To construct a comparable marketing/sales ratio for the OTC H_2 market, we compute cumulative advertising dollar expenditures (summed over the 10 advertising media) for each OTC H_2 and divide this by cumulative OTC H_2 revenues for each of the 3 years following launch.[43] Figure 1 presents the rather striking results for the OTC market. Later entrants have successively higher advertising/sales ratios. The ratio for Pepcid AC, the pioneer, is .41 in the year of launch. For Tagamet HB, the second entrant, it is .43; Zantac 75 and Axid AR have ratios of .53 and .67, respectively. Since advertising efforts are particularly intense immediately following product launch, it is not surprising that all four advertising/sales ratios decline over time. The

[42] See figure 7.7, p. 293, in Berndt *et al.*, Roles of Marketing, *supra* note 6.

[43] We present advertising/sales ratio as opposed to the level of advertising because of Dorfman and Steiner's insight that the profit-maximizing combination of price and advertising level for firms with market power is one whereby the advertising/sales ratio is equal to the ratio of the advertising elasticity of demand to the price elasticity of demand; see Robert A. Dorfman & Peter O. Steiner, Optimal Advertising and Optimal Quality, 44 Am. Econ. Rev. 826 (1954).

relationship between order of entry and the advertising/sales ratio persists 2 years after launch: first-mover Pepcid AC has the lowest value (.35), while the followers have higher ratios (.36 for Tagamet HB, .40 for Zantac 75, and .45 for Axid AR). Although the order-of-entry ranking persists 3 years after launch, the differences in the advertising/sales ratio among the four entrants diminish considerably over time: .32 for pioneer Pepcid AC, .34 for second entrant Tagamet HB, .35 for third entrant Zantac 75, and .36 for last entrant Axid AR. This reduction in differences over time is not surprising, since relative time on the market converges for the four OTCs with the passage of time.

This monotonic relationship between the advertising/sales ratio and order of entry supports the notion that consumers incur a switching cost for OTC medications, which is consistent with a first-mover advantage. This may also help explain the need for later entrants to invest more heavily in marketing to overcome incumbents' advantages. We examine the rationale behind the relationship between order of entry and marketing intensity further in Section VI.

An important aspect of rivalry in the Rx H_2 market involved the indications for which the FDA granted approval. Zantac Rx, for example, was the first H_2 to obtain approval for GERD (a severe form of heartburn), and having this approval allowed Zantac Rx detailers to expand their marketing efforts significantly by visiting offices of general practitioners and internists, not just the smaller number of gastroenterologists who treated ulcers. In the OTC H_2 market, a different but related rivalry developed that also involved FDA indication approvals. In April 1995, pioneer Pepcid AC received FDA approval not only for the treatment of episodic heartburn, but also for its prevention. Thus Pepcid AC could be marketed as a preemptive treatment that was used prior to eating spicy foods, for example. By contrast, when Tagamet HB received its initial FDA approval in June 1995, it was for the relief of symptoms of occasional heartburn, acid indigestion, and sour stomach, but not for their prevention. This placed Tagamet HB at a competitive disadvantage in its ability to market. The demand for preventative medication was likely to be very large, but Tagamet HB was preempted from marketing itself for prevention until it received a similar FDA approval for prevention on November 15, 1995.

In addition to its indication disadvantage, for Tagamet HB the initial dose was two 100-mg tablets, whereas the Pepcid AC dose was only one 10-mg tablet; in November 1996, Tagamet HB was able to change this to one 200-mg tablet per dose. Zantac 75 received FDA approval for only the relief of heartburn on December 19, 1995, while Axid AR received approval on May 9, 1996, for only the prevention of meal-induced heartburn, acid indigestion, and sour stomach.[44] Pepcid AC thus enjoyed two first-mover advantages in

[44] See the U.S. Food and Drug Administration, Approved Drug Products with Therapeutic

the OTC market: it was the first H_2 to obtain OTC approval from the FDA and the first to obtain approval for the prevention of heartburn, not just symptomatic relief. Although this dual first-mover advantage might have provided considerable benefits to Pepcid AC, the time differences in launch dates among the four OTCs were relatively small, and thus Pepcid AC may not have been able to exploit them as well as it would have if launch dates had been spread out over greater time intervals.

To describe sales developments for the OTC H_2s since their launch in 1995–96, we plot monthly days of therapy for each of the OTC H_2s in Figure 2, along with corresponding revenue shares in Figure 3. In interpreting these figures, recall first that the OTC prices are actual average consumer prices paid at mass merchandisers, food stores, and drugstores that use scanner checkout equipment and sell their chain store data to IRI. Thus, sales from convenience and other stores that do not employ scanner data are not included in the IRI data; also excluded are sales from stores that have scanning equipment but that are not part of chains selling their data to IRI. This implies that the OTC quantity and revenue data understate total U.S. sales. Second, in August 1996, at $1.60 and $1.53, Zantac 75 and Axid AR average daily prices were considerably higher than those for Pepcid AC ($1.31) and Tagamet HB ($1.26). As the average number of tablets per package increased over time, average daily prices fell for all four OTCs. By July 1999, there was little price dispersion: the average price for Axid AR was $1.09; for Zantac 75, $1.12; for Tagamet HB, $1.14; and for Pepcid AC, $1.16.

With this in mind, we now examine monthly sales units and revenue shares. As is seen in Figure 2, order-of-entry effects were apparently important in the OTC market, but they were not entirely invincible. First entrant Pepcid AC had been the market leader ever since its launch in June 1995, and last entrant Axid had sustained apparently permanent last-mover disadvantages. However, Zantac 75 was able to overtake Tagamet HB, the second mover in the OTC market, within 2 months of Zantac's launch. Zantac was unable to translate its Rx success into surmounting Pepcid AC's 10-month first-mover and indication approval advantages. In short, we observe some positive spillover effects from the Rx-to-OTC markets, but these appear to be limited.

A second result depicted in Figure 2 is that the OTC market for H_2s has become a large one. At the end of our sample in mid-1999, the four OTC products accounted for about 38 million patient-days of therapy per month (a figure biased downward for reasons discussed above), compared with about 70 million patient-days of Rx H_2 therapy sold to drugstores. Over-the-counter sales of the branded H_2s have therefore become a quite substantial component of brand equity, but the importance of OTC sales differs by brand. Over-the-counter patient-days of Pepcid AC therapy were about half those of

Equivalence Evaluations, in Electronic Orange Book (June 2000) (http://www.fda.gov/cder/ob/default.htm), for FDA approval dates of Rx and OTC versions of the drugs.

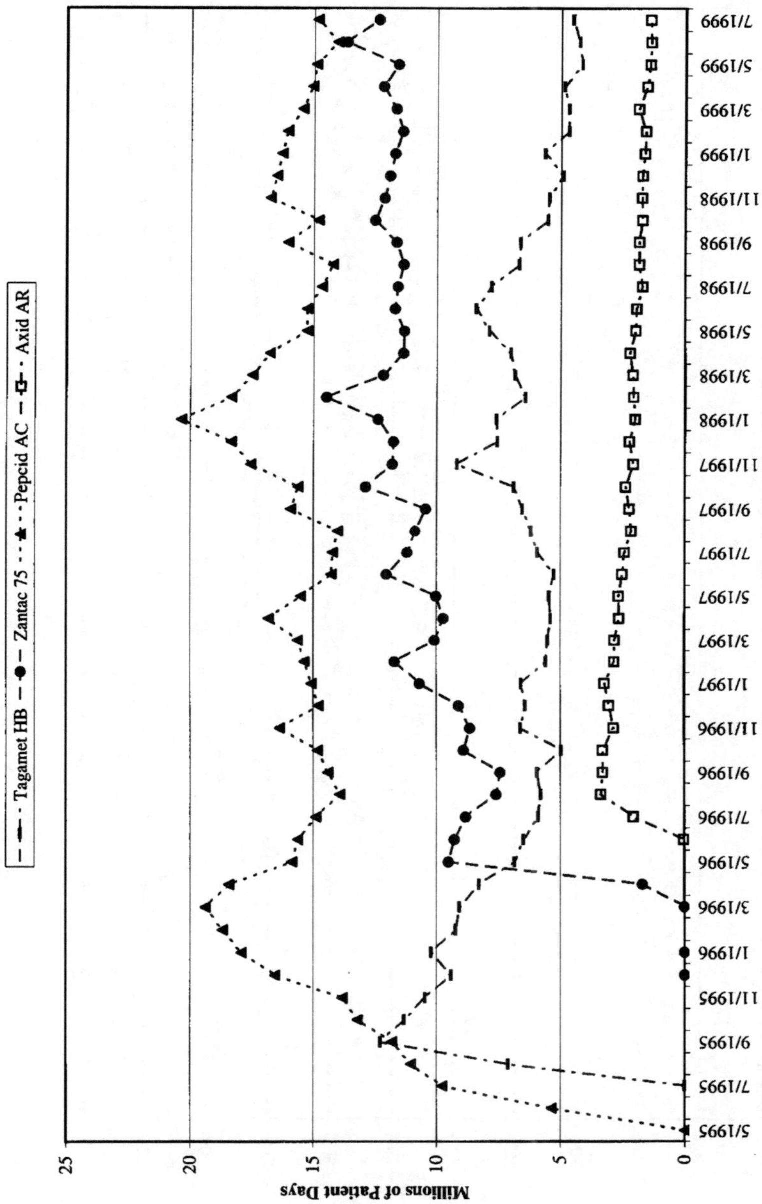

FIGURE 2.—Units of over-the-counter H_2 antagonists, monthly

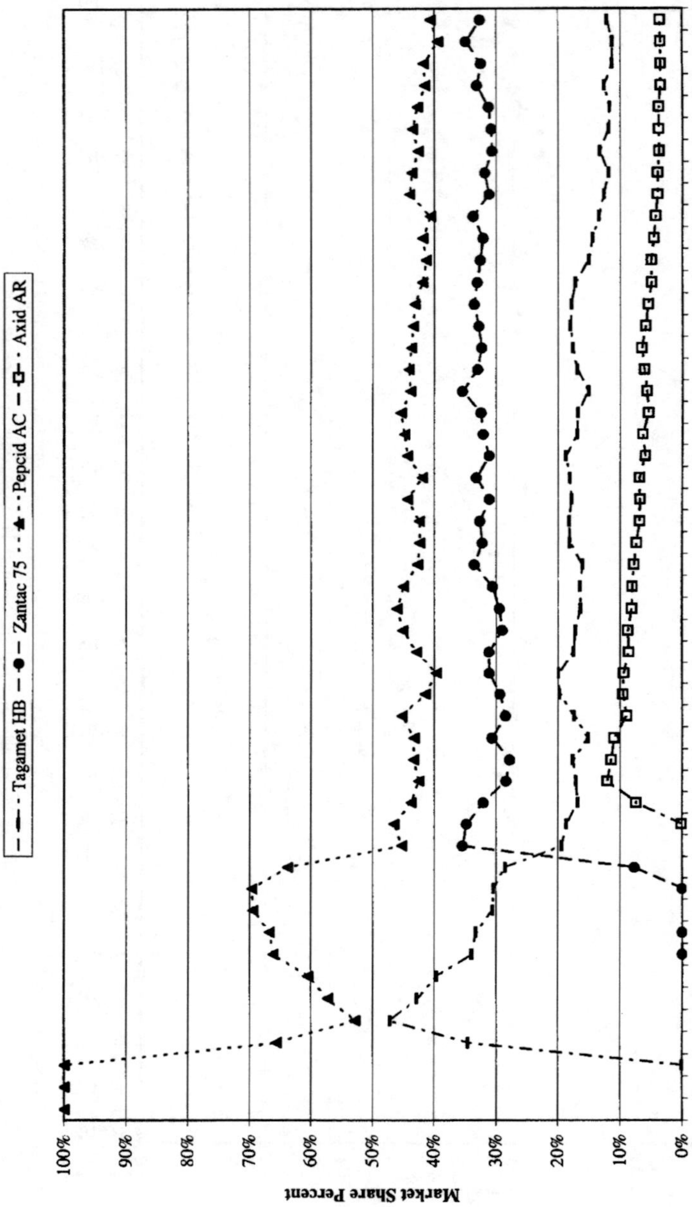

FIGURE 3.—Revenue shares of over-the-counter H_2 antagonists

Pepcid Rx. However, total days of therapy for Zantac 75, Tagamet HB, and Axid AR were only about 25–40 percent of those of their Rx (branded plus generic) sales. For Zantac and Tagamet, this implies brand equity that can persist even after the Rx product loses patent protection.

In Figure 3, we plot revenue shares for the four branded OTC H_2s. Given the information conveyed in Figure 2, it is not surprising that the revenue share of Pepcid AC was largest, hovering around 45 percent ever since mid-1996. The revenue share for Zantac 75 ranged from 28 percent to slightly under 35 percent and generally increased slowly but unsteadily over time. The launches of Zantac 75 and Axid AR appear to have hurt Tagamet HB. At the end of the sample time period in mid-1999, the Tagamet HB revenue share was about 12 percent, while that for Axid AR was 3–4 percent.[45]

We find, therefore, that order-of-entry and positive spillover effects between Rx and OTC brands contributed to success in the OTC market. Later entrants appeared to employ marketing instruments to mitigate earlier-entrant advantages. We assess this order-of-entry effect further in the regression analyses reported below. Consumer switching costs, imperfect information, and risk aversion may explain the high level of brand loyalty in the OTC drug market. Indeed, if asymmetric information and risk aversion are important in explaining high consumer switching costs, then Rx-to-OTC switches may be a good way to overcome the incumbent informational advantage in the OTC market. Specifically, by marketing the Rx version of a drug directly to consumers, producers may be able to exploit spillovers to its OTC version if the effects of advertising and brand-name capital are long-lived or signal quality. However, since we do not have data that would permit us to examine the informational content of marketing, detailed discussions of the informational value of marketing are outside the scope of this paper.

VI. Econometric Models of Impacts of Direct-to-Consumer Drugs and Traditional Marketing in the Prescription and Over-the-Counter H_2 Markets

With this descriptive analysis of order-of-entry effects, marketing efforts, and realized market shares of the OTC products as background, we now formulate testable hypotheses regarding the relationship between order of entry and marketing efforts. According to the Dorfman-Steiner[46] theorem, when profit-maximizing firms face downward-sloping demand curves, the optimal price and marketing efforts occur where the ratio of dollar marketing to sales equals the ratio of the marketing elasticity of demand to the (absolute value of the) price elasticity of demand. In the previous section, we reported that the cumulative advertising/sales ratios increased monotonically with or-

[45] The remaining market is composed of private-label OTC cimetidine.

[46] Dorfman & Steiner, *supra* note 43.

der of entry. If the price elasticities of demand were similar for all four products (or perhaps even greater for later entrants), then it follows that the marketing elasticity of demand must also increase with order of entry.

The above hypothesis may appear counterintuitive at first glance, but the intuition underlying the larger OTC DTC marketing elasticities for later entrants, ceteris paribus, is relatively simple. Let f_1' and f_2' be the marginal products of marketing for the first and second entrants, respectively. By definition, the marketing elasticity of demand can be written as $\alpha_i^M = f_i'(A_i/q_i)$, where A_i represents the level of marketing efforts and q_i represents the units sold for entrant i. If we evaluate entrants 1 and 2 at a common level of marketing efforts, then $\alpha_2^M > \alpha_1^M$ if and only if $f_2'/f_1' > q_2/q_1$. We would indeed expect $q_2 < q_1$ from first-mover advantages. If later entrants face smaller "penalties" in relative marginal product of marketing than in relative units sold, then $f_2'/f_1' > q_2/q_1$, and in that case later entrants will have larger marketing elasticities of demand (holding marketing efforts constant). Combined with the Dorfman-Steiner theorem and holding other things equal, we would then expect the marginal product from marketing efforts to become smaller for later entrants, as well as the marketing elasticity of demand to increase with order of entry. We examine the above hypothesis by adding interaction terms between marketing stocks and the order-of-entry variable to the traditional econometric demand model specification (see equations (2) and (3) below).

The underlying conceptual framework for our econometric analysis is very simple, and it is implicit rather than explicit. We build from the traditional economic theory of demand, mindful that in the Rx market, principal-agent issues involving physicians and patients and moral hazard resulting from the presence of insurance coverage complicate matters considerably.

In each of our regressions, we specify quantity demanded as a function of price, marketing efforts, and other factors. It is reasonable to expect that marketing efforts are long-lived, having sales impacts far beyond the month in which they are incurred. In previous research, it has been common to assume that the rate of depreciation of the impact of marketing efforts on sales is constant over time. We follow that tradition here, although research that generalizes the depreciation rate to allow it to increase as patent expiration approaches deserves high priority. We specify the marketing stock Z_t as a weighted sum of previous monthly marketing expenditure flows. According to the perpetual inventory method,

$$Z_t = (1 - \delta)Z_{t-1} + M_t, \tag{1}$$

where δ is the monthly depreciation rate and M_t is the new marketing expenditure incurred during month t. Thus, the marketing stock at the end of month t is the depreciation-adjusted amount from the previous period plus this month's new (inflation-adjusted) marketing efforts. If $\delta = 0$, then Z_t is simply the cumulative sum of all previous real marketing efforts, and if

$\delta = 1$, then the effects of this period's marketing efforts completely disappear at the end of the month and $Z_t = M_t$. In the econometric implementation, we estimate δ, rather than assume an a priori value. Further, we allow for different depreciation rates for DTC and physician-oriented marketing. Finally, we estimate demand models allowing price, quantity, and marketing all to be jointly determined, using instrumental variable methods.

A. *Shares within Over-the-Counter Drugs*

As a first step, we begin with factors affecting choice among the OTCs. The panel of OTC brands is an unbalanced one because of the different dates of product launch; for each OTC brand, the data end in May 1999. Although theoretical developments in the economic theory of demand now permit empirical specifications in which the number of alternative goods in the choice set changes over time, empirical implementations (based on multinomial logit or generalized extreme-value distributions) are few because of their computational complexity.[47] We follow the marketing and order-of-entry literature in which it has been traditional to specify the dependent and explanatory variables all relative to the pioneer in an unbalanced panel framework.[48]

Let QDAYOTC_{jt} be the number of days of therapy for OTC brand *j* in month *t;* PDAYOTC_{jt}, the corresponding price; ZOTCDTC_{jt}, the marketing stock of OTC marketing of brand *j* via DTC media; ZRXDTC_{jt}, the marketing stock of the Rx version of OTC drug *j* marketing on the basis of DTC media; and ZRXMD_{jt}, the marketing stock of the Rx version of OTC drug *j* marketing on the basis of physician-directed media. We define OTCORDER_j as the order of entry of OTC drug *j* in the OTC H_2 market, $\text{OTCORDER}_j \times \log(\text{ZRXMD}_j)$ as the interaction term between OTC order of entry and the log of relative physician-directed advertising stock of Rx drug *j*, $\text{OTCORDER}_j \times \log(\text{ZRXDTC}_j)$ as the interaction term between order-of-entry and the log of relative DTC advertising stock of Rx drug *j*, and $\text{OTCORDER}_j \times \log(\text{ZOTCDTC}_j)$ as the interaction term between order of entry and the log of relative advertising stock of OTC drug *j* to that of Pepcid AC. Given that the model framework involves variables measured relative to the first entrant, Pepcid AC, OTCORDER_j takes on values 2, 3, and 4.

[47] See, for example, Steven Berry, James Levinsohn, & Ariel Pakes, Automobile Prices in Market Equilibrium, 63 Econometrica 841 (1995); and Timothy F. Bresnahan, Scott Stern, & Manuel Trajtenberg, Market Segmentation and the Sources of Rents from Innovation: Personal Computers in the Late 1980s, 28 Rand J. Econ. S17 (1997).

[48] See Berndt *et al.*, Information, Marketing and Pricing, *supra* note 6; and Berndt *et al.*, Roles of Marketing, *supra* note 6.

We specify a regression equation having the form[49]

$$\begin{aligned}\ln\left(\frac{\mathrm{QOTCDAY}_{jt}}{\mathrm{QOTCDAY}_{\mathrm{PAC},t}}\right) = {} & a_0 + a_1 \times \ln\left(\frac{\mathrm{POTCDAY}_{jt}}{\mathrm{POTCDAY}_{\mathrm{PAC},t}}\right) \\ & + a_2 \times \ln\left(\frac{\mathrm{ZOTCDTC}_{jt}}{\mathrm{ZOTCDTC}_{\mathrm{PAC},t}}\right) \\ & + a_3 \times \ln\left(\frac{\mathrm{ZRXDTC}_{jt}}{\mathrm{ZRXDTC}_{\mathrm{PAC},t}}\right) \\ & + a_4 \times \ln\left(\frac{\mathrm{ZRXMD}_{jt}}{\mathrm{ZRXMD}_{\mathrm{PAC},t}}\right) \\ & + a_5 \times \mathrm{OTCORDER}_j \\ & + a_6 \times \mathrm{OTCORDER}_j \times \ln\left(\frac{\mathrm{ZOTCDTC}_{jt}}{\mathrm{ZOTCDTC}_{\mathrm{PAC},t}}\right) \\ & + a_7 \times \mathrm{OTCORDER}_j \times \ln\left(\frac{\mathrm{ZRXDTC}_{jt}}{\mathrm{ZRXDTC}_{\mathrm{PAC},t}}\right) \\ & + a_8 \times \mathrm{OTCORDER}_j \times \ln\left(\frac{\mathrm{ZRXMD}_{jt}}{\mathrm{ZRXMD}_{\mathrm{PAC},t}}\right) + \varepsilon_{jt},\end{aligned} \tag{2}$$

where PAC is the OTC pioneer Pepcid AC; j = Tagamet HB, Zantac 75, or Axid AR; and ε_{jt} is a random error term. Notice that the proportional effect of, say, a relative change in DTC marketing for an OTC product on its log market share in this interaction specification is equal to $a_2 + a_6 \times \mathrm{OTCORDER}_j$, and thus the effect of relative DTC marketing of an OTC product depends on that product's order of entry in the OTC market. Consistent with our hypotheses, we expect a_6 to be positive such that later entrants would face higher relative OTC DTC marketing demand elasticities. While we expect the marginal effect of order of entry on OTC demand to be negative (namely, later entrants have lower market shares than earlier entrants), we do not have any a priori assumptions regarding the signs of a_7 and a_8 (that is, the signs of the marginal effect of OTC order of entry on the cross-marketing elasticity of Rx drugs).

We "stack" the Tagamet HB, Zantac 75, and Axid AR observations, estimate the unbalanced panel by nonlinear least squares (NLS), and employ procedures to adjust for heteroskedasticity in standard errors.[50] Since by

[49] Results from initial regressions yielded unsatisfactory estimated coefficients on various variables capturing new FDA indication and dosing approvals for the OTC drugs. Since the differences in FDA indication approvals may already be captured by variations in advertising and pricing, and since the time differences between product launches were relatively minor, we excluded these FDA-related variables from further consideration.

[50] The sample size is 175 for NLS.

equation (1) the marketing stock variables depend on an unknown monthly deterioration rate δ, we perform a two-dimensional grid search over δ from 0 percent to 30 percent separately for physician-oriented and DTC marketing stocks, in steps of .5 percent, and then choose as our preferred model that combination of the δs and the remaining parameters that minimizes the mean square error.[51]

The within-OTC share model employs IRI scanner data for the OTC H_2s, IMS Health data on Rx physician-oriented marketing, and LNA data on DTC marketing of OTC and Rx products.

Column (1) of Table 1 shows the NLS regression results. The price elasticity is estimated to be −1.622 and is negative and significant ($p < .001$). The estimated monthly depreciation rates (on the basis of the grid search procedure) for physician-directed media and consumer-directed media are 10 percent and 13 percent, respectively. Relative OTC quantities demanded are positively related to physician-directed marketing stocks of their Rx brands with an elasticity that varies significantly with the order of entry.

Although the estimate of a_2 is insignificant, $a_2 + a_6 \times \text{OTCORDER}_j$ (that is, the effect of DTC marketing of the OTC drug on its demand) is positive and significant at all relevant values of OTCORDER_j. The relative OTC DTC marketing elasticities for OTC Tagamet, Zantac, and Axid are .176 ($p <$ .02), .318 ($p < .001$), and .460 ($p < .001$), respectively. The estimated relative elasticities of physician-directed marketing stocks are .163 (for Tagamet; $p < .001$), −.328 (for Zantac; $p < .001$), and −.819 (for Axid; $p < .001$). While there are positive spillovers from Rx physician-oriented marketing to an Rx-to-OTC switch for Tagamet, the spillover effects are negative for Zantac and Axid, which suggests OTC-Rx substitutability and cannibalization of Zantac and Axid OTC sales. In terms of spillovers from DTC marketing of the Rx version of the drug, we find small but still positive and significant spillovers for Zantac and Axid, but negative and insignificant spillovers for Tagamet. The relative elasticities for Zantac and Axid are .068 ($p < .001$) and .144 ($p < .001$), while for Tagamet the relative elasticity of DTC marketing of the Rx drug on OTC drug demand is −.008. By itself, the order-of-entry parameter estimate is also strong and significant. A joint F-test of the coefficients from the order-of-entry and interaction variables shows that these variables are significant ($p < .001$). Our findings therefore display multifaceted spillovers between marketing for the Rx drug and demand for the same-brand OTC drug. Marketing and order of entry play important roles in this market.

The NLS results are based on the assumption that regressors such as relative

[51] This yields numerically equivalent parameter estimates to an NLS estimator that repeatedly substitutes in for lagged values of $Z_{t-\tau}$ and thereby makes Z_t a weighted power series over all previous marketing flow expenditures. However, the standard errors from this grid search method are likely slightly underestimated.

TABLE 1

PARAMETER ESTIMATES FROM MARKET-SHARE MODELS FOR THE PRESCRIPTION (RX) AND OVER-THE-COUNTER (OTC) MARKETS

	EQUATION (2), OTC MARKET		EQUATION (3), RX MARKET	
	NLS (1)	2SLS (2)	NLS (3)	2SLS (4)
log(relative price)	−1.622** (.283)	−1.947** (.556)	.014 (.036)	−.441** (.061)
log(relative Rx physician-oriented marketing stock)	1.145** (.071)	.663** (.098)	1.467** (.091)	1.677** (.303)
log(relative Rx DTC marketing stock)	−.160** (.024)	−.169** (.023)	−.073** (.016)	−.082 (.067)
log(relative OTC DTC marketing stock)	−.108 (.093)	−.218 (.273)	−.004 (.008)	.012 (.013)
OTCORDER	−1.846** (.178)	−2.179** (.695)		
OTCORDER × log(relative Rx MD-oriented marketing stock)	−.491** (.039)	−.273** (.041)		
OTCORDER × log(relative Rx DTC marketing stock)	.076** (.010)	.072** (.010)		
OTCORDER × log(relative OTC DTC marketing stock)	.142** (.017)	.181** (.069)		
RXORDER			−.385** (.017)	−.330** (.019)
RXOFFPAT			−.002* (.001)	−.001 (.001)
Constant	1.508 (.968)	2.557 (2.786)	.556** (.050)	.409** (.092)
Depreciation rate for physician-oriented marketing (%)	10.0	25.0	.0	1.0
Depreciation rate for DTC marketing (%)	13.0	13.0	32.0	29.0
R^2	.961	.958	.774	.867
N	175	171	552	389

NOTE.—Estimated heteroskedasticity-robust asymptotic standard errors are in parentheses. NLS = nonlinear least squares; 2SLS = two-stage least squares; DTC = direct to consumer; MD = physician.

* Significant at the .05 level.

** Significant at the .01 level.

price and marketing investments are exogenous. But given the monopolistically competitive market structure for these OTC products, both pricing and marketing efforts are unlikely to be exogenously determined variables. Hence, we also estimate parameters in equation (2) using instrumental variables (two-stage least squares (2SLS)) and test for endogeneity using a Hausman specification test.

We employ two sets of exogenous variables as instruments. One group is common to all firms: log of average hourly earnings of production workers in pharmaceutical and advertising industries; log of producer price index of pharmaceuticals, cable television, network television, and outdoor advertising; a time counter; and quarterly indicators. The other group of instruments is firm specific: the number of months the Rx molecule has been off patent relative to the number of months Tagamet has been off patent, order of entry in the Rx market, log of the firm's DTC advertising stock for other non-H_2-antagonist stomach remedies relative to J&J Merck's DTC advertising stock for other non-H_2-antagonist stomach remedies, and log of the firm's DTC advertising stock for non-H_2-antagonist Rx products relative to Merck's DTC advertising stock for non-H_2-antagonist Rx products. We construct these stocks by assuming the monthly advertising depreciation rate to be 5 percent. We find systematic differences in the NLS and 2SLS estimates and reject the hypothesis that NLS is a consistent estimator of parameters in equation (2) ($\chi^2 = 30.91, p < .0001$).

Column (2) of Table 1 shows the 2SLS results.[52] The 2SLS and NLS results are generally qualitatively similar although quantitatively different. The price elasticity is estimated to be -1.947 and is negative and significant ($p < .002$). The estimated monthly depreciation rates (on the basis of the grid search procedure) for physician-directed media and consumer-directed media are 25 percent and 13 percent, respectively. The relative OTC quantities that are demanded are positively related to relative DTC marketing stocks for Zantac and Axid, but not for Tagamet. The estimated elasticity is .144 (for Tagamet), .324 (for Zantac, $p < .001$), and .505 (for Axid, $p < .001$). Consistent with Dorfman-Steiner's framework, we find that increasing advertising/sales ratios for later entrants correspond with their facing increasing OTC DTC marketing elasticities. Relative OTC quantities are also positively related to DTC marketing stocks of their Rx brands for Zantac (.047, $p < .001$) and Axid (.119, $p < .001$) but are negative for Tagamet ($-.025, p < .01$). On the other hand, relative quantities are negatively related to physician-directed marketing stocks of their Rx brands for Zantac ($-.157$, $p < .001$) and Axid ($-.430, p < .001$) but positively and significantly related to physician-directed marketing stocks of Rx Tagamet ($.116, p < .001$). Again, we find strong and significant order-of-entry effects.

[52] The sample size is 171 for 2SLS because data on advertising by the same firm for other products were not always available.

In summary, the various marketing elasticities depend systematically on order of entry. Prescription to over-the-counter spillovers involving both physician-directed and DTC marketing differ in sign depending on order of entry.[53] These multivariate results are consistent with the bivariate descriptive results reported earlier concerning the effects of order of entry on advertising intensity. Specifically, later entrants have higher relative OTC DTC marketing elasticities, and consistent with the Dorfman-Steiner theorem, they also have higher advertising/sales ratios. This is also consistent with the notion that later entrants face lower marginal returns on marketing and hence need to invest more in marketing relative to incumbents in order to reduce order-of-entry disadvantages.

B. Shares within the Prescription H_2 Markets

For the Rx market, we employ a similar approach to that used for the OTCs. Here, Tagamet is the pioneer, and variables for Rx drug *j* are measured relative to Tagamet (cimetidine). Let QRXDAY_{jt} and PRXDAY_{jt} be the quantity and price of a day of Rx therapy for drug *j*, and let RXOFFPAT_{jt} be the number of months the Rx drug has been off patent and faced generic competition; ZRXMD_{jt}, ZRXDTC_{jt}, and ZOTCDTC_{jt} are as defined earlier. We define RXORDER_j as the order of entry of Rx drug *j* in the Rx H_2 market and note that this variable takes on values of 2, 3, or 4.

With these variables defined, we specify the within-Rx H_2 regression as having the form

$$\begin{aligned}\ln\left(\frac{\text{QRXDAY}_{jt}}{\text{QRXDAY}_{\text{CIM},t}}\right) = {} & b_0 + b_1 \times \ln\left(\frac{\text{PRXDAY}_{jt}}{\text{PRXDAY}_{\text{CIM},t}}\right) \\ & + b_2 \times \ln\left(\frac{\text{ZOTCDTC}_{jt}}{\text{ZOTCDTC}_{\text{CIM},t}}\right) \\ & + b_3 \times \ln\left(\frac{\text{ZRXMD}_{jt}}{\text{ZRXMD}_{\text{CIM},t}}\right) \\ & + b_4 \times \ln\left(\frac{\text{ZRXDTC}_{jt}}{\text{ZRXDTC}_{\text{CIM},t}}\right) \\ & + b_5 \times \text{RXORDER}_j \\ & + b_6 \times (\text{RXOFFPAT}_{jt} - \text{RXOFFPAT}_{\text{CIM},t}) + u_{jt},\end{aligned} \tag{3}$$

[53] This hypothesis regarding spillovers involving physician-directed marketing and Rx-to-OTC switches could be explored further using another data set, namely, the National Ambulatory Medical Care Survey, to examine whether physician-directed marketing leads physicians to advise their patients to purchase OTC versions of the drug when it becomes available in non-Rx strength or whether instead physician-directed marketing induces physicians to prescribe Rx versions of the drug even when the non-Rx strength is available. Although the

where u_{jt} is a random error term.[54] We expect b_1 to be negative; namely, we expect relative units sold to vary negatively with relative prices, other things equal, although the presence of Rx drug insurance could dilute the expected negative relationship. We expect b_3 and b_4 to be positive, reflecting positive effects of relative physician-oriented and DTC marketing on relative Rx units sold. We do not have any a priori assumptions about the sign and magnitude of b_2 given the ambiguous spillover effects of DTC marketing of OTC brand on demand for the same-brand Rx drug. Although we expect b_5 to be negative, the expected sign of b_6 is ambiguous because of the combination of order-of-entry effects and generic entry (namely, early entrants generally faced earlier patent expiration).

Again we employ data from IRI, IMS Health, and LNA. Note that the Rx quantity and unit data for the two off-patent H_2s (Zantac and Tagamet) include generic sales. On the basis of a balanced monthly panel from January 1989 through June 2000, we estimate parameters in equation (3) by NLS and 2SLS (using the same instruments as described in the previous section).[55] Columns (3) and (4) of Table 1 report the corresponding results. A Hausman specification test again shows systematic differences in the coefficients from the NLS and 2SLS estimations ($\chi^2 = 162.45, p < .001$).

On the basis of the 2SLS specification, the estimated values of the monthly depreciation rate δ for physician-directed and consumer-directed marketing, using the grid search procedure, are 1 percent and 29 percent, respectively. Similar very low depreciation rates for physician-directed Rx marketing have been reported by Berndt and coauthors.[56] On the other hand, DTC marketing efforts depreciate much more rapidly in the Rx H_2 market than in the OTC H_2 segment. The price elasticity estimate of $-.441$ is small in absolute value, which reflects perhaps measurement error in the IMS Health Rx price measures (which exclude rebates) and the fact that prices paid by consumers can vary in ways that differ from price variation at the drugstore level.

These results imply that there appear to be fewer OTC-Rx marketing spillovers in the Rx market than in the OTC segment. Specifically, the relative quantities demanded of Rx H_2s are not significantly related to relative DTC marketing stocks of the same-brand OTC H_2 products nor to relative same-

---

advantage of this data set is its microeconomic observations (households and individuals), the sample sizes for these specific drugs are likely to be somewhat small, and coding errors between OTC and Rx versions of the same brand could create econometric difficulties. We therefore leave such research for another time.

[54] We did not include interaction terms between order-of-entry variables and marketing stocks because of the difficulty in interpreting those variables given a generic entry for Tagamet and Zantac and because of the greatly reduced role of marketing both preceding and following generic entry. On this, see Berndt, Kyle, & Ling, *supra* note 7.

[55] The sample size is 552 for NLS and 389 for 2SLS because of the lack of data for some of the instruments in the later time periods.

[56] Berndt *et al.*, Information, Marketing and Pricing, *supra* note 6; and Berndt *et al.*, Roles of Marketing, *supra* note 6

Rx-brand DTC marketing, but relative Rx quantities are strongly and positively related to the relative physician-oriented Rx marketing stocks (1.677, $p < .001$). As in Berndt and coauthors,[57] order-of-entry effects are negative and very strong ($-.330$, $p < .001$). Differences in months after loss of Rx patent expiration insignificantly affect the relative quantities demanded.

VII. Summary and Conclusions

The 1997 relaxation of restrictions on DTC marketing of Rx-only drugs in the United States has been accompanied by a substantial increase in DTC marketing efforts. In the mid-1990s there was also a marked increase in the number of previously Rx-only drugs approved by the FDA to be marketed under OTC status. In this paper, we have examined the impacts of DTC marketing, traditional physician-oriented detailing marketing, and other factors in affecting choice among the H_2-antagonist heartburn and antiulcer medications in the Rx-only and OTC markets. We have also examined spillovers between the Rx and OTC segments, as well as the relationship between order-of-entry effects and firms' marketing intensities.

We find that price and nonprice instruments (specifically marketing) play an important role in competitive rivalry among brands in the OTC market. Regarding marketing efforts, we find that DTC marketing of OTC brands has a substantial positive impact on own share in the OTC market segment and that for later entrants such as Zantac and Axid there is a significant and positive impact of DTC marketing of Rx brands on the share of same-brand OTC products. Therefore, deregulation of the DTC marketing of Rx products has spillover effects in the OTC market. Furthermore, for later OTC entrants Zantac and Axid, physician-oriented marketing of Rx brands has a negative and significant but relatively short-lived impact on the share of same-brand OTC products. Thus, for later entrants, physician-oriented Rx marketing cannibalizes their OTC sales. In summary, the sign and magnitude of marketing spillover effects depend on the marketing medium, the target audience, and the order of entry.

In contrast, DTC marketing of the same-brand OTC H_2 products appears to have no significant impact on the market shares for the same-brand Rx products, other things equal. Instead, only the relative physician-oriented marketing efforts of the H_2-antagonist brands have substantial and long-lived impacts on their own Rx shares. Marketing spillovers flow from Rx to OTC, but not from OTC to Rx.

One of the most interesting sets of findings in this study is the similarity of the relationships between order-of-entry effects and marketing intensities in the Rx and OTC market segments. Previous research in the Rx segment has shown that the ratio of cumulative marketing intensity (cumulative mar-

[57] Berndt *et al.*, Information, Marketing and Pricing, *supra* note 6.

keting efforts divided by cumulative sales) in the Rx segment increases monotonically with order of entry—the first entrant having the lowest intensity and successive entrants having higher marketing intensities. We observe the same general relationship in the OTC market. In addition, in the OTC market the magnitude of various marketing demand elasticities depends on their order of entry. An implication of this finding is that nonprice competition is very important in both the Rx and OTC segments. Specifically, while marketing is costly and may be less productive on the margin in increasing sales for later entrants, it is nonetheless an important tool in reducing earlier-entrant advantages. In this way, the deregulation of Rx DTC marketing enhances rivalry and facilitates competition.

Finally, while order-of-entry effects may be significant, they are not insurmountable, and there is some evidence of spillovers between the Rx and OTC markets. In particular, while the second Rx entrant, Zantac, was able to overcome the first-mover advantages of Rx Tagamet in the Rx market, neither of these brands was able to carry over its early-Rx-entrant advantages into a lead for its brand in the OTC market. Instead, first-OTC-entrant Pepcid AC was able to retain its first OTC entrant advantages till the end of our sample period in mid-1999. But over the same time period, the third OTC entrant, Zantac 75, was able to surpass second OTC entrant Tagamet HB and capture the second largest market share.

In future research, it will be useful to assess whether consumption spillovers (involving information obtained by others' consumption of a drug), which are observed in the Rx H_2 market, carry over to the OTC segment.[58] Future research might also usefully focus on modeling the depreciation of marketing efforts, particularly as a function of the age of the product and as patent expiration approaches.[59] Moreover, it would be useful to utilize more fully and explicitly recent developments in the economic theory of consumer demand that allow for consumer preference estimation even when the number of available products changes over time.[60] However, the existence of principal-agent and moral hazard issues, particularly strong in the Rx market, makes such research very difficult.

Finally, a very important set of issues, likely involving even more challenging modeling and measurement problems, involves examining the effects of DTC marketing not only on consumption patterns, but also on the health status of individuals. To the extent DTC marketing provides information of value to individuals concerning the prevalence of ailments and the availability

[58] Consumption externality effects at the individual brand and aggregate H_2 level are analyzed by Ernst R. Berndt, Robert S. Pindyck, & Pierre Azoulay, Consumption Externalities and Diffusion in Pharmaceutical Markets: Antiulcer Drugs, J. Indus. Econ. (forthcoming, 2003).

[59] See Ling, *supra* note 5.

[60] See, for example, Berry, Levinsohn, & Pakes, *supra* note 47; and Bresnahan, Stern, & Trajtenberg, *supra* note 47.

of medications to treat these ailments effectively, the benefits to consumers from deregulation of DTC marketing could be very substantial.

Bibliography

Berndt, Ernst R. "The U.S. Pharmaceutical Industry: Why Major Growth in Times of Cost Containment?" *Health Affairs* 20 (2001): 100–14.

Berndt, Ernst R.; Kyle, Margaret K.; and Ling, Davina. "The Long Shadow of Patent Expiration: Generic Entry and Rx-to-OTC Switches." Pp. 229–67 in *Scanner Data and Price Indexes*. National Bureau of Economic Research Series on the Conference on Research in Income and Wealth, edited by Robert C. Feenstra and Matthew D. Shapiro. Chicago: University of Chicago Press (for National Bureau of Economic Research), 2002.

Berndt, Ernst R.; Pindyck, Robert S.; and Azoulay, Pierre. "Consumption Externalities and Diffusion in Pharmaceutical Markets: Antiulcer Drugs." *Journal of Industrial Economics* (forthcoming 2003).

Berndt, Ernst R., et al. "Information, Marketing and Pricing in the U.S. Antiulcer Drug Market." *American Economic Review* 85 (1995): 100–105.

Berndt, Ernst R., et al. "The Roles of Marketing, Product Quality and Price Competition in the Growth and Composition of the U.S. Anti-ulcer Drug Industry." Pp. 277–322 in *The Economics of New Goods*. Studies in Income and Wealth, Vol. 58, edited by Timothy F. Bresnahan and Robert J. Gordon. Chicago: University of Chicago Press, 1997.

Berndt, Ernst R., et al. "An Analysis of the Diffusion of New Antidepressants: Variety, Quality and Marketing Efforts." *Journal of Mental Health Policy and Economics* 5 (2002): 3–17.

Berry, Steven; Levinsohn, James; and Pakes, Ariel. "Automobile Prices in Market Equilibrium." *Econometrica* 63 (1995): 841–90.

Bond, Ronald S., and Lean, David F. *Sales, Promotion, and Product Differentiation in Two Prescription Drug Markets*. Washington, D.C.: Staff Report of the Bureau of Economics of the Federal Trade Commission, Government Printing Office, 1977.

Bresnahan, Timothy F.; Stern, Scott; and Trajtenberg, Manuel. "Market Segmentation and the Sources of Rents from Innovation: Personal Computers in the Late 1980s." *RAND Journal of Economics* 28, Special Issue (1997): S17–S44.

Bucklin, Randolph E., and Gupta, Sunil. "Commercial Use of UPC Scanner Data: Industry and Academic Perspectives." *Marketing Science* 18 (1999): 247–73.

Caves, Richard E.; Whinston, Michael D.; and Hurwitz, Mark A. "Patent Expiration, Entry, and Competition in the U.S. Pharmaceutical Industry." *Brookings Papers on Economic Activity: Microeconomics* (1991): 1–48.

Dorfman, Robert A., and Steiner, Peter O. "Optimal Advertising and Optimal Quality." *American Economic Review* 44 (1954): 826–36.

Federal Trade Commission. *Advertising for Over-the-Counter Antacids: Final Staff Report and Recommendations*. Washington, D.C.: Bureau of Consumer Protection, 1983.

Frank, Richard G., and Salkever, David S. "Generic Entry and the Pricing of Pharmaceuticals." *Journal of Economics and Management Strategy* 6 (1997): 75–90.

Gemperli, Marcel P. "Rethinking the Role of the Learned Intermediary: The Effect of Direct-to-Consumer Advertising on Litigation." *Journal of the American Medical Association* 284 (2000): 2241.

Grabowski, Henry G., and Vernon, John M. "Brand Loyalty, Entry, and Price Competition in Pharmaceuticals after the 1984 Drug Act." *Journal of Law and Economics* 35 (1992): 331–50.

Guadagni, Peter M., and Little, John D. C. "A Logit Model of Brand Choice Calibrated on Scanner Data." *Marketing Science* 2 (1983): 203–38.

Henney, Jane E. "Challenges in Regulating Direct-to-Consumer Advertising." *Journal of the American Medical Association* 284 (2000): 2242.

Hesselgrave, Barbara. "Will Managed Care Embrace Rx-to-OTC Switches?" *Drug Topics*, June 2, 1997, pp. 13–17.

Huang, Alison J. "The Rise of Direct-to-Consumer Advertising of Prescription Drugs in the United States." *Journal of the American Medical Association* 284 (2000): 2240.

Hurwitz, Mark A., and Caves, Richard E. "Persuasion or Information? Promotion and the Shares of Brand Name and Generic Pharmaceuticals." *Journal of Law and Economics* 31 (1988): 299–320.

IMS Health. *Information Services Manual*. Plymouth Meeting, Penn.: IMS Health, 1998.

Information Resources, Inc. *Store Data Measures*. Waltham, Mass.: Information Resources, Inc., 1997.

King, Charles, III, et al. "Pepcid AC(A): Racing to the OTC Market." Case N9-500-073. Boston: Harvard Business School Publishing, February 4, 2000.

Leffler, Keith B. "Persuasion or Information? The Economics of Prescription Drug Advertising." *Journal of Law and Economics* 24 (1981): 45–74.

Ling, Davina. "Advertising, Competition and Prescription-to-Nonprescription Drug Switches in the U.S. Antacid Market." Unpublished xerolith. Cambridge, Mass.: Massachusetts Institute of Technology, Department of Economics, April 19, 1999.

McCarthy, Robert. "OTCs: The Wild Card in Cost-Effectiveness." *Business and Health* 17 (1999): 33–35.

Nelson, Philip K. "Advertising as Information." *Journal of Political Economy* 82 (1974): 729–54.

Nordenberg, Tamar. "Now Available without a Prescription." *FDA Consumer Magazine*, November 1996. http://www.fda.gov/fdac/features/996_otc.html.

Physicians' Desk Reference. Montvale, N.J.: Medical Economics Company, 2000.

Prevention Magazine. "National Survey of Consumer Reactions to Direct-to-Consumer Advertising" (report). Emmaus, Pa.: *Prevention Magazine*, 1999.

Robinson, William T.; Kalyanaram, Gurumurthy; and Urban, Glen L. "First-Mover Advantages from Pioneering New Markets: A Survey of Empirical Evidence." *Review of Industrial Organization* 9 (1994): 1–23.

Rosenthal, Meredith B., et al. "Promotion of Prescription Drugs to Consumers." *New England Journal of Medicine* 346 (2002): 498–505.

Rosenthal, Meredith B., et al. "Demand Effects of Recent Changes in Prescription Drug Promotion." In *Frontiers in Health Policy Research*, Vol. 6, edited by Alan M. Garber and David M. Cutler. Cambridge, Mass.: MIT Press (for National Bureau of Economic Research), 2003.

Schmalensee, Richard L. *The Economics of Advertising*. Amsterdam: North-Holland, 1972.

Schmalensee, Richard L. "Product Differentiation Advantages of Pioneering Brands." *American Economic Review* 72 (1982): 349–65.

Smith, Mickey C. "Rx-to-OTC Switches: Reflections and Projections." *Drug Topics*, July 20, 1998, p. 70.

STATA Reference Manual. STATA Reference Manual Release 6. Vol. 2. College Station, Tex.: STATA Press, 1999.

Stuart, Bruce, and Grana, James. "Are Prescribed and Over-the-Counter Medicines Economic Substitutes? A Study of the Effects of Health Insurance and Medicine Choices by the Elderly." *Medical Care* 33 (1995): 487–501.

Tanou, Elyse, and Burton, Thomas M. "More Firms 'Switch' Prescription Drugs to Give Them Over-the-Counter Status." *Wall Street Journal*, July 29, 1993, p. B1.

Temin, Peter. *Taking Your Medicine: Drug Regulation in the United States*. Cambridge, Mass.: Harvard University Press, 1980.

Temin, Peter. "Costs and Benefits in Switching Drugs from Rx to OTC." *Journal of Health Economics* 2 (1983): 187–205.

Temin, Peter. "Realized Benefits from Switching Drugs." *Journal of Law and Economics* 35 (1992): 351–69.

Urban, Glen L., et al. "Market Share Rewards to Pioneering Brands: An Empirical Analysis and Strategic Implications." *Management Science* 32 (1986): 645–59.

U.S. Food and Drug Administration. Center for Drug Evaluation and Research. "Approved Drug Products with Therapeutic Equivalence Evaluations." In *Electronic Orange Book*, October 2000. http://www.fda.gov/cder/ob/default.htm.

Wilkes, Michael S.; Bell, Robert A.; and Kravitz, Richard L. "Direct-to-

Consumer Prescription Drug Advertising: Trends, Impact and Implications." *Health Affairs* 19 (2000): 110–28.

Young, James Harvey. *The Medical Messiahs: A Social History of Health Quackery in Twentieth-Century America*. Princeton N.J.: Princeton University Press, 1967.

[22]

Empirical Research

Direct-to-Consumer Advertising of COX-2 Inhibitors: Effect on Appropriateness of Prescribing

Michele M. Spence
Kaiser Permanente
Stephanie S. Teleki
RAND
T. Craig Cheetham
Kaiser Permanente
Stuart O. Schweitzer
University of California, Los Angeles
Mirta Millares
Kaiser Permanente

Spending on direct-to-consumer advertising (DTCA) of prescription drugs has increased dramatically in the past several years. An unresolved question is whether such advertising leads to inappropriate prescribing. In this study, the authors use survey and administrative data to determine the association of DTCA with the appropriate prescribing of cyclooxygenase-2 (COX-2) inhibitors for 1,382 patients. Treatment with either a COX-2 or a traditional nonsteroidal anti-inflammatory drug (NSAID) was defined as appropriate or not according to three different definitions of gastrointestinal risk. Patients who saw or heard a COX-2 advertisement and asked their physician about the advertised drug were significantly more likely to be prescribed a COX-2 (versus a NSAID, as recommended by evidence-based guidelines) than all other patients. Findings also suggest that some patients may benefit from DTCA. The authors discuss the need for balanced drug information for consumers, increased physician vigilance in prescribing appropriately, and further study of DTCA.

Medical Care Research and Review, Vol. 62 No. 5, (October 2005) 544-559
DOI: 10.1177/1077558705279314

Keywords: *advertising; drug utilization; prescriptions; drugs; physician-patient relations*

During the past decade, pharmaceutical manufacturers have spent record amounts on direct-to-consumer advertising (DTCA) of prescription drugs. Spending levels have increased from an estimated $55 million in 1991 to $3.27 billion in 2003 (Wilkes, Bell, and Kravitz 2000; Humphreys and Boersig 2004). Evidence suggests that DTCA increases consumer demand for newer, more expensive drugs and that highly promoted drugs account for a substantial share of sales within their therapeutic class (National Institute for Health Care Management 1999, 2001; Levit et al. 2000; Zachry et al. 2002). Previous studies also have shown that patients' requests for heavily advertised drugs frequently result in prescriptions for those drugs, but the question remains whether such prescriptions are clinically appropriate (Mintzes et al. 2002; Aikin 2002; Weissman et al. 2003; Kravitz et al. 2005). The issue of appropriateness is crucial to the national debate about DTCA of prescription drugs (Batchlor and Laouri 2003).

We studied DTCA and appropriateness within the framework of nonsteroidal anti-inflammatory drugs (NSAIDs), a class of drugs that contains two subclasses: (1) traditional NSAIDs, such as ibuprofen and naproxen, and (2) a newer subclass known as *cyclooxygenase-2 inhibitors* (COX-2s). We focused on NSAIDs because these drugs are widely prescribed and because COX-2s have been heavily advertised, are more expensive than traditional NSAIDs, and are considered equally effective (not more effective) when compared with traditional NSAIDs for the treatment of pain and inflammation (National Institute for Health Care Management 2001; Emery et al. 1999; Morrison et al. 1999). We examined the impact of COX-2 DTCA on the likelihood of patients being prescribed either a COX-2 or a traditional NSAID according to evidence-based guidelines that recommend that the most appropriate use of COX-2s is among patients who are at high risk of gastrointestinal (GI) bleeding (Silverstein et al. 2000; Bombardier et al. 2000). Because of variation in patient response to treatment as well as in physician preferences, we used three different methods to identify GI bleeding risk.

This article, submitted to *Medical Care Research and Review* on December 23, 2003, was revised and accepted for publication on October 8, 2004.

The California HealthCare Foundation funded this research. The authors thank the following individuals for their review of this research at various stages: Linda B. Bourque, Mark S. Litwin, Thomas H. Rice, Sharon Levine, Les Zendle, and Marianne Laouri.

NEW CONTRIBUTION

This research provides an in-depth look at DTCA in a real-world setting. It addresses the issue of appropriateness within one class of drugs that have been heavily marketed to consumers. The relationship between patients' awareness of the advertisements, requests about advertised medications, and whether the prescribed medications were appropriate is explored using data from both surveys and administrative databases.

METHOD

This study was conducted at Kaiser Permanente (KP) Medical Care Program in Southern California, a nonprofit, group-model health maintenance organization (HMO) serving approximately three million members. The study was cross-sectional and included patients who were at least eighteen years old, were continuously enrolled in the health plan for at least one year, and had comparable prescription drug benefits during that time. Pharmacy databases were used to identify a stratified, random sample of 2,929 patients; half of these patients received a new prescription for celecoxib (brand name Celebrex) or rofecoxib (brand name Vioxx), and the other half received a new prescription for a traditional NSAID. To ensure that patients had interacted with a physician, the study included only those patients whose new prescription was filled within seven days of a physician office visit.

Data sources included survey responses and administrative database information. A mail survey was used to collect information on patient demographics, awareness of COX-2 DTC advertisements, and action resulting from such awareness. Patients received the survey three to six months after filling the initial prescription. The survey, available in English and Spanish, was mailed to patients in February 2001 and then was followed by a reminder postcard. Surveys were pilot tested on a group of KP patients (n = 9). The design and all procedures for this study were approved by the institutional review boards of KP Southern California and the University of California, Los Angeles.

MAJOR MEASURES

Patient awareness of COX-2 DTCA was measured by a series of survey questions. Patients were asked, "Have you ever seen or heard any advertisement for the drug Celebrex?" and "After you saw or heard the advertisement, did you ask your doctor about Celebrex?" Patients were asked the same questions about Vioxx. Responses were combined and grouped into two

TABLE 1 Appropriateness of Prescribing with Traditional NSAIDs and COX-2 Inhibitors, Assessed According to Three Methods of Defining Risk of Gastrointestinal Bleeding, 2001

	NSAID	*COX-2 Inhibitor*
Method 1: SCPMG clinical practice guideline		
SCORE levels 1–3	Appropriate (n = 528)	COX-2 instead of NSAID (n = 672)
SCORE level 4	NSAID instead of COX-2 (n = 18)	Appropriate (n = 121)
Method 2: Modified SCPMG clinical practice guideline		
SCORE levels 1–2	Appropriate (n = 423)	COX-2 instead of NSAID (n = 384)
SCORE level 3, 4	NSAID instead of COX-2 (n = 123)	Appropriate (n = 409)
Method 3: Laine criteria		
No criteria	Appropriate (n = 354)	COX-2 instead of NSAID (n = 273)
Met one or more criteria	NSAID instead of COX-2 (n = 206)	Appropriate (n = 549)

Source: Data from Kaiser Permanente Southern California/UCLA COX-2 DTCA Study.
Note: NSAID = nonsteroidal anti-inflammatory drug; COX-2 = cyclooxygenase-2; SCPMG = Southern California Permanente Medical Group; SCORE = Standardized Calculator of Risk for Events; DTCA = direct-to-consumer advertising.

categories: (1) saw or heard a COX-2 advertisement and asked a physician about the drug and (2) all others, which includes patients who did not see or hear an advertisement and those who saw or heard an advertisement but did not ask a physician about the drug.

The appropriateness measure was defined with respect to a patient's risk of GI bleeding. Patients were grouped into one of three categories: (1) prescribed a COX-2 instead of a traditional NSAID (i.e., not according to guideline), (2) prescribed a traditional NSAID instead of a COX-2 (i.e., not according to guideline), and (3) appropriately prescribed either a COX-2 or a traditional NSAID (i.e., according to guideline). Because clinical assessment may vary regarding severity of risk of GI bleeding, we used three different methods of defining this risk (see Table 1).

First, we used the definition of risk outlined in the clinical practice guideline endorsed by the Southern California Permanente Medical Group

(SCPMG), Method 1. This method uses the Standardized Calculator of Risk for Events (SCORE) tool, a scale developed by Stanford University researchers and validated in the KP population, to define GI risk (Singh 1998; Cheetham, Levy, and Spence 2003). The scale identifies patients at high risk for serious GI events associated with NSAID therapy (i.e., GI bleeding requiring hospitalization) on the basis of six factors. These factors include age, health status, type of arthritis, duration of prednisone use in past year, previous GI-related hospitalization, and previous GI side effects. Responses to the six factors are translated into one of four risk levels: level 1 indicates low risk, whereas level 4 indicates high risk for a NSAID-related GI event. According to the SCPMG guideline, patients at level 4 are at highest risk for a GI event and therefore are the most appropriate candidates for a COX-2; patients below level 4 are appropriately treated with a traditional NSAID (Kaiser Permanente 2001). With Method 1, patients at risk level 1, 2, or 3 are lower risk. If these patients received a traditional NSAID, they were classified as being appropriately prescribed according to the guideline. Only patients at risk level 4 who received a COX-2 were classified as being appropriately prescribed a COX-2.

For the second way of defining GI risk (Method 2), we allowed for a more liberal assessment of GI risk using the SCORE tool. In this method, patients at risk level 3 or 4 were considered at high risk for NSAID-related GI complications and were therefore the most appropriate candidates for a COX-2. Patients at risk levels 1 and 2 were classified as appropriately prescribed only if they received a traditional NSAID (versus a COX-2).

The third method for defining GI risk (Method 3) was based on criteria in a review article by Laine (2001). This method allowed for the most liberal assessment of GI risk. In Method 3, patients were considered at high risk for GI bleeding if they met one or more of the following criteria: history of ulcer or other GI event; older than age sixty-five; currently receiving anticoagulation therapy, corticosteroid therapy, or low-dose aspirin therapy; and history of severe rheumatoid arthritis. Method 3 classified patients as appropriately prescribed if they met at least one of the criteria and received a COX-2. Patients were also classified as appropriately prescribed if they did not meet any of the criteria and received a traditional NSAID.

The following covariates were also included in the analyses: patient age, gender, race, education, income, duration of membership in the health plan, health status (as measured by the chronic disease score), and relationship status (defined as living with spouse or partner, not living with spouse or partner, or not in a significant relationship). Patient chronic disease score was based on the measure developed by Clark et al. (1995) to assess disease severity. In addition, because prescribing patterns vary by physician characteristics (Eisenberg 1986), we included several covariates for the prescribing physician in the analyses. These covariates included physician age, gender, race, specialty, practice location, and tenure with the SCPMG. All patient and physician covariates are listed in Table 2.

STATISTICAL ANALYSIS

Multinomial logistic regression, a variant of logistic regression that allows use of a dependent variable with more than two categories, was used to examine predictors separately for each of the three methods. All models met the assumptions of multinomial logistic regression. Neither an evaluation of a correlation matrix nor additional tests of the model available in STATA version 7.0 revealed issues of multicollinearity. Interactions of DTCA awareness—crossed first with patient race and then with patient education—were evaluated but were not found statistically significant. Analysis of survey nonrespondents also was conducted to detect any statistically significant difference from survey respondents.

RESULTS

The overall survey response rate was 47 percent (1,382 of 2,929 patients). The response rate for the COX-2 group was 55 percent (822 of 1,499 patients); the response rate for the traditional NSAID group was 39 percent (560 of 1,430 patients). These rates were within the range anticipated for mail surveys (Bourque and Felder 1995; Aday 1996).

Table 2 shows the distribution of all variables for the analysis sample. About 20 percent of patients asked their physician about a COX-2 after seeing or hearing an advertisement. In general, the sample tended to be female, non-Hispanic white, and well educated. Most patients had been a KP member for at least two years, and 46 percent were at least sixty-five years old. Prescribing physicians tended to be middle-aged, male, non-Hispanic white, and practicing primary care medicine; 69 percent had practiced at KP for at least four years.

APPROPRIATENESS OF PRESCRIPTION BY DTCA AWARENESS

For Method 1, 78 percent of patients who saw or heard a COX-2 advertisement and asked were prescribed a COX-2 (instead of an NSAID, as the guideline recommends), versus 43 percent of all other patients (see Table 3). Twenty-one percent of patients who saw or heard a COX-2 advertisement and asked their physician were appropriately prescribed, versus 55 percent of all other patients. Compared to Method 1, there were more patients in Method 2

TABLE 2 Demographic Characteristics and Survey Results for 1,382 Patients in COX-2 Direct-To-Consumer Advertising (DTCA) Study, 2001

Item	n	%[a]
Awareness of COX-2 DTCA		
Did not see or hear DTCA or ask physician	1,110	80.32
Saw or heard DTCA and asked physician	272	19.68
Patient age		
Younger than 65	742	54.16
65 or older	628	45.84
Patient gender		
Male	471	34.11
Female	910	65.89
Patient race		
Non-Hispanic white	868	64.01
Other	488	35.99
Patient education		
High school graduate or less	422	31.12
Some college	506	37.32
College graduate or more	428	31.56
Patient income		
Less than $40,000	635	50.80
$40,000 or more	615	49.20
Patient length of membership in health plan		
Less than 2 years	210	15.20
2 to less than 6 years	612	44.28
6 years or more	560	40.52
Patient chronic disease score (continuous variable)		
M (*SD*)	2.09	0.85
Median	1.98	
Range	0.72 to 5.08	
Patient relationship status		
Living with spouse or partner	917	69.10
Not living with spouse or partner or not in a significant relationship	410	30.90
Physician age		
Younger than 36	302	24.65
36 to less than 51	658	53.71
51 years or older	265	21.63

(continued)

TABLE 2 (continued)

Item	n	%[a]
Physician gender		
Male	860	70.20
Female	365	29.80
Physician practice specialty		
Primary care	959	78.29
Specialty care	266	21.71
Physician practice location in SCPMG		
Metro	212	17.31
Valleys	190	15.51
Tri-central	283	23.10
Inland Empire	190	15.51
Orange County and San Diego	350	28.57
Physician race		
Non-Hispanic white	677	55.27
Other	548	44.73
Physician length of tenure with SCPMG		
Less than 4 years	383	31.27
4 years or more	842	68.73

Source: Data from Kaiser Permanente Southern California/UCLA COX-2 DTCA Study.
Note: SCPMG = Southern California Permanente Medical Group; COX-2 = cyclooxygenase-2.
a. Numbers may not add up to 1,382 for each variable because of missing data.

(53 percent) and Method 3 (67 percent) who were appropriately prescribed after seeing or hearing a COX-2 advertisement and asking their physician.

FACTORS ASSOCIATED WITH APPROPRIATENESS OF PRESCRIPTION

Table 4 presents regression results for the effect of COX-2 DTCA awareness on appropriateness after controlling for patient and physician characteristics. Other variables that were statistically significant in at least one model are discussed below but not presented in Table 4.

For all three methods of defining risk of GI bleeding, awareness of DTCA and asking a physician were significantly associated with being prescribed a COX-2 instead of an NSAID, compared to being appropriately prescribed either a COX-2 or an NSAID. Using Method 1, the odds of being prescribed a COX-2 instead of an NSAID for patients who saw or heard a COX-2 advertisement and asked their physician about the advertised drug were four times the

TABLE 3 Awareness of COX-2 DTCA and Appropriateness of Prescribing with Traditional NSAIDs and COX-2 Inhibitors Assessed According to Three Methods of Defining Risk of Gastrointestinal Bleeding, 2001

	Awareness of COX-2 DTCA			
	Saw or Heard DTCA and Asked Physician		*Did not see or Hear DTCA or ask Physician*	
Method	*Number*	*%*	*Number*	*%*
Method 1: SCPMG guideline*				
Appropriately prescribed	57	21.43	592	55.17
NSAID instead of COX-2	2	0.75	16	1.49
COX-2 instead of NSAID	207	77.82	465	43.34
Column total	266	100.00	1,073	100.00
Method 2: Modified SCPMG guideline*				
Appropriately prescribed	141	53.01	691	64.40
NSAID instead of COX-2	6	2.26	117	10.90
COX-2 instead of NSAID	119	44.74	265	24.70
Column total	266	100.00	1,073	100.00
Method 3: Laine criteria*				
Appropriately prescribed	183	67.28	720	64.86
NSAID instead of COX-2	10	3.68	196	17.66
COX-2 instead of NSAID	79	29.04	194	17.48
Column total	272	100.00	1,110	100.00

Note: DTCA = direct-to-consumer advertising; SCPMG = Southern California Permanente Medical Group; NSAID = nonsteroidal anti-inflammatory drug; COX-2 = cyclooxygenase-2.
*$p < .01$.

odds for all other patients. Using Methods 2 and 3, the odds of being prescribed a COX-2 for patients who saw or heard a COX-2 advertisement and asked their physician were three times the odds for all other patients. For all three methods (i.e., no matter how stringently GI bleeding risk was defined), patients who asked their doctor about COX-2s after seeing or hearing an advertisement were more likely to be prescribed a COX-2.

Awareness of DTCA and asking a physician was not significantly associated with prescribing an NSAID (as the guideline recommends) instead of a COX-2, compared to appropriate prescribing of either an NSAID or COX-2, using Method 1. However, using Methods 2 and 3, the odds of being prescribed a traditional NSAID for patients who both saw or heard a COX-2

TABLE 4 Predicting Appropriateness of COX-2 and Traditional NSAID Prescriptions Using Three Methods of Defining Gastrointestinal Risk, Using Odds Ratios, 2001

	Prescribed COX-2 Instead of NSAID vs. Appropriately Prescribed		*Prescribed NSAID Instead of COX-2 vs. Appropriately Prescribed*	
Awareness of COX-2 DTCA	*Odds Ratio*	*95% Confidence Interval*	*Odds Ratio*	*95% Confidence Interval*
Method 1: SCPMG clinical practice guideline[a]				
Saw or heard DTCA and asked physician	4.03	(2.77–5.87)*	1.14	(0.23–5.66)
Method 2: Modified SCPMG clinical practice guideline[b]				
Saw or heard DTCA and asked physician	3.05	(2.09–4.46)*	0.15	(0.06–0.39)*
Method 3: Laine criteria[c]				
Saw or heard DTCA and asked physician	3.15	(1.93–5.14)*	0.15	(0.07–0.31)*

Source: Data from Kaiser Permanente Southern California/UCLA COX-2 DTCA Study.
Note: The reference group for each method is "did not see or hear DTCA or ask physician." Regressions predicted appropriateness of prescribing. Regression analyses included all covariates listed in Table 2. Covariates significant at $p < .01$ are discussed in the text. Values in parentheses are done so to convey that the odds ratio is significant. DTCA = direct-to-consumer advertising; NSAID = nonsteroidal anti-inflammatory drug; COX-2 = cyclooxygenase-2; SCPMG = Southern California Permanente Medical Group.
a. $p < .001$, $n = 1{,}026$, pseudo $R^2 = 0.11$.
b. $p < .001$, $n = 1{,}026$, pseudo $R^2 = 0.15$.
c. $p < .001$, $n = 1{,}054$, pseudo $R^2 = 0.24$.
*$p < .01$.

advertisement and asked their physician about the advertised drug were one-seventh the odds for all other patients. Patients who were exposed to DTCA and asked their physician were less likely to be prescribed a traditional NSAID instead of a COX-2, as recommended by the guideline. In other words, they were more likely to be appropriately prescribed a COX-2.

In all three methods, physician specialty was a significant predictor of being prescribed a COX-2 (instead of an NSAID, as the guidelines recommend). Patients treated by specialists were approximately twice as likely to be prescribed a COX-2 as patients treated by generalists.

Additional variables were significant predictors in at least one model. For Methods 2 and 3 only, patient age was a significant predictor. Older patients were less likely to be prescribed a COX-2 and more likely to be prescribed a traditional NSAID. For methods 2 and 3, respectively, the odds of being prescribed a COX-2 (compared to being appropriately prescribed) for patients aged sixty-five years and older were one-quarter and one-tenth the odds for patients younger than sixty-five. Conversely, the odds of being prescribed a traditional NSAID for patients aged sixty-five years and older were four to five times the odds for patients younger than sixty-five. As expected, patients become more likely to be appropriate candidates for COX-2s with increasing age and therefore are less likely to be inappropriately prescribed a COX-2.

For Methods 2 and 3 only, the odds of being inappropriately prescribed a COX-2 (compared to being appropriately prescribed either a COX-2 or NSAID) for women were approximately twice the odds for men. Finally, for Method 1 only, sicker patients (i.e., those with higher chronic disease scores) were more likely to be prescribed a COX-2 instead of an NSAID.

ANALYSIS OF SURVEY NONRESPONDENTS

Survey nonrespondents and respondents were stratified by type of drug prescribed (COX-2 vs. traditional NSAID) and were compared with each other using available variables. Comparison of patients' age, gender, chronic disease score, and KP location showed that survey respondents and nonrespondents differed with respect to age. The mean age for survey respondents who received COX-2s was sixty-five, compared with fifty-nine for survey nonrespondents receiving these drugs. The mean age of survey respondents who received traditional NSAIDs was fifty-four, compared with forty-five for survey nonrespondents who received these drugs. This difference might be explained by the fact that older persons may be more likely to respond because they have more time to fill out surveys, are more interested in the topic, or both. From a statistical standpoint, survey respondents and nonrespondents in both drug groups also differed regarding chronic disease score, but these differences were not clinically meaningful; the average chronic disease score was approximately 2.0 for all groups included in comparisons.

DISCUSSION

We found that for all three methods, patients who saw COX-2 advertisements and asked their physician about COX-2s were more likely to be prescribed a COX-2 instead of an NSAID (compared to being appropriately prescribed either a COX-2 or an NSAID). This result indicates that DTCA may lead to inappropriate prescribing with costly medications. It has been suggested that one of the reasons for the divergence between routine medical practice and evidence-based recommendations is the marketing of newer, more costly agents compared with virtually no marketing for older, off-patent drugs (Fischer and Avorn 2004). The results found here provide evidence that at least in the case of COX-2s, DTCA is related to use that is inconsistent with three versions of recommended guidelines.

We also found that patients who were exposed to DTCA and asked their physician were less likely to be prescribed a traditional NSAID when the guidelines recommend that a COX-2 would be the appropriate choice of medication. This was the case for Methods 2 and 3, which were based on more liberal definitions of risk of GI bleeding. According to these methods, more patients were considered appropriately treated with a COX-2. This finding that patients who were exposed to COX-2 DTCA and asked their physicians were less likely to be prescribed a traditional NSAID instead of a COX-2 is consistent with the argument that DTCA may inform consumers, encourage doctor-patient communication, and consequently result in better, more appropriate care (Aikin 2002).

Patients who saw specialists were twice as likely to be prescribed a COX-2 as those seen by generalists. Specialists typically see patients on a referral basis and may be more likely to use treatments beyond the standard approach. Another plausible explanation could be that patients who see specialists may be more active in pursuing and paying attention to health care; as such, they may be more likely to notice drug advertisements and to ask their physician about advertised drugs.

We also found that women were more likely to be prescribed a COX-2 instead of an NSAID than men. This finding is consistent with past research indicating that some men may feel uncomfortable discussing their health concerns with a physician (Sandman, Simantov, and An 2000). It may be that because women tend to be more communicative about treatment preferences, they may be more likely to receive a prescription than men. Finally, sicker patients were more likely to be prescribed a COX-2. Perhaps physicians were using discretion in prescribing COX-2s for their sicker patients, even though these patients were not necessarily appropriate candidates according to the guideline.

STUDY LIMITATIONS

This research—conducted at a single HMO—may not be generalizable to a broader population. However, KP provides extensive patient education as well as balanced drug information to its physicians in an effort to promote appropriate drug prescribing. Therefore, our study may potentially underestimate the impact of DTCA on prescribing behavior in the broader population.

Our sample response rate was less than optimal and raises the possibility of nonresponse bias. Recall bias is another potential limitation. Patients might not have accurately remembered or reported the chronology of their exposure to DTCA.

Another potential limitation is that we sampled only patients who had received a prescription for either a traditional NSAID or a COX-2; patients who may have been exposed to DTCA or asked their physicians about COX-2s (or both) but never received either a COX-2 or a traditional NSAID were not included in the study. However, we deliberately selected a population for which the decision had been made to treat with medication (i.e., not through lifestyle change or other nonpharmacologic treatment). This patient population is targeted by COX-2 promotional efforts; appropriate prescribing in this population was therefore expected to be affected most by DTCA.

We also did not examine the impact of DTCA on other health outcomes or within different therapeutic categories. Behavioral changes attributable to DTCA and the impact of this promotion on treatment cost, medical use, and adverse events are important areas of future research.

Finally, this study focused on the patient's perspective and did not account for exposure of physicians to promotional activities by the pharmaceutical industry. Future research should explore the complex relationship between patients' and physicians' exposure to drug promotion and appropriate prescribing of advertised drugs.

CONCLUSION

From a business perspective, this study is consistent with what is already well known by advertisers: DTCA is a successful method of generating prescriptions. From societal and medical perspectives, however, success may be weighed differently (Andersen and Davidson 2001). With rising health care costs and limited financial resources, promotional strategies used by drug manufacturers may be considered successful only if they result in clinically appropriate prescriptions of the advertised drugs.

Appropriateness is a difficult concept to define and measure. DTCA frequently promotes drugs used for conditions where the measurement of appropriateness is especially elusive: pain, heartburn, allergies, sexual dysfunction, and mental health–related disorders. For COX-2s, we found that DTCA is a factor associated with overuse regardless of the way GI risk–related appropriateness is defined. Patients' exposure to DTCA was consistently associated with overuse of COX-2s, potentially leading to a wasteful use of resources. When appropriateness was broadly defined, we found that DTCA mitigates prescribing NSAIDs instead of COX-2s according to guideline, suggesting that some patients may benefit from such advertisements.

Our findings point to a need for balanced drug information and for both patients and physicians to be vigilant about the appropriateness of prescriptions for drugs that are heavily promoted to consumers. Our findings also raise questions regarding trade-offs. Are the potential benefits of DTCA worth the costs (in both human and financial terms) that may result from overuse? This is particularly relevant given that rofecoxib was withdrawn from the market by the manufacturer in September 2004 (Food and Drug Administration News 2004). A placebo-controlled trial for colon polyp prevention showed that use of rofecoxib increased patients' risk of cardiovascular disease (Merck Product News 2004). Is the public's health best served by marketing new drugs to consumers for which information on safety and efficacy is not well established? And once such information is known, are there more effective ways to inform patients who could appropriately benefit from new drug therapies without generating overuse? These are topics for future study.

REFERENCES

Aday, L. A. 1996. *Designing and conducting health surveys*. 2nd ed. San Francisco: Jossey-Bass.

Aikin, K. J. 2002. *Direct-to-consumer advertising of prescription drugs: Preliminary patient survey results*. Bethesda, MD: Food and Drug Administration.

Andersen, R. M., and P. L. Davidson. 2001. Improving access to care in America: Individual and contextual indicators. In *Changing the U.S. health care system*, edited by R. M. Andersen, T. H. Rice, and G. F. Kominski. San Francisco: Jossey-Bass, 3–30.

Batchlor, E., and M. Laouri. 2003. Pharmaceutical promotion, advertising, and consumers. *Health Affairs*. http://content.healthaffairs.org/cgi/reprint/hlthaff.w3.109v1.pdf.

Bombardier, C., L. Laine, A. Reicin, D. Shapiro, R. Burgos-Vargas, B. Davis, R. Day, M. Bosi Ferraz, C. J. Hawkey, M. C. Hochberg, T. K. Kvien, and T. J. Schnitzer. 2000. Comparison of upper gastrointestinal toxicity of rofecoxib and naproxen in patients with rheumatoid arthritis. *New England Journal of Medicine* 343 (21): 1520–28.

Bourque, L. B., and E. P. Fielder. 1995. *How to conduct self-administered and mail surveys*. Thousand Oaks, CA: Sage.

Cheetham, T. C., G. Levy, and M. Spence. 2003. Predicting the risk of gastrointestinal bleeding due to nonsteroidal anti-inflammatory drugs: NSAID electronic assessment of risk. *Journal of Rheumatology* 30 (10): 2241–44.

Clark, D. O., M. Von Korff, K. Saunders, W. M. Baluch, and G. E. Simon. 1995. A chronic disease score with empirically derived weights. *Medical Care* 33 (8): 783–95.

Eisenberg, J. M. 1986. *Doctors' decisions and the cost of medical care: The reasons for doctors' practice patterns and ways to change them*. Ann Arbor, MI: Health Administration Press Perspectives.

Emery, P., H. Zeidler, T. K. Kvien, M. Guslandi, R. Naudin, H. Stead, K. M. Verburg, P. C. Isakson, R. C. Hubbard, and G. S. Geis. 1999. Celecoxib versus diclofenac in long-term management of rheumatoid arthritis: Randomised double-blind comparison. *Lancet* 354:2106–111.

Fischer, M. A., and J. Avorn. 2004. Economic implications of evidence-based prescribing for hypertension. Can better care cost less? *Journal of the American Medical Association* 291 (15): 1850–56.

Food and Drug Administration News. 2004. FDA issues public health advisory on Vioxx as its manufacturer voluntarily withdraws the product. Available at http://www.fda.gov/bbs/topics/news/2004/NEW01122.html.

Humphreys, A., and C. Boersig. 2004. Tenth annual report on DTC: Consumer advertising fills the gap. *Med Ad News* 23 (6): 1, 40–53.

Kaiser Permanente Medical Care Program. 2001. COX-2 guidelines: NSAID GI risk strategizer. In *Drug formulary*, edited by Monica A. Yoshingaga, Mirta Millares, and Susan Nakahiro. Madison, OH: Lexi-Comp.

Kravitz, R. L., R. M. Epstein, M. D. Feldman, C. E. Franz, R. Azari, M. S. Wilkes, L. Hilton, and P. Franks. 2005. Influence of patients' requests for direct–to–customer advertised antidepressants. *Journal of the American Medical Association* 293(16): 1995-2002.

Laine, L. 2001. Approaches to nonsteroidal anti-inflammatory drug use in the high risk patient. *Gastroenterology* 120 (3): 594–606.

Levit, K., C. Cowan, H. Lazenby, A. Sensenig, P. McDonnell, J. Stiller, A. Martin, and the Health Accounts Team. 2000. Health spending in 1998: Signals of change. *Health Affairs* 19 (1): 124–32.

Merck Product News. 2004. Merck announces voluntary worldwide withdrawal of Vioxx. Available at http://www.merck.com/newsroom/press_releases/product/2004_0930.html.

Mintzes, B., M. L. Barer, R. L. Kravitz, A. Kazanjian, K. Bassett, J. Lexchin, R. G. Evans, R. Pan, and S. A. Marion. 2002. Influence of direct-to-consumer pharmaceutical advertising and patients' requests on prescribing decisions: Two-site cross-sectional survey. *British Medical Journal* 324:2 78–79.

Morrison, B. W., S. Christensen, W. Yuan, J. Brown, S. Amlani, and B. Seidenberg. 1999. Analgesic efficacy of the cyclooxygenase-2-specific inhibitor rofecoxib in post-dental surgery pain: a randomized, controlled trial. *Clinical Therapeutics* 21 (6): 943–53.

National Institute for Health Care Management. 1999. *Factors affecting the growth of prescription drug expenditures*. Available at http://www.nihcm.org/FinalText3.pdf.

———. 2001. *Prescription drugs and mass media advertising, 2000*. Available at http://www.nihcm.org/DTCbrief.pdf.

Sandman, D., E. Simantov, and C. An. 2000. *Out of touch: American men and the health care system: Commonwealth Fund Men's and Women's Health Survey Findings*. Available at http://www.cmwf.org/programs/women/sandman_outoftouch_374.pdf.

Silverstein, F. E., G. Faich, J. L. Goldstein, L. S. Simon, T. Pincus, A. Whelton, R. Makuch, G. Eisen, N. M. Agrawal, W. F. Stenson, A. M. Buss, W. W. Zhao, J. D. Kent, J. B. Lefkowith, K. M. Verburg, and G. S. Geis. 2000. Gastrointestinal toxicity with celecoxib vs. nonsteroidal anti-inflammatory drugs for osteoporosis and rheumatoid arthritis: The CLASS study, a randomized controlled trial. *Journal of the American Medical Association* 284 (10): 1247–55.

Singh, G., D. R. Ramsey, G. Triadafilopoulus, B. W. Brown, and R. R. Balise. 1998. GI score: A simple self-assessment instrument to quantify risk of serious NSAID-related GI complications in RA and OA. *Arthritis and Rheumatism* 41 (9): S75.

Weissman, J. S., D. Blumenthal, A. J. Silk, K. Zapert, M. Newman, and R. Leitman. 2003. Consumers' reports on the health effects of direct-to-consumer drug advertising. *Health Affairs*. http://content.healthaffairs.org/cgi/content/full/hlthaff.w3.82v1/DC1.

Wilkes, M. S., R. A. Bell, and R. L. Kravitz. 2000. Direct-to-consumer prescription drug advertising: Trends, impact, and implications. *Health Affairs* 19 (2): 110–28.

Zachry, W. M., M. D. Sheperd, M. J. Hinich, J. P. Wilson, C. M. Brown, and K. A. Lawson. 2002. Relationship between direct-to-consumer advertising and physician diagnosing and prescribing. *American Journal of Health-System Pharmacy* 59 (1): 42–49.

[23]

Expert Opinion

Monthly Focus: Pharmacoeconomics

Evaluation and review of pharmacoeconomic models

Joel W Hay
Department of Pharmaceutical Economics and Policy, University of Southern California, CA, USA

Difficult decisions as to whether to provide or withhold drug therapy to patients are needed to be made on a daily basis. These decisions should be based on carefully designed and constructed pharmacoeconomic models, with explicit and justifiable parameter values, validated by publication in peer-reviewed literature. This review describes and evaluates the common types of pharmacoeconomic models, modelling approaches and methods. It also discusses model quality, validity and usefulness.

Keywords: cost–benefit analysis, cost-effectiveness analysis, decision modelling, economic evaluations, pharmacoeconomic guidelines

Expert Opin. Pharmacother. (2004) 5(9):

1. Introduction

1.1 Background

Drugs are increasingly important to clinical decision making as newer therapies gain acceptance. With healthcare and pharmaceutical costs continuing to escalate, pharmacoeconomic analyses and models are becoming implicit or explicit requirements for drug use decision making [1]. Many countries have implemented formal pharmacoeconomic evaluation processes [2,3,101]. The Academy of Managed Care Pharmacy (AMCP) in the US has promulgated dossier requirements for drug formulary reimbursement in managed care organisations covering > 130 million Americans [4,5]. At the same time, the number of scientific papers and conferences using pharmacoeconomic models has exploded, with new scientific organisations and peer-reviewed journals devoting substantial focus on this field [6,7,102].

1.2 What are pharmacoeconomic models?

Pharmacoeconomic models are mathematical equation systems that apply economic analysis to value and rank alternative drug interventions [1,8]. Although the application of cost-effectiveness 'cost per life year saved' models to medical decisions goes back nearly 40 years [9], the term 'pharmacoeconomics' was coined by Lyle Bootman, Ray Townsend and William McGhan in their introductory textbook applying these health economic evaluation techniques to drug therapy [10].

All modelling entails abstraction from reality to capture essential details that are relevant to decisions, while ignoring details that add complexity without improving model reliability, validity or predictive accuracy. The archetype of good modelling practice was Copernicus' sixteenth century astronomical model of the solar system, replacing the Ptolemaic earth-centred model, and its complicated planetary precessions and loop-the-loops with a sun-centred model, with planets orbiting in simple ellipses. Although politically incorrect at the time, the Copernican model was more accurate and provided crucial new insights into astronomy that eventually led to Newton's laws of physical motion and to modern physics.

In fact, all real-world decisions, from what route to take to work to what asthma medicine to use, are based on either formal or informal decision models [11]. Even after a definitive outcomes trial on alternative drug treatments is completed, the decision-maker (physician, patient, formulary committee) must still extrapolate from the

Box 1. Key components of pharmacoeconomic model design.

Perspective
- What decision-maker framework is used to measure intervention costs and benefits?

Treatment comparisons
- What are the relevant interventions that must be compared?

Time horizon
- Over what time frame are comparative outcomes to be modelled?

Methodology
- Should the model be a decision tree model, Markov model, discrete event simulation model or some hybrid model type?

Data
- What is the source of data used to develop model parameters?

characteristics of the clinical trial study participants, study time frame and study circumstances to the relevant target population. Such extrapolations inevitably involve numerous simplifications and assumptions. Modelling allows the decision-maker to specify assumptions and parameter values in a formal and transparent manner, and to assess how sensitive results are to these assumptions and values [12]. Even though others may not agree with all model inputs, through model inspection, anyone can see which aspects of the inputs and findings are acceptable from their own perspective, and which need adjustment or refinement. Open and transparent models allow decision-makers to establish the value of obtaining better information to reduce areas of disagreement and uncertainty [13].

Pharmacoeconomic modelling involves both art and science. The modeller must choose the best information to use, given limited research resources. They must combine disparate data sources into a plausible representation of treatment alternatives, taking care to accurately extrapolate from known data to future time periods, patient categories, costs and/or treatment outcomes. Simplicity is preferable when possible. For example, in the early days of modelling the costs of the US HIV/AIDS epidemic, simple projections of HIV prevalence based on reported AIDS cases and known HIV incubation distributions, ultimately proved to be more accurate and reliable than official Centers for Disease Control and Prevention (CDC) HIV forecasts based on more complex biologically-grounded models of population mixing, disease transmission dynamics and prevalence of risky behaviours [14,15]. As the US HIV epidemic has stabilised and new therapies have altered HIV disease progression rates, more complex dynamic models are becoming more useful than simple models that were successful earlier [16].

Before any model parameters are chosen, there are many initial steps that affect model results substantially but are essentially subjective decisions (**Box 1**). Optimally, the modeller will choose the best approach based on the needs of the model user – the decision-maker. The modeller should first establish the decision-maker's 'perspective', as alternative perspectives (e.g., patient, provider, government, society) will imply large potential differences in the cost, health status and outcome valuations for 'treatment alternatives'. They must establish the relevant treatment comparisons. (e.g., is the analysis comparing all antihypertensives, or only β-blockers? Are they comparing a new drug against placebo or against the best available therapy?). They need to set a relevant analytical 'time horizon' (e.g., 30 days post-hospital discharge, 1 year and lifetime). They should choose an appropriate modelling 'methodology' (e.g., decision tree model, Markov model and Monte Carlo simulation model). Finally, they must decide what types of 'data' will best inform the model parameters. Will they use data from the literature, collect the data retrospectively or prospectively, or use a panel of experts to establish certain model parameter values?

Other approaches to pharmacoeconomic research besides modelling exist, including pharmacoeconomic demonstrations and outcomes trials, evaluation of retrospective databases, and syntheses of available pharmacoeconomic literature, but ultimately, the decision-maker will rely on assumptions to extrapolate beyond existing data or studies to specific patients. **Such extrapolations constitute an informal pharmacoeconomic model; even when as simple as the projection that outcomes observed in study populations will persist over time in non-study patients.**

1.3 Pharmacoeconomic modelling types

Although pharmacoeconomic models come in many variants and hybrids, there are four primary modelling genres: medical decision trees, Markov models, discrete event simulation/backwards induction models and Monte Carlo simulation models (**Table 1**). None are unique to pharmacoeconomics but all of them have specific advantages in pharmacoeconomic applications.

The most versatile modelling type is the medical decision tree model [17]. In this approach, all relevant outcomes, costs and health states are modelled graphically as sequential probabilistic branches from an initial state of health or medical intervention decision. By assigning costs, utilities, health state valuations or other outcome measures to each node and branch of costs or other outcomes along all potential paths, and then knowing the probability of each pathway, estimate the total expected cost, benefit, quality of life (QoL) or other expected outcomes for patients receiving each alternative. The example in **Figure 1** presents a simple decision tree model for comparing the cost-effectiveness of an implanted cardioverter defibrillator relative to conventional medical therapy for sudden death prevention in congestive heart failure patients [18].

Decision tree models are extremely flexible and can be used to model nearly any pharmacoeconomic decision process. The primary drawback is that the information requirements grow

Table 1. Pharmacoeconomic model types.

Model type	Description	Pros and cons
Decision tree models	Depicts patient health state changes with sequential probability branches from initial state or intervention	Pros: intuitive, very versatile and flexible, easy to depict clinical pathways graphically Cons: data requirements easily expand beyond available information, does not allow direct accounting of time spent in various states of health
Markov models	Depicts patient health state progression over multiple time cycles with fixed health state transition probabilities	Pros: all costs and outcomes easily calculated for every time interval, parameter uncertainty and sensitivity analysis easy to incorporate, parsimonious information requirements Cons: assumes that transition history does not matter, state transition probabilities are fixed over time
Discrete event simulation models	Depicts patient health state progression over multiple time cycles with variable health state transition probabilities	Pros: costs and outcomes calculated at each time interval, more realistic than fixed transition probability models Cons: can be difficult to compute results and sensitivity analyses, has greater data requirements
Monte Carlo simulation models	Depicts patient health state progression through computer simulation of multiple individuals with random pathways based on model probabilities	Pros: extremely flexible and realistic Cons: most computationally difficult, requires the most data

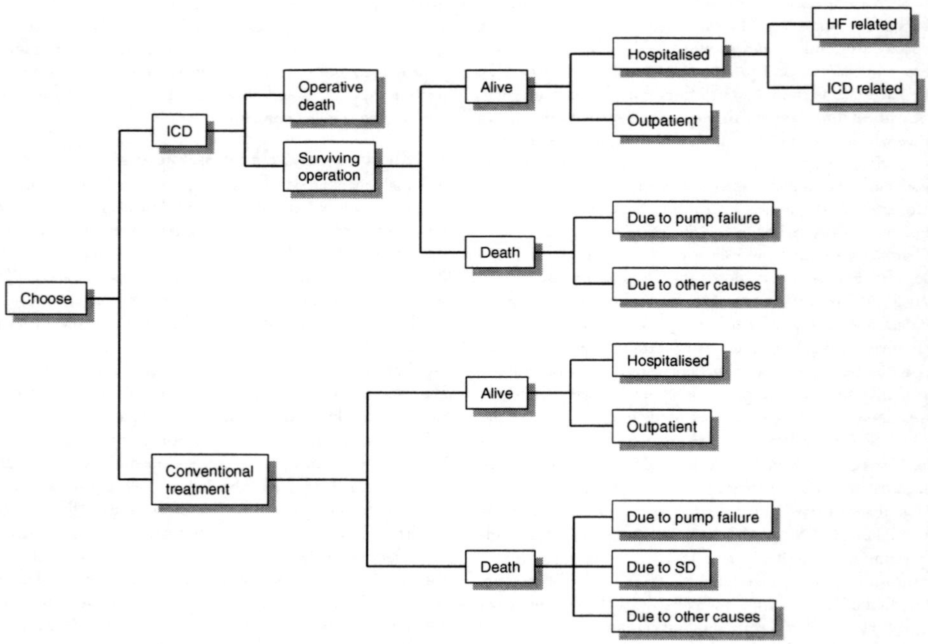

Figure 1. Decision tree for implanted cardioverter defibrillator compared to conventional therapy for sudden death prevention in congestive heart failure. Reprinted with permission from the *Journal of Cardiovascular Drugs and Therapy* [18].
HF: Heart failure; ICD: Implanted cardioverter defibrillator; SD: Sudden death.

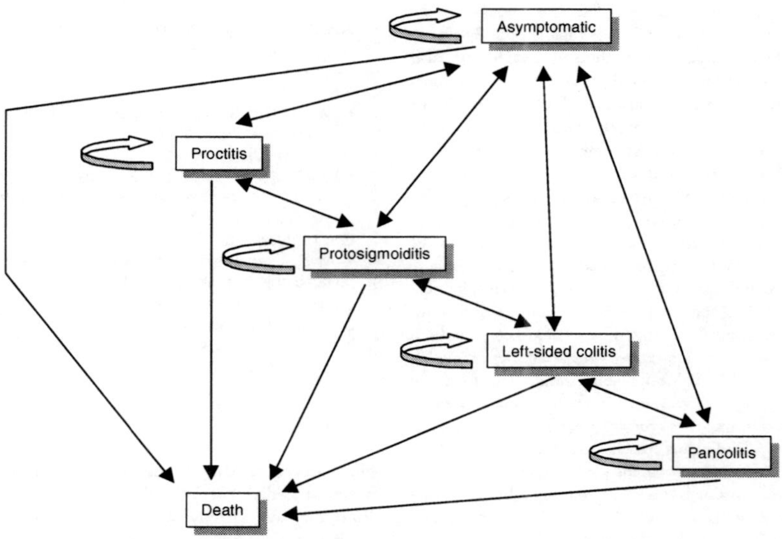

Figure 2. Markov model of potential health states and transitions for ulcerative colitis.

exponentially with the number and depth of decision tree branches. For this reason, decision tree models are best suited to shorter-term (e.g., acute care episodes) analyses, or to analyses that cannot be reduced to a smaller set of transition states in each model time period. Because adding a time dimension is *ad hoc* and cumbersome, decision tree models are not ideal in situations where time spent in alternative health states needs to be carefully tracked in order to measure costs, QoL or other outcomes.

Markov models explicitly capture event timing through periodic fixed length time cycles, with patients in a set of discrete health states during each cycle. After each cycle, patients transition probabilistically to other health states or remain in their current state. Markov models are frequently used in situations where a set of recurrent health states are observed (e.g., migraine headache, irritable bowel syndrome) or where patients progress over time through a sequence of definitive chronic disease stages (e.g., disease severity levels for diabetes, Alzheimer's disease or congestive heart failure), and each stage does not depend on prior progression history [19].

Figure 2 depicts a simple Markov model of health states and possible state transitions for patients with ulcerative colitis. Because health state transition probabilities only depend on a patient's health state in the current cycle, the Markov model is fully characterised by its cycle length and its health state transition probabilities. This makes it straightforward to compute and characterise the expected costs, QoL or other outcomes after any arbitrary number of time periods. From the example in **Figure 2**, patients can freely transit from each disease severity level to any other severity level, although many Markov models allow only progressive transitions to higher levels of disease severity, or transitions to end states such as death.

Discrete event simulation and backwards induction models are designed primarily to model lifetime or other chronic diseases in situations where Markov health state transition cycles are not practical, or where transition probabilities are not independent of time or past medical history [20-22]. Backwards induction models are similar in scope to discrete event simulation models but simpler and less general, as they impose a recursive structure on adjacent time intervals. In many circumstances, there is information on disease incidence, survival, QoL and costs for a range of age–gender cohorts (e.g., 5-year intervals) that change with age and prior medical history, thus rendering Markov models impractical. In such circumstances, one can split the patient's (expected) life into a finite number of discrete time periods and calculate the costs or other outcomes for all health states in each given time interval. Since there are numerous permutations of events and health states that are possible, the backwards induction model is analysed by starting in the final time interval (e.g., highest potential age category before death) and estimating the expected costs or other outcomes in that period, accumulating those outcomes backwards one period and adding those (appropriately discounted) final period outcomes, multiplied by the probability of surviving to the final period, to the expected outcomes in the penultimate time period. By repeating this 'backwards induction' method sequentially on each prior period, one eventually calculates all expected outcomes for all time intervals from the final period (e.g., end of life) to the first period (initial disease onset). This backwards induction approach either requires assignment of all appropriately discounted disease costs and other outcomes to the time period where they initially occur, so that only disease-free individuals transition forward to each subsequent time period, or requires iterative recalculation to ensure that the proportion of individuals in each disease state transitioning to the next period are consistent with future period calculations.

A final modelling approach, known as Monte Carlo simulation, can be applied to any of the modelling methods already described, or to arbitrary model structures or modelling hybrids [23,24]. With Monte Carlo simulation, instead of directly calculating expected outcomes based on model transition probabilities, one uses computer algorithms to simulate large numbers of individual patients progressing through the decision model. At each probabilistic transition point for each patient, a random value is drawn by computer, based on pre-assigned model probability distributions, to determine progression direction. The simulation is reiterated numerous times, intermediate and final patient transition frequencies are accumulated, and empirical averages and confidence intervals are calculated for all relevant outcomes. Like bootstrap estimation methods and other computer-intensive algorithms, Monte Carlo simulation models are becoming increasingly feasible, complex and realistic as computational power advances [25,26]. The advantage of Monte Carlo simulation models is that one can easily build more sophisticated stochastic processes than with models that rely only on probability expectations. One has to be careful to accurately reflect Monte Carlo simulation model precision and how it is affected by underlying parameter uncertainty and iteration frequency.

Box 2. Economic evaluation types differ by method for quantifying outcomes.

Cost-minimisation analysis
- Which alternative has the lowest cost? (Health state outcomes are not quantified)

Cost-effectiveness analysis
- Which alternative has the lowest cost in achieving the stated outcomes objective? (Health state outcomes are quantified in some fashion)

Cost-utility analysis
- Which alternative has the lowest cost in achieving the stated outcomes objective? (Health state outcomes are quantified in a utility index)

cost–benefit analysis
- Which alternative achieves the greatest net benefits minus costs? (Health state outcomes are quantified in monetary terms)

2. Pharmacoeconomic modelling issues

2.1 Which economic evaluation methods are best?

Although four methodologies are typically identified for pharmacoeconomic evaluation; cost–benefit analysis, cost-effectiveness analysis, cost-utility analysis and cost-minimisation analysis (**Box 2**), only the first two methods are substantive and distinct. Cost-minimisation analysis considers only intervention costs. It does not permit quantification of the outcomes associated with different interventions, and thus, has very limited application. Cost-utility analysis can be considered a special case of cost-effectiveness analysis, in which the outcome to be balanced against cost is a utility index value for each alternative intervention health states.

Any economic evaluation method will have embedded assumptions and implications for how the values of different individuals and population subgroups are weighted in the analysis [27-29]. Cost-effectiveness analysis predominates in pharmacoeconomic modelling, and is the evaluation approach recommended by the US Public Health Service Task Force Panel on Cost Effectiveness in Health and Medicine [27]. Their 'reference case' evaluation is a cost per quality adjusted life-year (QALY) outcomes analysis conducted from a societal perspective. This methodology is advocated because it does not require the analyst to assign monetary values to changes in risk of patient survival, pain, suffering or QoL. Moreover, as all QALYs are valued equally, irrespective of patient sociodemographic characteristics or patient privilege, status or fortune, the cost per QALY has a built-in egalitarian bias; particularly relative to cost–benefit analysis, which gives greater weight to outcomes occurring among those patients with greater economic resources [30].

Nevertheless, concerns exist with the cost per QALY evaluation method. It is only consistent with optimal healthcare resource allocation under very restrictive assumptions regarding patient utility and social welfare [31-35]. It is somewhat arbitrary as to which cost or outcomes to include in the cost per QALY analysis, and how to include them. There has been a debate about whether future non-medical costs or medical costs that are unrelated to the evaluation alternatives should be included in the cost-effectiveness analysis [33]. There are concerns that QALYs do not adequately capture employee productivity losses in some circumstances, or how productivity losses should be measured in cost-effectiveness analysis [36,37]. Moreover, some intervention effects could be just as easily allocated to either the numerator (costs) or the denominator (QALYs) with very different effects on the cost-effectiveness ratio. For example, consider a diabetes intervention (e.g., oral insulin) that eliminated the daily need of the patient to measure blood sugar and use self-injected insulin. The amount of time that the patient gained in reduced daily time for self-care could be subtracted from the indirect costs of disease treatment (numerator), or it could be added to the improved patient QoL (denominator). The resulting cost-effectiveness ratios could conceivably be very different and lead to different policy decisions, based on arbitrary accounting differences for treatment effects.

Cost–benefit analysis, or more precisel,y net-benefit analysis (benefits – costs), has long been preferred by economists, as it is easier to ground cost–benefit analysis in traditional utility theory and social welfare analysis, and it does not require ratios of outcome measures as with the cost-effectiveness method. Ratio measures are problematic for several reasons. Intervention A may have a very favourable cost-effectiveness ratio but be applicable to a rare disease and not produce many societal benefits whereas intervention B, for a common disease but with a less favourable cost-effectiveness ratio, may produce more total net benefits to society, and thus, should receive higher priority. Finally, given scarce resources, any healthcare decision-maker facing the task of ranking and allocating alternative healthcare interventions will ultimately have to establish an implicit monetary cost per QALY threshold value to decide which interventions are acceptable at the margin [38]. As a cost–benefit analysis does this explicitly, it fosters greater decision-making transparency and wider applicability.

A key shortcoming in cost–benefit analyses has been establishing monetary values for intervention health impacts. The cost-effectiveness method is inherently more egalitarian, as a cost–benefit analysis accepts existing wealth and income distributions in deciding how much people are willing to pay for alternative medical interventions. This is not an unambiguous advantage for the cost-effectiveness analysis method. Firstly, QALYs or other outcome measures that are based on the underlying life expectancy of the individual are not perfectly egalitarian. They have a definite bias favouring those patient categories with longer normal life expectancies, including Asians, Caucasians, younger patients, females and those without chronic disease; as QALYs gained through reducing disease in these populations will be relatively larger.

Secondly, in market economies, those with greater financial means are always able to command more resources, including healthcare. If the rich perceive that they are not getting medical services that they are willing to pay for, they will go elsewhere; either to black markets or to international healthcare providers. It can be argued that health insurance and government healthcare programmes already reflect the level of income and wealth redistribution for the provision of healthcare that each society is politically willing to assume, and that benefit estimates based on existing subsidised healthcare prices reflect societal willingness to pay at the margin. In any case, whether using cost-effectiveness or cost–benefit analysis, it is important to point out any distributional inequities resulting from different weighting of outcomes in patient subgroups, whether due to socioeconomic, demographic, medical history or to other factors.

In non-medical cost–benefit analyses, economists typically use revealed preference (RP) methods to determine benefit values – how much people are willing to pay for goods and services, usually through estimating demand functions with market data. Such an approach is impractical for most health improvements, as relevant markets either do not exist, or are heavily curtailed, regulated or distorted (e.g., the market for donor organs). Recent research in establishing benefit valuations has focused on the use of stated preference (SP) methodologies rather than RP methods.

SP methods involve asking subjects to rank or value alternative hypothetical health states in a series of choice experiments. When evaluated appropriately, such SP rankings are then convertible into preference and willingness-to-pay benefit measures. Current SP methods, particularly conjoint analysis, can be used to establish valid and reliable monetary valuations for healthcare interventions that can be incorporated into cost–benefit analyses [39,40]. Conjoint analysis is rigorously grounded in both economic utility theory and econometric estimation models with testable parameter restrictions, providing a direct assessment of consumer willingness-to-pay for treatment options in a framework that is resistant to subject 'response gaming'. It can be combined with data from RP studies to provide results that are more precise than either method separately. It has been used and validated in numerous private-sector and public-sector studies in many different fields of preference elicitation, and is growing rapidly in the healthcare evaluation literature [41].

The reliability and validity of SP value elicitation methods have been criticised as not being behaviourally accurate [42,43]. It is claimed that the artificial aspects of a hypothetical choice situation lead subjects to respond differently than in real life. Nevertheless, these methodological concerns apply as strongly to the health outcomes valuation methods used for measuring QALYs or alternative outcome measures used in cost-effectiveness analyses. It is very difficult to measure subject health state preferences without having them consider hypothetical trade-offs in artificial experimental settings.

2.2 How should model time horizons and discounting be handled?

Pharmacoeconomic models should base the analytical time horizon on the period in which the intervention has significant costs, health status or other outcome impacts. This is particularly difficult in lifetime chronic disease models, where available clinical trial data or treatment cost data seldom capture decades of therapeutic intervention [11]. Even if such lifetime data were available, cost, utilisation or clinical outcomes data that were decades old would often have limited relevance to decisions being made for patients anticipating treatment today, and over several decades into the future.

There have been controversies about time discounting in pharmacoeconomic models; how to convert future streams of costs, benefits or QALYs into comparable present value equivalents [27,44,45]. Many of these controversies stem from failure to recognise differences in the decision-maker perspective. Each perspective could plausibly imply different opportunity costs of time and possible differences in time trade-offs for costs and outcomes. A patient who cannot easily trade future health states for money or for present health states may have very different views and options for time discounting than a government concerned with treating generations of patients over time, or society as a whole, which is not constrained by government taxes and spending.

When considering a societal decision-maker, the Keeler–Cretin paradox and the Weinstein–Stason consistency argument are quite convincing in establishing the view that future costs and future health outcomes should be discounted using the same rate [27]. As Weinstein and Stason state '*It is the discounting of dollar costs, and the assumed steady-state relationship between (inflation-adjusted) dollars and health benefits, that mandates the discounting of health benefits as well as dollars*' [46].

A further counter-argument has been posited against the claim that future lives gained from medical intervention should not be discounted [47]. If an intervention saves a patient's life, it also saves the lives of all of the future generation offspring of that patient. If these future generation lives (or life years) cannot be discounted, then each potentially fertile patient represents an infinite number of potential future life years. This would make it impossible to choose between any patient or any healthcare intervention, since withholding healthcare from nearly anyone would have infinite potential expected cost. Using a 3% discount rate, under plausible assumptions about intergenerational fertility expectations, saving the life of a 20-year-old adult is equivalent to saving 1.91 discounted future intergenerational lives.

Generally, for pharmacoeconomic models done from a societal perspective, an annual discount rate of 1 – 5% is advocated. Even the UK government appears to have moved from recommending discounting only costs and not health outcomes to supporting a 3.5% discount rate for both costs and health outcomes in their reference case [48].

2.3 Pharmacoeconomic model parameter estimation

The four primary sources of pharmacoeconomic model parameter values are: literature review, prospective data analysis, retrospective data analysis and expert opinion (**Box 3**). In many situations, particularly for clinical parameters, relevant studies can be found in the published scientific literature or in other sources. Meta-analyses, systematic reviews and similar literature synthesis methods provide valuable techniques for combining information from different clinical trials and other data sources to generate more precise parameter estimates than can be obtained from any single article or clinical trial [49,50].

Systematic reviews require the analyst to prespecify which explicit inclusion and exclusion criteria will be applied to literature that is included in establishing model parameters. For example, in a systematic review, one might use clinical efficacy parameters taken only from peer-reviewed, English language publications based on double-blind, randomised, controlled trials. A systematic review is generally carried out to reduce the risk of subjective bias. If the analyst reports all literature search results from a prespecified set of reasonable inclusion and exclusion criteria, it is less likely that the resulting parameter estimates will exhibit bias. A meta-analysis is the data synthesis part of a systematic review. It will increase parameter precision where individual studies do not have enough power to detect a significant effect, as it includes more patients than any single constituent study. It produces more reliable results over a wider range of settings and contexts. Pharmacoeconomic models have generally not incorporated systematic review and meta-analysis methods as completely as possible, often using a non-systematic (*ad hoc*) approach to establishing base case parameter values from the available literature.

Box 3. Pharmacoeconomic model data sources.

Literature review
- Use systematic inclusion and exclusion criteria to decide which data available in the peer-reviewed or other literature is relevant to the analysis

Prospective data collection
- Use a prospectively designed and implemented study to obtain parameters of interest

Retrospective data collection
- Use data from a pre-existing study or database (e.g., insurance records, medical history records etc.) to obtain parameters of interest.

Expert opinion
- Obtain parameters of interest by polling experts in the relevant field.

Prospective analyses, particularly when based on randomised, controlled trials, are the most rigorous and internally valid approaches to establishing pharmacoeconomic parameter values [51]. Random assignment of study subjects to intervention alternatives ensures that costs, QoL and other outcome measure differences reflect true intervention differences, rather than artifacts of patient and/or provider selection bias. Because the analyst designs the prospective data collection instruments and sample in advance, whatever variables are needed can be captured with adequate precision. The drawbacks for prospective data collection studies are study costs, study time requirements and potential concerns about the external validity and generalisability of results [52].

It should be pointed out that merely piggybacking a pharmacoeconomic study on top of a typical clinical drug trial is often ineffective for capturing pharmacoeconomic parameters. Most Phase II and Phase III clinical trials are not well-suited or designed to capture valid and reliable pharmacoeconomic data. They are usually placebo-controlled, rather than employing active comparisons, they have built in patient selection, treatment protocols and medical utilisation patterns that are atypical in a real-world setting, and they are subject to Hawthorne effects – patients and providers do not behave the same as they would if they were not being studied.

Retrospective analyses have a different set of strengths and weaknesses than prospective studies [53-55]. They are limited to existing available data sets, such as insurance or government programme claims history or utilisation records. It is usually difficult to get retrospective cost or utilisation data that are linked to medical charts or other medical history information, so many aspects of patient health status and outcomes must be assessed indirectly. They have serious potential problems with patient and/or provider nonrandom selection of treatments, and require more sophisticated econometric analysis techniques than prospective studies [56]. Despite these drawbacks, retrospective data reflect real-world medical care utilisation and outcomes unburdened with study protocols. They are less expensive and easier to obtain than prospective studies, and are the only feasible available alternative for capturing pharmacoeconomic data in many circumstances.

In nearly all pharmacoeconomic models there are at least some parameters or modelling decisions that are not formally supported by literature or existing data. For these situations, the analyst is called on to use their best judgement, and to state the rationale clearly for the chosen parameter values and ranges. Even here, there is an opportunity to improve parameter precision by using 'expert opinion' to establish ranges for crucial unknown parameters. For example, in order to extend the cardiovascular disease risk reduction parameter beyond the time frame of existing statin clinical trials, one might assemble an expert panel of cardiologists, and choose the median value and parameter ranges based on their feedback. Even though no one knows what will happen to patients long beyond clinical trial timeframes, it would be difficult to contest the views of the best experts in that field. A variety of methods for systematically incorporating expert opinion into valid consensus estimates have been developed. The best-known of these is the Delphi method, which involved obtaining anonymous estimates from the various experts, providing feedback to them on group estimates and asking them to consider refining their estimates. This is iterated until the range of responses fails to converge further [57,103].

2.4 Incorporating uncertainty in pharmacoeconomic models

There are several sources of uncertainty in pharmacoeconomic models [27]. In fact, one of the most important contributions that models provide is to quantify which sources of uncertainty and parameter variation are crucial to model results, and which sources do not impact model findings. This allows policy makers to gauge the strength of confidence warranted for their decisions, and helps allocate research resources towards a better understanding of key model parameters.

Healthcare leads to uncertain patient outcomes, and nearly all pharmacoeconomic models use probability-weighted expected values to capture the inherent randomness in costs, health states and other model outcomes. There are also uncertainties because many parameters are not known precisely, or have different values for different decision-makers. For example, the true efficacy of a drug may only be estimated up to a certain level of precision, based on available clinical trial data. This type of uncertainty is defined as stochastic parameter uncertainty.

Some model parameters may be fully known or otherwise non-stochastic, but may still have variable effects on model results. For example, the rate of time discount might be set at 3% in the model, whereas a decision-maker in a different setting might rather use a 5% discount rate; or someone in another country may want to use different known hospital prices. Finally, the choice of the modelling framework and model structure itself will lead to uncertainty in model results.

Pharmacoeconomic models should be reported in terms of a 'base case' that reflects the best judgement of the analyst for all parameter values, with upper and lower bounds reflecting both stochastic and non-stochastic parameter uncertainty. The base case values are often chosen to reflect some mid-point, median or central tendency of available data or literature review results. However, the main criterion for the base case values should be the decision-maker's informed beliefs concerning parameter value plausibility, regardless of parameter data ranges.

Non-stochastic model parameters should be varied across their plausible ranges, with the results reported in either one-way or multi-way sensitivity analyses, depending on whether one or more parameters are varied at the same time. Sensitivity analyses should usually report best case and worse case scenarios for key model parameters. Threshold sensitivity analyses are used to show how much one or more parameters would have to change before the model results would imply a different policy conclusion.

In situations where model parameter means and standard errors (or other measures of precision) are available from the literature, clinical trials or other sources, there are several approaches to assessment of parameter uncertainty. A major issue in handling stochastic uncertainty relates to the philosophical distinction between Bayesian and classical frequentist analysis of random data [58]. In the traditional frequentist analysis, parameters are fixed and data are random, whereas in the Bayesian approach the converse is true. Frequentists use data to accept or reject hypotheses about parameter values or establish parameter confidence intervals. Bayesians use available data to estimate a 'posterior' parameter distribution, applying Bayes theorem to update and improve the precision of their prior beliefs about parameter values.

Bayesians have strong prior beliefs that their approach is superior, particularly in the context of healthcare decision making [59]. Nevertheless, most healthcare and pharmacoeconomic analysts remain unconvinced. Bayesian analysis has yet to establish a 'killer application' where the results are so superior to frequentist analysis that it becomes indispensable. Although Bayesian analysis is quite attractive on theoretical grounds, it adds a complicated set of new mathematical tools and jargon, making pharmacoeconomic models even less accessible to the unsophisticated user. Bayesian analysis often creates posterior statistical distributions that are too complex to even write down in closed form, and whereas these distributions can still be

Table 2. Alternative data sources for the declining exponential approximation of life expectancy method mortality calculations.

Data source example	Study population example	Estimated excess mortality rate
Mortality rate	56-Year-old men	Compound mortality rate – population mortality rate
Life-expectancy	56-Year-old men and women	1/(patient-specific life-expectancy) – 1/(population life-expectancy)
5-Year survival	55-Year-old men	-(1/5) (natural log of 5-year survival)
Median survival	56-Year-old men	= -0.693/(survival time)
Survival curve	56-Year-old men	Slope of negative log-survival curve

Adapted from [66].

evaluated using numerical approximation algorithms, the Bayesian analyst faces the daunting task of making these results intuitive and understandable by others. Moreover, the Bayesian analyst faces additional concerns if the assumed prior distributions or likelihood functions are mis-specified.

Assessing the impact of parameter uncertainty is a critical component of model development. Whether Bayesian or frequentist approaches are taken, probabilistic sensitivity analysis and Monte Carlo simulation methods should be used to evaluate the effects of changing stochastic model parameters on model results [60-62]. Ideally, one specifies a multivariate distribution for the stochastic parameters and simulates many repetitions of the model to establish confidence intervals for model findings. If one has individual-level data on costs and outcomes, bootstrap resampling methods are preferable, as these preserve the underlying empirical data structures [63].

However, parameter uncertainty is evaluated, it must be presented meaningfully. Because cost-effectiveness ratios have critical non-linearities (e.g., situations where the QALY denominator is zero or negative) cost-effectiveness ratios are often presented with 'acceptability curves', in which the cumulative probability of exceeding a given cost-effectiveness ratio is plotted against cost-effectiveness ratio thresholds [60]. This concern does not exist with cost–benefit analyses but one must still demonstrate how the multivariate parameter distribution impacts net benefit confidence interval estimates. Regression methods are useful for summarising the results of multivariate sensitivity analysis [64].

Pharmacoeconomic models typically use an approximate discrete time and discrete probability framework of analysis because of the limitations of available clinical and economic data. For example, although it is not possible to obtain national data on expected breast cancer survival for females 48 years of age, it may be feasible to obtain this information for females 45 – 50 years of age. These data limitations constrain the sorts of modelling approaches that can be employed. Continuous differential equations often employed in infectious disease epidemic modelling are seldom used in pharmacoeconomic models [16]. A frequently employed method for incorporating mortality and other event probabilities into pharmacoeconomic models is the declining exponential approximation of life expectancy (DEALE) methodology [65,66]. This approach, based on a constant hazard exponential survival model allows one to incorporate patient age- and gender-specific life-expectancies, disease-specific mortality, QoL changes and other parameters taken from various sources into a simple, flexible and consistent discrete probability model of intervention effects on disease, survival and other patient outcomes. As DEALE hazards can be varied for each discrete time period in the model, the constant hazard assumption is not as inflexible or unrealistic as it might initially appear. **Table 2** demonstrates the simplicity and flexibility of the DEALE methodology, showing how multiple alternative information sources can be used to estimate disease-specific hazard rates.

2.5 Pharmacoeconomic model quality, validity and usage guidelines

There are several international guidelines, recommendations and checklists for pharmacoeconomic model development and presentation [67-74]. Some of these are established by scientific organisations and peer-reviewed journals, some are established by healthcare reimbursement authorities and some are promulgated by the pharmaceutical industry. There is a fairly broad consensus on issues that are crucial to ensuring pharmacoeconomic modelling quality. Chiou *et al.* [75] developed and validated a conjoint analysis-based measure of pharmacoeconomic study quality scoring that is relatively easy to apply to pharmacoeconomic models reported in the literature [76]. The components and scoring weights of this quality index are shown in **Box 4**.

Pharmacoeconomic models are most useful and convincing when they are fully transparent to the user. Some peer-reviewed journals require that all models and data be made publicly available for others to test and evaluate. This is not always practical, as many pharmacoeconomic models contain proprietary or confidential information that cannot be fully released. Also, models are often written in complex software code. It would be excessively burdensome to require that every model be made fully user-friendly. A compromise recommended by the International Society for Pharmacoeconomics and Outcomes Research Pharmacoeconomic Modelling Task Force is '*...While the source code should generally remain the property of the modeller, reasonable requests for copies of models*

Evaluation and review of pharmacoeconomic models

Box 4. Criteria and weights selected for quality of health economics scale grading system*.

- Was the study objective presented in a clear, specific and measurable manner? (7)
- Were the perspective of the analysis (societal, third-party payer) and reasons for its selection stated? (4)
- Were variable estimates used in the analysis from the best available source (i.e., randomised control trial (best), expert opinion (worst)? (8)
- If estimates came from a subgroup analysis, were the groups prespecified at the beginning of the study? (1)
- Was uncertainty handled by: statistical analysis to address random events; sensitivity analysis to cover a range of assumptions? (9)
- Was incremental analysis performed between alternatives for resources and costs? (6)
- Was the methodology for data abstraction (including value health states and other benefits) stated? (5)
- Did the analytical horizon allow time for all relevant and important outcomes? Were benefits and costs that went beyond 1year discounted (3 – 5%) ,and justification given for the discount rate? (7)
- Was the measurement of costs appropriate, and the methodology for the estimation of quantities and unit costs clearly described? (8)
- Were the primary outcome measure(s) for the economic evaluation clearly stated and were the major short-term, long-term and negative outcomes included? (6)
- Were the health outcomes measures/scales valid and reliable? If previously tested valid and reliable measures were not available, was justification given for the measures/scales used? (7)
- Were the economic model (including structure), study methods and analysis, and the components of the numerator and denominator displayed in a clear transparent manner? (8)
- Were the choice of economic model, main assumptions and limitations of the study stated and justified? (7)
- Did the author(s) explicitly discuss direction and magnitude of potential biases? (6)
- Were the conclusions/recommendations of the study justified and based on the study results? (8)
- Was there a statement disclosing the source of funding for the study? (3)

Adapted from [75].
*Criteria weights (out of a total of 100) listed in parenthesis after each criterion.

with adequate user interface should be made available for peer review purposes, under conditions of strict security and protection of property rights' [74]. This is the approach taken by Value in Health and many other peer-reviewed journals in the field.

Model validation is a difficult and imperfect process. Internal validation is a necessary step but not sufficient. Certainly, all efforts should be undertaken to test and debug model equations, and to calibrate model predictions against available information from other models or external data. For example if a breast cancer screening model projects a 30% reduction in breast cancer deaths in the US population based on known screening patterns over the past decade, this should be matched against what becomes known about the observed change in actual breast cancer mortality. Often, the best way to catch logical flaws or other modelling problems is using one-way sensitivity analysis to set parameters at extreme values (even implausible values) and observe the resulting pattern of model results. 'Shake it 'til it breaks' is a good way to gain insights into model robustness. Porting the model to a new population subgroup or country, and checking the resulting predictions is another way to ensure internal consistency.

Pharmacoeconomic models will always be limited by their underlying scientific knowledge base. For example, recent negative clinical findings for oestrogen replacement therapy from the Women's Health Initiative trial have completely altered cost-effectiveness calculations for this intervention in ways that were not previously foreseen by clinicians or pharmacoeconomic modellers [77]. On the other hand, pharmacoeconomic models of statin therapy have stood the test of time reasonably well, primarily because early projections of statin therapeutic benefits based on Framingham risk reduction equations were somewhat conservative compared to the results of recent statin outcomes trials [20,78]. In situations where clinical trial data do not address longer term outcomes, or different patient subgroups pharmacoeconomic models can provide misleadingly precise estimates by assuming that observed relative risk reductions carry over directly beyond the bounds of the observed clinical trial results. While often plausible, this assumption is sometimes invalid.

One area where some pharmacoeconomic models have not done well is in projecting the benefits of cholinesterase inhibitor therapy for mild-to-moderate Alzheimer's disease patients beyond the short-term data available from existing medication clinical trials [79-82]. Extrapolated risk reductions do not have the hypothesised impact on institutionalisation and survival that these models predicted, and yet, these extrapolated benefits drove very favourable cost-effectiveness results. More recent findings do not confirm that short-term improvements in cognitive function are associated with longer term reductions in institutionalisation or progression of disability [83-85]. It is important to make fully clear what the impact of beyond-trial extrapolations is on model results [86,87]. In these cholinesterase inhibitor cost-effectiveness models, the unsubstantiated extrapolations accounted for the full estimated therapeutic benefits and created inappropriate policy implications.

A final issue in evaluating pharmacoeconomic model quality is the determination of what biases may have been implicitly or explicitly imposed on model development and result presentation. While all research is subject to possible bias, an obvious source of potential bias is the model research sponsor. One safeguard against this is to ensure that funding sources or other potential conflicts of interest are fully disclosed in model presentations and in submissions to journals. Another is the requirement established by the World Association of Medical Editors that participating journals require authors to affirm that sponsors had no control or censorship of submitted material [104].

Ultimately, pharmacoeconomic models should be judged on their intrinsic merits rather than *ad hominem* criteria such as sponsorship or authorship. Unfortunately, the editorial policy of the *New England Journal of Medicine* disagrees with this, and excludes all cost-effectiveness articles that are '*...by authors with any financial connections to companies whose products are featured prominently in the article (or their competitors)*' [88]. The policy of the *New England Journal of Medicine* is a minority view among scientific journals. As the Editors of the *Journal of Mental Health Policy and Economics* state [89]

> '*Exclusion of submitted [cost-effectiveness] manuscripts by authors who have a personal conflict of interests is not consistent with the aims of our Journal because the evaluation of the perspective that is under economic analysis and its implications for decision making are a fundamental part of the review process of this journal. The reviewers are able to judge the methods of the study and to check the reliability of authors' claims on the implications of the results for decision making.*'

Caveat emptor certainly applies to pharmacoeconomic models as it does to anything else. It is precisely the publication of pharmacoeconomic models based on existing guidelines in peer-reviewed scientific journals that ensures their credibility, validity and accuracy. It is much more likely that flaws in a pharmacoeconomic model submitted to a prominent scientific journal would be quickly discovered and discredited, usually prior to publication than in a model that was privately and confidentially shown to a managed care organisation formulary committee but never submitted for publication.

3. Expert opinion and discussion

Pharmacoeconomic models are not mathematical abstractions to demonstrate the analyst's intellectual prowess in stacking angels on the head of a pin. Every day, real-world decisions must be made with fixed budgets to either provide drug therapy to patients or withhold that therapy. Drug spending for one patient reduces resources available for the next patient. These decisions cannot wait for perfect information, or even for the next study. It is better that these decisions be informed by carefully constructed pharmacoeconomic models, with explicit parameter values open for inspection and validated through publication in the peer-reviewed literature, rather than by nameless or hidden bureaucrats reflecting their own prejudices.

Tremendous progress in methodological rigor and exciting new research directions have emerged for the development of pharmacoeconomic models over the past decade. This parallels the rapid growth of pharmaceuticals in the delivery of effective healthcare, and corresponding concerns about drug costs. It is likely that large-scale integrated healthcare delivery and medical history data systems will allow pharmacoeconomic microsimulation models of individual patient behaviour and outcomes that are vastly more sophisticated than today's models. The Medicare Modernisation Act will undoubtedly spur further substantial development in pharmacoeconomic modelling as the US federal government takes on the financial risk for managing drug therapy effectively and efficiently for millions of current and future retirees. In most other countries, concerns for the drug cost and utilisation requirements of rapidly ageing populations are already acute. Pharmacoeconomic modelling has a bright future, if for no other reason than the alternatives for social resource allocation are unsustainable in open societies. Even a flawed pharmacoeconomic model is better than an arbitrary and obscure medical decision process, if it leads to critical examination, open discussion and further research.

Acknowledgements

No research support provided for this paper. I appreciate review comments provided by Marc Botteman and Danielle Zammit. The views expressed are those of the author.

Bibliography

Papers of special note have been highlighted as either of interest (•) or of considerable interest (••) to readers.

1. LENS M, DAWES M: Economic evaluation in evidence based practice. *Expert Opin. Pharmacother.* (2002) 3(9):1239-1243.
2. Canadian Coordinating Office of Health Technology Assessment: *Guidelines for Economic Evaluation of Pharmaceuticals: Canada (2nd edn)*. CCOHTA Publications, Ottawa, Canada (1997).
3. KANAVOS P, TRUEMAN P, BOSILEVAC A: Can economic evaluation guidelines improve efficiency in resource allocation? The cases of Portugal, The Netherlands, Finland, and the United Kingdom. *Int. J. Technol. Assess. Health Care* (2000) **16**:1179-1192.
4. SULLIVAN SD, LYLES A, LUCE B, GRIGAR J: AMCP guidance for submission of clinical and economic evaluation data to support formulary listing in US health plans and pharmacy benefits management organizations. *J. Manag. Care Pharm.* (2001) 7(4):272-282.
5. OLSON BM, ARMSTRONG EP, GRIZZLE AJ, NICHTER MA: Industry's perception of presenting pharmacoeconomic models to managed

Evaluation and review of pharmacoeconomic models

care organizations. *J. Manag. Care Pharm.* (2003) 9(2):159-167.

6. ELIXHAUSER A, HALPERN M, SCHMIER J, LUCE B: Health Care CBA and CEA from 1991 to 1996: an updated bibliography. *Medical Care* (1998) 36(5 Suppl. 1):MS1-MS9.
• **A comprehensive evaluation of the literature up to 1996.**
7. ISPOR Ninth Annual International Meeting Contributed Presentation Abstracts. *Value Health* (2004) 7(3):219-393.
8. KIELHORN A, GRAF VON DER SCHULENBURG J-M: *The Health Economics Handbook.* Adis International, Chester, UK (2000).
9. KLARMAN HE, FRANCIS JO, ROSENTHAL GD: Efficient treatment of patients with kidney failure. *Medical Care* (1968) 6:48-54.
10. *Principles of Pharmacoeconomics.* Bootman JL, Townsend RJ, McGhan WF (Eds), Whitney Books Co., Cincinnati, OH, USA (1991).
• **A useful introductory textbook.**
11. BUXTON MJ, DRUMMOND M, VAN HOUT BA *et al.*: Modelling In economic evaluation: an unavoidable fact of life. *Health Economics* (1997) 6:217-227.
12. HAY J, JACKSON J: Methodological issues in conducting pharmacoeconomic evaluations–modeling studies. *Value Health* (1999) 2(3):78-81.
13. CLAXTON K: The irrelevance of inference: a decision-making approach to the stochastic evaluation of health care technologies. *J. Health Econ.* (1999) 18:341-364.
14. HAY J: Econometric issues in modeling the costs of AIDS. *Health Policy* (1989) 11(2):125-145.
15. HAY J, WOLAK F: A procedure for estimating the unconditional HIV infection distribution and its variability. *J. R. Stat. Soc. Ser. C. Appl. Stat.* (1994) 43(4):599-624.
16. BLOWER S, DOWLATABADI H: Sensitivity and uncertainty analysis of complex models of disease transmission: an HIV model as an example. *Intl. Stat. Rev.* (1994) 62(2):229-243.
17. BARR J, SCHUMACHER G: Decision analysis and pharmacoeconomics. In: *Principles of Pharmacoeconomics (2nd edn).* Bootman JL, Townsend RJ, McGhan WF (Eds), Whitney Books Co., Cincinnati, OH, USA (1996).
18. CHEN L, HAY J: Cost-effectiveness of implanted cardioverter defibrillator for sudden death prevention in congestive heart failure. *Cardiovasc Drugs Ther.* (2004) 18(2):161-170.
19. BRIGGS A, SCULPHER M: An introduction to Markov modeling for economic evaluation. *Pharmacoeconomics* (1998) 13(4):397-409.
• **A comprehensive introduction to Markov models.**
20. HAY J, WITTELS E, GOTTO A: An economic evaluation of lovastatin for cholesterol lowering and coronary artery disease reduction. *Am. J. Cardiol.* (1991) 67:789-796.
21. ETEMAD L, HAY J: Cost effectiveness analysis of pharmaceutical care in a Medicare drug benefit program. *Value Health* (2003) 6(4):425-435.
22. KARNON J: Alternative decision modelling techniques for the evaluation of health care technologies: Markov processes versus discrete event simulation. *Health Econ.* (2003) 12:837-848.
• **A useful contrast of Markov models and discrete event simulation models.**
23. LAW AM, KELTON WD: *Simulation Modeling and Analysis (3rd edn).* McGraw-Hill Higher Education, Boston, MA ,USA (2000).
• **A comprehensive text on simulation modelling.**
24. HUNINK M, GLASZIOU P, SIEGEL J *et al.*: *Decision Making in Health and Medicine. Integrating Evidence and Values.* Cambridge University Press, Cambridge, UK (2001).
• **A useful text on decision analysis methods.**
25. OBENCHAIN R, MELFI C, CROGHAN T, BUESCHING D: Bootstap analyses of cost effectiveness in antidepressant pharmacotherapy. *Pharmcoeconomics* (1997) 11:464-472.
• **An example of bootstrap confidence interval calculations.**
26. DOUBILET P, BEGG CB, WEINSTEIN MC, BRAUN P, MCNEIL BJ: Probabilistic sensitivity analysis using Monte Carlo simulation. A practical approach. *Med. Decis. Making* (1985) 5(2):157-177.
27. GOLD M, SIEGEL J, RUSSELL L, WEINSTEIN M: *Cost-Effectiveness in Health and Medicine.* Oxford University Press, New York, NY, USA (1996).
•• **The reference standard for cost-effectiveness analysis methodology.**
28. AVORN J: Benefit and cost analysis in geriatric care: turning age discrimination into health policy. *N. Engl. J. Med.* (1984) 310:1294-1301.
29. KRUPNICK AJ: *Valuing Health Outcomes: Policy Choices and Technical Issues.* Resources for the Future Report. Washington DC (2004).
• **A useful contrast of cost-effectiveness and cost–benefit methods.**
30. WAGSTAFF A: QALYs and the equity-efficiency trade-off. *J. Health Econ.* (1991) 10:21-41.
31. JOHANNESSON M: The relationship between cost-effectiveness analysis and cost–benefit analysis. Social Science and Medicine (1995) 41:483-489.
32. BLEICHRODT H, QUIGGIN J: Life cycle preferences over consumption and health: when is cost-effectiveness analysis equivalent to cost–benefit analysis? *J. Health Econ.* (1999) 18:681-708.
33. MELTZER D: Accounting for future costs in medical cost-effectiveness analysis. *J. Health Econ.* (1997) 16:33-64.
34. GARBER AM, PHELPS CE: Economic foundations of cost effectiveness analysis. *J. Health Econ.* (1997) 16:1-31.
•• **A fundamental assessment of the theoretical basis for cost-effectiveness analysis.**
35. KLOSE T: A utility-theoretic model for QALYs and willingness to pay. *Health Econ.* (2003) 12:17-31.
36. JOHANNESSON M, KARLSSON G: The friction cost method: a comment. *J. Health Econ.* (1997) 16:249-255.
37. KOOPMANSCHAP MA, RUTTEN FFH, VAN INEVELD BM, VAN ROIJEN L: The friction cost method for estimating the indirect costs of disease. *J. Health Econ.* (1995) 14:171-189.
38. DEVLIN N, PARKIN P: *Does Nice Have a Cost Effectiveness Threshold and What Other Factors Influence its Decisions: a Discrete Choice Analysis.* Dept of Economics Discussion Paper Series 03/01, City University of London, London, UK (2003).
39. LOUVIERE J, HENSHER D, SWAIT J: *Stated Choice Methods.* Cambridge University Press, New York, NY, USA (2000).
•• **A comprehensive textbook of SP methods.**

40. BINGHAM M, JOHNSON FR, MILLER D: Modeling choice behavior for new pharmaceutical products. *Value Health* (2001) **4**(1):1-13.

- **A useful application of SP methods to pharmaceuticals.**

41. HAY J: Conjoint analysis in pharmaceutical research. *J. Manag. Care Pharm.* (2002) **8**(3):206-209.

42. LLOYD AJ: Threats to the estimation of benefit: are preference elicitation methods accurate? *Health Econ.* (2003) **12**:393-402.

43. *Choices, Values and Frames*. Kahneman D, Tversky A (Eds). Cambridge University Press, New York, NY, USA (2000).

44. LAZARO A: Theoretical arguments for the discounting of health consequences where do we go from here? *Pharmacoeconomics* (2002) **20**(14):943-961.

45. GRAVELLE H, SMITH D: Discounting for health effects in cost benefit and cost effectiveness analysis. *Health Econ.* (2001) **10**(7):587-599.

46. WEINSTEIN M, STASON W: Foundations of cost-effectiveness analysis for health and medical practices. *N. Engl. J. Med.* (1977) **296**:716-721.

47. HAY J, ERNST R, MEISSNER C: Respiratory syncytial virus immune globulin: a cost effectiveness analysis. *Am. J. Manag. Care* (1996) **2**(2):851-861.

48. NATIONAL INSTITUTE FOR CLINICAL EXCELLENCE: *Guide to the Methods of Technology Appraisal*. London, UK (2004).

49. *Methods for Meta-Analysis in Medical Research*. Sutton AJ, Abrams KR *et al.* (Eds), Wiley Series in Probability and Statistics, New York, NY, USA (2000).

- •• **A valuable text on meta-analysis.**

50. GORDIS L: *Epidemiology*. WB Saunders Company, New York, NY, USA (1996).

51. RITTENHOUSE B, O'BRIEN B: Threats to the validity of pharmacoeconomic analyses based on clinical trial data. In: *Quality of Life and Pharmacoeconomics in Clinical Trials* (*2nd edn*). Spilker B (Ed), Lippincott-Raven Publishers, Philadelphia, PA, USA (1996).

52. EVANS C, CRAWFORD B: Data collection methods in prospective economic evaluations: how accurate are the results? *Value Health* (2000) **3**(4):277-286.

53. MOTHERAL B, BROOKS J, CLARK M *et al.*: A checklist for retrospective database studies: Report of the ISPOR task force on retrospective databases. *Value Health* (2003) **6**(2):90-97.

- **Describes many concerns and issues in retrospective data analysis.**

54. TERZA J: Estimating endogenous treatment effects in retrospective data analysis. *Value Health* (1999) **2**(6):429-434.

55. HAY J: Health care costs and outcomes: how should we evaluate real world data? *Value Health* (1999) **2**(6):417-420.

56. WOOLDRIDGE J: *Econometric Analysis of Cross Section and Panel Data*. MIT Press, Cambridge, MA, USA (2002).

- **A comprehensive advanced text on econometric methods relevant to pharmacoeconomics.**

57. OISHI S, MORTON S, MOORE A: Using data to enhance the expert panel process: Rating indications of alcohol-related problems in older adults. *Int. J. Technol. Assess. Health Care* (2001) **17**(1):125-136.

58. LUCE B, SHIH YCT, CLAXTON K: Introduction: Bayesian approach to technology assessment and decision making. *Int. J. Technol. Assess. Health Care* (2001) **17**(1):1-5.

59. WINKLER RL: Why Bayesian analysis hasn't caught on in healthcare decision making. *Int. J. Technol. Assess. Health Care* (2001) **17**(1):56-66.

- **An article supporting the application of Bayesian analysis in health care.**

60. BRIGGS AH, FENN P: Confidence intervals or surfaces? Uncertainty on the cost-effectiveness plane. *Health Econ.* (1998) **7**:723-740.

- •• **An innovative introduction to acceptability curves in cost-effectiveness analysis.**

61. BRIGGS AH: Handling uncertainty in cost-effectiveness models. *Pharmacoeconomics* (2000) **17**(5):479-500.

62. DOUBILET P, BEGG CB, WEINSTEIN MC, BRAUN P, MCNEIL BJ: Probabilistic sensitivity analysis using Monte Carlo simulation. A practical approach. *Med. Decis. Making* (1985) **5**(2):157-177.

63. OBENCHAIN RL: Resampling and multiplicity in cost-effectiveness inference. *J. Biopharm. Stat.* (1999) **9**(4):563-582.

64. HAY J: Economic models and sensitivity analysis. *Value Health* (1998) **1**(3):187-193.

- **A useful presentation of multivariate sensitivity analysis.**

65. BECK JR, PAUKER SG, KASSIRER JP: A convenient approach of life expectancy: Part I. Validation of the method. *Am. J. Med.* (1982) **73**:884-888.

- **A comprehensive presentation of the DEALE method.**

66. BECK JR, PAUKER SG, GOTTLIEB JE, KLEIN K, KASSIRER JP: A convenient approach of life expectancy: Part II. Use in medical decision-making. *Am. J. Med.* (1982) **73**:889-897.

67. GUYATT G, DRUMMOND M, FEENY D *et al.*: Guidelines for the clinical and economic evaluation of health care technologies. *Soc. Sci. Med.* (1986) **22**:393-408.

68. Economic analysis of health care technology. A report on principles. Task Force on Principles for Economic Analysis of Health Care Technology. *Ann. Intern. Med.* (1995) **123**:61-70.

69. CLEMENS K, TOWNSEND R, LUSCOMBE F *et al.*: Methodological and conduct principles for pharmacoeconomic research. Pharmaceutical Research and Manufacturers of America. *Pharmacoeconomics* (1995) **8**:169-174.

70. MENON D, SCHUBERT F, TORRANCE GW: Canada's new guidelines for the economic evaluation of pharmaceuticals. *Med. Care* (1996) **34**(12 Suppl.):DS77-DS86.

71. DRUMMOND MF, JEFFERSON TO: Guidelines for authors and peer reviewers of economic submissions to the BMJ. *Br. Med. J.* (1996) **313**:275-283.

72. WEINSTEIN MC, SIEGEL JE, GOLD MR *et al.*: Recommendations of the panel on cost-effectiveness in health and medicine. *JAMA* (1996) **276**:1253-1258.

73. ALBAN A, GYLDMARK M, PEDERSEN AV *et al.*: The Danish approach to standards for economic evaluation methodologies. *Pharmacoeconomics* (1997) **12**:627-636.

74. WEINSTEIN M, O'BRIEN B, HORNBERGER J *et al.*: Principles of good practice for decision analytic modeling in health-care evaluation: report of the ISPOR Task Force on Good Research Practices – Modeling Studies. *Value Health* (2003) **6**:9-17.

- •• **A consensus statement on good pharmacoeconomic modelling practices.**

75. CHIOU C-F, HAY J, WALLACE J *et al.*: Development and validation of a grading system for the quality of cost-effectiveness studies. *Med. Care* (2003) **41**:32-44.

•• **The first validated scoring system for pharmacoeconomic studies.**

76. OFMAN J, SULLIVAN S, NEUMANN P, CHIOU C-F, HENNING J, HAY J: Examining the value and quality of health economic analyses: implications of utilizing the QHES. *J. Manag. Care Pharm.* (2003) **9**(1):53-62.

77. YU YF, HAY JW,YU AP: Cost-effectiveness of long-term hormone replacement therapy (estrogen plus progestin) in healthy postmenopausal women for osteoporosis prevention. ISPOR Conference Abstract POS4. *Value Health* (2004) 7(3):296-97.

78. HAY J: Evaluating the cost-effectiveness of statins. *J. Manag. Care Pharm.* (2004) **10**(1):569-571.

79. HENKE CJ, BURCHMORE MJ: The economic impact of tacrine in the treatment of Alzheimer's disease. *Clin. Therapeut.* (1997) **19**:330-345.

80. LUBECK DP, MAZONSON PD, BOWE T: The potential impact of tacrine on expenditures for Alzheimer's disease. *Med. Interface* (1995) 7:130-138.

81. WIMO A, KARLSSON G, NORDBERG A, WINBLAD B: Treatment of Alzheimer's disease with tacrine – a cost analysis model. *Alzheimer Dis. Assoc. Disord.* (1997) **11**:191-200.

82. O'BRIEN B, GOEREE R, HUX M *et al.*: Economic evaluation of donepezil for the treatment of Alzheimer's disease in Canada. *Am. Geriatr. Soc.* (1999) 47(5):570-578.

83. AD2000 COLLABORATIVE GROUP: Long-term donepezil treatment in 565 patients with Alzheimer's disease (AD2000): randomised double-blind trial. *Lancet* (2004) **363**:2105-2115.

84. CLEGG A, BRYANT J, NICHOLSON T *et al.*: Clinical and cost effectiveness of donepezil, rivastigmine and galantamine for Alzheimer's disease. *The National Institute for Clinical Excellence*, London, UK (2000).

85. HAY J, ZAMMIT D: Alzheimer survival and nursing home free survival: Cognition, behavior and comorbities. *International Psychogeriatric Association 11th International Congress*, Chicago, IL, USA (2003) (Abstract 2361).

86. CLAXTON K, NEUMANN PJ, ARAKI S, WEINSTEIN MC: Bayesian value-of-information analysis: An application to a policy model of Alzheimer's disease. *Int. J. Technol. Assess. Health Care* (2001) 17(1):38-55.

• **An innovative assessment of the value of information in Alzheimer's disease treatment.**

87. NEUMANN PJ, HERMANN RC, KUNTZ KM *et al.*: Cost-effectiveness of donepezil in the treatment of mild or moderate Alzheimer's disease. *Neurology* (1999) **52**:1138-1145.

88. KASSIRER JP, ANGELL M: The journal policy on cost-effectiveness analysis. *N. Engl. J. Med.* (1994) **331**:669-670.

89. MOSCARELLI M, RUPP A: *J. Ment. Health Policy Econ.* (1998) **1**:105-107 (Editorial).

Websites

101. http://www.ispor.org/PEguidelines/index.asp ISPOR: Pharmacoeconomic Guidelines around the World. Accessed June 2004.

•• **An updated website showing the applicability of pharmacoeconomics for reimbursement in different countries.**

102. http://www.Adis.com Pharmacoeconomics. Accessed June 2004.

103. http://members.tripod.com/SSM_Delphi/delphi2.htm Accessed July 2004.

• **An introduction to the Delphi panel method.**

104. http://www.wame.org World Association of Medical Editors. Accessed June 2004.

Affiliation

Joel W Hay
Department of Pharmaceutical Economics and Policy, University of Southern California, USA
E-mail: JHay@usc.edu

Part III
Pricing

[24]

Journal of Economic Perspectives—Volume 16, Number 4—Fall 2002—Pages 45–66

Pharmaceuticals in U.S. Health Care: Determinants of Quantity and Price

Ernst R. Berndt

The U.S. pharmaceutical industry has again become the focus of considerable public attention and controversy, in part because of its highly visible sales growth, averaging around 12–13 percent annually over the last 15 years, along with its apparent high profitability.

To understand the economics underlying the pharmaceutical industry, the traditional microeconomic distinctions between short-, medium- and long-run costs turn out to be critical, as does the distinction between accounting and economic costs. Although the long-run supply of new pharmaceuticals depends critically on research and development efforts, in the short run, R&D costs are largely sunk or fixed, while the marginal costs of manufacturing another tablet of a developed drug are typically very small. For patent-protected branded pharmaceuticals, in most cases, prices are several times greater than short-run marginal production costs, thereby making short-run gross profit margin accounting measures for pharmaceuticals among the highest in all U.S. industries.

These different short- and long-run cost perspectives help one understand why the pharmaceutical industry is particularly vulnerable to public policies involving pricing. Although the conflict between static efficiency (price new drugs low, near short-run marginal cost) versus dynamic efficiency (price new drugs high, maintain incentives for innovation) is a deep and enduring one, as the costs of bringing new drugs to market have increased sharply in recent years, this tradeoff is becoming more severe. The resolution of this static versus dynamic efficiency conflict is likely the single most important issue facing the pharmaceutical industry over the next decade.

■ *Ernst R. Berndt is the Louis B. Seley Professor of Applied Economics, MIT Sloan School of Management, and Research Associate, National Bureau of Economic Research, both in Cambridge, Massachusetts.*

Table 1

Expenditures on Health Care Services and Supplies, Percentage Share by Category, 1960–2000

Category	*1960*	*1970*	*1980*	*1990*	*1995*	*1998*	*1999*	*2000*
Hospital care	36.9%	41.0%	43.5%	38.0%	36.1%	34.1%	33.4%	32.8%
Physician services	21.0	20.8	20.2	21.7	20.4	23.1	23.0	22.8
Prescription drugs	10.7	8.2	5.1	5.6	5.9	7.8	8.8	9.7
Nursing home care	3.2	6.2	7.6	7.5	7.8	8.0	7.6	7.3
All other	28.2	23.8	23.6	27.2	29.8	26.8	27.2	27.4

Notes: Data from the Centers for Medicare and Medicaid Services, National Health Accounts, various years. Expenditures exclude research and construction. "All other" includes dental and other professional services, home health care, nonprescription drugs and medical durables, vision products, net cost of private health insurance and government public health activities.

Pharmaceutical Expenditure Growth in Context

Prescription pharmaceuticals (hereafter, pharmaceuticals) account for a modest but increasingly important share of total U.S. health care expenditures. As shown in Table 1, between 1960 and 2000, hospital care has consistently been the single largest component of health care expenditures, ranging from 33 to 44 percent. Physician services has been the second largest component, accounting for approximately 20–23 percent of total health care expenditures. Although nursing home care was in third place during the 1980s and until about 1998, in 1999–2000 the relatively rapid sales growth of outpatient prescription pharmaceuticals propelled it into third place. By 2000, the outpatient pharmaceutical share constituted about 9.7 percent of total U.S. health care expenditures, slightly less than its 10.7 percent share back in 1960, but almost twice its 1980 share of 5.1 percent. This 9.7 percent share in 2000 translates into expenditures of $121.8 billion, or on average about $450 per person; for 2002, projected drug costs are $161 billion, or about $565 per person (⟨http://www.hcfa.gov/stats/NHE-Proj/proj2001/tables/t11.htm⟩). The distribution of drug expenditures across the entire population is quite skewed; for some chronically ill patients, the drug cost burden can be many times larger than the $565 average.

It is useful to decompose pharmaceutical expenditure growth into price growth of incumbent products, quantity growth of incumbent products and expenditures on new products. Although expenditures on pharmaceuticals grew at roughly similar average annual rates of 11.9 percent between 1987 and 1994 and 12.9 percent between 1994 and 2000, the primary driver of this spending growth differed in these two subperiods. As shown in Figure 1, from 1987 through 1994, price growth at 6.1 percent annually was responsible for slightly more than half of the 11.9 percent sales growth. However, from 1994 through 2000, price growth accounted for only about one-fifth of revenue growth (2.7 percentage points out of 12.9 percent), with the remaining four-fifths reflecting volume/mix changes

Figure 1
The U.S. Prescription Pharmaceutical Market Total Annual Sales Growth and its Sources

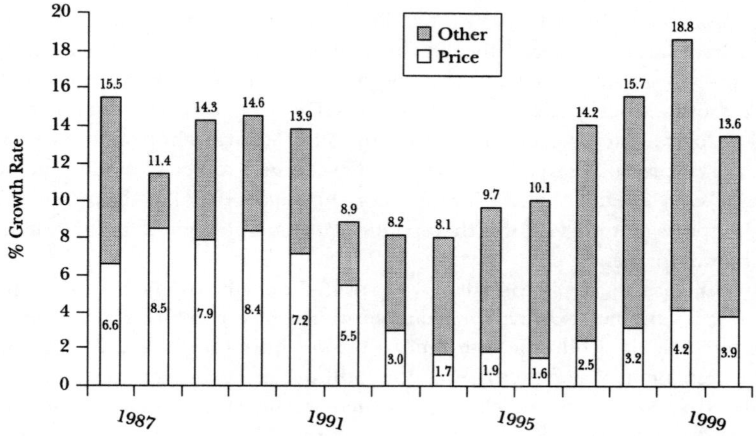

	Annual Averages		
	1987–2000	1987–1994	1994–2000
Sales Growth:	12.6%	11.9%	12.9%
Price Growth:	4.7%	6.1%	2.7%
Residual Growth:	7.9%	5.8%	10.2%

Source: IMS Health, Retail and Provider Perspective™, 2001.

in utilization rates for incumbent drugs, as well as expenditures on new pharmaceuticals. Hence, in recent years, price increases have been relatively less important, and instead, quantity growth—greater utilization of incumbent and new products—has been the primary driver of increased spending.

The relative importance of new products as drivers of total expenditure growth depends in part on how one defines "new drugs." IMS Health, a supplier of data on pharmaceutical use, defines a new product as any product launched during the twelve months ending with the last calendar quarter and having a new National Drug Classification code. Although a one-year window definition is rather narrow, it includes all new products, such as new generics, new branded products and new line extensions of existing molecules. While it would be preferable to have a new product definition that excluded new generic drugs having comparable branded presentations and strengths, spending on new generics is typically much less than that for new brands, and thus the IMS definition is a reasonable first-cut estimate of the impact of new products on drug spending. Using this definition of new products, IMS Health (2002) reports that from 1997 through 2000, expenditures on new drugs accounted for on average 42 percent of total spending growth, although in 2001, this share fell to about 20 percent as the number of new treatment approvals by the Food and Drug Administration decreased from a high of 53 in 1996 to 27 in 2000.

Some of the new drugs have involved novel generations of treatments obsolescing the old, vividly illustrating Schumpeter's notion of dynamic competition. The proton pump inhibitors (Prilosec, Prevacid, Aciphex and Protonix), for example, have largely replaced the previous generation's "wonder drugs," the H_2-antagonists (Tagamet, Zantac, Pepcid and Axid) for the treatment and prevention of ulcers and various gastrointestinal disorders. Due in large part to their increased safety or preferable side effect profiles, the new atypical antipsychotics such as Risperdal, Zyprexa, Seroquel and Geodon have largely replaced older generation products such as Haldol and Clozapine for the treatment of schizophrenia; IMS Health reports that in 2001, this therapeutic class had the highest annual spending growth at 33 percent.

In other cases, new products have provided effective therapies where previously few if any had existed: for example, the protease inhibitors for acquired immunodeficiency syndrome, the human growth hormone Protopin, and Viagra for the treatment of erectile dysfunction. Still others have been new entrants in already crowded therapeutic classes, but their manufacturers have claimed lower prices and greater cost-effectiveness: for example, Lipitor, a statin lipid-lowering agent that in 2001 was the top selling drug in the United States at $5.2 billion, and Protonix, a proton pump inhibitor.

A particularly remarkable class of new products has been the set of selective serotonin reuptake inhibitors, like Prozac, Zoloft, Paxil, Luvox and Celexa. Used initially primarily for the treatment of depression, these drugs have been shown to offset nonpharmaceutical medical costs by decreasing the intensity of costly psychotherapy (Berndt et al., 2002). Years after their initial launch in the late 1980s, developers of these drugs found new uses for the antidepressants, and now several have received FDA approval for the treatment of various anxiety disorders. Another antidepressant, Wellbutrin, has been approved for treatment of smoking cessation and is now manufactured in a lower dosage form and marketed under a different brand name, Zyban. While the new anxiety uses for the antidepressants would not be counted as new products by IMS Health, whereas Zyban likely would, it is clear that the pharmaceutical marketplace is a dynamic one, with both new products and new approved uses playing a very important role.

Major changes in the use of pharmaceuticals do not always involve newer drugs. The off-patent beta blockers, for example, along with other old blood pressure medications, are now routinely used in treatment following a heart attack, reducing morbidity and mortality associated with heart disease, decreasing the probability of a second heart attack and reducing costs of cardiovascular-related hospitalizations and surgeries (National Committee for Quality Assurance, ⟨http://www.ncqa.org⟩). By contrast, results from recent highly publicized randomized studies suggest that the widely practiced use of hormone replacement therapy to reduce cardiovascular disease in postmenopausal women may not only be ineffective, but may be harmful to certain women (Petitti, 2002).

This background suggests basic questions about quantity, price and value in

Table 2
Share of Prescription Drug Spending by Source of Payment, Selected Years, 1965–1998

Year	*Out-of-Pocket*	*Private Insurance*	*Medicaid*	*Other*
1965	92.6%	3.5%	0.0%	3.9
1970	82.4	8.8	7.6	1.2
1975	75.4	12.2	10.8	1.6
1980	66.0	20.1	11.7	2.2
1985	55.4	29.9	11.8	2.9
1990	48.3	34.4	13.5	3.8
1995	33.9	46.8	15.8	3.4
1996	31.6	48.8	16.1	3.5
1997	29.1	50.8	16.5	3.6
1998	26.6	52.7	17.1	3.6

Source: Report to the President: Prescription Drug Coverage, Spending, Utilization and Prices (Washington: DHHS, April 2000, Table 2-30).

the markets for prescription pharmaceuticals. What reasons explain the substantial increase in the quantity of prescription pharmaceuticals consumed since the mid-1990s? What factors affect the pricing of pharmaceuticals?

Increased Utilization of Pharmaceuticals

Although new products and new knowledge have surely had a substantial impact on the utilization of pharmaceuticals, here I instead focus on two of the more prosaic economic forces behind this quantity growth: increased drug insurance benefit coverage and enhanced marketing efforts, including in particular direct-to-consumer marketing.

Insurance coverage tends to increase consumption of medical services (for example, Newhouse, 1993, pp. 165–171). In this context, it is useful to examine third party drug insurance coverage, which has grown rapidly in the United States, particularly since 1990. As seen in Table 2, in 1965, only 3.5 percent of dollars spent for prescription pharmaceuticals were paid for by private insurance, while 92.6 percent came from consumers' out-of-pocket payments. In 1990, 25 years later, the private plus Medicaid insurance share had increased to 47.9 percent, about equal to the 48.3 percent from consumers' out-of-pocket payments. During the 1990s, the private plus Medicaid insurance share increased even more—to 62.6 percent in 1995 and 69.8 percent in 1998, even as the consumers' out-of-pocket share fell to 33.9 percent in 1995 and 26.6 percent in 1998.

In part, this expanded drug insurance coverage reflected an increasingly tight U.S. labor market in which employers provided more generous nonwage benefits to workers. But the increased drug benefit coverage also emanated from growth in the managed health care organizational form, which widely sought to attract insuree members by offering integrated drug and nondrug insurance coverage.

Growth in drug benefit coverage was also greatly facilitated by technological progress. Developments in information and telecommunications technologies made possible efficient and low-cost instantaneous processing of covered insurance transactions at retail pharmacies, replacing now antiquated "shoe box" methods by which insurees previously had been reimbursed for covered drug expenditures only after filling out various forms and providing proof of purchase. These technological developments also fostered the growth of new organizations—pharmaceutical benefit managers—that assisted payers and managed care organizations in part by closely monitoring prescription drug dispensing behavior in real time.

Until very recently, changes in the form of cost sharing between insurer and insuree have amplified the incentives that insurance provides to increase use of prescription drugs. Copeland (2000) reports that from 1990 to 1994, private health insurers increased pharmaceutical expenditures at an average annual growth rate of 17.3 percent, while consumers' out-of-pocket expenditures increased by only 4.8 percent per year. From 1994 to 1998, differentials in these average annual growth rates became even greater at 18.9 percent and 2.7 percent, respectively. With consumers directly footing an ever smaller marginal share of prescription drug costs, and insurers bearing the ever larger residual share, it is not surprising that the utilization of prescription drugs has increased dramatically.

In recent years, private third party insurers have attempted to control rising drug expenditures in a number of ways. One approach has been to steer use to preferred drugs on the insurer's list of approved medications (the "formulary"). During the early and mid-1990s, a common "two-tier" method was to charge consumers a low copayment for a generic drug (say, $5) and a higher copayment (like $10) for a branded drug in the same therapeutic class; in some relatively uncommon cases, a branded drug was not covered at all by the third party insurer, unless the physician provided evidence of medical necessity.

However, varying the copayments between generic and branded drugs in this two-tier formulary structure still meant that consumers typically faced no differential copayment among various brands within the same therapeutic class—even though to third party payers, the costs of various branded drugs within the same therapeutic class were not necessarily the same. Already by the early 1990s, private third party payers began to negotiate with brand drug manufacturers, offering them assured formulary access and/or preferential status on the payer's formulary in return for price discounts (rebates and chargebacks). To a brand manufacturer, being excluded from preferential status on a formulary could result in a substantial loss of market share. In this way, private third party payers exercised their power of exclusion to hold down drug prices and make aggregated demand for prescription pharmaceuticals more price elastic (Elzinga and Mills, 1997).

The ability of third party payers to obtain discounts from brand manufacturers was of course greatly affected by payers' perceived ability to influence the prescribing behavior of physicians. This ability to affect physician prescribing behavior varies among organizational forms. In staff-model health maintenance organizations, physicians' prescribing behavior can be influenced quite effectively, for in those organizations, physicians work solely for the organization that employs them, and drug prescriptions are dispensed primarily via in-house pharmacies. However, staff-model health maintenance organizations are now only a small part of the market; in the first six months of 2001, they accounted for less than 1 percent of all prescription drug expenditures. Instead, insurees have migrated toward more flexible preferred provider and independent practice association networks where control over physician prescribing behavior is less stringent. Most solo and group physician practices, for example, have contracts with more than one payer. Data from the 1996–1997 Community Tracking Survey of Physicians indicate that 61 percent of primary care physicians and 64 percent of specialists had contracts with six or more managed care organizations. When a physician is confronted with six or more distinct formularies, the result is often that the physician simply follows his or her own preferences, rather than tracking the formulary preferences of each patients' payer (Hellerstein, 1998). As a result, efforts by third party payers to control rising brand drug costs by focusing on physician prescribing behavior have had smaller effects than payers had hoped.

An alternative mechanism by which private payers have attempted to constrain rising pharmaceutical expenditures is to exert financial pressures on the patient (rather than the physician) by altering cost-sharing provisions between insurer and insuree. This involves changing the insuree's copayment (a fixed dollar amount) or coinsurance rate (a fixed percentage).

In the most recent formulary incarnations, called "three tier" formularies, many payers have not only raised the levels of patient copayments across both all generic and all brand prescriptions, but they have also implemented differential copayments amongst the various branded drugs within a given therapeutic class. In 2000, the average patient retail copayment for a generic (first tier) drug was \$7.17, that for preferred brands in a second tier was \$14.14, while that for all other nonpreferred brands on the third tier was \$27.35; these copayment levels represent successively larger percentage increases from 1998 levels across the three tiers, at 17 percent, 27 percent and 56 percent, respectively (*Takeeda-Lilly*, 2001).

Another recent phenomenon is using a separate and more attractive copayment structure to encourage mail order dispensing of certain drugs, particularly for medications used to treat long-term chronic conditions. On a per prescription basis, dispensing fees paid by insurers to mail order providers are only about half that paid retail pharmacies—on average \$1.15 vs. \$2.31 in 2000, down about 8 percent and 37 percent from 1995, respectively (*Takeeda-Lilly*, 2001). By shifting insurees needing long-term pharmaceutical treatment to mail order prescriptions (with, say, 90 days' supply rather than the usual retail pharmacy 30 days' supply), payers/insurers have been able to realize significant dispensing cost reductions per day of therapy. This use of mail order dispensing facilities by third party payers has of course exerted downward cost pressures on traditional retail pharmacy dispensing.

Three-tier formularies involving coinsurance (not copayment) have also grown recently. On average in 2000, the first, second and third tier coinsurance rates were 19, 21 and 42 percent for retail dispensing, respectively, and 18, 21 and (as expected, a much higher) 58 percent for mail order. Both three-tier formulary schemes have diffused rapidly. In 2000, three-tier copayment structures were offered by about 35 percent of employers surveyed, and three-tier coinsurance by 7 percent; the remaining 58 percent still had two-tier benefit designs. Some observers believe that because multiple-tier coinsurance schemes more finely and continuously affect consumers' marginal payments, they are increasingly likely to replace multiple-tier copayment designs. To date, very little is known about whether three-tier benefit design structures are more effective than the traditional two-tier schemes in shifting market shares among various medications, their impacts on overall drug expenditures and their effects on patients' health outcomes.

Aggressive Marketing Efforts

A second major factor affecting growth in prescription drug utilization is greater marketing efforts by pharmaceutical firms. The intensity and growth of marketing efforts by pharmaceutical firms in the last decade has generated considerable controversy, but little careful analysis.

For the U.S. pharmaceutical industry between 1996 and 2000, aggregate annual marketing to sales ratios ranged between 13.6 and 15.3 percent (Rosenthal et al., 2002a). To put this figure into perspective, it is instructive to consider a distinction between experience and search goods proposed by Nelson (1974). A pure search good does not require one's own consumption experience to gain reliable information on its traits; the potential purchaser need only examine its product specifications, which are often quantifiable. An example might be a DVD player or a credit card contract. By contrast, the characteristics and effectiveness of experience goods are largely idiosyncratic and unpredictable, so if a person wishes to obtain reliable information on the consumption aspects of a pure experience good, the person must consume it directly. Since for many pharmaceuticals, patient response in terms of efficacy, side effects and adverse interactions is idiosyncratic, pharmaceuticals often have the characteristics of experience goods. Nelson hypothesized that marketing-to-sales ratios would be greater for experience than for search goods, since with an experience good, sellers need to entice a consumer continuously to engage in a trial of the product and, to preempt defection to another product, remind the consumer of previous successful experiences.

Data on advertising/sales ratios are consistent with viewing prescription pharmaceuticals as experience goods. In 1998, advertising-sales ratios for primarily search good companies were relatively low: Home Depot, 1.6 percent; Phillips Electronics, 2.4 percent; American Express, 3.2 percent; Circuit City, 4.5 percent; Sony Corporation, 4.7 percent; and Intel, 5.8 percent. By contrast, 1998 ratios for experience good companies were as high if not higher than for pharmaceuticals: Ralston Purina, 14.9 percent; Wendy's International, 16.7 percent; Coors, 18.8 percent; McDonald's, 21.1 percent; Estee Lauder Cosmetics, 22.2 percent; Revlon, 24.0 percent; and L'Oreal, 26.5 percent (Berndt, 2001).

Perhaps more controversial is the relatively recent changing composition of pharmaceutical marketing efforts. Traditionally, pharmaceutical firms focused most of their marketing on physicians, either in the form of physician office visits by manufacturers' representatives (called "detailers," often dropping off product information and free samples) or by advertising in medical journals. Beginning in the early and mid-1990s, however, pharmaceutical firms greatly expanded their direct-to-consumer marketing efforts, not only in print media, but, especially, on television.

Although the aggregate marketing-to-sales ratio in the U.S. pharmaceutical industry was essentially unchanged at 14.1 percent in 1996 and 14.0 percent in 2000, the direct-to-consumer marketing-sales ratio rose from 1.2 to 2.2 percent between 1996 and 2000 (Rosenthal et al., 2002a). This one percentage point increase for direct-to-consumer marketing intensity came at the expense of the physician office-based detailing to sales ratio, which fell from 11.3 to 10.7 percent, and from the hospital-based plus medical journal advertising to sales ratio, which between 1996 and 2000, fell proportionally more from 1.1 to 0.6 percent. These changing ratios suggest, in keeping with the classic Dorfman-Steiner (1954) theorem, that elasticities of demand with respect to marketing increased for direct-to-consumer relative to other marketing instruments. Factors likely increasing the impact of direct-to-consumer marketing include the baby boom cohort becoming older and experiencing identifiable symptoms treatable with prescription drugs, as well as more general secular trends such as increased consumer empowerment.

It may not be coincidental, however, that direct-to-consumer advertising began to grow substantially in the early 1990s even as drug insurance benefits covered an ever larger proportion of all drug expenditures. Over time, the reach of direct-to-consumer marketing included an ever larger number of drug insurance beneficiaries, eventually reaching threshold levels where direct-to-consumer marketing became more profitable. With insured consumers paying relatively little at the margin for prescriptions, and with third party payers attempting to shift physician prescribing behavior toward the payers' formulary-preferred drugs, it is quite likely that direct-to-consumer marketing elasticities increased, at least relative to the elasticities of physician marketing.

An additional factor likely affecting direct-to-consumer marketing efforts is the Food and Drug Administration's 1997 clarification of what constituted "adequate provision" of information on radio and television advertising. The FDA's 1997 guidelines indicated that, in addition to meeting obligations requiring balanced information on benefits and risks, a necessary condition for fulfilling the adequate provision requirement was to refer in the broadcast to four sources from which consumers could obtain further information: their physician, a toll-free number, a print advertisement and a website. This clarification meant that pharmaceutical firms could now employ consumer-focused broadcast media more intensively in their marketing efforts, without fear of violating FDA marketing regulations.

While direct-to-consumer marketing has grown considerably, it is largely concentrated on a small portion of drugs. Rosenthal et al. (2002b) report that the median direct-to-consumer spending across drugs was zero between 1996 and 1999 and that in 2000, the top 20 advertised drugs accounted for about 60 percent of total direct-to-consumer marketing spending.

To date, very little research has been disseminated examining the effects of direct-to-consumer marketing on the sales of individual drugs within a therapeutic class, on sales of the entire class, and on health outcomes. Preliminary evidence suggests that direct-to-consumer marketing primarily increases total demand for a therapeutic class, with little shifting of market shares among the within-class individual products (Rosenthal et al., 2002b). One interpretation of this finding is consistent with the view that direct-to-consumer marketing encourages previously untreated patients to ask their physicians about treatment, but that the choice of a particular drug within a therapeutic class is determined primarily by other factors such as physician experience/preferences and by insurance coverage. Other things equal, brands having largest market share within a therapeutic class may therefore face the greatest incentive to increase direct-to-consumer marketing efforts, for they can expect to appropriate the corresponding share of increased class sales.

Summing Up Reasons Behind the Rise in Quantity Consumed

Currently there are no quantitative estimates of how much each possible factor contributed to the rise in consumption of prescription pharmaceuticals since the mid-1990s. My conjecture is that the rise in insurance coverage has been more important than increased marketing efforts, in part since aggregate marketing to sales ratios have been relatively constant, but these two factors interact positively. Moreover, both factors should be viewed in the larger context where significant new product introductions have replaced older therapies and expanded treatment possibilities, and where demographic changes led by baby boomers have increased overall demand for health care services.

In the future, if prescription drug insurance coverage is extended to the elderly via expanded Medicare benefits, I would expect a substantial insurance-induced growth in prescription drug utilization, but how large this effect would be is unclear. On the other hand, if in the future the U.S. labor market is not as tight as it has been in the last few years, one might expect to see private sector employers cut back on their contribution to drug cost-sharing, perhaps implementing greater patient copayments or coinsurance benefit design changes. This could have a substantial negative impact on growth in drug spending. It is also quite possible that employers will shift away from defined benefit schemes for drug coverage, where the insurance plan specifies what will be covered, and instead move toward defined contribution plans, where the plan specifies how much the employer will spend but gives employees greater choice in selecting prescription drug coverage. In such an environment, there could well be even greater incentives for pharmaceutical firms to increase direct-to-consumer marketing efforts.

Finally, a number of states are now considering implementation of formulary-like provisions in their Medicaid programs, specifying that certain branded drugs be designated as "preferred" and where physicians would need case-by-case authorization to prescribe nonpreferred brands. Notably, unlike the private sector, up until very recently, the states' Medicaid administrators have not utilized such prescription steering procedures. This may now change, and whether the states have authority to do so is being litigated. States are also attempting to expand drug coverage eligibility beyond current Medicaid criteria to the "near poor," thereby likely affecting both drug utilization and pricing.

The Pricing of Pharmaceuticals

The pricing of pharmaceuticals is complex and controversial. Nonetheless, basic economic theory provides many instructive insights. A useful starting point is to distinguish between prescription drugs that are patent-protected from those whose patent protection has expired.

For branded drugs, patent protection implies that the innovating firm has rights to market exclusivity for a limited time period; in many cases, an effective patent life is between 12 and 15 years, although this range can vary substantially according to the amount of time needed for FDA regulatory approval and other factors. Market exclusivity for a certain brand of a prescription pharmaceutical drug does not usually generate a pure monopoly situation, because most branded drugs face competition from other brands within a given therapeutic class. Within many therapeutic classes of drugs, a number of possible substitute medications exist, and in such cases, the market structure is more appropriately depicted by the differentiated product oligopoly framework. In such a setting, it is useful to envisage the optimal profit maximizing price as equaling marginal cost plus a positive margin, where the margin depends on benefits and attributes (including prices) of the firm's own drug relative to other drugs in the therapeutic class, on attributes of nondrug therapies, patient heterogeneity and other demand-side considerations. Since branded pharmaceuticals often have patent protection and oligopolistic differentiated products, one should expect this margin of price over marginal cost to be positive. But how large? What counts as marginal cost?

The Cost Structure of Pharmaceuticals

What one includes within marginal costs depends critically on the time period, as well as on the stage of the product life cycle. For pharmaceutical firms, R&D costs are very large and are increasing rapidly. A study released in November 2001 by the Tufts Center for the Study of Drug Development (⟨http://www.tufts.edu/med/csdd⟩) estimates that on average, it now costs about $802 million and takes 12 years to bring a new drug to market, including prepatent application R&D. This $802 million is more than twice the $350 million estimated a decade earlier, and in large part reflects increased costs of clinical development rather than basic R&D. In the long run, R&D costs are variable. Indeed, R&D costs are important choice variables affected by a variety of long-term expectations, including expectations concerning the future pricing and marketing environment. Once a drug is developed and ready to be marketed, however, these R&D costs become fixed or sunk. In the context of short-run pricing decisions, fixed or sunk R&D costs are essentially irrelevant.

For a drug that has already been developed and approved for marketing by the FDA, measures of marginal cost could include four categories: i) administrative activities; ii) production and manufacturing; iii) licensing royalties and fees, when the drug is licensed in; and iv) marketing efforts and other selling costs.

With respect to administrative activities, there are no important differences here between prescription drug firms and other multiproduct firms. In terms of production costs, once manufacturing plants are constructed and a drug has been developed, for many prescription drugs, the marginal costs of producing an additional tablet or capsule are very small—nickels, not dollars—although for some few pharmaceuticals, vaccines and, more commonly, biotech products, even short-run marginal production costs can be substantial relative to long-run costs. As with prepackaged software, short-run marginal production costs of pharmaceuticals are typically very small relative to long-run development costs, but for pharmaceuticals, the latter appear to have increased more sharply in recent years.

By contrast, when a pharmaceutical firm markets a drug that is licensed rather than is self-discovered or self-developed, licensing fees can be substantial. Reported royalty rates of 10–20 percent of revenues for licensed-in products are not unusual, depending in part on the point in the development process at which the product was originally licensed, and on cost-sharing arrangements during the discovery/development process. But for some products, the royalty rate can be even larger. Harris (2002), for example, reports that Merck receives a 32 percent royalty from net wholesale revenues of the sale of Prilosec by Astra Zeneca. From the vantage of the licensee, such licensing costs are variable, not fixed, even in the short run. It is worth noting that from an economic point of view, one could envisage a firm selling its own-discovered/own-developed drug to itself and charging itself a licensing fee (transfer price). In such cases, the existence of this opportunity cost could be viewed as a variable cost, although a proper assessment of the transfer price must exclude the possible impacts of double marginalization—upstream market power of the licensor combined with downstream market power of the licensee. This opportunity cost of licensing is but one more example of divergences between economic and traditional accounting measures of cost.

With respect to marketing costs, as noted earlier, the prescription drug industry's aggregate marketing to sales ratio has been relatively stable in the last five years, at roughly 15 percent. However, this 15 percent figure should be interpreted carefully.

One concern is that free samples account for about half of total (physician plus consumer-oriented) marketing efforts (Rosenthal et al., 2002a). But this cost calculation is based on valuing the free samples left physicians at their average retail price, not at the firm's marginal production costs. Unless all the free samples could have been sold at full retail price, this convention of how to account for costs of free samples substantially overstates the marketing costs of pharmaceutical firms.

Second, since marketing efforts are long-lived, marketing intensities vary dramatically over the product life cycle. In the first year following a new product launch, marketing expenditures are frequently greater than revenues for that product (Grabowski, Vernon and DiMasi, 2002). Such marketing efforts can be viewed as investments that pay benefits over time. In years following product launch, however, these launch marketing costs become fixed costs. During these postlaunch years, marketing intensities typically are much lower than in the launch year, although they may spike in certain circumstances, like following the publication of favorable findings in a medical journal, after the firm obtains FDA approval for marketing a new dosage of the product (for example, once a day versus twice a day), or obtains FDA approval for another medical condition. As patent expiration approaches, marketing efforts usually decline sharply, and following patent expiration, they are close to nil, since postpatent expiration benefits from any advertising induced utilization of the drug would be appropriated primarily by generic firms, rather than by the innovator brand (Berndt, Kyle and Ling, 2002).

Third, the durability of marketing effects, and the typical pattern of marketing intensity over the product life cycle, implies that while expectations concerning potential marketing costs and their sales impacts are important when making long-run decisions on whether to continue with R&D efforts for a drug in the pipeline, in the short run, only a portion of marketing costs are variable, and a very substantial portion are properly viewed as fixed. Recent shifts in marketing mix toward direct-to-consumer marketing, along with a relatively stable overall marketing-to-sales ratio, should have no material impact on short-run marginal costs, although they may shift demand curves outward.

Payers' Marginal Valuations of Drugs

Let us now turn to the demand side and consider marginal revenue. Marginal revenue reflects how a particular drug is valued in the marketplace, including considerations of efficacy, safety and tolerability, side effects, dosing convenience and risks of adverse interactions with other medications, all relative to other substitutable therapies and their prices.

A great deal of heterogeneity exists in the valuations patients place on drugs. Patients vary in their medical and functional responsiveness to a medication. Patients also vary in the values they attach to different characteristics of a drug; for example, some may care in particular about side effects, dosing convenience, the ability to keep functioning at work or to carry out activities of daily living when retired, or about a particular drug interaction. In considering a particular drug relative to other drug and nondrug therapies, the costs of physician office visits and hospitalizations will also be relevant. These costs vary not only within the U.S., but across countries as well. On the demand side, therefore, one should expect enormous heterogeneity in the marginal valuations of medications. This demand heterogeneity, together with low marginal production costs, creates incentives for targeted marketing efforts, as well as for nonuniform pricing.

Moreover, the entire demand schedule, and thus marginal revenue, also reflects the buying power of payers. In the U.S. private sector, buying power emanates not so much from sheer scale as from the ability of a potential buyer to exclude or downgrade a drug on the buyer's formulary (Ellison and Snyder, 2001). In countries in which purchasing power is concentrated in national or regional authorities, and in the United States for programs in which governments are major drug purchasers (like Medicaid), the legislated authority to decide on whether and how much to reimburse manufacturers for drugs creates considerable buying power for government payers.

Pricing with Demand Heterogeneity and Low Marginal Costs

Once a drug is developed and FDA approval has been obtained, for most branded drugs the profit-maximizing price is unlikely to be affected much by changes in the manufacturing cost component of variable costs.

One vivid illustration that branded drug prices do not depend materially on marginal manufacturing costs is the U.S. "flat price" phenomenon. A drug is flat priced when the price per tablet or capsule is essentially invariant over different amounts of the active pharmaceutical ingredient embodied within it. For many pharmaceuticals, costs of the active ingredient are the major component of variable manufacturing costs, more important than inert adhesives, stabilizers and other inert ingredients. Antidepressants are an example of flat-priced branded drugs. Berndt et al. (2000) report that in 1995–1996, mean costs to third party payers for Prozac 10 milligram and 20 milligram capsules were $2.00 and $2.02, for Paxil 20 mg and 30 mg tablets were $1.76 and $1.78 and for Zoloft 50 mg and 100 mg tablets were $1.86 and $1.91, respectively. Similar forms of flat pricing occur for the proton pump inhibitor therapeutic class, having well-known brand names of Prilosec (one of the world's largest selling drugs), Prevacid, Aciphex and Protonix, as well as in some other therapeutic classes.

With the same price being charged for different dosage strengths of the same branded molecule, it is clear that variations in manufacturing costs—reflecting the varying amount of active pharmaceutical ingredient contained in each tablet/capsule—do not significantly affect prices of patent-protected branded pharmaceuticals. What is being sold by the manufacturers is what patients and physicians value—benefit days of therapy embodied in the tablet/capsule, not milligrams of active pharmaceutical ingredient. This is somewhat analogous to certain other high-tech information technology products such as software, where the price reflects consumers' marginal valuations, not the marginal cost of reproducing compiled code by burning a CD-ROM, or of electronically shipping the software to the end-user, each of which is close to zero. For prescription drugs, as with prepackaged software (and, in some cases, telecommunications), the cost of bringing the first unit to market is extremely high, but the incremental manufacturing costs of making additional units are relatively minor. Price reflects marginal value, not marginal production cost.

It is puzzling why some drugs are flat-priced, whereas others are not. When a drug is flat-priced, incentives exist for the consumer/payer to cut the tablet in half—called "scoring." Kaiser Permanente once recommended that its insurees taking the antidepressant drug Zoloft score Pfizer's 100 mg tablet into two 50 mg tablets, thereby halving the effective price. Not all tablets can be scored, and in fact when manufactured in encapsulated rather than tablet form, they cannot be scored at all. While encapsulation protects a manufacturer from scoring, in some cases patients experience difficulties in ingesting a capsule, and thus encapsulating a drug is not always desirable on other grounds. Why are some flat-priced drugs manufactured in tablet form, thereby inviting scoring? Do these pricing practices reflect a type of two-part tariff, or some complex form of price discrimination? These questions merit further investigation.

It is also worth noting that once patents expire and significant generic entry occurs, the per tablet/capsule prices that generic manufacturers charge for different dosage strengths, while not quite proportional to the milligrams of active pharmaceutical ingredient contained in each tablet/capsule, do clearly rise with the active ingredient strength. This is what one would expect after patent expiration takes place, because competition among generic drug manufacturers should drive price close to marginal production costs (for generic firms, marketing costs are very small, since other generic firms could free-ride on any one firm's marketing efforts). In Europe, governmental purchasing authorities traditionally have reimbursed branded drug manufacturers for different strengths of the same drug in a manner clearly increasing in, but not quite proportional to, milligram strength. Doing so implicitly associates price variations with variations in marginal manufacturing costs. Although this reimbursement practice is the norm in Europe, it is now breaking down in Italy, where for some products flat pricing has begun to emerge.

Setting aside the curious issues of flat pricing, the pricing of branded pharmaceuticals is determined primarily by characteristics of demand. Outside the United States, most countries have national or regional purchasing bodies, with whom brand manufacturers negotiate a drug reimbursement price. In these contexts, both buyer and seller have significant but not necessarily equal market power. Once on the market, allowed price changes are frequently subject to national price controls. Hence, when negotiating for reimbursement prices with government buying authorities, the price at new product launch time is a critical economic variable for brand manufacturers.

For the United States, which accounts for not quite half of global branded prescription drug sales, empirical evidence is consistent with the notion that manufacturers price based primarily on marginal value. Lu and Comanor (1998), for example, report that the extent of therapeutic advance embodied in a new product is of greatest significance, with launch (list) prices of drugs representing important therapeutic gains being two or three times those of existing drugs used for the same purposes. New drugs that largely duplicate the actions of currently available products are typically priced at comparable levels, although the number of branded substitutes has a substantial negative impact on launch prices, reflecting competitive pressures.

Given a typical cost structure in which marginal short-run manufacturing costs are relatively minor, some marketing costs are variable but modest, and a demand side characterized by very substantial heterogeneity in marginal valuations, it is not at all surprising that with prescription drugs, the "law of one price" does not hold and that nonuniform pricing occurs, both within and between countries. Indeed, the multiplicity of prices observed for prescription drugs is similar to the range of prices in other industries with low marginal costs and heterogeneous demand, such as prepackaged software, financial data in electronic form and telecommunications.

Within the United States, the lowest prescription drug prices are typically negotiated by the Department of Veteran Affairs and the Department of Defense (Frank, 2001). Next lowest are prices to hospitals for inpatient prescription use only and to staff-model health maintenance organizations. Prices charged institutions such as health maintenance organizations (who reimburse pharmacies that dispense to their insurees) are typically discounted even less, and prices charged retail pharmacies for their cash-paying customers are discounted off "list" price the least. This general pattern of differential pricing is of course consistent with heterogeneity across purchaser groups in buying power and respective ability to move market share, although it also reflects legislated price control mechanisms.

International drug price comparisons are often fraught with difficulties in controlling for differences between list and transactions prices, for type of buyer group and for drug. Prescribing patterns also differ substantially across countries, implying that when constructing an aggregate price index, which countries' weights one employs has a critical impact. Danzon and Chao (2000) report that in any bilateral comparison with the United States, less than 60 percent of all molecules were dispensed in both countries. Nonetheless, drug manufacturers acknowledge the existence of price differences across countries, with the U.S. purchasers typically paying on average the highest brand prices and among the lowest for generics. Danzon (1997) provides a detailed Ramsey pricing interpretation of this phenomenon, arguing that by charging U.S. purchasers higher prices, pharmaceutical manufacturers can sell abroad to more price-sensitive customers at lower prices, thereby expanding worldwide access to drugs, yet still recouping large fixed R&D costs from their U.S. sales.

If nonuniform pricing is to be sustainable, then arbitrage between alternative buying groups cannot occur. In the United States, a variety of legal barriers block or limit such arbitrage. The Prescription Drug Marketing Act of 1987 explicitly prohibited hospitals from reselling to the general public prescription drugs purchased for inpatient use (obtained at very low prices from manufacturers), although hospitals could and do in fact have outpatient pharmacies, where the prescription drugs dispensed are purchased by the hospitals at the prices manufacturers charge other retail groups. The same legislation also made it illegal to reimport into the United States prescription drugs sold to purchasers outside the United States, other than for personal use. Much public attention has been focused recently on public officials sponsoring quick bus trips for senior citizens from northern U.S. states into Canada to fill prescriptions there at lower cost. A number of states are considering or already have passed legislation mandating that manufacturers extend U.S. customers the same prices charged in Canada, or a weighted average of prices in Canada and other countries. Related legislation has been introduced at the federal level. Since prescription drug tablets can be transported across national borders much more easily than other medical inputs, there has been no similar effort to ensure that U.S. physicians, U.S. hospitals and other U.S. health care providers charge Canadian prices as well. Although the empirical evidence is dated, Canadian prices of medical services such as physician services and hospital days seem generally lower than in the United States, except for nurses (Berndt, 2000).

A related prescription drug arbitrage situation exists within Europe. Traditionally, prices charged by brand manufacturers to government health care providers in the relatively poorer southern European countries have been considerably less than in northern Europe. This has led to the reselling of prescription drugs from southern to northern Europe, a phenomenon known as "parallel importing," which is now explicitly sanctioned by the European Union.

Branded pharmaceutical firms are vulnerable to price arbitrage and strongly oppose legislation that would require them to charge the same prices in the United States as abroad, particularly since U.S. sales account for almost half of global sales. Given the multitude of prices in the United States, how one would implement price parity is unclear. In the short run, such a law would likely result in reduced U.S. prices, but would be unlikely to be offset completely by raising prices abroad substantially, for existing products are often price controlled abroad. On a global basis, therefore, total revenues to manufacturers would be substantially adversely affected by such uniform pricing requirements. Over the medium term, were expected revenues to fall severely due to such policy changes, the likely result would be the termination of some existing R&D projects, especially those where, other things equal, the payoff is further in the distance. Preclinical research, which currently accounts for about 30 percent of out-of-pocket R&D costs, would be particularly susceptible to reduced revenue expectations. Over the longer term, expectations of reduced freedom to price in the United States would undoubtedly have a very substantial negative impact on all phases of drug R&D, and therefore would reduce the future supply of new products, decreasing price competition among them. While the magnitude of the long-run price elasticity of supply of prescription drugs is unknown, its positive sign can be safely assumed.

Although economic theory clearly implies that the R&D efforts of branded pharmaceuticals depend on long-run expectations, Scherer (2001) finds a surprisingly high short-run correlation between trend-adjusted R&D expenditures and trend-adjusted accounting gross profit margins for U.S. pharmaceutical firms from 1962–1996. This suggests that some long-run expectations may be affected considerably by relatively short-term experiences.

In public discussions, the pricing behavior of branded pharmaceuticals is often combined with comments concerning their profitability. Indeed, if one simply takes the ratio of annual accounting profits to annual sales, the U.S. branded pharmaceutical industry appears to be among the most profitable of all industries. However, given the large R&D costs and the considerable length of time between initial research and final product launch (for that minority of products who travel the full pipeline to FDA approval), it is critical that internal rate of return calculations incorporate the opportunity costs of R&D, else they considerably overstate profitability. In 1993, the U.S. Office of Technology Assessment reported that when drug manufacturers' R&D outlays were capitalized and amortized at plausible risk-adjusted rates, the industry's overall rate of return on invested capital in the 1970s and 1980s was found to exceed all-industry average returns by two to three percentage points. A subsequent 1998 study by the U.S. Congressional Budget Office found that when more aggressive generic entry assumptions were employed, reflecting U.S. generic entry experiences of the early 1990s, this excess return for branded U.S. pharmaceuticals was modestly reduced. The most recent profitability study by Grabowski, Vernon and DiMasi (2002) assesses returns for new drugs introduced into the United States between 1990 and 1994 and finds that the estimated mean return for the 118 new drug introductions was 11.5 percent, slightly greater than a real cost-of-capital of 11 percent. Hence, economic measures of profits and costs differ sharply from simple accounting measures. Were pharmaceuticals earning excess risk-adjusted returns on their investments, one would have expected mergers or acquisitions by other nondrug firms. Recent mergers and acquisitions involving pharmaceutical firms have instead involved other pharmaceutical or life sciences firms. An update and additional analyses of the pharmaceutical economic profitability calculations would provide a most useful evidentiary platform to inform current public discussions concerning the industry's pricing and profitability.

Patent Expiration and Brand-Generic Pricing

Since the GATT agreements of 1994, a U.S. patent provides market exclusivity rights for 20 years from the date the patent application was filed. Because clinical testing and Food and Drug Administration (FDA) approval generally follow patent filing, the effective patent life for prescription drugs is typically 12–15 years. Precisely when patent protection expires for branded pharmaceuticals is increasingly being litigated, in part because multiple patents involving product, production process and "method of use" often exist for a single molecule.

The 1984 Hatch-Waxman legislation made the entry of generic drugs at the expiration of the patent easier, because the generic entrant no longer needed to provide evidence concerning safety and efficacy of the drug, but instead needed only to document bioavailability and pharmaceutical equivalence with the brand product, as well as compliance with sound manufacturing provisions. The filing of an Abbreviated New Drug Application could now also take place prior to patent expiration, so that with FDA approval, entry of the generic drug could occur on the very day the brand patent expired.

With barriers to generic entry reduced, generic entry has been substantial. The generic share of prescription units dispensed has risen from 19 percent in 1984 to 33 percent in 1990, 42 percent in 1995 and stayed at 42–43 percent since then. Loss of market share to generic entrants has become increasingly rapid. In the late 1980s, after six months following initial generic entry, generics gained on average a 31 percent unit market share, but by the early 1990s this share increased to 44 percent (Grabowski and Vernon, 1996). With the rapid growth of pharmaceutical benefit management services, the loss of market share to generics has become even more rapid. Within two months after the August 2000 patent expiration for Merck's antihypertensive Vasotec, for example, generics gained 75 percent of prescription units in the formerly $2 billion U.S. annual sales market (Harris, 2002). Merck-Medco, the largest pharmaceutical benefit manager in the United States, claimed that within one week of the launch of generic forms of the antidepressant Prozac in August 2001, it achieved an 80 percent generic substitution rate (Pink Sheet, August 27, 2001, p. 8).

In a competitive market with free entry, one expects that entry will take place until price falls to marginal cost. Industry sources state that currently when there is only one generic entrant, the generic manufacturer's price relative to the brand is typically about 85 percent; with two manufacturers it decreases to 75 percent; and successive entrants competing on price continue to drive down the generic/brand relative price, in some cases to less than 10 percent. Although shift from brand to generic following loss of patent protection is increasingly rapid, the extent of generic entry still appears to be gradual (Berndt, Kyle and Ling, 2002). Why generic entry and price declines tend to be staggered, rather than fully coincident with patent expiration, is unclear.

Two other issues regarding brand-generic pricing merit attention. First, following loss of patent protection, brand products typically do not engage in price competition with generics, but instead raise average brand prices, targeting their product to that (ever smaller) market niche that remains brand loyal (for example, U.S. Congressional Budget Office, 1997). Second, at the retail level, relative generic/brand prices are typically higher than at the manufacturer or wholesale level. Retail chains can engage the various generic manufacturers of a molecule in price competition and purchase from the lowest price bidder. However, for retail cash (uninsured) customers, the brand price becomes an upper bound umbrella. As a result, absolute and relative margins for retailers selling to cash customers generally are larger for generics than for brands (Grabowski and Vernon, 1996). This is similar to the case of grocery stores and mass merchandisers, who typically realize greater margins from private label than nationally advertised branded products. For insured customers, payers benefit considerably from substituting to generics, and thus payers have often offered retail pharmacies larger dispensing fees for generic than brand prescription drugs. This difference is declining, however, and for 2000, its average has been estimated by *Takeeda-Lilly* (2001) to be only 5.6 percent ($2.44 for generics versus $2.31 for brands).

While passage of the Hatch-Waxman Act has undoubtedly increased generic entry and reduced prices of off-patent drugs, some other provisions of this legislation have had unintended consequences. When a generic firm files an Abbreviated New Drug Application with the FDA, it must certify either that a) the patent for the brand-name drug has expired; b) the patent for the brand-name drug will expire on a particular date, and the generic company does not seek to market its generic product before that date; or c) the patent for the brand-name drug is invalid or will not be infringed by the generic company's proposed product. If the generic firm certifies choice *c*, it must inform the brand manufacturer and provide explanations as to why it believes its generic drug either does not infringe upon the patent, or the patent is invalid. If in turn the brand manufacturer responds within 45 days by filing a patent infringement suit against the generic firm filing the application, then the FDA's approval of the generic's application is automatically stayed for 30 months or until there is a final decision in the patent case, whichever comes first. However, to encourage generic firms to challenge the legality of branded patents, if the potential generic entrant prevails against the brand in its certification of option *c*, then the generic is automatically granted an 180-day exclusivity period during which no other generic firm can market the same molecular product.

Notice that if the brand pharmaceutical firm files for patent infringement and loses, for six months following the decision there is only one generic competitor on the market, but if it does not challenge the generic on its *c* certification, it could face a much larger set of generic competitors. To the extent market share loss by the brand increases along with the number of generic entrants, a brand may be better off challenging and losing to the generic on its *c* certification than by not filing a patent infringement suit against the generic.

Currently there is considerable diversity among brand pharmaceutical firms in the aggressiveness with which they challenge generic companies' claims of patent expiration or patent validity (Harris, 2002). When the outcome of the contested *c* certification is uncertain, there are incentives to both the generic and brand to settle, with a possible outcome being delayed entry of the generic. Such a delayed entry results in a short-run loss in welfare for consumers and payers. This is apparently an unintended outcome of the Hatch-Waxman Act. Following allegations of collusion, recently the U.S. Department of Justice and the Federal Trade Commission have reached settlements with a number of brand and generic companies, in which they agree not to enter into agreements that delay generic entry. Legislation has also been introduced into Congress to amend relevant portions of the Hatch-Waxman Act.

Concluding Remarks

I have argued that the traditional microeconomic concepts of short-, medium- and long-run cost functions are critical in understanding the economics underlying observed variations in the prices and quantities of pharmaceuticals across space and time. I have also emphasized that the tradeoff between static (price new drugs low, near short-run marginal cost) and dynamic (price new drugs high, maintain incentives for innovation) is becoming increasingly severe, as the relative costs of bringing new drugs to market have increased sharply. This raises at least two questions. Has the recent substantial growth in the use of pharmaceuticals been on balance a good development for consumers? What types of novel incentive arrangements might help alleviate the increasingly severe conflict between static and dynamic efficiency?

A full discussion of either of these important questions is beyond the scope of this article. Regarding the first question, given the many factors other than medical care that affect an individual's health status over time, such as genetic factors and lifestyle, as well as interactions between drug and nondrug medical therapies, it is very difficult to isolate the health impacts of increased prescription drug utilization over the last decade from other developments. Nonetheless, for evidence suggesting that benefits of new pharmaceuticals are greater than their costs, see the articles in Iglehart (2001). For a contrarian view that much medical spending in the last six months of patients' lives has little if any positive impact, see Wennberg, Fisher and Skinner (2002). It is of course possible that both positions are correct. Regarding the second question on alternative patent and licensing policies, see Kremer (2000a, b) and the references cited there.

■ *The author gratefully acknowledges research support from the Massachusetts Institute of Technology Program on the Pharmaceutical Industry, extensive comments from the editors and from others too numerous to name. The author has served as a consultant to various branded pharmaceutical companies, to the Federal Trade Commission in a matter involving the generic drug industry and to several managed care organizations. The views expressed in this paper are the author's own and are not necessarily those of any of the entities or organizations with whom he has been associated.*

References

Berndt, Ernst R. 2000. "International Comparisons of Pharmaceutical Prices: What Do We Know, and What Does it Mean?" *Journal of Health Economics.* March/April, 19:2, pp. 283–87.

Berndt, Ernst R. 2001. "The U.S. Pharmaceutical Industry: Why Major Growth in Times of Cost Containment?" *Health Affairs.* March/April, 20:2, pp. 100–14.

Berndt, Ernst R., Margaret K. Kyle and Davina Ling. 2002. "The Long Shadow of Patent Expiration: Generic Entry and Rx to OTC Switches," in *Scanner Data and Price Indexes, NBER Series on the Conference on Research in Income and Wealth.* Robert C. Feenstra and Matthew D. Shapiro, eds. Chicago: University of Chicago Press for the National Bureau of Economic Research, forthcoming.

Berndt, Ernst R. et al. 2000. "Comparing SSRI Treatment Costs for Depression Using Retrospective Claims Data: The Role of Nonrandom Selection and Skewed Data." *Value in Health.* May/June, 3:3, pp. 208–21.

Berndt, Ernst R. et al. 2002. "The Medical Treatment of Depression, 1991–1996: Productive Inefficiency, Expected Outcome Variations, and Price Indexes." *Journal of Health Economics.* May, 21:3, pp. 373–96.

Copeland, Craig. 2000. "Prescription Drugs: Continued Rapid Growth." Washington, D.C., Employee Benefit Research Institute Notes, September.

Danzon, Patricia M. 1997. "Price Discrimination for Pharmaceuticals: Welfare Effects in the U.S. and the E.U." *International Journal of the Economics of Business.* November, 4:3, pp. 301–21.

Danzon, Patricia M. and Li-Wei Chao. 2000. "Cross-National Price Differences for Pharmaceuticals: How Large, and Why?" *Journal of Health Economics.* March/April, 19:2, pp. 159–96.

Dorfman, Robert and Peter O. Steiner. 1954.

"Optimal Advertising and Optimal Quality." *American Economic Review*. December, 44:5, pp. 826–36.

Ellison, Sara F. and Christopher M. Snyder. 2001. "Countervailing Power in Wholesale Pharmaceuticals." Working Paper 01-27, MIT Department of Economics, July.

Elzinga, Kenneth G. and David E. Mills. 1997. "The Distribution and Pricing of Drugs." *International Journal of the Economics of Business*. November, 4:3, pp. 287–99.

Frank, Richard G. 2001. "Prescription Drug Prices: Why Do Some Pay More Than Others Do?" *Health Affairs*. March/April, 20:2, pp. 115–28.

Grabowski, Henry and John Vernon. 1996. "Longer Patents for Increased Generic Competition in the U.S.: The Waxman-Hatch Act after One Decade." *PharmacoEconomics*. 10: Supplement 2, pp. 110–23.

Grabowski, Henry, John Vernon and Joseph DiMasi. 2002. "Returns on R&D for 1990s New Drug Introductions." Unpublished Working Paper, Duke University, Department of Economics, March.

Harris, Gardner. 2002. "Merck to Shed Medco, its Drug-Benefits Unit, in Bid to Boost Stock." *New York Times*. January 29, pp. A1, A8.

Hellerstein, Judith K. 1998. "The Importance of the Physician in the Generic versus Trade-Name Prescription Decision." *RAND Journal of Economics*. Spring, 29:1, pp. 108–36.

Iglehart, John K., ed. 2001. *The Value of Rx Innovation: A Primer from Health Affairs*. Millwood, Va.: Project HOPE.

IMS Health. 2002. "IMS Reports 16.9 Percent Growth in 2001 U.S. Prescription Sales." Available at ⟨http://www.imshealth.com/public/structure⟩.

Kremer, Michael. 2000a. "Creating Markets for New Vaccines. Part I: Rationale." NBER Paper No. 7716.

Kremer, Michael. 2000b. "Creating Markets for New Vaccines. Part II: Design Issues." NBER Working Paper No. 7717.

Lu, Z. John and William S. Comanor. 1998. "Strategic Pricing of New Pharmaceuticals." *Review of Economics and Statistics*. February, 80:1, pp. 108–18.

Nelson, Philip. 1974. "Advertising as Information." *Journal of Political Economy*. July/August, 82:4, pp. 729–54.

Newhouse, Joseph P. and the Insurance Experiment Group. 1993. *Free for All? Lessons from the RAND Health Insurance Experiment*. Cambridge, Mass.: Harvard University Press.

Petitti, Diana B. 2002. "Hormone Replacement Therapy for Prevention. More Evidence, More Pessimism." *Journal of the American Medical Association*. July 3, 288:1, pp. 99–101.

Rosenthal, Meredith B. et al. 2002a. "Promotion of Prescription Drugs to Consumers." *New England Journal of Medicine*. February 14, 346:7, pp. 498–505.

Rosenthal, Meredith B. et al. 2002b. "Demand Effects of Recent Changes in Prescription Drug Promotion," in *Frontiers in Health Policy Research, Volume 5*. Alan M. Garber, ed. Cambridge, Mass.: MIT Press for the National Bureau of Economic Research, forthcoming.

Scherer, F. Michael. 2001. "The Link Between Gross Profitability and Pharmaceutical R&D Spending." *Health Affairs*. September/October, 20:5, pp. 216–20.

Takeeda-Lilly Prescription Drug Benefit Cost and Plan Design Survey Report. 2001. Temple, Ariz.: Pharmacy Benefit Management Institute, Inc.

United States Congressional Budget Office. 1997. *How Increased Competition from Generic Drugs Has Affected Prices and Returns in the Pharmaceutical Industry*. Washington, D.C.: U.S. Government Printing Office.

United States Office of Technology Assessment. 1993. *Pharmaceutical R&D: Costs, Risks and Rewards*. Washington, D.C.: U.S. Government Printing Office.

Wennberg, John E., Elliott S. Fisher and Jonathan S. Skinner. 2002. "Geography and the Debate Over Medicare Reform." *Health Affairs*. Available online at ⟨http://www.healthaffairs.org/WebExclusives/Wennberg_Web_Excl_021302.htm⟩.

[25]

STRATEGIC PRICING OF NEW PHARMACEUTICALS

Z. John Lu and William S. Comanor*

Abstract—This paper provides empirical evidence on the leading factors affecting the prices of new pharmaceuticals, both at introduction and after 4, 6, and 8 years. Most important is the extent of therapeutic advance embodied in a new product. For drugs which represent important therapeutic gains, launch prices can be two or three times those of existing drugs used for the same purposes, while drugs that largely duplicate the actions of currently available products are typically priced at comparable levels. In addition, the number of branded substitutes has a substantial negative effect on launch prices, which reflects the importance of competitive pressures. Duplicate products thereby play an important economic role in pharmaceutical markets.

I. Introduction

THE PRICING of new pharmaceuticals has long been a source of controversy. When critics complain that prices are too high, particularly in relation to production costs, defenders respond that prevailing price levels are needed to fund enormous expenditures on research and development. In general, both positions compare prices to costs and ignore demand side considerations.[1]

We explore here an alternative set of determinants for the prices of new pharmaceutical products. In contrast to the standard arguments, we find that the primary explanatory factors are the therapeutic value of the product and the nature of competition in the relevant market.

Our analysis examines the pricing strategies used for newly patented pharmaceuticals. It covers 144 new drugs introduced in the United States between 1978 and 1987. We explore how the prices of patented new drugs are set relative to their existing substitutes and how these prices change over time.

II. Earlier Research on Pharmaceutical Prices

In the pharmaceutical industry, a patent is granted for a drug's novel chemical composition rather than its therapeutic properties. Many new pharmaceuticals receive patents despite their being functionally similar to existing drugs. As such, their introduction expands physicians' choices and can pose a competitive threat to established drugs with the same or similar indications. Nonetheless, the existing economic literature on the pharmaceutical industry has not adequately addressed the question of price competition among rival patented products. Indeed, in much of the literature, price competition is not considered until patents have expired and generic substitutes enter (Comanor (1986)).

An exception is the paper by Reekie (1978), which laid the foundation for much research in this area. Reekie examined the launching prices for new molecular entities (NMEs)[2] introduced into the U.S. market between 1958 and 1975. He found that, as a rule, new drugs representing important therapeutic advances are priced significantly above their existing substitutes, while imitators are priced much lower. For NMEs offering modest therapeutic gain and/or reduced side effects, the premium over existing substitutes is normally small. Hence, Reekie concluded that the proliferation of new patented drugs has not limited the extent of price competition. He also observed that over time, drugs with high introductory prices tend to have price reductions, whereas those with low introductory prices tend to show price increases.[3]

Weston (1979, 1982) also considered factors that affect drug prices. Like Reekie, he found that therapeutically innovative drugs are priced higher than existing substitutes, and imitative drugs are priced lower—a natural outcome of a competitive process that tends to equate quality-adjusted prices. In addition, he observed that the prices of innovative drugs decline as more competitors enter the therapeutic market, which leads to falling prices over time. He concluded: "the market success of a prescription medicine, other things being equal, is affected by its price relative to alternative products on the market" (1979, p. 85).

Suslow (1993) used a hedonic price model to estimate the shadow prices of diverse product attributes for a class of ulcer drugs. Her approach represented the first systematic attempt to use the method of hedonic prices to explain pharmaceutical price differences. An important finding is that over time, the quality-adjusted price for ulcer drugs increased significantly, if less than indicated by the unadjusted price index. In other words, although drugs introduced more recently are generally improved therapeutically, these gains do not account entirely for the higher prices that have been set.

III. Strategic Considerations

A. *Theoretical Literature*

An important early discussion of new product pricing is by Dean (1969), who distinguished between two strategies for pricing new products: skimming pricing and penetration pricing. Skimming is the strategy of setting a high initial price and then lowering it over time, while penetration is the

Received for publication Febuary 8, 1994. Revision accepted for publication October 30, 1996.

*Amgen, Inc., and University of California, respectively.

The authors are grateful to Anna Chen, M.D., for her considerable assistance in the preparation of the data set used in this paper, and to Richard Caves, Ted Frech, Rob Masson, Clement Krouse, F. M. Scherer, Michael Waldman, and Steven Wiggins for helpful comments on earlier drafts.

[1] For further discussion, see Comanor and Schweitzer (1995.)

[2] Each year hundreds of new drugs are approved for marketing by the Federal Drug Administration (FDA). Only a small fraction of them contain an active compound not yet marketed in the United States. They are called new molecular entities (NMEs) or new chemical entities (NCEs). The majority fall into the categories of new salt, new formulation, new indication, new combination, or generic duplicates of existing drugs.

[3] Similar patterns were observed for new drugs launched in the United Kingdom between 1962 and 1970; see Reekie (1977).

strategy of launching a new product at a low price and then raising it over time. Dean suggested that skimming is used for new products that offer significant advantages over existing ones, whereas penetration is more often employed for products that represent only marginal improvements over their established counterparts.

Dean's paper was followed by an extensive literature. A key paper is by Schmalensee (1982), who concluded that maximum profits are gained for "pioneering brands" that set a low introductory price which is followed by a higher regular price. He wrote: "this . . . low/high pricing sequence corresponds roughly to what is called 'penetration pricing' in the marketing and managerial economics literature" (p. 352). The critical factor, he argued, is buyers' lack of knowledge about a new product, which leads sellers to set low introductory prices to encourage use and build reputation.

Schmalensee also explored the optimal pricing strategy of a later entrant. While the preferred strategy turns on the particular structure of demand in the relevant market, he suggested that second entrants face a substantial disadvantage relative to their pioneering counterparts, so they need to set still lower launch prices to entice prospective consumers to purchase their product (pp. 353–358). Such firms need to follow an even more pronounced policy of setting low introductory prices followed by increases over time.

Like Schmalensee's study, Shapiro (1983) presumed the importance of buyers' perceptions of a new product in terms specifically of its quality level. He considered the effect of imperfect buyer information on product attributes for new "experience" goods, which are those whose users can determine product attributes only by using the product.

Dealing only with the optimal pricing strategy for a monopolist, Shapiro suggested that the extent of optimism or pessimism regarding a product is the critical factor. In the pessimistic case, the firm needs to build a reputation for its product, which is achieved by setting a low introductory price followed by a higher regular price. In the optimistic case, where consumers overestimate product quality, the firm will optimally "milk its reputation," which leads it to set a high launch price but then lower its price over time.

While these papers concern the role of buyer information regarding the product, they do not consider the informational content of the prices that are set. In contrast, other studies model prices as signals of product quality. For example, Bagwell and Riordan (1991) developed a model in which consumers have higher reservation prices for higher quality products but still a positive reservation price for a low-quality product. Their index of product quality turns on the extent to which new products embody an important advance over existing alternatives. They report that "firms signal high quality new products with prices that are above full information profit maximizing prices, [but also] . . . over time, as information about the product diffuses, the price distortion lessens or vanishes entirely." (p. 224) Thus, they predict opposite pricing strategies from those suggested above.

Finally, there is a third group of studies in which new product demand is characterized by a diffusion process, where the number of future buyers expands depending on the initial number of purchasers. As a result, sellers can increase future demand by setting lower current prices. The lower the introductory price, the faster the speed of diffusion, and the larger the number of consumers reached in the future. This suggests a strategy for all new products of setting low initial prices and increasing them over time.[4]

A striking feature of this literature is that very different results are obtained, depending on the particular assumptions made regarding the availability of information to prospective buyers and their response to it. In this study, we explore these matters empirically for the pricing strategies used with new pharmaceuticals.

B. *The Hypotheses*

Since new products typically compete with established drugs that are used for the same or similar purposes, competition often occurs among differentiated products with differing levels of buyer acceptance. In the context of address or spatial models of product differentiation (Eaton and Lipsey (1989)), the entrant's ability to attract buyers depends on its proximity in product space to existing products. New sellers can set higher prices when their products are more distant in product space from existing products, as long as there is a sufficiently large and inelastic demand.

Applied to pharmaceuticals, this conclusion means that new drugs will attract more demand when their characteristics are preferred by larger numbers of consumers, which generally requires that they provide a substantial therapeutic advance as compared to existing agents. But alternatively, if these products do not offer a therapeutic advance, they command lower prices. This consideration suggests that more improved products will have higher launch prices than their established rivals, while "me-too" or imitative products will not.

In addition, a new product's higher price may decline after introduction. The premiums will eventually attract additional rivals, so the originating firm will face increased competition in future years. Furthermore, because more therapeutically advanced drugs are likely to be accepted more rapidly due to their medical and scientific importance, introductory discounts are less needed to promote market penetration, and there is less occasion for increases to reach the product's equilibrium price. However, for new drugs that offer little therapeutic advantage over existing products, the need to build demand leads their sellers to set relatively low introductory prices but to raise them over time—the classic penetration strategy. We examine these conjectures in the

[4] See the diffusion model by Bass (1969) and also the studies by Robinson and Lakhani (1975) and Simon (1989, chap. 5).

analysis below, and we also investigate within each category of therapeutic advance whether pharmaceuticals introduced at higher relative prices have lower subsequent price increases.

Another factor that should affect the firm's choice of pricing strategy is the anticipated number of repeat purchases. Both Dolan and Jeuland (1981), and Rao (1984) demonstrate that penetration strategies are optimal when there are substantial prospects for repeat purchases. With pharmaceuticals, repeat purchases are less likely for drugs designed for acute than for chronic ailments. We therefore hypothesize that skimming strategies are more likely to apply in "acute" circumstances.

A further reason for setting lower introductory prices for drugs treating "chronic" conditions is that those illnesses are more pervasive among the elderly (Stuart et al. (1991)). Older patients generally have higher copayment rates for prescription drugs (Taylor (1993)), which reach 100% in the absence of insurance, and therefore are more price sensitive. For this reason also, the introductory prices of such drugs should be lower.

Prices are also affected by competitive conditions within particular markets. In pharmaceutical markets there are two distinct types of rivals. First, there are branded substitutes which typically embody different chemical compounds and enjoy patent protection; and second, there are generic versions of both new and existing products. Because of the substantial price differences between branded and generic products, we anticipate different price effects.

In the case of branded rivals, there are competing differentiated products, where each is preferred more or less strongly by different consumers according to their individual needs and the perceptions of their physicians. As more rivals enter the market, consumers find better substitution opportunities, demands become more elastic, and prices therefore decline. This result applies, for example, to a Bertrand equilibrium for markets with differentiated products (Krouse (1990, pp. 180–181)). In the empirical analysis we test this hypothesis.

With generic rivals, on the other hand, the interactions are more complicated. For the new drugs in our sample there are no direct generic rivals at introduction, but they are present for some substitute branded products. And generic competition appears for some new products following introduction.

The available evidence on the impact of generic competition on the prices charged for the original, branded compound is mixed. Caves et al. (1991) find a small decline in a branded drug's price following generic entry. However, Frank and Salkever (1995) find higher prices following the appearance of generic rivals as originating sellers accept the loss of buyers with more elastic demands and price accordingly.[5] Grabowski and Vernon (1992) on the other hand, report two significant positive and two significant negative coefficients for price trends of an original branded product following generic entry, out of 18 products studied.

However, our attention here is directed instead at a new product's launch price relative to that of an existing branded product now facing generic competition. In this context, a relevant matter is the significance of generic competition for the marketing efforts and product obsolescence of the existing drug. There is evidence of substantial declines in promotional efforts for branded products with impending or actual generic entry (Caves et al. (1991, pp. 39–42)). And there is also indication that sales decline even before generic substitutes appear: "the quantity of the branded drug sold . . . falls roughly 20 percent in the year of patent expiration and continues to decline at roughly 12 percent a year thereafter until [generic] entry occurs" (p. 42). Branded products with generic rivals are often approaching the ends of their product life cycles. Therefore, they become weaker rivals and present weaker constraints on the prices set for new products. As the returns from promotional activities decline with the appearance of generic rivals, there is less substitutability between that branded drug and the newly introduced one, which reduces the demand elasticity for the latter. Higher relative launch prices result, which we also test in the empirical analysis below.

In addition to effects on relative launch prices, we are also concerned with the impact of generic competition on price changes over time. Various studies have reported that generic drug prices decline as the number of these sellers increases (see Caves et al. (1991, pp. 36–37) and Wiggins and Maness (1995)). As this process continues, the original branded product is therefore an increasingly weak rival. Thus we examine whether price changes over time for new products are affected by changes in generic competition.

IV. Empirical Analysis

A. *Equations and Variables*

To investigate how prices for new drugs are set relative to existing substitute(s) and also how they change over time, we specify the following regression equations:

$$\begin{aligned} LRELP = {} & \beta_0 + \beta_1 RATEA + \beta_2 RATEB \\ & + \beta_3 ACUTE + \beta_4 LNUM(0) \\ & + \beta_5 [DGEN \text{ or } LPGN] + \epsilon \end{aligned} \tag{1}$$

$$\begin{aligned} LRATIO(t) = {} & \delta_0 + \delta_1 RATEA + \delta_2 RATEB \\ & + \delta_3 ACUTE + \delta_4 LNUM(t) \\ & + \delta_5 DALP + \delta_6 DBLP + \delta_7 DCLP \\ & + \delta_8 [DCHGEN(t) \text{ or } LCHPGN(t)] \\ & + e \end{aligned} \tag{2}$$

The variables are defined as follows:

LRELP = Natural logarithm of the ratio of the introductory price of a new drug to the aver-

[5] See Frank and Salkever (1992) and Hung (1994) for further discussion and evidence on this type of conduct.

age price of existing brand name substitutes

LRATIO(t) = Natural logarithm of the ratio of the real price, deflated by the consumer price index (CPI), of a new drug t years after introduction to its real introductory price (t = 4, 6, or 8)[6–8]

RATEA = Dummy variable that equals 1 if a new drug receives an FDA rating of A

RATEB = Dummy variable that equals 1 if a new drug receives an FDA rating of B

RATEC = Dummy variable that equals 1 if a new drug receives an FDA rating of C

ACUTE = Dummy variable that equals 1 if a new drug is indicated for an acute illness

LNUM(t) = Natural logarithm of the number of existing brand name substitutes after t years (t = 0, 4, 6, 8)

DALP = Interactive variable equaling the product of *RATEA* and *LRELP*

DBLP = Interactive variable equaling the product of *RATEB* and *LRELP*

DCLP = Interactive variable equaling the product of *RATEC* and *LRELP*

DGEN = Dummy variable that equals 1 if a brand name substitute has a generic rival at the time of the new product's introduction

DCHGEN(t) = Dummy variable that equals 1 if any brand name substitute has a generic rival after t years when there was none at the new product's introduction

LPGN = Natural logorithm of the percentage of brand name substitutes that have a generic rival at the new product's introduction, where the percentage is expressed as a whole number plus 1[9]

LINPGN = Product of the number of existing brand name substitutes at introduction and *LPGN*

LCHPGN(t) = Natural logarithm of the ratio of the percentage of brand name substitutes that have a generic rival after t years to the same percentage at the time of the new product's introduction, where the percentages are expressed as whole numbers plus 1 (t = 4, 6, 8)

We determine the price of a drug by one of four methods, depending on the means by which it is administered. For systemic drugs indicated in acute but nonemergency situations, it is the maximum recommended daily dosage multiplied by the unit price. For systemic drugs used in chronic conditions, it is the maximum recommended maintenance daily dosage multiplied by the unit price. The unit price is obtained by dividing the price for the largest pack size by its quantity. On average, the larger the pack size, the smaller the unit price, although the difference is small.

For topical agents such as creams, lotions, and ophthalmic solutions, the price is obtained by dividing the average wholesale price for the largest pack size by its weight or volume. Finally, for drugs used in emergency or life-threatening situations, price is the cost per course of treatment, such as per injection or per IV infusion.[10] The average price for existing substitutes is simply the mean value of each substitute's price. It would have been better to use the substitutes' market shares as weights, but the required data were not available.[11]

The therapeutic advance associated with a new drug is measured by the FDA ratings of new products:

Class A: Important therapeutic gain: Drug may provide effective therapy (by virtue of greatly increased efficacy or safety) for a disease not adequately treated or diagnosed by any marketed drug, or provide markedly improved treatment of a disease through improved efficacy or safety (including decreased abuse potential).

Class B: Modest therapeutic gain: Drug has a modest but real advantage over other available marketed drugs; for example, somewhat greater effectiveness, decreased adverse reactions, more convenient route of administration, etc.

Class C: Little or no therapeutic gain. Essentially duplicates in medical importance and therapy for one or more already existing drugs.

The FDA rankings have been subject to some criticism. Not only are assessments based on these rankings not internally consistent (Grabowski (1976, pp. 24–25)), but also they are made at the conclusion of the approval process and before the drug is used in practice. This second consideration can have an important effect on the appraisal of a new drug (Wardell et al. (1980)).

Because of these concerns, we compare the FDA rankings with those of two other studies that use panels of experts to determine the therapeutic advance from specific pharmaceuticals. Wardell and his colleagues surveyed 78 specialist physicians at the University of Rochester Medical Center, using their responses to divide new drugs into the same three categories defined by the FDA, and compared the two sets of results. Their most recent period, 1970 through 1976, is closest to our sample period, so we look primarily at drugs

[6] Let P^t be the nominal price for a new drug introduced in year t and ${}^rP_t$ the real price. By definition ${}^rP_t = P^t/\text{CPI}^t$. *RATIO*(4) = ${}^rP^{t+4}/{}^rP^t$ is the ratio of the real price 4 years after introduction to the real price at time of introduction. *RATIO*(6) and *RATIO*(8) are defined for 6 and 8 years, respectively. Therefore, when *RATIO* > 1, the real price has increased, whereas if *RATIO* < 1, the real price has fallen.

[7] Data for the CPI, with base year 1982, are from the Economic Report (1992).

[8] Equation (2) is estimated for three periods covering 4, 6 and 8 years after introduction.

[9] Because the logarithm of zero is undefined, we add 1 to the underlying values in order to use this transformation.

[10] Although the resulting prices refer to different quantity measures, they are homogeneous within treatment classes, which permits the determination of relative prices.

[11] Note that if the sales leader among these products sets an above-average price, as might occur, then the substitute product average price is understated. See footnote 19 for the relevance of this consideration.

introduced in those years. In their sample of 77 new pharmaceuticals, the Wardell panel reported a larger proportion incorporating modest therapeutic gains than did the FDA rankings: 49% against 38%. On the other hand, they found fewer new drugs with important gains: 16% as compared to 26%; and they found fewer with little or no gain: 30% rather than 36% (See Wardell et al. (1980, table III, p. 86)). Thus the FDA rankings have a larger variance than the Wardell rankings.

Schweitzer (1993) also employed panels of experts to determine "important" new drugs. His respondents included both American and French physicians. Requiring a modicum of agreement between the two groups before a drug is selected, he found a group of 32 drugs that met his criterion. Then, of products "thought to have been especially important, only 10 were designated A by the FDA; 13 were designated B; and 9 were designated C" (Schweitzer, (1993, p. 15)). In that study as well, there were important differences between therapeutic designations made after products have been used and those made by the FDA during the approval process.

These studies suggest that the FDA rankings may be a better index of therapeutic advance evaluated at introduction than subsequently, and also that there are likely to be measurement errors in the designations. Still they provide an independent source of information on this attribute, which has been used by other researchers (see in particular Reekie (1978)).

The variable *ACUTE* equals 1 if a new drug is indicated for an acute illness, but 0 when used for chronic conditions. In this study we define an acute condition as any ailment that generally lasts no more than three months. For many drugs it is straightforward to determine whether they are used in acute or chronic conditions, but for others it is not. Some drugs can be used in both conditions (e.g., many dermatological agents), but the recommended dosages are different depending on the usage. After consulting *Drug Facts and Comparisons,* we adopt the following rule: if a drug can be used in both acute and chronic conditions, only the dosage used in long-term treatment is selected to determine its daily cost, and it is assumed to be used for chronic conditions.

Finally, we measure competition from branded rivals by the number of brand name substitutes used for the same or similar purposes. But we have two variables for generic competition: the first is simply the presence or absence of a generic rival, and the second is the percentage of branded rivals with generic competition. As more branded products encounter generic competition, the perceived substitutability of these rivals may decline with attendant effects on the relative launch prices of new drugs.[12]

[12] We also test an alternate specification, which is an interaction variable between the number of branded substitutes and the logarithm of the percentage with generic competition.

B. The Data

To estimate the model, we compile a data set on 144 new molecular entities (NMEs) introduced into the U.S. market between 1978 and 1987. The names of NMEs introduced before 1984 along with their indications, the date of FDA approval, their therapeutic rating, and the normal means of administration were gathered from Food and Drug Administration (1985).[13] Data on NMEs introduced after 1984 are obtained from a study of drug lags between the United States and the United Kingdom (Lasagna et al. (1989))

Approximately 195 NMEs were launched between 1978 and 1987. From this number, we exclude about one fourth for various reasons. First, ten antineoplastic agents are deleted because these drugs are more frequently used in combination than alone. They are actually complements to established drugs rather than substitutes. Seven anesthetics are also excluded because their dosage requirement varies greatly among individual patients, depending on the conditions for which they are used. Drugs in other categories also have individualized dosage requirements, but the usual range is well defined and the maximum dosage can be computed more easily. A third category of excluded products consists of seven diagnostic devices because they are not therapeutic agents. Five contact lens products are also excluded for the same reason. Finally, 22 other drugs are eliminated because data on prices or other variables are not available for the entire period.

To find the appropriate substitutes for a new drug, we first consider generally the extent of substitutability among pharmaceutical products. Prior empirical studies grouped drugs into large therapeutic classes such as antibiotics or antihypertensives. Substitutability across these boundaries was then regarded as zero, while drugs within each class were viewed as perfect substitutes.

However, that definition of substitutability is far too broad. Within each therapeutic category, substitutes fall into smaller groups that are defined by a precise indication, side effect profiles, and mechanism of action. As the number of drugs in a therapeutic category increases, domains of high substitutability between them become smaller and smaller. For example, the first calcium channel blocker, Verapamil (Calan), faced competition from other drugs indicated in hypertension and angina pectoris, such as the beta blockers. When the second calcium channel blocker, Nifedipine (Procardia), was introduced, its main competitor was not the beta blockers but rather Verapamil. This is not to say that competition between calcium channel blockers and beta blockers no longer existed, but rather that competition within each subgroup of drugs was more intense. Including all products in a therapeutic category as substitutes of a new drug misrepresents the particular close substitutes of the drug and hence the extent of competition that it actually faces.

[13] The FDA has stopped rating the therapeutic improvement of new drugs, so more recent data are unavailable.

After consulting with several pharmacology references,[14] we define substitutability by the following criteria: substitutable drugs must have the same indication (e.g., antihypertension) and the same or similar route of administration.[15] In addition, mutually substitutable drugs must meet at least one of the following two criteria:

1. Their mechanisms of action are the same or similar (e.g., two different classes are beta blockers and ACE inhibitors).
2. They belong to the same broadly defined chemical class (e.g., antidepressants belonging to the class of tricyclic compounds). Usually drugs with a similar chemical structure or the same mechanism of action also share similar side effect profiles, although this is not always the case.

For most of the new drugs included in this study, substitutes were identified in this way. For a relatively few, the above criteria could not be met. The following alternative criteria are then applied:

1. They share the same indication.
2. Their routes of administration are the same or similar.
3. The older drug was the most commonly prescribed medicine among all that satisfy the first two requirements in the year immediately preceding the introduction of the new drug.

By checking comprehensive references published in various years, one can determine a "drug of choice" for a given illness at a particular time. Furthermore, *Pharmacy Times*, a monthly journal for pharmacists, publishes each April the names and rankings of the top 200 prescription drugs. These annual listings are also used to determine which of the existing drugs met the third criterion.

Using these criteria, 130 out of 144 NMEs were found with at least one branded substitute. For the remaining 14 drugs no substitute was identified. Appendix 1 lists the therapeutic classes from which close substitutes of new drugs are selected, and appendix 2 lists the NMEs for which there were no close substitutes at the time of introduction.[16]

For the drugs in our sample and also their close substitutes, we collected their average wholesale prices (AWP) from *Drug Topics Red Book*. To be sure, this source reports list prices rather than transaction prices, where the latter typically reflect discounts "off list" that are different for different buyers. If the structure of discounts is not widely different across products, then the AWP is an index of the many prices charged for the same product.[17]

Limited data on actual pharmacy acquisition costs (PAC) were obtained over a number of years for a small sample of nine products.[18] The simple correlation coefficients across time for each drug between PAC and AWP averaged 0.99; and the correlation coefficients between percentage changes in these variables for periods of four years or more averaged 0.90. However, we did find that larger discounts are typically given for older drugs. As a result, the price of a new drug relative to its older substitutes, as determined from AWP data, is likely to be understated and the reported rates of price increase are overstated.[19]

V. Empirical Findings

A. *Summary Statistics*

Tables 1 and 2 contain summary statistics for new drugs introduced from 1978 to 1987. On average, the more therapeutically significant a new drug is, as determined by the FDA ratings, the higher its relative price at introduction. The average relative launch price for A drugs is over 3, whereas for B and C drugs, it is just over 2 and 1, respectively. Since the standard deviations for relative introductory prices are large, the differences among the three classes are not statistically significant at conventional levels. Furthermore, the median price relatives reveal a similar pattern. In particular, the medium relative introductory price for C drugs is just below 1, indicating that on average imitative drugs are introduced at a similar price to existing drugs with the same indication.

During this period, a great majority of the new drugs rated A and B were introduced with premiums: 77% for A drugs and 79% for B drugs. On the other hand, a majority of drugs rated C were introduced with discounts: 51%. These patterns are similar to those reported by Reekie (1978) for an earlier period. Note also that drugs used for acute conditions tend to have higher premiums than those indicated for chronic conditions. This result applies to all three classes of new drugs.

Class A drugs also tend to have fewer substitutes over their life cycles. The reported average number of existing substitutes is 1 for such drugs, 2.63 for B drugs, and nearly 4 for C drugs. The average number of *additional* substitutes after eight years is 0.67 for A drugs, 2.05 for B drugs, and 1.80 for C drugs. This latter finding suggests that "imita-

[14] Goodman and Gilman's *Pharmacological Basis of Therapeutics* (1975, 1980, 1985, 1990), the American Medical Association (various editions), and, most helpful of all, *Drug Facts and Comparisons* (various editions).

[15] Administering a drug intravenously (IV) and intramuscularly (IM) are considered similar routes of administration for the purpose of this study, but IV and IM continuous infusions are not.

[16] These appendices are available from the authors upon request.

[17] The period covered in this study largely predates the rapid growth of managed care, which is relevant because it led to much greater price discounting. For this reason, the results presented here may not fully represent current conditions in pharmaceutical markets.

[18] Two of these products were excluded from the correlation analysis because there were fewer than four yearly observations for each of them.

[19] This empirical analysis is reported in Lu (1993, chap. 6). Note, however, that another factor may have the opposite effect and thereby ameliorate the understatement of the relative launch price variable. If the denominator of the *LRELP* variable is understated, as suggested in footnote 11, then *LRELP* itself is overstated.

TABLE 1.—SUMMARY STATISTICS FOR THREE TYPES OF NMEs

	Therapeutic Rating								
	A			B			C		
	Combined $n = 13$	Chronic $n = 10$	Acute $n = 3$	Combined $n = 48$	Chronic $n = 29$	Acute $n = 19$	Combined $n = 69$	Chronic $n = 53$	Acute $n = 16$
Relative launch price									
Mean	3.11 (2.47)	3.11 (2.76)	3.12 (0.88)	2.21 (2.53)	1.63 (1.14)	3.09 (3.65)	1.15 (0.78)	1.07 (0.80)	1.37 (0.68)
Median	2.47	2.07	2.97	1.35	1.19	1.72	0.97	0.94	1.23
Range	0.2–8.08	0.2–8.08	2.32–4.07	0.25–13.6	0.48–5.97	0.4–13.6	0.37–6.0	0.37–6.0	0.55–3.13
Average number of branded substitutes									
$t = 0$	1 (0)	1 (0)	1 (0)	2.63 (2.120)	2.66 (2.21)	2.58 (1.98)	3.78 (2.04)	3.81 (2.21)	3.67 (1.40)
$t = 4$	1.31 (0.63)	1.3 (0.67)	1.33 (0.58)	3.77 (2.97)	3.66 (3.09)	3.95 (2.95)	5.07 (2.65)	5.09 (2.84)	5.00 (1.97)
$t = 6$	1.25 (0.45)	1.22 (0.44)	1.33 (0.58)	4.54 (3.37)	4.37 (3.43)	4.79 (3.36)	5.47 (2.88)	5.52 (3.08)	5.31 (2.21)
$t = 8$	1.67 (0.71)	1.67 (0.82)	1.67 (0.58)	4.68 (3.21)	4.61 (3.29)	4.77 (3.22)	5.58 (2.92)	5.67 (3.10)	5.33 (2.35)
Ratio of substitutes with generic competition									
$t = 0$	0.15 (0.38)	0.20 (0.42)	0 (0)	0.19 (0.35)	0.17 (0.33)	0.21 (0.39)	0.20 (0.30)	0.20 (0.29)	0.20 (0.31)
$t = 4$	0.31 (0.43)	0.25 (0.42)	0.50 (0.50)	0.27 (0.36)	0.26 (0.33)	0.29 (0.42)	0.34 (0.32)	0.37 (0.31)	0.23 (0.31)
$t = 6$	0.38 (0.43)	0.33 (0.43)	0.50 (0.50)	0.27 (0.33)	0.29 (0.32)	0.23 (0.35)	0.40 (0.31)	0.45 (0.30)	0.23 (0.32)
$t = 8$	0.35 (0.35)	0.39 (0.38)	0.25 (0.35)	0.27 (0.32)	0.26 (0.27)	0.29 (0.39)	0.41 (0.32)	0.45 (0.29)	0.30 (0.37)

Notes: (1) n refers to the number of observations in the introductory period. The number of observations may be lower for later periods after introduction.
(2) Standard deviations are in parentheses.

tion" is not particularly common in the pharmaceutical industry.

While table 1 focuses on price relatives at the time of introduction, table 2 reports rates of change in product prices after accounting for the general rate of inflation. As indicated, the real price for a chronic A drug grew at the slowest pace, whereas that for a chronic C drug grew fastest. Eight years after introduction, the median real price for a chronic A drug had fallen by 14%, whereas the median real price for a chronic C drug had increased by more than 60%. Except for A drugs, real prices for chronic drugs rose faster than for acute drugs. The median price increase for acute B drugs was negative after both four and six years, indicating that the average real price for acute B drugs actually declines for a few years following introduction. We suspect that the discrepancy for A drugs as between chronic and acute drugs results from there being only three acute A drugs in the sample.

B. *Regression Results*

Tables 3 and 4 present the empirical results from estimating equations (1) and (2), respectively. Looking first at table 3, we find that the explanatory variables are all statistically significant with the expected signs, although only at the 10% level for A drugs. The intercept term represents C drugs used for chronic conditions. Compared with this baseline groups, the most therapeutically innovative drugs have the highest initial price premium as compared with their existing substitutes. The typical premium on B drugs is greater than for C drugs, but smaller than for A drugs. Drugs indicated for acute conditions also have larger premiums over their substitutes than chronic drugs.

Furthermore, the number of branded substitutes has a substantial negative effect on actual launch prices, which reveals the importance of competitive factors on the introductory price of new drugs. From the third equation, increasing

TABLE 2.—RATIOS OF INFLATION-ADJUSTED PRICES OVER 4, 6, AND 8 YEARS SINCE INTRODUCTION

FDA Rating	Type of Drug	Price Changes after 4 Years			Price Changes after 6 Years			Price Changes after 8 Years		
		Median	Means	Range	Median	Means	Range	Median	Means	Range
A	Chronic	0.87	0.92 (0.17)	0.68–1.19	0.86	0.96 (0.27)	0.63–1.32	0.86	1.02 (0.37)	0.59–1.53
	Acute	1.11	1.06 (0.23)	0.81–1.26	1.05	1.0 (0.39)	0.6–1.37	1.21	1.21 (0.16)	1.1–1.33
	Combined	0.87	0.95 (0.19)	0.68–1.26	0.91	0.97 (0.23)	0.6–1.37	0.98	1.07 (0.33)	0.59–1.53
B	Chronic	1.18	1.13 (0.16)	0.84–1.42	1.28	1.25 (0.20)	0.85–1.56	1.38	1.37 (0.23)	0.9–1.74
	Acute	0.95	1.0 (0.20)	0.79–1.59	0.98	1.08 (0.30)	0.75–1.91	1.3	1.25 (0.42)	0.69–2.1
	Combined	1.09	1.08 (0.19)	0.79–1.59	1.23	1.18 (0.26)	0.75–1.91	1.38	1.32 (0.32)	0.69–2.1
C	Chronic	1.26	1.26 (0.30)	0.68–2.01	1.40	1.49 (0.40)	0.74–2.45	1.61	1.74 (0.62)	0.71–3.7
	Acute	1.04	1.11 (0.26)	0.81–1.71	1.16	1.14 (0.34)	0.74–1.92	1.4	1.24 (0.39)	0.68–1.77
	Combined	1.22	1.23 (0.29)	0.68–2.01	1.38	1.41 (0.41)	0.74–2.45	1.55	1.62 (0.61)	0.68–3.7

Note: Standard deviations are in parentheses.

TABLE 3.—DETERMINANTS OF RELATIVE INTRODUCTORY PRICES

Constant	*RATEA*	*RATEB*	*ACUTE*	*LNUM(0)*	*DGEN*	*LPGN*
0.295 (2.32)[a]	0.374 (1.76)	0.267 (2.13)[b]	0.334 (2.75)[a]	−0.322 (3.75)[a]	—	—
R^2 = 0.27; adjusted R^2 = 0.25; N = 130						
0.230 (1.82)	0.388 (1.87)	0.293 (2.39)[b]	0.336 (2.84)[a]	−0.386 (4.45)[a]	0.332 (2.78)[a]	—
R^2 = 0.32; adjusted R^2 = 0.29; N = 130						
0.221 (1.76)	0.387 (1.88)	0.285 (2.34)[b]	0.335 (2.84)[a]	−0.376 (4.41)[a]	—	0.0857 (2.96)[a]
R^2 = 0.32; adjusted R^2 = 0.29; N = 130						

Notes: Values in parentheses are *t*-ratios.
[a] Statistically significant at the 1% level (two-tailed test).
[b] Statistically significant at the 5% level (two-tailed test).

TABLE 4.—DETERMINANTS OF RATES OF CHANGE OF REAL PRICES

	$t = 4$			$t = 6$			$t = 8$		
Constant	0.302 (6.56)[a]	0.295 (6.00)[a]	0.300 (6.23)[a]	0.490 (7.59)[a]	0.481 (6.99)[a]	0.486 (7.18)[a]	0.709 (7.12)[a]	0.686 (6.86)[a]	0.699 (7.00)[a]
RATEA	−0.339 (4.14)[a]	−0.337 (4.08)[a]	−0.339 (4.11)[a]	−0.491 (4.23)[a]	−0.490 (4.21)[a]	−0.491 (4.21)[a]	−0.562 (3.40)[a]	−0.578 (3.52)[a]	−0.578 (3.49)[a]
RATEB	−0.092 (2.15)[b]	−0.092 (2.12)[b]	−0.093 (2.16)[b]	−0.124 (2.14)[b]	−0.121 (2.08)[b]	−0.123 (2.12)[b]	−0.166 (1.95)	−0.166 (1.93)	−0.172 (2.01)[b]
ACUTE	−0.055 (1.33)	−0.052 (1.26)	−0.054 (1.29)	−0.146 (2.70)[a]	−0.140 (2.50)[b]	−0.143 (2.53)[b]	−0.132 (1.68)	−0.091 (1.10)	−0.101 (1.21)
DALP	−0.0072 (0.13)	−0.00809 (0.15)	−0.00735 (0.13)	−0.0104 (0.14)	−0.0134 (0.18)	−0.0117 (0.15)	−0.032 (0.33)	−0.0396 (0.42)	−0.0384 (0.40)
DBLP	−0.108 (2.50)[b]	−0.107 (2.47)[b]	−0.106 (2.46)[b]	−0.0978 (1.57)	−0.0980 (1.56)	−0.0982 (1.56)	−0.115 (1.33)	−0.123 (1.44)	−0.122 (1.42)
DCLP	−0.139 (2.66)[a]	−0.136 (2.57)[a]	−0.138 (2.62)[a]	−0.183 (2.66)[a]	−0.179 (2.57)[a]	−0.181 (2.61)[a]	−0.234 (2.48)[b]	−0.221 (2.35)[b]	−0.226 (2.38)[b]
LNUM(t)	−0.0769 (2.82)[a]	−0.0754 (2.74)[a]	−0.0765 (2.79)[a]	−0.100 (2.73)[a]	−0.100 (2.72)[a]	−0.101 (2.72)[a]	−0.158 (2.87)[a]	−0.182 (3.20)[a]	−0.178 (3.06)[a]
LCHPGN(t)	—	0.00439 (0.39)	—	—	0.00609 (0.41)	—	—	0.0337 (1.50)	—
DCHGEN(t)	—	—	0.0023 (0.05)	—	—	0.0102 (0.18)	—	—	0.836 (1.05)
R^2	0.25	0.25	0.25	0.32	0.32	0.32	0.29	0.31	0.30
Adjusted R^2	0.21	0.20	0.20	0.27	0.27	0.27	0.23	0.24	0.23
N	130	130	130	114	114	114	85	85	85

Notes: Values in parentheses are *t*-ratios.
[a] Statistically significant at the 1% level (two-tailed test).
[b] Statistically significant at the 5% level (two-tailed test).

the number of direct substitutes from one to two leads on average to a 38% decline in the ratio of a product's launch price to the average price of its predecessors; while increasing the number of substitutes from two to three leads to a 19% decline.

Competition from branded rivals has the expected depressing effect on launch prices, while generic competition apparently has the opposite effect. The second equation in table 3 includes a dummy variable for products whose rivals face generic competition, and as indicated there, its effect on average launch prices is strongly positive. We find a similar result when generic competition is measured by the percentage of branded substitutes with generic rivals.[20] These results suggest that firms set higher launch prices for new drugs when they face weakened competition from branded rivals, which frequently accompanies generic entry.

[20] When the impact of generic competition is measured by the interaction variable *LINPGN*, the estimated regression coefficient is 0.0163 with a *t* value of 2.19. While the remaining coefficients in the equation are similar to those reported above, this specification does not fit the underlying data quite as well as those reported in table 3; the adjusted R^2 is slightly lower at 0.27.

Turning to table 4, which deals with rates of price change following introduction, the primary explanatory variables are again statistically significant, except for B drugs after eight years. As anticipated, the estimated coefficients on A drugs are negative, while the coefficients on B drugs are also negative but with much smaller values. Furthermore, the estimated coefficients on A drugs are fairly close in value to the intercepts, although of opposite sign, which suggests that prices are fairly stable for these products. For B drugs, the estimated coefficients are much smaller, implying a slower pace of price increase. For C drugs, price changes are measured by the estimated intercept, which has a positive value in all cases.

The impact of competition from branded products is indicated by the coefficient of *LNUM*(*t*), which measures the number of direct substitutes after four, six, and eight years. These coefficients are negative and highly significant in all cases. More numerous rivals have the expected effect of slowing price increases.

Two variables reflect changes in generic competition from the level found at the new product's introduction. While the estimated coefficients are positive, they are never statistically significant. We conclude, therefore, that expanding generic competition has no significant effect on the rate of price increase for new products.

The remaining variables pertain to the relation between the introductory price relative and subsequent price changes for the three classes of products. The estimated coefficients are not significant for A drugs and inconsistent for B drugs, but clearly significant for C drugs. For those products, larger price increases were found among drugs introduced at relatively low levels. Finally, there is evidence that the prices of drugs used for acute conditions rise more slowly than for those indicated for chronic conditions.

These empirical results support the following conclusions. Therapeutically innovative drugs are generally introduced under a skimming strategy under which prices decline moderately over time. On the other hand, imitative drugs are typically launched under a penetration strategy which leads to an upward sloping price curve over time. When there are more branded substitutes, prices are lower, while generic competition leads typically to higher relative launch prices for new products although not to subsequent higher rates of price increase.

C. Dynamics of Drug Prices

Figures 1 and 2, which refer separately to acute and chronic conditions, summarize the price dynamics implicit in the estimated equations. The average price of existing substitutes in these diagrams is normalized to 1. The intercepts are then the median values of the price relatives for each type of drug. We multiply the median value of each explanatory variable in equation (2) by the relevant regression coefficient to obtain the values shown in these charts.[21]

FIGURE 1—REAL PRICES FOR NEW DRUGS INDICATED IN ACUTE CONDITIONS (SEMILOG SCALE)

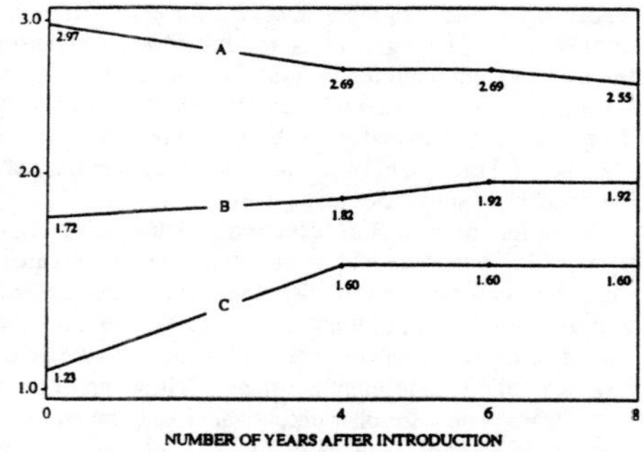

FIGURE 2—REAL PRICES FOR NEW DRUGS INDICATED IN CHRONIC CONDITIONS (SEMILOG SCALE)

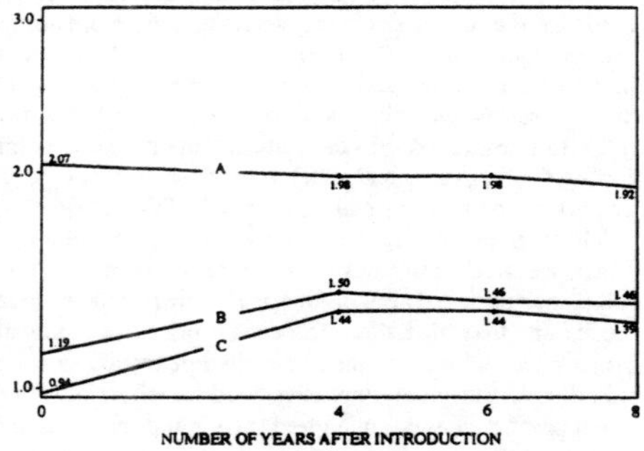

For drugs indicated for acute conditions, figure 1 reveals that real prices for A drugs decline somewhat over time, whereas real prices for C drugs increase slightly. For chronic drugs, the results are shown in figure 2. As pictured there, the real price for an A drug again declines, whereas the real price for a C drug generally increases.

VI. Conclusions and Policy Implications

Pharmaceutical price behavior appears to follow Dean's, (1969) original conjecture: a modified skimming strategy is pursued when launching a significant innovation, while a penetration strategy is used when introducing an imitative product. In our sample of new drugs, a great majority of class A and B drugs were launched with substantial price premiums over their existing substitutes, while a majority of

[21] In these computations, the change in generic competition is measured by *DCHGEN*(*t*).

class C drugs were launched at prices at or below those of their substitutes. Drugs indicated for acute conditions had larger premiums than those indicated for chronic illnesses, controlling for the degree of therapeutic advance. Over time, the average real price for an A drug declined slightly, while for a C drug, it increased substantially. The real price for a B drug rose more than that for an A drug but less than that for a C drug. And the extent of any price increase was limited by the number of substitutes in the market.

There has been public discussion of introducing regulations to limit the rate of pharmaceutical price increases to that of the consumer price index. In effect, such a regulation would discourage penetration strategies. The big losers would be the producers of "me-too" drugs, who would then have to follow a skimming strategy. These products are important avenues for pharmaceutical price competition. As our empirical results indicate, *both the introductory price and subsequent price increases are lower when there are more branded substitutes in the market.* Despite claims that prescribing physicians care little about prices, there is evidence that prices are lower when there are more competing products. Without the entry of close substitutes, the launch prices of innovative drugs would be higher, and also their prices would fall at a slower rate (or rise at a faster rate). Imitative products constitute an important competitive force in pharmaceutical markets and should not be disdained, as some policy makers have seen fit to do.[22]

These findings also suggest that total expenditures on pharmaceuticals may have little connection with rates of price change on existing products. The critical factor here is the extent to which the introductory prices of innovative drugs exceed those of their less therapeutically advanced substitutes. But more innovative products show few subsequent price increases, and indeed their real prices tend to fall after introduction. Furthermore, their introductory prices generally reflect the extent of their therapeutic advance. Our findings support the conclusion that higher expenditures on pharmaceuticals result primarily from the introduction of more effective products.

REFERENCES

American Medical Association, *Drug Evaluations* (Chicago, various years).

Bagwell, K., and M. H. Riordan, "High and Declining Prices Signal Product Quality," *American Economic Review* 81 (Mar. 1991), 224–239.

Bass, F. M., "A New Product Growth Model for Consumer Durables," *Management Science* 15 (1969), 215–227.

Caves, R. E., M. D. Whinston, and M. A. Hurwitz, "Patent Expiration, Entry, and Competition in the U.S. Pharmaceutical Industry," *Brookings Papers on Economic Activity: Microeconomics* (1991), 3–65.

Comanor, W. S., "The Political Economy of the Pharmaceutical Industry," *Journal of Economic Literature* 24 (Sept. 1986), 1178–1217.

Comanor, W. S., and S. O. Schweitzer, "Pharmaceuticals," in W. Adams and J. W. Brock (eds.), *The Structure of American Industry*, 9th ed. (Englewood Cliffs, NJ: Prentice-Hall, 1995), chap. 7, 177–196.

22 See the recent paper by the U.S. Commissioner of Food and Drugs, Kessler et al. (1994).

Dean, J. "Pricing Pioneering Products," *Journal of Industrial Economics* 17 (1969), 165–179.

Dolan, R., and A. Jeuland, "Experience Curves and Dynamic Demand Models: Implications for Optimal Pricing Strategies," *Journal of Marketing* 45 (Winter 1981), 52–62.

Drugs Facts and Comparisons (St. Louis, MO: Lippincott, Facts and Comparisons Division, 1977–1993).

Drug Topics Red Book (Montvale, NJ: Medical Economics Data, 1978–1993).

Eaton, B. C., and R. G. Lipsey, "Product Differentiation," in R. Schmalensee and R. W. Willig (eds.), *Handbook of Industrial Organization*, vol. I (North Holland: 1989), chap. 12, 723–768.

Economic Report of the President (Feb. 1992), table-B56, p. 361.

Food and Drug Administration, *New Drug Evaluation Statistical Report* (Washington, DC: Dept. of Health and Human Services, 1985).

Frank, R. E., and D. S. Salkever, "Pricing, Patent Loss, and the Market for Pharmaceuticals," *Southern Economic Journal* 59 (Oct. 1992), 165–179.

——— "Generic Entry and the Pricing of Pharmaceuticals," unpublished paper (Aug. 23, 1995).

Goodman, L., and L. Gillman. *The Pharmacological Basis of Therapeutics*, (New York: Macmillan, 1975, 1980, 1985, 1990).

Grabowski, H. G., *Drug Regulation and Innovation: Empirical Analysis and Policy Options* (Washington, DC: American Enterprise Institute, 1976).

Grabowski, H. G., and J. M. Vernon, "Brand Loyalty, Entry, and Price Competition in Pharmaceuticals after the 1984 Drug Act," *Journal of Law and Economics* 35 (Oct. 1992), 331–350.

Hung, C. S., "On Monopoly Power in a Differentiated Product Industry," *Review of Industrial Organization* 9 (Aug. 1994), 425–433.

Kessler, David A., Janet L. Rose, Robert J. Temple, Renie Shapiro, and Joseph P. Griffin, "Therapeutic Class Wars—Drug Promotion in a Competitive Marketplace," *New England Journal of Medicine* 331:20 (Nov. 17, 1994), 1350–1353.

Krouse, Clement G., *Theory of Industrial Economics* (Cambridge, MA: Basil Blackwell, 1990).

Lasagna, L., K. I. Kaiton, N. Mattison, and F. K. Northington, "The Drug Lag: An Update of New Drug Introductions in the U.S. and in the U.K., 1977 through 1987," *Clinical Pharmacology & Therapeutics* 46:2 (Aug. 1989), 121–138.

Lu, Z. J., "Strategic Pricing of Patented New Drugs," unpublished Ph.D. dissertation, University of California at Santa Barbara (Aug. 1993).

Pharmacy Times (various editions).

Rao, V. R., "Pricing Research in Marketing: The State of the Art," *Journal of Business* 57 (1984), 39–64.

Reekie, W. D., *Pricing New Pharmaceutical Products* (London, Croom Helm, 1977).

——— "Price and Quality Competition in the United States Drug Industry," *Journal of Industrial Economics* 26 (Mar. 1978), 223–237.

Robinson, B., and C. Lakhani, "Dynamic Pricing Models for New Product Pricing," *Management Science* 21 (June 1975), 1113–1122.

Schmalensee, R., "Product Differentiation Advantages of Pioneering Brands," *American Economic Review* 72 (June 1982), 349–365.

Schweitzer, S. O., "An International Comparison of the Approval of New Pharmaceuticals," Research Program in Pharmaceutical Economics and Policy, UCLA (Oct. 3, 1993).

Shapiro, C., "Optimal Pricing of Experience Goods," *Bell Journal of Economics* 14 (Autumn 1983), 497–507.

Simon, H., *Price Management* (Amsterdam: Elsevier, 1989).

Stuart, B., et al. "Patterns of Outpatient Prescription Drug Use among Pennsylvania Elderly," *Health Care Financing Review* 12:3 (Spring 1991), 61–72.

Suslow, V. Y., "Are There Better Ways to Spell Relief: A Hedonic Pricing Analysis of Ulcer Drugs," School of Business Administration, University of Michigan (Oct. 1993).

Taylor, T. N., "Factors Affecting Prescription Drug Utilization," The Upjohn Company (Jan. 1993).

U.S. Senate, Subcommittee on Antitrust and Monopoly. *Hearings on Competitive Problems in the Drug Industry*, pt. 5 (Washington, DC: U.S. Government Printing Office, 1968) p. 1566.

Wardell, W. M., J. DiRaddo, and M. Weintraub, "The Measurement of Therapeutic Value," *Journal of Clinical Pharmacology* 20 (Feb. 1980), 77–90.

Weston, J. F., "Pricing in the Pharmaceutical Industry," in R. I. Chien (ed.), *Issues in Pharmaceutical Economics* (Lexington, MA: D.C. Heath, 1979), 71–95.

———"A Survey of the Economics of the Pharmaceutical Industry with Emphasis on Economic Factors in Price Differentials," in *The Effectiveness of Medicines in Containing Dental Care Costs: Impact of Innovation, Regulation, and Quality* (Washington, DC: National Pharmaceutical Council, 1982), 29–46.

Wiggins, S. N., and R. Maness, "Price Competition in Pharmaceuticals: The Case of Anti-Infectives," unpublished paper (Mar. 1995).

[26]

A SIMPLE MODEL OF PHARMACEUTICAL PRICE DYNAMICS*

JAYANTA BHATTACHARYA *Stanford University* *and* *WILLIAM B. VOGT* *Carnegie Mellon University*

ABSTRACT

Branded pharmaceutical firms use price and promotional strategy to manage public knowledge about their drugs. We propose a dynamic theory of pharmaceutical pricing and conduct an exploratory empirical analysis inspired by the theory. Our theory predicts a pattern of increasing prices and decreasing promotional activities over a drug's life cycle. Prices are kept low and advertising levels high early in the life cycle in order to build public knowledge about the drug. As knowledge grows, prices rise and advertising falls. If the management of this stock is important enough, this tendency of prices to rise can overwhelm the price-decreasing effect of entry by generic competitors late in the drug life cycle. We argue that our theory of price dynamics explains empirical regularities in this industry.

I. INTRODUCTION

MOST industrial organization models of competition among firms predict that entry of a new competitor will result in a price decrease. In the market for pharmaceutical drugs, however, the price of a branded drug commonly rises after its patent expires and (lower priced) generic drugs enter the market.[1] The behavior of the original patent holder seems counterintuitive given the usual economic logic of competition.

In this paper, we present a new explanation for this stylized fact. The key to our explanation lies in the pharmaceutical company's dynamic demand management problem. Pricing and advertising strategies set today affect quan-

* Much of the work on this paper was completed while William Vogt was a John M. Olin visiting scholar at the Stigler Center for the Study of the Economy and the State, Graduate School of Business, University of Chicago, for which opportunity he is grateful. We thank Sam Peltzman, Gary Becker, Will Manning, the participants at the ELO and CHAS workshops at the University of Chicago, and the participants at the Health Economics Seminar at RAND for helpful comments. We also wish to thank IMS America for kindly providing the data.

[1] See Richard E. Caves, Michael D. Whinston, & Mark A. Hurwitz, Patent Expiration, Entry, and Competition in the U.S. Pharmaceutical Industry, Brookings Papers Econ. Activity: Microecon. 1 (1991); Henry G. Grabowski & John M. Vernon, Brand Loyalty, Entry, and Price Competition in Pharmaceuticals after the 1984 Drug Act, 35 J. Law & Econ. 331 (1992); and Richard G. Frank & David S. Salkever, Generic Entry and the Pricing of Pharmaceuticals (Working Paper No. 5306, Nat'l Bur. Econ. Res. 1995).

[*Journal of Law and Economics,* vol. XLVI (October 2003)]

tity demanded tomorrow. Patent expiry is an important event in the dynamic program shaping the firm's price and advertising path not only at and after expiry but before that point as well.

Because it is costly to learn about drugs, doctors' prescribing habits are sticky. Consequently, they possess an evolving stock of knowledge about each drug. A central problem for the pharmaceutical company is to shepherd this stock to its best advantage. At any point in time, low prices and high levels of advertising increase quantity demanded, but they also shift up demand at future times, since more doctors gain experience with and knowledge of the product.

Much of the relevant information about a drug is molecule specific rather than manufacturer specific. This means that, after patent expiry, generic entrants enjoy spillover benefits from physicians' stock of knowledge. This reduces the branded manufacturer's incentive to advertise and to keep prices low (both in the postexpiry period and in the run-up to patent expiry).

The solution to the pharmaceutical company's dynamic problem calls for rising prices and falling levels of advertising both before and after patent expiry as it first builds up and then exploits its drug's knowledge stock. There is a discontinuity at the point of patent expiry owing to the increased price competition that generic entry engenders.

In our story, despite the fact that branded prices continue to rise after patent expiry, it is still the case that patent expiry and generic entry have a salutary effect on prices. The price rise over the life cycle of the drug is caused by the pharmaceutical company's response to the inherent dynamics of demand. The price rise after generic entry is not caused by generic entry, as it would happen in any event.

II. Background

The literature on the effects of competition on drug pricing has a long history. In an examination of the effect of new products on the existing pharmaceutical prices, William Comanor[2] concludes that the introduction of new branded and patent-protected products can increase product differentiation in the marketplace and potentially increase prices. Peter Temin[3] agrees with this conclusion, although he uses a different (less theoretically grounded) argument. Sam Peltzman,[4] on the other hand, argues that even though new pharmaceutical products may be introduced at higher prices than the older drugs that are already on the market, the new drugs may nevertheless induce competitive effects that reduce overall drug prices.

[2] William S. Comanor, Research and Competitive Product Differentiation in the Pharmaceutical Industry in the United States, 31 Economica (n.s.) 372 (1964).

[3] Peter Temin, Taking Your Medicine: Drug Regulation in the United States (1980).

[4] Sam Peltzman, An Evaluation of Consumer Protection Legislation: The 1962 Drug Amendments, 81 J. Pol. Econ. 1049 (1973).

Jeffrey Perloff, Valerie Suslow, and Paul Seguin[5] develop a theoretical model of new drug introductions that potentially resolves the dispute among these papers. Following Steven Salop,[6] their model considers firm pricing decisions in a setting where drugs are spatially differentiated. When a new firm enters, whether the price of the existing product rises or falls depends on how closely substitutable the new drug is for the old one. In Bertrand pricing equilibrium, if the new drug is close in product space, then the prices of the old and new drugs will fall relative to the original price of the old drug. On the other hand, if the drugs are moderately differentiated, then drug prices might rise, even if the new and old firms do not collude.

While all of these papers focus on the entry of new and differentiated patented drugs, the recent empirical and theoretical literature on drug pricing tends to focus on the introduction of generic alternatives to branded drugs. Frederic Scherer[7] provides a concise summary of this literature.

Henry Grabowski and John Vernon[8] estimate that branded prices rise both before and after generic entry, albeit more slowly after entry. Conversely, Richard Caves, Michael Whinston, and Mark Hurwitz[9] estimate that the price of a branded drug falls about 2 percent after its patent expires. In a fixed-effects framework, Richard Frank and David Salkever[10] find that branded drug prices rise when generics enter. In a paper using a policy experiment in Germany, Nina Pavcnik[11] finds that the presence of generic drugs acts as a check on branded prices: when the German government enacted a policy exposing consumers to more of the financial consequences of choosing a higher priced drug, branded drug prices fell, and branded drug prices fell more for branded drugs facing more generic competition. Although these papers examine different sets of patented drugs at different times, all of them find that branded drug prices typically rise after patent expiry or fall only weakly. The empirical methodology in the paper by Grabowski and Vernon[12] is most similar to ours, and their results are quite similar to ours as well.

Frank and Salkever[13] present an explanation for the generic competition paradox. Their explanation has by and large become the accepted one for

[5] Jeffrey M. Perloff, Valerie Y. Suslow, & Paul J. Seguin, Higher Prices from Entry: Pricing of Brand-Name Drugs (Working Paper No. CPC99-003, Competition Pol'y Ctr., August 1995).

[6] Steven C. Salop, Monopolistic Competition with Outside Goods, 10 Bell J. Econ. 141 (1979).

[7] F. M. Scherer, Pricing, Profits, and Technological Progress in the Pharmaceutical Industry, 7 J. Econ. Persp. 97 (1993).

[8] Grabowski & Vernon, *supra* note 1.

[9] Caves, Whinston, & Hurwitz, *supra* note 1.

[10] Frank & Salkever, *supra* note 1.

[11] Nina Pavcnik, Do Pharmaceutical Prices Respond to Insurance? (Working Paper No. 7865, Nat'l Bur. Econ. Res., August 2000).

[12] Grabowski & Vernon, *supra* note 1.

[13] Richard G. Frank & David S. Salkever, Pricing, Patent Loss and the Market for Pharmaceuticals, 59 S. Econ. J. 165 (1992).

this puzzle.[14] In their story, the market for pharmaceuticals is segmented. There is a highly price-elastic hospital segment that responds to price changes in either the branded or generic drugs and a less elastic insured consumer segment that responds only to price changes in the branded drug. Before the entry of generics, the branded drug serves both segments; thus, the price elasticity it faces is a mixture of the price elasticities of the two segments. Upon generic entry, the branded drug loses the price-elastic segment to the generic drugs, and this lowers the elasticity of the branded drug's demand curve, which leads to an increase in price. The law of one price fails here because consumers value "quality" attributes associated with the branded drug such as persuasive advertising or perhaps the greater accumulated experience with the branded version.

In empirical work inspired by Frank and Salkever,[15] Scott Stern[16] estimates a nested logit model of demand in the market for gout drugs, for sedatives, and for oral diabetic therapies. He finds that the branded drug's demand becomes steeper with generic entry.

There is a related empirical literature concerning the measurement of pharmaceutical price indexes.[17] Ernst Berndt, Zvi Griliches, and Joshua Rossett[18] and Berndt and Paul Greenberg[19] find that the prices of branded pharmaceuticals rise over each drug's life cycle but that the rate of growth is slower immediately after introduction. Also, Gregory Kelly[20] finds that the prices of "new" drugs fall immediately after introduction. Because he is interested in updating price indexes for new products, his definition of new drugs includes generics.

There are a number of other papers in the pharmaceutical literature that emphasize parts of the dynamic demand management problem facing firms. However, none of these authors note that the solution to this demand management problem, without recourse to other phenomena, explains the generic competition paradox. Berndt and his coauthors[21] specify a model of knowl-

[14] For example, see Scherer, *supra* note 7; or Stern, *infra* note 16.

[15] Frank & Salkever, *supra* note 13.

[16] Scott Stern, When Entry Causes Prices to Rise: An Exploration of Product Demand in Pharmaceutical Markets (unpublished manuscript, Stanford Univ. 1995).

[17] We wish to thank an anonymous referee for suggesting the relevance of this literature to us.

[18] Ernst R. Berndt, Zvi Griliches, & Joshua G. Rossett, Auditing the Producer Price Index: Micro Evidence from Prescription Pharmaceutical Preparations, 11 J. Bus. & Econ. Stat. 251 (1993).

[19] Ernst R. Berndt & Paul E. Greenberg, An Updated and Extended Study of the Price Growth of Prescription Pharmaceutical Preparations, in Competitive Strategies in the Pharmaceutical Industry 35 (R. B. Helms ed. 1995)

[20] Gregory G. Kelly, Improving the PPI Sample for Prescription Pharmaceuticals, Monthly Lab. Rev., October 1997, at 10.

[21] Ernst R. Berndt *et al.*, Information, Marketing, and Pricing in the U.S. Antiulcer Drug Market, 85 Am. Econ. Rev. 100 (1995).

edge stock diffusion in the market for antiulcer medications. They find evidence that advertising by one firm in a therapeutic category increases demand for other drugs in the same category.

The (theoretical) approach of John Hudson[22] is most similar to ours. In his theory, lowering price reduces present profits but raises future demand by increasing the set of patients exposed to the drug. However, his framework does not consider advertising, patent expiry, or the shape of the optimal price path. In a similar paper, David Ridley[23] analyzes the effects of price controls in a market with intertemporal stickiness in demand and applies his model to the pharmaceutical industry.

The most recent paper in this vein is by Andrew Ching.[24] His theoretical model emphasizes learning as an explanation for the slow increase in generic market share after patent expiry. However, like Hudson,[25] he excludes advertising from the model. Most of his theoretical effort is aimed at analyzing price dynamics after patent expiry. When he does focus on the generic competition paradox, he relies on consumer heterogeneity to explain it.

In our paper, stickiness in demand is modeled rather abstractly via a "knowledge stock" variable. Closely related are the literatures on learning by using and switching costs,[26] which generate stickiness in demand in a more detailed micromodels of consumers. In the context of pharmaceuticals, Gregory Crawford and Matthew Shum[27] provide an empirical dynamic learning-by-using model. Andrea Coscelli[28] estimates the effect of physician and patient habit on prescription demand. Finally, in the rational addiction literature (see the paper by Gary Becker and Kevin Murphy,[29] for a start) intertemporal stickiness in demand arises directly out of individuals' utility functions as the marginal utility of future consumption rises in current consumption.

[22] John Hudson, Pricing Dynamics in the Pharmaceutical Industry, 24 Applied Econ. 103 (1992).

[23] David Ridley, The Wrong Prescription: Price Regulation in a Market with Consumer Start-Up Costs (Working paper, Duke Univ., Fuqua Sch. Bus. 2002).

[24] Andrew T. T. Ching, Dynamic Equilibrium in the U.S. Prescription Drug Market after Patent Expiration (unpublished manuscript, Univ. Minnesota, Dep't Econ. 2000).

[25] Hudson, *supra* note 22.

[26] For instance, see Paul Klemperer, Competition When Consumers Have Switching Costs: An Overview with Applications to Industrial Organization, Macroeconomics, and International Trade, 62 Rev. Econ. Stud. 515 (1995); and Edward E. Schlee, Buyer Experimentation and Introductory Pricing, 44 J. Econ. Behav. Org. 347 (2001).

[27] Gregory S. Crawford & Matthew Shum, Uncertainty and Learning in Pharmaceutical Demand (Working paper, Univ. Arizona, Dep't Econ., February 2003).

[28] Andrea Coscelli, The Importance of Doctors' and Patients' Preferences in the Prescription Decision, 48 J. Indus. Econ. 349 (2000).

[29] Gary S. Becker & Kevin M. Murphy, A Theory of Rational Addiction, 96 J. Pol. Econ. 675 (1988).

III. Model

Demand for the branded pharmaceutical product at each instant of time is $D^i(p, X)$. The price of the pharmaceutical is p, and the stock of knowledge about the pharmaceutical is X. Demand is indexed by $i \in \{B, A\}$, where B denotes the structure of demand before patent expiry and A denotes demand after patent expiry. We assume that demand is linear:

$$D^i(p, X) = \alpha_0^i - \alpha_p^i p + \alpha_X^i X. \tag{1}$$

Over time, the stock of knowledge evolves. We use a modified version of a standard "contagion" model of knowledge diffusion. The simple contagion model would have $\dot{X} = \rho_2 X(1 - X/M)$—knowledge diffuses quickly and at an accelerating rate early but then slows down as saturation occurs (X gets close to M). The contagion model essentially assumes that one comes to know about a drug by coming into contact with someone who already knows about it—whether or not they use the drug themselves. It seems likely that physicians who actually are using the drug are in a better position to impart knowledge. To reflect this, we include a term $\rho_1 D$ to allow knowledge diffusion to be positively affected by current use. Finally, pharmaceutical companies can impart knowledge directly via promotional activities, A. So the law of motion for knowledge is

$$\begin{aligned}\dot{X} &= A + \rho_1 D + \rho_2 X\left(1 - \frac{X}{M}\right) \\ &= A + \rho_1 D + \rho_2 X - \frac{\rho_2}{M}X^2 \qquad (2) \\ &= A + \rho_1 D + \rho_2 X - \rho_3 X^2.\end{aligned}$$

We assume a quadratic cost of promotional effort:

$$c(A) = \frac{1}{2\rho_4}A^2. \tag{3}$$

We make a number of additional assumptions on these functions:

A1: All parameters are positive.
A2: $r < \rho_2 + \frac{\rho_1\alpha_X}{2} + \frac{\alpha_X}{2\alpha_p}$.
A3: $\alpha_0^i > \alpha_p^i c$.
A4: $\alpha_0^B > \alpha_0^A$, $\alpha_p^B < \alpha_p^A$, $\alpha_X^B > \alpha_X^A$.

Assumptions 1 and 3 are regularity conditions. Assumption 1 imposes negatively sloping demand, costly promotion, and a variety of similar assumptions, and assumption 3 says that demand is high enough to make it worthwhile to produce the product at all. Assumption 2 restricts the interest rate r so that the firm does not discount the future too steeply.

Assumption 4 says that the effect of the expiry of a patent and subsequent generic entry is to reduce the level of the innovator's demand, increase the slope of the innovator's demand, and decrease the benefit of knowledge dissemination for the innovator's demand. The first two are quite standard—most oligopoly models would predict this change in a firm's residual demand upon the entry of a competitor. The last part of assumption 4 captures the knowledge externality discussed by Berndt and his colleagues[30]—since the generic and branded drugs have the same active ingredient(s), knowledge about the branded drug also provides knowledge about the generic drug.[31]

A. *The Innovator's Problem*

The instruments available to the firm to influence the path of sales are price and promotional effort. The firm solves the following problem:

$$\max_{\{p,A\}} \int_0^T \exp(-rt)[(p_t - c)D^B(p_t,X_t) - c(A_t)]$$

$$+ \int_T^\infty \exp(-rt)[(p_t - c)D^A(p_t,X_t) - c(A_t)],$$

$$\dot{X}_t = A_t + \rho_1 D_t^i + \rho_2 X_t - \rho_3 X_t^2,$$

$$D_t^i = \alpha_0^i - \alpha_p^i p_t + \alpha_X^i X_t,$$

$$X_t \geq 0,$$

$$X_0 = 0.$$

There are two epochs in the innovator's optimization problem. From time 0 to time T, there is a patent protecting the innovator's market, and the innovator acts as a monopolist. At time T, the patent expires, and from then on the innovator faces generic competition. This generic competition shifts the innovator's residual demand curve as described in assumption 4.

The stock of knowledge about the drug is X. We assume that this starts

[30] Berndt *et al.*, *supra* note 21.

[31] Notice we do not need to assume that the two drugs are identical or that knowledge about the branded drug is the same as knowledge about the generic drug, merely that knowledge about the branded drug spills over to some degree on demand for the generic.

out at zero when the drug is introduced, $X_0 = 0$. Furthermore, we assume that this stock cannot be negative.[32]

B. First-Order Conditions

The Hamiltonian associated with this dynamic program is

$$H^{CV} = (p - c)D(p, X) - c(A) + \lambda(A + \rho_1 D + \rho_2 X - \rho_3 X^2) + \mu \chi_{X=0}[A + \rho_1(\alpha_0 - \alpha_p p)]. \tag{4}$$

Thus, we are led to the following necessary conditions, which must hold for all t:

$$H_p^{CV} = 0 = (p - c + \rho_1 \lambda + \mu \chi_{X=0})D_p + D, \tag{5}$$

$$H_A^{CV} = 0 = c_A(A) - \lambda + \mu \chi_{X=0}, \tag{6}$$

$$\dot{\lambda} = r\lambda - (p - c)D_X + \lambda(\rho_1 D_X + \rho_2 - 2\rho_3 X), \tag{7}$$

$$\dot{X} = A + \rho_1 D + \rho_2 X - \rho_3 X^2, \tag{8}$$

$$X_0 = 0, \tag{9}$$

$$\mu \geq 0, \quad \text{and} \quad \mu \chi_{X=0}[A + \rho_1(\alpha_0 - \alpha_p p)] = 0. \tag{10}$$

Our choice of functional form for demand and cost of promotional effort ensures that H^{CV} is concave in p, A for each λ, so that the first-order conditions are sufficient for the problem of maximizing H^{CV} in p, A.

A key element of the solution to the problem is λ, the shadow price or value of knowledge. Its interpretation is the value to the firm of the stream of benefits associated with acquiring one more unit of X. In Appendix B, by solving the first-order conditions for A and p in terms of λ and X, we establish that, ceteris paribus,

[32] In order to impose the constraint, we require that $\chi_{X=0}(A + \rho_1 D) \geq 0$. The indicator variable, $\chi_{X=0}$, is equal to one any time X is zero. This constraint is equivalent to $\chi_{X=0}[A + \rho_1(\alpha_0 - \alpha_p p)] \geq 0$. Without any constraint, there is an undesirable potential solution to this problem. The firm could charge prices higher than the choke price and engage in negative promotion early in the program in order to drive X negative. The quadratic form (in X) of $\dot{X}$ would then set up a positive feedback causing X to go to negative infinity quickly. Later in the program, the firm could charge a price less than c to earn negative per unit profits on a large negative volume of sales, to earn large positive profits. To rule out this case, we need some constraint, and the positivity constraint on X is the easiest one.

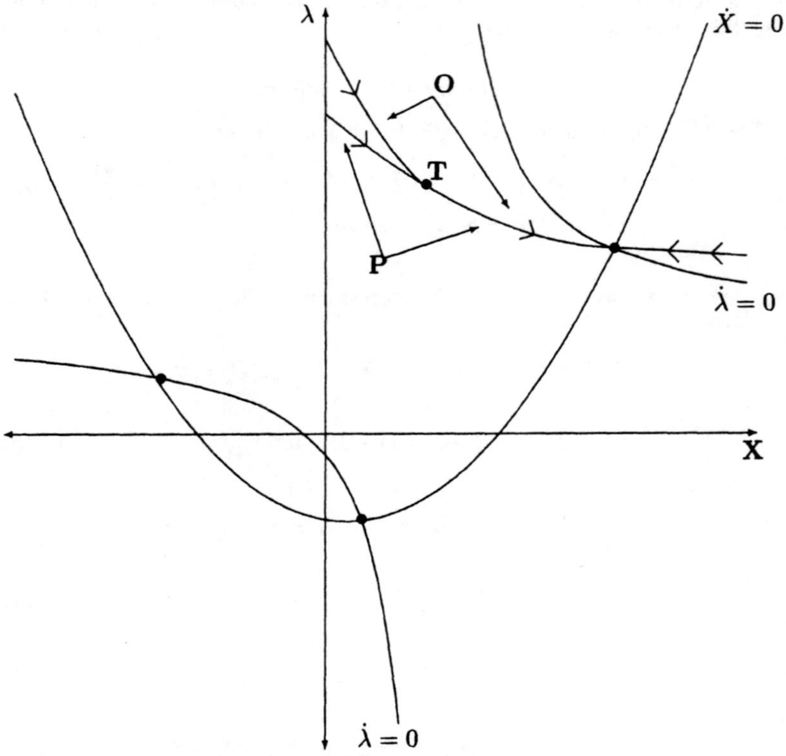

FIGURE 1.—Optimal paths, before and after

1. A is increasing in λ.
2. p is decreasing in λ.
3. p is increasing in X.

Advertising is increasing in λ since the firm will expend more effort to spread knowledge about its drug the more valuable is the knowledge. Since high demand increases the diffusion of knowledge, the firm will want to expand demand when knowledge is most valuable to it. Thus, it will charge a lower price when λ is higher. Finally, a large knowledge stock expands the level of demand, and the firm will tend to take advantage of this by charging a higher price so that p is increasing in X.

Given the time paths for λ and X, we would then have the optimal time path chosen by the firm for p and A. We solve for the optimal paths of λ

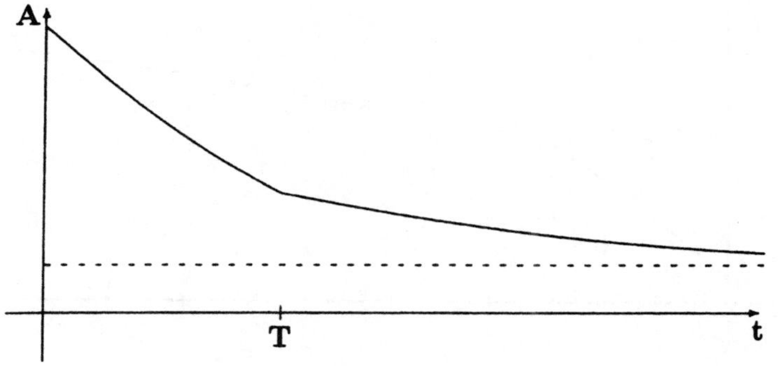

FIGURE 2.—Optimal path for *A*

and *X* via a phase diagram. The details of the analysis are confined in Appendix B. We summarize the results and their derivation here.

Figure 1 shows the optimal phase path for *X* and λ both before and after the expiry of the patent, which is labeled *T*. The path labeled *O* is the optimal path. At drug introduction, knowledge stock is zero and the firm begins at the λ-intercept of path *O*. As time elapses, the firm moves down path *O* until coming to rest at the steady state at the intersection of $\dot{X} = 0$ and $\dot{\lambda} = 0$.

The kink at point *T* is caused by patent expiry. At patent expiry, the rate of change of the knowledge stock drops discretely. Prior to patent expiry, two forces push λ down over time. First, as *X* accumulates, decreasing returns set in, making additional units less valuable. This process continues after the patent expires. Second, before patent expiry, with each passing moment, the firm knows that it will enjoy monopoly profits for a shorter period of time on each extra unit of knowledge. Thus, with each passing moment, each unit of *X* becomes less valuable. This second effect disappears at the moment of patent expiry.

So over the course of the drug life cycle, λ starts out high and then falls. While the drug is on patent, λ falls quickly. Then, when the drug loses its patent protection, λ begins to fall more slowly. Knowledge stock is continuously increasing over the course of the drug's life cycle. In the typical case, knowledge stock grows more slowly after patent expiry than before as the firm makes fewer investments in dissemination.

Figure 2 graphs the optimal path for advertising over a drug's life cycle. Before patent expiry, the value of additional knowledge diffusion is highest, thus promotional efforts are highest. As knowledge accumulates and patent expiry approaches, the value of incremental knowledge diffusion decreases and the firm reduces promotion. The rate of decrease decreases at the date of patent expiry.

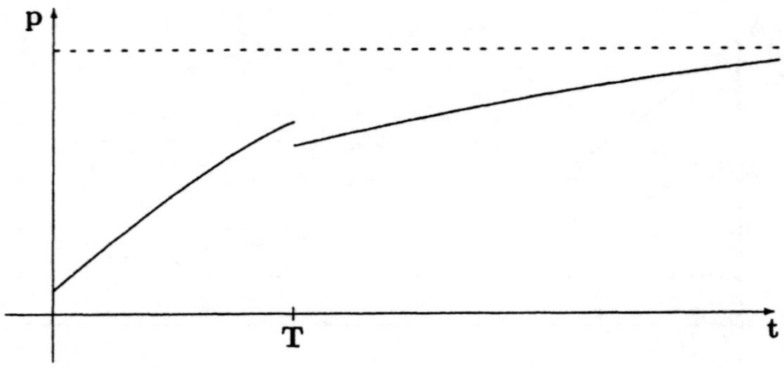

FIGURE 3.—Optimal path for p

Figure 3 graphs the optimal path for price. Early in the program, the firm establishes a low price to stimulate demand and therefore knowledge acquisition and diffusion. As time progresses, knowledge expands, which both reduces the long-run value of additional knowledge and increases the short-term returns to high prices. So prices rise quickly over time. When the patent expires, the branded firm's demand both shifts in and becomes more elastic. This pushes the firm to reduce prices discretely. In addition, the rate of growth of price decreases for the same reason that the decline in advertising slows—because $\dot{\lambda}$ drops at that point.

C. *Discussion*

In our model, the pharmaceutical firm's central dynamic problem is the management of physicians' information about its products. Knowledge is disseminated via word of mouth among physicians and via pharmaceutical company promotional effort. Word-of-mouth dissemination is enhanced when a large number of physicians use the drug. So the firm wishes to set a low price and exert high levels of promotional effort early in its program in order to build a stock of knowledge. As time passes, the buildup of the knowledge stock and the impending patent expiry erode the firm's incentive to disseminate knowledge, so its price rises and its level of promotional effort falls. After the patent has expired, the firm engages in steadily lower levels of promotional effort and steadily higher prices as the effect of the spillovers in knowledge between branded and generic drugs blunts its incentives to facilitate knowledge dissemination.

While we interpret X as the stock of physician knowledge, one might just as well reinterpret it as the stock of consumer knowledge or the union of the two. In that interpretation, A would include direct-to-consumer advertising

TABLE 1

COMPARISON OF THEORIES

	Frank & Salkever	Bhattacharya & Vogt
Assumptions:		
Horizon	Static	Dynamic
Demand	Segmented	Homogenous
Generic entry	Decreases |elasticity|	Increases |elasticity|
Predictions:		
p at entry	Increase	Decrease
p before entry	NA	Increasing quickly
p after entry	NA	Increasing slowly
Ads before	NA	Decreasing quickly
Ads after	NA	Decreasing slowly

NOTE.—Frank & Salkever = Richard G. Frank & David S. Salkever, Pricing, Patent Loss and the Market for Pharmaceuticals, 59 S. Econ. J. 165 (1992); Bhattacharya & Vogt = the present paper. NA = not applicable.

as well as detailing, journal advertising, and other activities directed at physicians.

D. *Comparison with Frank and Salkever's Study*

Frank and Salkever[33] provide a landmark contribution to the understanding of the generic competition paradox, and any new analysis must be compared with theirs.

First, our model differs from that of Frank and Salkever in its assumptions. Frank and Salkever assume, in a static model, that the innovator's demand curve becomes less elastic with the expiry of the innovating firm's patent. In contrast, in a dynamic model, we assume that demand becomes more elastic after patent expiry. This assumption is more consonant with the economist's typical intuition about the effect of entry on residual demand elasticity. To generate our price and promotional effort dynamics, we instead place the pharmaceutical firm's problem of managing knowledge about its product at the center of the model.

Second, our model differs from that of Frank and Salkever in its predictions. See Table 1 for a comparison of the two theories.

IV. EMPIRICS

We offer an exploratory analysis of the price and advertising paths of several drugs. Because of limitations of the sample and variables, this is a suggestive rather than a dispositive look at the predictions of our theory.

We sought a therapeutic class that had a number of patent expiries recently and that were important, both for patients and for pharmaceutical company

[33] Frank & Salkever, *supra* note 13.

TABLE 2

VARIABLE DESCRIPTIONS

Variable	Description
p	Price of the drug, $ per prescription
q	Quantity of the drug sold, 1,000s of prescriptions
Ads	Number of journal ads
Until	Quarters until patent expiry[a]
Onpat	Dummy for drug being on patent
Gener	Dummy for drug being a generic
Q	Aggregate quantity of the molecule sold

NOTE.—For each molecule in each quarter, there is one observation on the price of the branded drug, and after patent expiry, there is also one observation on the price of the generic version of the drug. Thus, in each quarter before patent expiry there is one observation per molecule, and in each quarter after there are two.

[a] This variable is negative after the patent expires and counts down with time.

revenues. The class we chose is β-blockers, which during our sample period were used principally as oral antihypertensive agents outside the hospital.

A. *Data*

Our principal data source is IMS America, a company that collects sales and other data for U.S. pharmaceutical markets. IMS kindly provided us with quarterly retail quantity and revenue data for our drugs. The drugs consist of all β-blockers that were on the market at any time during the sample period, from the fourth quarter of 1987 through the first quarter of 1993. These amount to 11 molecules.[34] IMS collects these data through retail pharmacy audits.

Each drug is sold in several different dosage levels, although all of the drugs we study are in oral form. For our analyses, we choose the most common dosage level for each drug. Unfortunately, in our data we are unable to distinguish different prescription sizes (for example, 30 tablets versus 90 tablets).

Patent expiry data were drawn from the Food and Drug Administration (FDA) Center for Drug Evaluation and Research's *Approved Drug Products with Therapeutic Equivalence Evaluations*,[35] also known as the FDA *Orange Book*. This source contains extensive information concerning date of approval, dosages approved, and the expiry dates of the relevant patents. Over our sample period, patents expired on four of our 11 drugs. We verified patent

[34] We have data for both branded and generic drugs of a particular chemical entity; however, the generic data as provided to us are not separated by manufacturer, so we are unable to separate "branded generics" from other generics.

[35] U.S. Department of Health and Human Services, Food and Drug Administration, Electronic Orange Book, http://www.fda.gov/cder/ob, visited December 2002.

TABLE 3

DESCRIPTIVE STATISTICS

Variable	Mean	Standard Deviation	25 Percent	75 Percent
p	27.90	7.67	25.60	32.30
q	991.53	1,065.56	113.00	1,898.50
Ads	1.62	3.14	.00	2.00
Until	4.87	15.71	−4.00	16.00
Onpat	.66			
Gener	.17			
Q	1,358.92	1,437.02	129.00	2,938.90

NOTE.—$N = 265$.

expiry dates by looking at the earliest date at which generics were sold for each molecule. In three of the four cases, generics entered within one quarter of patent expiry. Excluding the fourth, Penbutolol, has minimal effect on the results.

Descriptions of the variables used in our analyses appear in Table 2, and descriptive statistics for these variables appear in Table 3. We capture the time remaining until patent expiry in the variable Until. One could argue for defining Until in terms of the date of generic entry instead. The two definitions differ only for one drug, and our results are minimally affected by moving from one definition to the other.

Although such data exist, IMS did not share with us information on pharmaceutical promotional expenditures. Consequently, we developed a (rough) proxy for promotional effort by manually counting the number of journal advertisements for each drug in each quarter of our sample period. We counted ads in all issues of the *Journal of the American Medical Association*, the *New England Journal of Medicine*, and *Circulation*. The *Journal of the American Medical Association* and the *New England Journal of Medicine* are the two most widely read medical journals by American doctors, and *Circulation* is a widely read cardiology specialty journal.

B. *Specification*

1. Price and Advertising Dynamics

In order to examine the match between our model's predictions, shown in Table 1, and the evolution in the market for β-blockers, we regress prices and advertising effort on quarterly time-trend variables. Time is measured as quarters until patent expiry, with negative values denoting postexpiry quarters. In the regressions, the effect of the time trend is permitted to differ for the branded drug before and after expiry and is also permitted to differ between the branded and generic drugs. In addition, we include a dummy variable that indicates whether the drug is on patent. This last term permits the regression to pick up any discrete effect that patent expiry may have over and above a change in the trends. Finally, we include dummies for each branded drug and for each generic drug. Given that we include individual dummies and time until expiry, it is not possible to include a time trend, since it would be perfectly collinear with these.[36]

We estimate two different versions of the price trend regressions: one using price and one using log price as the dependent variable. We run each price regression twice using two different subsets of the β-blocker data. The first subset includes all 11 branded drugs and their generics, over the period between the fourth quarter of 1987 and the first quarter of 1993. This yields 265 separate drug-quarter observations, since some drugs are not present at the beginning of our observation period. The second subset includes just the four drugs that expire during the observation period and their generics. There are 104 separate drug-quarter observations in this subset. These are the only drugs for which we observe prices and advertising effort both before and after patent expiry.

Since there are several quarters with no advertising for some of the drugs, we are not able to run a log version of our advertising model. Like the price regressions, however, we run the advertising regression on two data subsets: all branded drugs and expiring branded drugs only. We run our advertising regressions using only observations from branded drugs, since generics never advertise in our sample. This leaves 221 separate drug-quarter observations in the first subset and 82 separate observations in the second.

All the price and advertising dynamics regressions are estimated using the generalized estimating equation procedure,[37] linear link function, and normal, AR(1) errors. The estimated results are asymptotically equivalent to generalized least squares with AR(1) errors. We have tried a variety of other error structures (both autoregressive and moving average) with lag depth of up to four quarters, and the results from those were not materially different from those reported here.

2. Demand Regressions

In addition to the price and advertising dynamics regressions, we estimate demand regressions. The purpose of these regressions is to characterize the relative importance of price, advertising, and knowledge stock on demand. We measure knowledge stock as total quantity of the molecule sold in the previous quarter. Molecule sales include both the branded and generic versions of the drugs. All the demand regressions include separate drug dummies for both branded and generic drugs.

[36] This problem is a familiar one in the analysis of panel data—it is impossible separately to identify cohort, age, and time effects in an unrestricted regression.

[37] See Kung-Yee Liang & Scott L. Zeger, Longitudinal Data Analysis Using Generalized Linear Models, 73 Biometrika 13 (1986).

TABLE 4

PRICE AND ADVERTISING DYNAMICS REGRESSIONS

	ALL DRUGS			EXPIRING DRUGS		
VARIABLE	p	$\ln p$	Ads[a]	p	$\ln p$	Ads[a]
Until	−.458	−.018	.057	−.239	−.009	.214
	(.093)	(.003)	(.084)	(.148)	(.005)	(.154)
Until × Onpat	−.104	.001	−.011	−.503	−.014	−.225
	(.105)	(.004)	(.094)	(.175)	(.006)	(.181)
Until × Gener	.349	.006		.243	.001	
	(.135)	(.005)		(.225)	(.008)	
Onpat	−.140	.010	.427	.292	.020	.190
	(.740)	(.029)	(.802)	(.831)	(.033)	(.884)
Drug × Gener	Yes	Yes	No	Yes	Yes	No
N	265	265	221	104	104	82

NOTE.—Standard errors are in parentheses. All regressions include drug dummy variables.
[a] Generic drugs are omitted from these regressions.

We estimate each of these two demand regression versions using ordinary least squares (OLS) and two-stage least squares. The motivation for the latter econometric technique is that our theory tells us that firms manipulate the key right-hand-side variables in our demand regression; that is, they choose price and advertising to manipulate the evolution of the knowledge stock. If this is correct, then price and ads will be endogenous.

Our instruments (detailed in Table 6) are largely related to the timing of drug introduction and patent expiry. As our theory demonstrates, these variables are integral to determining the firm's optimal pricing, advertising, and knowledge stock management strategy, so they are certainly correlated with the endogenous right-hand-side variables. We assume that these variables do not affect demand.[38] Also, because these variables depend on the vagaries of both the research and development process and the regulatory process, they are plausible instruments. Of course, in a model with endogenous research and development and control of the regulatory process by firms, these variables would be correlated with the unobserved determinants of demand.

C. *Results*

1. Pricing and Advertising Dynamics

Table 4 shows the results from the pricing and advertising dynamics regressions. The first three columns report results on the full sample, and the last three columns report results from the sample of drugs that went off patent

[38] In a model with forward-looking, informed consumers, this assumption would be untenable. What we have in mind is that the knowledge stock is resident in physicians and that they are constrained, by ethics or fear of malpractice suits, to provide the drug that is myopically best for each patient.

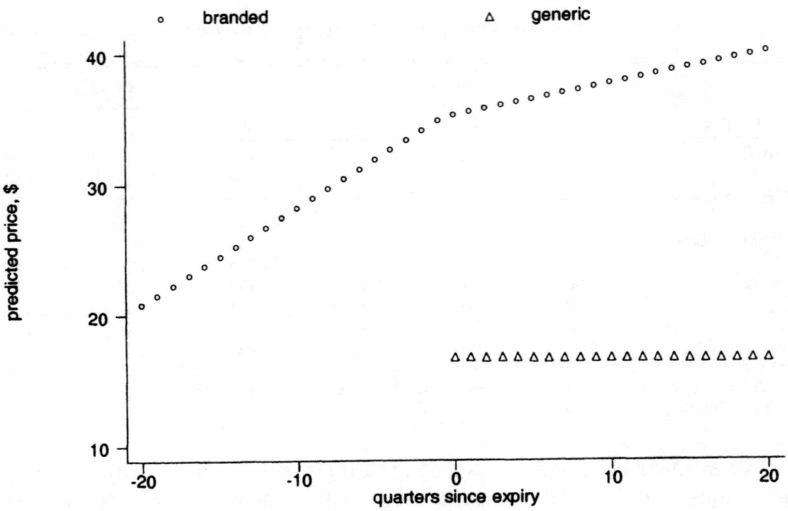

FIGURE 4.—Predicted price: expiring drugs

in our data. Looking at the fifth column, we see that price rises before patent expiry for the branded drug at a rate of about \$.74 (=.24 + .50) per quarter. At patent expiry, the price drops by \$.29 and thereafter rises by about \$.24 per quarter. Generic prices, by contrast, are roughly flat over time. The log specification and the specifications using all drugs confirm the basic results: branded prices are rising both before and after patent expiry, the rise is faster before expiry, and branded prices change little at the date of expiry. Figure 4 plots predicted values from the model of the fourth column for the average expiring drug.

To guard against our results being driven by the linear functional form assumption on the price dynamics, we estimated a smoothed version of this model. We smooth using the overlap polynomial method of Thomas MaCurdy, David Green, and Harry Paarsch.[39] Overlap polynomials are smooth spline functions that use the cumulative normal distribution rather than the step function to "turn on" and "turn off" the sections of the spline. This leads to an estimated function with derivatives of all orders. Details of the method can be found in the above-referenced papers.

For this application, we estimated an overlap polynomial in time since expiry. We estimate on the sample of expiring drugs, and we include a complete set of drug and generic-drug dummies as well as a dummy for

[39] Thomas MaCurdy, David Green, & Harry Paarsch, Assessing Empirical Approaches for Analyzing Taxes and Labor Supply, 25 J. Hum. Resources 415 (1990).

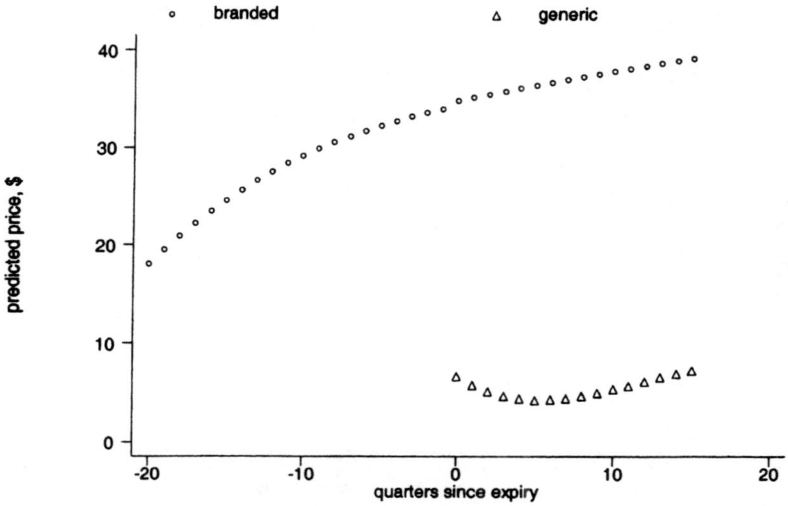

FIGURE 5.—Predicted price, smoothed: expiring drugs

being on patent. In essence, we estimate the model of the fifth column of Table 4 but with the time trend flexibly modeled. Knots are placed at time since expiry equal to 15, 7, 3, 0, −3, −10, −20, and a smoothing parameter of 25 is used. The spline functions in the reported results are levels (that is, zeroth-order polynomials), although we experimented with higher-order polynomials with similar results.

Results from this analysis appear in Figure 5. The basic results from the previous analysis continue to hold here. Price rises both before and after expiry, but faster before. Price changes very little at the time of patent expiry. Generic prices are lower than are branded, and the generic price trends up over time. The biggest difference between these results and the previous ones is in the behavior of generic prices shortly after expiry. Here they trend downward for about a year after expiry—evidently, generic entry happens gradually over about a year rather than all at once as our theory and our simpler empirical model assume.[40] This is consistent with prior work.[41]

[40] Under the Hatch-Waxman Act of 1984 decisions, the first generic entrant may enjoy a 6-month exclusivity period on the generic market if it successfully challenges the patent of the innovator. However, prior to 1997, only three generic entrants were granted such exclusivity. Between 1997 and 1999, only two more entrants were granted exclusivity. See, for example, Food and Drug Administration, Exclusivity Statistics, http://www.fda.gov/cder/present/dia-699/mu2-dia99/sld006.htm, visited April 2003.

[41] See Grabowski & Vernon, *supra* note 1; and David Reiffen & Michael R. Ward, Generic Drug Industry Dynamics (Working Paper No. 248, Fed. Trade Comm'n, Bur. Econ., February 2002).

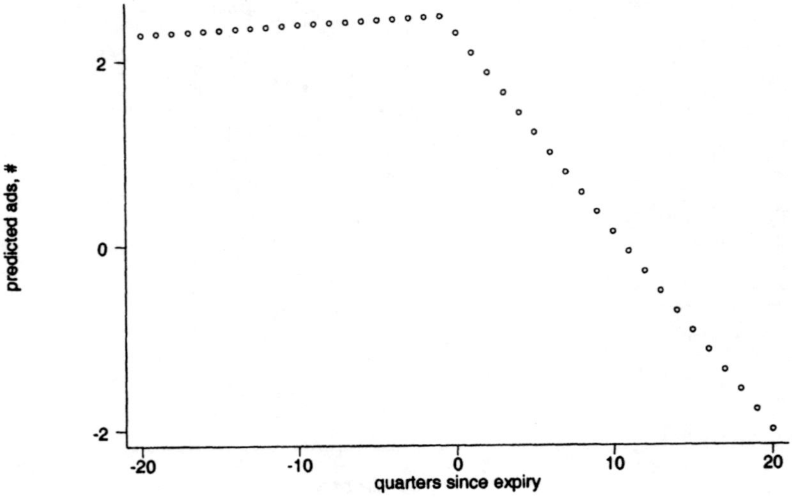

FIGURE 6.—Predicted ads: expiring drugs

Some previous work has found that some branded drug prices fall in the first few years after introduction.[42] Although prices in our sample rise over the first few years, this prior result is inconsistent with our theory, which predicts rising prices over the whole life cycle. A pattern of declining prices early in a drug's life cycle may be explained by signalling[43] or by consumers overestimating the imperfectly observable quality of the new drug.[44]

There is little of statistical significance in the advertising dynamics regression. In neither sample are there significant differences between the before and after expiry periods in levels or trends or jointly in levels and trends. A graph of the fit time path of ads appears in Figure 6.

2. Demand Regressions

Table 5 shows the results of the demand regressions using OLS. Equation (5.1) contains a simple demand specification in which quantity demanded depends on price, ads, knowledge stock (proxied by lagged aggregate molecule quantity), and drug dummies. Estimates from this equation have demand downward sloping but inelastic and show a strong effect of lagged on current

[42] See Z. John Lu & William S. Comanor, Strategic Pricing of New Pharmaceuticals, 80 Rev. Econ. & Stat. 108 (1998).

[43] See Kyle Bagwell & Michael H. Riordan, High and Declining Prices Signal Product Quality, 81 Am. Econ. Rev. 224 (1991).

[44] See Carl Shapiro, Optimal Pricing of Experience Goods, 14 Bell J. Econ. 497 (1983).

TABLE 5

DEMAND REGRESSIONS: ORDINARY LEAST SQUARES

Variable	Equation (5.1)	Equation (5.2)	Equation (5.3)
$\ln p$	−.704 (.113)	−1.433 (.192)	−1.431 (.175)
$\ln p$ × Onpat		1.011 (.212)	1.014 (.193)
$\ln p$ × Gener		.300 (.341)	−1.138 (.374)
Ads	.010 (.007)	.009 (.006)	.010 (.005)
$\ln Q(-1)$	.437 (.030)	.481 (.036)	.482 (.033)
$\ln Q(-1)$ × Onpat		−.029 (.027)	−.031 (.025)
$\ln Q(-1)$ × Gener		−2.216 (.262)	.372 (.444)
Onpat		−3.180 (.741)	−3.182 (.675)
Until × Gener			.077 (.011)
R^2	.990	.993	.994

NOTE.—The dependent variable is $\ln q$. All regressions include drug dummy variables and drug and generic interaction dummy variables. N = 250.

demand. Ads have no significant measured effect (although the point estimate is quite large), but this is not surprising given how noisy our measure for it is. All this is as our theory would predict.

To get at the more nuanced predictions of our theory, that branded demand should become more elastic after patent expiry and that branded demand should become less sensitive to the knowledge stock after expiry, we estimate the specification equation (5.2). Here the interaction between Onpat and price is positive, which shows that demand elasticity is estimated to be lower in absolute value prior to patent expiry. Furthermore, the beneficial effect of knowledge stock on branded demand is estimated to decline after expiry, although that result is not significant. Surprisingly, the demand for generics is estimated to be less elastic than the demand for branded drugs. Even more surprising, generic demand is estimated to have negative dependence on knowledge stock.

The surprising results in equation (5.2) are driven, we think, by a variable omitted from both the empirical work and our theory. Evidently, it takes time for knowledge about generics to diffuse. By our theory, generic demand should jump up immediately upon patent expiry. This does not happen in our data. Generic quantity increases gradually, which presumably reflects the diffusion of knowledge about the existence of generics or lags in pharmacies stocking generics. To allow for this effect, we construct equation (5.3). This specification contains a generic-specific time trend. Including the generic time trend provides more intuitive estimates. Generic demand is more elastic than branded demand. Generic drugs have positive spillover effects from the knowledge stock, and generic demand rises over time.

The two-stage least squares results appear in Table 6, and the contrast between the OLS and these results is modest. As one would expect, price elasticities of demand are estimated to be higher once the endogeneity of price is accounted for. Otherwise the results are quite similar. Equation (6.3)

TABLE 6

DEMAND REGRESSIONS: TWO-STAGE LEAST SQUARES

Variable	Equation (6.1)	Equation (6.2)	Equation (6.3)
$\ln p$	−.793 (.128)	−2.151 (.249)	−2.146 (.236)
$\ln p$ × Onpat		1.885 (.303)	1.916 (.287)
$\ln p$ × Gener		.986 (.410)	−1.211 (.494)
Ads	.020 (.012)	.024 (.012)	.032 (.012)
$\ln Q(-1)$	.433 (.031)	.500 (.039)	.507 (.037)
$\ln Q(-1)$ × Onpat		−.057 (.031)	−.066 (.030)
$\ln Q(-1)$ × Gener		−2.236 (.281)	.867 (.507)
Onpat		−6.097 (1.039)	−6.162 (.983)
Until × Gener			.097 (.013)
R^2	.990	.992	.993

NOTE.—The dependent variable is $\ln q$. The three equations include drug dummy variables and drug and generic interaction dummy variables. N = 250.

shows that price elasticity is higher for branded drugs after patent expiry. Also, knowledge stock has a larger beneficial effect on branded demand, and the difference between this effect before and after patent expiry is small, although in the "wrong" direction. Generic demand is more elastic than is branded demand, knowledge stock is beneficial to generics, and demand for generics rises over time.

V. CONCLUSION

We have presented a theoretical model that explains and adds nuance to the "stylized fact" that branded pharmaceutical prices rise in the face of generic entry. In our story, a pattern of price rising over time is generated by the firm's dynamic demand management problem—rising prices reflect the firm taking payoffs from earlier investments in knowledge stock. Generic entry causes an instantaneous price decline from the usual competitive effects; however, the same forces that push up branded prices before expiry also do so after expiry, and the (slower) upward trend reasserts itself.

Our empirical results are exploratory in nature and are imprecisely estimated; however, they provide suggestive confirmation of several aspects of our theory. First, prices and to a lesser extent advertising move as our theory predicts. The upward price trend is evident from the moment of introduction of the drug. Generic entry does not cause a measurable instantaneous effect on prices, but the trend growth in prices is muted after generics enter. Finally, the number of ads declines more quickly after patent expiry than before.

Our demand regressions also provide some confirmation for our theory. First, lagged demand, a proxy for knowledge stock, robustly influences contemporaneous demand. Second, branded demand becomes more elastic when patent protection lapses and generics enter.

APPENDIX A

TABLE A1

DRUGS STUDIED

Branded Name	Generic Name	Patent Expiry
Blocadrin	Timolol	April 1989
Brevibloc	Esmolol	June 2000
Cartrol	Carteolol	October 1994
Corgard	Nadolol	January 1993
Inderal LA	Propranolol	February 1996
Inderal	Propranolol	December 1984
Kerlone	Betaxolol	January 1999
Levatol	Penbutolol	December 1992
Lopressor, Lopressor IV	Metoprolol	December 1993
Satral	Acebutolol	December 1993
Tenormin	Atenolol	September 1991
Toprol	Metoprolol Tartarate	January 1995
Visken	Pindolol	September 1992

APPENDIX B

SOLUTION TO DYNAMIC PROGRAM

I. THE SOLUTION FROM T ON

We begin by analyzing the solution starting from time T. From T on, the problem is time invariant, and we will denote the initial stock of X at time T as K—this is the amount of knowledge accumulated over the interval $[0, T]$.

We draw the phase diagram for the unconstrained problem. Then we turn to the phase diagram in the presence of the constraint (see equation (10)).

A. *Phase Diagram, Unconstrained*

Ignoring the constraint, equation (6) can be solved immediately to give A as a function of λ as

$$A(\lambda) = (c_A)^{-1}(\lambda) = \rho_4\lambda. \tag{B1}$$

Similarly, equation (5) gives $p = p(\lambda, X)$:

$$p(\lambda, X) = \frac{1}{2}\left(c + \frac{\alpha_0 + \alpha_X X}{\alpha_p} - \rho_1\lambda\right). \tag{B2}$$

These solutions then may be substituted back into equation (7) and equation (8) to form a system of two autonomous differential equations. Then the initial condition on X, $X_0 = 0$, along with a condition on λ would often be enough to provide a solution.

Since there are neither initial nor final conditions for λ in this infinite horizon problem, there will be a large family of time paths consistent with these first-order conditions, and we will need to rule out all but one of them later.

Now we will substitute back into the laws of motion for X and λ. First, we consider $\dot{X}$ and substitute equation (B2) and equation (B1) into equation (8):

$$\begin{aligned} \dot{X} &= A + \rho_1 D + \rho_2 X - \rho_3 X^2 \\ &= \rho_4 \lambda + \frac{\rho_1}{2}(\alpha_0 + \alpha_X X - \alpha_p c + \alpha_p \rho_1 \lambda) + \rho_2 X - \rho_3 X^2 \\ &= \left(\rho_4 + \rho_1^2 \frac{\alpha_p}{2}\right)\lambda + \frac{\rho_1}{2}(\alpha_0 - \alpha_p c) + \left(\rho_2 + \alpha_X \frac{\rho_1}{2}\right) X - \rho_3 X^2. \end{aligned} \tag{B3}$$

Similarly, substituting into equation (7) yields

$$\begin{aligned} \dot{\lambda} &= r\lambda - (p - c)D_X - \lambda(\rho_1 D_X + \rho_2 - 2\rho_3 X) \\ &= \lambda\left(r - \frac{\rho_1 \alpha_X}{2} - \rho_2 + 2\rho_3 X\right) - \frac{\alpha_X}{2}\left(\frac{\alpha_0}{\alpha_p} - c\right) - \frac{\alpha_X^2}{2\alpha_p} X. \end{aligned} \tag{B4}$$

From the time of patent expiry on, this problem is an infinite-horizon, autonomous, discounted optimal control problem. We employ a phase diagram to solve the problem. We will look for a path leading to a steady state, so we solve equation (B3) for $\dot{X} = 0$ and equation (B4) for $\dot{\lambda} = 0$:

$$\begin{aligned} 0 &= \dot{X} \\ &= \left(\rho_4 + \rho_1^2 \frac{\alpha_p}{2}\right)\lambda + \frac{\rho_1}{2}(\alpha_0 - \alpha_p c) + \left(\rho_2 + \alpha_X \frac{\rho_1}{2}\right) X - \rho_3 X^2, \\ \lambda &= \frac{1}{\rho_4 + \rho_1^2 \alpha_p / 2}\left[\rho_3 X^2 - \left(\rho_2 + \alpha_X \frac{\rho_1}{2}\right) X - \frac{\rho_1}{2}(\alpha_0 - \alpha_p c)\right], \end{aligned} \tag{B5}$$

$$\begin{aligned} 0 &= \dot{\lambda} \\ &= \lambda\left(r - \frac{\rho_2 \alpha_X}{2} - \rho_2 + 2\rho_3 X\right) - \frac{\alpha_X}{2}\left(\frac{\alpha_0}{\alpha_p} - c\right) - \frac{\alpha_X^2}{2\alpha_p} X, \\ \lambda &= \frac{(\alpha_X/2)[(\alpha_0/\alpha_p) - c] + (\alpha_X^2/2\alpha_p)X}{r - (\rho_1 \alpha_X/2) - \rho_2 + 2\rho_3 X}. \end{aligned} \tag{B6}$$

The graph of $\dot{X} = 0$ has λ quadratic in X with a positive coefficient on the squared term, a negative coefficient on the linear term, and a negative λ-intercept. The graph of $\dot{\lambda} = 0$ is a negatively sloping hyperbola with a negative λ-intercept, a positive vertical asymptote, and a positive horizontal asymptote. In addition, it is easy to check that $\dot{X}_\lambda > 0$, $\dot{X}_X < 0$ near $\dot{X} = 0$ when the graph of $\dot{X} = 0$ is sloping up, $\dot{\lambda}_\lambda < 0$, and $\dot{\lambda}_X < 0$.

Figure B1 contains a phase diagram for this problem. First, let us find all of the steady states. Recall that $\dot{X} = 0$ is a convex parabola with a negative λ-intercept and that $\dot{\lambda} = 0$ is a negatively sloping hyperbola with a negative λ-intercept. Intersections of these two graphs are the steady-state levels of λ and X.

If the λ-intercept of $\dot{X} = 0$ is less than the λ-intercept of $\dot{\lambda} = 0$, then there are three intersections between the two graphs (this is the case pictured in Figure B1).

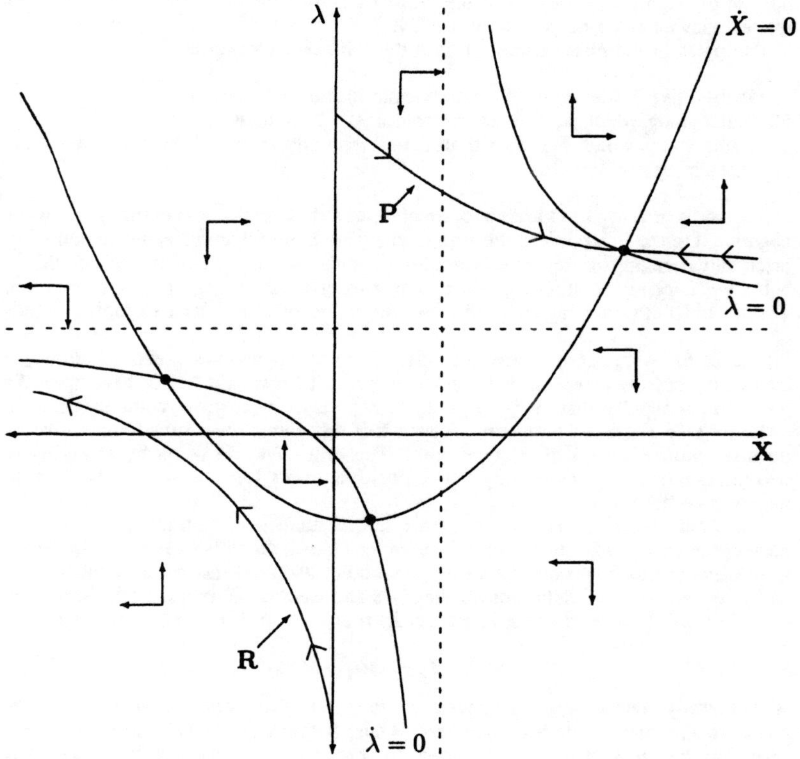

FIGURE B1.—Phase diagram for knowledge stock

One intersection must lie in the first quadrant. One intersection must lie in the second quadrant. The last intersection may lie either in the third or fourth quadrant, and we have drawn it in the fourth.

On the other hand, if the λ-intercept of $\dot{X} = 0$ is greater than the λ-intercept of $\dot{\lambda} = 0$, there is a single intersection between the two graphs: the one in the first quadrant.

In the next section, we will argue that the path labeled *P* is the solution. For now, consider path *R*. This is the type of potential solution we discussed in footnote 32. It eventually has the firm charging a negative price and earning negative per unit profits but making money by selling a large negative number of units.

B. Phase Diagram, with Constraint

Imposing the constraint that $X \geq 0$ affects only the parts of the phase plane in which *X* equals zero and $\dot{X}$ is less than zero. Thus, the affected portion of the phase plane is the λ-axis below the λ-intercept of $\dot{X} = 0$. The effects of the constraint are to make $\dot{X}$ equal to zero along that portion of the axis and to change the magnitude but not the sign of $\dot{\lambda}$. The half of the phase plane in which X is less than zero is no longer relevant since no path may reach it.

The paths in the phase plane fall into the following categories:

1. Path(s) like P leading to the steady state in the first quadrant.
2. Paths along which $\lambda, X \rightarrow +\infty$ monotonically eventually.
3. Paths along which λ is less than zero eventually forever (like S and all paths that dip below $\lambda = 0$).

The paths in category 3 are not optimal. Along these paths, λ eventually is always negative. On the $-\lambda$ portion, the firm is charging higher than the profit-maximizing price and engaging in negative promotion in order to reduce X. The firm could do better by charging the myopic profit-maximizing price and engaging in no promotion. This would both earn higher profits for any value of X and lead to higher values of X.

The paths in category 2 are not optimal. As X approaches positive infinity, it eventually becomes necessary for $p<c$ in order to maintain $\dot{X}>0$, because $\rho_3 X^2$ grows more rapidly than $\rho_2 X + \rho_1 \alpha_X X$, so $\alpha_0 - \alpha_p p$ must grow without bound in order to keep $\dot{X}$ greater than zero. A path like this cannot be optimal since it earns negative profits forever after some point. The firm could do better by engaging in myopic maximization eventually (since positive profits forever must be better than negative profits forever).

Since only the paths in category 1 are left, if there is an optimum, then it must correspond to a steady-state path like P. We can check that this path eventually leads to positive profits. Consider the steady-state point itself. At this point, λ equals zero and $\dot{X}$ equals zero by definition of steady state. Because $\dot{X}$ is quadratic, we know that $\dot{X}_X$ is less than zero at the larger (in X) root of $\dot{X} = 0$. It is also true that

$$\dot{\lambda} = r\lambda - (p - c)\alpha_X - \lambda(\dot{X}_X).$$

At the steady state in the first quadrant, λ is greater than zero. As we argue above, at the steady state, $\dot{X}_X$ is less than zero. Thus, both $r\lambda$ and $-\lambda\dot{X}_X$ are greater than zero. This means that for $\dot{\lambda}$ to be equal to zero it must be the case that $(p-c)$ is greater than zero. So, near the steady state, the firm is earning positive per period profits. Thus, on its face, a steady state path P could reasonably be optimal.

Along a path like P, λ is monotonically decreasing in time; that is, $\dot{\lambda}<0$. Similarly, X is monotonically increasing; that is, $\dot{X}>0$.

Also, we may characterize the behavior of price and promotional effort from T to infinity. Since A is an increasing function of λ and since it does not depend on X, we can conclude that A decreases along the optimal path. Similarly, since p is a decreasing function of λ and an increasing function of X and since $\dot{\lambda}<0$ and $\dot{X}>0$, we may conclude that p is increasing along the optimal path.

II. The Solution from 0 to T

The first-order conditions described in equations (5)–(10) must hold from 0 to T as well, of course. The difference is that, from 0 to T, α_0 is higher, α_p is higher, and α_X is lower. It is straightforward to verify that these conditions imply that λ is higher for each value of X. Also, since λ is decreasing in X and X is increasing over time, we can conclude that λ is higher before patent expiry than it is after.

Figure 1 shows a typical phase path for X and λ both before and after the expiry of the patent at the point labeled T. The path labeled O is the optimal path, and the path labeled P is (as in Figure B2) the optimal path with demand as it is after T. So

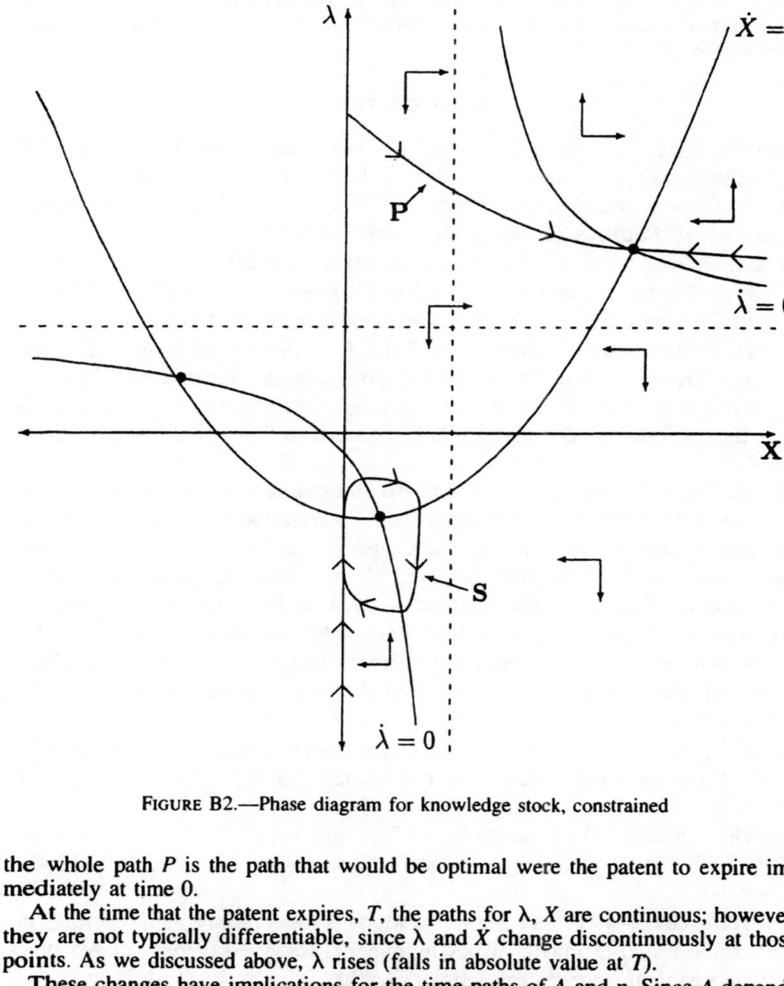

FIGURE B2.—Phase diagram for knowledge stock, constrained

the whole path P is the path that would be optimal were the patent to expire immediately at time 0.

At the time that the patent expires, T, the paths for λ, X are continuous; however, they are not typically differentiable, since λ and $\dot{X}$ change discontinuously at those points. As we discussed above, λ rises (falls in absolute value at T).

These changes have implications for the time paths of A and p. Since A depends positively on λ and only on λ, $\dot{A}$ rises (falls in absolute value) at time T. A typical optimal time path for A appears in Figure 2.

The case for p is not quite so simple. Since p depends negatively on λ and positively on X, $\dot{p}$ also depends negatively on λ and positively on $\dot{X}$. At time T, λ increases discontinuously (decreases in absolute value) and this tends to cause $\dot{p}$ to decrease.

$\dot{X}$ will decrease at time T. Consider the law of motion for X:

$$\dot{X} = A + \rho_1 D + \rho_2 X - \rho_3 X^2.$$

Since X and A are continuous, no discontinuous change in X may come from these. D does change discontinuously at T; however, it is easy to show that, under our assumptions, D may not rise at T. Thus, since $\dot{\lambda}$ rises and $\dot{X}$ falls at time T, $\dot{p}$ must fall at time T. It is equally easy to show that p falls at time T discontinuously. Figure 3 depicts the path of prices.

Bibliography

Bagwell, Kyle, and Riordan, Michael H. "High and Declining Prices Signal Product Quality." *American Economic Review* 81 (1991): 224–39.

Becker, Gary S., and Murphy, Kevin M. "A Theory of Rational Addiction." *Journal of Political Economy* 96 (1988): 675–700.

Berndt, Ernst R.; Bui, Linda; Reiley, David R.; and Urban, Glen L. "Information, Marketing, and Pricing in the U.S. Antiulcer Drug Market." *American Economic Review: Papers and Proceedings* 85 (1995): 100–5.

Berndt, Ernst R., and Greenberg, Paul E. "An Updated and Extended Study of the Price Growth of Prescription Pharmaceutical Preparations." In *Competitive Strategies in the Pharmaceutical Industry*, edited by Robert B. Helms, pp. 35–48. Washington, D.C.: American Enterprise Institute Press, 1995.

Berndt, Ernst R.; Griliches, Zvi; and Rossett, Joshua G. "Auditing the Producer Price Index: Micro Evidence from Prescription Pharmaceutical Preparations." *Journal of Business and Economic Statistics* 11 (1993): 251–64.

Caves, Richard E.; Whinston, Michael D.; and Hurwitz, Mark A. "Patent Expiration, Entry, and Competition in the U.S. Pharmaceutical Industry." *Brookings Papers on Economic Activity: Microeconomics* (1991): 1–48.

Ching, Andrew T. T. "Dynamic Equilibrium in the U.S. Prescription Drug Market after Patent Expiration." Unpublished manuscript. Minneapolis: University of Minnesota, 2000.

Comanor, William S. "Research and Competitive Product Differentiation in the Pharmaceutical Industry in the United States." *Economica* n.s. 31 (1964): 372–84.

Coscelli, Andrea. "The Importance of Doctors' and Patients' Preferences in the Prescription Decision." *Journal of Industrial Economics* 48 (2000): 349–69.

Crawford, Gregory S., and Shum, Matthew. "Uncertainty and Learning in Pharmaceutical Demand." Working paper. Tucson: University of Arizona, Department of Economics, February 2000.

Frank, Richard G., and Salkever, David S. "Pricing, Patent Loss and the Market for Pharmaceuticals." *Southern Economic Journal* 59 (1992): 165–79.

Frank, Richard G., and Salkever, David S. "Generic Entry and the Pricing of Pharmaceuticals." Working Paper No. 5306. Cambridge, Mass.: National Bureau of Economic Research, October 1995.

Grabowski, Henry G., and Vernon, John M. "Brand Loyalty, Entry, and Price Competition in Pharmaceuticals after the 1984 Drug Act." *Journal of Law and Economics* 35 (1992): 331–50.

Hudson, John. "Pricing Dynamics in the Pharmaceutical Industry." *Applied Economics* 24 (1992): 103–12.

Kelly, Gregory G. "Improving the PPI Sample for Prescription Pharmaceuticals." *Monthly Labor Review,* October 1997, pp. 10–17.

Klemperer, Paul. "Competition When Consumers Have Switching Costs: An Overview with Applications to Industrial Organization, Macroeconomics, and International Trade." *Review of Economic Studies* 62 (1995): 515–39.

Liang, Kung-Yee, and Zeger, Scott L. "Longitudinal Data Analysis Using Generalized Linear Models." *Biometrika* 73 (1986): 13–22.

Lu, Z. John, and Comanor, William S. "Strategic Pricing of New Pharmaceuticals." *Review of Economics and Statistics* 80 (1998): 108–18.

MaCurdy, Thomas; Green, David; and Paarsch, Harry. "Assessing Empirical Approaches for Analyzing Taxes and Labor Supply." *Journal of Human Resources* 25 (1990): 415–90.

Pavcnik, Nina. "Do Pharmaceutical Prices Respond to Insurance?" Working Paper No. 7865. Cambridge, Mass.: National Bureau of Economic Research, August 2000.

Peltzman, Sam. "An Evaluation of Consumer Protection Legislation: The 1962 Drug Amendments." *Journal of Political Economy* 81 (1973): 1049–91.

Perloff, Jeffrey M.; Suslow, Valerie Y.; and Seguin, Paul J. "Higher Prices from Entry: Pricing of Brand-Name Drugs." Working Paper No. CPC99-003. Berkeley: University of California, Berkeley, Institute of Business and Economic Research, Competition Policy Center, August 1995.

Reiffen, David, and Ward, Michael R. "Generic Drug Industry Dynamics." Working Paper No. 248. Washington, D.C.: Federal Trade Commission, Bureau of Economics, February 2002.

Ridley, David. "The Wrong Prescription: Price Regulation in a Market with Consumer Start-Up Costs." Working paper. Durham, N.C.: Duke University, Fuqua School of Business, 2002.

Salop, Steven C. "Monopolistic Competition with Outside Goods." *Bell Journal of Economics* 10 (1979): 141–56.

Scherer, F. M. "Pricing, Profits, and Technological Progress in the Pharmaceutical Industry." *Journal of Economic Perspectives,* Summer 1993, pp. 97–115.

Schlee, Edward E. "Buyer Experimentation and Introductory Pricing." *Journal of Economic Behavior and Organization* 44 (2001): 347–62.

Shapiro, Carl. "Optimal Pricing of Experience Goods." *Bell Journal of Economics* 14 (1983): 497–507.

Stern, Scott. "When Entry Causes Prices to Rise: An Exploration of Product Demand in Pharmaceutical Markets." Unpublished manuscript. Stanford, Calif.: Stanford University, 1995.

Temin, Peter. *Taking Your Medicine: Drug Regulation in the United States.* Cambridge, Mass.: Harvard University Press, 1980.

[27]

By Stuart O. Schweitzer and William S. Comanor

DOI: 10.1377/hlthaff.2009.0923
HEALTH AFFAIRS 30,
NO. 8 (2011): 1553-1561

Prices Of Pharmaceuticals In Poor Countries Are Much Lower Than In Wealthy Countries

Stuart O. Schweitzer (sschweit@ucla.edu) is a professor in the School of Public Health at the University of California, Los Angeles.

William S. Comanor is a professor in the School of Public Health at the University of California, Los Angeles, and is also a professor of economics at the University of California, Santa Barbara.

ABSTRACT Keeping pharmaceuticals affordable in poor countries is important for public health. Economic models suggest that manufacturers should be able to charge substantially lower prices in those markets than in industrialized countries without drastically reducing their profits. We report the results of a study of thirty drugs in twenty-nine countries, showing that many prices are already substantially discounted in middle-income and developing countries, compared to prices in the United States and other industrialized countries, and do not exceed long-run marginal costs. We also argue that the so-called peak load pricing model offers an economic foundation for fair drug pricing in the case of developing countries, and is a better solution than other pricing models to the problem of how to reduce drug prices in these countries to the level of manufacturers' marginal costs.

This paper addresses the issue of pharmaceuticals' affordability in developing countries and reports the empirical findings from our study of drug prices in twenty-nine countries between 2000 and 2007. If drug prices track income levels, then affordability should not limit access to pharmaceuticals in developing countries. However, if prices and income levels do not move in tandem, then the affordability of pharmaceuticals in poor countries could raise important health policy issues.

First, we review economic models that have been developed to explain price differences for the same or similar products. Second, we employ available data to determine how much drug prices are actually discounted below US prices in lower-income countries. We explore not only the extent of the discounting but also its prevalence across national markets.

Lastly, we consider parallel trade, which is frequently seen as a barrier to discounting drug prices. Parallel trade involves products sold to one country at a substantial discount that are then sold again—either back to the original country of manufacture or to another country where the products can substitute for comparable but higher-priced items. A full discussion of the theoretical basis for parallel trade and of the extent of that trade in practice is beyond the scope of this paper, but we offer some thoughts about the likely effect of parallel trade on prices in developing countries.

Patricia Danzon and Adrian Towse have discussed some of these issues.[1] Like them, we focus on pricing issues for drugs targeted at diseases found in both developed and developing countries rather than medicines required primarily in developing countries. Although we generally agree with Danzon and Towse's approach, there are important conceptual differences between us, which we discuss below.

Prices In Developing Countries

Three principal models have been used to explain why prices for the same products can vary across different markets. They are the price discrimination model, the Ramsey pricing model, and the peak load pricing model.

PRICE DISCRIMINATION AND RAMSEY PRICING MODELS The first and most prominent of these is the price discrimination model.[2] According to this model, firms maximize their profits by taking advantage of the elasticity of demand and charging consumers different prices according to what they are willing to pay. Consumers with low demand elasticity are those who continue to purchase the product despite increased prices. Firms charge them higher prices than consumers with high demand elasticity.

In some markets, however, the objective is to maximize the welfare of consumers and producers rather than to maximize profits. Various models of public utility pricing—of which the Ramsey pricing model is the best known—are based on this objective, which is considered particularly appropriate for public utilities and government entities. This approach is quite different from merely setting prices according to consumers' average income levels.

The principles of the Ramsey pricing model were originally put forth in 1927[3] but were extended in 1970.[4] This model holds that firms set prices to maximize the sum of revenues plus consumer surplus—that is, the differences between what the consumers pay and the higher amount that they would be willing to pay—as long as the firms are also able to earn profits at a predetermined level. A profit level might include the amount a firm needs to fund certain fixed costs, such as those related to research and development. As proponents of this model emphasize, charging prices that are equal to the marginal cost of production will not lead to the most desired outcomes if firms do not earn enough to support research and development.

Danzon and Towse conclude that combining differential pricing and Ramsey pricing is consistent with "economic efficiency" and with "standard norms of equity"[1(p201)] and therefore provides a conceptual basis for setting prices in developing countries. We disagree.

The authors acknowledge that the Ramsey pricing model says that "prices should differ across market segments in inverse relation to their demand [price] elasticities."[1(p202)] As a result, countries with less demand elasticity for pharmaceuticals should pay higher prices than those with more demand elasticity. However, this does not mean that prices are always lower where incomes are lower, because this would require that elasticity of demand is always higher in higher-income countries. This is not necessarily the case.

Another difficulty with applying the Ramsey pricing model to pharmaceuticals is that demand elasticities can reflect consumers' essential need for a product. As a result, this model leads to the conclusion that higher prices should be charged for more essential drugs, whose consumers are likely to have a lower demand elasticity, and lower prices should be charged for drugs whose consumers need them less.

In our judgment, that recommendation is perverse. For example, it could mean that the highest prices would be charged in poor countries with a very high prevalence of HIV that badly needed antiretroviral drugs, while countries with a lower prevalence that had less need for the drugs would pay lower prices for them. Interestingly, William Jack and Jean Lanjouw consider this same issue and reach a conclusion similar to ours. They find that this approach "prescribes that countries with greater needs should face higher prices."[5(p47)] However, they use this conclusion as the reason to recommend extending the use of the Ramsey model rather than rejecting it. This issue is important because many policy makers rely on Ramsey pricing principles despite their perverse implications.

PEAK LOAD PRICING MODEL Our alternative model, the peak load pricing model, relies more on cost than on demand. For this reason, we first briefly review the typical cost structure of large pharmaceutical firms.

▶ **TYPES OF COSTS:** There are three main categories of costs: production, research and development, and marketing costs. For the most part—uniformly with small-molecule drugs, although somewhat less so with biologics—production costs represent less than half of the total cost of the product. In contrast, research and development costs for new pharmaceuticals are often quite high; some experts estimate that they exceed $800 million on average for new products.[6] Finally, there are substantial marketing costs when a new product is introduced, largely because it can be costly to inform the medical practitioner community about its presence and characteristics.[7]

Some costs can be allocated to particular markets, while others apply equally to all markets. For example, some marketing is done only to certain populations. Similarly, production costs can be divided among specific markets according to the quantities sold there. On the other hand, research and development costs apply to all markets where a product is sold. The question here is how these costs should be allocated across different national markets.

▶ **ALLOCATING COSTS TO DIFFERENT MARKETS:** This question is particularly relevant for the peak load pricing model. That model was originally developed for public utilities, and its focus, like that of the Ramsey model, is on maximizing consumers' and producers' welfare rather than profits. In both traditional public utilities and the pharmaceutical industry, there are high fixed costs and low marginal or direct costs of production. For utilities, these fixed costs are typically the costs of building new capacity, while marginal costs are largely operating costs. For pharmaceutical companies, fixed costs are largely those of research and development, while marginal costs are primarily those related to manufacturing products.

For both utilities and pharmaceutical companies, sales in primary markets must cover their high fixed costs, but sales in secondary markets need not do so. That is, utilities need full capacity to meet the demand of consumers during peak periods, and no further capacity to satisfy the demand of off-peak users. Similarly, drug companies need to pay for research to develop pharmaceutical products for industrialized countries; they do not need to pay for any more research when they sell the same products in less developed countries.

The standard conclusion to be drawn from the peak load model is that peak users pay capacity and operating costs while off-peak users pay only operating costs.[8] Applying that conclusion to pharmaceutical markets implies that consumers in developed countries pay both their market-specific costs and the fixed costs of research and development, while consumers in less developed countries pay only the marginal production and distribution costs applicable to their markets. By this rule, the relevant production and marketing costs would be covered in each market, regardless of its average income level, while research and development costs would be paid only in the industrialized countries. Developing countries would obtain pharmaceuticals at their marginal cost.

▸ **INCOME DISTRIBUTION:** Jack and Lanjouw incorporate income distribution into their extension of Ramsey pricing rules, using the common assumption that the "marginal utility of income...decline[s] as income increases. That is, people get less benefit from an extra dollar as they become richer."[5(p51)] Therefore, Jack and Lanjouw acknowledge that optimal Ramsey prices can fall below marginal, or production, costs. However, they also observe that there are operational difficulties in applying that result and conclude that "as a practical matter, it may not be possible to implement prices [that are] lower than marginal costs."[5(p61)] As a result, their recommendations are the same as ours below.

▸ **PRODUCT AVAILABILITY:** We begin by assuming that the same or similar products are sold throughout the world. In other words, we assume that there are not two distinct sets of products, one for the industrialized regions of North America, Europe, and Japan, and the other for developing countries. This assumption is often but not always appropriate in the case of pharmaceuticals. Some products, such as those for certain neglected diseases, have only a small market in the industrialized world. However, demand is increasing rapidly in developing countries for treatments of diseases that are already common in industrialized countries.[9] As Lanjouw points out, "cancer and heart disease together account for 15 percent of all 'disability-adjusted life years' lost in the low and medium countries, [which] is four times higher than the disease burden due to malaria."[10(p109)] One reason for this change is increasing longevity in the developing world, which is leading to higher rates of cardiovascular disease, cancer, and other conditions. Another reason is the rapid growth in the size of the middle class in lower-income countries. As a result, the same pharmaceutical products are used in both developed and developing countries.

Although the peak load pricing model offers an economic foundation for fair drug pricing in developing countries, we do not suggest that it should also be applied to wealthy, industrialized countries. With the exception of the United States, these countries generally have well-developed systems for regulating pharmaceutical prices, in many cases including central government or quasi-government agencies that have power to bargain down prices. Even some US entities have the ability to bargain for or otherwise obtain lower pharmaceutical prices, such as the Department of Veterans Affairs and Medicaid. Our public utility pricing model is prescriptive only for pharmaceutical markets in developing countries and cannot easily be applied in more-advanced countries.

▸ **PATENT PROTECTION:** In a related proposal, Lanjouw suggests that pharmaceutical patents should apply to industrialized countries or developing countries, but not to both.[10] Presumably, innovative companies would prefer to have patent protection in developed countries because imitators could quickly develop generic equivalents that would greatly diminish innovators' profits. That would leave pharmaceutical markets in developing countries open to generic competition from the outset. Although that means prices in poorer countries would decline, there is no reason to believe that they would decline so much as to approach marginal costs. In the US market, the loss of patent protection leads to price declines of that magnitude only when there are a large number of generic versions of a product,[11,12] and there is little reason to expect that to happen except in the largest developing countries, such as India and China.

▸ **ACTUAL PRICE DIFFERENCES:** In this section

we consider actual drug pricing in relation to the peak load pricing model discussed above.

We examine here the extent to which drug prices actually differ across countries. Only a small number of studies have investigated this question, and few of them have looked specifically at price differences between developed and less developed countries.[13] An exception is a study by Frederick Schut and Peter van Bergeijk that compares average pharmaceutical prices in thirty-two countries, both industrialized and developing. The authors report a "strong positive relationship between price level and per capita GDP."[14(p1141)] We find a similar relationship. According to their analysis, "a 10% increase in per capita income [is] associated with on average 8% higher drug prices."[14(p1141)]

Study Data And Methods

We analyzed differences across countries in prices for three distinct categories of drugs: relatively new drugs that are still under patent; older drugs that have lost their patent protection and are therefore available generically; and drugs that the World Health Organization classifies as "essential"—that is, those drugs that satisfy the top-priority health care needs of a given population, based on disease prevalence, evidence about the safety and efficacy of the drugs, and comparative cost-effectiveness.[15] Products in this final group are typically older than those in either of the other two categories.

The drugs in our analysis were the leading sellers in the United States within each of the three categories. We included those drugs that were in the same category for each of the eight years from 2000 through 2007. Our sample consists of ten drugs in each category, for a total of thirty drugs (Exhibit 1). Because drug use patterns differ across countries, these drugs may not be the leading sellers in other countries.

We analyzed drug prices in all twenty-nine countries for which complete data on these drugs were available. Some of the countries are industrialized, others are middle-income, and still others are developing countries.[16] Exhibit 2 lists the countries according to their per capita gross domestic products in 2000.[17] In Exhibit 3 we provide average price indexes for each group of countries, relative to US prices.

We used data on drug sales and quantities[18] from the MIDAS data system of IMS Health, a widely used source of data on pharmaceutical sales,[16] for 2000–07. We calculated the average prices paid by retail distributors (except in China)[19] for the standard unit of a drug,[20] defining *average prices* as total sales to those distributors divided by the number of units sold. The average prices for each drug in each country are based on actual country sales, stated in both monetary values and standard physical units.[21] The price data do not include manufacturers' rebates.

Sales figures were expressed in local currency dollars, which IMS Health defines as local currency sales converted to US dollars at constant exchange rates. We aggregated sales and quantity data at the drug level. Thus, for those drugs that were sold by only one manufacturer, we computed prices from that seller's dollar and unit sales. For drugs sold by multiple manufacturers, we computed prices using dollar and unit sales aggregated across all of the manufacturers.

EXHIBIT 1

Leading-Selling Drugs In The United States By Category, 2000–07

Category	Drug
Patented	Carbamazepine
	Clarithromycin
	Diltiazem
	Estradiol
	Insulin human isophane
	Lansoprazole
	Losartan
	Medroxyprogesterone
	Tobramycin
	Triamcinolone acetonid
No longer patented	Amlodipine
	Amoxicillin
	Azithromycin
	Cetirizine
	Ciprofloxacin
	Enalapril
	Fluticasone
	Metformin
	Omeprazole
	Simvastatin
WHO essential drug	Acetylsalicylic acid
	Beclometasone
	Ethinylestradiol
	Hydrochlorothiazide
	Hydrocortisone
	Ibuprofen
	Norethisterone
	Pracetamol
	Ranitidine
	Salbutamol

SOURCE Authors' analysis of World Health Organization, IMS Health, and World Bank data (see Notes 15, 16, and 17 in text); and Food and Drug Administration. Orange Book, various editions.

Study Results

Our analyses show that drug prices tend to track per capita national income levels within each drug category (Exhibit 3). However, average price differences between industrialized and middle-income countries are largely due to higher drug prices in the United States.

For patented drugs, middle-income countries pay on average 52 percent of what industrialized countries pay, while developing countries pay 27 percent of the prices charged in industrialized countries. For drugs that are no longer patented, middle-income countries pay 71 percent and developing countries 41 percent of what industrialized countries pay, while for products on the World Health Organization's list of essential drugs, the figures are 28 percent and 6 percent. Thus, the average prices charged in developing countries for all three categories of drugs are much lower than those charged elsewhere.

More important is whether or not these discounts are deep enough that developing countries are paying the equivalent of marginal costs alone, as the peak load pricing model requires. To answer that question, we need estimates of the ratio of marginal cost to price for drugs that are still patented and those that no longer are. Fortunately, such estimates for patented drugs are available in the economic literature.

Once a drug's patent expires in the United States, generic versions enter most of the product's markets, and prices for the original and generic versions decline. Moreover, generic prices approach marginal costs when the number of generic producers is sufficiently large. Because of this process, generic prices in markets with large numbers of rival products have been used to estimate marginal costs.

Three studies report ratios of marginal cost, determined in this manner, to the price of products that are still patented. David Reiffen and Michael Ward "find that the implied ratio of marginal cost to pre-expiry branded prices when there are 11 or more firms is approximately 50 percent."[22(p44)] Richard Frank and David Salkever report that "with each additional [generic] entrant there is a fall in the average price of a generic product of between 5.6 percent and 7.2 percent."[23(p88)] Accordingly, increasing the number of generic producers from one to eleven

EXHIBIT 2

Countries Where US Leading-Selling Drugs Were Sold, 2000–07, By Gross Domestic Product (GDP)

Country	Per capita GDP (2000 US$)
United States	34,774
Switzerland	31,001
Netherlands	29,663
Canada	28,910
Australia	26,841
Germany	26,281
France	25,937
United Kingdom	25,673
Japan	25,274
Italy	24,431
Spain	22,296
Taiwan	20,156
Greece	18,588
Portugal	17,680
Saudi Arabia	17,212
Korea	15,547
Mexico	10,647
Poland	10,281
Turkey	8,150
Brazil	7,187
South Africa	6,552
Thailand	4,951
Tunisia	4,768
Egypt	3,860
Morocco	2,659
China	2,372
Philippines	2,333
India	1,452
French West Africa	1,418

SOURCE World Bank data (see Note 17 in text). **NOTES** French West Africa is an aggregation constructed by IMS Health (see Note 16 in text) comprising Benin, Burkina Faso, Cameroon, Côte d'Ivoire, Gabon, Guinea, Mali, Republic of the Congo, Senegal, and Togo. The World Bank does not list a per capita GDP for this aggregation, so we calculated that.

EXHIBIT 3

Income And Drug Prices By Country Group, 2007

		Drug price index by category of drug		
Country group	Mean per capita GDP	Patented	No longer patented	WHO essential drug
All industrialized	$38,803	61.9	88.3	47.9
United States	$45,778	100.0	100.0	100.0
Other industrialized	$34,322	37.4	80.9	14.4
Middle-income	$19,877	32.0	62.8	13.2
Developing	$4,515	16.6	36.0	2.9

SOURCE Authors' analysis of IMS Health data (see Note 16 in text). **NOTES** The drug price index is a Laspeyres index, calculated using observed prices in each country, multiplied by the importance (weight) of each product in the United States. Thus, the index shows whether prices in other countries are discounted below US prices, when comparing price indexes using the same weight for each product as in the United States. Because price indexes are calculated relative to the US prices, the price index for the United States is set at 100.0. The categories of countries and drugs are explained in the text. GDP is gross domestic product. WHO is World Health Organization.

would lead to a price reduction of more than 50 percent from the price of the original drug. And Richard Caves and colleagues find that with ten generic drug producers in a particular market, generic prices average fully 70 percent below the original price.[24]

PRICES IN THE UNITED STATES AND ELSEWHERE These benchmark figures can be compared with the price data in our study. Exhibit 3 shows that the average prices for patented drugs in developing countries are less than 20 percent of those in the United States, while prices in middle-income countries average 32 percent of US prices. These prices are thus below the benchmark estimates of US marginal costs. Although it is possible that marginal costs of pharmaceutical production are lower in developing or middle-income countries than in the United States, the effect of such reduced costs could not be large because most patented drugs are manufactured in industrialized countries. For these drugs, therefore, current prices outside the United States are generally lower than marginal costs.

It is more difficult to draw firm conclusions about the fairness of pricing for drugs that are no longer patented (Exhibit 3). Although for some of these products, prices in developing countries approach marginal costs, that is not always the case. For essential drugs, however, it is clear that prices are not higher than marginal costs. There is little indication, therefore, that average drug prices in developing and middle-income countries exceed the standard set by marginal costs.

Exhibit 3 also shows the large average price difference between the United States and the other industrialized countries combined. The latter countries receive discounts from US prices that are similar to those found in middle-income countries. In other words, the price discounts received in many middle-income countries are comparable to those received in industrialized countries apart from the United States.

It should be noted that US prices in Exhibit 3 are overstated because, as mentioned above, the data from IMS Health do not include manufacturers' discounts and rebates, which are quite common in the United States. Two estimates of the extent of this overstatement are available. Patricia Danzon and Michael Furukawa report that the average US price discount is about 8 percent of the "cash" price.[25] And calculations based on data collected by Families USA indicate an average discount of about 47 percent from the nondiscounted levels.[26] Although we have made no effort to reconcile these very different estimates, we believe that the correct value probably falls between the two.

DRUG PRICES AND AVERAGE COUNTRY INCOMES We carried out a regression analysis to estimate the relationship between pharmaceutical prices and average country incomes (Exhibit 4). Our data for thirty different drugs and twenty-nine different countries lend themselves to a estimating model that includes indicator variables for each year (2000 through 2007), country, and drug. We performed separate regressions for each of the three categories of drugs. Because the price variables were measured in logarithmic form, the coefficients could be interpreted as an elasticity—that is, the percentage price change associated with a 1 percent change in per capita gross domestic product.

For patented drugs, the estimated price elasticity is negative but not statistically significant. The negative sign indicates that higher prices are associated with lower average income, which is an economically perverse result. For the other two categories of drugs, however, the estimated elasticities are both positive and statistically significant, which indicates that prices are indeed higher where average incomes are greater.

Furthermore, these estimates suggest that drug prices increase by about 6 percent with a 10 percent increase in per capita income, instead of increasing at roughly the same rate. In other words, for most products that are no longer patented or are on the list of essential drugs, price discounts are larger in poorer countries, but these discounts do not generally reflect average national incomes.

EXHIBIT 4

Estimated Effects Of Countries' Average Incomes On Pharmaceutical Prices

Drug category	Elasticity of prices with respect to per capita GDP
Patented	−0.333
No longer patented	0.600[a]
WHO essential drug	0.607[b]

SOURCE Authors' analysis of IMS Health and World Bank data (see Notes 16 and 17 in text). **NOTES** Prices are per standard unit (see Note 20 in text). GDP is gross domestic product. [a]Significant at $p < 0.01$. [b]Significant at $p < 0.025$.

Parallel Trade

Parallel trade can make manufacturers reluctant to lower prices too much for products sold in less-developed countries because those products can be resold to more-developed countries—including the one where they were manufactured—undercutting the prices charged there. This concern applies primarily to drugs that are still patented because generic drug prices vary less across countries.

Thomas Bart estimates the extent of parallel trade in pharmaceuticals within the European Union at about €5.8 billion annually.[27] Countries with the largest market share of parallel-traded pharmaceuticals in 2002—the year of Bart's analysis—included the United Kingdom, with approximately 20 percent of its national total market (€2 billion) supplied through parallel trade, and Germany, with approximately 22 percent of its national market (€1.2 billion). Although parallel-traded drugs in large European countries frequently exceeded 10 percent of the market,[27] Bart's evidence is that these imports do not have a large impact on wholesale prices. However, he did not study parallel-traded drugs imported from outside the European Union.

PRICE EFFECTS The price effects of parallel trade in pharmaceuticals are influenced by the extent to which the participating importers undercut established prices. If importers are unable to expand their sales by lowering their prices further, they are unlikely to do so. Instead, importers are more likely to set prices that largely track those of their competitors. In that case, the price effects of parallel trade would be relatively minor.

The evidence on these issues is limited to trade within the European Union. Margaret Kyle and colleagues studied the effect of parallel trade there between 1993 and 2004 and report little indication of a link between parallel trade and subsequent reductions in drug prices.[28] Similarly, Panos Kanavos and coauthors find that parallel imports had little effect on prices for the twenty top-selling drugs in the European Union.[29] And in a study of imports of the statin drug simvastatin in three of the main parallel importing countries—Germany, the Netherlands, and the United Kingdom—between 1997 and 2002, Joan Costa-Font and Panos Kanavos find that the market share for imported simvastatin increased, but that price differences between imported and domestically produced versions were small.[30]

However, Mattias Ganslandt and Keith Maskus report that legalizing parallel trade in pharmaceuticals in Sweden in 1995 led to a 4 percent drop in average drug prices.[31] This finding suggests that parallel trade can still represent a substantial form of competition for drug manufacturers.

REDUCING PARALLEL TRADE Parallel trade can be controlled either by government action or by manufacturer behavior. Government regulation of pharmacists' profits—in Denmark, Germany, and Sweden, for example—has effectively reduced their incentive to purchase parallel imported drugs. Germany also has a limit on the volume of such drugs that a pharmacist can dispense.

Additionally, when profit margins are fixed, there is little demand for parallel imports that offer a lower price for an existing product. The Netherlands and the United Kingdom use "claw-back" mechanisms, in which any savings from the use of parallel imports are shared by the pharmacist and the government health authority.[32]

Pharmaceutical companies also can adopt strategies to limit the price effects of parallel imports. For example, marketing the same chemical compound under different names, or in different dosages or strengths, in different countries makes it harder for parallel traders to sell drugs manufactured for one country in another. Health care providers in a developed country used to prescribing the 25 mg version of a pill are likely to be reluctant to prescribe the 30 mg pill imported from a developing one.

Another corporate strategy to reduce parallel trade is to restrict sales to low-income countries from which products could be resold. In fact, Frank and Salkever report that pharmaceutical supply interruptions occur more frequently in countries that are important sources of drugs that are resold to higher priced markets.[23]

The available evidence on parallel trade suggests that its impact on manufacturers' revenue and price differentials is relatively modest. Because countries and manufacturers have ways to limit the trade's effects, it is not a major impediment to setting lower pharmaceutical prices in less-developed countries.

Conclusion

Because the availability of pharmaceuticals is increasingly essential for health, there are important reasons why prices should be lower in countries with lower incomes. Moreover, conventional economic models make a strong case that drug prices in such countries should not be greater than long-run marginal costs. Strikingly, we found that average drug prices in developing and middle-income countries did not exceed this benchmark.

One possible impediment to maintaining these price differentials between industrialized countries and those whose populations are less well off is the prospect of increased parallel trade, in which drugs that carry low prices in one country are resold to more-developed countries. However, we find that parallel trade is not a major threat to either manufacturers' revenue or to price discounts. Not only is the evidence of such effects weak, but various mechanisms are available to governments and manufacturers alike to ensure that drugs can be sold at lower prices in less-developed countries. ■

NOTES

1 Danzon PM, Towse A. Differential pricing for pharmaceuticals: reconciling access, R&D and patents. Int J Health Care Finance Econ. 2003; 3(3):183–205.

2 The conventional definition of price discrimination is that it "exists when two 'similar' products that have the same marginal cost to produce are sold by a firm at different prices." Armstrong M. Price discrimination. In: Buccirossi P, editor. Handbook of antitrust economics. Cambridge (MA): MIT Press; 2008. p. 433.

3 Ramsey FP. A contribution to the theory of taxation. Econ J (London). 1927;37(145):47–61.

4 Baumol WJ, Bradford DF. Optimal departures from marginal cost pricing. American Economic Review. 1970;60(3):265–83.

5 Jack W, Lanjouw JO. Financing pharmaceutical innovation: how much should poor countries contribute? World Bank Econ Rev. 2005;19(1):45–67.

6 DiMasi JA, Hansen RW, Grabowski HG. The price of innovation: new estimates of drug development costs. J Health Econ. 2003;22(2):151–85.

7 Leffler KB. Persuasion or information? The economics of prescription drug advertising. J Law Econ. 1981; 24(1):45–74.

8 Sherman R. Market regulation. Boston (MA): Pearson; 2008. p. 371.

9 Parker J. Burgeoning bourgeoisie. Economist. 2009 Feb 12:3–22.

10 Lanjouw J. A patent policy proposal for global diseases. Innovations. 2006;1(1):108–14.

11 Reiffin D, Ward MR. Generic drug industry dynamics. Rev Econ Stat. 2005;87(1):37–49.

12 Morton FM. Entry decisions in the generic pharmceutical industry. Rand J Econ. 1999;30(3):421–40.

13 A prominent study that considers only price differences among developed countries is Danzon PM, Chao LW. Cross-national price differences for pharmaceuticals: how large, and why? J Health Econ. 2000;19(2): 159–95.

14 Schut FT, van Bergeijk PAG. International price discrimination: the pharmaceutical industry. World Dev. 1986;14(9):1141.

15 We used the 2002 edition of the World Health Organization's list of essential drugs because this version appeared close to the beginning of our study period, and the design of the study required us to include drugs that were in a particular market class (patented, no longer patented, or essential) for the entire period. More recent lists of essential drugs are available, of course, but some of the drugs included in later years would not have been classified this way in the beginning of our data period. World Health Organization. WHO model list (revised April 2002): core list, explanatory notes, 12th ed. [Internet]. Geneva : WHO; 2002 Apr [cited 2011 Jul 29]. Available from: http://apps.who.int/medicinedocs/en/d/Jh3003e/3.html#Jh3003e

16 IMS Health. MIDAS. Danbury (CT): IMS Health; 2008

17 World Bank. Indicators [Internet]. Washington (DC): World Bank; [cited 2011 Jul 18]. Available from: http://data.worldbank.org/indicator/NY.GDP.PCAP.CD?page=1

18 The data on drug sales and quantities included retail transaction values and quantities for specific products by brand, form, strength, and package size.

19 Data for China are available only from hospital outpatient pharmacies. Because the largest proportion of pharmaceutical sales in China takes place in hospital outpatient departments, however, these hospital data are a good approximation for retail pharmacy data.

20 The standard unit is the smallest common dose of a drug: one tablet or capsule, for a solid drug taken orally; 5 ml for a syrup; and one ampoule or vial for a drug to be injected. Department of Commerce, International Trade Administration. Pharmaceutical price controls in OECD countries: implications for U.S. consumers, pricing, research and development, and innovation [Internet]. Washington (DC): The Department; 2004 Dec [cited 2011 Jun 23]. Available from: http://www.ita.doc.gov/drugpricingstudy

21 Although IMS Health (see Note 16) also provides sales by the number of grams of active ingredient, we did not employ these data because of the wide differences reported for grams per standard unit for certain products in some counties. More relevant is the fact that pharmaceutical prices are determined more by demand than by cost, and standard units are a better measure than grams of the quantities of products actually sold.

22 Reiffen D, Ward M. Generic drug industry dynamics. Rev Econ Stat. 2005;87:44.

23 Frank R, Salkever D. Generic entry and the pricing of pharmaceuticals. J Econ Manage Strategy. 1997;6:88.

24 Caves RE, Whinston MD, Hurwitz MA. Patent expiration, entry, and competition in the U.S. pharmaceutical industry. Brookings Papers on Economic Activity: Microeconomics. 1991:36.

25 Danzon PM, Furukawa MF. Prices and availability of pharmaceuticals: evidence from nine countries. Health Aff (Millwood). 2003;22: 521–36. DOI: 10.1377/hlthaff.w3.521.

26 Families USA reported the lowest prices from the Department of Veterans Affairs and the lowest Medicare Part D prices in November 2006 for the sixteen largest-selling drugs prescribed for seniors. Because the former prices represent negotiated prices through which discounts can be achieved, while the latter prices are set under rules that prevent the payer from negotiating prices, the difference between these two sets of prices is a valid estimate of the extent of discounting of pharmaceutical prices. Families USA [Internet]. Washington (DC): Families USA. Press release, New report shows Medicare drug plan prices are 58 percent higher than VA prices; 2007 Jan 9 [cited 2011 Jun 23]. Available from: http://www.familiesusa.org/resources/newsroom/press-releases/2007-press-releases/new-report-shows-medicare.html

27 Bart TN. Parallel trade of pharmaceuticals: a review of legal, economic, and political aspects. Value Health. 2008;11(5):996–1005.

28 Kyle MK, Allsbrook JS, Schulman KA. Does reimportation reduce price differences for prescription drugs? Lessons from the European Union. Health Serv Res. 2008;43(4): 1308–24.

29 Kanavos P, Costa-Font J, Merker S, Gemmill M. The economic impact of pharmaceutical parallel trade in European Union member states: a stakeholder analysis. London: London School of Economics and Political Science; 2004 Jan. (Special Research Paper).

30 Costa-Font J, Kanavos P. Constrained competition in parallel drug importation: the case of simvastatin in Germany, the Netherlands, and the United Kingdom. Gac Sanit. 2007;21(1):53–9. Spanish.

31 Ganslandt M, Maskus KE. Parallel imports and the pricing of pharmaceutical products: evidence from the European Union. J Health Econ. 2004;23(5):1035–57.

32 Kanavos P, Costa-Font J. Pharmaceutical parallel trade in Europe: stakeholder and competition effects. Economic Policy. 2005;20(44): 751–98.

ABOUT THE AUTHORS: STUART O. SCHWEITZER & WILLIAM S. COMANOR

Stuart O. Schweitzer is a professor in the School of Public Health, University of California, Los Angeles.

In this issue of *Health Affairs*, the study by Stuart Schweitzer and William Comanor finds that with low prices currently charged in many low- and middle-income countries, drug manufacturers are not making large profits in these markets. Yet even when drug prices do not exceed direct costs in these countries, drugs may still be unaffordable for large numbers of people.

The authors argue that the so-called peak load pricing model offers an economic foundation for fair drug pricing in the case of developing countries, and is a better solution than other pricing models to the problem of how to reduce drug prices in these countries to the level of manufacturers' marginal costs. Under that model, consumers in developed countries pay prices that cover both market-specific costs and the fixed costs of research and development, while consumers in less developed countries pay only the marginal production and distribution costs applicable to their market.

The coauthors came to study drug pricing in poor countries following a meeting between Schweitzer, an economist at the University of California, Los Angeles (UCLA), and Eli Lilly executives. The pharmaceutical executives "saw that this market could be both socially beneficial and profitable, but there was concern that drug price discounting might jeopardize their markets in industrialized countries," Schweitzer says. "We thought this would be a fruitful line of investigation."

In fact, this study does examine the prospect of increased parallel trade, in which drugs that carry low prices in one country are resold to more developed countries and therefore threaten manufacturers' revenue. But for various reasons, the authors conclude that the evidence of such effects is actually weak.

Schweitzer is a professor in the UCLA School of Public Health. His areas of expertise include pharmaceutical economics, health policy, and the international health industry, and he has published many articles and papers on these topics. He has a master's degree and a doctorate in economics from the University of California, Berkeley.

William S. Comanor is a professor at the University of California, Los Angeles and at the University of California, Santa Barbara.

Comanor is a professor in the School of Public Health at UCLA and is also a professor of economics at the University of California, Santa Barbara. He is an expert on the economics of research and development in the pharmaceutical industry and has published widely. He has a doctorate in economics from Harvard University.

[28]

ELSEVIER

Journal of Health Economics 19 (2000) 159–195

JOURNAL OF HEALTH ECONOMICS

www.elsevier.nl/locate/econbase

Cross-national price differences for pharmaceuticals: how large, and why?

Patricia M. Danzon *, Li-Wei Chao

Health Care Management Department, The Wharton School, University of Pennsylvania, 3641 Locust Walk, Philadelphia, PA 19104 USA

Received 1 October 1998; received in revised form 1 September 1999; accepted 1 November 1999

Abstract

Bilateral drug price and quantity indexes, based on comprehensive data for seven countries (US, Canada, France, Germany, Italy, Japan and the UK), refute the conventional wisdom that US drug prices are much higher than elsewhere, for Laspeyres (US-weighted) indexes. Previous drug-price comparisons are biased by unrepresentative samples and unweighted indexes. Quasi-hedonic regression shows that cross-national price differences reflect differences in product characteristics and in their implicit prices, which reflect the regulatory regime. Strict price regulation systematically lowers prices for older molecules and globally diffused molecules. Generic competition lowers prices in less-regulated regimes, which also have more price-elastic demand. © 2000 Elsevier Science B.V. All rights reserved.

1. Introduction

Accurate measurement of cross-national price differences for drugs is an important policy and research issue. Cross-national comparisons of drug prices are often used to evaluate the performance of different regulatory systems. The General Accounting Office's comparison of drug prices in the US relative to Canada and the UK concluded that US prices were 32% higher than Canada and 60% higher than the UK (U.S. General Accounting Office, 1992, 1994). The

* Corresponding author. Tel.: +1-215-898-5722; fax: +1-215-573-2157.
E-mail address: danzon@wharton.upenn.edu (P.M. Danzon).

PII: S0167-6296(99)00039-9

Minority Staff (U.S. House of Representatives, 1998) concluded that US prices were 70% higher than Canada and 102% higher than Mexico. These studies appear to support the view that US drug prices are much higher than the rest of the world's, and have contributed to proposals for drug price controls — for example, President Clinton's Health Security Act (U.S. Government Printing Office, 1993) and the Prescription Drug Fairness Act of 1999 (H.R. 644). In addition to these comparisons of average price levels, a growing number of countries, including Italy, Spain, the Netherlands, Canada, and Japan, use international comparisons in their regulation of prices for individual drugs.

Previous cross-national drug price comparisons have been biased due to the use of inappropriate index methods applied to small, non-random samples of branded products, omitting all generics. For example, the Minority Staff Report (1998) compared retail prices in the US relative to Canada or Mexico based on the unweighted average of the price ratios for 10 leading originator drugs, using a single pack per drug. The U.S. General Accounting Office (1992) US–Canada comparison reported the price in the US relative to the price in Canada for a market basket consisting of one pack of each of 121 leading brand products, unweighted. U.S. General Accounting Office (1994) used 77 products in its US–UK comparison. The OECD purchasing power parities (PPPs) for drugs and medical devices (OECD, 1993) are also based on small, unrepresentative samples for each country, use inappropriate imputation for missing prices and lack weights to reflect the relative importance of different products. [1]

The purpose of this paper is threefold. First, we report indexes of manufacturer-level drug prices for six countries — Canada, France, Germany, Italy, Japan and the UK — relative to the US, using more comprehensive data and more appropriate methods than those used in previous studies. Our sample is based on Intercontinental Medical Systems (IMS) data for all outpatient drug sales in 1992.[2] For all molecules that match across the countries under comparison, we compute a weighted average price per gram or price per dose, including all products in the molecule — originator, licensed, and generic — and all formulations, strengths and packs for each molecule. Using this more comprehensive sample, our Laspeyres (US quantity weighted) indexes for price per dose show foreign/US differences as follows: Canada +2.1%; Germany +24.7%; France −32%; Italy −13%; Japan −12%, and the UK −17%. Thus, with the expanded sample and weighted indexes, the differences across countries in average drug-price levels are not as great as suggested by previous studies that used small samples of leading branded products and unweighted averages.

[1] The retail prices used by the Minority Staff and OECD PPPs cannot provide a valid measure of manufacturer prices due to distribution margins and VAT, which differ across countries.

[2] Intercontinental Medical Systems (IMS) is a market research firm that collects data on drug sales worldwide.

Second, since estimates of price differences are very sensitive to the index measure used, we examine the factors inherent in these index measures that contribute to the different estimates. The ratio of each country's Paasche (own weighted) index relative to its Laspeyres (US weighted) index is consistently less than one, ranging from 0.32 for Germany to 0.67 for the UK. This tendency, for each country to appear cheaper using own-weighted indexes rather than comparison-weighted indexes is independent of whether the US or another country is used as the base. Known as the Gerschenkron effect, it has been found in indexes of intertemporal and cross-sectional price and quantity changes in other industries (for example, Gerschenkron, 1947; Gerschenkron and Erlich, 1951; Jonas and Sardy, 1972; Kravis et al. 1982; Van Ark et al. 1996).[3] The excess of Laspeyres indexes over Paasche indexes might simply reflect a substitution effect, assuming that consumers in each country use relatively more of those products that are relatively cheap in that country. However, the Bortkiewicz formula (von Bortkiewicz, 1922, 1924; Allen, 1975) shows that although a negative correlation between price and quantity relatives is necessary and sufficient for $P/L < 1$, the magnitude of the P/L differential also depends on the dispersion in price and quantity relatives:

$$P_{\mathrm{P}}/L_{\mathrm{P}} \equiv P_{\mathrm{Q}}/L_{\mathrm{Q}} \equiv 1 + (r_{xy} v_x v_y) \quad (1)$$

where r_{xy} is the weighted coefficient of correlation between price and quantity relatives, v_x is the weighted coefficient of variation of price relatives, and v_y is the weighted coefficient of variation of quantity relatives, with all components measured as deviations from the base-weighted index.

We estimate these components for our drug price distributions and find that the P/L differentials for drug prices are dominated by dispersion across molecules in each country's price and quantity relatives with the US. The coefficients of variation for price relatives v_x range from 0.72 in Canada to 14.6 in Japan. Thus, the effect of regulation (or other country-specific factors) is not simply to reduce all prices by a uniform percentage relative to unregulated US prices (in which case, v_x would be zero). By contrast, the correlation between price and quantity relatives r_{xy}, one possible measure of substitution effects, is negative but small, ranging from -0.001 in Japan to -0.106 in the UK.

The third purpose of this paper is to analyze the determinants of the variation in price relatives across molecules for each country relative to the US. We use quasi-hedonic regression to measure the contribution of product and market characteristics to prices in different countries, with a fully interacted model that permits intercepts and parameters (implicit prices of characteristics) to differ

[3] Most studies have attributed the Paasche/Laspeyres (P/L) discrepancy for intertemporal comparisons to intersectoral shifts that occur during the industrialization process. This hypothesis cannot explain our cross-national findings for drug prices.

across countries (for example, Kravis and Lipsey, 1971). This analysis finds that countries with strict price regulation (France, Italy, and Japan) systematically have lower prices for older molecules and for global products (a rough measure of therapeutic value), relative to less-regulated regimes such as the US and the UK. By contrast, generic competition operates as a more effective control on prices in less regulated regimes, particularly the US, which have both more generic competitors and more price competition between competitors than do regulated regimes. Given these systematic effects on relative prices of molecule age, therapeutic value and generics, an important implication for policy is that unbiased cross-national price comparison requires a sample that is representative along all these dimensions.

An important implication of our analysis for the methodology of price measurement is that standard hedonic regression methods do not strictly apply to measurement of cross-national drug price differences. Standard cross-area hedonic regression treats variation across areas in product characteristics as random, hence area intercepts can be interpreted as pure area effects (for example, Kokoski, 1991). However, in cross-country hedonic regression for drug prices, measured characteristics and their implicit prices are themselves influenced by each country's regulatory system, hence, differences in mean characteristics and their implicit prices are key to understanding the determinants of measured price differences. Country intercepts reflect only unmeasured country effects.

As noted earlier, there is considerable dispersion across molecules in the quantity relatives, $q_{j,\mathrm{S}}/q_{j,\mathrm{US}}$, which measure quantity consumed of each jth molecule in country S relative to the US. Indeed, the weighted coefficient of variation of quantity relatives is the single most important contributor to the differences between Laspeyres and Paasche indexes. We test whether differences across molecules in relative quantities can be partly explained by differences in their relative prices in country S, compared to the US. Our two-stage least squares estimates show significant negative own price elasticities (at the molecule level), ranging from -1.3 for the US, Canada, and Germany, to -0.36 for Italy. We conclude that there is some evidence of substitution towards molecules that are relatively cheap in each country, despite the low correlation between absolute price and quantity relatives r_{xy}, which partly reflects their right-skewed distributions. A full analysis of cross-national quantity differences is an important topic but beyond the scope of this paper.

The structure of the paper is as follows: Section 2 describes the data and methods. Section 3 reports Laspeyres and Paasche price and quantity indexes for the six countries relative to the US, and the Bortkiewicz decomposition into coefficients of correlation and variation. Section 4 reports quasi-hedonic regression analysis of log price relatives and estimates of demand elasticities. Section 5 uses the regression estimates to summarize the contribution of cross-national differences in product characteristics and their parameter effects to the mean price ratio for each country relative to the US. Section 6 concludes.

2. Data and methods

Accurate measurement of both cross-national and intertemporal price indexes for drugs is problematic because of the broad range of products, multidimensional quality and rapid technological change. Previous studies have focused on the measurement of intertemporal price change within the US. Berndt et al. (1993) show that fixed weight indexes, which delay the incorporation of new drugs, lead to upward biased measures of price inflation. Griliches and Cockburn (1994) address the problem of incorporating generic versions of old drugs. Suslow (1996) demonstrates the importance of quality differences, using hedonic regression applied to anti-ulcer drugs.

In the cross-national context, problems arising from diversity of products are more extreme. In our seven countries — Canada, France, Germany, Italy, Japan, the UK, and the US — less than one third of each country's molecules are present in all seven markets. Drugs with the same active ingredient may differ in dosage forms, strengths and packsizes across countries, and are produced by different manufacturers — originator, licensed, or generic producer — and sometimes in prescription and over-the-counter form. This diversity within and between countries implies a trade-off: if price comparisons are confined to products that are identical in chemical composition, manufacturer, formulation, strength and packsize, as attempted in previous studies, then only a small and unrepresentative sample of each country's products can be included, and most generics will be excluded. Most previous cross-national price comparisons (for example, U.S. General Accounting Office, 1992, 1994; Bureau European des Unions Consommateurs (BEUC), 1989a,b) have exacerbated this intrinsic problem of nonmatching products by intentionally selecting only leading branded prescription products.

This study draws data from a comprehensive IMS database of all drug sales through retail pharmacies between October 1991 and September 1992. We define a drug by active ingredient (molecule) and the anatomic therapeutic category (ATC) at the three-digit level (ATC3) to which the drug is classified, regardless of manufacturer or brand name. We report indexes for two samples. The bilaterally matched sample includes, for each country, all molecules that are available in both the US and the comparison country, ranging from 365 molecules for the Japan–US comparison to 438 for the Germany–US comparison. The global sample includes the 171 molecules that are available in all seven countries, hereafter "global molecules".[4] The price for each molecule is defined as a weighted average price,

[4] These bilateral and global samples are matched using molecule name and ATC3 as matching criteria. For a few molecules, different strengths and/or forms are classified by IMS to different ATCs, implying use for different indications. These are appropriately treated as distinct products because market and regulatory conditions may differ across ATCs. In fact, indexes based on the simple molecule, regardless of ATC, are very similar to those obtained from molecule/ATC3 matched samples presented in this paper.

based on all products in the molecule, including originator, licensed, generic and those OTC products that meet the sample selection criteria.[5] This weighted average price per molecule implicitly assumes that all products with the same active ingredient and for the same indication are perfect substitutes, regardless of originator/generic status, manufacturer, or prescription/OTC status. This assumption of perfect substitutability is consistent with practices of third-party payers in the US, Canada, Germany, Sweden, the UK, and other countries, who set a single reimbursement price for all generically equivalent products, regardless of real and perceived differences between originator and generic products (see Griliches and Cockburn, 1994).

Our prices are at the manufacturer level, except that the US price data do not reflect manufacturers discounts given directly to managed care and public purchasers, or sales through mail order, supermarkets, and HMOs. Similarly, the UK data do not reflect all discounts given to pharmacists.[6] Thus, IMS list prices for the US and the UK in 1992 may significantly overestimate actual manufacturer prices for certain products, as discussed further below. We use two measures, price per gram of active ingredient (KG) and price per IMS "standard unit" (SU). A standard unit is defined by IMS as one tablet, one capsule, 10 ml of a liquid, etc., and is a rough proxy for a dose. There is no perfect measure of a quality-constant course of drug therapy.[7] However, the advantage of standard units and grams is that they are defined for all formulations and packs, hence, our weighted average price for the molecule incorporates all forms and packs of that molecule. By contrast, previous cross-national drug price studies have compared prices for a single "representative" pack, for example, a pack of one hundred 250-mg tablets, sometimes with linear imputation where the same pack was not available in all countries. As shown below, since mean strength and packsize, and

[5] We exclude products with sales of less than 1000 packs or 1 kg of active ingredient, because of higher risk of sampling and reporting error. Multiple molecule drugs are excluded because the relative mix of the different molecules is not necessarily the same in all countries. Since OTC status is not identified, the sample includes some OTC products, and this is appropriate assuming they are good substitutes for prescription-bound products.

[6] In the US, between first quarter 1991 and 1993, the median best price discount declined from 24% to 14% for HMOs (U.S. General Accounting Office, 1994); the unweighted average best price discounts declined from 42% in first quarter 1991 to 33.4% in fourth quarter 1992 (U.S. Congressional Budget Office (CBO), 1996). For the UK, an April 1992 Department of Health Pharmacist Discount Enquiry showed generic prices on average 47.7% below the NHS drug tariff (of which 12.5% is the wholesale margin). Following deep reductions in NHS prices, an April 1993 Pharmacist Discount Enquiry found average discounts of only 26%.

[7] Other studies have used price per WHO defined daily dose (DDD), which is not available to us. DDDs are also imperfect because they are not defined to be equipotent units, do not necessarily correspond to actual daily doses, and ignore differences in duration of treatment (Danzon, 1996). Since DDDs for each drug are defined as grams per day, indexes based on DDDs should be similar to our indexes based on grams, if days of treatment are uniform across countries.

their implicit prices differ systematically across countries, serious bias can result from including only a single pack and using linear imputation based on price per pill in other packs if the selected pack is not available.[8]

Although we require only that the molecule/ATC3 match across countries, not the same manufacturer or packsize, nevertheless, over 40% of total retail pharmacy sales in Germany, France, Italy, and Japan do not match and cannot be included even in our larger, bilaterally matched samples. This heterogeneity in product-mix across countries implies that even the price indexes, which start with the universe of sales may be unavoidably biased because they are confined to matching molecules.

3. Laspeyres and Paasche price and quantity indexes

3.1. Price and quantity indexes

Table 1 reports price and quantity indexes for the two volume measures, standard units (SU) and grams (KG), for each of the six comparison countries relative to the US, using US weights (Laspeyres) and comparison country weights (Paasche). Also reported are the Paasche/Laspeyres ratios, which are identical for price and quantity indexes. The indexes in Parts A and B are, respectively, for bilaterally matched products and global products. The Laspeyres indexes, which may be most relevant from the US perspective since they use US weights, can be interpreted as a lower-bound estimate of how much the US might save by adopting another country's prices, assuming no change in US consumption patterns. The Paasche indexes provide an upper-bound estimate of potential savings, under the implausible assumption that the US would adopt the other country's consumption patterns, and that such changes in US prices and volumes would not affect R&D.

3.1.1. Price indexes

The Laspeyres indexes for price per standard unit show smaller price differences than reported in other studies: Canada and Germany, respectively, are 2.1% and 24.7% higher than the US; Japan, Italy, and the UK are respectively 11.6%, 12.9%, and 16.6% lower than the US; and France is 32.2% lower than the US. With the Paasche indexes, all countries appear to have lower prices than the US, ranging from 44% lower for the UK to 67% lower for France. Thus, both the magnitude and the rank ordering of price differentials depend on the weights. For given weights, the SU and KG indexes differ significantly for some countries, due to systematic difference in grams per standard unit. Strength per dose in Japan, for example, is typically weak, in part because doctors commonly prescribe several drugs to be taken together (polypharmacy). Japan thus appears 11.6% less

[8] Linear imputation can lead to bias because price per pill is not linear in packsize and both mean packsize and the price–packsize relation differ across countries (see Table 2 below).

Table 1
Pharmaceutical price indexes relative to US — 1992 molecule/ATC matching

a. Bilateral matches with US

Index/Variable		Canada	Germany	France	Italy	Japan	UK
Number of molecules		420	438	373	386	365	377
Laspeyres price index	(KG)	0.866	0.914	0.548	0.696	1.193	0.713
Laspeyres price index	(SU)	1.021	1.247	0.678	0.871	0.884	0.834
Paasche price index	(KG)	0.674	0.597	0.419	0.326	0.484	0.522
Paasche price index	(SU)	0.447	0.403	0.330	0.485	0.457	0.560
Laspeyres quantity index[a]	(KG)	1.320	1.145	2.122	2.353	1.019	1.026
Laspeyres quantity index[a]	(SU)	1.989	1.694	2.690	1.583	1.081	0.957
Paasche quantity index[a]	(KG)	1.027	0.748	1.621	1.103	0.414	0.752
Paasche quantity index[a]	(SU)	0.871	0.548	1.311	0.881	0.559	0.642
Population ratio (foreign/US)		0.103	0.244	0.218	0.220	0.473	0.219
Paasche/Laspeyres	(KG)	0.778	0.653	0.764	0.469	0.406	0.733
Paasche/Laspeyres	(SU)	0.438	0.323	0.487	0.557	0.517	0.671
r_{xy}	(KG)	−0.095	−0.006	−0.033	−0.011	−0.001	−0.106
v_x	(KG)	0.723	5.801	0.995	1.163	14.606	0.875
v_y	(KG)	3.241	9.972	7.154	42.262	77.209	2.872
r_{xy}	(SU)	−0.001	−0.008	−0.002	−0.027	−0.043	−0.047
v_x	(SU)	4.383	3.588	2.483	1.524	1.967	1.677
v_y	(SU)	124.321	24.664	129.718	10.758	5.689	4.172
$r_{xy} * v_x * v_y$	(KG)	−0.222	−0.347	−0.236	−0.531	−0.594	−0.267
$r_{xy} * v_x * v_y$	(SU)	−0.562	−0.677	−0.513	−0.443	−0.483	−0.329

b. All seven country matches

Index/Variable		Canada	Germany	France	Italy	Japan	UK
Number of molecules		171	171	171	171	171	171
Laspeyres price index	(KG)	0.857	0.887	0.576	0.696	1.163	0.708
Laspeyres price index	(SU)	0.983	1.193	0.701	0.910	0.943	0.883
Paasche price index	(KG)	0.699	0.589	0.427	0.302	0.792	0.553
Paasche price index	(SU)	0.694	0.362	0.364	0.543	0.479	0.630
Laspeyres quantity index[a]	(KG)	1.349	1.207	2.038	2.290	0.566	1.055
Laspeyres quantity index[a]	(SU)	1.358	1.966	2.392	1.276	0.936	0.927
Paasche quantity index[a]	(KG)	1.100	0.802	1.511	0.995	0.386	0.824
Paasche quantity index[a]	(SU)	0.959	0.596	1.242	0.761	0.476	0.661
Population ratio (foreign/US)		0.103	0.244	0.218	0.220	0.473	0.219
Paasche/Laspeyres	(KG)	0.815	0.664	0.741	0.435	0.681	0.781
Paasche/Laspeyres	(SU)	0.706	0.303	0.519	0.596	0.508	0.713
r_{xy}	(KG)	−0.094	−0.036	−0.035	−0.010	−0.044	−0.093
v_x	(KG)	0.569	0.919	0.925	1.102	1.863	0.892
v_y	(KG)	3.434	10.284	8.082	51.084	3.889	2.622
r_{xy}	(SU)	−0.034	−0.015	−0.020	−0.024	−0.061	−0.044
v_x	(SU)	2.009	1.809	1.102	1.467	1.942	1.804
v_y	(SU)	4.284	25.239	21.935	11.345	4.129	3.580
$r_{xy} * v_x * v_y$	(KG)	−0.185	−0.336	−0.259	−0.565	−0.319	−0.219
$r_{xy} * v_x * v_y$	(SU)	−0.294	−0.697	−0.481	−0.404	−0.492	−0.287

(continued on next page)

Table 1 (*continued*)

c. Contribution of sample and index methods to GAO price comparisons

	GAO full sample products @ GAO prices	GAO-IMS matched products @ GAO prices	GAO-IMS matched products @ IMS prices	GAO-IMS matched molecules @ IMS prices	IMS full sample molecules @ IMS prices
Canada–US price comparison using GAO list of drugs					
Mean of US price/mean of Canada price	1.337	1.313	1.106	1.260	1.611
Mean of price relatives (Canada = reference)	1.766	1.766	1.661	1.668	3.183
Mean of price relatives (US = reference)	0.746	0.770	0.812	0.831	2.709
Median of price relatives (Canada = reference)	1.433	1.355	1.282	1.289	1.196
Median of price relatives (US = reference)	0.698	0.738	0.781	0.776	0.836
Laspeyres price index (US = reference)	–	–	0.791	0.753	1.021
Paasche price index (US = reference)	–	–	0.768	0.717	0.447
Paasche price index (CA = reference)	–	–	1.263	1.327	0.979
r_{xy}	–	–	−0.060	−0.131	−0.001
v_x	–	–	0.388	0.498	4.383
v_y	–	–	1.277	0.729	124.321
N	121	85	88	77	420
UK–US price comparison using GAO list of drugs					
Mean of US price/mean of UK price	1.915	1.728	1.367	1.281	1.770
Mean of price relatives (UK = reference)	3.462	2.750	2.266	1.943	3.421
Mean of price relatives (US = reference)	0.552	0.583	0.738	0.841	1.191
Median of price relatives (UK = reference)	2.436	2.218	1.906	1.669	1.795
Median of price relatives (US = reference)	0.411	0.452	0.525	0.600	0.557
Laspeyres price index (US = reference)	–	–	0.698	0.740	0.834
Paasche price index (US = reference)	–	–	0.616	0.642	0.560
Paasche price index (UK = reference)	1.600[b]	–	1.433	1.352	1.199
r_{xy}	–	–	−0.113	−0.165	−0.047
v_x	–	–	0.851	0.818	1.677
v_y	–	–	1.227	0.980	4.172
N	77	56	57	56	377

[a]Adjusted for population.
[b]Reported in GAO Reports.

expensive than the US based on price per SU, but 19.3% more expensive based on price per KG, because more pills are required to yield a given total grams.

3.1.2. Quantity indexes

The quantity indexes in Table 1 are normalized by relative population size, so they can be interpreted as differences in quantity per capita. The Laspeyres SU indexes imply higher foreign consumption than the US for all countries except the UK — for example, France has quantity indexes more than twice the US level — whereas, Paasche indexes show other countries with lower per capita volume than the US, except France, which is at least 31% higher by all measures. Just as our price indexes show smaller cross-national differences than previously reported, so do our quantity indexes suggest smaller cross-national differences in per capita drug consumption.[9] Moreover, differences in KG quantity indexes are generally smaller than differences in SU indexes, suggesting that systematic differences in strength per pill are partially offset by differences in number of pills per capita. However, since our indexes are based on the subset of matching molecules, they do not support firm conclusions about differences in total drug consumption. In particular, the molecules included here are a smaller fraction of total drug sales for Germany, France, Italy, and Japan than for the UK, the US, and Canada.

3.1.3. Paasche / Laspeyres ratios

The Paasche/Laspeyres ratios are identical for price and quantity indexes and are all less than one, consistent with a Gerschenkron effect.[10] The P/L ratios for SU indexes range from 0.32 in Germany to 0.67 in the UK, whereas for KG indexes, the P/L ratios range from 0.41 in Japan to 0.78 in Canada. The generally lower P/L ratios for SU than for KG are consistent with the notion that systematic differences in strength per unit are partially offset by differences in number of units (more pills are consumed if strength per pill is low).

3.1.4. Global molecules

The price indexes for global molecules generally show slightly smaller price differences between countries than the indexes based on the larger, bilaterally matched samples. The Paasche/Laspeyres ratios are also generally (but not always) closer to unity for the global products than the bilateral products, suggesting less variation in consumption patterns for global drugs than for drugs that have less universal acceptance. Less cross-national price dispersion on global

9 For example, Burstall (1991) estimates per capita drug consumption by deflating total drug expenditures per capita by the Bureau European des Unions de Consommateurs (BEUC) (1989a,b) price indexes. This yields estimates of per capita volume, relative to the UK, of 3.06 for France, 2.06 for Italy and 1.53 for Germany, which are larger than most of the measures reported with our larger sample.

10 The choice of base country affects the magnitude but P/L ratios are always less than one.

products, particularly on price per SU, could reflect corporate strategies to maintain prices for global products within narrow bands in order to preempt parallel trade and/or regulatory cross-national spillovers; it could also reflect such regulatory spillover effects.[11]

3.1.5. Comparison with U.S. General Accounting Office (1992, 1994)

Table 1c illustrates the contribution of sample vs. methods to the difference between our estimates and those in U.S. General Accounting Office (1992, 1994), to the extent possible with our data. The GAO US–Canada comparison (U.S. General Accounting Office, 1992) reported the ratio of US price to Canadian price for a market basket consisting of one pack for each of 121 branded products; median price relatives were also reported. The GAO US–UK comparison (U.S. General Accounting Office, 1994) used one pack for each of 77 products and reported a Paasche index for the UK, that is, US weights applied to US/UK price relatives, which is the reciprocal of the Laspeyres index with US as base. We are not able to replicate perfectly the GAO analysis because of the GAO's sample of 121 drugs for Canada, we have data on only 85; of the GAO's 77 drugs for the UK, we have data on 56.[12] Our measure of price is a weighted average price per standard unit for all forms/strengths/packs for each product, whereas the GAO US–Canada study used the price per pack and the GAO US–UK study used price per pill based on a single pack.

In Table 1c, column 2 reports the GAO's results based on their data and methods. In column 3, we attempt to replicate their results using IMS data for the subsample of drugs that we can match. For the US–Canada comparison, we can confirm that our subsample yields estimates similar to the full GAO sample for the GAO index measure: the ratio of US price for the market basket relative to Canadian price in row 1 (mean US price/mean Canada price) is 1.337 for their full sample of 121 products (column 2)[13] and 1.313 for our subsample of 85 products (column 3). As a rough indicator of the effect of selecting a single pack, note that this unweighted mean US price/mean Canada price ratio falls from 1.31 to 1.106 when we substitute the IMS weighted average price per unit for all forms/strengths/packsizes (column 4) for GAO's single pack price (column 3). Column 5, which reports molecule level prices (weighted average over all

[11] Danzon (1997b) discusses manufacturers' incentives to reduce cross-national price differences in response to parallel trade and regulatory use of price comparisons.

[12] We attempted to match products in the IMS data to the GAO list, based on brand name and manufacturer. If the same manufacturer name could not be matched between the two countries, we substituted the same brand name product from a sole producer, if available. If this condition could not be met, the product is excluded from our sample.

[13] We are unable to explain the difference between our estimate of 1.337 and the 1.32 reported in US General Accounting Office (1992).

products), shows that adding generics to the GAO sample of products has little effect. However, expanding the sample to include matching molecules (column 6) changes the Canada–US Laspeyres index from 0.75 for the GAO subsample to 1.02 for the full sample of molecules. Thus, the selection of leading branded products is one major source of the bias in the US–GAO comparison.[14] Use of the ratio of unweighted mean prices adds a second major source of bias: for our full sample, the ratio of unweighted mean prices (mean US price/mean Canada price) is 1.61, whereas the Laspeyres index is only 1.02. The bias from using the mean of the price relatives is even larger and sign is indeterminate: mean price relative with Canada as base is 3.18, while mean price relative with US as base is 2.71!

For the UK, we cannot compute a UK-based Paasche index with our subsample of 57 products to compare to the GAO's index for their 77 product sample, because U.S. General Accounting Office (1994) does not report their weights. However, using the 57 GAO products and IMS average product prices and weights yields a UK-based Paasche index of 1.43, compared to 1.60 reported by GAO. Expanding the sample to include all matching molecules (column 6) reduces this index to 1.199, while the ratio of the unweighted means is 1.77. Again, the unweighted mean price relatives show sign reversal, with the US higher or lower than the UK, depending on the base.

Thus, the results for the UK, like those for Canada, show that both sample selection and using an unweighted index can each lead to bias of at least 20 percentage points; use of a single pack adds additional, smaller bias. The major source of sampling bias appears to be selection of leading branded products, not simply the exclusion of generics for those molecules that are multi-source. This is consistent with the finding of the U.S. General Accounting Office (1994) that substituting a generic, where available, for the branded product in their sample did not significantly affect their estimates. However, exclusion of generics would doubtless be a more significant factor for a comparison involving countries with very different generic shares, such as the US vs. France. The upward bias is exacerbated by use of unweighted means, which give undue weight to relatively high priced products. Comparisons based on unweighted price relatives (as in Minority Staff, 1998) are even more biased, extremely unstable and can reverse sign. This sign reversal results from the right-skew of the distributions of price relatives, which are bounded between zero and infinity, regardless of which country is the base.

[14] This selection bias appears to result from the GAO's selection of products that are leaders in large therapeutic categories: relative to the full sample, the molecules in the GAO subsamples for both Canada and the UK have slightly more generics per molecule, fewer substitute molecules in the therapeutic category, are relatively early entrants and have broader global diffusion. The P/L ratios for the GAO subsample are also closer to one, with much smaller variation in price and quantity relatives.

3.1.6. Comparison with Bureau European des Unions de Consommateurs BEUC (1989a,b)

For their study of drug prices in the 12 member states of the European Economic Community (EEC), the Belgian Consumers' Association (Bureau European des Unions de Consommateurs BEUC, 1989a) drew a sample of the 25 leading prescription drugs, by sales value, in each state in 1987, to which they added any omitted drugs that were in the top 10 by volume (volume unit unspecified). Drugs were matched across countries if they were produced by the same manufacturers or were the sole source product. Generics were explicitly excluded on grounds that: (1) prices differ across generic forms within a country, and (2) single generic products are rarely in the top 25 in terms of sales. Thus, the notion of substitutability between generic equivalents was ignored. Prices were imputed if products were missing, which was common — only 78 of the sample of 125 products (62%) were available in nine or more of the 12 countries — and where form/packsize did not match across countries. Most of the analyses focus on retail prices. The one comparison of manufacturer prices (retail minus an average distribution percentage) reports an index of the unweighted average price for the market basket relative to the EEC-average of 100. Normalizing this index relative to its UK value (since the EEC average includes countries that are not in our sample) yields the following: France 0.58, Italy 0.74, Germany 1.127 (based on Bureau European des Unions de Consommateurs BEUC, 1989a, Table 10). Thus, based on this unweighted average applied to a sample of brand-only prices, the UK — a country with a relatively large generic share — appears relatively costly. By contrast, our Laspeyres SU weighted indexes applied to our sample of all matching molecules, including generics, show the UK as second cheapest.[15] Bureau European des Unions de Consommateurs BEUC (1989b) extended this study to include the US, based on a sample of the 25 products for which they could find a perfect match. The retail price of this market basket of 25 products (unweighted and excluding VAT) showed the US at 1.28 of the UK index, compared to France 0.58, Italy 0.60, and Germany 1.24. These retail price indexes, which include distribution margins, are not strictly comparable to our manufacturer price indexes. Nevertheless, the general conclusion appears to hold, that comparisons that are based on an unweighted average of branded product prices only, excluding generics, tend to yield upward biased estimates of prices for relatively unregulated countries with large generic shares, notably the US, Germany and the UK, compared to France and Italy, which have strict price regulation and negligible generic shares.

[15] Dividing each country's Laspeyres SU index by the UK Laspeyres SU index yields: France 0.81, Italy 1.04, Germany 1.495. These cannot be interpreted as UK-based Laspeyres indexes because the Laspeyres index is not transitive. The Paasche indexes are less comparable because each country's Paasche index incorporates different, country-specific weights, so differences in the indexes reflect volumes as well as price differences.

3.2. Decomposition of Paasche / Laspeyres ratios

The Bortkiewicz formula (Eq. 1) shows that the Paasche/Laspeyres differential can be decomposed into three components: the coefficient of correlation between price and quantity relatives r_{xy} and the coefficients of variation of price and quantity relatives (v_x and v_y), all measured relative to the respective Laspeyres index (see Eq. 1). These measures, which are invariant to population differences, are reported in Table 1. The hypothesis that the P/L differences primarily reflect a substitution effect towards products that are relatively cheap in each country implies that the correlation coefficients between price and quantity relatives, r_{xy}, should be negative and large. In our data, r_{xy} is indeed negative but the magnitudes are too small to "explain" the P/L differences — ranging from -0.001 for Japan to -0.106 for the UK in the bilaterally matched samples, and from -0.01 in Japan to -0.094 in Canada for the global sample.

By contrast, v_x and v_y are large and dominate the Paasche/Laspeyres differentials. The range of v_x is larger for KG (from 0.72 for Canada to 14.61 for Japan) than for SU (from 1.52 for Italy to 4.38 for Canada). This greater uniformity in price relatives per dose than per gram is consistent with the hypothesis that manufacturers and/or regulators tend to set price per dose within an affordable range. The v_y is generally larger for SU (from 5.69 in Japan to 129.72 in Canada) than for KG (from 2.87 in the UK to 77.21 in Japan), suggesting that differences in strength per pill are partly offset by differences in number of pills. V_x and v_y are generally smaller for global products than for the bilaterally matched sample, consistent with less variation in prices and quantities for global, "high consensus" products than for the lower consensus drugs in the bilateral samples.[16]

This evidence, that v_x and v_y dominate the P/L discrepancy for cross-national price comparisons of pharmaceuticals, and that r_{xy} is relatively small, is consistent with Jonas and Sardy's (1972) findings for intertemporal quantity indexes for machinery in the US between 1889 and 1939. Like most previous studies, Jonas and Sardy (JS) focus on quantity indexes and attribute the P/L discrepancy to the process of industrialization, in which "the production of highly fabricated goods increases proportionately more than the production of slightly fabricated goods; and, at the same time, the relative prices of highly fabricated goods decrease". This hypothesis obviously cannot explain our finding of similar patterns in cross-national comparison of pharmaceutical prices. However, the JS finding that the P/L ratio increased with the lag between the base and the comparison periods suggests the related hypothesis, that P/L ratios should be closer to unity in countries with similar medical norms, notably, the US, the UK, and Canada. This

[16] For example, for the bilaterally matched molecules, five of the 12 values of v_y exceed 20 and three exceed 50, whereas for the global molecules only three of the 12 values of v_y exceed 20 and all but one are under 50.

assumes that use of a common language facilitates diffusion of medical research and consensus practices. Consistent with this, all four P/L ratios for global products for Canada and the UK are closer to unity than all but one of the eight ratios for the other countries.

Inspection of the data suggests that the high values for v_x and v_y partly reflect the extremely right-skewed distributions of both price and quantity relatives, which are bounded between zero and infinity. In our data, the distributions of price and quantity relatives pass tests for lognormality. Such departure from bivariate normality tends to bias Pearson correlation coefficients towards zero.[17] As shown in Table 1c, an important implication of this extreme skewness of the price relative distributions is that price comparisons that are based on unweighted means of price relatives are extremely sensitive to the sample and choice of base.

4. Multivariate analysis of price and quantity relatives

4.1. Theory

Section 3 demonstrated that, in any two-country comparison, there is a significant dispersion in relative prices and quantities across molecules and this dispersion leads to large divergence between Laspeyres and Paasche indexes. In this section, we examine the contribution of various product and market characteristics to the dispersion of price relatives, using quasi-hedonic regression. Our equations are quasi-hedonic for three reasons. First, in the standard hedonic approach to estimating cross-area price indexes, the main focus is on the area indicator variables, which can be interpreted as area-specific bilateral price indexes relative to the omitted area, controlling for product characteristics that are assumed to differ randomly across areas while the implicit prices of these characteristics are assumed invariant (for example, Kokoski, 1991). However, in our cross-national comparison of drug prices, both product characteristics and their implicit prices are expected to differ systematically across countries, reflecting the incentives and constraints of each country's regulatory and reimbursement environment. Thus, cross-country differences in mean product characteristics and their implicit prices are of direct interest as factors that contribute to systematic, cross-country differences in drug prices. Our country intercepts reflect only unmeasured country-specific effects, conditional on measured characteristics.

[17] The unweighted Pearson correlation coefficients between price and quantity relatives range from −0.006 for Canada/US to −0.07 for Italy/US. The same correlation coefficients for logged values are −0.55 and −0.35, respectively. The distribution-independent Spearman rank correlation coefficients are −0.35 and −0.26, respectively. Although these results with respect to extreme skewness pertain to the distribution of relative prices and quantities around zero, similar although less extreme patterns are found for distribution relative to the weighted mean, which is used in v_x and v_y.

Second, drug markets are imperfectly competitive because demand is influenced by such factors as insurance coverage, imperfect information, and physician prescribing, while supply is constrained by patents and regulation. Our quasi-hedonic regression coefficients are still implicit prices but cannot be interpreted as marginal values to consumers or marginal costs to producers.

Third, to capture the different impact of the imperfectly competitive market for pharmaceuticals in different countries, our price equations include measures of the extent of competition, although such measures would not belong in a pure hedonic equation. In countries that regulate prices, manufacturers and regulators presumably consider competitors prices in their negotiations over the regulated price. Moreover, since regulation sets a price ceiling but not a floor, price competition may still occur and is a hypothesis to be tested. Quality competition also occurs and may influence both unregulated and regulated prices. We therefore apply the same model to all countries, but test for cross-national differences in parameters.

The structural model, at the molecule level, is:[18]

$$P_{jkm} = P(\mathbf{Z}_{jkm}, G_{jk}, T_{jm}; R_j) \tag{2}$$

$$Q_{jkm} = Q(P_{jkm}, \mathbf{Z}'_{jkm}) \tag{3}$$

where P_{jkm} is the price of molecule k in therapeutic category m in country j, $\mathbf{Z}$ is a vector of quality and market characteristics, $\mathbf{Z}'$ is a subset of the these characteristics, G_{jk} is the number of generic competitors in molecule k in country j, T_{jm} is the number of therapeutic substitute molecules in category m in country j, and R_j is the (unobserved) regulatory regime in country j. For the quantity Eq. (3), the vector $\mathbf{Z}'$ includes only indicator variables for therapeutic category, to control for insurance and indication effects that may influence quantity directly. Thus, competition and most quality characteristics are not assumed to shift demand directly; rather, they influence quantity only indirectly through their effect on price.[19]

This simple model does not capture all relevant determinants of drug prices. First, demand in theory reflects incentives of patients, physicians and pharmacists. Our price measure is the manufacturer price, whereas the relevant price for patient demand is the patient's co-payment. In fact, in most countries in 1992, patient co-payments were low and often a fixed deductible per script, regardless of the product price (for example, in the UK, Germany), with total exemptions for the elderly, welfare recipients, etc. One exception is the US, where co-payments

[18] Danzon and Chao (1999) provide a more detailed analysis at the individual product level.

[19] Ellison et al. (1997) estimate a molecule-level demand system for four cephalosporins which includes own price and price of substitutes as the only explanatory variables. Price is treated as exogenous or instrumented by number of generic competitors, which is a restricted version of our model. Caves et al. (1991) report that aggregate molecule volume does not increase following generic entry, plausibly because a decline in promotion by originator firms offsets the effect of lower priced generics on volume.

varied from 0% to 100%, depending on health plan; overall, in 1992 roughly 50% of outpatient drug expenditure in the US was paid directly out-of-pocket (Levit et al., 1998). In 1992, physician incentives and constraints on drug choice were minimal, with few exceptions: fundholding physicians in the UK faced drug budgets; under reference pricing, German physicians had incentives to avoid products priced above the reference price, which applied primarily to multi-source products; and Japanese physicians were sensitive to the margin between the reimbursement and the acquisition cost (see below). Pharmacists did have incentives to be price sensitive in substituting between generically equivalent drugs in the US, the UK, and Canada. Since we lack data on these patient, physician, and pharmacy incentives for price-sensitivity, these unobserved characteristics might in theory influence both the unexplained country residuals and coefficients of some measured characteristics, as discussed below.

Second, manufacturer prices are regulated either directly or indirectly in all countries except in the US.[20] A rough categorization is that France, Italy, and Japan have strict price regulation, whereas Canada, Germany, and the UK have looser regulation. Specifically, France and Italy require approval of the manufacturer's price before a product becomes admitted for reimbursement. Subsequent price increases are rarely allowed and decreases may be mandated. In Japan, the manufacturer must obtain approval of the price for reimbursement at launch, and thereafter, the government sets the reimbursement price. However, since Japanese doctors dispense the drugs that they prescribe, drug manufacturers compete for market share by cutting actual price to increase the doctor's margin between reimbursement price and acquisition cost. The government revises downward the reimbursement prices every two (now one) years, based on surveys of manufacturer prices. In Canada, the Medicines Review Board monitors launch prices to assure that they are ''reasonable'', relative to foreign prices (for innovative products) or relative to existing product prices (for non-innovative products). Price increases are constrained to the general rate of inflation. Generic substitution is encouraged. The UK permits free pricing of new products, subject to the constraint that the rate of return from sales to the NHS on capital invested in the UK may not exceed a specified level; price increases require authorization. Reimbursement for multi-source, off-patent products is effectively a reference price system, where the Drug Tariff reimbursement price is based on supply prices of leading generics. Generic manufacturers compete by offering discounts off list prices, to increase the pharmacist's margin. The Drug Tariff price is periodically revised downward, but it reflects actual supply prices with a lag.[21] Germany had free pricing until

[20] This description outlines the regulatory systems as of 1992, the year of our data, which predates more recent important changes in several countries (see Danzon, 1997a).

[21] The NHS reimbursement to pharmacists includes a ''clawback'' (roughly 7%) which is intended to reflect the average discount below list prices.

1989, when reference pricing was introduced, focusing on multisource, off-patent products in Phase 1, extending to some therapeutic substitutes in Phases 2 and 3. Prices of non-reference priced products remained free until 1993. The expected effect of these regulatory characteristics on market attributes and coefficients is discussed below.

4.2. Variable definitions

4.2.1. Quality

Competition occurs on multiple dimensions of quality, and most regulatory systems take quality into account in setting prices. Hedonic regression would ideally include the characteristics that are of intrinsic value to consumers and regulators, in particular, therapeutic value and convenience. Since most of the relevant characteristics are not directly observable in our data, we include several proxy indicators for different dimensions of product quality.

A vector of binary indicators for one-digit therapeutic category (ATC1) controls for indication since, for example, cardiovascular drugs may, on the average, be more valuable than dermatologics. We use Global penetration, defined as the number of our seven countries in which the molecule is available, as a measure of therapeutic value. The implicit assumption is that, having incurred the fixed costs of drug development, a manufacturer will market a drug in any country in which its expected revenue exceeds the marginal cost of launch. Differences in Global penetration thus reflect differences in expected therapeutic value, assuming that expected revenue reflects expected value perceived by consumers and/or physicians and that the costs of launch are similar across products.[22] Molecule Age (months from the first product launch in country j to September 1992) is an inverse indicator of relative therapeutic value, assuming that recent molecules are on the average more effective than older molecules.[23] In these cross-sectional data, Molecule Age may also reflect life-cycle effects due to regulation and other factors.

Other quality indicators measure characteristics of the formulation. Strength per unit is included as a control. The expected sign is positive if the within-molecule

[22] Barral (1995) shows that global penetration is positively related to medical measures of therapeutic value. See also Thomas (1996) for a similar interpretation of this variable. Another, related interpretation is that products with high values of Global are products of multinational companies which may have economies of scale in diffusing products internationally, whereas products with low values of Global are more likely produced by smaller, local firms who may lack established connections in many countries but have political influence in regulated markets. These interpretations are related if multinational companies have higher hurdles for expected revenue in selecting the products that they take through development, compared to smaller companies.

[23] Molecule age is an inverse indicator of therapeutic value of a molecule, whereas individual product age is not expected to be related to therapeutic value because many new products are generic versions of old molecules.

effect (stronger products should be more effective, hence, receive higher prices) dominates the between-molecule effect (some very potent molecules have weak strength per pill but command high prices). The number of distinct formulation/strengths in the molecule (Form Codes) is an indicator of choice and convenience for patients, hence, is expected to be positively related to price.[24] Packsize (average number of units per pack) is expected to be inversely related to price per unit, if manufacturers pass on economies of scale in packaging. Since France, Italy, and Germany, have unit pack dispensing requirements, which prevent the pharmacist from splitting packs, average packsize is expected to be smaller, and competitive pressure to give volume discounts is expected to be lower in these countries than in the US, Canada, Japan, and the UK, where packsplitting is permitted and manufacturers offer large packs.

4.2.2. Competition

We include two measures of competition, recognizing that these are not product characteristics and hence, would not be appropriate for a pure hedonic regression under assumptions of competitive markets. Generic Competitors is the number of manufacturers of the molecule, including originators, licensees, parallel imports, and ''true'', post-patent generic entrants. Therapeutic Substitute Molecules in the ATC3 is a measure of therapeutic competitors, that is, compounds that are chemically distinct but are used to treat the same indication.[25] Price is expected to be more negatively related to generic competitors than to therapeutic competitors, because generics are closer substitutes and because pharmacists have strong incentives to be price-sensitive in regimes that permit generic substitution. To test for first mover advantage, we include the lag in months between this molecule's launch date and the launch of the first molecule in the ATC3 (molecule entry lag). The predicted sign is negative, if first mover advantage dominates product improvements that may be embodied in later molecules.

4.3. Specification

We use the log transform for prices and quantities, which are normally distributed after transformation. Log transforms of all explanatory variables are also used, since proportional effects are theoretically more plausible than linear

[24] Our variable is the maximum number of form/strengths for any manufacturer's product in the molecule. This is a lower bound on the total number of different form/strengths for the molecule if different manufacturers produce different form/strengths.

[25] In the IMS ATC classification system, the first letter indicates body part (e.g., C for cardiovasculars), and successive digits indicate narrower definitions of indication, mode of action or substance. Our measure of therapeutic substitutes is imperfect, because not all compounds in an ATC3 are equally good substitutes and drugs in different ATC3s may sometimes be substitutes.

effects. We estimate a fully interacted model that pools all countries but permits intercepts and coefficients to differ across countries:

$$\ln P_{kj} = \beta \ln \boldsymbol{X}_{kj} + \sum_{j=1}^{6} \delta_{kj} D_j \ln \boldsymbol{X}_{kj} + u_{kj} \tag{4}$$

where $j = 0, 1, \dots, 6$; $j = 0$ if country = US; $D_j = 1$ if country $= j$ and $j > 0$; 0 otherwise. The dependent variable, $\ln P_{kj}$, is the log price per standard unit for molecule k in country j, $\boldsymbol{X}$ is a vector of country-specific characteristics for that molecule in country j. In this form, δ_j measures country-specific implicit prices, that is, the difference between parameter effects for country j and for the US. Thus, each country's net implicit prices for characteristics are:

US	β
UK	$\beta + \delta_{UK}$
Canada	$\beta + \delta_{CN}$ etc.

This fully interacted model yields the same OLS coefficients as are obtained from separate regressions for each country. However, the pooled regression gives slightly different test statistics because the estimate of the residual variance σ_u^2 is based on the sum of squared residuals over all countries instead of being estimated separately for each country. The advantage of the pooled, interacted specification is that t-statistics for country interactions test directly for parameter differences across countries.

Table 2a reports results with the fully interacted model, which allows all parameters to differ across countries. Several of the coefficients are not significant at conventional levels, suggesting that the fully interacted model is too general and is not efficient. In Table 2b, we therefore report results from a constrained model that suppresses the interaction for those variables whose t-statistics in the fully interacted model were below unity. This imposes parameter equality for that variable in the comparison country and the US. The constraints improve efficiency but could impose bias if the constrained parameters are not truly identical. A test of the joint hypothesis, that the true value of the constrained parameters is zero, cannot be rejected, suggesting that any such bias is small.[26]

4.4. Empirical results: price equations

The parameter estimates in Table 2b confirm most of the basic hypotheses about effects of quality and market characteristics on price, but with significant differences across countries.

[26] The F statistic for the joint hypothesis that the constrained interactions are equal to zero is 0.67.

Table 2

a. Regression results for pharmaceutical prices — 1992 fully interacted model (*t*-statistics in parentheses) log price per standard unit, for molecule/ATC matched with US

Variable	US	CN	GE	FR	IT	JP	UK
Intercept	3.301 (8.592)	1.010 (1.603)	1.120 (1.681)	1.458 (2.115)	1.670 (2.483)	4.367 (5.672)	0.450 (0.661)
Quality							
Strength (ln)	0.125 (6.435)	−0.036 −(1.093)	0.084 (2.631)	0.002 (0.057)	0.052 (1.561)	−0.046 −(1.342)	−0.009 −(0.251)
Age (ln)	−0.190 −(3.516)	−0.116 −(1.372)	−0.212 −(2.438)	−0.434 −(4.916)	−0.394 −(4.643)	−0.719 −(6.833)	−0.340 −(3.658)
Form codes (ln)	0.282 (3.927)	−0.085 −(0.684)	0.114 (0.987)	−0.165 −(1.314)	−0.068 −(0.545)	−0.058 −(0.445)	−0.159 −(1.280)
Global (ln)	0.458 (4.680)	−0.226 −(1.286)	−0.430 −(2.352)	−0.648 −(3.020)	−0.830 −(3.921)	−0.683 −(3.704)	−0.150 −(0.732)
Packsize (ln)	−0.719 −(17.713)	−0.068 −(1.046)	0.170 (2.524)	0.027 (0.383)	0.032 (0.446)	0.029 (0.472)	0.126 (1.835)
Competition							
Generic competitors (ln)	−0.566 −(13.637)	0.110 (1.138)	0.188 (2.470)	0.629 (5.954)	0.770 (8.552)	0.693 (8.499)	0.329 (3.117)
Therapeutic substitute molecules (ln)	0.094 (1.389)	−0.103 −(0.910)	−0.314 −(3.109)	−0.233 −(2.086)	−0.193 −(1.877)	−0.128 −(1.237)	−0.247 −(2.272)
Therapeutic substitute molecule entry lag (ln)	−0.043 −(1.902)	0.017 (0.451)	0.084 (2.340)	0.050 (1.284)	0.039 (1.059)	0.057 (1.463)	0.063 (1.693)
Therapeutic categories							
A	−0.843 −(5.305)	0.209 (0.826)	0.195 (0.775)	0.796 (3.061)	0.810 (3.144)	0.648 (2.480)	0.390 (1.537)
B	−0.473 −(1.776)	0.332 (0.811)	0.440 (1.092)	0.725 (1.785)	0.699 (1.757)	0.555 (1.346)	0.351 (0.824)
D	−0.962 −(5.793)	0.133 (0.497)	0.442 (1.692)	0.689 (2.547)	0.924 (3.331)	−0.183 −(0.669)	0.356 (1.345)
G	0.345 (1.636)	−0.482 −(1.422)	−0.706 −(2.233)	0.028 (0.083)	−0.015 −(0.046)	−0.399 −(1.134)	−0.264 −(0.798)
H	−0.257 −(0.897)	−0.264 −(0.610)	0.616 (1.452)	0.676 (1.509)	0.296 (0.687)	0.298 (0.686)	0.243 (0.507)
J	0.625 (3.529)	−0.514 −(1.767)	−0.082 −(0.285)	−0.465 −(1.559)	0.032 (0.111)	−0.217 −(0.759)	0.155 (0.531)
L	0.727 (2.931)	−0.230 −(0.578)	0.407 (1.100)	−0.017 −(0.045)	0.077 (0.207)	0.375 (0.819)	0.034 (0.082)
M	−0.010 −(0.051)	0.166 (0.525)	−0.546 −(1.784)	−0.159 −(0.482)	−0.101 −(0.312)	−0.327 −(1.006)	0.292 (0.916)
N	0.193 (1.281)	−0.445 −(1.884)	−0.633 −(2.728)	−0.469 −(1.912)	−0.261 −(1.081)	−0.528 −(2.148)	−0.314 −(1.329)
P	−0.012 −(0.035)	−0.694 −(1.247)	−0.736 −(1.411)	−0.374 −(0.673)	−0.491 −(0.826)	−1.535 −(1.413)	−1.262 −(2.445)
R	−0.321 −(1.659)	−0.126 −(0.415)	0.029 (0.095)	0.374 (1.182)	0.424 (1.329)	0.238 (0.766)	0.307 (1.010)
S	−2.234 −(9.698)	−0.600 −(1.629)	−0.305 −(0.823)	0.140 (0.372)	0.533 (1.384)	0.222 (0.558)	0.026 (0.058)

$N = 2.987$

Adjusted $R^2 = 0.620$

b. Regression results for pharmaceutical prices — 1992 constrained model (*t*-statistics in parentheses) log price per standard unit, for molecule/ATC matched with US

Variable	US	CN	GE	FR	IT	JP	UK
Intercept	3.260 (10.334)	1.203 (2.428)	1.008 (1.769)	1.601 (2.726)	1.743 (3.203)	4.197 (6.266)	0.389 (0.742)
Quality							
Strength (ln)	0.124 (9.597)	−0.022 −(0.798)	0.089 (3.766)	–	0.052 (1.924)	−0.066 −(2.542)	–
Age (ln)	−0.184 −(3.660)	−0.150 −(2.056)	−0.216 −(2.665)	−0.443 −(5.219)	−0.387 −(4.863)	−0.690 −(6.906)	−0.354 −(3.953)
Form codes (ln)	0.273 (6.778)	–	–	−0.170 −(1.558)	–	–	−0.145 −(1.451)
Global (ln)	0.430 (5.163)	−0.241 −(1.493)	−0.341 −(2.016)	−0.645 −(3.170)	−0.820 −(4.102)	−0.617 −(3.589)	–
Packsize (ln)	−0.705 −(29.931)	−0.088 −(1.609)	0.180 (3.358)	–	–	–	0.106 (1.898)
Competition							
Generic competitors (ln)	−0.567 −(14.804)	0.097 (1.110)	0.231 (3.391)	0.645 (6.369)	0.756 (9.049)	0.674 (9.100)	0.322 (3.188)
Therapeutic substitute molecules (ln)	0.069 (1.326)	–	−0.279 −(3.118)	−0.216 −(2.189)	−0.188 −(2.135)	−0.144 −(1.616)	−0.200 −(2.137)
Therapeutic substitute molecule entry lag (ln)	−0.037 −(2.097)	–	0.074 (2.286)	0.041 (1.157)	0.037 (1.110)	0.057 (1.591)	0.056 (1.617)
Therapeutic categories							
A	−0.736 −(7.887)	–	–	0.704 (3.719)	0.694 (3.792)	0.572 (3.025)	0.237 (1.305)
B	−0.293 −(1.773)	–	0.272 (0.851)	0.555 (1.744)	0.510 (1.637)	0.403 (1.216)	–
D	−0.965 −(9.617)	–	0.486 (2.562)	0.704 (3.443)	0.910 (4.258)	–	0.316 (1.603)
G	0.275 (2.423)	−0.361 −(1.481)	−0.609 −(2.674)	–	–	−0.348 −(1.314)	–
H	−0.179 −(1.265)	–	0.593 (1.851)	0.600 (1.743)	–	–	–
J	0.611 (6.754)	−0.530 −(2.626)	–	−0.445 −(2.211)	–	–	–
L	0.742 (6.184)	–	0.436 (1.617)	–	–	–	–
M	0.021 (0.205)	–	−0.579 −(2.607)	–	–	−0.292 −(1.184)	–
N	0.216 (1.794)	−0.535 −(3.165)	−0.623 −(3.470)	−0.468 −(2.366)	−0.304 −(1.595)	−0.550 −(2.910)	−0.401 −(2.093)
P	−0.234 −(1.027)	−0.448 −(0.954)	−0.474 −(1.109)	–	–	−1.377 −(1.334)	−1.077 −(2.535)
R	−0.290 −(2.738)	–	–	0.351 (1.449)	0.389 (1.575)	–	0.237 (1.037)
S	−2.230 −(17.798)	−0.564 −(2.064)	–	–	0.482 (1.597)	–	–
$N = 2.987$							
Adjusted $R^2 = 0.622$							

(continued on next page)

Table 2 (*continued*)

c. Second stage of two-stage least squares (2SLS) regressions–pooled observations dependent variable: log of standard unit per capita (coefficients for non-US countries as difference from those for US) (coefficients for therapeutic category dummies omitted)

		US	CA	GE	FR	IT	JA	UK
Intercept	Coefficient *t*-stat (2SLS)	− 10.532 − (42.295)	0.744 (1.848)	0.381 (0.966)	1.745 (3.914)	1.923 (4.585)	0.498 (1.195)	− 0.059 − (0.140)
LPSU	Coefficient *t*-stat (2SLS)	− 1.294 − (16.556)	− 0.047 − (0.355)	− 0.130 − (0.831)	0.625 (4.250)	0.932 (6.312)	0.532 (3.961)	0.383 (2.508)

d. Coefficients of country intercepts with and without age and competition variables dependent variable: log of price per standard unit (*t*-statistics in parentheses)

		US	CA	GE	FR	IT	JA	UK
Intercept	Coefficient with age and competition $R^2 = 0.620$	3.301 (8.592)	1.010 (1.603)	1.120 (1.681)	1.458 (2.115)	1.670 (2.483)	4.367 (5.672)	0.450 (0.661)
Intercept	Coefficient without competition $R^2 = 0.602$	4.547 (13.678)	0.140 (0.251)	0.108 (0.181)	− 0.094 − (0.150)	0.201 (0.342)	2.995 (4.458)	− 0.799 − (1.344)
Intercept	Coefficient without age and competition $R^2 = 0.529$	3.156 (11.042)	0.202 (0.398)	− 0.954 − (1.928)	− 1.582 − (2.862)	− 0.643 − (1.183)	− 0.633 − (1.252)	− 1.784 − (3.416)

4.4.1. Quality

Price is inversely related to molecule age, consistent with the hypothesis that newer molecules offer improved therapeutic quality. The Age coefficient measures a pure age effect, controlling for number of generic and therapeutic competitors that increases with age. The molecule-age elasticity for the US is −0.18, with significant negative interactions for all countries that imply age elasticities ranging from −0.33 for Canada to −0.87 for Japan. The ranking of elasticities — more negative for France, Italy, and the UK than for Germany and Canada — is consistent with the fact that regulatory systems in the first three countries do not permit post-launch inflation adjustments, such that real prices fall over the life of the molecule, whereas, Canada permits a CPI increase. For Germany, declining prices over the life-cycle is consistent with other evidence (Danzon and Kim, 1996a,b) and may reflect spillover effects from other countries and/or the reference price system introduced in 1989, which initially targeted older molecules. The extreme negative age effects in Japan reflect the interaction between competition and regulation, and are consistent with other empirical evidence (Danzon and Kim, 1996a,b; Ikegami et al., 1998).

The elasticity of price with respect to Global penetration is 0.43 in the US, consistent with the joint hypothesis that global diffusion is an indicator of therapeutic value and that more effective drugs obtain higher prices in unregulated markets. The Global interactions are insignificant or small for other less regulated markets (UK, Canada, and Germany), but significantly negative for the strictly regulated countries. The net effect (US coefficient plus country-specific interaction) implies a negative price elasticity with respect to the therapeutic value (Global) for France (−0.22), Italy (−0.39), and Japan (−0.19).

Price is increasing in Strength per standard unit, as expected. The interaction is significantly negative for Japan, where the practice of polypharmacy may reduce the value of strong pills. Price is also positively related to the number of Forms available for the molecule, as expected, if range of formulations enhances convenience, effectiveness, and value. These effects do not differ significantly across countries. Price decreases with packsize, consistent with economies of scale in packaging that are (at least partially) passed on to purchasers.[27] Several of the 12 ATC1 category dummies are significant for the US, implying significant differences in the mean prices for different indications, relative to the omitted cardiovascular category, possibly due to differences in therapeutic value and/or average insurance coverage across therapeutic categories. Many country-interactions for

[27] The positive interaction for Germany may reflect the co-payment structure of a flat fee per script (DM3, except 0 for reference priced drugs), which created incentives for patients to prefer larger packs per prescription. In 1993, co-payments were related to the price of the drug; and in 1994, this co-payment schedule was based on packsize. For effects of packsize at the product level see Danzon and Chao (1999).

ATC1s are significant, implying that countries differ in medical norms and insurance for different types of drugs.

4.4.2. Competition

The US elasticity of molecule price with respect to Generic Competitors is −0.57, consistent with other evidence of generic competition in the US (Grabowski and Vernon, 1992; Ellison et al, 1997). The positive interactions imply that generic competition has a weaker but still negative net effect on molecule price in the less regulated markets: Canada (insignificantly different from the US), Germany (−0.34), and the UK (−0.25). However, the net effect of generics on molecule price is positive for France (0.08), Italy (0.19), and Japan (0.11). These positive elasticities are consistent with anecdotal evidence that multi-source suppliers in these countries are usually licensed co-marketers rather than competing generic manufacturers or minor "new" products that enter to obtain a higher regulated price.[28] Our estimates of the effects of generic competition on price may be subject to endogeneity bias, if generics entry is related to expected prices and expected prices are correlated with actual prices. In that case, our estimates are a lower bound for the competitive effects of generics on price.

Competition from therapeutic substitute molecules appears to have no significant effect on price in the US and Canada.[29] However, these list price data for the US do not reflect discounts given directly to manage care customers to gain preferred formulary status. Such competitive discounting is likely to be greatest in crowded therapeutic categories, leading us to underestimate the extent of therapeutic competition. Further downward bias is likely due to our inability to control for promotional expense and possible endogeneity of number of molecules in a class.[30] Number of therapeutic substitute molecules appears to have small but significant negative effects on price in France, Italy, Germany, and the UK, but the interpretation is unclear. Since France and Italy show no evidence of competitive effects of generics, which are closer substitutes, the most plausible explanation of the negative Therapeutic Substitute coefficients is that regulators use a form of implicit reference pricing, setting prices for new products based on prices of established products. The prices of these established products are inversely related to age because of regulatory constraints on inflation adjustments, as shown earlier.

[28] We follow IMS (and the manufacturer) in defining a new form — for example, a delayed release tablet — as a new product rather than a new form of an old product if it has a different product name. Thus Procardia XL is a distinct product from Procardia.

[29] Ellison et al. (1997) find fairly high cross-price elasticities between generic substitutes, smaller but sometimes significant elasticities between therapeutic substitutes in their study of cephalosporins in 1985–1991.

[30] If promotion has spillover effects that expands demand for the class, omitting a control for promotion would lead us to underestimate the effects of therapeutic substitutes on price. Similar bias may result if entry is positively related to expected prices which are positively correlated with observed prices.

Thus, this implicit price setting mechanism would result in the observed inverse relation between price and number of molecules in the class. For Germany and the UK, the negative Therapeutic Substitute coefficients findings may reflect competition or spillover effects of regulation from France and Italy, if parallel trade and international comparisons constrain price divergence across EU countries.

For the US and Canada, the significant negative Therapeutic Substitute Entry Lag coefficient implies that successive molecules enter at lower prices, with a 3.7% per month price reduction for each month of entry lag after the first molecule in a class.[31] This indicates competitive pricing by successive entrants that does not fully erode the first mover advantage. Other country interactions are generally positive, but significant only for Germany. Since the coefficients of number of therapeutic substitutes and therapeutic entry lag tend to be offsetting, the net effects of therapeutic substitutes depend on the combined effect, as discussed in Section 5.

4.4.3. Quantity equations

Table 2c reports price elasticities from the second stage of two-stage least squares estimates of the structural quantity equation (Eq. 3), which includes only ATC1 dummies in addition to (endogenous) price, with full interaction. All the right-hand-side variables in Eq. 4 (i.e., the variables in Table 2a) are used as instruments for price in the first stage. The price elasticity for the US is −1.29, with no significant difference for Canada or Germany. Elasticities are still negative but significantly smaller in absolute value in the UK (−0.91), Japan (−0.76), France (−0.67), and Italy (−0.36). These significant negative elasticities in the logs imply that the very low correlations between absolute prices and quantities in Table 1 are due to extreme values rather than to lack of an overall inverse relationship.

Our elasticity estimates are larger (in absolute value) than most prior estimates, and several factors may contribute. First, several previous studies (for example, Leibowitz et al., 1985) are based on aggregate expenditures, and hence, are expected to show less elastic demand than our measures, which reflect between-molecule substitution. Second, most prior studies estimate demand response to out-of-pocket price to consumers, whereas our manufacturer level prices are only roughly proportional to consumer prices, depending on proportionality of distribution margins, taxes and co-payment rates. Proportionality is most plausible for the US at this time and for some consumers in Canada, but not for the other countries. Thus, if price sensitivity were driven solely by consumer co-payments, we might expect small or zero quantity elasticities with respect to these manufacturer prices.

[31] Similarly, Boston Consulting Group (BCG) (1993) reports that late entrants enter at a price discount relative to the market leader, and that these discounts are greater in more crowded therapeutic categories.

Third, however, to the extent that demand decisions also reflect physician incentives, through indicative drug budgets, prescription monitoring by third party payers, etc., the full price is the relevant measure, not the consumer's co-payment. Fourth, to the extent that regulatory systems require price reductions if volume exceeds target levels, this imposes a spurious inverse relation between quantity and price that would bias up (in absolute value) the estimated price elasticity in countries with regulation.[32] Sorting out the contribution of these factors to the observed elasticities with respect to manufacturer price is an important topic for future research.

5. Accounting for price differentials: characteristics vs. parameters

We have shown that the relation between prices and product characteristics differs significantly across countries. In this section, we use the regression results in Table 2b to examine how far differences in mean values of these characteristics and their parameter effects can account for the (log) mean foreign/US price ratio. The (log) mean price relative for country j relative to the US can be written:

$$\ln R = \ln(P_j/P_u) = \ln P_j - \ln P_u = \ln \boldsymbol{X}_j \beta_j - \ln \boldsymbol{X}_u \beta_u + u_j - u_u \quad (5)$$

Comparing Eqs. (4) and (5):

$$\beta = \beta_u$$
$$\delta_j = \beta_j - \beta_u$$

or

$$\beta_j = \beta_u + \delta_j$$

Eq. (5) can thus be rewritten:

$$\ln R = (\ln \boldsymbol{X}_j - \ln \boldsymbol{X}_u)\beta_u + \ln \boldsymbol{X}_j \delta_j$$

The mean price ratio can thus be decomposed into two components. The first component or characteristics effect $(\ln \boldsymbol{X}_j - \ln \boldsymbol{X}_u)\ \beta_u$ reflects the difference in mean characteristics of our sample of drugs in country j, relative to the US, evaluated at US parameter values. The second component, $\ln \boldsymbol{X}_j\ (\beta_j - \beta_u) = \ln \boldsymbol{X}_j \delta_j$, is the country interaction or implicit price effect, which reflects the difference in implicit prices for characteristics in country j, compared to the US.[33] The country intercept estimates (with opposite sign) the unexplained country residual effects that are not explained by measured characteristics or their parameter effects. It also subsumes country effects for the omitted cardiovascular

[32] France applied a total revenue constraint "envelope globale" to certain products. The UK PPRS profit constraint implies a portfolio revenue constraint, given the capital base. For Italy (the Emilia Romagna region) for 1989–1993, Anessi (1997) estimates own price elasticities for individual cardiovascular products with respect to out-of-pocket prices to be −0.26 to −0.36.

[33] For application of a similar decomposition to wage differences, see Oaxaca (1973), Smith and Welch (1977), and Reimers (1983).

category. Cross-country differences in implicit prices for product characteristics are of interest, although in this pharmaceutical context, the standard interpretation of hedonic equations under assumptions of competitive equilibrium does not strictly apply. In an industry with significant fixed costs and imperfect competition, unregulated prices should approximate consumer valuations, rather than marginal costs. However, imperfect information and insurance may undermine this interpretation for pharmaceuticals and other medical services. In addition, in countries with regulation, monopsony government purchasers may drive prices towards marginal cost. The implicit characteristic prices presumably reflect the net effect of all these factors. Table 3 shows that differences in implicit prices are relatively more important than differences in mean product characteristics in accounting for mean price differences, at least for these matching products.

5.1. *Quality*

The main factors that tend to reduce drug prices in most other countries relative to the US are more negative returns to molecule age and to therapeutic value, as measured by global penetration. Returns to age and global penetration are most negative in France, Italy and Japan, which have the strictest price regulation (Table 3, column 7, ''parameter interactions''). Smaller but still negative age and global effects contribute to lower prices in Germany and Canada; only age effects are significant for the UK.[34] Smaller packs due to unit pack dispensing contribute to higher prices in other countries. But the overall effect of the quality variables (strength, age, forms, global, and packsize), including characteristics and parameter values, is to reduce prices significantly in the strictly regulated markets compared to the US, and to a lesser extent, the UK, Germany, and Canada. Differences in therapeutic mix (ATC1 dummies) and their parameter effects contribute very little to the overall mean price differences for these matching molecules, but this conclusion cannot necessarily be generalized to the full universe of drugs in each country.

5.2. *Competition*

The price-reducing effects of generic competition partially but not completely offset the more negative effects of age and global in the regulated countries. All other countries have fewer generic competitors per molecule than the US, and the price competitive effect of a given number of generic competitors is weaker

[34] The higher mean globalization score for foreign countries than for the US is an artifact of the bilaterally matched sample. Each non-US sample includes only drugs that are also available in the US, whereas the US sample includes all drugs that are available in at least one foreign country, and is therefore a larger sample. Other analysis (not reported here) shows that the fraction of sales that is attributable to global drugs is higher in the US than in France, Italy, Germany or Japan.

Table 3
Accounting for observed price ratios

Canada vs. US

Variable	US mean	CA mean	US parameter	CA parameter	Characteristic effects	Parameter interactions	Total
Strength	−3.1947	−3.2458	0.1242	−0.0217	−0.0064	0.0703	0.0639
Age of molecule	5.1501	5.2481	−0.1835	−0.1496	−0.0180	−0.7851	−0.8031
Forms	0.7942	0.7390	0.2729		−0.0151		−0.0151
Global	1.4675	1.6495	0.4297	−0.2406	0.0782	−0.3969	−0.3187
Packsize	4.2203	4.5254	−0.7052	−0.0877	−0.2151	−0.3967	−0.6118
Quality subtotal					−0.1763	−1.5085	−1.6848
Generic competitors	1.0400	0.5584	−0.5674	0.0965	0.2732	0.0539	0.3271
Therapeutic substitute molecules	1.9829	1.8350	0.0693		−0.0103		−0.0103
Therapeutic substitute molecule entry lag	3.9194	3.7744	−0.0367		0.0053		0.0053
Competition subtotal					0.2683	0.0539	0.3222
Therapeutic categories subtotal					0.0112	−0.2029	−0.1916
Residual subtotal	1.0000	1.0000	3.2600	1.2031	0.0000	1.2031	1.2031
Total: log of observed price ratios							−0.3510

Germany vs. US

Variable	US mean	GE mean	US parameter	GE parameter	Characteristic effects	Parameter interactions	Total
Strength	−3.1947	−3.1998	0.1242	0.0891	−0.0006	−0.2851	−0.2857
Age of molecule	5.1501	5.4017	−0.1835	−0.2156	−0.0462	−1.1648	−1.2109
Forms	0.7942	0.8158	0.2729		0.0059		0.0059
Global	1.4675	1.6532	0.4297	−0.3408	0.0798	−0.5634	−0.4836
Packsize	4.2203	3.7189	−0.7052	0.1799	0.3536	0.6691	1.0227
Quality subtotal					0.3925	−1.3441	−0.9516
Generic competitors	1.0400	0.7627	−0.5674	0.2306	0.1573	0.1759	0.3332
Therapeutic substitute molecules	1.9829	2.2971	0.0693	−0.2794	0.0218	−0.6418	−0.6201
Therapeutic substitute molecule entry lag	3.9194	4.4072	−0.0367	0.0738	−0.0179	0.3254	0.3075
Competition subtotal					0.1612	−0.1406	0.0206
Therapeutic categories subtotal					0.0491	−0.0955	−0.0464
Residual subtotal	1.0000	1.0000	3.2600	1.0076	0.0000	1.0076	1.0076
Total: log of observed price ratios							0.0303

France vs. US

Variable	US mean	FR mean	US parameter	FR parameter	Characteristic effects	Parameter interactions	Total
Strength	−3.1947	−3.3296	0.1242		−0.0168		−0.0168
Age of molecule	5.1501	5.2840	−0.1835	−0.4429	−0.0246	−2.3402	−2.3648
Forms	0.7942	0.5656	0.2729	−0.1704	−0.0624	−0.0964	−0.1587
Global	1.4675	1.7235	0.4297	−0.6449	0.1100	−1.1115	−1.0015
Packsize	4.2203	3.2359	−0.7052		0.6942		0.6942
Quality subtotal					0.7005	−3.5481	−2.8476
Generic competitors	1.0400	0.4293	−0.5674	0.6450	0.3466	0.2769	0.6234
Therapeutic substitute molecules	1.9829	2.1812	0.0693	−0.2157	0.0137	−0.4706	−0.4568
Therapeutic molecule entry lag	3.9194	4.2098	−0.0367	0.0413	−0.0107	0.1739	0.1632
Competition subtotal					0.3496	−0.0198	0.3298
Therapeutic categories subtotal					0.0352	0.1050	0.1402
Residual subtotal	1.0000	1.0000	3.2600	1.6015	0.0000	1.6015	1.6015
Total: log of observed price ratios							−0.7761

Italy vs. US

Variable	US mean	IT mean	US parameter	IT parameter	Characteristic effects	Paramter interactions	Total
Strength	−3.1947	−3.2587	0.1242	0.0520	−0.0079	−0.1694	−0.1774
Age of molecule	5.1501	5.2171	−0.1835	−0.3871	−0.0123	−2.0197	−2.0320
Forms	0.7942	0.6336	0.2729		−0.0438		−0.0438
Global	1.4675	1.7256	0.4297	−0.8203	0.1109	−1.4155	−1.3046
Packsize	4.2203	3.1055	−0.7052		0.7861		0.7861
Quality subtotal					0.8330	−3.6046	−2.7716
Generic competitors	1.0400	0.5657	−0.5674	0.7562	0.2692	0.4277	0.6969
Therapeutic substitute molecules	1.9829	2.2460	0.0693	−0.1876	0.0182	−0.4213	−0.4031
Therapeutic molecule entry lag	3.9194	4.1805	−0.0367	0.0367	−0.0096	0.1536	0.1440
Competition subtotal					0.2778	0.1600	0.4378
Therapeutic categories subtotal					0.0862	0.1814	0.2677
Residual subtotal	1.0000	1.0000	3.2600	1.7429	0.0000	1.7429	1.7429
Total: log of observed price ratios							−0.3232

(continued on next page)

Table 3 (*continued*)

Japan vs. US

Variable	US mean	JA mean	US parameter	JA parameter	Characteristic effects	Parameter interactions	Total
Strength	−3.1947	−3.4937	0.1242	−0.0655	−0.0371	0.2289	0.1917
Age of molecule	5.1501	5.3882	−0.1835	−0.6900	−0.0437	−3.7178	−3.7615
Forms	0.7942	0.8079	0.2729		0.0037		0.0037
Global	1.4675	1.6679	0.4297	−0.6167	0.0861	−1.0286	−0.9425
Packsize	4.2203	5.2774	−0.7052		−0.7454		−0.7454
Quality subtotal					−0.7363	−4.5175	−5.2539
Generic competitors	1.0400	0.8107	−0.5674	0.6739	0.1301	0.5463	0.6764
Therapeutic substitute molecules	1.9829	2.3063	0.0693	−0.1444	0.0224	−0.3331	−0.3107
Therapeutic molecule entry lag	3.9194	3.9518	−0.0367	0.0570	−0.0012	0.2251	0.2239
Competition subtotal					0.1513	0.4384	0.5897
Therapeutic categories subtotal					0.0719	−0.0446	0.0272
Residual subtotal	1.0000	1.0000	3.2600	4.1970	0.0000	4.1970	4.1970
Total: log of observed price ratios							−0.4400

UK vs. US

Variable	US mean	UK mean	US parameter	UK parameter	Characteristic effects	Parameter interactions	Total
Strength	−3.1947	−3.2369	0.1242		−0.0052		−0.0052
Age of molecule	5.1501	5.3195	−0.1835	−0.3535	−0.0311	−1.8805	−1.9116
Forms	0.7942	0.7728	0.2729	−0.1449	−0.0058	−0.1120	−0.1178
Global	1.4675	1.7103	0.4297		0.1043		0.1043
Packsize	4.2203	3.9501	−0.7052	0.1060	0.1906	0.4185	0.6091
Quality subtotal					0.2527	−1.5740	−1.3212
Generic competitors	1.0400	0.3624	−0.5674	0.3220	0.3845	0.1167	0.5012
Therapeutic substitute molecules	1.9829	1.9842	0.0693	−0.2000	0.0001	−0.3969	−0.3968
Therapeutic molecule entry lag	3.9194	3.8916	−0.0367	0.0556	0.0010	0.2163	0.2173
Competition subtotal					0.3856	−0.0639	0.3217
Therapeutic categories subtotal					0.0829	−0.0058	0.0771
Residual subtotal	1.0000	1.0000	3.2600	0.3887	0.0000	0.3887	0.3887
Total: log of observed price ratios							−0.5337

(except for Canada). However, the overall price-increasing effect of generic competition (i.e., the effect of fewer generics plus the effect of weaker price competition among generics in non-US countries) ranges from 0.62 in France to 0.70 in Italy, which is much smaller in magnitude than the negative molecule age effect (from −2.03 in Italy to −3.76 in Japan) or the negative global effect (from −0.94 in Japan to −1.30 in Italy). Note that these characteristics are related: incentives for generic entry are weak where demand is not price sensitive and where regulated originator prices decline with molecule age, hence, are very low by the time of patent expiry. The combined effect of therapeutic substitute molecules and therapeutic substitute entry lag contributes little to explaining the magnitude of cross-national price differences, although in general the combined effect is to reduce prices in other countries relative to the US (insignificant difference for Canada). As discussed earlier, this effect is more plausibly attributed to regulation than to competition, at least for France, Italy and Japan.

5.3. Unmeasured effects

The country intercepts can be interpreted as conditional estimates of country price differentials, controlling for measured characteristics and their implicit prices that are themselves influenced by regulation. These country intercepts are positive and significant in all countries except the UK. This implies that predicted values based solely on measured characteristics are below actual values, but that this is partially offset by positive, country-specific effects due to unmeasured factors, such as insurance. As an alternative, unconditional measure, Table 2d reports the country intercepts for (a) the full specification in Table 2a; (b) omitting the competition variables; and (c) omitting molecule age and competition variables, which appear to be the characteristics that are most affected by regulation. When competition alone is omitted, all the country interactions are insignificant except Japan, which is still positive. When molecule age is also omitted, the country interactions for Germany, France, and the UK, are significantly negative, while Canada, Italy, and Japan are not significantly different from the US.

Thus, the country intercepts from quasi-hedonic regression for drug prices, which in theory, might offer an approach to measuring cross-national price differences that controls for product differences, are in fact extremely sensitive to specification. For some countries, these measures differ in both magnitude and sign from the Laspeyres and Paasche indexes in Table 1. This is a further evidence of the sensitivity of drug price comparisons to methods used. Improving these estimates from hedonic regression is the subject of ongoing research.

6. Conclusions

We have demonstrated that the conventional view, that drug prices are much higher in the US than in other countries, is biased due to the small, unrepresentative samples and inappropriate methods used in prior studies. Indexes based on a comprehensive sample that include generics show smaller cross-national differences in the average cost of drug therapy, at manufacturer prices, than implied by previous studies. However, this analysis has also demonstrated the sensitivity of cross-national price comparisons to the methods used, including sample selection, weights, unit of measure, and index. Laspeyres indexes consistently exceed Paasche indexes, by up to 50 percentage points in some cases. These differences reflect in part the right-skewed distributions of price and quantity relatives for each bilateral comparison. Although specific magnitudes would change if a country other than the US were used as the base, the Paasche/Laspeyres divergence remains, due to dispersion of relative prices and quantity across products.

The dispersion of relative prices across products in any bilateral comparison reflects both differences in product characteristics for the matching molecules and differences in market characteristics, particularly the extent of competition between generic equivalents. Differences in mean characteristics are generally less important than differences in implicit prices for these characteristics. The main factors tending to lower prices in other countries, relative to the US, are lower prices for older molecules and for therapeutic value, as measured by global penetration. These negative returns to age and therapeutic value are particularly strong in the countries with strict price regulation — France, Italy and Japan — and are consistent with the structure of their regulatory systems. On the other hand, generic competition is more effective at lowering prices in the US and in the less stringently regulated markets (Canada, Germany, and the UK) than the more regulated markets (France, Italy, and Japan). Demand elasticities estimated from regression analysis are significantly negative for all countries, but are more negative in the US and the other less regulated countries than for the strictly regulated countries.

The main conclusion from this analysis is that any generalizations about relative prices for drugs in different countries are tentative at best, because of the diversity of products, prices, and volumes, which makes conclusions very sensitive to the sample and methods. The safe conclusion is that results will be systematically biased if the comparison is based on a sample that is unrepresentative with respect to either age of molecules, extent of globalization or generic share. Much remains unexplained about the factors that contribute to cross-national price differences. Although we have identified certain factors — returns to age, therapeutic merit, and competition — nevertheless, controlling for these measured factors leaves large unmeasured country effects. The contribution of insurance structure and other factors to these unexplained differences is an important subject for future research.

This analysis also has implications for the use of international price comparisons to regulate domestic prices. The conclusions depend on the objectives, but in any case, there are no simple answers. One possible objective of such external referencing is to achieve an average domestic price level that is comparable to the average price level in the comparison countries. This objective will not be achieved by comparing prices of individual new branded products at launch, on a product-by-product basis, because post-launch price paths diverge due to country-specific regulatory and competitive environments. A theoretically more appropriate comparison would use the discounted present value of expected prices over the molecule life-cycle. Most countries with external referencing use as their benchmark the unweighted median, mean, or minimum price in the market basket drawn from the comparison countries. We have shown that such unweighted measures are extremely sensitive to the sample selected, particularly if the comparison is based on a single pack of a single manufacturer. However, although weighting would in theory, reduce the instability, there are no obvious appropriate weights for such multilateral comparisons of prices of a single product. If different countries apply external referencing to the same products, but use different benchmark countries or different weights, then, each country's perspective on the same distribution of relative prices will yield a different conclusion about their relative price level.

A second possible regulatory objective is to set price differences across countries to achieve appropriate per capita contributions to the joint costs of pharmaceutical R&D, based on Ramsey pricing principles (Danzon, 1997b). For this objective, the appropriate comparison is the discounted present value of expected revenue per capita over the originator product's life-cycle, which takes into account cross-national differences in per capita quantity as well as price over the life-cycle, for example, due to different post-patent generic penetration rates across countries.[35] Further research is necessary on both theory and practical empirical measures, if international comparisons are to be used to achieve the desired price levels for consumers and returns for manufacturers.

Acknowledgements

This research was supported by a grant from Pfizer to the University of Pennsylvania for the study of international price comparisons. Li-Wei Chao also received support from Public Health Service grants (T32-HS000009 and F32-HS00085-01) from the AHCPR. We also thank IMS International for supplying the data. Conclusions do not necessarily reflect the views of the research sponsors.

References

Allen, R.G., 1975. Index Numbers in Theory and Practice. Aldine Publishing, Chicago.

Anessi, E.P., 1997. The effect of user charges on the utilization of prescription medicines in the Italian National Health Service. Unpublished doctoral dissertation, The Wharton School, University of Pennsylvania, Philadelphia.

[35] Danzon and Kim (1996a,b).

Barral, P.E., 1995. Twenty Years of Pharmaceutical Research Results throughout the World (1975–1994). Fondation Rhone-Poulenc Sante, Paris.

Berndt, E.R., Griliches, Z., Rosett, J.G., 1993. Auditing the producer price index: micro evidence from prescription pharmaceutical preparations. Journal of Economics and Business Statistics 11 (3), 251–264.

Boston Consulting Group (BCG), 1993. The Changing Environment for US Pharmaceuticals. Boston Consulting Group, New York.

Bureau European des Unions de Consommateurs (BEUC), 1989a. Drug Prices and Drug Legislation in Europe. Belgian Consumers' Association, Brussels.

Bureau European des Unions de Consommateurs (BEUC), 1989b. Testimony before the US Senate Special Committee on Aging. Oral Testimony, November 16.

Burstall, M.L., 1991. Europe after 1992: implications for pharmaceuticals. Health Affairs, 157–171, Fall.

Caves, R.E., Whinston, M.D., Hurwitz, M.A., 1991. Patent expiration, entry, and competition in the U.S. pharmaceutical industry. In: Brookings Papers on Economic Activity: Microeconomics. pp. 1–66.

Danzon, P.M., 1996. Defined daily doses for pharmaceuticals. Working paper, University of Pennsylvania, The Wharton School, Philadelphia.

Danzon, P.M., 1997a. Price Regulation in the Pharmaceutical Industry: National vs. Global Interests. The AEI Press, Washington, DC.

Danzon, P.M., 1997b. Price discrimination for pharmaceuticals: welfare effects in the US and the EU. International Journal of the Economics of Business 4 (3), 301–322.

Danzon, P.M., Chao, L.W., 1999. Does regulation drive out competition in markets for pharmaceuticals. Journal of Law and Economics, (Forthcoming).

Danzon, P.M., Kim, J.D., 1996. Price indexes for pharmaceuticals: how accurate are international comparisons. Working paper, University of Pennsylvania, The Wharton School, Philadelphia.

Danzon, P.M., Kim, J.D., 1996. Life-cycle returns to pharmaceuticals: a cross-national comparison. Working paper, University of Pennsylvania, The Wharton School, Philadelphia.

Ellison, S.F., Cockburn, I., Griliches, Z., Hausman, J., 1997. Characteristics of demand for pharmaceutical products: an examination of four cephalosporins. RAND Journal of Economics 28 (3), 426–446.

Gerschenkron, A., 1947. The Soviet indices of industrial production. Review of Economics and Statistics 34, 217–226.

Gerschenkron, A., Erlich, A., 1951. A Dollar Index of Soviet Machinery Output 1927–28 to 1937. The Rand Corporation R-197, Santa Monica.

Grabowski, H.G., Vernon, J.M., 1992. Brand loyalty, entry and price competition in pharmaceuticals after the 1984 Act. Journal of Law and Economics 35 (2), 331–350.

Griliches, Z., Cockburn, I., 1994. Generics and new goods in pharmaceutical price indexes. American Economic Review 84 (5), 1213–1232.

Ikegami, N., Ikeda, S., Kawai, H., 1998. Why medical care costs in Japan have increased despite declining prices for pharmaceuticals. PharmacoEconomics 14 (Suppl. 1), 97–105.

Jonas, P., Sardy, H., 1972. The Gerschenkron effect: a re-examination. Review of Economics and Statistics 52, 82–86.

Kokoski, M.F., 1991, New research on interarea consumer price differences. Monthly Labor Review July, 31–34.

Kravis, I.B., Heston, A., Summer, R., 1982. World Product and Income: International Comparisons of Real Gross Products, Statistical Office of the United Nations and the World Bank. Johns Hopkins University Press, Baltimore.

Kravis, I.B., Lipsey, R.E., 1971. International price comparisons by regression methods. In: Griliches, Z. (Ed.), Price Indexes and Quality Change: Studies in New Methods and Measurement. Harvard University Press, Cambridge, pp. 150–179.

Leibowitz, A., Manning, W., 1985. The demand for prescription drugs as a function of cost-sharing. Social Science and Medicine 21 (10), 1063–1069.
Levit, K., Cowan, C., Braden, B., 1998. National health expenditures in 1997: more slow growth. Health Affairs 17 (6), 99–110.
Oaxaca, R., 1973. Male–female wage differences in urban labor markets. International Economic Review 14, 693–709.
OECD, 1993. PPP-GK Results. OECD, Washington, DC.
Reimers, C., 1983. Labor market discrimination against Hispanic and black men. The Review of Economics and Statistics 65 (4), 570–579.
Smith, J.P., Welch, F.R., 1977. Black–white male wage ratios: 1960–70. American Economic Review 67, 323–338.
Thomas, L.G. II, 1996. Industrial policy and international competitiveness in the pharmaceutical industry. In: Helms, R.B. (Ed.), Competitive Strategies in the Pharmaceutical Industry. The AEI Press, Washington, DC, pp. 107–129.
U.S. Congressional Budget Office (CBO), 1996. How the Medicaid Rebate on Prescription Drugs Affects Pricing in the Pharmaceutical Industry. January 1996.
U.S. General Accounting Office, 1992. Prescription Drugs: Companies Typically Charge More in the United States than in Canada. GAO/HRD 92-110.
U.S. General Accounting Office, 1994. Prescription Drugs: Companies Typically Charge More in the United States than in the United Kingdom. GAO/HEHS 94-29.
U.S. Government Printing Office, 1993. Health Security Act (HR 3600 IH/S 1757).
U.S. House of Representatives, Committee on Government Reform and Oversight, 1998. Minority Staff Report, Prepared for Rep. Thomas A. Allen. Prescription Drug Pricing in the 1st Congressional District in Maine: An International Price Comparison (October 24, 1998).
Van Ark, B., Monnikhof, E., Timmer, M., 1996. Prices, Quantities and Productivity in Industry: A Study of Transition Economies in a Comparative Perspective. National Bureau of Economic Research.
von Bortkiewicz, L., 1922. Zweck und struktur einer preisindexzahl. Nordisk Statistik Tidskrift 1.
von Bortkiewicz, L., 1924. Zweck und struktur einer preisindexzahl. Nordisk Statistik Tidskrift 3.

Part IV
Regulation

[29]

Studies in American Political Development, 21 (Fall 2007), 149–180.

Policy Tragedy and the Emergence of Regulation: The Food, Drug, and Cosmetic Act of 1938

Daniel Carpenter, *Department of Government Harvard University*
Gisela Sin, *Department of Political Science University of Illinois*

It is now a commonplace assertion among scholars of regulation to say that new regulatory statutes follow "crises," "tragedies," or "scandals." The content and form of these critical events varies considerably. They include acts of journalism or research such as the publication of the Nader Report (which purportedly led to new federal automobile safety regulations) or Upton Sinclair's *The Jungle* (which eased the path for the Pure Food and Drugs Act of 1906). They include instantaneous disasters such as the Union Carbide gas leak in Bhopal, India, as well as slowly materializing epidemics like the thousands of horrific birth defects that resulted from widespread use of the sedative thalidomide in Europe and Australia in the late 1950s. As Lawrence Rothenberg describes this argument, it amounts to a meta-narrative of the origins of regulation, an alternative to capture theory. In the tragedy narrative of regulation, "public opinion becomes energized by some dramatic event or condition illustrating the pitfalls of a market's unobstructed operation; the outcry spurs elected officials to promulgate governmental regulation." This story, as he notes, is at least as old as the work of Marver Bernstein and Anthony Downs.[1]

So widely held is the claim that regulation follows from crisis that it remains virtually unexamined in empirical and historical analyses. The connection between "critical" events and the legislation that supposedly follows from them is vague, the implied causal mechanisms either poorly described or altogether evanescent. This unfortunate state of empiricism prevails widely, but not for lack of theoretical guidance. A decades-old body of literature in political science and sociology has confronted the issue of how supposed exogenous "conditions" become pressing "problems" for which public-sector engagement is appropriate and feasible. Operative metaphors in these literatures include "agenda-setting" in political science and "problem definition" in sociology. Spurred and represented largely by the work of political scientist John

We are grateful to Nancy Bermeo, Amy Bridges, Barry Burden, Ballard Campbell, Brandice Canes-Wrone, Margaret Carr, Mark Graber, Patricia Keenan, Ken Kersch, Marc Law, Michael Neblo, Tom Romer, Stephen Skowronek, Keith Whittington and two anonymous reviewers for helpful comments. We also profited from engaging, in-depth conversations with Rick Hall, Scott James and Theda Skocpol, and we thank Scott James for providing us with relevant congressional voting data and district- and state-level measures for the 1930s. We thank audiences at the University of Michigan RWJ Health Policy Seminar Series (January 2002), the Harvard University American Politics Research Workshop (September 2002), the Social Science History Association meetings (October 2002), the Midwest Political Science Association and the Princeton University APD Conference. Carpenter thanks the Robert Wood Johnson Foundation Investigator Awards in Health Policy Research, the Robert Wood Johnson Foundation Scholars in Health Policy Program, and the National Science Foundation (SES-0076452) for research support. All errors and interpretations are our own.

1. See Rothenberg, *Politics, Organizations and Regulation: Interstate Trucking Regulation at the ICC* (Ann Arbor: University of Michigan Press, 1994), 40. Marver Bernstein, *Regulating Business by Independent Commission*, (Princeton, NJ: Princeton University Press, 1955); see also Downs, *Inside Bureaucracy* (Boston: Little, Brown, 1967). On automobile safety-regulation, see Jerry L. Mashaw and David L. Harfst, *The Struggle for Auto Safety* (Cambridge, MA: Harvard University Press, 1990).

 ISSN 0898-588X/07 $15.00

Kingdon, these analyses direct our attention to the endogeneity of "problems" in need of policy "solutions." Significant policy change usually requires the simultaneous alignment of a "solution stream" with a "problem stream" and the "political stream." A policy tool (solution) becomes matched to a crisis (problem) at a time when political conditions favor action.[2]

As Deborah Stone has recognized, the alignment of policy streams and solution streams, of technologies with crises, often requires direct human action in the form of a causal story. Politicians, voters and organized interests must believe a counterfactual. Had the proposed technology (policy change) been in place, the problem would not have happened or would have been ameliorated. The counterfactual is then transformed into a prediction about the future. If the policy technology is adopted, future problems of the sort recently experienced will disappear or decline in severity or frequency. Stone observes the existence of a politics of claims-making about events, with political actors aligned and ready to "deliberately portray" conditions and issues "in ways calculated to gain support for their side."[3]

American politics and regulatory struggles are full of such stories, but many of them lack particularity. How specifically is an event transformed into a focusing event? Who does the focusing and the framing, to which audiences and with which mechanisms? From what soup of contending proposals, from what solution stream, does the eventual policy emerge? In this article, we elaborate the dynamics of agenda setting, problem definition and the formation of causal stories by means of historical political science. We examine one of the most important regulatory statutes in American and indeed global history—the Food, Drug, and Cosmetic Act of 1938. The 1938 act gives the U.S. Food and Drug Administration (FDA) sole authority to determine the ex ante marketability of any pharmaceutical product. Along with the Durham-Humphrey Amendments of 1951, the 1938 act also undergirds mandatory prescriptions in the United States. Taken together, these statutes put pharmaceutical consumers at second remove from an ethical drug they wish to consume. In order for an American patient to consume most drugs, the FDA must first approve them, and then the consumer's doctor must prescribe them. The premarket review provisions of the 1938 legislation have been emulated the world over, and institutions structured upon this rationale now govern pharmaceutical research, development, and marketing in the European Union and its member nations, in Australia, Brazil, Canada, India, Israel, Japan, South Africa, South Korea, and many other nations.

By most accounts, the Food, Drug, and Cosmetic Act of 1938 issued from crisis. Historians have traditionally attributed the 1938 Food, Drug, and Cosmetic Act to some combination of New Deal forces and the sulfanilamide tragedy of 1937, which occurred when the anti-infective drug, "Dr. Massengill's Elixir Sulfanilamid," caused 107 deaths and became the subject of national controversy.[4] This is not to deny that other interpretations are possible. More recently, other scholars including political scientist Harry Marks have argued that the law conforms to an industry capture explanation, as the rulemaking that occurred after the Act's passage largely conformed to the wishes of the organized pharmaceutical industry.[5]

The Idea of Policy Tragedy. In the particular creation of modern pharmaceutical regulation—and as a more general allegory for policy change—the combination of event, framing, and policy solution is well represented by the combined performative and political metaphor of a "policy tragedy." In a policy tragedy, someone has been harmed, and wrongly so. The "victim" may be individual or collective, and the latter is often represented by the former in the manner of an exemplar or "poster child." A culprit (often the system, perhaps represented by a single individual, or corporation or government actor) is responsible in a causal, nearly criminal fashion. The public (the tragedy's "chorus") points a finger at essential and observable features of the regulatory regime, the status quo, as causing or failing to prevent the harm or injustice in question. Yet in a policy tragedy,

2. John Kingdon, *Agendas, Alternatives and Public Policies*, Second Edition (New York: Longman Classics in Political Science, 2003), esp. chap 5 and 94–100. The streams metaphors appear in chap. 4, 86–88. We thank an anonymous reviewer for pressing the importance of these passages upon us and for some of the language we use to describe Kingdon's argument. Other salient contributions to this literature include Deborah A. Stone, "Causal Stories and the Formation of Policy Agendas," *Political Science Quarterly* 104 (1989): 281–300; Frank R. Baumgartner and Bryan D. Jones, *Agendas and Instability in American Politics* (Chicago: University of Chicago Press, 1993); Jones and Baumgartner, *The Politics of Attention: How Government Prioritizes Problems* (Chicago: University of Chicago Press, 2005), esp. chap. 3. An important generator of much of the sociological literature is Stephen Hilgartner and Charles L. Bosk, "The Rise and Fall of Social Problems: A Public Arenas Model," *American Journal of Sociology* 94 (1988): 53–78.

3. Stone, "Causal Stories and the Formation of Policy Agendas," 281–82, 293.

4. Charles O. Jackson, *Food and Drug Legislation in the New Deal* (Princeton, NJ: Princeton University Press, 1970). James Harvey Young, *The Medical Messiahs: A Social History of Health Quackery in Twentieth-Century America* (Princeton, NJ: Princeton University Press, 1967).

5. Harry M. Marks, "Revisiting 'The Origins of Compulsory Drug Prescriptions,'" *American Journal of Public Health* 85 (1995): 109–15; Peter Temin, *Taking Your Medicine: Drug Regulation in the United States* (Cambridge, MA: Harvard University Press, 1980). For a more extended argument about the ideas animating therapeutic reform in the United States, see Marks, *The Progress of Experiment: Science and Therapeutic Reform in the United States, 1900–1990* (New York: Cambridge University Press, 1997).

unlike the criminal or judicial realm, the culprit is not to be punished but reformed. The ultimate causal inference concerns policy, and it is drawn by the choral public and its representatives, even as it may be preceded and assisted by the lessons drawn and publicized by political elites, media organizations, and other actors. By assigning emotive weight and causal rationality to an episode—by linking the harm with a condition, and by spinning the counterfactual that the harm would not have occurred (and will not occur henceforth) with appropriate reform—the construction of policy tragedies can align the problem and solution streams of agenda-setting.[6]

Policy tragedies are historical and political products. They are complex combinations of the (intended) results of political framing and storytelling and the (often unintended) results of everyday portrayals of facts by popular media and public officials.[7]

As scholars have long recognized, history is no more owned by official chroniclers than is religion by the highest priests. There is an element of indeterminacy and contingency in agenda-setting that historical political science must recognize. We need not embrace relativism to acknowledge that in everyday life, as well as in formal politics, any set of facts is amenable to numerous (though often finitely many) interpretations. Hence it is useful to distinguish between the concept of an *episode*, a sequence of brute facts of the situation that are relatively consensual, and a *tragedy*, which may be conceived as a particular narrative linking the facts of the episode together, in such a way as to generate "lessons."

Tragedies are woven from episodes (or sequences of facts) when human agents engage in framing, selective highlighting, and distillation of facts to present a sense-making portrait of history that also includes policy lessons for the action of others. The fundamental "facts" of an episode constrain the possible interpretations, but they often leave open more than one alternative story to tell. Echoing and elaborating upon Kingdon's work, we observe that certain episodes become tragedies and crises only when powerfully situated political actors convert a sequence of facts into a narrative with ready-made lessons for public and political consumption. Nothing about this process implies a lie of any sort. The process is about selective emphasis—drawing attention to some features of the problem rather than others—and not fabrication.

Key to our account is whether the stories embedded in policy tragedies have lessons. We may think of a lesson as a prescription for action or policy, a prescription which follows a story sequentially, and a prescription whose truth, allure or persuasive value depends heavily upon the story told. Lessons can be taken as ammunition for the course and continuation of policy debates. Lessons if sufficiently powerful can change the course of politics and policy making. These lessons are often implicit; a story may be told in such a way as to suggest strongly to its audience that a certain action be taken or avoided. In other cases, the explicit lessons are part of the story, woven into it. Most narratives converting episodes to tragedies, we think, embed both implicit and explicit lessons.[8]

Because lessons are part of a larger political sphere in which claims and proposals are bandied about, one might fairly wonder how well narrative lessons compete with statistical lessons, philosophical lessons or other forms of argumentation. One potential answer lies in the nature of beliefs and memory. Beliefs about social phenomena often reside not in abstract representations (a demand curve, the proletariat) or estimates (the rate of inflation, the added death risk from smoking), but in stories. One of many reasons for the persistence of narrative is the active role of imagination and prospecting in memory construction. In some ways, stories are often more evocative, more vivid, and more memorable to a wider range of people than are other forms of data. In other ways, stories better lend themselves to the simulation of future events that have mental and emotional relevance for those involving in making new policy.[9]

Multivocality, Framing and the Power of Implicit Narrative. An episode is converted into a tragedy when there is an identifiable change in the way that the story is told from one time to another. The facts can

6. The notion of tragedy and the role of the chorus that we have in mind are taken from Greek tragedy, in particular Sophocles' *Oedipus Rex* and *Antigone*, G. M. Kirkwood, "The Dramatic Role of the Chorus in Sophocles," *Phoenix* 8 (1954): 1–22.

7. Kingdon, *Agendas, Alternatives and Public Policies*, 94–100; Stone maintains a tighter focus on inferential patterns following the events and patterns that are interpreted, such that "causal argument is at the heart of problem definition" ("Causal Stories and the Formation of Policy Agendas," 299). On the selective introduction or emphasis of political dimensions as akin to an act of framing, see William H. Riker, *The Art of Political Manipulation* (New Haven, CT: Yale University Press, 1986).

8. In health politics, see Thomas R. Oliver, "Ideas, Entrepreneurship, and the Politics of Health Care Reform," *Stanford Law and Policy Review* 3 (1991): 160–80; Oliver and Pamela Paul-Shaheen, "Translating Ideas into Actions: Entrepreneurial Leadership in State Health Care Reform," *Journal of Health Politics, Policy, and Law* 22 (1997): 721–88.

9. The notion of lessons as implicit and symbolic stands in contrast to the emphasis of Deborah Stone upon more rigorous causal argumentation, including the use of epidemiology and statistics in administrative, judicial, and legislative politics ("Causal Stories and the Formation of Policy Agendas," 291, 297–99). On the notion of active memory construction, see Daniel L. Schacter, *The Seven Sins of Memory: How the Mind Forgets and Remembers* (Boston: Houghton Mifflin, 2001); Schachter and Donna Rose Addis, "Constructive Memory: The Ghosts of Past and Future," *Nature* 445 (2007).

limit the range of possible interpretations and narratives to only a few; however, they can also create multivocal possibilities. Although only a finite number of stories can be told, the number of possible stories is almost always greater than one. The agent can emphasize some features of the episode without fabricating. Hence the multiplicity of possible stories is not unlike the problem of underdetermination in statistical modeling. It remains fundamentally different in that for competing narratives there exists no clear "information criterion" or "model success statistic" with which people can consensually choose one framing over another.[10]

Framing is active and passive. Events that are later interpreted as a "tragedy" do not come to public attention undigested. Or, as Kingdon remarked, "Problems are not self-evident by the indicators." They require "focusing events." Much of the distillation process occurs directly, and consciously and strategically. Yet much of it occurs in ways that cannot be traced to active and conscious manipulation. The conscious or unconscious adding of a certain word or image to dialogue may invert the preexisting framing of an event and portray its winners and losers in new, more compelling or more forgettable ways.[11]

Victimhood, Policy Beneficiaries, and the Target Populations of Regulation. We note, finally, that in policymaking and policy tragedies, the narrative must embed a representation of the victim or the beneficiary (or both). If a policy solution is to be a credible response to a tragedy, then the victim whose fate could have been saved or improved must be accessible to public understanding and empathy. Put differently, the potential beneficiaries of the policy must be either identifiable (as in distributive politics) or imaginable (as in the politics of collective welfare). Scholars of welfare policy have described this dynamic as one of the social construction of "target populations." Exactly how deserving or benefit-worthy the imputed targets of a policy are depends upon factors such as race, gender, ethnicity, age, and observed behavior. A focus on policy tragedy links the social construction of target populations in regulation to the political construction of victimhood in regulatory crises.[12]

We hope that our narrative demonstrates the allure of a productive nexus between the collective endeavor of American political development and the scholarship of agenda-setting. To political scientists, sociologists, and other students of agenda-setting and framing, the tale spun here is at turns both familiar and surprising. It is familiar because it echoes and tangibly embodies much of the theoretical architecture of modern political science and institutional sociology. Yet the narrative offers surprises because most agenda-setting accounts lack the historical particularity and contingency to which American political development scholarship is attentive. What is missing from many agenda-setting accounts is an elaboration of the possible frames, the role of particular situated actors in shaping the agenda, a symbolic analysis of particular tragedies—how they were interpreted, what sorts of emotions and rhetoric were summoned, how the tragedies set in motion a contest of causal and symbolic interpretation—and their yield of specific regulatory products (statutes, rules, administrative actions). Agenda-setting and symbolic analyses bring to American political development a useful battery of ideas and methods. Yet with its focus on durable shifts in authority, upon institutional formation and upon state actors, American political development brings useful technologies and concepts to the study of historical agenda-setting, tools that have been too little deployed in agenda-setting research.[13]

10. We have in mind a notion of multivocality like that in Victor Turner, *The Forest of Symbols* (Ithaca, NY: Cornell University Press, 1967). See also John F. Padgett and Christopher K. Ansell, "Robust Action and the Rise of the Medici, 1400–1434," *American Journal of Sociology* 98 (1993): 1259–319. The relevance of these themes for American political development scholars is helpfully elaborated in Adam D. Sheingate, "Political Entrepreneurship, Institutional Change, and American Political Development," *Studies in American Political Development* 17 (2003): 185–203. The classic Bayesian criterion for distinguishing among alternative models of statistical histories appears in Gideon Schwarz, "Estimating the Dimension of a Model," *Annals of Statistics* 6 (1978): 461–64.

11. Kingdon *Agendas, Alternatives and Public Policies*, 94. Much of the work on framing in political science is restricted to the era of television news; Shanto Iyengar, *Is Anyone Responsible? How Television Frames Political Issues* (Chicago: University of Chicago Press, 1991); Robert C. Entman, *Projections of Power: Framing News, Public Opinion, and U.S. Foreign Policy* (Chicago: University of Chicago Press, 2004). Hence American political development scholarship could be helpful in revealing patterns of issue framing before the latter twentieth century.

12. Anne Schneider and Helene Ingram, "Social Construction of Target Populations: Implications for Politics and Policy," *American Political Science Review* 87 (1993): 334–47; Robert Lieberman, "Comment: Social Construction," *American Political Science Review* 89 (1995) 437–41. See more recently Martin Gilens, *Why Americans Hate Welfare* (Chicago: University of Chicago Press, 1998); in this sense of deservingness, Theda Skocpol's *Protecting Soldiers and Mothers* (Cambridge, MA: Harvard University Press, 1992) can be reinterpreted as a story about the historical construction of target populations for early American welfare policy.

13. On state actors and their strategies for institutional and policy reform, see Eric A. Nordlinger, *On the Autonomy of the Democratic State* (Cambridge, MA: Harvard university Press, 1981), as well as the more synthetic treatment of Karen Orren and Stephen Skowronek, *The Search for American Political Development* (New York: Cambridge University Press, 2004). For instance, one strand of agenda-setting research has employed quantitative analysis of problems, as seen for example in Baumgartner and Jones, *Agendas and Instability in American Politics*; Jones and Baumgartner, *The Politics of Attention.* In health policy, see Elizabeth Armstrong, Daniel Carpenter and Marie Hojnacki, "Whose Deaths Matter? Mortality, Advocacy and Attention to Disease in the Mass Media," *Journal of Health Politics, Policy and Law* 31 (2006): 729–72. Yet historical analysis has been largely left aside from much of this literature; for a partial exception see Oliver and Paul-Shaheen, "Translating Ideas into Actions."

I. Linking Crises and Regulation

The claim that regulation follows certain critical events (either actual events or journalistic exposes) is common to historians of numerous fields of regulation. Scholars ranging from Oscar Anderson to James Harvey Young and Daniel Carpenter have partially ascribed final passage of the Pure Food and Drugs Act of 1906 to publication of Upton Sinclair's *The Jungle*, an expose of substandard hygienic practices in Chicago meat packing plants that sold more than a million copies in the first year of its printing. Scholars from Paul Quirk ("The Food and Drug Administration") to Milton Friedman (*Free to Choose*) have noted that the thalidomide tragedy of the late 1950s eased the passage of the 1962 Kefauver-Harris Amendments to the 1938 Food, Drug, and Cosmetic Act, which substantially tightened FDA drug approval standards. Pundits and scholars alike have noted the correspondence between events and legislation in cases ranging from Three Mile Island and nuclear facility regulation, to Love Canal and toxic waste cleanup laws, and to visible pollution and environmental regulation. Consider, for instance, Evan Ringquist's assessment of the origins of environmental regulation:

> Environmental regulation exploded on to the national agenda in the late 1960s. *Like most regulatory policies*, environmental regulation is profoundly affected by crises or focusing events external to the regulatory environment itself. Following a series of focusing events, from the publication of *Silent Spring* in 1962 to the outbreak of drinking water contamination in Milwaukee in 1993, federal responsibilities in environmental protection have grown to include the regulation of air and water pollution, solid wastes, hazardous wastes, noise and radiation pollution, pesticides, and most toxic chemicals traded in interstate commerce.[14]

We cite Ringquist here because his argument is much clearer than those of other scholars who point to crises or tragedies as a cause of regulation. He posits a specific mechanism—the process of "focusing"—by which a certain event or publication might induce governments to pass new regulatory statutes and create new regulatory agencies. The other term used in the regulation literature is that of "outcry," a signifier for a change in public opinion that is induced by critical events.

Even so, it is not clear how the process of focusing necessarily implies any direct connection to the political processes by which regulation is produced. Do "focusing" events lead "outcrying" voters to demand new forms of regulation by exposing failures or imperfections in the marketplace? Do politicians observe these events and anticipate voter reaction, taking up and passing new forms of regulation in order to minimize the effect of these events upon their re-election outcomes? If so, *which officials*—legislators, executives, judges, administrators—are most induced to take new action?

Or consider different mechanisms. Do well-informed (and well-heeled) interest groups or agencies take up the aegis of reform after critical events or tragedies? Might they, with the help of favorable media coverage, attempt to frame the event in such a way that voters and politicians are led inexorably from the fact of the event to certain policy conclusion, from a positive fact to a normative prescription for change? Or is it the case that critical events and tragedies give cover to rent-seeking interests who can frame self-serving legislation as publicly beneficial, as a solution to the crisis?

Another puzzle is that many episodes potentially worthy of the appellation *tragedy* or *crisis* occur, but clearly not all of them have focusing power or lead to new regulation. There were numerous deaths and widespread morbidity reported from use of patent medicines in the 1920s and 1930s, yet none of these but the sulfanilamide episode led to meaningful and sustained reform. Devastating mining accidents were a feature of the industrial landscape from the mid-nineteenth century through the twentieth; however, not until the 1950s through the 1970s did stringent mining safety regulation get enacted. Although it lies outside of the realm of economic regulation, neither the 1999 shooting at a Columbine, Colorado, high school, nor numerous other school-related shootings has, at this writing, led to broad-based reform of any state's gun laws.[15]

Our criticism of existing scholarship, then, is not that it gets the account wrong. Ringquist and other scholars are, we think, probably correct to point to

14. Oscar E. Anderson, *The Health of a Nation: Harvey W. Wiley and the Fight for Pure Food*, (Chicago, University of Chicago Press, 1958); James Harvey Young, *Pure Food* (Princeton, NJ: Princeton University Press, 1990); Carpenter, *The Forging of Bureaucratic Autonomy*, (Princeton, NJ: Princeton University Press, 2001), chap. 8. Quirk, "The Food and Drug Administration," in *Regulatory Agencies*, ed. James Q. Wilson (Washington, DC: Brookings Institute Press, 1980). Evan Ringquist, "Environmental Protection Regulation," in *Regulation and Consumer Protection: Politics, Bureaucracy and Economics*, ed. Kenneth J. Meier, E. Thomas Garman, and Lael Keiser, 3d ed. (Houston, TX: Dame Publications, 1998). See also Ringquist's assessment of the rise of environmental concern in the late 1960s:

> Beginning in the late 1960s, a series of focusing events (e.g., the Torrey Canyon and Santa Barbara oil spills, Ohio's Cuyahoga River catching fire, the original Earth day celebration in 1970) radically changed the environment surrounding pollution control regulation. By 1970, public opinion polls showed that environmental protection was the most frequently cited public problem. (Ibid., 150)

15. To render the point another way, consider the *absence* of tragedy-based politics in Scott C. James's skillful retelling of the creation of independent regulatory commissions in the United States; James, *Presidents, Parties and the State: A Party System Perspective on Democratic Regulatory Choice* (New York: Cambridge University Press, 2000).

the Cuyahoga fire and Carson's *Silent Spring* as events which have some causal relationship to the emergence of more stringent environmental regulation in the late 1960s and 1970s. Our concern is rather narrative specificity. What is it about focusing events, tragedies, and crises that induces politicians to consider and pass new legislation? Scholars generally lack any sort of causally and narratively specific account of the historical and political mechanisms by which such new forms of regulation are traceable to critical events.

A Counterfactual Condition. We believe that the traceability of legislative or regulatory change to a specific event (and to a framing of that event) requires that a particular form of counterfactual be true or at least strongly defensible. Speaking hypothetically, let us say that the analyst observes an *event,* a framing of that event (*frame*), and a subsequent regulatory change (a *regulation*). The event and the frame may be combined conceptually into a single object, the *event-frame.* In order for the political scientist or political historian to argue cogently and persuasively that the event induced the change in some causal sense, *it must be the case that, in the absence of the event-frame match, the new regulation in question would not have materialized, would not have materialized when it materialized, or would not have materialized in the form that it materialized.* Causal inference may not be possible or desirable in many cases, but if it is to be relied upon, the analyst must go further than this statement. Since new regulations in republican and democratic systems are the result of particular processes of institutional action, then the relationship between the event, the event-frame and the eventual regulation must satisfy one or more of the following conditions:

1. In the absence of the event and the event-frame, the proposed regulation would not have become part of the policy agenda.[16]
2. In the absence of the event and the event-frame, certain crucial votes would have been cast against the regulatory change, or for some competitive alternative, such that the final law would not have materialized.
   (a) In the absence of the event and the event-frame, public opinion regarding the proposed regulatory change would have remained in favor of the status quo or insufficiently supportive of change.
   (b) In the absence of the event and the event-frame, an executive actor would have either vetoed the final law or would have refrained from lobbying in such a way as to have eased its passage.
   (c) In the absence of the event and the event-frame, certain lobbying organizations (interest groups, civic organizations, or bureaucracies) would have refrained from lobbying in such a way as to have eased the law's passage.[17]
3. In the absence of the event and the event-frame, a different law would have been passed.

Note that a given event and a given frame may satisfy more than one of these conditions. To the degree that more than one of the statements is satisfied, the narrative connecting the event will always be more complex. We do not regard narrative complexity as a weakness of any account—it is more commonly a strength—but we believe that the analyst should call attention to it when present.

The 1938 Act as a Canonical Example. Previous accounts of the 1938 Food, Drug, and Cosmetic Act have pointed uniformly to the sulfanilamide tragedy as perhaps the principal causal factor in the passage of a new law. Charles Jackson, who has authored the most thorough monograph on the 1938 law, writes that the "Elixir Sulfanilamide disaster . . . for the first time really brought about a heated public demand for legislation." James Harvey Young, probably the most prolific historian to write on the history of food-and-drug legislation and the patent-medicine industry in the United States, writes that in response to the sulfanilamide deaths, "The public, shocked into a new awareness that the [1906] law had loopholes, urged Congress to remedy the fault." Speaking more generally of the history of food and drug regulation, Young writes that "The thalidomide near-disaster, like the meat-packing scandals of 1906 and the sulfanilamide tragedy of 1937, forced the Congress to enact a major new protective law." The FDA's staff historians have ratified this conventional wisdom, suggesting that the sulfanilamide tragedy "propelled the bill itself through Congress."[18]

This is not to deny that other interpretations of Act have been advanced. Harry Marks argues that the law conforms better to a capture account of regulation along the lines of Gabriel Kolko's interpretation of

16. We do not intend to advance a specific concept of the policy agenda here, save that it might include the agenda of a particular committee, the president, party leaders for the congressional majority, or some other crucial actor.

17. This is not an exhaustive list of the counterfactual statements whose truth could be used as evidence to support a causal relationship between an event and a new law, but covers some of the dominant alternatives.

18. Jackson, *Food and Drug Legislation,* 218; Young, *Medical Messiahs,* 186, 418. John P. Swann, "History of the FDA" (adapted from George Kurian, ed., *A Historical Guide to the U.S. Government* (New York: Oxford University Press, 1998), at www.fda.gov/oc/history/historyoffda/section2.html (accessed August 15, 2007).

Progressive Era regulatory laws. Marks shows that organized pharmaceutical companies extracted noteworthy concessions in the writing of the 1938 act, and were perhaps even more successful in seeing their interests met in post-1938 administrative rulemaking by the FDA. Marks's evidence is fresh, interesting and undoubtedly merits further exploration. Yet it is questionable whether his evidence truly supports a standard capture account. For one, businesses might be politically successful in blunting the force of a new regulatory statute, but this fact (even if well established) falls well short of evidence for capture. The essential notion behind a capture account is that existing or large producers are able to design regulation to function as an entry barrier against smaller or potential competitors. A second reason to doubt Marks's argument is that, as Jackson points out, most business lobbying was of a defensive nature: "The support [of the 1938 law] by many segments of the affected trades was forced as a defensive reaction." Patent medicine and established pharmaceutical manufacturers were alike aligned against FDA-strengthening legislation before 1935.[19] Resigned to the inevitability of a new regulatory statute after November 1937, organized pharmaceutical manufacturers tried their best to blunt a law while supporting the general reform initiative.

Marks's arguments notwithstanding, no historian of whom we are aware is willing to weave the narrative of food and drug regulation in the late 1930s without pointing to the sulfanilamide tragedy as a central if not historically necessary event in the reform process. Again, however, these existing accounts are lacking in narrative and causal specificity, making it difficult to trace the new law directly to the act. Jackson's claim that the law brought about a "heated public demand" for legislation, while plausible, remains unsupported by evidence from correspondence, media coverage, polling data and the like. Young's similar claim that the public was "shocked" by the tragedy and subsequently pressed for a new law is similarly devoid of empirical support. Consider the possibility that politicians responded to the tragedy by anticipating public reaction or by considering the loopholes of the 1906 law themselves, *without prompting or communication from the public.* Neither Jackson nor Young offers any evidence to disprove this hypothesis. Or consider what the nefarious concepts of *public, public outcry*, and *public opinion* mean in these accounts. Was there a genuine public outcry for reform in the sense that it was distributed widely among citizens of all classes, all geographic sections, all ages, both parties, and both sexes following the sulfanilamide deaths? Jackson, Young and other authors refer to a "public outcry" and "public pressure" without specifying whence or from whom the voices came.

We investigate these questions below. In order to understand the policy tragedy of sulfanilamide and the food-and-drug-regulation reform initiative of the 1930s, one must comprehend the economic and social context of the markets and commodities that politicians sought to regulate. We begin with a brief look at the early twentieth-century market for proprietary medicines.

II. Proprietary Medicines and the "Right of Self-Medication"

Two related forces had opposed passage of FDA-strengthening legislation: the proprietary medicine industry, and votaries of the doctrine of *self-medication.* These twin pillars of nineteenth-century health practice were mutually sustaining. The proprietary medicine industry was premised upon behavioral alternatives to professional medical practice and counsel. The doctrine of self-medication, centuries old but waning, was viable only in the presence of purchasable medications to which the consumer had relatively unimpeded access.

Proprietary drugs (or patent medicines) have long been described in highly anachronistic terms, as "nostrums" marketed by "snake-oil peddlers," or as products whose manufacture and sale are equated with quackery. Such language might imply that the market for such medicines was a trifling sideshow to the emergence of medically prescribed pharmaceutical products in the economic history of the West. Indeed, nothing could be further from the truth. The market for patent medicines in the United States grew from the colonial period and, by the early twentieth century, accounted for hundreds of millions of dollars in annual sales. Such products accounted for millions of dollars in advertising revenue in periodicals and medical journals nationwide, including the *Journal of the American Medical Association,* which depended heavily upon patent medicine ads until 1905.[20]

It is difficult to demarcate patent medicines from their more legitimated "non-patent" counterparts. Patent medicines were just as likely *not* to have received a federal patent as to have one. Until the mid-twentieth century, patent medicines were commonly prescribed by fully licensed and board-certified physicians, and they were frequently listed on official pharmacopoeia. The operative distinction became clearer in the late 1800s, when pharmaceutical companies began restricting their advertising to doctors and began to list the contents of their

19. Jackson, *Food and Drug Legislation,* 206. Jackson provides abundant evidence that organized pharmaceutical interests were opposed to reform of the 1906 law at 68, 79, 95, 104, 107, 112, 119, 123. We provide additional narrative and quantitative evidence against capture and rent-seeking accounts below.

20. James Harvey Young, *The Toadstool Millionaires* (Princeton, NJ: Princeton University Press, 1961). See also Young's *Medical Messiahs.*

medications on the sides of the bottles. Thus proprietary medicines were usually distinguished by (1) the absence of chemical or pharmacological information on their labels and (2) their heavy reliance upon direct-to-consumer advertising.[21]

Over the course of the nineteenth century the market for proprietary medicines—which ranged from novel pharmacological concoctions to filling empty pharmaceutical containers with water or grain alcohol and reselling them—exploded in size.[22] An 1804 New York drug catalog listed some 80 or 90 names of patent medicines, but by 1858 the number of products ranged from 500 to 1,500, depending upon the estimate used. By 1905, *Druggist's Circular* listed more than 28,000 patent medicines; a year later, congressional testimony put the estimate at 50,000. By 1859, the proprietary medicine business was valued in census figures at $3,500,000 in annual revenues. By 1904, that revenue estimate reached $74,500,000, a figure which, by 1912, had increased by approximately 60 percent to more than $110 million. By mid-century, congressional investigators estimated annual revenues of the proprietary medicine industry at $1 billion to $2 billion.

The set of drugs marketed as patent medicines varied widely in their composition and therapeutic claims. They included Robert Harper's "Cuforhedake Brane-Fude," a "brain food" supplement containing a dangerous combination of alcohol and acetanilid whose title subtly offered to cure headaches.[23] Anti-impotence medications and sexual stimulation drugs with names such as "Persenico" and "Revivio" were very common. Within ten days of consuming "Persenico" the patient would have success "in combating neurasthenic impotence, pre-senility, low vitality, and general nervous ailments, particularly . . . of sexual origin." The love-sex hormone "Revivio" offered men the chance to "improve your vigor." Those suffering from gastrointestinal constipation or "piles" could purchase, with a money-back guarantee, "Dr. Young's Rectal Dilators." The dilators purportedly used "natural methods" to strengthen rectal muscles by "imitating Nature's own process."

These medications had far more pervasive effects of might be implied by the morbid historical curiosity that they inspire today. There were at least three deleterious outcomes of the widespread marketing of these drugs. The first was *equilibrium fraud*. Consumers were buying products with the belief that they held curing power when in fact they usually held none or were in fact harmful to health. With the possible exception of aspirin (whose contents were usually published) and several analgesics, no widely sold patent medicine of the late-nineteenth to early-twentieth century was later shown to have significant marginal clinical curative power for its consumers.[24] Perhaps worse, many patent medicines were associated with high toxicity and other safety hazards. Most "soothing tonics" for babies and children were laced with alcohol, opium, or some combination of the two. "Gouraud's Oriental Face Cream" led to "genuine facial beauty," but government investigators later learned that it did so by imparting significant mercury to its consumers, thereby inducing skin discoloration.

The truly severe harm associated with proprietary medicines concerned not hazards in the medicines themselves but the treatment foregone by their consumption. There were two rational or semi-rational mechanisms that engendered such an outcome. First, knowledgeable consumers would often forgo the opportunity to consume even legitimate pharmaceutical products out of awareness of the hazards associated with fraudulent varieties. Second, and most important, for every consumer trying to reduce morbidity and/or mortality by consuming a non-curative patent medicine, valuable medical treatment was forfeited. In some cases, consumers would experiment with different drug products until they found something that worked for them. Even in cases where they eventually happened upon a remedy with true curative value, their consumption of other patent medicines in this auto-experimental process usually implied a serious delay in effective treatment. In other cases, superstitious learning led to an even worse outcome. In cases where the consumer's ailment would have gone away on its own, the consumer often wrongly reasoned that the patent medicine had in fact cured a disease, a conclusion which induced further consumption of the drug, and (via observation and informational transmission through interpersonal networks) heightened consumption by others.[25]

The staying power of patent medicines in the United States and other Western nations was linked to a set of beliefs about the relationship between individual agents and the curing of disease. The philosophy or ideology of self-medication or *auto-therapy* was centuries old and linked to organized challenges to the medical and pharmacological professions. The set of movements intertwined with these beliefs is far

21. Young, *Medical Messiahs*, chap. 2.

22. The information in the following two pages is taken from Young, *Medical Messiahs*, chaps. 2–3; and Jackson, *Food and Drug Legislation*, 127–28.

23. Compounds containing acetanilid were suspected in at least twenty-two deaths in 1905 (Young, *Medical Messiahs*, 6). Acetanilid mimicked opiates, inducing overdoses and lending themselves to addictive consumption.

24. The most recent example was Laetrile, a highly touted cancer remedy that occasioned great controversy in the 1970s and 1980s. Subsequent studies showed Laetrile not to have had any effects, and its current use by cancer patients is negligible.

25. Jackson, *Food and Drug Legislation*, 96. For a theoretical and empirical argument that such pathological learning is common in consumer evaluations of doctor quality and pharmaceutical efficacy, see Jishnu Das, "Do Patients Learn About Doctor Quality? Theory and Evidence from India," (Ph.D. diss., Harvard University, 2001); and Daniel Carpenter, "A Simple Theory of Placebo Learning with Self-Remitting Diseases," unpub. mss., 2005.

too diverse and complex to be discussed here, but it suffices to note that the social, economic and political authority of organized medicine came at the expense of organized homeopathy, chiropractic practice, holistic medicine and other movements. The emergence of a national market for proprietary drugs was in some ways akin to, in other ways vastly different from, these movements. Patent medicine makers commonly advertised their drugs as a means of avoiding the expense and personal intrusion occasioned by a visit to the doctor. (The latter point explains why patent medicines were popular among women living under cultural norms of Victorian domesticity, and among men seeking treatment for gonorrhea and syphilis.) Yet patent medicines competed powerfully with alternative medicine and indeed drove out of business many nineteenth- and twentieth-century practitioners of the (non-medical) healing arts.[26]

The set of specific beliefs described by the *right of self-medication* emerged with greater cultural force during the antebellum period and continued in force through the early 1900s. At their core, claims for the primacy or privileged status of self-medication depended upon beliefs in consumer autonomy and judgment.[27] Votaries of self-medication frequently voiced their support for stronger labeling disclosure requirements for drug manufacturers, in part out of the belief that "the intelligent layman" needed maximal information to render an informed pharmaceutical purchasing decision. Yet the supporters of auto-therapy usually disdained state and federal regulatory measures. One of the most relevant political implications of their ethic was a time-honored right of self-medication. In operation, this included the absolute liberty of the consumer or patient to purchase any and all medications for the amelioration of his or her ailments. Whatever the disease, and whatever the purported cure, the layman should be able to exercise his own scientific judgment in drug purchasing decisions.[28]

The proprietary medicine industry entered the twentieth century almost completely unregulated. Aside from some state-level statutes passed to regulate food in the 1880s and 1890s, no government regulation of the proprietary medicine market existed. The signal change in Progressive-Era regulation of drugs came in 1906, when Dr. Harvey Wiley of the USDA's Bureau of Chemistry successfully completed a twenty-year campaign to pass a federal food and drug regulation bill. The 1906 law gave USDA power to seize articles of manufacture deemed "fraudulent" or falsely advertised, and prodigious cooperation between Wiley and officials at the Post Office Department was successful in prosecuting hundreds of cases in the Progressive period. Yet such cases were always prosecuted *ex post*, and the associated penalties were minimal. Robert Harper's marketing of "Brane-Fude," for instance, brought him a fine of $700. Compared with the $2 million in profits he had made on the product, it was a trifling fine.

Whether due to the unevenness of state regulation or the greater staying power of self-medication ideologies in the South, southern states provided, by the 1930s, a truly comfortable home for many firms in the proprietary medicine industry. Indeed, the proprietary medicine industry was characterized by some exclusively regional markets. Some nostrums sold in California were virtually unheard of on the in the East, and many more drugs marketed in southern states were generally unavailable or not widely purchased in states outside the former Confederacy.

III. The Emergence of New Regulatory Alternatives: Bureaucratic Agenda-Setting and the Power of Organized Women

Calls for a revision of the 1906 Pure Food and Drugs Act were largely unrelated to changes in the proprietary medicine industry or to consumer tragedies of the 1920s and early 1930s. Instead, two forces—the FDA (backed by Roosevelt administration officials in the Department of Agriculture) and organized women's groups—exercised strong leverage in pressing for changes to the 1906 law. One of their principal successes was finding able legislative sponsors, principally Senator Royal Copeland (D–NY) and Representative Virgil Chapman (D–KY). From 1934 to 1937, Copeland in particular authored a succession of bills that would have substantially strengthened the FDA.

FDA officials had long been disappointed with the operation of the 1906 act, repeatedly lamenting that manufacturers were able to exploit loopholes in the statute, that successfully prosecuted proprietary manufacturers quickly relabeled their products and entered the market again, and that dangerous and worthless medications were entering the market. Patent medicine manufacturers circumvented the labeling and fraud restrictions of the 1906 act by veiling their therapeutic claims (hence "Cuforhedake") or by removing information from the label altogether.

The first bill addressing these problems, S. 1944 (introduced in December 1933), was authored by FDA personnel and sponsored by Copeland. Along with its successors, S. 2800 and S. 5 (both introduced in 1934), S. 1944 attempted to rein in the patent medicine industry. S. 1944 required disclosure of ingredients on labels, removed the 1906 act's requirement that the FDA had to prove intent to defraud in order to seize shipments of a good, gave

26. Paul Starr, *The Social Transformation of American Medicine* (New York: Basic Books, 1982); Marks, *Progress of Experiment.*

27. We sidestep the term "patient autonomy" here as it is a more recent concept and assumes the existence of a professional-patient relationship, a relationship which the ethic of self-medication often challenged or rejected altogether.

28. Jackson, *Food and Drug Legislation,* 79, 114.

the FDA power to seize multiple shipments of misbranded goods, and rendered advertisers and manufacturers alike legally liable for fraudulent claims. The bill also gave to the FDA power over pharmaceutical advertising. S. 2800 and S. 5 relaxed many of these provisions, in particular by introducing judicial constraints on seizures and by relaxing the formula disclosure provisions of earlier bills. As the legislation progressed through congress, debates over labeling, seizure and advertising regulation would attract the greatest energy and debate.

Administrative leaders at the FDA, most notably Walter Campbell and Paul Dunbar—careerists who had trained under USDA Chief Chemist Harvey Wiley before 1910—made use of three strategies in advancing the case for strengthening the 1906 act. First, they allied with friendly forces in the Roosevelt administration, most notably Rexford Tugwell. Tugwell was FDR's assistant secretary of agriculture and perhaps the most powerful liberal voice in the administration in the early 1930s. He desired for the pharmaceutical industry a system of industrial oversight not unlike that envisioned in the National Recovery Administration (NRA) or antitrust law, where "fair and responsible competition" would be a primary policy goal. His continued support of FDA-strengthening legislation was crucial in light of a salient fact about the food and drug regulatory struggle: *Roosevelt was not supportive of the FDA's or of Copeland's efforts.* At a general level, the president was generally uninterested in regulatory measures and more interested in laws specifically aimed at economic recovery and national infrastructure. More specifically, Royal Copeland was a New Deal dissident, and New Dealers in Congress and the administration resented his sponsorship of the bill.[29]

The FDA's second stratagem was a skilled and indirect publicity campaign aimed at demonstrating the hazards of adulterated food and medicines to the nation's press. The FDA had been prevented from direct lobbying and publicity efforts in the Deficiency Appropriations Act of 1919, yet the FDA found creative ways to circumvent this rule, distributing pamphlets such as the one entitled *Why We Need a New Pure Food Law* and making radio talks on S. 2800. FDA Information Officer Ruth Lamb successfully invited press outlets to give fresh attention to Copeland's first Senate bill (S. 1944), and she used her own time and money to author a popular book on the hazards of patent medicines entitled *The American Chamber of Horrors* (1936).[30]

The FDA's third strategy was one that required coordination but not persuasion. FDA officials drew upon their decades-old alliances with women's groups and organized consumer unions. Two women's groups—the General Federation of Women's Clubs (GFWC) and the Women's Christian Temperance Union (WCTU)—were instrumental in lobbying for the 1906 act. As Theda Skocpol and Elizabeth Clemens have argued, the GFWC and the WCTU were some of the most powerful lobbies of their time, almost single-handedly waging successful campaigns for mothers' pensions and child-labor laws. Joining the women's groups, moreover, was the increasingly assertive and powerful Consumers' Research (CR). CR was founded in 1929 with 1,000 members and by 1933 had ballooned to 45,000 members. As Jackson describes the union, "CR's influence and significance far exceeded its actual membership. The organization served as a coordinating body for congressional and other sympathizers of consumer legislation." Rexford Tugwell found "astounding" the "receptive attitude of the general public" toward CR.[31]

Despite the seemingly favorable circumstances—an overwhelming Democratic majority in Congress with pro-regulation impulses, a Democratic president, supportive women's groups and a well-coordinated rhetorical campaign—several factors combined to blunt the FDA's initiative for food and drug law reform in the mid-1930s. The first was well-organized and well-represented opposition from the affected industries. As Jackson describes the rise of opposition, "Many existing trade bodies were turned almost immediately into vehicles of resistance. Especially militant were the Proprietary Association [PA] and the United Medicine Manufacturers of America [UMMA]." The PA and UMMA sponsored protest gatherings, radio advertisements, and coordinated petition campaigns against FDA-strengthening bills. The manufacturers found able legislative defenders such as Senators Josiah Bailey (D–NC) and Arthur Vandenberg (R–MI).[32]

Two other difficulties were related less to the opponents of reform than to its supporters. Rexford Tugwell was the lightning rod of the early Roosevelt administration, was disliked by rural Democrats and conservatives, and his visible association with the Copeland bill soon become a serious liability for the FDA. Opponents of S. 2800 and S. 1944 sounded alarms of "Tugwellmania" and referred to the Copeland measure as "the Tugwell bill." A New Deal dissident whom administration Democrats resented, Copeland himself was perhaps a more serious liability, at least early on. FDR withheld endorsement for his

29. See Jackson, *Food and Drug Legislation*, 63–65, 84, 118. Ruth Deforest Lamb, *American Chamber of Horrors: The Truth About Food and Drugs* (New York: Farrar & Rinehart, 1935).

30. For an informative summary of these efforts, see Gwen Kay, "Healthy Public Relations: The FDA's 1930s Legislative Campaign," *Bulletin of the History of Medicine* 75 (2001): 446–87. Kay makes shrewd use of the Ruth Lamb Atkinson Papers collection at Vassar College.

31. Carpenter, *Forging of Bureaucratic Autonomy*, chap. 8; Skocpol, *Protecting Soldiers and Mothers*; Elizabeth Clemens, *The People's Lobby* (Chicago: University of Chicago Press, 1998); Jackson, *Food and Drug Legislation*, 20–21.

32. Jackson, *Food and Drug Legislation*, 38–39.

home state's senator in the 1934 midterm elections and made no secret of the fact. Roosevelt loyalists in the Democratic Party, including Alben Barkley and other southerners, were determined to keep Copeland an arm's length away from political or moral victories on food and drug regulation.

Opponents of reform landed an apparent deathblow in 1935, when the Senate passed Copeland's S. 5, but only after attaching the infamous "Bailey amendment," which vitiated the measure. The Bailey amendment prohibited the FDA from regulating any aspect of pharmaceutical advertising and would give all such control to the Federal Trade Commission (FTC). From the vantage of the 1906 law, this was a step backwards for the FDA. Even under the Progressive Era statute, the FDA had at least *ex post* control over fraudulent advertising. Once Bailey's amendment was approved, S. 5 passed the Senate but was doomed from criticisms from both the left and the right. S. 5 then died in the House by an overwhelming 190–70 vote.

Roll call votes are available for three crucial votes on the Senate measure in the 74th Congress (1935–1936), and we analyze these votes here to test for the impact of observed ideology, party, region and organized interests. The first two votes were on procedural measures to reconsider an amendment that had been attached to S. 5 during committee. Those who favored a stronger FDA wanted to revisit the committee's decisions and voted "yes" on this measure. The third vote was a vote on the Bailey amendment prohibiting the FDA from regulating pharmaceutical advertising. Proponents of reform voted "no" on this measure, while most opponents of reform voted to pass it.[33]

We conduct probit regressions of these three votes in the 74th Congress. Our regressors are chosen to unearth patterns of support for FDA-strengthening regulation before the sulfanilamide disaster. We first include two general measures of ideology or voting propensity, namely first and second-dimension D-NOMINATE scores. We also include the senator's party (1 if Democrat) and the underlying Democratic strength of his constituency, measured by the percentage of vote for FDR in the 1932 election. To this we add a variable measuring the shift in voter support for FDR from 1932 to 1936 as a way of measuring political trends within each state. We also include demographic and economic variables measuring the state's rate of unemployment in 1930, the percentage of its residents between the ages of 18 and 20 in school, the percentage of its residents who were illiterate as defined by the Census, and the percentage of its residents who were African-American. These variables capture salient political, social, economic and cultural features of states, features we include as controls in the hopes of properly estimating the contribution of ideology and business influence in a well-specified statistical representation of voting. To these we add a "South" dummy variable indicating the states of former Confederacy. We do not attempt to attach expectations to these variables and their coefficient estimates. The ethic of self-medication, for instance, interacted in complicated ways with literacy and education. The illiterate and less educated were more easily misled by patent medicine promoters and sellers, and they were less aware of more legitimized health treatments. Yet the more educated and more literate were also more able to read the newspapers and pamphlets in which patent medicines were sold to the public. Literacy and education could, at this time, be a double-edged sword in the genesis and reproduction of health fraud.[34]

To test industry capture and rent-seeking hypotheses, we employ two variables measuring the presence of organized patent-medicine and pharmaceutical manufacturers in a state. The first measures the number of industry members of the Proprietary Association whose headquarters were in a state. The second measures the number of primary (above associate) members of the United Medicine Manufacturers' Association whose headquarters were in a state. Table 1 gives the summary statistics for these and other variables used in our analyses.

The vote regressions in Table 2 suggest several factors. First, the first dimension D-NOMINATE score has a negative coefficient estimate in the first two regressions and a positive estimate in the third. Since higher scores indicate more conservative members, this result implies that more liberal senators were more likely to vote for the first two measures and less likely to vote for the third. Conditioning on this effect, Democrats appear to be slightly more likely to vote against FDA-strengthening legislation, but these coefficient estimates are statistically indistinguishable from zero. The variables measuring support for FDR are also insignificant, suggesting that underlying Democratic support in one's constituency did not, net of other factors, induce more or less support for reform.

A key result from the Table 2 regressions is that rent-seeking hypotheses are strongly rejected. The variable measuring UMMA firms headquartered in a state is negatively associated with "yes" votes for the first two reconsideration measures and positively

33. Some friends of reform who were also favorable to increased FTC jurisdiction of the economy voted for the Bailey amendment as well. The FTC had powerful friends in the House, not least among Brandeisian liberals who saw the commission as the best hope for a Progressive policy of economy-wide central management and antitrust. This was the wisdom of Bailey's measure, to have split economic liberals from the FDA by sending them headlong into an embrace with the Commission.

34. On NOMINATE-based methods and their application to American political history, see Keith Poole and Howard Rosenthal, *Congress: A Political-Economic History of Roll-Call Voting* (New York: Oxford University Press, 1998).

Table 1. Descriptive Statistics for Selective Variables

Variable	Valid N	Mean (Std Error)	Min	Max
Towns to which *Massengill's Elixir Sulfanilamide* was shipped, 1937	48 states	8.10 (14.10)	0	61
Confirmed Deaths from *Elixir Sulfanilamide*, 1937	48 states	1.89 (4.24)	0	21
Percentage of State Population African-American, 1930 Census	48 states	9.51 (13.63)	0.06	50.23
Percentage of Population Illiterate (Census Definition), 1930 Census	48 states	4.65 (3.94)	0.79	14.92
Percentage of State Population 18–20 in School, 1930 Census	48 states	22.89 (5.11)	14.31	33.62
Percentage of State Employable Workers Unemployed, 1930 Census	48 states	4.33 (1.71)	1.27	8.19
Retail Value-Added as a Percentage of Whole Value-Added, 1930 Census	48 states	118.42 (71.41)	40.16	373.73
Number of Proprietary Association Firms Headquartered in State, 1935	48 states	4.06 (10.33)	0	67
Number of UMMA Firms Headquartered in State, 1935	48 states	2.35 (4.08)	0	17
Percentage of Two-Party Presidential Vote for FDR, 1932	48 states	59.74 (17.76)	23.76	100
First-Dimension D-NOMINATE SCORE, 74th Senate	106 Senators	−0.15 (0.34)	−0.717	0.763
Vote on First S. 5 Reconsideration Measure, 1935	75 votes	0.54 (0.50)	0	1
Vote on Second S. 5 Reconsideration Measure, 1935	67 votes	0.58 (0.50)	0	1
Vote on Bailey Amendment, 1935	73 votes	0.52 (0.50)	0	1

associated with votes for the Bailey amendment. In other words, pharmaceutical interests aligned themselves against the legislation, and their legislative representatives followed suit. The variable measuring state-level presence of proprietary manufacturers is insignificant at the $p < 0.05$ level in all regressions.[35] In addition, senators from states with higher unemployment rates were more likely to support the reconsideration measure, which may reflect anticipated effects of tighter regulation upon proprietary manufacturers in the state. This result is not, however, predicted by a rent-seeking perspective.

Rent-seeking and industry capture explanations are not, then, supported by our probit regressions. Indeed, a hypothesis which runs *counter* to the capture perspective receives strong support. Affected industries, particularly the organized pharmaceutical firms that would have benefited from removed proprietary competition, nonetheless agitated against the legislation, and their representatives were more likely to vote against FDA-strengthening measures.

Indeed, pharmaceutical and proprietary opponents of the Copeland bill won the early battles. While the 1936 election confirmed FDR's popularity, strengthened the hand of liberals in the Democratic Party, and solidified Democratic congressional majorities, it did not generate added momentum for passage of new pharmaceutical regulation. Perhaps the most important reason was the rise of the Conservative Coalition in Congress, a cross-party alliance of southern Democrats and Republicans that frustrated many of Roosevelt's legislative initiatives through voting and through control of the House Rules Committee. For this reason, the challenge for Copeland and FDA officials was all the greater. Some of the most steadfast opponents of regulatory reform had just become more institutionally formidable.[36]

35. The coefficient estimate for the PA measure does achieve significance at the $p < 0.10$ level in the model for the first reconsideration vote, but this is due to the fact that this measure is highly correlated (rho = 0.5598) with the UMMA measure. Once the UMMA measure is removed, the coefficient estimate for the PA measure in this model switches sign and becomes insignificant ($b = -0.00029$; $z = -0.019$). This is not true for the UMMA measure, which remains negative and statistically significant in the first two models and positive and statistically significant in the third model when the PA measure is removed.

36. James T. Patterson, *Congressional Conservatism and the New Deal* (Lexington: University of Kentucky Press, 1967); Eric Schickler, *Disjointed Pluralism* (Princeton, NJ: Princeton University Press, 2001).

Table 2. Probit Analyses of Three Votes on S. 5 (Senate Votes, 74th Congress)

	[Senate Votes, 74th Congress]		
Variable	S. 5 Amendment Reconsideration [4/1/1935]	S. 5 Amendment Reconsideration [4/2/1935]	Bailey Amendment [4/8/1935]
Constant	1.8371 (1.5636)	**3.8839** (1.8262)	−1.7690 (1.4917)
D-NOMINATE 1-D	**−2.0944** (0.8531)	**−2.6960** (1.0643)	**1.8166** (0.8019)
D-NOMINATE 2-D	−1.3916 (0.8194)	0.3583 (1.1096)	0.3844 (0.8613)
Party (Democrat = 1)	−0.7572 (0.6857)	−1.3627 (0.8369)	1.0947 (0.6750)
Percentage of State Vote for FDR, 1932	−0.0041 (0.0206)	0.0169 (0.0250)	0.0081 (0.0185)
Change in % of State for FDR, 1932–1936	−0.0103 (0.0321)	−0.0471 (0.0386)	−0.0177 (0.0250)
% of State Population African-American	−0.0445 (0.0396)	−0.0429 (0.0492)	0.0153 (0.0377)
% of State Population Illiterate	−0.1166 (0.0790)	**−0.2109** (0.0924)	0.1061 (0.0818)
% of State Population Educated	−0.0879 (0.0494)	**−0.2119** (0.0683)	0.0370 (0.0469)
% of State "Gainful Workers" Unemployed	**0.4181** (0.1327)	**0.5893** (0.1736)	−0.0815 (0.1134)
Retail Sales as % of Wholesale	−0.0010 (0.0026)	−0.0009 (0.0028)	−0.0007 (0.0025)
South	**2.1259** (0.9639)	1.1556 (1.5649)	−0.8767 (0.8770)
Number of Proprietary Association firms in state	0.0375 (0.0215)	0.0311 (0.0245)	−0.0179 (0.0178)
Number of UMMA firms in state	**−0.2596** (0.0829)	**−0.2888** (0.0929)	0.0882 (0.0541)
N (df)	83 (69)	75 (61)	81 (67)
LLF	−43.512	−33.796	−49.307
Pseudo-R^2	0.2417	0.3396	0.1139

Notes: Asymptotic standard errors in parentheses. Bold coefficient estimate implies statistical significance at $p < 0.05$ (two-tailed test). UMMA firms and PA firms variables correlated at 0.5598. Removal of UMMA firms variable results in negative but insignificant estimate on PA firms variable.

IV. The Sulfanilamide Episode of 1937

In the summer of 1937, Royal Copeland confided to friends and colleagues that S. 5, along with other hopes for strengthening the FDA's power over the pharmaceutical market, was dying. Months later, the FDA began to hear reports of several deaths in Tulsa, Oklahoma, associated with a proprietary drug called "Elixir Sulfanilamide," an anti-infective drug manufactured by the patent medicine concern Dr. Massengill, of Bristol, Tennessee (Figure 1). FDA officials began investigating the Tulsa deaths, but as they did so, a number of other reports of mortality and morbidity, many of them among children, were making rounds in medical and regulatory and medical networks.

Dr. Massengill's Elixir Sulfanilamide was manufactured as part of a larger trend toward the use of sulfanilamides in the 1930s. Popular in Europe for the treatment of common colds, pneumonia and other infections, sulfanilamide was now making its way into many medicines manufactured in the U.S. FDA officials therefore suspected that the problem lay not in the sulfanilamide itself but rather in the elixir solution in which it was suspended for pharmacological delivery. Dr. Massengill's solvent, as it turned out, was diethylene glycol, which remains an essential ingredient in antifreeze and is highly toxic even in small doses.

Dr. Massengill's Elixir Sulfanilamide began to ship to localities from three distribution points—New York City, Bristol, and San Francisco—in September 1937. By late October, seventy-three persons had perished in ways that doctors could directly attribute to having consumed the elixir. Another twenty deaths were suspected to be related to the drug, but the FDA and doctors lacked

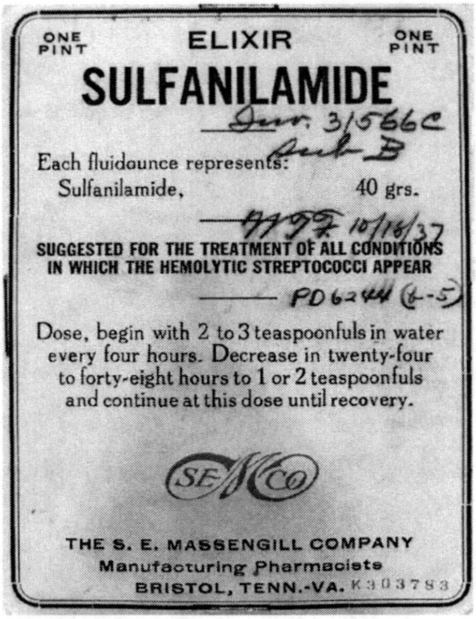

Fig. 1. An Elixir Sulfanilamide Label, 1937 (RG 246, National Archives).

sufficient autopsy evidence to make a direct link in these cases. In the fall of 1937, an emergency session of the Congress called upon the Department of Agriculture (USDA) to make a report regarding the tragedy, and the secretary published a highly detailed report of the deaths that was cited repeatedly in the press and in congressional testimony. At the end of this document, the USDA published a map showing all of the shipment points to which the elixir had been distributed, as well as all localities in which any deaths occurred, as well the number of deaths occurring in a locality. A reproduction of this map appears in Figure 2.

As it turns out, the deaths from sulfanilamide were not as widely distributed, and the public outcry was not as broad, as blunt scholarly descriptions would have us believe. Jackson reports that "Fatalities took place in fifteen states, as far east as Virginia and as far west as California."[37] Yet he fails to mention that most of the deaths occurred in southern and border states, and that some states of the former Confederacy were spared relative to others. There were six deaths in East St. Louis, Illinois, and another eight in Charleston, South Carolina. Louisiana experienced no fatalities, while Oklahoma experienced eleven, and Mississippi witnessed twenty-one. Part of the problem is that the map, which is in the legislative archives of the House of Representatives, was not published with the secretary's report. As a result, USDA officials and members of Congress saw the map, but the public (as far as we can tell) did not. Yet the concentration of deaths (and shipments) suggests something about the mechanisms by which the drug was propagated through a large population of consumers. The prescription and consumption of elixir sulfanilamide was probably dependent upon local referral networks and the idiosyncratic practices of individual physicians.

In order to get a richer understanding of the sulfanilamide tragedy, we conducted maximum likelihood count regressions of the number of deaths and the number of towns receiving shipments of elixir sulfanilamide, using two different levels of geographic aggregation (state and county). These analyses appear in Table 3, which reports the results of four negative binomial regression analyses. In each analysis, one of two variables—(a) the number of towns receiving shipment in a county/state or (b) the number of deaths in a county/state—is regressed upon several economic and demographic variables. These include all of the measures used earlier to proxy for education, literacy, racial composition of the population, unemployment, and retail/wholesale composition of the local economy. To these, plus the South dummy used earlier, we add the percent of the population that is in a classified "rural" area (farm and non-farm) and the log of value-added in manufacturing (a measure of aggregate wealth). The rural measure in particular is one that we hope will help to characterize some of the information networks that may have influenced prescription and consumption of elixir sulfanilamide.

The count regression analyses show that the Massengill Company was more likely to ship elixir sulfanilamide to the South, to areas where the population was less educated, and both (1) to areas that were characterized by greater manufacturing value-added and (2) areas with more population in rural residence. The percentage population rural variable is insignificantly related to shipments and deaths in the county-level analyses, but significantly related in the state analyses. The reason probably has to do with the large number of rural counties in Southern and middle Western states, which have many more counties per state than do eastern and Pacific Coast states. Conditioned on the number of towns receiving shipment, deaths were unassociated with all of the variables in our analyses except the South dummy, a result that might simply imply that consumption conditional on shipment was higher in southern states than in non-southern states.

The brute facts of the sulfanilamide episode, then, were as follows. A product called "Elixir of Sulfanilamide-Massengill" was manufactured and distributed. Many consumed it after prescription as an antibiotic or as a treatment for venereal disease. Use

37. Jackson, *Food and Drug Legislation*, 159.

Fig. 2. Distribution of Massengill's Elixir Sulfanilamid (USDA Report to Congress, 1937).

Table 3. Negative Binomial Regression Analyses of Shipments and Deaths From Elixer Sulfanilamide, 1937

Variable	Shipments [State]	Shipments [County]	Deaths [State]	Deaths [County]
Constant	**−22.1858** (5.2501)	**3.1175** (0.7132)	**−24.7381** (13.4956)	**−8.8145** (3.1772)
% of State Population African-American	0.0437 (0.0347)	0.0008 (0.0048)	**0.1523** (0.0864)	0.0226 (0.0182)
% of State Population Illiterate	−0.1239 (0.1308)	0.0122 (0.0165)	−0.2928 (0.3153)	−0.0180 (0.0703)
% of State Population Educated	−0.0148 (0.0440)	**−0.0240** (0.0116)	0.0812 (0.1072)	0.0581 (0.0357)
% of State "Gainful Workers" Unemployed	0.4039 (0.2483)	0.0563 (0.0405)	**1.6160** (0.6824)	0.0090 (0.1910)
Retail Value-Added as % of Wholesale Value-Added	−0.0096 (0.0058)	0.0000 (0.0000)	**−0.0498** (0.0229)	0.00001 (0.00004)
South	1.0747 (0.7243)	**1.3139** (0.1801)	0.5197 (1.3894)	**2.5361** (0.8599)
ln(Value-Added Manufacturing)	**1.3668** (0.2731)	**0.1326** (0.0463)	0.6521 (0.6214)	0.0717 (0.2082)
% of County Population Rural (farm & non-farm)	**0.1056** (0.0278)	−0.0040 (0.0041)	**0.1936** (0.0816)	−0.0143 (0.0179)
Number of towns receiving sulfanilamide shipments	—	—	**0.0450** (0.0225)	**3.2789** (0.4907)
ln(dispersion) [se]	**−0.1738** (0.2973)	**0.6520** (0.1962)	**0.3268** (0.4598)	**2.4090** (0.2354)
N	48	2563	48	2563
LLF	−109.488	−976.328	50.799	−167.010

of the medicine was most common in the upper-country South (Tennessee) and in the plains Midwest (southern Illinois, Oklahoma), and appears to have been disproportionately common among African Americans. People became seriously ill from its consumption, and, by late October 1937, at least seventy-three of these had died. The FDA, assisted by state and local health officials and the American Medical Association, commenced an effort to secure as much of the compound as possible before any more as consumed.

V. Sulfanilamide from Episode to Tragedy: The FDA and the National Media

How did the deaths resulting from elixir sulfanilamide use reach news organizations, Congress, and the public? How was the episode distilled into a tragedy, and what were the lessons of that tragedy?

The first reports of illness and death resulting from elixir sulfanilamide came not to the FDA but the American Medical Association. On 11 October 1937, Dr. James Stevenson, president of the Tulsa (Oklahoma) County Medical Society, sent a telegram to the AMA's Chemical Laboratory, stating that six deaths had occurred after prescription and administration of the elixir. Communications between the AMA and Tulsa area physicians continued, and the AMA Chemical Laboratory messaged immediately for a shipment of the Elixir, which the Massengill Company promptly sent. Upon cursory analysis and laboratory tests with experimental animals, the Chemical Laboratory concluded that diethylene glycol and not sulfanilamide was the causative factor in the deaths. Based upon this information, as well as new and independent reports of deaths coming from East St. Louis, Illinois, the Editor of *JAMA* issued a public warning on 2 October then again on 18 October, which also appeared in the 23 October issue of *JAMA*.[38]

38. "Sulfanilamide—A Warning," *Journal of the American Medical Association (JAMA)*, 109 (1937). Paul Nicholas Leech (Director, AMA Chemical Laboratory), "Elixir of Sulfanilamide-Massengill," Special Article from the AMA Chemical Laboratory, *JAMA* 109 (1937): 1531.

On 14 October 1937, three days after the initial Tulsa inquiry at the AMA, the first word of elixir sulfanilamide deaths reached the FDA. On 16 October, an FDA investigator telegraphed headquarters with news that nine persons in the Tulsa area had died there from taking the elixir. From this point forward, and for about three weeks, reporting of the deaths was shared by the FDA and the American Medical Association. There was a degree of mutual dependence in this reporting. The Administration relied upon AMA reports and its own investigators; the AMA relied upon FDA reports and its own information from networks of physicians.[39]

The AMA's 18 October warning was reported a day later in various newspapers, using Associated Press wire reports. The *Washington Post*'s title and subtitle were exemplary:

Venereal Disease 'Cure' Kills 8 of 10 Patients in Oklahoma
Sulfanilamide, Hailed as Remedy, Used in Fatal Preparation; Doctors Blame Other Drug;
Firms Seeks to Recover 375 Cases on Market.[40]

As *Post*'s headline suggests, the very initial accounts of sulfanilamide deaths never mentioned the FDA. The AMA had broken the story, and it was the manufacturer Massengill and not the FDA to which was attributed the attempt to remove Elixir Sulfanilamide from the market.

Additional insight into the character of the deaths can be gleaned from attention to the details of these early accounts. Although the elixir had been prescribed for various conditions, early reports described it as a "Venereal Disease Cure." This was true in many cases, leading individual physicians to refuse to reveal the names of their patients to whom they had prescribed the elixir. Connected with this stigma, the early discussion of the drug and its using population also had subtle racial undertones. In the initial *JAMA* report, an AMA reporting chemist noted "In the last several days I have seen four deaths in patients using a product called "Elixir of Sulfanilamide" and sold by Massengill & Company. These patients, all Negroes, were treated by a Dr. Weathers of East St. Louis, Ill." Dr. Morris Fishbein, editor of *JAMA*, had made an implicit reference to young black males purchasing the drug as a venereal disease cure when he stated that "the association had learned of widespread purchases in one city by youths attempting to treat themselves for venereal disease."[41]

By the end of the week (Saturday, 23 October), and certainly by the end of October 1937, the primary source of information on the sulfanilamide episode had become Campbell and the FDA. With the FDA feeding daily reports of its search and investigation activities to the Associated Press, media attention turned to the mounting death toll and whether the FDA could "round up" the medicine "in time" to save those who, with the elixir still in their medicine cabinets, were still at risk. Newspaper stories told of FDA officials working late nights and weekends to inform the public, of commandeering airplanes and academic chemists to search far and wide for remaining samples of the drug, and generally of a vast, nationwide operation centered in the FDA.

Seizure of Deadly 'Elixir' Saves Marylander as U.S.
Hastens to Check Toll
Already at 29

> Death in Salisbury, Md., from the use of the drug "elixir of sulfanilamide" was narrowly averted yesterday while airplanes and chemists hastily drafted into service failed to save nine lives in other parts of the Nation.
>
> . . .
>
> From coast to coast, in large cities like New York and backwoods communities of the South, West and Midwest, field agents are desperately fighting against time to save lives of potential victims who have the elixir in their medicine cabinets.
>
> With only four of these drug detectives available to cover Alabama, Mississippi, Louisiana and two-thirds of Texas, airplanes were chartered yesterday for the sake of speed. "We have never had an outbreak like this," said Campbell, whose office in the south building of the Department of Agriculture is the nerve center of the life-and-death roundup.
>
> "The only thing we are concerned with is taking the compound out of circulation, removing it from wholesale houses, drug stores, homes and wherever else it may be." (*Washington Post*, 23 October 1937)

NEAR END OF CHASE FOR DEADLY ELIXIR.
Government Agents Hope to Recover Today
the last of 700 Bottles.

> A nationwide race with death, seeking recovery of more than 700 bottles, mostly pints, of a new liquid medicine named elixir of sulfanilamide, which has already caused thirty-six verified deaths, was described today at the headquarters of the American Medical Association.
>
> Every agent of the United States Food and Drug Administration is scouring the country to recover the bottles, said Dr. Morris Fishbein, spokesman of the medical association. By some time tomorrow, according to J. O. Clarke of the

39. On the AMA's dependence on the FDA, see Leech, "Elixir," *JAMA* 109 (1937): 1539. On the FDA's dependence on the AMA, see *Report of the Secretary*, Sen. Doc. 124; Charles Dunn, *Federal Food, Drug, and Cosmetic Act*, 1317.

40. *Washington Post*, 19 Oct. 1937, 3. See also "'Elixir' Fatal to 14 in West is Seized Here," *Washington Post*, 20 Oct. 1937, 1.

41. O. E. Hagebusch, M.D., "Necropsies of Four Patients Following Administration of Elixir of Sulfanilamide-Massengill," in "The Chemical Laboratory," *JAMA* 109 (1937): 1537. Statement attributed to Fishbein in "Venereal Disease 'Cure' Kills 8 of 10 Patients in Oklahoma," *Washington Post*, 19 Oct. 1937, 3.

Food and Drug Administration, it is hoped that all the outstanding shipments will be recovered. (*New York Times*, 25 October 1937)

Nurse, Herself a Victim, Saves Six from "Elixir."

While 200 agents of the Federal drug office yesterday scoured the Nation for bottles of deadly sulfanilamide and diethylene "elixir" still unaccounted for, Evelyn Sharborough, a pretty 28-year old nurse in Mount Olive, Miss., was caring for six patients surviving from 13 who were treated with the mixture.

...

In Washington officials of the food and drug administration spent Sunday within reach of telephones. Dr. J. J. Durrett, chief of the drug section, said the list of verified deaths from the elixir still stood at 37. (*Washington Post*, 25 October 1937)[42]

FDA officials wasted little time in trying to frame the episode as evidence of the weakness of the 1906 laws and its patchwork of supplementary regulations. Technically nothing in the elixir sulfanilamide disaster implied that the Massengill Company had broken a single law. There was little basis in federal statute for prosecuting Bristol. The only charge against Massengill that stuck was an arcane mislabeling charge, namely that "elixir" implied alcoholic content yet "Elixir Sulfanilamide" contained no alcohol. On 19 October, just the second day of media reporting on the sulfanilamide deaths, Walter Campbell noted that only a thread of the current law prohibiting misbranding allowed the Administration to round up the elixir. Campbell said that the fatalities "are new evidence of the need for tightening the Nation's food and drug laws and predicted legislation to that end will be pressed at the coming session of Congress, in spite of failure to enact loophole plugs in the last few years."[43] By the end of the week, a tidy bundle of facts and policy recommendations were consistently and almost imperceptibly bandied about news reports, including the fact that the elixir had violated federal law only by being misbranded:

Need for New Drug Laws Cited.

...

Calling attention to the need for drastic tightening up of the Federal food and drug laws, toward which numerous bills have been introduced, but none enacted, Bureau Chief Campbell and Dr. Durrett cited the following handicaps in the present emergency:

Intervention of the Food and Drug Administration is justified only because of the alleged misbranding, the "elixir" on the label being challenged, and not because the liquid contained poison.

Even though the preparation is known to have death-dealing properties, the Federal Government cannot legally make a seizure unless it has been shipped across a state line.

Confiscation of a bottle whose seal has been broken cannot be made.[44]

Along with Campbell, Durrett, and their FDA associates, there were two other voices distilling policy lessons from the sulfanilamide episode. The first was Morris Fishbein of the AMA. In the *Journal*'s 23 October editorial, he drew larger policy implications from the sulfanilamide episode:

The possibilities are unlimited because we are here concerned with a preparation not standardized by any reliable agency, semisecret in composition and apparently hastily rushed into the market to meet an overenthusiastic reception of a new remedy. This tragic experience should be a final warning to physicians relative to the prescribing and administration of this type of preparation.

Despite the presence of organizational distrust between the AMA and the FDA, Fishbein himself proved to be one of the FDA's biggest supporters.[45]

A resounding political echo began to boom from the second voice, the national women's organizations who had long befriended the FDA. In a letter to her members on 28 October 1937, League of Women Voters President Marguerite M. Wells declared that the sulfanilamide events "point tragically to the need for Federal legislation ensuring a governmental check on such products before they are distributed to a helpless public." Like other women's organization officials, she blamed "special interests" for Congress' failure to pass legislation revising and strengthening the 1906 act.[46]

One week after the first media reports of deaths, observers commonly agreed that reform was likely.

42. Gerald G. Gross, "Seizure of Deadly 'Elixir' Saves Marylander as U.S. Hastens to Check Toll Already at 29," *Washington Post*, 23 Oct. 1937, 1; "Near End of Chase for Deadly Elixir," *New York Times*, 25 Oct. 1937, 21; "Nurse, Herself a Victim, Saves Six from 'Elixir,'" *Washington Post*, 25 Oct. 1937, 2.

43. Gerald G. Gross, "Seizure of Deadly 'Elixir' Saves Marylander as U.S. Hastens to Check Toll Already at 29," *Washington Post*, 23 Oct. 1937, 1. For journalistic repetition of these arguments, almost verbatim from FDA pronouncements, see for example "Control of Drugs [editorial]," *Washington Post*, 26 Oct. 1937. Jackson, *Food and Drug Legislation*, 156–57.

44. Gerald G. Gross, "Seizure of Deadly 'Elixir' Saves Marylander as U.S. Hastens to Check Toll Already at 29," *Washington Post*, 23 Oct. 1937, 2.

45. Jackson describes the American Medical Association as only partially supportive of FDA-strengthening legislation throughout the 1930s (*Food and Drug Legislation*, 211). This is consistent with his account, but shows Fishbein to be an exception to the organizational pattern of the AMA.

46. "Plea for U.S. Regulation follows 'Elixir' Deaths," *Washington Post*, 29 Oct. 1937, 9.

Yet despite the intensive media attention to the deaths and to the FDA's hunt for the elixir, nothing in the bills that had yet been floated before Congress contained a pre-market review provision of the sort to which Fishbein and Wells alluded. There was no sustained call for a gatekeeping clause or any form of regulatory licensure. The *Washington Post* editorial page noted the political status quo on 26 October 1937:

> it seems certain that the current sulfanilamide incident will insure, at least, some improvement in food and drug regulation. The pending bill would broaden the definitions of, and put teeth into the penalties for, adulteration. It would also permit prosecution for misrepresentation, without requiring proof of fraudulent intent, as at present. It would not provide for Federal analysis and licensing of proprietary medicine as has worked so successfully in the case of vaccines. But even without this, it would be expected to prevent deaths similar to the "elixir" tragedies.[47]

The *Post* editorial revealed how far the FDA, Congress, organized interests, and the organized public were from agreeing upon any form of gatekeeping provision. While it was certain that "improvement" would come, the *Post*'s best guess was that licensure of patent medicines would not be among those improvements.

Had the elixir sulfanilamide story died out in late October 1937, it is quite possible that no premarket provision would have accrued to the FDA in the 1930s. Yet the sulfanilamide story endured, for several reasons. First, the deaths had occurred while Congress was out of session, and when the second session of the 75th Congress resumed in November 1937, FDA officials and Royal Copeland seized an opportunity to place the episode and its tragic meaning at the center of the legislative agenda. Second, the reports of deaths were still trickling in, creating something of a news cycle and fastening reporters to FDA officials week after week.

Ironically, the first synthesized report issued on the elixir sulfanilamide deaths was issued not by the FDA but in the *Journal of the American Medical Association* on 6 November 1937. The AMA's Chemical Laboratory, under the direction of Paul Nicholas Leech, commissioned a team of investigators from the University of Chicago and Johns Hopkins University and assessed the physiological effects of administration of three treatments: (1) diethylene glycol alone, (2) sulfanilamide alone (not suspending in diethylene glycol) and (3) repeated dosages of Elixir Sulfanilamide-Massengill. The results were unequivocal; diethylene glycol and not sulfanilamide was to blame for the deaths and illnesses.[48] Yet Leech (and probably Morris Fishbein) added language extolling the FDA's effort in securing unconsumed shipments of the elixir.

> Deaths and clues of deaths were reported to the American Medical Association headquarters by various press services, by information received from physicians, and chiefly clues from the Food and Drug Administration. The latter organization placed a tremendous force of inspectors in the field. It obtained a list of approximately 700 shipments from the manufacturer. The inspectors then traced every shipment to its final destination. If the bottle had been opened, they inquired to whom it had been dispensed. It was in this manner that most of the deaths were traced after the original reports from Tulsa and East St. Louis.[49]

Leech and Fishbein's acknowledgement was more than symbolic, for it pointed to a wider transformation in public responsibility for information provision in the wake of the elixir deaths. By the second week of November, when the Senate had reconvened and had asked (in Senate Resolution 194) the secretary of agriculture to issue a report on the deaths resulting from use of the elixir, the FDA's role in information provision about the episode had eclipsed that of the AMA. News reports of the elixir episode now mentioned the FDA almost exclusively, the AMA hardly at all. And the AMA, too (as Leech's editorial thanks to the Administration suggests) also relied heavily upon the FDA's reporting for its analysis. By November 1937, the agency had cornered a near monopoly on information about the deaths and the elixir.

Walter Campbell and the Wallace Report. From the very earliest stages of the sulfanilamide episode, Walter Campbell and his FDA associates saw an opportunity to add a pre-market licensing provision to the nation's food and drug statute. On 19 October, Campbell issued a press release advocating for a "[g]overnmental licensing system." The release was largely ignored at the time, but Campbell kept up his campaign more quietly. In correspondence with Clark Gavin, managing editor of *National Consumer News*, Campbell confided on 28 October that,

> In my opinion, full and complete public protection can be guaranteed against the preparation and sale of harmful medicines only by the adoption of proper preventative measures. Such products, in my judgment, should be marketed under Governmental supervision. This would require legislation authorizing control by the issuance of licenses . . . . a Governmental licensing system, at least for new and potent medicines, probably will be required if the tragic experiences growing out

47. "Control of Drugs."
48. Leech, "Elixir," *JAMA* 109 (1937): 1531–39.
49. Ibid., 1539.

> of the sale and use of this poisonous elixir of sulfanilamid are not to be repeated.[50]

To underscore the point that support and publicity from mouthpieces such as Gavin's magazine and other consumerist outlets would be necessary for passage of FDA-strengthening legislation, Campbell added a sober prognosis of the prospects for near-term reform. Citing "powerful opposition to the enactment of a food and drug bill" he argued that "The promptness with which legislative action may be contemplated, and the adequacy of the law passed, will depend in large measure, if not entirely, upon the extent and the aggressiveness of consumer interests displayed."[51]

Campbell's next stratagem was to turn to Royal Copeland and the Senate. On 26 October, Copeland wrote Campbell and asked whether S. 5 as currently written would have prevented the elixir sulfanilamide episode. On 29 October, Campbell replied with a vivid and reasoned negative.

> To seize these hastily concocted and untried preparations after discovery of their lethal effect, or to prosecute the manufacturer criminally, is not enough. It is our view that the bill [S. 5] should be amended to require a license from the Government preliminary to the distribution of all drugs containing any potent ingredient or combination of ingredients, the use of which has not become well established in medical practice.
> In the interest of safety, society has required that physicians be licensed to practice the healing art. Pharmacists are licensed to compound drugs. Even steamfitters, electricians and plumbers are required to have licenses. Certainly a requirement that potent proprietary medicines be manufactured under license can be justified on the ground of public safety.[52]

Campbell then closed the letter with a promise of full cooperation in drafting appropriate legislation.

> I recognize the extreme difficulty that there may be in drafting suitable language for the amendment I am recommending. We shall be glad to make ourselves available for any help we can be of to you, to the Legislative Counsel, or to others whom you may ask to work on the problem.[53]

The next crucial step, perhaps *the* crucial step as far as Congress and much of the reading public was concerned, was the release of Secretary of Agriculture Henry A. Wallace's report on the deaths. From the very first page of the report, Wallace and his FDA colleagues distilled one overwhelming lesson from the tragedy: the absolute necessity of pre-market review of drugs to assess their safety profile:

> Before the "elixir" was put on the market, it was tested by the firm for flavor but not for its effect on human life. The existing Food and Drugs Act does not require that new drugs be tested before they are placed on sale.
> ... Since the Federal Food and Drugs Act contains no provision against dangerous drugs, seizures had to be based on a charge that the word elixir implies an alcoholic solution, whereas this product was a diethylene glycol solution. Had the product been called a solution, rather than an elixir, no charge of violating the law could have been brought.
> ... The fatal "elixir" was rushed onto the market without adequate test to determine whether or not diethylene glycol may be safely used as a solvent for sulfanilamide, despite previously published reports in scientific literature showing that diethylene glycol might be dangerous when taken internally. A few simple and inexpensive tests on experimental animals would have quickly demonstrated the toxic properties of both diethylene glycol and the "elixir."[54]

Wallace's report began with this "executive summary" of the sulfanilamide story. The implied causal inference was clear. Not only did elixir sulfanilamide cause at least seventy-three deaths, but deficiencies in the process by which the drug was brought to market, *which were equivalent to deficiencies in the 1906 law,* also caused those deaths. Just as clear as the implied causal story was the counterfactual: "A few simple and inexpensive tests," the sort that would be performed by the company before marketing and analyzed in a pre-market review process by the FDA, would quickly have evinced the elixir's "toxic properties." Translation: with a pre-market review process, none of this would have happened.

The structure of the Wallace report also laid bare the nature of the tragedy and the FDA's intended policy solutions (see Table 4). It proceeded, not unlike a court brief, from facts to conclusions in a near deductive manner. The USDA report started on its strongest footing, dealing first those facts of a scientific character, then the facts of historical and legal ones. It then proceeded methodically to limitations of the 1906 statute and suggestions for

50. Walter G. Campbell to Clark Gavin, Managing Editor, *National Consumer News* (New York), 28 Oct. 1937; USDA-FDA Press Release, "Death-Dealing Drug," 19 Oct. 1937; encl. in Campbell to Gavin ltr, National Archives I, RG 46, HR75A.

51. Ibid.

52. Campbell to Copeland, 29 Oct. 1937; National Archives I, RG 46, HR75A; underlining in original.

53. Ibid.

54. U.S. Department of Agriculture, *Report of the Secretary of Agriculture on Deaths Due to Elixir Sulfanilamide-Massengill, Submitted in Response to Senate Resolution 194 of November 16, 1937,* Senate Document No. 124, 75th Congress, Second Session (Washington, D.C.; GPO). Original typescript in National Archives I, RG 46, SEN75A-F674; parts repr. in Dunn, *Federal Food, Drug, and Cosmetic Act,* 1317, 1319. The paragraphs above (except for the last) appear on the first page of the original typescript.

Table 4. Subject Headings in the USDA's Report on Elixir Sulfanilamide (November, 1937)

HOW THE "ELIXIR" WAS PRODUCED
THE FOOD AND DRUG ADMINISTRATION STEPS IN
THE PROBLEM BEFORE PHYSICIANS AND PHARMACISTS
EFFECTS OF THE DRUG
ACTION UNDER THE LAW
LIMITATIONS OF THE LAW
RECOMMENDATIONS FOR LEGISLATION

reform. It was also succinct, consuming twenty-three pages of double-spaced text.[55]

For several reasons, the Wallace report rendered the sulfanilamide tragedy even more evocative and memorable than it had been. First, USDA officials and news reports connected the deaths together in a way that wove the entire affair into a single narrative, making it ready for consumption by news hungry reporters and editors. Some portions of the narrative were particularly vivid, even visually so. Only a few deaths were among young children who had taken the drug to combat an infection. Yet one of these was the single most publicized death, both in congressional debates, in USDA reports, and (from what we can tell) newspaper coverage of the sulfanilamide episode. The most widely known story was prompted by a letter from Mrs. Maise Nidiffer of Tulsa—whose six-year-old daughter Joan died from taking the drug—to President Roosevelt. Nidiffer wrote of her daughter's harrowing death, "her little body tossing to & fro ... & that little voice screaming with pain and it seems as tho it drive me insane [*sic*]." She pleaded with the president that he would "take steps to prevent such sales of drugs that will take little lives & leave such suffering behind and such a bleak outlook on the future as I have tonight." Along with the letter she enclosed a photograph of her smiling but now deceased child, a print that made its way into several newspaper reports and into the USDA report on the tragedy (Figure 3). In the entire reporting on the deaths due to elixir sulfanilamide, the Joan Nidiffer story did not (so far as we can tell) surface until the Wallace report.[56]

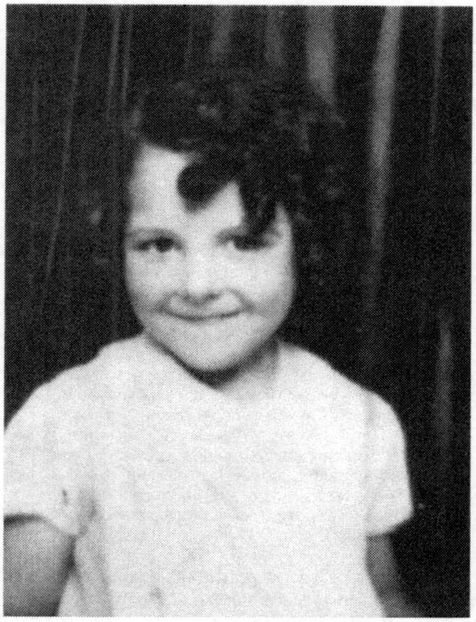

Fig. 3. The Joan Nidiffer Photo, in Report of the Secretary of Agriculture, 1937.

Maise Nidiffer's letter and the photograph of her daughter impelled and expressed the conversion of episode to tragedy. Together, text and image took what had been a series of scattered deaths among patients—many of them syphilitic black men—and purged it of blackness, of sexual maturity, and of social isolation. The victim of American policy failure was now a daughter connected to a mother and a loving family, a smiling white child who could not be said to have courted the agony that sulfanilamide wreaked upon her body.

In the pages immediately following the Nidiffer letter and the photo of the elixir's adorable young victim, the FDA turned immediately to the decisive action it took under the current law and the existing limitations of that law. Then, bringing the report to its culmination, Wallace issued four policy

55. These headings are reported as they appear in the typescript version sent to Congress, which appears in the Senate Committee files, typescript *Report to the Secretary of Agriculture on Deaths due to Elixir Sulfanilamide-Massengill*, National Archives I, RG 46, SEN75A–F674. All words were in capitals and all titles were center-justified as they appear here.

56. Maise Nidiffer to President Franklin D. Roosevelt, 8 Nov. 1937; copy in typescript *Report of the Secretary of Agriculture on Deaths due to Elixir Sulfanilamide-Massengill*, National Archives I, RG 46, SEN75A-F674. Jackson reports that the Nidiffer story was "widely distributed," and that, by the spring of 1938, it "had even become part of the [Agriculture] Secretary's report to Congress on the drug disaster" (*Food and Drug Legislation*, 163, 184). In fact the USDA's inclusion of the photo seems to have preceded popular media coverage of the girl's death; see Jackson's discussion of the May 1938 issue of *Survey Graphic*, which reprinted the letter (ibid., 184).

recommendations.[57] The department first offered an explicit argument for licensure, not of firms, but of products. And the Wallace report reflected the carefully chosen words of Walter Campbell in his letter to Copeland of a month earlier.

> 1. License control of new drugs to insure that they will not be generally distributed until experimental and clinical tests have shown them to be safe for use.
> ... It is the Department's view that no other form of control will effectively safeguard the public from the dangers of premature distribution of new drugs. To increase the penalties for violations and to require label disclosure of ingredients would be helpful, but by no means fully adequate.
> In the interest of safety society has required that physicians be licensed to practice the healing art. Pharmacists are licensed to compound and dispense drugs. Electricians, plumbers and steam engineers pursue their respective trades under license. But there is no such control to prevent incompetent drug manufacturers from marketing any kind of lethal potion.

The first USDA suggestion seemed innocent enough, but it stood as the most far-reaching licensure provision to be enacted for any agency during the New Deal. The bills leading to the National Industrial Recovery Act (NIRA) of 1933 had proposed licensure of firms prior to market entry, but this idea was scrapped long before the bills came to a vote. Beyond this, the pre-market review provision that Wallace was calling for would give Congress (and ultimately the FDA) power to define what a new drug is.

However broad the power to define new drugs would be, there was a problem with relying on pre-market review alone. Drugs already on the market were not coverable under a licensure statute. So Wallace asked for FDA authority to prohibit these outright.

> 2. Prohibition of drugs which are dangerous to health when administered in accordance with the manufacturer's directions for use. This would provide a more appropriate basis of action than that on which proceedings were instituted against the "elixir." A number of dangerous drugs are not on the market against which not even a trivial charge of violation can be made.

When passed, this provision and the pre-market review procedure would foretell the deathblow of the patent medicine industry in the United States. Not long in following were stringent labeling requirements, such that every adverse effect of which the manufacturer had prior evidence must be stated on the label.

> 3. Requirement that drug labels bear appropriate directions for use and warnings against probable misuse. Much injury results from insufficient directions and from lack of warning against overdosage, or administration to children, or use in disease conditions where the drug is dangerous, or the possibility of drug addiction.

Finally, FDA officials received their long-sought wish of a compulsory disclosure requirement for all ingredients (inactive as well as active) on the label of the drug. Diethylene glycol, after all, had not been the active ingredient in "Elixir Sulfanilamide-Massengill," just a solvent. And as the report stated, this provision was intended to serve as much as a control on foreign firms as on domestic patent medicine manufacturers.

> 4. Prohibition of secret remedies by requiring that labels disclose fully the composition of the drug. Many foreign countries now impose this requirement. Many drugs manufactured in the United States are exported to such countries under labels bearing such disclosure. The same drugs are sold to our citizens under labels that give no hint of their composition.

Henry Wallace's report has long since disappeared from public memory, relegated to congressional and USDA archives and the appendices of aging legal histories of the 1938 legislation. Yet it is no understatement to say that Wallace's document forms the originary basis of modern pharmaceutical regulation in the United States and much of the industrialized world. The four enumerated powers—(1) pre-market review requirements, (2) prohibition (or withdrawal authority), (3) labeling regulation, and (4) compulsory disclosure of all drug contents (active and inactive)—have become assumed and core legal features of pharmaceutical markets ranging from European national economies and the European Union to Japan, India, Australia, Canada, and South Africa. While crucial provisions and procedures have been added to these powers, the origins of government gatekeeping authority over the pharmaceutical marketplace can, in many respects, be traced to this document.

More immediately, Wallace's report occasioned the biggest single flood of news reporting since the original deaths were reported. Headlines from New York and Washington area papers were noteworthy in their attribution of a drive or demand for new legislation that the Wallace report, the elixir deaths and the FDA's successful "roundup" of the drug had now created.

57. These appear on pages 21–24 of the typescript in the Archives; repr. in Dunn, *Federal Food, Drug, and Cosmetic Act*, 1326–27.

COPELAND ASKS CURB ON ELIXIR. Joins Wallace in Move for Tighter Law. AIMS TO PROTECT PUBLIC. Secretary of Agriculture has 4-Point Program to Guard Lives.

FEDERAL ROUNDUP OF ELIXIR REVIVES DRUG BILL DRIVE. Copeland Backs Wallace Rules as Secretary Tells How Deaths Were Stopped.

Elixir Deaths Result in Demand for Law.[58]

On the House floor, Edward Herbert Rees (R–KS) complained that,

> newspapers and periodicals are crowded with information and of incidents where individuals and companies have taken advantage of people by the hundreds and the thousands, by falsification of advertising and adulteration as well as misbranding of foods and medicines.[59]

In this respect, the reaction to the disaster was not simply confined to the actual deaths but also to fear of numerous medications marketed under the title of "elixir," as well as fear of other sulfanilamide drugs that were not suspended in a diethylene glycol solution. Worried consumers flooded FDA investigators and county and state medication societies with questions about whether they had taken a deadly medication, or whether anything in their medicine cabinet was safe. For this reason, the pattern of *shipments* of Elixir Sulfanilamide Massengill was just as important politically as the pattern of *deaths* it caused. Virtually every town that received at least one shipment of Massengill's elixir later hosted several or more FDA investigators, state food and drug regulators, members of state and local presses, and visitors from local and state medical societies.[60]

The success of the FDA in quickly ridding the country of the elixir shipments was notable and noted. By December 1937, FDA officials had removed 99.2 percent of the 240 gallons of the elixir that were originally sent out in September. In his *Federal Food and Drug Laws—Leaders Who Achieved their Enactment and Enforcement,* Fred B. Linton offered a horrifying counterfactual: had the entire shipment of Dr. Massengill's Elixir Sulfanilamide been consumed, and had deaths occurred in the same proportion as they had to earlier levels of consumption, over 4,500 persons would have died from the elixir.[61]

58. Story headings taken, respectively, from *New York Sun,* 26 Nov. 1937; *New York Post,* 26 Nov. 1937; *Washington Daily News,* 26 Nov. 1937, 28. Copies of all three stories are available from clipping in Copeland Papers, Bentley Historical Library, University of Michigan, Ann Arbor, Michigan.

59. *Congressional Record,* 24 Nov. 1937, 549–50; repr. in Dunn, *Federal Food, Drug, and Cosmetic Act,* 771–72.

60. Jackson, *Food and Drug Legislation,* 159–60.

61. Jackson, *Food and Drug Legislation in the New Deal* Ibid., 160.

VI. The Sulfanilamide Tragedy and the Passage of the Food, Drug, and Cosmetic Act of 1938

The media reporting in the wake of the Wallace report bespoke a much deeper transformation (Figure 4). In late October 1937, even with the national news craze over the mounting death toll and the FDA's hunt for the remaining elixir bottles, there was no discussion of a gatekeeping provision. The Wallace report not only introduced this possibility, it also established the idea as the dominant alternative to the status quo. The USDA report tied the threads from news coverage, private experience (Joan Nidiffer), medical investigation, regulatory detail, and other features together into a story that made sense—a story in which the moral of policy reform followed narratively from the apparently brute facts. Media coverage of the momentum for new legislation now attributed the demand and drive for a new law to the elixir deaths, the Wallace report, and the quickness with which federal agents had tracked down the sulfanilamide supply and had removed it from the marketplace.[62]

In this light, Royal Copeland's introduction of a pre-market review provision was a *reaction* to the USDA's proposals, not a forerunner. Wallace's report was the first official proposal for gatekeeping authority. None of Copeland's bills had a gatekeeping provison before the report, and Copeland's first bill after the report wrote the USDA's recommendations in to a proposed law.

On 1 December 1937, Copeland introduced a new measure to replace S. 5. Copeland's S. 3073 had many of the provisions of S. 5, but added the pre-market review provision in Section 505, which remains today the basis for FDA review of new drugs. The bill required manufacturers to supply the USDA with records of their clinical and non-clinical experiments, a list of the drug's ingredients, a plan for manufacturing practices, and examples of labels. The secretary of agriculture would then certify the drug for sale or give reason why the drug was refused marketability. A proprietary trade journal warned that, under S. 3073, "the Food and Drug Administration would become absolute dictator, the overlord of the drug industry."

In February 1938, Copeland's S. 3073 was considered again in the Senate. Women's groups and public health leagues now lobbied intensively for its passage, and their rhetoric made the clear the centrality of the Wallace report in the new deliberations. The Public Health Federation recorded itself as "heartily in favor of the recommendations of the

62. "'Elixir' Deaths Result in Demand for Law," *Washington Daily News,* 26 Nov. 1937, 8; "Federal Roundup of Elixir Revives Drug Bill Drive," *New York Post,* 26 Nov. 1937; "Copeland Asks Curb on Elixir," *New York Sun,* 26 Nov. 1937. All in scrapbooks, Royal Copeland Papers, Bentley Historical Library, University of Michigan.

Secretary of Agriculture, to protect the public against drugs like elixir of sulphanilamide."[63] It passed the Senate again, and again unanimously, and was combined with S. 5 into a new S. 5, which went to the House, where the Commerce Committee, chaired by Clarence Lea (D–CA), again stalled the bill. The Lea Committee reported the House's version of the bill in April 1938, but with at least two significant differences from the Senate version. First, the Senate version provided explicitly for the regulation of combination drugs—bundles of drugs which were individually already on the market, but which were possibly new as a combination—whereas the House did not provide for regulation of these products. Patent medicine interests could exploit this loophole, it was feared, by selling combination products which, by virtue of their components' previous marketing, would bypass the FDA review process.

The second amendment to emerge from the Lea Committee was something of a poison pill that threatened the entire measure. Lea's committee attached a provision requiring the secretary of agriculture to respond to any suit against any regulation by withholding the entire enforcement of the regulation until court review, and conduct public hearings in response to any suit brought by a private party. The ostensible source of this amendment was the apple-growing interests of Washington State, who had been burned by tightened restrictions on lead arsenic in their pesticide sprays. It was later claimed by the *St. Louis Post Dispatch* that patent medicine makers and Washington farmers had secretly agreed to the court review provision as a means of killing Copeland's bill. The minority of the House committee, led by Kentucky Democrat Virgil Chapman, expressed its fear that "the bill, if enacted with this [court] review provision, will not any substantial improvement over the terms of the present law." An *Emporia Gazette* editorialist lamented that "it is a pity the good things in the bill have no chance of being put into operation." Reform supporters seemed now convinced that the court review provision had vitiated entirely the gatekeeping procedures of the bill. As a coalition of fourteen women's groups stated, "We are convinced that this proposal for judicial review of regulations more than offsets the improvements over the present law contained in this bill." Representative John Coffee (D–WA) echoed this position when he asked "If the right to sell poison unbranded is a vested right—since when?"[64]

In House debates in April and June 1938, the elixir tragedy loomed large. Coffee invoked the Wallace report's "excellent recommendations" and lamented that the bill reported by the Lea Committee had followed Wallace's suggestions "but in part." He gestured poignantly to "such utterly needless and inexcusable tragedies" as the elixir disaster, "Shall we have to wait for another hundred deaths before we get proper preventative measures?" Jerry Joseph O'Connell (D–MT), with echoes of Maise Nidiffer's letter, shifted the focus from apple-grower interests to the elixir victims.

> This [court review] section, as written, is decidedly for the benefit of the producer and not for the consumer.
>
> It has been stated that the issue here is whether you are going to wipe out the investment of these poor apple growers, but I contend that the issue in this court review section and the issue in this bill is whether you are going to permit these young children and men and women to be killed by spurious patent medicines and by all the fake drugs and cures that are flooding the market today, which are far more involved in this bill than the question of the production of apples.
>
> The question further is whether little children are going to die in vain and whether all this agitation over such poisonous deaths is to be in vain. The question is whether we are going to wipe all that out now in order to help a few apple growers in this country. I maintain that human life is far more important than profits.
>
> Are we going to legislate for the great benefit of the American people and for the consumers of the United States or are we going to legislate for this little group?[65]

S. 5 passed the House with the court-review provision intact. The end result of the provision, had it passed both chambers, would have wrought significant change in U.S. administrative law. No longer would courts be limited to reviewing administrative rules ex post; instead, rules would have to survive court review before they could ever take hold. USDA officials rightly foresaw that the court review provision was an invitation to endless delay of effective regulation by interminable lawsuits and complaints. In a composite letter of 22 April 1938, and sent to the House, representatives of fourteen women's

63. Bleecker Marquette (Executive Secretary, Public Health Federation, Cincinnati, Ohio) to Chairman, Committee on Commerce, U.S. Senate, February 21, 1938; NA, RG 46, SEN 75A-E1, "Papers relating to specific bills," "with respect to S. 3073."

64. *Minority Views to Accompany S. 5.*, April 21, 1938; House of Representatives, 75th Congress, Third Session, Report 2139, Part 2; reprinted in Dunn, 834. William Allen White, "The Drug Pirates," *Emporia Gazette*, April 21, 1938; in Extension of Remarks by John H. Coffee, CR 83 (May 20, 1938) appendix, p. 9515; reprinted in Dunn, 839. On the continued attention of women's groups to the progress of the bill, see Mrs. William Dick Sporborg, "Organized Women Keep Close Watch on Food-Drug Act," *New York Tribune*, April 10. 1938.

65. Coffee and O'Connell qtd. in Dunn, *Federal Food, Drug, and Cosmetic Act*, 873, 946–47.

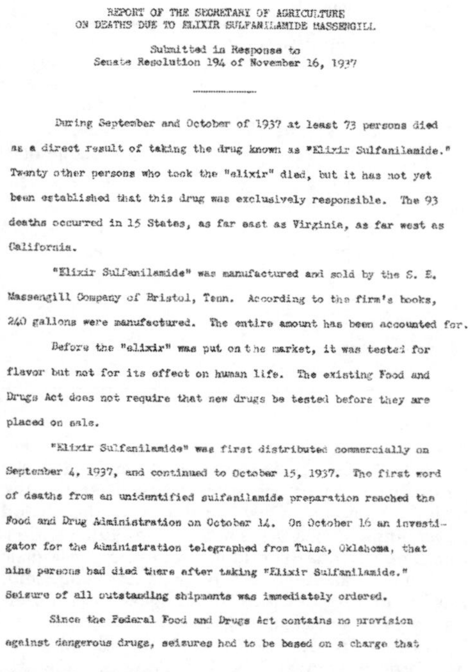

REPORT OF THE SECRETARY OF AGRICULTURE
ON DEATHS DUE TO ELIXIR SULFANILAMIDE MASSENGILL

Submitted in Response to
Senate Resolution 194 of November 16, 1937

During September and October of 1937 at least 73 persons died as a direct result of taking the drug known as "Elixir Sulfanilamide." Twenty other persons who took the "elixir" died, but it has not yet been established that this drug was exclusively responsible. The 93 deaths occurred in 15 States, as far east as Virginia, as far west as California.

"Elixir Sulfanilamide" was manufactured and sold by the S. E. Massengill Company of Bristol, Tenn. According to the firm's books, 240 gallons were manufactured. The entire amount has been accounted for.

Before the "elixir" was put on the market, it was tested for flavor but not for its effect on human life. The existing Food and Drugs Act does not require that new drugs be tested before they are placed on sale.

"Elixir Sulfanilamide" was first distributed commercially on September 4, 1937, and continued to October 15, 1937. The first word of deaths from an unidentified sulfanilamide preparation reached the Food and Drug Administration on October 14. On October 16 an investigator for the Administration telegraphed from Tulsa, Oklahoma, that nine persons had died there after taking "Elixir Sulfanilamide." Seizure of all outstanding shipments was immediately ordered.

Since the Federal Food and Drugs Act contains no provision against dangerous drugs, seizures had to be based on a charge that

Fig. 4. The Wallace Report of 1937—Progenitor of Modern Pharmaceutical Regulation.

groups threatened to lobby President Roosevelt to veto the measure entirely.[66]

The FDA, Wallace, and Copeland saw their final triumph in the House-Senate conference committee that reported a consensual version of the bill on 11 June 1938. The court-review provision was dropped, and the conferees made it clear that the secretary of agriculture could promulgate regulations to define combination drugs as new drugs. After unanimous passage in both chambers, Roosevelt signed the bill into law on 25 June 1938.

For historical purposes, an essential puzzle is this: Why did Congress move from unanimous Senate support of a weaker bill in the first session of the 75th Congress (May–August 1937) to a generally unanimous approval of a stronger bill in the second session of the 75th Congress (April–June 1938)? There are several possible explanations other than the thalidomide tragedy, not least a host of possible narratives connected to the 1936 general election and perhaps the impending 1938 midterms. We discuss these below. Before examining this transition, however, we note that the voting data with which we can do so is rather limited. We have none of the House votes at our disposal, and all we know about the final outcome of the Senate is that it was unanimous.

Yet voting data are not the sort of data needed (much less sufficient) to address this question. We know that the 75th Senate passed a weaker version of regulation in its first session (1937), and a stronger version of regulation with gatekeeping authority for the FDA in its second session (1938). In both cases the House served to defeat or delay passage of the Senate legislation. What changed was not voting patterns but the *content* of the proposed legislation. What is needed to explain the 1938 legislation and its difference from 1937 bills, then, is not voting analysis but narrative.[67]

Perhaps the easiest and starkest comparison can be conducted between the 1937 and 1938 versions of S. 5. This is something of a "test" of the effects of thalidomide—and in particular the Administration's framing of the episode—upon the legislation of the 75th Congress.

As the comparison in Table 5 suggests, virtually nothing else changed in the legislation from the S. 5 passed in 1937 to the final 1938 act. The electoral composition of the legislature was identical, the leadership of Congress and of the relevant committees were identical, the votes were identical, and all of the other provisions affecting food, cosmetics, inspection and seizure authority remained the same.

The tabular analysis, then, allows us to answer the counterfactual evidence posed earlier. In the absence of the sulfanilamide tragedy—the episode framed by the FDA and converted into a tragedy with specific political lessons—the 1938 Food, Drug, and Cosmetic Act would not have contained a pre-market review provision.

What of the 75th Congress? Several possibilities related to the 1936 election are evident as partial explanations for the 1938 legislation, in the sense that the composition of the 75th Congress may have been a necessary condition for the 1938 act's passage. It might be that many or most of the opponents from the 74th Congress were replaced by more liberal, pro-regulatory members. Another possibility is that increased competition from liberal Democrats in the home states and districts of

66. Wallace: "It is the Department's considered judgment that it would be better to continue the old law in effect than to enact S. 5 with this provision." Women's groups: "Unless this section providing for judicial review is struck out, the undersigned organizations must oppose the enactment of the measure." (Letter repr. in House debate; Dunn, 845). On the veto threat, see remarks of John Coffee in the *Congressional Record*, reprinted in ibid., 876; also Richard L. Stokes, "Dispute Over Alleged Joker in Drug Act in Conference May Cause Measure to Fail," *St. Louis Post-Dispatch*, 8 Jun. 1938; repr. in Dunn, *Federal Food, Drug, and Cosmetic Act*, 1012.

67. And because the 1938 bill became *more* legally stringent than the 1937 bills, median voter dynamics (a softening of the legislation from the first to the second session of the 75th Congress) cannot explain the transformation.

Table 5. Comparison of S. 5 before and after Sulfanilamide Tragedy and Wallace Proposal

Bill	S. 5 (1937)	Campbell-Wallace Proposal	S. 5 (1938)
Congress	75th	75th	75th
Session of Congress	First	Btw 1st and 2nd	Third
Final passage in Senate	Unanimous	NA	Unanimous
Provision for Cosmetics Regulation	Yes	Kept	Yes
Advertising Regulation	Yes	Kept	Yes
Primary Advertising Regulation with FTC	Yes	Kept	Yes
Multiple Seizure Authority (all commodities)	Yes	Kept	Yes
Pre-market Review Provision [Section 505 (a)–(c)]	No	Proposed	Yes

conservative opponents may have led otherwise recalcitrant conservatives who remained in the 75th Congress to adopt a more pro-regulatory stance, as a way of making peace with FDR or to demonstrate to concerned voters that they could be friendly to some kind of consumer protection regulation.

While considering this, it is important to note the backdrop of the 75th Congress. It is significant that the 75th Congress was famous not for its liberalism but for its conservatism, namely the institutional emergence of the Conservative Coalition and its hostile takeover of the House Rules Committee. This coalition effectively frustrated many of Roosevelt's New Deal initiatives. Figure 5 sheds some light upon the possibility of change in the composition of the Senate. Using measures of congressional ideology that are directly comparable over time, we observe that the Senate became only marginally more "liberal" in its voting propensity from the 74th Congress to the 75th Congress. This difference, moreover, is not statistically significant.[68]

Part of what happened was a partisan transformation. The Democratic majority in the Senate went from 69–25 in the 74th Congress to 76–16 in the 75th Congress. In order for this shift to help explain the movement in regulation voting, however, it must have been the case that opponents of S. 5 were more likely to be replaced than those senators voting for it. We create a "replacement" variable scored 1 if a senator voting on FDA-related legislation in the 74th Senate was replaced and 0 if not. We then regress this variable on the votes for the three bills analyzed in Table 2. The t-statistics are -1.45 and -2.16 for the recommitment measures and -0.09 for the Bailey amendment. Only in the case of the second recommitment measure is there a significant relationship. There is indeed nothing resembling a systematic pattern here, and the votes on the Bailey amendment, which killed S. 5 in the 74th Congress, are entirely unrelated to replacement dynamics.

Of course, replacement and ideological shifts can only provide context. The 75th Congress, after all, passed a weakened reform initiative in 1937, before the sulfanilamide tragedy. So, too, FDR had lashed out at the Copeland measure in a press conference on 23 February. The Commerce Committee had dramatically weakened S. 5 and, while it then passed the Senate, it did so over the objections of Copeland, the FDA, and consumers' and women's groups. To make matters worse, the Senate in March 1937 passed the Wheeler-Lea Act giving control over all advertising regulation to the Federal Trade Commission. In the House, meanwhile, Copeland's much-weakened Senate measure was pigeonholed in the Senate Commerce Committee. The upshot of these developments is that the 75th Congress was, until the sulfanilamide tragedy, acting more conservatively on matters related to pharmaceuticals than was the 74th.

FDR's broadsides against the Copeland measure in February 1937—Copeland was the most vigorous Senate opponent of the President's court-packing plan—suggest one other thing. The shift in legislative fortunes for FDA-strengthening legislation was not one induced by FDR's warming to the Copeland bill. If FDR did warm to stronger FDA regulation of patent medicines and pharmaceuticals, this was a shift directly related to the fall 1937 tragedy.

A Southern Deathblow: The Geographic Burden of Elixir Sulfanilamide. While it appears that the sulfanilamide episode registered on a nationwide consciousness

68. The congressional ideology measures are chamber medians from the DW-NOMINATE score. Indeed, the Democrats of the 75th Congress were, by the DW-NOMINATE measure, less liberal in their voting behavior in the 75th Congress than in the 73rd (and the 72nd), during which Copeland's bill was under consideration. Nor is there appreciable change in the Republican median.

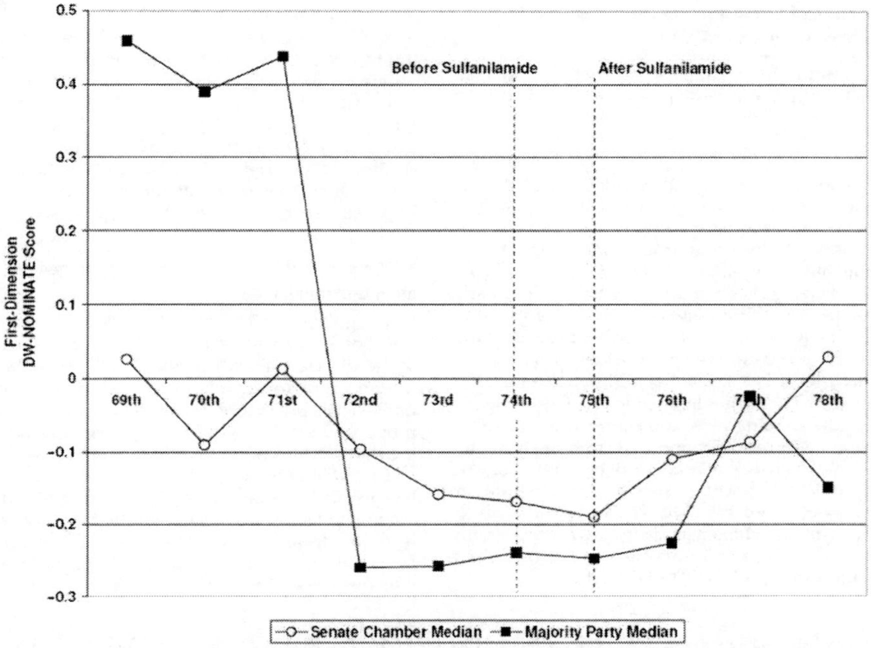

Fig. 5. Changes in DW-NOMINATE Medians, 69th–78th Congresses (Senate).

and agenda, it is also true (see Section VII and Tables 6–7) that the sulfanilamide deaths were somewhat geographically concentrated. In a way that seems symbolic now but was evident to few at the time, the pattern of elixir shipments, deaths and subsequent FDA visits struck in the very region that housed the most vocal defenders of the right of self-medication, and of the patent medicine industry. *Newsweek* reported that FDA officials were morbidly "jubilant" over the fact that the elixir was produced in the district of Carroll Reece (R–TN), a consistent and vocal opponent of FDA-strengthening legislation. The concentration of sulfanilamide deaths in Tennessee was also noted by Senator Josiah Bailey, a Senate foe of Copeland's measure who received mail asking him to change his stance on regulation "so to make impossible a repetition of the recent Sulfanilamide tragedy."[69]

There is some narrative evidence to support a more specific hypothesis, namely that the sulfanilamide deaths may have peeled Southern members of the anti-regulatory coalition from its ranks and have moderated their opposition to FDA control. In the last, very brief Senate debate on S. 3073 in May 1938, Arthur Vandenberg still expressed his reservations about the measure, but Josiah Bailey, who was the most vociferous and public opponent of earlier reform bills, did not (even though he was apparently on the floor).[70]

69. *Newsweek*, 22 Nov. 1937; FDA Scrapbooks, vol. 17. Cited in Jackson, *Food and Drug Legislation*, 165. Letter to Bailey: Mecklenburg [TN] Medical Association to Bailey, 20 Mar. 1938, Bailey Papers; cited in Jackson, *Food and Drug Legislation*, 163.

70. One possibility is that the sulfanilamide tragedy pushed the Senate over a "tipping point" by splitting the nascent Conservative Coalition. In this scenario, the tragedy's imagery, combined with the geographical distribution of deaths and shipments, removed more liberal members of the opposition from the coalition and converted them into issue-specific supporters of FDA-strengthening legislation. If those who broke from the ranks of the opposition, and those who broke ranks earlier, were more likely to have sulfanilamide shipments and deaths in their constituencies, then a geographical account of sulfanilamide's impact would receive additional support. Of course, had there been a non-unanimous vote on the final bill in the Senate or the House, we could have regressed changes in votes on the distribution of the deaths and shipments themselves. We would like to observe a series of endorsements, announced vote intentions, observable acts of participation, or some similar measurable index of support for a new law in such a way that individual support for a new measure could be gauged during the fall of 1937. For an excellent example of such a research methodology, see Richard L. Hall, *Participation in Congress* (New Haven, CT: Yale University Press, 1997).

Table 6. Bivariate Correlation between Shipments of Elixir Sulfanilamide and D-NOMINATE 1-D

Correlation for Total Sample [n = 106]	**−0.3156**
Correlation for South Only [n = 27]	**−0.5169**

An explanation centered upon the framing of sulfanilamide plausibly accounts for the shift in votes from a divisive battle over a weak bill to stronger support for a vigorous law. It does, moreover, perform better than the available alternatives, which are irreconcilable with the anti-regulatory posture struck by the early 75th Congress. It is fully consistent with our argument, though not necessary to it, to hypothesize that the tragedy convinced everybody—whether their constituency was affected or not—that additional regulation was needed. The symbolic character of the tragedy made a gate-keeping provision more palatable to all those who had previously opposed strengthening the FDA, in part because neither Copeland nor Tugwell nor anyone else had written such a provision into any seriously considered bill. The key, in our analysis, is that the symbolic character was in part intentionally framed, emphasized and presented to the organized public and Congress by USDA-FDA officials.

Hardcore opponents of FDA authority continued to speak out against the Copeland legislation, implying that the unanimity observed in the vote was not indicative of a full embrace of the 1938 Act by all those who voted for it. Although the final House margin of passage was "overwhelming" (but also unreported), FDA opponents there continued a vigorous defense of the right of self-medication and loudly voiced their worries about the continued accretion of bureaucratic power to federal agencies.

VII. Conclusion: Lessons of the Policy Tragedy of Elixir Sulfanilamide

New regulations often follow tragedies, but not reflexively so. The reason that scholars and pundits call some adverse events "tragedies" and that others fail to enter the annals of popular and recorded history is that active political agents seek to frame and reinterpret episodes into tragedies. Of course, this process is loaded with unintended consequences and is rarely one in which any single agent takes full control. But because the FDA possessed a near monopoly on information relating to sulfanilamide and the deaths resulting from it, the conversion of sulfanilamide from episode to tragedy was in large measure the effective work of a single organization. Our analysis

Table 7. The Relationship between Sulfanilamide Shipment Incidence and Anti-Regulatory Propensity, 1937 (Senate Votes, 74th Congress)

	[Senate Votes, 74th Congress]		
Variable	S. 5 Amendment Reconsideration [4/1/1935]	S. 5 Amendment Reconsideration [4/2/1935]	Bailey Amendment [4/8/1935]
Sample vote on bill	"Nay" voters	"Nay" voters	"Yea" voters
Bivariate Correlations			
Correlation btw Shipments and D-NOMINATE 1-D	**−0.3366**	−0.2474	**−0.3485**
Correlation btw Deaths and D-NOMINATE 1-D	**−0.3234**	−0.1937	**−0.2825**
Correlation btw Shipments and Predicted Yes Vote	**0.2173**	**0.3742**	0.0443
Correlation btw Deaths and Predicted Yes Vote	0.1038	**0.2554**	0.1511
Univariate Regressions			
Regression of D-NOMINATE 1-D on Shipments	**−0.0118** (0.0054)	−0.0195 (0.0140)	**−0.0082** (0.0034)
Regression of D-NOMINATE 1-D on Deaths	**−0.0373** (0.0179)	−0.0249 (0.0230)	−0.0282* (0.0146)
Regression of " Yea" Probability on Shipments	0.0035 (0.0026)	**0.0112** (0.0050)	0.0004 (0.0013)

Notes: Asymptotic standard errors in parentheses. Bold estimate implies statistical significance at $p < 0.05$ (two-tailed test). * implies statistical significance at $p < 0.10$. "Univariate regressions" always include a constant term. "Predicted Yea Votes" and "Predicted Nay Votes" based on Table 2 models.

of the policy tragedy of sulfanilamide generates historical conclusions that may have broader application in the analysis of American political development.

1. *The Debility of Capture.* One of our strongest conclusions is a negative one. Rent-seeking and industry capture explanations of the 1938 Food, Drug, and Cosmetic Act fare poorly in explaining either the process of agenda-setting or the votes on regulatory legislation. Indeed, our analyses support not merely the null hypothesis that affected industries were uninvolved in buying protection from the legislative process, but the *opposite* conclusion that affected industries, including and especially those who stood to profit from entry barriers that would be created in the 1938 act, were opposed to new regulation. Both narratively and statistically there is consistent support for this claim.

This is not to deny the importance of the organized pharmaceutical industry and patent medicine associations in shaping the legislation and (perhaps) its administrative implementation. The emergence of American pharmaceutical regulation did witness business influence, particularly in successful attempts by industry allies before the fall of 1937 to weaken, sidetrack, or altogether gut the USDA's legislative proposals. Yet if business influence is observed, industry capture—the rigging of regulation by economic "incumbents" in order to restrict competition and create a marketplace with rents—is not.[71]

2. *The Political Timing of Episode and its Conversion to Tragedy.* Second, the timing of the sulfanilamide tragedy allows us to gain some perspective on its precise contribution to the new regulation. The sulfanilamide deaths occurred *after* FDA leaders had, through steady and entrepreneurial political action, established an FDA-strengthening measure as the dominant alternative to the status quo. By the autumn of 1937, there was already a relatively structured debate between those who favored the existing body of law accumulated from the 1906 Pure Food and Drugs Act (or a slightly modified version thereof that would have given the Federal Trade Commission more power), and those who favored a bill that would have given the FDA broader regulatory authority over cosmetic and pharmaceutical products. In other words, the sulfanilamide tragedy did not "spur elected officials to promulgate governmental regulation," as historian Charles Jackson has argued. Many features of the regulation had been proposed and refined before the deaths occurred. It was *because* of this context, not in spite of it, that the 1938 law passed.

With attention to the timing of the reform, the substantive political move that centers the narrative of American pharmaceutical regulation can also be understood. The most significant feature of the 1938 act was its inclusion of a gatekeeping provision—allowing pre-market rejection by the FDA of any drug intended to be introduced into interstate commerce the United States. Comparing legislation passed by one house of Congress, and before the tragedy, to legislation passed after the tragedy, we observe a crucial difference in the appearance, for the first time, of a provision for pre-market review of pharmaceuticals. Underlying voting patterns did not shift appreciably. It is the content of the bill that changed.[72]

Because the FDA was successfully able to frame the sulfanilamide episode as exemplary of the defects of existing law, and as an instance in which the agency acted quickly and forcefully within its limited capacities, the sulfanilamide tragedy induced a change in the policy agenda. The form of regulatory legislation considered by Congress changed unalterably, as House and Senate leaders, at the prompting of FDA officials, attached a gatekeeping provision (Section 505 (a)–(c)) to the food and drug bill. The tragedy also shifted preferences among previously reluctant Southern Democrats and conservative Republicans, leading them to abandon the rhetoric of self-medication, to drop their resistance to FDA-strengthening legislation and to take up and pass the core legislation comprising the 1938 Act. Since 1937–1938 coincides with the emergence of a "conservative coalition" of southern Democrats and Republicans in Congress, the timing of the tragedy was particularly powerful.

Yet it is also worth reflecting on the historical context. The sulfanilamide tragedy occurred when the Senate and House were already well informed about alternative regulatory measures facing them. In both chambers of Congress, the FDA had found able and energetic sponsors for drug reform (Copeland and Virgil Chapman). Much of the costly work of building coalitions behind legislation had already been accomplished. Had the sulfanilamide tragedy occurred at another *time,* when FDA regulation as the dominant alternative to the status quo was not advanced by bureaucratic leaders, the Act would either not have passed or would have taken a much different form. In this respect, we can with some

71. David Vogel, *Fluctuating Fortunes: The Political Power of Business in America* (New York: Basic Books, 1989); Daniel Carpenter, "Protection without Capture: Product Approval by a Politically Responsive, Learning Regulator," *American Political Science Review* 98 (2004): 613–31.

72. It is in this respect that the case of American pharmaceutical regulation offers some methodological instruction. Note here that historically-oriented students of politics can combine narrative methods and agenda-setting methods by attending to the timing of the event in question. This follows Paul Pierson, "Not Just What but When: Timing and Sequence in Political Processes," *Studies in American Political Development* 14 (2000): 72–92. This interpretation of voting and bills stands in partial contrast to characterizations of Senate voting that we made in an earlier version of this article.

confidence reject the counterfactual that, had the sulfanilamide tragedy *not* occurred, regulatory reform in food and drugs would not have been on the agenda in the 75th Congress. It indeed was on the agenda of the 75th Congress in the spring of 1937. This is not to say that pharmaceutical regulation was warmly embraced by that legislature. What the sulfanilamide tragedy did, once distilled by USDA-FDA rhetoric, was to change the specific legislative agenda from regulation without licensure to regulation with licensure.

3. *Framing: The Inversion of Victimhood, the Admixture of Race and Innocence.* The third conditional feature of the tragedy concerns not its timing but its framing. In part due to the thorough and relentless efforts of FDA officials to turn and frame the sulfanilamide episode to the agency's advantage, in part due to media coverage (which relied heavily upon the FDA's information), two social facts became attached to the sulfanilamide episode. These facts and the episode constitute the "event-frame" match that propelled a more muscular version of FDA-strengthening legislation through the 75th Congress. First, the tragedy was seen as a nationwide disaster affecting primarily white victims, especially children. In fact, most of the sulfanilamide deaths occurred in the upper-country South and lower Midwest, and African-Americans were probably disproportionately affected by consumption of the elixir. Second, the FDA acted quickly to remove the entire product supply from the market, and its careful yet trumpeting presentation of this action both vaulted its reputation and left politicians and consumer advocates decrying weaknesses in the 1906 law. These were not fully consistent tenets, and the ultimate success of the FDA's activity was to bundle them into a logical, sense-making whole.

Perhaps the most striking reframing of the episode came in the way that first the USDA, then the 75th Congress and the American media, inverted the status of chemical victimhood and reframed the "target population" of pharmaceutical regulation. Whereas the early medical reports described a drug popular among mature men, many of them black, many of whom were seeking a quick and private treatment for syphilis, the Administration had, by the late autumn of 1937, morphed the exemplar of a sulfanilamide victim, and the visible casualty of policy failure, into the darling face of Joan Nidiffer. The victimhood of American policy failure had been inverted, from black, male, and possibly sexually licentious, to white, virginal and deserving. Although the contribution of the Nidiffer story to the act's passage is impossible to know with causal precision, it merits reflection that, in the 1937 and 1938 congressional debates, not one of the black male, rural male, or syphilis patient consumers of sulfanilamide was mentioned as a tragedy.

It is important, then, to consider how other advocates interpreted the sulfanilamide tragedy and how they read its lessons into rather different policy implications and statutory proposals. One of them was embedded in Charles Wesley Dunn's proposal to add another misbranding charge to any medicine that had not, before its market entry, proved its therapeutic claims. This would have changed the FDA's authority and the basis of a "misbranding" charge, but federal regulation of medicines would still have been regulation *ex post* approval, as it was from 1906 to 1938. Dunn's alternative proposal would have recognized the severity of the sulfanilamide episode but would not have gleaned from the tragedy the necessity of explicitly preventative measures.

Another set of alternative framings—admittedly less concrete and quite manifold—were all the other versions of the Copeland bill that had received serious consideration before October 1937. When the *Washington Post* and other news outlets waxed prophetic on the likelihood of new legislation, their editors had in mind the S. 5 that had passed the Senate in the first session of the 75th Congress, but which had stalled in the House. That bill, too, lacked a gatekeeping provision.

Our general conclusion, then, is that crises can in fact "lead to" or "cause" regulation, but the way in which they do so is politically contingent on the action of framing, an action that no one actor can entirely control. There is nothing in our argument or the primary evidence suggesting that anyone in the Food and Drug Administration deliberately or consciously misrepresented any feature of the sulfanilamide episode. Some features of the sulfanilamide affair were in fact tailor-made for re-interpretation. Some facts and sequences lend themselves to the production of lessons more than others do. Throughout the FDA was constrained by some "factual" features of the sulfanilamide episode. What its officials did—quite skillfully, it now appears—is to emphasize some features of the law more than others.

The policy tragedy of sulfanilamide also demonstrates the power of causal stories that are not backed up by statistics and logical argumentation, but are instead supported by logic that remains inescapably implicit, emotive, and moral. Storytelling and tragedy-weaving exercise a particular hold upon the political imagination, so much so that a narrative or a moving picture can be more persuasive than a research article. While the authority of statistical argumentation in modern politics is not in doubt, that authority is continually challenged by more symbolic and interpretive forms of policy argument.[73]

4. *The Role of the Audience.* An essential feature of a tragedy is the presence of a judgmental audience.[74]

73. Again, this feature of the narrative of the origins of American pharmaceutical regulation distinguishes it from the sort of model offered in Stone, "Causal Stories and the Formation of Policy Agendas."

74. Many thanks to Chip Heath for pressing this point. We take responsibility for its use here.

In Sophocles' *Antigone*, it is the public chorus that interjects its assessments in the unfolding of the drama and, at the end, this same chorus distills lessons from the events of the preceding narrative. The tragic framing of the sulfanilamide episode was, throughout, dependent upon audiences in medical journals, in national and regional newspapers, and, most important, in Congress. Like the choruses of Sophocles and Euripides, these were not passive audiences. Morris Fishbein and Royal Copeland actively inserted their judgment and energy into the struggle over food and drug law reform. Yet the fundamental reshaping of the narrative of elixir sulfanilamide was accomplished by federal officials in the USDA. The crucial features of the USDA's framing were three: (1) its exposure of apparent weaknesses in existing law, (2) its conversion of victimhood from black to white, from maturity to childhood, and (3) its equation of such undeserved sulfanilamide deaths with tragedies that could and must be explicitly prevented through licensure.

5. *Bureaucracy and the Interpretative Monopoly.* It is, finally, worth remembering that a government agency, one well equipped to reveal and interpret the sulfanilamide affair, acted as the narrator of record in this story. In the act of framing, privileged access to the facts that are being distilled can generate greater authority and credibility of the interpretation produced. If she has monopolistic access to information about the case or events that others do not have, the agent can offer selective portrayal and selective emphasis, without being easily challenged on the facts.

This feature of the sulfanilamide tragedy helps to inform contemporary understanding of bureaucratic politics. Agencies often possess immense informational advantages, particularly when the facts in question are intimately known only by those who administer the specifics of policy. This has been of particular advantage to bureaucratic actors who wish to change policy not only through "standard" administrative means, but through the legislative process itself and in particular through to weaving of a coherent and alluring narrative that supports particular policy changes. In some respects, then, the making of the 1938 Food, Drug, and Cosmetic Act stands as another instantiation of bureaucratic autonomy, though different from notions recently advanced in institutional political science.[75]

The endeavors of Walter Campbell, Royal Copeland, and Henry Wallace are forgotten now. Yet they shaped the American and global history of medicine and pharmaceutical development for decades in ways that have yet to be appreciated, and perhaps never will. Their actions amount to a form of political innovation, a feat shared in this case between a career bureaucrat (Campbell), an administrator emerging as a national politician (Wallace), and a career legislator (Copeland).[76] The saga of American pharmaceutical regulation and its origins demonstrates that political innovation and entrepreneurship, in its most powerful and enduring moment, consists in symbolic politics—in the interpretation, framing and public distillation of observable history.

BIBLIOGRAPHY: SELECTED PRIMARY SOURCE

Archival and Manuscript Collections Consulted

Records of the *American Civil Liberties Union*, Seeley Mudd Special Collections Library, Princeton University, Princeton, New Jersey.

Records of the *American Medical Association Council on Drugs*, Archives of the American Medical Association, Chicago, Illinois.

Royal *Copeland* Papers, Bentley Historical Library, University of Michigan, Ann Arbor, Michigan.

Records of the *Committee on Interstate and Foreign Commerce*, U.S. House of Representatives, RG 233, National Archives I

Records of the *Committee on Manufactures*, U.S. Senate, RG 46, National Archives I

Records of the *Committee on Commerce*, U.S. Senate, RG 46, National Archives I

Morris *Fishbein* Papers, University of Chicago Archives and Special Collections Library, Chicago, Illinois.

Records of the *Food and Drug Administration*, RG 88, National Archives II

Historical Health Fraud and Alternative Medicine Collection, Archives of the American Medical Association, Chicago, Illinois.

Mayo Authors Publications Series, Mayo Foundation History of Medicine Library, Mayo Clinic, Rochester, Minnesota

Records of the *Secretary of Agriculture*, RG 16, National Archives II

Harvey Washington *Wiley* Papers, Manuscript Division, Library of Congress, Washington, D.C.

Government Documents and Official Prints

Food, Drugs and Cosmetics. Hearings before a Subcommittee of the Committee on Commerce, United States Senate,

75. Patrick Roberts, "FEMA and the Prospects for Reputation-Based Autonomy," *Studies in American Political Development* 20 (2006): 57–87.

76. Sheingate, "Political Entrepreneurship, Institutional Change, and American Political Development," in *Formative Acts: American Politics in the Making*, eds. Stephen Skowronek and Matt Glassman (Philadelphia: University of Pennsylvania Press, 2007).

73rd Congress, Second Session, on S. 1944. 7–8 December 1933. (Washington, DC: Government Printing Office).

Foods, Drugs and Cosmetics. Hearings before the Committee on Commerce, United States Senate, 73rd Congress, Second Session, on S. 2800. 27 February–3 March 1934. (Washington, DC: Government Printing Office).

Foods, Drugs and Cosmetics. Hearings before a Subcommittee of the Committee on Commerce, United States Senate, 74th Congress, First Session, on S. 5. March 2, 8, and 9, 1935. (Washington, DC: Government Printing Office).

Foods, Drugs and Cosmetics. Hearings before a Subcommittee of the Committee on Interstate and Foreign Commerce, United States House of Representatives, 74rh Congress, First Session, on H.R. 6906, H.R. 8805, H.R. 8941, and S. 5. 22, 24, 25, 29, 30, 31 July, 6, 7, 8, 9, 10, 12 August 1935. (Washington, DC: Government Printing Office).

[30]

THE JOURNAL OF INDUSTRIAL ECONOMICS 0022-1821
Volume LI June 2003 No. 2

CONSUMPTION EXTERNALITIES AND DIFFUSION IN PHARMACEUTICAL MARKETS: ANTIULCER DRUGS*

ERNST R. BERNDT,† ROBERT S. PINDYCK,† AND PIERRE AZOULAY‡

We examine the role of consumption externalities in the demand for pharmaceuticals at both the brand level and over a therapeutic class of drugs. Externalities emerge when use of a drug by others affects its value, and/or conveys information about efficacy and safety to patients and physicians. This can affect the rate of market diffusion for a new entrant, and can lead to dominance of one drug despite the availability of close substitutes. We use data for H_2-antagonist antiulcer drugs to estimate a dynamic demand model and quantify these effects. The model has three components: an hedonic price equation that measures how the aggregate usage of a drug, as well as conventional attributes, affect brand valuation; equations relating equilibrium market shares to quality-adjusted prices and marketing levels; and diffusion equations describing the dynamic adjustment process. We find that consumption externalities influence both valuations and rates of diffusion, and that they operate at the brand and not the therapeutic class level.

I. INTRODUCTION

We examine the diffusion process characterizing a set of pharmaceutical innovations: H_2-antagonist antiulcer drugs, which avoid costly hospitalizations and surgeries, and also are effective in treating rather common ailments such as heartburn. We treat the origins of these innovations as largely exogenous, and focus on demand-side factors that affect long-run market saturation, not only for the overall therapeutic class, but also for particular brands within the class. In particular, we examine consumption externalities, i.e., ways in which the demand for a branded pharmaceutical by

*The research leading to this paper was supported by the National Science Foundation through grants to Berndt and Pindyck, and by MIT's Program on the Pharmaceutical Industry. Our thanks to Winnie Choi and Ornsiri Rungruxsirivorn for their outstanding research assistance, and to Iain Cockburn, Clint Cummins, Neil Gandal, Austan Goolsbee, Zvi Griliches, Jerry Hausman, Andrea Shepard, and seminar participants at Columbia University, MIT, Tel Aviv University, and the NBER for helpful comments. This is a shorter version of our NBER Working Paper of the same title, and was initially prepared in honor of Zvi Griliches' 20 years as Director of the NBER Productivity Program.

†Authors' affiliations: Sloan School of Management, Massachusetts Institute of Technology, Cambridge, MA, USA.
email: erberndt@mit.edu
email: rpyndyck@mit.edu
‡Graduate School of Business, Columbia University, New York, NY, USA.
email: pierre.azoulay@columbia.edu

patients and physicians depends on the number of other patients that have taken or are taking the drug.

Consumption externalities arise when the use of a drug by others influences perceptions about its efficacy, safety, and 'acceptability,' and thus affects its valuation and rate of adoption. Unlike computer software and telecommunications systems where consumption externalities stem from direct external benefits, in pharmaceutical markets these externalities are largely informational in nature: The widespread use of a drug may convey information about its safety and efficacy, and, for physicians, may imply 'accepted practice' and hence greater immunity to malpractice lawsuits.[1] For example, the fact that a drug has been widely used may be evidence that it is efficacious relative to its side effects and risks. Or, physicians might conclude that the probability of a malpractice suit is lower when a widely used drug is prescribed, whatever the actual efficacy and risks of the drug.

If they are strong enough, consumption externalities could lead to the dominance of one drug — not necessarily the most efficacious or safest — despite the availability of close substitutes. Consumption externalities also affect the rate at which a new product diffuses into the market: As more people use the product, word-of-mouth communication increases, accelerating the rate at which others become aware of it. In either case, the result can be a market outcome that is inefficient.[2]

We distinguish between externalities that influence consumers' valuations of a drug, and those that influence the rate of diffusion in the market.[3] Consumers' valuations are affected when the use of a drug by others influences its perceived efficacy and safety. One of our goals is to identify and quantify the magnitude of this effect. A second goal is to assess the importance of past sales as a determinant of the rate of product diffusion.

Pharmaceutical markets are usually bounded in terms of therapeutic classes of drugs, the members of which are substitutes. Thus it is important to distinguish between consumption externalities at two levels. The first is

[1] There is evidence of this dependence from early sociological studies of the diffusion of new drugs and medical technologies; see, e.g., Coleman, Katz, and Menzel (1966). For a recent study of the effects of potential malpractice liability on physician behavior, see Kessler and McClellan (1996). Temin (1980) has shown that physicians do not have well-organized information on the comparative effectiveness and riskiness of substitute drugs, and make decisions based largely on the customary behavior of other doctors.

[2] This is analogous to inefficient herd behavior resulting from informational externalities in technology adoption and investment decisions. The inefficiency arises when agents rationally try to free ride on the information generated by the adoption decisions of others; see, e.g., Scharfstein and Stein (1990) and Bikhchandani, Hirshleifer, and Welch (1998). Goolsbee and Klenow (1999) present evidence of very similar spillover effects in consumers' purchases of home computers. Gandal, Kende, and Rob (2000) estimate a dynamic demand model of technology adoption for compact disc players and CD titles.

[3] Decisions to utilize a drug can be made or influenced by both patients and physicians. We do not try to differentiate their roles in the adoption decision, and include both when we refer to 'consumers'.

with respect to a therapeutic class, e.g., H_2-antagonist antiulcer drugs, SSRI antidepressants, or cholesterol-lowering drugs. We expect that physicians may be more willing to prescribe and patients to take a drug the more the drug's therapeutic class has been 'accepted,' where 'acceptance' can be measured at least in part by the number of other people that have taken drugs in that class. The second is with respect to a specific brand of drug within a therapeutic class: Physicians and patients may be more willing to use Zantac (as opposed to Tagamet, Axid, or Pepcid) the greater is its 'acceptance,' as measured by market share or cumulative sales.

Although we focus on demand, the issues we examine have broad implications for the structure and performance of pharmaceutical markets, as well as other markets in which buyers decide whether to adopt new products or technologies. For example, consumption externalities may give firms the incentive to compete very aggressively in the early stages of market evolution, to try to win a future position with substantial market power. Even if externalities do not affect consumers' valuations of a product, an initially large market share can lead to 'tipping' by affecting the rate of diffusion: If a product's rate of diffusion depends positively on the number of consumers already using it, the firm with an initial market share advantage could increase that advantage as the market saturates.

When they occur at the brand level, consumption externalities can create an incentive to price low initially and advertise heavily, and later convey market power to the owner of a dominant brand. They also affect the reward for being first to market, making it worthwhile to invest heavily to accelerate R&D. Conversely, when they occur at the therapeutic class level, they can create second-mover advantages, whereby later entrants free-ride on the information and awareness generated by the pioneering brand. If this effect dominates, firms might find it optimal to arrive second on the market, and try to develop a drug with better attributes (e.g., fewer side effects) than those of the first mover.[4]

We focus on a particular therapeutic class, namely the H_2-antagonist antiulcer drugs: Tagamet, Zantac, Pepcid, and Axid. These drugs comprise a well-defined market because they all function in roughly the same way by causing the stomach to produce less hydrochloric acid. They differ in dosing frequency, side effects, and interactions with other drugs, but for most patients they could readily be substituted for each other. Our analysis covers the time period from 1977, when Tagamet was first introduced, through 1993, the year before Tagamet lost patent protection and two years before

[4] Indeed, as we will see, this appears to be the case with H_2-antagonist antiulcer drugs. Zantac arrived second but with better attributes than first-mover Tagamet, and soon attained a dominant share of the market. For discussions of first-mover advantages in prescription drug markets, see Bond and Lean (1977), and Berndt, Bui, Reilly, and Urban (1995, 1997). For an empirical study of pricing strategies in these markets, see Lu and Comanor (1998).

over-the-counter versions of the H_2-antagonist drugs were introduced. Prilosec, a proton-pump inhibitor used to treat similar disorders, was introduced in the United States in 1989. However, until 1995, the FDA required Prilosec to carry a warning on its label concerning safety in long-term treatment, so it was not a strong substitute for the H_2-antagonist drugs.

Because the four drugs were introduced sequentially, this data set allows us to address important issues related to brand diffusion and competition. How important, for example, is the first-mover advantage resulting from an 'installed base' of patients? How does that installed base affect a brand's rate of diffusion, and substitution across brands? What portion of a drug's value can be attributed to brand-level versus therapeutic class-level consumption externalities? We can also examine strategic issues specific to this industry. Zantac was introduced at a higher price than Tagamet and had the disadvantage of being a 'second mover,' but overtook Tagamet in sales after about four years. To what extent was this due to Zantac's better attributes and higher level of marketing?

Our model has three components. First, we estimate an hedonic price equation that accounts for the price impacts of objective attributes such as the number of side effects, dosing, etc. We also include cumulative lagged sales of a brand and/or the therapeutic class as additional attribute variables. This allows us to measure the importance of a drug's past usage, as well as conventional attributes, as components of its current value.

Second, we use the quasi-residuals from this hedonic price index as a quality-adjusted price and, based on data for the last four years of our sample, estimate an equilibrium model of brand shares. During this period we can reasonably expect that all four brands have fully diffused through the market, so we can measure the equilibrium dependence of sales on relative (quality-adjusted) prices and marketing levels.

Third, we estimate a set of dynamic diffusion equations that explains the adjustment of sales to their equilibrium, or saturation, levels. These endogenous saturation levels depend on prices, advertising levels, and population, and thus change over time as these variables evolve. Rates of diffusion for the brands depend indirectly on drug attributes through the hedonic residuals, as well as on prices and marketing efforts. But rates of diffusion also depend directly on past sales of the therapeutic class and/or the particular brand, reflecting learning and word-of-mouth effects. Thus, variables reflecting past sales can affect rates of diffusion and equilibrium market shares through multiple channels.

This approach has the virtue that it fits the data quite well: Dynamic simulations of the model yield time paths for brand sales that track the actual time paths very closely. However, this goodness of fit comes at the expense of structural assumptions that we impose to identify key parameters (e.g., that the last four years of our sample represents a period of market equilibrium). This framework is discussed in the next section. Section 3 discusses the data and estimation methods. Estimates of the hedonic price equations, the equilibrium share model, and the dynamic diffusion equations are presented and discussed in Sections 4, 5, and 6 respectively. Section 7 presents simulation results, and Section 8 concludes.

II. MODELLING PHARMACEUTICAL DEMANDS

As explained above, the past sales of a drug can affect its current demand by directly affecting its value to consumers, and by increasing awareness of the drug's existence and thereby accelerating its rate of diffusion. Our model, which accounts for these two mechanisms at both the therapeutic class and brand levels, is structured as follows.

First, perceptions of a drug's efficacy, safety, and medical 'acceptability' are essentially perceptions of its quality, so if past sales of a drug affect these perceptions, they should affect the drug's quality-adjusted price. This suggests that one could estimate the perceived value of a drug's past sales from an hedonic price regression that includes a variable such as past sales in addition to other product attributes. Of course, one could argue that the significance of measures of past sales reflects switching costs rather than consumption externalities. Based on discussions with physicians, however, it is our understanding that during the 1977–1993 time frame of our data, most patients were prescribed H_2 drugs for less than a year. Thus the growth in sales reflects a growing influx of new rather than long-term continuing patients. Given the preponderance of short-term treatments, it is unlikely that an observed dependence of price on past sales is due largely to switching costs.

Thus we begin by estimating an hedonic price equation using an (unbalanced) panel of prices and attributes for the four H_2-antagonist drugs. Included among the attributes are measures of the numbers of patients that are taking or have taken the drug in the past.[5] We thereby test whether variables that reflect the acceptance of a drug help to explain prices as expected, and we estimate their contribution to perceived value. Also, we employ the quasi-residuals of this hedonic regression as a quality-adjusted price in the other two components of our model.

Second, using the hedonic quasi-residuals, along with data on brand advertising, we estimate equations for the equilibrium market shares of the four brands. To do this, we use data only for the last 4 years of our sample, when the market was mature and adjustment to equilibrium was largely complete. Because the number of drugs on the market changed during the years prior to this period, we use a multinomial logit model. This restricts the

[5] Gandal (1994) and Brynjolfsson and Kemerer (1995) employed such an approach to estimate magnitude and value of network effects in spreadsheet software programs. Berndt, Cockburn, and Griliches (1996), Cockburn and Anis (2001), and Suslow (1996) have estimated hedonic price indexes of pharmaceutical products, but did not test for the presence of consumption externalities.

equilibrium cross-price elasticities to be the same for drugs with equal shares, but yields partial (i.e., subject to a constant total industry demand) own-price and advertising elasticities that depend on market shares but not on the number of drugs in the market. Using these equilibrium share equations, we calculate *fitted equilibrium shares* for the entire sample period. For example, we calculate what the Tagamet and Zantac equilibrium shares would have been in, say, 1985, when these were the only drugs on the market.

An alternative and less restrictive approach would involve estimating a share model with unadjusted prices and all the attributes. We investigated this alternative, but found that during the equilibrium time period there is simply not enough variability in the attributes to identify parameters. Moreover, we also used a nested model to test whether adding attributes to our baseline specification adds explanatory power, and found that it does not.

Third, we estimate a set of dynamic diffusion equations for the four individual brands. These equations explain changes in the sales of a particular brand in terms of adjustment to that brand's equilibrium share of an industry saturation level (which is estimated), where the adjustment is partly due to the influence of an 'installed base' of patients that are using or have used the drug, and partly independent of that base. Furthermore, the installed base is measured both with respect to the entire therapeutic category and with respect to the individual brand. In this way we estimate the relative importance of category-specific versus brand-specific spillover effects on the rate of diffusion.

This three-step approach has the distinct disadvantage that it imposes strong structural assumptions — most notably that we can identify a period of market equilibrium. An alternative approach would be to substitute functional expressions for the brands' equilibrium shares directly into the diffusion equations, and then estimate those equations over the entire sample. We have pursued that approach, but found that it is not possible to precisely identify key parameters. By imposing identifying assumptions, our three-step approach has a number of advantages. First, it lets us measure the importance of spillover effects as a component of perceived value, and in terms of its influence on the rate of product diffusion. Second, we can model the structure of inter-brand competition in a parsimonious way, without the usual problem of having to sacrifice the dynamic aspects of demand. Third, the three parts of the model each provide information regarding a different aspect of demand, and allow us to address questions raised in the Introduction, such as the extent to which Zantac's performance can be attributed to its better attributes and higher rate of advertising.

(i). *Hedonic Price Equation*

We estimate hedonic price equations that relate the price of product i at time t, p_{it}, to a set of measured quality characteristics, C_{it}, a set of time dummy variables, D_t, and two measures of product acceptance: the depreciated stock of cumulative patient days of therapy of brand i up to time t, XS_{it}, and the corresponding depreciated stock for the therapeutic class as a whole, XS_t. We employ both linear and semi-log specifications. The linear specification is

$$(1) \qquad P_{it} = C'_{it}\beta + D'_t\gamma + \omega_1 XS_{i,t-1} + \omega_2 XS_{t-1} + \eta_{it},$$

where β, γ, and ω contain parameters to be estimated, and η is a stochastic disturbance term. The depreciated stock of cumulative patient days of therapy is computed as

$$(2) \qquad XS_{it} = \sum_{\tau=0}^{t} (1-\delta)^{\tau} X_{i,t-\tau},$$

and similarly for XS_t, but using $X_t = \Sigma_i X_{it}$. Here, δ is a monthly depreciation rate and $X_{i,t-\tau}$ is sales of patient days of therapy of drug i in month $t-\tau$. As discussed in Section 3, we set $\delta = .05$.

To obtain measures of quality-adjusted prices, we compute the quasi-residual:

$$(3) \qquad P_{it} = p_{it} - C'_{it}\hat{\beta} - \hat{\omega}_1 XS_{i,t-1} - \hat{\omega}_2 XS_{t-1}.$$

Note that variations in P_{it} over time and across products net out the impacts of quality differences, including valuations of past sales as measured by $XS_{i,t}$ and XS_t.

(ii). *Equilibrium Shares*

We use a simple multinomial logit model to describe equilibrium brand shares. Denoting the quantity share of brand i at time t by s^*_{it}, equilibrium shares are given by

$$(4) \qquad \log\left(\frac{s^*_{it}}{s^*_{T,t}}\right) = \lambda_{i0} + \lambda_1(p_{it} - p_{T,t}) + \lambda_2(X_{it} - X_{T,t})$$
$$+ \lambda_3(\text{MINSTK}_{it} - \text{MINSTK}_{T,t}) + \epsilon_{it},$$

where i = Z (Zantac), A (Axid), and P (Pepcid), $s^*_{T,t}$ is the equilibrium share of Tagamet, p_{it} is the drug price (the dependent variable in eqn. (1)), X_{it} is the set of drug attributes included in the hedonic equation, and MINSTK_{it} is the depreciated stock of detailing minutes, our measure of marketing. Variation in patient and physician 'tastes' occurs through the error term ϵ_{it}.

Since this demand system includes brand-specific effects λ_{i0}, the λ_2 coefficients have to be identified off longitudinal variation. Unfortunately, there is not enough time-series variation to identify these coefficients during the equilibrium period. As a result, we estimate the more restricted model:

$$\text{(5)} \qquad \log\left(\frac{s_{it}^*}{s_{T,t}^*}\right) = a_{i0} + a_1(P_{it} - P_{T,t}) + a_3(\text{MINSTK}_{it} - \text{MINSTK}_{T,t}) + \epsilon_{it},$$

where P_{it} is the quasi-residual from eqn. (3). Under the assumption that consumers' valuation of attributes do not change over the sample period, then eqn. (5) reduces to eqn. (4).

This parsimonious model imposes restrictions on equilibrium demands — for any two drugs, cross-price elasticities with respect to a third drug can differ only to the extent that the first two have different market shares. In our case these restrictions are less problematic: There are only four products in the market, and they are close substitutes. The difference between any two H_2 drugs is far smaller than the difference between, say, a Ford Escort and a Lexus, so there is less need to use the more complex approach of Berry, Levinsohn and Pakes (1995). Also, note that this demand model does not include an outside good. The reason is that our dynamic diffusion equations explain the adjustment to an *endogenous* saturation level X_t^* (see below), and thus account for consumers' outside treatment options.

(iii). *Saturation Levels*

Given estimates of equilibrium shares, we can determine saturation levels for each brand, i.e., the level of sales that a brand would reach once in equilibrium. These saturation levels vary over time for two reasons. First, the equilibrium market shares on which they depend change as relative quality-adjusted prices and advertising levels evolve. Note that even if nominal prices, attributes, and advertising levels were fixed, equilibrium shares could still change because changing cumulative sales affects quality-adjusted prices. Second, brand saturation levels also depend on the saturation level for sales of the overall therapeutic category, which varies as the population grows and as the average industry price changes.

We denote the industry saturation level by X_t^*, and we model it as a function of the average industry quality-adjusted price $\bar{P}_t$, the total stock of depreciated detailing minutes for the industry MINSTKTOT_t, and population POP_t:

$$\text{(6)} \qquad \log X_t^* = b_0 + b_1 \log \bar{P}_t + b_2 \log \text{POP}_t + b_3 \log \text{MINSTKTOT}_t$$

Given the equilibrium shares s_{it}^* and this industry saturation level, the saturation level for each brand is just $X_{it}{}^* = s_{it}{}^* X_t{}^*$.

(iv). *Dynamic Diffusion Equations*

The third part of our model is a set of equations describing product diffusion at the brand level, i.e., how sales of each brand, X_{it}, approach the saturation level $X_{it}^* = s_{it}^* X_t^*$. These equations are not derived from a formal dynamic optimization model, in part because of difficulties of dealing with moral hazard (due to insurance) and principal-agent issues (the physician-patient relationship) without transaction-level data. Instead, we adapt a set of models that have been widely used in marketing studies of new product diffusion, in a way that allows us to distinguish among alternative sources of sales growth.[6] Specifically, we work with versions of the generalized logistic equation:

$$(7) \qquad \frac{dX_t}{dt} = \alpha(X_t^* - X_t) + \beta X_t(X_t^* - X_t),$$

and the generalized Gompertz equation:

$$(8) \qquad \frac{dX_t}{dt} = \alpha(\log X_t^* - \log X_t) + \beta X_t(\log X_t^* - \log X_t).$$

The first term on the right-hand side of eqns. (7) and (8) represents sales growth (towards the saturation level) that is independent of usage of the drug by others. (It may be due to advertising, a willingness of physicians to experiment with a new drug, etc.) The second term represents sales growth that is due to the influence of current sales (and in our specification below, past sales). As discussed above, the saturation level X_t^* will vary over time as prices, demographics, and levels of marketing activity change.

If $\alpha = 0$ and X_t^* is constant, the solutions to both of these equations are S-shaped 'saturation' curves, where sales first increase slowly, then accelerate, and finally level out as X_t approaches X_t^*. If $\alpha > 0$, sales can accelerate faster early on, because sales growth is not dependent solely on current or past sales. If X_t^* is not constant, i.e., the saturation level is varying over time, sales pursue a moving target.[7]

We adapt these diffusion equations by noting that the saturation level for brand i is given by $s_{it}^* X_t^*$, where s_{it}^* is the equilibrium share of brand i (which in turn is a function of relative prices and advertising levels). In order to allow for consumption externalities at both the brand and the therapeutic

[6] For an overview of diffusion models of this type and their application, see Mahajan and Muller (1979), Mahajan, Muller, and Bass (1990), and Geroski (2000).

[7] As a referee pointed out, an S-shaped diffusion curve could also result if consumers' valuations were normally distributed and quality-adjusted prices were declining over time. As shown in Figure 4, however, during this time period quality-adjusted prices were generally rising.

category levels, we estimate the following two discrete-time versions of the continuous-time diffusion processes above:

$$(9)\qquad X_{it} - X_{i,t-n} = \left[\log(\hat{s}^*_{it}X^*_t) - \log X_{i,t-n}\right] \cdot \left[C_i + \sum_{k=2}^{12} \theta_k m_{kt} + d_0 \mathrm{XS}_{t-n} + d_1 \mathrm{XS}_{i,t-n}\right]$$

and

$$(10)\qquad X_{it} - X_{i,t-n} = \left[\log(\hat{s}^*_{it}X^*_t) - \log X_{i,t-n}\right] \cdot \left[C_i + \sum_{k=2}^{12} \theta_k m_{kt} + d_0 \log \mathrm{XS}_{t-n} + d_1 \log \mathrm{XS}_{i,t-n}\right]$$

The parameters d_0 and d_1 measure the effects of industry-level and brand-specific spillovers, respectively, on the rate of diffusion of each brand. Note that when estimating these equations, we use both the in-sample and out-of-sample *fitted* values of the equilibrium shares, $\hat{s}^*_{it}$. The industry saturation level, X^*_t, is endogenous, and is given by eqn. (6).

III. DATA AND ESTIMATION

Here we briefly summarize the construction of our data set. (Much of our data are described in more detail in the Data Appendix of Berndt, Bui, Reiley, and Urban (1997).)

To aggregate over the various strengths and presentational formulations of each drug, we divide monthly sales in total milligrams of active ingredient by the recommended daily dosage, in milligrams, for duodenal ulcer treatment. This yields patient days of therapy X_{it}, expressed in millions. By 1993, total monthly sales was about 120 million patient days of therapy, which is roughly equivalent to 4 million patients. To obtain the nominal price per day of patient therapy, we divide total revenue from sales of drug i in month t by X_{it}. We deflate this nominal price by the Producer Price Index for finished goods (1982 = 1.00) to obtain the real price for drug i in 1982 dollars. In 1993, the average real price was about \$1.50 per patient day of therapy. Both price and quantity measures refer to sales from wholesalers to retail drug stores, as computed by IMS America.

Our measure of marketing effort is the number of minutes that physicians in the United States were 'detailed' by pharmaceutical sales representatives, obtained from IMS America. In the 1990s, monthly minutes of detailing varied from about 40,000 to 250,000 across products and over time. We construct a cumulative depreciated stock of detailing minutes, MINSTK_{it}, for each brand. This stock is expressed in millions of minutes, and is computed analogously to eqn. (2), with $\delta = .05$, which is approximately the rate estimated in Berndt *et al.* (1997) and King (1997). Also, we performed a grid search for δ by repeatedly estimating the equilibrium share equations using generalized method of moments estimation (GMM). The GMM objective function is quite flat over values of δ between 0.02 and 0.08, and has two local minima; the value of 0.05 lies midway between those minima.

To compute the quality-adjusted average price for the H_2 class, $\bar{P}_t$, we weight each of the products on the market at that time by the average patient-day share during the period. These average shares are computed separately for epochs when there were two, three, and four H_2 products on the market. We also compute a *total* level of advertising for the therapeutic class, MINSTKTOT_t, by summing MINSTK_{it} over all four products.

We used several quality characteristics in our hedonic equations. The first, DOSAGE, is the number of tablets normally required per day. When Zantac appeared in 1983, it had twice-a-day dosage, in contrast to Tagamet's four-times-a-day version. Lower DOSAGE implies higher quality, because it leads to greater patient compliance. Note that the DOSAGE variable changes over time as manufacturers obtained FDA approval to market more convenient dosages, which ultimately became once-a-day formulations for all four brands.

These drugs have also differed in terms of the medical conditions for which they obtained FDA marketing approval (the 'approved indications'). Zantac was the first H_2-antagonist to obtain approval for GERD (gastroesophageal reflux disease), a common ailment whose symptoms vary from mild heartburn to intense pain. Although all four H_2-antagonists had obtained approval at product launch date for active duodenal ulcer treatment, FDA approval times varied for active gastric ulcer treatment, duodenal ulcer maintenance treatment, and stress ulcer prophylaxis. We compute SUMATT as the sum of the indications, other than GERD and active duodenal ulcer treatment, for which the drug had FDA approval.

Another important attribute of prescription drugs is the extent to which they might interact adversely with other medications. For each H_2-antagonist we construct a variable, INTER, that sums up the number of major drugs with which it had adverse interactions, as reported in annual editions of *Physicians' Desk Reference*. By late 1993, Tagamet had registered ten adverse interactions, while Zantac, Pepcid, and Axid had either zero or one.

Finally, we construct a monthly time counter, TIME, starting at one in August 1977, and take U.S. population data from the U.S. Census Bureau web site, www.census.gov (in millions of people).

Figure 1 shows monthly sales of each drug. Although Tagamet was the pioneer and only H_2-antagonist drug on the market for six years, Zantac captured market share rapidly following its entry in July 1983. Total industry sales continued to increase after Zantac's entry, but Tagamet's sales began to fall after peaking at about 46 million patient days in April 1984.

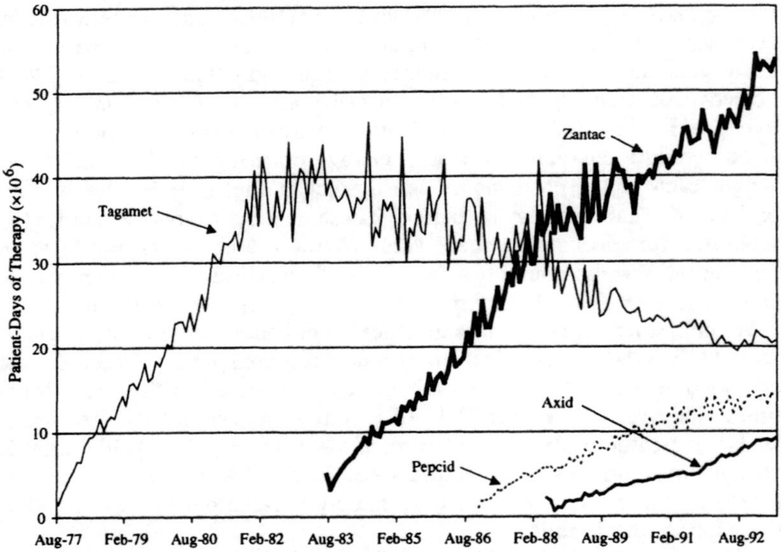

Figure 1
Monthly Sales for H_2-Antagonist Drugs

Tagamet's share continued to decline when Pepcid and Axid entered, but these drugs were far less successful than Zantac; Pepcid's share one year after entry was only about 8 percent, and Axid's 4 percent. By the end of our sample in May, 1993, Zantac held about a 55-percent market share, Tagamet 21 percent, Pepcid 15 percent, and Axid 9 percent.

Tagamet's real (quality-unadjusted) price gradually decreased from about $1 per day at entry to $0.80 per day when Zantac entered. As shown in Figure 2, Zantac entered with a large price premium over Tagamet, and thereafter the prices of *both* Zantac and Tagamet rose over time. The prices of Pepcid and Axid were between those of Zantac and Tagamet.

Finally, Figure 3 shows the depreciated stock of detailing minutes for each brand, computed using a monthly depreciation rate of 5 percent. The stocks for all four brands rose steadily most of the time that they were on the market, but Tagamet's fell during the last two years, perhaps in expectation of the imminent loss of patent protection in May 1994.

The data used to estimate the hedonic and brand diffusion equations form an unbalanced panel, while those used for the equilibrium share equations form a balanced panel. We estimate the parameters of the hedonic price equation by ordinary least squares, and compute heteroscedasticity-consistent and ARMA(2,2) serial correlation-consistent standard errors. We estimate the logit equations for the equilibrium brand shares three ways:

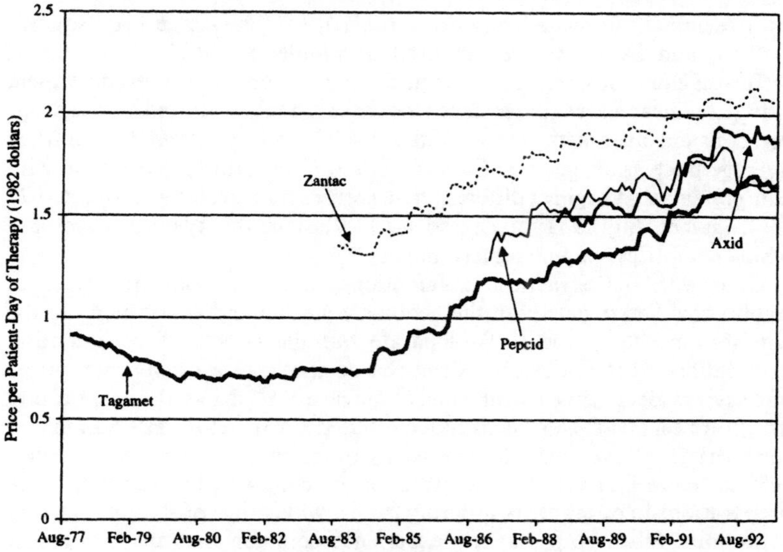

Figure 2
Real Prices of H_2-Antagonist Drugs

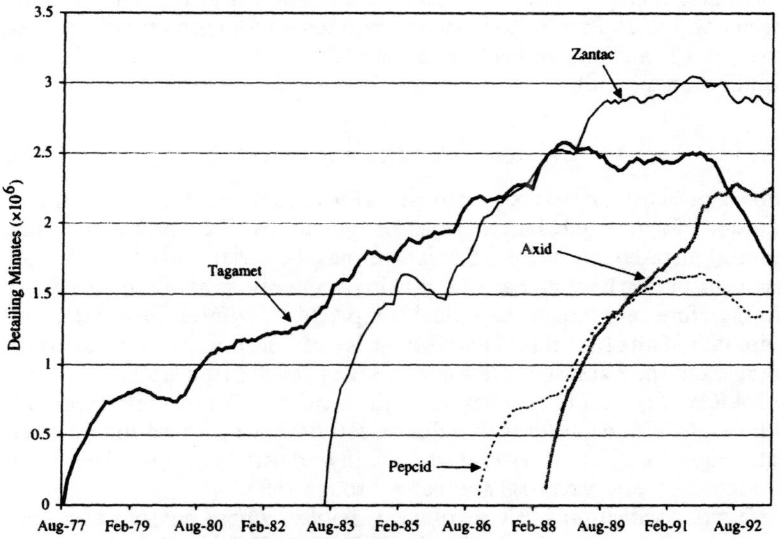

Figure 3
Detailing Stocks for H_2-Antagonist Drugs ($\delta = 5\%$)

as a seemingly unrelated regression (SUR), by three-stage least squares (3SLS), and by generalized method of moments (GMM). The brand diffusion equations are nonlinear in the parameters, so we estimate them using nonlinear least squares. Since the share weights of the individual drugs are constant arithmetic means within each epoch, we treat the industry average price as exogenous. For each brand *i*, we form the vectors X_i with components that begin at different time periods for each *i* (e.g., August 1977 for Tagamet, July 1983 for Zantac, etc.). We stack the X_i's into a vector X which comprises our unbalanced panel.

Even with our structural assumptions, we must confront issues of unobserved heterogeneity in the hedonic equation and endogeneity in the equilibrium share model. To separate out the effects of consumption externalities from unobserved drug characteristics, we use *hospital* prices and sales as identifying instruments. In the case of H_2 drugs, the hospital and drugstore segments can be considered independent. Hospitals administer these drugs intravenously to emergency room patients in order to reduce acid secretion induced by severe trauma. By contrast, drugstores sell oral preparations to outpatients suffering from a wide range of stomach-related conditions. Since both markets experience common manufacturing cost shocks, hospital prices and sales are likely to be strongly correlated with drugstore prices and sales, but uncorrelated with unobserved determinants of drugstore demand.

Table 1 shows summary statistics for the variables used in the model. Part A includes aggregate industry variables, and Parts B to E include brand-specific variables. Part F shows summary statistics for each brand's market share, price, and marketing for the last 53 months of our sample (the 'equilibrium' period).

IV. HEDONIC PRICE EQUATIONS

Table 2 presents the results of estimating linear and semi-log hedonic price equations for our unbalanced panel of four drugs. We first estimate the hedonic price equation by OLS. There may be serial correlation in the residuals, but we have no basis for making assumptions about its structure. We therefore re-estimate the model using GMM, with an instrument set composed of all of the right hand side variables. The point estimates do not change, but the *t*-statistics are robust to the presence of heteroscedasticity and ARMA(2,2)-serial correlation in the residuals. All of the regressions include annual and quarterly time dummies (not shown). These dummies are highly significant, and show that real, quality-adjusted prices fell from 1977 through 1981, and then rose gradually through 1993.

We work with four basic attribute variables, whose construction and interpretation was discussed in Section 3: GERD, SUMATT, INTER, and DOSAGE. As can be seen from the table, GERD, INTER, and DOSAGE

TABLE I
SUMMARY STATISTICS

	Mean	Std Dev	Minimum	Maximum
A. *Industry Variables (Nobs = 188)*				
X_t (patient-days/month, $\times 10^6$)	51.75	25.57	3.773	99.05
XS_t (cumul. patient-days, $\times 10^6$)	1028.4	619.7	7.715	2099.3
$\bar{P}_t$ (quality-adjusted avg. price)	1.562	0.215	1.155	1.914
$\bar{p}_t$ (real avg. price, 1982$)	1.206	0.441	0.688	1.930
POP_t (U.S. population, $\times 10^6$)	237.3	10.34	219.4	256.2
MIN_t (detailing minutes, $\times 10^6$)	0.249	0.171	0.019	0.604
$MINSTKTOT_t$ (ind. tot. stock min., $\times 10^6$)	4.173	3.107	0.263	9.268
B. *Tagamet (Nobs = 188)*				
X_{it} (patient-days/month, $\times 10^6$)	27.52	9.087	3.773	46.42
XS_{it} (cumul. patient-days, $\times 10^6$)	615.0	259.0	7.715	872.6
P_{it} (quality-adjusted price)	1.562	0.232	1.155	2.004
p_{it} (real price, 1982$)	1.056	0.328	0.688	1.700
MIN_{it} (detailing minutes, $\times 10^6$)	0.094	0.036	0.019	0.199
$MINSTK_{it}$ (stock of minutes, $\times 10^6$)	1.727	0.656	0.263	2.576
$GERD_{it}$ (GERD dummy)	0.133	0.340	0.000	1.000
$SUMATT_{it}$ (other approved indications)	1.612	0.873	0.000	3.000
$INTER_{it}$ (# adverse drug interactions)	7.096	3.617	0.000	10.00
$DOSAGE_{it}$ (daily dosing frequency)	2.516	1.164	1.000	4.000
C. *Zantac (Nobs = 117)*				
X_{it} (patient-days/month, $\times 10^6$)	30.42	14.20	4.190	54.27
XS_{it} (cumul. patient-days, $\times 10^6$)	537.8	337.9	11.92	1093.2
P_{it} (quality-adjusted price)	1.733	0.108	1.533	1.961
p_{it} (real price, 1982$)	1.770	0.239	1.309	2.129
MIN_{it} (detailing minutes, $\times 10^6$)	0.133	0.036	0.048	0.212
$MINSTK_{it}$ (stock of minutes, $\times 10^6$)	2.289	0.667	0.704	3.049
$GERD_{it}$ (GERD dummy)	0.718	0.452	0.000	1.000
$SUMATT_{it}$ (other approved indications)	1.530	0.794	0.000	2.000
$INTER_{it}$ (# adverse drug interactions)	0.145	0.354	0.000	1.000
$DOSAGE_{it}$ (daily dosing frequency)	1.342	0.476	1.000	2.000
D. *Pepcid (Nobs = 77)*				
X_{it} (patient-days/month, $\times 10^6$)	9.173	3.693	1.947	14.61
XS_{it} (cumul. patient-days, $\times 10^6$)	141.7	86.62	4.740	284.0
P_{it} (quality-adjusted price)	1.695	0.177	0.417	1.892
p_{it} (real price, 1982$)	1.616	0.123	1.286	1.844
MIN_{it} (detailing minutes, $\times 10^6$)	0.075	0.023	0.031	0.131
$MINSTK_{it}$ (stock of minutes, $\times 10^6$)	1.211	0.389	0.295	1.645
$GERD_{it}$ (GERD dummy)	0.234	0.426	0.000	1.000
$SUMATT_{it}$ (other approved indications)	1.727	0.448	1.000	2.000
$INTER_{it}$ (# adverse drug interactions)	0.000	0.000	0.000	0.000
$DOSAGE_{it}$ (daily dosing frequency)	1.000	0.000	1.000	1.000
E. *Axid (Nobs = 59)*				
X_{it} (patient-days/month, $\times 10^6$)	4.926	2.344	0.704	9.207
XS_{it} (cumul. patient-days, $\times 10^6$)	65.16	41.80	4.568	146.6
P_{it} (quality-adjusted price)	1.778	0.090	1.630	1.964
p_{it} (real price, 1982$)	1.680	0.169	1.456	1.943
MIN_{it} (detailing minutes, $\times 10^6$)	0.114	0.024	0.069	0.217
$MINSTK_{it}$ (stock of minutes, $\times 10^6$)	1.647	0.517	0.427	2.277
$GERD_{it}$ (GERD dummy)	0.390	0.492	0.000	1.000
$SUMATT_{it}$ (other approved indications)	1.000	0.000	1.000	1.000
$INTER_{it}$ (# adverse drug interactions)	1.000	0.000	1.000	1.000
$DOSAGE_{it}$ (daily dosing frequency)	1.000	1.000	1.000	1.000
F. *Balanced Panel, 1989–1993 (Nobs = 53)*				
S_{it}–Tagamet	0.293	0.059	0.212	0.407
S_{it}–Zantac	0.519	0.018	0.478	0.550
S_{it}–Pepcid	0.130	0.023	0.079	0.169

(*continued overleaf*)

TABLE I (continued)

	Mean	Std Dev	Minimum	Maximum
S_{it}-Axid	0.058	0.023	0.011	0.094
P_{it}-Tagamet	1.854	0.093	1.709	2.004
P_{it}-Zantac	1.808	0.086	1.673	1.961
P_{it}-Pepcid	1.738	0.106	1.542	1.892
P_{it}-Axid	1.790	0.088	1.630	1.964
$MINSTK_{it}$-Tagamet	2.343	0.221	1.713	2.538
$MINSTK_{it}$-Zantac	2.895	0.099	2.535	3.049
$MINSTK_{it}$-Pepcid	1.450	0.154	1.030	1.645
$MINSTK_{it}$-Axid	1.758	0.415	0.914	2.277

are all highly significant and have the expected signs; SUMATT is usually insignificant, and has the wrong sign, which may reflect the fact that much prescribing is 'off-label,' i.e., permitted but not formally approved by the FDA.[8]

Each equation also has one or two variables that measure the effects of past sales at the brand-specific and therapeutic category levels. The first variable, $XS_{i,t-1}$, is the depreciated stock of past sales of brand *i*, calculated using a monthly depreciation rate of 5 percent. The second variable, XS_{t-1}, is the corresponding depreciated stock of past sales for the therapeutic category. Note in Table 2 that the brand-specific variable XS_{t-1} is always positive and highly significant in both the linear and semi-log versions, while the variable for the therapeutic category, $XS_{i,t-1}$, is insignificant. We infer from this that the use of a drug by others affects its valuation, and that this effect operates at the brand rather than the therapeutic class level.[9]

To see the magnitude of this effect, consider column (1) in Table 2, where the coefficient on $XS_{i,t-1}$ is about 0.00018. Just prior to Zantac's introduction in August 1983, Tagamet had a depreciated stock of past sales of 786 million patient days. Had this figure been about 200 million (25 percent) less, the value of Tagamet would have been reduced by \$0.036 (i.e., 200×0.00018), or about 5 percent of its approximately \$0.75 price at that

[8] It is unclear whether marketing effort should be included in the hedonic equation. One could argue that our measures of consumption externalities fully incorporate the effects of marketing and other informational investments. In our data, the simple correlation between XS_{it} and $MINSTK_{it}$ is 0.802, 0.954, 0.849, and 0.945 for the four brands, suggesting that it would be very difficult to estimate the separate effects of marketing efforts and consumption externalities as components of the hedonic price. However, when we instead included in the hedonic equation the residual of a simple regression of the stock of detailing minutes on the stock of patient days (the brand-specific consumption externality measure), the results were little affected.

[9] To check on whether the lagged quantity variable was correlated with the hedonic disturbance term, we instrumented past sales using cumulative hospital sales. We ran a Hausman test for exogeneity of past sales and could not reject the null hypothesis for each of the six specifications. To explore possible strategic pricing, we also ran regressions adding as a regressor the number of firms competing in the market that month, initially as a single count variable, and then as three dummy variables for the duopoly, three-firm, and four-term epochs. The parameter estimates on these variables were always insignificant.

TABLE II
HEDONIC PRICE EQUATION

	A. *Dependent Variable* = P_{it}			B. *Dependent Variable* = *log* P_{it}		
	(1)	(2)	(3)	(4)	(5)	(6)
Const.	1.3535 (18.82)	1.4152 (18.44)	1.3919 (17.64)	0.5113 (7.47)	0.5467 (7.45)	0.5387 (7.21)
$GERD_{it}$	0.1816 (10.72)	0.2320 (13.48)	0.1820 (10.71)	0.1245 (10.50)	0.1418 (13.40)	0.1247 (10.48)
$SUMATT_{it}$	−0.0159 (−0.98)	0.0163 (1.11)	−0.0156 (−0.97)	−0.0061 (−0.49)	0.0050 (0.46)	−0.0059 (−0.48)
$INTER_{it}$	−0.0452 (−16.62)	−0.0375 (−14.37)	−0.0452 (−16.59)	−0.0286 (−14.33)	−0.0259 (−14.56)	−0.0285 (−14.29)
$DOSAGE_{it}$	−0.1158 (−6.83)	−0.1194 (−7.41)	−0.1157 (−6.83)	−0.1555 (−9.63)	−0.1566 (−9.91)	−0.1554 (−9.64)
$XS_{it}(-1)$	0.1758×10^{-3} (5.49)		0.1753×10^{-3} (5.48)	0.6030×10^{-4} (2.72)		0.5998×10^{-4} (2.71)
$XS_t(-1)$		0.4804×10^{-3} (1.79)	0.4265×10^{-3} (1.50)		0.0239×10^{-3} (1.45)	0.3054×10^{-3} (1.34)
R^2	0.966	0.960	0.967	0.970	0.969	0.970
Zantac Price Premium	$0.01	$0.35	$0.30	$0.04	$0.27	$0.25

Note: All regressions include annual and quarterly time dummies; NOB = 441; *t*-statistics (from heteroscedasticity-consistent and ARMA(2,2) serial-correlation consistent standard errors) in parentheses. Zantac price premium is the estimated quality-adjusted price of Zantac minus that of Tagamet at the time of Zantac's entry in July 1983, based on attribute differences with Tagamet. (The actual deflated price difference was $0.615.)

time. This implies a brand-specific valuation elasticity of 0.2 (0.05/0.25), which is positive but modest. The semi-log hedonic equation yields even smaller elasticities. In all of the calculations that follow, we use Model (1) of Table 2, i.e., the linear hedonic equation.

Figure 4 shows quality-adjusted real prices for the four drugs. The sharp movements in these prices are largely due to changes in the drugs' attributes. For example, increases in the quality-adjusted price of Tagamet during 1980–82 are due to findings of additional interactions with other drugs that reduced its effective quality. The sharp drops in the price of Tagamet in January 1985 and January 1987 are due to changes in dosing from four daily doses to two, and then to one. Zantac's quality-adjusted price also dropped in January 1987 because its daily dosing dropped from two to one. Pepcid's quality-adjusted price dropped in December 1991 when it received approval for treatment of GERD.

Note that at the time of Zantac's entry in 1983, its quality-adjusted price was close to that of Tagamet. This can help us understand the pricing of Zantac. Ignoring quality differentials, Zantac was priced about 61 cents above Tagamet (in 1982 dollars). One might argue that this higher price was intended to signal higher quality. Zantac indeed had quality advantages over Tagamet, in particular fewer interactions and less frequent dosing. However, it also had a disadvantage insofar as Tagamet's installed base gave Tagamet a perceived value premium. Our hedonic equation implies

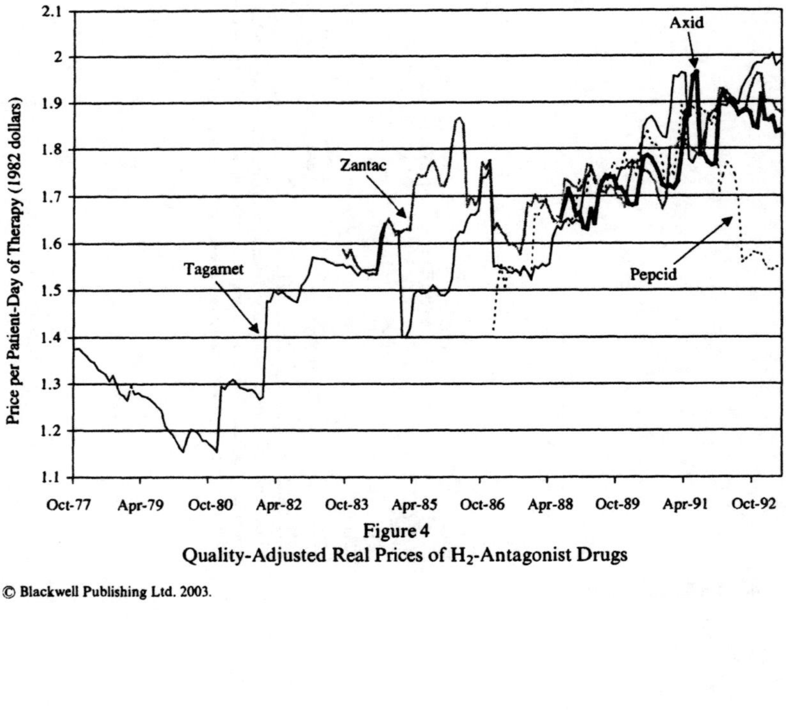

Figure 4
Quality-Adjusted Real Prices of H_2-Antagonist Drugs

that Zantac had a 72-cent advantage from its better dosing and interaction profile, and a 12-cent disadvantage from the consumption externality, implying a net price premium of only $61 - 72 + 12 = 1$ cent.

V. EQUILIBRIUM SHARE EQUATIONS

Using the hedonic equation (1) from Table 2, we construct quasi-residuals that represent quality-adjusted prices for each brand. With these quasi-residuals, along with the depreciated stock of detailing minutes for each brand, we estimate a multinomial logit model using the last 53 months of data for our sample. During this period, all four brands were well established and their efficacy and side-effects were well known. Thus it is reasonable to impose the identifying assumption that the market was in equilibrium during this period, so that any changes in market shares were due to changes in prices and marketing efforts.

Because price and marketing levels are likely to be endogenous, we need a set of instrumental variables for consistent estimation. We use four instruments: (i) the log of the wage rate in the pharmaceutical industry, (ii) the PPI for intermediate goods, (iii) the cumulative stocks of detailing minutes for each of the four firms on all their *other* products (calculated the same way as $MINSTK_{it}$), and (iv) quality-adjusted prices for each of the firms for H_2-antagonist drugs *sold to hospitals.*[10] Note that the first two of these instruments vary only over time, and the second two vary over time and across drugs.

Estimation results are in Table 3. Columns (1) and (2) show the SUR and 3SLS estimates, respectively. A Hausman specification test on the 3SLS estimates fails to reject exogeneity of price and advertising; the test statistic is 6.486 ($p = 0.090$). This failure to reject exogeneity is not due to a problem of using weak instruments. In the first-stage regressions, both individual t-tests and joint F-tests on whether parameters of the overidentifying instruments are zero were decisively rejected. Column (3), our preferred model, is estimated by GMM, with t-statistics based on heteroscedasticity-consistent and ARMA(1,1) serial-correlation-consistent standard errors. The J-statistic used to test the overidentifying restrictions is 16.618; with 10 degrees of freedom (five instruments, including the constant, times three equations, minus five parameters), the p-value is 0.093.

Table 3 also shows price and detailing elasticities computed at the point of means for the 1989–1993 sample period. Focusing on column (3), note that the own-price elasticities are in the range of about –0.3 to –0.6. These elasticities are based on holding the total quantity of H_2-antagonist drugs constant when the price of a single drug changes, i.e., they only reflect

[10] We also used hospital *quantity sales* as an additional instrument, with no change in the results.

TABLE III
ESTIMATES OF EQUILIBRIUM LOGIT MARKET SHARES, 1989-1993

		(Omitted Share is Tagamet, NOBS = 53) (1) SUR	(2) 3SLS	(3) GMM
Intercept–Zantac		0.1983 (10.47)	0.1937 (10.14)	0.2055 (14.89)
Intercept–Pepcid		−0.0817 (−3.33)	−0.0788 (−3.16)	−0.0957 (−4.31)
Intercept–Axid		−1.1067 (−73.38)	−1.1045 (−71.23)	−1.1047 (−87.50)
a_1		−0.2889 (−4.76)	−0.3129 (−4.90)	−0.3442 (−5.91)
a_2		0.7634 (32.08)	0.7697 (31.53)	0.7414 (43.12)
R^2		0.78/0.81/0.96	0.78/0.81/0.96	0.77/0.81/0.96
ϵ_P	Tagamet	−0.385 (−4.757)	−0.417 (−4.897)	−0.459 (−5.908)
	Zantac	−0.250 (−4.757)	−0.271 (−4.897)	−0.298 (−5.908)
	Pepcid	−0.435 (−4.757)	−0.471 (−4.897)	−0.518 (−5.908)
	Axid	−0.485 (−4.757)	−0.525 (−4.897)	−0.577 (−5.908)
ϵ_{MIN}	Tagamet	1.286 (32.078)	1.297 (31.534)	1.249 (43.119)
	Zantac	1.057 (32.078)	1.066 (31.534)	1.027 (43.119)
	Pepcid	0.958 (32.078)	0.966 (31.534)	0.930 (43.119)
	Axid	1.258 (32.078)	1.268 (31.534)	1.222 (43.119)

Note: For models (1) and (2), *t*-statistics (from heteroscedasticity-consistent standard errors) are in parentheses. For model (2), the Hausman test statistic for exogeneity of price and advertising is 6.486 (p = 0.090). For model (3), the *t*-statistics are from heteroscedasticity-consistent and ARMA(1,1) serial-correlation-consistent standard errors; the *J*-statistic for the test of overidentifying restrictions is 16.618, df = 10, p = 0.083. The price and advertising elasticities are computed at the point of means for the 1989–1993 sample period.

substitution within the therapeutic category, so the *total* own-price elasticities will be larger in magnitude. The estimated detailing elasticities are close to unity, which might seem large. After launch ramp-up, the advertising-to-sales ratio for these drugs was about 15 to 20 percent, so even if the own-price elasticities were −1, the advertising elasticity should be about 0.2 if the marginal cost of detailing were constant. (Detailing accounted for about 80 percent of total pharmaceutical marketing.) It is likely, however, that the marginal cost of detailing rises sharply as it becomes increasingly difficult for detailers to get additional minutes of physicians' time, and is much higher than the average cost. This is consistent with our large elasticity estimates.

As can be seen from Table 3, our elasticity estimates are robust to the choice of estimation method. Although not shown in the table, both the price and detailing elasticities are also robust to the monthly depreciation rate used to compute the stock of detailing minutes. Depreciation rates between 2 percent and 8 percent yield very little change in the parameter estimates or the optimized value of the GMM objective function.

Using column (3) from Table 3, we construct fitted values of equilibrium shares for the four drugs. By 'equilibrium shares,' we mean the shares that each of these drugs would have had at any point in time had the market already reached equilibrium. For the months prior to 1989, we generate out-of-sample backcasts of the equilibrium shares. For example, let k denote the number of drugs competing in the market at a point in time. We can write the fitted shares from model (3) in Table 3 as

$$(11)\qquad \hat{s}^*_{it}(k) = \frac{\exp(\delta_{it})}{1 + \sum_{j=1}^{k} \exp(\delta_{jt})}$$

where $\delta_{it} = \hat{a}_{i0} + \hat{a}_1(P_{it} - P_{T,t}) + \hat{a}_2(\text{MINSTK}_{it} - \text{MINSTK}_{T,t})$, and the subscript T denotes Tagamet.

To check our identifying assumption that the last 53 months represents an equilibrium period, we re-estimated the share model over a period that begins six months earlier, and then six months later. The resulting elasticity estimates were essentially unchanged. Also, to test the assumption that the market was in equilibrium during this period, we examined whether the residuals of the demand system exhibited any brand-specific time trends. In a model that also included drug and year effects, we were unable to reject the hypothesis that the brand-specific time trends were individually or jointly equal to zero.

VI. DIFFUSION EQUATIONS

The third component of our model is a set of equations describing the diffusion of the brands as they approach their equilibrium levels. We estimate modified Gompertz equations (9) and (10), using the hedonic quasi-residuals and equilibrium shares described above.[11]

These equations explain the *change* in sales; at issue is how large a time interval this change should represent. In principle, we could estimate a model describing monthly changes in sales. However, it is unclear whether the accounting of sales in the data is free of lags, and there is high-frequency noise due to ordering and stocking decisions by drugstores, so we use three-month changes in sales.[12] Also, we estimate models in which the depreciated stock of past sales (of the brand and the therapeutic category) are in linear and in logarithmic form. Estimation is by NLS, combining the data for the four brands to form an unbalanced panel. The results are shown in Table 4.

Note that individual brand prices affect the average quality-adjusted price for the therapeutic category, $\bar{P}_t$, which in turn affects the industry saturation level. In addition, *relative* prices affect brand saturation levels through the equilibrium shares. Finally, the long-run own-price elasticity for the

[11] We also estimated logistic versions of the model, with little change in the results.

[12] We also estimated the model using one-month and six-month changes. The results using six-month changes are very close to those reported here, but one-month changes yield a worse fit.

therapeutic category is given by the estimated coefficient, b_1, and ranges from –0.3 to –0.9. The total own-price elasticity for each individual brand is

$$E_i^P = \frac{\partial \log s_i^*}{\partial \log P_i} + b_1 \bar{s}_{i4} = a_1(1 - s_i^*)P_i + b_1 \bar{s}_{i4}$$

Likewise, the total detailing elasticity for each individual brand is given by

$$E_i^A = \frac{\partial \log s_i^*}{\partial \log \text{MINSTK}_i} + b_3 \frac{\text{MINSTK}_i}{\text{MINSKTOT}}$$
$$= a_2(1 - s_i^*)\text{MINSTK}_i + b_3 \frac{\text{MINSTK}_i}{\text{MINSKTOT}}$$

Here, $\bar{s}_{i4}$ is the average share of drug i during the period in which all four drugs are present.

In this model, consumption externalities attributable to past sales of the therapeutic category are captured by the coefficient d_0, while those attributable to past sales of the individual brand are captured by d_1. Note that d_1 is positive and significant, while d_0 is insignificant. We infer from this that the effect of past consumption on the rate of product diffusion occurs primarily at the brand level.

TABLE IV
BRAND DIFFUSION EQUATIONS NOBS = 429

Past Sales	(1) XS_{t-3}	(2) $\log[XS_{t-3}]$		(1)	(2)
C_{Tagamet}	0.5307 (1.25)	–2.6602 (–1.76)	**Elasticity Estimates**		
C_{Zantac}	2.6309 (1.46)	–3.1004 (–1.11)	ϵ_P (Tagamet)	–0.7569 (–3.73)	–0.8202 (–2.76)
C_{Pepcid}	4.2109 (1.46)	–2.0477 (–0.68)	ϵ_P (Zantac)	–0.8266 (–2.46)	–0.9388 (–1.84)
C_{Axid}	5.1534 (1.50)	–3.9436 (–1.35)	ϵ_P (Pepcid)	–0.6490 (–5.38)	–0.6770 (–4.39)
d_0	–0.0024 (–1.04)	0.0612 (0.13)	ϵ_P (Axid)	–0.6357 (–6.08)	–0.6483 (–5.73)
d_1	0.0180 (4.04)	1.3585 (4.57)			
b_0	–26.887 (–2.41)	–49.474 (–3.05)	ϵ_{MIN} (Tagamet)	1.3104 (36.74)	1.2794 (28.45)
b_1	–1.0205 (–1.59)	–1.2366 (–1.26)	ϵ_{MIN} (Zantac)	1.1021 (31.48)	1.0639 (21.87)
b_2	5.7040 (2.73)	9.8617 (3.25)	ϵ_{MIN} (Pepcid)	0.9677 (38.60)	0.9487 (31.42)
b_3	0.2182 (2.92)	0.1069 (0.87)	ϵ_{MIN} (Axid)	1.2672 (39.29)	1.2442 (32.65)
R^2	0.293	0.200			

Note: In each model, the consumption externality is $\text{CE}_t = \text{XS}_t$ or $\log[\text{XS}_t]$, and $\text{CE}_{it} = \text{XS}_{it}$ or $\log[\text{XS}_{it}]$. We estimate the following model by nonlinear least squares, using data for the four brands, combined to form an unbalanced panel:

$$X_{it} - X_{it-3} = [\log(\hat{s}_{it}^* X_t^*) - \log X_{it-3}] \cdot \left[C_i + \sum_{k=2}^{12} \theta_k m_{kt} + d_0 \text{CE}_{t-3} + d_1 \text{CE}_{it-3}\right]$$

where $\log X_t^* = b_0 + b_1 \log \bar{P}_t + b_2 \log \text{POP}_t + b_3 \log \text{MINSTKTOT}_t$. The $\hat{s}_{it}^*$'s are the fitted equilibrium market shares from model (3) of Table 4, adjusted to account for the number of competing brands in each of the 4 epochs. The m_{kt}'s are a set of monthly time dummies whose coefficients θ_k are not reported. Numbers in parentheses are t-statistics from heteroscedasticity-consistent standard errors.

Table 4 also shows estimated *total* own-price and detailing elasticities. The price elasticities are on the order of –0.65 to –0.94, and the detailing elasticities are 1 to 1.3. Given that marginal production cost for these antiulcer drugs is very small (about 10 cents to 20 cents per daily dose), we would expect the own-price elasticities to be close to –1 if producers maximize profits, so our estimated price elasticities seem somewhat low. As explained earlier, the large detailing elasticities may reflect a rising marginal cost of detailing.

VII. SIMULATIONS

Simulations of the complete model are used for two purposes. First, in-sample simulations test the model's validity: Using historical values for the attributes, prices, advertising levels, and population, we can solve for all of the other variables endogenously in a dynamic framework, and compare the results to the actual data. Second, we use the model to simulate the effects of alternative strategies for pricing, detailing, and quality improvement.

Because the model is highly nonlinear, the convergence and stability of the simulations are sensitive to initial conditions. To deal with this, we simulate the full model using the actual values of sales for each brand for the first 12 months following the entry of the brand.

Figure 5 shows the simulated and actual sales for all four brands. The simulated series comes from a dynamic simulation in which real prices,

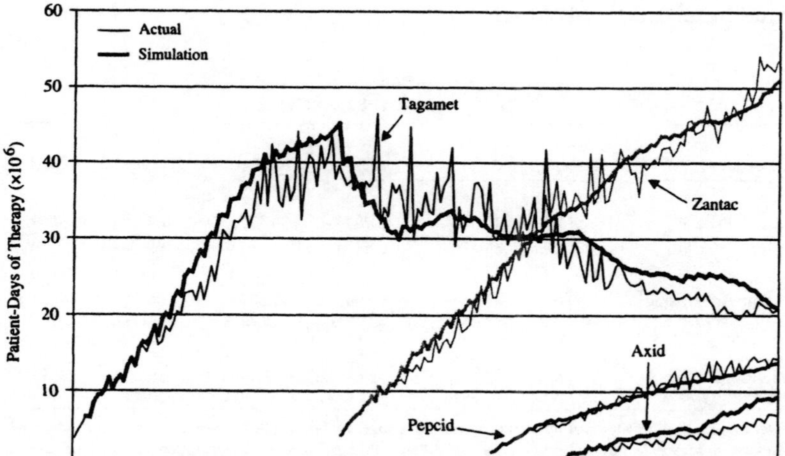

Figure 5
Full Simulation of Brand Sales versus Actual

detailing minutes, attribute levels, and population are exogenous, and all other variables (quality-adjusted prices and average price, equilibrium shares, the industry saturation level, and sales of each brand) are solved for endogenously. Note that overall, the simulated values are very close to the actual values.

We also use the model to simulate three different changes in market conditions:

- We set Zantac's nominal price in each month equal to that of Tagamet.
- We set Zantac's detailing minutes in each month equal to that of Tagamet.
- We reduced d_1, the coefficient in the brand diffusion model that determines the impact of past sales on the rate of growth of current sales, by 50 percent (from 0.018 to 0.009).

The results of these simulations are summarized in Table 5, which shows the change in sales for each brand (the experiment minus the base case) in May 1993, and the resulting change in cumulative profits for Zantac and Tagamet.

Because Zantac had better attributes than Tagamet, setting Zantac's nominal price equal to Tagamet's makes its quality-adjusted price lower than Tagamet's. The result is that Zantac's sales are about 20 percent higher, because its lower quality-adjusted price results in an increase in its equilibrium share. However, the sales of Tagamet, Pepcid, and Axid are also higher than in the base case simulation. The reason is that even though their equilibrium *shares* are lower, the average industry price is now lower, so that the industry saturation level, X_t^*, is higher, which outweighs the equilibrium share reductions.

TABLE V
SIMULATION EXPERIMENTS

	May 1993					
Experiment	ΔX_T	ΔX_Z	ΔX_P	ΔX_A	$\Delta\Sigma\Pi_T$	$\Delta\Sigma\Pi_Z$
(1)						
Zantac Price at	1.5733	10.784	0.7073	0.1710	268.21	−669.6
Tagamet Level	6.87%	22.3%	5.05%	2.79%	5.07%	−11.0%
(2)						
Zantac Advertising	5.8974	−13.548	2.9091	1.0013	306.54	−662.2
at Tagamet Level	26.0%	−27.88%	22.34%	16.25%	5.79%	−10.7%
(3)						
Coefficient d_1	3.5294	−3.5837	−1.6551	−3.1595	−106.12	−882.3
Reduced by 50%	15.7%	−7.39%	−12.8%	−52.9%	−2.02%	−14.4%

Note: ΔX_Z is the difference (absolute and percentage change) in Zantac sales between the experiment and the base case, in May 1993. Similarly, ΔX_T, ΔX_P, and ΔX_A are the differences in Tagamet, Pepcid, and Axid sales in May 1993. $\Delta\Sigma\Pi_Z$ is the aggregate change in gross profit for Zantac under the simulation experiment compared to the base case simulation, and $\Delta\Sigma\Pi_T$ is the aggregate change in gross profit for Tagamet. In Experiment (2), we use an average cost per minute of detailing, which varies from $3.76 in 1983 to $8.09 in 1993, to calculate the savings in reduced advertising expenditures for Zantac.

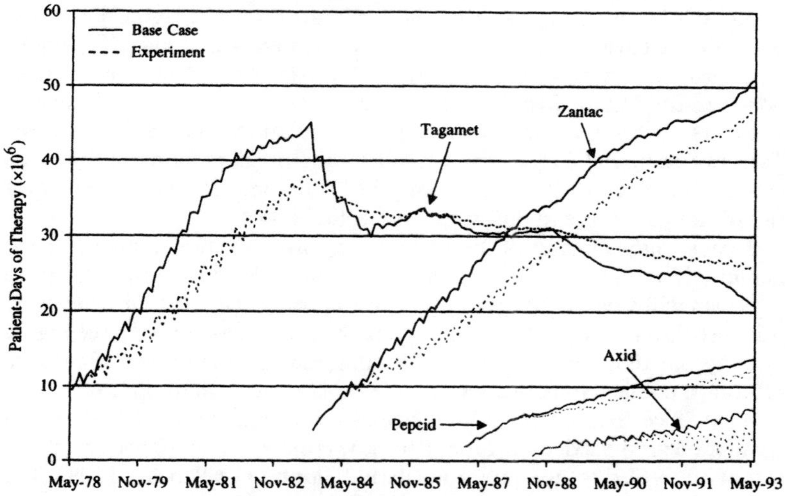

Figure 6
Coefficient d_1 Set Equal to 50 Percent of Estimated Value

Next, we set Zantac's detailing level equal to Tagamet's. Recall that Zantac detailed much more heavily than Tagamet, so in effect we are decreasing Zantac's detailing. The result is that Zantac's sales are much lower by the end of the period, and the sales of Tagamet, Axid, and Pepcid are all higher. This is due to the large estimates (about 1.0) of the advertising elasticities of demand in the equilibrium share model. Table 5 shows the impact on Zantac's cumulative gross profits, ignoring production costs (which are small), but accounting for detailing costs, which are estimated annually from aggregate pharmaceutical industry data.[13] Observe that although Zantac's detailing expenditures drop, its sales drop by so much that its cumulative profits fall by almost $700 million.

Lastly, we evaluate the effect of past sales on the rate of brand diffusion. This effect is captured by the coefficient d_1 in the diffusion equations; note from column (1) of Table 4 that the estimated value for d_1 is 0.0180. We

[13] We used average 'Cost per Call' data, estimated each year for the entire pharmaceutical industry by IMS (IMS, 1996, pp. 7–47 and A-20), from a survey of manufacturers who estimate the cost of keeping a representative 'in the field'—salary, bonus, car, insurance, expenses, training, etc. IMS indicates that, on average, a call involves from two to four 'product details,' i.e., individual products discussed by the sales representative. In addition to the number of detailing minutes for each drug, we have data on the number of details per month for each drug. Aggregating these two series to the level of the H_2-antagonist class and assuming that each 'call' comprises three 'details,' we compute an average annual cost per detailing minute from 1977 to 1993. In 1982 dollars, this average cost increases from $3.28 in 1977 to $8.09 in 1993.

reduce this by half, i.e., to 0.0090. The results are shown in Figure 6. Because past sales of Tagamet now contribute less to the growth of sales, Tagamet's sales grow much more slowly than in the base case. The same is true, however, for Zantac, Pepcid, and Axid. As a result, by late 1984 Tagamet's sales are *higher* than in the base case simulation. As Table 5 shows, Tagamet's cumulative gross profits fall by about $25 million, but Zantac's cumulative gross profits fall by nearly $900 million. Thus past sales play a significant role in brand diffusion and profitability.

Because our estimates of total own-price elasticities are all below one in magnitude (see Table 4), simulations of unilateral or multilateral price increases will yield higher profits. It thus appears that all four firms were pricing below their optimal levels. Although prices rose over time (see Figure 2), why did they not rise faster? Pharmaceutical pricing has often been subject to political pressure, which may explain lower-than-optimal prices.

What if *all* four firms had advertised more than they did? We ran a simulation in which detailing for all firms was increased by 10 percent above actual values during the equilibrium period, January 1989 to April 1993. The cumulative percentage changes in each firm's profits over the 53 months, accounting for the cost of the added detailing, were 0.36 percent for Tagamet, 2.80 percent for Zantac, –4.05 percent for Pepcid, and –2.77 percent for Axid. Much of these differences is due to differences in market shares; note from eqn. (6) that *any* increase in detailing increases the *industry* saturation level, so firms will benefit in proportion to their shares. Part of these differences is due to different detailing elasticities, as shown in Table 4. That is why Pepcid suffers a greater loss in profits than Axid, even though its market share is larger.

VIII. CONCLUSIONS

In order to examine the ways in which consumption externalities influence the demands for prescription drugs, we have estimated a three-stage model of quality-adjusted prices, equilibrium market shares and saturation levels, and rates of brand diffusion. Consumption externalities are captured by introducing the depreciated stock of past sales, for the brand and for the therapeutic class, in both an hedonic price equation and an equation for brand diffusion. The resulting model fits the data well — dynamic simulations yield time paths for brand sales that track the actual time paths very closely. Furthermore, we are able to identify the sources of consumption externalities, and measure their magnitudes.

We find that consumption externalities operate at the brand-specific level. Although statistically significant, their economic importance is mixed. In our hedonic equations, past sales contribute to the value of a brand, but only explain a few percent of that value. However, past sales have an economically significant effect on the rate of diffusion. Our simulations imply that had the magnitude of the effect of past sales been 50 percent smaller, Zantac would have earned $882 million less in gross profits, an amount roughly equivalent to three months of 1992 sales.

These results have important strategic implications. Our hedonic price equations suggest that pioneering firms benefit (in terms of consumer valuation) by being first to market and establishing a large installed base before another firm enters, but that this effect is modest. On the other hand, we find that rates of diffusion can be accelerated by a larger brand-specific installed base. Thus, even if the ultimate saturation level for a second entrant is close to that of a first entrant with similar attributes, the more rapid rate of diffusion can result in much greater profits.

In the case of antiulcer drugs, consumption externalities were not large enough to prevent the second entrant from overcoming the pioneering brand. Our results shed light on Zantac's success. It derived little benefit from the information about H_2-antagonists generated by Tagamet: free-riding from inter-brand consumption externalities is negligible. Instead, delayed entry allowed Glaxo to introduce a product with better quality attributes. This, together with an unusually large amount of detailing, allowed Zantac to overcome the limited first-mover advantage that Tagamet obtained from its installed base of patients.[14]

REFERENCES

Berndt, Ernst R., *The Practice of Econometrics: Classic and Contemporary*, Reading, MA: Addison-Wesley Publishing Company, 1991.

Berndt, Ernst R., Cockburn Iain and Griliches Zvi, 'Pharmaceutical Innovations and Market Dynamics: Tracking Effects on Price Indexes for Antidepressant Drugs,' *Brookings Papers on Economic Activity: Microeconomics* 1996, 133–188.

Berndt, Ernst R., Bui Linda T., Reiley David H. and Urban Glen L., 'The Roles of Marketing, Product Quality, and Price Competition in the Growth and Composition of the U.S. Antiulcer Drug Industry,' in *The Economics of New Goods*, T. Bresnahan and R. Gordon, eds., University of Chicago Press, 1997, 277–322.

Berndt, Ernst R., Bui Linda T., Reiley David H. and Urban Glen L., 'Information, Marketing, and Pricing in the U.S. Antiulcer Drug Market,' *American Economic Review Papers and Proceedings*, May 1995, 85.

Berndt, Ernst R., Pindyck Robert S. and Azoulay Pierre, 'Consumption Externalities and Diffusion in Pharmaceutical Markets: Antiulcer Drugs,' NBER Working Paper No. 7772, June 2000.

Berry, Steven T., Levinsohn James and Ariel Pakes, 'Automobile Prices in Market Equilibrium,' *Econometrica*, 1995, 60(4), 889–917.

[14] Anecdotal evidence suggests that these features are not unique to the antiulcer drug market. In the anti-hypertensive market, for example, Merck introduced its ACE Inhibitor Vasotec later than Bristol Myers-Squibb's pioner, Capoten. As recounted by Werth (1994), p. 58: 'Merck had put scores of chemists on the task of improving [Capoten], then followed up with a withering sales campaign so effective that it ended up beating Squibb in the market even though Capoten was launched first and was much the same drug'.

Bikhchandani, Sushil, Hirshleifer David and Welch Ivo, 'Learning from the Behavior of Others: Conformity, Fads, and Informational Cascades,' *Journal of Economic Perspectives*, Summer 1998, 12, 151–170.

Bond, Ronald S. and Lean David F., *Sales, Promotion, and Product Differentiation in Two Prescription Drug Markets*, Staff Report of the Bureau of Economics of the Federal Trade Commission, February, 1977.

Brynjolfsson, Erik and Kemerer Chris F., 'Network Externalities in Microcomputer Software: An Econometric Analysis of the Spreadsheet Market,' *Management Science*, December 1996, 42, 1627–1647.

Cockburn, Iain and Anis Aslam H., 'Hedonic Analysis of Arthritis Drugs,' Chapter 11 in David M. Cutler and Ernst R. Berndt, eds., *Medical Care Output and Productivity*, Chicago: University of Chicago Press for the National Bureau of Economic Research, 2001, 439–458.

Coleman, James S., Katz Elihu and Menzel Herbert, *Medical Innovation: A Diffusion Study*, Indianapolis: Bobbs-Merrill, 1966.

Ellison, Sara Fisher, Cockburn Iain, Griliches Zvi and Hausman Jerry, 'Characteristics of Demand for Pharmaceutical Products: An Examination of Four Cephalosporins,' *RAND Journal of Economics*, Autumn, 1997, 28, 426–446.

Gandal, Neil, 'Hedonic Price Indexes for Spreadsheets and an Empirical Test for Network Externalities,' *RAND Journal of Economics*, Spring, 1994, **25**, 160–170.

Gandal, Neil, Kende Michael and Rob Rafael, 'The Dynamics of Technological Adoption in Hardware/Software Systems: The Case of Compact Disc Players,' *RAND Journal of Economics*, Spring, 2000, 31, 43–61.

Geroski, P. A., 'Models of Technology Diffusion,' *Research Policy*, 2000, **29**, 603–625

Goolsbee, Austan and Klenow Peter J., 'Evidence on Network and Learning Externalities in the Diffusion of Home Computers,' NBER Working Paper No. 7329, Sept. 1999.

IMS America, *Information Services Manual*, Philadelphia, 1996.

Kessler, Daniel and McClellan Mark, 'Do Doctors Practice Defensive Medicine?' *Quarterly Journal of Economics*, May, 1996, 20, 353–390.

King, Charles III, 'Empirical Studies of Marketing, Product Differentiation, Pricing and Competition,' Ph.D. dissertation, Massachusetts Institute of Technology, June, 1997.

Lu, Z. John and Comanor William S., 'Strategic Pricing of New Pharmaceuticals,' *Review of Economics and Statistics*, February, 1998, 80, 108–118.

Mahajan, Vijay and Muller Eitan, 'Innovation Diffusion and New Product Growth Models in Marketing,' *Journal of Marketing*, Fall, 1979, 43, 55–68.

Mahajan, Vijay, Muller Eitan and Bass Frank M., 'New Product Diffusion Models in Marketing: A Review and Directions for Research,' *Journal of Marketing*, 1990, 54, 1–26.

Scharfstein, David and Stein Jeremy, 'Herd Behavior and Investment,' *American Economic Review*, June, 1990, 80, 465–479.

Suslow, Valerie Y., 'Measuring Quality Change in the Market for Anti-Ulcer Drugs,' Chapter 4 in Robert M. Helms, ed., *Competitive Strategies in the Pharmaceutical Industry*, Washington, DC, American Enterprise Institute: AEI Press, 1996, 49–72.

Temin, Peter, *Taking Your Medicine: Drug Regulation in the United States*, Harvard University Press, 1980.

Werth, Barry, *The Billion-Dollar Molecule*, New York: Simon and Schuster, 1994.

[31]

Journal of Health Economics 29 (2010) 856–865

Contents lists available at ScienceDirect

Journal of Health Economics

journal homepage: www.elsevier.com/locate/econbase

Price and welfare effects of a pharmaceutical substitution reform

David Granlund [a,b,*]

[a] The Swedish Retail Institute (HUI), 103 29 Stockholm, Sweden
[b] Department of Economics, Umeå University, 901 87 Umeå, Sweden

ARTICLE INFO

Article history:
Received 26 April 2009
Received in revised form 26 July 2010
Accepted 6 August 2010
Available online 19 August 2010

JEL classification:
D40
I11
L65

Keywords:
Drugs
Generic competition
Equivalent variation
Demand estimation

ABSTRACT

The price effects of the Swedish pharmaceutical substitution reform are analyzed using data for a panel of all pharmaceutical product sold in Sweden in 1997–2007. The price reduction due to the reform was estimated to average 10% and was found to be significantly larger for brand-name pharmaceuticals than for generics. The results also imply that the reform amplified the effect that generic entry has on brand-name prices by a factor of 10. Results of a demand estimation imply that the price reductions increased total pharmaceutical consumption by 8% and consumer welfare by SEK 2.7 billion annually.

1. Introduction

In October 2002, the Swedish pharmaceutical market was reformed. The reform requires pharmacists to substitute the cheapest available generic (or parallel-imported product) for the prescribed pharmaceutical product in cases when neither the physician nor the consumer opposes substitution. The reform was supposed to lower pharmaceutical costs directly, as prescribed pharmaceuticals were replaced with cheaper versions, and indirectly, through increased price competition. To contain rising pharmaceutical costs, similar reforms have been introduced in many European countries and American states.

The Swedish substitution reform has increased consumers' information about available cheaper substitutes and has made it easier to substitute the prescribed pharmaceutical with a cheaper substitute. It has also increased consumers' copayments for choosing products other than the cheapest version. All of these characteristics of the substitution reform have contributed to making consumers more price sensitive, which, in turn, may have contributed to increased price competition and thus lower pharmaceutical prices.

The main purpose of this paper is to estimate how the Swedish substitution reform has affected pharmaceutical prices, through its effect on price competition. This is done separately for generics, brand-name products that faced generic competition at the time of reform, brand-name products that did not face generic competition at that time, and a group of products belonging to none of these groups (*Others*). Based on this, one can calculate how much more current pharmaceutical consumption would have cost without the reform. Since current pharmaceutical consumption levels would not be the same without the price effects of the reform, this is not a very exact measure of the importance of the reform. I therefore quantify the importance of the reform's price effects in terms of equivalent variation, and to this end, I estimate price and income elasticities for pharmaceuticals. Equivalent variation answers the question of how much consumers would have had to receive in extra income in order to obtain the same utility level without the reform's price effects, as they now obtain with the reform's price effects, and are used as welfare measure in this paper.

Only a few studies have estimated the price effects of substitution reforms. Granlund and Rudholm (2007) estimated that the Swedish substitution reform, in its first 4 years, reduced the unweighted average prices by 4% for both generics and brand-name pharmaceuticals facing generic competition. These results were obtained by using a specification that allowed prices to gradually adjust to the reform. They obtained significantly smaller effects when they estimated a specification without an adjustment process

* Correspondence address: Department of Economics, Umeå University, 901 87 Umeå, Sweden. Tel.: +46 8 7627282; fax: +46 8 6797606.
E-mail address: david.granlund@econ.umu.se.

0167-6296/$ – see front matter © 2010 Elsevier B.V. All rights reserved.
doi:10.1016/j.jhealeco.2010.08.003

and concluded that it was important to account for the adjustment. The results of Granlund and Rudholm, though, cannot be used to estimate savings and welfare effects caused by increased price competition, since the reform effect is likely correlated with product sales values, for which they did not account. Using pharmaceutical price index data from 16 OECD countries, Buzzelli et al. (2006) estimated that substitution reforms lowered pharmaceutical prices by 3%. They did, however, not investigate whether or not prices were gradually adjusted to the reforms.[1] This paper contributes to this literature by, for example, providing the first test of whether or not a substitution reform also affects pharmaceuticals that do not face generic competition.

A few related papers estimate price and income elasticities for pharmaceuticals on an aggregated level; for example, Alexander et al. (1994), that examine how the demand for all pharmaceuticals (and not just a single product or group of products) is affected by changed income and pharmaceutical prices (and not just out-of-pocket costs) on a national level. As discussed by Getzen (2000), elasticities vary with the level of analysis, since elasticities on different levels are affected by partly different decisions. The results of the present paper are therefore not directly comparable to price and income elasticities estimated on a micro-level. The present paper also relates to studies evaluating welfare effects of different reforms, for example Watal (2000) and Chaudhuri et al. (2006), which both estimated the welfare losses caused from enforcing pharmaceutical patents in India.

This paper contributes to the literature analyzing the effect of generic entry on brand-name pharmaceutical prices, by studying how a substitution reform influences this effect. To my knowledge, this has never been studied before. The empirical results in the literature analyzing the price effects of generic entry are mixed. On one hand, Caves et al. (1991) found that the initial entry of generic products led to a reduction in brand-name prices. Similarly, Wiggins and Maness (1994) and Lu and Comanor (1998) found that the number of generic products had a negative effect on brand-name prices. On the other hand, Grabowski and Vernon (1992) and Frank and Salkever (1997) reported that brand-name prices rose in response to generic entry. One explanation of this is that generic entry reduces the own-price elasticity of brand-name products (Frank and Salkever, 1992, 1997). Frank and Salkever (1992) also demonstrated that, if consumers become more price sensitive, under reasonable conditions this will increase the downward pressure exerted by generic entry on brand-name prices.

The next section describes the context and the substitution reform. In section three, I discuss the empirical approach, first, for estimating the reform's effects on prices, and second, regarding the welfare measure and the demand function. Section 3 also contains some descriptive statistics. In Section 4, I present the results of the various estimations and in Section 5 I discuss other possible welfare effects. Finally, the paper's conclusions are presented in Section 6.

2. Swedish pharmaceutical benefits scheme

Subsidies have covered a large part of the pharmaceutical costs for Swedish consumers ever since pharmaceutical benefits scheme was introduced in 1955.[2] Since January 1997, a step-wise copayment structure for pharmaceuticals has been used to limit consumers' pharmaceutical costs. At first, consumers paid all costs up to SEK 400 per 12-month period, 50% of the cost from SEK 400–1200, 25% from SEK 1200–2800, and 10% from SEK 2800–3800; after this level, all costs in the period were covered by subsidies.[3] As of 1 June 1999, all these break-points were increased by SEK 500, but have since remained unchanged.

Before the substitution reform, a reference price system, introduced in January 1993, was in effect. Reference prices were set to 110% of the cheapest available substitute products, and costs exceeding these reference prices were not included in the maximum annual copayment limit (RFFS, 1992:20; RFFS, 1996:31).

2.1. The substitution reform

The substitution reform came into effect on 1 October 2002 and replaced the reference price system. This reform requires pharmacists to inform consumers whether substitute products are available, and that the cheapest available substitute product would be provided within the Swedish pharmaceutical benefits scheme.[4] The pharmacist must also inform consumers that they can buy the prescribed pharmaceutical product instead of the cheapest substitute if they pay the price difference themselves. Finally, the substitution reform requires that pharmacists substitute the cheapest available generic (or parallel-imported product) for the prescribed pharmaceutical product in cases when neither the prescribing physician prohibits the substitution for medical reasons, nor the consumer chooses to pay the price difference between the prescribed and the generic alternative. In cases where the physician prohibits the substitution for medical reasons, the consumer is still reimbursed.

Three characteristics of the substitution reform may have contributed to making consumers more price sensitive, which in turn has resulted in more generic substitution and lower pharmaceutical prices. First, the substitution reform lowered the transaction cost of generic substitution, since before the substitution reform it was recommended that the physicians be contacted before substituting products if they had not explicitly consented to substitution on the prescriptions. Second, when substitution is presented as an option (as it always should be after the substitution reform) consumers gain information about that cheaper substitutes exist and can easily gain information also about price differences between the pharmaceutical substitutes. Finally, under the substitution reform, only costs up to 100% of the cheapest substitutable product were contained by the pharmaceutical benefit scheme, compared with 110% in the reference price system. This increased the consumer's out-of-pocket costs for choosing to buy the prescribed pharmaceutical by 0–10% of the price of the cheapest generic version, depending on the patient's copayment rate.

According to a theoretical model presented by Granlund and Rudholm (2007), the substitution reform likely has a greater effect on prices for brands that face generic competition than for generics. The intuition is that, while the fact that the substitution reform made consumers more cross-price sensitive works for lower prices in both product groups, the substitution reform also increases the demand for generics at the expense of the demand for brand-name products, which likely reduces the incentives for generics to lower

[1] The National Corporation of Swedish Pharmacies et al. (2003, 2004) aimed to assess the savings due to increased price competition, but did not account for expiring patents or price-trends in their reports and based their estimates on a non-representative sample consisting of the substances with the largest sales values.

[2] The sources used in this section are SFS (1981):49 and the government bills dealing with changes in this law. These bills are listed at www.notisum.se/rnp/sls/fakta/a9810049.htm, 30 October 2008.

[3] All monetary values in this paper (except those regarding copayments cited in this section) are deflated by the CPI and expressed in 2007 prices. The average exchange rates in 2007 were USD/SEK = 6.76 and EUR/SEK = 9.25 (the Riksbank).

[4] The Swedish Medical Products Agency defines a product as a substitute if it has the same active substance, strength, and form (e.g. pills or oral fluid) as the prescribed product, and if its package sizes can approximately sum up to the prescribed quantity.

their prices but increases the likelihood of price cuts for brand-names.

Brand-name products without generic competition are likely affected less by the substitution reform than other brands, but should still be affected. At least some of these products are substitutes for pharmaceuticals subject to generic competition and hence face lower demand as the prices of these pharmaceuticals drop, which – depending on the shape of their demand functions – might cause price cuts. Patent-protected pharmaceuticals might also be directly affected by the substitution reform, since many of them face competition from cheaper parallel-imported pharmaceuticals.

The prices in the *Others* group, consisting, for example, of vitamins and/or minerals, is expected to be affected relatively little by the substitution reform, since few of these products have what the Swedish Medical Products Agency considers to be close substitutes.

2.2. Price setting and distribution

Throughout the study period, for a pharmaceutical to be included in the benefits scheme, its price had to be authorized, before October 2002 by the National Social Insurance Board and thereafter by the Pharmaceutical Benefits Board. It was easier for pharmaceutical firms to get Pharmaceutical Benefits Board approvals of price reductions than price increases, except if the new price did not exceed the price of the most expensive exchangeable product.[5] This fact, together with pharmaceutical firms' incomplete information about the reactions of physicians, consumers and other pharmaceutical firms to the substitution reform, gave firms an incentive to adjust their prices gradually after the substitution reform of October 2002. Since the exception means that most generics could increase their prices as easy as they could reduce them, one might expect fastest price adjustments for generics; but, since their brand-competitors likely will not adjust their price immediately, neither will the generics.

Throughout the study period, pharmaceuticals were sold through a nationwide government owned monopoly, the National Corporation of Swedish Pharmacies, which paid and charged uniform prices nationwide for each pharmaceutical product.

3. Methods and materials

3.1. Estimating the substitution reform's effects on prices

The substitution reform's effects on prices are estimated using monthly data, from January 1997 through October 2007, provided by IMS Sweden for all pharmaceuticals sold in Sweden. The reform effects were estimated separately for *Generics*,[6] brand-name pharmaceuticals that faced generic competition at the time of reform (*BrandC*),[7] brand-name pharmaceuticals that did not face generic competition at that time (*BrandM*), and a group of products belonging to none of these groups (*Others*), using the following specification:

$$\ln Price_{it} = \beta_1 D_t + \beta_2 \left[\frac{D_t}{(t-R)^{\mu}} \right] + \beta_3 GC_{it} + \beta_4 Trend_t + \theta_i + \varepsilon_{it}. \quad \text{(R1)}$$

The dependent variable is the natural logarithm of the price per package paid by the National Corporation of Swedish Pharmacies, and thus charged by the pharmaceutical companies, for product i in month t. Product refers to the most detailed observation unit: for example, if a brand and a generic firm market two package sizes each of the same pharmaceutical, they are treated as four separate products even if the two firms' package sizes are the same.

D is an indicator variable taking the value of one after the substitution reform, that is, in October 2002 and thereafter. $D/(t-R)$, where $t-R$ is the number of months from the reform time, is included to capture the adjustment process. Here, the parameter μ measures the curvature of the adjustment process.

GC_{it} is a dummy that takes the value of 1 from the first month product i faces generic competition and is only included for the two brand-name populations. By comparing the GC_{it} coefficient between the two brand populations, I can examine how the substitution reform has affected the price effect of generic competition.[8]

A trend variable (*Trend*) is included to account for possible common price trends. Finally, product-specific fixed effects (θ_i) are included. These capture all the time-invariant differences in price levels between pharmaceutical products and thus make it possible to use the natural logarithm of the price per package as the dependent variable.

By letting the prices adjust gradually to the substitution reform, the estimation approach used here follows Granlund and Rudholm (2007). The specification assumes that the potential price adjustment was largest directly after the substitution reform and gradually decreased as time passed. This is a logical assumption, since pharmaceutical firms' knowledge of physicians', consumers' and other pharmaceutical firms' reactions to the substitution reform likely increased fastest directly after the substitution reform when the knowledge level was lowest. However, it is difficult to make any a priori assumptions about the speed of this process, so μ is allowed to be determined by the data.

This specification of the adjustment is likely to give good estimates of the substitution reform effects in the study period. It is, however, unsuitable for out-of-sample predictions (at least, for predictions into the far future), since the specification assumes that – unless the adjustment is instantaneous (i.e., $\beta_2 = 0$) – the adjustment will continue indefinitely. An alternate approach sometimes used in reform evaluations is to let the trend slope change with the reform. This is reasonable when evaluating reforms that might indeed change the trend slope, but when considering a reform like that examined here, which presumably will result in a new long-term price level but not a new long-term price trend, the risk of this approach is that it will ascribe price changes unrelated to the substitution reform, to the reform effect.[9]

[5] The Pharmaceutical Benefits Board is required to decide whether to approve price cuts as soon as possible, but is allowed 90 days (or under some circumstances 150 days) to handle applications for price increase (SFS, 2002:687). Firms must justify price increases, but not price reductions. Also, the Pharmaceutical Benefits Board is restrictive in allowing price increases and only allows an increase if special reasons exist (LFNFS, 2003:1).

[6] The generics group also includes so-called branded generics. Branded generics are generic versions of the pharmaceutical product which are sold under their own product name, while other generics are sold under the substance name, usually followed by the company name.

[7] A product is defined as facing generic competition if at least one generic or branded generic has the same active substance, strength, and form (e.g. pills or oral fluid) as the product. Since, for example, a product comprising 20 pills can be replaced by two packages of 10 pills each, a brand-name product is defined as facing generic competition even if its package size differs from that of its generic competitors.

[8] Generic competition directly followed expiring patent on many products which suggests that much of the variation in GC_{it} is exogenous in the sense that it is explained by expiring patents rather than price changes of the brand-name products. In the absence of strong, truly exogenous instruments, it is preferable to treat this variable as exogenous rather than employing an instrumental variable method.

[9] These changes could be caused, for example, by the introduction of new pharmaceuticals that lower the demand for pharmaceutical for which they are substitutes and by changes in pharmaceutical markets in other countries (e.g., regarding price-controls).

As mentioned above, the break-points in the pharmaceutical benefits scheme were increased by SEK 500 in June 1999. One might expect that this would have made consumers more price sensitive by increasing their copayment rates, which, in turn, might have encouraged pharmaceutical firms to lower their prices. However, due to the construction of Swedish pharmaceutical benefits scheme and due to the skewed distribution of consumers' pharmaceutical consumption, most of the pharmaceuticals were bought by consumers who, regardless of this increase, had zero marginal cost for pharmaceuticals.[10] Therefore, this change likely had, at most, minor effects on prices. Estimations including controls for the increased break-points, and for delayed responses to this increase and to the benefits scheme changes of January 1997, indicated no price effects and gave only marginally different results for the parameters of interest, so these results are not reported.

Letting the parameter estimates differ between the four pharmaceutical groups will improve the efficiency of the estimators, if these groups are differently affected by the substitution reform, and makes it possible to test, for example, whether the substitution reform also affected the prices of pharmaceuticals for which there are no generic substitutes. To do this by splitting the population, instead of by using interaction variables, keeps the models non-linear in only one variable – the adjustment variable $D/(t-R)$ – which allows the specification to be easily estimated using a grid-search estimation strategy. This method is employed for each model by setting μ equal to values ranging from 0 to 5 and then estimating the remaining parameters using a Prais–Winsten estimator that corrects for first-order serial correlation in the error terms. Finally, likelihood values were used to discriminate between the different parameter values. The likelihood values were also used to calculate 95% confidence intervals for the adjustment parameter, μ.

In all estimations, the observations are assigned weights that equal the products' total sales values in the study period; if the reform effects are correlated with sales values, this is necessary when estimating how the substitution reform affected the pharmaceutical price levels. As for price indexes, there are several alternate sets of weights that can be used, so I have reported the results obtained also when using pre-reform sales as weights.

3.2. Demand and welfare estimation

Hausman (1981) demonstrated that knowledge of the uncompensated (i.e., the Marshallian) demand function is all that is needed to establish an exact measure of the welfare effects caused by changed prices. The welfare effects can be expressed either in terms of compensating variation (CV) or, as here, in terms of equivalent variation (EV).

In this context, the EV formula derived by Hausman is written:

$$\mathrm{EV} = -\left\{ \frac{(1-\gamma_2)}{(1+\gamma_1)I^{\gamma_2}} [p_{ref} Q(P_{ref}, I) - P_{alt} Q(P_{alt}, I)] + I^{(1-\gamma 2)} \right\}^{1/(1-\gamma_2)} + I,$$

where γ_1 is the price elasticity of demand and γ_2 is the income elasticity of demand, both of which must be estimated. P_{ref} is the index for pharmacies' selling prices of pharmaceuticals, and P_{alt} is given by $P_{alt} = P_{ref}(1 - ARE)$. *ARE* is short for the average reform effect and is obtained by weighting together the predicted reform effects for the four pharmaceutical groups. The difference between the coefficient of GC_{it} after and before the substitution reform in October 2002 is treated as part of the reform effects. Finally, Q(.) is the predicted annual pharmaceutical demand at various price levels and I is annual income.

If both the price and the income elasticity equal zero, the EV measures equal the extra amount that consumption after the substitution reform would have cost without the price-lowering effect of the substitution reform. Since P_{ref} is an index for the full prices of pharmaceuticals, and not only the out-of-pocket prices paid by the consumers, the EV will measure the welfare effects of the price cuts for the whole consumer-side of the market, both directly for the consumers and for the insurers. The cost of the pharmaceutical benefits scheme is still paid for by the consumers – in the Swedish case, by income taxes – but the distinction is still important if, for example, one wishes to consider the distributional effects of the substitution reform.

Bear in mind that the reform effects are estimated using the pharmacies' purchase prices. Nevertheless, I have still chosen to use the pharmacies' selling prices in the EV measures and in estimating the price elasticity (γ_1). The justification is that pharmaceutical demand is most closely related to the selling prices. If the pharmacies' margins are affected by the substitution reform, however, the choice may cause an inconsistency in the EV measures. As reported in Section 4, the Pharmaceutical Benefits Board has allowed increased margins because the substitution reform has increased pharmacies' costs. However, it is impossible to know whether some of these increases would have been allowed in any case, even without the substitution reform, and then justified on other grounds. In Section 4, I therefore focus on the EV measures obtained by assuming that margins were unaffected by the substitution reform, but also report EV measures obtained by adjusting the average reform effect (*ARE*) in line with the margin changes justified by the substitution reform.

Since I want to calculate the EV for the substitution reform that has affected the entire pharmaceutical market, and not just the prices of a few drugs, the price and income elasticity should be estimated on an aggregated level.[11] Since the elasticities might differ between countries, the estimation should preferably be done using Swedish data. As mentioned above, no cross-sectional variation in pharmaceutical prices was allowed in Sweden in the study period, implying that the demand function (or at least the price elasticity) must be identified using only variation over time. As discussed below, several difficulties are associated with this, so I will also calculate the EV measures based on demand estimates made for other countries.

The uncompensated pharmaceutical demand in Sweden are estimated using aggregated quarterly data provided by the National Corporation of Swedish Pharmacies, the Riksbank, and Statistics Sweden. The estimations are preformed using the following two specifications:

$$\Delta \ln Q_t = \alpha + \gamma_1 \Delta \ln P_t + \gamma_2 \Delta \ln I_t + \gamma_3 \Delta Trend_t + \sum_{q=2}^{4} \theta_q \Delta Quarter_{qt} + \gamma_4 \Delta Hoard_t + \varepsilon_t, \qquad \text{(D1)}$$

[10] Data from the county of Västerbotten show that 54–61% of the pharmaceuticals in 2000 were bought by consumers, who had reached the new highest break-point of the insurance before, or on, the current purchasing occasion. Since at the time of purchasing, consumers are on average approximately 6 months into the 12-month insurance period, a higher share than this had a marginal cost of zero after the reform as well.

[11] Deriving the price elasticity of aggregated consumption from demand estimates based on product level data is unfeasible since it would require the estimation of all relevant cross-price elasticities between the nearly 15,000 pharmaceutical products.

$$\ln Q_t = \alpha + \gamma_1 \ln P_t + \gamma_2 \ln I_t + \gamma_3 Trend_t + \sum_{q=2}^{4} \theta_q Quarter_{qt} + \gamma_4 Hoard_t + \gamma_5 \ln Q_{t-1} + \gamma_6 \ln Q_{t-4} + \varepsilon_t, \quad (D2)$$

where both are inspired by a specification in Alexander et al. (1994). Q_t is defined as the pharmacies' total purchase of pharmaceuticals in quarter t, measured in SEK per 1000 inhabitants and working day, and divided by an index for pharmacies' purchase prices. P_t is the index for pharmacies' selling prices of pharmaceuticals and I is GDP per capita in SEK 1000. *ln* indicates that the natural logarithms of the variables are used and Δ indicates that the first differences of the variables are used (e.g., $\Delta \ln Q_t = \ln Q_t - \ln Q_{t-1}$). A trend variable is included and complemented by three quarter-dummies, since Andersson et al. (2007) report that there are seasonal variations in the sales values of pharmaceuticals.[12]

The variable *Hoard* is included to capture the hoarding that is observed in the quarters before increases in the patients' copayment shares and the corresponding decline in sales in the quarters directly after the changes. For a quarter after changed rules that increased patients' copayment shares, *Hoard* equals the percentage increase in the consumer price index for pharmaceuticals compared with the preceding quarter; *Hoard* equals the negative value of that increase for a quarter preceding such a change and 0 otherwise. Hence, the parameter for this variable will estimate the demand shift between subsequent quarters induced by stockpiling. When calculating the consumer price index for pharmaceuticals, Statistics Sweden ignores the fact that the consumers' copayment shares are decreasing functions of pharmaceutical prices. The effects of changed pharmaceutical prices on consumer prices are therefore exaggerated in the consumer price index for pharmaceuticals. This might result in some measurement error of *Hoard* and more severe measurement errors in the index itself, so it is not included in the specifications.

According to Dickey–Fuller tests, it cannot be rejected that the time series $\ln Q$, $\ln P$ and $\ln I$ have unit roots. Since this non-stationarity might result in spurious regression it should be addressed. In this paper, two alternate approaches, each with different flaws and merits, are used to address non-stationarity. The first is to make a first-difference transformation, specification (1), and the second is to include lagged vales of pharmaceutical consumption, specification (2). The choice to include the first and fourth lags ($\ln Q_{t-1}$ and $\ln Q_{t-4}$) is based on the Akaike information criterion (Greene, 2003, Chapter 8).

Both specifications ensure that the error terms are stationary and that the results are therefore not spurious. The first specification addresses the non-stationarity of all variables and is suitable for estimating short-term effects. However, if $\ln P$ is endogenous, this approach is difficult to use since it is inherently hard to find strong instruments for the first-difference of $\ln P$. Regarding the second specification, it should be noted that the coefficients for lagged consumption can easily capture the effects of omitted variables and therefore should not be interpreted as estimates of persistency in pharmaceutical consumption. Hence, the long-term effects cannot be estimated using this specification.[13] Due to the auto-regressive processes of $\ln P$ and $\ln I$, there is also a risk that some of the effects of these variables will be attributed to the coefficients for lagged pharmaceutical consumption. A conclusion that can be drawn from this discussion is that the second specification is useful in investigating whether or not $\ln P$ is endogenous, but if $\ln P$ is not endogenous, or only weakly so, the first specification is preferable.

Endogeneity has been discussed previously in this context. For example, Reekie (1978) assumed that sellers of pharmaceuticals set prices each period and offer to sell indefinitely large amounts at that price in the period, arguing that prices are therefore determined largely by non-demand-related factors and thus can be treated as exogenous. It should, however, be noted that even if prices are predetermined, as they are on the Swedish market, demand expectations might play a role in the price setting, which might cause some endogeneity problems.

The specifications are estimated using both OLS and IV estimators and the error terms are allowed to be correlated within calendar years. In the IV estimations, $\ln P$ is instrumented with its second and fourth lag and with the first and second lag of the variable $\ln TCW$. *TCW* is the total competitiveness weights index, which measures the value of the Swedish crown (SEK) against a basket of other currencies. The lags of $\ln TCW$ are included as instruments mainly to capture the sharp declines in the value of the Swedish crown that occurred when it was devaluated in September 1981 (−10%) and October 1982 (−16%) and when Sweden abandoned the fixed exchange rate in November 1992, which resulted in a depreciation of approximately 21% within 3 months. These events were likely unexpected when pharmaceutical prices were set and therefore likely caused price changes. Several other instruments, and combination of instruments, have also been tested. The choice of instrument-set is based on the Kleibergen–Paap weak identification statistic, which measures the strength of the instruments, and the Hansen J statistic, which tests the validity of the instruments.

3.3. Descriptive statistics

Table 1 presents descriptive statistics for the variables used when estimating the reform effects on prices. The means of ln *Price* are not easily comparable between the four groups since they represent the prices of very heterogeneous products. Still, it is not surprising to find the highest average in the *BrandM* population, consisting of brand-name pharmaceuticals that did not face generic competition 1 October 2002 when the substitution reform came into effect.

Table 1
Weighted means of variables used in the price estimations.

Variable	*Generics*	*BrandC*	*BrandM*	*Others*
ln *Price*	4.56	5.22	6.80	5.79
D	0.52	0.46	0.53	0.50
GC	0.00	0.81	0.04	0.00
Trend	69.80	65.01	70.91	68.23
Observations	228 730	83 462	405 086	152 708
Products	4232	989	6267	3216
Market share	0.13	0.09	0.65	0.13

Note: The products' total sales values in the study period are used as weights.

[12] The main differences between these specifications and the one in Alexander et al. (1994) are that I do not take the natural logarithm of the trend variable, since this would mean that the percentage change in the pharmaceutical consumption is assumed to decline with time, and that I either make a first-difference transformation or include lagged consumption. I have also estimated a specification similar to that of Alexander et al., and then obtained results similar to theirs, but concluded that the results likely were spurious, since statistical tests suggested that the included time series were non-stationary and not cointegrated.

[13] I have tried to estimate long-term elasticities using error-correction models, but failed to obtain reliable estimates, likely because $\ln Q$, $\ln P$ and $\ln I$ are not cointegrated; at least a residual-based test provides no support for cointegration.

Table 2
Means of variables used in the demand estimations.

Variable	Level	First-difference
ln *Q*	3.34	0.02
ln *P*	5.35	−0.01
ln *I*	4.12	0.00
Trend	56.5	1.00
Hoard	0.00	0.00
ln *TCW*	4.71	0.00
Observations	112	111

Note: No data are missing, so 25% of the observations are from each quarter.

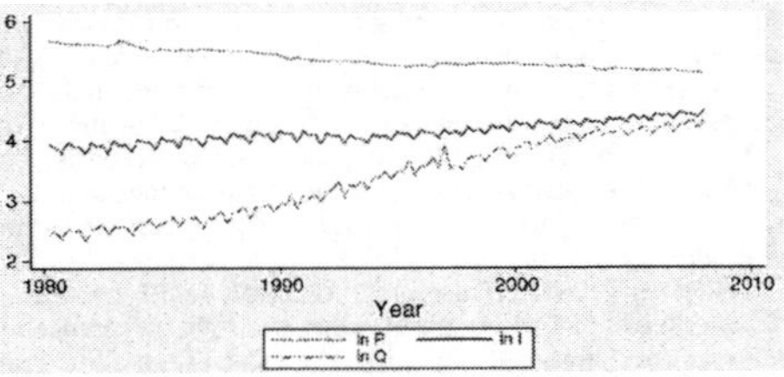

Fig. 1. Depictions of three time series used in the demand estimations.

In the *BrandM* population 810 of the 6267 products gained generic competition at some time after the substitution reform, but Table 1 shows that the weighted frequency of observations facing competition is only 4%. In the *BrandC* population, consisting of brand-name pharmaceuticals that faced generic competition at the time of reform, 364 of the 989 products gained generic competition first after the beginning of the study period, but the weighted frequency of observations without competition is only 19%. The market shares show that *BrandM* is by far the most important population in terms of sales values.Descriptive statistics for the variables used in the demand specifications are given in Table 2. Fig. 1 illustrates how the three main variables have changed over time, indicating, for example, that there is seasonal variation in both GDP per capita and the purchase of pharmaceuticals.

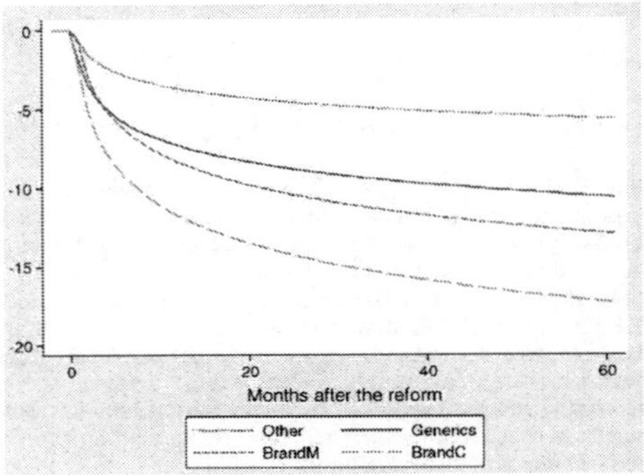

Fig. 2. Estimated reform effects.

4. Results

4.1. Estimated reform effects

Table 3 first reports the predicted instantaneous effect of the substitution reform (Ref_{inst}), the mean reform effect for October 2002 through October 2007 (Ref_{mean}), and the reform effect as of the last month of the study period (Ref_{end}). These three all express the percentage effects the substitution reform has had on pharmaceutical prices in each population. Ref_{inst} equals $100 * \exp(\beta_1 + \beta_2) - 1]$ and does not depend on μ, since $t - R$ takes the value of one in the first month of the substitution reform (October 2002), while Ref_{mean} and Ref_{end} are calculated also using the estimates of μ in accordance with specification (R1). The substitution reform effects at different points in time are also illustrated in Fig. 2.

The estimates of Ref_{mean} indicate that the substitution reform has had significant effects on the prices in all pharmaceutical groups in the study period. The largest relative price cut, 14%, is found in the population of brands that faced generic competition at the time of the substitution reform (*BrandC*); the second largest amounts to 10% and is found for brands that lacked generic competition at that time (*BrandM*). A comparison of the estimates

Table 3
Estimation results, percentage effect on prices.

	Generics	*BrandC*	*BrandM*	*Others*
Ref_{inst} (β_2, μ)	−1.98**	−2.45**	−0.76**	−0.62**
	(−2.32:−1.65)	(−2.72:−2.17)	(−0.96:−0.57)	(−0.80:−0.43)
Ref_{mean} (β_1, β_2, μ)	−8.72**	−13.97**	−10.26**	−4.52**
	(−9.83:−7.62)	(−14.86:−13.08)	(−10.83:−9.68)	(−5.17:−3.86)
Ref_{end} (β_1, β_2, μ)	−11.22**	−17.31**	−12.95**	−5.68**
	(−11.99:−9.23)	(−18.41:−16.20)	(−13.66:−12.23)	(−6.50:−4.85)
GC (β_3)		−0.45*	−4.78**	
		(−0.81:−0.10)	(−5.22:−4.35)	
$Trend$ (β_4)	0.15**	0.33**	0.21**	0.62**
	(0.13:0.18)	(0.25:0.42)	(0.20:0.23)	(0.59:0.64)
$D/(t-R)$ (μ)	2.9^{-4}**	2.3^{-4}**	1.5^{-4}**	2.3^{-4}**
	(0.0<:8.5^{-3})	(0.0<:7.0^{-3})	(0.0<:1.4^{-3})	(0.0<:6.0^{-3})
Observations	224,498	82,472	398,800	149,490
Products	4191	988	6236	3175
Log likelihood	273,402	155,962	572,372	298,956

Notes: The products' total sales values in the study period are used as weights.
Robust 95% confidence intervals are shown in parentheses. The confidence intervals for μ are ot symmetrical, which is expected, since a value of μ equaling zero leads to an empirical model here the adjustment variable equals the reform indicator variable.

* Significance at 5% levels.

** Significance at 1% levels.

Table 4
Estimation results for pharmaceutical demand, multiplied by 100.

	Specification D1	Specification D2	
	OLS (first-diff.)	OLS	IV
$\ln P$	−75.83**	−32.86*	−35.23*
	(−130.51:−21.15)	(−57.56:−8.16.)	(−64.71:−5.75.)
$\ln I$	45.49*	8.14	10.11
	(8.75:82.24)	(−28.39:44.66)	(−23.23:43.45)
Trend#	1.08*	−0.10	−0.14
	(0.18:1.98)	(−0.55:0.35)	(−0.61:0.34)
$Quarter_2$	4.01**	3.11**	3.04**
	(2.40:5.64)	(1.05:5.17)	(1.20:4.87)
$Quarter_3$	−7.36**	−9.69**	−9.46**
	(−11.50:−3.23)	(−14.27:−5.11)	(−13.81:−5.11)
$Quarter_4$	−2.60	6.34**	6.23**
	(−5.47:0.27)	(2.20:10.47)	(2.85:9.61)
Hoard	−0.30**	−0.52**	−0.53**
	(−0.50:−0.10)	(−0.84:−0.21)	(−0.82:0.24)
$\ln Q_{t-1}$		59.99**	60.23**
		(47.94:72.05)	(48.95:71.51)
$\ln Q_{t-4}$		35.09**	35.48**
		(25.42:44.76)	(26.51:44.46)
Observations	111	108	108
AIC	−341.58	−365.48	−365.45
R^2	0.8642	0.9955	0.9955
Kleibergen–Paap			30.32
Hansen J (*P*-value)			0.22

Notes: Robust 95% confidence intervals are shown in parentheses.
Note that *Trend* only becomes a constant in the first-difference specification.
* Significance at 5% percent levels.
** Significance at 1% percent levels.

for *GC* in these two populations reveals another reform effect: the price effect of getting generic competition goes from being merely −0.45% before the substitution reform to −4.78% after the substitution reform. Together, these results for brand-name pharmaceuticals indicate that the eventual reform effect for those brands that gained generic competition sometime after the substitution reform is similar in size to the effect for those that faced generic competition before the substitution reform.

The lowest estimated average reform effect is −5% for *Others* while the estimated average reform effect is −9% for *Genercs*. Using the market shares from Table 1 as weights, the average reform effect over the four pharmaceutical groups is −9.87% (95% CI −10.29:−9.45) or −9.66% (95% CI −10.07:−9.24) when the effect on *GC* is not included.

The results also clearly indicate that the pharmaceutical firms had not fully adjusted their prices to the substitution reform already by October 2002: for the different populations, the instantaneous price cuts were 1–2%, compared with declines of 6–17% by the end of the study period. This conclusion is also strengthened by the fact that both β_2 and μ differ significantly from zero. As expected, the results indicate that the adjustment was fastest for Generics.

The estimates for μ assume values below 0.001 in all populations which results in correlations between D and $D/(t-R)\mu$ of above 0.99. Due to these high correlations, the estimates for β_1 and β_2 should not be interpreted separately and are therefore not reported. Fortunately, these high correlations do not affect the reliability of the joint effect of D and $D/(t-R)\mu$ within the study period (Verbeek, 2008, Chapter 2). The estimates of Ref_{inst}, Ref_{mean}, and Ref_{end} as well as the predictions depicted in Fig. 2 are thus still reliable and retain small confidence intervals despite these correlations.

The time trend estimate is positive in all populations and largest for *Others*. When the products' pre-reform sales values are used as weights, instead of the sales values for the entire study period, Ref_{mean} shrinks in absolute size for Generics and for *BrandM* to −6.86% and −9.31%, while it increases in absolute size to −15.89% for *BrandM* and to −5.91% for *Others*. In total, the weighted average reform effect is reduced in absolute size by half a percentage point.[14]

4.2. Estimated demand and welfare effects

The first column of Table 4 presents the OLS results for specification (1) (the first-difference), while the second and third columns present the OLS and IV results for specification (2). No strong and valid instruments are found for $\Delta \ln P$, so the IV results for the first-difference specification are not reported.

Let us start by noting that the estimates obtained using specification (1) differ quite substantially from those obtained using specification (2). This is expected, since the estimates of specification (1) describe how changes in the independent variable affect the change in demand, while the estimates of specification (2) – given the high coefficients for lagged consumption – more or less describe how the level of the independent variable affects the change in demand. As discussed above, the coefficients for lagged consumption can easily capture the effects of omitted variables and should therefore not be interpreted as estimates of persistence in pharmaceutical consumption.

The OLS and IV estimates for specification (2) differ less from each other. If prices are endogenous, one would expect the OLS estimate in the second column to be larger than the IV estimate

[14] The weighted average reform effect is considerably larger when using a specification that allows the slope of the time trend to change at the time of the substitution reform. There is, however, reason to believe that this specification is inappropriate. Quite apart from the reasons mentioned previously in the text, the results obtained using this specification cast doubt on its validity. For example, the results for brands indicate that the reform effect is of the same size irrespective of whether or not the product faces generic competition.

for ln *P* Table 4 shows that this is the case, but the difference is quite small and not statistically significant. The difference might still indicate that there is an endogeneity problem, but the problem seems small in relation to the problem caused by including lagged consumption. Therefore, I view the results for specification (1) as the most reliable ones, and will focus my discussion on these estimates.

The price and income elasticity estimates for specification (1) are both significantly different from zero and have the expected signs, indicating that consumption decreases with prices but increases with income. The results for specification (1) also indicate a considerable seasonal variation, and growth over time, in pharmaceutical demand. The estimate of −0.003 for the variable *Horad* suggests that a change in pharmaceutical benefits scheme that increases consumer prices for pharmaceuticals by 10% is preceded by a temporary increase of 3% in the demand.

Based on the estimated reform effects one can calculate that, without the price-lowering effect of the substitution reform, Sweden's pharmaceutical consumption after the substitution reform would have cost on average SEK 2.80 billion more per year in the study period. This can be compared with total Swedish pharmaceutical sales that averaged SEK 25.50 billions during this period, but this is not a very exact measure of the importance of the substitution reform, since the pharmaceutical consumption would have been lower without the price-lowering effect of the substitution reform.

A better measure is equivalent variation (EV). Using the price and income elasticities of specification (1), the average annual EV measure in the study period is estimated to be SEK 2.68 billion. The increase in welfare is estimated to be SEK 1.80 billion in 2003 and SEK 3.30 billion in 2006. Using a real discount rate of 3%, the present value in 2002 of the welfare effects for October 2002 through October 2007 amounts to SEK 12.42 billion.

Since the estimates reported in Table 4 are not very robust, I have also calculated the EV measures using other values for the price and income elasticities. Zero is a logical upper bound for the price elasticity and gives a present value of the welfare effects of SEK 12.96 billion. Economic theory provides no natural lower bound for the price elasticity; instead I report that the present value becomes SEK 12.05 billion when the price elasticity is set to −1.31 (the lower limit of the 95% confidence interval of specification (1)), and SEK 10.86 billion when it is set to −3.25 (the estimate reported by Alexander et al.).[15] The EV measures are only marginally affected by the income elasticity: if the income elasticity is set to 1.55 (the estimate reported by Alexander et al.), the present value remains at SEK 12.42 billion, and if it is set to 0 it becomes SEK 0.01 billion higher.

The welfare estimate reported above measures the value for the whole consumer-side of the market, both directly for the consumers and for the insurers. That the estimated price elasticity is above −1 implies that the substitution reform has reduced pharmaceutical expenditures. The average reduction for October 2002 through October 2007 is 2.5% and the present value of the reduced expenditures amounts to SEK 3.00 billion. In this period, approximately 75% of the pharmaceutical expenditures were paid by the insurer (the National Corporation of Swedish Pharmacies). This means that the insurers' costs have decreased by approximately SEK 2.25 billion (75% of the SEK 3.00 billion, actually somewhat more than this due to the non-linear construction of Swedish pharmaceutical benefits scheme), meaning that approximately SEK 10 billion of the discounted welfare improvement accrues directly to the consumers.

In view of increased costs due to the substitution reform, the Pharmaceutical Benefits Board allowed the National Corporation of Swedish Pharmacies to increase its annual margins by SEK 56 million in 2003, and by an additionally SEK 20 million in 2006 (National Corporation of Swedish Pharmacies, 2003; Pharmaceutical Benefits Board, 2005). If the estimated average reform effect is adjusted for these increases, the estimated average annual EV measure shrinks from SEK 2.68 billion to SEK 2.62 billion and the discounted welfare effect goes from SEK 12.42 billion to SEK 12.15 billion.

5. Other welfare effects

The substitution reform of October 2002 of course has other welfare effects besides those on the consumer-side in the form of reduced prices. Below, I briefly discuss other important welfare effects, though it is beyond the scope of this paper to provide estimates of these.

The substitution of cheaper versions for prescribed pharmaceuticals has not only led to increased price competition but also to direct savings. A rough estimate of these savings is SEK 0.6 billion per year.[16] There are, however, reasons not to consider the entire savings as constituting a welfare improvement for consumers. Andersson et al. (2005) and Granlund and Rudholm (2008) reported that significant shares of Swedish consumers refused substitution and paid extra to get the prescribed instead of the generic (or parallel-imported) pharmaceutical, indicating that they viewed the substitutes as inferior. Similarly, the Medical Products Agency (2004) reports that some consumers feel generic substitutes are less effective than brand-name pharmaceuticals; generic substitution might therefore affect patient willingness to follow physician recommendations. Generic substitution might also increase the risk that some consumers confuse different drugs.

Since the substitution reform has made consumers and physicians more familiar to generic pharmaceuticals, it might have affected physicians' prescribing pattern. Generic substitution might also have increased the costs for the Pharmaceutical Benefits Board, which must make more decisions regarding price changes, and for physicians, who might have to answer questions about generic substitution from their patients.[17]

The total producer surplus of the pharmaceutical firms has clearly been reduced by the substitution reform: the revenues have declined and the costs have increased due to higher quantities. Some generic producers have likely benefited from the substitution reform due to increased market shares, while the profits of brand-name producers have been affected most negatively. Generic substitution also reduces the expected profits arising from new pharmaceuticals and thus the incentive to invest in research

[15] I share the opinion of Alexander et al., who found their estimate on −3.25 very surprising. If pharmaceutical products are substitutes for each other, the own-price elasticity of individual products should be below that of pharmaceuticals as a group. This, in combination with pharmaceutical firms' high mark-ups over marginal cost, suggests that a price elasticity of −3.25 is not in accordance with the behavior of well-informed profit-maximizing pharmaceutical firms: such an elastic demand suggests that the firms could raise profits by reducing prices. For example, if the price elasticity of a firm's products is −3, a price cut of 1% would increase revenues by nearly 2%. If the marginal costs are constant, this would raise the variable costs by 3% and thus increase the firms profit if the variable costs are <2/3 of the revenues.

[16] This estimate is obtained by extrapolating to the whole of Sweden from data for the county of Västerbotten for January 2003–October 2006; see Granlund (2009) for a description of this data. The National Corporation of Swedish Pharmacies et al. (2003) estimated these savings to be SEK 0.5 billion based on national data for the first 6 months after the reform.

[17] Andersson et al. (2006) investigated physicians' opinions on and experiences of the Swedish substitution reform.

and development. However, since the Swedish pharmaceutical market is small from a global perspective, this effect is also small.

6. Discussion

In this paper, the Swedish substitution reform was estimated to have reduced the average price of pharmaceuticals during October 2002 through October 2007 by 10%. The reform effect was found to be significantly greater for brand-name than for generic products. The results also suggest that the substitution reform amplified the effect of generic entry on brand-name prices by a factor of 10. This in turn has contributed to the reform effect being of similar size for brand-name products, irrespective of whether a product gained generic competition before or after the substitution reform.

The results confirm the conclusion of Granlund and Rudholm (2007), that pharmaceutical firms gradually adjusted their prices after the substitution reform, and that prices of generics were reduced less than those of brands that faced generic competition is in accordance with their theoretical predictions. The estimated reform effects reported here, however, were significantly larger than those obtained by Granlund and Rudholm. One important explanation is that the observations here were weighted to obtain estimates of welfare effects due to increased price competition. This paper also differs from Granlund and Rudholm (2007) by, for example, studying the effects on all pharmaceutical products sold in Sweden, by using longer time series, and by studying the effect on the prices charged by the pharmaceutical firms, instead of those charged by the pharmacies.

The reform effects reported here are also considerably larger than those that Buzzelli et al. (2006) estimated for 16 OECD countries. This difference could be because the Swedish substitution reform was more successful in reducing prices than were the substitution reforms of the other 15 countries Buzzelli et al. studied. The difference could also be because I, unlike them, used a specification that allowed for gradual price adjustments after the substitution reform.

The results of this paper support the theoretical predictions of Frank and Salkever (1992) by indicating that the effect of generic competition changes significantly when consumers become more price sensitive, as they did with the Swedish substitution reform. How a substitution reform influences the effects of generic entry has, to my knowledge, never been tested before.

The price elasticity was estimated to −0.76, which is more negative than most price elasticities for pharmaceuticals reported in the literature, but not directly comparable to many of those, since they measure the elasticities of pharmaceutical demand with respect to out-of-pocket prices for pharmaceuticals. If physicians' prescribing behavior is also affected by the costs to the insurers, this reduces the effect that changed copayments have on pharmaceutical demand. The price elasticity estimate is, however, considerably less negative than that reported by Alexander et al. (1994). The income elasticity of 0.45 indicates that pharmaceutical consumption is a necessity in the short run. This can be compared with the long-term estimate reported by Alexander et al. (1994) and those summarized by Getzen (2000), indicating that pharmaceuticals and healthcare on a national level are a luxuries. One explanation of these differences is that pharmaceutical demand reacts slowly to changes in income. The estimations of the demand for pharmaceuticals were, however, troubled by the non-stationarity of the key variables, so these elasticity estimates should be interpreted with caution. Fortunately, the welfare estimates expressed in equivalent variation are not very sensitive with respect to price and income elasticities, so the present value of the welfare effects remains between SEK 12 and 13 billion for reasonable values of the elasticities.

To conclude, this paper has demonstrated that the substitution reform has reduced pharmaceutical prices considerably. Even though more research is needed into other consequences of the substitution reform, the substitution reform has likely been welfare improving from a Swedish perspective. The result may differ from a global perspective, since most brand-name producers are located outside Sweden and since consumers all over the world are affected by reduced incentives for pharmaceutical research and development.

Acknowledgements

I am grateful to Kenneth Carling, Reza Mortazavi, Niklas Rudholm, two anonymous reviewers and participants in seminars at Dalarna and Örebro Universities and participants at the Swedish Workshop on Competition Research in 2009 for their helpful comments and suggestions, and to the Swedish Competition Authority for a research grant that supported the work. I wrote most of this paper while I was a guest researcher at Dalarna University and whish to thank them for their hospitality. I also wish to thank IMS Sweden, the National Corporation of Swedish Pharmacies, the Riksbank and Statistics Sweden for providing the datasets.

References

Alexander, D.L., Flynn, J.E., Linkins, L.A., 1994. Estimates of the demand for ethical pharmaceutical drugs across countries and time. Applied Economics 26, 821–826.

Andersson, K., Sonesson, C., Petzold, M., Carlsten, A., Lönnroth, K., 2005. 2005 What are the obstacles to generic substitution? An assessment of the behaviour of prescribers patients and pharmacies during the first year of generic substitution in Sweden. Pharmacoepidemiology and Drug Safety 14, 341–348.

Andersson, K., Jörgensen, T., Carlsten, A., 2006. Physicians' opinions and experiences of the Pharmaceutical Benefits Reform. Scandinavian Journal of Public Health 34, 654–659.

Andersson, K., Bergström, G., Petzold, M.G., Carlsten, A., 2007. Impact of a generic substitution reform on patients' and society's expenditure for pharmaceuticals. Health Policy 81, 376–384.

Buzzelli, C., Kangasharju, A., Linnosmaa, I., Valtonen, H., 2006. Impact of generic substitution on pharmaceutical prices and expenditures in OECD countries. Journal of Pharmaceutical Finance Economics and Policy 15, 41–62.

Caves, R.E., Whinston, M.D., Hurwitz, M.A., 1991. Patent expiration, entry and competition in the U.S. pharmaceutical industry: an exploratory analysis, Brookings Paper of Economic Activity, Microeconomics, pp. 1–66.

Chaudhuri, S., Goldberg, P.K., Jia, P., 2006. Estimating the effects of global patent protection in pharmaceuticals: a case study of quinolones in India. American Economic Review 96, 1477–1514.

Frank, R.G., Salkever, D.S., 1992. Pricing, patent loss and the market for pharmaceuticals. Southern Economic Journal 59, 165–179.

Frank, R.G., Salkever, D.S., 1997. Generic entry and pricing of pharmaceuticals. Journal of Economics and Management Strategy 6, 75–90.

Getzen, TE, 2000. healthcare is an individual necessity and a national luxury: applying multilevel decision models to the analysis of healthcare expenditures. Journal of Health Economics 19, 259–270.

Grabowski, H.G., Vernon, J.M., 1992. Brand Loyalty, entry and price competition in pharmaceuticals after the 1984 drug act. Journal of Law and Economics 35, 331–350.

Granlund, D, 2009. Are private physicians more likely to veto generic substitution of prescribed pharmaceuticals? Social Science and Medicine 69, 1643–1650.

Granlund, D., Rudholm, N., 2007. Consumer information and pharmaceutical prices: theory and evidence, Umeå Economic Studies 709, Umeå University. Forthcoming in Oxford Bulletin of Economics and Statistics.

Granlund, D., Rudholm, N., 2008. Consumer loyalty in the Swedish pharmaceutical market, Umeå Economic Studies 742, Umeå University.

Greene, W.H., 2003. Econometric Analysis, 5th ed. Prentice Hall, New York.

Hausman, J., 1981. Exact consumer's surplus and deadweight loss. American Economic Review 71, 662–676.

Lu, Z.J., Comanor, W.S., 1998. Strategic pricing of new pharmaceuticals. Review of Economics and Statistics 80, 108–118.

LFNFS, 2003:1. Läkemedelsförmå nsnämndens föreskrifter om ansökan och beslut hos Läkemedelsförmå nsnämnden [The Pharmaceutical Benefits Board's regulations about application and decisions at the Pharmaceutical Benefits Board] (in Swedish).

Medical Products Agency, 2004. Biverkningsrapporter i samband med utbyte av läkemedel [Reports of side-effects in connection with exchange of pharmaceuticals]. Stockholm (in Swedish).

National Corporation of Swedish Pharmacies, 2003. Bokslutskommuniké 2002 [Annual report communiqué 2002]. Stockholm (in Swedish).
National Corporation of Swedish Pharmacies, The Federation of Swedish County Councils, The Pharmaceutical Benefits Board, 2003. Utbyte av läkemedel – En uppföljning av de första sex må naderna med den nya reformen [Substitution of pharmaceuticals – the first 6 months with the new reform]. Stockholm (in Swedish).
National Corporation of Swedish Pharmacies, The Federation of Swedish County Councils, The Pharmaceutical Benefits Board, 2004. Utbyte av läkemedel – En uppföljning av de första 15 må naderna med läkemedelsreformen [Substitution of pharmaceuticals – the first 15 months of the substitution reform]. Stockholm (in Swedish).
Pharmaceutical Benefits Board, 2005. Höjd marginal för apoteket [Increased margins for the Pharmacy]. Stockholm (in Swedish).
Reekie, W.D., 1978. Price and quality competition in the United States drug industry. Journal of Industrial Economics 26, 223–237.
RFFS, 1992:20. Riksförsäkringsverkets föreskrifter om fastställande av pris på läkemedel [The National Social Insurance Board's regulations for establishing prices for pharmaceuticals]. (in Swedish).
RFFS. 1996:31. Riksförsäkringsverkets föreskrifter om fastställande av pris på läkemedel m.m. [The National Social Insurance Board's regulations for establishing prices for pharmaceuticals etc.] (in Swedish).
SFS, 1981:49. Lag om begränsning av läkemedelskostnader, m.m. [Law (1981:49) concerning limitations of pharmaceutical costs, etc.] (in Swedish).
SFS, 2002:687. Förordning om läkemedelsförmå ner m.m. [Ordinance (2002:687) on Pharmaceutical Benefits, etc.] (in Swedish).
Watal, J., 2000. Pharmaceutical patents, prices and welfare losses: policy options for India under the WTO TRIPS agreement. World Economy 23, 5–21.
Verbeek, M, 2008. Modern Econometrics, 3rd ed. John Wiley and Sons Ltd., West Sussex.
Wiggins, S.N., Maness, R., 1994. Price competition in pharmaceutical markets. Department of Economics, Texas A&M University. Unpublished manscript.

[32]

HEALTH ECONOMICS
Health Econ. **16**: 653–665 (2007)
Published online in Wiley InterScience (www.interscience.wiley.com). DOI: 10.1002/hec.1263

IF IT AIN'T BROKE, DON'T PRICE FIX IT: THE OFT AND THE PPRS

ADRIAN TOWSE*
Office of Health Economics, London, UK

SUMMARY

The Office of Fair Trading (OFT) Report on the UK Pharmaceutical Price Regulation Scheme (PPRS) recommends that when the current five-year PPRS expires in 2010 it be replaced with 'value-based pricing' which involves pre-launch centralised government price setting based on a cost-per-QALY threshold plus periodic *ex post* reviews. I examine the validity of the OFTs criticisms of the existing PPRS, review its proposals and propose an alternative way forward. I conclude that PPRS has performed well as a procurement bargain between industry and the UK government. It does not, however, incentivise efficient *relative* prices. That is not its job. I identify a number of problems with the OFT proposals. I recommend that key elements of a reformed UK pharmaceutical environment for 2010 should include an expanded role for HTA but with companies retaining freedom to set prices at launch; HTA use targeted via a contingent value of information approach; a retained backstop PPRS, perhaps moving to an RPI-X type control; the use of risk sharing and non-linear pricing arrangements; measures to ensure more effective therapeutic switching at local level; and measures to improve the take up of cost-effective treatments.

Received 9 May 2007; Accepted 25 May 2007

KEY WORDS: regulation; pharmaceuticals; cost-effectiveness; profit control; value of information

One of the UK's two competition bodies, the Office of Fair Trading (OFT), has produced over 1000 pages of analysis of the UK Pharmaceutical Price Regulation Scheme (PPRS) in an 18-month 'market study' (OFT, 2007a). The study is one of a number in public procurement (DotEcon, 2004). It examines whether the PPRS is effective in meeting its high-level objectives, or whether there is a case for reform (para 1.2). Another key objective for the OFT was to improve the terms of debate about '*pharmaceutical pricing and reimbursement, not just in the UK, but internationally*' (para 1.16). The OFT concludes that more regulation is needed because there are demand side problems in the NHS, not because of an absence of competition on the supply side. This case for regulation is therefore very different from that found in regulated activities in economic sectors such as communications, energy, transport and water where lack of competitive supply is the problem.

The OFT proposes the abandonment of the 50-year-old PPRS in 2010 in favour of a new regime of government 'product-by-product' price setting based on 'value' which it claims will incentivise companies to undertake R&D to find the cost-effective treatments NHS patients need. It sounds promising but is the OFT analysis accurate and is there any 'beef' in these proposals? A number of questions arise which can be grouped into the following:

- What are we trying to achieve?
- Is the 'old' PPRS failing to do this?
- Will the OFT's proposals help?
- Given the answers to these questions, what is the way forward?

*Correspondence to: Office of Health Economics, 12 Whitehall, London SW1A 2DY, UK. E-mail: atowse@ohe.org

WHAT ARE WE TRYING TO ACHIEVE?

Health-care systems and their pricing and reimbursement systems (which typically focus on input price and recommendations for or against the use of specific medicines in some or all groups of patients) should be trying to achieve two things from the use of pharmaceuticals:

- an efficient use of the medicines currently available – static efficiency. This involves addressing questions such as:
    - are the prices 'right', i.e. do they reflect opportunity costs?
    - given prices and budgets, are pharmaceuticals being used within a condition or patient group in the most cost-effective way, i.e. are we achieving productive efficiency?
    - are we treating the conditions and patients that society most cares about, i.e. given input prices and cost-effectiveness are we achieving allocative efficiency? For those who believe a QALY is a QALY there is no distinction between productive and allocative efficiency; for the rest of us this matters.
- to stimulate the development of new cost-effective medicines – dynamic efficiency. This requires a combination of:
    - revenues (i.e. price multiplied by volume) for current medicines that send the appropriate signals about the revenues the system is willing to spend on valuable new treatments;
    - any other incentives (or disincentives) to compensate for any under- or overpayment through the pricing and reimbursement system.

Estimating the cost of R&D is a particular problem for pharmaceuticals because of high failure rates, long development times (10–12 years) and the global joint sunk cost characteristics of R&D. Not only is there a large divergence between short-run marginal costs (Philipson and Jena, 2005) and long-run marginal costs for individual drugs, it is necessary to account for the resource cost of failures and early development work that was not product specific (DiMasi *et al.*, 2003). Revenues from individual drugs tend therefore to bear little relation to their short-run costs and returns are highly skewed (Grabowski *et al.*, 2002). From a societal perspective what matters is the ability of companies to achieve *ex post* returns on product portfolios where social value exceeds social cost, or for enough companies to keep believing *ex ante* that they will achieve a return on socially useful R&D investments.

More controversial issues are: (1) the role if any that P&R systems should play in trying to attract pharmaceutical industry investment to a specific location; and (2) the extent to which it is appropriate to reward innovation *per se*.

IS THE 'OLD' PPRS FAILING?

Context

The UK government does not set drug prices or (with a few exceptions) dictate use via positive or negative lists. It uses indirect methods. The PPRS acts as a constraint on branded drug prices and profits. Local prescribers informed by HTA seek to maximise health outcomes given local budgets. In recent years, new HTA institutions (the National Institute for Health and Clinical Excellence (NICE), the Scottish Medicines Consortium (SMC) and the All Wales Medicines Strategy Group (AWMSG)) have been put in place to provide strong direction on the cost-effective use of drugs and (in the case of NICE) other technologies. However, there is often slow take up of technologies that are recommended for use. There are high rates of generic prescribing and a strong competitive generics industry.

DOI: 10.1002/hec

The PPRS is a unique scheme both in the realm of pharmaceutical price regulation and more generally of government regulation and procurement. The objectives of the scheme (DoH, 2004) are to:

- secure the provision of safe and effective medicines for the NHS at reasonable prices;
- promote a strong and profitable pharmaceutical industry capable of such sustained research and development expenditure as should lead to the future availability of new and improved medicines; and
- encourage the efficient and competitive development and supply of medicines to pharmaceutical markets in this and other countries.

The PPRS is an agreement negotiated every 5 years between industry and government, within a statutory framework. It includes periodic price cuts. The last one-off price cut (part of the 2005 Scheme) was 7%. Key elements are:

1. A profit cap with banded upper (lower) rates of return to provide for paybacks and price cuts (increases).
2. Price freedom for NCEs at launch followed by a price freeze, i.e. once set the price cannot be increased in nominal terms. This means NHS prescribers can begin using the product as soon as the company launches it following licensing approval.
3. Price modulation, which allows companies to increase the prices of some products provided they reduce the prices of others such that the expected overall volume-weighted revenue is the same. (This enables companies with product portfolios to adjust to competitive circumstances – i.e. their revenues would otherwise be falling – at cost neutrality to the NHS.)

Theoretical problems

It is thus a hybrid scheme combining a profit cap and a price control. It is easy for economists to dislike it – and many do. The major theoretical problems are:

1. Return on capital (profit cap) regulation can lead to inefficiency around the allowable rate of return and the treatment of costs.
   (a) There is an incentive to overinvest ('gold plate') capital if the return offered exceeds the cost of capital (Averch and Johnson, 1962). But the PPRS regulates accounting rates of profit, not economic rates of return, (Edwards *et al.*, 1987). As R&D is not capitalised but expensed, the largest asset of the industry does not appear on the balance sheet. The accounting rate of profit *needs* to be above the economic return. It cannot be assumed (as the OFT implies) that the 21% accounting rate of profit is above the cost of capital.
   (b) Any rate of return set is an average. Different R&D projects will in reality have different (systematic and hence undiversifiable) risks. This may reflect the science, the chances of successful commercialisation or the stage at which the project is at – 'operational gearing' (Myers, 1999). The OFT argues that an average return encourages low-risk, low-value product investment. This ignores the impact of competition and of HTA as I discuss below.
   (c) There is a danger of 'cost plus', as costs are allowed before profit. However, as the OFT notes the PPRS uses a combination of allowances not related to actual spend and costs that the DH can disallow. It benchmarks companies against each other in a form of yardstick competition (Shliefer, 1985). OXERA modelled the potential impact on accounting and economic returns of different levels of costs and allowances, and treatments of R&D (OFT, 2007b). It found some offsetting effects which suggests that the DH and industry are well aware of the 'swings and roundabouts' when they negotiate.

DOI: 10.1002/hec

2. Regulating an industry with joint costs in only one of its geographical markets produces cost allocation issues (verification of costs and of allocations). The OFT identifies particular issues around the treatment of transfer pricing. These clearly need to be tackled.
3. Danger of 'regulatory capture' i.e. the DH is too close to the industry to do its job properly. The OFT does not explicitly address this, but it looks at component parts which might include:
   (a) There is not enough challenge. The OFT does not suggest this – and indeed congratulates the DH on its application of the Scheme.
   (b) DH is compromised by its desire to keep UK investment – I return to this.
   (c) The profit cap does not bite – to a large part reflecting the issue with transfer pricing referred to above. The OFT assumes that because no company has been in 'payback' since 2005 this means that the cap is ineffective. The reverse could also be the true – a desire to avoid profit cap penalties influences pricing behaviour or another binding constraint (e.g. the impact of HTA on new product pricing) means the profit cap is providing a 'backstop'.
   (d) Overall UK price levels. The OFT implies that UK brand prices are high. The DH figures for 2005 (in the OFT Report) show the UK as the fourth highest out of 10 EU countries. (These figures exclude Sweden which has brand prices above the UK derived from an HTA process the OFT supports.) The OFT ignores the key driver of relative prices identified by the DH – exchange rate movements. A recalculation of the 2005 numbers using the Treasury-commissioned estimate of a sterling/euro equilibrium exchange rate of 1.37 euros to the £ (Wren-Lewis, 2003) puts the UK as the eighth lowest out of the 10 EU countries. This makes sense. A combination of parallel trade and restrictions on UK price increases after launch means companies set UK launch prices with a view to expected euro/£ exchange rates over the lifetime of the product. We are also yet to assess the impact of UK HTA on UK relative prices. Recent work (Danzon and Furukawa, 2006) on biological drug prices concludes '*that prices for biologics are relatively low in the United Kingdom...*'
4. Modulation links markets. A company competing in more than one market could 'cross subsidise' price at the expense of companies competing in only one. However, existing competition law protects companies from predatory pricing by competitors, irrespective of PPRS rules.

Nature of competition for innovation

The OFT argues that in the UK, companies choose to bring 'me too' type products to the NHS market because they are low risk and get an excessive reward under the PPRS. This reflects a misunderstanding of the R&D process and implies that the PPRS somehow guarantees a return irrespective of the quality of the product – which it does not. R&D processes have changed. There is plenty of R&D-based competition with many new entrants into the R&D process (Cockburn, 2004). Evidence shows potential market size has a direct impact on drug and vaccine development (Acemoglu and Linn, 2003; Finkelstein, 2003; Lichtenberg and Walsfogel, 2003). Scientific advances in the understanding of disease mechanisms now lead to several companies competing to find ways of exploiting that knowledge. Competition in translational research is stimulated by advances in basic research. This can lead to several products getting to a new therapy market shortly after one another. This change is reflected in the reduced time between the first and the subsequent entrants (Towse and Leighton, 1999).

DiMasi and Paquette (2004) found that by the time the first-in-class product enters most 'follow-on' products are already in late stages of clinical development. They concluded that '*The development histories of entrants to new drug classes suggest that development races better characterise new drug development than does a model of post hoc imitation. Thus, the usual distinctions drawn between breakthrough and 'me-too' drugs may not be very meaningful.*' A science-driven competitive process leads

DOI: 10.1002/hec

to companies seeking breakthrough products but often ending up with *de facto* 'me toos.' These drugs do, however, provide value to payers and to patients through one or more of: competing in the provision of information; competing on price; or competing for different sub-groups of patients within the disease area (Wertheimer *et al.*, 2001; OHE, 2005). Of course this requires a 'demand side' that sends the right signals and is able to exploit these effects.

Attracting investment

The OFT argues that the PPRS has not been effective in attracting R&D and manufacturing investment as '*the scheme does not contain any systematic incentives to locate investments within the UK.*' (para 3.35), and any attempt to incorporate such goals would 'be contrary to EC legislation' (para 3.70). This is not a new finding – the EU Commission, other Member State governments and companies have all been through the wording of the Scheme to check this.

Is it legitimate to use a P&R regime to attract investment? Will it be successful? Claxton has argued it is not legitimate (Claxton, 2007). It is not obvious why this is the case. Government procurement often has an industrial policy objective. Industrial policy is often misguided – witness 50 plus years of intervention in the UK motor industry – but in pharmaceuticals it has assisted the UK in getting 10% of global R&D investment with only 3% of global sales. It could be argued that any industrial policy funding should be identified separately, and not come out of the health budget. There is a case for this in principle. But when the P&R climate influences investment this is difficult.

The OFT concludes that it will not be successful in practice. Only the science base and clinical research infrastructure matter. It does not recognise the 'intangible' value of the PPRS. The long-term 'sunk' nature of pharmaceutical investment means that there are opportunities for governments as buyers to behave opportunistically. The stability of the PPRS reinforces the reputation of the UK government as not prone to opportunistic 'hold up' of the pharmaceutical industry once it has sunk costs into R&D and the UK economy. Most R&D investment is 'footloose.' There are other places it could go. For rational reasons, companies will seek to avoid rewarding countries with regulatory regimes that have policy instability, or attempt free riding on R&D, provided it does not cost them (the companies) too much. When good science can be found in more than one country the business environment will become a factor in investment location (NERA, forthcoming).

Relative prices

The OFT sees the central problem with the PPRS as being no mechanism for ensuring that relative prices reflect value – '*neither the profit cap nor the price cut helps to secure prices that reflect the therapeutic value of the drugs...to the NHS.*' This is true – assessing value is done elsewhere in the system – although not well according to the OFT.

The reality is that the PPRS has performed well as a procurement bargain between industry and the UK government. It does not incentivise efficient *relative* prices. That is not its job. Will the OFT's proposals tackle this efficiently?

WILL THE OFT'S PROPOSALS HELP?

The OFT proposes that when the current five-year PPRS expires in 2010, government and industry work towards a new one replacing profit control with a version of something it calls 'value-based pricing' (VBP), which involves *ex ante* centralised government price setting based on a cost-per-QALY threshold plus periodic *ex post* reviews. More specifically the OFT proposes:

1. All new products are subject to a NICE/SMC/AWMSG *ex ante* review, i.e. before launch. The review identifies appropriate prices given evidence on expected costs and effects and an agreed cost-per-QALY threshold.

DOI: 10.1002/hec

2. Prices are set by the Department of Health on the basis of this review. At a later stage the OFT envisage the HTA and pricing roles would be combined in a new independent UK-wide body.
3. When a therapy class has significant new evidence, a new entrant, or a patent expiry, a new review is conducted and prices adjusted accordingly.
4. Prices can go down or up as a consequence of the review.
5. At a patent expiry of product A:
   (a) The price of the originator brand of A is reduced automatically to 25% above the price of generic versions of A.
   (b) The prices of competing brands (B, C) go down to 50% above the generic price of A, unless they can show advantages over drug A.
6. The use of risk sharing and non linear pricing agreements to help set the right prices.
7. Continuation of the PPRS as a negotiated 5-year agreement in order to maintain stability, albeit with the existing profit cap/price control arrangements replaced by an agreed VBP framework (reflecting (1)–(6) above) including a cost-per-QALY threshold.
8. A fixed drug budget.

The OFT also considers a purely *ex post* version of VBP, in which companies are free to set prices subject to post-launch reviews at which point the government adjusts prices. It rejected this option because it anticipates poor take up of products by the NHS in the absence of a review at launch.

I have a number of concerns about the OFT's recommendations.

What is value-based pricing?

Prices need to reflect appropriate resource costs. In normal markets companies set prices to maximise profits. The prices customers are prepared to pay reflect the value to them. The marginal group of customers pays prices more or less equal to the value they receive. Intramarginal customers gain consumer surplus. Companies remain in the market in the long run if all costs are covered. Investment takes place if *ex ante* revenues are expected to provide a return that takes account of the risk associated with the project. Competition reduces prices towards costs. How close prices get to costs depends on the degree of competition which in part depends on product differentiation. Products with unique attributes can command premium prices – limited by consumer willingness to pay for these attributes given where else they can spend their money. In this sense, it is hard to think of prices not reflecting value for very long. Customers will walk away.

In the case of pharmaceuticals, the NHS provides insurance cover to patients. There are principal–agency problems. Patient demand will tend to be inelastic. They are not paying. Prescribers have budgets and so should look for value to exceed or equal price. HTA is intended to provide a payer assessment of cost-effectiveness, i.e. of NHS willingness to pay. The real issue is how NHS medicine markets should *adjust* to bring price and value into line, i.e. through price or through volume or a combination. The OFT assumes adjustment should or can only take place through price. If prices do not reflect value at current volumes, it assumes prices rather than volumes are wrong.

Demand side failures

As the OFT recognises '*The PPRS works in conjunction with a wide range of mechanisms and institutions designed to encourage cost effective prescribing at local and national level.*' The problem is that the OFT thinks these mechanisms do not work. Hence, it sets out an agenda that replaces them with central price setting. GPs can carry on handing out the pills but no one expects them to have any responsibility for getting value for money. The OFT's main plank of evidence is a GP survey of 1000 GPs testing their awareness of the relative prices of medicines within six major therapeutic groups. It found that '*GP's ability to rank branded drugs in order of price proved to be no better than chance.*' (Box 2.3 and Annexe C). This is quite consistent with previous studies on the subject (DH/ABPI, 2002; Ryan *et al.*, 1992, 1996; Silcock *et al.*, 1997) and while discouraging does not, contrary to OFT's evident belief, prove a lack of price sensitivity on the demand side of the NHS medicines market. English GPs are influenced in their prescribing by NICE, practice formularies and Primary Care Trust (PCT) advisers, among other factors. As long as someone with influence in this process understands cost-effectiveness it is unnecessary for individual GPs to be price aware.

Of course the demand side is a long way from working as well as it needs to. The NAO (2007) Report on prescribing identified the characteristics of PCTs that had been successful in pursuing value for money prescribing. The OFT is right to point out that centralisation of HTA reduces duplication of effort and provides scale economies. But local awareness of value for money remains essential for three reasons:

- HTA recommendations are implemented locally. Prescribing volumes have to adjust up or down. UK take up of new medicines identified by NICE as cost-effective is slow. The OFT, unfortunately, has nothing to say on the take up of products that are recommended under its VBP system. Cooksey (2006) proposes the use of 'Knowledge Transfer' teams within the NHS to speed uptake of cost-effective technologies. Adelphi Consulting (2006) in its work on take up for the MISG identified what successful PCTs did.
- Central guidance cannot cover everything. Even if it did local choices still have to be made. There will not be enough money in the budget to do everything that is deemed cost-effective or necessary by the centre. Hence, the debate over the relevant cost-effectiveness threshold to use (Culyer *et al.*, 2007) and renewed interest in Programme Budgeting techniques to help understand efficient choice at the (local) margin.
- Centralisation can lead to information loss (local experience of the product, local priorities and opportunity cost in terms of the projects given up to fund central decisions are unknown or ignored) with consequential errors.

The OFT implies that an inefficient demand side is wasting money. It states '*we identified over £500m of expenditure in 2005 that could have been put to more cost effective uses. For one drug alone we estimate that the use of more value-reflective prices could potentially have saved £350million in that year*' (page 4). Yet the OFT knew at the time of writing (February 2007) that the savings from substituting use of generic simvastatin in the place of Lipitor were much lower. NHS statin prescribing had become more efficient through national (incentivised) targets following NICE guidance in January 2006, a subsequent BMJ editorial, and more aggressive PCT pursuit of generic substitution. The NHS was driving a search for savings that was not dependent on increased knowledge of the relative prices of all statins by individual GPs (Keyworth and Yarrow, 2007).

Government price setting

Government price setting introduces major additional uncertainty into the R&D process. The UK has slow product uptake. Now price is to be subject to potential opportunistic (but understandable) attempts by the government to keep NHS costs down. This is not a stable business environment. The OFT draws on a number of other countries where it thinks there are working models the UK can adapt. Its prime candidate is the LFN in Sweden. However, LFN states that 'another important aspect of the Swedish reimbursement system is that we do not negotiate prices. We look upon the price as an integrated part of the cost-effectiveness analysis. If the price is too high there will be no cost-effectiveness' (LFN, 2007). LFN also argues it is not eager to force the price down as much as possible, for three reasons. First, they do not believe that it is really possible for a government agency to efficiently set prices. Second, they do not want to regulate the pharmaceutical market more than necessary. And third, a reimbursement system that uses cost-effectiveness from a societal perspective can play an important role when it comes to

DOI: 10.1002/hec

stimulating innovations. It makes far more sense to let companies set prices in the knowledge that the NHS will use HTA effectively to decide whether or not to use products and in which groups of patients.

Use of QALYs

The OFT proposals mean that the cost-per-QALY calculation would become the sole criterion for price determination and drug rationing within the NHS. It is not clear that QALYs are ready to move from being a key influencer to sole determinant. Concerns include:

- how to derive a cost-per-QALY threshold? If this is to reflect societal preferences these may vary between disease area and patient group. If it is to reflect the opportunity cost of the health gain from interventions efficiently displaced (i.e. those that are least efficient) in the NHS by funding a new treatment then there has to be a way of discovering this information. However, as the OFT suggests, some element of stability is required if the threshold is to provide long-term signals of society's willingness to pay for innovation. There are trade-offs to be made which can in part be informed by research currently underway on societal preferences and the cost-effectiveness of existing NHS programmes. The resulting figure has to be 'sold' to the public as well as to industry and the NHS;
- the ability of the QALY to accurately reflect the impact on patient morbidity and willingness to 'trade' quality and length of life – particularly in disease areas such as cancer where life expectancy may be short. The QALY assumption of a constant willingness to trade length of life against quality of life does not seem to hold in these circumstances;
- the need to take a more societal perspective on costs and benefits, including the productivity benefits of getting people back to work. The OFT indicate NICE should move in this direction – and it is right to do so, but this is not straight forward. There are difficult methodological and measurement issues;
- the consistency of QALY estimates depending on the method of elicitation used. As Kind puts it 'The research agenda remains substantial.' (Kind, forthcoming).

Efficient use of HTA

HTA resources in the UK are scarce and the NHS has many needs. The Cooksey (2006) Report identified priorities, recommending (page 102) '*expanding the HTA programme to*:

- *strengthen the commissioned workstreams for primary research, clinical trials and themed call programmes*;
- *...diagnostic tests*;
- *follow up on research recommendations from NICE* (see 35);
- *...medical devices...*;
- *improve Knowledge Transfer...*;
- *augment HTA clinical trials infrastructure*.'

The OFT's desire to significantly expand the use of HTA to cover all new drugs is hard to justify. Indeed any detailed consideration of proportionality is absent. HTA should be expanded and used where it can offer greatest value – that may well involve more effort with drugs but the OFT proposal to cover all drugs not just 'at launch' but with regular re-reviews is unlikely to make sense. I recommend below a contingent value of information approach to the use of HTA.

Pre-launch emphasis

The OFT opt for a pre-launch review. Yet even with improved Phase III development programmes or adoption of the Cooksey (2006) proposal for a 'new drug development pathway' with 'conditional

DOI: 10.1002/hec

licensing' at the end of Phase II giving earlier access to the market, earlier review by NICE followed up by 'the use of real-world data' through use of NHS IT and patient registries, it is hard to see how definitive and quick decisions can be made at launch. Claxton (2007) and Griffin *et al.* (2007) argue that more has to be done pre-launch because manufacturers have little incentive to undertake additional work if their product has been authorised and because there are issues around conducting RCTs when products have already been recommended for use in the NHS. Within a formal value of information framework they argue that if there is no opportunity to collect information post-launch to resolve uncertainties around the mean cost-effectiveness estimate then manufacturers must either supply information pre-launch that reduces this uncertainty or accept a lower price that provides an acceptable expectation that the product will be cost-effective in use. However, it is not obvious that post-launch data collection is of limited value and most RCTs *are* conducted post-launch. The challenge is to find an acceptable level of data to enable a pre-launch view to be taken where needed and to enable requirements for post-launch assessment to be specified.

Static versus dynamic efficiency

The OFT propose that prices should reflect cost-effectiveness at the marginal patient group using the cost-per-QALY threshold. Where there are choices, i.e. different sub-groups have different cost-effectiveness ratios, then the DH and the company would negotiate whether to go for a lower price and serve all patient sub-groups or a higher price and restrict use to a subset of patients. This is of course what happens now – except that companies decide the price and HTA bodies recommend which patient sub-groups it should be used in. Claxton (2007) argues that this could lead to perfect price discrimination (for example, by a refusal to undertake sub-group analysis and the setting of price at the cost-per-QALY threshold) and the appropriation of all the value of the innovation by the manufacturer until patent expiry, at which point prices fall if there is a competitive generic market and all of the surplus comes to the NHS. The reality is that sub-group analysis can be done on an *ad hoc* basis by HTA bodies, and companies take a high risk if they refuse to undertake it. More importantly:

- it is highly unlikely that all of the consumer surplus will accrue to the innovator during patent life;
- there is no right answer as to where to draw the line. The more of the surplus that accrues to the innovator, the greater the incentives for future innovation and health gain. However, the greater the surplus that accrues to the NHS, the greater the immediate health gain. Evidence suggests that the societal gains from pharmaceuticals and other health technologies have been high (Philipson and Jena, 2005; Murphy and Topel, 2003).

Therapeutic reference pricing?

The post-launch reviews proposed by the OFT resemble a form of therapeutic reference pricing (TRP) in which price regulation refuses on principle to recognise any differential value of products within a therapy class. The impact of this on the innovation process I set out earlier cannot be overstated. Subsequent entrants cannot get a price premium even if their products are better for patients, and once the first product comes off-patent the prices of follow-on products are forced down by an automatic formula so reducing the effective patent life of the follow-on product. As Pammolli and Riccaboni (2004) put it:

> some cost containment initiatives recently implemented or under study across the world could permanently and adversely affect competition in the industry. For example, convergence toward price control schemes such as reference pricing for on patent drugs within broad equivalency classes would reduce expected revenues from horizontal product differentiation and would reinforce first-mover advantages, which would in turn lead to higher concentration....All in all, international convergence toward price control and reference pricing for innovative drugs would have negative

DOI: 10.1002/hec

effects on industry structure and innovation. A new industry landscape would take shape, but one that might look quite different from what policy makers originally had in mind.

The OFT would no doubt argue that its proposals to force down all brand prices in a therapeutic category to a small premium over the first off-patent generic is not TRP, because if there are differences they can be reflected in price premiums. The evidence from elsewhere in the world is that this is rarely done. The fundamental problem is the OFT's insistence that all adjustment should be through price. If a product is no longer value for money across a broad spectrum of patients because a competitor product is now off-patent, then *volume* should adjust and use be restricted to any patient sub-groups where it is still cost-effective. The company may choose to reduce price to retain competitiveness in the broader population. That is a commercial judgement for it to make.

Treatment of off-patent products

As we have noted above, the UK has a competitive generics market and its continuation is essential if the NHS is to maximise the benefits of innovation. The OFT's proposals to bring down originator and competitor brand prices reduce the incentives for generic companies. Indeed Sweden and Australia have moved away from linked systems because they impacted on their ability to get low price generics.

Rewarding innovation per se

The OFT argues that it would not be efficient to reward products with higher prices than justified on cost-per-QALY grounds alone just because they were innovative *per se*, i.e. pioneering in a disease area. It seems to argue this on grounds of practicality – how could an efficient mechanism be designed – rather than principle. This is important as there is a case for such an approach. In all markets there are externalities from use. Early adopters typically pay high prices and the experience gained enables better products to be developed or existing ones to be better used. These benefits accrue to subsequent users Suppose there were no early adopters? If there are (on average) systematic later benefits from use of (say) a first-in-class product, then it makes sense to subsidise early use. Use is (in effect) buying an option on access to future technology. An analogous situation is where we know that evaluative research on one product will almost provide an externality in terms of building up a knowledge base from which it then becomes easier to assess the value of other products. Of course, there is a difference between knowing that in principle an effect could be there and finding evidence to support a credible policy rule.

Fixed drug budget

The OFT proposal for a fixed drug budget is nonsensical. Maximising overall NHS efficiency requires switching input mix as required to maximise health gain (Garrison and Towse, 2003). It claims that such an arrangement may be helpful to companies because innovations will only compete with other innovations for access to treatment. (In effect there will be a shadow cost-per-QALY for medicines that is different – higher or lower depending on where the threshold is set – from the rest of the NHS.) It seems more likely that it sees such a fixed budget as protection for the NHS from increased pharmaceutical spend. This suggests a lack of confidence in its proposed VBP system to deliver efficient relative prices and use of drugs.

WHAT IS THE WAY FORWARD?

Strengthening the 'demand side'

The UK NHS needs to improve its arrangements for medicines procurement and use by continuing to tackle the 'demand side' failures that led to the development of the PPRS as a regulatory procurement

DOI: 10.1002/hec

tool. This involves not only more use of HTA but enabling PCTs and prescribers to get better value for money, both through local priority setting and through effective use of medicines deemed cost-effective.

A backstop PPRS

The PPRS should remain as a 'backstop' control but only until it is clear that the 'demand side' is robust enough to ensure value for money use of drugs. Those products subject to HTA reviews could be treated differently within the PPRS. The option of moving from a profit cap/price control scheme to an RPI-X type control as used in UK utility regulation could be explored (Vickers and Yarrow, 1988). It had previously been thought unsuitable for pharmaceuticals because it cannot address new products (Cave and Towse, 1997; Bloom and Van Reenen, 1998). Use of a separate HTA process could leave a residual RPI-X control on older and niche medicines.

A contingent appraisal process

A critical issue is the effective use of HTA given the resource constraints and the availability of information at launch and post-launch (Buxton, 2006). Towse and Buxton (2006) identified the need for more analyses of a wider range of technologies within the resource constraints on appraisals (financial and/or the availability of time and of skilled researchers). They set out several actions, in particular the:

- '*development of a more contingent appraisal process where the level of analytical effort is more closely related to the nature of the decision problem*;
- *use of value of information (VoI) methods to determine the relevant level of complexity in particular cases*;
- *use of VoI to determine which technologies to appraise*;
- *use of 'MS type' risk sharing schemes involving additional data collection with payment contingent on actual patient outcomes. This can allow adoption of technologies despite high levels of remaining uncertainty*.'

Elements of reform

Key elements of a reformed UK pharmaceutical environment for 2010 should therefore include:

- an expanded role for HTA but with companies retaining freedom to set prices at launch and HTA use targeted at major products with a mix of at-launch and post-launch reviews. The choice of products to review, and timing of reviews to be determined using a contingent approach;
- the retention of a backstop profit cap/price control PPRS scheme perhaps moving to an RPI-X type control;
- the use of risk sharing and non-linear pricing arrangements. These could be negotiated centrally or locally;
- measures to ensure more effective therapeutic switching at local level when new products enter, there is new information about cost-effectiveness, or a major product comes off-patent. The NHS is getting better, but there is still substantial health gain and cash savings to be made from a more rapid adjustment of prescribing volumes;
- measures to improve the take up of cost-effective treatments. This has to involve a combination of support for local priority setting and for more effective use of clinical guidelines for the management of patients.

DOI: 10.1002/hec

The objective is to tackle relative prices, volumes (efficient levels of use) and the absolute level of prices, within a framework that provides rewards for innovation and a stable procurement environment for the industry – albeit one where there is a determined search for value for money.

ACKNOWLEDGEMENTS

The Office of Health Economics is supported by an annual grant from the Association of the British Pharmaceutical Industry. The views expressed by the author in this paper are not those of the OHE or the ABPI.

REFERENCES

Acemoglu D, Linn J. *Market Size in Innovation: Theory and Evidence from the Pharmaceutical Industry*. Massachusetts Institute of Technology: Cambridge, MA, 2003; *Working Paper 03-33*, Massachusetts Institute of Technology, Department of Economics Working Paper Series.

Adelphi Consulting. 2006. *Qualitative Analysis of Variation in Uptake of Medicines across the NHS in England*. A Report prepared for the Technical Group of the Partnership Workstream of the Ministerial Industry Strategy Group. Department of Health and Association of the British Pharmaceutical Industry. http://www.dh.gov.uk/en/Publicationsandstatistics/Publications/PublicationsPolicyAndGuidance/DH_065198

Averch H, Johnson L. 1962. Behaviour of the firm under regulatory constraint. *American Economic Review* **52**: 1052–1069.

Bloom N, Van Reenen J. 1998. Regulating drug prices: where do we go from here? *Fiscal Studies* **19**: 321–342.

Buxton M. 2006. Economic evaluation and decision making in the United Kingdom. *PharmacoEconomics* **24**: 1133–1142.

Cave M, Towse A. 1997. *Regulating Prices Paid by the NHS for Medicines Supplied by the UK-Based Pharmaceutical Industry*. Briefing No. 34. Office of Health Economics: London.

Claxton K. 2007. OFT, VBP: QED? *Health Economic* **16**(6): 545–558.

Cockburn I. 2004. The changing structure of the pharmaceutical industry. *Health Affairs* **23**(1): 10–22.

Cooksey D. 2006. *A Review of UK Health Research Funding*. The Stationery Office: London.

Culyer AJ, McCabe C, Briggs A, Claxton K, Buxton M, Akehurst R, Sculpher M, Brazier J. 2007. Searching for a threshold, not setting one: the role of the National Institute of Health and Clinical Excellence. *Journal of Health Services Research and Policy* **12**(1): 56–58.

Danzon PM, Furukawa MF. 2006. Prices and availability of biopharmaceuticals: an international comparison. *Health Affairs* **25**(5): 1353–1362.

Department of Health. 2004. *The Pharmaceutical Price Regulation Scheme 2005*. Department of Health: London.

Department of Health and the Association of the British Pharmaceutical Industry. 2002. *PPRS: The Study into the Extent of Competition in the Supply of Branded Medicines to the NHS*. Department of Health: London.

DiMasi J, Paquette C. 2004. The economics of follow-on drug research and development. trends in entry rates and the timing of development. *PharmacoEconomics* **22**(2): 1–14.

DiMasi JA, Hansen RW, Grabowski HG. 2003. The price of innovation: new estimates of drug development costs. *Journal of Health Economics* **22**: 151–185.

DotEcon. 2004. Assessing the impact of public sector procurement on competition. *Report for the Office of Fair Trading*, vol. 1. Office of Fair Trading, London, OFT742a, September.

Edwards JSS, Kay JA, Mayer CP. 1987. *The Economic Analysis of Accounting Profitability*. Oxford University Press: Oxford.

Finkelstein A. 2003. Health policy and technological change: evidence from the vaccine industry. *NBER Working Paper No. 9460*, National Bureau of Economic Research, Cambridge, MA.

Garrison L, Towse A. 2003. The drug budget silo mentality in Europe: an overview. *Value in Health* **6**(s1): S1–S9.

Grabowski H, Vernon J, Di Masi J. 2002. Returns on research and development for 1990s new drug introductions. *PharmacoEconomics* **20**(3): 11–29.

Griffin S, Claxton K, Palmer S, Sculpher MJ. 2007. Dangerous omissions: the consequences of ignoring decision uncertainty. *Medical Decision Making* **27**(1): E8.

Keyworth T, Yarrow G. 2007. *Review of the Office of Fair Trading's Market Study of the Pharmaceutical Price Regulation Scheme*. Regulatory Policy Institute: Oxford.

Kind P. forthcoming. Putting the 'Q' in QALYs. In *The Influence of Alan Williams*, Mason A, Towse A (eds). Radcliffe: Oxford.

LFN (Pharmaceutical Benefits Board). 2007. *The Swedish Pharmaceutical Reimbursement System – A Brief Overview*. LFN: Solna.

Lichtenberg FR, Walsfogel J. 2003. *Does misery love company? Evidence from pharmaceutical markets before and after the Orphan Drug Act. Working Paper 9750*, National Bureau of Economic Research, Cambridge, MA.

Murphy KM, Topel RH (eds). 2003. *Measuring the Gains from Medical Research: An Economic Approach*. The University of Chicago Press: Chicago.

Myers S. 1999. Measuring pharmaceutical risk and the cost of capital. In *Risk and Return in the Pharmaceutical Industry*, Sussex J, Marchant N (eds). Office of Health Economics: London; 59–76.

NAO Report. 2007. *Prescribing Costs in Primary Care*. Report by the Comptroller and Auditor General, HC 454 Session 2006-7, The Stationery Office, London, May.

NERA. forthcoming. *Key Factors in Attracting Internationally Mobile Investments by the Research-Based Pharmaceutical Industry*. Report to the UK Ministerial Industry Strategy Group. http://www.dh.gov.uk/en/Publicationsandstatistics/Publications/PublicationsPolicyAndGuidance/DH_065198

Office of Fair Trading. 2007a. *The Pharmaceutical Price Regulation Scheme. An OFT Market Study*. Office of Fair Trading: London.

Office of Fair Trading. 2007b. Annexe I modelling of profitability. *The Pharmaceutical Price Regulation Scheme. An OFT Market Study*. Office of Fair Trading: London.

OHE Consulting. 2005. *The Many Faces of Innovation*. A Report for The European Federation of Pharmaceutical Industries and Associations (EFPIA). OHE Consulting: London. http//:www.efpia.org/Objects/2/Files/Manyfacesofinnovation.pdf

Pammolli F, Riccaboni M. 2004. Market structure and drug innovation. *Health Affairs* **23**: 48–50.

Philipson TJ, Jena AB. 2005. Who benefits from new medical technologies? Estimates of consumer and producer surpluses for HIV/AIDS drugs. *Forum for Health Economics & Policy* **9**: Article 3. http://www.bepress.com/fhep/biomedical_research/3

Ryan M, Yule B, Bond C, Taylor R. 1992. Knowledge of drug costs: a comparison of general practitioners in Scotland and England. *British Journal of General Practice* **42**: 6–9.

Ryan M, Yule B, Bond C, Taylor R. 1996. Do physicians perceptions of drug costs influence their prescribing. *Pharmacoeconomics* **9**: 321–331.

Shliefer A. 1985. A theory of yardstick competition. *Rand Journal of Economics* **16**: 319–327.

Silcock J, Ryan M, Bond C, Taylor R. 1997. Changes in Scottish general practitioners attitudes and knowledge in respect of prescribing costs between 1986 and 1995. *European Journal of General Practice* **2**: 168–170.

Towse A, Buxton M. 2006. *Notes on a Conference in Honour of Bernie O'Brien. Three Challenges to Achieving Better Analysis for Better Decisions: Generalisability, Complexity and Thresholds*. OHE Briefing No. 42. Office of Health Economics: London.

Towse A, Leighton T. 1999. The changing nature of NCE pricing of second and subsequent entrants. In *Risk and Return in the Pharmaceutical Industry*, Sussex J, Marchant N (eds). Office of Health Economics: London; 91–105.

Vickers J, Yarrow G. 1988. *Privatisation. An Economic Analysis*. The MIT Press: Cambridge, MA.

Wertheimer A, Levy R, O'Connor T. 2001. Too many drugs? The clinical and economics value of incremental innovations. *Investing in Health: The Social and Economic Benefits of Health Care Innovation* **14**: 77–118

Wren-Lewis S. 2003. *Estimates of Equilibrium Exchange Rates for Sterling Against the Euro*. EMU Study. HM Treasury, London.

DOI: 10.1002/hec

[33]

The Timing of Drug Approvals in the United States and Abroad

An understanding of the international diffusion of new pharmaceuticals is important because the market for pharmaceuticals is so international, as was noted in Chapter 7. This trend in multinational ownership of pharmaceutical firms and their worldwide research and development (R&D) and sales efforts have accelerated with the formation of multinational trade blocs in both North America (the North American Free Trade Association, or NAFTA) and Europe (the European Union, or EU) and the likelihood of similar blocs in South-East Asia (ASEAN by 2020) and South America (Mercosur, or Common Market of the South). Furthermore, the timing of new drug approvals has important implications for a nation's overall health status, health expenditures, and social equity.

The drug approval process in any country involves a balancing of conflicting social objectives: safety and access. Thus the approval process in any country will inevitably be criticized by those who would like to shift priorities one way or the other.

The United States has a widely respected but stringent review process overseen by the Food and Drug Administration (FDA) of the Department of Health and Human Services. The FDA sets out guidelines for basic research and animal testing that must be met before human tests can begin. Once human tests are allowed, they take place in progressively larger phases so that dangerous products will be recognized before large numbers of subjects are exposed. The process has worked well, generally, but criticism of the delay has led to numerous reforms that seem to be effective in reducing the approval time.

There is also concern that the regulatory delays in the United States put American patients at risk, relative to those in other countries. A number of researchers have asked whether the United States suffers from a "drug lag." While some studies claim that there *is* such a lag, new research has found that *every* country experiences lags in approving important drugs, and the United States is relatively quick, compared to other major countries.

We conclude the chapter with some recommendations on the regulatory review process that might shorten the review without jeopardizing the safety of patients.

The Timing of Pharmaceutical Approvals and Health Policy

The timing of approval of new pharmaceuticals is actually the result of two timing decisions: when the pharmaceutical developer files a drug's New Drug Application (NDA), and the length of the FDA's review process. Firms would like the review completed as quickly as possible in every market, with large markets meaning more to the firm financially than small markets. But there are strategic considerations, as industry leaders know which countries have particularly stringent review processes, which have lenient ones, and which countries are dependent on other countries to indicate an acceptable drug. Countries with a rigorous approval process require more lengthy testing and documentation, which slows down the preapproval process and, of course, delays the NDA filing. The two events, filing an NDA and approving a drug, are not entirely independent events: firms will delay filing in a stringent country until absolutely all the evidence is in and can be presented. Firms may even wait intentionally until a drug has been in use successfully in another country before filing in the stringent country.

The approval of new pharmaceuticals by a country's regulatory authority involves a balancing of two conflicting objectives: assuring the population access to the latest therapeutic agents available, while protecting patients from the risk of dangerous products. The two goals conflict because speeding access inevitably entails allowing approval of some drugs that turn out to be harmful. Avoiding any drugs that might be dangerous, however, would slow access to drugs that are later found to be safe and effective. This balancing is accomplished in the United States with a drug approval process that explicitly values both safety and efficacy. The process can be stopped at any point if findings suggest either lack of safety or efficacy. The FDA's recent interest in expanding post-marketing surveillance, which allows a new drug to be marketed while the medical community is alerted to watch for signs of harm caused by the drug, is an attempt to shift the balance toward access while accepting greater risk. Underlying the approval dilemma is the existence of uncertainty as to a drug's true benefit and risk.

Ideally, each country will adopt those drugs whose benefit–risk profile is favorable relative to its preference for access and risk. But errors are inevitably made, with "bad" drugs occasionally approved[1] and "good" drugs not approved. Errors of the former kind may result in recalls and withdrawals, whereas errors of the latter type result in frustration on the part of physicians and add fuel to the political fire to reduce the FDA's authority.

One would expect countries to be internally consistent in the speed of their approval process depending on their relative preference for safety and access. Countries that are particularly risk averse, for example, would be expected to be slow in approving new drugs, while waiting to learn of other countries' experience. These countries would lag behind countries that tend to favor access. A nation's preference of safety over access may vary over time, but one would expect to observe consistent patterns of lags across countries, with some countries tending to lead in the approval "race," while others follow behind. The importance of a drug enters into the timing decision because of the expected benefit that such a drug may confer upon the population. Especially important drugs will be expected to produce greater benefit, for a given level of risk, than drugs that follow on, or mimic others. The approval process may be inconsistent in the case of unimportant, me-too, drugs. On the one hand approval might come quickly because the more closely they are related to existing drugs, the less new risk they pose. On the other hand, the closer they are to existing drugs, the less benefit they will confer, and the less pressure there is to approve them rapidly. For important drugs, however, one would expect much more consistency in the relative approval times among countries, with corresponding leads or lags dependent on countries' relative balance between acceptance of risk and benefit.

The Drug Approval Process in the United States

Upon completion of toxicological and safety testing in animals, drug companies are required to file a Investigational New Drug (IND) application with the FDA prior to any human testing. An IND application contains the drug sponsor's research plans, details of manufacturing processes, and results of laboratory and animal tests to date. The clinical section contains a detailed description, or protocol, of the initially planned clinical trials and a general overview of the studies that will follow. The manufacturing section describes the facilities, equipment, and techniques the sponsor will use to produce the drug (U.S. Congress, OTA 1993).

Unless the FDA disapproves the IND application within a 30-day period, it is automatically approved and clinical tests can begin. For administrative purposes and as a means of prioritizing its work, the FDA rates each drug for which an IND is received according to the drug's novelty and the agency's subjective judgment of the drug's therapeutic potential. Until 1992, the FDA used a five-category rating system of therapeutic importance: *A* for important therapeutic gain; *B* for modest therapeutic gain; *C* for little or no therapeutic gain; *AA* for AIDS designation; and *V* for a designated orphan drug (described later in this chapter). Beginning in 1992 the rating scheme was changed to include only two categories, *P* (Priority) for the most important drugs, and *S* (Standard) for all other drugs.

Phase I Trials

Phase I studies are small trials (generally less than 100 participants), usually involving only healthy volunteers, to assess safety and see how the body absorbs and eliminates the drugs and to document the response it produces.[2] At this point the drug company must once again decide whether to continue with the project. On the basis of information accumulated up to this point, the company tries to determine whether the product is of sufficient quality to warrant the investment of the necessary resources to market the product. In addition, the company will try to estimate the manufacturing costs of the drug (Faust 1971). This will often be the first attempt to estimate these costs because it is the first stage at which an accurate description of the actual drug product is available.

During phase I trials, the FDA can impose a clinical hold by which it prohibits the study from proceeding or stops a trial that has started for reasons of safety or because of a sponsor's failure to accurately disclose the risk of study to investigators. Sponsors can request to release a clinical hold by submitting an official response addressing all pertinent issues identified in the clinical hold (U.S. Department of Health and Human Services [USDHHS] 2003a). The FDA then has 30 days to respond to such requests. Although the FDA routinely provides advice in such cases, investigators may choose to ignore any advice regarding the design of phase I studies in areas other than patient safety.

At this point, the clinician is instrumental in reevaluating the number of patients necessary for the clinical tests, the length of time that each testing stage will require, the specific information that will have to be developed to prove efficacy for the compound, the likelihood that such information can be developed, and the overall and yearly expenditure estimates for the project (Wiggins 1981).

Phase II Trials

Phase II trials are conducted to obtain preliminary data on the effectiveness of the drug for a particular indication or indications in patients with the disease or condition. This phase of testing also helps determine the common short-term side effects and risks associated with the drug. Phase II studies are typically well controlled, closely monitored, and conducted in a relatively small number of patients, usually involving several hundred people. Various doses of the drug are compared so that the large phase III trials can test the most successful dosage. The groups selected consist of patients for whom the drug is intended to be of benefit. Under the 1962 FDA Amendments, substantial evidence of efficacy in the intended use of the drug is required before marketing approval can be granted. The FDA does not specify the trial design, but the design most likely to show significant effect of the drug is to compare it to an inert substance, a placebo. Although studies comparing the experimental drug to other drugs on the market are possible, they entail more risk for the sponsor (for example, if the experimental drug is less effective than the other drug the sponsor will certainly have difficulty marketing the new product) and without a placebo control group efficacy will *still* not be determined because of the "placebo effect," with some patients feeling improvement just because they are taking what they think is a drug. Thus is most FDA trials are limited to the experimental drug compared to a placebo. The other aspect of study design is that studies should be blind to reduce the likelihood of bias. A study is *single blind* if the patient does not know whether he or she is receiving the active drug or the placebo. A study is *double blind* if even the investigator does not know which patients are receiving the experimental drug. Therefore, most clinical trials are randomized, double-blind, experimental–placebo studies.

When successful, phase II trials usually provide the first significant evidence of efficacy. Additional safety data are also obtained during this phase and usually through concurrent animal studies.

During these trials, corporate management will take a great deal of interest in drugs under development, and request detailed information consisting of the drug's expected manufacturing cost, price, expected sales at different prices, estimated length of time for the drug to reach market, and development costs that are likely to be incurred through the marketing stage (Wiggins 1981). This updated information is used to make better decisions about which drugs should be candidates for further testing and which drugs should be dropped. Considering that four out of every five drugs entering phase I testing do not clear human testing and gain regulatory approval for marketing (PHRMA 2006), it is important for research management to assess the continued feasibility of the drug to prevent any further financial loss to the company.

Phase III Trials

The third, and final, premarketing clinical development phase involves large-scale controlled clinical trials of a drug's safety and effectiveness in hospital and outpatient settings at the dose and route that will subsequently be marketed. The larger sample sizes, ranging from several hundred to several thousand patients, increase the likelihood that actual benefits will be found to be statistically significant. In both phase II and phase III trials, the FDA can impose a clinical hold if a study is unsafe (as in phase I) or if the protocol is clearly deficient in design in meeting its stated objectives. Phase III studies are used to gather precise information on the drug's effectiveness for specific indications, determine whether the drug produces a broader range and severity of adverse effects than those exhibited in the smaller study population of phase I and phase II studies, and identify the best way of administering and using the drug for the purpose intended. This information forms the basis for deciding on the content of the product label and package insert if the drug is approved (U.S. Congress, OTA 1993). Important pharmacokinetic and pharmacodynamic properties of a drug product appear on the label under specific sections in a format and language recommended by the FDA (Marroum and Gobburu 2002).

In recent years, there has been increased attention to obtaining good dose–response information and assessing need for modifying treatment in demographic (age, gender, race) and concomitant disease (renal or hepatic function abnormalities) subgroups and assessing drug–drug interaction during clinical trials (Temple 2002). Debate has arisen over whether separate clinical trials should be conducted in children; however, enlisting children in clinical trials raises issues of increased risk and informed consent (Sharav 2003). Underrepresentation of minority groups in clinical trials has also become a recent focus. This issue may affect the generalizability and/or external validity of the trial findings, which may have important repercussions for the safety and efficacy of the new drug in addition to reducing the opportunities for subgroup analysis (Hussain-Gambles 2003).

New Drug Application

The FDA has two subagencies that regulate and monitor the pharmaceutical research process: the Center for Drug Evaluation and Research (CDER) and the Center for Biologics Evaluation and Research (CBER). Drug sponsors seeking marketing approval for a new chemical, antibiotic, hormone, or enzyme drug product file a New Drug Application (NDA) with the CDER. Biotechnological drug products and vaccines must file two applications with the CBER: a product license application (PLA) covering the drug, and an establishment license application (ELA) covering the facilities manufacturing the product.

The CDER has 60 days from the date a company submits an NDA to decide if it contains sufficient information for the agency to conduct a substantive review. The process of review is carried out by the Review Division, and the results are given to the Division Director. If there are any disagreements over the strength of scientific evidence for the drug, the NDA moves up one level to the Office Director for more consideration. If disagreement continues, the director of CDER will review the application and proposed FDA decision (USDHHS 1990).

Once the agency reaches agreement, the Review Division Director sends a letter to the company explaining its decision. The FDA's approval letter can either approve the product for market or declare that the agency would approve the drug once the company addresses concerns about its effectiveness or safety (called an "Approvable Letter"). Alternatively, the letter can state that the drug is "unapprovable" (U.S. Congress, OTA 1993). The company has 10 days to respond to either an approvable or unapprovable letter, providing information on its attempt to correct the problem(s) stated in the FDA letter. If the sponsor does not respond within 10 days, the FDA automatically withdraws the NDA (21 C.F.R. sec 314.105). Most NDAs require at least one such amendment by the company.

By law, the FDA must complete its review of an NDA within 180 days, although with each amendment, an additional 180 days are granted (21 C.F.R.sec 314.60). Even with the extensions, however, actual review time exceeds the statutory allowances. Data from the FDA indicate that the 26 new drugs approved in 2002 took an average of 17.8 months in review (Pharmaceutical Research and Manufacturers of America 2003). While still exceeding 180 days, this average is noticeably shorter than it was a decade ago when the FDA reported that the 23 NDAs for new molecular entities approved in 1990 took an average of 30 months to approve (USDHHS 1990).

The CBER review process for new products is similar to that of the CDER, although more emphasis is placed on the safety and quality of the processes and facilities used to produce a biological drug. Also in contrast to the CDER's NDA review process, there are no statutory limits on the amount of time CBER reviewers may take to complete their review of PLAs and ELAs (U.S. Congress, OTA 1993).

Postapproval Research

Federal regulation requires manufacturers selling drugs in the United States to notify the FDA periodically about the performance of their products. This surveillance is designed to detect uncommon, yet serious, adverse reactions typically not revealed during premarketing testing. Physicians are encouraged to report adverse events through the FDA's MedWatch program. If serious problems with a drug show up when the number of patients taking a drug is very large or the time period is long enough, valuable information can be learned. Phase IV trials were originally thought of as part of a compromise that allowed new drugs to be approved in an expedited fashion before all of the phase III trials had been completed. In return for approving drugs that might be dangerous, the FDA stipulated that many of these drugs would be more thoroughly studied in phase IV trials. There was increased risk of danger, but if the drug was safe, patients would have earlier access to them. Manufacturers of prescription medical products are required by regulation to submit adverse event reports to the FDA, which in turn uses this information to update drug labeling and, on rare occasions, to reevaluate the approval or marketing decision. In addition to the voluntary reporting program (MedWatch), the FDA is empowered to require structural surveillance of approved and marketed drugs. Most postapproval studies are less than a year in length. In some cases, postapproval monitoring is especially important because phase III trials were purposely made smaller or more brief than normal. This is done frequently in the case of HIV/AIDS drugs, for instance, because of the urgency of the medical problem. These additional studies usually include usage in children and drug interactions (U.S. Congress, OTA 1993). Today few phase IV trials are required of manufacturers, and there appears to be lax oversight of them, so that many that are authorized are never undertaken (*New York Times* 2004).

Since the early 1960s and the thalidomide tragedy, we have come a long way in improving drug safety, while speeding access to new products. Preapproved drug testing is far more rigorous (and expensive) than before and the ability of the FDA to review NDAs efficiently has also improved. In the international context, firms are now able to use some European and Japanese drug trial data (see Recent Initiatives, below), thereby reducing the amount of overlapping testing that is required.

In 2004 the FDA was involved in two drug recalls that some say demonstrate that the agency is inadequately weighing safety issues as it deliberates drug approvals. The appropriate weighing of safety and access is complicated because the two goals are in mutual conflict with one another. Safety is, of course, an important goal of a nation's drug regulatory system, but the only way to ensure safety is to increase the cost of drug approval by lengthening the drug approval process and increasing the sample size of phase III investigations. A few examples illustrate how difficult this strategy can be. In the 1960s diethylstilbesterol (DES) was prescribed for pregnant women to ease morning sickness. The drug appeared to be innocuous, having no visible effect on either the mother or the newborn. But when the offspring reached puberty some of them began to exhibit serious abnormalities in their reproductive system. The detective work of finding the cause of these abnormalities among teenagers was daunting, and only after lengthy investigation was the problem tracked back to the drug that the children's mothers had taken. From a policy standpoint, the DES story was very difficult. The effects of the drug were not only felt in the next generation from that actually taking the drug, but only after some dozen years! Imagine designing clinical trials that would have detected this side effect.

Recent Initiatives to Expedite Drug Approvals

The regulatory process described above is often criticized by the pharmaceutical industry as being unduly stringent and excessively lengthy, and is commonly cited as a major cause of the increased costs associated with drug R&D. The time between an IND application and an NDA filing rose from 2.5 years in the 1960s to 5 years by 1997 (Lesney 2000). And the time from synthesis of a compound to an NDA approval rose from 8 to 15 years during the same period (DiMasi et al. 1994). Pressure to speed the FDA's review process has also come from organized patient groups, such as people with HIV/AIDS. They frequently point out that for rapidly progressing, terminal conditions, the risk of an inadvertent approval of a bad drug has less significance, and the weighing of risks should favor access far more than it generally does.

In response, the White House Council on Competitiveness and the FDA proposed several initiatives aimed at reducing the time required to move a drug from clinical testing through marketing approval. First, drug sponsors could begin phase I clinical testing without receiving IND status from the FDA. Instead, institutional review boards (IRBs) at hospitals or other medical institutions that administer the trials would review and monitor them. Second, the FDA could approve drugs for life-threatening diseases for which no alternative therapy exists on the basis of limited evidence of safety and efficacy. Sponsors could collect and provide the full complement of such evidence after the drug was approved. The third proposal was that the FDA could contract with outside experts in academia and other institutions to review pieces of NDAs in which the FDA expected little scientific controversy. Finally, the FDA could look to foreign drug approval systems with sufficiently high standards to warrant U.S. approval on the basis of an approval in these other countries (Stanley 1981; U.S. Congress, OTA 1993). Some of these proposals have been implemented.

The FDA has issued new rulings allowing for earlier access to INDs for patients with life-threatening or serious illnesses and accelerated review of NDAs. Under accelerated review, the CDER can make urgently needed drugs available for distribution sooner. For accelerated approval, a drug has only to show a positive effect on a disease marker or intermediate end point rather than a final outcome. For example, the FDA spent an estimated 8 staff-years, or $600,000, for expedited approval of zidovudine, or Retrovir, marketed to treat AIDS (USDHHS 1995). In expanded-access protocols, drugs treating patients' conditions for which no real alternatives exist are closely monitored by both the sponsor and CDER. In addition, the International Conference on Harmonization (ICH) was created to promote efficiency in clinical trials and human testing between the European Union, Japan, and the United States. The ICH has developed a Common Technical Document (CTD) to document the proceedings and findings of clinical trials (Molzon 2003). By July 2003, the CTD was required by the European Union and Japan and strongly recommended by the FDA. The CTD is meant to provide a common form for submitting and transferring valuable information in an effort to streamline the international review process. These and other efforts to streamline the review process appear to have had some success. The FDA approved 21 new molecular entities in 2003, of which 9 were classified as priority and 12 were classified as standard. The mean approval times for priority and standard approvals in 2003 were 6.7 months and 23.1 months, respectively. This represents a marked decrease in approval times in the last 10 years, when the mean approval times for priority and standard approvals in 1992 were 14.9 months and 27.2 months, respectively.

Another initiative, approved by Congress in 1992, was the Prescription Drug User Fee Act (PDUFA) (Public Law 102–571). This initiative was designed to allow the agency to increase resources devoted to approval review to shorten regulatory review times. The two main provisions of the PDUFA are (1) a system of per-application user fees that fund increases in the reviewer staff at the CDER, and (2) an incentive structure whereby the legislation is renewed only if the FDA meets specified performance goals (Carpenter 2004). When a company seeks FDA approval for a new drug or biologic prior to marketing, it must submit an application along with a fee to support the review process (USDHHS 2004). In addition, companies pay annual fees for each manufacturing establishment and for each prescription drug product marketed. Under the PDUFA, industry provides the funding in exchange for FDA agreement to meet drug-review performance goals, which emphasize timeliness.

Since 1992, the PDUFA has been reauthorized twice: by the Food and Drug Modernization Act of 1997 and again by the Public Health Security and Bioterrorism Preparedness and Response Act of 2002. Fees began at $100,000 for each NDA or PLA/ELA. By 2004, the fee schedule increased to $573,500 for an application requiring clinical data, and $286,750 for an application not requiring clinical data or a supplement requiring clinical data (USDHHS 2003b). Since enactment of the PDUFA, review times for drugs have greatly decreased to 13 months in 2002 (Carpenter 2004).

Is There a U.S. Drug Lag?

Whether the United States lags behind other countries to an unacceptable degree is an important political issue, and concern that the United States consistently approves drugs later than other countries frequently leads to criticism of the FDA. Although the literature on delays in drug availability in the United States relative to other countries is large, it is unfortunately contradictory (Andersson 1992a). There is wide variation in methodology across studies, and even definitions of measures of access to new pharmaceuticals differ from one study to another. Furthermore, the definition of which pharmaceuticals to include in the comparative studies lacks uniformity, and the sample of drugs in many of the studies is not well designed to answer the questions posed. The question of changing access over time has been a major policy focus of many international studies, but time periods vary across the studies, with many covering only a narrow span of time.

Most international studies have compared drug approvals in the United States to those in the United Kingdom. The question of whether the United States has a drug lag was first asked by Wardell (1973), who analyzed the approval of every drug eventually approved by the United States or the United Kingdom from 1962 to 1971. He then updated the study to include drugs approved through 1976 (Wardell 1978). These studies found that drug approvals in the United States did lag behind those in the United Kingdom, and that the situation had worsened in the latter period. Wardell looked both at the failure of one country to (ever) approve a drug that the other had approved and at the delay in one country's approval relative to that of the other. Andersson (1992a) has defined the former as the "absolute" drug lag, and the latter as the "relative" drug lag. Others have also found evidence to support Wardell's original finding of a U.S. drug lag (Grabowski and Vernon 1977, Grabowski 1980, Berlin and Jonsson 1986, Kaitin 1989, Kaitin et al. 1989, Burstall 1991, Reichert and Healy 2001). Additionally, Grabowski and Vernon (1977) and Grabowski (1980) found the lag to be increasing over time. But the Grabowski study looked at *all* drugs introduced in the United States, and the Grabowski and Vernon study looked only at drugs discovered in the United States. Consideration of all drugs ever introduced merges both important and unimportant drugs and fails to distinguish between different lag patterns for the two types of products. But considering only U.S. discoveries is overly restrictive for an industry as multinational as pharmaceuticals, where both research and marketing are international activities of all major firms and many important drugs are developed by foreign drug companies.

Simmons (1974) suggested that the apparent U.S. lag could be explained by the inclusion in the analysis of unimportant drugs, which were not as readily available in the United States. Coppinger et al. (1989) also criticized the finding of a U.S. drug lag, and showed that when discontinued drugs were omitted from the study, together with introductions of unimportant drugs and those that took place prior to 1977, the United States no longer appeared to have a drug lag relative to the United Kingdom. Parker (1989) found evidence of a drug lag in the United States, but observed that it had declined over time. Parker's analysis, however, included all drugs that were introduced from 1970 to 1983, and measurement of lags based on *all* drugs approved by a country might be biased upward because drugs that are related to existing products (so-called me-too drugs) may find earlier approval because much of the pre-market testing has already been done. Andersson (1992b) looked at approval times in seven industrialized countries, but considered all 553 drugs introduced in Sweden between 1960 and 1987. The study found that the United Kingdom and West Germany were quicker in approving new drugs, with the United States, Sweden, France, Italy, and Norway lagging. But because the study considered such a large number of products, including unimportant as well as important drugs, it is difficult to interpret the significance of the findings.

Several authors have attempted to restrict their analyses to important drugs, recognizing that limited access to drugs without substantial therapeutic impact does not impose the same kind of hardship on patients as it would for more innovative drugs. DeHaen (1975) discussed "major" drugs but did not define the term. He analyzed the absolute drug lag for five countries over a short time period (1967–1973) and concluded that all countries show lags behind one another, and the United States is not alone in restricting access to new pharmaceuticals. In Parker's multinational study of drug approvals, he considered only drugs that were approved in at least three countries out of his 18-country sample, suggesting that approval by multiple countries validates a drug's importance (Parker 1984). This is also the approach taken by Berlin and Jonsson (1986) and by Andersson (1992b), who refer to "consensus" in their studies of absolute drug lag. But a drug's approval by many countries in a sample is not necessarily an indication that it is important. It may merely mean that there is consensus as to its safety and efficacy. In fact, if drug approvals *were* correlated with importance, studies of the absolute drug lag would be meaningless because drugs that were not eventually widely approved would be, by definition, unimportant. Hass (1983) approached the question of importance by considering top-selling drugs for inclusion in his study of drug approvals by 11 industrialized countries. But sales is an incomplete proxy for importance, because drugs that are not approved for marketing in major markets (such as the United States) will find their worldwide sales reduced, together with their apparent importance.

Analysis of the timing of drug approvals also illustrates important differences between the drug approval systems used in various countries. FDA approval identifies a drug as safe and effective and allows it to be marketed in the United States. But in other countries the process is more complex. In France, for example, the cost of prescribed drugs is reimbursed by the Social Security system and so the approval and marketing decisions are separated (Weintraub 1982). The Commission d'autorisation de mise sur le marche (AMM) conducts the scientific review, analogous to that of the U.S. FDA. The approved drug's dossier then goes to the Commission de la Transparence, which conducts a joint clinical and economic assessment. The product will be covered by Social Security only after this commission has determined the price and level of reimbursement. Approval by the Commission de la Transparence, therefore, determines the date at which a new product can be effectively marketed.

Figure 9.1 shows the lag in approval (in months) for 32 drugs found to have been particularly important at the time of their introduction in both France and the United

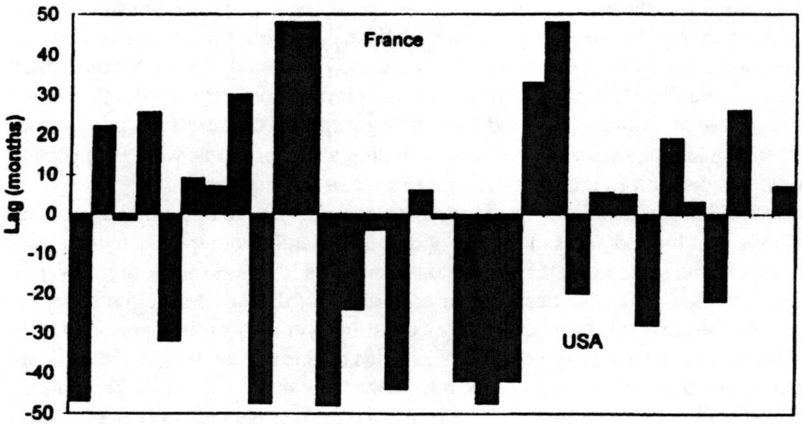

Figure 9.1. Approval delays: France and the United States (in months). *Source*: Schweitzer (1996).

States by panels of physicians and pharmacists in each country (Schweitzer 1996). Bars above the line imply an earlier French approval (a positive U.S. lag), while those below the line signify an earlier U.S. approval (a negative U.S. lag). The drugs are shown chronologically, in order of U.S. approval.

The distribution of the lags appears strikingly random, with both countries having many, and frequently very long, lags. The United States approved 16 drugs first, and France approved 15 first. There was one tie. Four of the American approvals occurred more than 48 months after the approval by France, and three of the French approvals were delayed as much. Furthermore, these delayed approvals for the United States were very long, with three lags greater than 90 months, and one of them greater than 100 months. The mean of the United States lags was 42.2 months (SE = 34.2), while it was only 25.4 months for France (SE = 22.0).

An approach for analysis of the timing of drug approvals is continued in work by Schweitzer and colleagues (1985), Grabowski (1988), and Grabowski and colleagues (1992). These authors studied lags in access to new pharmaceuticals to Medicaid recipients in states with drug formularies and found wide variation in access across states. They quantified the lag by constructing an index of a product's availability during an initial 4-year marketing period beginning after the drug is first approved by one state. This 4-year period is arbitrary, but represents the idea that a drug's real contribution will be made during its first 4 years of use. After this time, other drugs or treatments are likely to be introduced that will supplant it. This is a useful approach for study of the U.S. international drug lag.

Additional analysis of approvals was done using the 4-year initial marketing period, the approach used previously to study access to new drugs in state Medicaid programs. The proportion of this 4-year period during which a new drug was available in each country is a meaningful measure of its accessibility in each lagging country because it emphasizes the period of time during which the drug was especially new and had the fewest competitors. The proportion of accessibility during this 48-month period for each drug is termed the Drug Availability Index (DAI) and ranges from 0.00 (implying that a drug was not approved within 4 years of its approval in the lead country) to 1.00 (for the leading country). Analysis of the DAI between the United States and France shows that France is slightly quicker in approving drugs than the United States (Schweitzer 1996). The mean DAI for all drugs for France is 0.77 (SE = 0.33), and for the United States, 0.67 (SE = 0.41). The difference between each country's DAI is less pronounced than the difference between the mean lags measured in months because the DAI truncates the lags at 48 months. Neither of the differences is significant at the $P = 0.05$ level.

The frequency distributions of the lag times are similar for the United States and France, implying that each country has frequent and substantial approval lags. This observation is consistent with the observation made by DeHaen (1975), that all countries have drug lags.

A multiple regression analysis was performed to see if the U.S. DAI could be explained by the simultaneous effect of each drug's therapeutic class (cardiac, digestive system, etc.), year, and initial FDA rating of the drug's innovativeness, given by the FDA at the beginning of the review process. One might expect the rating to predict speed of approval, if the FDA were to concentrate its resources on those drugs that held the promise of bringing especially large clinical benefits. The multivariate analysis explains a very small proportion of the variation in U.S. DAI, however, indicating that neither therapeutic classification, FDA designation, nor time explains the U.S. DAI relative to that of France.

There is no consistent evidence that the drug approval process in the United States is slower than that of France. Although the average lag for U.S. approvals, measured in months, is longer than it is for France, the proportion of time during the initial marketing period when new drugs are available, measured by the DAI, is not significantly higher for the United States than for France. Furthermore, the data suggest that the U.S. approval process may have improved during the 1980s relative to that of France, but the number of important drugs approved in this later period is small, so the change is not statistically significant. Contrary to the initial hypotheses, U.S. approval was not quicker than that of France for drugs that the FDA had designated especially innovative, nor was it faster for cardiovascular drugs, in spite of public focus on heart disease as this nation's leading cause of death. This finding is consistent with that of Andersson (1992a), who also found approval times to be unrelated to a drug's therapeutic class or the FDA rating of therapeutic innovativeness.

A study of the timing of important new drug approvals by the G-7 countries plus Switzerland found similarly large variation in approval times across country (Schweitzer et al. 1996). The sample of drugs included in this study was somewhat expanded from the earlier French–United States comparison to include 34 drugs, based as before on concurrence between the French and American panels of physicians and pharmacists. The average monthly lag for each country is shown in Table 9.1.

Switzerland had the fastest approvals, on average, followed by France and the United States, while Italy and Germany were the slowest of the countries studied. Despite the apparently large differences between some of the countries, the variance of the lag was so large for each country that the differences were not generally statistically significant. Consistent with previous findings, the approval lags for all countries varied greatly. And equally important, all countries had long lags in approving many of the important drugs. Even in Switzerland, with the overall

Table 9.1. Average Monthly Approval Lag, by Country

Country	Lag (Months)
Canada	65.35
France	42.62
Germany	72.24
Italy	69.22
Japan	64.00
Switzerland	28.35
United States	50.53
United Kingdom	61.53

Source: Adapted from Schweitzer et al. (1996).

earliest approvals, the average approval was over 2 years later than the approval by the first country in the sample. The implication of this analysis of speed of the drug approval process in countries with similar review mechanisms and criteria is far from clear, for the wide variation in the timing of drug approvals is left unexplained. The variation is especially surprising when one realizes that all the drugs studied are thought to have been important at the time the approval decisions were made.

There are many reasons why a country may lag behind another in approving new drugs. One reason is that pharmaceutical companies may be slow in filing for approval in a particular country. Often this is due to the strategy of waiting until additional data are available before starting an application process expected to be especially rigorous. If firms delay the application because of a perceived need to compile a more complete dossier in one country than is required in another, resulting lags are indicative of different societal preferences regarding access and risk among countries. Nonetheless, these lags ought to be consistent across drugs. The inconsistent pattern of time lags evident from the various studies suggests that the difference in length of approval process in many countries, including the United States, is not due to differences in social preferences but to variation in the approval process itself.

This variation in delay of new important drug approvals is so large that it is possible that patients are frequently denied useful therapies. Whether or not this is the case depends on the likelihood of decision errors (i.e., dangerous drugs being approved, or beneficial drugs being denied approval). A case study approach directed at these decision errors is undoubtedly a useful line of future inquiry.

One approach for improving the efficiency of the FDA might be for it to consider expanding its fast-track approval system, currently applied to HIV/AIDS drugs, to all drugs thought to be therapeutically important, even if this results in greater delays for approvals of less important drugs. Of course, the success of this strategy is contingent upon improving the agency's ability to forecast drug importance.

Notes

1. If one considers the approval process to be a screening test, with a positive finding representing appearance of a problem, and a negative test implying no problem, approval of a bad drug is a false-negative result, while denying a good drug is a false-positive one. This analysis is more thoroughly developed by Intriligator (1996).
2. For cancer drugs, however, phase I trials involve cancer patients, not healthy individuals.

References

Andersson F. 1992a. The drug lag issue: the debate seen from an international perspective. *International Journal of Health Services* 22:53–72.

Andersson F. 1992b. The international diffusion of new drugs: a comparative study of seven industrialized countries. *Journal of Research in Pharmaceutical Economics* 4(2):43–62.

Berlin H and Jonsson B. 1986. International dissemination of new drugs: a comparative study of six countries. *Managerial and Decision Economics* 7:235–242.

Burstall ML. 1991. Europe after 1992: implications for pharmaceuticals. *Health Affairs*, Fall, 157–171.

Carpenter DP. 2004. The political economy of FDA drug review: processing, politics, and lessons for policy. *Health Affairs* 23:52–63.

Coppinger PL, Peck CC, and Temple RJ. 1989. Understanding comparisons of drug introductions between the United States and the United Kingdom. *Clinical Pharmacology and Therapeutics* 46:139–145.

DeHaen P. 1975. The drug lag—does it exist in Europe? *Drug Intelligence and Clinical Pharmacy* 9:144–150.

DiMasi JA, Seibring FM, and Lasagna L. 1994. New drug development in the United States from 1963 to 1992. *Clinical Pharmacology and Therapeutics* 55:15.

Faust R. 1971. Project selection in the pharmaceutical industry. *Research Management* 14:46–55.

Grabowski HG. 1980. Regulation and the international diffusion of pharmaceuticals. In RB Helms (ed), *The International Supply of Medicines: Implications of U.S. Regulatory Reform*. Washington, DC: American Enterprise Institute for Public Policy Research.

Grabowski HG. 1988. Medicaid patients' access to new drugs. *Health Affairs* 7(5):102–114.

Grabowski HG, Schweitzer SO, and Shiota R. 1992. The effect of Medicaid formularies on the availability of new drugs. *PharmacoEconomics* 1(Suppl):32–40.

Grabowski HG and Vernon JM. 1977. Innovation and invention—consumer protection regulation in ethical drugs. *American Economic Review* 67:359–364.

Hass AE Jr. 1983. Where drug marketing patterns are similar. *Medical Marketing and Media* 18:78–83.

Hussain-Gambles M. 2003. Ethnic minority under representation in clinical trials. Whose responsibility is it anyway? *Journal of Health Organ Management* 17(2):138–143.

Intriligator MD. 1996. Drug evaluations: type I vs. type II errors. Presented before the UCLA Seminar in Pharmaceutical Economics and Policy, Working Paper #96–2.

Kaitin K. 1989. Reply to "Understanding Comparisons of Drug Introductions between the United States and the United Kingdom." *Clinical Pharmacological Therapeutics* 46:146–148.

Kaitin K, Mattison N, Northington FK, and Lasagna L. 1989. The drug lag: an update of new drug introductions in the United States and in the United Kingdom, 1977 through 1987. *Clinical Pharmacological Therapeutics* 46:121–138.

Lesney M. 2000. What about the FDA? *Modern Drug Discovery* 3(8):29–33.

Marroum PJ and Goburu J. 2002. The product label: how pharmacokinetics and pharmacodynamics reach the prescriber. *Clinical Pharmacokinetics* 41(3):161–169.

Molzon J. 2003. The common technical document: the changing face of the new drug application. *Nature Reviews/Drug Discovery* 2:71–71.

New York Times. 2004. Looking for adverse drug effects. November 27.

Parker JES. 1984. *The International Diffusion of Pharmaceuticals*. London: Macmillan.

Parker JES. 1989. Who has a lag? *Managerial and Decision Economics* 10:299–309.

Pharmaceutical Research and Manufacturers of America. 2006. *Pharmaceutical Industry Profile 2006*. Washington, DC: Pharmaceutical Research and Manufacturers of America.

Pharmaceutical Research and Manufacturers of America. 2003. *Pharmaceutical Industry Profile 2003*. Washington, DC: Pharmaceutical Research and Manufacturers of America.

Reichert J and Healy E. 2001. Biopharmaceuticals approved in the EU 1995–1999: a European Union–United States comparison. *European Journal of Pharmaceuticals and Biopharmaceuticals* 51:1–7.

Schweitzer SO. 1996. An international comparison of the approval of new drugs. In Heller D and Geisler E (eds), *Managing Technology in Healthcare*. Boston: Kluwer.

Schweitzer SO, Salehi H, and Boling N. 1985. The social drug lag. *Social Science and Medicine* 21(10)1077–1082.

Schweitzer SO, Schweitzer ME, and Sourty-LeGuellec M-J. 1996. Is there a United States drug lag? The timing of new pharmaceutical approvals in the G-7 countries and Switzerland. *Medical Care Research and Review* 53(2):162–178.

Sharav VH. 2003. Children in clinical research: a conflict of moral values. *American Journal of Bioethics* 3(1):InFocus.

Simmons HE. 1974. The drug regulatory system of the United States Food and Drug Administration: a defense of current requirements for safety and efficacy. *International Journal of Health Services* 4:95–107.

Stanley GR. 1981. Use of foreign data in a new drug application. *Food Drug Cosmetic Law Journal* 36:340–344.

Temple R. 2002. Policy developments in regulatory approval. *Statistics in Medicine* 21:2939–2948.

U.S. Congress, Office of Technology Assessment (OTA). *Pharmaceutical R&D: Costs, Risks, and Rewards*. OTA-H-522. Washington, DC: Government Printing Office.

[USDHHS] U.S. Department of Health and Human Services, Food and Drug Administration. 1990. *From Test Tube to Patient: New Drug Development in the U.S., and FDA Consumer Special Report*. DHHS Publ. No. (FDA) 90-3168. Washington, DC: Government Printing Office, 1990.

[USDHHS] U.S. Department of Health and Human Services, Food and Drug Administration. 1995. *Benefit Vs. Risk: How CDER Approves New Drugs. FDA Consumer Special Report on New Drug Development in the United States*. Washington, DC: Government Printing Office, January.

[USDHHS] U.S. Department of Health and Human Services. 2003a. Agency information collection activities: proposed collection; comment request; guidance for industry on submitting and reviewing complete responses to clinical holds. *Federal Register* 68(76):19545–19546. Washington, DC: Government Printing Office, April 21.

[USDHHS] U.S. Department of Health and Human Services. 2003b. Food and Drug Administration Establishment of Prescription Drug User Fee Rates for Fiscal Year 2004. *Federal Register* 68(148):45249–45352. Washington, DC: Government Printing Office, August 1.

[USDHHS] U.S. Department of Health and Human Services, Food and Drug Administration. *n.d. Prescription Drug User Fees—Overview*. http://www.fda.gov/oc/pdufa/overview.html.

Wardell WM. 1973. Introduction of new therapeutic drugs in the United States and Great Britain: an international comparison. *Clinical Pharmacology and Therapeutics* 14:773–790.

Wardell WM. 1978. The drug lag revisited: comparison by therapeutic area of patterns of drugs marketed in the United States and Great Britain from 1972 through 1976. *Clinical Pharmacology and Therapeutics* 24:499–524.

Weintraub M. 1982. The French drug approval process. *Journal of Clinical Pharmacology* 22(5&6):213–222.

Wiggins SN. 1981. Product quality regulation and new drug introductions: some new evidence from the 1970s. *Review of Economics and Statistics* 63(4):615–619.